The Developing Person

Through Childhood and Adolescence

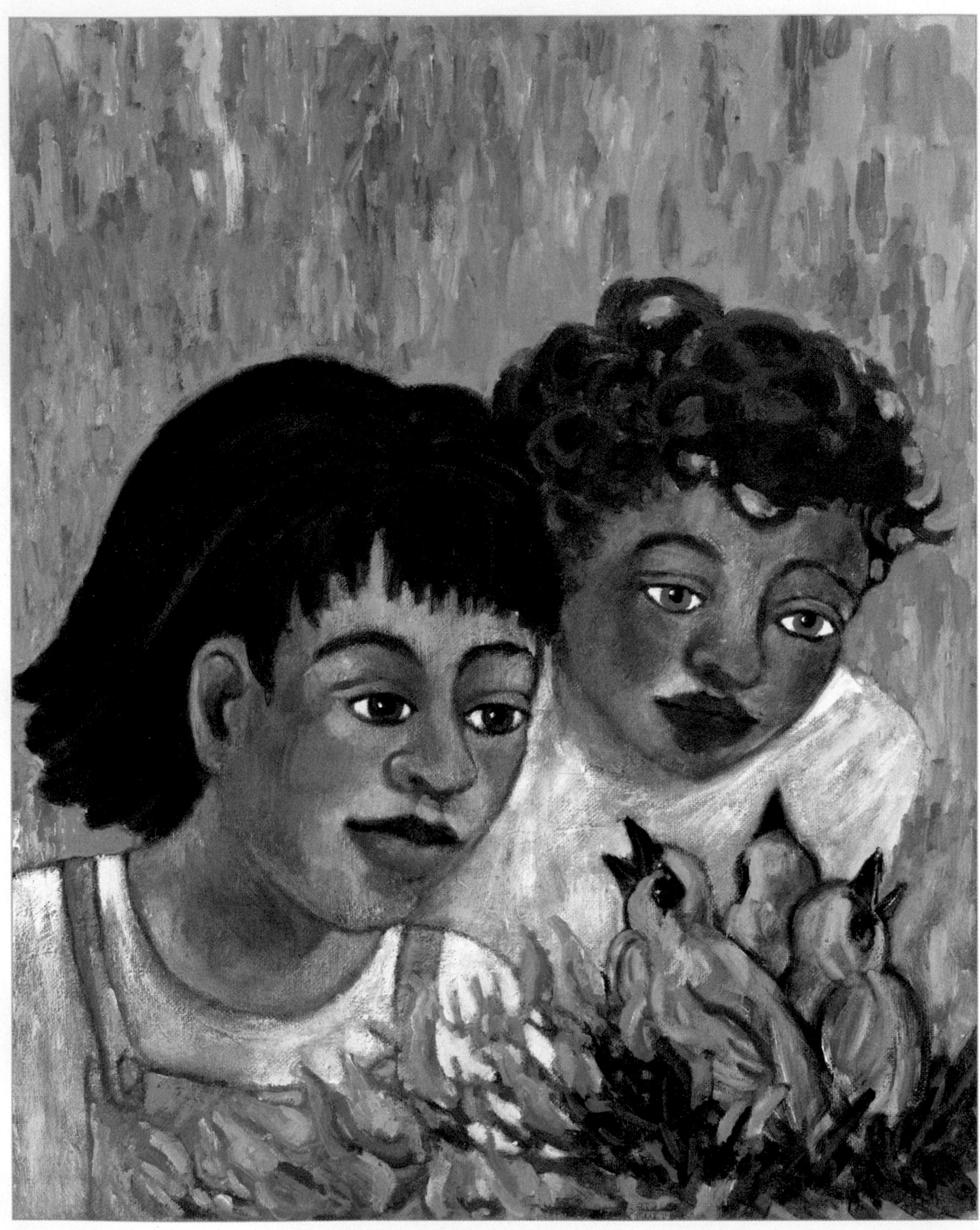

Christian Pierre captures the essence of child development in her cover paintings. ***Discovery of a Bird's Nest*** (front cover) shows that to a child, life is expansive and bright; adults might see the nestlings as small and insignificant and the sky as dark. The message of ***Sunset Together*** (back cover) is that children see life as best viewed with anticipation and hope, in the company of a friend.

The Developing Person

Through Childhood and Adolescence

EIGHTH EDITION

Kathleen Stassen Berger

Bronx Community College

City University of New York

WORTH PUBLISHERS

Publisher: Catherine Woods

Executive Editor: Jessica Bayne

Developmental Editor: Cecilia Gardner, Tom Churchill

Marketing Manager: Amy Shefferd

Supplements and Media Editor: Sharon Merritt

Associate Managing Editor: Tracey Kuehn

Project Editor: Vivien Weiss

Art Director and Cover Designer: Barbara Reingold

Interior Designer: Lissi Sigillo

Layout Designer: Paul Lacy

Associate Designer: Lyndall Culbertson

Senior Illustration Coordinator: Bill Page

Illustrations: Todd Buck Illustration and TSI Graphics

Photo Manager: Christine Buese

Photo Researcher: Donna Ranieri, Vikii Wong

Production Manager: Barbara Anne Seixas

Composition: TSI Graphics

Printing and Binding: RR Donnelley

Cover Art: Christian Pierre, *Discovery of a Bird's Nest* (front) and *Sunset Together* (back)

Library of Congress Control Number: 2008929725

ISBN-13: 978-1-4292-1647-0

ISBN-10: 1-4292-1647-6

ppbk. ISBN-13: 978-1-4292-2080-4

ppbk. ISBN-10: 1-4292-2080-5

Printed in the United States of America

Third printing

Worth Publishers

41 Madison Avenue

New York, NY 10010

www.worthpublishers.com

Credit is given to the following sources for permission to use the photos indicated:

Part Openers

Corbis, pp. vii, ix, xxx

Babystock/Jupiter Images, pp. vi, ix, x, 128, 217

Polka Dot Images/Jupiter Images, pp. vi, xi, 218, 307

Nonstock/Jupiter Images, pp. vi, xi, 308, 403

Brand X Pictures/Jupiter Images, pp. vii, xii, 404, 503

Chapter Openers

Tony Savino/The Image Works, pp. ix, 2

Shu-Tung-Unep/Peter Arnold, pp. ix, 36

David M. Phillips/Photo Researchers, Inc., p. 64

Rick Gomez/Corbis, pp. x, 96

Marcus Mok/Jupiter Images, pp. x, 130, 217

BananaStock/Jupiter Images, pp. x, 160, 217

Bruce Yuan-Yue Bi/Lonely Planet, pp. 186, 217

Blend Images/Jupiter Images, pp. 220, 307

Alloy Photography/Veer, pp. xi, 248, 307

Taxi/Getty Images, pp. xi, 276, 307

Eric Wheater/Lonely Planet Images, pp. xii, 310, 403

Nonstock/Jupiter Images, pp. 336, 403

Sean Sprague/The Image Works, pp. xii, 370, 403

Michael Prince/Corbis, pp. xii, 406, 503

Image 100/Jupiter Images, pp. xiii, 438, 503

John Powell/Topham/The Image Works, pp. 470, 503

Robert Harding/Getty Images, p. 504

ABOUT THE AUTHOR

Kathleen Stassen Berger received her undergraduate education at Stanford University and Radcliffe College, earned an M.A.T. from Harvard University and an M.S. and Ph.D from Yeshiva University. Her broad experience as an educator includes directing a preschool, teaching philosophy and humanities at the United Nations International School, teaching child and adolescent development to graduate students at Fordham University, teaching undergraduates at Montclair State University in New Jersey and at Quinnipiac University in Connecticut, and teaching inmates earning paralegal degrees at Sing Sing Prison.

For the past 35 years, Berger has taught at Bronx Community College of the City University of New York. She has taught introduction to psychology, child and adolescent development, adulthood and aging, social psychology, abnormal psychology, and human motivation. Her students—who come from many ethnic, economic, and educational backgrounds and who have a wide range of interests—consistently honor her with the highest teaching evaluations. Her own four children attended New York City public schools, one reason that she was elected as president of Community School Board in District Two.

Berger is also the author of *The Developing Person Through the Life Span* and *The Developing Person Through Childhood*. Her developmental texts are currently being used at nearly 700 colleges and universities worldwide and are available in Spanish, French, Italian, and Portuguese as well as English. Her research interests include adolescent identity, immigrants, and bullying, and she has contributed articles on developmental topics to the *Wiley Encyclopedia of Psychology*. Berger's interest in college education is manifest in articles published by the American Association for Higher Education and the National Education Association for Higher Education. She continues to teach and learn with every semester and every edition of her books.

BRIEF CONTENTS

CONTENTS

PART III
Early Childhood 219

PART IV
Middle Childhood 309

Preface

My Youngest at 8 Months When I look at this photo of Sarah, I see evidence of Mrs. Todd's devotion. Sarah's hair is washed and carefully brushed, her jumper and blouse are clean and pressed, and the carpet and step-stool are perfect equipment for standing practice. Sarah's legs—chubby and far apart—indicate that she is not about to walk early; but, given all these signs of Mrs. Todd's attention to caregiving, it is not surprising, in hindsight, that my fourth daughter was my earliest walker.

Each year, each day, and even each hour is a gift, to be filled with joy and work. This book is a gift too, at least to me.

To be specific, my interest in development began in earnest when our first two children (Bethany and Rachel) were infants. As a young professor, I often told anecdotes of their early days; some of those stories appear in this book. A few years later, our third baby (Elissa) cried and needed a walk; I walked with her into a meeting that led to this book. Our fourth child (Sarah) was conceived only after this text was widely adopted and we realized we could afford another child. She is another gift from this book.

My reading and study for the first seven editions helped me many times as I mothered my four through infancy, childhood, and adolescence. Most important was deciding when to intervene and when to let them learn for themselves. For instance, I was active in their elementary school, but I withheld my critique of Rachel's dyed red hair. Now all four are college graduates, with careers that make me proud. One is newly married; none are parents. Their development is one reason this eighth edition is the first to include an epilogue on emerging adults.

Gifts come from the wider community of social scientists as well, which I try to transmit to you. Globalization, neuroscience, dynamic systems, and genetic analysis provide new insights. The integration of mind and body is now better understood; specifics about the brain and about heredity are in every chapter.

Teaching and writing remain my life's work and passion, and I am grateful to share my work with many current and future colleagues. I strive to make this text

A Woman Now Two young girls participate in the traditional coming-of-age ceremony in Japan. Their kimonos and hairstyles are elaborate and traditional, as is the sake (rice wine) they drink. This is part of the ceremony signifying passage from girlhood to womanhood.

challenging and accessible, remembering that my own students propelled me to write it. They deserved a book that respected their intellect and experiences, without making development seem dull or obscure. Readers of this book will become tomorrow's leaders. I hope you find this book a useful gift toward compassion and wisdom.

To learn more about this text, including topics that are new to this edition, read on. Or you can turn to Chapter 1, and begin your developmental study.

New Material

"Another edition? Is there really anything new to include?"

When I hear that question, I am taken aback. So much is new since the last edition that it is hard to know where to start. We know more about genetics, about brain development, about infant day care, about friendship, about schools. No page is unchanged. Indeed, probably no paragraph remains untouched.

One change overall is increased attention to culture, with examples from many nations, as well as many comparisons between ethnic, economic, and gender groups in North America and in other parts of the world. Another change throughout is a dynamic-systems approach (a key term in Chapter 1). You won't see "dynamic systems" as a phrase in every chapter, but the underlying ideas of that approach pervade the text.

Developmental science is an exciting, evolving area of study. Not only are thousands of research studies published each year, but new concepts emerge that deepen our understanding of contemporary children. The most compelling of these concepts and the best of this research are integrated into this text. Every chapter has been updated to add new material on topics from *mirror neurons* (Chapter 1) to *language development* (Chapter 6) to *childhood obesity* (Chapter 11) to *cyberbullying* (Chapter 15).

CHRIS STOWERS / GETTY IMAGES

On the Edge Wearing no helmet, moving against traffic, and riding a racing bike among buses and trucks—these are a thrilling combination for bicycle messengers, almost all of whom are emerging-adult men.

Revised Chapters on Adolescence and a New Epilogue on Emerging Adulthood

I have been particularly impressed with the conceptual changes and longitudinal research that provide new insight into adolescence and emerging adulthood. As a result, I have carefully reorganized and revised the three chapters on adolescence; I also added a new epilogue on the period from age 18 to age 25. Highlights include new discoveries about the adolescent brain (e.g., the prefrontal cortex is not fully mature until the early 20s), the onset of puberty, and a more nuanced view of sexual identity. Also new is the dramatic cohort shift in emerging adulthood—once a time for settling down, but now a time for exploring, learning, and risk taking. Many college students are themselves emerging adults who are not quite ready to embrace adulthood. The new epilogue addresses this transitional age group, which has become the focus of a burgeoning area of research—a dramatic example of the impact of human experience on our research and theories.

Extensive Coverage of Brain Development

Beyond organizational changes, every page of this text reflects new research and theory. Brain development is the most obvious example, with every trio of chapters including a section on the brain. A sampling of this material is listed below:

Mirror neurons, pp. 17–18
A View from Science: Depression and the Brain, pp. 18–19
Neurological influences on ADHD, p. 60

Prenatal brain development, pp. 100–103
Effects of anoxia on the brain, pp. 118–119
Brain development during infancy, pp. 135–141
Sensation, perception, and brain development, pp. 142–143
Reflexes, pp. 145–146
Brain development and motor skills, pp. 146–147
Measuring brain activity, pp. 167–168
Information processing: Affordances and memory, pp. 168–174
Brain maturation and the emotions during infancy, pp. 191–192
Brain development in early childhood, pp. 225–231
Speed of thought, pp. 225–226
Connecting the brain's hemispheres, pp. 226–227
Planning and analyzing, pp. 227–229
Emotions, pp. 229–231
Brain maturation and theory of mind, p. 259
Role of prefrontal cortex in emotional regulation, p. 281
Gender differences in brain development, pp. 299–300, 303–304
Brain development in middle childhood, pp. 321–326
Advances in brain functioning, pp. 321–322
Measuring the mind, pp. 323–326
Information processing in middle childhood, pp. 342–347
HPA axis, HPG axis, and puberty, pp. 408–411
Brain development during adolescence, pp. 439–443
Brain maturation in emerging adulthood, p. 513

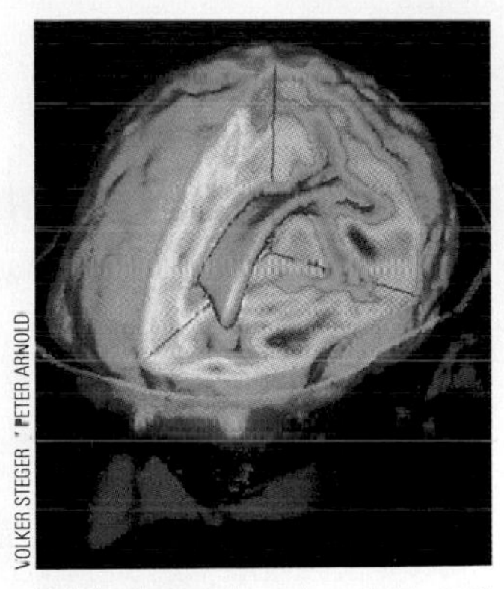
VOLKER STEGER / PETER ARNOLD

fMRI when talking (see Table 6.2).

Technique

fMRI (functional magnetic resonance imaging)

Use

Measures changes in blood flow anywhere in the brain (not just the outer layers).

Limitations

Signifies brain activity, but infants are notoriously active, which can make fMRIs useless.

New Research Design Feature

A new element appears in this edition to highlight the scientific basis of the study of development. Throughout the text, Research Designs appear in the margin, keyed to a study cited in the adjacent text; they explain more about the participants, methods, and limitations of that study. Students are encouraged to read the original studies, which also reveal the many ways—via statistics, hypotheses, and research findings—in which scientists test, substantiate, and sometimes reject their original assumptions.

New Focus for Boxed Features

Not only has developmental study changed, but students have changed as well. This edition reflects that, too. In response to instructors and students, two series of boxes emphasize how the concepts of developmental science affect—and are affected by—human life. "A View from Science" highlights research that shapes theory, practice, and application. "A Personal Perspective" focuses on the experiences of real people, including my own family. In addition, each chapter begins with a personal example.

Research Design

Scientists: Lloyd D. Johnston, Patrick M. O'Malley, Jerald G. Bachman, and John E. Schulenberg.

Publication: Monitoring the Future is online. Print copies are available from the National Institute on Drug Abuse, in Bethesda, Maryland.

Participants: In 2007, 48,000 students in 403 high schools, throughout the United States.

Design: Beginning in 1975, scientists from the University of Michigan surveyed adolescents each year, asking about drug use, drug availability, and personal attitudes. The basic questions have remained the same, with new drugs added (e.g., Vicodin, OxyContin). Data are reported by age, sex, ethnicity, and region.

Major conclusion: Over the 32 years of the survey, drug use declined, rose, and recently declined again. New drugs continue to appear, and sometimes old drugs become more popular again. Use is more affected by attitudes than by availability.

Comment: This study tracks many cohort changes within the United States. Interested readers should access the latest reports online. Note that other nations often show different patterns and that Monitoring the Future does not usually include high school dropouts.

Content Changes to the Eighth Edition

Like all sciences, child and adolescent development is built on the foundation of past learning. Every edition of a textbook must necessarily restate many facts and concepts—stages and ages, norms and variations, dangers and diversities, classic

Lighting Up These kindergartners in Buenos Aires may be exhibiting mirror neurons at work as they get ready to join other fans in cheering on Argentina's soccer team in a match against Peru.

NATACHA PISARENKO / AP

theories and fascinating applications. However, new discoveries and innovative theories continually change the study of development, and these, too, must be included. As a result, no page in this eighth edition is exactly what it was in the seventh edition, much less the first. Highlights of this updating appear below.

Part I: The Beginnings
1. Introduction

- Recent findings about mirror neurons lead into a new boxed feature, "A View from Science: Depression and the Brain."
- The discussion of the five characteristics of development has been reorganized to reflect the multifaceted richness of developmental science, including a new table entitled "The Five Characteristics of Development."
- A new subsection "zooms in" to focus on genetic and neurological influences on development and "zooms out" to consider social contextual influences.
- New research on language acquisition among deaf children offers an example of the difference-equals-deficit error.

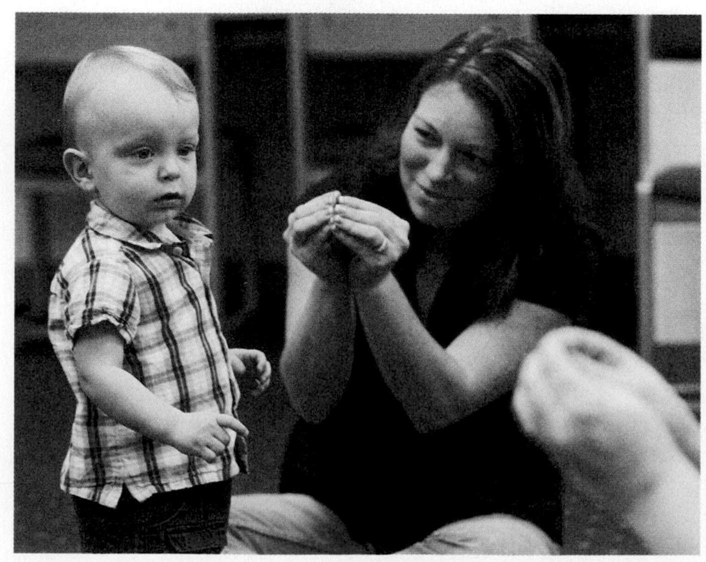

Happy Talk Ty's mother and the teacher demonstrate the sign for "more" in a sign-language class at the public library in Hudson, Florida. Ty takes the lesson very seriously: Learning language in any form is crucial for 1-year-olds.

NEWSCOM

2. Theories of Development

- New research on the influences of nature and nurture in ADHD is covered extensively.
- The chapter begins and ends with a personal anecdote about one of my daughters, which is viewed through the lens of each of the major theories discussed in the chapter.

3. Heredity and Environment

- The major section on the genetic code has been updated and reorganized to include twin research and reproductive technology.
- A new boxed feature discusses the controversy about the use of genetic tests to detect psychological disorders.

4. Prenatal Development and Birth

- The discussion of birth complications stresses the development of low-birthweight infants.
- The revised discussion of teratogens focuses on protective measures.

Part II: The First Two Years

5. The First Two Years: Biosocial Development

- The explanation of growth norms has been expanded.
- Updates to the research on brain development and functioning are featured in the discussions of exuberance and pruning, language acquisition, and plasticity.
- Ethnic and cultural variations in development are emphasized, including differences in sensory development, motor skills development, and sleeping patterns.
- Statistics on childhood diseases worldwide have been updated, highlighting the success of immunization.

6. The First Two Years: Cognitive Development

- Restructured discussion of Piaget's theory includes recent research.
- The discussion of information processing has been updated and expanded, including a new subsection on aspects of memory.
- The sections on language acquisition and theories of language learning have been extensively revised.

7. The First Two Years: Psychosocial Development

- A brand-new section on toilet training discusses how various theories and cultures view this process.
- The presentation of self-awareness focuses sharply on self-recognition and the self-conscious emotions.
- A new major section examines the connection between brain maturation and emotional development, including discussions of differentiation of emotions, the genesis of social impulses, and responses to stress.
- The role of fathers in children's development is updated and expanded, recognizing direct and indirect influences.

Part III: Early Childhood

8. Early Childhood: Biosocial Development

- Recent research is covered that shows the neurological and cultural bases of impulsiveness and perseveration.
- The discussion of motor skills has been expanded to include modern environmental hazards, especially toxic pollutants.

9. Early Childhood: Cognitive Development

- Piaget's and Vygotsky's views of how young children think and learn are combined in a major text section, for easier comparison and contrast.

- The discussion of language ends with a section emphasizing constant change—both children's adaptability in acquiring language and the way languages themselves change to suit the times.

10. Early Childhood: Psychosocial Development

- Gender differences in emotional regulation are highlighted, incorporating recent findings about brain maturation.
- Morality is discussed in a separate major section, covering aggression and the emergence of a sense of right and wrong.

Part IV: Middle Childhood

11. Middle Childhood: Biosocial Development

- A new discussion has been added on children's health habits.
- The discussion of childhood obesity has been expanded to include its international prevalence and major causes (genetics, parenting practices, and social influences).
- The coverage of autistic spectrum disorders has been updated.

12. Middle Childhood: Cognitive Development

- A new boxed feature, "A View from Science: Explicit Instruction vs. Discovery Learning," describes a major experiment that explored the effectiveness of discovery learning.
- Language is now a major section, covering the expansion of vocabulary and the impact and methods of second-language learning.
- The concluding section, "Teaching and Learning," has been reorganized to include discussions of immigrant and low-income children, gender and international differences in achievement (with new tables on norms and expectations), the reading and math wars, and cultural influences on education.

13. Middle Childhood: Psychosocial Development

- The discussion of internal psychosocial changes and external sociocultural influences has been completely reorganized and expanded.
- A new section on the development of self-concept and self-esteem has been added.

MARY KNOX MERRILL/ THE CHRISTIAN SCIENCE MONITOR / GETTY IMAGES

Smiling Faces Sometimes Everyone in this group is an immigrant, born far from their current home in Burlington, Vermont. Jean Luc Dushime escaped the 1994 genocide in Rwanda, central Africa, when he was 14. He eventually adapted to his new language, climate, surroundings, and culture. Today he helps immigrant children make the same transition.

AP PHOTO / LAS CRUCES SUN-NEWS, VLADIMIR CHALOUPKA

Sacred Thread Every religion has some ritual in which young people make a public commitment to their faith. These Hindu boys are receiving the *jenoi,* a sacred thread that they will wear all their lives. In this initiation ceremony, they shave their heads, wear new robes, and vow to pray three times a day and to study the Vedas, or scriptures.

- A new section on children's moral questioning and moral reasoning has been added.
- The discussion of friendship has been expanded.

Part V: Adolescence

14. Adolescence: Biosocial Development

- The discussion of hormonal activity has been expanded, including the role of leptin in the onset of puberty.
- A new section on nutrition discusses common dietary deficiencies and the causes, symptoms, and treatment of eating disorders.
- A new subsection introduces recent research on changes in body rhythms in adolescence and the neurological roots of those changes.

15. Adolescence: Cognitive Development

- Neurological development in adolescence and its influence on adolescent thinking are now highlighted.
- The discussions of education in middle school and high school are now combined in a new major section, "Teaching and Learning."
- A new subsection on the vocational options of those not bound for college has been added.
- A new subsection on high school dropouts has been added, incorporating recent research.
- "A Personal Perspective: James, the High-Achieving Dropout," illustrates the dynamics that can lead to the decision to drop out of school.

16. Adolescence: Psychosocial Development

- The material on sexual/gender identity and political/ethnic identity has been updated and expanded.
- "Cliques and Crowds" discusses the functions of these groups and the influence they have on adolescents' lives.
- "Sexuality" now covers everything from how adolescents learn about sex to new statistics on sexual activity among U.S. teenagers and a new discussion of the challenges facing homosexual youth.
- The coverage of delinquency has been expanded and includes a new boxed feature, "A Personal Perspective: A Feminist Looks at the Data."

EPA / CORBIS

A Proud Teacher "Is it possible to train a cockroach?" This hypothetical question, an example of formal operational thought, was posed by 15-year-old Tristan Williams of New Mexico. In his award-winning science project, he succeeded in conditioning Madagascar cockroaches to hiss at the sight of a permanent marker. (His parents' logical reasoning about having 600 cockroaches living in their home is not known.)

Epilogue: Emerging Adulthood

- Mirroring the organizational structure of the book as a whole, this entirely new epilogue highlights the physical, cognitive, and psychosocial changes that occur between the ages of 18 and 25.
- The epilogue emphasizes the robust health and vitality of emerging adulthood, and also considers the dangers to health posed by drugs, alcohol, and sexually transmitted diseases.
- New neurological research is presented, including the ongoing development of the prefrontal cortex and its impact on cognition.
- The section on psychosocial development focuses on relationships, especially on changing family connections, new and old friendships, and the development of romances (including cohabitation).

Ongoing Features

Many characteristics of this book have been acclaimed since the first edition and have been retained in this revision.

Writing that Communicates the Excitement and Challenge of the Field

An overview of the science of human development should be lively, just as people are. Each sentence conveys tone as well as content. Chapter-opening vignettes bring student readers into the immediacy of development. Examples and explanations abound, helping students make the connections among theory, research, and their own experiences.

Coverage of Diversity

Multicultural, international, rich and poor, infant and grandparent, male and female, birth and puberty, gay and straight, normal and pathological—all these words and ideas are vital to appreciating how we all develop. Research uncovers surprising commonalities and notable differences: We are all the same, yet each of us is unique.

BJORN SVENSSON / ALAMY

Toy Guns for Boys, Cinderella for Girls Young boys throughout the world are the ones who aim toy guns, while young girls imagine themselves as a princess. The question is why: Are these young monks in Laos responding to biology or to culture?

Beginning with the discussion of "all kinds of people" in Chapter 1, each chapter highlights the possibilities and variations of human life during childhood and adolescence. New research on family structures, immigrants, bilingualism, and ethnic differences in health are among the many topics that illustrate variations. The discussions of culture and diversity throughout this new edition encourage awareness of, and then respect for, human differences. Examples and research findings from many parts of the world are not add-on highlights or boxes, but are integral throughout, as the following list of diversity-related section titles and discussions makes clear:

Including all kinds of people, pp. 4–5
Nature–nurture controversy, pp. 5, 59–61
Culture and development, pp. 13–16
Sociocultural theory, pp. 49–52
International data on IVF and adoption, pp. 73–75
Gender and culture in alcoholism, pp. 83–84
International variations in vision problems, pp. 83–84
International differences in rates of certain birth defects, p. 107
Pediatric AIDS in developed and developing nations, pp. 111–112
Birth practices in developing nations, pp. 116–118
Low-birthweight rates in various countries, pp. 119–120
Cultural variations in social support to prevent birth complications, pp. 122–123
Cultural variations in co-sleeping practices, p. 134
Abandoned Romanian children adopted in the U.S. and western Europe, p. 141
Ethnic variations in development of motor skills, pp. 148–149
Cultural differences in rates of sudden infant death syndrome, pp. 153–154
Cultural factors affecting language development during the first two years, pp. 177–179
Cultural variations in toilet training, pp. 194–195
Ethnotheories, p. 199
Cultural ideas about proximal and distal parenting, pp. 199–200
A Personal Perspective: "Let's Go to Grandma's" (example of child-rearing practices), p. 201
Cultural differences in attachment, p. 206
Latino fathers, p. 209
Infant day care: International comparisons, p. 210
Cultural variations in growth patterns in early childhood, pp. 222–223
Theory of mind in various cultures, pp. 259–260
Learning two languages, pp. 264–266
Early-childhood education in Reggio-Emilia, Italy, pp. 269–270
Culture and emotional control, p. 280
Cultural differences in play, pp. 284–285
Cultural variations in parenting styles, pp. 290–291
Sociocultural theory on gender roles, p. 303
Childhood obesity as an international problem, pp. 317–318
Cultural influences on cognition in Zimbabwe and Brazil, pp. 341–342
Second-language learning and instruction, pp. 349–352
National variations in school curricula, pp. 355–359
Education in Japan, p. 365
A culture clash in Canadian education, pp. 365–367
Self-esteem as an American value, pp. 375–376
Diversity in family structure and function, pp. 383–385, 387–388
Study of bullying in Norway's schools, p. 397

Cultural influences on children's values, pp. 400–401
Ethnic differences in age of puberty, pp. 415–416
Cultural and religious variation in sexual activity during adolescence, pp. 423–424
Achieving ethnic identity in adolescence, pp. 475–476
Cultural values and adolescent independence, p. 479
Immigrant youth and peer support, pp. 483–485
Romances, straight and gay, pp. 486–487
Cultural differences in adolescent suicide, pp. 495–497
Emerging adulthood in developed nations, pp. 505–506
Falling birth rates worldwide, pp. 507–508

Up-to-Date Coverage

My mentors taught me to be curious, creative, and skeptical. I eagerly read and critique thousands of journal articles and books on everything from autism to zygosity. The recent explosion of research in neuroscience and genetics has challenged me, once again, first to understand and then to explain many complex findings and speculative leaps. My students continue to ask questions and share their experiences, always providing new perspectives and concerns.

Topical Organization Within a Chronological Framework

The book's basic organization remains unchanged except for one important addition. The first four chapters begin the book with coverage of definitions, theories, genetics, and prenatal development. These chapters function not only as a developmental foundation but also as the structure for explaining the life-span perspective, including plasticity, nature and nurture, multicultural awareness, risk analysis, the damage–repair cycle, family bonding, and many other concepts that yield insights for human development.

The other four parts correspond to the major periods of child development. Each part contains three chapters, one for each of the three domains: biosocial, cognitive, and psychosocial.

Then comes the new epilogue on emerging adulthood, which serves to restate the basic principles of development, using examples that resonate with current students.

The topical organization within a chronological framework is a useful scaffold for students' understanding of the interplay between age and domain. The chapters are color-coded with tabs on the edge of each right-hand page. The pages of the biosocial chapters have green tabs, the cognitive chapters have purple tabs, and the psychosocial chapters have pink tabs.

Pedagogical Aids

Each chapter ends with a summary, a list of key terms (with page numbers indicating where the word is introduced and defined), key questions, and application exercises designed to encourage students to apply concepts to everyday life. Key terms appear in boldface type in the text; they are defined in the margins and again in a glossary at the back of the book. The outline on the first page of each chapter and the system of major and minor subheads facilitate the survey-question-read-write-review (SQ3R) approach.

In this edition, we have added many subordinate heads to help students readily appreciate the structure of the discussion and perceive connections between topics. A "Summing Up" feature at the end of each main section allows students

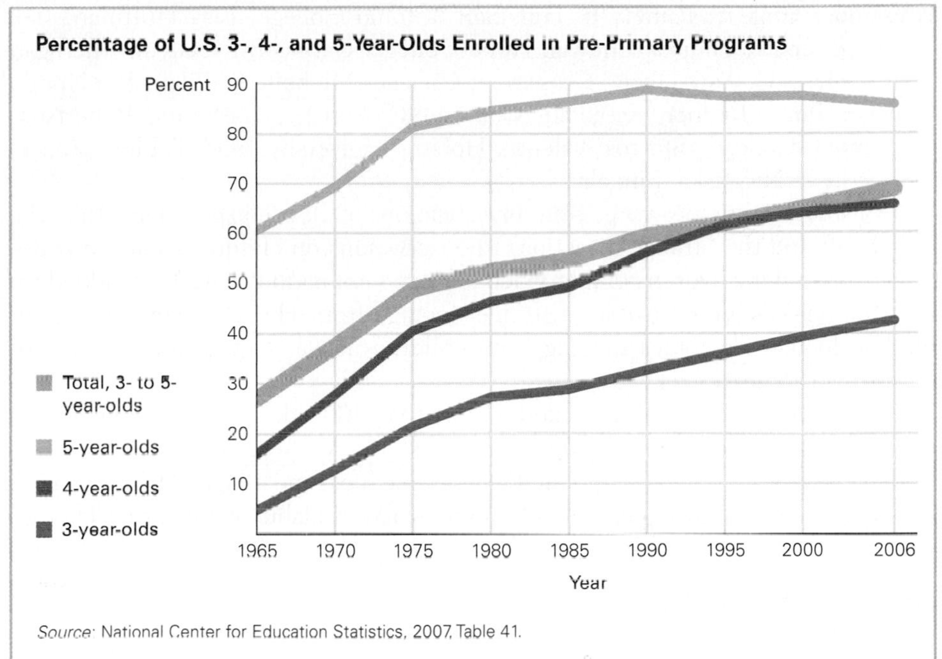

FIGURE 9.5

Changing Times As research increasingly finds that preschool education provides a foundation for later learning, more and more young children are enrolled in educational programs.

Observation Quiz (see answer, page 270). Which age group experienced the most dramatic increase in preschool attendance from 1965 to 1975?

to pause and reflect on what they've just read. "Observation Quizzes" inspire readers to look more closely at certain photographs, tables, and graphs. The "Especially for . . ." questions in the margins, many of which are new to this edition, apply concepts to situations that may confront parents and other people in development-related roles and careers, such as nurses, educators, day-care providers, psychologists, and social workers.

Especially for Nurses (see response, page 243): While weighing a 4-year-old, you notice several bruises on the child's legs. When you ask about them, the child says nothing and the parent says the child bumps into things. What should you do?

Photographs, Tables, and Graphs that Are Integral to the Text

Students learn a great deal from this book's illustrations because Worth Publishers encourages authors to choose the photographs, tables, and graphs and to write captions that extend the content. Appendix A furthers this process by presenting a chart or table for each chapter that contains detailed data for further study. (This Preface offers a selection of this edition's illustrations.)

Supplements

As an instructor myself, I know that supplements can make or break a class. Students are much more media savvy than they once were; we have new online materials to help them learn. Please look at the Video Tool Kit for both students and instructors. It helps you (and them) understand the field. In addition, DevelopmentalPortal is now offered with this book. These and other supplements are described below.

Video Tool Kit

The Video Tool Kit takes a technological leap forward in this edition: The materials are available online. The Tool Kit was prepared by a talented team of instructors, including: Victoria Cross, University of California, Davis; Sheridan Dewolf,

Grossmont College; Pamela B. Hill, San Antonio College; Lisa Huffman, Ball State University; Thomas Ludwig, Hope College; Cathleen McGreal, Michigan State University; Amy Obegi, Grossmont College; Michelle L. Pilati, Rio Hondo College; Tanya Renner, Kapiolani Community College; Catherine Robertson, Grossmont College; Stavros Valenti, Hofstra University; and Pauline Zeece, University of Nebraska, Lincoln.

The student activities range from investigations of classic experiments (like the visual cliff and the Strange Situation) to observations on children's play and adolescent risk taking. Dozens of new video clips and animations have been added for this edition—including classic historical footage from Harry Harlow and spellbinding footage on topics ranging from children in war to the development of empathy in adolescence.

For instructors, the Tool Kit includes more than 400 video clips and animations, along with discussion starters and PowerPoint slides. All these videos can be downloaded (as MPEGs or close-captioned QuickTime files) and assigned to students. A selection of the 150 most popular video clips is also available on CD or DVD.

DevelopmentPortal

This is the complete online gateway to all student and instructor resources available with the textbook. DevelopmentPortal brings together the video tool kits, the eBook, and powerful assessment tools. Created by psychologists and master teachers, DevelopmentPortal includes powerful diagnostic quizzes to focus study where it is needed most and an assignment test that allows instructors to construct and administer tests and quizzes.

The quiz bank (featuring more than 80 questions per chapter) that powers the student assessment was written by Rebecca Griffiths, College of the Sequoias. These questions are not from the test bank! They can be used for review and assessment.

eBook

The interactive eBook fully integrates the complete text and its electronic study tools in a format that instructors and students can customize—all at a significantly lower price than the printed text. It offers access from any Internet-connected computer; quick, intuitive navigation to any section, subsection, or printed book page number; a notes feature that allows any page to be customized; a full-text search; text highlighting; and a searchable glossary.

The Companion Web Site

Edited by Catherine Robertson (Grossmont College), the companion Web site (at www.worthpublishers.com/berger) is an online educational setting for students and instructors. It is free, and tools on the site include: interactive Flashcards in both English and Spanish; a Spanish-language glossary; quizzes; annotated Web links; and Frequently Asked Questions About Development. A password-protected Instructor Site offers a full array of teaching resources, including PowerPoint slides, an online quiz gradebook, and links to additional tools.

Journey Through Childhood Videos

Bringing observational learning to the classroom, this video series allows students to watch and listen to real children as a way of amplifying their reading of the text.

Journey Through Childhood offers vivid footage of people of all ages from around the world (North America, Europe, Africa, Asia, and South America), as seen in everyday environments (homes, hospitals, schools, and offices) and at major life transitions (birth, marriage, divorce, being grandparents).

Interviews with prominent developmentalists—including Charles Nelson, Barbara Rogoff, Ann Peterson, and Steven Pinker—are integrated throughout to help students link research and theory to their experiences. Interviews with social workers, teachers, and nurses who work with children and adolescents give students direct insight into the practical challenges and rewards of their professions. One hour of unedited footage helps students sharpen their observation skills.

Child and Adolescent Development Telecourse

Stepping Stones, developed by Coast Learning Systems and Worth Publishers, teaches the fundamentals of child and adolescent development. The course also explores the variety of individual and developmental contexts that influence development, such as socioeconomic status, culture, genetics, family, school, and society. Each video lesson includes specific examples interwoven with commentary by subject-matter experts. In addition, there are video lessons on the whole child, and special topics such as the role of the father, abuse and neglect, school, and challenges for teens.

Instructor's Resources

This collection of resources, written by Richard O. Straub (University of Michigan, Dearborn), has been hailed as the richest instructors' aid in developmental psychology. This manual features chapter-by-chapter previews and lecture guides, learning objectives, springboard topics for discussion and debate, handouts for student projects, and supplementary readings from journal articles. Course-planning suggestions, ideas for term projects, and a guide to media are also included.

Study Guide

The *Study Guide* by Richard O. Straub helps students evaluate their understanding and retain their learning longer. Each chapter includes a review of key concepts, guided study questions, and section reviews that encourage students' active participation in the learning process. Two practice tests and a challenge test help them assess their mastery of the material.

PowerPoint Slides

A number of different presentation slides prepared by Madeleine L. Tattoon (Riverside Community College) are available on the Web site or on the *Instructor's Resources* CD-ROM. There are two prebuilt PowerPoint slide sets for each text chapter—one featuring chapter outlines, the other featuring all chapter illustrations. These slides can be used as is or customized to fit individual needs. Video presentation slides provide an easy way to connect chapter content to the selected video clip and to follow each clip with discussion questions designed to promote critical thinking. In addition, Professor Tattoon has produced a set of enhanced lecture slides focusing on key themes from the text and featuring tables, graphs, and figures.

Overhead Transparencies

This set of 50 full-color transparencies consists of key diagrams, charts, graphs, and tables from the textbook.

Test Bank and Computerized Test Bank

The test bank, extensively revised by Rod Fowers (Highline Community College) and Rosemary McCullough (University of New England) includes more than 90 multiple-choice and 70 fill-in, true-false, and essay questions for each chapter. Each question is keyed to the textbook by topic, page number, and level of difficulty.

The Diploma computerized test bank, available on a dual-platform CD-ROM for Windows and Macintosh, guides instructors step-by-step through the process of creating a test. It allows them to add an unlimited number of questions; to edit, scramble, or resequence items; to format a test; and to include pictures, equations, and media links. The accompanying gradebook enables instructors to record students' grades throughout the course and includes the capacity to sort student records, view detailed analyses of test items, curve tests, generate reports, add weights to grades, and more.

The CD-ROM is also the access point for Diploma Online Testing, which allows instructors to create and administer secure exams over a network or over the Internet. In addition, Diploma has the ability to restrict tests to specific computers or time blocks. Blackboard- and WebCT-formatted versions of each item in the Test Bank are available on the CD-ROM.

Thanks

I'd like to thank those academic reviewers who have read this book in every edition and who have provided suggestions, criticisms, references, and encouragement. They have all made this a better book. I want to mention especially those who have reviewed this edition:

Elizabeth Ann Adams, *College of Southern Nevada*
Gary Anderson, *Camosun College*
Pamela Auburn, *University of Houston, Downtown*
Denise Berg, *Santa Monica College*
Kathleen Bey, *Palm Beach Community College*
Jennifer Briffa, *Merritt College*
Jessica Carpenter, *Elgin Community College*
Tabitha Dell'Angelo, *The College of New Jersey*
Albert Gardner, *University of Maryland*
Eugene Geist, *Ohio University*
Andrew Getzfeld, *New York University*
Judi Gibian-Mennenga, *Harper College*
Toni Harris, *Virginia State University*
Jessica Jablonski, *Richard Stockton College*
Mark Jacobs, *Palomar College*
Marguerite D. Kermis, *Canisius College*
Sarah M. Kern, *The College of New Jersey*
Deborah Laffranchini, *Modesto Junior College*
Richard Langford, *University of Hawaii, West O'ahu*
Laura Manson, *Santa Monica College*
Michael K. Meyerhoff, *Harper College*
Robin Musselman, *Lehigh Carbon Community College*
Jane Ogden, *East Texas Baptist University*
Tiffany A. Parker, *Southeast Missouri State University*
Merryl (Missi) Patterson, *Austin Community College*
Amy K. Resch, *Citrus College*
Janet Weinstein-Zanger, *Endicott College*
Herkie Lee Williams, *El Camino College, Compton Center*

The editorial, production, and marketing people at Worth Publishers are dedicated to meeting the highest standards of excellence. Their devotion of time, effort, and talent to every aspect of publishing is a model for the industry. I particularly would like to thank: Stacey Alexander, Jessica Bayne, Christine Buese,

Tom Chao, Tom Churchill, Cele Gardner, Lorraine Klimowich, Tom Kling, Tracey Kuehn, Sharon Merritt, Katherine Nurre, Donna Ranieri, Babs Reingold, Barbara Seixas, Amy Shefferd, Walter Shih, Ted Szczepanski, Vivien Weiss, Vikii Wong, and Catherine Woods.

Dedication

This edition is dedicated to the new generation of the world's children, who must cope with challenges unknown to their parents, and to all the adults who guide them. I am awed at each child's ability to survive and even thrive, overcoming problems (such as globalization, greed, and family disruption) and hoping for the future. I am hopeful, too.

Kathleen Stassen Berger

Kathleen Stassen Berger

New York, August 2008

The Developing Person

Through Childhood and Adolescence

The Beginnings

CHAPTER 1

CHAPTER 2

CHAPTER 3

CHAPTER 4

PART I

The science of human development has many beginnings.

Chapter 1 introduces what we study, why, and how, explaining some research strategies and methods used to understand how people grow and change.

Chapter 2 introduces theories of development to focus our study. It describes three grand theories and two emergent ones, all of which lay the foundation for hundreds of other theories and thousands of observations.

Chapter 3 traces the interaction of nature (heredity) and nurture (environment). Chemical instructions on the genes and chromosomes influence everything from the thickness of toenails to the swiftness of brain waves, from quick temper to memory for faces. Genes never act alone, so Chapter 3 also examines some of the effects of education, child rearing, and culture on a person's development.

Chapter 4 details the biological start of each developing person, from one dividing cell to a newborn's birth. Together these four chapters begin our study of human development.

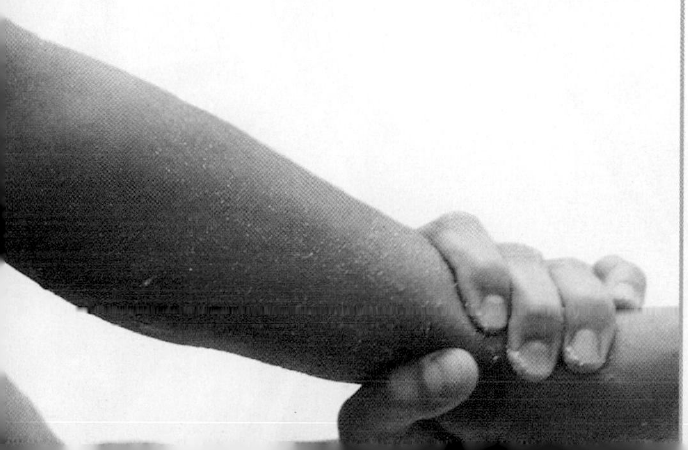

1

CHAPTER OUTLINE

Introduction

My student, Gloria, was upset. Her daughter, only 16 years old, was no longer a virgin. Worse, Gloria didn't know that until, during a parent–teen discussion group at her church, her daughter announced to the entire group that she had had sex.

"I should have known. A counselor told me she would have early sex and use drugs, just like I did."

I was horrified by this—not by the daughter's sexual activity but by the counselor's prediction. I knew that Gloria had been drug-free for years and was married to a man she loved. She brought him to meet me: He was a caring stepfather to her teenage daughter and the father of her two younger children.

I learned that the counselor worked in middle school, where she had met once with Gloria four years earlier, when her daughter was a rebellious 12-year-old.

"The counselor told us that my daughter would follow my example."

Perhaps Gloria had misunderstood the counselor. But it's more likely that neither the counselor nor Gloria understood development, correlation, or ethics—all of which are explained in this chapter. I assured Gloria that families, cultures, and individuals change as time goes on, that no past history locks in the future. As you learn about the terms, methods, and processes of human development, remember that the past is prologue, not conclusion. This chapter is an introduction to the true nature of development.

Defining Development

The **science of human development** *seeks to understand how and why people—all kinds of people, everywhere, of every age—change over time.* Developmentalists recognize that growth is *multidirectional, multidisciplinary, multicontextual, multicultural,* and *plastic.* All these terms will be explained in this chapter, but first we need to delve deeper into the elements of the basic definition of developmental science: the how and why of development, the kinds of people included, and the observation of change over time.

science of human development The science that seeks to understand how and why people of all ages and circumstances change or remain the same over time.

Understanding How and Why

First, developmental study is a *science* (Bornstein & Lamb, 2005). It depends on theories, data, analysis, critical thinking, and sound methodology—just like every other science. And like all scientists, developmentalists ask questions and seek answers, trying to ascertain "how and why"—that is, trying to discover the processes of development and the reasons for those processes.

Science cannot decide the purpose of life; we need philosophy or religion for that (National Academy of Sciences, 2008). Literature and art can also provide insight beyond the scientific experiment. But "the empirical sciences will show us the way, the means, and the obstacles" involved in making life what we want it to be (Koops, 2003, p. 18).

empirical Based on observation, experience, or experiment; not theoretical.

To say that something is **empirical** means that it is based on data, on many experiences, on demonstrations, on facts. Without empirical evidence followed by applications, human life might be "solitary, poor, nasty, brutish, and short," as it was for most people before the scientific revolution (Hobbes, 1651/1997).

Only 50 years ago, parents were forbidden to visit their hospitalized children, schoolteachers regularly hit their students, and millions of children died of diseases that are now rare. In the United States in 1954, about 3 of every 100 newborns died before age 5; in 2004, 99 of every 100 survived at least until age 10 (U.S. Bureau of the Census, 2007). Scientific research, conclusions, and then applications promote children's survival, health, and happiness.

As you surely realize, facts themselves can be misinterpreted. Because the study of development is a science, it is based on *objective* evidence. Because it concerns human life and growth, it is also laden with *subjective* perceptions, which are open to bias. This interplay of the objective and the subjective, of the universal and the personal, makes developmental science a challenging, fascinating, and even transformative study.

For example, adults have heartfelt opinions about what pregnant women should eat, how (or even whether) crying infants should be comforted, when toddlers should be toilet trained, where children should go to school, whom teenagers should befriend. These views, like all opinions, are subjective.

Scientists seek to move past that subjectivity, to progress from opinion to truth, from wishes to outcomes. To avoid unexamined opinions and rein in personal biases, scientists follow the four basic steps of the **scientific method:**

scientific method A way to answer questions that requires empirical research and data-based conclusions.

hypothesis A specific prediction that is stated in such a way that it can be tested and either confirmed or refuted.

1. *Begin with curiosity.* On the basis of theory, prior research, or a personal observation, pose a question.
2. *Develop a hypothesis.* Form the question into a **hypothesis,** a specific prediction that can be tested.
3. *Test the hypothesis.* Design and conduct research to gather empirical evidence (data).
4. *Draw conclusions.* Use the evidence to support or refute the hypothesis.

This text describes many conclusions reached via the scientific method. Opinions —from researchers, from the author of this text, from your own interpretations— also enter into the equation because no human can be entirely objective. This introduction should help you recognize opinions when they arise, alerting you to seek evidence.

replication The repetition of a study, using different participants.

Developmentalists begin with curiosity and then seek the facts, drawing conclusions only after careful research. Indeed, **replication**—the repetition of a study, using different participants—is often a fifth step, needed before conclusions are accepted by the scientific community. Since scientists are human, some prejudices lurk in what they decide to study and how they study it. The goal, however, is to be as objective as possible, in order to help all people develop their potential. The scientific method is discussed in more detail later in this chapter.

Including All Kinds of People

As the second element of our definition indicates, developmental science includes *all kinds of people*—young and old; rich and poor; of every ethnicity, background, sexuality, culture, and nationality. Developmental research begins with individuals, not groups, although group influences on individuals (such as culture and nationality) are considered as well. For that reason, we will soon highlight how each person's own culture, historical background, and economic status influence his or her individual development. The challenge is to identify universalities and differences and then describe them in ways that simultaneously unify and distinguish each human being.

Both the universal and the unique are evident in each developing person. For example, your father's father's father was once a boy who never sent a text message, was not vaccinated against chicken pox, and did not fear nuclear war. That much is universal, relevant to understanding great-grandfathers. Also universal is that his life affects you, even if you never knew him. None of his descendants is totally untouched (for better or worse) by his values and behavior. Further, about 12 percent of your genes were his as well, including, if you are male, his Y chromosome.

AP PHOTO / HIDAJET DELIC

All the Same, All Different At first glance, all these boys look the same, in age, background, religion, ethnicity, and experience. They have fled war-torn Kosovo and are shown resting at a refugee center near Sarajevo, Bosnia. A closer look reveals that each of them, like every other human, is unique in background and experience.

Yet your great-grandfather is (or was) unique. No one exactly like him will ever live again. His effect on you depends on dozens of other factors, again unique to you. Your study of development will help you discover his influence, perhaps helping you fight or follow his lead, but he might be one reason why you laugh, or learn, or believe as you do.

The Nature–Nurture Controversy

This example highlights a great puzzle of development, the *nature–nurture controversy*. **Nature** refers to the influence of genes that people inherit. **Nurture** refers to environmental influences, beginning with the health and diet of the embryo's mother and continuing lifelong, including family, school, community, and society. Both nature and nurture affect everyone, always, but how much and in what ways are hotly disputed.

nature A general term for the traits, capacities, and limitations that each individual inherits genetically from his or her parents at the moment of conception.

nurture A general term for all the environmental influences that affect development after an individual is conceived.

The nature–nurture controversy has many other names, among them *heredity versus environment* and *maturation versus learning*. Under whatever name, the basic question is: How much of any characteristic, behavior, or pattern of development is the result of genes and how much is the result of experience?

Note the question is "how much," not "which," because both genes and the environment affect every characteristic. Nature and nurture are always contributing to every aspect of development. Further, each contribution always affects the others. Thus, genes elicit a certain kind of nurture, and that nurture in turn affects the genes. This is most evident when a temperamentally difficult child is quick to cry in anger. That response may cause the parents to be more punishing, and that punishment may strengthen the angry responses of the child. Thus nature affects nurture, and then nurture affects nature (Moffitt et al., 2006; Reiss et al., 2000).

Consequently, when developmentalists study "all kinds of people," they search for generalities, for universals. But they also remember that each person's unique combination of nature and nurture means that information about one person—say, a 10-year old Chinese girl—may help us understand other girls, or other Chinese, or other 10-year-olds, but does not necessarily apply to any other 10-year-old Chinese girl. It is a mistake to consider anyone of any gender, nationality, or age as identical to the others.

Difference Is Not Necessarily Deficit

A worse mistake would be to consider every deviation a problem. Something that is odd, weird, or rare may be merely odd, weird, or rare—and not problematic at all. Every human tends to think that his or her way of child rearing, of believing, of being is best. That tendency has many benefits; it is helpful to think that our ways are good. But if one way is best, are other ways worse? Is that mother I heard yelling at her child in the supermarket (which I would never do) wrong and ignorant, perhaps abusive? If I decided she was, I would be committing a **difference-equals-deficit error.** Such mistakes are one reason we need science. Differences are not necessarily wrong or right; the scientific method is needed for accurate assessments of deviations from the norm.

difference-equals-deficit error The mistaken belief that a deviation from some norm is necessarily inferior to behavior or characteristics that meet the standard.

The error of assuming that a difference is a deficit may be made clearer with an example. It was once widely assumed that children with disabilities were not only different, but deficient—unable to behave normally and to learn what able children could. Since they were pitied and excluded from most schools, data supported this assumption. For instance, deaf children could not talk, read, or even think as well as other children could.

Their problems were particularly glaring with regard to reading, since fluency in language precedes fluid reading; because deaf children had few words, they could not recognize words when they saw them on the page. If they were admitted to school, their teachers tried to make them as similar to hearing children as possible: Normal language (speech) was taught, and the use of sign language was forbidden. However, when researchers stopped assuming that differences were deficits, they discovered that sign language activates the language areas of infant brains and that deaf children can communicate as well, and as quickly, as hearing children. If deaf infants are taught appropriately, their intellect matches that of other children (Schick et al., 2007). Some even become fluent in reading the printed word (Goldin-Meadow & Mayberry, 2001).

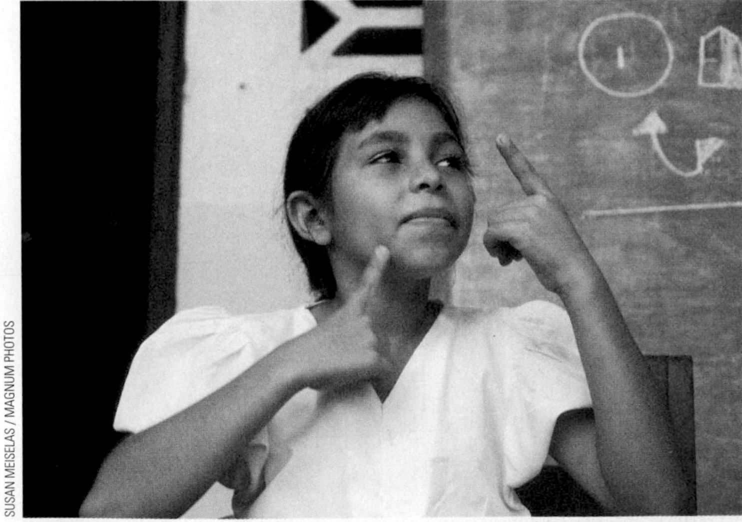

SUSAN MEISELAS / MAGNUM PHOTOS

Just Different, Not Deficient A young girl uses Nicaraguan Sign Language, invented in the 1970s by children at the school for the deaf that she attends in Managua. Sign language conveys meaning perfectly well and is not inferior to speech, as most educators once assumed.

A surprise was discovered at a boarding school for deaf children in Nicaragua. The teachers never used sign language, but the children themselves developed gestures to express complex ideas (including grammatical devices such as placement and movement of finger signs), creating an elaborate sign language that was improved by each new generation of deaf children who came to the school (Senghas et al., 2004). This indicated advanced intelligence that no one had expected the children to have. Similarly, other studies find some deaf children to be extraordinarily expressive, perceptive, and creative. Their difference may be an asset, not a liability, in many areas of life (Marschark & Spencer, 2003).

Currently, some hearing parents teach their hearing babies sign language, hoping to accelerate the child's later learning (Goodwyn et al., 2000). Researchers find that all children learn better when they use gestures as well as words (Cook et al., 2008). Education is being transformed by such discoveries—advances that were not expected when differences were assumed to be deficits.

Observing Changes over Time

The third crucial element in the definition of developmental science is the issue of whether individuals *change or remain the same over time.* The science of human development studies all the transformations and consistencies of human life, from

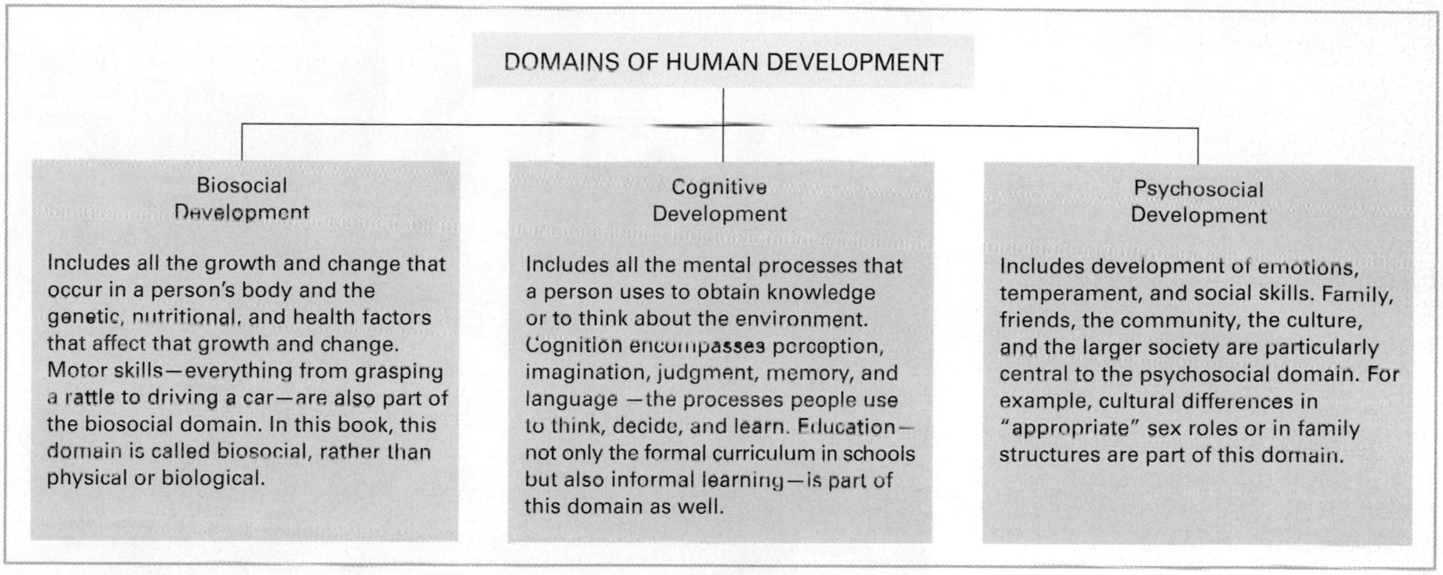

DOMAINS OF HUMAN DEVELOPMENT		
Biosocial Development	Cognitive Development	Psychosocial Development
Includes all the growth and change that occur in a person's body and the genetic, nutritional, and health factors that affect that growth and change. Motor skills—everything from grasping a rattle to driving a car—are also part of the biosocial domain. In this book, this domain is called biosocial, rather than physical or biological.	Includes all the mental processes that a person uses to obtain knowledge or to think about the environment. Cognition encompasses perception, imagination, judgment, memory, and language —the processes people use to think, decide, and learn. Education—not only the formal curriculum in schools but also informal learning—is part of this domain as well.	Includes development of emotions, temperament, and social skills. Family, friends, the community, the culture, and the larger society are particularly central to the psychosocial domain. For example, cultural differences in "appropriate" sex roles or in family structures are part of this domain.

FIGURE 1.1

The Three Domains The division of human development into three domains makes it easier to study, but remember that very few factors belong exclusively to one domain or another. Development is not piecemeal but holistic: Each aspect of development is related to all three domains.

the very beginning to the very end. Sometimes developmentalists even analyze each fraction of a second, determining, for example, that a barely perceptible change in a newborn's facial expression reflects a parent's fleeting glance (Lavelli & Fogel, 2005). More often years, not milliseconds, are analyzed, revealing unexpected twists and turns.

One way in which developmentalists try to divide life into segments is by using chronology, considering each age (infancy, early childhood, and so on) as a separate stage of growth. Another way is by considering three domains of development—*biosocial, cognitive,* and *psychosocial*—that roughly correspond to biology, psychology, and sociology, or body, mind, and social world. (Figure 1.1 provides a detailed description of each domain.)

Even when developmentalists use such divisions, they recognize that each stage affects the others; there is a "reciprocal connection between age-focused developmental specialties [such as infancy, childhood, adolescence, adulthood]" (Baltes et al., 2006, p. 644). Similarly, every type of development touches on all three domains; they all occur simultaneously in each person. For example, although language learning is primarily cognitive, babies start speaking because of a combination of *biosocial development* (maturation of the brain and vocal cords), *cognitive development* (understanding of connections between things and words), and *psychosocial development* (reactions to others' responses). Further, development at every age builds on what has gone before and previews what is to come. Thus, first words are spoken at about age 1, but those words depend on attention from the caregiver in the first months of life, and they provide a foundation for reading at age 5 and beyond.

Dynamic Systems

The interactions of ages (for example, prenatal and postnatal life), domains (body and mind), and people (parent and child) are central to the study of development. One way to highlight this is to take a **dynamic-systems approach,** which

dynamic-systems approach A view of human development as an ongoing, ever-changing interaction between the physical and emotional being and between the person and every aspect of his or her environment, including the family and society.

AP PHOTO / JIM MONE

Dynamic Interaction A dynamic-systems approach highlights the ever-changing impact that each part of a system has on all the other parts. This classroom scene reflects the eagerness for education felt by many immigrants, the reticence of some boys in an academic context, and a global perspective (as demonstrated by the world map). These facets emerge from various systems—family, gender, and culture—and they have interacted to produce this moment.

Observation Quiz (see answer, page 10): What country is this?

Especially for Future Teachers (see response, page 10): Does the classroom furniture shown in the photograph above affect instruction?

stresses the fluctuations and transitions that occur constantly throughout life. In this view, developmental science is "the dynamic synthesis of multiple levels of analysis" (Lerner et al., 2005, p. 38).

The word *systems* captures the idea that a change in one part of a person, family, or society affects all the other aspects because each part is connected. Applying the dynamic-systems approach to human development is a "relatively new" effort (Thelen & Smith, 2006, p. 258), but this perspective has aided natural scientists for decades. They have long recognized that systemic change over time is the nature of life:

> Seasons change in ordered measure, clouds assemble and disperse, trees grow to certain shape and size, snowflakes form and melt, minute plants and animals pass through elaborate life cycles that are invisible to us, and social groups come together and disband.
>
> *[Thelen & Smith, 2006, p. 271]*

Many Directions

At the beginning of the chapter, we noted the five basic characteristics of development. Now we can explain the first of those five terms: Development is *multidirectional,* which literally means "many directions." A multidirectional approach contrasts with an exclusively *linear* (meaning "in a straight line," or one-dimensional) approach, which assumes that continuity is always evident. By using a dynamic-systems approach, developmentalists have gathered data indicating that almost all human change shows not only accelerations and decelerations (which may be linear) but also curves, zigzags, and sudden stops.

Many people assume that children's development—both physical and mental—follows a straight, linear growth pattern. Yet multidirectional influences apply even to something as simple as height, not only over the years (babies and adolescents grow faster than children, adults stop growing and then shrink) but also over the months (more growth occurs in summer) and even over the hours (faster growth occurs during sleep).

It is apparent that development follows many paths—up and down, stable or erratic, backtracking or leaping forward. There is evidence for simple growth, radical transformation, improvement, and decline as well as for continuity—day to day, year to year, and generation to generation (see Figure 1.2). A gain and a loss may occur together, and a loss may lead to a gain, or vice versa (Baltes et al., 2006).

One way to express this variability is to acknowledge continuity and discontinuity. **Continuity** refers to characteristics that are stable over time; **discontinuity** refers to characteristics that are unlike those that came before. Both continuity (as with biological sex or temperament) and discontinuity (as with speaking a new language or quitting an addictive drug) are evident in each person's life and with each human characteristic.

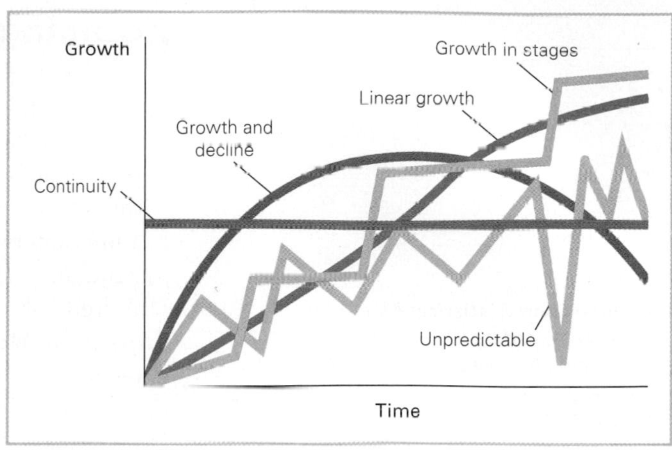

FIGURE 1.2

Patterns of Developmental Growth Many patterns of developmental growth have been discovered by careful research. Although linear (or near-linear) progress seems most common, scientists now find that almost no aspect of human change follows the linear pattern exactly.

IQ (intelligence quotient, explained in detail in Chapter 11) is a much-studied example. Usually, a person's IQ scores show continuity: A 3-year-old of normal intelligence is likely to become a normally intelligent 13-year-old and 33-year-old. However, for some children, IQ scores rise and fall and then rise again over time (Caspi et al., 1996; Dietz et al., 2007; Hoekstra et al., 2007). The same is true for almost every trait.

Although change is multidirectional, the paths of development are not random. For instance, if IQ scores rise, it is usually because of some change in circumstances, such as an improvement in the home or school.

Developmentalists seek to understand the patterns of change at various ages and for various reasons. For this effort, another pair of concepts—critical period and sensitive period—are useful. A **critical period** is a time when certain things *must* occur for normal development. For example, the fetus develops arms and legs, hands and feet, fingers and toes, each on a particular day between 21 and 50 days after conception. If this critical period for limb development is disrupted, then the child never develops normal extremities. In one tragic episode, between 1957 and 1961, thousands of pregnant women in 30 nations took a new prescription sedative called thalidomide during this critical period, and their babies were born with missing or deformed extremities.

At certain points during early childhood, there may be a **sensitive period,** when a particular development occurs most easily. One example is language. If children do not master a first language during the sensitive period between ages 1 and 3 years, they may still do so later (hence this is not a critical period), but they will have more difficulty. Similarly, some (but not all) researchers believe that the years before puberty may be a sensitive period for learning a second or third language, although not every scholar agrees this is the case (Birdsong, 2006; Hershensohn, 2007).

continuity Signifies developments over time that appear to persist, unchanging, from one age to the next. Parents might recognize the same personality traits in their grown children that they saw in them as infants.

discontinuity Signifies developments that appear quite different from those that came before. A person, or a researcher, might believe that "everything changed" when school started or when puberty began, for instance.

critical period A time when a particular type of developmental growth (in body or behavior) must happen. If the critical period passes without that growth, the person will never grow in that particular way.

sensitive period A time when a certain type of development is most likely to happen and happens most easily. If that development does not occur during that sensitive period, it could still occur later. For example, early childhood is considered a sensitive period for language learning.

SUMMING UP

Human development can be studied in many ways because each person is unique as well as similar to every other human being. The scientific study of development begins with curiosity and then follows a specific sequence, from hypothesis to data collection to conclusions that are based on empirical evidence, not on wishful thinking or prejudice.

Nature and nurture always interact. A dynamic-systems approach finds continuity as well as discontinuity, erratic change as well as linear progress, gains as well as losses throughout life. Development is multidirectional, with the specific directions varying by domain, by individual, and by time. ■

Zooming In and Zooming Out

The science of human development has been stretched in opposite directions over the past few decades. Developmentalists are delving more deeply into developing persons and looking more broadly at the contexts around them, as if adjusting a photographer's lens or a computer screen to zoom in to the neurons and genes within each person and to zoom out to the surrounding contexts.

One example of this deeper and broader investigation is apparent in the plans for the next edition of the guidelines for classifying psychological disorders. Hundreds of psychiatrists are drafting the fifth edition of the ***Diagnostic and Statistical Manual of Mental Disorders*** (DSM), a guide used to diagnose psychological problems. The fifth edition is not projected to be published until 2011, but experts already agree that it will differ in two ways from the fourth edition (APA, 2000): It will include more material on genetics and on human relationships (Beach et al., 2006). These changes for DSM-V reflect the new understanding of development. We must consider what we learn about genetic makeup (zooming in) and also what we learn about social contexts (zooming out).

Diagnostic and Statistical Manual of Mental Disorders (DSM) The American Psychiatric Association's official guide to the diagnosis (not treatment) of mental disorders.

Especially for Science Majors (see response, page 12): Do "zooming in" and "zooming out" now occur in the natural sciences as well as in the social sciences?

Many Disciplines

Scientists from many academic disciplines, each with his or her unique perspective, have always contributed to the study of human development; together their contributions provide a full view of the whole person. Thus the science of human development is *multidisciplinary;* this second of the five characteristics is necessitated by the complexity of each life.

Many forces pull scientists to stick to a narrow discipline (zooming in), researching one activity of one species at one age. A tight focus provides detailed understanding of, for instance, the rhythms of vocalization among 3-month-old infants, or the way schoolchildren learn to add, or the effects of alcohol on adolescent mice. (Each of these topics has been studied extensively, and the results inform later sections of this book.)

However, developmentalists are constantly reminded that each person develops simultaneously in every domain, always affected by both broader contexts (zooming out, as with culture) and tiny molecules (such as genetic codes). Consequently, many more disciplines besides the three primary ones (biology, psychology, and sociology) contribute to the science of human development. Neuroscience, history, medicine, education, genetics, political science, economics, demography, anthropology, and others make development a multidisciplinary study. As one expert explains, "The study of development is a huge community enterprise that spans generations and many disciplines" (Moore, 2002, p. 74). Multidisciplinary research is necessary because humans develop simultaneously in many domains, in multifaceted contexts, and in diverse cultures.

➤Answer to Observation Quiz (from page 8): The Three Somali girls wearing headscarves may have thrown you off, but these first-graders attend school in Minneapolis, Minnesota, in the United States. Clues include the children's diversity (few countries are as multiethnic as the United States; this particular school has students from 17 nations), the children's clothing (obviously Western), and—for the sharp-eyed—the flag near the door.

➤Response for Future Teachers (from page 8): Yes. Every aspect of the environment affects what happens within that space. In this classroom, tables and movable chairs foster group collaboration and conversation—potent learning methods that are difficult to achieve when desks and seats are bolted to the floor in rows and the teacher sits or stands at the front of the room.

The need to consider many levels of development has been emphasized by a leading scholar, Urie Bronfenbrenner, who recommended an **ecological-systems approach** to developmental study (1977). He argued that, just as a naturalist studying an organism examines the *ecology,* or the interrelationship of the organism and its entire environment, developmentalists need to examine all the systems that surround the development of each person.

ecological-systems approach The view that in the study of human development, the person should be considered in all the contexts and interactions that constitute a life.

Bronfenbrenner described three nested levels that affect each person (diagrammed in Figure 1.3): *microsystems* (elements of the immediate surroundings, such as a child's family and peer group), *exosystems* (local institutions, such as school and church), and *macrosystems* (the larger social setting, including cultural values, economic policies, and political processes).

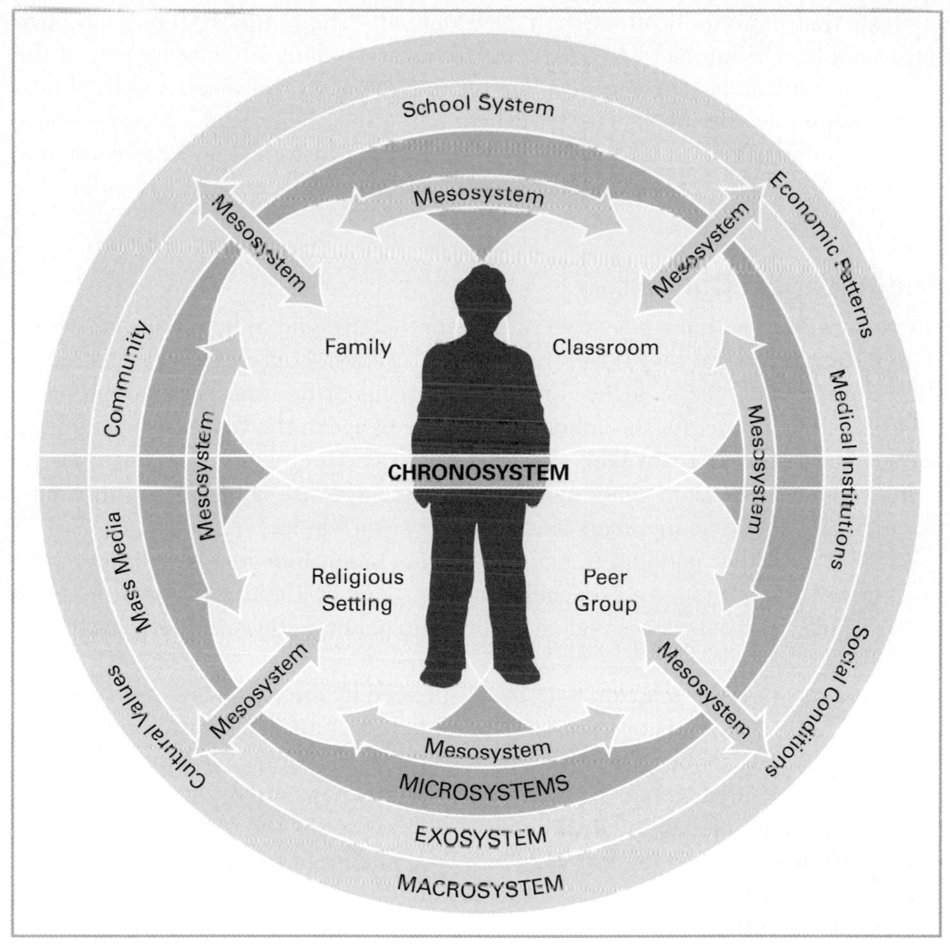

FIGURE 1.3

The Ecological Model According to developmental researcher Uric Bronfenbrenner, each person is significantly affected by interactions among a number of overlapping systems, which provide the context of development. *Microsystems*—family, peer groups, classroom, neighborhood, house of worship—intimately and immediately shape human development. *Mesosystems* refer to interactions among systems, as when parents coordinate their efforts with teachers to educate the child. Surrounding and supporting the microsystems are the *exosystems,* which include all the external networks, such as community structures and local educational, medical, employment, and communications systems, that influence the microsystems. Influencing all three of these systems is the *macrosystem,* which includes cultural values, political philosophies, economic patterns, and social conditions. Bronfenbrenner added a fifth system, the *chronosystem,* to emphasize the importance of historical time, and now the entire concept is called *bioecological,* to include biology.

Recognizing the importance of historical conditions, Bronfenbrenner described the *chronosystem* (literally, "time system"), which affects the other three systems. He also appreciated the dynamic interaction of the microsystem, exosystem, and macrosystem, and he named a fifth system, the *mesosystem,* which connects systems. One example of a mesosystem is the interface between home and school, including various communication processes between a child's parents and teachers (such as letters home, parent–teacher conferences, phone calls, back-to-school nights). Another mesosystem is made up of all the connections between a person's work and family life. These include not only the direct impact of family-leave policies and work hours but also such indirect connections as unemployment rates, minimum wage standards, and hiring practices, each of which may affect the children of a family.

Throughout his life, Bronfenbrenner emphasized studying humans in natural settings, as they actually live their lives, including their physical well-being. He renamed his approach *bioecological theory* to take the role of biology (zooming in) into account (Bronfenbrenner & Morris, 2006).

Social Contexts

One crucial way to consider a broader perspective on each person (to zoom out) is to take a *multicontextual* approach. This is the third characteristic of developmental science. As bioecological theory emphasizes, humans develop within dozens of contexts that profoundly affect their development. The family system is an obvious example. The interactions between parents and among siblings are part of the context in which each person develops. Family contexts are discussed in almost every chapter in this book. Here we highlight two other social contexts whose influence may not be as obvious as the family's: the historical and the economic contexts. A multicontextual understanding of development requires consideration of both of these.

The Historical Context

cohort A group of people who were born at about the same time and thus move through life together, experiencing the same historical events and cultural shifts at about the same age.

All persons born within a few years of one another are said to be a **cohort,** whose shared age means that they travel through life together. Each person is affected by the values, events, technologies, and culture of his or her era. For example, attitudes about war differ for the cohorts who came of age in the United States during World War II, the Vietnam War, and the Gulf War. Much attention is paid to the beliefs of the baby-boom generation because its large size is having an unusually powerful impact on its members and on society as a whole.

If you doubt that national trends and events touch individuals, consider your first name—a word chosen especially for you. Look at Table 1.1, which lists the most popular names for boys and girls born into cohorts 20 years apart, beginning in 1927.

Your name and your reaction to it are influenced by the era. If you wish you had another name, blame history, not your parents. Of course, the historical context includes attitudes about gender. Throughout the past century, parents of all backgrounds have tended to give boys more traditional names than girls. And in the United States, ethnic and biblical names (such as Jacob—near the top every year since 1999 but number 367 in 1962) have become more popular than traditional names (such as Robert, which was first or second every year until 1954, but fell to number 47 in 2007).

Interesting data about names come from contemporary Hispanic families in Los Angeles (Sue & Telles, 2007). More newborn boys are given Spanish names, such as Carlos and José, than girls, who are likely to be named like their non-Hispanic playmates, with names such as Emily or Ashley rather than Ana Maria or Consuela.

VINCE DE WITT / STOCK, BOSTON

Not the Typical Path This woman's lifelong ambition is to walk the 2,160-mile Appalachian Trail from Maine to Georgia. She is considerably more active than the average member of her cohort.

"And this is Charles, our web-master."

Computer Expert in a Baseball Cap Cohort differences become most apparent when new technology appears. Which age group is most likely to download music onto iPods or to send text messages on cellular phones?

➤Response for Science Majors (from page 10): Yes. Every science has become deeper (zooming in) and broader (zooming out) in recent decades. For example, biology now zooms in to study micro RNA (tiny transcription factors that affect DNA) and zooms out to examine climate change (a global phenomenon that occurs not only from year to year but also over millennia).

TABLE 1.1

Which First Names for U.S. Girls and Boys Were Most Popular in 1927, 1947, 1967, 1987, and 2007?

Year	Top Five Girls' Names	Top Five Boys' Names
______	Mary, Dorothy, Betty, Helen, Margaret	Robert, John, James, William, Charles
______	Lisa, Kimberly, Michelle, Mary, Susan	Michael, David, James, John, Robert
______	Emily, Isabella, Emma, Ava, Madison	Jacob, Michael, Ethan, Joshua, Daniel
______	Linda, Mary, Patricia, Barbara, Sandra	James, Robert, John, William, Richard
______	Jessica, Ashley, Amanda, Jennifer, Sarah	Michael, Christopher, Matthew, Joshua, David

Source: Social Security Administration Web site, http://www.ssa.gov/OACT/babynames/; retrieved June 17, 2008.

Guess First If your answers, in order from top to bottom, were 1927, 1967, 2007, 1947, and 1987, you are excellent at detecting cohort influences. If you made a mistake, perhaps that's because the data are compiled from applications for Social Security numbers during each year, so the names of those who did not get a Social Security number are omitted.

Socioeconomic Status

Social scientists who study family economics rely on **socioeconomic status,** abbreviated **SES.** (Sometimes SES is used to refer to a person's standing in society, or social class, as in "middle class" or "working class.") SES involves much more than money (Gershoff et al., 2007). It includes occupation, education, and place of residence. The SES of a U.S. family consisting of, say, an infant, an unemployed mother, and a father who earns $15,000 a year would be low if the wage earner was an illiterate dishwasher living in a crowded tenement; but it would be much higher if the wage earner was a postdoctoral student living on campus and teaching part time. As this example illustrates, SES includes advantages and disadvantages, opportunities and limitations, past history and future prospects—all of which affect housing, nutrition, material possessions, knowledge, and habits. Although a low income obviously limits a person, other factors (such as education) can make the chances of emerging from poverty better or worse.

socioeconomic status (SES) A person's position in society as determined by income, wealth, occupation, education, place of residence, and other factors.

From a multicontextual viewpoint, it is not surprising that the economic and historical contexts interact. For example, life expectancy for newborns in the United States is strongly influenced by prenatal care, infant nutrition, abuse prevention in childhood, and automobile and driver regulations—all of which have improved over recent decades. Among the results of these improvements are a reduction in the death rate and an increase in the average life span. However, according to a study that divided neighborhoods into tenths, from the lowest to the highest average incomes, improvements have benefited people living in wealthier communities more than others (Singh & Siahpush, 2006; see Figure 1.4).

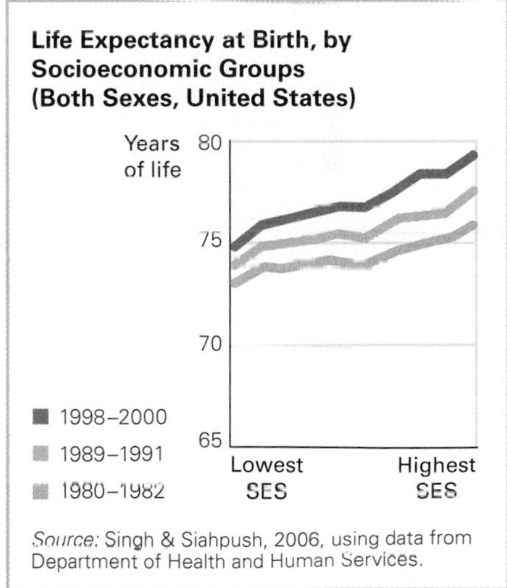

FIGURE 1.4

The Rich Live Longer For every cohort, an increase in income means improved health and longer life. Life expectancy for people at the lowest SES level has increased by only about a year over the past 20 years, while the richest cohort has gained four years.

Although all social scientists acknowledge the power of the economic context, exactly how potent SES is thought to be is affected partly by the particular social science discipline (sociologists believe SES is more influential than geneticists do) and partly by national origin (Europeans believe it is more difficult to escape childhood SES than North Americans do) (Alesina & Edward, 2004). Those differences are among the reasons developmentalists are *multidisciplinary* and *multicontextual,* as you just learned, and *multicultural,* as we now explain.

Culture and Development

People in different cultures hold varied views of development, and from the very beginning humans are profoundly affected by the cultures that surround them.

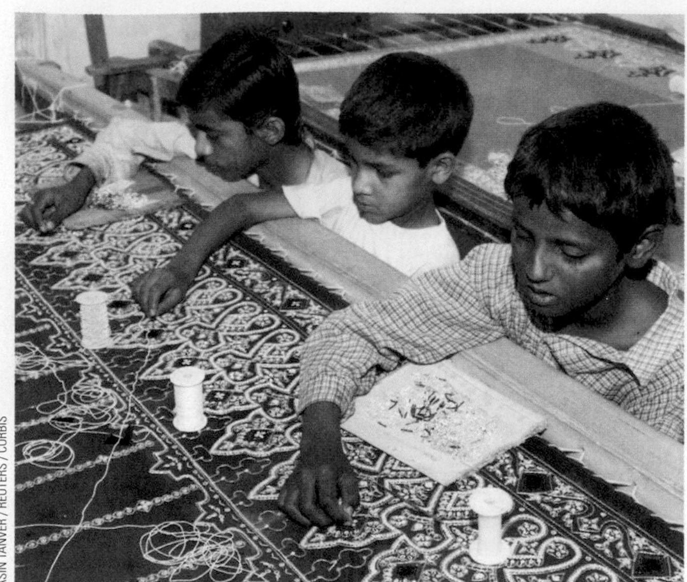

ASIN TANVER / REUTERS / CORBIS

Culturally Acceptable Putting very young children to work is still a widespread custom in many parts of the world. The International Labor Organization estimates that, worldwide, 246 million children aged 5 to 17 are employed—often at very low wages. The children pictured here are working in an embroidery shop in Pakistan.

Observation Quiz (see answer, page 16): Why are they using only their right hands?

Thus "the most basic universal condition of infancy is that all children live in culture. . . . Human infants do not survive outside of culture" (Nelson, 2007, p. 59). To understand what is universal and what is unique about each person's development, it is crucial to consider diverse cultural influences. This requirement has given rise to the fourth characteristic of developmental science: It is *multicultural*.

When social scientists use the term *culture*, they refer to the "patterns of behavior that are passed from one generation to the next . . . [and] that serve as the resources for the current life of a social group" (Cole, 2005, p. 49). The social group may be citizens of a nation, residents of a region within a nation, members of an ethnic group, people living in one neighborhood, or even students in a college class.

Any group may have its own culture—its own values, customs, clothes, dwellings, cuisine, and assumptions. Culture affects every action—indeed, every thought. Thus, to understand anyone's development, scientists zoom out to consider the cultures in which that person is immersed. Have you ever wondered why some of your classmates use highlighters, study in the library, and call professors by their first names, while others do not? The answer may be culture.

A recent technique to measure prejudice is called the *Implicit Association Test*, which measures the milliseconds of hesitation as people categorize others by race, gender, and so on (Baron & Banaji, 2006). The fact that unconscious biases show up in such a measure reveals that cultural assumptions affect everyone, even unconsciously.

Children resist and adults abandon some cultural traditions and values when historical, economic, geographical, or family circumstances change (Smedley & Smedley, 2005). Developmentalists now take a *multicultural* (many cultures) approach, not a merely *cross-cultural* (across cultures) approach. The term *multicultural* recognizes that the dynamic changes each person undergoes are influenced by many different cultural variables. Culture is not confined to customs and objects; rather it is a system that gives meaning, happiness, and direction to life (Matsumoto, 2007). Therefore, everyone is affected by many cultures, rejecting

AP PHOTO / CHARLES REX ARBOGAST

The Culture of Poverty In this southern Illinois neighborhood, littered yards are part of a "culture of poverty" that also includes poor nutrition, substandard housing, and an average life expectancy of 52 years.

Observation Quiz (see answer, page 16): A 13-year-old is in this photo, trying to garden. Can you find her?

some parts of one culture and accepting some parts of others. Cultures themselves are dynamic, not static—they are always changing as people change.

Ethnicity and Race

Confusion arises whenever people—scientists or nonscientists—refer to ethnic groups, races, cultures, and socioeconomic classes, because these categories overlap. The preceding discussion and the following definitions may dispel this confusion.

People of an **ethnic group** share certain attributes, almost always including ancestral heritage and often national origin, religion, culture, and language (Whitfield & McClearn, 2005). (*Heritage* refers to customs and traditions passed down from elders; *national origin* refers to the place where one's ancestors were born.) Ethnic categories arise from history, sociology, and psychology, not from biology.

The term **race,** in contrast, has been used to categorize people on the basis of biology, particularly outward appearance. However, appearance is not a reliable indicator of biological differences. For instance, about 95 percent of the genetic differences between one person and another occur *within,* not between, supposed racial groups. Skin color is often considered the most salient racial marker, but genetic variation is particularly apparent among dark-skinned people whose ancestors were African (Tishkoff & Kidd, 2004). Race is misleading as a biological category. Instead, race is a **social construction,** an idea created by society.

Social constructions are not without power, however: Perceived racial differences lead to discrimination, and racial identity affects cognition (see the discussion of *stereotype threat* in Chapter 15). As one team of psychologists expressed it, "Race is a social construction wherein individuals [who are] labeled as being of different races on the basis of physical characteristics are often treated as though they belong to biologically defined groups" (Goldston et al., 2008, p. 14). Differential treatment is a potent influence on development.

When comparing people of many cultural backgrounds, it is apparent that racial categories are fluid and variable. Racial boundaries were crucial for North Americans during the nineteenth century but are not so important for South Americans in the twenty-first century (Spickard, 2007). People of Arab ancestry are "White" in the United States but "non-White" in England, another social construction that is changing.

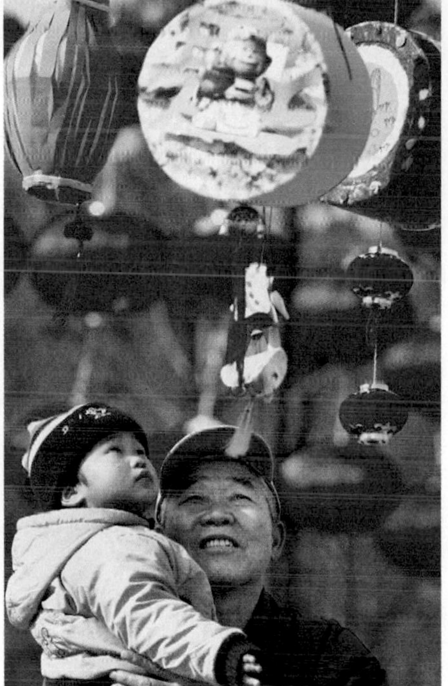

ZHOU GUANGLI / XINHUA PRESS / CORBIS

Heritage Aloft At least 10 major ethnic groups make up China's population of more than a billion. This man shows his grandson the multicolored lanterns displayed on Lantern Day in Hangzhou. Other nations, and other parts of China, have no Lantern Day festival, but all have special traditional celebrations of their own.

ethnic group People whose ancestors were born in the same region and who often share a language, culture, and religion.

race A group of people who are regarded by themselves or by others as distinct from other groups on the basis of physical appearance.

social construction An idea that is built on shared perceptions, not on objective reality. Many age-related terms, such as *childhood, adolescence, yuppie,* and *senior citizen,* are social constructions.

REUTERS / JEFF J MITCHELL

No Raisins? For centuries at St. Andrews University in Scotland, new students gave seniors a pound of raisins or else got dunked in a fountain. Wine has replaced raisins, and foam is sprayed instead of water—but on Raisin Monday a social construction lives on.

➤Answer to Observation Quiz (from page 14): They are actually using both hands. The left hand pulls the needle from underneath. Note that they work in rhythm—to keep up the pace as well as to avoid getting in each other's way.

➤Answer to Observation Quiz (from page 14): A teenager named Carolyn, in an orange shirt, is at the far left.

Ethnic Groups and Social Class

To further complicate categorization, SES overlaps with ethnicity and race, and culture influences all three. One careful study found many health differences among Americans of African, Asian, European, and Hispanic heritage living in New England, but on deeper analysis, at least half of those differences could be traced to SES (Krieger et al., 2005). Efforts to disentangle SES, ethnicity, and culture always find substantial overlap among them.

One example of the interaction of SES and ethnicity is found in sleep patterns. As described in detail in Chapter 5, where an infant sleeps—in which bed, in which room, and so on—varies markedly among people of various cultures and incomes. Similarly, all school-age children benefit from getting enough sleep, but disturbed sleep takes a greater toll if the child is low income and African American (Buckhalt et al., 2007).

Genetic Codes and Brain Activity

Genes affect everything, including most psychological disorders. So does the individual's environment. By zooming out, developmental researchers can shed light on the effects of nurture—the individual's family and social context. By zooming in, they can add to our understanding of nature—the individual's inborn characteristics. And, as we shall see, they almost always find that nature and nurture interact.

The MAOA Gene and Violence

One of the human problems that developmentalists continually seek to understand is why some young people become violent, hurting others as well as themselves. Zooming out has revealed many factors in the social context that contribute to this problem, including past child abuse and current SES. The violent delinquent is often a boy who was beaten in childhood and who now lives in a violent, drug-filled, crowded neighborhood (Maas et al., 2008).

Yet some boys who live under such conditions, past and current, nonetheless avoid becoming violent. Zooming in to look at genes and brain factors helps explain how this happens. Each person has about 3 billion pairs of genetic messages, on about 20,000 genes. Most genes are the same for every mammal, but occasionally a gene can be inherited in more than one version. All this is explained in Chapter 3, but for now you need to understand just one example. One genetic variant occurs in the code for an enzyme, monoamine oxidase A (MAOA), which affects chemicals in the brain called *neurotransmitters.* This gene comes in two versions, one producing higher levels of the enzyme than the other. Both versions are quite normal; about a third of all people whose genes have been analyzed have the lower-MAOA version.

FIGURE 1.5

Genetic Origins for Violent Crime Two variables—parental treatment and a variant of the gene that produces the enzyme MAOA—interact to affect the likelihood that a child will commit a violent crime. Of the boys in the "probable maltreatment" category, 10 percent were convicted of a violent crime if their MAOA level was high, but 26 percent were convicted if their MAOA was low.

Observation Quiz (see answer, page 18): Which combination of the two variables is most protective against violent criminality?

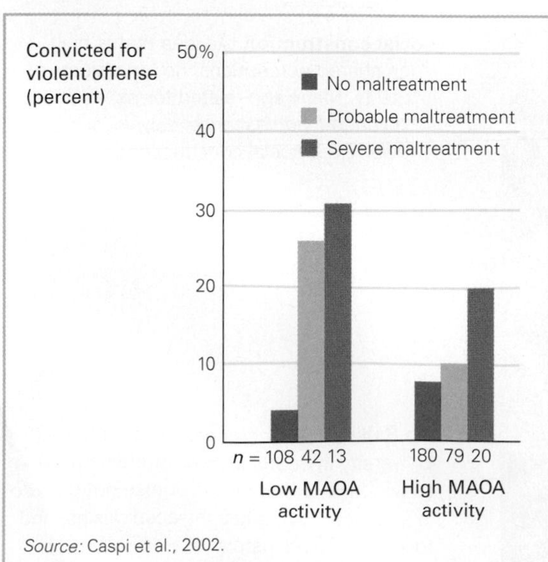

One study began with virtually every child born in Dunedin, New Zealand, between April 1, 1972, and March 31, 1973. They and their families were examined on dozens of measures from early childhood on. One measure was whether or not the children were maltreated. Another measure was which variant of the MAOA gene they had inherited. Boys who were mistreated by their parents were about twice as likely to be overly aggressive (to develop a conduct disorder, to be violent, to be antisocial, and eventually to be convicted of a violent crime) if they had the low-MAOA gene instead of the high-MAOA gene (Caspi et al., 2002) (see Figure 1.5).

Does this mean that becoming a violent criminal is genetic? No. As Figure 1.5 shows, *if* they were not maltreated, boys with the low-MAOA gene were more likely to become law-abiding, peaceable adults. Of course, all parents should treat their children well, but if the child is a boy with this gene, the effects of parenting can be extreme.

Mirror Neurons

In addition to looking at the interplay of the social context and genetic factors, developmentalists can zoom in to understand each person as never before, using new measures of brain activity. For example, about a decade ago, neuroscientists noticed that parts of a monkey's brain responded to actions the monkey observed as if the actions were being performed by the monkey itself. Thus, when one monkey watched another reach for a piece of fruit, the same brain areas were activated in both monkeys. This response originated in the F5 area of the monkey premotor cortex, where certain brain cells, dubbed **mirror neurons,** were found (Rizzolatti & Craighero, 2004).

mirror neurons Brain cells that fire both when an individual performs an action and when the individual observes the same action performed by someone else.

The implications of this discovery quickly crossed disciplines and species. Scientists "turned to the human brain and found neural activity that mirrors not only the movement but also the intentions, sensations, and emotions of those around us" (G. Miller, 2005, p. 945). Another researcher agrees that "the human mirror neuron system may allow us to go beyond imitating the observed motor acts of others to infer their intentions and perhaps even their states of mind" (Coward, 2008, p.1494). As "cognitive science meets neurophysiology" (Garbarini & Adenzato, 2004, p. 100), researchers have demonstrated that human mirror neurons probably affect learning and thinking.

An observer's mirror neurons are especially likely to respond if the person understands what he or she observes. For example, when people who are already experts in dance or in martial arts watch someone else perform those skills, the brains of the observers light up in the areas that would be activated if they themselves were performing (Calvo-Merino et al., 2005).

Scientists in many disciplines are trying to understand the implications and limitations of this discovery (Rizzolatti & Sinigaglia, 2008; Soekadar et al., 2008). Mirror neurons may be relevant to such topics as cultural transmission, autism, language learning, and sympathy for other people. These neurons are present in children and even in babies—which makes developmentalists speculate that the

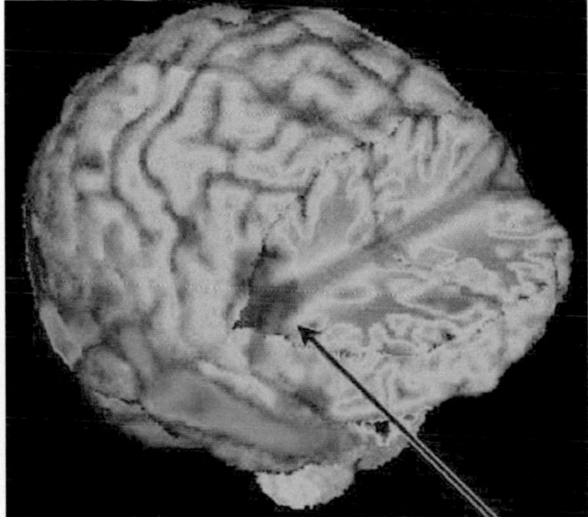

NATACHA PISARENKO / AP

Lighting Up In the photograph at left, the arrow points to a web of neurons that are activated not only when a monkey uses motor abilities (as in reaching for a banana) but also when the monkey sees another perform that action. At right, these kindergartners in Buenos Aires may be exhibiting mirror neurons at work as they get ready to join other fans in cheering on Argentina's soccer team in a match against Peru.

➤Answer to Observation Quiz (from page 16): Low MAOA (surprisingly) and no maltreatment is the most protective combination.

action of mirror neurons is one reason young children learn so quickly (Chen et al., 2004; Lepage & Théoret, 2006).

Many scientists believe that infants develop their own emotions as they watch the emotional expressions of others (Tronick, 2007). This may include learning to become depressed, as the following feature suggests.

a view from science

Depression and the Brain

One reason that ongoing discoveries in genetics and neuroscience are thrilling to many developmentalists is that they reveal the importance of nongenetic influences. This may seem paradoxical, because every person's genes are set at conception, 38 weeks before birth, and basic brain structures are formed prenatally, beginning in the third week after conception.

But the same research that has found the power of the 20,000 or so human genes (half of them for brain development) also finds that nutrition, education, and child rearing are crucial; they enhance or dampen the effect of every gene. This is especially true for emotions, impulses, and anxieties, all of which originate in the brain and develop during childhood (Fries & Pollak, 2007; Johnson, 2007).

Consider research on depression. There is no doubt that depression is partly genetic—a matter of brain chemicals that pervade some people's central nervous systems and make them feel sad and uninterested in life. There is also no doubt that depression is developmental, with rates of depression increasing and decreasing at certain points of the life span (Kapornai & Vetró, 2008). For instance, depression suddenly increases in early adolescence, particularly among girls, who are about four times as likely to be depressed as younger children of either sex. Remember the need for multicontextual and multicultural understanding, however. Depression is not solely genetic, and its patterns are not purely biological.

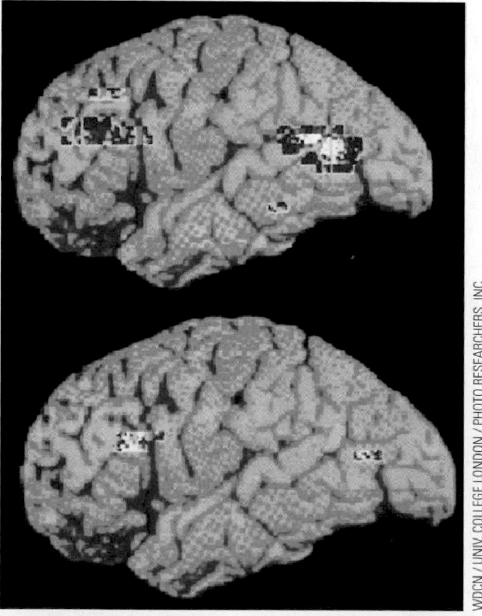

WDCN / UNIV. COLLEGE LONDON / PHOTO RESEARCHERS, INC.

Red Means Stop At top, the red areas on this PET scan show abnormally low metabolic activity and blood flow in a depressed person's brain, in contrast to the normal brain at bottom.

Depressed mothers smile and talk to their infants less, and the infants become less active and verbal. The connection between maternal and infant depression does not prove that the mother's behavior *caused* the infant's depression. The infants may have inherited a tendency toward depression from their mothers, or the causal connection may start with an unresponsive infant who makes the mother depressed, instead of vice versa. Many experts, however, are convinced that maternal depression precedes infant depression. One who has investigated mother–infant interaction for decades relates that he once

> asked nondepressed mothers of 3-month-old infants to simulate depression for 3 minutes. The mothers were asked to speak in a monotone, to keep their faces flat and expressionless, to slouch back in their chair, to minimize touch, and to imagine that they felt tired and blue. The infants . . . reacted strongly, . . . cycling among states of wariness, disengagement, and distress with brief bids to their mother to resume her normal affective state. Importantly, the infants continued to be distressed and disengaged . . . after the mothers resumed normal interactive behavior.
>
> [*Tronick, 2007, p. 306*]

Research over the years of early childhood finds that a mother's pattern during the first six years of her child's life—for example, going from severe to less severe depression—is echoed by her child. A 1-year-old who is depressed and whose mother is also depressed is likely to still be depressed at age 6 if the mother still is, but is likely to be much happier if the mother's mood has lifted.

One detailed study traced this connection in multiple ways (Ashman et al., 2008). Various measures were first taken when the children were 14 months old, and these measures were repeated at ages 2, 3½, 4½, and 6½. The researchers found that children of mothers whose depression decreased were less aggressive or hyperactive (as rated by their teachers on such observations as "hits other children" and "does not work quietly") than children whose mothers were continually depressed.

Included were measures of heart and brain activity. The 6-year-olds of depressed mothers were physiologically different from the children of nondepressed mothers. Hearts and brains showed that the pattern of the mother's depression over the years had a major impact. If the mother's life circumstances (her relationship with her husband, for instance) improved, she became less depressed. So did her child.

The researchers note that "consistent with previous research, contextual risk factors such as low marital satisfaction and high family conflict were found to mediate the relationship between maternal depression and child behavior measures" (Ashman et al., 2008, p. 74). The authors suggest that the child's home environment might actually change "children's patterns of brain activity as well as their behavioral outcomes" (p. 75).

Every "view from science" has practical implications. Here the lesson is that babies learn about emotions from the reactions of their caregivers (see Chapter 7). If a mother appears depressed, someone else could help her infant by playing happily with the baby every day.

Plasticity

Research on genetics has broadened our understanding of **plasticity,** the idea that, throughout life, humans can be molded (like plastic). An appreciation of plasticity is the fifth characteristic of developmental science. Developmentalists have long believed that plasticity applies to social learning (people can learn new habits). More recently, they have come to believe that plasticity is evident in academic learning as well (illiterate adults can learn to read).

plasticity The idea that abilities, personality, and other human traits can change over time. Plasticity is particularly evident during childhood, but even older adults are not always "set in their ways."

Discoveries in genetics and neuroscience suggest that plasticity may even occur for biologically based traits. The MAOA gene, discussed earlier, is probably not the only one that creates possibilities for both good and ill (Belsky et al., 2007). Plasticity does not mean that anyone can become anything; there are biological, brain-based, and genetic limits on every aspect of growth. But plasticity does mean that each person has potential that is not evident at birth, as I know from my nephew David.

Especially for Doctors and Nurses (see response, page 21): Can immunization protect an embryo?

a personal perspective

Plasticity and My Nephew David

In the spring of 1967 in rural Kentucky, an epidemic of rubella (German measles) reached two more people: my sister-in-law, who had a sore throat for a couple of days, and the embryo she was carrying, who was damaged for life. My nephew was born that November.

"We had our baby," my brother phoned to tell me.

"Wonderful! Boy or girl?" I asked.

"Boy. David. . . . He has some problems. He is scheduled for heart surgery tomorrow. Both eyes have thick cataracts. And more."

"Oh, no! I am so sorry."

"Don't worry. It's not genetic. It won't happen to your baby."

I was heartsick for my brother and his wife, but he was worried that I might find the news stressful, since I was pregnant myself. I soon learned that my baby was fine, but David was not. He required immediate heart surgery, and early removal of one of his cataracts destroyed vision in that eye.

David was born in Appalachia. His father is a professor and his mother is a nurse. Their social, cultural, and economic contexts encouraged them to seek help. They called a counselor, who told them how to help David learn. One instruction was to put him on a large rug to play. If he crawled off the rug, they should say "No" and place him back in the middle. He would learn to use his sense of touch to explore without bumping into walls.

As I watched David grow, I saw that the rubella affected every part of his body, including his jaw, spine, feet, and brain. At age 3, David could not yet talk, chew solid food, use the toilet, coordinate his fingers, or walk normally. An IQ test showed him to be severely mentally retarded. Fortunately, although deafness is common in children with rubella syndrome, David could hear. He learned to talk; his first word, at age 4, was *dada*. By age 5, a new round of surgery repaired his heart and removed the cataract on the other eye, allowing some vision.

By then, the social construction that children with severe disabilities are unteachable was changing. David was enrolled in four schools. Two were for children with cerebral palsy; one of them offered morning classes and the other was open only in the afternoon. Both were closed on Fridays, so on those days David attended a school for the mentally retarded. On Sundays he went to church school—his first experience with "mainstreaming" (the social construction that children with special needs should learn in the same classrooms as other children).

At age 7, David entered regular public school. His motor skills were poor (he had difficulty controlling a pencil), his efforts to read were limited by his faulty vision, and his social skills were impaired (he pinched other children).

By age 10, David had made great strides. He had skipped a year of school and was a fifth-grader. He could read—with a magnifying glass—at the eleventh-grade level. He was kind to everyone. Outside school, he began to learn a second language, play the violin, and sing in the choir. He eventually went to college.

David (at right in the photograph, with his brothers) now works as a translator of German texts. He enjoys doing translations because, he says, "I like providing a service to scholars, giving them access to something they would otherwise not have" (personal communication, 2007). He recently reported that he is

> generally quite happy, but secretly a little happier lately . . . because I have been consistently getting a pretty good vibrato when I am singing, not only by myself but in congregational hymns in church. [I asked what vibrato is; he explained:] When a note bounces up and down within a quarter-tone either way of concert pitch, optimally between 5.5 and 8.2 times per second."

GREG STASSEN

Amazing. David is both knowledgeable and happy, and he continues to develop his skills. He also has a wry sense of humor. When I told him that I wasn't progressing as fast as I wanted to in revising this text, even though I was working every day, he replied, "That sounds just like a certain father I know."

The rubella damage will always be with David, limiting his development. Plasticity does not mean that everything is possible. But biology is not destiny, and medicine can and does save lives and fix problems. One of David's eyes is glass, and he wears a back brace to help his posture. As his aunt, I have watched him defy pessimistic predictions. David is a testament to plasticity, demonstrating that no human is entirely, inevitably, restricted by past experiences. He also embodies the other four characteristics of development, summarized in Table 1.2.

TABLE 1.2

Five Characteristics of Development

Characteristic	Application in David's Story
Multidirectional. Change occurs in every direction, not always in a straight line. Gains and losses, predictable growth, and unexpected transformations are evident.	David's development seemed static (or even regressive, as when early surgery destroyed one eye) but then accelerated each time he entered a new school or college.
Multidisciplinary. Numerous academic fields—especially psychology, biology, education, and sociology, but also neuroscience, economics, religion, anthropology, history, medicine, genetics, and many more—contribute data and insights.	Two disciplines were particularly critical: medicine (David would have died without advances in surgery on newborns) and education (special educators guided him, from the first time he crawled on the rug through specialized preschools and mainstreaming).
Multicontextual. Human lives are embedded in many contexts, including historical conditions, economic constraints, and family patterns.	The high SES of David's family made it possible for him to receive daily medical and educational care. His two older brothers protected him.
Multicultural. Many cultures—not just between nations but also within them—affect how people develop.	Appalachia has a particular culture, including acceptance of people with disabilities and willingness to help families in need. Those aspects of that culture benefited David and his family.
Plasticity. Every individual, and every trait within each individual, can be altered at any point in the life span. Change is ongoing, although it is neither random nor easy.	David's measured IQ changed from about 40 (severely mentally retarded) to about 130 (far above average), and his physical disabilities became less crippling as he matured.

SUMMING UP

Developmental science increasingly includes consideration of the biochemical and sociological influences on a person—two areas that were less significant for earlier researchers. This change has required greater multidisciplinary study, as well as increased emphasis on the many contexts and cultures in which development occurs. As Bronfenbrenner's bioecological approach emphasizes, cohort, culture, and socioeconomic status affect each person's development, and biological factors are always influential. Ethnicity, race, and poverty all impact development as well, with much variation and overlap. Although many constraints affect development, people alter and transcend their demographic categories, demonstrating plasticity: Change is possible throughout life. ■

➤Response for Doctors and Nurses (from page 19): No and yes. Embryos cannot be vaccinated, but immunization can prevent the spread of disease and keep a pregnant woman healthy.

Applying the Scientific Method

We have already stressed that the goal of developmental science is to apply the scientific method in order to reach conclusions based on evidence, not wishful thinking, and thereby build our understanding of the natural and social environment. We begin with curiosity, then ask questions, test hypotheses, gather evidence, and draw conclusions. Now we look at some of the ways in which this is accomplished.

Testing Hypotheses

Remember that once a scientist has posed a question or issue to study, the next step is to form a hypothesis, which is an explicit idea to be tested. The tests may either confirm or refute the hypothesis. In either case, the research has been successful. There are four common ways to test hypotheses: observations, experiments, surveys, and case studies.

Observation

Scientific observation requires the researcher to observe and record behavior systematically. Observations often occur in a natural setting, such as at home, in a school, or in a public park, because such settings encourage people to behave as they usually do. In order not to interfere with the participant's natural behavior, the observer tries to be as unobtrusive as possible.

scientific observation A method of testing a hypothesis by unobtrusively watching and recording participants' behavior in a systematic and objective manner, in a natural setting, in a laboratory, or in searches of archival data.

Observation can also be done in a laboratory or in searches of archival data, such as historical records of births and deaths. You saw an example earlier in the chapter: the U.S. Social Security Administration's record of the names given to newborns over the past century. Observation of that archive revealed the most popular names for babies in a series of cohorts, as listed in Table 1.1.

Some researchers have used observation to understand the questions that children ask. The questions may reveal mistaken logic, as when a 4-year-old boy, seeing a grave being dug in a cemetery, said, "It is only the naughty people who are buried, isn't it, because auntie said all the good people went to heaven" (quoted in Harris, 2000, p. 168). When he was told that everyone is buried, he said, "Oh, heaven must be underground or they couldn't get there."

One researcher decided to explore children's questions in more detail (Chouinard, 2007). She trained parents (all from California, of many ethnic groups) to record every question their children asked. These parental observations revealed that the average child asked two or three questions *per minute.* Most of the questions were designed to gather information, and the parents usually answered as best they could, sometimes adding more information than the child had asked for. This finding was replicated by other research in the United States.

Observation has one major limitation, however: It does not indicate what *causes* people to do what they do. As this researcher explained, "We cannot draw conclusions about causality from these data. . . . [T]here is no evidence that any

Can They See Her? No, and they cannot hear each other. This scientist is observing three deaf boys through a window that is a mirror on the other side. Her observations will help them learn to communicate.

ALAMY

experiment A research method in which the researcher tries to determine the cause-and-effect relationships between two variables by manipulating one (called the *independent variable*) and then observing and recording the resulting changes in the other (called the *dependent variable*).

independent variable In an experiment, the variable that is introduced to see what effect it has on the dependent variable. (Also called *experimental variable*.)

dependent variable In an experiment, the variable that may change as a result of whatever new condition or situation the experimenter adds. In other words, the dependent variable *depends* on the independent variable.

experimental group A group of participants in a research study who experience some special treatment or condition (the independent variable).

comparison group/control group A group of participants in a research study who are similar to the experimental group in all relevant ways but who do not experience the experimental condition (the independent variable).

of the information that children get from asking questions actually goes in, and is used for some purpose, and accomplishes some goal" (Chouinard, 2007, p. 82).

The Experiment

The **experiment** is the research method that scientists use to establish cause. In the social sciences, experimenters typically give people a particular treatment, or expose them to a specific condition, and then note whether their behavior changes.

In technical terms, the experimenters manipulate an **independent variable** (the treatment or special condition, also called the *experimental variable*). They note whether the independent variable affects the specific behavior they are studying, called the **dependent variable** (which, in theory, *depends* on the independent variable). Thus, the independent variable is the new, special treatment; the dependent variable is the result of that treatment. The purpose of an experiment is to find out whether an independent variable affects the dependent variable. Statistics are often used to analyze the results; see Table 1.3 for explanations of some common statistical measures (none of which is perfect).

To make sure a change in the dependent variable is caused by the independent variable, experimenters often compare two groups of participants: One gets the special treatment, and the other, similar in every relevant way, does not. Thus, in a typical experiment (as diagrammed in Figure 1.6), two groups of participants are studied: an **experimental group,** which receives a particular treatment (the independent variable), and a **comparison group** (also called a **control group**), which does not.

TABLE 1.3

Statistical Measures Often Used to Analyze Research Results

Measure	Use
Effect size	Indicates how much one variable affects another. Effect size ranges from 0 to 1: An effect size of 0.2 is called small, 0.5 moderate, and 0.8 large.
Significance	Indicates whether the results might have occurred by chance. A finding that chance would produce the results less than 5 times in 100 is significant at the 0.05 level. A finding that chance would produce the results once in 100 times is significant at 0.01; once in 1,000 times is significant at 0.001.
Cost-benefit analysis	Calculates how much a particular independent variable costs versus how much it saves. This is particularly useful to analyze public spending. For instance, one cost-benefit analysis showed that an expensive preschool program cost $15,166 per child (in 2000 dollars) but saved $215,000 by age 40, in reduced costs of special education, unemployment, prison, and other public expenses (Belfield et al., 2006).
Odds ratio	Indicates how a particular variable compares to a standard, set at 1. For example, one study found that, although less than 1 percent of all child homicides occurred at school, the odds were similar for public and private schools. The odds of such deaths occurring in high schools, however, were 18.47 times that of elementary or middle schools (set at 1.0) (MMWR, January 18, 2008).
Factor analysis	Zooming in and zooming out, we can see hundreds of variables that could affect any behavior. In addition, many variables (such as family income and parental education) may overlap. To take this into account, analysis reveals variables that can be clustered together to form a factor, which is a composite of many variables. For example, SES might become one factor, child personality another.
Meta-analysis	A "study of studies." Researchers use statistical tools to synthesize the results of previous, separate studies. Then they analyze the accumulated results, using criteria that weight each study fairly. This approach improves data analysis by combining the results of studies that used so few participants that the conclusions did not reach significance.

Sources: Alasuntari et al., 2008; Duncan & Magnuson, 2007; Hubbard & Lindsay, 2008.

Who Participates? For all these measures, the characteristics of the people who participate in the study (formerly called the subjects, now called the participants) are important, as is the number of people who are studied. Even a tiny effect size that could be applied to a large population may indicate a useful benefit. For example, the effect size of exercise on heart health is small, but millions of lives would be saved if everyone walked at least an hour a day.

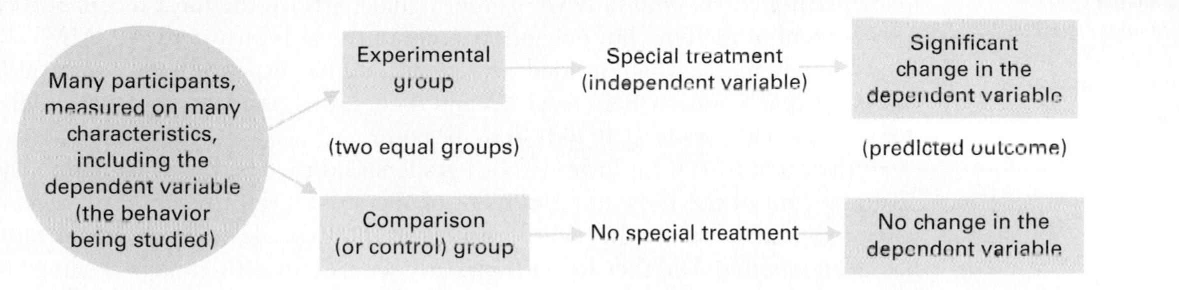

Procedure:

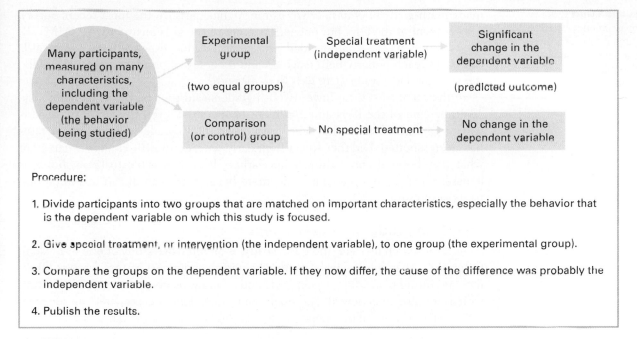

1. Divide participants into two groups that are matched on important characteristics, especially the behavior that is the dependent variable on which this study is focused.

2. Give special treatment, or intervention (the independent variable), to one group (the experimental group).

3. Compare the groups on the dependent variable. If they now differ, the cause of the difference was probably the independent variable.

4. Publish the results.

FIGURE 1.6

How to Conduct an Experiment The basic sequence diagrammed here applies to all experiments. Many additional features, especially the statistical measures listed on page 22 and various ways of reducing experimenter bias, affect whether step 4, publication, occurs. (Scientific journals reject reports of experiments that were not rigorous in method and analysis.)

Observation Quiz (see answer, page 24): Does the experimental group always change?

Remember what the researcher on children's questions wrote: "We cannot draw conclusions about causality from these data." Consequently, she followed up with an experiment (Chouinard, 2007). Young children were asked to guess which of two pictured objects (a cat or a ball, a spoon or a cup, a rose or a daisy) was hidden in a box. Half of the children (the control group) were not allowed to ask questions; they just had to guess. The other half (the experimental group) could ask questions if they wished. Most of the experimental group generated appropriate questions (such as, for the cat or the ball, "Does it roll?"). The data showed that, in six trials, the children in the control group guessed correctly about three out of six times (as would be expected by chance), but the children in the experimental group got more than five of their six guesses right. This experiment showed causality, because the questions led to answers that the children used to guess correctly. Thus, children ask questions to learn, and they listen to the answers.

The application from such research is that adults should answer preschoolers' questions, even though the average child may ask more than a hundred questions per hour. Children learn from the answers to their questions.

Especially for Nurses (see response, page 24): In the field of medicine, why are experiments conducted to test new drugs and treatments?

The Survey

A third research method is the **survey.** Information is collected from a large number of people by interview, questionnaire, or some other means. This is a quick and direct way to obtain data. However, getting valid survey data is not easy, for many reasons. Among those reasons are that some people refuse to answer and others present themselves as they would like to be perceived, not as they really are.

survey A research method in which information is collected from a large number of people by interviews, written questionnaires, or some other means.

A large group of adolescents, representative of all high school students in the United States, are asked dozens of questions every two years, including this one: "Have you had sexual intercourse before age 13?" Every time, more than twice as

➤Answer to Observation Quiz (from page 23): No. Note the word *predicted.* The hypothesis is that change will occur for the experimental group but not the control group, but the reason for doing the experiment is to discover whether that prediction does indeed come true.

many ninth-grade boys answer yes as ninth-grade girls. In the most recent survey, 13.5 percent of the boys but only 4.9 percent of the girls answered yes (MMWR, June 6, 2008, p. 21). That lopsided sex ratio is puzzling, especially since more girls than boys reach puberty before age 13 and their sexual partners are usually older, not younger. Do boys brag, or girls deny, or both?

In the same survey, far fewer twelfth-graders said they had had sex before age 13 (6 percent of the boys and 2 percent of the girls), even though in a previous survey, conducted when the same cohort were ninth-graders, much higher rates had been reported. Did they forget their early sex? Are twelfth-graders ashamed of what they boasted about three years earlier? It is impossible to know, but it is apparent that surveys may not be accurate because of such distortions in participants' responses.

The Case Study

case study A research method in which one individual is studied intensively.

A fourth research method, the **case study,** is an intensive study of one individual. Often the researcher begins by asking the person about past history, current thinking, and future plans. Other people (friends, family, teachers) who know the individual are also interviewed. Although some questions are prepared in advance, follow-up questions allow deeper understanding of each particular case.

Social workers, detectives, and clinical psychologists use case studies professionally, trying to understand the particular influences and characteristics of a person so that the professional can find services, solve a crime, or help the person overcome a problem. Often practitioners present a case study to their colleagues for insight and suggestions. For example, an organization called *Zero to Three* published a book of case studies written by workers who promoted infant mental health (Shirilla & Weatherston, 2002). One case focused on Dee, an unmarried Michigan mother living in a shelter, and her newborn son, Darrell. Dee's foster mother, Mrs. Hill, had thrown her out because she was pregnant. The infant-health worker writes of one visit:

> Darrell was just waking up when I arrived. Dee took him out of his crib and set him on the floor. The room felt cold, and he was wearing a very lightweight cotton wrapper that was too small. . . . Dee didn't seem aware of the cold or Darrell and went on to tell me that she might drop out of school. It was Mrs. Hill's idea to go to school, anyway, and . . .
>
> "She's just a mean old lady! And she has all my winter clothes. She won't give them back to me. I had a beautiful red wool coat that she gave me last Christmas. I have nothing to wear now, and I'm cold."
>
> I responded, "You need a warm winter coat to wrap around you. I know that you really want that red wool coat. Have you asked her to look for it?"
>
> "She says she can't find it. She probably gave it to somebody else."
>
> "It's not fair, Dee. . . . You need a coat to keep you warm." . . .
>
> By now Darrell was crawling very competently between us. She noticed him, touched his legs and exclaimed, "You're cold! You need a warmer outfit on."
>
> She quickly found a clean, heavier stretchy suit. "I don't want my baby to get sick!"
>
> *[Weatherston, 2002, p. 194]*

➤Response for Nurses (from page 23): Experiments are the only way to determine cause-and-effect relationships. If we want to be sure that a new drug or treatment is safe and effective, an experiment must be conducted to establish that the drug or treatment improves health.

Should the worker have asked Dee to dress Darrell more warmly or called Mrs. Hill about the red coat? She did not. Her approach may have been wise because, years later, Darrell and his mother—unlike most similar pairs—were living together in a house. He was doing well in a magnet school; she had a steady job.

Case studies can illustrate developmental ideas. But one case cannot be a primary research source, because what is true for Dee or your mother or my nephew may not be true for anyone else. At best, a case study raises hypotheses that need more formal exploration, exemplify a general finding, or provide an example that might be instructive. Before conclusions are accepted by the scientific community, observations and experiments are necessary.

Studying Change over Time

Developmental scientists use the methods just described—observations, experiments, surveys, and case studies—but they must also track ongoing development. Therefore, they include the effects of aging in their study. Usually they accomplish this by using one of three basic research designs: cross-sectional, longitudinal, or cross-sequential (summarized graphically in Figure 1.7).

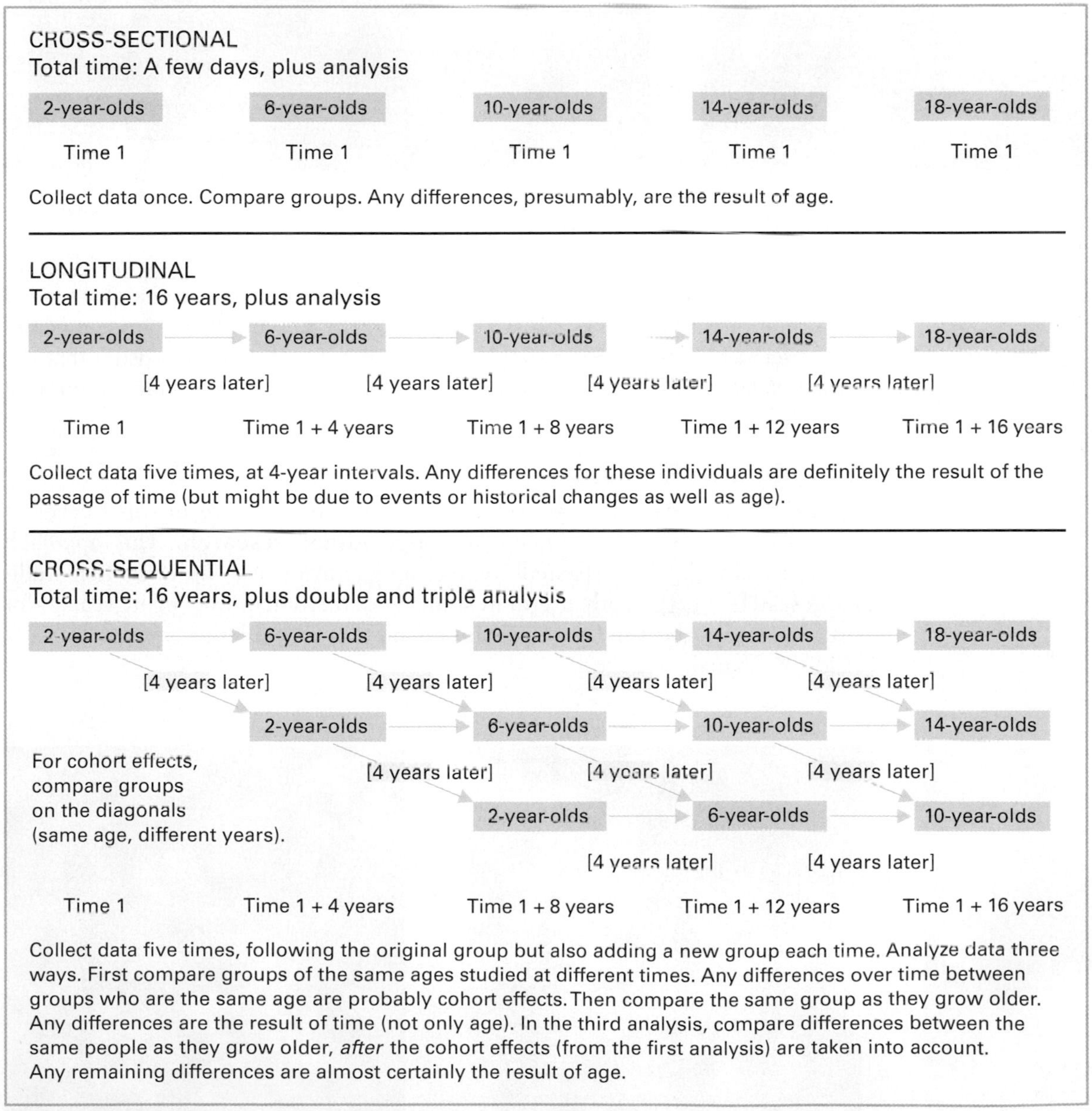

CROSS-SECTIONAL
Total time: A few days, plus analysis

2-year-olds	6-year-olds	10-year-olds	14-year-olds	18-year-olds
Time 1	Time 1	Time 1	Time 1	Time 1

Collect data once. Compare groups. Any differences, presumably, are the result of age.

LONGITUDINAL
Total time: 16 years, plus analysis

2-year-olds	→ 6-year-olds	→ 10-year-olds	→ 14-year-olds	→ 18-year-olds
	[4 years later]	[4 years later]	[4 years later]	[4 years later]
Time 1	Time 1 + 4 years	Time 1 + 8 years	Time 1 + 12 years	Time 1 + 16 years

Collect data five times, at 4-year intervals. Any differences for these individuals are definitely the result of the passage of time (but might be due to events or historical changes as well as age).

CROSS-SEQUENTIAL
Total time: 16 years, plus double and triple analysis

2-year-olds	→ 6-year-olds	→ 10-year-olds	→ 14-year-olds	→ 18-year-olds
	[4 years later]	[4 years later]	[4 years later]	[4 years later]
	2-year-olds	→ 6-year-olds	→ 10-year-olds	→ 14-year-olds
For cohort effects, compare groups on the diagonals (same age, different years).		[4 years later]	[4 years later]	[4 years later]
		2-year-olds	→ 6-year-olds	→ 10-year-olds
			[4 years later]	[4 years later]
Time 1	Time 1 + 4 years	Time 1 + 8 years	Time 1 + 12 years	Time 1 + 16 years

Collect data five times, following the original group but also adding a new group each time. Analyze data three ways. First compare groups of the same ages studied at different times. Any differences over time between groups who are the same age are probably cohort effects. Then compare the same group as they grow older. Any differences are the result of time (not only age). In the third analysis, compare differences between the same people as they grow older, *after* the cohort effects (from the first analysis) are taken into account. Any remaining differences are almost certainly the result of age.

FIGURE 1.7

Which Approach Is Best? Cross-sequential research is the most time-consuming and most complex approach, but it also yields the best information about development. This is one reason why hundreds of scientists conduct research on the same topics, replicating one another's work—to gain some of the advantages of cross-sequential research without having to wait all those years.

PURESTOCK / ALAMY

JON FEINGERSH / DRR.NET

Compare These with Those The apparent similarity of these two groups in gender and ethnic composition makes them candidates for cross-sectional research. Before we could be sure that any difference between the two groups is the result of age, we would have to be sure the groups are alike in other ways, such as socioeconomic status and religious affiliation. Even if two groups seem identical in everything but age, there may be unknown differences.

cross-sectional research A research design that compares groups of people who differ in age but are similar in other important characteristics.

longitudinal research A research design in which the same individuals are followed over time and their development is repeatedly assessed.

Cross-Sectional Research

The most convenient, and thus most common, way to study development is with **cross-sectional research.** Groups of people who differ in age but share other important characteristics (such as education, SES, and ethnicity) are compared. Cross-sectional design seems simple enough, but it is difficult to ensure that the various age groups being compared are similar in every important background variable.

Longitudinal Research

To help discover whether age itself, not cohort differences, results in a developmental change, scientists undertake **longitudinal research.** This approach involves collecting data repeatedly on the same individuals as they age. Longitudinal research is particularly useful in studying development over many years—for instance, from the time participants are newborns until they are adolescents (Elder & Shanahan, 2006).

(FIRST 5 PICTURES) © VISCHER FAMILY ARCHIVE / THE IMAGE WORKS

Six Stages of Life These photos show Sarah-Maria, born in 1980 in Switzerland, in infancy (age 1), early childhood (age 3), the school years (age 8), adolescence (age 15), emerging adulthood (age 19), and adulthood (age 27).

TABLE 1.4

Some Findings from Longitudinal Research

- *Adjustment to parents' divorce.* Negative effects linger, sometimes even into middle age, but not for everyone (Amato & Afifi, 2006; Hetherington & Kelly, 2002).
- *Preventing delinquency.* Patient parenting at age 5, using conversation rather than physical punishment, decreases the likelihood of delinquency 10 years later (Pettit, 2004).
- *The effects of day care.* The quality and extent of nonmaternal care in infancy and early childhood are less influential than the mother's warmth and responsiveness or coldness and rejection (NICHD, 2005).
- *Parenting difficult babies.* Although some babies are difficult (crying, irregular), responsive and encouraging parenting results in better than average development by first grade (Belsky et al., 2007; Stright et al., 2007).
- *The stability of personality.* Early temperament and childhood personality predict later personality in adolescence and beyond, although some change is always possible (Kagan, 2007; McCrae & Costa, 2003; Roberts et al., 2007).

You already read about the links among MAOA, child maltreatment, and adult criminality. That was one of hundreds of findings from a longitudinal study of an entire cohort in Dunedin, New Zealand. Some other surprising findings of longitudinal research are given in Table 1.4.

Longitudinal research has several drawbacks. Over time, participants may withdraw, move to an unknown address, or die. These losses can skew the final results if those who disappear are unlike those who stay (and they usually are). Another problem is that participants become increasingly aware of the questions or the goals of the study and therefore may change in ways that most people do not.

Probably the biggest problem comes from the changing historical context. Science, popular culture, and politics alter life experiences, and those changes limit the current relevance of data collected on people born decades ago. Meanwhile, having to wait for analysis of the effects of longitudinal research may mean that findings come too late to help people living now. For example, dozens of new chemicals, drugs, and additives given to young children might cause cancer in middle age or might be perfectly safe. It takes about 50 years for longitudinal research to tell us which.

© SARAH-MARIA VISCHER / THE IMAGE WORKS

Cross-Sequential Research

cross-sequential research A hybrid research method in which researchers first study several groups of people of different ages (a cross-sectional approach) and then follow those groups over the years (a longitudinal approach). (Also called *cohort-sequential research* or *time-sequential research.*)

Cross-sectional and longitudinal research each have advantages that compensate for the other's disadvantages. Scientists use the two together, often with complex statistical analysis (Hartmann & Pelzel, 2005). The simplest combination is **cross-sequential research** (also referred to as *cohort-sequential research* or *time-sequential research*). With this design, researchers study several groups of people of different ages (a cross-sectional approach) and follow all of them over the years (a longitudinal approach).

A cross-sequential design can compare findings for a group of, say, 18-year-olds, with findings for the same individuals at age 8, as well as with findings for groups who were 18 a decade or two earlier and groups who are 8 years old now (see Figure 1.7). Cross-sequential research thus allows scientists to disentangle differences related to chronological age from those related to historical period.

Especially for Future Researchers (see response, page 30): What is the best method for collecting data?

SUMMING UP

Scientists use many methods to study human development. Each method is useful; none is perfect. Researchers observe people unobtrusively, and they conduct experiments under controlled conditions. They may survey hundreds or even thousands of people; they may study one case in detail.

Since developmentalists need to understand change over time, and also need to apply findings to current concerns, researchers undertake cross-sectional, longitudinal, and cross-sequential research. Every method has strengths and weaknesses. A hypothesis must be tested several ways—and with various statistical safeguards—before the scientific community accepts a research conclusion. ■

Cautions from Science

There is no doubt that the scientific method illuminates and illustrates human development as nothing else does. Facts, hypotheses, and possibilities have all emerged that would not be known without science; people of all ages are healthier and more capable than they were in previous generations because of it. For example, far more parents hold their preterm infants, more young children look at books, more third-graders use computers, and more teenagers finish high school today than a century ago. Science is one reason.

Developmental scientists also discover which historical changes are not beneficial. Television, divorce, shift work, and lead paint are less benign than people once thought.

Although the benefits of science are many, so are the pitfalls. We now describe three of them: misinterpreting data, overdependence on numbers, and unethical practices.

Correlation and Causation

correlation A number indicating the degree of relationship between two variables, expressed in terms of the likelihood that one variable will (or will not) occur when the other variable does (or does not). A correlation is not an indication that one variable causes the other, only that the two variables are related.

Probably the most common mistake made in the interpretation of research is the confusion of correlation with causation. A **correlation** exists between two variables if one variable is more (or less) likely to occur when the other does. (Anything that can vary is called a *variable.*) A correlation is *positive* if both variables tend to increase together or decrease together, *negative* if one variable tends to increase while the other decreases, and *zero* if no connection is evident. (Try taking the quiz in Table 1.5.)

To illustrate: From birth to age 9, there is a positive correlation between age and height (children grow taller as they grow older), a negative correlation between age

TABLE 1.5

Quiz on Correlation

Two Variables	Positive, Negative, or Zero Correlation?	Why? (Third Variable)
1. Ice cream sales and murder rate	________	________
2. Learning to read and number of baby teeth	________	________
3. Adult gender and number of offspring	________	________

For each of these three pairs of variables, indicate whether the correlation between them is positive, negative, or nonexistent. Then try to think of a third variable that would determine the direction of the correlation. The correct answers are printed upside down below.

and amount of sleep (children sleep less as they grow older), and zero correlation between age and number of toes. None of these correlations are surprising, but many other correlations are unexpected. For instance, first-born children are more likely to develop asthma than are later-born children, teenage girls have higher rates of mental health problems than do teenage boys, and newborns born to immigrants weigh more than do newborns of nonimmigrants. (All these correlations are discussed later.)

Correlations are easy to misinterpret. The mantra *correlation is not causation* is taught to every social scientist, yet researchers are still tempted to assume that one variable causes another. For instance, a longitudinal study found a correlation between teenagers' listening to music with degrading sex themes (with males depicted as sexually insatiable studs and women as mindless sex objects) and sexual intercourse before age 20 (see Table 1.6). Although the authors of this study say that they cannot be certain of the direction of effects, because correlation is not causation, they write that

> reducing the amount of degrading sexual content in popular music, or reducing young people's exposure to music with this type of content, could delay initiation of intercourse. . . . Intervention possibilities include reaching out to parents of adolescents, to teens, and to the recording industry.
>
> *[Martino et al., 2006, p. 439]*

The researchers suggest that lyrics glorifying uncommitted sex encourage teenagers to have sex without first building a relationship. Some readers of this study objected. One criminal justice professor at the University of Massachusetts wrote:

> The fact that sexually active kids listen to music with a sexual content should not be surprising. Did we expect they would listen to Mozart's Requiem?
>
> *[Siegel, 2006]*

TABLE 1.6

Correlates of First Sexual Intercourse Before Age 20

Variable	Correlation
Listening to degrading sexual music	0.36*
Having friends who will approve of sex	0.39
Having parents who know where teen is	–0.30
Engaging in heavy petting before age 15	0.47

*The correlation between music and first intercourse remained significant and positive after other factors were taken into account.
Source: Martino et al., 2006.

Answers:
1. Positive; third variable: heat
2. Negative; third variable: age
3. Zero; each child must have a parent of each sex; no third variable

Research Design

Scientists: Six researchers, sponsored by the RAND Corporation.

Publication: *Pediatrics* (2006). This study was also reported in many news stories.

Participants: Total of 1,461 U.S. teenagers, randomly selected to be representative of all U.S. teens.

Design: Teenagers were interviewed by phone, three times over three years, and asked which of 16 popular music groups they listened to. Coders rated whether songs contained sexually degrading lyrics. Some participants refused to answer questions about sex, but responses of 938 who were virgins when the study began were analyzed.

Major conclusion: Listening to sexually degrading music, but not other teen music about sex, encourages teenagers to have sexual intercourse.

Comment: This is a correlational study. The longitudinal sequence (music, then intercourse) prompted the conclusions, but others disagree about the relationship between the variables.

With correlation, there is always the possibility that the direction of causality is the opposite of the one hypothesized or that a third variable may be the underlying cause. Did that happen here? (See the Research Design.) Alternative explanations from each domain for the connection between having early sex and listening to sex-themed music include the following:

- *Biosocial.* Some teenagers have high levels of testosterone (a hormone that increases in adolescence, especially for boys), which drives them to seek sexual experiences and explicitly sexual music. Sexual intercourse may be the result of those hormones (a third variable).
- *Cognitive.* Some teenagers seek sexual experiences, and they find music to reinforce their values. (This explanation for the correlation suggests the opposite causal direction from the authors' assumption.)
- *Psychosocial.* Teenagers idolize some music stars—they go to concerts, watch videos, buy posters. They seek to emulate their idol's lifestyle, which may include sexual activities. Listening to music is a by-product of this idolization (a third variable).

Each of these three explanations is possible, as is the original one. Many other hypotheses could be formulated based on other variables already mentioned, such as genes, SES, and culture. Correlation indicates connection, not cause.

Quantity and Quality

A second caution concerns how much scientists should rely on data produced by **quantitative research** (from the word *quantity*). Quantitative research data can be categorized, ranked, or numbered and thus can be easily translated across cultures. People are asked questions with quantifiable answers—for example, whether they agree or disagree with a statement (only two choices) or whether they do something well, not well, or not at all (three choices). One example of quantitative research is the use of children's school achievement scores to measure the effectiveness of education.

quantitative research Research that provides data that can be expressed with numbers, such as ranks or scales.

Since quantities can be easily summarized, compared, charted, and replicated, many scientists prefer quantitative research. Statistics require numbers. Quantitative data are said to provide "rigorous, empirically testable representations" (Nesselroade & Molenaar, 2003, p. 635). However, when data are reduced to categories and numbers, some nuances and individual distinctions are lost. Many developmental researchers thus turn to **qualitative research** (from *quality*), asking open-ended questions, reporting answers in narrative (not numerical) form, allowing "a rich description of the phenomena of interest" (Hartmann & Pelzel, 2005, p. 163). Consider this example. A group of kindergartners began a playground "grass war" triggered by freshly mown grass and a boy who hit a girl named Carlotta.

qualitative research Research that considers qualities instead of quantities. Descriptions of particular conditions and participants' expressed ideas are often part of qualitative studies.

> The grass war now escalates, with girls and boys on both sides becoming involved. In fact, all but a few of the 5-year-old group I am observing are now in the grass war. The war continues for some time until Marina [one of the children] suggests to the children in our group that they make peace. Marina with several children behind her marches up to the boy who hit Carlotta and offers her hand in peace. The boy responds by throwing grass in Marina's face . . . over the objections of another boy who is in his group. Marina stands her ground after being hit with the grass. The second boy pulls his friend aside and suggests that they make peace. The other boy is against the proposal, but eventually agrees and the two then shake hands with Marina. Marina then returns to our group and declares, "Peace has been established." The two groups now meet for a round of handshaking.
>
> *[Corsaro & Molinari, 2000, p. 192]*

➤Response for Future Researchers (from page 28): There is no best method for collecting data. The method used depends on many factors, such as the age of participants (infants can't complete questionnaires), the question being researched, and the time frame.

Notice that this is scientific observation. The researcher did not intervene. His neutrality allowed him to witness young children, on their own, resolving a conflict.

Could this observation be expressed in numbers? Since the weapon was grass, not sticks and stones, would this interaction be categorized as a conflict or not? A girl was the peacemaker and a boy started the fight, a gender difference that would be lost in a quantitative study. This particular incident happened in Italy. Does that matter? Without more research, we do not know if either the gender difference or the Italian location is relevant.

Qualitative research reflects cultural and contextual diversity and complexity. But it is also more vulnerable to bias and harder to replicate. Imagine how many years of kindergarten observation would be needed to locate a large enough sample of spontaneous grass wars to determine whether gender is relevant.

Especially for People Who Have Applied to College or Graduate School (see response, page 33): Is the admissions process based on quality or quantity?

Developmentalists use both quantitative and qualitative methods. Sometimes they translate qualitative research into quantifiable data, sometimes using qualitative studies to suggest hypotheses for quantitative research, always taking care not to leap to conclusions from one small study (Hartmann & Pelzel, 2005).

Ethics in Research

The most important caution for all scientists, especially those who study children, is to ensure that their research meets the ethical standards of their field. Each academic discipline and professional society involved in the study of human development has a **code of ethics** (a set of moral principles) and a scientific culture that protect the integrity of research. As an example, the standards of the Society for Research in Child Development (2007) are listed in Table 1.7.

code of ethics A set of moral principles that members of a profession or group are expected to follow.

TABLE 1.7

The SRCD's Ethical Standards for Research with Children
1. No procedures can be used that harm a child, physically or psychologically.
2. Children must be fully informed of the procedures of the study, must consent, and can stop at any time.
3. Parents must also be fully informed, and allowed to opt out at any time with no penalty.
4. Additional consent must be obtained from anyone else (such as teachers) whose interaction with the child is to be studied.
5. Incentives (such as toys or money) to participate cannot be excessive.
6. If deception about the goal is necessary, the procedures must be explained in advance, and the deception explained when the study is complete.
7. Confidential records (with names or other identifying material) can be accessed only with permission.
8. Any promises to children or parents must be honored.
9. If the investigator discovers anything that harms the child's well-being (such as abuse), parents or other experts must be told so they can help the child.
10. If unforeseen consequences occur, the investigator must repair any harm and change the procedures.
11. All information must be kept in confidence.
12. Participants must be fully informed immediately following the research.
13. Results must be carefully reported to parents and participants.
14. Investigators should be mindful of the social, political, and human implications of their research.
15. The highest standard of scientific integrity and honesty must be followed.
16. Members can be expelled from the Society for Research in Child Development for personal misconduct, such as a felony conviction.

Especially for Future Researchers and Science Writers (see response, page 34): Do any ethical guidelines apply when an author writes about the experiences of family members, friends, or research participants?

Ethical standards and codes have become more stringent as scientists have become increasingly concerned that "research is not only valid and useful, but also ethical" (Lindsay, 2000, p. 20). Most educational and medical institutions have an *Institutional Research Board* (IRB), a group charged with permitting only ethical research. Although IRBs often slow down scientific study, some research done before they existed was clearly unethical, especially when children, members of minority groups, prisoners, and animals were involved (Blum, 2002; Washington, 2006).

Protection of Research Participants

Researchers must ensure that participation is voluntary, confidential, and harmless. In Western nations, this entails "informed consent" of the participants and, if children are involved, of the parents. In some other nations, consent may be sought from village elders or heads of families, as well as, of course, the research participants themselves (Doumbo, 2005).

The need to protect participants is especially obvious with children, but the same principles apply no matter what the age of the participants (Gilhooly, 2002). These include explaining the purposes and procedures of the study in advance, obtaining written permission to proceed, and allowing the participants to stop at any time. As one leading scientist explains:

> All scientists need to be very careful about how evidence was obtained. . . . [They must have] considerable self-awareness as well as a reaffirmation of the old virtues of honesty, skepticism, and integrity.
>
> *[Bateson, 2005, p. 645]*

Implications of Research Results

Once a study has been completed, additional ethical issues arise. Scientists are obligated to report research results as accurately and completely as possible, without distorting the results to support any political, economic, or cultural position.

An obvious breach of ethics is to "cook" the data, arranging the numbers so that a particular conclusion seems the only reasonable one. Deliberate falsification is rare; it leads to ostracism from the scientific community, dismissal from a teaching or research position, and, sometimes, criminal prosecution.

A more insidious danger is the unintentional slanting of research results through flaws in the methodology, whether in the design, the collection methods, or the analysis of the data. To prevent this, scientific training, collaboration, and replication are crucial. Numerous precautions are built into methodology, several of which have already been explained. In addition, scientific reports in professional journals include (1) details of the study to allow for replication, (2) a section describing the limitations of the findings, and (3) alternative interpretations of the results.

There is an additional ethical concern. Standard 14 in Table 1.7 holds that "investigators should be mindful of the social, political, and human implications of their research." What does it mean to be "mindful" of the implications of research?

In one study, a group of college students who listened to Mozart before taking a cognitive test scored higher than another group who heard no music (Rauscher et al., 1993; Rauscher & Shaw, 1998). The researchers reported this finding, but they did not stress the limitations of the study. They should have been more mindful, because this "Mozart effect" was wildly misinterpreted: The governor of Georgia ordered that all babies born in his state be given a free Mozart CD in order to improve their intelligence, and Florida passed a law requiring every state-funded infant day-care center to play classical music (Bruer, 1999).

In fact, the initial research did not use infants. In a later study that did use children, Mozart did not fare as well as more child-oriented music (Schellenberg et al., 2007). The original results could not be replicated (Crncec et al., 2006; McKelvie & Low, 2002). False hopes were raised and money spent because the researchers, and those who interpreted the research, were not "mindful of the implications" of their original work.

➤Response for People Who Have Applied to College or Graduate School (from page 31): Most institutions of higher education emphasize quantitative data—the SAT, GRE, GPA, class rank, and so on. Decide for yourself whether this is fairer than a more qualitative approach.

What Should We Study?

Every reader of this book should consider the most important ethical concern of all: Are scientists answering the questions that are crucial to human development?

- Do we know enough about prenatal nutrition and drugs to protect every fetus?
- Do we know enough about the effects of poverty to enable everyone to be healthy?
- Do we know enough about sexual behavior to eliminate AIDS, unwanted pregnancy, and sex abuse?
- Do we know enough about education to enable every child to learn basic skills, morals, and social values?

The answer to all these questions is a resounding *NO*. The reasons are many, including that each of these questions touches on controversial topics, which makes some researchers avoid them and few funders support them. Yet ethical standards go beyond caring for participants, ensuring confidentiality, and reporting research honestly. Developmentalists also have an obligation to study topics that are of major importance for the human family. Many people suffer because these questions go unanswered or are not even asked.

The next cohort of developmental scientists will build on what is known, mindful of what needs to be explored. As you read this book, follow the first step of the scientific method: Begin with curiosity and ask many questions. You will find some answers, and you will also help the next generation of scientists determine "What should we study?"

SUMMING UP

Science has helped people in many ways over the past century, contributing to longer and happier lives. However, there are several potential pitfalls in scientific research. For instance, although correlations are useful, people may mistakenly assume that they prove cause, not simply connection. Quantitative research is more objective and easier to replicate than qualitative research, but it loses the nuances that qualitative research can reveal. Scientists follow codes of ethics to make sure they fully inform research participants and safeguard their well-being. Research codes have become more stringent in recent years. Scientists also must be "mindful of implications," which means they must take care that results are not misinterpreted. The most urgent developmental issues are controversial and therefore difficult to study objectively or to report honestly. That is precisely why further scientific research is needed. ■

SUMMARY

Defining Development

1. The study of human development is a science that seeks to understand how people change or remain the same over time. As a science, it begins with questions and hypotheses, and then uses various methods to gather empirical data. Finally, researchers draw conclusions based on the evidence.

2. All kinds of people, of every age, culture, and background, are studied by developmental scientists. One goal is to find the universal patterns of human growth, while recognizing that each person is unique.

3. The universality of human development and the uniqueness of each individual's development are both evident in nature (the genes) and nurture (the environment); no person is quite like another.

4. A dynamic-systems approach to development emphasizes that change is ongoing in life, with each part of development affecting every other part. Change is *multidirectional,* sometimes linear, but more often following a nonlinear path. Both continuity (sameness) and discontinuity (sudden shifts) are evident.

Zooming In and Zooming Out

5. To understand development requires research and insights from many academic disciplines. This *multidisciplinary* approach includes some disciplines (such as genetics) that focus on internal biological factors and others (such as economics) that look at larger social forces.

6. A bioecological approach, first explained by Urie Bronfenbrenner, notes that each person is situated within larger systems of family, school, community, and culture. Building on that perspective, developmentalists now take a *multicontextual* approach to development, aware that each person develops within many contexts.

7. Certain experiences or innovations shape people of each cohort, because they are members of a particular generation who share the experience of significant historical events. A person's socioeconomic status also affects development lifelong.

8. Closely related to the multicontextual approach is the *multicultural* approach. This recognizes that culture has a profound effect on development—people form cultures, and cultures, in turn, shape people.

9. Paradoxically, recent findings from genetics confirm the importance of context and culture. For example, children who inherit specific tendencies (for violence or depression, for instance) develop in quite different ways, depending on their family context.

10. Children learn through imitation, perhaps via the action of mirror neurons, as well as through direct family or cultural guidance. Throughout life, human development is *plastic,* which means that it is possible for individuals to change in important ways.

Applying the Scientific Method

11. Commonly used research methods are scientific observation, the experiment, the survey, and the case study. Statistical analysis helps with interpretation of data, especially when an independent and dependent variable are studied in an experiment. A case study may provoke thought, but it is the least likely of the research methods to produce conclusions that generalize to other people.

12. To study change over time, scientists use three research designs: cross-sectional research (comparing people of different ages), longitudinal research (studying the same people over time), and cross-sequential research (combining the two other methods). Each has advantages and disadvantages.

Cautions from Science

13. A correlation shows that two variables are related. However, it does not prove that one variable causes the other: The relationship of variables may be opposite to the one expected, or both may be the result of a third variable.

14. In qualitative research, information is reported without being quantified and thus is not translated into numbers. Qualitative research best captures the nuance of individual lives, but quantitative research is easier to replicate, interpret, and verify.

15. Ethical behavior is crucial in all the sciences. Not only must participants be protected, but results must be clearly reported and interpreted. Scientists must be mindful of the implications of their research.

16. Appropriate application of scientific research depends partly on the training and integrity of the scientists. The most important ethical question is whether scientists are designing, conducting, analyzing, publishing, and applying the research that is most critically needed.

➤Response for Future Researchers and Science Writers (from page 32): Yes. Anyone you write about must give consent and be fully informed about your intentions. They can be identified by name only if they give permission. For example, family members gave permission before anecdotes about them were included in this text. My nephew David read the first draft of his story (see pages 19–20) and is proud to have his experiences used to teach others.

KEY TERMS

science of human development (p. 3)
empirical (p. 4)
scientific method (p. 4)
hypothesis (p. 4)
replication (p. 4)
nature (p. 5)
nurture (p. 5)
difference-equals-deficit error (p. 6)
dynamic-systems approach (p. 7)
continuity (p. 9)
discontinuity (p. 9)
critical period (p. 9)
sensitive period (p. 9)
Diagnostic and Statistical Manual of Mental Disorders (DSM) (p. 10)
ecological-systems approach (p. 10)
cohort (p. 12)
socioeconomic status (SES) (p. 13)
ethnic group (p. 15)
race (p. 15)
social construction (p. 15)
mirror neurons (p. 17)
plasticity (p. 19)
scientific observation (p. 21)
experiment (p. 22)
independent variable (p. 22)
dependent variable (p. 22)
experimental group (p. 22)
comparison group/control group (p. 22)
survey (p. 23)
case study (24)
cross-sectional research (p. 26)
longitudinal research (p. 26)
cross-sequential research (p. 28)
correlation (p. 28)
quantitative research (p. 30)
qualitative research (p. 30)
code of ethics (p. 31)

KEY QUESTIONS

1. What does it mean to say that the study of human development is a science?

2. Give an example of a social construction. Why is it a construction, not a fact?

3. What is the difference between an ethnic group and a culture?

4. What are some cohort differences between you and your parents?

5. Why does the fact that SES and ethnic differences overlap pose a problem?

6. What are the differences between scientific observation and ordinary observation?

7. In what ways can surveys be considered the opposite of case studies?

8. Why would a scientist conduct a cross-sectional study?

9. Why would people refuse to participate in a research study or quit before a study was finished?

10. Cite two probable correlations (positive and negative) regarding how you spend your time.

11. What are the disadvantages and advantages of qualitative research?

12. What is one additional question about development that should be answered?

APPLICATIONS

1. It is said that culture is pervasive but that people are unaware of it. List 30 things you did *today* that you might have done differently in another culture.

2. How would your life be different if your parents were much higher or lower in SES than they are?

3. Design an experiment to answer a question you have about human development. Specify the question and the hypothesis, and then describe the experiment, including the sample size and the variables. (Look first at Appendix B.)

2

CHAPTER OUTLINE

Theories of Development

"She needs a special school. She cannot come back here next year," Elissa's middle school principal said to us.

My husband and I were stunned. The principal thought that our wonderful daughter, a bright and bubbly (Martin called her "frothy") seventh grader, was learning-disabled. We knew that Elissa was disorganized—frequently misplacing homework, getting lost coming home from school, forgetting which class met on which day—but she was articulate and a good reader. We never imagined she was unable to function in a regular school. We sought theories—to help us organize our confused and jumbled thoughts and observations, to lead to action.

This chapter describes five major theories that are central to the study of development. Three of these theories are called "grand," because they guided thousands of social scientists throughout the twentieth century. Two are called "emerging," because they are newer, less coherent, but insightful for current scholars. At the end of this chapter, we illustrate applications of theories, first by discussing ADHD (attention-deficit/hyperactivity disorder) and then by returning to Elissa's story.

Grand Theories

In the first half of the twentieth century, two opposing theories—psychoanalytic theory and behaviorism (also called *learning theory*)—began as general theories of psychology and later were applied specifically to human development. By mid-century, cognitive theory had emerged, and it became the dominant seedbed of research hypotheses. All three theories are "grand" in that they are comprehensive, enduring, and widely applied (McAdams & Pals, 2006).

Psychoanalytic Theory

Inner drives and motives, many of them irrational, originating in childhood, and unconscious (hidden from awareness), are crucial concepts in **psychoanalytic theory.** These basic underlying forces are thought to influence every aspect of thinking and behavior, from the smallest details of daily life to the crucial choices of a lifetime.

psychoanalytic theory A grand theory of human development that holds that irrational, unconscious drives and motives, often originating in childhood, underlie human behavior.

SUSAN LAPIDES / DESIGN CONCEPTIONS

Childhood Sexuality The girl's interest in the statue's anatomy may reflect simple curiosity, but Freudian theory would maintain that it is a clear manifestation of the phallic stage of psychosexual development, when girls are said to feel deprived because they lack a penis.

Freud's Ideas

Psychoanalytic theory originated with Sigmund Freud (1856–1939), an Austrian physician who treated patients suffering from mental illness. He listened to their accounts of dreams and fantasies, thought deeply about Greek drama and primitive art, and constructed an elaborate, multifaceted theory still admired by many today (e.g., Merlino et al., 2007).

According to Freud, development in the first six years occurs in three stages, each characterized by sexual pleasure centered on a particular part of the body. In infancy, the erotic body part is the mouth (the *oral stage*); in early childhood, it is the anus (the *anal stage*); in the preschool years, it is the penis (the *phallic stage*), a source of pride and fear among boys and a reason for sadness and envy among girls. Then come *latency* and, beginning at adolescence and lasting lifelong, the *genital stage* (see Table 2.1).

Freud maintained that at each stage, sensual satisfaction (from stimulation of the mouth, anus, or penis) is linked to major developmental needs and challenges. Each stage includes its own potential conflicts. For instance, according to Freud, how people experience and resolve these conflicts—especially those related to weaning, toilet training, and sexual pleasure—determines personality patterns because "the early stages provide the foundation for adult behavior" (Salkind, 2004, p. 125).

A psychoanalytic interpretation would be that adults may be stuck in unconscious struggles rooted in a childhood stage if they smoke cigarettes (stuck in the oral stage) or keep careful track of money (anal) or are romantically attracted to much older partners (phallic). For all of us, childhood fantasies and memories remain powerful throughout life. If you have ever wondered why lovers call each other "baby" or why many people refer to their spouse as their "old lady" or "sugar daddy," then Freud's theory provides an explanation: The parent–child relationship is the model for all intimacy.

Researchers interested in attachment theory have further developed this idea, building on the notion that early relationships between parent and child echo throughout life. These researchers have found that "infant attachment history" predicts numerous aspects of intimate relationship functioning (Sroufe et al., 2005, p. 203), including romance (Mikulincer & Goodman, 2006).

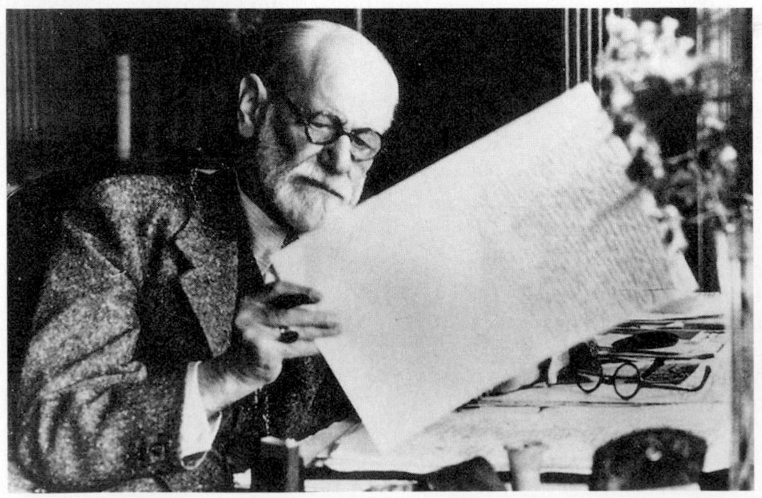

AKG / PHOTO RESEARCHERS, INC.

Freud at Work In addition to being the world's first psychoanalyst, Sigmund Freud was a prolific writer. His many papers and case histories, primarily descriptions of his patients' bizarre symptoms and unconscious sexual urges, helped make the psychoanalytic perspective a dominant force for much of the twentieth century.

Erikson's Ideas

Many of Freud's followers became famous theorists themselves. The most notable in the field of human development was Erik Erikson (1902–1994).

Erikson never knew his biological father. He spent his childhood in Germany, his adolescence wandering through Italy, and his emerging adulthood in Austria, working with Freud's daughter Anna. He married an American, and he fled just before the Nazis came to power in Germany in 1933. Once in the United States, he continued his interest in various cultures: He studied Harvard students, Boston children at play, and Native Americans.

In both his life and his work, Erikson was immersed in the study of cultural diversity, social change, and psychological crises. Among his many writings was a massive case study of Mahatma Gandhi (Erikson, 1969), who was born in India, was educated in Britain, practiced law in South Africa, and led the nonviolent revolution that helped India gain independence.

Erikson described eight developmental stages, each characterized by a challenging developmental crisis (summarized in Table 2.1). He named two polarities at each stage. For instance, he characterized the crisis of the third stage (ages 3 to 6) as initiative versus guilt. He recognized a wide range of potential resolutions of each crisis between the polar opposites; indeed, he believed that, for most people, development at each stage leads to neither extreme but to something in between.

CORBIS

What's in a Name?—Erik Erikson As a young man, this neo-Freudian changed his last name to the one we know him by. What do you think his choice means? (See the caption to the next photograph.)

TABLE 2.1

Comparison of Freud's Psychosexual and Erikson's Psychosocial Stages

Approximate Age	Freud (Psychosexual)	Erikson (Psychosocial)
Birth to 1 year	*Oral Stage* The lips, tongue, and gums are the focus of pleasurable sensations in the baby's body, and sucking and feeding are the most stimulating activities.	*Trust vs. Mistrust* Babies either trust that others will care for their basic needs, including nourishment, warmth, cleanliness, and physical contact, *or* develop mistrust about the care of others.
1–3 years	*Anal Stage* The anus is the focus of pleasurable sensations in the baby's body, and toilet training is the most important activity.	*Autonomy vs. Shame and Doubt* Children either become self-sufficient in many activities, including toileting, feeding, walking, exploring, and talking, *or* doubt their own abilities.
3–6 years	*Phallic Stage* The phallus, or penis, is the most important body part, and pleasure is derived from genital stimulation. Boys are proud of their penises; girls wonder why they don't have one.	*Initiative vs. Guilt* Children either want to undertake many adultlike activities *or* internalize the limits and prohibitions set by parents. They feel either adventurous *or* guilty.
6–11 years	*Latency* Not really a stage, latency is an interlude during which sexual needs are quiet and children put psychic energy into conventional activities like schoolwork and sports.	*Industry vs. Inferiority* Children busily learn to be competent and productive in mastering new skills *or* feel inferior, unable to do anything as well as they wish they could.
Adolescence	*Genital Stage* The genitals are the focus of pleasurable sensations, and the young person seeks sexual stimulation and sexual satisfaction in heterosexual relationships.	*Identity vs. Role Confusion* Adolescents try to figure out "Who am I?" They establish sexual, political, and vocational identities *or* are confused about what roles to play.
Adulthood	Freud believed that the genital stage lasts throughout adulthood. He also said that the goal of a healthy life is "to love and to work."	*Intimacy vs. Isolation* Young adults seek companionship and love *or* become isolated from others because they fear rejection and disappointment. *Generativity vs. Stagnation* Middle-aged adults contribute to the next generation through meaningful work, creative activities, and/or raising a family, *or* they stagnate. *Integrity vs. Despair* Older adults try to make sense out of their lives, either seeing life as a meaningful whole *or* despairing at goals never reached.

GIDEON MENDEL / CORBIS

Who Are We? The most famous of Erikson's eight crises is the identity crisis, during adolescence, when young people find their own answer to the question "Who am I?" Erikson did this for himself by choosing a last name that, with his first name, implies "son of myself" (Erik, Erik's son). These children in Northern Ireland may be smoking because their search for identity is taking place in a sociocultural context that allows an unhealthy path toward adulthood.

As you can see from Table 2.1, Erikson's first five stages follow the same sequence as Freud's stages and include the same core concepts. Erikson, like Freud, believed that the problems of adult life echo the conflicts of childhood. For example, an adult who has difficulty establishing a secure, mutual relationship with a life partner may never have resolved the first crisis of early infancy, trust versus mistrust. However, Erikson's stages differ significantly from Freud's: They emphasize family and culture, not sexual urges.

For Erikson, the resolution of each crisis depends on the interaction between the individual and the social environment constructed by the family and culture. In the stage of initiative versus guilt, for instance, children between ages 3 and 6 often want to undertake activities that exceed their abilities or that overstep the limits set by their parents. They jump into swimming pools, put their shirts on backward, make cakes with their own recipes. Such initiatives may lead to pride or failure, with failure perhaps producing guilt.

The resolution of the initiative-versus-guilt crisis depends on how the child seeks independence, how the parents react, and what the society expects. As an example, some families and cultures encourage 5-year-olds to be assertive, seeing them as creative spirits, whereas others call them "rude" or "fresh" if they insist on getting their own way. Lively 5-year-olds in the more tolerant culture are more likely than children in the stricter culture to resolve the crisis of this stage by feeling good about their assertiveness.

Especially for Teachers (see response, page 43) Your kindergartners are talkative and always moving. They almost never sit quietly and listen to you. What would Erik Erikson recommend?

Children internalize, or accept, the responses of their parents, peers, and cultures, and those internalized reactions persist throughout life. Even in late adulthood, one person may be bold and outspoken while another fears saying the wrong thing—all because they resolved their initiative-versus-guilt stage in opposite ways.

Both Erikson and Freud emphasized the first years of life, and both considered early conflicts when they sought to explain later problems. This is the main criticism of psychoanalytic theory, especially from behaviorists, whose ideas we will now examine.

Behaviorism

The second grand theory, **behaviorism,** arose in direct opposition to the psychoanalytic emphasis on unconscious, hidden urges (described in Table 2.2). Such urges could not be quantified, and the raw material for Freud's theories came from his patients and from Greek drama, which did not seem scientific. Early in the twentieth century, John B. Watson (1878–1958) argued that if psychology was to be a science, psychologists should examine only what they could see and measure: behavior, not thoughts and hidden urges. In Watson's words:

> Let us limit ourselves to things that can be observed, and formulate laws concerned only with those things. . . . We can observe behavior—what the organism does or says.
>
> *[Watson, 1924/1998, p. 6]*

According to Watson, if psychologists focus on behavior, they will realize that anything can be learned. He wrote:

> Give me a dozen healthy infants, well-formed, and my own specified world to bring them up in and I'll guarantee to take any one at random and train him to become any type of specialist I might select—doctor, lawyer, artist, merchant chief, and yes, even beggar-man and thief, regardless of his talents, penchants, tendencies, abilities, vocations, and race.
>
> *[Watson, 1924/1998, p. 82]*

Other psychologists, especially in the United States, thought that Watson's emphasis on learning was insightful. They found it difficult to use the scientific method to verify the unconscious motives and drives that Freud had described (Cairns & Cairns, 2006). Some of them developed behaviorism as a way to study actual behavior, objectively and scientifically.

behaviorism A grand theory of human development that studies observable behavior. Behaviorism is also called *learning theory* because it describes the laws and processes by which behavior is learned.

ARCHIVES OF THE HISTORY OF AMERICAN PSYCHOLOGY, THE UNIVERSITY OF AKRON

An Early Behaviorist John Watson was an early proponent of learning theory whose ideas are still influential today.

Laws of Behavior

For every individual at every age, from newborn to centenarian, behaviorists seek the overarching laws that govern how simple actions and environmental responses shape such complex actions as reading a book or making a family dinner. Behaviorists are also called *learning theorists,* because they believe that all behavior is learned step by step. Then the learned behaviors become habits that people repeat without much thought, which is true for at least half of what we do (Neal et al., 2006).

Especially for Teachers (see response, page 43) Same problem as previously (talkative kindergartners), but what would a behaviorist recommend?

TABLE 2.2

Psychoanalytic Theory vs. Behaviorism

Area of Disagreement	Psychoanalytic Theory	Behaviorism
The unconscious	Emphasizes unconscious wishes and urges, unknown to the person but powerful all the same	Holds that the unconscious not only is unknowable but also may be a destructive fiction that keeps people from changing
Observable behavior	Holds that observable behavior is a symptom, not the cause—the tip of an iceberg, with the bulk of the problem submerged	Looks only at observable behavior—what a person does rather than what a person thinks, feels, or imagines
Importance of childhood	Stresses that early childhood, including infancy, is critical; even if a person does not remember what happened, the early legacy lingers throughout life	Holds that current conditioning is crucial; early habits and patterns can be unlearned, even reversed, if appropriate reinforcements and punishments are used
Scientific status	Holds that most aspects of human development are beyond the reach of scientific experiment; uses ancient myths, the words of disturbed adults, dreams, play, and poetry as raw material	Is proud to be a science, dependent on verifiable data and carefully controlled experiments; discards ideas that sound good but are not proven

The specific laws of learning apply to **conditioning,** the processes by which responses become linked to particular stimuli. There are two types of conditioning: classical and operant.

conditioning According to behaviorism, the processes by which responses become linked to particular stimuli and learning takes place. The word *conditioning* is used to emphasize the importance of repeated practice, as when an athlete *conditions* his or her body to perform well by training for a long time.

More than a century ago, Russian scientist Ivan Pavlov (1849–1936), after winning the Nobel Prize for his work on animal digestion, noted that his experimental dogs drooled not only when they saw and smelled food but also when they heard the footsteps of the attendants who brought the food. This observation led Pavlov to perform his famous experiments, conditioning dogs to salivate when they heard a specific sound.

Pavlov began by sounding a tone just before presenting food. After a number of repetitions of the sound-then-food sequence, dogs began salivating at the sound even when there was no food. This simple experiment demonstrated **classical conditioning** (also called *respondent conditioning*), by which a person or animal is conditioned to associate a neutral stimulus with a meaningful stimulus, gradually responding to the neutral stimulus with the same response as to the meaningful one.

classical conditioning The learning process in which a meaningful stimulus (such as the smell of food to a hungry animal) is connected with a neutral stimulus (such as the sound of a bell) that had no special meaning before conditioning. Also called *respondent conditioning.*

The most influential North American behaviorist was B. F. Skinner (1904–1990). Skinner agreed with Watson that psychology should focus on the scientific study of behavior, and he agreed with Pavlov that classical conditioning explains some behavior. However, Skinner believed that another type of conditioning, **operant conditioning** (also called *instrumental conditioning*), is crucial, especially in complex learning. In operant conditioning, animals behave in a particular way and a response occurs. If the response is useful or pleasurable, the animal is likely to repeat the behavior. If the response is painful, the animal is not likely to repeat the behavior.

operant conditioning The learning process by which a particular action is followed by something desired (which makes the person or animal more likely to repeat the action) or by something unwanted (which makes the action less likely to be repeated). Also called *instrumental conditioning.*

SOVFOTO

A Contemporary of Freud Ivan Pavlov was a physiologist who received the Nobel Prize in 1904 for his research on digestive processes. It was this line of study that led to his discovery of classical conditioning.

Observation Quiz (see answer, page 46): In appearance, how is Pavlov similar to Freud, and how do both look different from the other theorists pictured?

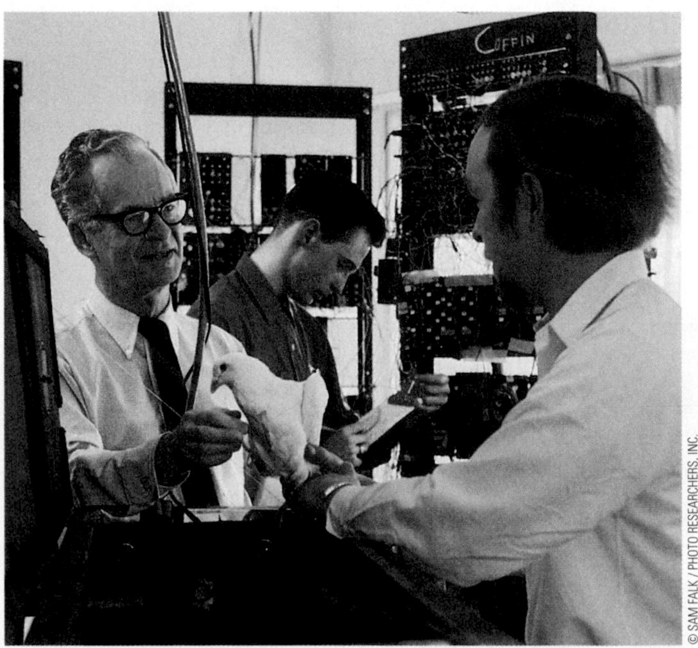

© SAM FALK / PHOTO RESEARCHERS, INC.

Rats, Pigeons, and People B. F. Skinner is best known for his experiments with rats and pigeons, but he also applied his knowledge to human problems. For his daughter, he designed a glass-enclosed crib in which temperature, humidity, and perceptual stimulation could be controlled to make her time in the crib enjoyable and educational. He wrote about an ideal society based on principles of operant conditioning, where, for example, workers in less desirable jobs would earn greater rewards.

Pleasant consequences are sometimes called "rewards," and unpleasant consequences are sometimes called "punishments." Behaviorists hesitate to use those words, however, because what people commonly think of as a punishment can actually be a reward, and vice versa. For example, parents punish their children by withholding dessert, by spanking them, by not letting them play, by speaking harshly to them, and so on. But a particular child might dislike the dessert. In that case, being deprived of it is actually a reward, not a punishment. Another child might not mind a spanking, especially if he or she craves parental attention. In that family, the intended punishment (spanking) is actually a reward (attention).

Any consequence that follows a behavior and makes the person (or animal) likely to repeat that behavior is called a **reinforcement,** not a reward. Once a behavior has been conditioned, humans and other creatures will repeat it even if reinforcement occurs only occasionally.

reinforcement A technique for conditioning behavior in which that behavior is followed by something desired, such as food for a hungry animal or a welcoming smile for a lonely person.

Similarly, punishment makes a creature less likely to repeat a certain action. Almost all daily behavior, from combing your hair to joking with friends, can be understood as a result of past operant conditioning, according to behaviorists.

This insight has practical application for parents: Early parenting is considered crucial, because it teaches habits that may endure. For instance, if parents want their child to share, and their infant offers them a gummy, half-eaten cracker, they should take the gift with apparent delight and then return it, smiling. Adults should never pull at a toy a child is holding—this just encourages the child to hold on tight. (Strangers sometimes did that with my children, teaching them possessiveness—a lesson I didn't want my children to learn.)

The science of human development has benefited from behaviorism. The theory's emphasis on the origins and consequences of observed behavior led researchers to realize that many actions that seem to be genetic, or to result from deeply rooted emotional problems, are actually learned. And if something is learned, it can be unlearned. No longer are "the events of infancy and early childhood . . . the foundation for adult personality and psychopathology," as psychoanalysts believed (Cairns & Cairns, 2006, p. 117). People *can* change, even in old age.

That makes behaviorism a very hopeful theory. It encourages scientists to find ways to eliminate destructive behaviors, among them temper tantrums, phobias, and addictions. Many teachers, counselors, and parents use behaviorist techniques to break undesirable habits and teach new behaviors (Kazdin, 2001). Tantrums cease, phobias disappear, addicts recover, and so on, although not always as easily as the theory predicts.

Like all good theories, both behaviorism and psychoanalytic theory have led to hypotheses and scientific experiments, such as those described in the following.

➤Response for Teachers (from page 40): Erikson would note that the behavior of 5-year-olds is affected by their developmental stage and by their culture. Therefore, you might design your curriculum to accommodate active, noisy children. Initiative should be encouraged and guilt avoided, for the most part.

➤Response for Teachers (from page 41): Behaviorists believe that anyone can learn anything. If your goal is quiet, attentive children, begin by reinforcing a moment's quiet or a quiet child, and soon all the children will be trying to remain attentive for several minutes at a time.

a view from science

What's a Mother For?

Why do children love their mothers, even if their mothers are cruel or unresponsive? Is it because their mothers fed or comforted them when they were infants? To explore such questions, scientists need theories; then they need data to disprove or confirm their theories.

Both behaviorism and psychoanalytic theory originally hypothesized that mothers are loved because they satisfy the newborn's hunger and sucking needs. In other words, "the infant's attachment to the mother stemmed from internal drives which triggered activities connected with the libations of the mother's breast. This belief was the only one these two theoretical groups ever had in common" (C. Harlow, 1986). During infancy, mothers were for feeding, and not much else.

Physicians in every hospital were taught that germs caused disease, so they assumed that mothers who kissed and hugged their babies would "spoil" and sicken them. As a consequence, a hundred years ago, orphanages and hospitals kept babies clean and well fed but forbade caregivers to caress them because "human contact was the ultimate enemy of health" (Blum, 2002, p. 35).

In the 1950s, Harry Harlow (1905–1981), a psychologist who studied learning in monkeys, observed something surprising.

> We had separated more than 60 of these animals from their mothers 6 to 12 hours after birth and suckled them on tiny bottles. . . . During the course of our studies we noticed that the laboratory-raised babies showed strong attachment to the folded gauze diapers which were used to cover the . . . floor of their cages.
>
> *[Harlow, 1958, p. 673]*

In fact, the infant monkeys seemed more attached to the cloth diapers than to their bottles. This was contrary to the two prevailing theories. Psychoanalytic theory predicted that infants would love whatever satisfied their oral needs, and behaviorism predicted that infants would cherish whatever provided food—in this case bottles, not their floorcloths.

Harlow raised eight infant monkeys with no other animals but with two "surrogate" (artificial) mothers, both mother-monkey size. One surrogate was made of bare wire and the other was covered by soft terrycloth. Half of the baby monkeys were fed by a bottle stuck through the chest of the cloth "mother," the other four by a bottle on the wire "mother" (see the Research Design).

Harlow measured how much time each infant monkey spent clinging to each of the two surrogates. To his surprise, even the four babies that fed from the wire mother clung to the cloth mother, going to the wire mother only when hunger compelled them to do so (see Figure 2.1). Then Harlow put an unfamiliar mechanical toy into each infant's cage. The monkeys immediately sought comfort from their cloth mother, clinging to the soft belly with one forepaw and then timidly exploring the new object with the other. Monkeys confronted by the same toy with access only to the wire mother were terrified—freezing, screaming, shivering, hiding, urinating. Harlow concluded that mothering is not primarily about feeding but about what he called "contact comfort" or "love."

Harlow's experiments are a classic example of the usefulness of theories. Because he knew what theories predicted about love and comfort, Harlow was intrigued by the monkeys' attraction to

Research Design

Scientists: Harry Harlow and many others.

Publication: Reprinted in *Learning to Love: The Selected Papers of H. F. Harlow* (1986), edited by Clara Mears Harlow.

Subjects: Eight infant rhesus monkeys born in Harlow's laboratory.

Design: The monkeys were raised from birth in separate cages, each with two "surrogate mothers": one made of bare wire and the other of wire covered with terrycloth. Half the monkeys were fed by a bottle stuck onto the wire mother, the other half by a bottle stuck onto the cloth mother. Harlow recorded how much time the monkeys spent feeding from and clinging to each mother.

Major conclusion: Monkeys, and presumably all primate infants, need "contact comfort," the warm and soft reassurance of a mother's touch.

Comment: Many design problems are apparent: too few subjects, ethical questions about treatment of animals, and uncertainty about whether data on lab-reared, socially isolated rhesus monkeys applies to humans, or even to other primates in nature. However, the results of this experiment were so dramatic that it has been replicated and revised by dozens of other researchers. Harlow's research revolutionized child care.

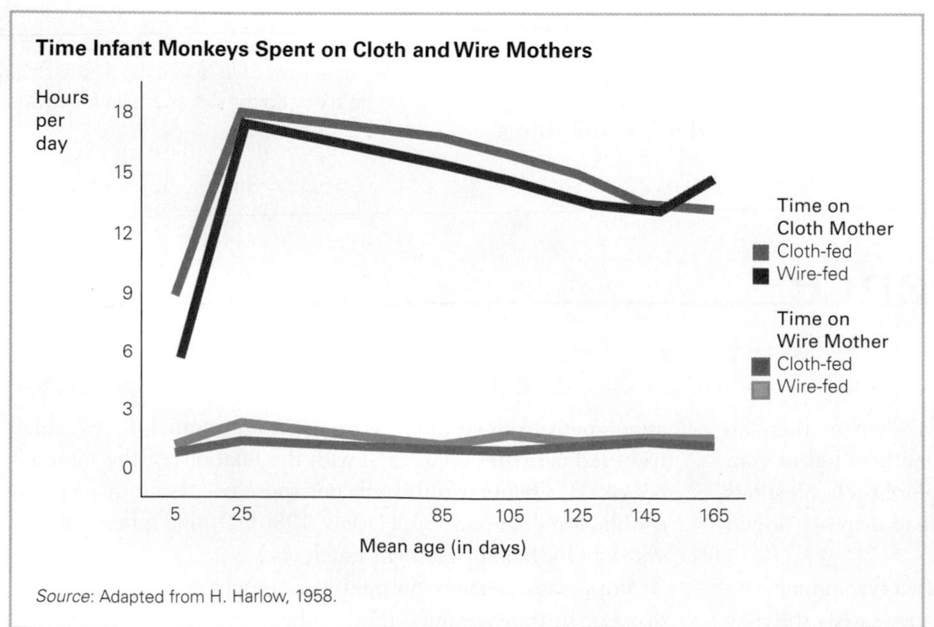

FIGURE 2.1

Softer Is Better During the first three weeks of Harlow's experiment, the infant monkeys developed a strong preference for the cloth-covered "mothers." That preference lasted throughout the experiment, even among the monkeys who were fed by a wire-covered mother.

Observation Quiz (see answer, page 46): At five days, how much time did the wire-fed monkeys (compared with the cloth-fed monkeys) spend on the cloth mothers?

the gauze diapers covering the floors of their cages. That led to closer observation, a hypothesis, a clever series of experiments, and some amazing results.

This research revolutionized the treatment of sick or motherless children. Even very tiny, fragile preterm infants now have contact with their parents, typically including very gentle touch—and they live happier and healthier lives because of it (see Chapter 4).

Clinging to "Mother" Even though it gave no milk, this "mother" was soft and warm enough that infant monkeys spent almost all their time holding on to it. Many infants, some children, and even some adults cling to a familiar stuffed animal when life becomes frightening. According to Harlow, the reasons are the same: All primates are comforted by something soft, warm, and familiar to the touch.

HARLOW PRIMATE LABORATORY, UNIVERSITY OF WISCONSIN

Social Learning

Originally, behaviorists believed that all behavior arose from a chain of learned responses, the result of classical and operant conditioning. One refinement of behaviorism came from evidence (from humans as well as from monkeys) that social creatures appreciate one another's touch, warmth, reassurance, and example.

This revision is called **social learning theory** (see Figure 2.2). Its central premise is that humans can learn from observing others, without personally experiencing any reinforcement. We learn from other people because we are social beings. We grow up in families, we learn from friends and teachers, we love and hate and admire other people—even when we wish we were more independent.

An integral part of social learning is **modeling,** in which people observe what someone else does and then copy it. Even hairstyles and dance steps are copied from others—which explains why they change with each generation.

Modeling is far more complex than simple imitation because people model only some actions, of some individuals, in some contexts. Generally, modeling is likely when the observer is uncertain or inexperienced and when the model is admired, powerful, nurturing, or similar to the observer (Bandura, 1986, 1997).

For example, some children are never personally abused but see their parents hit each other. Some of these children become adults who are violent with their romantic partners, while others are careful to avoid such behavior. Both of these opposite responses support social learning theory; they show the continuing impact of the original example. One child identified with the abuser and the other with the victim; as a result, each learned a different lesson.

As this example shows, social learning is connected to perceptions and interpretations. It is also related to self-understanding, social reflection, and **self-efficacy,** a feeling of self-confidence that people develop when they have high aspirations and notable achievements (Bandura, 2006).

Self-efficacy explains a paradox found in recent research: Parents who do not believe in their own efficacy, and who think their babies are strong-willed, are stricter and less responsive than other parents. Why? The explanation from social learning theory is that their own parents probably never let them develop a strong sense of themselves, so they still feel ineffective (Guzell & Vernon-Feagans,

social learning theory An extension of behaviorism that emphasizes the influence that other people have over a person's behavior. Even without specific reinforcement, every individual learns many things through observation and imitation of other people.

modeling The central process of social learning, by which a person observes the actions of others and then copies them.

self-efficacy In social learning theory, the belief of some people that they are able to change themselves and effectively alter the social context.

Learning occurs through:

- **Classical conditioning** Through association, neutral stimulus becomes conditioned stimulus.
- **Operant conditioning** Through reinforcement, weak or rare response becomes strong, frequent response.
- **Social learning** Through modeling, observed behaviors become copied behaviors.

FIGURE 2.2

Three Types of Learning Behaviorism is also called "learning theory" because it emphasizes the learning process, as shown here.

PHOTOGRAPHER'S CHOICE / GETTY

JEFFREY DUNN / MIRA.COM / DRR.NET

Social Learning in Action Social learning validates the old maxim "Actions speak louder than words." If the moments here are typical for each child, the girl on the left is likely to grow up with a ready sense of the importance of this particular chore of infant care. Unfortunately, the girl on the right may smoke tobacco like her mother—even if her mother warns her not to do so.

Observation Quiz (see answer, page 48): What shows that these children imitate their parents?

2004). According to this theory, the parents of these ineffective parents probably punished them in childhood when they tried to assert themselves. Therefore, following their parents' example, they never developed self-efficacy.

Current versions of social learning theory incorporate elements of two other major theories, cognitive and sociocultural (Bandura, 2006). Indeed, as you will soon learn, the five theories may overlap in practice (see page 59).

➤Answer to Observation Quiz (from page 42): Both are balding, with white beards. Note also that none of the other theorists in this chapter have beards—a cohort difference, not an ideological one.

Cognitive Theory

The third grand theory, **cognitive theory,** emphasizes the structure and development of thought processes. According to this theory, thoughts and expectations profoundly affect attitudes, beliefs, values, assumptions, and actions. Cognitive theory dominated psychology in the last decades of the twentieth century. During that time it branched into new areas of cognitive understanding, including *information-processing theory,* which focuses on the step-by-step process of intellectual development from perception to expression (described in Chapter 6).

cognitive theory A grand theory of human development that focuses on changes in how people think over time. According to this theory, our thoughts shape our attitudes, beliefs, and behaviors.

➤Answer to Observation Quiz (from page 44): Six hours, or one-third less time. Note that later on, the wire-fed monkeys (compared with the cloth-fed monkeys) spent equal, or even more, time on the cloth mothers.

The patriarch of cognitive theory was Jean Piaget (1896–1980), a Swiss scientist trained in biology. He became interested in the science of human thinking when he was hired to field-test questions for a standardized IQ test. Although Piaget's job was to determine at what age children could answer various questions correctly, it was the *incorrect* answers that caught his attention. How children think is more revealing, Piaget concluded, than what they know; process, not product, is important.

YVES DEBRAINE / BLACK STAR

Would You Talk to This Man? Children loved talking to Jean Piaget, and he learned by listening carefully—especially to their incorrect explanations, which no one had paid much attention to before. All his life, Piaget was absorbed with studying the way children think. He called himself a "genetic epistemologist"—one who studies how children gain knowledge about the world as they grow up.

Piaget's interest grew as he observed his own three infants, recording what they did

TABLE 2.3

Piaget's Periods of Cognitive Development

Age Range	Name of Period	Characteristics of the Period	Major Gains During the Period
Birth to 2 years	Sensorimotor	Infants use senses and motor abilities to understand the world. Learning is active; there is no conceptual or reflective thought.	Infants learn that an object still exists when it is out of sight (*object permanence*) and begin to think through mental actions.
2–6 years	Preoperational	Children think magically and poetically, using language to understand the world. Thinking is *egocentric,* causing children to perceive the world from their own perspective.	The imagination flourishes, and language becomes a significant means of self-expression and of influence from others.
6–11 years	Concrete operational	Children understand and apply logical operations, or principles, to interpret experiences objectively and rationally. Their thinking is limited to what they can personally see, hear, touch, and experience.	By applying logical abilities, children learn to understand concepts of conservation, number, classification, and many other scientific ideas.
12 years through adulthood	Formal operational	Adolescents and adults think about abstractions and hypothetical concepts and reason analytically, not just emotionally. They can be logical about things they have never experienced.	Ethics, politics, and social and moral issues become fascinating as adolescents and adults take a broader and more theoretical approach to experience.

at what age. He realized that babies are much more curious and thoughtful than other psychologists had imagined. Later he studied hundreds of schoolchildren.

From this work Piaget developed the central thesis of cognitive theory: How people think changes with time and experience, and thought processes always affect behavior. Piaget maintained that cognitive development occurs in four major periods, or stages: *sensorimotor, preoperational, concrete operational,* and *formal operational* (see Table 2.3). These periods are age-related, and, as you will see in later chapters, each period fosters particular ways of thinking and acting (Inhelder & Piaget, 1958; Piaget, 1952b).

Intellectual advancement occurs because humans seek **cognitive equilibrium**—that is, a state of mental balance. An easy way to achieve this balance is to interpret new experiences through the lens of preexisting ideas; this is called *assimilation.* For example, infants discover that new objects can be grasped in the same way as familiar objects, and adolescents explain the day's headlines as support for their existing worldviews.

Sometimes, however, a new experience is jarring and incomprehensible. Then the individual experiences cognitive disequilibrium, an imbalance that initially creates confusion. As Figure 2.3 illustrates, disequilibrium leads to cognitive growth because people must adapt their old concepts. Piaget describes two types of adaptation:

- *Assimilation,* in which new experiences are interpreted to fit into, or assimilate with, old ideas
- *Accommodation,* in which old ideas are restructured to include, or accommodate, new experiences

cognitive equilibrium In cognitive theory, a state of mental balance in which people are not confused because they can use their existing thought processes to understand current experiences and ideas.

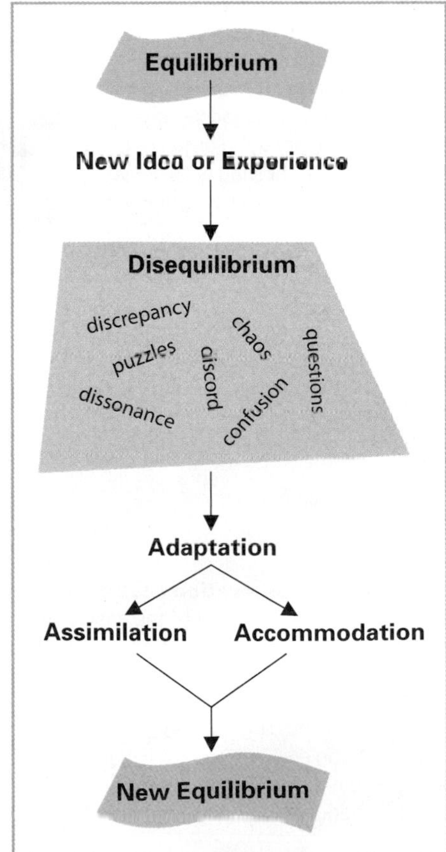

FIGURE 2.3

Challenge Me Most of us, most of the time, prefer the comfort of our conventional conclusions. According to Piaget, however, when new ideas disturb our thinking, we have an opportunity to expand our cognition with a broader and deeper understanding.

© IGAL JUSIDMAN

(a)

(b)

RANDY DUCHAINE, BROOKLYN, NY

(c)

PHOTODISC / PUNCHSTOCK

(d)

How to Think About Flowers A person's stage of cognitive growth influences how he or she thinks about everything, including flowers. *(a)* To 7-month-old Maya, in the sensorimotor stage, flowers are "known" through pulling, smelling, and even biting. *(b)* At the concrete operational stage, children become more logical. This boy can understand that flowers need sunlight, water, and time to grow. At the adult's formal operational stage, flowers can be part of a larger, logical scheme—either to earn money *(c)* or to cultivate beauty *(d)*. Thinking is an active process from the beginning of life until the end.

Accommodation requires more mental energy than assimilation, but it is sometimes necessary because new ideas and experiences may not fit into existing cognitive structures. Accommodation produces significant intellectual growth, including advancement to the next stage of cognitive development.

For example, if your mother says she will do something you never expected (depending on your mother, this might be studying karate or ballet, voting for a conservative or a socialist), you will experience cognitive disequilibrium. Adaptation is necessary. You might *assimilate* by deciding she didn't mean it. Or you might *accommodate* by expanding and revising your concept of your mother—and you might grow intellectually as a result.

Ideally, when people disagree, adaptation is mutual. For example, parents are often startled by their adolescents' strong opinions—perhaps that heroin should be legalized or that cigarettes should be outlawed. Parents may grow intellectually if they revise their concepts, and adolescents may grow if they incorporate their parents' opinions.

➤Answer to Observation Quiz (from page 46): The obvious part of the answer is that one girl is feeding her doll and the other is pretending to smoke a cigarette, but modeling goes far beyond that. Notice that the first girl is holding her spoon at exactly the same angle as her mother is holding hers and that the positions of the second girl's hand, fingers, and arm mirror her mother's.

According to cognitive theory, intellectual growth is active, responsive to clashing ideas and challenging experiences, not dependent on maturation (as psychoanalytic theory suggests) or repetition (as behaviorism holds).

SUMMING UP

The three major developmental theories originated almost a century ago, each pioneered by men who developed theories so comprehensive and creative that they deserve to be called "grand." Each theory has a different focus: emotions (psychoanalytic theory), actions (behaviorism), and thoughts (cognitive theory) (see Figure 2.4).

Freud and Erikson thought it was important to understand unconscious drives and early experiences in order to understand personality and actions. Behaviorists instead stress experiences in the recent past, especially learning by association, by reinforcement, and by observation. Cognitive theory holds that we need to appreciate how people think in order to understand them. According to Piaget, the way people think changes with age as their brains mature and their experiences challenge their past assumptions. ■

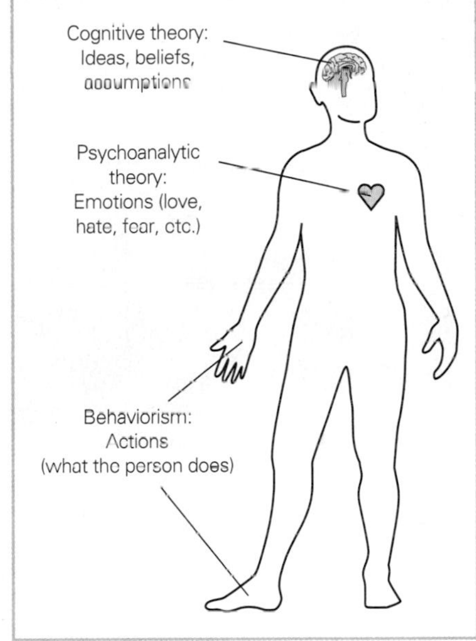

FIGURE 2.4

Major Focuses of the Three Grand Theories This simplified figure emphasizes that, while all three of the grand theories recognize that thoughts, emotions, and actions interact within each person, each theory focuses on a different aspect of the person.

Emergent Theories

You have surely noticed that the grand theorists were all men, born more than a hundred years ago, whose biological and academic ancestors were from western Europe and North America. These background variables undoubtedly limited their perspective. (Of course, female, non-Western, and contemporary theorists are limited by their backgrounds as well.)

Two new theories have emerged that, unlike the grand theories, are multicultural and multidisciplinary, developed not only by men of European ancestry but also by many non-Western, non-White, and female scientists. One, *sociocultural theory*, draws on research in education, anthropology, and history. The other, *epigenetic theory*, arises from biology, genetics, and neuroscience. Their wide-ranging multicultural and multidisciplinary approach makes these theories particularly pertinent to our study.

Neither emergent theory has yet developed a comprehensive, coherent explanation of all of human development, of how and why people change. However, both provide significant and useful frameworks that lead to better understanding. That is precisely what good theories do.

Sociocultural Theory

Although "sociocultural theory is still emerging" (Rogoff, 1998, p. 687), many developmentalists believe that "individual development must be understood in, and cannot be separated from, its social and cultural-historical context" (Rogoff, 2003, p. 50). The central thesis of **sociocultural theory** is that human development results from the dynamic interaction between developing persons and the society and culture that surround them.

sociocultural theory An emergent theory that holds that development results from the dynamic interaction of each person with the surrounding social and cultural forces.

Cultural Variations

Consider this question: What should you do if your 6-month-old daughter starts to fuss? You could give her a pacifier, turn on a musical mobile, change her diaper, prepare a bottle, rock her, sing a lullaby, offer a breast, shake a rattle, ask for help, or close the door and walk away. Each is the right thing to do in some cultures but not in others. In fact, in some cultures parents are warned not to "spoil" their

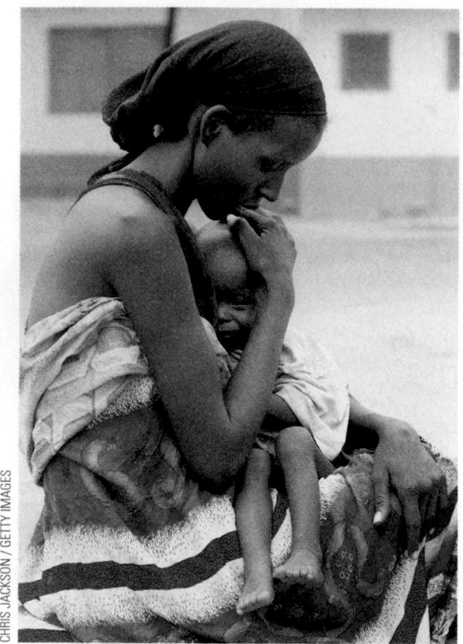

CHRIS JACKSON / GETTY IMAGES

The Comfort of Close Contact Many cultures encourage parents to soothe babies by holding them close, as this mother in Kenya is doing. Her baby is malnourished, but he has a good chance of recovering; she has carried him miles to find food, and their strong bond is healthy for both of them.

guided participation In sociocultural theory, a technique in which skilled mentors help novices learn not only by providing instruction but also by allowing direct, shared involvement in the activity. Also called *apprenticeship in thinking.*

crying babies by picking them up, while in others they are told that parents who let their babies cry are abusive and neglectful.

Often we consider culture to be a widespread set of values, as when we contrast "American" with "Asian" culture. In fact, however, cultures vary from town to town, as found in a study of two central African groups, the Aka and the Ngandu. The Aka were more likely to hold their infants, and the babies fussed, smiled, and vocalized less than the Ngandu babies (Hewlett et al., 1998). Which approach is better? Any answer you give (including "both" and "neither") is rooted in your culture.

Few adults realize how much their responses are shaped by culture. Societies provide not only customs but also tools and theories. For instance, some places have no pacifiers, bottles, or mobiles—or even diapers or doors. The tools available for reacting to a crying baby profoundly affect parents and infants in ways that echo throughout life. Possessions and privacy are valued much more in some cultures than in others, a value learned in infancy.

The pioneer of the sociocultural perspective was Lev Vygotsky (1896–1934), a psychologist from the former Soviet Union. Vygotsky studied cognitive competency among the diverse peoples of his huge nation, as well as among children who were mentally retarded. He studied how Asian farmers used tools, how illiterate people understood abstract ideas, and how children learned in Moscow. In his view, each person learns from the more skilled members of the community (Vygotsky, 1934/1986).

Novices must acquire whatever knowledge and capabilities their society requires. This is best accomplished through **guided participation:** Tutors (not only those designated to teach, but also friends and strangers who know more than the novice) engage learners in joint activities. They offer instruction and, beyond that, "mutual involvement in several widespread cultural practices with great importance for learning: narratives, routines, and play" (Rogoff, 2003, p. 285).

Each of us begins life knowing nothing about our culture, which includes such basic knowledge as how and what to eat, when to express emotions, and even how to communicate. Guided participation (also called *apprenticeship in thinking*) is a central concept of sociocultural theory. Much learning is informal, social, and pervasive.

One of my students recently came to my office with her young son, who eyed my candy dish but held tightly to his mother's hand.

"He can have one if it's all right with you," I whispered.

She nodded and told him, "Dr. Berger will let you have one piece of candy."

He smiled shyly and quickly took one.

"What do you say?" she prompted.

"Thank you," he replied, glancing at me out of the corner of his eye.

"You're welcome," I said.

In that brief moment, all three of us were engaged in guided participation. We were surrounded by cultural traditions and practices, including my role as professor, the fact that I have an office and a candy dish (a custom that I learned from one of my teachers), and the authority of the parent. This mother had taught her son to say "thank you," as some families do and others don't. Specifics differ, but all adults teach children skills they may need in their society. My mother taught me to say "you're welcome" in response to "thank you," although I did not know what it really meant.

Especially for Nurses (see response, page 53) Using guided participation, how would you teach a young child who has asthma to breathe with a nebulizer?

Social interaction is pivotal in sociocultural theory (Wertsch & Tulviste, 2005). This contrasts with the way the grand theories view learning: They see learning as depending primarily on either the student or the teacher, not on both simultaneously. In guided participation, neither student nor teacher is passive; they learn from each other, through conversations and activities that they engage in together (Karpov & Haywood, 1998).

The concept that cultural patterns and beliefs are *social constructions* (explained in Chapter 1) is easy for sociocultural theorists to grasp. They believe that socially constructed ideas are no less powerful than physical or emotional constraints. For example, for centuries, women were not allowed to work as firefighters. Reasons centered on their physical limitations (they were too weak to pull hoses) and questions about their judgment (they were too emotional to deal with emergencies). There are female firefighters now, so these objections were not valid; the social climate had allowed this view of a woman's abilities to persist. In other words, the social reasons were more powerful than the reality.

Values shape development, even though values are constructed. This point was stressed by Vygotsky, who believed that mentally and physically disabled children should be educated (Vygotsky, 1925/1994). That belief has taken hold in U.S. culture in the past 30 years, revolutionizing the education of children with special needs (Rogoff, 2003).

The Founder of Sociocultural Theory Lev Vygotsky, now recognized as a seminal thinker whose ideas on the role of culture and history are revolutionizing education and the study of development, was a contemporary of Freud, Skinner, Pavlov, and Piaget. Vygotsky did not attain their eminence in his lifetime, partly because his work, conducted in Stalinist Russia, was largely inaccessible to the Western world and partly because he died young, at age 38.

The Zone of Proximal Development

According to sociocultural theory, whether people are learning a manual skill, a social custom, or a language, the basic process is the same. A teacher (parent, peer, or professional) must locate the learner's **zone of proximal development,** which consists of the skills, knowledge, and concepts that the learner is close ("proximal") to acquiring but cannot yet master without help.

Through sensitive assessment of the learner, the teacher engages the student in a "process of joint construction," and they work together until the student attains the particular new knowledge or skill in question (Valsiner, 2006). The teacher must avoid two opposite dangers: boredom and failure. Some frustration is permitted, but the learner must be actively engaged, never passive or overwhelmed (see Figure 2.5).

zone of proximal development In sociocultural theory, a metaphorical area, or "zone," surrounding a learner that includes all the skills, knowledge, and concepts that the person is close to acquiring but cannot yet master without help.

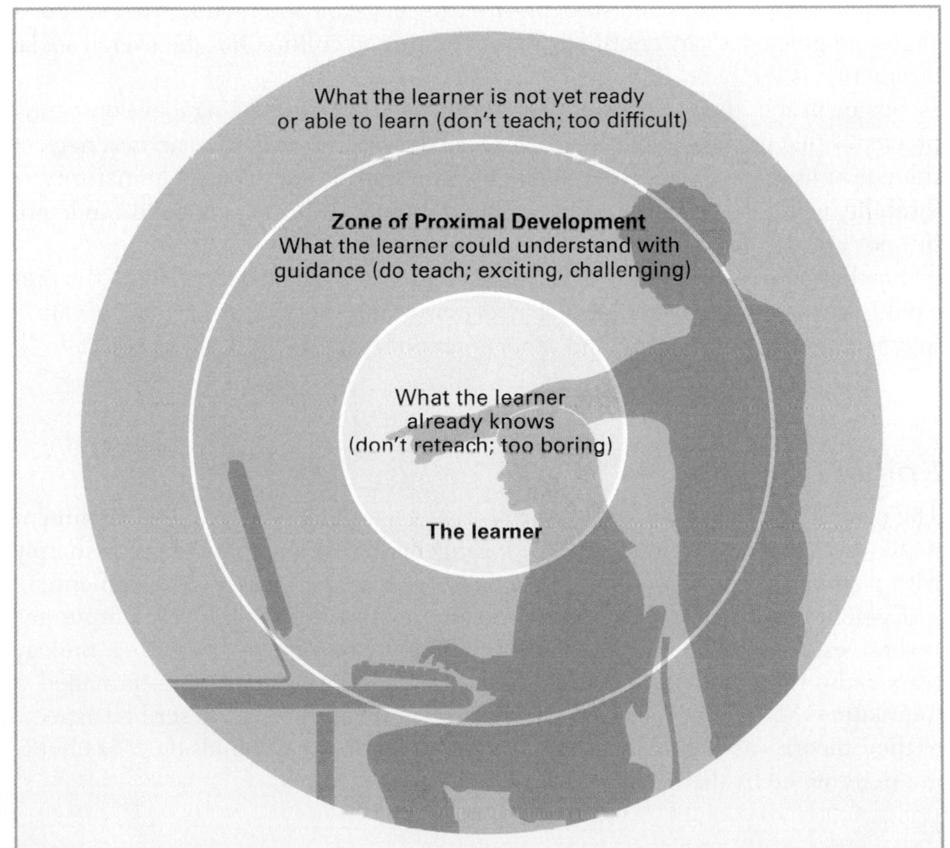

FIGURE 2.5

The Magic Middle Somewhere between the boring and the impossible is the zone of proximal development, where interaction between teacher and learner results in knowledge never before grasped or skills not already mastered. The intellectual excitement of that zone is the origin of the joy that both instruction and study can bring.

ARIEL SKELLEY / BLEND IMAGES / DRR.NET

Learning to Ride Although they are usually not aware of it, children learn most of their skills because adults guide them carefully. The moment captured here is the product of many moments of guided participation.

To make this seemingly abstract process more concrete, consider an example: a father teaching his son to ride a bicycle.

1. He begins by rolling the child along, supporting his weight while telling him to keep his hands on the handlebars, to push the right and left pedals alternately in rhythm, and to look straight ahead.
2. As the son becomes more comfortable and confident, the father begins to roll him along more quickly, praising him for steadily pumping.
3. Within a few lessons, Dad is jogging beside the boy, holding on only to the back of the seat.
4. When the father senses that his son could maintain his balance by himself, he urges the boy to pedal faster. The father lets go but remains ready to take hold again.
5. Finally, the moment comes when the boy is riding on his own.

Note that this is not instruction by preset rules. Sociocultural learning is active and interactive. No child learns to ride a bike by reading and memorizing written instructions, and no good teacher merely repeats a prepared lesson.

Because each student has personal traits, experiences, and aspirations, education must be individualized with personal encouragement. Learning styles vary: Some children need more assurance than others; some learn best by looking, others by hearing. A mentor needs to sense when and whether support or freedom is needed and how peers can help (they are sometimes the best mentors). Teachers know how the zone of proximal development expands and shifts.

Excursions into and through the zone of proximal development (such as the boy prompted to say "thank you" or learning to balance on a bike) are commonplace for all of us. Mentors, attuned to ever-shifting abilities and motivation, continually urge a new level of competence. Learners ask questions, show interest, and demonstrate progress, thus guiding and inspiring the mentors. When education goes well, both teachers and students are fully engaged and productive. Particular skills and processes vary enormously from culture to culture, but the overall social interaction is the same.

Especially for Teachers (see response, page 54) Following Vygotsky's precepts, how might you teach reading to an entire class of first-graders at various skill levels?

Sociocultural theorists have been criticized for overlooking developmental processes that are not primarily social. Vygotsky's theory, in particular, may neglect the power of genes to guide development, especially if neurological immaturity or disability makes some learning impossible (Wertsch, 1998). Every child can learn, but not every child can learn anything at any moment.

Furthermore, while culture is pervasive, and informal teachers abound, the prevailing sociocultural values are not necessarily the most desirable: Such values may include racism, sexism, and other forms of bias. We all learn these as well, even when we do not realize it.

Epigenetic Theory

epigenetic theory An emergent theory of development that considers both the genetic origins of behavior (within each person and within each species) and the direct, systematic influence that environmental forces have, over time, on genes.

The central idea of **epigenetic theory** is that genes interact with the environment to allow development (Gottlieb, 2003). Epigenetic development contrasts sharply with *preformism,* the theory that genes determine every aspect of development.

Epigenetic theory is the newest developmental theory, but it incorporates several established bodies of research. Many disciplines—including biology (especially the principles of evolution), genetics, and chemistry—provided a foundation. Many psychologists, including Erikson and Piaget, described aspects of their theories as *epigenetic,* recognizing that development builds on genes but is not determined by them.

Several specialties within the social sciences—especially *sociobiology* (the study of how individuals within society seek to pass along their genetic heritage), *evolutionary psychology* (the study of the inherited patterns of behavior that were once adaptive), and *ethology* (the study of animals in their natural environments)—stress the interaction of genes and the environment. In other words, sociobiology, evolutionary psychology, and ethology are all epigenetic disciplines.

➤Response for Nurses (from page 50): You would guide the child in the zone of proximal development, where teacher and child interact. Thus, you might encourage the child to prepare the nebulizer (by putting in the medicine, for instance) and then breathe through it yourself, taking turns with the child.

With, On, and Around the Genes

What, then, is new about the epigenetic theory of development? One way to answer that question is to consider the word *epigenetic* itself. It is formed from the root word *genetic* and the prefix *epi-*.

Genetic Effects *Genetic* refers to the entire genome, which includes the following:

1. The genes that make each person (except monozygotic twins) genetically unique
2. The genes that distinguish our species as human
3. The genes that all animals share

The first of these three categories of genes captures most of our attention. Some genes are called *polymorphic* (literally, "having many forms") because the basic gene is transmitted with small variations in the code (more on this in Chapter 3), and these variations account for many of our individual differences. Polymorphisms determine how curly our hair is and how easy it is for us to learn the multiplication tables. Indeed, all variable psychological as well as all physical traits—from bashfulness to blood type, from moodiness to metabolism, from vocational aptitude to voice tone—are influenced by genes in their many forms. Even how religious a person is, or whether we marry, or which candidate gets our vote is genetically influenced (Bouchard et al., 2004).

Humans tend to focus on minor differences between one person and another, but most genes are of the second or third type—genes that distinguish our species as human and genes that all animals share. These genes contain the instructions that make all humans develop two legs and all mammals develop eyes and legs.

Even the timing of developmental change is genetic: Humans walk and talk at about 1 year and can reproduce after puberty because genes switch on those abilities (unless something is terribly wrong). Obviously, whether a person actually talks or has a baby depends on much more than genes, but genes make such achievements possible at certain ages. Thus, half of epigenetic theory is about the power of genes.

Environmental Effects The other half of the word *epigenetic* is equally important. The prefix *epi-* means "with," "around," "before," "after," "on," or "near." Thus, *epigenetic* refers to all the surrounding factors that affect the expression of genetic influences. Those factors stop some genes before they have any effect, and they give other genes extensive influence.

Some factors (such as injury, temperature, and crowding) retard or halt genetic expression; some factors (such as nourishing food, loving care, and freedom to play) facilitate it. In "epigenetic programming . . . environmental effects on . . . health or behavior are mediated through altered gene expression," and vice versa (Moffitt et al., 2006, pp. 5–6).

Epigenetic theory puts the two halves together in one word to signify this inevitable interaction between genes and the environment. This is illustrated by the diagram in Figure 2.6, which was first published in 1992 by Gilbert Gottlieb, a leading proponent of epigenetic theory. This simple diagram, with arrows going up

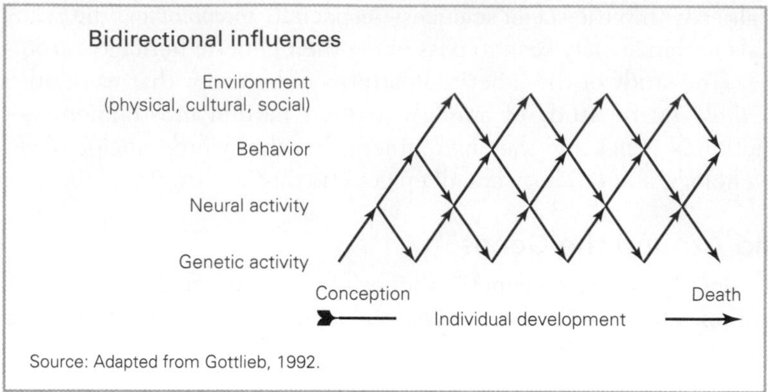

FIGURE 2.6

An Epigenetic Model of Development Notice that there are as many arrows going down as going up, at all levels. Although development begins with genes at conception, it requires that all four factors interact.

Observation Quiz (see answer, page 56): According to this diagram, does genetic influence stop at birth?

and down over time, has been redrawn and reprinted dozens of times to emphasize that dynamic interaction begins at conception and continues throughout each person's life (Gottlieb, 1992).

Epigenetic effects are easier to notice in lower animals than in people (Koolhaas et al., 2006). For example, the color of an animal's fur is genetically determined, but environment causes some rabbit species to have white fur in cold climates and brown fur in warm ones.

Even biological sex can be epigenetic. Alligator eggs become males when the nest temperature is 34°C or above during days 7 to 21 of incubation; they hatch as females at nest temperatures of 28–31°C (Ferguson & Joanen, 1982). For humans, the age of the parents correlates with the sex of their child, an epigenetic effect. (Teenagers conceive more boys than older adults do.)

As development progresses, each person proceeds along the course set by earlier genetic–environmental interactions, which allow a range of possible outcomes called the *reaction range*. Thus, some toddlers cannot become musical masters because that is above the range of their inherited potential. But they still have a range of possible reactions to music, depending on their experiences—from being an avid listener to being indifferent.

Some aspects of development become less plastic, or changeable, with age (Baltes et al., 2006), which explains why certain prenatal conditions (e.g., drug or alcohol use by a pregnant woman) can damage the brain and body of a fetus far more than they damage the woman herself. However, even in adulthood contexts can change inherited patterns.

The Example of Drug Addiction Dramatic evidence of this comes from drug addiction. A person's potential to become addicted is genetic. That potential can be realized—a genetically vulnerable person becomes an addict or an alcoholic—if the person repeatedly consumes an addictive substance. Someone who does not inherit the same genetic predisposition may consume the substance and not form an addiction. Thus, addiction is epigenetic, the outcome of the interaction of genes and environment. Even monozygotic twins (who have the same genes) can differ in whether or not they become alcoholics because of differences in their environments (Moffitt et al., 2006).

Once people become addicted to a particular drug, something in their biochemistry and brain makes them hypersensitive to that drug. For example, one drink makes a nonalcoholic pleasantly tipsy but awakens a powerful craving in an alcoholic. The role of experience in drug addiction has been demonstrated in countless experiments (Crombag & Robinson, 2004). Nonetheless, as one team of researchers explains:

➤**Response for Teachers** (from page 52): First of all, you wouldn't teach them "to read"; you would find out each child's skill level and what he or she was capable of learning next, tailoring instruction to each child's zone of proximal development. For some this might be letter recognition; for others, comprehension of paragraphs they read silently. Second, you wouldn't teach the whole class. You would figure out a way to individualize instruction, maybe by forming pairs, with one child teaching the other; by setting up appropriate computer instruction; or by having parents or ancillary teachers work with small groups of three or four children.

> Within the epigenetic model, each intermediary phenotype [genetic manifestation] is an outcome as well as a precursor to a subsequent outcome contingent on the quality of person–environment interactions. . . . Sudden shifts . . . can occur. . . . [For example,] 86 percent of regular heroin users among soldiers in Vietnam abruptly terminated consumption upon return to the United States (Robins, Helzer, & Davis, 1975). In effect, a substantial change in the environment produced a major phenotype change.
>
> [*Tarter et al., 1999, p. 672*]

The fact that most addicted soldiers were able to kick the heroin habit permanently astonishes anyone who has watched an addict get "clean" and then relapse time after time. The conventional explanation for an addict's repeated relapses is that, once a person is addicted, the biochemical pull of the drug is too strong to resist. However, the example of the Vietnam veterans suggests that the biochemical (and genetic) aspect of addiction does not work in isolation; the social context (*epi-*) is powerful as well—a point confirmed by more recent research (Baker et al., 2006).

Thus, a crucial aspect of epigenetic theory is that genes never function alone; their potential is not actualized unless certain *epi-* factors occur. For example, many disorders—including schizophrenia, autism, antisocial personality disorder, and some forms of depression—have a genetic component. But none are purely genetic. All are epigenetic: The severity (and even the existence) of the psychopathology depends on environment as well as on genes (Krueger & Markon, 2006; Moffitt et al., 2006).

People who inherit a particular variant of one gene (called the short allele of 5-HTT) have a higher than average risk of becoming depressed. However, even people who have this variant do not usually become depressed unless they are maltreated as children or experience stressful events as adults (Caspi et al., 2003). Culture also matters: In one study of Russian women, those who had attempted suicide were less, not more, likely to have the short allele than the others (Gaysina et al., 2006). Epigenetic effects again.

Genetic Adaptation

So far we have described epigenetic factors that affect individuals. Epigenetic factors also affect groups of people and entire species. It is apparent that over billions of years there has been "continual reorganization of epigenetic and genetic determinants." That makes it foolhardy to try to understand species development (even of lower organisms) as solely genetic, transmitted without change over eons (Newman & Müller, 2006, p. 61).

Selective adaptation is ongoing. Genes that increase the chances of survival and reproduction are the most likely to be passed on. In the same way, selective adaptation makes destructive genes increasingly rare: If a particular gene killed every child who inherited it, no one born with that gene would survive to pass it on to the next generation.

selective adaptation The process by which humans and other species gradually adjust to their environment. This process is based on the frequency with which a particular genetic trait in a population increases or decreases over generations; that frequency depends on whether or not the trait contributes to the survival and reproductive ability of members of that population.

To see how this works, imagine that an unusual genetic variant makes it more likely that a child will grow up and reproduce. About half of that child's offspring will inherit the same gene as their fortunate father or mother. They, too, will reproduce, and thus that beneficial gene will become more common with each succeeding generation. Eventually, almost everyone will have that gene and the entire population will thrive.

Whether a gene is beneficial, harmful, or neutral depends on the particular environment in which it operates (or fails to operate). For instance, allergy to bee stings is genetic, but inheriting it is no problem if the person's neighborhood

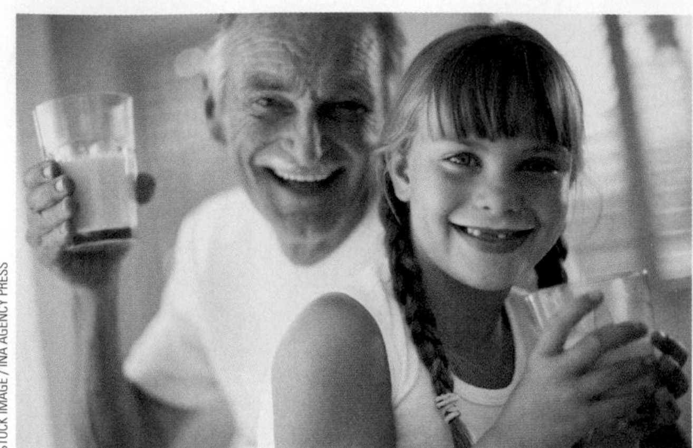
STOCK IMAGE / INA AGENCY PRESS

Got Milk! Many people in Sweden (like this pair) and the other Scandinavian countries regularly drink cow's milk and digest it easily. That may be because their ancient occupation of cattle herding coincided with a genetic tendency toward lactose tolerance.

has no bees and the person does not travel to areas that do have them. Likewise, complex genetic traits depend on the context for their impact. For example, people who inherit fearfulness have an advantage in a hostile environment (they may escape attack) but not in a benign one (they may miss the benefits of social contact because they avoid other people). Many genes may be either benign or destructive, depending on the environment (Belsky et al., 2007).

Specialized bills (for birds) or teeth (for mammals) perhaps emerged first as a mutation and became so useful that more and more birds or mammals inherited and then passed along that gene. Thus, a woodpecker's strong, narrow bill pries insects out of the bark of trees, and a duck's broad, rounded bill strains food from water. Because of genes, "a duck out of water" is a dead duck.

Human differences can also be traced to selective adaptation. Research suggests that all humans may originally have been lactose-intolerant, getting sick if they drank cow's milk. However, in regions where dairy farming was introduced thousands of years ago, a few people had a gene that produced an enzyme that helped them digest cow's milk. They became healthier than the others, so they had more children. In fact, the genetic variant that allows digestion of cow's milk appeared independently in several cattle-herding populations and spread among those people (Gibbons, 2006).

For tribes and clans as well as for individuals, the interaction of genes and environment affects the chances of survival. Genetic variations are needed when conditions change. In that situation, if no member of a species has inherited some variants of genes needed for adaptation to that change, the entire species may disappear. About 90 percent of all species that ever existed have become extinct, partly *because* each of those species eventually reached a point where none of its members could adapt to changed conditions (Buss et al., 1998).

Thus far, humans have adapted well, surviving in dramatically diverse climates and ecosystems. The world's debate about global warming, for example, has shifted from whether or not it exists (the scientific evidence clearly indicates that it does) to who will survive the environmental changes. The interplay of genetic inheritance and specific environment will no doubt be a deciding factor.

Epigenetic theory suggests that adaptation occurs for all living creatures, no matter where and how they live (Fish, 2002). Consider humans and chimpanzees: These two species share 99 percent of their genes, yet there are about a million times more humans alive at this moment than chimpanzees. That 1 percent genetic difference includes several characteristics that have enabled humans to survive and multiply at a greater rate than chimpanzees. One reason is that humans have longer legs than chimpanzees, which makes it easier to walk long distances on two legs. This bipedal (two-legged) locomotion increased mobility, so humans (but not chimps) could journey from Africa to distant fertile regions. Humans are the only mammals that have traveled, reproduced, and thrived on every landmass of the world (except Antarctica).

Some aspects of epigenetic theory are widely accepted, including one that helps us understand why human children and parents love each other: It originates with the genes (Hofer, 2006). Children depend for survival on a decade or more of adult care; so for the human species to survive, children and parents must become attached to each other. Consequently, babies instinctively smile at faces, and a newborn's physical appearance (that round, bald head and those tiny toes) stirs almost any adult's protective affection.

➤Answer to Observation Quiz (from page 54): No. Arrows originating with genetic activity extend throughout development until death.

Over the millennia, unloved infants were likely to die and thus never have children of their own; therefore, parent–child affection, which contributed to an infant's survival, became adaptive and widespread among the population. A mother's love is strengthened by the secretion of oxytocin, the hormone that triggers birth—an example of selective adaptation that I know well.

a personal perspective

My Beautiful, Hairless Babies

In the beginning, infants accept help from anyone. This was a good survival strategy during the centuries when women regularly died in childbirth. By crawling age, infants are emotionally attached to their caregivers—another good survival tactic. Infants who stayed near caregivers were unlikely to be lost in a blizzard or eaten by an animal in the jungle—and thus survived to have children of their own (Taylor, 2006).

Likewise, adults are genetically disposed to nurture babies. Logically, no reasonable person would choose sleepless nights, dirty diapers, and years of self-sacrifice. Yet billions of adults undergo substantial pain and expense in order to be parents.

As the mother of four, I have been surprised by the power of genetic programming many times. With my first-born, I asked my pediatrician whether Bethany wasn't one of the most beautiful, perfect babies he had ever seen.

"Yes," he said, with a twinkle in his eyes, "and my patients are better looking than the patients of any other pediatrician in the city."

When my second child was 1 day old, the hospital offered to sell me a photograph of her—hairless, chinless, and with swollen eyelids. I glanced at it and said no, because the photo didn't look at all like her—it made my beautiful Rachel look almost ugly. I was similarly enamored of Elissa and Sarah, my third and fourth daughters.

However, I am not only a woman who loves her children; I am also a woman who loves her sleep. On one predawn morning, as I roused myself yet again to feed Sarah, I asked myself why I had chosen for the fourth time to add someone to my life who I knew would deprive me of my precious slumber. The answer, of course, is that some genetic instincts are even stronger than the instinct for personal comfort.

UNEP / SAY BOON FOO / THE IMAGE WORKS

Open Wide Caregivers and babies elicit responses from each other that ensure survival of the next generation. The caregiver's role in this vital interaction is obvious, but ethology has shown that infants starve if they do not chirp, meow, whine, bleat, squeal, cry, or otherwise signal hunger—and then open their mouths wide when food arrives. Both the baby birds and the baby human obviously know what to do.

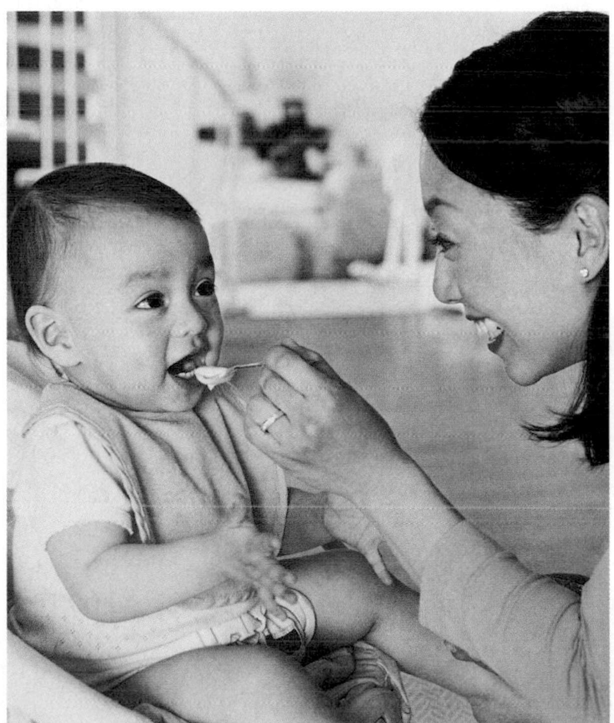

DIGITAL VISION / PUNCHSTOCK

SUMMING UP

Both of the emergent theories combine insights, data, and methods from many academic disciplines and take into account current research and techniques. However, they point in opposite directions. Sociocultural theory looks outward, to the overarching social, historical, and cultural patterns that affect communities, families, and, ultimately, individuals. Sociocultural theory emphasizes that social and cultural groups transmit their values and skills to children through the zone of proximal development, which differs for each learner. By contrast, epigenetic theory begins by looking inward, at thousands of genes, and then moves outward to incorporate the environmental factors that directly affect the expression of those genes. Epigenetic theory includes both individual genetic transmission and centuries-old, species-wide adaptation. ■

Useful Application of Theories

Each major theory discussed in this chapter has contributed a great deal to our understanding of human development (see Table 2.4):

- Psychoanalytic theory has made us aware of the impact of early-childhood experiences on subsequent development, whether these experiences are remembered or not.
- Behaviorism has shown the effect that immediate responses, associations, and examples have on learning.
- Cognitive theory reveals how thoughts, beliefs, and intellectual frameworks affect every aspect of our development.
- Sociocultural theory reminds us that human development is embedded in a rich and multifaceted cultural context, which is evident in every social interaction.
- Epigenetic theory emphasizes the interaction between genetic instructions and surrounding contexts.

In order, these five theories focus on: early childhood, environment, mind, culture, and genes. No comprehensive view of development can ignore any of these factors.

Each theory has also faced severe criticism. Psychoanalytic theory has been faulted for being too subjective; behaviorism, for being too mechanistic; cognitive theory, for undervaluing cultural diversity; sociocultural theory, for neglecting

TABLE 2.4

Five Perspectives on Human Development

Theory	Area of Focus	Fundamental Depiction of What People Do	Relative Emphasis on Nature or Nurture?
Psychoanalytic theory	Psychosexual (Freud) or psychosocial (Erikson) stages	Battle unconscious impulses and overcome major crises	More nature (biological, sexual impulses, and parent–child bonds)
Behaviorism	Conditioning through stimulus and response	Respond to stimuli, reinforcement, and models	More nurture (direct environment produces various behaviors)
Cognitive theory	Thinking, remembering, analyzing	Seek to understand experiences while forming concepts and cognitive strategies	More nature (person's own mental activity and motivation are key)
Sociocultural theory	Social context, expressed through people, language, customs	Learn the tools, skills, and values of society through apprenticeships	More nurture (interaction of mentor and learner, within cultural context)
Epigenetic theory	Genes and factors that repress or encourage genetic expression	Develop impulses, interests, and patterns inherited from ancestors	Begins with nature; nurture is also crucial, via nutrients, toxins, and so on

individual initiative; and epigenetic theory, for neglecting the human spirit. Some people consider all the major theories to be variations on the universal human experience (McAdams & Pals, 2006); others see them as "fundamentally irreconcilable" (Wood & Joseph, 2007, p. 57).

Every **developmental theory** is a systematic statement of principles that provide a coherent framework for understanding how and why people change as they grow older. Theories connect facts and observations with patterns and explanations, weaving the details of life into a meaningful whole.

developmental theory A group of ideas, assumptions, and generalizations that interpret and illuminate the thousands of observations that have been made about human growth. A developmental theory provides a framework for explaining the patterns and problems of development.

As an analogy, imagine building a house. A person could have a heap of lumber, nails, and other materials, but without a blueprint or construction drawings, the heap cannot become a house. Observations of human development are essential raw materials, but theories are needed to put them together. To be more specific:

- Theories lead to pivotal hypotheses, each of which becomes "a direct test of a question" (Salkind, 2004, p. 14).
- Theories generate discoveries.
- Theories offer practical guidance. As Kurt Lewin (1943) once quipped, "Nothing is as practical as a good theory."

Most developmentalists prefer an **eclectic perspective.** That is, rather than adopt any one theory exclusively, they make selective use of all of them. Sometimes they severely criticize or ignore one theory or another, but they remain open to surprises from scientific research that cause rethinking and new theorizing.

eclectic perspective The approach taken by most developmentalists, in which they apply aspects of each of the various theories of development rather than adhering exclusively to one theory.

An eclectic approach (not tied to any one theory) is beneficial because everyone, scientists as well as laypeople, tends to be biased. It is easy to dismiss alternative points of view, but using all five theories opens our eyes and minds to aspects of development that we might otherwise ignore.

Whatever their limitations, developmental theories illuminate life's myriad experiences and events time and time again. Development is dazzling and confusing, but without scientific theory and data, ideology and prejudice can easily obscure reality. One illustration of this comes from the dispute that has echoed through every decade of developmental study: the nature–nurture controversy.

The Nature-Nurture Controversy

Remember from Chapter 1 that an enduring dispute about human development is the nature–nurture controversy. As you can see from Table 2.4, each of the five theories of development has a somewhat different take on this issue. All acknowledge that the interactions of child and parent, genes and the environment—not nature or nurture alone—lead to development. This interaction is complex, with

> feedback loops swirling in all directions, all inextricably intertwined. . . . Both nature and nurture now have seats at the theoretical table, and so the really hard work now begins—to specify, in nitty gritty detail, exactly how the many biological and social environmental factors identified by recent theories weave together.
>
> *[Lippa, 2002, pp. 197, 206]*

Theories help with this "really hard work." Imagine a parent and a teacher discussing a child's behavior. Each suggests a possible explanation that causes the other to say, "I never thought of that." Having five theories is like having five very perceptive observers. All five are not always on target, but it is certainly better to use alternate theories to expand perception than to stay stuck in one narrow groove. A hand functions best with five fingers, even though some fingers are more useful than others. The five theories differ in how and when they see nature and nurture interacting. Since no simple formula describes the nature–nurture combination, it is helpful to consider many perspectives.

STEVE LISS / TIME LIFE PICTURES / GETTY IMAGES

Jitterbug Marty, a 9-year-old diagnosed with attention-deficit/hyperactivity disorder, dances energetically in his room. Like all children with ADHD, he is overactive during every waking moment and wherever he is.

The Very Active Child Some children seem always active, running around or restless even when they should be still. They are impulsive, unable to attend to anything for more than a moment. These are symptoms of attention-deficit/hyperactivity disorder, or ADHD (American Psychiatric Association, 2000). The symptoms and treatment of ADHD are discussed in Chapter 11; here we will look at how developmental theorists emphasize nature or nurture as the cause of this condition (Gatzke-Kopp & Beauchaine, 2007; Nigg, 2006; Valera et al., 2007).

Several facts support the idea that ADHD is genetic. Children with ADHD share the following characteristics:

- They are usually boys who have male relatives with the same problem.
- They are overactive in every context, at home as well as at school.
- Their brain structures differ from those of other children.
- They are often calmed by stimulants, such as Ritalin, Adderall, and even coffee.

This last fact convinces many: Since biochemical treatment works, the cause of ADHD must be biochemical—that is, essentially, "nature" (Faraone et al., 2005)—and thus many researchers seek better drugs, believing that nature is the cause of the disorder (e.g., Lopez, 2006).

But wait. There is also evidence that something in the environment is the cause:

- The rapid increase in diagnosis of ADHD (from 1 percent of all U.S. children 50 years ago to 5 percent today) cannot be genetic, since selective adaptation takes centuries.
- Many environmental factors correlate with ADHD, including crowded homes, television, lead, prenatal stress, food additives, and rigid teaching (e.g., Bateman et al., 2004; Pineda et al., 2007).
- The incidence of ADHD varies markedly from place to place, even when the child population is from the same genetic stock (Polanczyk & Rohde, 2007).
- Many children outgrow ADHD, functioning as normal adults.

Weighing Nature Against Nurture The more closely we look, the more confusing the data become. For instance, if one monozygotic twin is hyperactive, the other twin is also likely to be (evidence for the effect of nature) but is not always (evidence for the effect of nurture) (Lehn et al., 2007; Wood et al., 2007). This dispute is not academic: Some people passionately believe that ADHD is overdiagnosed and children are overdrugged because experts put too much emphasis on nature as the cause; others think underdiagnosis is the problem (Sciutto & Eisenberg, 2007).

Many other issues in development—including birth defects, drug use, aggression, reading and math education, delinquency, and suicide—are treated differently if one believes more in nature than in nurture, or vice versa. Ideology and ignorance often add to polarization. As one scholar, using the example of aggression, points out: "Individual differences in aggression can be accounted for by genetic or socialization differences, with politically conservative scientists tending to believe the former and more liberal scientists the latter" (M. Lewis, 1997, p. 102). Many developmental issues become weapons in cultural wars. It is crucial to step back, using more than one theory to avoid getting stuck on one side or the other in a political battle.

"Opinions shift back and forth between extreme positions" on nature versus nurture (W. Singer, 2003, p. 438). Because false assumptions lead to contradictory and even harmful policies, it is critical to use scientific inquiry and data as a buffer between opinions and conclusions.

How can we avoid extremes, resist the pull of ideology, and overcome bias? Consider theory! Actually, consider more than one theory, and use theory to suggest more possibilities and perspectives, which in turn will lead to new hypotheses to be explored. This approach is widely used in research into ADHD, resulting in an integrative, multimodel approach to treating the problem.

Developmental Theory and Elissa's Story

Now let us return to my daughter Elissa, whose supposed need for a special school was the story that began this chapter. My husband and I did not decide to choose between nature and nurture. We considered all five perspectives.

Because of psychoanalytic theory, we took Elissa to a psychiatrist, who told us that our family dynamics had created the problem and that Elissa herself was compensating amazingly well, developing social skills to compensate for the difficulties she was experiencing with the learning demands of school. This assured us that at least she was doing well in some ways.

Inspired by behaviorism, we began to be quite specific in reinforcing the desired behavior. For example, instead of accepting that she would forget what assignments she had, we checked her homework list and sat with her, praising her as she did each task. We also devised tools to help her, such as attaching her bus pass to her bookbag.

Cognitive theory says that perceptions are crucial. Our perception was altered after talking with the principal, whose opinion we sought to change. We saw Elissa's behavior in a new light, and so did Elissa, especially after she spent a day as a visiting student in a special school, with other children with learning disabilities.

Sociocultural explanations focus on the context, and here my husband and I realized that the school had not done all it could have done for Elissa. We wrote an impassioned letter to the principal, reminding her of the school's mission to teach every student instead of rejecting our daughter. At the same time, we changed the microsystem for Elissa: We got her a tutor and enlisted other family members to help us and her.

Finally, epigenetic theory focuses on genes, and Martin and I were startled to recognize that we were also disorganized by nature. That's why we were stunned at the principal's words: We had accepted Elissa's disability as quite normal. Epigenetic theory also notes that genetic tendencies can be channeled and overcome;

that view encouraged us to make all the changes mentioned above. We had great hopes, since despite our newly acknowledged genetic deficits, we were quite happy and successful adults.

The result of all this was that Elissa earned A's on her final exams that year, and the school grudgingly allowed her to return "just for one more year." By the middle of eighth grade, she was doing so well that they forgot they had said she could not stay for high school. Recently, Elissa was valedictorian of her law school class; as a young adult, she is quite happy and successful, like her parents.

Which theory and action worked? It is impossible to know. As you remember from Chapter 1, one case does not prove anything. However, to this day, I am glad that we took an eclectic approach, using many strategies from many theories for many reasons. Something worked—and that shows that theories can be useful, personally as well as academically.

SUMMING UP

As the nature–nurture controversy makes clear, theories are needed to suggest hypotheses, to spur investigation, and, finally, to arrive at answers, so that objective research can replace personal assumptions. Theories are not true or false, but they serve to move the scientific process forward from the first step (ask a question) to the last (draw conclusions). Given the impact of some applications (e.g., the widespread medication of children with ADHD), such progress is sorely needed. ■

SUMMARY

Grand Theories

1. Psychoanalytic theory emphasizes that human actions and thoughts originate from unconscious impulses and childhood conflicts. Freud theorized that sexual urges arise during three stages of childhood development: oral, anal, and phallic. Parents' reactions to conflicts associated with their children's erotic impulses have a lasting impact on personality, according to Freud.

2. Erikson's version of psychoanalytic theory emphasizes psychosocial development, specifically as societies, cultures, and parents respond to children. Erikson described eight successive stages of psychosocial development, each involving a developmental crisis that occurs as people mature within their context.

3. Behaviorists, or learning theorists, believe that scientists should study observable and measurable behavior. Behaviorism emphasizes conditioning—a learning process. The process of conditioning occurs lifelong, as reinforcement and punishment affect behavior.

4. Social learning theory recognizes that much of human behavior is learned by observing the behavior of others. The basic process is modeling. Children are particularly susceptible to social learning, but all of us learn to be more or less effective because of social influences.

5. Cognitive theorists believe that thought processes are powerful influences on human attitudes, behavior, and development. Piaget proposed that children's thinking develops through four age-related periods, propelled by an active search for cognitive equilibrium.

Emergent Theories

6. Sociocultural theory explains human development in terms of the guidance, support, and structure provided by cultures and societies. For Vygotsky, learning occurs through social interactions, when knowledgeable members of the society guide learners through their zone of proximal development.

7. Epigenetic theory begins with genes, powerful and omnipresent, affecting every aspect of development. Genes are always affected by environmental influences, from prenatal toxins and nutrients to long-term stresses and nurturing families and friends. This interaction can halt, modify, or strengthen the effects of the genes within the person and, via selective adaptation over time, within the species.

Useful Application of Theories

8. Psychoanalytic, behavioral, cognitive, sociocultural, and epigenetic theories have each aided our understanding of human development, yet no one theory is broad enough to describe the full complexity and diversity of human experience. Most developmentalists are eclectic, drawing on many theories.

9. Each theory can shed some light on almost every developmental issue. One example is the nature–nurture controversy. All researchers agree that both genes and the environment influence all aspects of development, but the specific applications that stem from an emphasis on either nature or nurture can affect people in opposite ways. More research is needed, and theories point toward questions that need to be answered.

KEY TERMS

psychoanalytic theory (p. 37)
behaviorism (p. 41)
conditioning (p. 42)
classical conditioning (p. 42)
operant conditioning (p. 42)
reinforcement (p. 43)
social learning theory (p. 45)
modeling (p. 45)
self-efficacy (p. 45)
cognitive theory (p. 46)
cognitive equilibrium (p. 47)
sociocultural theory (49)
guided participation (p. 50)
zone of proximal development (p. 51)
epigenetic theory (p. 52)
selective adaptation (p. 55)
developmental theory (p. 59)
eclectic perspective (p. 59)

KEY QUESTIONS

1. How might a psychoanalytic theorist interpret a childhood experience, such as the arrival of a new sibling?

2. How can behaviorism be seen as a reaction to psychoanalytic theory?

3. According to behaviorism, why might some teenagers begin smoking cigarettes?

4. According to Piaget's theory, what happens when a person experiences cognitive disequilibrium?

5. What would a teacher influenced by Vygotsky do?

6. How might sociocultural theory explain how students behave in class?

7. How might epigenetic theory explain the behavior of a pet dog or cat?

8. How might genetic diversity help a species survive?

9. Why are most developmentalists said to be eclectic?

10. Why does it make a difference whether hyperactivity stems primarily from nature or primarily from nurture?

APPLICATIONS

1. Developmentalists sometimes talk about "folk theories," which are theories developed by ordinary people, who may not know that they are theorizing. Choose three sayings commonly used in your culture, such as (from the dominant U.S. culture) "A penny saved is a penny earned" or "As the twig is bent, so grows the tree." Explain the underlying assumptions, or theory, that each saying reflects.

2. Behaviorism has been used to change personal habits. Think of a habit you'd like to change (e.g., stop smoking, exercise more, watch less TV). Count the frequency of that behavior for a week, noting the reinforcers for each instance. Then, and only then, try to develop a substitute behavior by reinforcing yourself for it. Keep careful records; chart the data over several days. What did you learn?

3. The nature–nurture debate can apply to many issues. Ask three people to tell you their theories about what factors create a criminal and how criminals should be punished or rehabilitated. Identify which theory described in this chapter is closest to each explanation you are given.

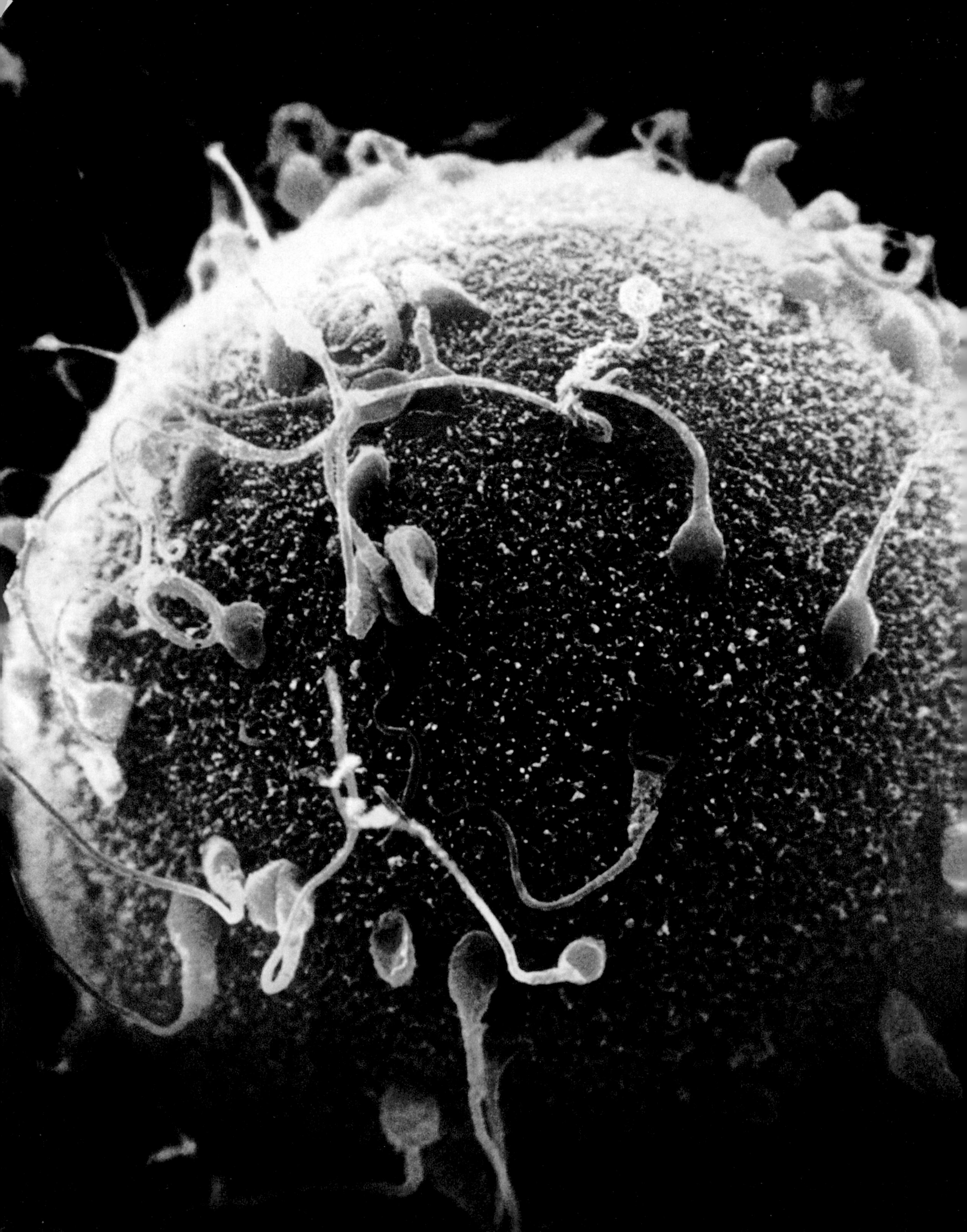

3

CHAPTER OUTLINE

Heredity and Environment

As I came to pick up Rachel from school, another mother pulled me aside. She whispered that Rachel had fallen on her hand and that her little finger was probably broken. My daughter was happily playing, but when I examined her finger, I saw that it was crooked. Trying to avoid both needless panic and medical neglect, I consulted my husband. He smiled and spread out his hands, revealing the same bend in his little finger. Aha! An inherited abnormality, not an injury. But why had I never noticed this before?

That bent finger is one small example of millions of genetic surprises in human development, most of which usually go unnoticed unless a problem appears. This chapter anticipates and explains some of those mysteries, going behind the scenes to reveal not only what genes are but also how they work. Genetics raises many ethical issues, and we will explore those, too. First, the basics.

The Genetic Code

You already know that your genes affect every aspect of your development and that they came from your parents and will be passed on to your children. But before we explore some of the intricacies of these facts, let us remember that a person is much more than a set of genetic instructions.

Although life begins with genes, development is dynamic, ongoing, and interactional. Each person is unlike any other, not only because of the unique instructions locked in DNA but also because of all the personal, social, and cultural influences that affect each person lifelong.

Conception, birth, growth, puberty, and death are pivotal developments that are powerfully affected by genes. Genes dictate that the maximum life span for mice is 4 years; for humans, 122 years; and for tortoises, 150 years (Crews, 2003). But for most of us, the social context is also crucial. In 2008, the average Japanese man lived to 78, the average African American man lived to 60, and the average man in Angola lived to about 38 (U.S. Bureau of the Census, 2007). All, or virtually all, of the reasons for those differences in life span are environmental; that is, they are related more to social influences, such as diet and medical care, than to genes.

To understand development, we must begin with genes. But never forget that your genetic heritage describes possibilities (you could live to 122, as the longest-lived human did) but does not determine outcomes (you probably won't).

What Genes Are

We begin by reviewing some biology. All living things are made up of tiny cells. The work of these cells is done by *proteins.* Each cell manufactures certain proteins according to instructions stored by molecules of **deoxyribonucleic acid (DNA)** at the heart of each cell. DNA molecules are stored on a **chromosome.**

deoxyribonucleic acid (DNA) The molecule that contains the chemical instructions for cells to manufacture various proteins.

chromosome One of the 46 molecules of DNA (in 23 pairs) that each cell of the human body contains and that, together, contain all the genes. Other species have more or fewer chromosomes.

gene A section of a chromosome and the basic unit for the transmission of heredity, consisting of a string of chemicals that are instructions for the cell to manufacture certain proteins.

Humans have 23 pairs of chromosomes (46 in all), which contain the instructions to make all the proteins that a person needs (see Figure 3.1). One member of each pair of chromosomes is inherited from each parent. Each pair of chromosomes is distinct, so they are designated pair 1, pair 2, and so on up to pair 23.

The instructions in the 46 chromosomes are organized into units called genes, with each **gene** (about 20,000 in all for a human) usually located at a particular place on a pair. Each gene contains the chemical recipe for making a specific protein (Brooker, 2009).

What exactly is a protein? A protein is composed of a sequence of chemicals, a long string of *amino acids,* which are the building blocks of life. The recipe for manufacturing a protein consists of instructions for stringing together the right amino acids in the right order.

These instructions are transmitted to the cell via four chemicals, called *bases,* that arrange themselves in pairs: These chemicals are adenine, thiamine, cytosine, and guanine (abbreviated A, T, C, and G). The bases pair up in only four possible ways (A-T, T-A, C-G, and G-C), and each of these is referred to as a base pair. Humans

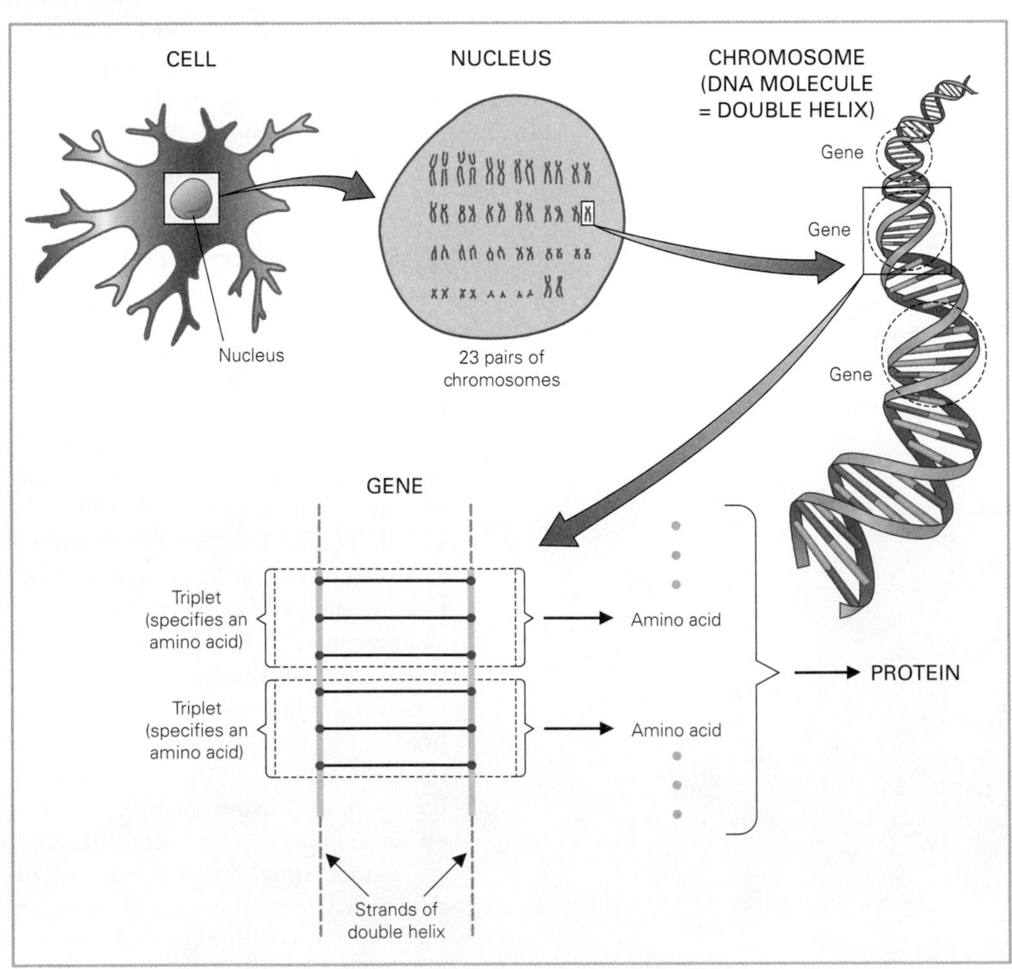

FIGURE 3.1

How Proteins Are Made The genes on the chromosomes in the nucleus of each cell instruct the cell to manufacture the proteins needed to sustain life and development.

have more than 3 billion base pairs, which are arranged in triplets on the 20,000 genes. A triplet is simply a section of a gene that contains three base pairs.

Most genes have thousands of base pairs in triplets arranged in a specific order, and this arrangement constitutes the codes for making the 20 types of amino acids needed for development of a human being. Sometimes, however, the codes can vary, so some genes have a few base pairs that differ from other versions of that gene. These genes are called *polymorphic* ("many shapes"), and each variation is called an **allele** of that gene. Most alleles cause only minor differences (such as the shape of an eyebrow), but some cause more notable differences (such as the amount of the MAOA enzyme in the body, as you read in Chapter 1).

allele Any of the possible forms in which a gene for a particular trait can occur.

Everyone has some significant alleles. Variations in base pairs (called SNPs—single-nucleotide polymorphisms) are not rare, nor are extra repetitions of a piece of a gene, or sometimes of a whole gene. As one expert said, "What's cool is that we are a mosaic of pieces of genomes. None of us is truly normal" (Eichler, quoted in Cohen, 2007, p. 1315).

The entire packet of instructions to make a living organism is called the **genome.** There is a genome for every species of plant and animal and for every individual in every species. Each person (except some monozygotic twins) has a slightly different genome, but the human genome is 99.9 percent the same for any two persons. Our genetic similarities far outweigh our differences.

genome The full set of genes that are the instructions to make an individual member of a certain species.

To recap: The human genome contains about 20,000 genes on 46 chromosomes, using 3 billion base pairs of four chemicals to instruct the cells to produce 20 amino acids that create the proteins to make each person unique, yet similar to all other humans. These numbers may be confusing, but the total is awe-inspiring. As one expert explains:

Especially for Scientists (see response, page 69) A hundred years ago, it was believed that humans had 48 chromosomes, not 46; 10 years ago, it was thought that humans had 100,000 genes, not 20,000 or so. Why?

> If each triplet is considered a word, this sequence of genes is . . . as long as 800 Bibles. If I read the genome out to you at the rate of one word per second for eight hours a day, it would take me a century. . . . This is a gigantic document, an immense book, a recipe of extravagant length, and it all fits inside the microscopic nucleus of a tiny cell that fits easily upon the head of a pin.
>
> [Ridley, 1999, p. 7]

Another amazing part of human genetics is how genes work together to make a person, as we now explain (Klug et al., 2008).

The Beginnings of Life

Development begins at conception, when a male reproductive cell, or *sperm* (plural: *sperm*), penetrates the membrane of a female reproductive cell, or *ovum* (plural: *ova*). Each human reproductive cell, or **gamete,** contains 23 chromosomes, half of a person's 46.

gamete A reproductive cell; that is, a sperm or ovum that can produce a new individual if it combines with a gamete from the other sex to make a zygote.

Thus, although most cells in every man's body have two chromosomes of each kind (two of pair 10, for instance), each of his sperm has only one chromosome of that pair. About half the time it would be the chromosome number 10 he inherited from his mother, and half the time it would be the chromosome 10 he inherited from his father. The same is true for each female gamete, or ovum.

The particular member of each chromosome pair on a given gamete is random. That means each person can produce 2^{23} different gametes—more than 8 million versions of his or her own 46 chromosomes. A given couple could have billions of children, each unlike the others because of differences in the particular sperm and ovum that created them. That is only the beginning of human diversity. At conception, some genes reshuffle, and some triplets and pairs of bases are added or deleted. And, of course, experiences from conception onward differ as well

Matching Genes

When conception occurs in the usual way, some of several million sperm find their way through the vagina, cervix, and uterus and then into a fallopian tube (oviduct), where they find an ovum if the woman has recently ovulated (usually about 14 days before her next menstrual period). If a sperm encounters an ovum and penetrates its outer shell, the nuclei of the two cells may form a new living cell called a **zygote.** Two cells have literally become one, and that zygote is unlike the cells of either parent.

zygote The single cell formed from the fusing of two gametes, a sperm and an ovum.

At that moment, the father's chromosomes match up with the mother's chromosomes, so that the zygote contains 23 pairs of chromosomes, arranged in father/mother pairs. The genes on those 46 chromosomes constitute the organism's genetic inheritance, or **genotype,** which endures throughout life, repeated in almost every cell. (Sometimes a zygote has more or fewer than 46 chromosomes, a problem we will discuss later in the chapter.)

genotype An organism's entire genetic inheritance, or genetic potential.

In 22 of the 23 pairs of human chromosomes, each chromosome is closely matched to the other. Each of these 44 chromosomes is called an *autosome* (*auto* means "self") to indicate that it is independent of the 23rd pair of chromosomes, which are called the sex chromosomes.

Each autosome, from chromosome number 1 to chromosome number 22, contains hundreds of genes in the same positions and sequence; this allows each gene on each autosome to match up with its counterpart from the other parent at conception. If the gene from one parent is exactly like the gene from the other parent, that gene pair is said to be *homozygous* (literally, "same-zygote").

However, the match is not always letter perfect, because the two parents might have different alleles of a particular gene. If the code of a gene from one parent differs from the code of its counterpart from the other parent, that gene pair is said to be *heterozygous* ("different-zygote").

Rarely, a gene has no counterpart on the other autosome and one gene stands alone. But more than 99.9 percent of the genes on the 22 pairs of chromosomes find a match, usually a homozygotic match but sometimes a heterozygotic one.

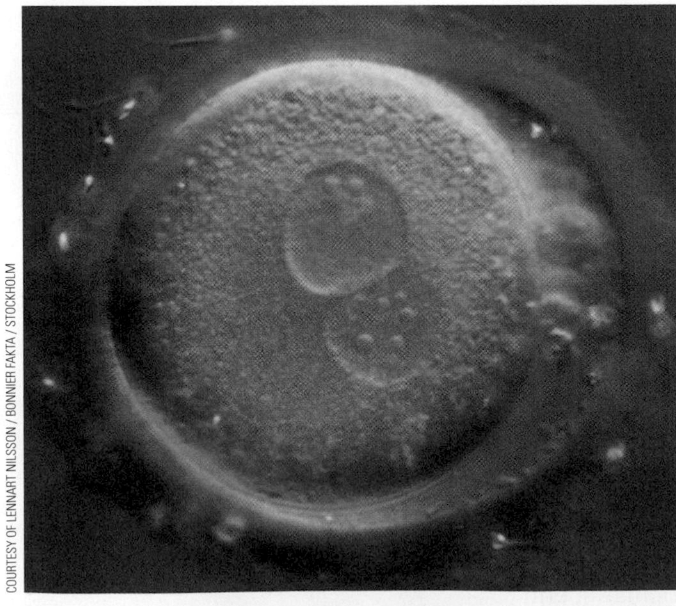

COURTESY OF LENNART NILSSON / BONNIER FAKTA / STOCKHOLM

The Moment of Conception This ovum is about to become a zygote. It has been penetrated by a single sperm, whose nucleus now lies next to the nucleus of the ovum. Soon, the two nuclei will fuse, bringing together about 20,000 genes to guide development.

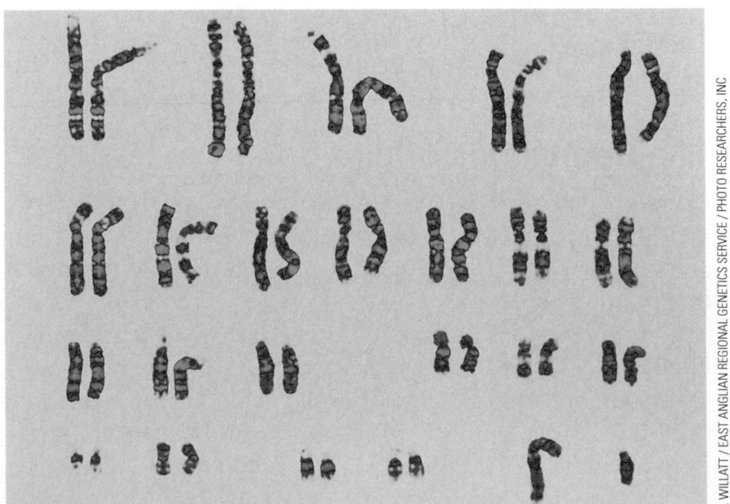

L. WILLATT / EAST ANGLIAN REGIONAL GENETICS SERVICE / PHOTO RESEARCHERS, INC

Mapping the Karyotype A *karyotype* portrays a person's chromosomes. To create a karyotype, a cell is grown in a laboratory, magnified, and then usually photographed. The photo is cut into pieces and rearranged so that the matched pairs of chromosomes are lined up from largest (*top left*) to smallest (*bottom row, fourth pair from the left*). Shown at the bottom right is the 23rd chromosome pair: These two do not match, meaning that this karyotype shows a male (XY).

Genetic diversity, although small in the grand scheme of all the genes that make humans one species, is beneficial to the human race overall. Indeed, diversity is one reason humans have survived for millennia, while many other species have gone extinct. As an example, some people have genes that protect against AIDS. A few people seem immune to HIV because of a specific allele, a small difference in the code of one gene (Little, 2002). Such differences also allowed a few of our ancestors to survive tuberculosis, malaria, the Black Death, and other scourges that took the lives of millions.

➤Response for Scientists (from page 67): There was some scientific evidence for the wrong numbers (e.g., chimpanzees have 48 chromosomes), but the reality is that humans tend to overestimate many things, from the number of genes to their grades on the next test. Scientists are very human: They are inclined to overestimate until the data prove them wrong.

SUMMING UP

The fusion of two gametes (sperm and ovum) creates a zygote, a tiny one-celled creature that has the potential to develop into a human being. One way to describe that process is chemically: DNA is composed of four chemicals that pair up; three of those pairs (a triplet) direct the formation of an amino acid; amino acids in a particular sequence make up proteins; and proteins make a person. Another way to describe it is with numbers: The genetic code for a human being consists of about 3 billion base pairs of amino acids on about 20,000 genes in 46 chromosomes, half from the mother and half from the father. All humans have very similar genes, but the few differences—alternative forms of genes called alleles—not only make each human distinct but create diversity that allows the human race to survive. ■

Sex, Multiple Births, and Fertility

The basics of chromosomes and genes, just explained, hold true for all living creatures. However, many people care passionately about certain details of heredity: whether a zygote will become a boy or a girl, whether a single baby or twins will be born, and whether a particular couple is fertile or not. These details make little difference to the biological survival of the human species overall (when many couples are infertile, other couples tend to have larger families), but they are crucial to the psychological well-being of many individuals. Accordingly, we explain them now.

Male or Female?

Remember that each human reproductive cell, or gamete (an ovum for a woman, a sperm for a man), contains only 23 chromosomes rather than 23 *pairs* of chromosomes. Therefore, because a woman's **23rd pair** of chromosomes **(XX)** is composed of two X chromosomes, when this pair divides to form two ova, each ovum will contain one X chromosome. Because a man's 23rd pair of chromosomes **(XY)** contains one X and one Y chromosome, when it divides to produce two sperm, one sperm will have an X chromosome and one will have a Y chromosome. The X chromosome is bigger and has more genes, but the Y chromosome has a crucial gene, called SRY, that directs a developing fetus to make male organs. Thus, the sex of a baby depends on which kind of sperm penetrates the ovum—a Y sperm with the SRY gene, creating a boy (XY), or an X sperm, creating a girl (XX) (see Figure 3.2).

23rd pair The chromosome pair that, in humans, determines the zygote's (and hence the person's) sex. The other 22 pairs are autosomes, the same whether the 23rd pair is for a male or a female.

XX A 23rd chromosome pair that consists of two X-shaped chromosomes, one each from the mother and the father. XX zygotes become females.

XY A 23rd chromosome pair that consists of an X-shaped chromosome from the mother and a Y-shaped chromosome from the father. XY zygotes become males.

The natural sex ratio at birth is close to 50/50. This ratio is affected by serious adversity (such as famine), when males are less likely to be conceived and more likely to be spontaneously aborted (that is, miscarried). For some species, environmental conditions dramatically tilt the sex ratio. In certain reptiles, for instance, the temperature in the nest during incubation can produce almost all males or almost all females (Quinn et al., 2007).

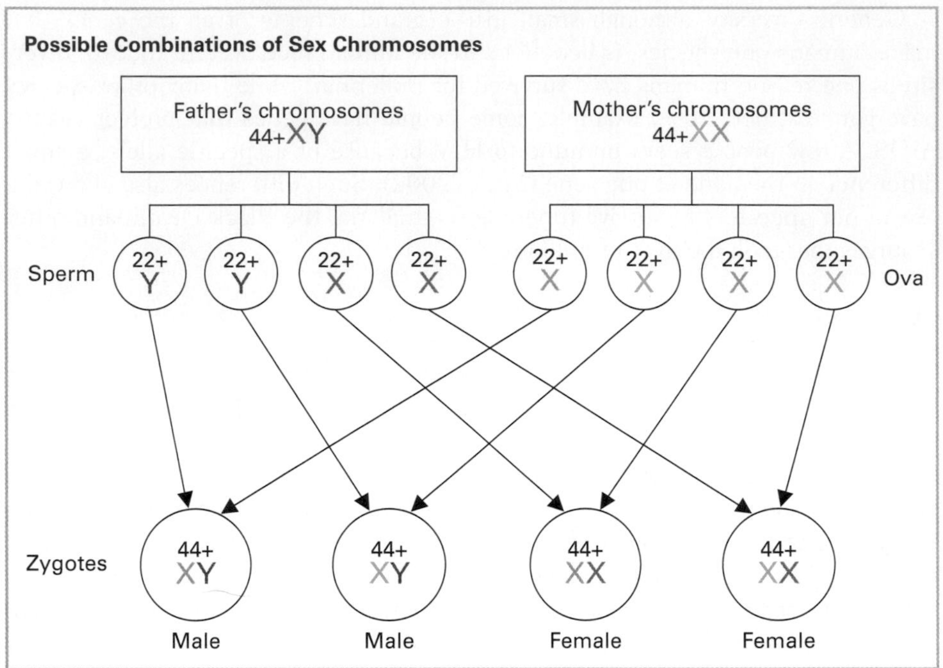

FIGURE 3.2

Determining a Zygote's Sex Any given couple can produce four possible combinations of sex chromosomes; two lead to female children and two, to male. In terms of the future person's sex, it does not matter which of the mother's Xs the zygote inherited. All that matters is whether the father's Y sperm or X sperm fertilized the ovum. However, for X-linked conditions it matters a great deal, because typically one, but not both, of the mother's Xs carries the trait.

Observation Quiz (see answer, page 72): In the chapter-opening photograph (page 64), can you distinguish the Y sperm from the X sperm?

Until a century ago, it was thought that women, not men, determined the sex of offspring. Now scientists understand genetics better and realize that it is the inheritance of an XX or an XY chromosome that determines sex. This understanding has led to the development of several ways to affect the sex ratio. One method is sperm-sorting, changing the proportion of X and Y sperm before insemination. For cattle, this technique is almost always successful at creating cows or steers, as desired; for humans, it works about 80 percent of the time.

Another method is to analyze the chromosomes of an embryo or fetus (as the developing person is called before birth) and then abort pregnancies of the "wrong" sex. This was a common practice in some cities in China, as an unexpected consequence of a policy begun in 1990. A "one child per couple" campaign to reduce poverty succeeded, but some couples opted to make sure their only child was a boy. Since 1993, the Chinese government has forbidden prenatal testing to determine sex, but "the law has been spottily enforced" (French, 2005, p. 3). For instance, in the city of Guiyang, only 75 girls are born for every 100 boys (French, 2005).

The United Nations opposes sex selection, and some nations—China, India, Australia, and Canada among them—outlaw it unless it is used to prevent the birth of a child with severe disabilities (such as hemophilia, which affects only boys). Other nations, including the United States, allow it.

One expert wrote that, worldwide, more than 100 million XX fetuses have been aborted in "gendericide" because their parents did not want a girl (Sharma, 2008). Defending this practice, one doctor said, "Reproductive choice is a very personal matter. If it's not going to hurt anyone, we go ahead and give them what they want" (Steinberg, cited in Grady, 2007). This is one of many ethical questions raised by new technology.

Twins

Giving parents "what they want" has often involved infertility treatments. One result is thousands of pairs of twins (and many sets of triplets and quadruplets) who would never have been conceived naturally (see Figures 3.3 and 3.4). These

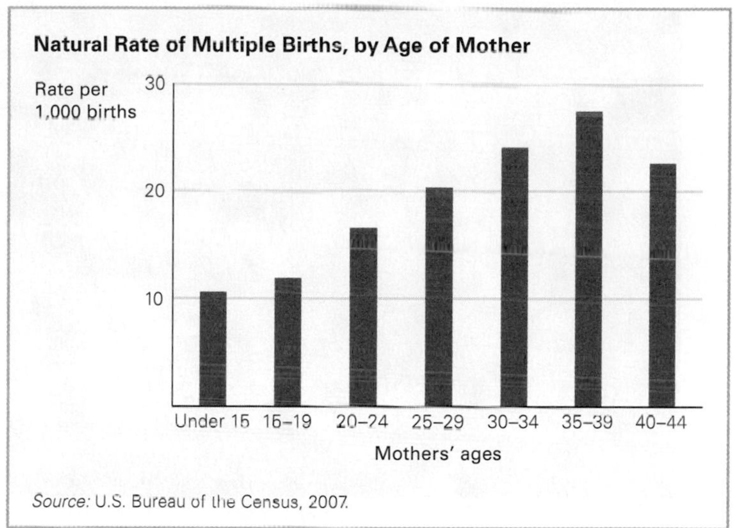

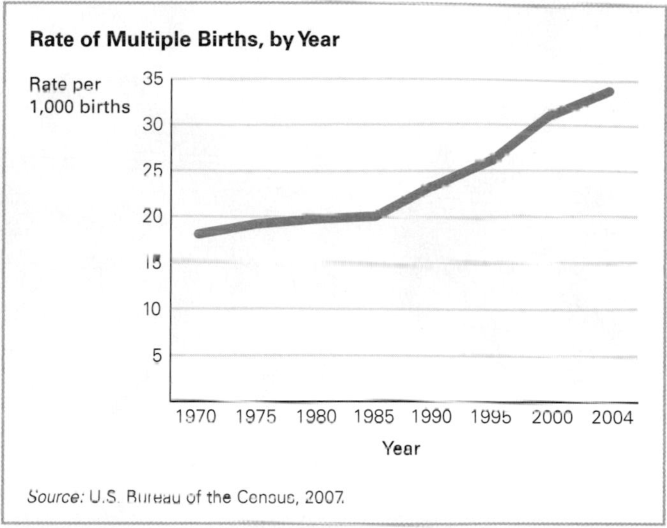

FIGURE 3.3

More Twins Born as Mothers Age This graph (based on 1971 data) shows the natural rate of multiple births in the United States. Other data show that African American women are more likely to spontaneously ovulate two ova; thus, they have more twins than the overall rates shown here. Hispanic and Asian American women are less likely to produce two ova at once, so they have a lower rate of multiple births. All women, however, are more likely to have twins in their 30s than in their teens.

FIGURE 3.4

More Twins Than Ever Historically in the United States, twins were born about once in every 20 births. The advent of assisted reproductive technology (ART) led to a dramatic increase in multiple births. Currently about 1 in every 15 of the youngest Americans is a multiple.

Observation Quiz (see answer, page 73): If 34 in 1,000 births is a multiple, isn't that 1 in 29, not 1 in 15?

multiple births are genetically no more similar to each other than are any other siblings born to the same parents. Let us take a closer look at twins, and then consider how so many more twins have come to be born in recent years.

Monozygotic Twins

You will remember that a zygote is the cell that is formed when a sperm and an ovum unite. Although every zygote is genetically unique, about once in 250 human conceptions, the zygote not only duplicates but splits apart completely before differentiation (sometimes more than once), creating two, or four, or even eight separate zygotes, each identical to that first single cell. (An incomplete split of the zygote creates *conjoined twins,* formerly called Siamese twins.)

If each of these separated cells implants and grows, multiple births occur. One separation results in **monozygotic (MZ) twins,** who are also called *identical twins.* Two or three separations create monozygotic quadruplets or octuplets. (The word *monozygotic* comes from the combination of *mono,* which means "one," and *zygote.*)

monozygotic (MZ) twins Twins who originate from one zygote that splits apart very early in development. (Also called *identical twins.*) Other monozygotic multiple births (such as triplets and quadruplets) can occur as well.

Because monozygotic multiples originate from the same zygote, they begin life with the same genotype—with identical genetic instructions for physical appearance, psychological traits, vulnerability to diseases, and everything else. This genetic similarity continues lifelong, although occasionally one of the zygotes repeats or deletes part of the genetic code, allowing some genetic difference. Being an MZ twin has some advantages. One is that a monozygotic twin can donate a kidney for surgical implantation in the other twin with no risk of organ rejection.

Development starts with genes, and the codes are set within hours after conception, but prenatal and postnatal environments are crucial influences on every individual. Variations in these environments allow monozygotic twins to be not quite identical. For example, monozygotic twins differ in birthweight because of

DAVID YOUNG-WOLFF / PHOTOEDIT

JOHNER IMAGES / GETTY IMAGES

Same Birthday, Same (or Different?) Genes Twins who are of different sexes or who have obvious differences in personality are dizygotic, sharing only half of their genes. Many same-sex twins with similar temperaments are dizygotic as well. One of these twin pairs is dizygotic; the other is monozygotic.

Observation Quiz (see answer, page 74): Can you tell which pair is monozygotic?

where each implanted in the mother's uterus. Parents may treat such twins differently—some favoring the larger one, some the smaller—and that will affect each child (Caspi et al., 2004; Piontelli, 2002).

Developmentalists study monozygotic twins because when these twins differ, the difference can be attributed to a post-zygote influence. For example, 13-year-old monozygotic twins, Brian and Jason, are part of one family, so their nature (as MZ twins) is identical and much of their environment is shared. Both boys have Asperger syndrome (a developmental disorder explained in Chapter 11), but the impact varies. Brian is shy and socially awkward, in ways that are quite common for 13-year-olds. His Asperger syndrome might have escaped detection were it not for Jason, who displays much more noticeable symptoms. Jason "fails miserably" in social interaction, and his "stilted conversations typically include inappropriate questions and comments" (Bower, 2006, p. 106). Why is one monozygotic twin so much more impaired than the other? A likely cause is that Brian breathed nor-

➤Answer to Observation Quiz (from page 70): Probably not. The Y sperm are slightly smaller, which can be detected via scientific analysis (some cattle breeders raise only steers using such analysis), but visual inspection, even magnified as in the photo, may be inaccurate.

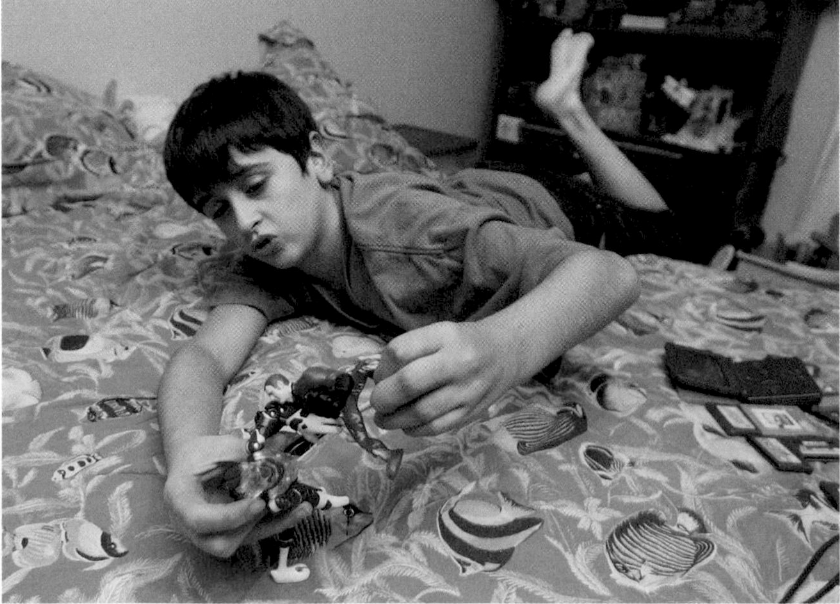

JOHN AMIS / AP

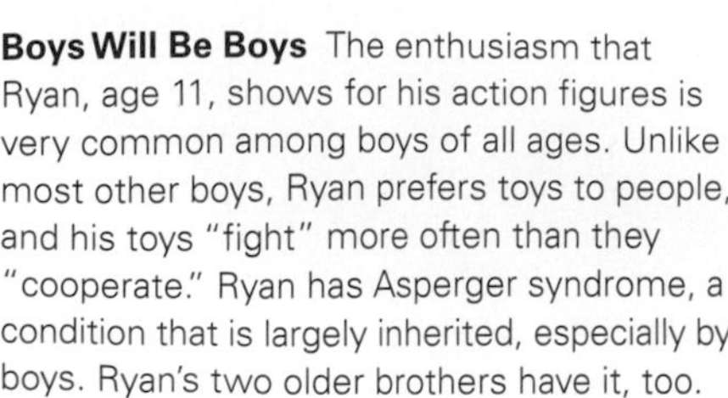

Boys Will Be Boys The enthusiasm that Ryan, age 11, shows for his action figures is very common among boys of all ages. Unlike most other boys, Ryan prefers toys to people, and his toys "fight" more often than they "cooperate." Ryan has Asperger syndrome, a condition that is largely inherited, especially by boys. Ryan's two older brothers have it, too.

mally at birth but Jason did not breathe for several seconds. Lack of oxygen may have damaged Jason's brain.

Dizygotic Twins

When naturally conceived, about two-thirds of twins are **dizygotic (DZ) twins,** also called *fraternal twins.* They began life as two separate zygotes created by the fertilization of two ova by two sperm at roughly the same time. (Usually, only one ovum is released per month, but sometimes two or more ova become available for fertilization.)

dizygotic (DZ) twins Twins who are formed when two separate ova are fertilized by two separate sperm at roughly the same time. (Also called *fraternal twins.*)

The incidence of dizygotic twins varies by ethnicity and age. For example, DZ twins occur naturally about once in every 11 births among Yoruba women from Nigeria, once in 100 births among British women, and once in 700 births among Japanese women (Gall, 1996; Piontelli, 2002). Women in their late 30s are twice as likely as women in their early 20s to have DZ twins. Multiple ovulation is also genetic, which is why twins "run in families," inherited via the X chromosome. That also explains why twins are sometimes said to "skip a generation." A man who has a twinning X will not father twins because he does not ovulate, but his daughters (who inherit his X) might.

➤Answer to Observation Quiz (from page 71): Each multiple birth produces at least two babies, so twice as many children are twins as there are pregnancies that produce twins.

Like all siblings from the same parents, DZ twins have about half of their genes in common. And like any other siblings, they can look quite similar or they can differ markedly in many ways (including sex). Some look so much alike that genetic tests are necessary to determine that they are indeed dizygotic.

Assisted Reproduction

Many adults want to become parents but are unable to reproduce when they wish. Between 20 and 30 percent of all couples are troubled by **infertility,** which is defined as the inability to conceive after at least a year of trying.

infertility The inability to conceive after at least a year of trying to do so via sexual intercourse.

The lowest rates of infertility are among emerging adults (age 18–25) who have avoided drugs and sexually transmitted infections and who live in medically advanced nations. The highest rates worldwide are among couples over age 35 in sub-Saharan Africa.

About one-third of all infertility problems originate with women and one-third with men; the final one-third are of unknown origin (Orshan, 2008). For that reason, counseling and medical intervention usually involve both partners (Covington & Burns, 2006).

Many infertile couples who obtain counseling decide to become parents by adopting a child. Adoption is less common than it was 50 years ago. Because contraception, abortion, and single parenthood have all become more widespread, far fewer newborns are available for adoption in developed nations. As a result, more international adoptions occur—about 20,000 per year in the United States since 2000 (Gross, 2007).

The national origin of babies adopted by U.S. couples varies over time, as economies and laws change. For example, South Korea was once the main source, the birthplace of thousands of U.S. adoptees. Now fewer than 5 percent of international adoptees are from Korea. Currently, almost a third are from Ethiopia or Guatemala (see Figure 3.5).

In developed nations, infertile couples often turn to medical intervention, or **assisted reproductive technology (ART),** to help them conceive. One simple treatment for some cases of female infertility is to use drugs to cause ovulation; this often causes several ova to be released and multiple births to occur. If the male is infertile, sperm from a donor may be inserted into the female partner's uterus, in a process called *artificial insemination,* which has been in use for 50 years.

assisted reproductive technology (ART) A general term for the techniques designed to help infertile couples conceive and then sustain a pregnancy.

Major Countries of Origin for U.S. International Adoptees, 2007

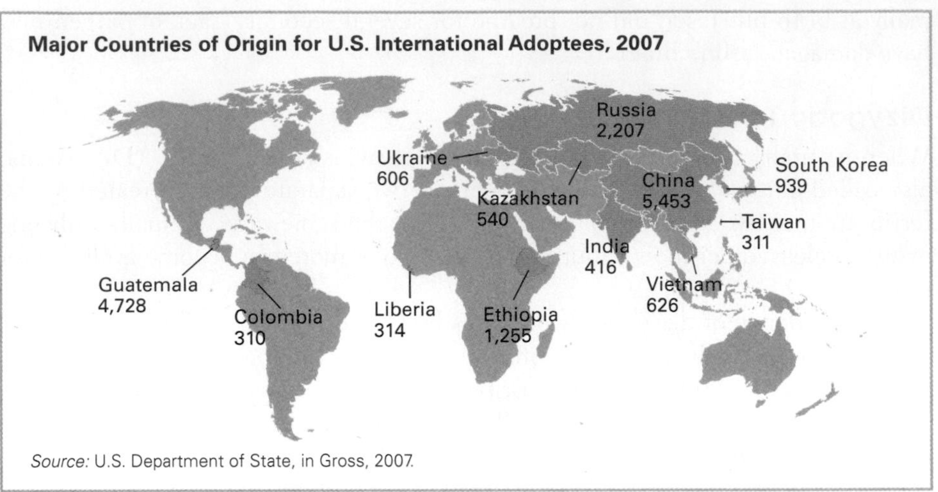

Source: U.S. Department of State, in Gross, 2007.

FIGURE 3.5

Why Vietnam but Not Indonesia? This map shows the top 12 nations from which infants (more girls than boys) were adopted into the United States in 2007. Decisions depend more on politics and culture than on population size or poverty: Many of the poorest and most populous nations (e.g., Indonesia, Nigeria, and Brazil) do not allow international adoptions.

In Vitro Fertilization

Increasingly common are various techniques that begin with **in vitro fertilization (IVF).** In this process, ova are surgically removed from a woman and mixed with sperm. If fertilization occurs, viable zygotes begin to duplicate in vitro, which literally means "in glass" (i.e., in a glass laboratory dish).

in vitro fertilization (IVF) Fertilization that takes place outside a woman's body (as in a glass laboratory dish). The procedure involves mixing sperm with ova that have been surgically removed from the woman's ovary. If the combination produces a zygote, it is inserted into the woman's uterus, where it may implant and develop into a baby.

Currently, a typical IVF cycle also uses *intra-cytoplasmic sperm injection (ICSI)*, in which one sperm is inserted into one ovum. IVF sidesteps problems with ovulation and blocked fallopian tubes. ICSI solves the problem of too few active sperm—problematic because conception requires thousands of sperm to swim to the ovum, even though only one succeeds in penetrating the ovum. ICSI is also used when a man is HIV-positive and his wife is HIV-negative. Such couples use condoms for sexual intercourse, but sperm can be collected and washed in the laboratory to rid them of the virus before being inserted into an ovum (Kato et al., 2006).

Risks and Benefits

Only about one-third of all IVF cycles produce a pregnancy, since implantation does not always occur. Nonetheless, since the world's first "test-tube baby" was born in England in 1978, IVF has produced more than a million infants in almost all nations; currently, 1 percent of all U.S. newborns are conceived this way (MMWR, June 8, 2007).

Some infertile adults may achieve conception and birth with the assistance of donated sperm, donated ova, or a donated womb. (These are said to be "donated" because it is illegal to profit from providing such services, although compensation is allowed.) Thus, it is possible for a newborn to have five parents: a genetic mother, a genetic father, a gestational mother, and a couple who paid for the services of the other three.

Complications and birth defects increase with IVF, especially when several zygotes are implanted at once (MacKay et al., 2006; Shevell et al., 2005). Low-birthweight twins or triplets are the outcome of almost half of all IVF pregnancies in the United States (MMWR, June 8, 2007).

Also in the United States, primarily because of ART, triplet births have increased by 500 percent since 1970; twin births have almost doubled in that time (U.S. Bureau of the Census, 2007). Hundreds of thousands of couples who thought they could never have any children now have two or three—often to their delight but to the distress of many scientists, as described in the following (Newton et al., 2007).

➤Answer to Observation Quiz (from page 72): The Japanese American girls are the monozygotic twins. If you were not sure, look at their teeth, their eyebrows, and the shape of their faces, compared with the ears and chins of the boys.

a view from science

IVF and Multiple Births

If you were infertile and wanted a baby, would you try IVF? If your answer is yes, knowing that each IVF cycle requires surgery and is costly (about $40,000, with marked variation from clinic to clinic), would you want several zygotes inserted at once to increase the chances of multiple births? Most infertile couples say yes; most developmentalists wish they would say no.

A pregnancy with more than one fetus increases the risk of complications for the mother, including high blood pressure and emergency cesarean birth. The babies are also likely to have problems, because the more fetuses that share a womb, the smaller, less mature, and more vulnerable each one is. Multiples are born small and early: on average, twins three weeks early; triplets, six weeks; and quadruplets, nine weeks.

All their lives, multiple-birth babies have higher rates of disease and disabilities; they develop more slowly and form weaker social bonds than equally small single babies; and they have higher rates of early death (Feldman & Eidelman, 2004). All of this is a burden on parents, of course, and also on the society that must pay more in health care for the average twin than for the average single-born child.

This cost-benefit analysis has convinced some governments to take action on IVF and ART. Finland allows only two zygotes to be implanted after in vitro fertilization. The limit is three in Norway and four in several other nations. In Belgium, the government pays only for single-embryo transfers, a policy that has halved that country's rate of twin births (Ombelet, 2007).

In the United States, couples pay for IVF (no public money is used) and can request as many embryos to be inserted as possible. If more than two embryos implant, many doctors recommend that some be selectively aborted in order to give the remaining ones a better chance of a healthy birth. A clash between scientific recommendations and personal wishes often results. As scientists have found ways to accomplish what earlier scientists could not, they have also uncovered complex new social and moral issues (Covington & Burns, 2006; Dooley et al., 2003).

SUMMING UP

Genes carried on the 23rd pair of chromosomes determine biological sex. Zygotes with an XX at the 23rd pair become female and those with an XY become male. Thus, when a man's chromosomes divide to make sperm, some are X and some are Y, and that determines whether the newborn will be a boy or girl. Twins are monozygotic (identical) if one zygote splits to create two separate organisms; they are dizygotic if two separate ova are fertilized by two sperm. The rate of dizygotic twins (and other multiples) is increasing because of assisted reproduction. Couples who are infertile have many ways to have children, including international adoption and IVF (in vitro fertilization). ■

From One Cell to Many

As already explained, when sperm and ovum combine into a zygote, they establish the *genotype*—all the genes that the developing person has. Creation of an actual person from one cell involves several complex processes of duplication of genetic information, cell division, and differentiation of cells into different types.

Some genes on the genotype are ignored and others amplified in the formation of the **phenotype,** which is the actual appearance and manifest behavior of the person. We begin by describing the early development of that one original cell, the zygote.

phenotype The observable characteristics of a person, including appearance, personality, intelligence, and all other traits.

New Cells, New Functions

Within hours after conception, the zygote begins *duplication* and *division.* First, the 23 pairs of chromosomes duplicate, forming two complete sets of the genome. These two sets move toward opposite sides of the zygote; the single cell splits neatly down the middle into two cells, each containing the entire original genetic code. These two cells duplicate and divide, becoming four, which duplicate and divide, becoming eight, and so on, all within one organism (except for monozygotic multiples).

By the time you (or I, or any other person) were born, your original one-celled zygote had become about 10 trillion cells. By adulthood, people have more than 100 trillion cells. But no matter how large the total number, no matter how much division and duplication occur, almost every cell carries an exact copy of the complete genetic instructions inherited by the one-celled zygote. This explains why DNA testing of any body cell, even from a drop of blood or a snip of hair, can identify "the real father," "the guilty criminal," or "the long-lost brother."

The fact that every cell in the embryo contains the developing human's complete genetic code does not mean that any cell could become a person—far from it. At about the eight-cell stage, a third process, *differentiation,* is added to duplication and division. In differentiation, cells begin to specialize, taking different forms and reproducing at various rates, depending on where they are located in the developing body. As one expert explains, "We are sitting with parts of our body that could have been used for thinking" (Gottlieb, 2002, p. 172).

Stem Cells

As a result of this specialization and differentiation, cells change soon after conception from being *stem cells,* able to produce any type of cell, to being able to become only one kind of cell. Specialization causes some cells to be part of an eye, others part of a finger. All cells carry the same genetic information, but specialized cells can no longer be stem cells.

Thousands of scientists are trying to find a way to make cells switch back to being stem cells. One group may have succeeded. They started with a skin cell from the tail of a mouse that had been genetically programmed, by elimination of a particular gene, to have sickle-cell anemia (Hanna, et al., 2007). They then treated that tail cell with viruses to make it revert to a stem cell. They added the missing gene and then put that treated cell back into the mouse. Success: The genetic disease was overcome by the healthy stem cell. This method is not yet safe for humans (and may not be safe for mice), but it is a step toward therapeutic use of stem cells.

Some genes include codes for activation of certain processes at a particular time in the life span, which explains why puberty occurs when it does, as well as why young children do not think or act like older ones. The ability to think about abstractions, to plan ahead, or even to learn to talk are beyond children whose brains are not yet genetically primed for such accomplishments (Marcus, 2004).

Many Factors

Keep in mind that "genes merely produce proteins, not mature traits" (Gottlieb, 2002, p. 164). In other words, the genotype instigates body and brain formation, but the phenotype (the visible traits and behaviors) depends on many genes and on the environment. Most traits are **polygenic** (affected by many genes) and **multifactorial** (influenced by many factors).

polygenic Referring to a trait that is influenced by many genes.

multifactorial Referring to a trait that is affected by many factors, both genetic and environmental.

A zygote might have the genes for becoming, say, a musical genius, but that potential will not be realized without the contributions of many other factors. Some of those factors are in the genome itself, because

> genes occupy only about 1.5 percent of the genome. The other 98.5 percent, dubbed "junk DNA," now appears to produce transcription of its genetic code, boosting the raw information output of the genome to about 62 times what the gene alone would produce.
>
> [Barry, 2007, p. 154]

Many of these biological factors are studied by thousands of geneticists, in many nations. Other factors are environmental; these are studied by other scientists. Almost daily, new discoveries reveal the multifactorial complexity of human development.

Gene–Gene Interactions

Many new discoveries have followed the completion of the **Human Genome Project** in 2001. One of the first surprises of the project was the discovery that humans have far fewer than the 100,000 genes previously thought. The total is actually between 18,000 and 23,000; the precise number is elusive because—another surprise—it is not always easy to figure out where one gene starts and another ends (Barry, 2007).

Human Genome Project An international effort to map the complete human genetic code. This effort was essentially completed in 2001, though analysis is ongoing.

Another surprise is the similarity of the genes of all living creatures. For example, the *Pax6 gene* directs the formation of the eyes of flies, mice, and people; if the Pax6 gene is missing in any creature, eyes do not form (Pratt & Price, 2006). Another gene produces the legs of a butterfly, a cat, a centipede, and a person. Chimpanzees have 48 chromosomes versus 46 for humans, but nonetheless humans and chimpanzees have 99 percent of their genes in common.

The genetic similarity among living creatures might make you wonder what accounts for the differences. The answer lies partly in that "junk DNA" around the genes (lower creatures have far less of it) and partly in the 100 or so "regulator" genes, which influence thousands of other genes (Marcus, 2004). Regulator genes direct formation of a creature who talks, walks, and thinks as humans do, and the material around the genes facilitates transcription (message sending) of the DNA.

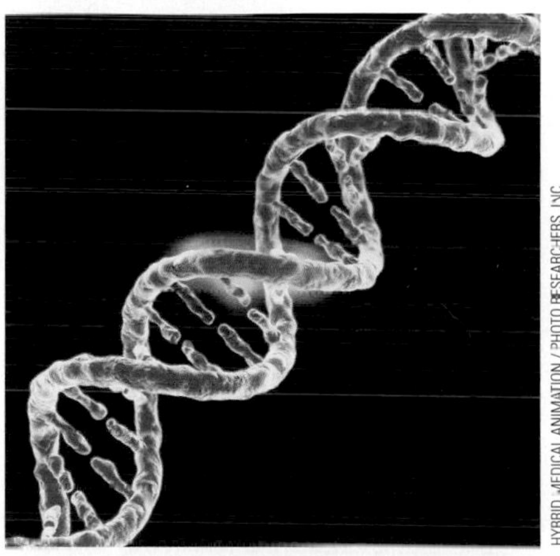

HYBRID MEDICAL ANIMATION / PHOTO RESEARCHERS, INC

Twelve of Three Billion Pairs This is a computer illustration of a small segment of one gene, with several triplets. Even a small difference in one gene, such as a few extra triplets, can cause major changes in the phenotype of a person.

Probably the crucial difference between humans and other creatures is in the brain. Adult brain size (about 1,400 cubic centimeters) is remarkably similar among humans worldwide, especially when compared with the small brains (about 370 cubic centimeters) of the chimpanzees (Holden, 2006). Of course, bigger animals (elephants) have bigger brains, but the proportion of brain to body is significantly greater for humans than for other creatures.

Another surprise from the Human Genome Project is that humans differ in many genetic ways from each other. Although more than 99 percent of the base pairs of the human genome are identical for all humans, minor variations in alleles, deletions, and duplications result in genetic interactions that render each person unique. To better understand how genes interact, it helps to understand additive, dominant, and recessive genes.

Additive Heredity

Some alleles are called **additive genes** because their effects *add up* to influence the phenotype. When genes interact additively, the trait they produce reflects the contributions of all the genes that are involved. Height, hair curliness, and skin color, for instance, are usually the result of additive genes. Indeed, height is affected by an estimated 100 genes, each contributing a small amount, some to make a person a little taller than average, some a little shorter (Little, 2002).

additive gene A gene that has several alleles, each of which contributes to the final phenotype (such as skin color or height).

Most people have ancestors of various heights, hair curliness, skin color, and so on, so a child's phenotype may not reflect the parents' phenotypes, although it always reflects their genotypes. My daughter Rachel (with the crooked little finger) is of average height, shorter than either my husband or me but taller than either of her grandmothers. She apparently inherited from us some of her grandmothers' genes for relatively short height.

Especially for Future Parents (see response, page 79): Suppose you wanted your daughters to be short and your sons to be tall. Could you achieve that?

Remember, a child inherits half of his or her genes from one parent and half from the other. How any additive trait turns out depends partly on the interactions of all the genes a child happens to inherit. Some genes amplify or dampen the effects of other genes, but each additive gene contributes something. For instance, the SRY gene on the Y chromosome produces male hormones. One effect of these hormones is to make boys taller. Therefore, even if a brother and sister happened to inherit identical height genes (unlikely, but possible), the boy (XY) would still grow to be several inches taller than the girl (XX).

Dominant–Recessive Heredity

Some alleles are not additive. This does not matter with homozygotic pairs, in which both genes provide the same instructions. It does matter with heterozygotic pairs, because the genes in these pairs don't exactly match; thus, their instructions differ. In one nonadditive form of heredity, alleles interact in a **dominant–recessive pattern,** meaning that one allele, the *dominant gene,* is more influential than the other, the *recessive gene.*

dominant–recessive pattern The interaction of a pair of alleles in such a way that the phenotype reveals the influence of one allele (the dominant gene) more than that of the other (the recessive gene).

Most recessive genes are harmless and produce only minor distinctions. For example, blue eyes are determined by a recessive allele and brown eyes by a dominant one, which means that couples who are discordant for eye color will have brown-eyed children—unless the parent with brown eyes is a carrier of the blue-eyes gene. Or two brown-eyed parents could have a blue-eyed child if both adults have the recessive blue-eyes gene.

Many recessive traits are not completely hidden and are influenced by other genes as well. This is evident even with eye color: Hazel eyes reflect a recessive blue-eyes gene.

Blood Types Sometimes the dominant gene controls the expression of a characteristic. A person with a recessive gene that is not expressed in the phenotype is said to be a **carrier** of that gene. The recessive gene is *carried* on the genotype but does not act to influence the phenotype. For example, the gene for blood type B is dominant and the gene for blood type O is recessive, which means that a person whose genotype is BO would have B blood type (and could receive a transfusion of B blood) and would be a carrier of O (irrelevant for transfusion).

carrier A person whose genotype includes a gene that is not expressed in the phenotype. Such an unexpressed gene occurs in half of the carrier's gametes and thus is passed on to half of the carrier's children, who will most likely be carriers, too. Generally, only when such a gene is inherited from both parents does the characteristic appear in the phenotype.

An additional blood factor is Rh, which can be positive or negative. The Rh-negative blood factor is recessive, so a person whose genetic pair for blood factor contains one Rh-positive gene *and* one Rh-negative gene would have Rh-positive blood. (Some of the complex relationships of blood genotype and phenotype are shown in Appendix A, p. A-3.) Blood type can include more than a dozen additional factors, which is why DNA detection often begins with blood samples.

With blood transfusion, it is a person's phenotype, not his or her genotype, that matters, and scientists are working to increase the precision of blood typing (Quill, 2008). For reproduction, however, the blood genotype may be crucial. For instance, if a zygote happens to inherit the Rh-positive factor from the father and the Rh-negative factor from the mother (who has the double recessive for that trait), and if the mother was exposed earlier to Rh-positive blood, she might have developed antibodies that destroy the Rh-positive blood of her fetus. Once, millions of babies were stillborn as a consequence of this clash. Now that the problem has been recognized and medicine has found ways to halt antibody production, such deaths have become rare.

X-Linked Genes A special case of the dominant–recessive pattern occurs with genes that are **X-linked,** that is, located on the X chromosome. If an X-linked gene is recessive—as are the genes for most forms of color blindness, many allergies, several diseases, and some learning disabilities—the fact that it is on the X chromosome is critical (see Table 3.1).

X-linked Referring to a gene carried on the X chromosome. If a boy inherits an X-linked recessive trait from his mother, he expresses that trait because the Y from his father has no counteracting gene. Girls are more likely to be carriers of X-linked traits but are less likely to express them.

Since the Y chromosome is much smaller than the X, an X-linked recessive gene almost never has a dominant counterpart on the Y. For this reason, recessive

TABLE 3.1

The 23rd Pair and X-Linked Color Blindness

X indicates an X chromosome with the X-linked gene for color blindness

23rd Pair	Phenotype	Genotype	Next Generation
1. XX	Normal woman	Not a carrier	No color blindness from mother
2. XY	Normal man	Normal X from mother	No color blindness from father
3. XX	Normal woman	Carrier from father	Half her children will inherit her X. The girls with her X will be carriers; the boys with her X will be color-blind.
4. XX	Normal woman	Carrier from mother	Half her children will inherit her X. The girls with her X will be carriers; the boys with her X will be color-blind.
5. XY	Color-blind man	Inherited from mother	All his daughters will have his X. None of his sons will have his X. All his children will have normal vision, unless their mother also had an X for color blindness.
6. XX	Color-blind woman (rare)	Inherited from both parents	Every child will have one X from her. Therefore, every son will be color-blind. Daughters will be only carriers, unless they also inherit an X from the father, as their mother did.

traits carried on the X affect the phenotypes of sons more often than those of daughters (who have another X, which usually has the dominant, normal gene). This explains, for instance, why 20 times as many boys as girls have color blindness, an X-linked disorder (McIntyre, 2002). (See Table 3.1.)

More Complications

As complex as the preceding explanation may seem, it simplifies the actual mechanism of genetic interaction by making genes appear to be separately functioning entities. But remember that genes merely direct the creation of 20 types of amino acids, which combine to produce thousands of proteins, which then form the body's structures and direct biochemical functions. Beginning at conception and continuing throughout life, the proteins of each cell interact with other proteins, nutrients, and toxins (Allis et al., 2007).

For any living creature, the outcome of all the interactions involved in heredity is difficult to predict. A small alteration in the sequence of base pairs of a gene or several extra repetitions in one triplet may be inconsequential or may cascade to create a major developmental problem. One reason prediction is difficult is that many early genetic interactions are seemingly a matter of chance.

Sometimes one half of a gene pair switches off during prenatal development, allowing the other to become dominant. When and why this happens is, at the moment, unpredictable; the very fact that it happens is a new discovery (Gimelbrant et al., 2007). Not quite as new is the understanding that one of a female's X chromosomes becomes inactive about 10 days after conception. It seems random whether the inactive X is the one from the mother or the father, and usually it does not matter much.

However, a few genes have different effects depending on whether they come from the mother or the father. This phenomenon is known as *imprinting*. The two best-known examples of imprinting are Prader-Willi syndrome and Angelman

➤**Response for Future Parents** (from page 77): Yes, but you wouldn't want to. You would have to choose one mate for your sons and another for your daughters, and you would have to use sex-selection methods. Even so, it might not work, given all the genes on your genotype. More important, the effort would be unethical, unnatural, and possibly illegal.

syndrome. Both result in cognitive impairment, and both are caused by a deletion of the same small part of chromosome 15. However, if that deletion occurs on the father's chromosome 15, the child (boy or girl) will develop Prader-Willi syndrome and become, among other things, obese and slow moving. But if it occurs on the mother's chromosome 15, the child will inherit Angelman syndrome and be thin and hyperactive.

SUMMING UP

After conception, the one-celled zygote begins duplication and division, following genetic instructions to form an embryo and, eventually, a person. Although most instructions are the same for every human, even for every mammal, some genes make humans distinct from other animals (especially in the brain), and a few genes make each person unique. Some genes are additive, some dominant, some recessive. All are affected by the environment, beginning at conception. Each person's phenotype (expressed characteristics) reflects his or her genotype (genetic inheritance) in complex ways; it is quite possible for a couple to produce a child whose phenotype is unlike that of either parent. ■

Genotype and Phenotype

The main goal of this chapter is to help every reader grasp the complexity of the relationship between genotype and phenotype. For the past 100 years, thousands of scientists have struggled to grasp this complexity.

At the beginning of the twentieth century, enthusiasm for genetics led to *eugenics* (literally, "good genes"), the idea that selective breeding was needed to improve the human race. That idea led to programs of forced sterilization of people who were thought to have "bad genes," a travesty that occurred not only in Nazi Germany but in other countries as well, including the United States.

In reaction to that horror, by mid-century social scientists were stressing the power of child rearing (nurture) over genetics (nature), a notion bolstered by behaviorism (see Chapter 2). Then research on twins began to accumulate, finding that monozygotic twins raised in separate households nonetheless shared many traits. The importance of genes was reaffirmed.

Research Design

Scientists: David Reiss, Jenae M. Neiderhiser, E. Mavis Hetherington, and Robert Plomin.

Publication: *The Relationship Code* (Harvard University Press, 2000), as well as many journals.

Participants: 720 families, each with two children aged 10–18 with varied genetic links: monozygotic twins, dizygotic twins, full siblings, half-siblings, and unrelated siblings with biological and stepparents.

Design: Dozens of checklists, interviews, and observations, including longitudinal measures, were used to indicate emotions and cognitive abilities of parents and adolescents, as well as their interactions. Extensive analysis was undertaken to distinguish genetic and environmental effects.

Major conclusion: Genes have a strong impact on every characteristic, but family structure and parental style modify genetic influence.

Comment: By including siblings with so many kinds of relationships to each other and to their parents, with multiple, longitudinal measures, this study untangles some complex nature–nurture interactions.

Current Consensus

In the past two decades, thousands of scientists in many nations have studied innumerable children, including stepsiblings, adopted siblings raised together, biological siblings raised apart, and twins, monozygotic or dizygotic, raised together or apart (e.g., Reiss et al., 2000; see the Research Design). Scientists currently exploring genotype and phenotype use tools and strategies that were once unavailable (including molecular analysis, mouse genomes, linkage studies, advanced statistics, and brain scans) to understand the inheritance of psychological as well as physical traits. Developmentalists today accept four generalities that were surprising when first reported (Ellis & Bjorklund, 2005; Miller et al., 2006; Plomin et al., 2003; Rutter, 2006):

1. Genes affect every aspect of behavior, including social interactions and intellectual abilities.
2. Most environmental influences on children raised in the same home are *not* shared.

3. Each child's genes elicit responses that shape development. In other words, children's upbringing and social environment are often partly the result of their genes.
4. Throughout life, in a process called *niche-picking,* people choose friends and environments that are compatible with their genes; thus, genetic influences *increase* with age.

As you learn more about the interactions among genetic and nongenetic influences, always remember to distinguish between a person's *genotype,* or genetic *potential,* and his or her *phenotype,* the actual *expression* of that genetic potential in the person's appearance, health, intelligence, and behavior.

Everyone carries genes that are not expressed in the phenotype. Only rarely is one gene, or even one pair of genes, the direct cause of a disorder (some instances are described below), but many combinations of genes affect the phenotype, additively or in some other way. There are many genes linked to schizophrenia, for instance. One reason for the various types of schizophrenia—and for variations in its severity in individuals—is that each person has different combinations of genes, all of which vary in expression (Harrison & Weinberger, 2005). Each person also has unique experiences, of course, and experience affects everything in a person's life, including the expression of mental illness.

About half of all genes affect the brain but not the rest of the body. Thus, thousands of genetic combinations, in which each gene has the potential for small but measurable effects, influence personality patterns and cognitive skills. The specifics depend on other genes, on family, and on culture (Vogler, 2006). As part of a study called the Hapmap Project, a team of eight scientists, working to decipher the coding variations of 11 million alleles, put it this way:

> Many different genes distributed throughout the human genome contribute to the total genetic variability of a particular complex trait, with any single gene accounting for no more than a few percent of the overall variability.
>
> [Hinds et al., 2005, p. 1079]

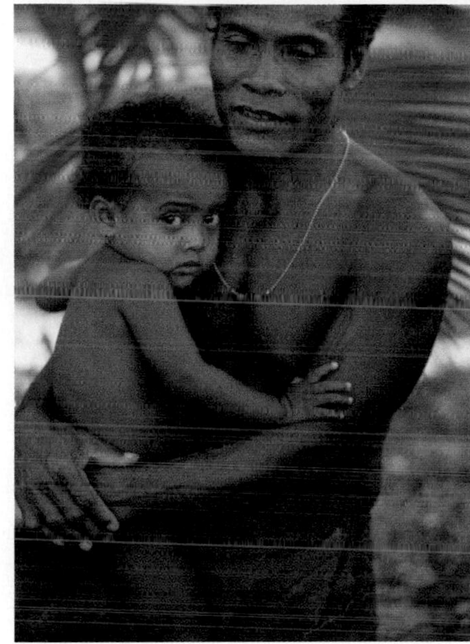

CORBIS / THE PURCELL TEAM

Shyness Is Universal Inhibition is a psychological trait that is influenced by genetics. It is more common at some ages (late infancy and early adolescence) and in some gene pools (natives of northern Europe and East Asia) than others. But every community includes some individuals who are unmistakably shy, such as this toddler in Woleai, more than 3,000 miles west of Hawaii.

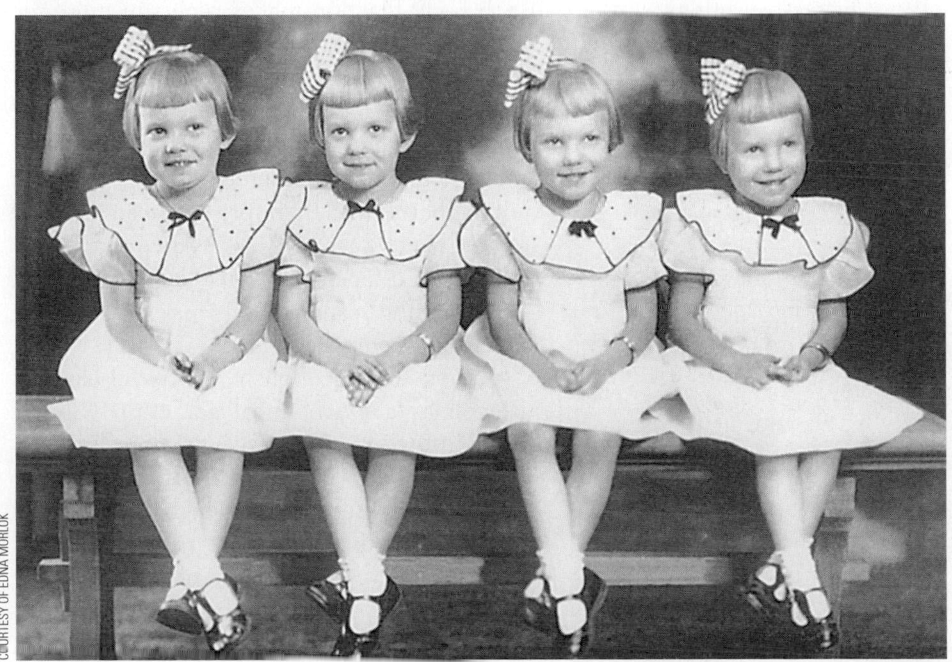

COURTESY OF EDNA MORLOK

Too Cute? This portrait of the Genain sisters was taken 20 years before they all developed schizophrenia. However, from their identical hair ribbons to the identical position of their feet, it is apparent that their unusual status as quadruplets set them apart as curiosities. Could their life in the spotlight have nurtured their potential for schizophrenia? There is no way to know for sure.

Thus, when something is "genetic," that does not mean that its genetic origins are substantial, fixed, or unalterable. It means that it is part of a person's basic foundation, affecting many aspects of life but determining none (Rutter, 2006). Rachel's little finger, mentioned in the chapter's opening, was the product of genes, but it might have not been crooked if her prenatal environment had been different.

Every trait, action, and attitude has a genetic component: Without genes, no behavior could exist. But without environment, no gene could be expressed. Now we examine two complex traits: addiction and visual acuity. As you read about two specific expressions of those traits (alcoholism and nearsightedness), you will see that understanding the progression from genotype to phenotype has many practical uses.

Alcoholism

At various times, drug addiction, including addiction to alcohol, has been considered a moral weakness, a social scourge, a personality defect, or some combination of the three. Addicts were locked up in jails or in mental institutions. Some nations tried to stop alcoholism by making alcohol illegal, as the United States did from 1919 to 1933, and most nations have laws forbidding use of certain drugs, as well as taxes to discourage the use of others.

Genetics of Alcoholism

Especially for Future Drug Counselors (see response, page 84): Is the wish for excitement likely to lead to addiction?

Nonaddicts have long wondered why addicts don't "just quit." Now we know that inherited biochemistry makes people vulnerable to various addictions. Anyone can abuse drugs and alcohol, but genes create an addictive pull that can be overpowering, extremely weak, or something in between (Heath et al., 2003).

Alcoholism has been studied for decades. Current thinking is that "genetic vulnerability [to alcoholism is] likely to be conferred by multiple genes of small to modest effects, possibly only apparent in gene–environment interactions" (Enoch, 2006, p. 193). Physiological reactions to alcohol vary, just as reactions to prescription drugs and many foods vary. Some drinkers become sleepy, others nauseated, others aggressive, others euphoric. Each body reaction makes a person more, or less, likely to have another drink.

Proof of the role of genes comes from the brain patterns of alcoholics' sons who have never consumed alcohol. Their brains differ from the brains of sons of nonalcoholics. The way bodies digest and metabolize alcohol allows some people to "hold their liquor" better and therefore to abuse alcohol. Others (notably many East Asians) sweat and become red-faced after just a few sips, an embarrassing response that may lead people to abstain instead.

Early Death or Long Life? Jerzy Skibo is a Polish farmer pausing to enjoy his lunch of sausage, cheese, and wine. This diet could be unhealthy if he is genetically vulnerable to heart disease or alcoholism. Or he might have protective genes and live to age 100, as some Polish farmers do.

RAYMOND GEHMAN / CORBIS

Genetically, alcoholism is a psychological as well as a biochemical addiction (Enoch et al., 2006), and both aspects are influenced by genes. Certain personality traits (a quick temper, sensation seeking, high anxiety) encourage drinking and drug taking. Certain contexts, such as fraternity parties, make it hard to avoid drinking; other contexts, such as a church social in a "dry" county, make it hard to drink.

Gender and Culture in Alcoholism

Gender also mitigates or increases susceptibility to alcoholism, depending on culture. For biological reasons (body size, fat composition, genes for metabolism), women become drunk on less alcohol than men do. In Japan, although women have the same genes as men for metabolizing alcohol, they drink only about a tenth as much. But when Japanese women live in the United States, their average alcohol consumption increases about fivefold (Higuchi et al., 1996). Obviously, gender, culture, and cohort all affect the contexts that encourage or discourage alcoholism.

Culture is particularly crucial. If people inherit genes that predispose them to alcoholism but live where alcohol is unavailable (in rural Saudi Arabia, for example), the genotype will never be expressed in the phenotype. Similarly, if alcohol-prone children grow up where alcohol is abundant but belong to a religious group that disapproves of drinking (such as Seventh-Day Adventists in California), they may escape their genetic tendency. Nature *and* nurture are required to create an alcoholic.

Visual Acuity

Both age and genes are powerful influences on vision. First consider age. Newborns cannot focus more than 2 feet away; children see better each year until about age 8; many adolescents develop nearsightedness (myopia) when their eyeball shape changes.

Heritability of Nearsightedness

Now consider genes. A study of British twins found that the Pax6 gene, which governs eye formation, has many alleles that make people somewhat nearsighted (Hammond et al., 2004). This research found heritability of almost 90 percent, which means that if one monozygotic twin is nearsighted, the other twin will almost always be nearsighted, too.

Heritability is a statistic that indicates only what percentage of the variation in a particular trait *within a particular population,* in a particular context and era, can be traced to genes. For example, the heritability of height is very high—about 95 percent—in nations in which children receive good medical care and ample nourishment; it is only about 20 percent in nations in which many children are malnourished. Thus, the 90 percent heritability of nearsightedness among British children does not necessarily apply elsewhere.

heritability A statistic that indicates what percentage of the variation in a particular trait within a particular population, in a particular context and era, can be traced to genes.

International Variations

In some places, visual problems are caused almost entirely by hazards in the environment. In many African nations, heritability of visual acuity is close to zero because nutrition, not genes, is the primary reason some children see better than others. The most dramatic example occurs when children lack vitamin A. More than 100,000 African children have poor sight for that very reason (West & Sommer, 2001). Scientists are working to develop a strain of maize (a dietary staple in Africa) that is high in vitamin A. If they succeed, heritability will increase as eyesight improves (Harjes et al., 2008).

What about children who are well nourished? Is their visual acuity entirely inherited? Multicultural research indicates that it is not. In Singapore, Taiwan, and Hong Kong, a surge in childhood myopia has been called an epidemic. The first published research on this phenomenon appeared in 1992, when scholars noticed a significant change in the results of army-mandated medical exams of all 17-year-old males in Singapore: 43 percent were nearsighted in 1990, compared with only

REUTERS / KIM KYUNG-HOON / LANDOV

Good Students These young Korean children are already learning to read a second language, Chinese. They are probably also advanced in math and science, compared with 8-year-olds in the United States. Their accomplishments may have come at a price: Many of them are nearsighted.

26 percent a decade earlier (Tay et al., 1992). Further studies found that the prevalence of nearsightedness in children increased in Taiwan from 12 percent at age 6 to 84 percent at age 17; in Singapore, from 28 percent at age 6 to 44 percent at age 9; in Hong Kong, from 10 percent at age 7 to 60 percent at age 10 (cited in Grosvenor, 2003).

Not every scholar is convinced that "myopia is increasing at an 'epidemic' rate, particularly in East Asia" (Park & Congdon, 2004, p. 21). A complication is that most of this research is cross-sectional (see Chapter 1), and, since nearsightedness increases with puberty, some of these increases may be the result of maturation. It is also possible that some of these children were already nearsighted by age 6 or so but had not yet been diagnosed.

The fact remains that the dramatic increase in nearsightedness among children in these nations is far greater than the increase among children outside East Asia. Furthermore, the parents of these same children are much less likely to be nearsighted, which suggests that nurture, not nature, is at play. What could the environmental cause be?

One possible culprit is often suggested: an increase in study time. In Chapter 12, you will learn that, unlike their parents, contemporary East Asian children are amazingly proficient in math and science, partly because they spend more time doing schoolwork than their parents did and more than Western children do. As their developing eyes focus on the pages in front of them, they may lose acuity for objects far away—which is exactly what nearsightedness means.

Ophthalmologists suggest that if Asian children spent more time outside playing, walking, or relaxing in daylight, fewer of them might need glasses (Goss, 2002; Grosvenor, 2003). As one expert concludes, "The extremely rapid changes in the prevalence of myopia and the dependence of myopia on the level of education indicate that there are very strong environmental impacts" on Asian children's vision (Morgan, 2003, p. 276).

A true experiment to test this hypothesis would be unethical. No scientist would randomly divide children into an experimental and a control group, with one group forbidden to play outside and the other group forbidden to study. But a study of 10- to 12-year-olds in Singapore found a correlation between nearsightedness (measured by optometric exams) and high achievement, especially in language (presumably reflecting more reading). You learned in Chapter 1 that correlation is not causation, but the odds ratio of 2.5 and a statistical significance of 0.001 strongly suggest a causal link (Saw et al., 2007).

➤Response for Future Drug Counselors (from page 82): Maybe. Some people who love risk become addicts; others develop a healthy lifestyle that includes adventure, new people, and exotic places. Any trait can lead in various directions. You need to be aware of the connection so that you can steer your clients toward healthy adventures.

Practical Applications

Some applications of the genotype–phenotype interaction are obvious. We know, for instance, that every disorder has a genetic component; therefore, parents need not blame their child rearing or their children for every problem that arises. If parents know each other's family history, or if they know that a particular child inherited a particular risk factor, they can avoid some recrimination and needless punishment.

Practical steps may also become clear. For instance, if alcoholism is in the genes, parents can keep alcohol away from their home and children. If nearsightedness runs in the family, parents can make sure that children spend time each day playing outdoors.

Of course, nondrinking and outdoor play are recommended for every child, as are dozens of other behaviors—such as flossing the teeth, saying thank you, getting enough sleep, eating vegetables, and writing thank-you notes. However, no child can do everything, and no parent can enforce every proper action. Awareness of genes helps parents set reasonable priorities, take constructive action, and avoid needless blame.

As you probably realize, this is not simple. Heritability refers to groups, not individuals. If a particular child is nearsighted, the nature–nurture ratio is elusive. Nurture cannot always overcome nature. However, every characteristic is partly genetic and partly not. Plasticity (see Chapter 1) is possible. Genes are not destiny.

Forgetting this fact can lead to dire consequences. Consider baseball superstar Mickey Mantle, who mistakenly thought that his "bad genes" were his fate, not a warning (Jaffe, 2004). Most of his male relatives died before they reached middle age, including his father, who died of cancer at age 39. Mantle concluded that he would die young, too. He ignored another genetic threat: Most of his male relatives were heavy drinkers of alcohol. Knowing his family history, Mantle could have avoided alcoholism by never starting to drink. In that case, his phenotype would not have reflected an aspect of his genotype. Instead he became "a notorious alcoholic, [because he] believed a family history of early mortality meant he would die young" (Jaffe, 2004, p. 37). At age 46 Mantle reportedly said, "If I knew I was going to live this long, I would have taken better care of myself." Despite a last-minute liver transplant, liver damage killed him at age 63—15 years short of the average life expectancy for a man of his era.

SUMMING UP

Genes affect every trait—whether it be a wonderful characteristic, such as a wacky sense of humor; a fearsome one, such as a violent temper; or a quite ordinary one, such as the tendency to be bored. The environment affects every trait as well, in ways that change as maturational, cultural, and historical processes unfold. Genetic expression can be directed or deflected, depending on the culture and the society as well as on the individual and the family. This is apparent in alcoholism, nearsightedness, and almost every other physical or psychological condition. All have genetic roots, developmental patterns, and environmental triggers. Knowing this can help people circumvent genetic tendencies for many forms of destructive behavior and disability. ■

Chromosomal and Genetic Abnormalities

We now focus on abnormalities that are caused by an identifiable problem, such as an extra chromosome or a single harmful gene. Such abnormalities are relevant to our study of development for three reasons:

- They provide insight into the complexities of nature and nurture.
- Knowing their origins helps limit their effects.
- Information combats the prejudice that surrounds such problems.

Information is needed as much for families dealing with a loved one's abnormality as for the affected individuals themselves. Infants born with genetic and chromosomal problems are much more likely to live into adulthood now than was the case a few decades ago. This development raises emotional and cognitive issues for their parents and siblings that are not yet well understood (Lewis et al., 2006).

GETTY (TAXI)

Is She the Baby's Grandmother? No. Women over age 40 now have a higher birth rate than women that age did just a few decades ago. Later-life pregnancies are more likely to involve complications, but the outcome is sometimes what you see here: a gray-haired mother thrilled with her happy, healthy infant.

mosaicism A condition in which an organism has a mixture of cells, some normal and some with an odd number of chromosomes or a series of missing genes.

Down syndrome A condition in which a person has 47 chromosomes instead of the usual 46, with three rather than two chromosomes at the 21st position. People with Down syndrome typically have distinctive characteristics, including unusual facial features, heart abnormalities, and language difficulties. (Also called *trisomy-21*.)

Not Exactly 46

Usually each sperm and each ovum has 23 chromosomes, and the zygote they create has 46. However, some gametes have a chromosomal abnormality: more or fewer than 23 chromosomes. One variable that correlates with chromosomal abnormalities is the parents' age, particularly the age of the mother. A possible explanation for an abnormal number of chromosomes is this: Since ova begin to form before a girl is born, older mothers have older ova that are more likely to split 22–24 instead of 23–23.

Chromosomal abnormalities can also occur after a zygote has formed, in the first days after conception. In a condition called **mosaicism,** cell duplication and division may produce a person with a mixture of cells, some with 46 chromosomes, some not.

Chromosomal problems are not rare: About 5 to 10 percent of all zygotes have more or fewer than 46 chromosomes (Brooker, 2009). Far fewer—less than 1 percent—are actually born, primarily because most such zygotes never duplicate, divide, and differentiate (Moore & Persaud, 2003). Many of those that begin to develop are spontaneously aborted early in pregnancy or aborted by choice when the parents learn about the abnormality. If such a fetus survives all this, birth itself is hazardous: About 5 percent of stillborn (dead-at-birth) babies have more than 46 chromosomes (Miller & Therman, 2001).

Once in about every 200 births, a viable infant is born with 45, 47, or, rarely, 48 or 49 chromosomes. Each of these abnormalities leads to a recognizable *syndrome,* a cluster of distinct characteristics that tend to occur together. Usually the cause is that three chromosomes occupy a particular location instead of the usual two, a condition called a *trisomy.*

Down Syndrome

Down syndrome is the most common extra-chromosome condition that may allow the fetus to survive. Down syndrome is also called *trisomy-21* because a person with this condition has three copies of chromosome 21.

The chances that a baby will be born with Down syndrome increase with the mother's age. According to one estimate, a 20-year-old woman has about 1 chance in 800 of carrying a fetus with Down syndrome; a 39-year-old woman, 1 in 67; and a 44-year-old woman, 1 in 16 (see Appendix A, p. A-3).

Some 300 distinct characteristics can result from the presence of that third chromosome 21. No individual with Down syndrome is quite like another, either in symptoms or in severity, for four reasons:

1. Some are mosaic, having some cells with 46 chromosomes and others with 47.
2. Only part of the extra chromosome 21 may be present.
3. Each person's environment is different, from conception onward.
4. Genes on other chromosomes affect those extra genes on the 21st chromosome.

Despite this variability, most people with trisomy-21 have specific facial characteristics—a thick tongue, round face, slanted eyes—as well as distinctively formed hands, feet, and fingerprints. Many also have hearing problems, heart abnormalities, muscle weakness, and short stature. They are usually slower to develop intellectually, especially in language (Cohen, 2005). Their eventual intellect varies: Some are severely retarded; others are of average or even above-average intelligence—although this is difficult to determine because many resist conventional testing (Cuskelly et al., 2002).

Many young children with trisomy-21 are sweet-tempered and less likely to cry or complain than are other children. This may become a liability if a child with Down syndrome gets less adult attention and thus less opportunity to learn, or if

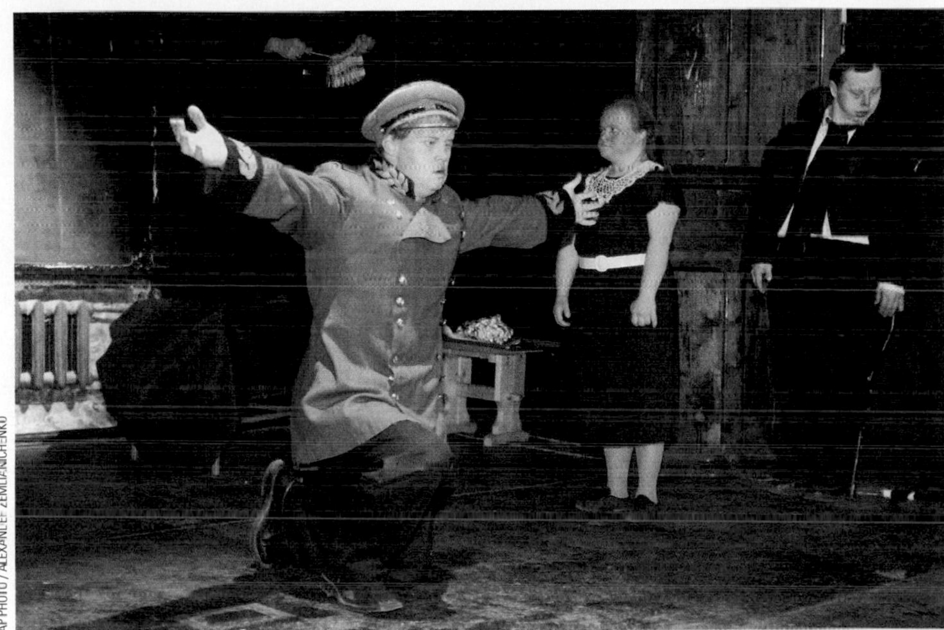

AP PHOTO / ALEXANDER ZEMLIANICHENKO

Great Theater A leading man named Sergei Makarov, shown here acting in a Gogol play, is extraordinarily talented. He is a member of Moscow's Theater of Simple Souls, all of whom have Down syndrome. Does "simple souls" evoke pity? No need; a film starring Makarov won the top prize in Russia's national film festival in 2006.

the child uses ineffective social strategies with other children (Wishart, 2007).

Adults with Down syndrome age faster than other adults, with the ailments of aging usually setting in at about age 30. By middle adulthood, they usually develop Alzheimer's disease, which severely impairs their communication skills. Serious heart and lung ailments result in a higher midlife death rate than that of other adults (Esbensen et al., 2007).

This generally pessimistic description, however, does not reflect the actual experience of everyone with Down syndrome. Some become happy young adults. One advised others:

> You may have to work hard, but don't ever give up. Always remember that you are important. You are special in your own unique way. And one of the best ways to feel good about yourself is to share yourself with someone else.
>
> *[Christi Todd, quoted in Hassold & Patterson, 1999]*

REUTERS / CLAUDIA DAUT

Universal Happiness All young children delight in painting brightly colored pictures on a big canvas, but this scene is unusual for two reasons: Daniel has trisomy-21, and this photograph was taken at the only school in Chile where normal and special-needs children share classrooms.

Abnormalities of the 23rd Pair

Every human has at least 44 autosomes and one X chromosome; a zygote cannot develop without those 45. However, about 1 in every 500 infants has only one X and no Y (the X stands alone) or has three or more sex chromosomes, not just two (Hamerton & Evans, 2005).

Having an odd number of sex chromosomes impairs cognitive and psychosocial development as well as sexual maturation. The specifics depend on the particular configuration as well as on other genetic factors (Mazzocco & Ross, 2007).

Most embryos with only one sex chromosome are not viable. There is one exception, however: *Turner syndrome* is a condition in which a person has only an X chromosome. It affects only girls (because there is no Y with an SRY gene), and it results in their having underdeveloped female organs and other anomalies.

The most common condition in which a person has three sex chromosomes instead of two is *Klinefelter syndrome,* which affects only boys with two X chromosomes

Especially for Future Doctors (see response, page 88): Might a patient who is worried about his or her sexuality have an undiagnosed abnormality of the sex chromosome?

➤Response for Future Doctors (from page 87): That is highly unlikely. Chromosomal abnormalities are evident long before adulthood. It is quite normal for adults to be worried about sexuality for social, not biological, reasons. If necessary, you could test the karyotype, but that is probably needlessly alarmist.

and one Y chromosome (XXY). Such a boy will be a little slow in elementary school, but not until age 12 or so—when the double X keeps his penis from growing and causes fat to accumulate around his breasts—does it become clear that something is wrong.

For boys with XXY, supplemental hormones can alleviate some physical problems, and special education aids learning—an example of nurture compensating for nature. Other children with too many sex chromosomes, such as XYY or XXX, are quite rare and usually have specific disabilities.

TABLE 3.2

Common Genetic Diseases and Conditions

Name	Description	Prognosis	Probable Inheritance	Incidence*	Carrier Detection?†	Prenatal Detection?
Albinism	No melanin; person is very blond and pale	Normal, but must avoid sun damage	Recessive	Rare overall; 1 in 8 Hopi Indians is a carrier	No	No
Alzheimer's disease	Loss of memory and increasing mental impairment	Eventual death, often after years of dependency	Early onset—dominant; after age 60—multifactorial	Fewer than 1 in 100 middle-aged adults; perhaps 25 percent of all adults over age 85	Yes, for some genes; ApoE4 allele increases incidence	No
Cancer	Tumors that can spread	With early diagnosis and treatment, most are cured; without them, death usually within 3 years	Multifactorial; almost all cancers have a genetic component	More than half of all people develop some form of cancer; about one-fourth die of it	No	No
Cleft palate, cleft lip	The two sides of the upper lip or palate are not joined	Correctable by surgery	Multifactorial	1 in every 700 births; more common in Asian Americans and American Indians	No	Yes
Club foot	The foot and ankle are twisted	Correctable by surgery	Multifactorial	1 in every 200 births; more common in boys	No	Yes
Cystic fibrosis	Mucous obstructions, especially in lungs and digestive organs	Most live to middle adulthood	Recessive gene; also spontaneous mutations	1 in 3,200; 1 in 25 European Americans is a carrier	Sometimes	Yes, in most cases
Diabetes	Abnormal sugar metabolism because of insufficient insulin	Early onset (type 1) fatal without insulin; for later onset (type 2), variable risks	Multifactorial; for later onset, body weight is significant	Type 1: 1 in 500 births; more common in American Indians and African Americans. Type 2: 1 adult in 6 by age 60	No	No
Deafness (congenital)	Inability to hear from birth on	Deaf children can learn sign language and live normally	Multifactorial; some forms are recessive	1 in 1,000 births; more common in people from Middle East	No	No
Hemophilia	Absence of clotting factor in blood	Death from internal bleeding; blood transfusions prevent damage	X-linked recessive; also spontaneous mutations	1 in 10,000 males; royal families of England, Russia, and Germany had it	Yes	Yes
Hydrocephalus	Obstruction causes excess fluid in the brain	Brain damage and death; surgery can make normal life possible	Multifactorial	1 in every 100 births	No	Yes
Muscular dystrophy (30 diseases)	Weakening of muscles	Inability to walk, move; wasting away and sometimes death	Recessive or multifactorial	1 in every 3,500 males develops Duchenne's	Yes, for some forms	Yes, for some forms

*Incidence statistics vary from country to country; those given here are for the United States. All these diseases can occur in any ethnic group. Many affected groups limit transmission through genetic counseling; for example, the incidence of Tay-Sachs disease is declining because many Jewish young adults obtain testing and counseling before marriage.
†"Yes" refers to carrier detection. Family history can also reveal genetic risk.

Gene Disorders

Everyone carries alleles that *could* produce serious diseases or handicaps in the next generation (see Table 3.2). Because most genes contribute only a small amount to a disorder and because the human genome was just recently mapped, the exact impact of each allele implicated in multifactorial disorders is not yet known (Hinds et al., 2005). However, much is known about single-gene disorders, which have been studied for decades (Miller et al., 2006), and we turn to them next.

Observation Quiz (see answer, page 90): Is there any ethnic group that does not have a genetic condition that is more common among its members than among the general population?

Name	Description	Prognosis	Probable Inheritance	Incidence*	Carrier Detection?†	Prenatal Detection?
Neural-tube defects (open spine)	Anencephaly (parts of the brain missing) or spina bifida (lower spine not closed)	Anencephalic—severe retardation; spina bifida—poor lower body control	Multifactorial; folic acid deficit and genes	Anencephaly—1 in 1,000 births; spina bifida—3 in 1,000; more common in Welsh and Scots	No	Yes
Phenylketonuria (PKU)	Abnormal digestion of protein	Mental retardation, preventable by diet begun by 10 days after birth	Recessive	1 in 100 European Americans is a carrier, especially Norwegians and Irish	Yes	Yes
Pyloric stenosis	Overgrowth of muscle in intestine	Vomiting, loss of weight, eventual death; correctable by surgery	Multifactorial	1 male in 200, 1 female in 1,000; less common in African Americans	No	No
Rett syndrome	Neurological developmental disorder	Boys die at birth. At 6–18 months, girls lose communication and motor abilities	X-linked	1 in 10,000 female births	No	Sometimes
Schizophrenia	Severely distorted thought processes	No cure; drugs, hospitalization, psychotherapy ease symptoms	Multifactorial	1 in 100 people develop it by early adulthood	No	No
Sickle-cell anemia	Abnormal blood cells	Possible painful "crisis"; heart and kidney failure; treatable with drugs	Recessive	1 in 11 African Americans and 1 in 20 Latinos are carriers	Yes	Yes
Tay-Sachs disease	Enzyme disease	Healthy infant becomes weaker, usually dying by age 5	Recessive	1 in 30 American Jews and 1 in 20 French Canadians are carriers	Yes	Yes
Thalassemia	Abnormal blood cells	Paleness and listlessness, low resistance to infections, slow growth	Usually recessive, occasionally dominant	1 in 10 Americans from southern Europe, northern Africa, or south Asia is a carrier	Yes	Yes
Tourette syndrome	Uncontrollable tics, body jerking, verbal outbursts	Appears at about age 5; worsens then improves with age	Dominant, but variable penetrance	1 in 250 children	Sometimes	No

Sources: Benacerraf, 2007; Briley & Sulser, 2001; Butler & Meaney, 2005; Haydon, 2007; Hemminki et al., 2008; Klug et al., 2008; McKusick, 2007; Mange & Mange, 1999; K. L. Moore & Persaud, 2007; Shahin et al., 2002.

Dominant-Gene Disorders

Most of the 7,000 *known* single-gene disorders are dominant (always expressed). They are known because they are easy to notice—their dominant effects are apparent in the phenotype. With a few exceptions, severe dominant disorders are rare because people who have such disorders rarely have children and thus the gene dies with them.

One exception is *Huntington's disease,* a fatal central nervous system disorder caused by a genetic miscode—more than 35 repetitions of a particular triplet. Unlike most dominant traits, the effects of Huntington's disease do not begin until middle adulthood. By that time, a person could have had several children, half of whom would inherit the same dominant gene (Bates et al., 2002).

Another exception is *Tourette syndrome,* which is relatively common because it is not disabling (Olson, 2004). About 30 percent of those who inherit the syndrome exhibit recurrent, uncontrollable tics and explosive verbal outbursts, which usually begin at about age 6. The remaining 70 percent have milder symptoms, such as an occasional twitch that is barely noticeable or a postponable impulse to clear their throat (Olson, 2004). (Many children and adults *without* this syndrome also have such symptoms.)

A person with mild Tourette syndrome might curse and tremor when alone but behave normally in public. Girls who have the Tourette genotype only rarely express it with the obvious tics and verbal explosions of young boys. Tourette syndrome is age-related: It often first appears at school age and sometimes disappears in adolescence.

Fragile X Syndrome

Several genetic disorders are sex-linked, or carried on the X chromosome. Males are thus more likely to be significantly affected by such conditions because they have only one X chromosome, whereas a female's second X chromosome may override the expression of a sex-linked disorder. One such disorder is called **fragile X syndrome;** it is caused by a single gene that has more than 200 repetitions of one triplet (Plomin et al., 2003). (Some repetitions are normal, but not this many.)

fragile X syndrome A genetic disorder in which part of the X chromosome seems to be attached to the rest of it by a very thin string of molecules. The cause is a single gene that has more than 200 repetitions of one triplet.

The cognitive deficits caused by fragile X syndrome are the most common form of *inherited* mental retardation (many other forms, such as trisomy-21, are not inherited). In addition to having cognitive deficits, children with fragile X syndrome often have emotional problems, such as being very shy or very aggressive, with poor social skills (Hagerman & Hagerman, 2002).

Although fragile X syndrome is an X-linked, single-gene disorder, the exact inheritance pattern is unknown. It does seem that repetitions increase when the affected X chromosome is passed from one generation to the next, and more repetitions lead to more disabilities.

Specific symptoms vary markedly (Cornish et al., 2007). About two-thirds of females with the fragile X gene are normal; one-third show some mental deficiency. Of males who inherit a fragile X, about 20 percent seem unaffected, about 33 percent are somewhat retarded, and the rest are severely retarded. Many of the people most severely disabled by fragile X syndrome also exhibit symptoms of autism (see Chapter 11). If a man with a fragile X is normal, half the sons of his daughters (his grandsons) will probably be significantly impaired because the number of repetitions increases with each generation. But predictions are imperfect because the transmission pattern varies.

➤**Answer to Observation Quiz** (from page 89): No. As you see, many major ethnic groups are mentioned in Table 3.2. In fact, even much smaller groups whose members tend to marry within the group also have higher rates of particular conditions.

Recessive-Gene Disorders

Most recessive disorders are on autosomes and thus are not X-linked. Examples include cystic fibrosis, thalassemia, and sickle-cell anemia, all of which are equally common and devastating in males and females (see Table 3.2). About 1 in 12 North Americans is a carrier for one of these three conditions. That high incidence occurs because, although the double-recessive pattern is lethal, one recessive gene is protective (Brooker, 2009).

For example, carriers of the sickle-cell trait are less likely to die of malaria, which is still prevalent in central Africa. Their descendants in North America, including about 10 percent of all African Americans, carry a gene that they do not need. Similarly, cystic fibrosis is more common among people whose ancestors came from northern Europe; carriers may have been protected from cholera.

Sometimes a person who carries a lethal gene has many descendants who marry each other. If both members of such a couple are carriers themselves, their children have one chance in four of inheriting the double recessive and thus the disease. For instance, many descendants of Ashkenazi Jews from one eastern European region have inherited the recessive Tay-Sachs gene. If two carriers marry each other, the Tay-Sachs gene is more likely to be expressed in their children. A child with Tay-Sachs disease begins to show symptoms at about 6 months; the disorder causes blindness, deafness, paralysis, and, ultimately, death by age 4 or 5. (A screening test is available to help limit the spread of this deadly condition.)

Tay-Sachs disease is also common among another group with high rates of intermarriage, the French Cajuns in Louisiana. Similarly, members of the Old Order Amish sect of eastern Pennsylvania have unusually high rates of a particular form of dwarfism. Just about everyone of every ethnicity is a carrier for some recessive disease, but it is relatively uncommon for two carriers of the same condition to marry; and unless that happens, the genotype never appears in the phenotype.

Especially for Historians (see response, page 92): Some genetic diseases may have changed the course of history. For instance, the last czar of Russia had four healthy daughters and one son with hemophilia. Once called the royal disease, hemophilia is X-linked. How could this rare condition have affected the monarchies of Russia, England, Austria, Germany, and Spain?

SUMMING UP

Many zygotes include an odd number of chromosomes or genes for a serious hereditary condition. Most of these zygotes never grow, or they are aborted spontaneously long before birth. However, some people with trisomy-21 (Down syndrome) or an odd number of sex chromosomes (such as Turner syndrome or Klinefelter syndrome) survive. They have physical and cognitive impairments, but some are able to lead fairly normal lives. Dominant genetic diseases are uncommon, but almost everyone carries a rare gene for a serious recessive condition. Occasionally, a single recessive gene is protective (e.g., the sickle-cell trait protects against malaria), promoting the survival of its carriers and thus increasing the likelihood of a marriage between two carriers. They have one chance in four of conceiving a child with the disease. ■

Genetic Counseling and Testing

Until recently, couples blamed witches or fate, not genes or chromosomes, after the birth of a child with a disorder. Today, often long before they marry, many young adults worry about passing on genetic conditions to their children. It seems that everyone has a relative with a serious condition, and everyone wonders if their children will inherit it.

Who Should Get Counseling, and When?

Genetic counseling provides facts and helps prospective parents discuss sensitive issues regarding their risk of passing along harmful conditions to their children. It includes testing, listening, and explaining by professional counselors. Counselors must be carefully trained, because many people, especially when considering

genetic counseling Consultation and testing by trained experts that enable individuals to learn about their genetic heritage, including harmful conditions that they might pass along to any children they may conceive.

➤Response for Historians (from page 91): Hemophilia is a painful chronic disease that (before blood transfusions became feasible) killed a boy before adulthood. Though rare, it ran in European royal families, whose members often intermarried, which meant that many queens (including England's Queen Victoria) were carriers of hemophilia and thus were destined to watch half their sons die of it. All families, even rulers of nations, are distracted from their work when they have a child with a mysterious and lethal illness. Some historians believe that hemophilia among European royalty was an underlying cause of the Russian Revolution of 1917 as well as of the spread of democracy in the nineteenth and twentieth centuries.

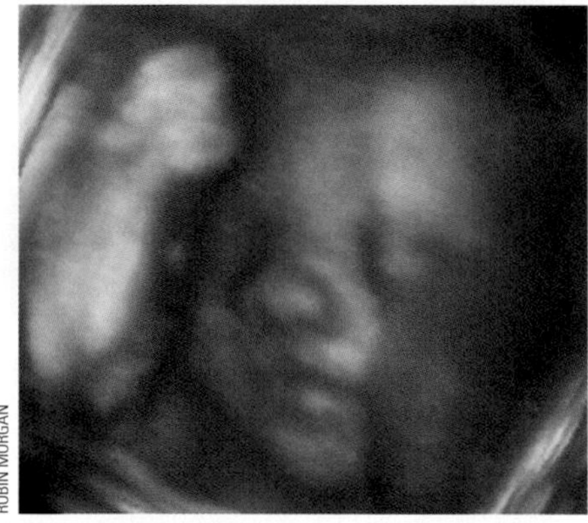

ROBIN MORGAN

There's Your Baby For many parents, their first glimpse of their future child is an ultrasound image. This is Alice Morgan, 63 days before birth.

phenylketonuria (PKU) A genetic disorder in which a child's body is unable to metabolize an amino acid called phenylalanine. The resulting buildup of phenylalanine in body fluids causes brain damage, progressive mental retardation, and other symptoms.

personal and emotionally laden information, need help understanding such concepts as "risks" and "probability" (O'Doherty, 2006).

Preconception, prenatal, or even prenuptial (before marriage) genetic testing and counseling are recommended for the following people:

- Individuals who have a parent, sibling, or child with a serious genetic condition
- Couples who have had several spontaneous abortions (miscarriages) or stillbirths
- Couples who are infertile
- Couples from the same ethnic group, particularly if they are related to each other
- Women over age 35 and men over age 40

Genetic counselors try to follow two ethical guidelines. First, tests are kept confidential, beyond the reach of insurance companies and public records. Second, decisions are made by the clients, not by the counselors. These guidelines are not always easy to follow.

One particular quandary arises when genetic tests on children with disabilities reveal that the husband is not the child's biological father. Counselors vary in how they handle this situation (Lucast, 2007).

A more general dilemma occurs when couples decide on a course of action that the counselor does not recommend. The professional's job is to explain the facts and risks, including probabilities and projections, and then allow couples to make their own choices.

Is Knowledge Always Power?

Genetic counselors, scientists, and the general public usually favor genetic testing, reasoning that having some information is better than having none. However, high-risk individuals (who might hear bad news) do not always want to know, especially if the truth might jeopardize their marriage, their insurance coverage, or their chance of parenthood.

One notable example occurs with people whose mother or father died of Huntington's disease, which means they have a 50/50 risk of developing the condition themselves. Many do not want to know their status unless they are contemplating parenthood. Those who learn that they do *not* have the gene often have a more difficult time coping with the news, psychologically, than do their siblings who develop the disease (Skirton & Patch, 2002). Their difficulty may arise from "survivors's guilt," some people's reaction to the realization that they have escaped a horrible fate that a loved one (in this case, a parent and often a sibling) suffer.

Accurate information may cause anxiety instead of relieving it. Testing before conception provides odds, not absolutes, so it leaves prospective parents unsure about whether their child would be healthy. Testing during pregnancy may result in parents having to choose between abortion and bearing a severely handicapped child. Testing after birth may cause parents to be less affectionate with a child, thus making the problem worse (Twomey, 2006).

Sometimes testing is recommended and even legally required. This is the case for **phenylketonuria (PKU).** Newborns with the double-recessive gene for PKU become severely retarded if they consume phenylalanine, a substance found in many foods. But if they maintain a diet free of that amino acid, they develop almost normally (Hillman, 2005). Society benefits with each child saved from harm, but the burden of maintaining the diet falls on the parents, who never imagined that the birth of a child would necessitate such care.

Dozens of other conditions are often tested for (specifics vary by state and nation). Although many developmentalists advocate testing because early diagnosis can mitigate many conditions, individualized counseling is also recommended when parents have various specific needs and inclinations. One study of the testing of newborns showed that some parents wanted only objective facts while others wanted emotional support. Parents were distressed if they sought one of these services but received the other (Tluczek et al., 2006).

Before conception, prospective parents' reactions to genetic testing vary enormously. Some high-risk individuals refuse testing. Others with the same risk choose testing and then sterilization. Still others take their chances, some accepting that they may have a seriously ill child and some deciding to abort the fetus if testing reveals the presence of a genetic defect.

Many factors require careful counseling, especially because misinformation abounds. Consider the experience of one of my students. A month before she became pregnant, Jeannette had a rubella vaccination. Hearing this, her prenatal care doctor told her that

> my baby would be born with many defects, his ears would not be normal, he would be mentally retarded. . . . I went home and cried for hours and hours. . . . I finally went to see a genetic counselor. Everything was fine, thank the Lord, thank you, my beautiful baby is okay.
>
> *[Jeannette, personal communication, 2008]*

ROBERT SPENCER / THE NEW YORK TIMES

"The Hardest Decision I Ever Had to Make" That's how this woman described her decision to terminate her third pregnancy when genetic testing revealed that the fetus had Down syndrome. She soon became pregnant again with a male fetus that had the normal 46 chromosomes, as did her two daughters and her fourth child, not yet born. Many personal factors influence such decisions. Do you think she and her husband would have made the same choice if they had had no other children?

Decisions about each child affect other children in the family, other relatives, and society as a whole (McConkie-Rosell & O'Daniel, 2007). Some people want tests for psychological disorders as well as physical ones, but counselors seldom recommend such testing, as the following explains.

a view from science

Genetic Testing for Psychological Disorders

Might your genes increase your chances of developing a psychological disorder—say, schizophrenia, dementia, bipolar disorder, autism, or addiction? If so, should you seek genetic testing to learn more? The Human Genome Project has accelerated the discovery of genes that add small bits to our store of risk data regarding every psychological condition. This growing knowledge has increased the demand from some members of the public to undergo genetic testing for such illnesses. For the most part, scientists refuse to conduct such tests. Let's briefly explore this area of controversy.

In Chapter 1's discussion of MAOA and antisocial personality, you read that psychological disorders are multifactorial: Genes increase vulnerability, but the environment is crucial. As another example, consider schizophrenia, a devastating condition that distorts thought and gives rise to hallucinations, delusions, garbled talk, and irrational emotions. When one monozygotic twin develops schizophrenia, about half the time the other identical twin will also develop the disorder (Harrison & Weinberger, 2005). For dyzygotic twins and other siblings, the risk is much lower—about 12 percent—but higher than the 1 percent incidence among people who have no relatives with schizophrenia. This leaves no doubt that genes are one factor.

Yet dozens of environmental conditions also correlate with schizophrenia. These include undernutrition of the mother during pregnancy, birth during the summer, use of psychoactive drugs in adolescence, emigration to another nation as a young adult, and family emotionality during adulthood. Because environment is crucial and many potentially contributing genes remain to be identified, few scientists think people would benefit from genetic testing for schizophrenia.

Another example is testing for the ApoE4 allele (that is, allele 4 of the ApoE gene), which is associated with Alzheimer's disease (Marx, 2007). Compared to people without that allele, a person with one ApoE4 allele has 8 times the risk of developing Alzheimer-type dementia in old age, and a person with two such alleles has 20 times the risk. Many researchers in gerontology test for ApoE4, but almost none tell the participants the results of those tests. They reason that the information might do more harm than good, especially since some people with the double allele never develop Alzheimer's disease and some people without it do. The test results do not change anything; they may simply add to the worry of people who have the allele and bring false assurance or survivor's guilt to people who do not.

For every condition, including unusual talents, learning abilities, and diseases, the interaction of genes and the environment makes development unpredictable, even if the genes are known. Some people with sickle-cell anemia suffer terribly and then die young, while others live satisfying lives, with occasional painful crises that can be weathered. Much depends on the family and social context as well as on interventions yet to be discovered (Gustafson et al., 2006). Genes are part of every human story, influencing every page, but they never determine the plot or the final paragraph.

SUMMING UP

Genetic testing can relieve many worries and increase the proportion of healthy children. However, information about risks and consequences is not always benign. Many people believe that prospective parents should know what genes they carry; some high-risk individuals and parents of children with serious ailments are not so sure. The costs and benefits of testing vary by disease: Some tests merely estimate the risk of a disease for which no cure is available (e.g., Alzheimer's disease); other tests are quite accurate and make it possible to avert a severe disability (e.g., PKU). Counselors try to explain facts and probabilities with compassion; the final decision about whether or not to have a baby is made by the couple, not the counselor. ■

SUMMARY

The Genetic Code

1. Genes are the foundation for all development, first instructing the living creature to form the body and brain, and then regulating thought and behavior. Human conception occurs when two gametes (an ovum and a sperm, each with 23 chromosomes) combine to form a zygote, 46 chromosomes in a single cell.

2. Genes and chromosomes from each parent match up to make the zygote. The match is not always perfect, because of genetic variations called alleles.

Sex, Multiple Births, and Fertility

3. The sex of an embryo depends on the sperm: A Y sperm creates an XY (male) embryo; an X sperm creates an XX (female) embryo. Every cell of every living creature has the unique genetic code of the zygote that began that life. The human genome contains about 20,000 genes in all.

4. Twins occur if a zygote splits into two separate beings (monozygotic, or identical, twins) or if two ova are fertilized by two sperm (dizygotic, or fraternal, twins). Monozygotic multiples are genetically the same. Dizygotic multiples have only half of their genes in common, as do all other siblings who have the same parents.

5. Fertility treatments, including drugs and in vitro fertilization, have led not only to the birth of millions of much-wanted babies but also to an increase in multiple births, which have a higher rate of medical problems.

From One Cell to Many

6. Genes interact in various ways, sometimes additively, with each gene contributing to development, and sometimes in a dominant–recessive pattern. Environmental factors influence the phenotype as well.

7. The environment interacts with the genetic instructions for every trait, even for physical appearance. Every aspect of a person is almost always multifactorial and polygenic.

8. The first few divisions of a zygote are stem cells, capable of becoming any part of a person. Then cells differentiate, specializing in a particular function.

9. Combinations of chromosomes, interactions among genes, and myriad influences from the environment all assure both similarity and diversity within and between species. This aids health and survival.

Genotype and Phenotype

10. Environmental influences are crucial for almost every complex trait, with each child as well as each culture experiencing different environments.

11. Some people are genetically susceptible to alcoholism and nearsightedness, but nongenetic factors affect every condition. Cultural differences in the rates of both of these problems are dramatic evidence for the role of nurture.

12. Knowing the impact of genes and the environment can be helpful. People are less likely to blame someone for a characteristic that is inherited, but realizing that someone is at risk of a serious condition helps with prevention.

Chromosomal and Genetic Abnormalities

13. Often a gamete has fewer or more than 23 chromosomes. The result is a zygote with an odd number of chromosomes.

14. Usually zygotes with other than 46 chromosomes do not develop. The main exceptions are three chromosomes at the 21st location (Down syndrome, or trisomy-21) or an odd number of sex chromosomes. In such cases, the child has physical and cognitive problems but can live a nearly normal life.

15. Everyone is a carrier for genetic abnormalities. Usually those conditions are recessive (not affecting their phenotype). If dominant, the trait is usually mild, varied, or inconsequential until late adulthood. If being a carrier for a genetic abnormality, such as the sickle-cell trait, is protective, then that gene can become widespread in a population.

Genetic Counseling and Testing

16. Genetic testing and counseling can help many couples learn whether their future children are at risk for a chromosomal or genetic abnormality. Genetic testing usually provides information about risks, not actualities. Couples, counselors, and cultures differ in the decisions they make.

KEY TERMS

deoxyribonucleic acid (DNA) (p. 66)
chromosome (p. 66)
gene (p. 66)
allele (p. 67)
genome (p. 67)
gamete (p. 67)
zygote (p. 68)
genotype (p. 68)
23rd pair (p. 69)
XX (p. 69)
XY (p. 69)
monozygotic (MZ) twins (p. 71)
dizygotic (DZ) twins (p. 73)
infertility (p. 73)
assisted reproductive technology (ART) (p. 73)
in vitro fertilization (IVF) (p. 74)
phenotype (p. 75)
polygenic (p. 76)
multifactorial (p. 76)
Human Genome Project (p. 77)
additive gene (p. 77)
dominant–recessive pattern (p. 78)
carrier (p. 78)
X-linked (p. 78)
heritability (p. 83)
mosaicism (p. 86)
Down syndrome (p. 86)
fragile X syndrome (p. 90)
genetic counseling (p. 91)
phenylketonuria (PKU) (p. 92)

KEY QUESTIONS

1. What are the relationships among proteins, genes, chromosomes, and the genome?

2. How and when is the sex of a zygote determined? Why is the ratio of boy babies to girl babies significant?

3. Which method of identifying a criminal do you think is most accurate: a lineup of suspects, a confession, a fingerprint match, or DNA identification? Why?

4. Genetically speaking, how similar are people to each other and to other animals?

5. Sometimes parents have a child who looks like neither of them. How does that happen?

6. What are the differences among monozygotic twins, dizygotic twins, other siblings, and clones?

7. From the prospective parents' perspective, what are the advantages and disadvantages of adoption versus ART?

8. Explain how the course of alcoholism or nearsightedness is affected by nature and by nurture.

9. What are the causes and effects of Down syndrome?

10. Why is genetic counseling a personal decision and usually confidential?

11. Genetic testing for various diseases is much more common now than it once was. What are the advantages and disadvantages?

APPLICATIONS

1. Pick one of your traits, and explain the influences that both nature *and* nurture have on it. For example, if you have a short temper, explain its origins in your genetics, your culture, and your childhood experiences.

2. Many adults have a preference for a son or a daughter. Interview adults of several ages and backgrounds about their preferences. If they give the socially preferable answer ("It does not matter"), ask how they think the two sexes differ. Listen and take notes—don't debate. Analyze the implications of the responses you get.

3. Draw a genetic chart of your biological relatives, going back as many generations as you can, listing all serious illnesses and causes of death. Include ancestors who died in infancy. Do you see any genetic susceptibility? If so, how can you overcome it?

4. List a dozen people you know who need glasses (or other corrective lenses) and a dozen who do not. Are there any patterns? Is this correlation or causation?

4

CHAPTER OUTLINE

Prenatal Development and Birth

My friend Judy, who taught history at the United Nations School, habitually contrasted the broad sweep of global history and the immediate, local particulars. She did this even when she was pregnant, rubbing her belly and saying, "Statistically, this is probably a Chinese boy."

Judy was right. The majority of newborns are male (about 52 percent), and more of them (about 25 percent) are Chinese than any other ethnicity. Given Judy's personal particulars (her age, her genes), no one was surprised when she gave birth to a European American girl. Judy herself seemed awestruck, repeatedly recounting tiny details, as if no baby like hers had ever appeared before. She was right about that, too.

Judy's situation illustrates the dual themes of this chapter. Every topic—prenatal development, possible toxins, birthweight, medical assistance, parent–infant bonding—is directly relevant to the 150 million babies born on earth each year. Universal patterns are described. Yet each pregnancy and birth is unique. This chapter includes generalities and variations. Learn all you can—and if you have a baby, expect to be awed by your personal miracle.

From Zygote to Newborn

The most dramatic and extensive transformation of the entire life span occurs before birth. To make prenatal development easier to study, pregnancy is often divided into three main periods. The first two weeks are called the **germinal period;** the weeks from the third through the eighth are the **embryonic period;** the months from the ninth week until birth are the **fetal period.** (Alternative terms related to the phases of pregnancy are discussed in Table 4.1.)

germinal period The first two weeks of prenatal development after conception, characterized by rapid cell division and the beginning of cell differentiation.

embryonic period The stage of prenatal development from approximately the third through the eighth week after conception, during which the basic forms of all body structures, including internal organs, develop.

fetal period The stage of prenatal development from the ninth week after conception until birth, during which the organs grow in size and mature in functioning.

Germinal: The First 14 Days

You learned in Chapter 3 that the one-celled *zygote* soon begins to duplicate, divide, and differentiate (see Figure 4.1). When the cells take on distinct characteristics and gravitate toward particular positions relative to one another, the entire cell mass—still very fragile and tiny—is called a **blastocyst.**

blastocyst A cell mass that develops from the zygote in the first few days after conception.

TABLE 4.1

Timing and Terminology

Popular and professional books use various phrases to segment pregnancy. The following comments may help to clarify the phrases used.

- *Beginning of pregnancy:* Pregnancy begins at conception, which is also the starting point of *gestational age*. However, the organism does not become an *embryo* until about two weeks later, and pregnancy does not affect the woman (and cannot be confirmed by blood or urine testing) until implantation. Paradoxically, many obstetricians date the onset of pregnancy from the date of the woman's last menstrual period (LMP), about 14 days *before* conception.
- *Length of pregnancy:* Full-term pregnancies last 266 days, or 38 weeks, or 9 months. If the LMP is used as the starting time, pregnancy lasts 40 weeks, sometimes expressed as 10 lunar months. (A lunar month is 28 days long.)
- *Trimesters:* Instead of *germinal period, embryonic period,* and *fetal period,* some writers divide pregnancy into three-month periods called *trimesters*. Months 1, 2, and 3 are called the *first trimester;* months 4, 5, and 6, the *second trimester;* and months 7, 8, and 9, the *third trimester.*
- *Due date:* Although doctors assign a specific due date (based on the woman's LMP), only 5 percent of babies are born on that exact date. Babies born between three weeks before and two weeks after that date are considered "full term" or "on time." Babies born earlier are called *preterm;* babies born later are called *post-term*. The words *preterm* and *post-term* are more accurate than *premature* and *postmature*.

placenta The organ that surrounds the developing embryo and fetus, sustaining life via the umbilical cord. The placenta is attached to the wall of the pregnant woman's uterus.

implantation The process, beginning about 10 days after conception, in which the developing organism burrows into the placenta that lines the uterus, where it can be nourished and protected as it continues to develop.

About a week after conception, the blastocyst, now consisting of more than 100 cells, separates into two distinct masses. The outer cells form a shell that will become the **placenta** (the organ that develops within the pregnant woman's uterus to protect and nourish the developing creature), and the inner cells form the nucleus that will become the embryo.

The first task of the outer cells is to achieve **implantation**—that is, to embed themselves in the nurturing environment of the uterus. Implantation occurs about 10 days after conception and is hazardous (K. L. Moore & Persaud, 2003). At least 60 percent of all natural conceptions and 70 percent of all in vitro conceptions fail to implant (see Table 4.2).

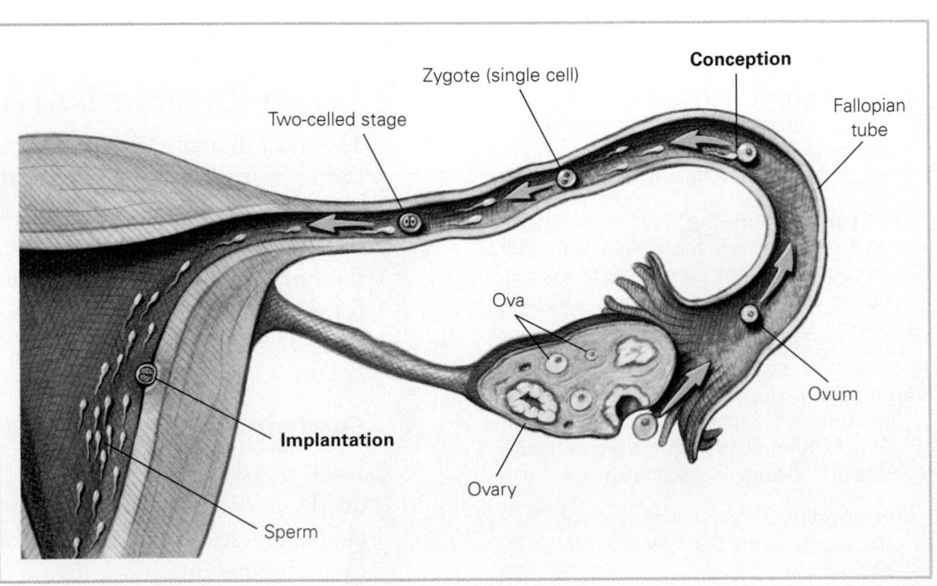

FIGURE 4.1

The Most Dangerous Journey In the first 10 days after conception, the organism does not increase in size because it is not yet nourished by the mother. However, the number of cells increases rapidly as the organism prepares for implantation, which occurs successfully about a third of the time.

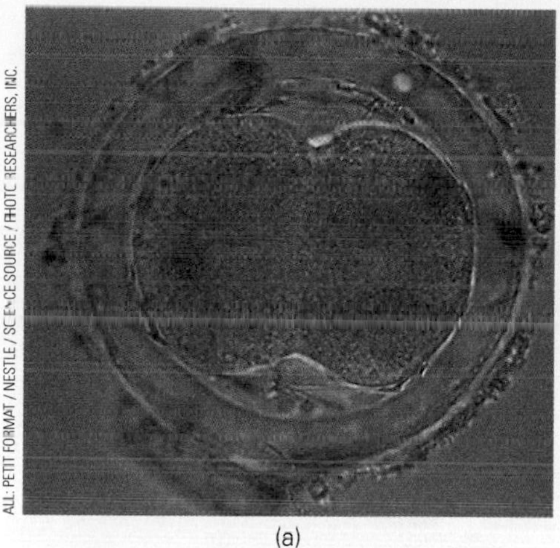
(a)

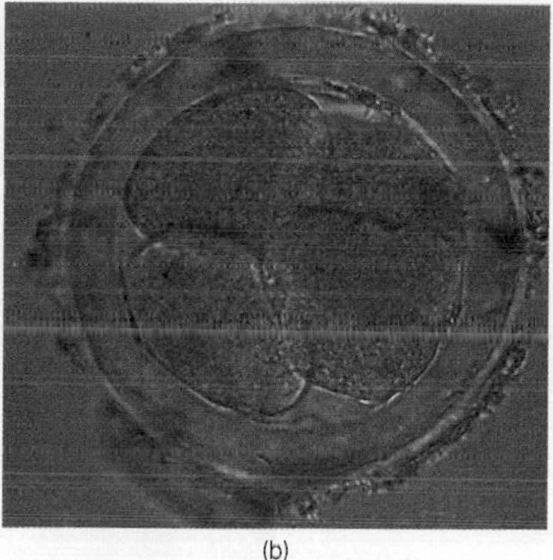
(b)

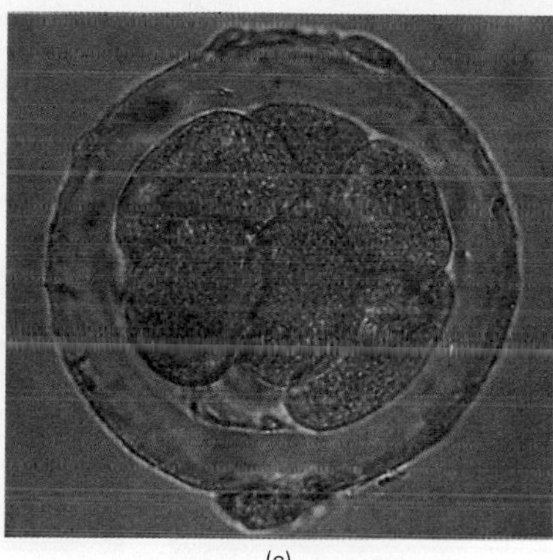
(c)

First Stages of the Germinal Period The original zygote as it divides into (*a*) two cells, (*b*) four cells, and (*c*) eight cells. Occasionally at this early stage, the cells separate completely, forming the beginning of monozygotic twins, quadruplets, or octuplets.

TABLE 4.2

Vulnerability During Prenatal Development

The Germinal Period
At least 60 percent of all developing organisms fail to grow or implant properly and thus do not survive the germinal period. Most of these organisms are grossly abnormal.

The Embryonic Period
About 20 percent of all embryos are aborted spontaneously, most often because of chromosomal abnormalities.

The Fetal Period
About 5 percent of all fetuses are aborted spontaneously before viability at 22 weeks or are stillborn, defined as born dead after 22 weeks.

Birth
About 31 percent of all zygotes grow and survive to become living newborn babies.

Sources: Bentley & Mascie-Taylor, 2000; K. L. Moore & Persaud, 2003.

Embryo: From the Third Through the Eighth Week

The start of the third week initiates the *embryonic period,* when the former blastocyst becomes a distinct being—not yet recognizably human but worthy of a new name, **embryo.** The first sign of a human body structure appears as a thin line (called the *primitive streak*) down the middle of the embryo. This line becomes the *neural tube* 22 days after conception and eventually develops into the *central nervous system*—the brain and spinal cord (K. L. Moore & Persaud, 2003).

embryo The name for a developing human organism from about the third through the eighth week after conception.

The head begins to take shape in the fourth week, as eyes, ears, nose, and mouth start to form. Also in the fourth week, a minuscule blood vessel that will become the heart begins to pulsate, making the cardiovascular system the first to show any activity.

By the fifth week, buds that will become arms and legs appear. The upper arms and then forearms, palms, and webbed fingers form. Legs, feet, and webbed toes, in that order, emerge a few days later, each with the beginning of a skeletal structure. Then—52 and 54 days after conception, respectively—the fingers and toes separate.

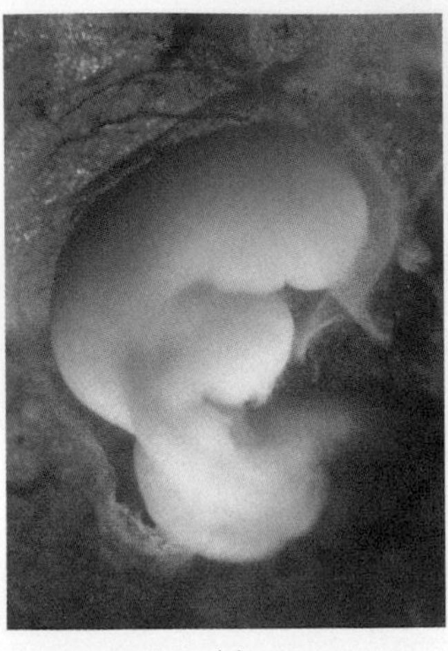

(a)

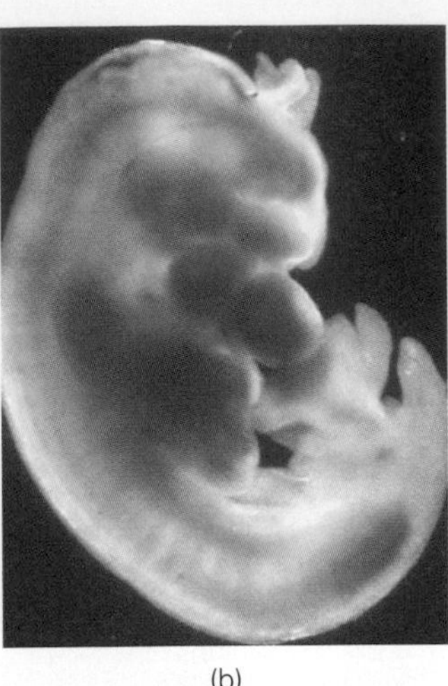

(b)

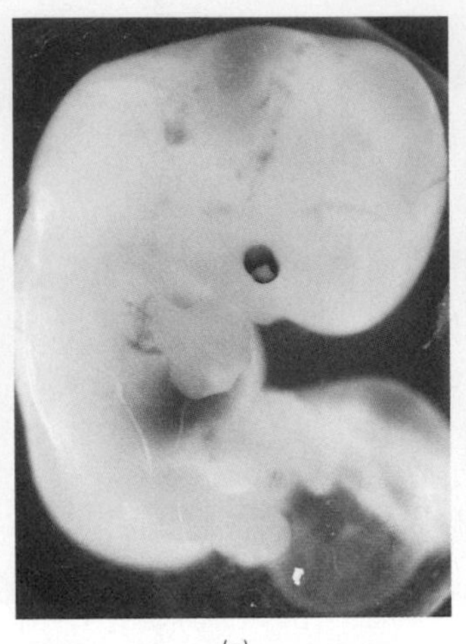

(c)

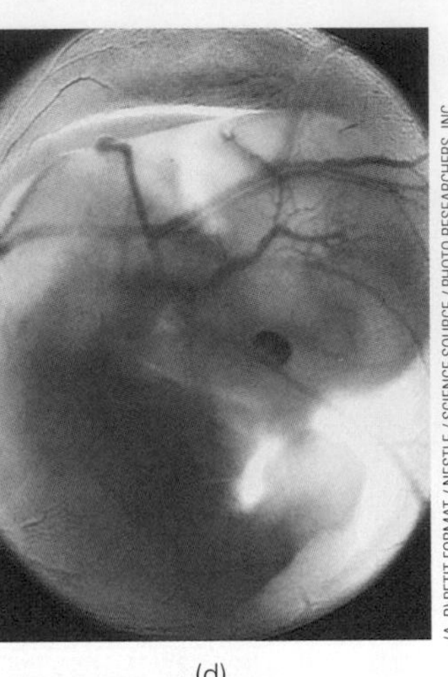

(d)

The Embryonic Period *(a)* At 4 weeks past conception, the embryo is only about 1/8 inch (3 millimeters) long, but already the head (*top right*) has taken shape. *(b)* At 5 weeks past conception, the embryo has grown to twice the size it was at 4 weeks. Its primitive heart, which has been pulsing for a week now, is visible, as is what appears to be a primitive tail, which will soon be enclosed by skin and protective tissue at the tip of the backbone (the coccyx). *(c)* By 7 weeks, the organism is somewhat less than an inch (2½ centimeters) long. Eyes, nose, the digestive system, and even the first stage of toe formation can be seen. *(d)* At 8 weeks, the 1-inch-long organism is clearly recognizable as a human fetus.

At the eighth week after conception (56 days), the embryo weighs just one-thirtieth of an ounce (1 gram) and is about 1 inch (2½ centimeters) long. The head has become rounded, and the features of the face are formed. The embryo has all the basic organs and body parts of a human being, including elbows and knees, nostrils and toes, and a unisex structure called the *indifferent gonad.* It moves frequently, about 150 times an hour (Piontelli, 2002).

Fetus: From the Ninth Week Until Birth

fetus The name for a developing human organism from the start of the ninth week after conception until birth.

The developing organism is called a **fetus** from the start of the ninth week after conception until birth. During the fetal period, it develops from a tiny, sexless creature smaller than the last joint of your thumb to a 7½-pound, 20-inch (3,400 grams, 51 centimeters) boy or girl.

The Third Month

Especially for Biologists (see response, page 102): Many people believe that the differences between the sexes are primarily sociocultural, not biological. Is there any prenatal support for that view?

If an embryo is male (XY), the SRY gene on the Y chromosome commands that male sexual organs develop; with no such command, the indifferent gonad develops into female sex organs. By the 12th week, the genitals are fully formed and are sending hormones to the developing brain.

Although most functions of the brain are gender-neutral, many (but not all) neuroscientists believe that hormones cause some sex differences in brain organization by mid-pregnancy (Neave, 2008). This has been shown in birds and lower animals; it may be true for people as well.

At the end of the third month, the fetus has all its body parts, weighs approximately 3 ounces (87 grams), and is about 3 inches (7.5 centimeters) long. Early prenatal growth is very rapid, but there is considerable variation from fetus to fetus, especially in body weight (K. L. Moore & Persaud, 2003). The numbers just given—3 months, 3 ounces, 3 inches—are rounded off for easy recollection. (For those who use the metric system, "100 days, 100 millimeters, 100 grams" is similarly useful.)

Despite the variations, some aspects of third-month growth are universal. The 3-month-old fetus is too small to survive outside the womb, and the organs are not yet functioning. However, all the body structures are in place.

The Middle Three Months: Preparing to Survive

In the fourth, fifth, and sixth months, the heartbeat becomes stronger and the cardiovascular system becomes more active. Digestive and excretory systems develop. Fingernails, toenails, and buds for teeth form, and hair grows (including eyelashes).

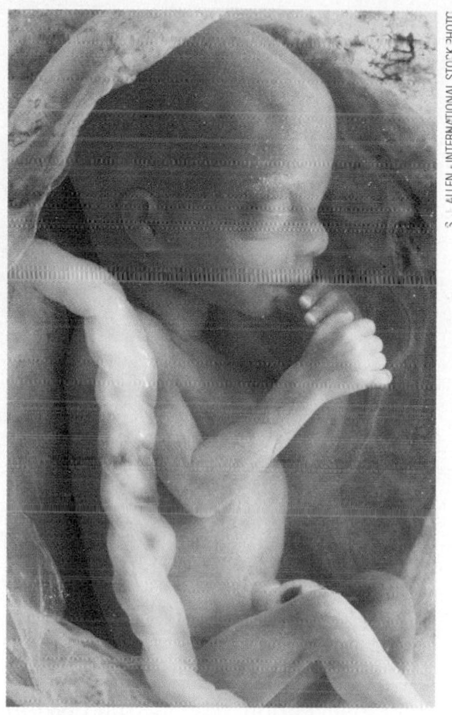

S. J. ALLEN / INTERNATIONAL STOCK PHOTO

The Fetus At the end of 4 months, the fetus, now 6 inches long, looks fully formed but out of proportion—the distance from the top of the skull to the neck is almost as long as that from the neck to the rump. For many more weeks, the fetus must depend on the translucent membranes of the placenta and umbilical cord (the long white object in the foreground) for survival.

Observation Quiz (see answer, page 103): Can you see eyebrows, fingernails, and genitals?

Brain Development Amazing as body growth is, the brain's development during this time is even more impressive. It increases about six times in size and develops many new neurons, or brain cells (in a process called *neurogenesis*), and synapses (*synaptogenesis*), which are connections between neurons. The neurons begin to organize themselves, some dying, some extending long axons to distant neurons (Kolb & Whishaw, 2003). Brain growth and neurological organization continue for years, as you will see in later chapters (in which we discuss neurons, synapses, and axons more fully).

Advances in fetal brain functioning are critical to attainment of the **age of viability,** the age at which a preterm newborn can survive. That's because the brain regulates basic body functions, such as breathing and sucking. With advanced medical care, the age of viability is about 22 weeks after conception, although most babies born this early weigh under 500 grams (less than a pound), and those who live are often severely disabled because the brain does not develop as well outside the uterus. (For a summary of information about preterm birthweights, see Table 4.7 on page 119.)

age of viability The age (about 22 weeks after conception) at which a fetus may survive outside the mother's uterus if specialized medical care is available.

Babies born before 22 weeks of gestation do not survive. This barrier has not been broken even with sophisticated respirators and heart regulators, probably because maintaining life requires some brain response (Paul et al., 2006). Fifty years ago, babies born at 23–26 weeks also died, but their survival rate has improved dramatically—about two-thirds live (Kelly, 2006; Wilson-Costello et al., 2007).

Preterm Newborns However, such preterm infants are vulnerable. A study that compared 8-year-olds who had been born very early with others who had been born full term (at 35–40 weeks) found that 20 percent of the preterm children had cerebral palsy, 41 percent had some degree of mental retardation, and only 20 percent had no disabilities (Marlow et al., 2005).

Modern medical care has reduced the proportion of 22- to 28-week-old newborns who die before birth, but mortality and morbidity rates for this group have not improved over the past decade. That somber statistic has led one team to suggest that neonatal care has reached its limits (Paul et al., 2006).

At about 28 weeks, brain-wave patterns include occasional bursts of activity that resemble the sleep–wake cycles of a newborn, and heart rate and body movement become reactive, not random, decreasing when the fetus needs rest. Because of brain and organ maturation, most babies born at 28 weeks develop normally.

Can He Hear? A fetus, just about at the age of viability, is shown fingering his ear. Such gestures are probably random; but, yes, he can hear.

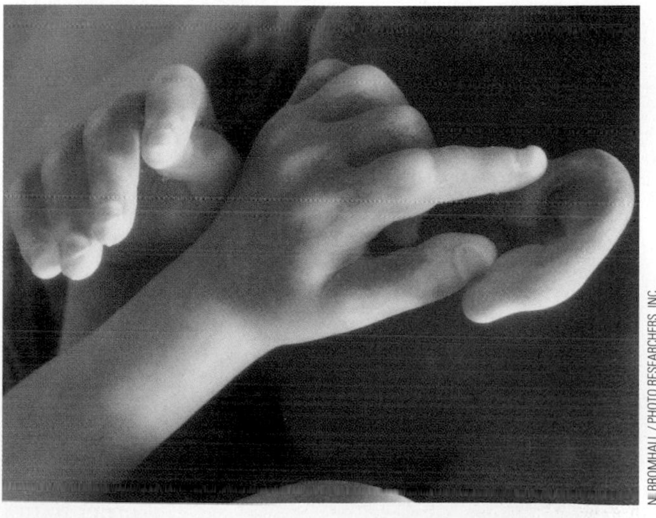

NI BROMHALL / PHOTO RESEARCHERS, INC.

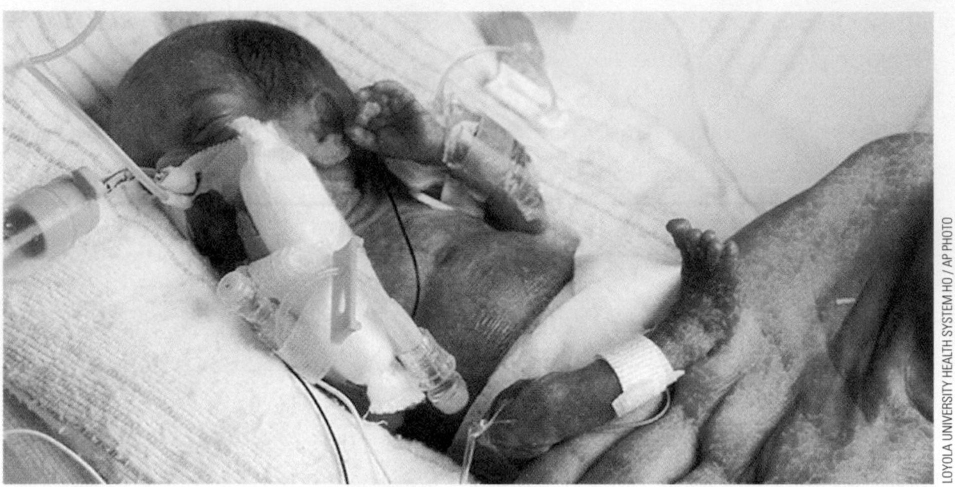

LOYOLA UNIVERSITY HEALTH SYSTEM HO / AP PHOTO

One of the Tiniest Rumaisa Rahman was born after 26 weeks and 6 days weighing only 8.6 ounces (244 grams). Nevertheless, she has a good chance of living a full, normal life. Rumaisa gained 5 pounds (2,270 grams) in the hospital and then, 6 months after her birth, went home. Her twin sister, Hiba, who weighed 1.3 pounds (590 grams) at birth, had gone home two months earlier. At their one-year birthday, the twins seemed normal, with Rumaisa weighing 15 pounds (6,800 grams) and Hiba 17 (7,711 grams) (CBS News, 2005).

Weight is significant, although not as significant as brain maturity. By 28 weeks, the typical fetus weighs about 3 pounds (1.3 kilograms), and its chances of survival are 95 percent.

Weight is an imprecise indicator for maturity. For babies who are genetically small or who gain less weight because they are twins, the critical variable is time since conception. This is true even in countries in which prenatal care results in fewer preterm infants than in the United States. For instance, a study of adolescents in Spain found that those who were born at 34 weeks were intellectually indistinguishable from those born full term (38 weeks), but those born before 28 weeks had brain abnormalities and a lower average IQ (Narberhaus et al., 2007).

A very tiny preterm infant who survives makes headlines. Amillia Taylor was born in October 2006 after only 21 weeks and six days in the uterus—a new record (Wingert, 2007). Since she was conceived via IVF, Amillia's gestational age was actually 22 weeks. She weighed just 10 ounces (284 grams) and measured a mere 9½ inches (24 centimeters). Her survival was aided by her sex (girls survive more often) and birthplace (a specialized neonatal facility in Miami).

The Final Three Months: From Viability to Full Term

For a fetus to reach the age of viability simply means that life outside the womb is *possible*. Each day of the final three months of prenatal growth improves the odds, not merely of survival but of a healthy and happy baby.

A viable preterm infant born in the seventh month is a tiny creature requiring intensive hospital care and life-support systems for each gram of nourishment and for every shallow breath. By contrast, after nine months or so, the typical full-term infant is a vigorous person, ready to thrive at home on mother's milk—no expert help, oxygenated air, or special feeding required.

The critical difference between a fragile preterm baby and a robust newborn is maturation of the neurological, respiratory, and cardiovascular systems. In the final three months of prenatal life, brain waves indicate responsiveness; the lungs expand and contract, using the amniotic fluid as a substitute for air; and heart valves, arteries, and veins circulate the fetal blood.

Fetal weight gain in the last three months is about 4½ pounds (2,040 grams). This increase ensures adequate nutrition to the developing brain and protects against severe malnutrition in the last trimester, which would reduce learning ability and health lifelong (Jones & Devoe, 2005). The brain grows rapidly toward the end of pregnancy (Malinger et al., 2006). At full term, human brain growth is so extensive that the *cortex* (the brain's advanced outer layer) forms several folds in order to fit into the skull (see Figure 4.2).

➤**Response for Biologists** (from page 100): Only one of the 46 human chromosomes determines sex, and the genitals develop last in the prenatal sequence. Sex differences are apparent before birth, but they are relatively minor.

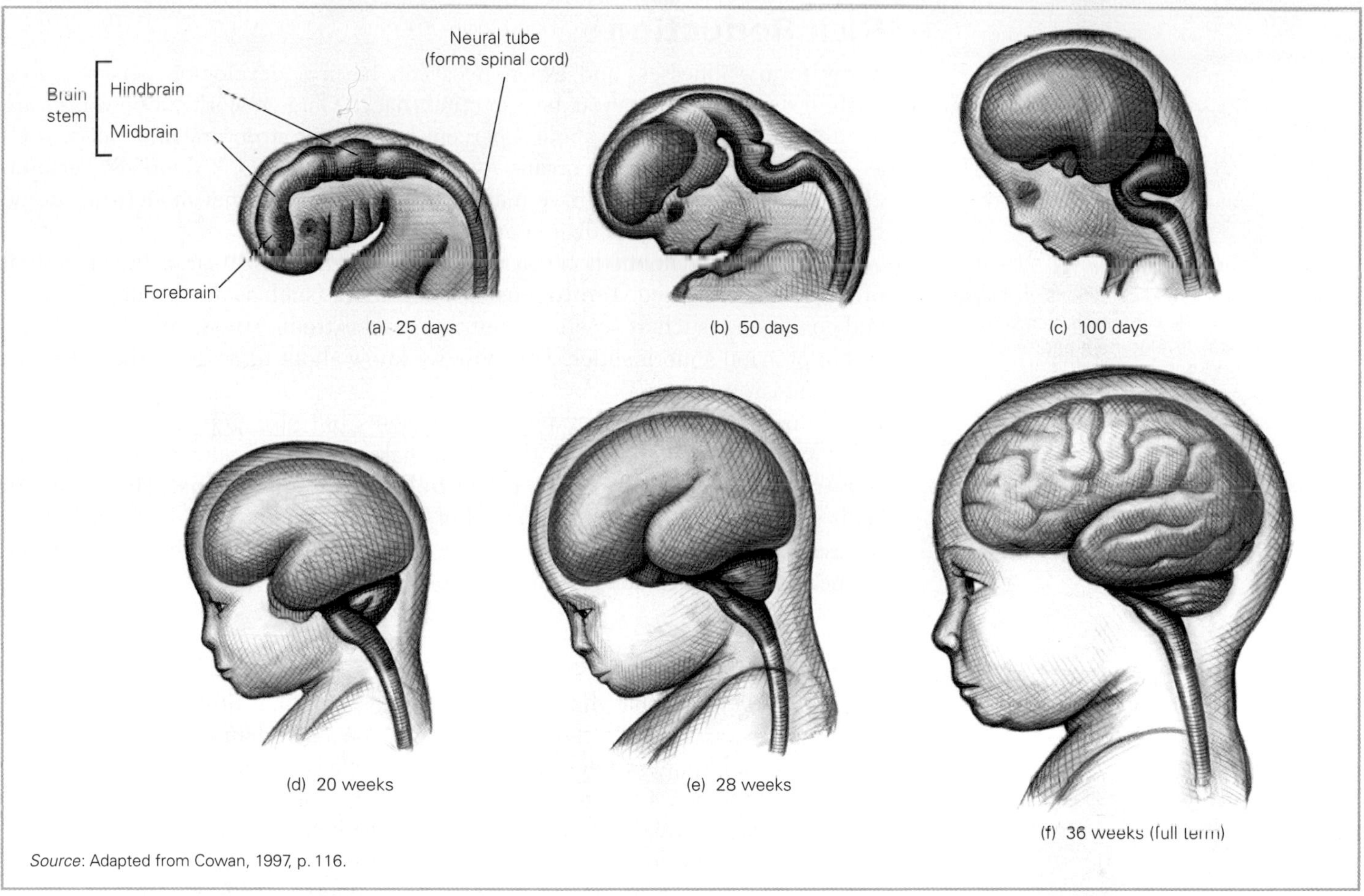

Source: Adapted from Cowan, 1997, p. 116.

FIGURE 4.2

Prenatal Growth of the Brain Just 25 days after conception (*a*), the central nervous system is already evident. The brain looks distinctly human by day 100 (*c*). By the 28th week of gestation (*e*), at the very time brain activity begins, the various sections of the brain are recognizable. When the fetus is full term (*f*), all the parts of the brain, including the cortex (the outer layer), are formed, folding over one another and becoming more convoluted, or wrinkled, as the number of brain cells increases.

The relationship between mother and child intensifies during the final three months, for the fetus's size and movements make the pregnant woman very aware of it. In turn, the fetus becomes aware of the mother's sounds (voice and heartbeat), smells (via amniotic fluid), and behavior (Aslin & Hunt, 2001). Regular walking is soothing, and sudden noises cause the fetus to jump.

When the mother is highly fearful or anxious, the fetal heart beats faster and body movements increase (DiPietro et al., 2002). Research from many scientists suggests that maternal stress can affect the fetal nervous system, influencing the child's responses to threat lifelong (Austin et al., 2005; Kapoor et al., 2006; Viltart & Vanbesien-Mailliot, 2007).

SUMMING UP

In two weeks of rapid cell duplication, differentiation, and finally implantation, the one-celled zygote becomes a blastocyst and then a many-celled embryo. The embryo develops the beginning of the central nervous system (3 weeks), a heart and a face (4 weeks), arms and legs (5 weeks), hands and feet (6 weeks), and fingers and toes (7 weeks), while the inner organs take shape. By 8 weeks, all the body structures, except male and female organs, are in place. Fetal development proceeds rapidly. A weight gain of about 2 pounds (900 grams) and brain maturation make viability possible by about 22 weeks. Further development of the brain, lungs, and heart makes the full-term, 35- to 40-week-old newborn ready for life. ■

➤**Answer to Observation Quiz** (from page 101): Yes, yes, and no. Genitals are formed, but they are not visible in this photo. The object growing from the lower belly is the umbilical cord.

Risk Reduction

Many toxins, illnesses, and experiences can harm a developing person before birth. If this topic alarms you, bear in mind that the large majority of newborns are healthy and capable. Only about 3 percent have major structural anomalies, such as cleft palate, malformed organs, or missing limbs (K. L. Moore & Persaud, 2003); another 10 percent have minor physical problems that modern medicine can treat, such as an extra digit or an undescended testicle.

teratogens Agents and conditions, including viruses, drugs, and chemicals, that can impair prenatal development and result in birth defects or even death.

Prenatal development is not a dangerous period to be feared but a natural process to be protected. **Teratogens** are substances (such as drugs and pollutants) and conditions (such as severe malnutrition and extreme stress) that increase the risk of prenatal abnormalities. The more we know about teratogens, the better we are able to avoid them.

behavioral teratogens Agents and conditions that can harm the prenatal brain, impairing the future child's intellectual and emotional functioning.

Teratogens cause not only physical problems but also impaired learning and behavior. Teratogens that harm the brain, making a child hyperactive, antisocial, learning-delayed, and so on, are called **behavioral teratogens.** The origins of such problems are difficult to trace, but about 20 percent of all children have behavioral difficulties (usually not noticed until years after birth) that *could* be connected to damage done during the prenatal period.

Determining Risk

It was once believed that the placenta screened out all harmful substances. Then two tragedies occurred. In the first, doctors on an Australian military base traced an increase in blindness among newborns to rubella (German measles) contracted by pregnant women a few months earlier (Gregg, 1941, in Persaud et al., 1985). Scientists realized that some diseases during pregnancy could harm a fetus.

The second episode was mentioned in Chapter 1: A sudden increase in the number of infants born with missing or deformed arms and legs in the late 1950s was traced to the mothers' use of a new sedative called thalidomide (Schardein, 1976). Scientists realized that exposure to drugs taken by the mother could also harm a fetus.

teratology The study of birth defects.

risk analysis The science of weighing the potential effects of a particular event, substance, or experience to determine the likelihood of harm. In teratology, risk analysis attempts to evaluate everything that affects the chances that a particular agent or condition will cause damage to an embryo or fetus.

The effort to understand what triggered such damage gave rise to **teratology,** the study of the causes and effects of birth defect abnormalities. Teratology is a science of **risk analysis,** of weighing the chances that a particular teratogen will affect the fetus. More than 10,000 studies of animals and people have shown that hundreds of teratogens exist. These include not just diseases and drugs but also chemicals widely used in daily life; stressful events; trace chemicals and minerals in food, water, and air; vitamin deficiencies; and even maternal exhaustion.

All teratogens increase the *risk* of damage, but none of them *always* cause damage. Critical prenatal factors—timing, dosage, and genes—are described here. Some postnatal influences—such as early care and attachment—are discussed in the three chapters on infancy (Chapters 5, 6, and 7).

Timing of Exposure

One crucial factor is timing—the age of the developing organism when it is exposed to the teratogen. Some teratogens cause damage early in prenatal development, when a particular part of the body is forming. Thalidomide, for example, stopped or impaired the formation of arms and legs if the mother took the drug in weeks 6 or 7, but it caused no damage if it was taken after week 9.

You learned in Chapter 1 that the time of greatest susceptibility is called the *critical period.* As you can see in Figure 4.3, each body structure has its own critical period. The entire six weeks of the embryonic stage can be called a critical

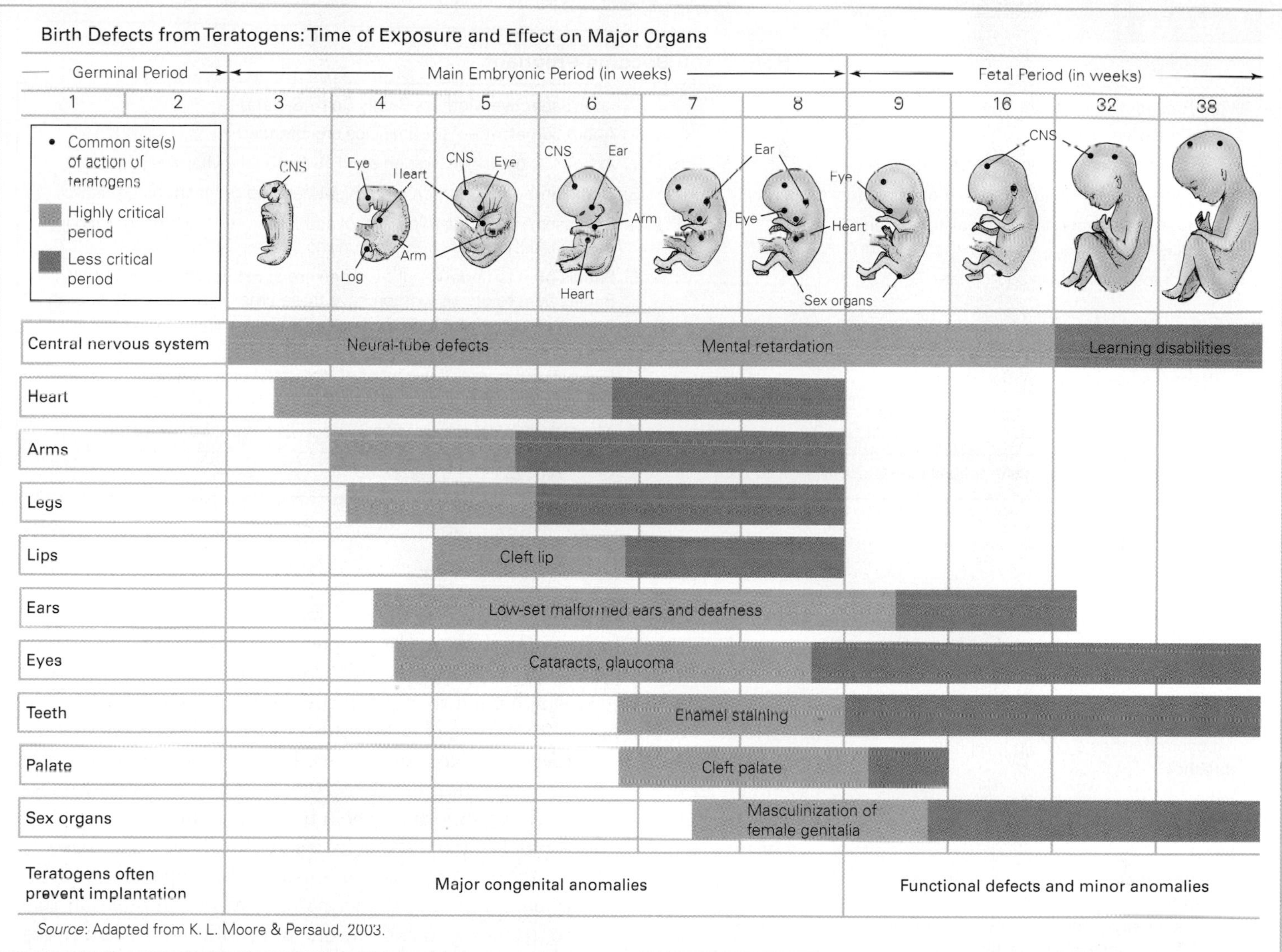

FIGURE 4.3

Critical Periods in Human Development The most serious damage from teratogens (*orange bars*) is likely to occur early in prenatal development. However, significant damage (*purple bars*) to many vital parts of the body, including the brain, eyes, and genitals, can occur during the last months of pregnancy as well.

period for physical structure and form, with the specifics varying somewhat week by week (K. L. Moore & Persaud, 2003).

Because the early days are critical, most obstetricians today recommend that *before* pregnancy, all couples get counseling, stop using recreational drugs (especially alcohol), and update their immunizations (Kuller et al., 2001). In addition, a prospective mother should make sure her body is ready by eating a balanced diet, with extra folic acid and iron. Not all women follow these recommendations; see Table 4.3.

Since the brain continues to grow throughout prenatal development, there is no safe period for behavioral teratogens. Teratogens that cause preterm birth or low birthweight (notably cigarettes) are particularly harmful in the second half of pregnancy; but, for many reasons, women should stop smoking or ingesting any drugs and should start eating well and taking prenatal vitamins before conceiving.

TABLE 4.3

Before You Become Pregnant

What Prospective Mothers Should Do	What Prospective Mothers Really Do (U.S. data)
1. Plan the pregnancy.	1. About 60 percent of pregnancies are intended.
2. Take a daily multivitamin with folic acid.	2. About 40 percent of women aged 18 to 45 take vitamins.
3. Avoid binge drinking (defined as 4 or more drinks in a row).	3. One-eighth of all women who might become pregnant binge-drink.
4. Update immunizations against all teratogenic viruses, especially rubella.	4. Because of laws regarding school admission, most young women in the United States are well immunized.
5. Gain or lose weight, as appropriate.	5. Babies born to underweight women are at risk for low birthweight. Babies born to obese women have three times the usual rate of birth complications. About half of all women begin pregnancy at an appropriate weight.
6. Reassess use of prescription drugs.	6. Eighty-five percent of pregnant women take prescription drugs (not counting vitamins).
7. Maintain exercise habits.	7. Most women do not exercise, especially in the third trimester.

Sources: Downs & Hausenblas, 2007; Suellentrop et al., 2006; Tsai et al., 2007.

Amount of Exposure

threshold effect A situation in which a certain teratogen is relatively harmless in small doses but becomes harmful once exposure reaches a certain level (the threshold).

interaction effect The result of a combination of teratogens. Sometimes the risk of harm is greatly magnified when an embryo or fetus is exposed to more than one teratogen at the same time.

Especially for Nutritionists (see response, page 109): Is it beneficial that most breakfast cereals are fortified with vitamins and minerals?

A second important factor is the dose and/or frequency of exposure. Some teratogens have a **threshold effect;** that is, they are virtually harmless until exposure reaches a certain level, at which point they "cross the threshold" and become damaging (Reece & Hobbins, 2007). Indeed, a few substances are beneficial in small amounts but fiercely teratogenic in large quantities. For example, vitamin A is an essential part of the prenatal diet, but more than 10,000 units per day may be too much and 50,000 units can cause abnormalities in body structures.

For most teratogens, experts hesitate to specify a safe threshold. One reason is the **interaction effect,** when one teratogen intensifies the impact of another. Alcohol, tobacco, and marijuana interact, doing more harm in combination than any one of them does alone. Ironically, using any one of these three makes a pregnant woman likely to use the others as well.

Another irony is that many beneficial substances also carry some risk. This has recently been highlighted in a controversy over the U.S. government's recommendation that pregnant women limit their consumption of fish in order to avoid ingesting certain toxic minerals, especially mercury, that fish have absorbed. But a British study found that fish contains nutrients that benefit the fetal brain. This study concluded that the risk that a pregnant woman would reduce her child's intelligence by limiting fish consumption was higher than the risk of causing birth defects by eating fish contaminated by mercury (Hibbeln et al., 2007).

Genetic Vulnerability

A third factor that determines whether, and to what extent, a specific teratogen will be harmful is the developing organism's genes (Mann & Andrews, 2007). Several lines of evidence suggest that genes may be crucial.

- Dizygotic (fraternal) twins, who are exposed to the same teratogens but have only half their genes in common, are born with different abnormalities. This suggests the existence of both protective and vulnerable genes.
- Cleft lip, cleft palate, and club foot are more common in some families. This suggests genetic vulnerability (Botto et al., 2004; Hartl & Jones, 1999).

- International comparisons of rates of birth defects find some marked differences that do not seem environmental (World Health Organization, 2003). For example, Japan has low rates of many birth defects but three times as many newborns with cleft lip as Canada.

Genes are also known to affect the likelihood of neural-tube defects (see Table 3.2, pages 88–89). Both spina bifida and microcephaly are more common in some ethnic groups (specifically, among infants of Irish, English, and Egyptian descent) and less common in others (most Asian and African groups). The reason is that some groups have more carriers of an allele that decreases utilization of folic acid (Mills et al., 1995). If every pregnant woman consumed extra folic acid, then embryos with this allele would get enough of this B vitamin to develop normally.

Since the genes of the fetus are unknown, and the central nervous system begins to form in the third week after conception, all women are urged to take a daily multivitamin with folic acid as a precaution *before* becoming pregnant. Only a third of U.S. women do so (Suellentrop et al., 2006), but a 1996 U.S. law and a 1998 Canadian one require that folic acid be added to cereal and bread manufactured in those countries. As a result of these laws, folic acid consumption in the United States has increased by 50 percent, and neural-tube defects have decreased by 26 percent (Bentley et al., 2006; MMWR, September 13, 2002). In Europe, where no folic acid fortification has occurred, neural-tube defects have not decreased (Botto et al., 2005).

In some cases, genetic vulnerability is related to the sex of the developing organism. Generally, males (XY) are at greater risk. That is one explanation for the more frequent spontaneous abortion of male than of female fetuses. In addition, boys have more birth defects, learning disabilities, and other problems caused by behavioral teratogens; here, again, genes are implicated.

Protective Measures

Because of the many variables involved, the impact of teratogens cannot be predicted before mid-pregnancy (and usually not even then) for individuals. However, much is known about how risks can be reduced. Table 4.4 lists some teratogens and their effects, as well as preventive measures.

Some pregnant women are exposed to the teratogens listed in the table with no evident harm, and some defects occur even though the woman avoided all known teratogens while pregnant. As a precaution, women are advised to avoid drugs, chemicals in pesticides (including bug spray), construction materials (including solvents), and cosmetics (including hair dye) *before* getting pregnant.

Such advice is easy to give but not easy to follow. Even doctors should be more careful. A study (see the Research Design) of 152,531 births in eight U.S. health maintenance organizations (HMOs) found that doctors wrote an average of three prescriptions per pregnant woman, including drugs that had not been proven safe during pregnancy (prescribed for 38 percent) and drugs with proven risks (prescribed for 5 percent) (Andrade et al., 2004).

Some of those drugs with proven risks (3.4 percent) were in the Food and Drug Administration's category D, which are drugs that are sometimes harmful but may be worth the risk when the harm of not taking them is greater. Some antiepileptic drugs and antidepressants are in this category. Since severely depressed women do not eat right or sleep enough, many doctors believe that carefully prescribed antidepressants are warranted during pregnancy (L. Cohen et al., 2006).

However, a few of the prescribed drugs (1 percent) were in category X, which should *never* be taken by pregnant women because they are proven teratogens and

Research Design

Scientists: Susan Andrade and others.

Publication: *American Journal of Obstetrics and Gynecology* (2004).

Participants: 152,531 women who gave birth from 1996 to 2000.

Design: Computer search of records from eight HMOs for prescriptions written for these participants between the date of the first prenatal visit and the delivery date.

Major conclusion: Many doctors prescribe drugs for pregnant women that are not known to be safe.

Comment: This method avoids the possibility of women or doctors forgetting or denying drug use during pregnancy. However, some of the women may not have taken the drugs that were prescribed for them, either by their own choice or on advice from a physician. Follow-up research is needed to establish a correlation between birth defects and drugs prescribed.

TABLE 4.4

Teratogens: Effects of Exposure and Prevention of Damage

Teratogens	Effects on Child of Exposure	Measures for Preventing Damage
Diseases		
Rubella (German measles)	In embryonic period, causes blindness and deafness; in first and second trimesters, causes brain damage	Get immunized before becoming pregnant
Toxoplasmosis	Brain damage, loss of vision, mental retardation	Avoid eating undercooked meat and handling cat feces, garden dirt
Measles, chicken pox, influenza	May impair brain functioning	Get immunized before getting pregnant; avoid infected people during pregnancy
Syphilis	Baby is born with syphilis, which, untreated, leads to brain and bone damage and eventual death	Early prenatal diagnosis and treatment with antibiotics
AIDS	Baby may catch the virus. If so, illness and death are likely during childhood.	Prenatal drugs and cesarean birth make AIDS transmission rare
Other sexually transmitted infections, including gonorrhea and chlamydia	Not usually harmful during pregnancy but may cause blindness and infections if transmitted during birth	Early diagnosis and treatment; if necessary, cesarean section, treatment of newborn
Infections, including infections of urinary tract, gums, and teeth	May cause premature labor, which increases vulnerability to brain damage	Get infection treated, preferably before becoming pregnant
Pollutants		
Lead, mercury, PCBs (polychlorinated biphenyls), dioxin, and some pesticides, herbicides, and cleaning compounds	May cause spontaneous abortion, preterm labor, and brain damage	Most common substances are harmless in small doses, but pregnant women should still avoid regular and direct exposure, such as drinking well water, eating unwashed fruits or vegetables, using chemical compounds, eating fish from polluted waters
Radiation		
Massive or repeated exposure to radiation, as in medical X-rays	In the embryonic period, may cause abnormally small head (microcephaly) and mental retardation; in the fetal period, suspected but not proven to cause brain damage. Exposure to background radiation, as from power plants, is usually too low to have an effect.	Get sonograms, not X-rays, during pregnancy; pregnant women who work directly with radiation need special protection or temporary assignment to another job
Social and Behavioral Factors		
Very high stress	Early in pregnancy, may cause cleft lip or cleft palate, spontaneous abortion, or preterm labor	Get adequate relaxation, rest, and sleep; reduce hours of employment; get help with housework and child care
Malnutrition	When severe, may interfere with conception, implantation, normal fetal development, and full-term birth	Eat a balanced diet (with adequate vitamins and minerals, including, especially, folic acid, iron, and vitamin A); achieve normal weight before getting pregnant, then gain 25–35 lbs (10–15 kg) during pregnancy
Excessive, exhausting exercise	Can affect fetal development when it interferes with pregnant woman's sleep or digestion	Get regular, moderate exercise
Medicinal Drugs		
Lithium	Can cause heart abnormalities	Avoid all medicines, whether prescription or over-the-counter, during pregnancy unless they are approved by a medical professional who knows about the pregnancy and is aware of the most recent research
Tetracycline	Can harm the teeth	
Retinoic acid	Can cause limb deformities	
Streptomycin	Can cause deafness	
ACE inhibitors	Can harm digestive organs	
Phenobarbital	Can affect brain development	
Thalidomide	Can stop ear and limb formation	

TABLE 4.4 *(continued from page 108)*

Teratogens: Effects of Exposure and Prevention of Damage

Teratogens	Effects on Child of Exposure	Measures for Preventing Damage
Psychoactive Drugs		
Caffeine	Normal use poses no problem	Avoid excessive use: Drink no more than three cups a day of beverages containing caffeine (coffee, tea, cola drinks, hot chocolate)
Alcohol	May cause fetal alcohol syndrome (FAS) or fetal alcohol effects (FAE) (see A View from Science, page 110)	Stop or severely limit alcohol consumption during pregnancy; especially dangerous are three or more drinks a day or five or more drinks on one occasion
Tobacco	Increases risk of malformations of limbs and urinary tract, and may affect the baby's lungs	Stop smoking before and during pregnancy
Marijuana	Heavy exposure may affect the central nervous system; when smoked, may hinder fetal growth	Avoid or strictly limit marijuana consumption
Heroin	Slows fetal growth and may cause premature labor; newborns with heroin in their bloodstream require medical treatment to prevent the pain and convulsions of withdrawal	Get treated for heroin addiction before becoming pregnant; if already pregnant, gradual withdrawal on methadone is better than continued use of heroin
Cocaine	May cause slow fetal growth, premature labor, and learning problems in the first years of life	Stop using cocaine before pregnancy; babies of cocaine-using mothers may need special medical and educational attention in their first years of life
Inhaled solvents (glue or aerosol)	May cause abnormally small head, crossed eyes, and other indications of brain damage	Stop sniffing inhalants before becoming pregnant; be aware that serious damage can occur before a woman knows she is pregnant

Note: This table summarizes some relatively common teratogenic effects. As the text makes clear, many individual factors in each pregnancy affect whether a given teratogen will actually cause damage and what that damage might be. This is a general summary of what is known; new evidence is reported almost daily, so some of these generalities will change. Pregnant women or women who want to become pregnant should consult with their physicians.
Sources: Mann & Andrews, 2007; O'Rahilly & Müller, 2001; Reece & Hobbins, 2007; Shepard & Lemire, 2004; L.T. Singer et al., 2002.

safer alternatives are available (Andrade et al., 2004). In fairness to the doctors, though, some of their patients may not have told them (or even known) that they were pregnant.

Pregnant women are not always cautious enough themselves. A nationwide survey has found that some women acknowledge smoking (14 percent) and drinking (5 percent) during the last three months of their pregnancies (Suellentrop et al., 2006). No doctor would condone that.

Does society have a role in these situations? Should any doctor who prescribes a category X drug for a pregnant woman be banned from medical practice? Should any pregnant woman who drinks or smokes, or anyone who goes along with such behavior (husbands, bartenders, store owners), be arrested?

Before we examine these questions, remember what you learned about the scientific method in Chapter 1. A hypothesis is tested in many ways, and conclusions are considered tentative until valid replication has been done. Most research on teratogens has been done with mice; harm to humans is rarely proven to the satisfaction of every scientist. Definitive proof may take decades. For example, DES, a drug that was intended to prevent miscarriages, was prescribed for many pregnant women during the 1960s. Only when their children became adults was it found that prenatal exposure to DES caused cancer and other problems with sex organs. Now consider the following View from Science.

➤**Response for Nutritionists** (from page 106): Useful, yes; optimal, no. Some essential vitamins are missing (too expensive), and individual needs differ, depending on age, sex, health, genes, and eating habits. The reduction in neural-tube defects is good, but many women do not benefit because they don't eat cereal or take vitamin supplements before becoming pregnant.

a view from science

Jail Those Drunken Women?

Alcohol in high doses is a proven teratogen. Proof did not come easy; 40 years ago drinking alcohol during pregnancy was believed to be harmless. But some obstetricians noted that some patients who drank heavily while they were pregnant had babies with distorted faces, including small eyes and a thin upper lip.

Those newborns became mentally retarded, impulsive, and hyperactive children. This combination of signs and symptoms was named **fetal alcohol syndrome (FAS).** Later, researchers also identified a milder condition called **fetal alcohol effects (FAE),** which is marked by problems with emotions and cognition in older children whose mothers drank heavily during pregnancy (Streissguth & Conner, 2001).

Experiments with mice and monkeys, as well as natural experiments with alcoholic women worldwide—including, recently, South Africa (May et al., 2005)—have left no doubt about the correlation between maternal drinking and fetal harm. Such replication has convinced scientists that women who drink heavily during pregnancy are risking the health of their babies.

However, as with every teratogen, the link is not always present: Not every child whose mother drinks develops FAS or FAE (Streissguth, 2007).

It is not known how much alcohol, if any, a pregnant woman can safely drink before putting her fetus at risk. Most doctors in the United States (although not in Europe) advise pregnant women to abstain completely from alcohol. Since 1998, four U.S. states—North and South Dakota, Wisconsin, and Oklahoma—have authorized "involuntary commitment" (jail or forced residential treatment) for pregnant women who drink. Many doctors, social workers, and the American Medical Association fear that the threat of such punishment might cause women who most need prenatal care to avoid getting it.

Scientists are cautious about recommending action in this area. To punish women before harm has become evident or without establishing the actual cause of harm is contrary to the scientific method, which seeks proof. But does caution have to mean that millions of children will be allowed to suffer impairment? If a pregnant woman you knew ordered a glass of wine, would you try to stop her?

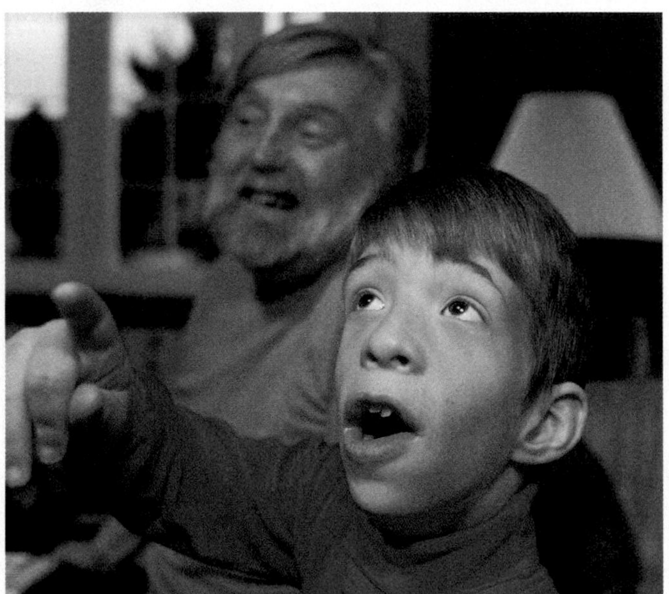

Yes, But . . . An adopted boy points out something to his father—a positive interaction between the two. The shapes of the boy's eyes, ears, and upper lip indicate that he was born with fetal alcohol syndrome (FAS). Scientists disagree about the strength of the correlation between FAS and drinking alcohol during pregnancy.

fetal alcohol syndrome (FAS) A cluster of birth defects, including abnormal facial characteristics, slow physical growth, and retarded mental development, that may occur in the child of a woman who drinks alcohol while pregnant.

fetal alcohol effects (FAE) A condition in which a child has been exposed to alcohol before birth and has some signs of fetal alcohol syndrome, including emotional and cognitive problems, but does not meet all the necessary criteria to be diagnosed with that disorder.

sonogram An image of an unborn fetus (or an internal organ) produced by using high-frequency sound waves (ultrasound).

Benefits of Prenatal Care

Early prenatal care has many advantages (Reece & Hobbins, 2007). Chief among them is protection against teratogens—learning what medicines to avoid and what foods to eat, for instance. Dozens of tests for substances in a pregnant woman's blood and urine are routinely done at every stage of pregnancy to diagnose problems (see Table 4.5). A **sonogram** (an ultrasound image of the fetus) is regularly done to reveal whether the fetus is developing normally.

Only a few decades ago, most twins came as a surprise to their parents at birth. No more: A sonogram reveals how many fetuses a woman is carrying. This can be lifesaving information. For instance, about 15 percent of all twins share a placenta and a bloodstream, so it is possible for one fetus to get too much nourishment (and to die of an overworked heart) while the other gets too little (and dies of malnutrition). Now this problem can be detected on a sonogram and usually treated in mid-pregnancy (Sakata et al., 2006).

Further, if her fetus is growing slowly, a woman can remedy some causes, such as poor nutrition, night employment, long hours of standing, stress, and exhaustion (Croteau et al., 2006). Prenatal care alerts the woman and her care provider to many other possible problems (anemia, hypertension, diabetes) that can be mitigated.

Early prenatal care can also prevent fetal exposure to some deadly teratogens. For example, a fetus will not be infected with syphilis or HIV if its mother is diagnosed and treated early on. Only a decade ago, 26 percent of women with HIV passed the virus on to their fetuses, many of whom suffered and died of AIDS in childhood. Today, routine early diagnosis of HIV (at least in the Americas and Europe) leads to treatment that can prevent prenatal transmission (McDonald et al., 2007; Read et al., 2007).

Especially for Social Workers (see response, page 113): When is it most important to convince women to be tested for HIV: a month before pregnancy, a month after conception, or immediately after birth?

TABLE 4.5

Methods of Postconception Testing

Method	Description	Risks, Concerns, and Indications
Pre-implantation testing	After in vitro fertilization, one cell is removed from each zygote at the four- or eight-cell stage and analyzed.	Not entirely accurate. Requires surgery, in vitro fertilization, and rapid assessment. This delays implantation and reduces the likelihood of successful birth. It is used only when couples are at high risk of known, testable genetic disorders.
Tests for pregnancy-associated plasma protein (PAPPA) and human chorionic gonadotropin	Blood tests are usually done at about 11 weeks to indicate levels of these substances.	Indicate normal pregnancy, but false-positive or false-negative results sometimes occur.
Alpha-fetoprotein assay	The mother's blood is tested for the level of alpha-fetoprotein (AFP), now usually done at mid-pregnancy; often combined with other blood tests and repeat sonogram.	Indicates neural-tube defects, multiple embryos (both cause high AFP), or Down syndrome (low AFP). Normal levels change each week; interpretation requires accurate dating of conception.
Sonogram (ultrasound)	High-frequency sound waves are used to produce a "picture" of the fetus as early as 8 weeks. Sonograms are more accurate later in pregnancy to detect less apparent problems, to confirm earlier suspicions, and to anticipate birth complications.	Reveals problems such as a small head or other body malformations, excess fluid accumulating on the brain, Down syndrome (detected by expert, looking at neck of fetus), and several diseases (for instance, of the kidneys). Estimates fetal age and reveals multiple fetuses, placental position, and fetal growth, all of which are useful in every pregnancy. Sometimes sex is apparent. No known risks, unlike the X-rays that it has replaced.
Chorionic villi sampling (CVS)	A sample of the chorion (part of the placenta) is obtained (via sonogram and syringe) at about 10 weeks and analyzed. Since the cells of the placenta are genetically identical to the cells of the fetus, this can indicate many chromosomal or genetic abnormalities.	Provides the same information as amniocentesis but can be performed earlier. Not 100 percent accurate. Causes a spontaneous abortion (rare).
Amniocentesis	About half an ounce of the fluid inside the placenta is withdrawn (via sonogram and syringe) at about 16 weeks. The cells are cultured and analyzed.	Spontaneous abortion is now very rare (less than 0.05 percent). Detects chromosomal abnormalities and other genetic and prenatal problems. The amniotic fluid also reveals the sex of the fetus. Is done later in pregnancy than other tests, and it takes a week before results are known.

Sources: Eddleman et al., 2006; Malone et al., 2005; K. L. Moore & Persaud, 2003; Reece & Hobbins, 2007; Wright et al., 2006.

AP PHOTO

The Legacy of AIDS Orphanages have closed in developed nations because they are no longer needed. In contrast, the need for orphanages is increasing in many parts of the developing world, where AIDS has orphaned 11 million children, according to UNICEF data. The children photographed here are in an orphanage in Zimbabwe. Some of them may have inherited the AIDS virus from their parents.

As a result, pediatric AIDS is disappearing in North America and Europe. However, it is still increasing in most of Africa, where prenatal care is scarce and antiviral drugs are rarely available and affordable. Furthermore, the social stigma of HIV/AIDS in some communities causes some husbands and families to abandon pregnant women who are HIV-positive. That possibility makes women afraid to be tested and treated for the virus. In Botswana and South Africa, some doctors avoid even telling pregnant women their diagnosis (Epstein, 2007).

Even in developed nations, some prenatal tests create stress. About 20 percent of the time, the first sonogram or blood tests suggest that more tests are needed. Most such warnings are false positives, test results that indicate a birth defect may be present when the fetus is actually fine. It is also possible to get a false negative, a test result that shows no problem when a defect actually exists. Usually, the cut-off scores for various prenatal tests are set to produce more false positives than false negatives, but in either case, prenatal testing can strain a marriage. Consider Martha and John.

a personal perspective

"What Do People Live to Do?"

John and Martha, graduate students at Harvard, were expecting their second child. Martha was four months pregnant, and her initial prenatal screening revealed an abnormally low level of alpha-fetoprotein (AFP), which could indicate that the fetus had Down syndrome. It was too early for amniocentesis, a more definitive test, so another blood test was scheduled to double-check the AFP level.

John met Martha at a café after a nurse had drawn the second blood sample but before the laboratory reported the test result. Later, Martha wrote about their conversation.

> "Did they tell you anything about the test?" John said. "What exactly is the problem?" . . .
>
> "We've got a one in eight hundred and ninety-five shot at a retarded baby."
>
> John smiled, "I can live with those odds."
>
> I tried to smile back, but I couldn't. . . . I wanted to tell John about the worry in my gut. I wanted to tell him that it was more than worry—that it was a certainty. Then I realized all over again how preposterous that was. "I'm still a little scared."
>
> He reached across the table for my hand. "Sure," he said, "that's understandable. But even if there is a problem, we've caught it in time. . . . The worst case scenario is that you might have to have an abortion, and that's a long shot. Everything's going to be fine."
>
> . . . "I might *have to have* an abortion?" The chill inside me was gone. Instead I could feel my face flushing hot with anger.

"Since when do you decide what I *have to* do with my body?"

John looked surprised. "I never said I was going to decide anything," he protested. "It's just that if the tests show something wrong with the baby, of course we'll abort. We've talked about this."

"What we've talked about," I told John in a low, dangerous voice, "is that I am pro-choice. That means I decide whether or not I'd abort a baby with a birth defect. . . . I'm not so sure of this."

"You used to be," said John.

"I know I used to be." I rubbed my eyes. I felt terribly confused. "But now . . . look, John, it's not as though we're deciding whether or not to have a baby. We're deciding what *kind* of baby we're willing to accept. If it's perfect in every way, we keep it. If it doesn't fit the right specifications, whoosh! Out it goes.". . .

John was looking more and more confused. "Martha, why are you on this soapbox? What's your point?"

"My point is," I said, "that I'm trying to get you to tell me what you think constitutes a 'defective' baby. What about . . . oh, I don't know, a hyperactive baby? Or an ugly one?"

"They can't test for those things and—"

"Well, what if they could?" I said. "Medicine can do all kinds of magical tricks these days. Pretty soon we're going to be aborting babies because they have the gene for alcoholism, or homosexuality, or manic depression. . . . Did you know that in China they abort a lot of fetuses just because they're female?" I growled. "Is being a girl 'defective' enough for you?"

"Look," he said, "I know I can't always see things from your perspective. And I'm sorry about that. But the way I see it, if a baby is going to be deformed or something, abortion is a way to keep everyone from suffering—*especially* the baby. It's like shooting a horse that's broken its leg. . . . A lame horse dies slowly, you know? . . . It dies in terrible pain. And it can't run anymore. So it can't enjoy life even if it doesn't die. Horses live to run; that's what they do. If a baby is born not being able to do what other people do, I think it's better not to prolong its suffering."

". . . And what is it," I said softly, more to myself than to John, "what is it that people do? What do we live to do, the way a horse lives to run?"

[Beck, 1999, pp. 132–133, 135]

The second AFP test came back low but in the normal range, "meaning there was no reason to fear that [the fetus] had Down syndrome" (Beck, p. 137).

John thought they had decided to abort a Down syndrome fetus, but his response as they waited for test results had Martha "hot with anger." As Chapter 3 explains, genetic counselors help couples discuss their choices *before* becoming pregnant, but John and Martha had no counseling because they hadn't planned this pregnancy and they were at low risk for any problems, including chromosomal ones.

Amniocentesis later revealed that the second AFP was a false negative. The fetus had Down syndrome after all.

Before they conceive, many couples discuss the circumstances under which they would consider abortion. But many are much less certain about that decision once pregnancy occurs. We will return to Martha and John at the end of this chapter.

SUMMING UP

Risk analysis is a complex but necessary aspect of prenatal development, especially because the placenta does not protect the fetus from all hazards, such as diseases, drugs, and pollutants. Many factors reduce risk, including the mother's good health and adequate nutrition before pregnancy and early prenatal care (to diagnose and treat problems and to teach the woman how to protect her fetus). Risk is affected by dose, frequency, and timing of exposure to teratogens, as well as by the fetus's genetic vulnerability. Prenatal testing often reassures the prospective parents but may reveal severe problems that require difficult decisions. ■

➤Response for Social Workers (from page 111): Testing and then treatment are useful at any time, because women who know they are HIV-positive are more likely to get treatment, reduce risk of transmission, and avoid pregnancy. If pregnancy does occur, early diagnosis is best. Getting tested after birth is too late for the baby.

Birth

For a full-term fetus and a healthy mother, birth can be simple and quick. At some time during the last month of pregnancy, most fetuses change position, turning upside down so that the head is low in the mother's pelvic cavity. They are now in position to be born in the usual way, head first.

About 1 in 20 babies does not turn and is positioned to be born "breech," that is, buttocks or, rarely, feet first. Obstetricians or midwives sometimes manually turn such fetuses before birth or recommend a cesarean section (described below),

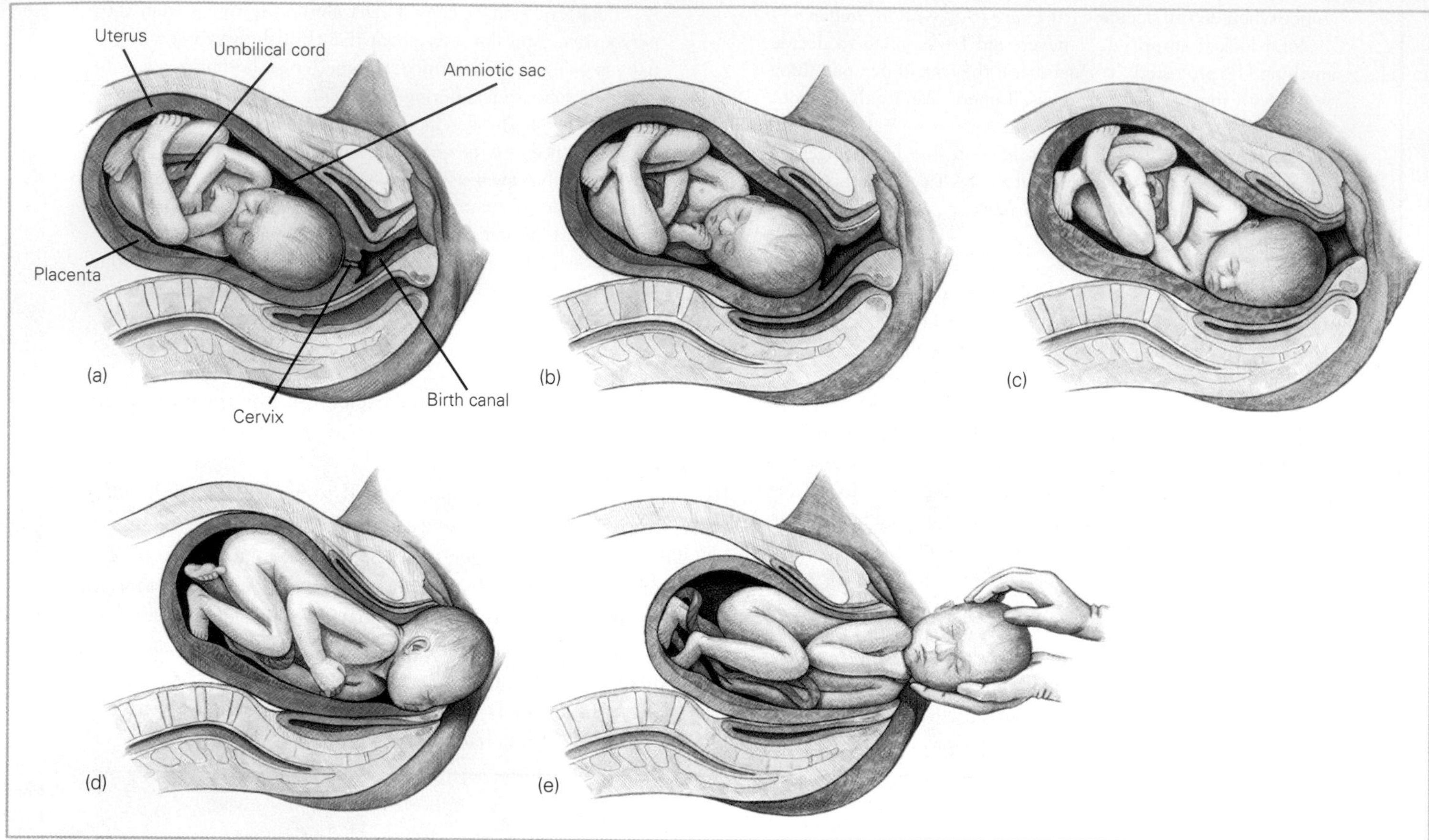

FIGURE 4.4

A Normal, Uncomplicated Birth *(a)* The baby's position as the birth process begins. *(b)* The first stage of labor: The cervix dilates to allow passage of the baby's head. *(c)* Transition: The baby's head moves into the "birth canal," the vagina. *(d)* The second stage of labor: The baby's head moves through the opening of the vagina ("crowns") and *(e)* emerges completely.

Observation Quiz (see answer, page 117): In drawing *(e)*, what is the birth attendant doing as the baby's head emerges?

because breech babies may get insufficient oxygen during labor (Reece & Hobbins, 2007). Worse and very rare is a *transverse lie,* when the fetus is sideways, in which case vaginal birth is impossible.

Usually about 38 weeks after conception, the fetal brain signals the release of certain hormones that trigger the woman's uterine muscles to contract and relax, starting active labor. Uterine contractions gradually become strong and regular and begin to occur less than 10 minutes apart.

The baby is born, on average, after 12 hours of active labor for first births and 7 hours for subsequent births (K. L. Moore & Persaud, 2003), although it is not unusual for labor to take twice, or half, that long. Women's birthing positions also vary—sitting, squatting, lying down, or even immersed in warm water. Figure 4.4 shows the sequence of stages in the birth process.

The Newborn's First Minutes

Most newborns begin to breathe as soon as their heads emerge, even before the birth process is complete. Those first breaths cause the infant's color to change from bluish to pinkish as oxygen begins to circulate. Hands and feet are the last body parts to turn pink. ("Bluish" and "pinkish" refer to the blood color, visible beneath the skin, and apply to newborns of all skin colors.) The eyes open wide; the tiny fingers grab; the tinier toes stretch and retract. The newborn is instantly, zestfully ready for life.

Nevertheless, there is much to be done. Mucus in the baby's throat is removed, especially if the first breaths seem shallow or strained. The umbilical cord is cut to detach the placenta, leaving the navel, or "belly button." The placenta is then

TABLE 4.6

Criteria and Scoring of the Apgar Scale

	Five Vital Signs				
Score	Color	Heartbeat	Reflex Irritability	Muscle Tone	Respiratory Effort
0	Blue, pale	Absent	No response	Flaccid, limp	Absent
1	Body pink, extremities blue	Slow (below 100)	Grimace	Weak, inactive	Irregular, slow
2	Entirely pink	Rapid (over 100)	Coughing, sneezing, crying	Strong, active	Good; baby is crying

Source: Apgar, 1953.

expelled. If birth is assisted by a trained health worker—as are 99 percent of the births in industrialized nations and about half of all births worldwide—newborns are weighed, examined to make sure no problems require prompt medical attention, and wrapped to preserve body heat.

In developed nations, the **Apgar scale** is a quick and widely used way for birth attendants to assess the baby's condition (see Table 4.6). The examiner checks five vital signs—heart rate, breathing, muscle tone, color, and reflexes—at one minute and again at five minutes after birth, assigning each a score of 0, 1, or 2 and totaling all five scores (Moster et al., 2001). A total score of 10 is ideal.

The five-minute Apgar score is the crucial one. An Australian study found that at one minute, many healthy newborns look blue (0 on the Apgar for that characteristic) because they are low on oxygen—with a saturation rate of 63 percent or less—but the blood level of oxygen quickly rises to 90 percent or more (Kamlin et al., 2006). If the five-minute total score is 7 or above, all is well.

If the score is below 7, the infant needs help. If the score is below 4, the newborn is in critical condition and "Dr. Apgar" may be paged, a call that alerts the neonatalist on duty to rush to the delivery room. Fortunately, most newborns get a score of 7 or above, which reassures the new parents, who cradle their newborn and congratulate each other.

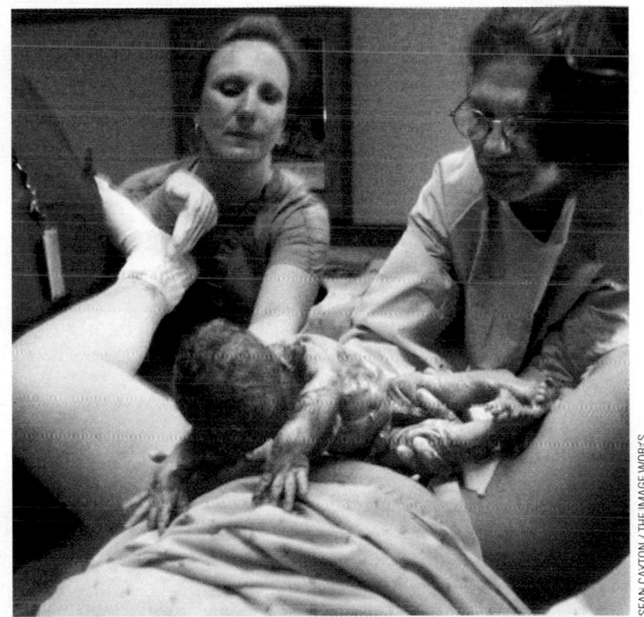

SEAN CAYTON / THE IMAGE WORKS

No Doctor Needed In this Colorado Springs birthing center, most babies are delivered with the help of nurse-midwives. This newborn's bloody appearance and bluish fingers are completely normal; an Apgar test at five minutes revealed that the baby's heart was beating steadily and that the body was "entirely pink."

Variations

How closely any given birth matches the foregoing description depends on the parents' preparation for birth, the physical and emotional support provided by birth attendants, the position and size of the fetus, and the customs of the culture. In developed nations, births usually include drugs to dull pain or speed contractions, sterile procedures, and various hospital protocols to ensure readiness for emergencies and to avoid lawsuits.

Medical Intervention

In about 31 percent of births in the United States, a **cesarean section** is performed (Hamilton et al., 2007). In this surgical procedure, also called a *c-section* or simply *section,* the fetus is removed through incisions in the mother's abdomen and uterus. The rate of surgical birth varies markedly from place to place, with many developed nations having far fewer cesareans than the United States but others having more (see Figure 4.5).

Apgar scale A quick assessment of a newborn's body functioning. The baby's color, heart rate, reflexes, muscle tone, and respiratory effort are given a score of 0, 1, or 2 twice—at one minute and five minutes after birth—and each time the total of all five scores is compared with the ideal score of 10 (which is rarely attained).

cesarean section A surgical birth, in which incisions through the mother's abdomen and uterus allow the fetus to be removed quickly, instead of being delivered through the vagina. (Also called *c-section* or simply *section*.)

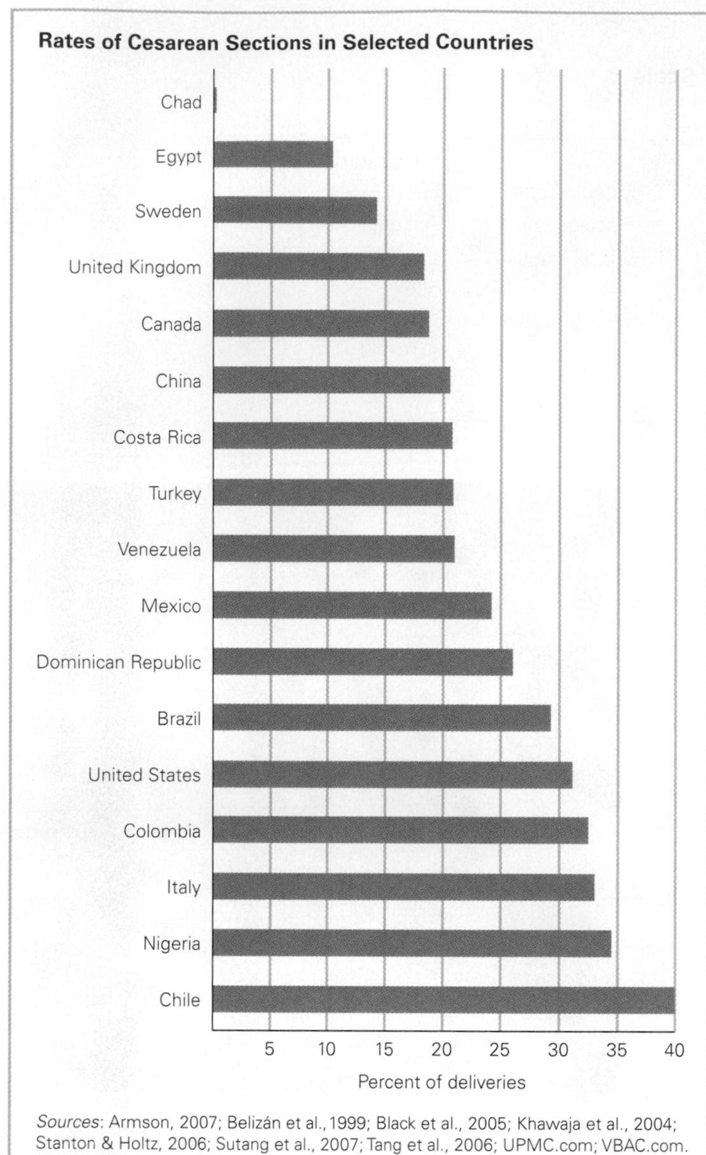

Sources: Armson, 2007; Belizán et al., 1999; Black et al., 2005; Khawaja et al., 2004; Stanton & Holtz, 2006; Sutang et al., 2007; Tang et al., 2006; UPMC.com; VBAC.com.

FIGURE 4.5

Too Many Cesareans or Too Few? Rates of cesarean deliveries vary widely from nation to nation. In general, cesarean births are declining in North America and increasing in Africa. Latin America has the highest rates in the world (note that 40 percent of all births in Chile are by cesarean), and sub-Saharan Africa has the lowest (the rate in Chad is less than half of 1 percent). The underlying issue is whether some women who should have cesareans do not get them, while other women have unnecessary cesareans.

If serious organic abnormalities are evident, surgery is often warranted: Microsurgery on tiny hearts, lungs, and digestive systems has become amazingly successful in recent years. Specialized feeding, warmth, and extra oxygen are also available to the newborn when needed. Seventy years ago, 5 percent of all newborns in the United States died (De Lee, 1938). Today almost every newborn lives. The death rate in the first days of life is only 1 in 200, with that one almost always in critical condition at birth because of an obvious problem, such as extremely low birthweight or massive birth defects.

In developed nations, newborns are routinely tested for various diseases. If a problem is confirmed by further testing, parents and medical staff can begin protective measures (such as the diet to prevent PKU, explained in Chapter 3) (MMWR, October 15, 2004). Just as during prenatal testing, false positives may cause needless worry, and even correct tests may reveal problems that cannot be treated. Nonetheless, most professionals, including those involved with the March of Dimes, advocate testing all newborns for dozens of conditions (Green et al., 2006).

Every year worldwide, obstetricians, midwives, and nurses save millions of lives—of mothers as well as of infants. Indeed, a lack of medical attention during childbirth and illegal abortions is the major reason motherhood is still hazardous in the least developed nations; about 1 in 16 women in sub-Saharan Africa dies of complications from abortion or birth (Kruk et al., 2008).

However, intervention is not always best for mother and child. In Pelotas, Brazil, most births are by cesarean (82 percent for private patients in 2004). The rate of low-birthweight infants in that region of Brazil is rising (from 11 to 16 percent in 10 years) because some infants are delivered by cesarean before they are ready (Barros et al., 2005). In general, cesareans are easier on the fetus, and quicker for doctor and mother, but increase the rate of birth complications in later pregnancies (Getahun et al., 2006).

Birth in Developing Nations

In the United States, only 1 percent of births take place at home—about half by choice and half because of unexpectedly rapid labor. In contrast, most births worldwide occur at home. Sometimes such births seem amazingly simple and pain-free. Here is a description of a home birth in Ghana:

> Huddled in a corner of the hut, [Emefa, a woman in labor,] was lying on the floor. . . . She lay curled into a small ball on her left side, her pregnant and contracting uterus protruding from her thin frame. No sound came from her. No sound came from the midwife either. She was seated in the corner of the dark, hot, hut, waiting. Suddenly, Emefa gave a low whimper and hauled herself into a sitting and then squatting position. The midwife crept over to her and gently supported Emefa's back as she bore down. No words, no commands, no yelling. . . . The baby's head appeared gradually, slowly making its progress into the world. . . . A soft whoosh and the baby's body was born into the steady and confident hands of the midwife. And still there was no sound. The baby did not

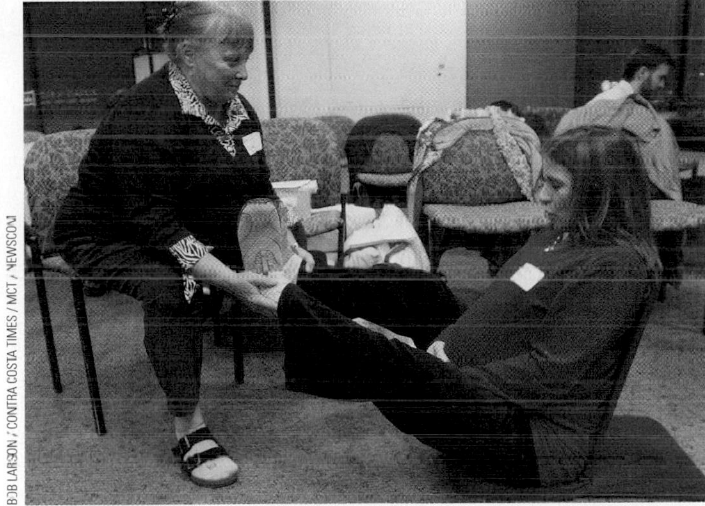
BOB LARSON / CONTRA COSTA TIMES / MCT / NEWSCOM

AP PHOTO / LYNNE SLADKY

The Same Situation, Many Miles Apart: Preparing for Birth Both of these pregnant women are carrying twins, but their prognoses are quite different. The American woman in Lamaze class (*left*) is practicing breathing during labor. The pregnant woman in Afghanistan (*right*) and her doctors discuss why labor will be induced: One of her twins is not developing normally. Neither is expected to live. Virtually all newborns in developed nations survive; the Afghani woman has already lost two children at birth.

Observation Quiz (see answer, page 119): Is the woman at left in the left-hand photo the pregnant woman's doctor?

> cry, not because there was any problem, but because it was a gentle birth. The baby was breathing as he was handed to his mother.
>
> *[Hiller, 2003, p. 3]*

Infants delivered at home, no matter what the culture, are usually quite normal and healthy, but any complications can become more serious if the mother must wait for emergency medical help (Pang et al., 2002). As modern medicine is introduced in many regions of the world, a clash often develops between traditional home births attended by a midwife and hospital births attended by an obstetrician: Home births risk complications, and hospital births risk too much intervention. All too often, women must choose one or the other, rather than combining the best features of each. An example of such a combination is reported regarding the Inuit people of northern Canada:

> Until thirty or forty years ago every woman, and most men, learned midwifery skills and knew what to do to help at a birth if they were needed. . . . They helped the woman kneel or squat on caribou skins, and tied the cord with caribou sinews. . . . Since the 1950s, as the medical system took control in the belief that hospital birth was safer, more and more pregnant women were evacuated by air to deliver in large hospitals in Winnipeg and other cities. . . . Around three weeks before her due date a woman is flown south to wait in bed and breakfast accommodation for labor to start, and to have it induced if the baby does not arrive when expected. Anxious about their children left at home, mothers became bored and depressed.
>
> . . . Women . . . deliver in a supine position [on the back] instead of an upright one, which was part of their tradition, and also describe being tied up while giving birth. Many women say that children who have been born in a hospital are different and no longer fit into the Inuit lifestyle. . . . Several new birth centres have now been created [in the Inuit homeland] and nurse-midwives are bringing in traditional midwives as assistants during childbirth, training some Inuit midwives to work alongside them, and at the same time learning some of the old Inuit ways themselves.
>
> *[Kitzinger, 2001, pp. 160–161]*

➤**Answer to Observation Quiz** (from page 114): The birth attendant is turning the baby's head after it has emerged; doing this helps the shoulders come out more easily.

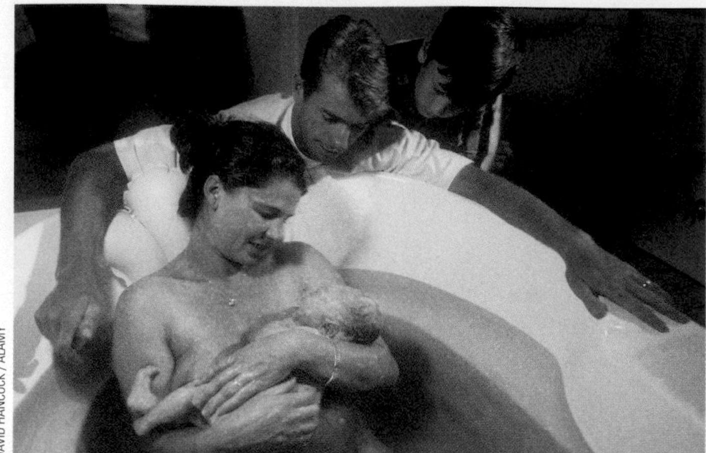

DAVID HANCOCK / ALAMY

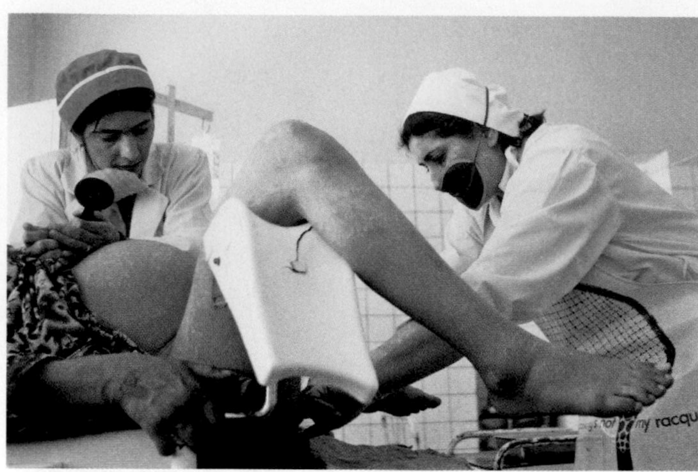

NATALIE BEHRING / ONASIA.COM

The Same Situation, Many Miles Apart: Back to Basics The physical process of giving birth is the same for all women, but the circumstances vary widely. Many Western women are forgoing the traditional hospital birth in favor of such methods as water birth (*left*). For women in many developing countries, meanwhile, a sanitary hospital birth would be an improvement—but the hospitals cannot afford even basic supplies. In a delivery room in Afghanistan (*right*), the doctor is wearing a cooking apron instead of surgical scrubs and an eye mask over her mouth.

Another example of a traditional custom incorporated into a modern birth is the presence of a **doula.** Long a fixture in many Latin American countries, a doula is a woman who helps other women with labor, delivery, breast-feeding, and newborn care. Increasing numbers of women in North America now hire a professional doula to perform these functions, and some hospitals provide doula support (Mottl-Santiago et al., 2008).

From a developmental perspective, such combinations of traditional and modern birthing practices are excellent. Some practices in every culture are helpful and some are harmful to development; a thoughtful combination of traditional and modern is likely to be an improvement over a wholesale rejection of one or the other.

doula A woman who helps with the birth process. Traditionally in Latin America, a doula was the only professional who attended childbirths. Now doulas are likely to work alongside a hospital's medical staff to help mothers through labor and delivery.

Birth Complications

A *birth complication* is anything in the newborn, the mother, or the birth process itself that requires special medical attention. When a fetus is already at risk because of a genetic abnormality or exposure to a teratogen, when a mother is unusually young, old, small, or ill, or when labor occurs too soon, birth complications become more likely.

Complications are usually part of a sequence of events and conditions that begin long before birth and may continue for years. This means that prevention and treatment must be ongoing. We focus now on lack of oxygen, one of the most serious complications, and low birthweight, one of the most common.

Anoxia

Anoxia literally means "no oxygen." Inadequate oxygen during birth can kill the infant or cause brain damage if it lasts longer than a few seconds. The use of some forms of anesthesia during the birth process was discontinued because they slowed down the delivery of oxygen to the fetus or made it more difficult for a newborn to breathe on its own.

anoxia A lack of oxygen that, if prolonged during birth, can cause brain damage or death to the baby.

Cerebral palsy (difficulties with movement and speech resulting from brain damage) was once thought to be caused solely by birth procedures: excessive pain medication, slow breech birth, or delivery by forceps (an instrument used to pull the fetus's head through the birth canal). In fact, however, cerebral palsy often results from genetic vulnerability, worsened by teratogens and a birth in which anoxia occurs.

cerebral palsy A disorder that results from damage to the brain's motor centers. People with cerebral palsy have difficulty with muscle control, so their speech and body movements are impaired.

A pair of monozygotic twins were mentioned in Chapter 3, one of whom had a much more severe case of Asperger syndrome than the other. That twin also experienced anoxia at birth: Doctors needed to give him oxygen and clear mucus from his throat before he started breathing on his own. That is the likely explanation for his more severe brain damage. Similarly, it is thought that some people develop schizophrenia as the result of a bout of anoxia at birth. In both disorders, the underlying problem is genetic, but anoxia can further stress the immature brain.

Anoxia has many causes and is always risky; that's why the fetal heart rate is monitored during labor and why a newborn's color is one of the five criteria on the Apgar scale. How long a fetus can experience anoxia without suffering brain damage depends on genes, weight, neurological maturity, drugs in the bloodstream (either taken by the mother before birth or given by the doctor during birth), and a host of other factors.

➤**Answer to Observation Quiz** (from page 117): No; she is the pregnant woman's mother. Doctors are unlikely to attend their patients' Lamaze classes, but every pregnant woman in the class is supposed to have a helper—usually the baby's father, but sometimes a close relative or friend.

Low Birthweight

The World Health Organization defines **low birthweight (LBW)** as a body weight of less than 2,500 grams (5½ pounds) at birth. The smallest LBW babies are further grouped into **very low birthweight (VLBW),** a weight of less than 1,500 grams (3 pounds, 5 ounces), and **extremely low birthweight (ELBW),** a weight of less than 1,000 grams (2 pounds, 3 ounces). Table 4.7 correlates these weights with the stages of prenatal development.

The rate of LBW varies widely from nation to nation (see Figure 4.6). The U.S. rate of 8.2 percent in 2005 has been rising steadily over the past two decades and is now higher than it has been in more than 30 years (see Figure 4.7).

Remember that fetal body weight normally doubles in the last trimester of pregnancy, with a typical gain of almost 2 pounds (900 grams) occurring in the final three weeks. Thus, in a **preterm birth,** defined as occurring 3 or more weeks before the standard 38 weeks have elapsed, the baby usually (though not always) is LBW.

low birthweight (LBW) A body weight at birth of less than 5½ pounds (2,500 grams).

very low birthweight (VLBW) A body weight at birth of less than 3 pounds, 5 ounces (1,500 grams).

extremely low birthweight (ELBW) A body weight at birth of less than 2 pounds, 3 ounces (1,000 grams).

preterm birth A birth that occurs 3 or more weeks before the full 38 weeks of the typical pregnancy have elapsed—that is, at 35 or fewer weeks after conception.

TABLE 4.7

AT ABOUT THIS TIME: Average Prenatal Weights*

Period of Development	Weeks After Conception	Weight (Nonmetric)	Weight (Metric)	Notes
End of embryonic period	8	1/30 oz.	1 g	This is the most common time for spontaneous abortion (miscarriage).
End of first trimester	13	3 oz.	85 g	
At viability (50/50 chance of survival)	22	20 oz.	570 g	A birthweight less than 2 lb., 3 oz. (1,000 g) is considered extremely low birthweight (ELBW).
End of second trimester	26–28	2–3 lb.	900–1,400 g	Less than 3 lb., 5 oz. (2,500 g) is very low birthweight (VLBW).
End of preterm period	35	5½ lb.	2,500 g	Less than 5½ lb. (2,500 g) is low birthweight (LBW).
Full-term	38	7½ lb.	3,400 g	Between 5½ and 9 lb. (2,500–4,000 g) is considered normal weight.

*To make them easier to remember, the weights are rounded off (which accounts for the inexact correspondence between metric and nonmetric measures). Actual weights vary. For instance, a normal full-term infant can weigh between 5½ and 9 pounds (2,500 and 4,000 grams); a viable infant, especially one of several born at 26 or more weeks, can weigh less than shown here.

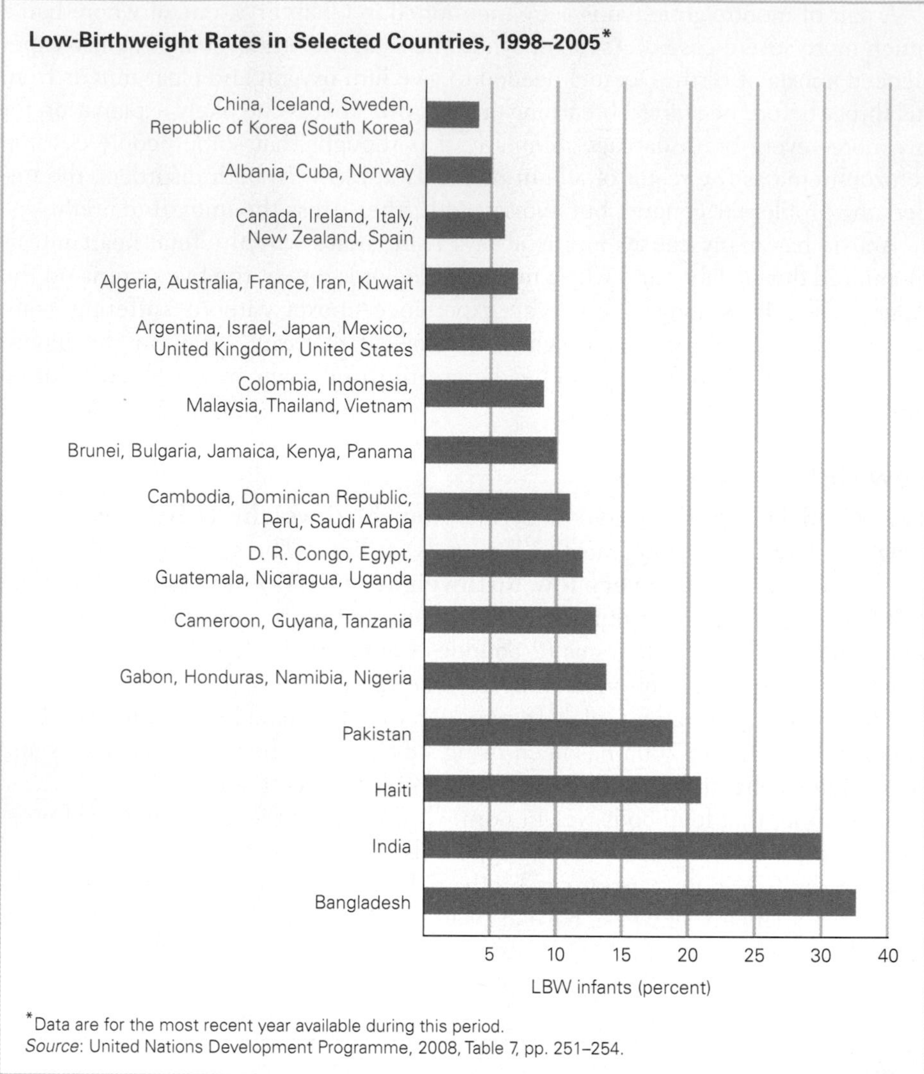

FIGURE 4.6

Low Birthweight Around the World The LBW rate is often considered a reflection of a country's commitment to its children as well as a reflection of its economic resources.

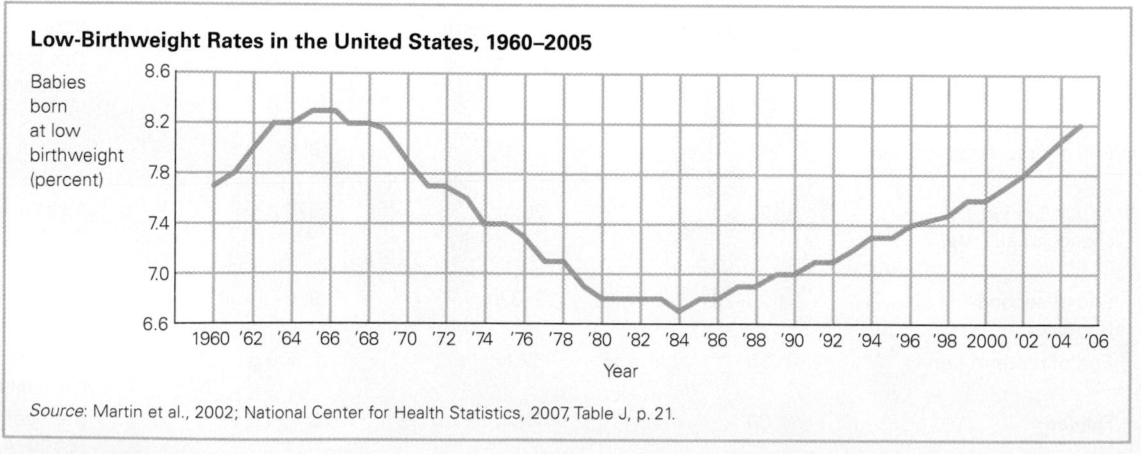

Observation Quiz (see answer, page 122): In what year was 1 out of every 13 U.S. babies (7.5 percent) born weighing less than 5½ pounds (2,500 grams)?

FIGURE 4.7

Not Improving The LBW rate is often taken to be a measure of a nation's overall health. In the United States, the rise and fall of this rate are related to many factors, among them prenatal care, maternal use of drugs, overall nutrition, and number of multiple births.

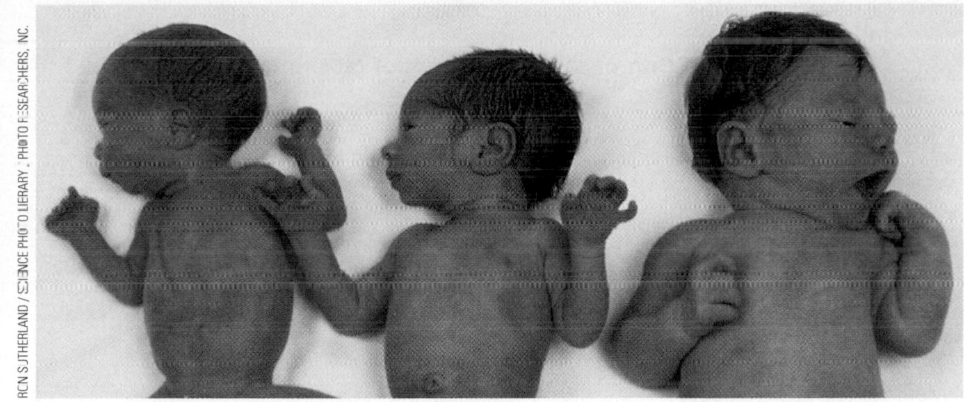

RON SUTHERLAND / SCIENCE PHOTO LIBRARY / PHOTO RESEARCHERS, INC.

Which Baby Is Oldest? The baby at the left is the oldest, at almost 1 month; the baby at the right is the youngest, at just 2 days. Are you surprised? The explanation is that the 1-month-old was born 9 weeks early and now weighs less than 5½ pounds (2,500 grams); the 2-day-old was full term and weighs almost 8 pounds (3,600 grams). The baby in the middle, born full-term but weighing only 2 pounds (900 grams), is the most worrisome. Her ears and hands are larger than the preterm baby's, but her skull is small; malnutrition may have deprived her brain as well as her body.

Although most preterm babies are LBW because they missed those final weeks of weight gain, some babies are underweight because they gained weight too slowly throughout pregnancy. They are called *small for dates* or **small for gestational age (SGA).** An underweight SGA infant causes more concern than an underweight preterm birth, because SGA signifies impairment during prenatal development.

small for gestational age (SGA) A term for a baby whose birthweight is significantly lower than expected, given the time since conception. For example, a 5-pound (2,265-gram) newborn is considered SGA if born on time but not SGA if born two months early. (Also called *small for dates.*)

If a sonogram reveals slow fetal growth, the pregnant woman is alerted to try to remedy the problem (stop drinking and smoking, eat more, find a less stressful job). But if nothing can be done, birth may be induced early or a cesarean performed in order to prevent the neurological consequences of continued slow growth. Newborns who are *both* preterm and SGA make up the most rapidly increasing category of low-birthweight infants (Ananth et al., 2003).

Normally, in the first months outside the womb, a low-birthweight infant exhibits "catch-up growth," gaining weight faster than average. However, a significant number of SGA infants do the opposite and undereat. They are then likely to be diagnosed with "failure to thrive"; these babies are at high risk of becoming mentally slow and physically small (Casey et al., 2006).

Causes of SGA include problems with the placenta or umbilical cord, as well as maternal illness. However, maternal drug use is a far more common reason. Every psychoactive drug slows fetal growth. Tobacco is the worst and the most prevalent cause of SGA, implicated in 25 percent of all LBW births worldwide. Smoking among pregnant women is declining in the United States but rising in many other nations, especially in Asia. Consequently, the rates of LBW shown in Figure 4.6 may increase.

Prescription drugs can also cause low birthweight. For instance, antidepressants double the incidence of both preterm and SGA infants (Källén, 2004). Some pregnant women need drugs to stave off serious depression, but, as with many measures already mentioned (cesarean sections, genetic testing, anesthesia), the costs and benefits to mother and fetus need to be analyzed case by case (Cohen et al., 2006).

Every psychoactive drug, including prescribed medicines and legal drugs (such as alcohol and nicotine), crosses the placenta and may make a newborn jittery and irritable—signs that the infant is withdrawing from that drug. If the mother is heavily addicted (as with heroin or methadone), the newborn may need to be given some of the drug in order to ease withdrawal.

Another common reason for slow fetal growth is maternal malnutrition. Women who begin pregnancy underweight, who eat poorly during pregnancy, or who gain less than 3 pounds (1,400 grams) per month in the last six months are more likely

Research Design

Scientists: Gordon C. S. Smith and four other British researchers.

Publication: *American Journal of Public Health* (2007).

Participants: All 84,701 women in Scotland who had their first child between 1991 and 2001, except those with multiple births, stillbirths, or births after 43 weeks of gestation.

Design: Correlation of mother's weight in early pregnancy with birth outcome.

Major conclusion: Obese women have significantly more elective preterm deliveries (usually because the physician insists), and thus more ELBW infants. The reason is usually preeclampsia (a serious complication during pregnancy), which halts at delivery.

Comment: Although overweight women are less likely to have a spontaneous preterm birth, obese women risk pregnancy complications. Ideally, women should be neither too thin nor too fat when pregnancy begins.

TABLE 4.8

Risking Birth Complications: Impact of Mother's Weight

	Incidence of Complication (Percent)			
BMI (Body Mass Index)*	Preeclampsia†	Spontaneous Preterm Births	Elective Preterm Births	ELBW Newborns
Less than 20 (underweight)	2.2%	5.3%	2.5%	0.4%
20–24.9 (healthy weight)	3.0	3.6	2.3	0.3
25–29.9 (overweight)	4.9	3.3	2.7	0.4
30–34.9 (obese)	7.4	3.1	3.6	0.4
More than 35 (morbidly obese)	10.0	3.0	5.0	1.0

*For an explanation of *BMI*, see p. 000.
†A disease of pregnancy; includes high blood pressure.
Source: G. C. S. Smith et al., 2007.

to have an underweight infant. Ironically, obese women (those with a BMI of 30 or more; see Chapter 14) also are at higher risk of having ELBW infants because they are more likely to experience serious pregnancy complications, such as preeclampsia, that require preterm delivery (G. C. S. Smith et al., 2007) (see Table 4.8). The healthiest pregnancies occur in women who are neither too thin nor too heavy. This conclusion came from a study of all the first births in Scotland over a decade (see the Research Design).

Malnutrition (not age) is the primary reason teenage girls often have small babies (Zeck et al., 2008). If they eat haphazardly and poorly, their diet cannot support their own growth, much less the growth of another developing person. Unfortunately, many of the risk factors just mentioned—underweight, undereating, underage, and drug use—tend to occur together.

Finally, as you remember from Chapter 3, multiple births are usually LBW. Assisted reproductive technology (ART) has dramatically increased the rate of multiples and thus of LBW (Pinborg et al., 2004). Half of all in vitro births are multiples.

Social Support

None of the factors that impede or interrupt prenatal growth are inevitable. Quality of medical care, education, culture, and social support affect every developing person before birth, via their impact on the pregnant woman.

The importance of these factors is made starkly evident in data from Gambia, a poor nation in Africa. Preterm births are most common (17 percent) in July, when many women are working long hours in the fields. SGA births are more common (31 percent) in November, the end of the "hungry season," when most women have been undernourished for three months or more (Rayco-Solon et al., 2005).

Fathers and other relatives, neighbors, cultures, and clinics can markedly reduce the risk of birth complications. For example, the rate of low birthweight and other problems among immigrant families is lower than the overall North American rate, probably because the families of pregnant women are more likely to make sure that they do not smoke, drink, or undereat (Auger et al., 2008).

In contrast, there is a high rate of birth complications among U.S.-born women of African American descent, even when they are well nourished, do not use drugs, and obtain good prenatal care. One explanation is that the racism of the larger society adds stress to their lives that they cannot shake off, a factor that takes a toll on

➤**Answer to Observation Quiz** (from page 120): In 1998. After having declined, the LBW rate began an upward climb in the mid-1980s.

African Americans' health overall (Geronimus et al., 2006). Genetic vulnerability is another possibility, but it's unlikely; women born in Africa or the Caribbean who give birth in the United States do not have as many birth complications.

Mothers, Fathers, and a Good Start

Birth complications can have a lingering impact on the new family, depending partly on the sensitivity of hospital care and on the home. LBW babies are more likely to become overweight and have health problems, particularly heart problems (Hack et al., 2002). This correlation may exist because the infants experienced high levels of stress hormones in their early days or perhaps because their parents fed them more or raised them differently from other children.

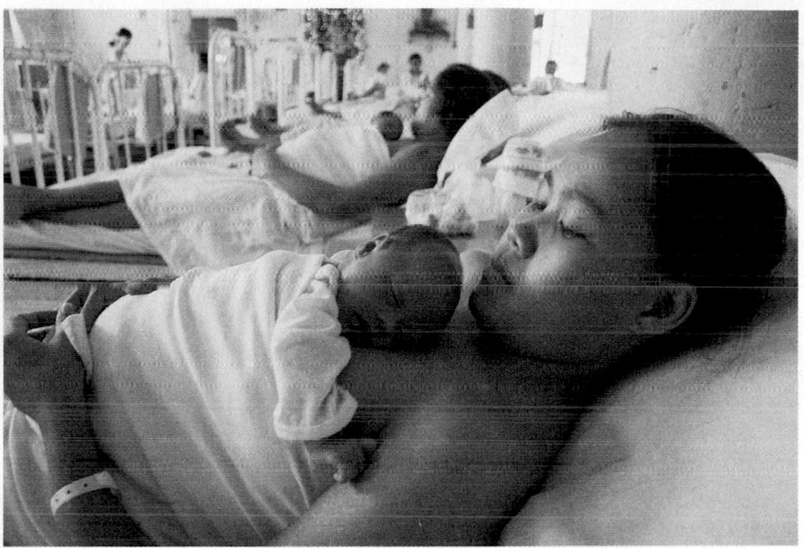

ALEX BALUYUT / ONASIA.COM

A Beneficial Beginning These new mothers in a maternity ward in Manila are providing their babies with kangaroo care.

To reduce stress, even when a newborn must stay in the hospital for weeks after birth, the parents are encouraged to help with early caregiving, not only because it benefits the baby but because they, too, are deprived and stressed (Eriksson & Pehrsson, 2005). When the infant's survival and normality are in doubt, many parents feel inadequate, sad, guilty, or angry. Such emotions become more manageable when the parents gain confidence by touching and caring for their vulnerable newborn.

One way to achieve parental involvement is through a procedure called **kangaroo care,** in which the mother of a low-birthweight infant spends at least an hour a day holding her newborn between her breasts, skin-to-skin, allowing the tiny baby to hear her heart beat and feel her body heat. Fathers also can cradle newborns next to their chests.

kangaroo care A form of child care in which the mother of a low-birthweight infant spends at least an hour a day holding the baby between her breasts, like a kangaroo that carries her immature newborn in a pouch on her abdomen.

One comparison study (Feldman et al., 2002) in Israel found that kangaroo-care newborns slept more deeply and spent more time alert than did infants who received standard care. By 6 months of age, infants who had received kangaroo care were more responsive to their mothers. These findings could be the result of either improved infant maturation or increased maternal sensitivity, but either way, this is good news. Other research confirms the benefits of kangaroo care (Ludington-Hoe et al., 2006; Tallandini & Scalembra, 2006).

Another way parents can help their newborn is through *massage therapy,* gently stroking their preterm infant several times a day. Tiny babies who are caressed seem less irritable and more relaxed (Hernandez-Reif et al., 2007). Massage of newborns is routine in many nations; it is an innovation in the United States.

All humans are social creatures, interacting with their families and their societies. Accordingly, prenatal development and birth involve not only the fetus but also the mother, father, and many others. As you have already read, a woman's chance of avoiding risks during pregnancy depends partly on her family, her ethnic background, and the nation where she lives.

Help from Fathers

Fathers can be crucial in the effort to produce a healthy baby. A supportive father-to-be helps a mother-to-be stay healthy, well nourished, and drug-free. Neither education nor employment correlates with decreased alcohol consumption during pregnancy: Marriage does (MMWR, April 5, 2002). Thus, when it comes to alcohol, husbands seem to help their wives abstain. Overall, a woman's drug consumption and nutrition during pregnancy are powerfully affected by her husband's health habits.

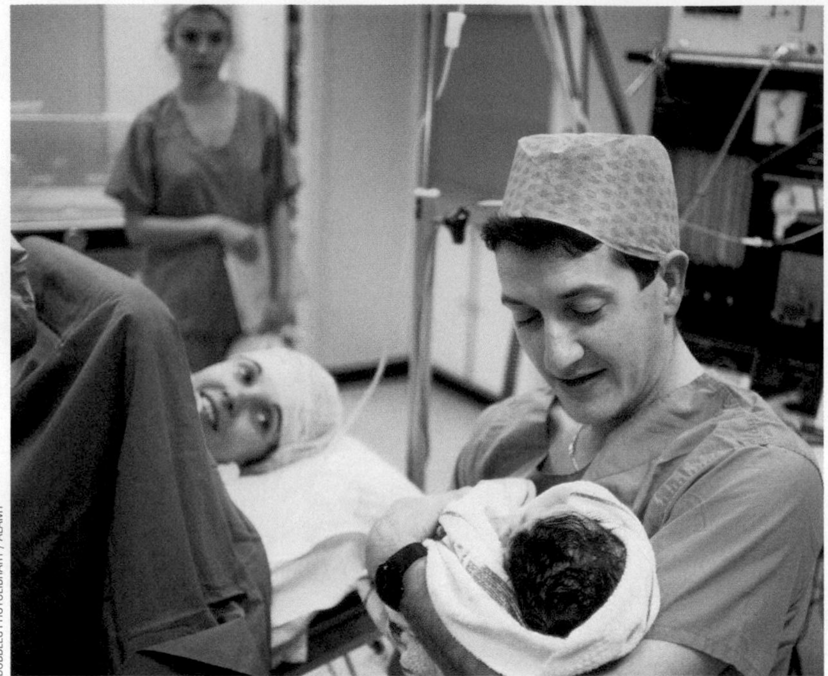

BUBBLES PHOTOLIBRARY / ALAMY

His Baby, Too This new father's evident joy in his baby illustrates a truism that developmental research has only recently reflected: Fathers contribute much more than just half their child's genes.

An alternate explanation for the correlation between marriage and healthy newborns is that pregnancies within marriage are more often wanted and planned by both parents; that fact in itself encourages both the pregnant woman and her husband to make sure she takes care of herself. Only about half of all U.S. pregnancies are planned; women who are young and unwed are particularly unlikely to become pregnant intentionally.

Not only by example, but also more directly, fathers and other family members can decrease or increase a mother's stress, which in turn affects her circulation, diet, rest, and digestion and, ultimately, the fetus. One study in northern India found that 18 percent of fathers-to-be abused their wives during pregnancy; the result was a doubling of the rate of fragile newborns and infant death (Ahmed et al., 2006).

Another way to interpret this research is to note that 82 percent of fathers-to-be took good care of their wives. In fact, many men are attentive and helpful to their pregnant wives, even when the wives are demanding and unhappy.

The need for social support is mutual. Fathers need reassurance, just as mothers do. Levels of cortisol, a stress hormone, correlate between expectant fathers and mothers: When one parent is stressed, the other often is, too (Berg & Wynne-Edwards, 2002), as the following illustrates.

a personal perspective

"You'd Throw Him in a Dumpster"

Remember John and Martha, the young couple whose amniocentesis revealed that their fetus had Down syndrome, or trisomy-21? Martha decided to have the baby, but they had never really discussed the issue. One night at 3:00 A.M., Martha, seven months pregnant, was crying uncontrollably. She told John she was scared.

> "Scared of what?" he said. "Of a little baby who's not as perfect as you think he ought to be?"
>
> "I didn't say I wanted him to be perfect," I said. "I just want him to be normal. That's all I want. Just normal."
>
> "That is total bullshit. . . . You don't want this baby to be normal. You'd throw him in a dumpster if he just turned out to be normal. What you really want is for him to be superhuman."
>
> "For your information," I said in my most acid tone, "I was the one who decided to keep this baby, even though he's got Down's. You were the one who wanted to throw him in a dumpster."
>
> "How would you know?" John's voice was still gaining volume. "You never asked me what I wanted, did you? No. You never even asked me. . . ."
>
> *[Beck, 1999, p. 255]*

This episode ended well, with a long, warm, and honest conversation between the two prospective parents. Both parents learned what their fetus meant to the other, a topic that had been taboo until that night. Adam, their future son, became an important part of their relationship.

John and Martha's experience is not uncommon: During pregnancy or in the days after birth, it is not unusual for couples to experience a lack of communication and/or the sudden eruption of previously unexpressed emotions. Honest discussion between expectant or new parents is difficult, especially because birth raises powerful memories from childhood and irrational fears about the future. Some fathers disappear, either literally or by increasing their work hours.

Yet open and intimate communication is crucial if a couple is to form a **parental alliance,** a cooperative working relationship between two parents who raise their child together. The need for a parental alliance is evident in an unexpected, yet common, consequence of birth: postpartum depression.

parental alliance Cooperation between a mother and a father based on their mutual commitment to their children. In a parental alliance, the parents agree to support each other in their shared parental roles.

Postpartum Depression

In the days, weeks, and even months after birth, between 10 and 15 percent of U.S. women experience **postpartum depression** (MMWR, April 11, 2008), a sense of inadequacy and sadness (called *baby blues* in the mild version and *postpartum psychosis* in the most severe form) (Perfetti et al., 2004). These rates are for the United States; some other nations have higher rates. For example, rates in Pakistan were 36 percent on a standard postpartum scale (Husain et al., 2006).

postpartum depression A new mother's feelings of inadequacy and sadness in the days and weeks after giving birth.

A mother with postpartum depression finds normal baby care (feeding, diapering, bathing) to be very burdensome, and she may have thoughts of neglecting or abusing the infant. Postpartum depression that lasts more than a few weeks can have a long-term impact on the child, so it should be diagnosed and treated as soon as possible.

The father's reaction is crucial when a mother experiences postpartum depression. His active caregiving helps the baby to thrive and the mother to recover. However, some fathers become depressed themselves after the birth. Even if the mother is not depressed, the father's depression is likely to affect the baby. One study found that sons of fathers who were depressed after their birth had notable behavior problems as toddlers (Ramchandani et al., 2005).

From a developmental perspective, some causes of postpartum depression predate the pregnancy (such as preexisting depression, financial stress, or marital problems); others occur during pregnancy (women are more often depressed two months before birth than two months after); and still others are specific to the infant (health, feeding, or sleeping problems) and to the birth (Ashman & Dawson, 2002; Jones, 2006).

SHEHZAD NOORANI / PETER ARNOLD, INC.

A Teenage Mother This week-old baby, born in a poor village in Myanmar (Burma), has a better chance of survival than he might otherwise have had, because his 18-year-old mother has bonded with him.

Bonding

Focusing on the parents' emotions raises the question: To what extent are the first hours after birth crucial for the **parent–infant bond,** the strong, loving connection that forms as parents hold, examine, and feed their newborn? It has been claimed that this bond develops in the first hours after birth when a mother touches her naked baby, just as sheep and goats must immediately smell and nuzzle their newborns if they are to nurture them (Klaus & Kennell, 1976).

However, research does not find that early skin-to-skin contact is essential for humans (Eyer, 1992; Lamb, 1982). Unlike sheep and goats, most other mammals do not need immediate contact for parents to nurture their offspring. In fact, substantial research on monkeys begins with *cross-fostering,* a strategy in which newborns are removed from their biological mothers in the first days of life and raised by another female or even a male. A strong and beneficial relationship sometimes develops (Suomi, 2002).

parent–infant bond The strong, loving connection that forms as parents hold, examine, and feed their newborn.

Most developmentalists hope that mothers, fathers, and newborns strengthen their relationship in the hours and days after birth. That is a good foundation for the difficult days, nights, and years ahead. But bonding immediately after birth is neither necessary nor sufficient for a strong parental alliance and for parent–child attachment throughout life.

Especially for Scientists (see response, page 126): Research with animals can benefit people, but it is sometimes used too quickly to support conclusions about people. When does that happen?

➤Response for Scientists (from page 125): Animal research tends to be used too quickly whenever it supports an assertion that is popular but has not been substantiated by research data, as in the social construction about physical contact being crucial for parent–infant bonding.

SUMMING UP

Most newborns weigh about 7½ pounds (3,400 grams), score at least 7 out of 10 on the Apgar scale, and thrive without medical assistance. Although modern medicine has made maternal or infant death and serious impairment less common in advanced nations, many critics deplore the tendency to treat birth as a medical crisis instead of a natural event. Developmentalists note that birth complications are rarely the consequence of birth practices alone; prenatal problems are usually involved.

Many factors in the family, the fetus's genetic makeup, and social conditions lead to low birthweight, a potentially serious and increasingly common problem. Postpartum depression is not rare, but, again, factors operating before and after birth affect how serious and long-lasting this problem is. Human parents and infants seem to benefit from close physical contact following the birth, but it is not essential for emotional bonding. The family relationship begins before conception, may be strengthened by the birth process, and continues lifelong. ■

SUMMARY

From Zygote to Newborn

1. The first two weeks of prenatal growth are called the germinal period. During this period, the single-celled zygote develops into a blastocyst with more than 100 cells, travels down the fallopian tube, and implants itself in the lining of the uterus. Most zygotes do not develop.

2. The period from the third through the eighth week after conception is called the embryonic period. The heart begins to beat, and the eyes, ears, nose, and mouth begin to form. By the eighth week, the embryo has the basic organs and features of a human, with the exception of the sex organs.

3. The fetal period extends from the 9th week until birth. By the 12th week, all the organs and body structures have formed. The fetus attains viability at 22 weeks, when the brain is sufficiently mature to regulate basic body functions. Babies born before the 26th week are at high risk of death or disability.

4. The average fetus gains approximately 4½ pounds (2,000 grams) during the last three months of pregnancy and weighs 7½ pounds (3,400 grams) at birth. Maturation of brain, lungs, and heart ensures survival of more than 99 percent of all full-term babies born in developed nations.

Risk Reduction

5. Some teratogens (diseases, drugs, and pollutants) cause physical impairment. Others, called behavioral teratogens, harm the brain and therefore impair cognitive abilities and personality tendencies.

6. Whether a teratogen harms an embryo or fetus depends on timing, amount of exposure, and genetic vulnerability. To protect against prenatal complications, good public and personal health practices are strongly recommended.

7. Many methods of prenatal testing inform pregnant couples how the fetus is developing. Such knowledge can bring anxiety and unexpected responsibility as well as welcome information.

Birth

8. Birth typically begins with contractions that push the fetus, head first, out of the uterus and then through the vagina. The Apgar scale, which rates the neonate's vital signs at one minute and again at five minutes after birth, provides a quick evaluation of the infant's health.

9. Medical intervention can speed contractions, dull pain, and save lives. However, many aspects of medicalized birth have been criticized as impersonal and unnecessary. Contemporary birthing practices are aimed at finding a balance, protecting the baby but also allowing more parental involvement and control.

10. Birth complications, such as unusually long and stressful labor that includes anoxia (a lack of oxygen to the fetus), have many causes. Long-term handicaps, such as cerebral palsy, are not inevitable for such children, but careful nurturing from their parents may be needed.

11. Low birthweight (under 5½ pounds, or 2,500 grams) may arise from multiple births, placental problems, maternal illness, malnutrition, smoking, drinking, drug use, and age. Compared with full-term newborns, preterm and underweight babies experience more medical difficulties. Fetuses that grow slowly (and thus are small for gestational age, or SGA) are especially vulnerable.

12. Kangaroo care is helpful when the newborn is of low birthweight. Mother–newborn interaction should be encouraged, although the parent–infant bond depends on many factors in addition to birth practices.

13. Many women feel unhappy, incompetent, or unwell after giving birth. Postpartum depression gradually disappears with appropriate help; fathers are particularly crucial to the well-being of mother and child, although they also are vulnerable to depression.

KEY TERMS

germinal period (p. 97)
embryonic period (p. 97)
fetal period (p. 97)
blastocyst (p. 97)
placenta (p. 98)
implantation (p. 98)
embryo (p. 99)
fetus (p. 100)
age of viability (p. 101)
teratogens (p. 104)
behavioral teratogens (p. 104)
teratology (p. 104)
risk analysis (p. 104)
threshold effect (p. 106)
interaction effect (p. 106)
fetal alcohol syndrome (FAS) (p. 110)
fetal alcohol effects (FAE) (p. 110)
sonogram (p. 110)
Apgar scale (p. 115)
cesarean section (p. 115)
doula (p. 118)
anoxia (p. 118)
cerebral palsy (p. 118)
low birthweight (LBW) (p. 119)
very low birthweight (VLBW) (p. 119)
extremely low birthweight (ELBW) (p. 119)
preterm birth (p. 119)
small for gestational age (SGA) (p. 121)
kangaroo care (p. 123)
parental alliance (p. 125)
postpartum depression (p. 125)
parent–infant bond (p. 125)

KEY QUESTIONS

1. What are the major differences between an embryo at 2 weeks and at 8 weeks after conception?

2. What are the factors in achieving viability?

3. Since almost all fetuses born at 30 weeks survive, why don't women avoid the last month of pregnancy by having an elective cesarean at that time?

4. Which maternal behavior or characteristic seems most harmful to the fetus: eating a diet low in folic acid, drinking a lot of alcohol, or being HIV-positive? Explain your answer.

5. How much influence do husbands and mothers have on pregnant women? Explain your answer.

6. How have medical procedures helped *and* harmed the birth process?

7. What are the differences between a typical pregnancy and birth in Africa and a typical one in the United States?

8. Why do hospitals encourage parents of fragile newborns to provide some care, even if the newborn is in critical condition?

9. Name four causes of low birthweight. What can be done to prevent each one?

10. What can be done to relieve the effects of postpartum depression on the mother, the father, and the infant?

APPLICATIONS

1. Go to a nearby greeting-card store and analyze the cards about pregnancy and birth. Do you see any cultural attitudes (e.g., variations depending on the sex of the newborn or of the parent)? If possible, compare those cards with cards from a store that caters to another economic or cultural group.

2. Interview three mothers of varied backgrounds about their birth experiences. Make your interviews open-ended—let them choose what to tell you, as long as they give at least a 10-minute description. Then compare and contrast the three accounts, noting especially any influences of culture, personality, circumstances, or cohort.

3. People sometimes wonder how any pregnant woman could jeopardize the health of her fetus. Consider your own health-related behavior in the past month—exercise, sleep, nutrition, drug use, medical and dental care, disease avoidance, and so on. Would you change your behavior if you were pregnant? Would it make a difference if your family, your partner, or you yourself did not want a baby?

The First Two Years

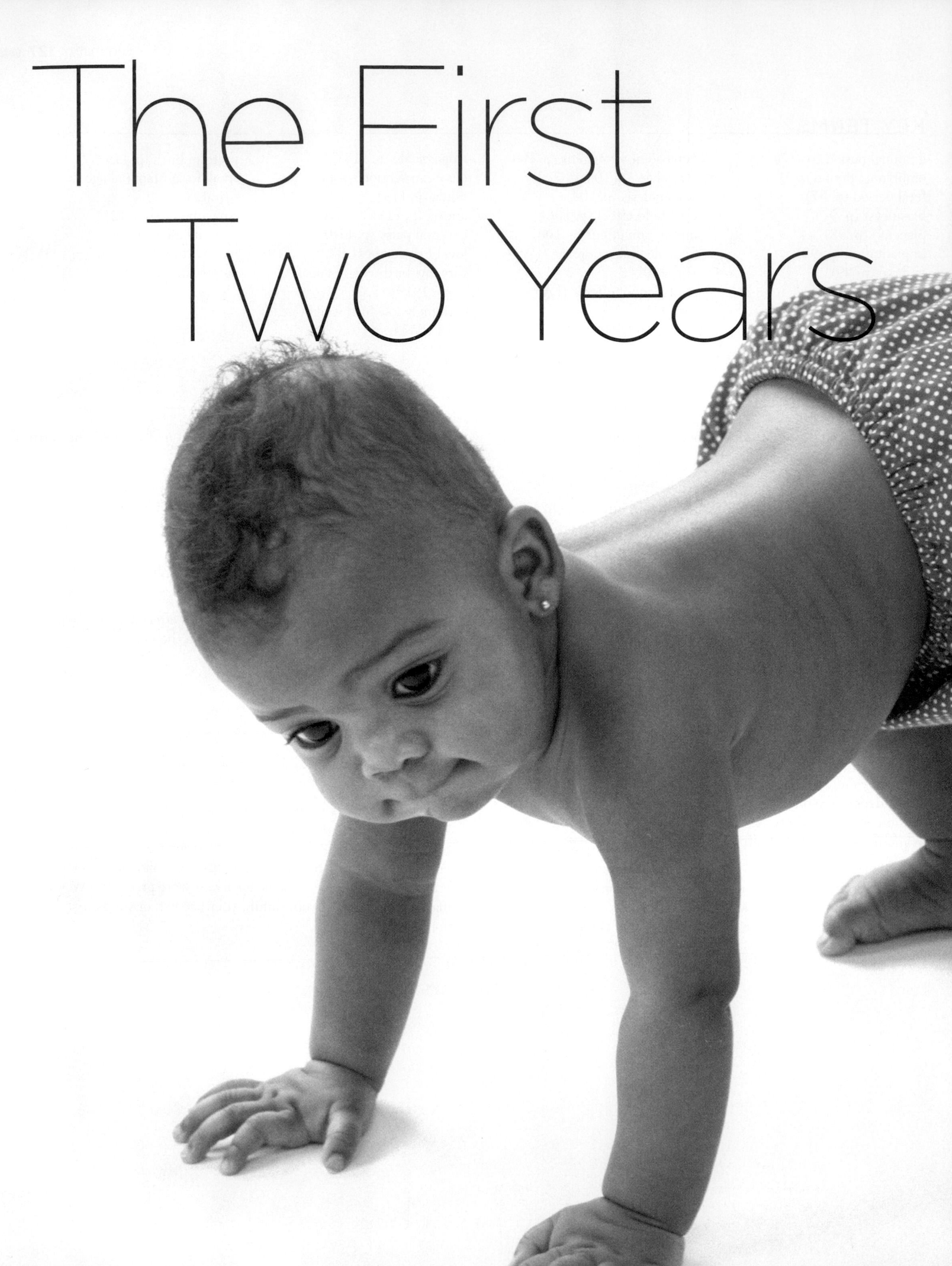

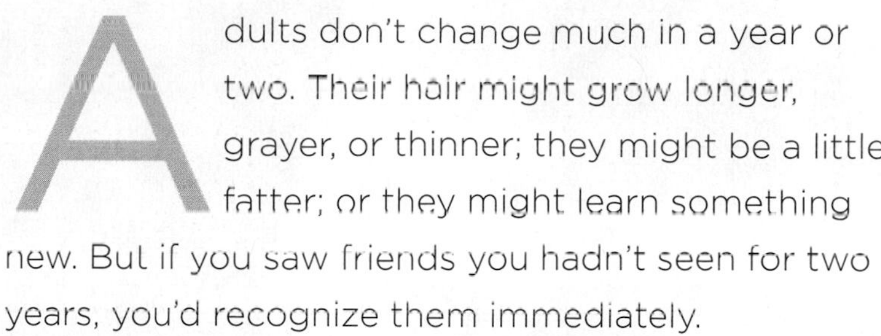

PART II

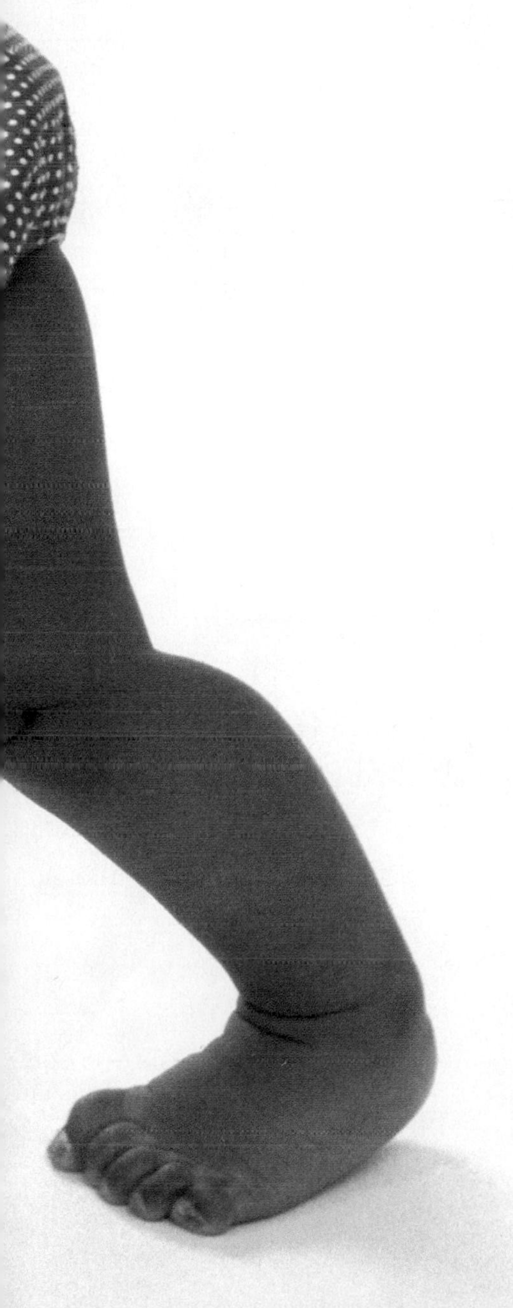

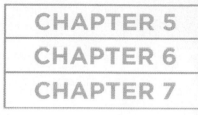

Adults don't change much in a year or two. Their hair might grow longer, grayer, or thinner; they might be a little fatter; or they might learn something new. But if you saw friends you hadn't seen for two years, you'd recognize them immediately.

By contrast, if you cared for a newborn every single day for a month, went away for two years, and then came back, you might not recognize him or her, because the baby would have quadrupled in weight, grown taller by more than a foot, and sprouted a new head of hair. The child's behavior would have changed, too. Not much crying, but some laughter and fear—including fear of you.

A year or two is not much compared with the 75 or so years of the average life span. However, in two years newborns reach half their adult height, learn to talk in sentences, and come to express almost every emotion—not just joy and fear but also love, jealousy, and shame. The next three chapters describe these radical and awesome changes.

5

CHAPTER OUTLINE

HAZEL HANKIN

My Youngest at 8 Months When I look at this photo of Sarah, I see evidence of Mrs. Todd's devotion. Sarah's hair is washed and carefully brushed, her jumper and blouse are clean and pressed, and the carpet and stepstool are perfect equipment for standing practice. Sarah's legs—chubby and far apart—indicate that she is not about to walk early; but, given all these signs of Mrs. Todd's attention to caregiving, it is not surprising, in hindsight, that my fourth daughter was my earliest walker.

The First Two Years: Biosocial Development

Our first child, Bethany, was born when I was earning my PhD. I paid close attention to developmental norms, such as "sitting by 6 months, walking and talking by 12." At 14 months, Bethany had not taken any steps. Like many developmentalists, I decided that genes were more influential than parenting. My hypothesis was confirmed when my next two children, Rachel and Elissa, were slow to walk.

When my youngest, Sarah, was born, I hired a full-time caregiver, Mrs. Todd, from Jamaica. I cautioned her that Berger children begin to walk late.

"Sarah will be walking by one year," Mrs. Todd told me.

"We'll see" I replied, confident of my genetic understanding.

Mrs. Todd bounced baby Sarah on her lap, day after day, and spent hours giving her "walking practice" to Sarah's great delight. Sarah took her first step at 12 months, a humbling lesson for me.

This chapter describes the first two years in the development of body and brain—the physical growth, muscle control, and cortex maturation that make the toddler a much different person from the newborn. Variations abound, some genetic and some contextual, including—as I now believe—many that stem from the influence of cultures and caregivers.

Body Changes

In infancy, growth is so fast, and the consequences of neglect are so severe, that gains need to be closely monitored. Medical checkups, including measurement of height, weight, and head circumference, occur every few weeks at first in order to ascertain whether an infant is progressing as expected.

Body Size

Exactly how rapidly does growth typically occur? You saw in Chapter 4 that at birth the average infant weighs 7½ pounds (3,400 grams) and measures about 20 inches (51 centimeters). This means that the typical newborn weighs less than a gallon of milk and is about as long as the distance from a large man's elbow to the tips of his fingers.

Infants typically double their birth weight by the fourth month and triple it by age 1. Physical growth then slows, but it is still rapid. By 24 months, most children weigh almost 30 pounds (13.5 kilograms) and are between

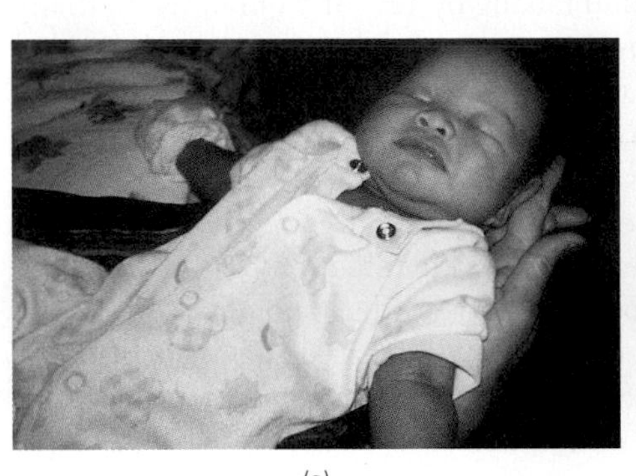
(a)

(b)

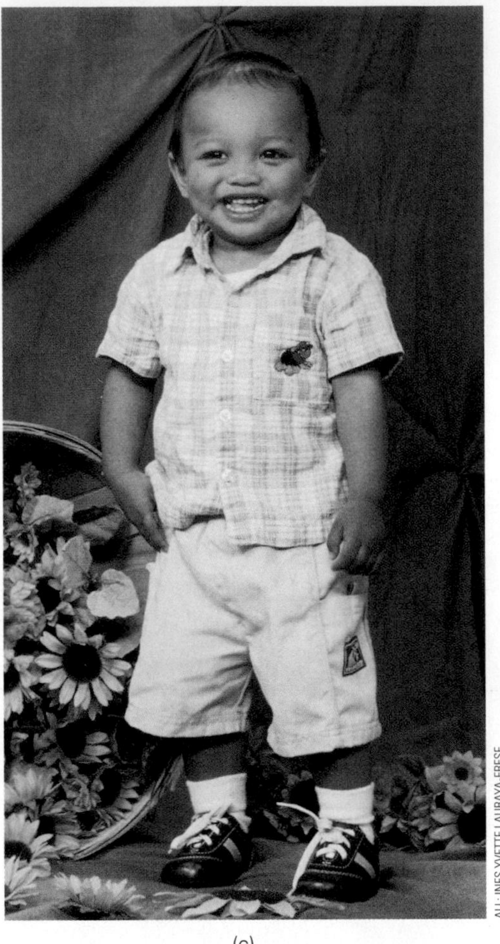
(c)

ALL: INES YVETTE LAURAYA-ERESE

Both Amazing and Average Juwan's growth from (*a*) 4 months to (*b*) 12 months to (*c*) 24 months is a surprise and delight to everyone who knows him. At age 2, this Filipino American toddler seems to have become a self-assured, outgoing individual, obviously unique. Yet the norms indicate that he is developing right on schedule—weight, teeth, motor skills, and all.

32 and 36 inches (81–91 centimeters) tall. This means that 2-year-olds are already half their adult height and about 20 percent of their adult weight, four times as heavy as they were at birth. (See Appendix A, pages A-6, A-7.)

Much of the weight increase in the early months is fat, which provides insulation for warmth and a store of nourishment. Small babies usually experience "catch-up growth" to gain those advantages. Stored nutrition keeps the brain growing even when teething or the sniffles interfere with eating. When nutrition is temporarily inadequate, the body stops growing but the brain does not—a phenomenon called **head-sparing** (Georgieff & Rao, 2001; Yeung, 2006). (Chronic malnutrition is discussed later in this chapter.)

head-sparing A biological mechanism that protects the brain when malnutrition affects body growth. The brain is the last part of the body to be damaged by malnutrition.

norm An average, or standard, measurement, calculated from the measurements of many individuals within a specific group or population.

percentile A point on a ranking scale of 0 to 100. The 50th percentile is the midpoint; half the people in the population being studied rank higher and half rank lower.

Each of the numbers in the previous paragraphs is a **norm,** an average or standard for a particular population. This chapter also began by citing a norm (walking by 12 months). Norms must be carefully interpreted. The "particular population" here is a representative sample of North American infants. Infant norms differ for infants from other continents.

To keep norms in perspective, it helps to understand percentiles, which range from zero to 100 for any variable within a population. The 50th **percentile** is the midway point and thus is exactly average, with half the people above it and half below it. (Bethany was advanced in vocabulary at 14 months, at the 80th percentile, which is one reason I was not too worried about her walking.)

A child of average weight would be close to the 50th percentile. Some children would be heavy (above the 75th percentile) and some quite light (below the 25th). Half the children would be outside the 25th–75th percentile norm. They might be quite healthy although not average.

The advantage of calculating percentiles is that children can be compared not only to others the same age but also to themselves at different times. Thus, a child whose weight *and* height are both at the 90th percentile at birth and again at 6 months is fine; so is a child whose height and weight are both consistently at the 20th percentile.

Percentiles sometimes suggest that worry is appropriate. A newborn who is at the 50th percentile in height and weight (about 21 inches and 7½ pounds) but later is at the 40th percentile in height and the 80th percentile in weight may be showing signs of future obesity. Those specific percentiles (40 and 80) are not worrisome in and of themselves, but the combination is a warning. Pediatricians and nurses notice when a child is far from the norm, but, as in this example, they pay closer attention to *changes* from earlier rankings.

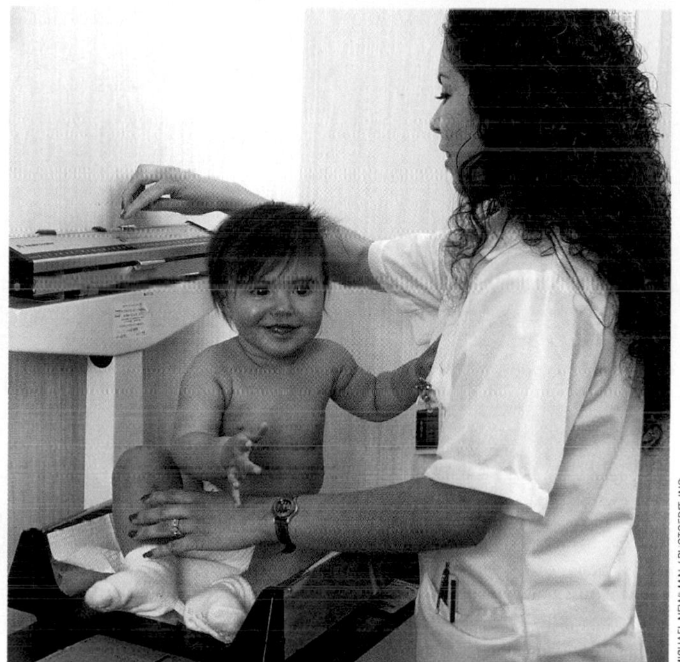

MICHAEL NEWMAN / PHOTOEDIT, INC.

The Weigh-In At her 1-year well-baby checkup, Blair sits up steadily, weighs more than 20 pounds, and would scramble off the table if she could. Both Blair's development and the nurse's protective arm are quite appropriate.

Sleep

New babies spend most of their time sleeping, about 17 hours or more a day. Those who are well fed and full term actually sleep more than the preterm ones, since they have less need to wake up every two hours to eat.

Throughout childhood, regular and ample sleep correlates with normal brain maturation, learning, emotional regulation, and psychological adjustment in school and within the family (Bates et al., 2002; Sadeh et al., 2000). Children who wake up often or easily or who sleep too little usually have physical or psychological problems. Lifelong, sleep deprivation can cause health problems, and vice versa (Murphy & Delanty, 2007).

REM sleep Rapid eye movement sleep, a stage of sleep characterized by flickering eyes behind closed lids, dreaming, and rapid brain waves.

Maturation and Sleep Patterns

Over the first months, the relative amount of time spent in each type or stage of sleep (deep, shallow, dreaming) changes. Newborns dream a lot; about half their sleep is **REM sleep** (rapid eye movement sleep), characterized by flickering eyes, dreaming, and rapid brain waves. Dreaming declines over the early weeks, as does "transitional sleep," the dozing, half-awake stage. At 3 or 4 months, quiet sleep (also called slow-wave sleep) increases markedly.

By about 3 months, the various states of waking and sleeping become more evident. Thus, although newborns often seem half asleep, neither in deep sleep nor wide awake, by 3 months most babies have periods of alertness when they are neither hungry nor sleepy and periods of deep sleep when even loud noises do not rouse them.

Sleep patterns are affected by birth order, diet, and child-rearing practices, as well as by brain maturation. Babies who are

DAVID YOUNG-WOLFF / PHOTOEDIT, INC.

Dreaming, Dozing, or Sound Asleep? Babies spend most of their time sleeping.

fed cow's milk and cereal sleep more soundly, which is not necessarily a good thing, as will be discussed later. If parents respond to predawn cries with food and play, babies learn to wake up night after night—again, not necessarily a good thing.

First-born infants typically "receive more attention" (Bornstein, 2002, p. 28), which may be why they have more sleep problems than later-borns. Such problems may be more troubling for parents than for infants. This does not render them insignificant, however; sleep-deprived parents may provide less attention than a baby needs (Bayer et al., 2007).

Developmentalists agree that insisting that an infant conform to the parents' sleep–wake schedule can be frustrating and, in some cases, harmful to the infant, whose brain patterns and digestion are not ready for adult sleep patterns. However, when children frequently interrupt the adults' sleep, the parents may experience ill effects. Ideally, families interact and adapt so that every member's basic needs are met.

Co-Sleeping

co-sleeping A custom in which parents and their children (usually infants) sleep together in the same bed.

One question for many parents is: Where should infants sleep? Parents hear contradictory advice about the practice called **co-sleeping,** in which parents and infants sleep together in the same bed (Hormann, 2007). In the end, most parents choose a sleeping arrangement because it conforms to the customs of their culture, not because any particular arrangement is universally considered best (Tamis-LeMonda et al., 2008).

Most parents in Asia, Africa, and Latin America favor co-sleeping. Traditionally, Western parents put their infants to sleep in a crib in a separate bedroom, unless the family does not have a spare room. However, co-sleeping is becoming increasingly common in Western families. A survey of British parents found that half of them slept with their infants some of the time (Blair & Ball, 2004). A study of California families found that about a third practiced co-sleeping from birth; about one-fourth of couples put newborns in another room but allowed their toddlers to sleep with them; slightly less than half kept their offspring in separate bedrooms throughout childhood (Keller & Goldberg, 2004).

Breast-feeding is more common with co-sleeping, but so is sudden infant death (Ruys et al., 2007). Co-sleeping poses a greater risk if the adult is drugged or drunk, and thus in danger of "overlying" the baby. One expert suggests that sleeping in the same room is beneficial but bed-sharing is not, especially if the adult bed is soft and has comforters and blankets, thus increasing the baby's risk of suffocation (Alm, 2007). Another expert considers bed-sharing to be safe:

> Mothers instinctively take up a protective posture when sharing a bed with their infants, lying in a fetal position with their lower arm above the infant's head and the infant lying within around 20–30 centimeters [about 10 inches] from the mother's chest. The position of the mother's thighs prevents the baby from sliding down the bed.
>
> *[Wailoo et al., 2004, p. 1083]*

A crucial issue is sleep deprivation. A videotape analysis found that co-sleeping infants wake up twice as often (six times a night) as solo-sleeping infants (three times), but co-sleepers get just as much sleep as solo sleepers because they go back to sleep more quickly (Mao et al., 2004). One of the main reasons for co-sleeping is that parents get more sleep if they do not need to be fully roused to feed the baby during the night.

Especially for New Parents (see response, page 138): You are aware of cultural differences in sleeping practices, and this raises a very practical issue: Should your newborn sleep in bed with you?

Sleeping patterns are like other aspects of infant care: Many different paths can lead to normal child development. Extreme fears about different sleeping arrangements are probably unwarranted. Most infants develop well no matter where they sleep.

SUMMING UP

Birthweight doubles, triples, and quadruples by 4 months, 12 months, and 24 months, respectively. Height increases by about a foot (about 30 centimeters) in the first two years. Such norms are useful as general guidelines, but individual percentile rankings over time indicate whether a particular infant is growing normally. Sleep becomes regular, dreaming less common, and distinct sleep–wake patterns develop, usually including a long night's sleep by age 1. By age 2, time spent dreaming decreases to about what it is for an older child. Cultural and caregiving practices influence norms, schedules, and expectations, especially in regard to where the infant should sleep. ■

Brain Development

Recall that the newborn's skull is disproportionately large. That's because it must be big enough to hold the brain, which at birth is already 25 percent of its adult weight. The neonate's body, by comparison, is typically only 5 percent of the adult weight. By age 2, the brain is almost 75 percent of adult brain weight; the child's total body weight is about 20 percent of its adult weight (see Figure 5.1).

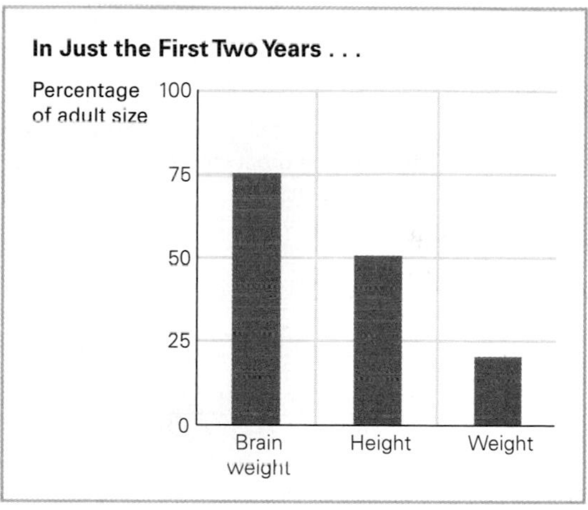

FIGURE 5.1

Growing Up Two-year-olds are barely talking and are totally dependent on adults, but they have already reached half their adult height and three-fourths of their adult brain size. This is dramatic evidence that biosocial growth is the foundation for cognitive and social maturity.

Connections in the Brain

Head circumference provides a rough idea of how the brain is growing, which is why medical checkups include measurement of the skull. The distance around the head typically increases about 35 percent (from 13 to 18 inches, or from 33 to 46 centimeters) within the first year.

Much more significant (although harder to measure) are changes in the brain's communication system. To understand this, we review the basics of neurological development (see Figure 5.2).

Basic Brain Structures

The brain's communication system begins with nerve cells, called **neurons.** Most neurons are created before birth, at a peak production rate of 250,000 new brain cells per minute in mid-pregnancy (Purves et al., 2004). In infancy, the human

neuron One of the billions of nerve cells in the central nervous system, especially the brain.

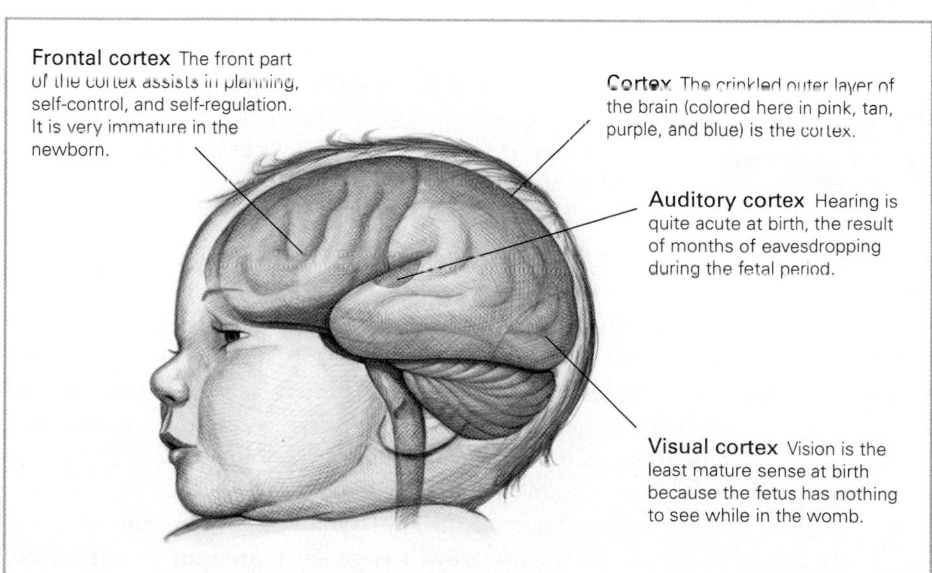

Frontal cortex The front part of the cortex assists in planning, self-control, and self-regulation. It is very immature in the newborn.
Cortex The crinkled outer layer of the brain (colored here in pink, tan, purple, and blue) is the cortex.
Auditory cortex Hearing is quite acute at birth, the result of months of eavesdropping during the fetal period.
Visual cortex Vision is the least mature sense at birth because the fetus has nothing to see while in the womb.

FIGURE 5.2

The Developing Cortex The infant's cortex consists of four to six thin layers of tissue that cover the brain. It contains virtually all the neurons that make conscious thought possible. Some areas of the cortex, such as those devoted to the basic senses, mature relatively early. Others, such as the frontal cortex, mature quite late.

brain has billions of neurons. Some neurons are deep inside the brain or in the *brain stem,* a region that controls automatic responses such as heartbeat, breathing, temperature, and arousal. About 70 percent of neurons are in the **cortex,** the brain's six outer layers (sometimes called the *neocortex*). The cortex is crucial for humans, as the following facts make clear (Kolb & Whishaw, 2008):

cortex The outer layers of the brain in humans and other mammals. Most thinking, feeling, and sensing involve the cortex. (Sometimes called the *neocortex.*)

axon A fiber that extends from a neuron and transmits electrochemical impulses from that neuron to the dendrites of other neurons.

dendrite A fiber that extends from a neuron and receives electrochemical impulses transmitted from other neurons via their axons.

synapse The intersection between the axon of one neuron and the dendrites of other neurons.

transient exuberance The great increase in the number of dendrites that occurs in an infant's brain during the first two years of life.

- About 80 percent of the human brain material is in the cortex.
- In other mammals, the cortex is proportionally smaller. Nonmammals have no cortex.
- Most thinking, feeling, and sensing occurs in the cortex, although other parts of the brain are also active.

Various areas of the cortex specialize in particular functions. For instance, there is a visual cortex, an auditory cortex, and an area dedicated to the sense of touch for each body part—even for each finger of a person or, in rats, for each whisker (Barnett et al., 2006). Regional specialization within the cortex occurs not only for motor skills and senses but also for particular kinds of cognition.

One of the fascinating aspects of brain specialization is that a certain part of the brain (called the *fusiform face area*) seems dedicated to perception of faces. In newborns, this area is activated not only by real faces but also by visual stimuli (e.g., pictures) that look like faces. The infant's experiences refine perception in this area, so 6-month-olds recognize their mothers and fathers, examine the faces of strangers, and no longer pay careful attention to monkey faces (Johnson, 2005).

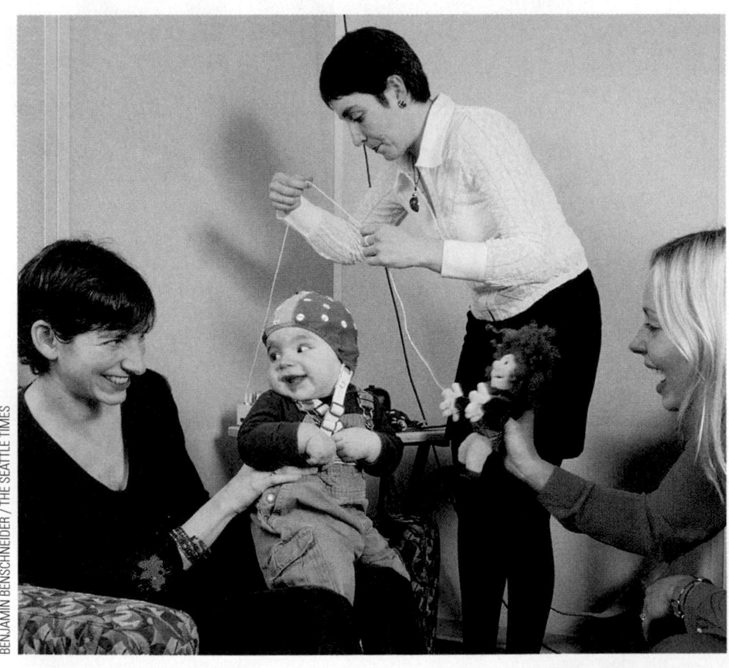

BENJAMIN BENSCHNEIDER / THE SEATTLE TIMES

Electric Excitement Milo's delight at his mother's facial expressions is visible, not just in his eyes and mouth but also in the neurons of the outer layer of his cortex. Electrodes map his brain activation region by region and moment by moment. Every month of life up to age 2 shows increased electrical excitement.

Within and between brain areas, neurons are connected to other neurons by intricate networks of nerve fibers called **axons** and **dendrites** (see Figure 5.3). Each neuron has a single axon and numerous dendrites, which spread out like the branches of a tree. The axon of one neuron meets the dendrites of other neurons at intersections called **synapses,** which are critical communication links within the brain.

To be more specific, neurons communicate by sending electrochemical impulses through their axons to synapses, to be picked up by the dendrites of other neurons. The dendrites bring the message to the cell bodies of their neurons, which, in turn, convey the message via their axons to still other neurons.

Axons and dendrites do not touch at synapses. Instead, the electrical impulses in axons typically cause the release of chemicals called *neurotransmitters,* which carry information from the axon of the sending neuron, across the *synaptic gap,* to the dendrites of the receiving neuron, in a rapid sequence that is speeded up by a process called *myelination* (described in Chapter 8).

Transient Exuberance and Pruning

At birth, the brain contains more than 100 billion neurons, more than any person will ever use (de Haan & Johnson, 2003). By contrast, the newborn's brain has far fewer dendrites and synapses than the person will eventually possess. During the first months and years, rapid growth and refinement in axons, dendrites, and synapses occur, especially in the cortex. Dendrite growth is the major reason that the brain weighs three times as much at age 2 as at birth (Johnson, 2005).

An estimated fivefold increase in the number of dendrites in the cortex occurs in the 24 months after birth; about 100 trillion synapses are present by age 2 (Schwartz & Begley, 2002). This early growth is called **transient exuberance,**

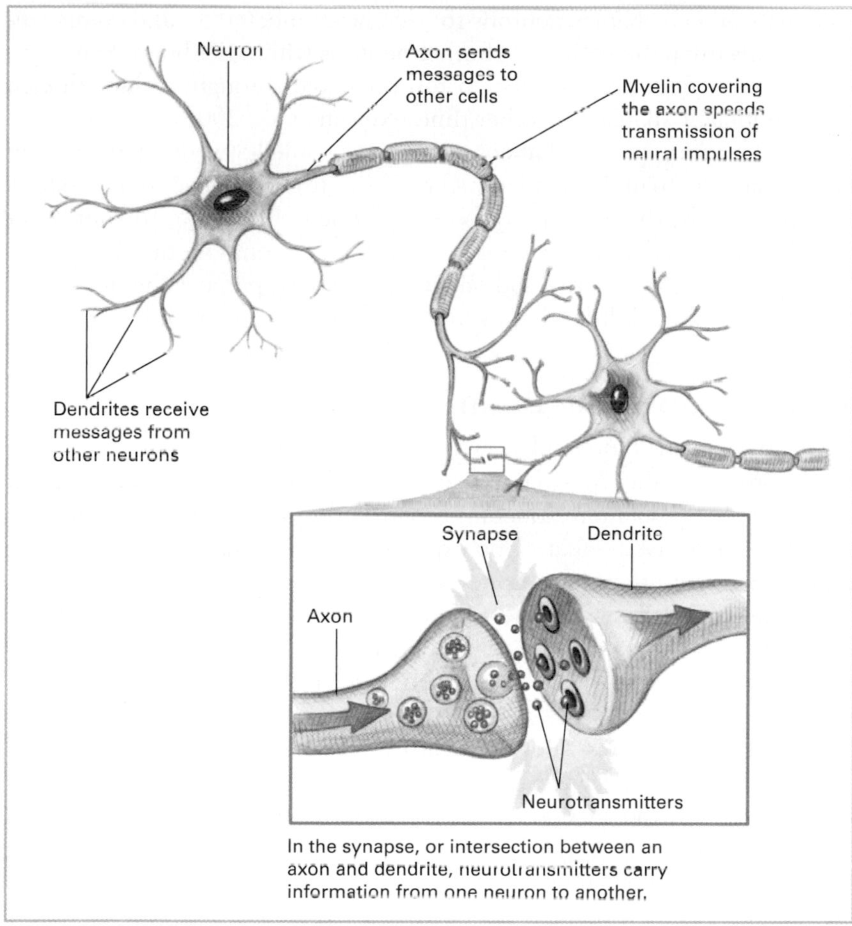

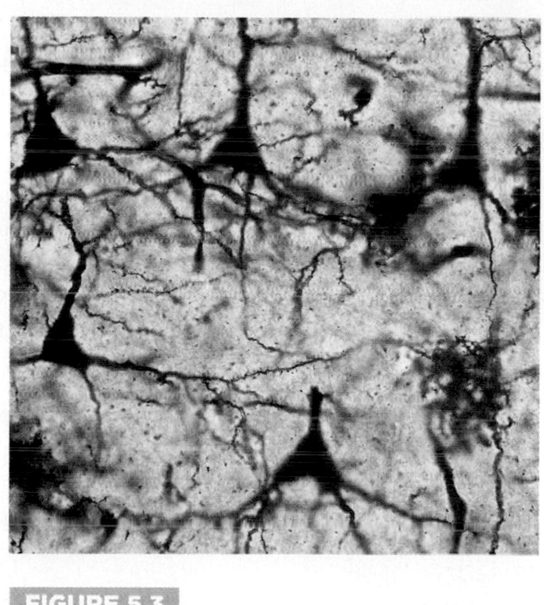

FIGURE 5.3

How Two Neurons Communicate The link between one neuron and another is shown in the simplified diagram at left. The infant brain actually contains billions of neurons, each with one axon and many dendrites. Every electrochemical message to or from the brain causes thousands of neurons to fire simultaneously, each transmitting the message across the synapse to neighboring neurons. The electron micrograph directly above shows several neurons, greatly magnified, with their tangled but highly organized and well-coordinated sets of dendrites and axons.

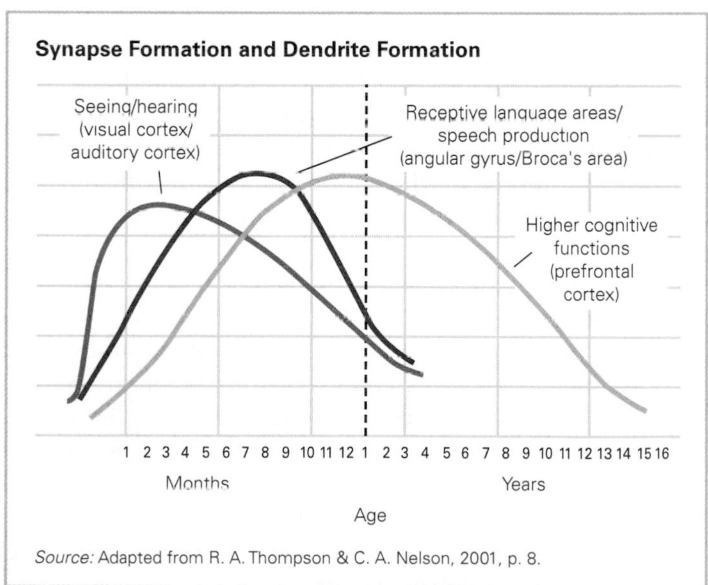

FIGURE 5.4

Brain Growth in Response to Experience These curves show the rapid rate of experience-dependent synapse formation for three functions of the brain (senses, language, and analysis). After the initial increase, the underused neurons are gradually pruned, or inactivated, as no functioning dendrites are formed from them.

Observation Quiz (see answer, page 138): Why do both "12 months" and "1 year" appear on the "Age" line?

because the expanded growth of dendrites is only temporary (transient), followed by *pruning* (see Figure 5.4), in which unused neurons and misconnected dendrites atrophy and die (Barinaga, 2003). (This process is called *pruning* because it resembles the way a gardener might prune a rose bush by cutting away some stems to enable more, or more beautiful, roses to bloom.)

➤Response for New Parents (from page 134): From the psychological and cultural perspectives, babies can sleep anywhere as long as the parents can hear them if they cry. The main consideration is safety: Infants should not sleep on a mattress that is too soft, nor should a baby sleep beside an adult who is drunk or drugged or sleeps very soundly. Otherwise, the family should decide for itself where its members would sleep best.

Transient exuberance enables neurons to become connected to, and communicate with, a greatly expanding number of other neurons within the brain. Synapses, dendrites, and even neurons continue to form and die throughout life, though more rapidly in infancy than at any other time (Nelson et al., 2006).

Thinking and learning require that connections be made between many parts of the brain. For example, to understand any word in this text, you need to understand the surrounding words, the ideas they convey, and how they relate to your other thoughts and experiences. Babies' brains have the same requirement, although at first they have few experiences to build on, and the various parts of the brain have not yet developed to the adult level or even to the level of a 2-year-old.

Experience Shapes the Brain

➤Answer to Observation Quiz (from page 137): "One year" signifies the entire year, from day 365 to day 729, and that is indicated by its location between "12 months" and "2 years."

The specifics of brain structure and growth depend on genes as well as on experience, which produces the "postnatal rise and fall" of synapses (de Haan & Johnson, 2003, p. 5). Soon after exuberant expansion, some dendrites wither away because they are underused—that is, no experiences have caused them to send a message to the axons of other neurons.

Strangely enough, this loss increases brainpower by promoting a more intricate organization of existing connections. The "increasing cognitive complexity of childhood is related to a loss rather than a gain of synapses" (de Haan & Johnson, 2003, p. 8).

Further evidence of the benefit of cell death comes from the damage caused by "a persistent failure of normal synapse pruning" (Irwin et al., 2002, p. 194). This is one of the symptoms of the genetic disorder called fragile X syndrome (described in Chapter 3). Because their brains have not undergone normal pruning, children with fragile X syndrome become mentally retarded; their dendrites are too dense and too long, which makes thinking very difficult for them.

Stress and the Brain

The brain produces cortisol and other hormones in response to stress. Cortisol production is evident in infants and continues throughout life (Adam et al., 2007).

An unfortunate example of the effect of experience in brain development occurs when the brain produces an overabundance of stress hormones early in life (which happens, for instance, when an infant is frequently terrified). When this occurs, the brain becomes incapable of normal stress responses. Later, that person's brain may either overproduce stress hormones, making the person hypervigilant (always on the alert), or underproduce them, making the person emotionally flat (never happy, sad, or angry).

A kindergarten teacher might notice that one child becomes furious or terrified at a mild provocation and another child seems indifferent to everything. Why? In both cases, the underlying cause could be excessive stress-hormone production in infancy, which changed the way those particular children's brains respond to stress.

Necessary and Possible Experiences

Scientist William Greenough has identified two experience-related aspects of brain development (Greenough et al., 1987):

experience-expectant brain functions Brain functions that require certain basic common experiences (which an infant can be expected to have) in order to develop normally.

- **Experience-expectant brain functions.** Certain basic functions of the brain require basic experiences in order to develop, just as a tree requires water. Those basic experiences are part of almost every infant's life, and thus almost every human brain develops as it should. Brains need such experiences and expect them.

- **Experience-dependent brain functions.** Some brain functions may or may not develop, depending on whether the infant has certain experiences. These experiences happen to infants in some families and cultures but not in others.

experience-dependent brain functions Brain functions that depend on particular, variable experiences and that therefore may or may not develop in a particular infant.

The basic, expected experiences *must* happen for normal brain maturation to occur, and they almost always do. The human brain is designed to expect them and needs them for growth. For example, in deserts and in the Arctic, on isolated farms and in crowded cities, almost all babies have things to see, objects to manipulate, and people to love them. As a result, their brains develop normally.

In contrast, dependent experiences *may* happen; because of them, one brain differs from another. Particular experiences vary, such as which language a baby hears or how its mother reacts to frustration. *Depending* on the particular experiences it has, an infant's brain becomes structured and connected one way or another, as some dendrites grow and neurons thrive while others die. Consequently, all people are similar, but each person is unique, because each has particular early experiences.

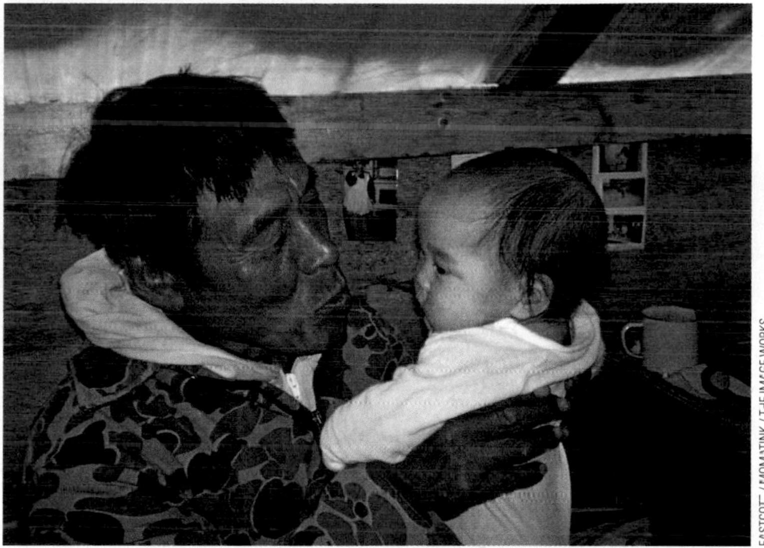

EASTCOTT / MOMATINK / THE IMAGE WORKS

Let's Talk Infants evoke facial expressions and baby talk, no matter where they are or which adults they are with. Communication is thus experience-expectant: Young human brains expect it and need it.

Observation Quiz (see answer, page 140): Are these two father and daughter? Where are they?

This distinction can be made for all mammals. Some of the most persuasive research into this issue has been done with songbirds. All male songbirds have a brain region dedicated to listening and reproducing sounds (experience-expectant), but each species in a particular locality learns to produce a slightly different song (experience-dependent). Birds are genetically designed to develop the neurons that they need, which might be neurons dedicated to learning new songs (canaries) or to finding hidden seeds (chickadees). Both of these functions require experiences that circumstances offer to some birds but not to others (Barinaga, 2003).

In unusual situations, knowledge of which developmental events are experience-expectant is helpful. For example, proliferation and pruning occur at about 4 months in the visual and auditory cortexes, so infants are eager to see and listen. For this reason, remedies for blind or deaf infants (such as surgery, eyeglasses, cochlear implants, or hearing aids) should be provided early in life to prevent atrophy of the brain regions that expect sights and sounds (Leonard, 2003). Thus, deaf infants whose deficits are recognized and remediated in the early months become more proficient at understanding and expressing language than infants with the same deficits whose remedy occurs later. Brain expectancy is the critical difference (Kennedy et al., 2006).

If early visual or auditory neuronal connections are not made, then the visual or auditory cortex of the brain may become dedicated to other senses, such as touch. That is why it is easier for a blind person to read Braille than for a seeing person, because blind people often have more brain cells dedicated to the sense of touch (Pascual-Leone & Torres, 1993).

The language areas of the brain develop most rapidly between 6 and 24 months, so infants need to hear a lot of speech in order to speak fluently. In fact, speech heard toward the end of the first year helps infants recognize the characteristics of their local language before they utter a word (Saffran et al., 2006).

The last part of the brain to mature is the **prefrontal cortex,** the area for anticipation, planning, and impulse control. It is virtually inactive in early infancy but gradually becomes more efficient over the years of childhood and adolescence

prefrontal cortex The area of cortex at the front of the brain that specializes in anticipation, planning, and impulse control.

(Luciana, 2003). Thus, telling an infant to stop crying is pointless, because the infant cannot decide to stop crying—such decisions require brain functions that are not yet present.

shaken baby syndrome A life-threatening injury that occurs when an infant is forcefully shaken back and forth, a motion that ruptures blood vessels in the brain and breaks neural connections.

Some adults shake a baby to stop its crying—an act that can have devastating effects on an infant's brain. This can cause **shaken baby syndrome,** a life-threatening condition that occurs when an infant is shaken back and forth, sharply and quickly, so that the brain rebounds against the skull. The violent shaking stops the crying, because blood vessels in the brain rupture and neural connections break; the result is often permanent brain damage, coma, or death. In the United States, more than one in five children hospitalized for maltreatment are suffering from shaken baby syndrome (Rovi et al., 2004).

Implications for Caregivers

What does early brain development mean for caregivers? First, early brain growth is rapid and dependent on experience. This means that caressing a newborn, talking to a preverbal infant, and showing affection toward a toddler may be essential to help them develop their full potential. If such experiences are missing from the child's early weeks and months, lifelong damage may result.

Second, each brain region follows a sequence of growing, connecting, and pruning. It is pointless to provide some forms of stimulation before the brain is ready. Adults should follow the baby's curiosity. Infants respond most strongly and positively to whatever their brains need; that is why very young babies like to look at and listen to musical mobiles, strangers on the street, and, best of all, their enthusiastic caregivers.

self-righting The inborn drive to remedy a developmental deficit.

This preference reflects **self-righting,** the inborn drive to remedy deficits. Infants with few toys develop their brains by playing with whatever is available. They do not need the latest educational playthings; their brains will develop normally with ordinary human interaction. One-year-olds cannot appreciate blocks with letters and numbers on them; just don't keep them in a dark, quiet place all day long.

Human brains are designed to grow and adapt; they retain some plasticity throughout life, but plasticity is especially apparent in the beginning during the most sensitive time for brain growth (Baltes et al., 2006; Erzurumlu et al., 2006). Brains protect themselves from overstimulation; that's why overstimulated babies cry or sleep. They also adjust to understimulation, responding to minimal experiences by developing new connections (Greenough, 1993).

Neuroscientists once thought that brains were influenced *solely* by genes and prenatal influences. The opposite assumption was held by many social scientists, who thought that environment was all that mattered. Cultures (according to anthropologists) or societies (according to sociologists) or parents (according to psychologists) could be credited or blamed for a child's every emotion and action.

➤Answer to Observation Quiz (from page 139): The man's straight black hair, high cheekbones, and weather-beaten face indicate that he is an Indian from North or South America. Other clues pinpoint the location. Note his lined, hooded jacket and the low, heat-conserving ceiling of the house—he is an Inuit in northern Canada. A father's attention makes a baby laugh and vocalize, not look away, so this man is not the 6-month-old baby's father. She is being held by a visiting friend of the family.

Now most scientists, especially developmentalists, take a multidisciplinary approach that incorporates both neuroscience and social science (Nelson et al., 2006). They believe that plasticity is an "inherent property of development" (Johnson, 2005, p. 189), but they also know that there are biological limitations on growth.

As you remember from Chapter 1, humans have *sensitive periods,* during which particular kinds of development are primed to occur (Baltes et al., 2006). The first two years of life are a sensitive period for many aspects of brain development, a time during which the brain needs some experiences to develop normally. The following explains this experience-expectant time in detail.

a view from science

Plasticity and Deprivation

The developmental community was stunned and saddened in 1970 by the discovery of a 13-year-old girl named Genie, who had spent most of her childhood alone in a room in her family's Los Angeles home. Her father, who was severely disturbed, kept Genie tied to a chair, never hearing human speech or feeling love. After she was rescued, Genie responded to affection and learned to speak, but she never developed normally

Most developmentalists concluded that her normal experiences came too late; her brain had already passed the sensitive period for development of many abilities. Her care after rescue did not compensate for, or even properly respond to, her emotional deprivation (Rymer, 1994).

But Genie was just one person. Perhaps she had been born brain-damaged and that was why, as a teenager, she did not have the basic skills that most people take for granted. Or her treatment itself may have been inhumane.

To explore these possibilities, Marion Diamond, William Greenough, and their colleagues raised some "deprived" rats alone in small, barren cages and other "enriched" rats in large cages with other rats as well as toys. At autopsy, the brains of the enriched rats were found to be larger and heavier, with more dendrites (D. Diamond et al., 1988; Greenough & Volkmar, 1973). Many other researchers with other mammals confirmed this phenomenon: Isolation and sensory deprivation harm the developing brain, and a complex social environment enhances neurological growth (Curtis & Nelson, 2003).

Such experiments are unthinkable with humans, but in the 1980s Romanian dictator Nicolae Ceausesçu conducted a chilling natural experiment. Wanting to increase his country's population, he paid parents a bonus for each newborn, forbade birth control, and outlawed abortions.

As a consequence of these policies, illegal abortions became the leading cause of death for women age 15 to 45 (Verona, 2003), and more than 100,000 children were abandoned to crowded, impersonal state-run orphanages (D. E. Johnson, 2000). These children suffered "severe and pervasive restriction of human interactions, play, conversation, and experiences" (Rutter & O'Connor, 2004, p. 91).

Ceausesçu was ousted and killed in 1989. During the next two years, thousands of Romanian children from these orphanages were adopted by North American and western European families who believed that "lots of love and good food would change the skinny, floppy waif they found in the orphanage into the child of their dreams" (D. E. Johnson, 2000, p. 154).

All the Romanian adoptees experienced catch-up growth, becoming taller and gaining weight until they reached normal size (Rutter & O'Connor, 2004). However, many were emotionally damaged: They were overfriendly, or angry, or frightened (Chisholm, 1998). The children who fared best were adopted before 6 months of age (Rutter, 2006).

For scientists who expected dire consequences, the news was generally good: "The human infant has built-in 'buffers' against early adversity" (O'Connor et al., 2000). Self-righting was apparent. By age 11, most children adopted by 6 months were quite normal.

However, some of the children never recovered. No further gains occurred after age 6, except for the most severely impaired children, who were still below average. The 11-year-olds who had been adopted after they were 6 months old scored an average of 85 on the WISC IQ test, 15 points below normal. Deprivation was evident, particularly in language and social interaction—abilities controlled by the cortex.

Neither dire nor sunny predictions about maltreated children are accurate. A team of scientists who have devoted their lives to studying impaired children advise: "Be skeptical about 'miracle' cures of severely affected individuals which appear in the media, or even in scientific journals, while recognizing that partial amelioration can occur in individual cases" (Clarke & Clarke, 2003, p. 131).

Further research in Romania concludes that infants develop best in their own families, second best in foster families, and much worse in institutions (Nelson et al., 2006). All infants need basic love and stimulation to become the persons their genes potentially enable them to become. Head-sparing, plasticity, self-righting, catch-up growth, and experience-expectant events all compensate for the many imperfections and lapses of human parenting, but they cannot overcome extreme early deprivation completely.

AP / WIDE WORLD PHOTOS

A Fortunate Pair Elaine Himelfarb (shown in the background), of San Diego, California, is shown here in Bucharest to adopt 22-month-old Maria.

SUMMING UP

Brain growth is rapid during the first months of life, when dendrites and the synapses within the cortex increase exponentially. By age 2, the brain has already reached three-fourths of its adult weight. Shrinkage of underused and unconnected dendrites begins in the sensory and motor areas and then occurs in other areas. Although some brain development is maturational, experience is also essential—both the universal experiences that almost every infant has (experience-expectant brain functions) and the particular experiences whose nature depends on the child's family or culture (experience-dependent brain functions). ■

Especially for Social Workers (see response, page 144): An infertile couple in their late 30s asks for your help in adopting a child from eastern Europe. They particularly want an older child. How do you respond?

Sensation and Movement

You learned in Chapter 2 that Piaget called the first period of intelligence the *sensorimotor* stage, emphasizing that cognition develops from the senses and motor skills. The same concept—that infant brain development depends on sensory experiences and early movements—underlies the discussion you have just read.

For that reason, within hours of a baby's birth, doctors and nurses make sure the infant's vital organs are functioning, assessing basic senses and motor responses. Many of them use the *Brazelton Neonatal Assessment Scale,* which measures 26 items of newborn behavior (such as cuddling, listening, and self-soothing) as well as several reflexes. Now we describe the sequence in which these abilities—all very immature at birth—develop.

The Five Senses

Every sense functions at birth. Newborns have open eyes, sensitive ears, and responsive noses, tongues, and skin. Throughout their first year, infants use these senses to sort and classify their many experiences. Indeed, "infants spend the better part of their first year merely looking around" (Rovee-Collier, 2001, p. 35). They also listen, smell, taste, and touch anything they can.

You may have noticed that very young babies seem to attend to everything, but without much focus or discrimination. For instance, they smile at almost anyone and put almost anything in their mouths (Adolph & Berger, 2005). Why are they not more cautious? Because sensation precedes perception.

sensation The response of a sensory system (eyes, ears, skin, tongue, nose) when it detects a stimulus.

perception The mental processing of sensory information when the brain interprets a sensation.

Sensation occurs when a sensory system detects a stimulus, as when the inner ear reverberates with sound or the retina and pupil of the eye intercept light. Thus, sensations begin when an outer organ (eye, ear, nose, tongue, or skin) meets anything that can be seen, heard, smelled, tasted, or touched.

Perception occurs when the brain notices and processes a sensation. Perception occurs in the cortex, usually as the result of a message from one of the sensing organs—a message based on past experience that suggests a particular sensation might be worth interpreting (Diamond, 2007).

Some sensations are beyond comprehension. A newborn does not know that the letters on a page might have significance, that Mother's face should be distinguished from Father's, or that the smells of roses and garlic have different connotations. Perceptions require experience, either direct experience or messages from other people.

Infant brains are attuned to their own social experiences, especially to social experiences that are repeated, and they try to make sense of these experiences (Leonard, 2003). Thus, a newborn named Emily has no idea that *Emily* is her name, but she has the brain and auditory capacity to hear sounds in the usual speech range (not the high-pitched sounds that only dogs can hear) and an inborn preference for repeated patterns.

At about 4 months, when her auditory cortex is rapidly creating and pruning dendrites, the repeated word *Emily* is perceived as well as sensed. Further, that sound emanates from the people Emily has learned to love (Saffran et al., 2006).

Before 6 months, Emily may open her eyes and turn her head when her name is called. It will take many more months before she tries to say "Emmy" and still longer before she knows that *Emily* is indeed her name.

Thus, cognition follows perception, when people think about what they have perceived. (Later, cognition no longer requires sensation: People imagine, fantasize, hypothesize.) The sequence of comprehension, from sensation to perception to cognition, requires first that an infant's sense organs function. No wonder the parts of the cortex dedicated to the senses develop rapidly: Their development is the prerequisite for human intellect.

Especially for Parents of Grown Children (see response, page 145): Suppose you realize that you seldom talked to your children until they talked to you and that you never used a stroller or a walker but put them in cribs and playpens. Did you limit their brain growth and their sensory capacity?

Hearing

The sense of hearing develops during the last trimester of pregnancy and is already quite acute at birth (Saffran et al., 2006). Certain sounds trigger reflexes in newborns, even without conscious perception. Sudden noises startle them, making them cry; rhythmic sounds, such as a lullaby or a heartbeat, soothe them and put them to sleep.

A newborn's hearing can be checked with advanced equipment, as is done at most hospitals in North America and Europe, although only a small proportion (less than 1 percent) of newborns have hearing problems severe enough to benefit from early remediation (Calevo et al., 2007). Normally, even in the first days of life, infants turn their heads toward the source of a sound. It takes some learning before they can accurately pinpoint exactly where the sound came from, but they already sense and begin to perceive what they hear (Saffran et al., 2006).

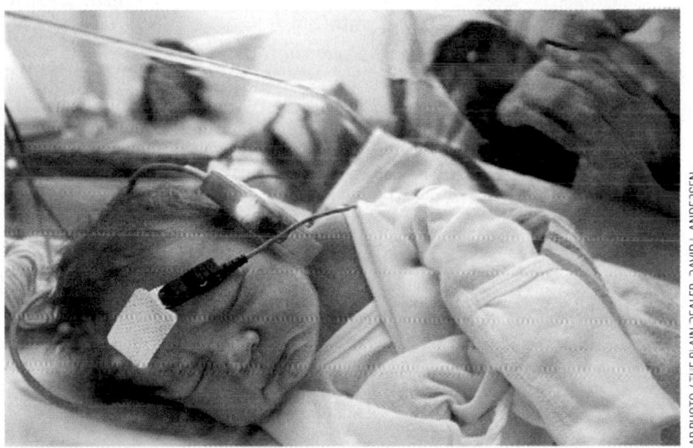

AP PHOTO / THE PLAIN DEALER, DAVID I. ANDERSEN

Before Leaving the Hospital As mandated by a 2004 Ohio law, 1-day-old Henry has his hearing tested via vibrations of the inner ear in response to various tones. The computer interprets the data and signals any need for more tests—as is the case for about 1 baby in 100. Normal newborns hear quite well; Henry's hearing was fine.

Young infants are particularly attentive to the human voice, developing rapid comprehension of the rhythm, segmentation, and cadence of spoken words long before comprehension of their meaning. As time goes on, sensitive hearing combines with brain development to distinguish patterns of sounds and syllables.

Infants become accustomed to the rules of their language, such as which syllable is usually stressed (various English dialects have different rules), whether changing voice tone is crucial (as in Chinese), whether certain sound combinations are repeated, and so on. All this is based on very careful listening to human speech, even speech that is not directed toward them and is uttered in a language they do not yet understand.

Seeing

Vision is the least mature sense at birth. Although the eyes open in mid-pregnancy and are sensitive to bright light (if the pregnant woman is sunbathing in a bikini, for instance), the fetus has nothing much to see. Newborns are "legally blind"; they focus only on objects between 4 and 30 inches (10 and 75 centimeters) away (Bornstein et al., 2005).

Soon experience combines with maturation of the visual cortex to improve the ability to see shapes and then notice details. By 2 months, infants look more intently at a human face and, tentatively and fleetingly, smile in response to it.

Over time, visual scanning becomes more organized, extensive, and efficient; it centers on important points. Thus, 3-month-olds look more closely than younger

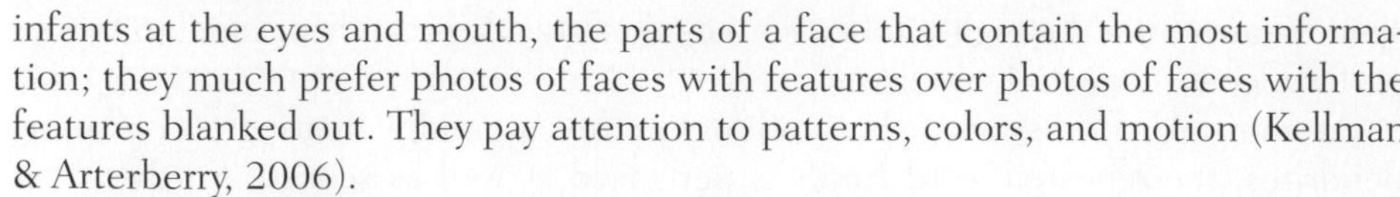

infants at the eyes and mouth, the parts of a face that contain the most information; they much prefer photos of faces with features over photos of faces with the features blanked out. They pay attention to patterns, colors, and motion (Kellman & Arterberry, 2006).

binocular vision The ability to focus the two eyes in a coordinated manner in order to see one image.

Binocular vision is the ability to coordinate the two eyes to see one image. Because using both eyes together is impossible in the confines of the womb, many newborns seem to focus with one eye or the other, or to use their two eyes independently, so that they momentarily look wall-eyed or cross-eyed. At about 14 weeks, binocular vision appears quite suddenly, probably because the underlying brain mechanisms are activated, allowing both eyes to focus on one thing (Atkinson & Braddick, 2003).

➤Response for Social Workers (from page 142): Tell them that such a child would require extra time and commitment, more than a younger adoptee would. Ask whether both are prepared to cut down on their working hours in order to meet with other parents of international adoptees, to obtain professional help (for speech, nutrition, physical development, and/or family therapy), and to help the child with schoolwork, play dates, and so on. You might encourage them instead to adopt a special-needs child from their own area, to become foster parents, or to volunteer at least 10 hours a week at a day-care center. Their response would indicate their willingness to help a real—not imagined—child. If they demonstrate their understanding of what is required, then you might help them adopt the child they want.

Smelling, Tasting, and Touching

As with vision and hearing, the senses of smell, taste, and touch function at birth and rapidly adapt to the social world. For example, one study found that a taste of sugar calmed 2-week-olds but had no effect on 4-week-olds—unless it was accompanied by a reassuring look from a caregiver (Zeifman et al., 1996). Another study found that sugar is a good pain reliever for newborns (Gradin et al., 2002).

Similar adaptation occurs for the senses of smell and touch. As babies learn to recognize their caregiver's smell and handling, they relax only when cradled by their familiar caregiver, even when their eyes are closed. The ability to be comforted by touch is one of the important "skills" tested in the Brazelton Neonatal Assessment Scale. Although almost all newborns respond to massage and cuddling, over time they perceive whose touch it is and what it communicates. For instance, 12-month-olds respond differently to their mother's touch according to whether it is tense or relaxed (Hertenstein & Campos, 2001).

The entire package of the five senses furthers two goals: social interaction (to respond to familiar caregivers) and comfort (to be soothed amid the disturbances of infant life). Infants even adapt the senses of pain and motion (which are not counted along with the five senses because no body part is dedicated to them) for socialization and comfort.

The most important experiences are perceived with all the senses. Breast milk, for instance, is a mild sedative, so the newborn literally feels happier at the mother's breast, connecting pleasure with taste, touch, smell, and sight.

Because infants respond to motion as well as to sights and sounds, many new parents soothe their baby's distress by rocking, carrying, or even driving (with the baby in a safety seat) while humming a lullaby; here again, infant comfort is con-

Learning About a Lime As with every other normal infant, Jacqueline's curiosity leads to taste and then to a slow reaction, from puzzlement to tongue-out disgust. Jacqueline's responses demonstrate that the sense of taste is acute in infancy and that quick brain reactions are still to come.

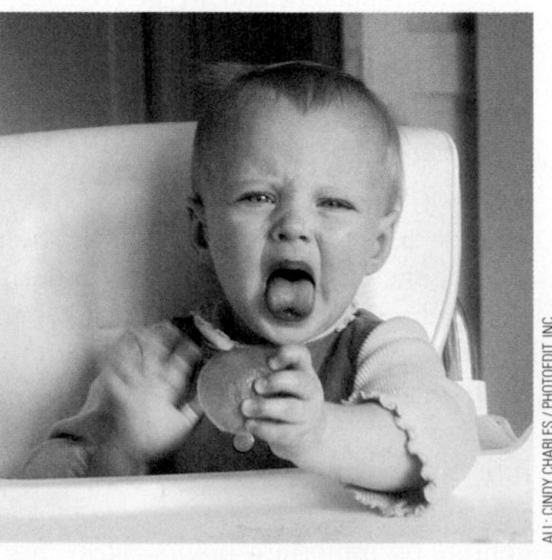

ALL: CINDY CHARLES / PHOTOEDIT, INC.

nected with social interaction. Another soothing activity involves carrying the infant in a sling while vacuuming the carpet: Steady noise, movement, and touch combine to soothe distress. In sum, infants' senses are immature, but they function quite well to help babies join the human family.

Motor Skills

We now come to the most visible and dramatic advances of infancy, those that ultimately allow the child to "stand tall and walk proud." Thanks to ongoing changes in size and proportion and to increasing brain maturation, infants markedly improve their **motor skills,** which are the abilities needed to move and control the body.

motor skill The learned ability to move some part of the body, in actions ranging from a large leap to a flicker of the eyelid. (The word *motor* here refers to movement of muscles.)

Reflexes

Newborns can move their bodies—curl their toes, grasp with their fingers, screw up their faces—but these movements are not under voluntary control. Strictly speaking, the infant's first motor skills are not really skills but reflexes. A **reflex** is an involuntary response to a particular stimulus. Newborns have dozens of reflexes, 18 of which are mentioned in *italics* below. Three sets of reflexes are critical for survival:

reflex An unlearned, involuntary action or movement emitted in response to a particular stimulus. A reflex is an automatic response that is built into the nervous system and occurs without conscious thought.

- Reflexes that maintain oxygen supply. The *breathing reflex* begins in normal newborns even before the umbilical cord, with its supply of oxygen, is cut. Additional reflexes that maintain oxygen are reflexive *hiccups* and *sneezes,* as well as *thrashing* (moving the arms and legs about) to escape something that covers the face.
- Reflexes that maintain constant body temperature. When infants are cold, they *cry, shiver,* and *tuck in their legs* close to their bodies, thereby helping to keep themselves warm. When they are hot, they try to *push away* blankets and then stay still.
- Reflexes that facilitate feeding. The *sucking reflex* causes newborns to suck anything that touches their lips—fingers, toes, blankets, and rattles, as well as natural and artificial nipples of various textures and shapes. The *rooting reflex* causes babies to turn their mouths toward anything that brushes against their cheeks—a reflexive search for a nipple—and start to suck. *Swallowing* is another important reflex that aids feeding, as are *crying* when the stomach is empty and *spitting up* when too much has been swallowed too quickly.

Other reflexes are not necessary for survival but are important signs of normal brain and body functioning. Among them are the following:

- *Babinski reflex.* When infants' feet are stroked, their toes fan upward.
- *Stepping reflex.* When infants are held upright with their feet touching a flat surface, they move their legs as if to walk.
- *Swimming reflex.* When they are laid horizontally on their stomachs, infants stretch out their arms and legs.
- *Palmar grasping reflex.* When something touches infants' palms, they grip it tightly.
- *Moro reflex.* When someone startles them, perhaps by banging on the table they are lying on, infants fling their arms outward and then bring them together on their chests, as if to hold on to something, while crying with wide-open eyes.

➤Response for Parents of Grown Children (from page 143): Probably not. Experience-expectant brain development is programmed to occur for all infants, requiring only the stimulation that virtually all families provide—warmth, reassuring touch, overheard conversation, facial expressions, movement. Extras such as baby talk, music, exercise, mobiles, and massage may be beneficial but are not essential.

Many reflexes are tested at birth, because they indicate both normal brain development and genetic temperament. Cultural differences *may* originate from

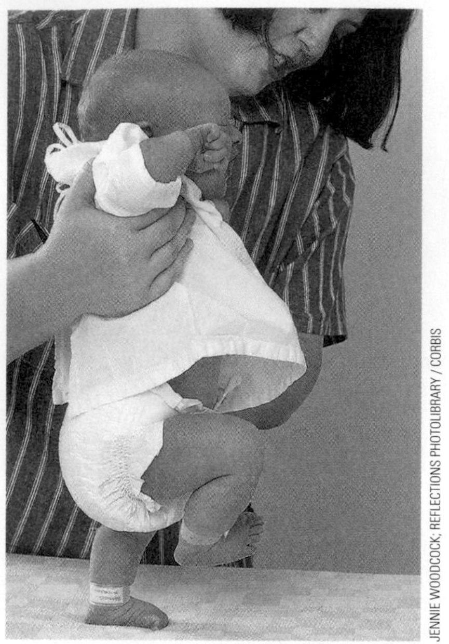

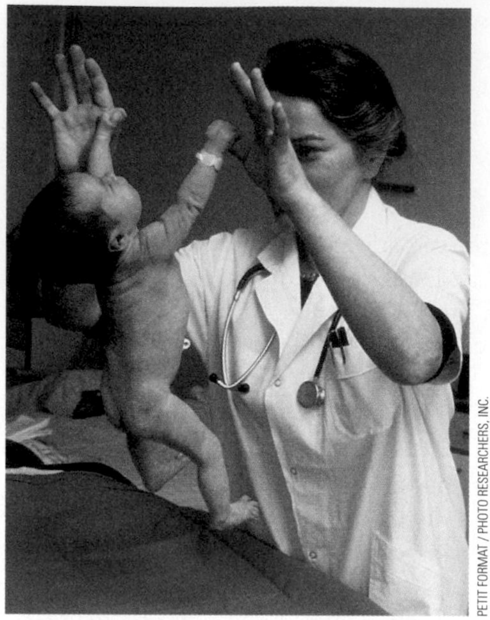

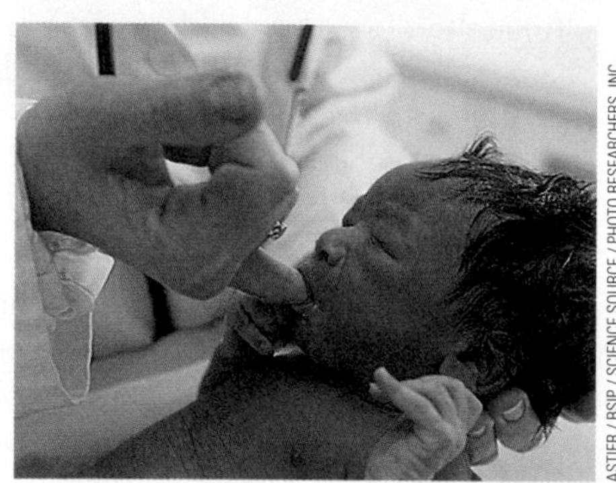

Never Underestimate the Power of a Reflex For developmentalists, newborn reflexes are mechanisms for survival, indicators of brain maturation, and vestiges of evolutionary history. For parents, they are mostly delightful and sometimes amazing. Both of these viewpoints are demonstrated by three star performers: A 1-day-old girl stepping eagerly forward on legs too tiny to support her body, a newborn grasping so tightly that his legs dangle in space, and a newborn boy sucking peacefully on the doctor's finger.

temperamental differences. For instance, some researchers report that reflexive thrashing and crying when a cloth covers the face is typical for European infants but not Chinese ones, who often will simply turn their heads to escape the cloth. In general, Chinese infants are less active than European babies in their reflexive responses; the difference may be primarily either genetic or environmental, as prenatal care, birth practices, diet, and early postnatal care are all different for Chinese and European babies (Kagan & Snidman, 2004).

Gross Motor Skills

gross motor skills Physical abilities involving large body movements, such as walking and jumping. (The word *gross* here means "big.")

Deliberate actions that coordinate many parts of the body, producing large movements, are called **gross motor skills.** These emerge directly from reflexes. Crawling is one example. Newborns placed on their stomachs reflexively move their arms and legs as if they were swimming. As young infants gain muscle strength, they start to wiggle, attempting to move forward by pushing their arms, shoulders, and upper bodies against the surface they are lying on. Usually by 5 months or so, they become able to use their arms, and then legs, to inch forward on their bellies. This is a gross motor skill.

Between 8 and 10 months after birth, most infants can lift their midsections and crawl (or *creep,* as the British call it) on "all fours," coordinating the movements of their hands and knees in a smooth, balanced manner (Adolph et al., 1998). Crawling is experience-dependent. Some normal babies never do it, especially if the floor is cold, hot, or rough, or if they have always slept on their backs (Pin et al., 2007).

It is not true that babies *must crawl* to develop normally. All babies figure out some way to move before they can walk (inching, bear walking, scooting, creeping, or crawling), but many resist "tummy time" by rolling over and fussing to indicate that they do not want crawling practice (Adolph & Berger, 2005).

Sitting also progresses gradually, as it depends on developing the muscles that steady the heavy top half of the body. By 3 months, most babies have enough muscle control to be lap-sitters if the lap's owner provides supportive arms. By about 6 months, they can sit unsupported.

Walking progresses from reflexive, hesitant, adult-supported stepping to a smooth, coordinated gait. Some children step while holding on at 9 months, stand alone momentarily at 10 months, and walk well, unassisted, at 12 months. Three factors combine to allow toddlers to walk (Adolph et al., 2003):

- *Muscle strength.* Newborns with skinny legs or infants buoyed by water make stepping movements, but 6-month-olds on dry land do not; their legs are too chubby for their underdeveloped muscles.
- *Brain maturation within the motor cortex.* The first leg movements—kicking (alternating legs at birth and then kicking both legs together or one leg repeatedly at about 3 months)—occur without much thought or aim. As the brain matures, deliberate leg action becomes possible.
- *Practice.* Unbalanced, wide-legged, short strides become a steady, smooth gait after hours of practice.

Once the first two developments have made walking possible, infants become passionate walkers, logging those needed hours of practice. They take steps on many surfaces, with bare feet or wearing socks, slippers, or shoes. They hate to be pushed in their strollers when they can walk:

> Walking infants practice keeping balance in upright stance and locomotion for more than 6 accumulated hours per day. They average between 500 and 1,500 walking steps per hour so that by the end of each day, they have taken 9,000 walking steps and traveled the length of 29 football fields.
>
> *[Adolph et al., 2003, p. 494]*

RICK GOMEZ / MASTERFILE

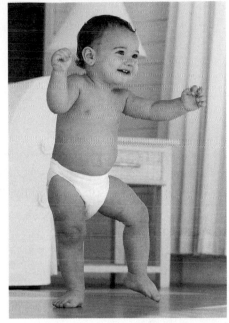

Bossa Nova Baby? This boy in Brazil demonstrates his joy at acquiring the gross motor skill of walking, which quickly becomes dancing whenever music plays.

Fine Motor Skills

Small body movements are called **fine motor skills.** Hand and finger movements are fine motor skills, enabling humans to write, draw, type, tie, and so on. Movements of the tongue, jaw, lips, feet, and toes are fine movements, too.

fine motor skills Physical abilities involving small body movements, especially of the hands and fingers, such as drawing and picking up a coin. (The word *fine* here means "small.")

Actually, mouth skills (tongue, jaw, lips) precede finger skills by many months, and skillful grabbing with the feet sometimes precedes grabbing with the hands (Adolph & Berger, 2005). However, hand skills are most valued in adult society and every culture encourages them, so every child practices them. By contrast, skilled spitting or chewing is not praised, so even blowing bubbles with gum is not practiced very much.

Regarding finger skills, newborns have a strong reflexive grasp but seem to lack hand and finger control. During their first 2 months, babies excitedly stare and wave their arms at objects dangling within reach. By 3 months of age, they can usually touch an object, but they cannot yet grab and hold on unless it is placed in their hands, partly because their eye–hand coordination is limited.

By 4 months, infants sometimes grab, but their timing is off: They close their hands too early or too late, and their grasp tends to be of short duration. Finally, by 6 months, with a concentrated, deliberate stare, most babies can reach for, grab at, and hold onto almost any object that is of the right size. They can hold a bottle, shake a rattle, and yank a sister's braids.

Once reaching is possible, babies practice it enthusiastically. In fact, "from 6 to 9 months, reaching appears as a quite compulsive behaviour for small objects presented within arm's reach" (Atkinson & Braddick, 2003, p. 58).

Toward the end of the first year and throughout the second, finger skills improve, as babies master the pincer movement (using thumb and forefinger to pick up tiny objects) and self-feeding (first with hands, then fingers, then utensils). In the second year, grabbing becomes more selective (Atkinson & Braddick, 2003).

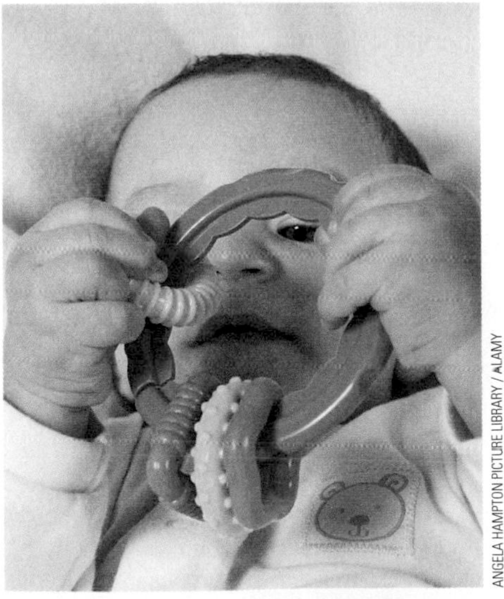

ANGELA HAMPTON PICTURE LIBRARY / ALAMY

Mind in the Making Pull, grab, look, and listen. Using every sense at once is a baby's favorite way to experience life, generating brain connections as well as commotion.

Toddlers learn when not to pull at sister's braids, or Mommy's earrings, or Daddy's glasses. However, as you will learn in the next chapter, the curiosity of the "little scientist" may overwhelm inhibition.

Ethnic Variations

All healthy infants develop skills in the same sequence, but they vary in the age at which they acquire them. Table 5.1 shows age norms for gross motor skills, based on a large, representative, multiethnic sample of U.S. infants. Generally speaking, when infants are grouped by ethnicity, African Americans tend to develop these skills earlier than Hispanic Americans, who develop them earlier than European Americans. Internationally, the earliest walkers in the world are in Uganda, where well-nourished and healthy babies walk at 10 months, on average. Some of the latest walkers are in France.

TABLE 5.1

AT ABOUT THIS TIME: Age Norms (in Months) for Gross Motor Skills

Skill	When 50% of All Babies Master the Skill	When 95% of All Babies Master the Skill
Sit, head steady	3 months	4 months
Sit, unsupported	6	7
Pull to stand (holding on)	9	10
Stand alone	12	14
Walk well	13	15
Walk backward	15	17
Run	18	20
Jump up	26	29

Note: As the text explains, age norms are approximate and are affected by culture and cohort. These are U.S. norms, mostly for European American children. Mastering skills a few weeks earlier or later is not an indication of health or intelligence. Mastering them very late, however, is a cause for concern.

Source: Coovadia & Wittenberg, 2004; based primarily on Denver II (Frankenburg et al., 1992).

Observation Quiz (see answer, page 150): Which of these skills has the greatest variation in age of acquisition? Why?

What accounts for this variation? The power of genes is suggested not only by ethnic differences but also by evidence from identical twins, who begin to walk on the same day more often than fraternal twins do. Striking individual differences are apparent in infant strategies, effort, and concentration in mastering motor skills, again suggesting something inborn in motor-skill achievements (Thelen & Corbetta, 2002).

But genes are only a small part of most ethnic differences. Cultural patterns of child rearing can affect sensation, perception, and motor skills. For instance, early reflexes are less likely to fade if culture and conditions allow extensive practice. This principle has been demonstrated with legs (the stepping reflex), hands (the grasping reflex), and crawling (the swimming reflex). Senses and motor skills are part of a complex and dynamic system in which practice counts (Thelen & Corbetta, 2002).

For example, Jamaican caregivers provide rhythmic stretching exercises for their infants as part of daily care; their infants are among the world's youngest

Safe and Secure Like this Algonquin baby in Quebec, many American Indian infants spend hours each day on a cradle board, to the distress of some non-Native adults until they see that most of the babies are quite happy that way. The discovery in the 1950s that Native American children walked at about the same age as European American children suggested that maturation, not practice, led to motor skills. Later research found that most Native American infants also received special exercise sessions each day, implying that practice plays a larger role than most psychologists once thought.

walkers (Adolph & Berger, 2005). Other cultures discourage or even prevent infants from crawling or walking. The people of Bali, Indonesia, never let their infants crawl, for babies are considered divine and crawling is for animals (Diener, 2000). Similar reasoning appeared in colonial America, where "standing stools" were designed for children so they could strengthen their walking muscles without sitting or crawling (Calvert, 2003).

By contrast, the Beng people of the Ivory Coast are proud when their babies start to crawl but do not let them walk until at least 1 year. Although the Beng do not recognize the connection, one reason for this prohibition may be birth control: Beng mothers do not resume sexual relations until their baby begins walking (Gottlieb, 2000).

Variation in the timing of the development of motor skills is normal, but a pattern of unusually slow development suggests that the infant needs careful examination.

SUMMING UP

The five senses (seeing, hearing, smelling, tasting, touching) function quite well at birth, although hearing is far superior to vision, probably because of experience: The fetus has much more to hear than to see. After birth, vision develops rapidly; binocular vision emerges at about the 14th week. Quite sensitive perception from all sense organs is evident by 1 year. The senses work together and are particularly attuned to human interaction.

Motor skills begin with survival reflexes but quickly expand to include various body movements that the infant masters. Infants lift their heads, then sit, then stand, then walk and run. Sensory and motor skills follow a genetic and maturational timetable, but they are also powerfully influenced by experiences—guided by caregivers and culture—and by practice, which infants do as much as their immature and top-heavy bodies allow. ■

Public Health Measures

Public health refers to the wellness of an entire population. Many laws (aimed at preventing contagious diseases, for instance), policies (aimed at protecting the water supply, say), and cultural norms (promoting or discouraging breast-feeding, for example) are aspects of public health. Personal health practices, such as a parent's decision to take a baby to the doctor, are affected by public health measures.

Although precise worldwide statistics are unavailable, at least 9 billion children were born between 1950 and 2008. About 2 billion of them died before age 5. Although 2 billion is far too many, twice as many would have died without public health practices.

Especially beneficial are measures that provide preventive care, including childhood immunization, clean water, and adequate nutrition. One particular medical treatment, *oral rehydration therapy* (giving restorative liquids to children who are sick and have diarrhea), saves 3 million young children *per year,* most of them in developing nations; the therapy is helpful in developed nations as well (Spandorfer et al., 2005).

Another relatively simple and inexpensive disease-prevention measure in malaria-prone areas involves providing bed nets treated with insect repellent. Children who sleep under these nets are much less likely to die of malaria, which is transmitted through mosquito bites and kills about a million people (mostly children) a year (Roberts, 2007).

Most children in every nation now live to adulthood (UNICEF, 2006). In the healthiest nations, 99.9 percent who survive the first month (when the sickest and

➤**Answer to Observation Quiz** (from page 148): Jumping up, with a three-month age range for acquisition. The reason is that the older an infant is, the more impact culture has.

smallest newborns die) live to age 15. Even in the least healthy nations, where a few decades ago half the children died, now about three-fourths live (see Table 5.2).

Immunization

Measles, whooping cough, pneumonia, and other illnesses were once familiar childhood killers. Although these diseases can still be fatal, especially for malnourished children, they are now rare among children in developed nations. Children are protected by **immunization,** which primes the body's immune system to resist a specific contagious disease. Immunization is said to have had "a greater impact on human mortality reduction and population growth than any other public health intervention besides clean water" (J. P. Baker, 2000).

immunization A process that stimulates the body's immune system to defend against attack by a particular contagious disease. Immunization may be accomplished either naturally (by having the disease) or through vaccination (often by having an injection).

When people catch a contagious disease, their immune system produces antibodies to prevent a recurrence. In a person who has not had the disease, a vaccine —a small dose of inactive virus (often administered via an injection, or "shot," in the arm but sometimes by wearing a patch, swallowing, or inhaling)—stimulates the production of antibodies against that disease. Some details about various vaccines are given in Table 5.3. (Immunization schedules, giving the ages at which children and adolescents should be vaccinated, appear in Appendix A, page A-4.)

TABLE 5.2

Deaths of Children Under Age 5 in Selected Countries

Country	Number of Deaths per 1,000
Singapore	3*
Iceland	3*
Japan	4†
Italy	4*
Sweden	4
Spain	5†
Australia	5†
United Kingdom	6†
Canada	6
New Zealand	6†
United States	7†
Russia	18†
Vietnam	19*
China	27†
Mexico	27†
Brazil	33†
Philippines	33†
India	74†
Nigeria	194
Afghanistan	257
Sierra Leone	282

* Reduced by at least one-third since 1990.
† Reduced by half since 1990.
Source: UNICEF, 2006.

This table shows the number of deaths per 1,000 children under age 5 for 20 of the 192 members of the United Nations. Most nations have improved markedly on this measure since 1990. Only when war destroys families and interferes with public health measures (as it has in Afghanistan and Sierra Leone) are nations not improving.

Dramatic Successes

Stunning successes in immunization include the following:

- Smallpox, the most lethal disease for children in the past, was eradicated worldwide as of 1971. Vaccination against smallpox is no longer needed. Emergency workers are immunized as a precaution against bioterrorism, not because a normal outbreak is anticipated.
- Polio, a crippling and sometimes fatal disease, has become very rare. Widespread vaccination, begun in 1955, has led to the elimination of polio in most nations (including the United States). Just 784 cases worldwide were reported in 2003. In the same year, however, rumors about the safety of the polio vaccine halted immunization in northern Nigeria; consequently, polio reappeared in West Africa in 2004, and there were 1,948 cases worldwide in 2005 (Arita et al., 2006).
- Measles (rubeola, not rubella) is disappearing worldwide, thanks to a vaccine developed in 1963. Prior to that time, 3 million to 4 million cases were reported each year in the United States alone (CDC, 2007). Only 37 cases occurred in the United States in 2007 (MMWR, February 29, 2008). One reason for the decline is the introduction of a new method of vaccinating against measles by inhalation rather than injection; this inhalation method is now widely used in Mexico.
- A recent success is a newly developed vaccine against rotovirus, which causes infant diarrhea and kills half a million children a year (Glass & Parashar, 2006).

Immunization protects children not only from diseases but also from serious complications, including deafness, blindness, sterility, and meningitis. Sometimes the aftereffects of a childhood illness do not become apparent until decades later. Childhood mumps, for instance, is associated with a doubled risk of schizophrenia in adults (Dalman et al., 2008).

Furthermore, each vaccinated child stops the spread of the disease and thus protects others, including people who cannot be safely immunized. Newborns may die if they catch a disease; the fetus of a pregnant woman who contracts rubella (German measles) may be born blind, deaf, and brain-damaged; adults

TABLE 5.3

Details About Vaccinations: United States

Vaccine	Year of Introduction*	Peak Annual Disease Total*	2007 Total†	Consequences of Natural Disease*†	Percent of Children Vaccinated (U.S.)†	Known Vaccine Side Effects†
Chicken pox (varicella)	1995	4 million (est.)	34,507	Encephalitis (2 in 10,000 cases), bacterial skin infections, shingles (300,000 per year)	90.0	Fever (1 in 10 doses); mild rash (1 in 20 doses)
DTaP					84.5	Seizures (1 in 14,000), crying, for 3 hours or more (1 in 1,000), fever of 105°F or higher (1 in 16,000)
Diphtheria	1923	206,939	0	Death (5 to 10 in 100 cases), muscle paralysis, heart failure		Adult Td (tetanus and diphtheria) vaccine may cause deep, aching pain and muscle wasting in upper arms
Tetanus	1927	1,560 (est.)	20	Death (1 in 10 cases), fractured bones, pneumonia		
Pertussis	1926 (whole cell) 1991 (acellular)	265,269	8,739	Death (2 in 1,000 cases), pneumonia (10 in 100 cases), seizures (1 to 2 in 100 cases)		Brain disease (0 to 10 in 1 million doses—whole-cell vaccine only)
H influenzae (Type B) (childhood) (all serotypes)	1985	20,000 (est.)	2,231	Death (2 to 3 in 100 cases), meningitis, pneumonia, blood poisoning, inflammation of epiglottis, skin or bone infections	92.6	Redness, warmth, or swelling at injection site (1 in 4); fever of 101°F or higher (1 in 20)
IPV (inactivated) polio vaccine)	1955; improved version used in U.S. since 1987	21,269	0	Death (2 to 5 in 100 cases in children), respiratory failure, paralysis, postpolio syndrome	92.6	Soreness and redness at injection site
MMR					92.3	Seizure caused by fever (1 in 3,000 doses); low platelet count (1 in 30,000 doses)
Measles	1963	894,134	30	Encephalitis (1 in 1,000 cases), pneumonia (6 in 100 cases), death (1 to 2 in 1,000 cases), seizure (6 to 7 in 1,000 cases)		Temporary joint pain and stiffness (1 in 4 teenaged girls and women)
Mumps	1967	152,209	715	Deafness (1 in 20,000 cases), inflamed testicles (20 to 50 in 100 postpubertal males)		
Rubella	1969	56,686	11	Blindness, deafness, heart defects, and/or mental retardation in 85 percent of children born to mothers infected in early pregnancy		
PCV7 (pneumococcal conjugate vaccine)† (childhood)	2000	93,000 (est.)	20,000 (2005 est.)	Death or serious illness caused by meningitis, pneumonia, blood poisoning, ear infections		Fever over 100.4°F (1 in 3); redness, tenderness, or swelling at injection site (1 in 4)

Sources: *Lieu et al., 2000; †Centers for Disease Control and Prevention Web site (www.cdc.gov/vaccines), accessed September 17, 2008.

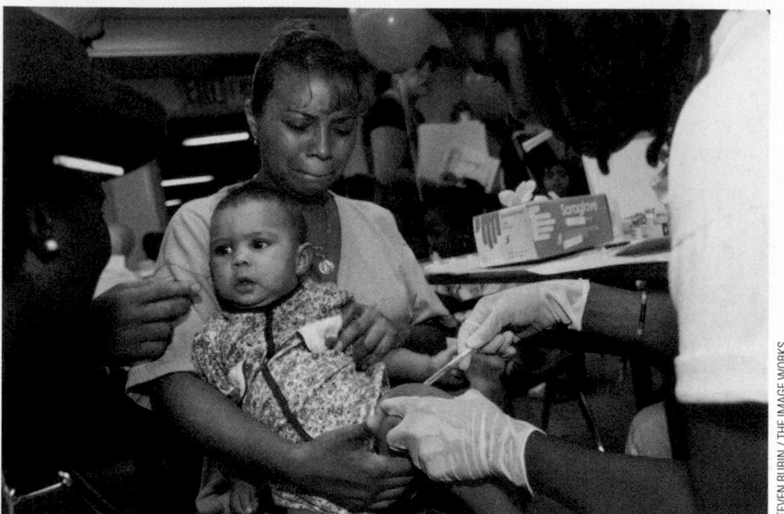

STEVEN RUBIN / THE IMAGE WORKS

Look Away! The benefits of immunization justify the baby's brief discomfort, but many parents still do not appreciate the importance of following the recommended schedule of immunizations.

who contract mumps or rubeola may become quite ill; and adults who have impaired immune systems (because they are HIV-positive, very old, or undergoing chemotherapy, for example) can die from "childhood" diseases.

Problems with Immunization

Parents do not always make sure their children get vaccinated on the recommended schedule. In the United States, although most 2-year-olds are fully immunized, only one-third get all their vaccinations on time (Mell et al., 2005). One reason for this casual attitude is that parents do not notice if their child does *not* get seriously ill. One doctor, who wants people to pay more attention to disease prevention, laments, "No one notices when things go right" (Bortz, 2005, p. 389).

Especially for Nurses and Pediatricians (see response, page 154): A mother refuses to have her baby immunized because she wants to prevent side effects. She wants your signature for a religious exemption. What should you do?

Unfortunately, even "minor" diseases can sometimes kill. One Kansas father, age 36, caught varicella (chicken pox) from his 9-year-old daughter. He suffered numerous complications and died on March 9, 2002 (MMWR, June 13, 2003). No one in his family had been vaccinated. (Unlike most other states, Kansas did not require varicella immunization for school entry). The 9-year-old was the carrier, but the parents, school, pediatrician, and lawmakers were also part of the problem. Before the vaccine, more than 100 people in the United States died each year from chicken pox and 1 million were itchy and feverish for a week (Nguyen et al., 2005).

Many parents are concerned about potential side effects of vaccinations. For example, in recent years many parents were alarmed by reports that the MMR (measles-mumps-rubella) vaccine caused autism, but that hypothesis has been repeatedly disproved (Shattuck, 2006). The risks posed by the diseases are far greater than the risks from immunization (as Table 5.3 indicates). A review of the published research concludes: "The data demonstrate consistently that the overall benefit of vaccinations ranks among the foremost achievements in modern public health" (Dershewitz, 2002).

More than 1 million children in developing nations die each year because effective vaccines against AIDS, malaria, cholera, typhoid, and shigellosis are not yet ready for widespread use (Russell, 2002). Another 2 million to 3 million die each year from diphtheria, tetanus, and measles because they have not been immunized against those diseases (Mahmoud, 2004); 100,000 children in India died in 2005 from measles alone (Dugger, 2006).

Sudden Infant Death Syndrome

Infant mortality worldwide has plummeted in recent years (see Figure 5.5). Several reasons have already been mentioned: advances in newborn care, better nutrition, access to clean water, and widespread immunization. Another reason is that fewer babies are dying of unknown causes, especially **sudden infant death syndrome (SIDS).**

sudden infant death syndrome (SIDS) A situation in which a seemingly healthy infant, at least 2 months of age, suddenly stops breathing and dies unexpectedly while asleep.

Still, some young infants who appear healthy—already gaining weight, learning to shake a rattle, starting to roll over, and smiling at their caregivers—die unexpectedly in their sleep. If autopsy and careful investigation find no apparent cause of death, the diagnosis is SIDS (Byard, 2004).

In 1990 in the United States, about 5,000 babies died of SIDS—about 1 infant in 800. Canada, Great Britain, Australia, and virtually every European and South American nation experienced a similar rate.

Careful data collection revealed surprising ethnic differences. Babies of Asian descent were far less likely than babies of European or African descent to succumb to SIDS. *Before* a worldwide campaign to reduce the risk, only 1 baby in 3,000 in Hong Kong died of SIDS, compared with 1 baby in 200 in New Zealand (Byard, 2004).

Within ethnic groups, low socioeconomic status (SES) increases the rate of SIDS, but poverty did not explain these notable ethnic differences. For example, Bangladeshi families in England are often quite poor, yet their babies almost never die of SIDS. For decades, pediatricians made the same mistake that I made with Bethany's late walking (see page 131): They thought that genes caused the difference, which meant there was nothing they or their patients could do.

Fortunately, as multicultural awareness increased, so did a closer look at infant-care practices. Bangladeshi infants in England are almost always breast fed, and they sleep surrounded by family members, hearing noises and feeling the comforting touch of their caregivers. They do not sleep deeply for long. By contrast, their traditional British age-mates slept in their own private spaces, never co-sleeping. Those "long periods of lone sleep may contribute to the higher rates of SIDS among white infants" (Gantley et al., 1993).

Similarly, Chinese mothers not only breast-feed but also tend periodically to their sleeping babies, caressing a cheek or repositioning a limb. Another difference was observed: Chinese infants sleep on their backs.

Especially for Police Officers and Social Workers (see response, page 155): If an infant died suddenly, what would you look for to distinguish SIDS from homicide?

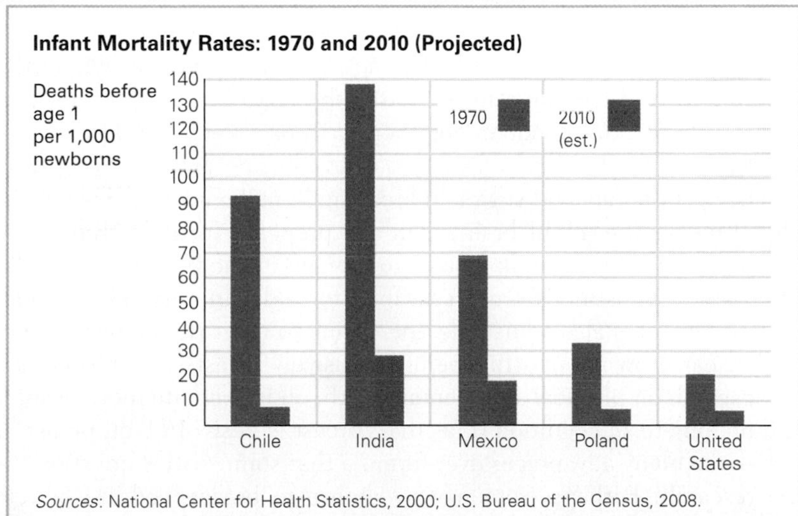

FIGURE 5.5

More Babies Are Surviving Improvements in public health—better nutrition, cleaner water, more widespread immunization—over the past three decades have meant millions of survivors.

Critical Thinking Question (see answer, page 155): The United States seems to be doing very well in reducing infant deaths. Can you suggest another way to present the U.S. data that would lead to another impression?

JOHN VINK / MAGNUM PHOTOS

Sleeping Like a Baby It's best to lay babies on their backs to sleep—even if it's in a hammock in a Cambodian temple.

Some doctors began to advise parents to put their infants to sleep on their backs, not their stomachs. Parents worried that the back-sleeping babies would choke, but some heeded the advice. Their babies did not choke.

SIDS rates began to decrease in every nation, especially those where stomach- or side-sleeping had been the norm. Rates fell to 1 in 1,000 in New Zealand, for instance. In the United States, in the four years between 1992 and 1996, stomach-sleeping decreased from 70 to 24 percent, and the SIDS rate dropped from 1.2 to 0.7 per 1,000, a "remarkable success" (Pollack & Frohna, 2001).

"Back to sleep" (the public awareness slogan) does not prevent all SIDS deaths. Low birthweight, overdressed infants, low SES, formula-feeding, and teenage parenthood are still risk factors (Byard, 2004). Maternal smoking is a particular risk (Anderson et al., 2005), and certain brain patterns correlate with SIDS deaths (Paterson et al., 2006).

Protective factors in addition to back-sleeping include breast-feeding and pacifier use (Li et al., 2006), which may help by strengthening infants' breathing reflexes. It also helps to be born in the spring, perhaps because babies born then have fewer bedclothes in summer, when they are 2 to 6 months old (the time of highest SIDS deaths).

Nutrition

The importance of nutrition in babies' development has been indirectly noted throughout this chapter. You read that pediatricians closely monitor early weight gain, that head-sparing protects the brain from temporary undernourishment, that oral rehydration prevents childhood diarrhea from being fatal, that breast-feeding reduces the risk of SIDS. Now, we focus directly on how infants are fed.

Breast Is Best

For most newborns, good nutrition starts with mother's milk. *Colostrum,* a thick, high-calorie fluid, is secreted by a woman's breasts for about the first three days following the birth of her child. After that, the breasts begin to produce milk, the ideal infant food (see Table 5.4). Compared with cow's milk, human milk is sterile, at body temperature, with iron, vitamins, and other nutrients for brain and body.

Babies who are exclusively breast-fed are less likely to get sick, because breast milk provides them with antibodies against any disease to which the mother is immune. Breast-feeding also decreases the risk of many diseases that appear in childhood and adulthood, among them asthma, obesity, and heart disease (Oddy, 2004).

The specific fats and sugars in breast milk make it more digestible, and probably better for the infant brain, than any prepared formula (Riordan, 2005). The composition of breast milk adjusts to the age of the baby; breast milk for premature babies is distinct from breast milk for older infants. The quantity of breast milk produced is also adjustable, increasing to meet the demand: Twins and even triplets can grow strong while being exclusively breast-fed for months.

Research on physical and mental health, on immediate mother–infant bonding, and on long-term cognition finds that "breast is best." In fact, breast milk appears to have so many advantages over formula that some critics question the validity of the research: Perhaps women who choose to breast-feed are better caregivers, which might explain the superior situation of breast-fed babies. In the United

➤Response for Nurses and Pediatricians (from page 152): It is very difficult to convince people that their method of child rearing is wrong, although, given what you know, you should try. In this case, listen respectfully and then describe specific instances of serious illness or death from a childhood disease. Suggest that the mother ask her grandparents if they knew anyone who had polio, tuberculosis, or tetanus (they probably did). If you cannot convince this mother, do not despair: Vaccination of 95 percent of toddlers helps protect the other 5 percent. If the mother has deeply held religious reasons, talk to her clergy adviser, if not to change the mother's mind, at least to understand her perspective.

TABLE 5.4

The Benefits of Breast-Feeding

For the Baby
Balance of nutrition (fat, protein, etc.) adjusts to age of baby
Breast milk has micronutrients not found in formula
Less infant illness: including allergies, ear infections, stomach upsets
Less childhood asthma
Better childhood vision
Less adult illness, including diabetes, cancer, heart disease
Protection against measles and all other childhood diseases, since breast milk contains antibodies
Stronger jaws, fewer cavities, advanced breathing reflexes (less SIDS)
Higher IQ, less likely to drop out of school, more likely to attend college
Later puberty, less prone to teenage pregnancy
Less likely to become obese, hypertensive by age 12
For the Mother
Easier bonding with baby
Reduced risk of breast cancer and osteoporosis
Natural contraception (with exclusive breast-feeding, for several months)
Pleasure of breast stimulation
Satisfaction of meeting infant's basic need
No formula to prepare; no sterilization
Easier travel with the baby
For the Family
Increased survival of other children (because of spacing of births)
Increased family income (because formula and medical care are expensive)
Less stress on father, especially at night (he cannot be expected to feed the baby)

Sources: Beilin & Huang, 2008; DiGirolamo et al., 2005; Oddy, 2004; Riordan, 2005.

States, a survey finds that parents of breast-fed babies are more likely to be married, college graduates, or immigrants (Gibson-Davis & Brooks-Gunn, 2006; see the Research Design).

Other researchers find that bottle-feeding may sometimes be better, such as when the mother is HIV-positive or uses toxic or addictive drugs. Even then, however, breast milk may be best. In some African nations, HIV-positive women are encouraged to breast-feed exclusively, because their infants' risk of catching the virus from breast milk is less than their risk of dying from infections, diarrhea, or malnutrition as a result of occasional bottle-feeding (Cohen, 2007). Formula is acceptable only if it is "feasible, affordable, sustainable, and safe" (WHO, 2000).

Virtually all doctors worldwide recommend exclusive breast-feeding for the first four to six months. Some hospitals help implement breast-feeding by putting the infant to the breast within an hour after birth, avoiding any bottle-feeding, and allowing the baby to room with the mother (Murray et al., 2007). Contrary to the assumption that breast-feeding is instinctive for mothers, it involves some learning—hard to find if hospitals and family members do not encourage it.

After six months, other foods can be added—especially cereals and bananas, which are easily digested and provide the iron and vitamin C that older infants need. Breast milk should be part of the diet for a year (or longer, if mother and baby wish).

➤Response for Police Officers and Social Workers (from page 153): An autopsy, or at least a speedy and careful examination by a medical pathologist, is needed. Suspected foul play must be either substantiated or firmly rejected—so that the parents can be arrested or warned about conditions that caused an accident, or can mourn in peace. Careful notes about the immediate circumstances—such as the infant's body position when discovered, the position of the mattress and blankets, the warmth and humidity of the room, and the baby's health—are crucial. Further, although SIDS victims sometimes turn blue and seem bruised, they rarely display signs of specific injury or neglect, such as a broken limb, a scarred face, an angry rash, or a skinny body.

➤Answer to Critical Thinking Question (from page 153): The same data could be presented in terms of rate of reduction in infant mortality. Chile's projected rate in 2010 is less than 10 percent of what it was in 1970—much better than the projected U.S. rate, which in 2010 is 30 percent of what it was in 1970. (Other data show that about 25 developed nations have lower infant mortality rates than the United States.)

Research Design

Scientists: Christina Gibson-Davis and Jeanne Brooks-Gunn.

Publication: *American Journal of Public Health* (2006).

Participants: A study called Fragile Families surveyed about 5,000 new mothers from 75 U.S. hospitals.

Design: Mothers and fathers were asked about their social status (e.g., education, marriage, immigration, income, employment) and breast-feeding, with assurance of confidentiality. Questions were asked of both parents soon after birth and again of the mothers a year later.

Major conclusion: A mother's decision to start and continue breast-feeding is affected by many aspects of her social context. U.S.-born mothers are less likely to breast-feed.

Comment: This finding is for a population often omitted from other surveys. It confirms that having a husband and being educated are significant correlates of breast-feeding.

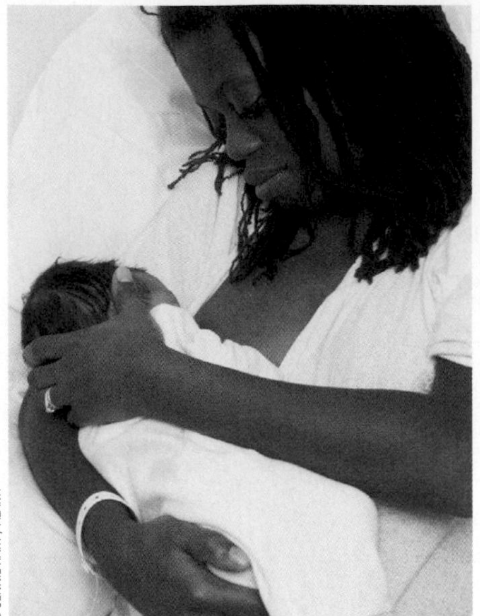

© JENNIE HART / ALAMY

© W.LAYER / PETER ARNOLD, INC.

Observation Quiz (see answer, page 158) What three differences do you see between these two breast-feeding women—one in the United States and one in Madagascar?

The Same Situation, Many Miles Apart: Breast-Feeding Breast-feeding is universal. None of us would exist if our foremothers had not successfully breast-fed their babies for millennia. Currently breast-feeding is practiced worldwide, but it is no longer the only way to feed infants, and each culture has particular practices.

Babies who do not get enough sunlight may need additional vitamin D—whether through supplemental drops or pills or cereal and milk—to prevent the crooked leg growth of rickets (Stokstad, 2003). Light skin absorbs vitamin D from sun exposure more readily than dark skin does, so dark-skinned infants in cold climates are at particular risk of vitamin D deficiency.

In developing nations, breast-feeding dramatically reduces infant death. In the United States and worldwide, more than 90 percent of infants are breast-fed at birth, but only 36 percent are exclusively breast-fed for the first six months. By their second birthday, half of the world's infants (especially in poor nations) are still being fed some breast milk, usually at night (UNICEF, 2006).

Whether or not a new mother continues to breast-feed for six months depends a great deal on her experiences in the first week, when encouragement and practical help are most needed (DiGirolamo et al., 2005). Fathers' attitudes and support are often crucial to successful breast-feeding. Ideally, nurses visit new parents at home for several weeks; such visits (routine in some nations, rare in others) increase the likelihood that breast-feeding will continue (Coutinho et al., 2005).

Malnutrition

protein-calorie malnutrition A condition in which a person does not consume sufficient food of any kind. This deprivation can result in several illnesses, severe weight loss, and even death.

Protein-calorie malnutrition occurs when a person does not consume sufficient food of any kind. Roughly 9 percent of the world's children suffer from "wasting," being severely and chronically malnourished because they do not get adequate calories, especially calories from protein (UNICEF, 2006). These 9 percent are very short for their age and underweight for their height.

Many more children are too short *or* too underweight (two or more standard deviations below the average well-nourished child). According to this criterion, between 25 and 30 percent of the world's children are malnourished (UNICEF, 2006), which is far too large a percentage but an improvement over five years ago (Serageldin, 2002).

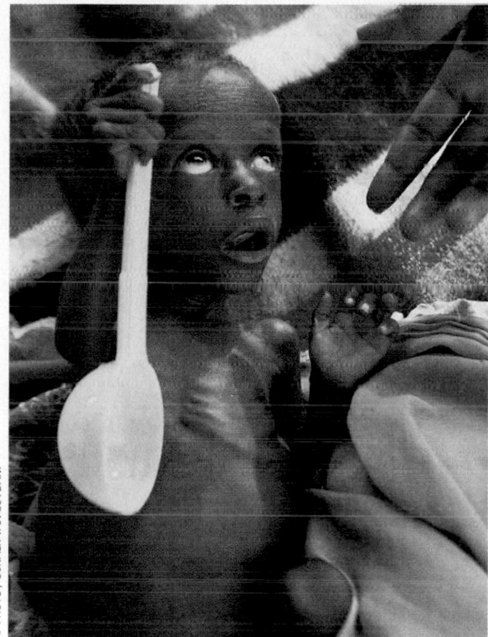

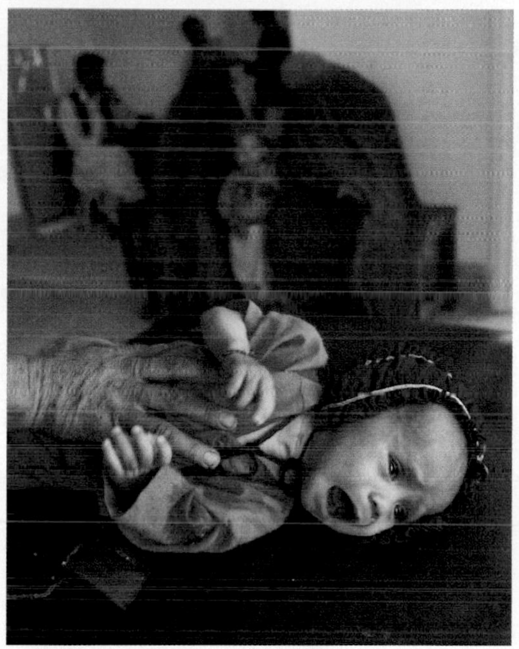

The Same Situation, Many Miles Apart: Children Still Malnourished Infant malnutrition is common in nations at war (like Afghanistan, *at right*) or with crop failure (like Niger, *at left*). UNICEF relief programs reach only half the children in either nation. The children in these photographs are among the lucky ones who are being fed.

To measure a particular child's nutritional status, compare weight and height with the detailed norms presented in Appendix A, pages A-6 and A-7, and look at the child's percentile rankings from birth on. A child may simply be genetically short or thin, but a decline in percentile ranking during the first two years is an ominous sign.

Chronically malnourished infants and children suffer in three ways (Adejuyigbe et al., 2008; United Nations World Food Program, 2008):

- Their brains may not develop normally. If malnutrition has continued long enough to affect the baby's height, it may also have affected the brain.
- Malnourished children have no body reserves to protect them against common diseases. About half of all childhood deaths occur because malnutrition makes a childhood disease lethal.
- Some diseases result directly from malnutrition.

The worst disease directly caused by malnutrition is **marasmus.** Growth stops, body tissues waste away, and the infant victim eventually dies. Prevention of marasmus begins long before birth, with good nutrition for the pregnant woman. Then breast-feeding on demand (eight or more times a day) and frequent checkups to monitor the baby's weight can stop marasmus before it begins. Infants who show signs of "failure to thrive" (they do not gain weight) can be hospitalized and treated before brain damage occurs.

marasmus A disease of severe protein-calorie malnutrition during early infancy, in which growth stops, body tissues waste away, and the infant eventually dies.

Malnutrition after age 1 may cause **kwashiorkor.** Ironically, *kwashiorkor* means "a disease of the older child when a new baby arrives"—signifying cessation of breast-feeding and less maternal attention. In kwashiorkor, the child's growth is retarded; the liver is damaged; the immune system is weakened; the face, legs, and abdomen swell with fluid (edema); the energy level is reduced (so malnourished children play less); and the hair becomes thin, brittle, and colorless.

kwashiorkor A disease of chronic malnutrition during childhood, in which a protein deficiency makes the child more vulnerable to other diseases, such as measles, diarrhea, and influenza.

➤Answer to Observation Quiz (from page 156): The babies' ages, the settings, and the mothers' apparent attitudes. The U.S. mother (*left*) is indoors in a hospital and seems attentive to whether she is feeding her infant the right way. The mother in Madagascar (*right*) seems confident and content as she feeds her older baby in a public place, enjoying the social scene.

SUMMING UP

Many public health practices save millions of infants each year. Immunizing children, putting infants to sleep on their backs, and breast-feeding are simple yet lifesaving steps. These are all affected by culture, but they are called public health measures rather than parental practices when they are encouraged by national policies.

An underlying theme of this chapter is that healthy biological growth is the result not simply of genes and nutrition but also of a social environment that provides opportunities for growth: lullabies and mobiles for stimulating the infant's senses, encouragement for developing the first motor skills, and protection against disease. Each aspect of development is linked to every other aspect, and each developing person is linked to family, community, and world. ■

SUMMARY

Body Changes

1. In the first two years of life, infants grow taller, gain weight, and increase in head circumference—all indicative of development. The norm at birth is 7½ pounds in weight, 20 inches long (about 3,400 grams, 51 centimeters). Birthweight doubles by 4 months, triples by 1 year, and quadruples by 2 years, when toddlers weigh about 30 pounds (13½ kilograms).

2. Sleep gradually decreases over the first two years. As with all areas of development, variations in sleep patterns are normal, caused by both nature and nurture. In developed nations, co-sleeping is increasingly common for very young infants, and many developmentalists consider it a harmless, or even beneficial, practice.

Brain Development

3. The brain increases dramatically in size, from about 25 to 75 percent of adult weight, in the first two years. Complexity increases as well, with transient exuberance of cell growth, development of dendrites, and formation of synapses. Both growth and pruning aid cognition.

4. Experience is vital for dendrites and synapses to link neurons. In the first year, the parts of the cortex dedicated to the senses and motor skills mature. If neurons are unused, they atrophy, and the brain regions are rededicated to processing other sensations. Normal stimulation, which almost all infants obtain, allows experience-expectant maturation.

5. Most experience-dependent brain growth reflects the varied, culture-specific experiences of the infant. Therefore, one person's brain differs from another's. However, in the basic capacities that humans share—emotional, linguistic, and sensory—all normal infants are equally capable.

Sensation and Movement

6. At birth, the senses already respond to stimuli. Prenatal experience makes hearing the most mature sense. Vision is the least mature sense at birth, but it improves quickly. Infants use their senses to strengthen their early social interactions.

7. Newborns have many reflexes, including the survival reflexes of sucking and breathing. Gross motor skills are soon evident, from rolling over to sitting up (at about 6 months), from standing to walking (at about 1 year), from climbing to running (before age 2).

8. Fine motor skills are difficult for infants, but babies gradually develop the hand and finger control needed to grab, aim, and manipulate almost anything within reach. Experience, time, and motivation allow infants to advance in all their motor skills.

Public Health Measures

9. About 2 billion infant deaths have been prevented in the past half-century because of improved health care. One major innovation is immunization, which has eradicated smallpox and virtually eliminated polio and measles in developed nations.

10. Sudden infant death syndrome (SIDS) once killed about 5,000 infants per year in the United States and thousands more worldwide. This number has been reduced by half since 1990, primarily because researchers discovered that putting infants to sleep on their backs makes SIDS less likely. If mothers stopped smoking, hundreds more infants would survive.

11. Breast-feeding is best for infants, partly because breast milk helps them resist disease and promotes growth of every kind. Most babies are breast-fed at birth, but less than half are exclusively breast-fed for 6 months, as most doctors worldwide recommend.

12. Severe malnutrition stunts growth and can cause death, both directly through marasmus or kwashiorkor and indirectly through vulnerability if a child catches measles, an intestinal disorder, or some other illness.

KEY TERMS

head-sparing (p. 132)
norm (p. 132)
percentile (p. 132)
REM sleep (p. 133)
co-sleeping (p. 134)
neuron (p. 135)
cortex (p. 136)
axon (p. 136)
dendrite (p. 136)
synapse (p. 136)
transient exuberance (p. 136)
experience expectant brain functions (p. 138)
experience-dependent brain functions (p. 139)
prefrontal cortex (p. 139)
shaken baby syndrome (p. 140)
self-righting (p. 140)
sensation (p. 142)
perception (p. 142)
binocular vision (p. 144)
motor skill (p. 145)
reflex (p. 145)
gross motor skills (p. 146)
fine motor skills (p. 147)
immunization (p. 150)
sudden infant death syndrome (SIDS) (p. 153)
protein-calorie malnutrition (p. 156)
marasmus (p. 157)
kwashiorkor (p. 157)

KEY QUESTIONS

1. In what aspects of development (at any age) would it be best to be at the 10th, 50th, and 90th percentiles? Give an example for each.

2. How might stress hormones affect later development?

3. Why is pruning an essential part of brain development?

4. What is the relationship between the cortex and dendrites?

5. What are the differences in the visual abilities of a newborn and a 3-month-old?

6. How acute is hearing before birth, at birth, and over the first year?

7. Why would parents encourage early (before 12 months) or late (after 12 months) walking?

8. In what ways does immunization save lives?

9. What are the signs of malnutrition?

10. Since breast-feeding is best, why do most North American mothers bottle-feed their 6-month-olds?

11. When is it better *not* to breast-feed an infant?

APPLICATIONS

1. Immunization regulations and practices vary, partly for social and political reasons. Ask at least two faculty or administrative staff members what immunizations students at your college must have and why. If you hear "it's a law," ask why that law is in place.

2. Observe three infants (whom you do not know) in public places such as a store, playground, or bus. Look closely at body size and motor skills, especially how much control each baby has over legs and hands. From that, estimate the age in months, and then ask the caregiver how old the infant is. (Most caregivers know the infant's exact age and are happy to tell you.)

3. *This project can be done alone, but it is more informative if several students pool responses.* Ask 3 to 10 adults whether they were bottle-fed or breast-fed and, if breast-fed, for how long. If anyone does not know, or if anyone expresses embarrassment about how long they were breast-fed, that itself is worth noting. Is there any correlation between adult body size and mode of infant feeding?

DR. DONALD SHIELDS
W.

6

CHAPTER OUTLINE

The First Two Years: Cognitive Development

Uncle Henry, my aunt's husband, boasted that he did nothing with his three children—all boys—until they were smart enough to talk. He may have found a good excuse to avoid diapering, burping, and bathing, but his beliefs about cognition were wrong. Babies are smart from the first days of life, and they communicate quite well long before they say their first words.

Uncle Henry missed his children's most impressive cognitive accomplishments. His sons grew up devoted to their mother, and when they became fathers, they were intimately involved in their own infants' lives. The research and conclusions presented in this chapter help explain all this.

We begin with Piaget's framework for observing the intellectual progression over the first two years, from newborns who know nothing about the world to toddlers who can make a wish, say it out loud, and blow out their birthday candles. We describe some specific research on early cognition, including a theoretical approach (information processing) and specific methods (habituation, brain scans) that have shown preverbal infants to be avid learners. We end by asking how early cognitive accomplishments, particularly the acquisition of language, occur.

Sensorimotor Intelligence

Jean Piaget, who was introduced in Chapter 2, was "arguably the most influential researcher of all times within the area of cognitive developmental psychology" (Birney et al., 2005, p. 328). Contrary to most people of his day (including my Uncle Henry), Piaget realized that infants are smart and active learners, adapting to experience—and Piaget believed that adaptation is the core of intelligence.

Piaget described four distinct periods of cognitive development. The first begins at birth and ends at about 24 months. Piaget referred to cognition during this period as **sensorimotor intelligence** because infants learn through their senses and motor skills. This two-year-long period is subdivided into six stages (see Table 6.1).

sensorimotor intelligence Piaget's term for the way infants think—by using their senses and motor skills—during the first period of cognitive development.

Stages One and Two: Primary Circular Reactions

In every aspect of sensorimotor intelligence, the brain and the senses interact. Sensation, perception, and cognition cycle back and forth (circling round and round) in what Piaget called a circular reaction. The first two stages of

primary circular reactions The first of three types of feedback loops in sensorimotor intelligence, this one involving the infant's own body. The infant senses motion, sucking, noise, and other stimuli, and tries to understand them.

sensorimotor intelligence involve **primary circular reactions,** which involve the infant's own body.

Stage one, called the *stage of reflexes,* lasts only for a month. It includes senses as well as reflexes, the foundation of infant thought. Reflexes become deliberate; sensation leads to perception and then to cognition. Sensorimotor intelligence begins.

As reflexes adjust, the baby enters stage two, *first acquired adaptations* (also called the stage of first habits). Adaptation includes both *assimilation* and *accommodation* (see Chapter 2), which people use to understand their experience. Infants adapt their reflexes, which become deliberate actions as repeated responses provide information about what the body does and how a particular action feels.

Here is one example. Newborns suck anything that touches their lips; sucking is one of the strongest reflexes. By about 1 month, infants start to adapt their reflexive sucking. Some items require not just assimilation but also accommodation: Pacifiers need to be sucked without the reflexive tongue-pushing and swallowing that natural nipples require. This adaptation is a sign that infants have begun to interpret their perceptions; as they accommodate to pacifiers, they are "thinking."

After several months, additional adaptation of the sucking reflex is evident. The infant's cognitive responses include: Suck some things to soothe hunger, suck some for comfort, and never suck others (fuzzy blankets, large balls).

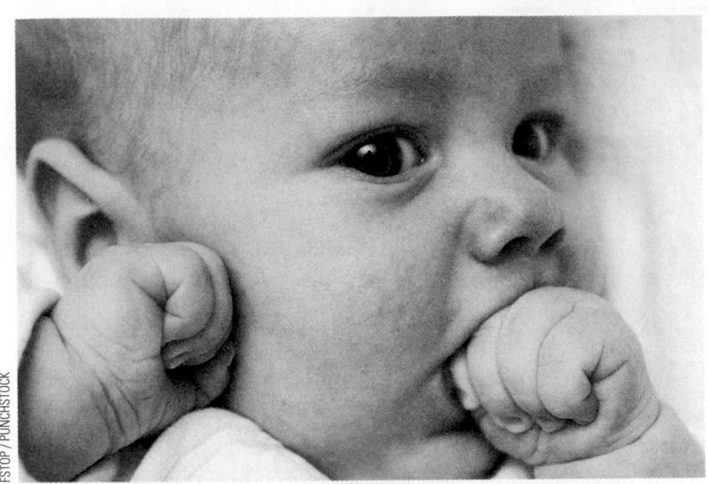

FSTOP / PUNCHSTOCK

Time for Adaptation Sucking is a reflex at first, but adaptation begins as soon as an infant differentiates a pacifier from her mother's breast or realizes that her hand has grown too big to fit into her mouth. This infant's expression of concentration suggests that she is about to make that adaptation and suck just her thumb from now on.

TABLE 6.1

The Six Stages of Sensorimotor Intelligence

For an overview of the stages of sensorimotor thought, it helps to group the six stages into pairs. The first two stages involve the infant's responses to its own body.

Primary Circular Reactions	
Stage One (birth to 1 month)	*Reflexes*: sucking, grasping, staring, listening.
Stage Two (1–4 months)	*The first acquired adaptations*: accommodation and coordination of reflexes. Examples: sucking a pacifier differently from a nipple; grabbing a bottle to suck it.
The next two stages involve the infant's responses to objects and people.	
Secondary Circular Reactions	
Stage Three (4–8 months)	*Making interesting sights last*: responding to people and objects. Example: clapping hands when mother says "patty-cake."
Stage Four (8–12 months)	*New adaptation and anticipation*: becoming more deliberate and purposeful in responding to people and objects. Example: putting mother's hands together in order to make her start playing patty-cake.
The last two stages are the most creative, first with action and then with ideas.	
Tertiary Circular Reactions	
Stage Five (12–18 months)	*New means through active experimentation*: experimentation and creativity in the actions of the "little scientist." Example: putting a teddy bear in the toilet and flushing it.
Stage Six (18–24 months)	*New means through mental combinations*: considering before doing provides the child with new ways of achieving a goal without resorting to trial-and-error experiments. Example: before flushing, remembering that the toilet overflowed the last time, and hesitating.

Adaptation is apparent when babies are not hungry but want the reassurance of rhythmic sucking. Then they suck a pacifier, or, if their reflexes have not adapted to a pacifier (because one was not offered), they suck their thumbs, fingers, or knuckles. Once an adaptation is successful, it sticks. If parents of a 3-month-old thumb-sucker decide that a pacifier would be more attractive, it is too late. The infant has already acquired an adaptation of sucking and will refuse a substitute. People of all ages tend to be set in their ways for cognitive reasons; this is an early example.

Especially for Parents (see response, page 167): When should parents decide whether to feed their baby only by breast, only by bottle, or using some combination? When should they decide whether or not to let their baby use a pacifier?

Stages Three and Four: Secondary Circular Reactions

In stages three and four of sensorimotor intelligence, development advances from primary circular reactions (which involve the baby's own body) to **secondary circular reactions,** which go beyond the baby's body to involve other people and objects. The infant responds to other people, to toys, and to any other object that he or she can touch or move.

secondary circular reactions The second of three types of feedback loops in sensorimotor intelligence, this one involving people and objects. Infants respond to other people, to toys, and to any other object they can touch or move.

During stage three (age 4 to 8 months), infants attempt to produce exciting experiences, *making interesting events last.* Realizing that rattles make noise, for example, they wave their arms and laugh whenever someone puts a rattle in their hand. The sight of something that normally delights an infant—a favorite toy, a smiling parent—can trigger active efforts for interaction.

Stage four (8 months to 1 year) is called *new adaptation and anticipation,* or "the means to an end," because babies think about a goal and how to reach it. Often they ask for help from their caregivers (fussing, pointing, gesturing) to accomplish what they want.

Thinking is more innovative in stage four than it was in stage three because adaptation is more complex. For instance, instead of always smiling at Daddy, an infant might assess Daddy's mood first and then try to engage him in a favorite game. Stage-three babies merely understand how to continue an experience. Stage-four babies initiate and anticipate experiences.

New Directions

A 10-month-old girl who enjoys playing in the bathtub might see a bar of soap, crawl over to her mother with it as a signal to start her bath, and then remove her clothes to make her wishes crystal clear—finally squealing with delight when the bath water is turned on. Similarly, if a 10-month-old boy sees his mother putting on her coat to leave, he might try to stop her or drag over his own jacket to signal that he wants to go with her.

These examples reveal *goal-directed behavior*—that is, purposeful action. The baby's obvious goal-directedness stems from (1) an enhanced awareness of cause and effect, (2) memory for actions already completed, and (3) understanding of other people's intentions (Behne et al., 2005; Willatts, 1999). Such cognitive awareness coincides with the new motor skills needed to achieve goals (e.g., crawling, walking); both developments are the result of brain maturation (Adolph & Berger, 2006).

ESBIN-ANDERSON / THE IMAGE WORKS

Talk to Me This 4-month-old is learning how to make interesting sights last: The best way to get Daddy to respond is to vocalize, stare, smile, and pat his cheek.

Object Permanence

Piaget thought that babies first understand a concept called **object permanence** at about 8 months. Object permanence refers to the awareness that objects or people continue to exist when they can no longer be seen, touched, or heard.

object permanence The realization that objects (including people) still exist when they can no longer be seen, touched, or heard.

LAURA DWIGHT

Where's Rosa? At 18 months, Rosa knows all about object permanence and hiding. Her only problem here is distinguishing between "self" and "other."

Other researchers agreed that a goal-directed search for toys that have fallen from the baby's crib, rolled under a couch, or disappeared under a blanket does not begin to emerge until about 8 months, just as Piaget indicated. However, many current scientists question Piaget's interpretations, as the following explains.

a view from science

Object Permanence Revisited

Before Piaget, it was assumed that infants understood objects just as adults do. Piaget demonstrated that assumption to be wrong. In Piaget's simple experiment, an adult shows an infant an interesting toy, covers it with a lightweight cloth, and observes the infant's response. The results:

- Infants younger than 8 months do not search for the object (by removing the cloth).
- At about 8 months, infants search immediately after the object is covered but seem to forget about the object if they have to wait a few seconds.
- By 2 years, children fully understand object permanence, progressing through six stages of ever-advancing cognition (Piaget, 1954).

As you learned in Chapter 1, the scientific method includes (1) *replication* (thousands of scientists in dozens of nations have replicated Piaget's work, using his original research design) and (2) *questioning* the conclusions of published research. Piaget claimed that failure to search for a hidden object meant that infants have no concept of object permanence. Researchers question whether other immaturities, such as imperfect motor skills or fragile memory, could mask an infant's understanding that objects still exist when they are no longer visible (Cohen & Cashon, 2006; Ruffman et al., 2005).

Apparently they can. As one researcher points out, "Amid his acute observation and brilliant theorizing, Piaget . . . mistook infants' motor incompetence for conceptual incompetence" (Mandler, 2004, p. 17). A series of clever experiments, in which objects seemed to disappear behind a screen while researchers traced eye movements and brain activity, revealed some inkling of object permanence in infants as young as 4½ months (Baillargeon & DeVos, 1991; Spelke, 1993).

The specific finding that contradicted Piaget is that, long before 8 months, infants showed surprise (by staring longer, for instance) when an observed object vanished behind a screen, or became two objects, or moved in an unexpected way. Their surprise (evidenced by longer stares) suggests they had developed an understanding of object permanence, in that the infants seemed to think the observed object still existed behind the screen (Baillargeon, 1994).

Further exploration of infant cognition came from a series of experiments in which 2-, 4-, and 6-month-olds watched balls moving behind a screen, sometimes disappearing, sometimes reemerging in a smooth path, sometimes reemerging in the wrong place (Johnson et al., 2003). The 2-month-olds showed no awareness of anything odd, no matter what the balls did; the 4-month-olds showed signs that they knew something was amiss; the 6-month-olds demonstrated (with attentive stares) that they expected the balls to move in the usual way and were surprised when they didn't.

The idea that such surprise indicates object permanence is accepted by some scientists, who believe that "infants as young as 2 and 3 months of age can represent fully hidden objects,"

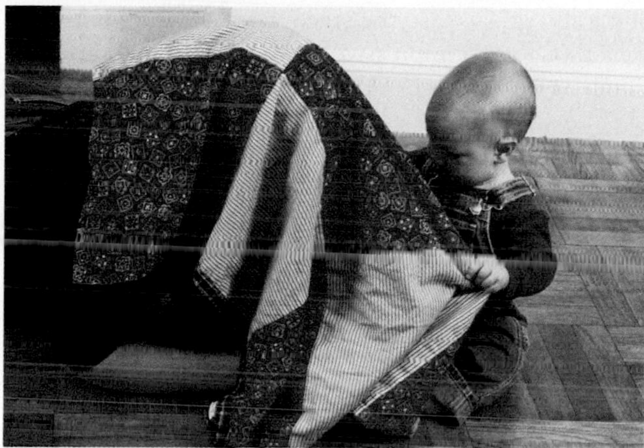

Peek-a-Boo The best hidden object is Mom under an easily moved blanket, as 7-month-old Elias has discovered. Peek-a-boo is fun from about 7 to 12 months. In another month, Elias will search for more conventionally hidden objects. In a year or two, his surprise and delight at finding Mom will fade.

BOTH LAURA DWIGHT

but it is not accepted by everyone. Other scientists hold a "more traditional view" that only infants of "8 and 9 months can do so" (Cohen & Cashon, 2006, p. 224).

Nonetheless, this research provides caregivers with many practical suggestions. If very young infants fuss because they want something they see but cannot have (your keys, a cigarette, a piece of candy), all an adult needs to do to stop the fussing is to put the object out of sight. For toddlers, however, merely hiding a forbidden object is not enough. It must be securely locked up or thrown away, and even then, the child might cry.

The fact that object permanence develops gradually also lets caregivers know that some games, such as peek-a-boo and hide-and-seek, are too advanced at some ages but great fun at others. Peek-a-boo elicits gales of laughter from 8-month-olds.

Stages Five and Six: Tertiary Circular Reactions

In their second year, infants start experimenting in thought and deed, first in the opposite sequence—acting first and perhaps thinking later. **Tertiary circular reactions** begin when 1-year-olds take their first independent actions to discover the properties of other people, animals, and things.

Infants no longer respond simply to their own bodies (primary reactions) or to other people or objects (secondary reactions). They initiate new exploration, in a pattern more like a spiral than a closed circle.

The first stage of tertiary circular reactions, Piaget's stage five (age 12 to 18 months), is called *new means through active experimentation.* Building on the accomplishments of stage four, infants become more expansive and creative in their goal-directed and purposeful activities. Toddlerhood is a time of active exploration, when babies delight in squeezing all the toothpaste out of the tube, taking apart the iPod, uncovering the anthill.

Piaget referred to the stage-five toddler as a **"little scientist"** who undertakes, "in scientific language, the 'experiment in order to see'" (Piaget, 1962, p. 266). The "little scientist's" devotion to discovery is familiar to every adult scientist—and to every parent.

Finally, in the sixth stage (age 18 to 24 months), toddlers begin to anticipate and solve simple problems by using *mental combinations,* an intellectual experimentation that supersedes the active experimentation of stage five. Thankfully, the sequence sometimes begins with thought (especially if an adult previously said that something was forbidden), and then action occurs.

In the sixth stage, children are able to combine two ideas. For instance, they know that a doll is not a real baby and they also know that a doll can be belted into

tertiary circular reactions The third of three types of feedback loops in sensorimotor intelligence, this one involving active exploration and experimentation. Infants explore a range of new activities, varying their responses as a way of learning about the world.

"little scientist" The stage-five toddler (age 12 to 18 months) who experiments without anticipating the results, using trial and error in active and creative exploration.

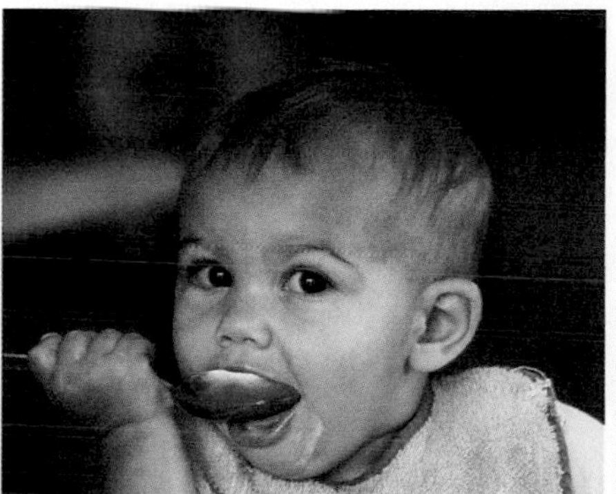

MEYER RANGELL / THE IMAGE WORKS

Bib and Bath Learning to use eating utensils is a cognitively stimulating experience that is largely a matter of trial and—often messy—error. A "little scientist" in action!

Especially for Parents (see response, page 168): One parent wants to put all the breakable or dangerous objects away because a toddler is now able to move around independently. The other parent says that the baby should learn not to touch certain things. Who is right?

deferred imitation A sequence in which an infant first perceives something that someone else does and then performs the same action a few hours or even days later.

LWA-DANN TARDIFF / CORBIS

I'm Listening This 14-month-old is a master at deferred imitation. He knows how to hold a cell phone and what gestures to use as the "conversation" goes on.

habituation The process of getting used to an object or event through repeated exposure to it.

a stroller and taken for a walk. This is also the stage when toddlers put two words together to express a new thought, an impressive intellectual accomplishment.

Because they can combine ideas, stage-six toddlers think about consequences, hesitating a moment before yanking the cat's tail or dropping a raw egg on the floor. Their strong impulse to discover sometimes overwhelms reflection; they do not always choose wisely. But at least thought precedes action.

Being able to use mental combinations makes it possible for a child to pretend. A toddler might sing to a doll before tucking it into bed. This is in marked contrast to the younger infant (who treats a doll like any other toy, throwing or biting it) or to the stage-five toddler (who tries to pull off the head, arms, and legs to see what is inside).

Piaget describes another stage-six intellectual accomplishment, involving both thinking and memory. **Deferred imitation** occurs when infants copy behavior they noticed hours or even days earlier (Piaget, 1962). A classic example is Piaget's daughter, Jacqueline, who observed another child

> who got into a terrible temper. He screamed as he tried to get out of a playpen and pushed it backward, stamping his feet. Jacqueline stood watching him in amazement, never having witnessed such a scene before. The next day, she herself screamed in her playpen and tried to move it, stamping her foot lightly several times in succession.
>
> *[Piaget, 1962, p. 63]*

Piaget and Modern Research

Infants reach the various stages of sensorimotor intelligence earlier than Piaget predicted. Not only do many 5-month-olds show surprise when object permanence seems invalid, but many babies pretend and defer imitation before 1 year (Bauer, 2006; Jones & Herbert, 2006; Meltzoff & Moore, 1999).

Piaget underestimated infant cognition because he based his conclusions on what he saw his own infants do. Direct observation of only three children is a start, but no contemporary researcher would stop there. Given the immaturity and variability of babies, dozens of infants must be studied in creative yet logical ways in order to draw valid conclusions. For instance, to prove that object permanence occurred before 6 months, Renée Baillargeon (2000) listed 30 studies that reached that conclusion.

When studying infants, there are always problems with "fidelity and credibility" (Bornstein et al., 2005, p. 287). To overcome these issues, modern researchers use innovative statistics, designs, sample sizes, and strategies that were not available to Piaget (Hartmann & Pelzel, 2005).

Boredom as a Research Method

For the past several decades, hundreds of studies have depended on a research method called **habituation** (from the word *habit*). Habituation is the process of getting used to an experience after repeated exposure, as when the school cafeteria serves macaroni day after day or when infants repeatedly encounter the same sound, sight, or toy. Evidence of habituation is loss of interest (or, for macaroni, loss of appetite).

Using habituation as a research strategy involves repeating one stimulus until babies lose interest, and then presenting another, slightly different stimulus (a new sound, sight, or other sensation). Babies can indicate in many ways—a longer gaze; a faster or slower heart rate; more or less muscle tension; a change in the rate, rhythm, or pressure of suction on a nipple—if they detect a difference between the habitual stimulus and the new one. Subtle indicators are recorded by technology (eye-gaze cameras, heart monitors, brain scans) that did not exist in Piaget's time.

By inducing habituation and then presenting a new stimulus, scientists have learned that even 1-month-olds can detect the difference between a *pah* sound and a *bah* sound, between a circle with two dots inside it and a circle without any dots, and much more. Babies younger than 6 months perceive far more than Piaget imagined.

➤Response for Parents (from page 163): Both decisions should be made within the first month, during the stage of reflexes. If parents wait until the infant is 4 months or older, they may discover that they are too late. It is difficult to introduce a bottle to a 4-month-old who has been exclusively breast-fed or a pacifier to a baby who has already adapted the sucking reflex to a thumb.

Measuring the Brain

Techniques to measure brain activity (see Table 6.2) (Johnson, 2005) have proven that babies are thinking long before they talk. In functional magnetic resonance imaging, or **fMRI,** scanning equipment records a burst of electrical activity within the brain, which indicates that neurons are firing; researchers conclude that a particular stimulus has been noticed and processed. Using such advanced methods, scientists are convinced that infants have memories, goals, and mental combinations in advance of Piaget's stages.

fMRI Functional magnetic resonance imaging, a measuring technique in which the brain's electrical excitement indicates activation anywhere in the brain; fMRI helps researchers locate neurological responses to stimuli.

Indeed, early brain development is wide-ranging: Dendrites proliferate, and pruning is extensive (as described in Chapter 5). The first years of life are filled

TABLE 6.2

Some Techniques Used by Neuroscientists to Understand Brain Function

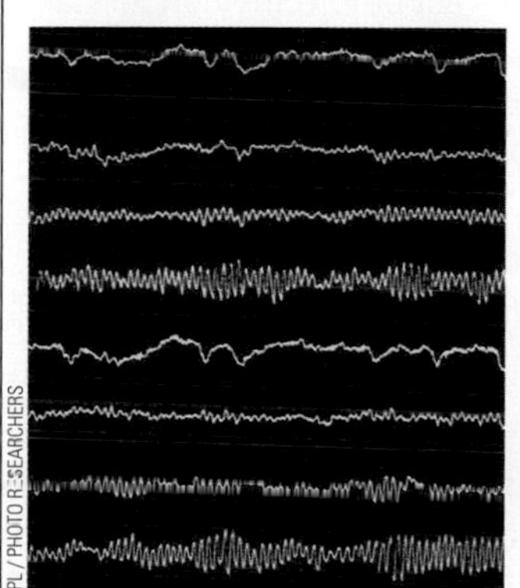
SPL / PHOTO RESEARCHERS

EEG, normal brain

Technique
EEG (electroencephalogram)

Use
Measures electrical activity in the top layers of the brain, where the cortex is.

Limitations
Especially in infancy, much brain activity of interest occurs below the cortex.

©2001 UNIVERSITY OF WASHINGTON, INSTITUTE FOR LEARNING AND BRAIN SCIENCES

ERP when listening

Technique
ERP (event-related potential)

Use
Notes the amplitude and frequency of electrical activity (as shown by brain waves) in specific parts of the cortex in reaction to various stimuli.

Limitations
Reaction within the cortex signifies perception, but interpretation of the amplitude and timing of brain waves is not straightforward.

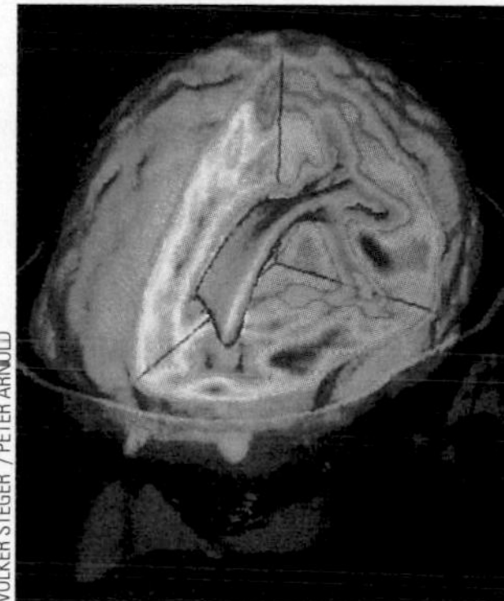
VOLKER STEGER / PETER ARNOLD

fMRI when talking

Technique
fMRI (functional magnetic resonance imaging)

Use
Measures changes in blood flow anywhere in the brain (not just the outer layers).

Limitations
Signifies brain activity, but infants are notoriously active, which can make fMRIs useless.

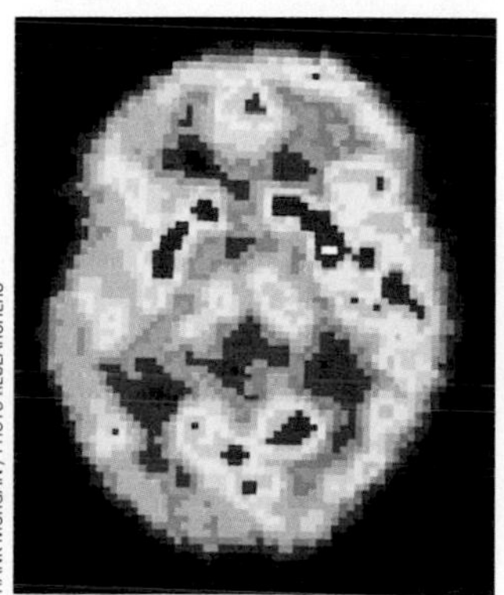
HANK MORGAN / PHOTO RESEARCHERS

PET scan of sleep

Technique
PET (positron emission tomography)

Use
Also (like fMRI) reveals activity in various parts of the brain. Locations can be pinpointed with precision, but PET requires injection of radioactive dye to light up the active parts of the brain.

Limitations
Many parents and researchers hesitate to inject radioactive dye into an infant's brain unless a serious abnormality is suspected.

For both practical and ethical reasons, these techniques have not been used with large, representative samples of normal infants. One of the challenges of neuroscience is to develop methods that are harmless, easy to use, and comprehensive for the study of normal children. A more immediate challenge is to depict the data in ways that are easy to interpret.

➤**Response for Parents** (from page 166): It is easier and safer to babyproof the house, because toddlers, being "little scientists," want to explore. However, it is important for both parents to encourage and guide the baby, so it is preferable to leave out a few untouchable items if that will help prevent a major conflict between husband and wife.

with mental activity and may be prime time for cognitive development (Johnson, 2005). Overall, researchers have compiled "ample data to suggest that learning and memory are correlated with changes in the brain at multiple levels" (Nelson et al., 2006, p. 17). Brain scans of normal infants are difficult and costly, but all the evidence so far indicates that babies are avid learners.

In fact, discoveries of intellectual changes based on infants' experiences have given developmentalists a new worry: People might think that the first years are the *only* ones for brain growth. Not so. As 20 leading developmentalists explain, the

> focus on "zero to three" as a critical or particularly sensitive period is highly problematic, not because this isn't an important period for the developing brain, but [because] . . . attention to the period from birth to 3 years begins too late and ends too soon.
>
> *[National Research Council and Institute of Medicine, 2000, p. 7]*

SUMMING UP

Piaget discovered, described, and then celebrated active infant learning, which he described in six stages of sensorimotor intelligence. Babies use their senses and motor skills to gain an understanding of their world, first with reflexes and then by adapting through assimilation and accommodation. Although Piaget was a respected pioneer, object permanence, pursuit of goals, and deferred imitation all develop earlier in infancy than he realized. The infant is a "little scientist," not only at age 1, as Piaget described so well, but even in the first months of life. Infants sometimes act before they understand, but thinking may develop before motor skills can execute thoughts. ■

Information Processing

Piaget was a "grand" theorist; he described shifts in the nature of cognition in terms of stages from years 0 to 2, 2 to 6, 6 to 12, and 12 on. His sweeping overview contrasts with **information-processing theory,** a perspective modeled on computer functioning, including input, memory, programs, calculation, and output.

information-processing theory A perspective that compares human thinking processes, by analogy, to computer analysis of data, including sensory input, connections, stored memories, and output.

Although there are many versions of information-processing theory, they all share one feature: a belief that a step-by-step description of the mechanisms of thought adds insight to our understanding (Munakata, 2006). Human information processing begins with input picked up by the senses; proceeds to brain reactions, connections, and stored memories; and concludes with some output.

Especially for Computer Experts (see response, page 171): In what way is the human mind not like a computer?

For infants, the output might be moving a hand to uncover a toy (object permanence), saying a word (e.g., *mama*) to signify recognition, or simply glancing briefly at a photograph (habituation). Instead of the newborn who cries reflexively in hunger, a slightly older infant might perceive a bottle, remember that it relieves hunger, reach for it, and then suck from it.

Older infants are much more thoughtful and effective than newborns because their information-processing ability is more advanced. Researchers have demonstrated that these advances occur week by week in the first year. This is contrary to the discontinuity described by Piaget when he theorized that such advances occurred in distinct stages (Cohen & Cashon, 2006).

With the aid of the neuroscience techniques described in Table 6.2, information-processing research has found impressive intellectual capacities in the infant. For example, concepts and categories seem to develop in the infant brain by about 6 months (Mandler, 2007; Quinn, 2004). Also in the middle of the first year, infants manifest a basic understanding of cause and effect. When they see one object bump into another, launching the second one, they understand that the first object caused the second to move (Cohen & Cashon, 2006).

The information-processing perspective helps tie together many aspects of infant cognition. We review two of these now: affordances and memory. Affordances concern perception (or, by analogy, input). Memory concerns brain organization and output (again by analogy, information storage and retrieval).

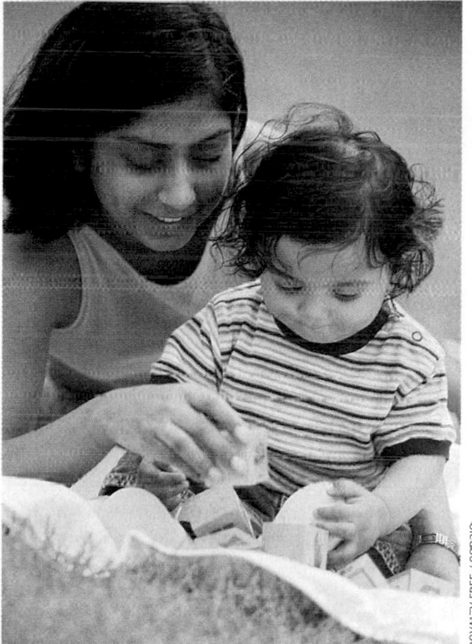

Baby in Charge As this mother no doubt realizes, for her toddler, playing with blocks affords touching, stacking, and tossing them, not trying to identify the letters and numbers on them.

ROYALTY-FREE / CORBIS

Affordances

Remember, perception is the mental processing of information that arrives at the brain from the sensory organs. It is the first step of information processing, the input to the brain. One of the puzzles of development is that two people can have discrepant perceptions of the same situation, not only interpreting it differently but actually observing it differently.

Concepts from the Gibsons

Decades of thought and research led Eleanor and James Gibson to conclude that perception is far from automatic (E. Gibson, 1969; J. Gibson, 1979). Perception —for infants, as for the rest of us—is a cognitive accomplishment that requires selectivity: "Perceiving is active, a process of obtaining information about the world. . . . We don't simply see, we look" (E. Gibson, 1988, p. 5).

The Gibsons contend that the environment (people, places, and objects) *affords,* or offers, many opportunities for perception and for interaction with what is perceived (E. Gibson, 1997). Each of these opportunities is called an **affordance.** Which particular affordance is perceived and acted on depends on four factors: sensory awareness, immediate motivation, current level of development, and past experience.

affordance An opportunity for perception and interaction that is offered by a person, place, or object in the environment.

Selective Perception As a simple example, consider the affordances of a lemon. It may be perceived as something that affords smelling, tasting, touching, viewing, throwing, squeezing, and biting (among other things). Each of these affordances is further perceived as offering pleasure, pain, or some other emotional response.

Which of the affordances of a lemon is perceived and acted upon depends on the four factors just mentioned: sensations, motives, age, and experience. Consequently, a lemon elicits quite different perceptions from an artist about to paint a still life, a thirsty adult, and a teething baby wanting something to gnaw on. Indeed, in some cultures, a lemon is rarely perceived, and thus a stray lemon on the ground would offer no affordance at all.

Clearly, a person's age affects what affordances he or she sees. A toddler's idea of what affords running might be any unobstructed surface—a meadow, a long hallway in an apartment building, or a road. To an adult eye, the degree to which these places afford running may be restricted by such factors as a bull grazing in the meadow, neighbors along the hallway, or traffic on the road. Moreover, young children love to run, so they notice affordances for running. By contrast, many adults prefer to stay put—so they do not perceive whether running is afforded or not.

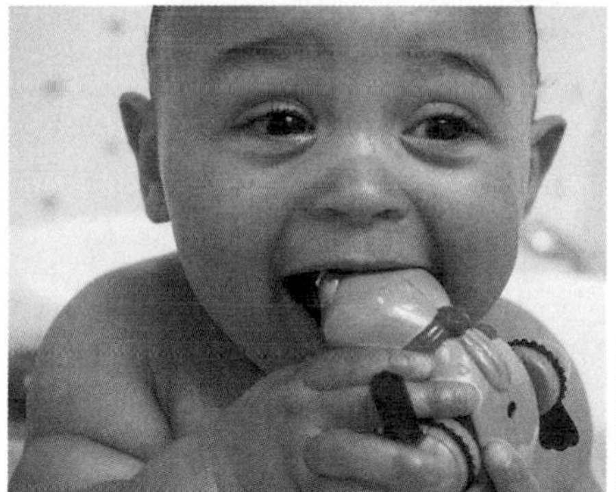

Chewable? Motivation is crucial for affordances. This baby's toy was designed to afford pulling, but he is teething, so he is motivated to recognize that it also affords chewing.

BSIP / PHOTOTAKE USA

Research on Early Affordances As their information processing improves over the first year, infants become quicker to recognize affordances. A detailed study traced the responses of infants of different ages to eight different displays on a TV screen (Courage et al., 2006; see the Research Design). These scientists measured, among other things, how many times the infants glanced away from the displays, how long their most extensive look lasted, and how their heart rate may have changed.

Research Design

Scientists: Mary L. Courage, Greg D. Reynolds, and John E. Richards.

Publication: *Child Development* (2006).

Participants: One hundred infants aged 14, 20, 26, 39, and 52 weeks (20 at each age). None had birth complications or known disabilities. Each was tested sitting in the mother's lap.

Design: Babies saw eight displays on a TV monitor, four of them motionless (a face, dots, triangles and lines, a *Sesame Street* scene) and the other four showing the same objects in motion. Duration of looking was measured in seconds by researchers who did not know what the babies saw, and heart rate was measured via an electrocardiogram (EEG).

Major conclusions: Look time and heart rate varied by age and display. Moving displays captured attention more than static ones; human forms were more attractive than geometric designs. The youngest babies often just stared blankly (and showed almost no slowing of heart rate), while the older babies glanced, glanced away, and then looked more closely. Age differences suggested advances in processing; the oldest babies were most "stimulus dependent"—that is, most influenced by the specifics of what they saw.

Comment: This study provides rich data on age and information processing, including one table with 360 data points —72 at each age. This richness complicates analysis, but because the study compares heart rate, look time, age, and display, its conclusions are more reliable.

The older infants were quicker to process the display and decide whether it was interesting—a sign of better information processing. For example, the 14-week-olds looked at static dots for 10 seconds at a time, the 20-week-olds for 6 seconds, and babies from 26 to 52 weeks for only 5 seconds.

Developmental trends were apparent, especially for the most interesting display, which was a video from *Sesame Street*. Babies stared at this video for an average of 18 seconds (usually one long look) when they were 14 weeks old, 10 seconds at 26 weeks, and then back up to 15 seconds at 52 weeks. According to the researchers, not only was input more quickly perceived with greater age (hence shorter looks for less interesting things) but cognitive processing also advanced (hence more intense looks at *Sesame Street*) (Courage et al., 2006).

Affordances are sought by infants of every age. For instance, in one study, 9- to 12-month-olds were presented with unknown objects that rattled, rang, squeaked, or were silent. They decided what noise the object afforded on the basis of whether the object's shape was similar to that of another noise-making object they had already seen.

By 12 months, they also used vocabulary. They were told the name of a noise-making object, and they then predicted what noise another object would make based on its name (Graham et al., 2004). (Even for adults, a rose by any other name may not afford smelling.)

In another experiment, 12- to 24-month-olds watched adults look at or bend a laminated photograph and then followed the example, either looking at or bending it themselves. They did not yet know that photos are primarily for viewing, so they used whichever affordance they had been shown (Callaghan et al., 2004).

The Visual Cliff The fact that experience affects which affordances are perceived is quite apparent in studies of depth perception. This research began with an apparatus called the **visual cliff,** which was designed to provide the illusion of a sudden dropoff between one horizontal surface and another (see photograph). Mothers were able to urge their 6-month-olds to wiggle toward them over the supposed edge of the cliff, but even with mothers urging, 10-month-olds fearfully refused to budge (E. Gibson & Walk, 1960).

Researchers once thought that a visual deficit, namely inadequate depth perception, prevented young babies from seeing the drop. According to this hypothesis, as the visual cortex became more mature, 8-month-olds could see that crawling into the gap afforded falling.

Later research (using advanced technology) disproved that interpretation. Even 3-month-olds notice a drop: Their heart rate slows and their eyes open wide when they are placed over the cliff. But until they can crawl, they do not realize that crawling over an edge affords falling, potentially with a frightening and painful result.

The infant's awareness of the affordance of the visual cliff depends on past experience. The difference is in processing, not input; in affordance, not mere perception. The same sequence happens with walking: Novice walkers are fearless and reckless; experienced walkers are more cautious and deliberate (Adolph & Berger, 2005).

visual cliff An experimental apparatus that gives an illusion of a sudden dropoff between one horizontal surface and another.

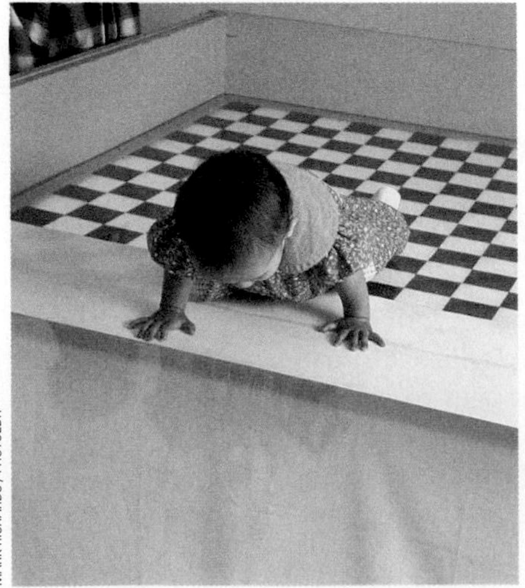

MARK RICHARDS / PHOTOEDIT

Depth Perception This toddler in a laboratory in Berkeley, California, is crawling on the experimental apparatus called a visual cliff. She stops at the edge of what she perceives as a dropoff.

Movement

Despite all the variations from one infant to another in the particular affordances they perceive, all seek to understand two kinds of affordances. Babies pay close attention to things that move and to people. This was demonstrated by the study of the eight TV displays mentioned earlier: Motion was more interesting than static displays, and people were more interesting than dots (Courage et al., 2006).

Especially for Parents of Infants (see response, page 173): When should you be particularly worried that your baby will fall off the bed or down the stairs?

Perception that focuses on movement and change is called **dynamic perception.** Infants love motion. As soon as they can, they move their bodies—grabbing, scooting, crawling, walking. To their delight, they realize that such motions change what the world affords them. As a result, infants work hard to master each successive motor activity (Adolph & Berger, 2005).

dynamic perception Perception that is primed to focus on movement and change.

Other creatures that move, especially infants' own caregivers, are among the best sources of pleasure, again because of dynamic perception. It's almost impossible to teach a baby not to chase and grab any moving creature, including a dog, a cat, or even a cockroach.

Infants' interest in motion and action was examined in another experiment that sought to learn what affordances were perceived by babies too young to talk or walk (van Hof et al., 2008). A ball was moved at various speeds in front of infants aged 3 to 9 months. Most tried to touch or catch the ball as it passed within reach. However, marked differences appeared in their perception of the affordance of "catchableness." Sometimes younger infants did not reach for slow-moving balls yet tried (unsuccessfully) to grasp the faster balls. They successfully touched the ball in only about 20 percent of their tries.

LLI SEER / IMAGE BANK

One Constant, Multisensual Perception From the angle of her arm and the bend of her hand, it appears that this infant recognizes the constancy of the furry mass, perceiving it as a single entity whether it is standing still, rolling in the sand, or walking along the beach.

By contrast, the 9-month-olds knew when a ball afforded catching. They grabbed the slower balls and refused to try for the very fast ones; their success rate was almost 100 percent. This result "follows directly from one of the key concepts of ecological psychology, that animals perceive the environment in terms of action possibilities or affordances" (van Hof et al., 2008, p. 193).

People

The other universal principle of infant perception is **people preference.** This characteristic may have evolved over the centuries because humans of all ages survived by learning to attend to, and rely on, one another. As you remember from Chapter 5, all human senses are primed to respond to social stimuli (Bornstein et al., 2005); this topic is further explored in Chapter 7. Here we focus on the development of people preference as a marker of cognition. Infants find novelty of most objects and experiences increasingly attractive as their thinking advances, but when it comes to people, they prefer familiarity. Infants soon recognize their regular caregivers and expect certain affordances (comfort, food, entertainment) from them.

people preference A universal principle of infant perception, consisting of an innate attraction to other humans, which is evident in visual, auditory, tactile, and other preferences.

Affordances of Caregivers Very young babies are particularly interested in the emotional affordances of their caregivers, using their limited perceptual abilities and intellectual understanding to respond to smiles, shouts, and other behaviors. Infants connect facial expression with tone of voice long before they understand language. This ability has led to an interesting hypothesis:

> Given that infants are frequently exposed to their caregivers' emotional displays and further presented with opportunities to view the affordances (Gibson, 1959, 1979) of those emotional expressions, we propose that the expressions of familiar persons are meaningful to infants very early in life.
>
> [*Kahana-Kalman & Walker Andrews, 2001, p. 366*]

➤Response for Computer Experts (from page 168): In dozens of ways, including speed of calculation, ability to network across the world, and vulnerability to viruses. In one crucial way the human mind is better: Computers wear out within a few years, while human minds keep working until death.

Building on earlier research by other scientists on infant perception, researchers Ronit Kahana-Kalman and Arlene Walker-Andrews presented infants with two moving images on one video screen. Both images were of a woman; one was their mother and the other was a stranger. In one image the woman visibly expresses joy; in the other, sorrow.

Each presentation of the two images was accompanied by an audiotape of that woman's happy *or* sad talk. Previous studies had found that 7-month-olds can reliably match emotional voices with the appropriate facial expressions. At that age, but not earlier, they looked longer at strangers whose voices and faces expressed the same emotions.

Some infants in Kahana-Kalman and Walker-Andrews' experiment were only 3½ months old. When they did not know the woman, they failed to match the verbal emotion with the facial expression. In other words, when the face was that of a stranger, these young infants did not look longer at the happy face when they heard happy talk or the sad face when they heard the sad voice. That result was expected from previous research.

Especially for Parents (see response, page 174): This research on early affordances suggests a crucial lesson about how many babysitters an infant should have. What is it?

Smiling at Mommy However, when the 3½-month-olds saw their own mother on the video (two images, happy and sad) and heard her happy or her sad voice, they correctly matched visual and vocal emotions. They looked longest at their happy mothers talking in a happy way, but they also looked at their sad mothers when they heard their mother's sad voice—an amazing display of connecting speech and facial expressions.

The researchers noticed something else as well. When these infants saw and heard their happy mothers, they smiled twice as fast, seven times as long, and much more brightly (with cheeks raised as well as lips upturned) than for the happy strangers (Kahana-Kalman & Walker-Andrews, 2001). Experience had taught them that a smiling mother affords joy, while the affordances of a smiling stranger are more difficult to judge.

He Remembers! In this demonstration of Rovee-Collier's experiment, a young infant immediately remembers how to make the familiar mobile move. (Unfamiliar mobiles do not provoke the same reaction.) He kicks his right leg and flails both arms, just as he learned to do several weeks ago.

Observation Quiz (see answer, page 174): How and why is this mobile unlike those usually sold for babies?

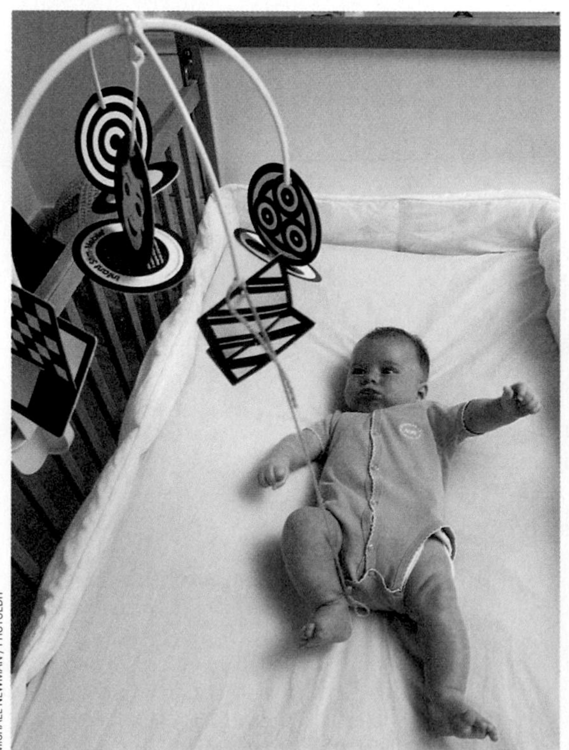

MICHAEL NEWMAN / PHOTOEDIT

Memory

Processing and remembering events requires a certain amount of experience and brain maturation. For example, repeated experiences of Mother bringing food is likely to be remembered; one time when Grandma did so is forgotten.

Even with repetition, infants have great difficulty storing new memories in their first year, and older children are often unable to describe one-time events that occurred when they were younger. One reason has to do with language ability: People use words to store (and sometimes distort) memories, so preverbal children have difficulty with recall (Richardson & Hayne, 2007).

However, a series of experiments has revealed that very young infants *can* remember, even if they cannot later put their memories into words. Memories are particularly evident when:

- Experimental conditions are similar to real life.
- Motivation is high.
- Retrieval is strengthened by reminders and repetition.

The most dramatic evidence for infant memory comes from innovative experiments in which 3-month-olds were taught to make a mobile move by kicking their legs (Rovee-Collier, 1987, 1990). The infants lay on their backs, in their own cribs, connected to a mobile by means of a ribbon tied to one foot (see photograph).

Virtually all the infants began making some occasional kicks (as well as random arm movements and noises) and realized, after a while, that kicking made the mobile move. They then kicked more vigorously and frequently, sometimes laughing at their accomplishment. Each kick added pleasure, a repeated experience. So far, this is no surprise—self-activated movement is highly reinforcing to infants, part of dynamic perception.

When some infants had the mobile-and-ribbon apparatus reinstalled in their cribs *one week later,* most started to kick immediately; this reaction indicated that they remembered their previous experience. But when other infants were retested *two weeks later,* they began with only random kicks. Apparently they had forgotten what they had learned—evidence that memory is fragile early in life.

➤Response for Parents of Infants (from page 171): Constant vigilance is necessary for the first few years of a child's life, but the most dangerous age is from about 4 to 8 months, when infants can move but do not yet fear falling over an edge.

Reminders and Repetition

The lead researcher, Carolyn Rovee-Collier, developed another experiment that demonstrated that 3-month-old infants *could* remember after two weeks *if* they had a brief reminder session before being retested (Rovee-Collier & Hayne, 1987). A **reminder session** is any experience that helps people recollect an idea, a thing, or an experience.

reminder session A perceptual experience that is intended to help a person recollect an idea, a thing, or an experience, without testing whether the person remembers it at the moment.

In this particular reminder session, two weeks after the initial training, the infants watched the mobile move but were *not* tied to it and were positioned so that they could *not* kick. The next day, when they were again connected to the mobile and positioned so that they *could* move their legs, they kicked as they had learned to do two weeks earlier. Watching the mobile move on the previous day revived their faded memory. The information about making the mobile move was stored in their brains; they needed processing time to retrieve it. The reminder session provided that time.

Other research finds that repeated reminders are more powerful than single reminders (Bearce & Rovee-Collier, 2006). Photographs and videos also help consolidate early memories (Sheffield & Hudson, 2006).

A Little Older, a Little More Memory

After about 6 months, infants can retain information for longer periods of time than younger babies can, with less training, repetition, or reminding. Toward the end of the first year, many kinds of memory, including that involved in deferred imitation, are apparent (Meltzoff & Moore, 1999; Morgan & Hayne, 2007). For example, suppose a 9-month-old watches someone playing with a toy he or she has never seen before. The next day, if given the toy, the 9-month-old is likely to play with it in the same way as he or she had observed. (Younger infants do not.)

By the middle of the second year, toddlers remember and reenact more complex sequences. In one study, 16- and 20-month-olds watched an experimenter put a doll to bed, make a party hat, and clean a table (Bauer & Dow, 1994). For each activity, the experimenter used props and gave a brief "instruction" for performing each step. For instance, to clean the table, the experimenter wet it with water from a white spray bottle, saying, "Put on the water"; wiped the table with a paper towel, saying, "Wipe it"; and threw the towel in a wooden trash basket, saying, "Toss it." A week later, most toddlers carried out the sequence when they heard "Put on the water. Wipe it. Toss it." They did what they had witnessed, even when the props were different (e.g., a clear spray bottle, a sponge, and a plastic garbage can). This behavior shows that they were remembering concepts, not merely imitating actions.

NANCY SHEEHAN / PHOTOEDIT

Memory Aid Personal motivation and action are crucial to early memory, and that is why Noel has no trouble remembering which shape covers the photograph of herself as a baby.

Many other experiments also show that toddlers are thinking conceptually, not just repeating what they have experienced. The neurons of the brain change to reflect children's experiences and memories even in the first years of life (Bauer, 2007).

Aspects of Memory

Mapping brain activity patterns through fMRI and PET scans reveals that one region of the brain is devoted to memory for faces and others to memory for sounds, events, sights, phrases, and much more. Several additional brain regions also participate in these various memories. Gradual brain maturation and growth help to explain why some kinds of memories are better consolidated in infancy than others (de Haan, 2007).

An important developmental distinction can be made between *implicit memory,* which involves memories that remain hidden until a particular stimulus brings them to mind (like the reminder sessions with the mobile), and *explicit memory,* which involves memories that can be recalled on demand. Explicit memories are usually verbal, and thus "although explicit memory *emerges* sometime between 6 and 12 months, it is far from fully developed" (Nelson et al., 2006, p. 23).

➤Response for Parents (from page 172): It is important that infants have time for repeated exposure to each caregiver, because infants adjust their behavior to maximize whatever each particular caregiver affords in the way of play, emotions, and vocalization. Parents should find one steady babysitter rather than several.

The particular part of the brain that explicit memory depends on is the *hippocampus* (see Chapter 8), which is present at birth but very immature until about age 5 or 6. It is no surprise that this age coincides with the beginning of formal education, because 5- and 6-year-olds are much better at memorizing than are younger children. But implicit memories begin much earlier, which may explain why some people, places, and smells seem familiar or emotionally evocative to you, but you don't know why.

Infants probably store within their brains many emotions and sensations that they cannot readily retrieve, whereas memories of motion (dynamic perception) are remembered once that particular action is cued by the context (as when the infants remembered how to kick to make the mobile move). Once they understand words, a verbal reminder aids retrieval, even after a delay (Bauer, 2006).

➤Answer to Observation Quiz (from page 172): It is black and white, with larger objects—designed to be particularly attractive to infants, not to adult shoppers.

SUMMING UP

Infant cognition can be studied using the information-processing perspective, which analyzes each component of how thoughts begin and how they are organized, remembered, and expressed. Infant perception is powerfully influenced by particular experiences and motivation, so the affordances perceived by one infant may differ from those perceived by another. Memory depends on both experience and brain maturation. That is why memory is fragile in the first year (although it can be triggered by dynamic perception and reminders) and becomes more evident in the second year (although many types of memory remain quite fragile). ■

Language: What Develops in the First Two Years?

The acquisition of language, with its thousands of words, idiomatic phrases, grammar rules, and exceptions, differentiates *Homo sapiens* from all other species.

No other species has anything even approaching the elaborate networks of neurons—all the brain structures—that support the 6,000 human languages. Already by age 2, the human ability to communicate far surpasses that of adults of every other species. Here we describe the specific steps in early language learning and then confront the puzzle that scientists have not yet unraveled: How do infants learn to use language?

The Universal Sequence

The timing of language acquisition varies; the most advanced 10 percent of 2-year-olds speak more than 550 words, and the least advanced 10 percent speak fewer than 100 words—a fivefold difference (Merriman, 1999). (Some possible explanations for this disparity are discussed at the end of this chapter.) But, although timing varies, the sequence is the same worldwide (see Table 6.3).

Even deaf children who, with the help of cochlear implants, become able to hear before age 3 follow the sequence, again with different timing. Although they get a late start, they often catch up to their age-mates within a year or so because the process of language learning accelerates (Ertmer et al., 2007).

CORBIS / ANTHONY BANNISTER

Too Young for Language? No. The early stages of language are communication through noises, gestures, and facial expressions, very evident here between this !Kung grandmother and granddaughter.

Listening and Responding

Infants begin learning language before birth, via brain organization and auditory experiences during the final prenatal months. Newborns look closely at facial expression and prefer to hear speech over other sounds. Infants demonstrate early preferences for the sights and sounds that humans use to communicate. By 6 months, infants can distinguish, just by looking at someone's mouth movements (without sound), whether that person is speaking their native language or not (Weikum et al., 2007).

Careful analysis has found that how adults interact with babies is distinct in many ways from adult-only interaction (Falk, 2004). For instance, adults talk to babies with higher pitch, simpler words, repetition, exaggerated tone, and varied speed. This special language form is sometimes called *baby talk,* since it is talk

TABLE 6.3

AT ABOUT THIS TIME: The Development of Spoken Language in the First Two Years

Age*	Means of Communication
Newborn	Reflexive communication—cries, movements, facial expressions
2 months	A range of meaningful noises—cooing, fussing, crying, laughing
3–6 months	New sounds, including squeals, growls, croons, trills, vowel sounds
6–10 months	Babbling, including both consonant and vowel sounds repeated in syllables
10–12 months	Comprehension of simple words; speechlike intonations; specific vocalizations that have meaning to those who know the infant well. Deaf babies express their first signs; hearing babies also use specific gestures (e.g., pointing) to communicate.
12 months	First spoken words that are recognizably part of the native language
13–18 months	Slow growth of vocabulary, up to about 50 words
18 months	Naming explosion—three or more words learned per day. Much variation: Some toddlers do not yet speak.
21 months	First two-word sentence
24 months	Multiword sentences. Half the toddler's utterances are two or more words long.

*The ages of accomplishment in this table reflect norms. Many healthy children with normal intelligence attain these steps in language development earlier or later than indicated here.
Source: Bloom, 1993, 1998; Fenson et al., 2000; Lenneberg, 1967.

STOCK CONNECTION DISTRIBUTION / ALAMY

Lip-Reading Communication begins in early infancy. Infants closely watch speakers' mouth movements and facial expressions. By this baby's age, 5 months, bilingual infants can tell by looking who is speaking French and who is speaking English.

directed toward babies; it is also sometimes called *motherese,* since mothers universally speak it. Both these terms have misleading implications, so scientists prefer the more formal term **child-directed speech.**

child-directed speech The high-pitched, simplified, and repetitive way adults speak to infants. (Also called *baby talk* or *motherese.*)

No matter what it is called, child-directed speech fosters early language learning. Even at 7 months, infants begin to recognize words, but only words that are highly distinctive (Singh, 2008). For instance, they might distinguish the words *bottle, dog,* and *mama* before they can differentiate words that sound much more alike—such as *baby, Bobbie,* and *Barbie.*

Infants respond to adult noises and expressions (as well as to their own internal pleasures and pains) with a variety of vocal sounds. Responses gradually expand beyond crying and cooing. By 4 months, most babies will also squeal, growl, gurgle, grunt, croon, and yell, telling everyone within earshot what is on their minds.

Also within the first months, listening becomes more selective. Not only do infants prefer child-directed speech, they like alliterative sounds (Hayes & Slater, 2008), in which a letter or syllable is repeated; they also love songs, which are typically filled with rhymes, repetition, and varied pitch (Schön et al., 2008). Think of the alliteration in your favorite lullaby ("Rock-a-*b*ye *b*aby," for example) and you will recognize that speech to babies emphasizes simple sounds more than content.

Babbling

babbling The extended repetition of certain syllables, such as *ba-ba-ba,* that begins when babies are between 6 and 9 months old.

At between 6 and 9 months, babies begin to repeat certain syllables (*ma-ma-ma, da-da-da, ba-ba-ba*), a phenomenon referred to as **babbling** because of the way it sounds. Babbling is experience-expectant; all babies do it, even deaf ones—at least at first. Responses from other people encourage babbling (remember, this is the age of "making interesting events last"). Deaf babies stop babbling (because they cannot hear responses) and hearing babies continue. All babies make rhythmic gestures, waving their arms as they babble, again in response to the actions of others (Iverson & Fagan, 2004). Toward the end of the first year, babbling begins to sound like the infant's native language; infants imitate the accents, consonants, and other aspects of the language that they hear.

Especially for Nurses and Pediatricians (see response, page 178): The parents of a 6-month-old have just been told that their child is deaf. They don't believe it, because, as they tell you, the baby babbles as much as their other children did. What do you tell them?

Videotapes of deaf infants whose parents use sign language with them show that 10-month-olds use about a dozen distinct hand gestures in a repetitive manner similar to babbling. All babies express concepts with gestures sooner than with speech (Goldin-Meadow, 2006).

Parents of many hearing babies use hand signs to allow early communication months before the first spoken words (Pizer at al., 2007). For example, adults sign "I love you" accompanied by smiles of affection, and soon babies sign it back.

Happy Talk Ty's mother and the teacher demonstrate the sign for "more" in a sign-language class at the public library in Hudson, Florida. Ty takes the lesson very seriously: Learning language in any form is crucial for 1-year-olds.

NEWSCOM

Pointing is an advanced gesture that requires understanding another person's perspective. Most animals cannot interpret pointing; most humans can do so at 10 months. This is one of the intriguing aspects of human development, since pointing indicates a strong preference for social interaction (Tomasello et al., 2007).

First Words

Finally, at about 1 year of age, the average baby communicates with a few words. Usually, caregivers understand the first word before strangers do, which makes it hard for researchers to pinpoint exactly what a 12-month-old can say. For example, a 13-month-old named Kyle knew standard words such as *mama,* but he also knew *da, ba, tam, opma,* and *daes,* which his parents knew to be, respectively, "downstairs," "bottle," "tummy," "oatmeal," and "starfish" (yes, that's what *daes* meant!) (Lewis et al., 1999).

In the first months of the second year, spoken vocabulary increases very gradually, at a rate of perhaps one new word a week. However, 6- to 15-month-olds learn meanings rapidly; they understand about 10 times more words than they speak (Schafer, 2005; Snow, 2006).

The first words soon take on nuances of tone, loudness, and cadence that are precursors of the first grammar. A single word can convey many messages by the way it is spoken. Imagine meaning in "Dada!" and "Dada?" and "Dada." Each is a **holophrase,** a single word spoken in such a way that it expresses a complete, meaningful thought (Tomasello, 2006).

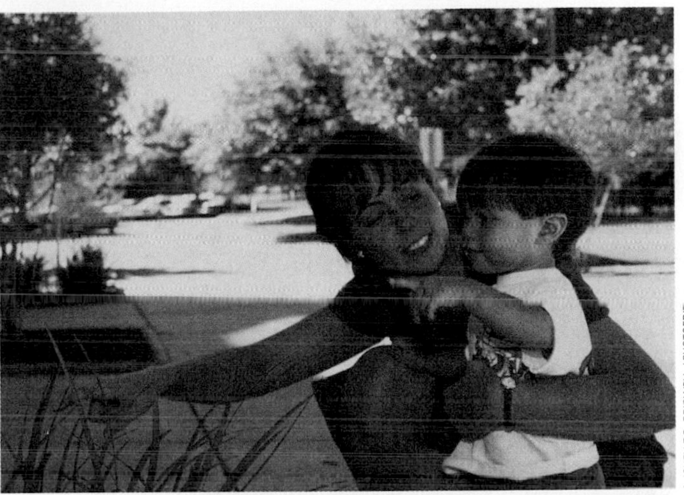

MICHELLE D. BRIDWELL / PHOTOEDIT

Show Me Where Pointing is one of the earliest forms of communication, emerging at about 10 months. As Carlos's mother demonstrates, accurate pointing requires a basic understanding of social interaction, because the pointer needs to take the observer's angle of vision into account.

Intonation (variation of tone and pitch) is extensive in babbling and again in holophrases at about 18 months, with a dip in between (at about 12 months). At that one-year point, infants seem to reorganize their vocalization from universal to language-specific (Snow, 2006). They are no longer just singing and talking to themselves (babbling) but communicating with others (uttering holophrases).

The Naming Explosion

Once vocabulary reaches about 50 *expressed* words (as distinct from understood words, which are far more extensive), it builds rapidly, at a rate of 50 to 100 words per month; 21-month-olds say twice as many words as 18-month-olds (Adamson & Bakeman, 2006). This language spurt is called the **naming explosion,** because many of the early words are nouns, although the word *noun* refers to a linguistic category, not an infant's vocabulary, which includes noun-like adjectives (e.g., "bouncing" uttered by itself can mean "ball") (Waxman & Lidz, 2006).

holophrase A single word that is used to express a complete, meaningful thought.

naming explosion A sudden increase in an infant's vocabulary, especially in the number of nouns, that begins at about 18 months of age.

In almost every language, the name of each significant caregiver (often *dada, mama, nana, papa, baba, tata*), sibling, and sometimes pet is learned between 12 and 18 months (Bloom, 1998). (See Appendix A, p. A-4.) Other frequently uttered words refer to the child's favorite foods (*nana* can be *banana* as well as *grandma*) and to elimination (*pee-pee, wee-wee, poo-poo, ka-ka, doo-doo*).

No doubt you have noticed that all these words have a similar structure: two identical syllables, each a consonant followed by a vowel sound. Many more words follow that pattern—not just *baba* but also *bobo, bebe, bubu, bibi*. Others are slightly more complicated—not just *mama* but also *ma-me, ama,* and so on.

Especially for Caregivers (see response, page 179): A toddler calls two people "Mama." Is this a sign of confusion?

Cultural Differences

Cultures and families vary a great deal in how much child-directed speech children hear. Some parents read to their infants, teach them signs that communicate, and respond to every noise as if it is an attempt to talk. Others are much less verbal, using gestures, touch, and tone, saying "Hush" and "No" instead of repeating words that the toddler says.

The idea that children should be "seen but not heard" is contrary to the emphasis on communication in many U.S. families. However, it is widespread among other families, including some Latino families in the United States (Cabrera et al., 2006), and among many fathers, especially those of low SES (Lamb, 2004).

Since I am a mother with a particular SES and cultural background, it is no surprise that I spoke, sang, and read to my children before age 1. But as a developmental scientist, I know that some assumptions about child care are social constructions, not adaptive in every culture and cohort. Although many families appreciate a talkative child, many other families do not.

JORGEN SCHYTTE / PETER ARNOLD

Where in the World? Different cultures influence children's language learning in different ways. Children who spend a lot of time with adults receive abundant exposure to the unique speech patterns of their culture.

Observation Quiz (see answer, page 181): What elements in this photograph suggest cultural differences between this family and most European or North American ones?

Verb-Friendly Languages Although all new talkers say names, use similar sounds, and say more nouns than any other part of speech, the ratio of nouns to verbs and adjectives varies from place to place. For example, by 18 months, English-speaking infants use relatively more nouns but fewer verbs than Chinese or Korean infants do. Why?

One explanation goes back to the language itself. Chinese and Korean are "verb-friendly," in that verbs are placed at the beginning or end of sentences and are thus easier to learn. In English, verbs occur in various positions within sentences, and their forms sometimes change in illogical ways (e.g., *go, went, gone, will go*). This irregularity makes English verbs harder to learn than nouns (Gentner & Boroditsky, 2001).

An alternative explanation for cultural differences in the proportion of nouns and verbs considers the entire social context: Playing with a variety of toys and learning about dozens of objects are crucial in North American culture, whereas East Asian cultures emphasize human interactions—specifically, how one person responds to another. Accordingly, North American infants are expected to name many objects, whereas Asian infants are expected to encode social interactions into language. Thus, a Chinese toddler might learn the Chinese equivalent of *come, play, love, carry, run,* and so on before a Canadian one learns these words. This is the result of experience, not genes. A toddler of Chinese heritage, growing up in an English-speaking Canadian home, has the same language-learning patterns as other Canadian toddlers.

➤Response for Nurses and Pediatricians (from page 176): Urge the parents to begin learning sign language immediately and investigate the possibility of cochlear implants. Babbling has a biological basis and begins at a specified time, in deaf as well as hearing babies. However, deaf babies eventually begin to use gestures more and to vocalize less than hearing babies. If their infant can hear, sign language does no harm. If the child is deaf, however, non-communication may be devastating.

Concepts and Language Every language has some concepts that are easy and some that are hard for infants. English-speaking infants confuse *before* and *after;* Dutch-speaking infants misuse *out* when it refers to taking off clothes; Korean infants need to learn two meanings of *in* (Mandler, 2004). Learning adjectives is easier in Italian and Spanish than in English or French because of patterns in those languages (Waxman & Lidz, 2006). Specifically, adjectives can stand by themselves without the nouns. If I want a blue cup from a group of multicolored cups, I would ask for "a blue cup" or "a blue one" in English but simply "uno azul" (a blue) in Spanish. Despite such variations, in every language, infants demonstrate impressive speed and efficiency in acquiring both vocabulary and grammar (Bornstein et al., 2004).

In comparing cultures, it is crucial to remember that language encodes cultural values and social constructions (Chiu et al., 2007). If a child is more referential (saying words that refer to objects) than expressive (saying words that refer to emotions), that preference reflects the values and priorities of the parents.

Putting Words Together

grammar All the methods—word order, verb forms, and so on—that languages use to communicate meaning, apart from the words themselves.

Grammar includes all the methods that languages use to communicate meaning. Word order, prefixes, suffixes, intonation, verb forms, pronouns, and other parts of speech—all of these are aspects of grammar. Grammar is obvious when two-word combinations begin, at about 21 months. These sentences follow the word order "Baby cry" or "More juice," rather than the reverse. Soon the child is combining three words, usually in subject–verb–object order in English (for example, "Mommy read book"), rather than any of the five other possible sequences of those words.

A child's grammar correlates with the size of his or her vocabulary (Snow, 2006). The child who says "Baby is crying" is advanced in language development compared with the child who says "Baby crying" or simply the holophrase "Baby" (Dionne et al., 2003). Comprehension advances as well. Their expanding knowledge of both vocabulary and grammar helps toddlers understand what others are saying (Kedar et al., 2006).

Sometimes listening to two languages slows down grammar, as children take longer to understand how words should be combined. However, "development in each language proceeds separately and in a language-specific manner" (Conboy & Thal, 2006, p. 727).

Children can master two languages, but the crucial variable is how much speech in both languages the child hears. If children know that a particular person speaks only one language, then by age 2 they will answer accordingly. Most young bilingual children have parents who also are bilingual, and these children mix vocabularies and switch grammars because they expect the parents to be able to understand.

➤Response for Caregivers (from page 177): Not at all. Toddlers hear several people called "Mama" (their own mother, their grandmothers, their cousins' and friends' mothers) and experience mothering from several people, so it is not surprising if they use "Mama" too broadly. They will eventually narrow the label down to the one correct person.

Theories of Language Learning

Worldwide, people who are not yet 2 years old already use language well. Their acquisition of language is so impressive that, by adolescence, some of them compose lyrics or deliver orations that move thousands of their co-linguists. How is language learned so easily and so well?

Answers come from three schools of thought, each of which is connected to a theory—namely, behaviorism, epigenetic theory, and sociocultural theory. The first says that infants learn language because they are directly taught, the second that infants naturally understand language, and the third that social impulses propel infants to communicate.

Parents and teachers want children to speak fluently, but no one wants to waste time teaching something that infants either cannot learn or will learn on their own. Which theory should guide them?

Theory One: Infants Need to Be Taught

The seeds of the first theory were planted more than 50 years ago, when the dominant theory in North American psychology was behaviorism, or learning theory. The essential idea was that all learning is acquired, step by step, through association and

Especially for Nurses and Pediatricians (see response, page 181): Bob and Joan have been reading about language development in children. They are convinced that language is "hardwired," so they need not talk to their 6-month old son. How do you respond?

WOLFGANG KAEHLER / CORBIS

Cultural Values If they are typical of most families in the relatively taciturn Otavalo culture of Ecuador, these three children hear significantly less conversation than children elsewhere. In most Western cultures, that might be called maltreatment. However, each culture encourages the qualities it values, and verbal fluency is not a priority in this community. In fact, people who talk too much are ostracized and those who keep secrets are valued, so encouragement of talking may constitute maltreatment in the Otavalo culture.

Research Design

Scientists: Helen Raikes, Barbara Alexander Pan, Gayle Luze, Catherine S. Tamis-Lamonda, Jeanne Brooks-Gunn, Jill Constantine, et al.

Publication: *Child Development* (2006).

Participants: From 17 Early Head Start programs, 2,581 mother–infant pairs were interviewed. All were low income; 26 percent were married; 53 percent were high school graduates. About a third each were Americans of European, African, and Hispanic heritage.

Design: When the infants were 14, 24, and 36 months old, their language ability was measured and the mothers were asked how often they read to them and how many books the babies had. The children's language abilities were compared to 15 variables.

Major conclusions: Being read to correlated with language, but early reading (at 14 months) was not as strong a predictor of future language scores as were two other factors, maternal warmth and education. By 36 months, children whose mothers read to them often were quite verbal.

Comment: The size and diversity of this sample add to confidence in the conclusions. Being read to as a baby is one of many factors that foster language. Various details of this study could be used to support all three theories of language learning discussed here.

reinforcement. Just as Pavlov's dogs learned to associate a sound with the presentation of food (see Chapter 2), behaviorists believe that infants associate objects with words they have heard often, especially if reinforcement occurs.

B. F. Skinner (1957) noticed that spontaneous babbling is usually reinforced. Typically, every time the baby says "ma-ma-ma-ma," a grinning mother appears, repeating the sound as well as showering the baby with attention, praise, and perhaps food. These affordances of mothers are exactly what infants want. To achieve that, babies repeat those sounds, and, via operant conditioning, talking begins.

Most parents worldwide are excellent instructors, responding to their infants' gestures and sounds (Gros-Louis et al., 2006). Even in preliterate societies, parents use child-directed speech, responding quickly with a high-pitched voice, short sentences, stressed nouns, and simple grammar—exactly the techniques that behaviorists would recommend.

The core ideas of this theory are the following:

- Parents are expert teachers, although other caregivers help them teach children to speak.
- Frequent repetition of words is instructive, especially when they are linked to daily life.
- Well-taught infants become well-spoken children.

Behaviorists note that some 3-year-olds converse in elaborate sentences; others just barely put one simple word with another. Such variations correlate with the amount of language teaching the child receives and, eventually, with adult intelligence (Fagan et al., 2007). Parents of the most verbally adept children teach language throughout infancy—singing, explaining, listening, responding, and reading to them every day, even before age 1 (Raikes et al., 2006; see the Research Design).

In one large study in Australia, parents who provided extensive language exposure before age 1 had children who spoke early and well (Reilly et al., 2006). In a detailed U.S. study, researchers analyzed the language that mothers (all middle-class) used with their preverbal infants, aged 9 to 17 months (Tamis-Lamonda et al., 2001).

Variation was evident in both studies. In the U.S. study, one mother never imitated her infant's babbling; another mother imitated 21 times in 10 minutes, babbling back as if in conversation. Overall, mothers were most likely to describe things or actions (e.g., "That is a spoon you are holding—spoon"). The range was vast: In 10 minutes, one mother gave only 4 descriptions, while another provided her baby with 33 descriptions.

The frequency of maternal responsiveness at 9 months predicted infants' language many months later (see Figure 6.1). It was

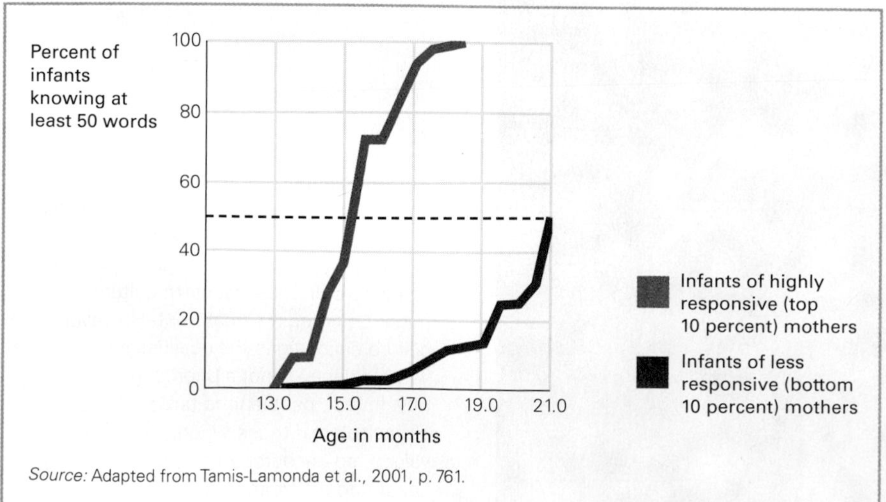

Source: Adapted from Tamis-Lamonda et al., 2001, p. 761.

FIGURE 6.1

Maternal Responsiveness and Infants' Language Acquisition Learning the first 50 words is a milestone in early language acquisition, as it predicts the arrival of the naming explosion and the multiword sentence a few weeks later. Researchers found that the 9-month-old infants of highly responsive mothers (top 10 percent) reached this milestone as early as 15 months. The infants of nonresponsive mothers (bottom 10 percent) lagged significantly behind.

not that noisy infants, whose genes would soon make them start talking, elicited more talk. Some quiet infants had mothers who talked a lot—suggesting play activities, describing things, and asking questions. Quiet infants with talkative mothers usually became talkative later on.

This research is in keeping with the behaviorist theory that adults teach language and infants learn it. According to this perspective, if adults want children who speak, understand, and (later) read well, they must talk to their babies.

Theory Two: Infants Teach Themselves

A contrary theory holds that language learning is innate; adults need not teach it. The seeds of this perspective were planted soon after Skinner proposed his theory of verbal learning. Noam Chomsky (1968, 1980) and his followers believe that language is too complex to be mastered merely through step-by-step conditioning. While behaviorists focus on variations among children in their vocabulary size, Chomsky focuses on similarities in language acquisition.

Noting that all young children master basic grammar at about the same age, Chomsky cited this *universal grammar* as evidence that humans are born with a mental structure that prepares them to incorporate some elements of human language—for example, the use of a raised tone at the end of an utterance to indicate a question. Chomsky labeled this hypothesized mental structure the **language acquisition device,** or **LAD.** The LAD enables children to derive the rules of grammar quickly and effectively from the speech they hear every day, regardless of whether their native language is English, Thai, or Urdu.

Other scholars agree with Chomsky that infants are innately ready to use their minds to understand and speak whatever language is offered. This idea does not strip languages and cultures of their surface differences in sounds, grammar, and almost everything else; the point is that "language is a window on human nature, exposing deep and universal features of our thoughts and feelings" (Pinker, 2007, p. 148).

The various languages of the world are all logical, coherent, and systematic. Infants are primed to grasp the particular language they are exposed to, making caregiver speech "not a 'trigger' but a 'nutrient'" (Slobin, 2001, p. 438). There is no need for a trigger, according to theory two, because words are "expected" by the developing brain, which quickly and efficiently connects neurons to support whichever particular language the infant hears.

Research supports this perspective as well. As you remember, newborns are primed to listen to speech (Vouloumanos & Werker, 2007), and all infants babble *ma-ma* and *da-da* sounds (not yet referring to mother or father). No reinforcement or teaching is needed; infants merely need dendrites to grow, mouth muscles to strengthen, neurons to connect, and speech to be heard.

Nature also provides for deaf infants. All 6-month-olds, hearing or not, would rather look at sign language than at nonlinguistic pantomime. For hearing infants, this preference disappears by 10 months, because their affinity for gestural language is no longer needed (Krentz & Corina, 2008). Deaf infants are signing by then.

Theory Three: Social Impulses Foster Infant Language Learning

The third theory is called *social-pragmatic* because it perceives the crucial starting point to be neither vocabulary reinforcement (behaviorism) nor the innate connection (epigenetic) but rather the social reason for language: communication. According to this perspective—which is an extension of sociocultural theory—infants communicate in every way they can because humans are social beings, dependent on one another for survival, well-being, and joy.

➤Answer to Observation Quiz (from page 170): At least four elements are unusual in today's Western families: large size (four children), a child held in the mother's lap to eat (i.e., no high chair for the baby), the father pouring for everyone, and the fact that the whole family, including teenagers, is eating together. A fifth aspect, that they are *all* drinking Coke, is more typical in Africa than in North America. This family lives in Mozambique.

language acquisition device (LAD) Chomsky's term for a hypothesized mental structure that enables humans to learn language, including the basic aspects of grammar, vocabulary, and intonation.

➤Response for Nurses and Pediatricians (from page 179): While much of language development is indeed hardwired, many experts assert that exposure to language is required. You don't need to convince Bob and Joan of this point, though—just convince them that their baby will be happier if they talk to him.

BRAND X PICTURES / ALAMY

Not Talking? No words yet, but this boy communicates well with Dad, using eyes, mouth, and hands. What are they telling each other?

The Social Newborn Newborns look searchingly at human faces and listen intently to human voices because they seek to respond to emotions, not because they want to know content. By 9 months, infant brain patterns and heart rates indicate attention when people talk to them, again without understanding content but with awareness that they are the focus of attention (Santesso et al., 2007).

It is the emotional messages of speech, not the words, that are the focus of early communication. In one study, people who had never heard English (Shuar hunter-farmers living in remote foothills of the Andes Mountains in Ecuador) listened to tapes of North American mothers talking to their babies. The Shuar successfully distinguished among speech conveying comfort, approval, attention, and prohibition, without knowing any of the words (Bryant & Barrett, 2007).

It is easy to believe that early communication is primarily social. Before age 1, infants vocalize, babble, gesture, listen, and point—with an outstretched little index finger that is soon accompanied by a very sophisticated glance to see if the other person is looking at the right spot (Tomasello et al., 2007). These and many other examples show that communication is the servant of social interaction (Bloom, 1998; Hoehl et al., 2008).

The Social Toddler Here is an experiment. Suppose an 18-month-old is playing with an unnamed toy and an adult utters a word. Does the child connect that word to the toy? A behaviorist's learning-by-association prediction would be yes, but the true answer is no. When toddlers played with a fascinating toy and adults said a word, the toddlers looked up, figured out what the adult was looking at, and assigned the new word to that, not to the fascinating toy (Baldwin, 1993). This supports theory three: The toddlers were socially focused.

Another study also suggests social learning. Many 1-year-olds enjoy watching television, becoming absorbed in programs like *Teletubbies,* but they probably do not learn much from it. In a controlled experiment, 1-year-olds learned vocabulary much better when someone taught them in person rather than on a video. This suggests personal, social language acquisition, not impersonal learning (Krcmar et al., 2007).

According to theory three, then, social impulses—not explicit teaching or brain maturation (as in the first two perspectives, respectively)—lead infants to learn language, "as part of the package of being a human social animal" (Hollich et al., 2000). They seek to understand what others want and intend, and therefore "children acquire linguistic symbols as a kind of by-product of social action with adults" (Tomasello, 2001, p. 135).

A Hybrid Theory

Which of these three perspectives is correct? As you can see, each position has been supported by research. Scholars have attempted to integrate all three perspectives. In one monograph based on 12 experiments designed by eight researchers (Hollich et al., 2000), the authors presented a hybrid (which literally means "a new creature, formed by combining other living things") of previous theories.

They noted that children learn language to do numerous things—indicate intention, call objects by name, put words together, talk to family members, sing to themselves, express their wishes, remember the past, and much more. Therefore, the scientists hypothesize that learning some aspects of language is best explained by one theory at one age and other aspects by another perspective at another age.

For example, the name of the family dog may be learned by association and repetition, with family members and eventually the dog itself reinforcing the name, a behaviorist process. However, the distinction between *cat* and *dog* may reflect a neurological predilection (epigenetic), which means that the human brain may be genetically wired to differentiate those species. The very fact that infants allow themselves to be licked by a dog may reflect an inborn joy in social interaction (sociopragmatic).

Which theory do you think explains the fact that the 6-month-old's ability to hear a difference in sounds predicts that child's ability to talk at 13 months, 18 months, and 24 months? This could be the result of listening to many words (behaviorist), of inborn potential (epigenetic), or of social impulses (sociocultural). After intensive study, the scientists who reported that the ability to hear differences leads to speaking proficiently endorsed a hybrid theory, concluding that "multiple attentional, social and linguistic cues" contribute to early language (Tsao et al., 2004, p. 1081).

In another study supporting the hybrid theory, 10-month-old infants looked at objects, presented in pairs, that they had never seen before. One of each pair was fascinating to babies and the other was boring, specifically "a blue sparkle wand . . . [paired with] a white cabinet latch . . . a red, green, and pink party clacker . . . [paired with] a beige bottle opener" (Pruden et al., 2006, p. 267). The experimenter said a made-up name (not an actual word), and then the infants were tested to see if they assigned the word to the object that had the experimenter's attention (the dull one) or the one that was interesting to the child. Remember that 18-month-old toddlers in an earlier experiment chose the object that the experimenters looked at. However, this time 10-month-olds seemed to assign the word to the fascinating object, not the dull one.

These researchers interpreted their experiment as supporting the idea that *how* language is learned depends on the age of the child as well as on the particular circumstances. Behaviorism works to explain language acquisition for young children, social learning for slightly older ones. As the research team expressed it: "The perceptually driven 10-month-old becomes the socially aware 19-month-old" (Pruden et al., 2006, p. 278).

It makes logical and practical sense for nature to provide several paths toward language learning and for various theorists to emphasize one or another (Sebastián-Gallés, 2007). Indeed, although child-directed speech is an ideal way for children to learn, some cultures do not encourage adults to talk to preverbal infants. Fortunately, an alternate route is available: Babies learn from overhearing adults speak to each other (Floor & Akhtar, 2006; Soderstrom, 2007). Each mode of learning may be preferred or more efficient in some stages, cultures, and families, but virtually all children learn to communicate with the words and grammar of their native tongue (Bornstein et al., 2004).

Language acquisition theories and researchers need to take all kinds of development into account. Many do. As one expert concludes:

> In the current view, our best hope for unraveling some of the mysteries of language acquisition rests with approaches that incorporate multiple factors, that is, with approaches that incorporate not only some explicit linguistic model, but also the full range of biological, cultural, and psycholinguistic processes involved.
>
> *[Tomasello, 2006, p. 292–293]*

Infants are active learners not only of language, as just outlined, and of the concepts explained in the first half of this chapter but also of the motor skills detailed in Chapter 5 and the social and emotional understanding to be described in Chapter 7. Uncle Henry was very much mistaken.

Especially for Educators (see response, page 184): An infant day-care center has a new child whose parents speak a language other than the one the teachers speak. Should the teachers learn basic words in the new language, or should they expect the baby to learn the majority language?

➤Response for Educators (from page 183): Probably both. Infants love to communicate, and they seek every possible way to do so. Therefore, the teachers should try to understand the baby, and the baby's parents, but should also start teaching the baby the majority language of the school.

SUMMING UP

From the first days of life, babies attend to words and expressions, responding as well as their limited abilities allow—crying, cooing, and soon babbling. Before age 1, they understand simple words and communicate with gestures. At 1 year, most infants speak. Vocabulary accumulates slowly at first, but then more rapidly with the naming explosion and with the emergence of the holophrase and the two-word sentence.

The impressive language learning of the first two years can be explained in many ways. One theory contends that caregivers must teach language, reinforcing the infant's vocal expressions. Another theory relies on the idea of an inborn language acquisition device, a mental structure that facilitates the acquisition of language as soon as maturation makes that possible. A third theory stresses social interaction, implying that infants learn language because they are social beings. A hybrid model combines all three of these theories. Because infants vary in culture, learning style, and social context, the hybrid theory acknowledges that each of the other theories may have some validity at different points in the acquisition of language. ■

SUMMARY

Sensorimotor Intelligence

1. Piaget realized that very young infants are active learners, seeking to understand their complex observations and experiences. Adaptation in infancy is characterized by sensorimotor intelligence, the first of Piaget's four stages of cognitive development. At every time of their lives, people adapt their thoughts to the experiences they have.

2. Sensorimotor intelligence develops in six stages—three pairs of two stages each—beginning with reflexes and ending with the toddler's active exploration and use of mental combinations. In each pair of stages, development occurs in one of three types of circular reactions, or feedback loops, in which the infant takes in experiences and tries to make sense of them.

3. Reflexes provide the foundation for intelligence. The continual process of assimilation and accommodation is evident in the first acquired adaptations, from 1 to 4 months. The sucking reflex accommodates the particular nipples and other objects that the baby learns to suck. Over the next year, infants become more goal-oriented, creative, and experimental as "little scientists."

4. Infants gradually develop an understanding of objects in their first two years of life. As shown in Piaget's classic experiment, infants understand object permanence and begin to search for hidden objects at about 8 months. Other research finds that Piaget underestimated the cognition of young infants.

Information Processing

5. Another approach to understanding infant cognition is information-processing theory, which looks at each step of the thinking process, from input to output. The perceptions of a young infant are attuned to the particular affordances, or opportunities for action, that are present in the infant's world.

6. Objects that move are particularly interesting to infants, as are other humans. Objects as well as people afford many possibilities for interaction and perception, and therefore these affordances enhance early cognition.

7. Infant memory is fragile but not completely absent. Reminder sessions help trigger memories, and young brains learn motor sequences long before they can remember with words. Memory is multifaceted; explicit memories are rare in infancy.

Language: What Develops in the First Two Years?

8. Eager attempts to communicate are apparent in the first year. Infants babble at about 6 to 9 months, understand words and gestures by 10 months, and speak their first words at about 1 year.

9. Vocabulary begins to build very slowly until the infant knows approximately 50 words. Then a naming explosion begins. Toward the end of the second year, toddlers begin putting two words together, showing by their word order that they understand the rudiments of grammar.

10. Various theories attempt to explain how infants learn language as quickly as they do. The three main theories emphasize different aspects of early language learning: that infants must be taught, that their brains are genetically attuned to language, and that their social impulses foster language learning.

11. Each of these theories seems partly true. The challenge for developmental scientists has been to formulate a hybrid theory that uses all the insights and research on early language learning. The challenge for caregivers is to respond appropriately to the infant's early attempts to communicate.

KEY TERMS

sensorimotor intelligence (p. 161)
primary circular reactions (p. 162)
secondary circular reactions (p. 163)
object permanence (p. 163)
tertiary circular reactions (p. 165)
"little scientist" (p. 165)
deferred imitation (p. 166)
habituation (p. 166)
fMRI (p. 167)
information processing theory (p. 168)
affordance (p. 169)
visual cliff (p. 170)
dynamic perception (p. 171)
people preference (p. 171)
reminder session (p. 173)
child-directed speech (p. 176)
babbling (p. 176)
holophrase (p. 177)
naming explosion (p. 177)
grammar (p. 178)
language acquisition device (LAD) (p. 181)

KEY QUESTIONS

1. Why is Piaget's first period of cognitive development called sensorimotor intelligence? Give examples.

2. Give examples of some things that adults learn via sensorimotor intelligence.

3. What does the active experimentation of the stage-five toddler suggest for parents?

4. Why are some researchers concerned that so much emphasis is being placed on early brain development?

5. How do researchers figure out whether an infant has a concept of something even if the infant cannot talk about it yet?

6. What does research on affordances suggest about cognitive differences between one infant and another?

7. Why would a child remember very little about experiences in infancy?

8. What indicates that toddlers use some grammar?

9. How do deaf and hearing babies compare in early language learning?

10. How would a caregiver who subscribes to the behaviorist theory of language learning respond when an infant babbles?

11. According to the sociocultural theory of language learning, what might explain why an 18-month-old is not yet talking?

12. What does the hybrid model of language learning suggest to caregivers?

APPLICATIONS

1. Elicit vocalizations from an infant—babbling if the baby is under age 1, using words if older. Write down all the baby says for 10 minutes. Then ask the primary caregiver to elicit vocalizations for 10 minutes, and write these down. What differences are apparent between the baby's two attempts at communication? Compare your findings with the norms described in the chapter.

2. Piaget's definition of intelligence is adaptation. Others consider a good memory or an extensive vocabulary to be a sign of intelligence. How would you define intelligence? Give examples.

3. Many educators recommend that parents read to babies even before the babies begin talking. What theory of language development does this reflect?

4. Test an infant's ability to search for a hidden object. Ideally, the infant should be about 7 or 8 months old, and you should retest over a period of weeks. If the infant can immediately find the object, make the task harder by pausing between the hiding and the searching or by secretly moving the object from one hiding place to another.

7

CHAPTER OUTLINE

The First Two Years: Psychosocial Development

As I sat on a crowded subway car, a young woman boarded with an infant, about 8 months old, in one arm and a heavy shopping bag on the other. She stood in front of me, trying to steady herself as the train started to move. "Can I help?" I asked. Wordlessly she handed me . . . the baby. I began softly singing a children's song. The baby was quiet, neither crying nor smiling, keeping her eyes intently on her mother. We traveled for about 10 minutes, with the baby wary but not crying, and with me wondering why I was holding a living human being rather than the mother's shopping bag.

Adults express cultural and personal values as they provide various experiences for infants, and each individual reacts with his or her particular emotions. That is the basis of psychosocial development. I was happy the baby on my lap was quiet. I did not expect her to smile, as she was about the age when infants recognize strangers as such. All three of us were part of a psychosocial interaction; our reactions were affected by our ages, past experiences, and circumstances.

This chapter opens by tracing infants' emotions as their brains mature and their experiences accumulate over the first two years. Then we review the five major theories that were first described in Chapter 2, focusing on how each describes psychosocial development during infancy. Toilet training, temperament, and ethnotheories are included in that section. This leads to an exploration of caregiver–infant interaction, particularly the concepts of *synchrony, attachment,* and *social referencing*—all pivotal to psychosocial development. For each of these aspects of caregiving, we consider fathers as well as mothers.

We then weigh the pros and cons of infant day care (a common experience for babies worldwide), paying special attention to its impact on psychosocial development. The chapter ends with practical suggestions for stimulating the healthy emotional growth of very young children. That subway mother may have made a wise choice in handing me her baby—just not the choice I would have expected.

TABLE 7.1

AT ABOUT THIS TIME: Ages When Emotions Emerge

Age	Emotional Expression
Birth	Crying; contentment
6 weeks	Social smile
3 months	Laughter; curiosity
4 months	Full, responsive smiles
4–8 months	Anger
9–14 months	Fear of social events (strangers, separation from caregiver)
12 months	Fear of unexpected sights and sounds
18 months	Self-awareness; pride; shame; embarrassment

As always, culture and experience influence the norms of development. This is especially true for emotional development after the first 8 months.

Emotional Development

Within the first two years, infants progress from reactive pain and pleasure to complex patterns of social awareness (see Table 7.1). This is the period of life with "high emotional responsiveness" (Izard et al., 2002, p. 767), expressed in speedy, uncensored reactions—crying, startling, laughing, raging—and, by toddlerhood, complex responses, from self-satisfied grins to mournful pouts.

Infants' Emotions

At first there is pleasure and pain. Newborns look happy and relaxed when fed and drifting off to sleep. They cry when they are hurt or hungry, are tired or frightened (as by a loud noise or a sudden loss of support), or are suffering from *colic,* the recurrent bouts of uncontrollable crying and irritability that afflict about a third of all infants in the early months.

Smiling and Laughing

social smile A smile evoked by a human face, normally evident in infants about 6 weeks after birth.

Soon, additional emotions become recognizable (Lavelli & Fogel, 2005). Curiosity is evident as infants distinguish the unusual from the familiar. Happiness is expressed by the **social smile,** a smile evoked by a human face at about 6 weeks. Soon laughter appears, at about 3 or 4 months. Infants worldwide express social joy (at people, not just things) between 2 and 4 months (Konner, 2007).

The sound of a baby's laugh pleases most adults, which is one reason parents, and even adept strangers, encourage it. Among the Navajo, whoever brings forth that first laugh gives a feast to celebrate that the baby is becoming a person (Rogoff, 2003). Laughter builds as curiosity does; a typical 6-month-old laughs loudly upon discovering new things, particularly social experiences that have the right balance between familiarity and surprise, such as Daddy making a funny face.

GERI ENGBERG / THE IMAGE WORKS

Friendship Begins Emotions connect friends to each other—these two 1-year-olds as well as friends of any age. The shared smiles indicate a strong social connection. What will they do next?

Anger and Sadness

Anger is evident at 6 months, usually triggered by frustration. It is most apparent when infants are prevented from reaching a graspable object they want or moving as they wish (Plutchik, 2003). Infants hate to be strapped in, caged in, closed in, or even just held tightly on someone's lap when they want to explore.

Anger in infancy is a healthy response to frustration, unlike sadness, which also appears in the first months. Sadness indicates withdrawal and is accompanied by an increase in the body's production of *cortisol,* a stress hormone (Lewis & Ramsay, 2005).

It is more difficult to conduct reliable hormone assays with infants than with older people, so not all the hormonal changes that accompany infant emotions are known. However, the fact that sadness is accompanied by signs of stress indicates that sorrow is not a superficial emotion for infants. Many researchers believe that the infant brain is shaped by the early social emotions, particularly sadness and fear (Fries & Pollak, 2007; Johnson, 2007).

stranger wariness An infant's expression of concern—a quiet stare, clinging to a familiar person, or sadness—when a stranger appears.

separation anxiety An infant's distress when a familiar caregiver leaves, most obvious between 9 and 14 months.

Fear

Fully formed fear in response to some person, thing, or situation (not just distress at a surprise) emerges at about 9 months and then rapidly becomes more frequent as well as more apparent (Witherington et al., 2004). Two kinds of social fear are obvious:

- **Stranger wariness,** which an infant expresses by no longer smiling at any friendly face and by crying if an unfamiliar person moves too close, too quickly
- **Separation anxiety,** which an infant expresses in tears, dismay, or anger when a familiar caregiver leaves

Separation anxiety is normal at age 1, intensifies by age 2, and usually subsides after that. If it remains strong after age 3, it is considered an emotional disorder (Silverman & Dick-Niederhauser, 2004).

Many 1-year-olds fear not just strangers but also anything unexpected, from the flush of a toilet to the pop of a jack-in-the-box, from the closing of elevator doors to the tail-wagging approach of a dog. With repeated experiences and caregiver reassurance, older infants might themselves enjoy flushing the toilet (again and again) or calling the dog (crying if the dog does *not* come).

JOURNAL-COURIER / TIFFANY HERMON / THE IMAGE WORKS

Stranger Wariness Becomes Santa Terror For toddlers, even a friendly stranger is cause for alarm, especially if Mom's protective arms are withdrawn. The most frightening strangers are men who are unusually dressed and who act as if they might take the child away. Ironically, therefore, Santa Claus remains terrifying until children are about 3 years old.

Toddlers' Emotions

Many emotions that emerge in the first months of life take on new strength at about age 1 (Kagan, 2002). Throughout the second year and beyond, anger and fear typically become less frequent but more focused, targeted toward infuriating or terrifying experiences. Similarly, laughing and crying become louder and more discriminating.

New emotions appear toward the end of the second year: pride, shame, embarrassment, and guilt (Witherington et al., 2004). These emotions require an awareness of other people. They emerge from family interactions, influenced by the culture (Mesquita & Leu, 2007). For example, pride is encouraged in North American toddlers ("You did it all by yourself"—even when that is untrue), but Asian families discourage pride and cultivate modesty and shame (Rogoff, 2003).

By age 2, children can display the entire spectrum of emotional reactions. They have been taught which expressions of emotion are acceptable in their culture and which are not (Saarni et al., 2006). For example, if a toddler holds on tightly to his mother's skirt and hides his face when a friendly but strange dog approaches, the

Especially for Nurses and Pediatricians (see response, page 192) Parents come to you concerned that their 1-year-old hides her face and holds onto them tightly whenever a stranger appears. What do you tell them?

self-awareness A person's realization that he or she is a distinct individual, whose body, mind, and actions are separate from those of other people.

mother could hastily pick the child up or bend down to pet the dog. The mother's response encourages fear or happiness the next time a dog appears.

Self-Awareness

In addition to social interactions, another foundation for emotional growth is **self-awareness,** the realization that one's body, mind, and actions are separate from those of other people (R. A. Thompson, 2006). At about age 1, an emerging sense of "me" and "mine" leads to a new consciousness of others. As one developmentalist explains:

> With the emergence of consciousness in the second year of life, we see vast changes in both children's emotional life and the nature of their social relationships. . . . The child can feel . . . self-conscious emotions, like pride at a job well done or shame over a failure.
>
> *[M. Lewis, 1997, p. 132]*

Very young infants have no sense of self—at least of *self* as most people define it (Harter, 2006). In fact, a prominent psychoanalyst, Margaret Mahler, theorized that for the first 4 months of life infants see themselves as part of their mothers. They "hatch" at about 5 months and spend the next several months developing a sense of self as separate from their mothers (Mahler et al., 1975). The period from 15 to 18 months "is noteworthy for the emergence of the *Me-self,* the sense of self as the *object* of one's knowledge" (Harter, 1998, p. 562).

Mirror Recognition

In a classic experiment (M. Lewis & J. Brooks, 1978), babies aged 9–24 months looked into a mirror after a dot of rouge had been surreptitiously put on their noses. If the babies reacted by touching their noses, that meant they knew the mirror showed their own faces. None of the babies less than 12 months old reacted as if they knew the mark was on them (they sometimes smiled and touched the dot on the "other" baby in the mirror). However, those between 15 and 24 months usually showed self-awareness, touching their own noses with curiosity and puzzlement.

Self-recognition in the mirror test as well as in photographs usually emerges at about 18 months, at the same time as two other advances: pretending and using first-person pronouns *(I, me, mine, myself, my).* Some developmentalists connect self-recognition with self-understanding (e.g., Gallup et al., 2002), although "the interpretation of this seemingly simple task is plagued by controversy" (Nielsen et al., 2006, p. 166).

Mirror, Mirror This toddler clearly recognizes herself in the reflection in the mirror, and her careful combing indicates that she also knows that her culture admires long hair in females.

Observation Quiz (see answer, page 192): This little girl may end up tangling her hair instead of smoothing it. Besides the comb, what else do you see that she might misuse?

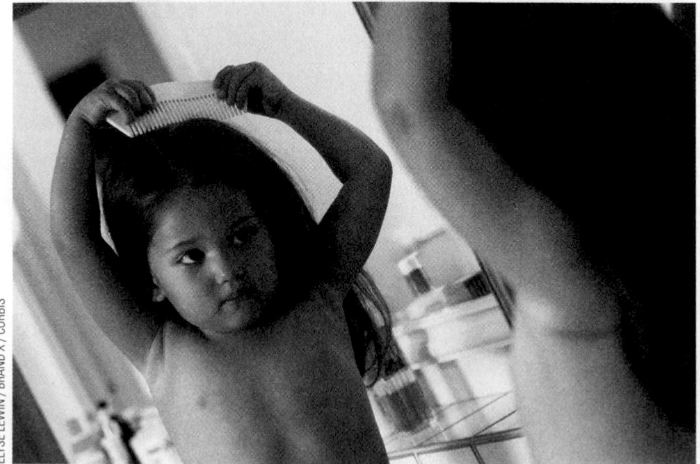

ELYSE LEWIN / BRAND X / CORBIS

For example, one study found that self-recognition in the mirror test *negatively* correlated with embarrassment when a doll's leg fell off (it had been rigged to do so) as each toddler played with it (Barrett, 2005). Particularly for boys, 17-month-olds who recognized themselves were *less* embarrassed at this mishap and more likely to tell the examiner about it. Does a sense of self at this age diminish shame as it increases pride?

Perhaps. Pride seems to be linked to the maturing self-concept, not necessarily to other people's opinions or actions (Barrett, 2005). If someone tells a toddler, "You're very smart," the child may smile but usually already feels smart—and thus is already pleased and proud. Telling toddlers that they are smart, strong, or beautiful may even be unhelpful (Kelley et al., 2000). It may undercut their self-awareness, making it seem as if pride comes from pleasing other people.

Brain Maturation and the Emotions

Brain maturation is involved in all the emotional developments just described. There is no doubt that varied experiences, as well as good nutrition, promote both brain maturation and emotional development. Nor is there any doubt that emotional reactions begin in the brain (Johnson, 2007).

As explained in Chapter 6, fMRI and PET scans of infant brains are notoriously difficult, expensive, and open to various interpretations. However, developmentalists agree that infants' emotional development is directly connected to brain development in two areas, social awareness and reactions to stress.

More subtle connections between brain architecture and emotional expression, as in mirror neurons (see Chapter 1) or in fear responses to stress, are still speculative. Research has not yet pinned down the connections, sequences, or ages at which advances in brain development might foster more advanced emotions (although 3 months and 8 months have been suggested as pivotal).

Synesthesia

One topic of great interest is the relationship between brain maturation and the differentiation of emotions. Research on infant senses suggests that such differentiation originates in the brain.

For older children and adults, it is known that *synesthesia*—the stimulation of one sensory stimulus to the brain (sound, sight, touch, taste, or smell) by another—is at least partly genetic. Synesthesia is often connected to creativity and is unusual (Barnett et al., 2008).

For infants, however, synesthesia seems common, because the boundaries between the sensory parts of the cortex are less distinct. For a newborn, textures seem associated with vision and sounds with smells; and the infant's own body seems associated with the bodies of others. The sensory connections are called cross-model perception; the interpersonal connections may become the basis for early social understanding (Meltzoff, 2007).

The tendency of one part of the brain to activate another also seems to occur with the emotions. An infant's cry can be triggered by pain, fear, tiredness, or excitement; laughter can turn to tears for reasons that adults do not understand. Note that the pattern is quite different for older children and adults, who usually cry only in sadness (and sometimes not even then). Infant emotions are less predictable than adult ones because of the way their brains are activated. Compared with infants, the toddlers' targeted and self-aware emotions (described earlier) may result from their advances in brain specialization.

Social Impulses

Most developmentalists agree that the social smile and the first laughter appear as the cortex matures (Konner, 2007). The same is probably true for nonreflexive fear, self-awareness, and anger. The maturation of a particular part of the cortex (the anterior cingulate gyrus) is directly connected to emotional self-regulation, which allows the child to moderate these emotions (Posner et al., 2007).

One important aspect of the infant's emotional development is that particular people (typically those the infant sees most often) begin to arouse specific emotions. This is almost certainly the result of brain development, as a sequence of neurons that fire together become more closely and quickly connected in the brain.

All infant emotional reactions depend partly on memory, which, as Chapter 6 explained, is fragile in the first months and gradually improves as dendrites and axons connect. No wonder toddlers (but not young infants) get angry quickly when a teasing older sibling approaches them or react with fear when entering the

➤Response for Nurses and Pediatricians (from page 190): Stranger wariness is normal up to about 14 months. This baby's behavior actually sounds like secure attachment!

➤Answer to Observation Quiz (from page 190): Perfume. She might splash too much of her mother's perfume on herself, reeking instead of wafting.

doctor's office. They can now remember the last time someone prevented them from doing what they wanted or the shot the doctor gave them last month.

Stress

As already mentioned in Chapter 5, excessive stress impairs the brain, particularly in areas associated with emotional development (Adam et al., 2007). Brain imagery and cortisol measurements have proven that the hypothalamus, the part of the brain that regulates various bodily functions and hormone production, is affected by chronic early stress; it may grow more slowly than in nonstressed infants. (The hypothalamus is discussed further in Chapter 8.)

Some research finds that children of teenage mothers experience more stress, even at 4 months of age (Azar et al., 2007). Teenage mothers sometimes neglect or abuse their babies, although as you will see in the next chapter, most parents of every age provide adequate care. Early motherhood is a risk factor, increasing the chances for maltreatment. Abuse certainly has long-term consequences for a child's emotional development, and high levels of stress hormones are one sign of emotional impairment.

The specifics of how maltreatment harms the infant brain are difficult to prove, for obvious ethical reasons. However, it is known that the brains of older children who have been maltreated respond abnormally not only to stress but also to photographs of frightened people (Gordis et al., 2008; Masten et al., 2008). These abnormal neurological responses begin in infancy.

This research has important applications. Everything should be done to prevent excessive stress in infants, even when no evidence of maltreatment exists. One obvious way is to help new mothers, but the role of fathers may also be crucial. When the father of a baby delivered via cesarean section provides *kangaroo care,* holding the newborn against his naked chest (see Chapter 4), that baby tends to cry less and to be more relaxed (Erlandsson et al., 2007). Throughout early development, the father's behavior toward the mother affects her stress level, and her state of high or low stress is then transmitted to the baby (Talge et al., 2007).

A Case of Abnormal Emotional Development

The developmental progression just reviewed describes the usual sequence, the result of caregivers' attention and brain maturation. The usual, however, is not inevitable. One father writes about his third child, Jacob, whose brain did not propel him along the usual path.

> [My wife, Rebecca, and I] were convinced that we were set. We had surpassed our quota of 2.6 children and were ready to engage parental autopilot. I had just begun a prestigious job and was working 10–11 hours a day. The children would be fine. We hired a nanny to watch Jacob during the day. As each of Jacob's early milestones passed, we felt that we had taken another step toward our goal of having three normal children. We were on our way to the perfect American family. Yet, somewhere back in our minds we had some doubts. Jacob seemed different than the girls. He had some unusual attributes. There were times when we would be holding him and he would arch his back and scream so loud that it was painful for us.
>
> *[Jacob's father, 1997, p. 59]*

As an infant, Jacob did not relate to his parents (or to anyone else). His parents paid little heed to his emotional difficulties, focusing instead on physical development. They noted that Jacob sat up and walked on schedule, and whenever they "had some doubts," they found excuses, telling themselves that "boys are different." As time went on, however, their excuses fell short. His father continues:

> Jacob had become increasingly isolated [by age 2]. I'm not a psychologist, but I believe that he just stopped trying. It was too hard, perhaps too scary. He couldn't figure out what was expected of him. The world had become too confusing, and so he withdrew from it. He would seek out the comfort of quiet, dark places and sit by himself. He would lose himself in the bright, colorful images of cartoons and animated movies.
>
> *[Jacob's father, 1997, p. 62]*

Something had to be done, as Jacob's parents eventually realized. They took him at age 3 for evaluation at a major teaching hospital. He was seen by at least 10 experts, none of whom were encouraging.

The diagnosis was "pervasive developmental disorder," a catchall diagnosis of emotional abnormalities that can include autism (discussed in Chapter 11). His despairing parents were advised to consider residential placement because Jacob would always need special care and, with Jacob living elsewhere, they would not be constantly reminded of their "failure." This recommendation did not take into account the commitment that Jacob's parents, like most parents, felt toward their child.

Yet, despite their commitment, they had ignored signs of trouble, overlooking their son's sometimes violent reaction to being held. The absence of smiling and of social reactions should have raised an alarm. The father's use of the word *autopilot* to describe his and his wife's approach to parenting shows that he realized this in hindsight. Later in this chapter, you will learn the outcome.

SUMMING UP

Newborns seem to have only two simple emotions, distress and contentment, which are expressed by crying or looking happy. Very soon curiosity and obvious joy, with social smiles and laughter, appear. By the second half of the first year, anger and fear are increasingly evident, especially in reaction to social experiences, such as encountering a stranger. In the second year, as infants become self-aware, they express emotions connected to themselves, including pride, shame, embarrassment, and guilt, and emotions about other people. The normal (and universal) course of maturation makes these emotions possible at around 18 months, but context and learning affect the timing, frequency, and intensity of their expression. Underlying all emotional development is brain maturation and the connections between neurons, although many specifics remain to be discovered. ■

Theories of Infant Psychosocial Development

Each of the five major theories described in Chapter 2 has a distinct perspective on the origin and significance of infants' emotions. This section includes discussion of several current and crucial research areas: toilet training, temperament, and ethnotheories. All three are outgrowths of these five theories, but consideration of each topic illustrates the application of theories. This demonstrates again the role of theory in science—to spark further study.

Psychoanalytic Theory

Psychoanalytic theory connects biosocial and psychosocial development and emphasizes the need for responsive maternal care. Both major psychoanalytic theorists, Sigmund Freud and Erik Erikson, described two distinct early stages. Freud (1935, 1940/1964) wrote about the *oral stage* and the *anal stage*. Erikson (1963) called his first stages *trust versus mistrust* and *autonomy versus shame and doubt*.

Especially for Nursing Mothers (see response, page 196): You have heard that if you wean your child too early, he or she will overeat or become an alcoholic. Is it true?

Freud: The Oral and Anal Stages

According to Freud (1935), the first year of life is the *oral stage,* so named because the mouth is the young infant's primary source of gratification. In the second year, with the *anal stage,* the infant's main pleasure comes from the anus—particularly from the sensual pleasure of bowel movements and, eventually, the psychological pleasure of controlling them.

Freud believed that both the oral and anal stages are fraught with potential conflicts that have long-term consequences. If a mother frustrates her infant's urge to suck—by weaning the infant too early, for example, or preventing the child from sucking on fingers or toes—the child may become distressed and anxious, eventually becoming an adult with an *oral fixation.* Such a person is stuck (fixated) at the oral stage and therefore eats, drinks, chews, bites, or talks excessively, in quest of the mouth-related pleasure denied in infancy.

Similarly, if toilet training is overly strict or if it begins before the infant is mature enough, parent–infant interaction may become locked into a conflict over the toddler's refusal, or inability, to comply. The child becomes fixated and develops an *anal personality*—as an adult, seeking self-control with an unusually strong need for regularity in all aspects of life. This aspect of Freud's theory has been studied in detail and, ultimately, refuted (Sears et al., 1976). Other ideas about the optimal timing and method of toilet training, and their impact on the child, are discussed in the following.

a view from science

Toilet Training: How and When?

A century ago, parents typically began toilet training infants in the first month of life (Accardo, 2006). Then psychoanalytic theory influenced parents to postpone toilet training until the child was ready, thus avoiding conflict and the potential development of "anal personalities." The child would decide when to begin.

Some U.S. scientists, in rejecting the psychoanalytic view, have proposed an alternative schedule for toilet training that is based on behaviorist principles and is said to take only one day (Azrin & Foxx, 1974). In this method, children drink quantities of their favorite juice; sit on the potty with a parent nearby to keep them happy, entertained, and in place; and then, when the inevitable occurs, are praised and rewarded. They soon learn to head for the potty whenever the need arises.

One comparison study found that this behaviorist approach was often effective for older children with serious disabilities. However, this study also found that many methods of toilet training succeeded with normal children. No method seemed to result in marked negative emotional consequences (Klassen et al., 2006).

It is true that later training, initiated by the child, tends to succeed more quickly. One study followed hundreds of toddlers whose parents began toilet-training them between ages 1½ and 3 years. Early starters took about a year to be completely toilet trained (doing everything without help), while later starters took only about three months (Blum et al., 2003). Other research in industrialized nations found that the particular age at which success becomes likely depends more on the child's bladder size and sleep habits (which vary a great deal among children) than on the culture (Jansson et al., 2005).

REUTERS / JOSE MIGUEL GOMEZ / LANDOV

All Together, Now Toddlers in an employees' day-care program at a flower farm in Colombia learn to use the potty on a schedule.

Psychoanalytic theory on toilet training has been undermined by cross-cultural surveys. Researchers have found that toilet training occurs "in very diverse ways . . . at different ages, with different degrees of attention and harshness" (Rozin, 2007, p. 405). In some cultures, parents are expected to toilet-train their infants by 6 months; in others, parents do not train their children at all because toddlers train themselves by watching slightly older children and imitating what they do.

Variations are also evident within cultures. A survey found that some U.S. parents thought toilet training should begin as early as 6 months, others as late as 4 years. The preferred age was affected by the parents' level of education: More years of education correlated with expectations of later training (Horn et al., 2006).

The more educated parents may have been influenced by Barry Brazelton, a leading U.S. pediatrician who writes about child development. He believes that toilet training should begin when the child is cognitively, emotionally, and biologically "ready." That is usually around age 2 for daytime training and age 3 or older for nighttime dryness (Brazelton & Sparrow, 2006).

As with many other child-rearing issues, many recommendations and practices related to toilet training reflect value judgments. Brazelton writes:

> As a society, we are far too concerned about pushing children to be toilet trained early. I don't even like the phrase "toilet training." It really should be toilet learning.
>
> *[Brazelton & Sparrow, 2006, p. 193]*

Rejecting this relaxed, child-centered approach, some Western parents prefer to start potty training very early. One U.S. mother began training her baby just 33 days after birth. She noticed when her son was about to defecate, held him above the toilet, and had trained him by 6 months (Sun & Rugolotto, 2004).

The view from contemporary science is that the "best" age to start training depends on what the goal is. If the goal is to foster the child's independence and autonomy, with as little parental interference as possible, then it makes sense to wait until the sense of self is well developed. But if the goal is to have a well-trained infant, and if the parents are patient and willing to respond to subtle signs that defecation is imminent, then starting early makes sense (Accardo, 2006).

Erikson: Trust and Autonomy

According to Erikson, the first crisis of life is **trust versus mistrust,** when infants learn whether the world can be trusted to satisfy their basic needs. Babies feel secure when food and comfort are provided with "consistency, continuity, and sameness of experience" (Erikson, 1963, p. 247). If social interaction inspires trust and security, the child (and later the adult) will confidently explore the social world.

trust versus mistrust Erikson's first psychosocial crisis. Infants learn basic trust if the world is a secure place where their basic needs (for food, comfort, attention, and so on) are met.

The next crisis is called **autonomy versus shame and doubt.** Toddlers want autonomy (self-rule) over their own actions and bodies. If they fail to gain it, they feel ashamed of their actions and doubtful about their abilities.

autonomy versus shame and doubt Erikson's second crisis of psychosocial development. Toddlers either succeed or fail in gaining a sense of self-rule over their own actions and bodies.

Like Freud, Erikson believed that problems arising in early infancy could last a lifetime, creating an adult who is suspicious and pessimistic (mistrusting) or who is easily shamed (insufficient autonomy). These traits could be destructive or not, depending on the norms and expectations of the culture. Some cultures (including that of the United States) encourage independence and autonomy; in others (for example, in China), "shame is a normative emotion that develops as parents use explicit shaming techniques" to encourage children's loyalty and harmony within their families (Mascolo et al., 2003, p. 402). Westerners expect toddlers to go through the stubborn and defiant "terrible twos"; parents elsewhere expect toddlers to be docile and obedient. Thus, autonomy is prized in the United States, but it is considered immature by many other peoples of the world (Morelli & Rothbaum, 2007).

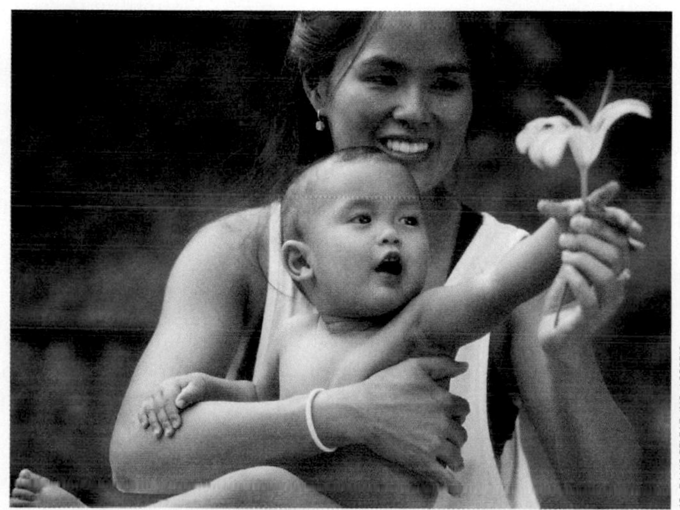

JOSE LUIS PELEAZ, INC./CORBIS

A Mother's Dilemma Infants are wonderfully curious, as this little boy demonstrates. Parents, however, must guide as well as encourage the drive toward autonomy. Notice this mother's expression as she makes sure her son does not crush or eat the flower.

➤**Response for Nursing Mothers** (from page 194): Freud thought so, but there is no experimental evidence that weaning, even when ill timed, has such dire long-term effects.

Behaviorism

From the perspective of behaviorism, emotions and personality are molded as parents reinforce or punish a child's spontaneous behaviors. Behaviorists believe that if parents smile and pick up their infant at every glimmer of a grin, he or she will become a child—and later an adult—with a sunny disposition. They believe the opposite is also true. The early behaviorist John Watson expressed this idea in strong terms:

> Failure to bring up a happy child, a well-adjusted child—assuming bodily health—falls squarely upon the parents' shoulders. [By the time the child is 3] parents have already determined . . . [whether the child] is to grow into a happy person, wholesome and good-natured, whether he is to be a whining, complaining neurotic, an anger-driven, vindictive, over-bearing slave driver, or one whose every move in life is definitely controlled by fear.
>
> *[Watson, 1928, pp. 7, 45]*

social learning Learning that is accomplished by observing others.

Later behaviorists noted that infants also experience **social learning,** which is learning that is accomplished by observing others. Albert Bandura conducted a classic experiment: Children watched an adult hitting a rubber Bobo clown with a mallet and then treated the doll the same way (Bandura, 1977). In this experiment, 4-year-old children had good reason to follow the example; they had been deliberately frustrated by being told they could not play with some attractive toys and were then left alone with a mallet and the Bobo doll. Both boys and girls pounded and kicked Bobo.

Since that experiment, developmentalists have demonstrated that social learning occurs throughout infancy and childhood (Morris et al., 2007; Nielsen, 2006). In many families, toddlers express emotions in various ways—from giggling to cursing—and in much the same way as their parents or older siblings do. A boy might develop a hot temper, for instance, if his father's outbursts seem to win respect from his mother.

Note that behaviorist theory emphasizes the role of parents, especially mothers, as does psychoanalytic theory. Freud thought that the mother is the young child's first and most enduring "love object," and behaviorists stress the power that a mother has over her children. In retrospect, this focus on mothers seems too narrow. The other three major theories reflect more recent research and the changing historical context. Fathers, siblings, and other caregivers matter.

Cognitive Theory

Cognitive theory holds that thoughts and values determine a person's perspective. Early experiences are important because beliefs, perceptions, and memories make them so, not because they are buried in the unconscious (psychoanalytic theory) or burned into the brain's patterns (behaviorism).

working model In cognitive theory, a set of assumptions that the individual uses to organize perceptions and experiences. For example, a person might assume that other people are trustworthy and be surprised by evidence that this working model of human behavior is erroneous.

Infants use their early relationships to develop a **working model,** a set of assumptions that become a frame of reference that can be called on later in life (Bretherton & Munholland, 1999; R. A. Thompson & Raikes, 2003). It is called a "model" because these early relationships form a prototype, or blueprint, for later relationships; it is called "working" because, while usable, it is not necessarily fixed or final.

Ideally, infants develop "a working model of the self as valued, loved, and competent" and "a working model of parents as emotionally available, loving, sensitive and supportive" (Harter, 2006, p. 519). However, reality does not always conform to the ideal. A 1-year-old girl might develop a working model, based on her parents' inconsistent responses to her, that people are unpredictable. All her life she will apply that model to every new person she meets. Her childhood relationships will be insecure, and in adulthood she might always be on guard against further disappointment.

To use Piaget's terminology, that girl has developed a cognitive *schema* to organize her perceptions of other people. According to cognitive theory, a child's *interpretation* of early experiences is crucial, not necessarily the experiences themselves (Schaffer, 2000).

The hopeful message from cognitive theory is that people can rethink and reorganize their thoughts, developing new working models that are more positive than their original ones. Our mistrustful girl can learn to trust if her later experiences—such as marriage to a faithful and loving husband—provide a new model.

Epigenetic Theory

As you remember from Chapter 2, epigenetic theory holds that every human characteristic is strongly influenced by each person's unique genotype. Thus, a child might be happy or anxious not because of early experiences (as the three grand theories would say) but because of inborn predispositions. A person's DNA remains the same from conception on, no matter how his or her emotions are blocked (psychoanalytic theory), reinforced (behaviorism), or interpreted (cognitive theory).

Temperament

Among each person's genetic predispositions are the traits of **temperament,** defined as "constitutionally based individual differences" in emotions, activity, and self-regulation (Rothbart & Bates, 2006, p. 100). "Constitutionally based" means that these traits originate with nature (genes), although they are influenced by nurture.

temperament Inborn differences between one person and another in emotions, activity, and self-regulation. Temperament is epigenetic, originating in genes but affected by child-rearing practices.

Temperament is similar to personality. Some researchers believe that the two constructs overlap (e.g., Caspi & Shiner, 2006). Generally, however, personality traits (e.g., honesty and humility) are considered to be primarily learned, whereas temperamental traits (e.g., shyness and aggression) are considered to be primarily genetic. Even though temperamental traits originate with the genes, preceding child-rearing practices and the learning of cultural values, their expression is modified by experience (Rothbart & Bates, 2006).

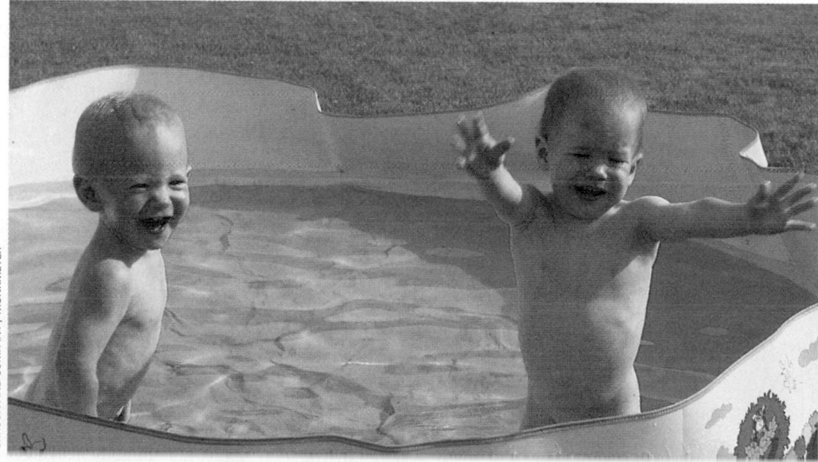

Twins They were born on the same day and now are experiencing a wading pool for the first time.

Observation Quiz (see answer, page 198): Are these twins monozygotic or dizygotic?

The New York Longitudinal Study

In laboratory studies of temperament, some infants experience events that have been designed to be frightening. Four-month-olds might see spinning mobiles or hear unusual sounds. Older babies might confront a noisy, moving robot or a clown who quickly moves close. At such experiences, some children laugh (and are classified as "easy"), some cry ("difficult"), and some are quiet ("slow to warm up") (Fox et al., 2001; Kagan & Snidman, 2004). These categories come from a classic study called the *New York Longitudinal Study* (NYLS). Begun in the 1960s, the NYLS was the first among many large studies to recognize that each newborn has distinct inborn traits.

LEONG KA TAI / MATERIAL WORLD

Which Sister Has a Personality Problem? In Mongolia, females are expected to display shyness as a sign of respect to elders and strangers. Consequently, if the younger of these sisters is as shy as she seems, her parents are less likely to be distressed about her withdrawn behavior than the typical North American parent would be. Conversely, they may worry about the boldness of her older sister.

Although temperament begins in the brain, it is difficult to detect via brain scans, so most of the research uses parents' reports and direct observation. In order to avoid merely reflecting the parents' hopes and biases, researchers ask for specifics, seeking what are called "operational" definitions. As the NYLS researchers explain:

> If a mother said that her child did not like his first solid food, we . . . were satisfied only when she gave a description such as "When I put the food into his mouth he cried loudly, twisted his head away, and let it drool out."
>
> [*Chess et al., 1965, p. 26*]

According to the NYLS, by 3 months, infants manifest nine temperamental traits that can be clustered into four categories (the three described above and a fourth category of "hard to classify" infants). The proportion of infants in each category was as follows:

- Easy (40 percent)
- Difficult (10 percent)
- Slow to warm up (15 percent)
- Hard to classify (35 percent)

The NYLS found that temperament often changes in the early weeks but becomes increasingly stable by age 3 or so. Children with extreme temperaments (perhaps very difficult or very easy) are likely to become adolescents and young adults with the same traits (Guerin et al., 2003).

The Big Five

Big Five The five basic clusters of personality traits that remain quite stable throughout life: openness, conscientiousness, extroversion, agreeableness, and neuroticism.

Other researchers began by studying adult personality traits and came up with the **Big Five** (whose first letters form the memorable acronym *OCEAN*). They are listed here with the characteristics that define them:

- Openness: imaginative, curious, welcoming new experiences
- Conscientiousness: organized, deliberate, conforming
- Extroversion: outgoing, assertive, active
- Agreeableness: kind, helpful, easygoing
- Neuroticism: anxious, moody, self-critical

The Big Five traits are found in many cultures, among people of all ages, although the proportions in each category differ by age and nationality. (McCrae & Costa, 2003). The Big Five are more complex than the easy/difficult/slow-to-warm-up classifications; but an infant high in agreeableness might be classified as easy, one high in neuroticism would be difficult, and so on.

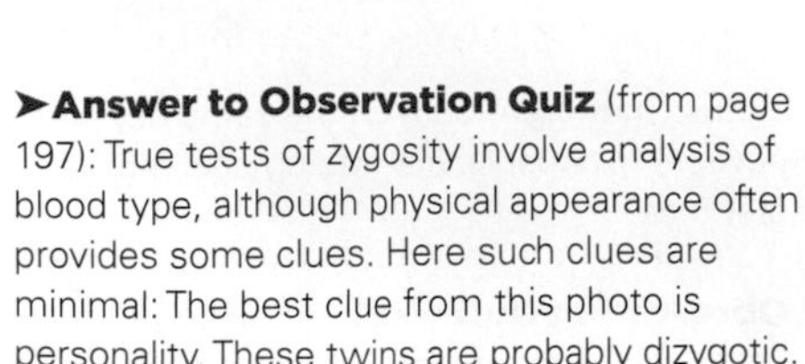

➤Answer to Observation Quiz (from page 197): True tests of zygosity involve analysis of blood type, although physical appearance often provides some clues. Here such clues are minimal: The best clue from this photo is personality. These twins are probably dizygotic.

Sociocultural Theory

No one doubts that "human development occurs in a cultural context" (Kagitcibasi, 2003, p. 166). The crucial question is *how much* influence culture has. Sociocultural theorists argue that the influence is substantial, that the entire social and cultural context has a major impact on infant–caregiver relationships and thus on infants' development.

Ethnotheories

An **ethnotheory** is a theory that is embedded in a particular culture or ethnic group. Usually the group members are unaware that theories underlie their customs. However, as you have already seen with breast-feeding and co-sleeping in Chapter 5, many child-rearing practices arise from ethnotheories (H. Keller et al., 2006).

ethnotheory A theory that underlies the values and practices of a culture but is not usually apparent to the people within the culture.

This is true for emotional development as well. For example, if a culture's ethnotheory includes the idea that ancestors are reincarnated in the younger generation, then "children are not expected to show respect for adults, but adults [are expected to show respect] for their reborn ancestors." Such cultures favor indulgent child-rearing practices, with no harsh punishments. "Western people perceive [these cultures] as extremely lenient" (Dasen, 2003, pp. 149–150).

Especially for Linguists and Writers (see response, page 201): U.S. culture has given rise to the term *empty nest,* signifying an ethnotheory about mothers whose children live elsewhere. What cultural values are expressed by that term?

Remember that cultures change over time, in response to changing contexts. This was confirmed by one study of the ethnotheories of grandmothers and mothers of 3-month-olds (Lamm et al., 2008). The grandmother–mother pairs were from four contexts: urban Germany, urban India, and urban and rural Cameroon, West Africa. Women in each nation held ethnotheories different from those of the women in the other nations. In all four cultures, generational differences were apparent, with the mothers valuing autonomy more than the grandmothers.

The generation gap was smallest, however, in the two cultures that were most different. Among urban Germans, the grandmothers tended to agree with the mothers in valuing autonomy; among rural Africans, the mothers tended to agree with the grandmothers in valuing compliance. The greatest mother–grandmother attitude gap was in urban Cameroon, probably because recent social change there has been dramatic and the traditions and values learned by the grandmothers differed markedly from those learned by the mothers (Lamm et al., 2008).

JOHN WARBURTON-LEE / DANITA DELIMONT AGENCY / DDB.NET

No Distance Between Them This Namibian mother holds her child very close and has massaged his whole body with butterfat and red ochre. Touch and caress, more than words and toys, express love in a proximal culture.

Proximal and Distal Parenting

Another ethnotheory involves a culture's ideas about how much parents should carry and cuddle their infants. **Proximal parenting** involves being physically close to a baby, often holding and touching. **Distal parenting** involves keeping some distance—providing toys, feeding by putting finger food within reach, and talking face to face instead of communicating by touch. Caregivers who are convinced that one of these approaches to parenting is better than the other are expressing an ethnotheory, although usually they simply respond without being aware that they are practicing proximal or distal parenting.

A longitudinal study comparing child rearing among the Nso people of Cameroon and among Greeks in Athens found marked differences between the two cultures in proximal and distal parenting (H. Keller et al., 2004). The researchers videotaped 78 mothers as they played with their 3-month-olds. Coders (who did not know the study's hypothesis) rated the style of play as either proximal (e.g., carrying, swinging, caressing, exercising the child's body) or distal (e.g., face-to-face talking) (see Table 7.2 and the Research Design).

proximal parenting Caregiving practices that involve being physically close to a baby, with frequent holding and touching.

distal parenting Caregiving practices that involve remaining distant from a baby, providing toys, food, and face-to-face communication with minimal holding and touching.

The Nso mothers were proximal parents, holding their babies all the time and almost never using toys or bottles. The Greek mothers were distal parents,

Research Design

Scientists: A team of six from three nations (Germany, Greece, Costa Rica).

Publication: *Child Development* (2004).

Participants: A total of 90 mothers participated when their babies were 3 months old and again when they were 18 months old (32 from Cameroon, 46 from Greece, 12 from Costa Rica). In Greece and Costa Rica, researchers recruited mothers in hospitals. In Cameroon, permission was first sought from the local leader, and then announcements were made among local people.

Design: First, mothers played with their 3-month-olds, and that play was videotaped and coded for particular behaviors. Fifteen months later, the toddlers' self-recognition was assessed with the rouge test, and compliance with preset maternal commands was measured. The mother's frequency of eye contact and body contact with the infant at 3 months was compared with the toddler's self-awareness and compliance at 18 months.

Major conclusion: Toddlers with proximal mothers were more obedient but less self-aware; toddlers with distal mothers tended to show the opposite pattern.

Comment: This is one of the best comparison studies of child-rearing practices in various cultures. Families differed in income and urbanization; these variables need to be explored in other research.

Especially for Pediatricians (see response, page 202): A parent complains that her child refuses to stay in the car seat, spits out disliked foods, and almost never does what she says. How should you respond?

TABLE 7.2

Play Patterns in Rural Cameroon and Urban Greece

		Amount of Time Spent in Play (percent)	
Age of Babies	Type of Play	Nso, Cameroon	Athens, Greece
3 months	Held by mother	100	31
3 months	Object play	3	40
	Toddler Behavior Measured		
18 months	Self-recognition	3	68
18 months	Compliance (without prompting)	72	2

Source: Adapted from Keller et al., 2004.

using objects almost half the time and holding their babies less than the Nso parents did.

The researchers hypothesized that proximal parenting would result in toddlers who were less self-aware but more compliant—traits needed in an interdependent and cooperative society such as rural Cameroon. By contrast, distal parenting might result in toddlers who are self-aware but less obedient—traits needed in modern Athens, where independence, self-reliance, and competition are highly valued.

The predictions were accurate. At 18 months, the same children were tested on self-awareness (via the rouge test) and compliance with parents' instructions. The African toddlers didn't recognize themselves in the mirror but were compliant; the opposite was true of the Greek children.

Replicating their own work, these researchers studied a dozen mother–infant pairs in Costa Rica. In that Central American nation, caregiver–infant distance was midway between the Nso and the Greeks, as was later toddler behavior. The researchers reanalyzed all their data, child by child. They found that, even apart from culture, proximal or distal play at 3 months was highly predictive of toddler behavior. In other words, Greek mothers who, unlike most of their peers, were proximal parents had more obedient toddlers (H. Keller et al., 2004). The same results were found by a longitudinal study of German fathers (Borke et al., 2007).

As this research suggests, every aspect of early emotional development interacts with cultural ideas of what is appropriate, and those ideas are expressed in parental actions. Other research has found that separation anxiety is more evident in Japan than in Germany, because Japanese infants "have very few experiences with separation from the mother," whereas in Germany "infants are frequently left alone outside of stores or supermarkets" while their mothers shop (Saarni et al., 2006, p. 237).

From the beginning of life, some emotions are dampened and others are fueled by family responses, as influenced by culture. We noted earlier that infants become angry when they are restrained. Some Western parents rarely hold their infants except to restrain them (and the purpose of the restraint is often to enforce a separation between the parent and the infant). Parents force their protesting toddlers to sit in strollers, to ride in car seats, to stay in cribs and playpens or behind gates—all examples of distal parenting.

If toddlers do not lie down quietly to allow diapers to be quickly changed (and few do), some parents simply hold the protesting child down to get the task done quickly. Compare this approach to that of Roberto's parents, who used nursing (very proximal) and the threat of separation to get their son to wear pants.

a personal perspective

"Let's Go to Grandma's"

There are many good ways to raise a child. As I listen to my students who are parents, raise my own children, and read about parents elsewhere, I realize that children develop well with diverse practices. Here is one example.

Mayan parents from Mexico and Guatemala believe that children should not be forced to obey their parents. Roberto, at 18 months, did not want to wear a diaper.

> "Let's put on your diaper . . . Let's go to Grandma's . . . We're going to do an errand." This did not work, and the mother invited Roberto to nurse, as she swiftly slipped the diaper on him with the father's assistance. The father announced, "It's over."
>
> *[Rogoff, 2003, p. 204]*

When my own toddlers refused to put on some garment, I either pulled on their clothes as they protested or let them remain undressed. My response depended on my energy level and whether there was some social reason they needed to be clothed. Either way, someone won and someone lost. Self-assertion, not cooperation, was the result. Not the case for Roberto's mother, although she felt

> increasing exasperation that the child was wiggling and not standing to facilitate putting on his pants. Her voice softened as Roberto became interested in the ball, and she increased the stakes: "Do you want another toy?" They [father and mother] continued to try to talk Roberto into cooperating, and handed him various objects, which Roberto enjoyed. But still he stubbornly refused to cooperate with dressing. They left him alone for a while. When his father asked if he was ready, Roberto pouted "nono!"
>
> After a bit, the mother told Roberto that she was leaving and waved goodbye. "Are you going with me?" Roberto sat quietly with a worried look. "Then put on your pants, put on your pants to go up the hill." Roberto stared into space, seeming to consider the alternatives. His mother started to walk away, "OK then, I'm going. Goodbye." Roberto started to cry, and his father persuaded, "Put on your pants then!" and his mother asked, "Are you going with me?"
>
> Roberto looked down worriedly, one arm outstretched in half a take-me gesture.
>
> "Come on, then," his mother offered the pants and Roberto let his father lift him to a stand and cooperated in putting his legs into the pants and in standing to have them fastened. His mother did not intend to leave; instead she suggested that Roberto dance for the audience. Roberto did a baby version of a traditional dance.
>
> *[Rogoff, 2003, p. 204]*

This is an example of an ethnotheory that "elders protect and guide rather than giving orders or dominating" (Rogoff, 2003, p. 205). A second ethnotheory is apparent as well: The parents readily used deception to get their child to do what they wanted.

If I had urged my daughter to let me dress her so that she could go out with me and she had then complied, I would have kept my promise and taken her out. I value truth-telling and promise-keeping; I would rather tell someone that her hat is ugly than lie and say I think it's attractive (although I usually stay quiet). But some cultures value harmony more than honesty and would consider me needlessly insulting. My way is merely my way, not necessarily the best way.

SUMMING UP

The five major theories differ in their explanations of the origins of early emotions and personality. Psychoanalytic theory stresses the mother's responses to the infant's needs for food and elimination (Freud) or for security and independence (Erikson). Behaviorism also stresses caregiving—especially as parents reinforce the behaviors they want their baby to learn or as they thoughtlessly teach unwanted behaviors.

Learning is also crucial in cognitive theory—not the moment-by-moment learning of behaviorism, but the infant's self-constructed concept, or working model, of the world. Epigenetic theory begins with inherited temperament and then describes how that inborn temperament is shaped. Sociocultural theory also sees an interaction between nature and nurture but emphasizes that the diversity of nurture explains much of the diversity of emotions. According to sociocultural theory, child-rearing practices arise from ethnotheories, implicit and unexpressed but very powerful. ■

➤Response for Linguists and Writers (from page 199): The implication is that human mothers are like sad birds, bereft of their fledglings, who have flown away.

➤Response for Parents of Toddlers (from page 200): Remember the origins of the misbehavior—probably a combination of the child's inborn temperament and the parent's distal parenting. Blended with ethnotheory, all contribute to the child's being stubborn and independent. Acceptance is more warranted than anger. On the other hand, this parent may be expressing hostility toward the child—a sign that intervention may be needed. Find out.

Especially for Nurses (see response, page 204): Parents come to you with their fussy 3-month-old. They say that they have read that temperament is "fixed" before birth, and they are worried that their child will always be difficult. What do you tell them?

goodness of fit A similarity of temperament and values that produces a smooth interaction between an individual and his or her social context, including family, school, and community.

The Development of Social Bonds

All the theories of development agree that healthy human development depends on social connections. You have already seen the importance of social bonds in numerous examples, including the abnormal behavior of emotionally deprived Romanian orphans (Chapter 5) and the social exchanges required for language learning (Chapter 6). Emotions elicit social reactions; infants are happier and healthier when other people (especially their mothers) are nearby. Now we look closely at infant–caregiver bonds, beginning with the overall "fit" between baby and caregiver and then more specifically at three phases of social development: synchrony, attachment, and social referencing.

Variations Among Infants

One longitudinal study of infant temperament (Fox et al., 2001) identified three distinct types—positive (exuberant), negative, and inhibited (fearful)—among its 4-month-old participants. The researchers followed each group, taking laboratory measures, mothers' reports, and brain scans at 9, 14, 24, and 48 months.

Half of the participants did not change much, reacting the same way and having similar brain-wave patterns when confronted with frightening experiences all four times they were tested. The other half altered their responses as they grew older. Fearful infants were most likely to change, and exuberant infants least likely (see Figure 7.1). That speaks to the influence of child rearing on inborn temperament: Adults coax frightened children to be braver but encourage exuberant children to stay happy.

Goodness of Fit

This study and many others show that the interaction between cultural influences and inherited traits shapes behavior, particularly in the first years of life. Whatever their child's temperament, parents need to find a **goodness of fit**—that is, a temperamental adjustment that allows smooth infant–caregiver interaction. With a good fit, parents of difficult babies build a close relationship; parents of exuberant, curious infants learn to protect them from harm; parents of slow-to-warm-up toddlers give them time to adjust. Note that the parents need to do most of the adjusting, as is evident in this example of a man and his daughter:

> Kevin is a very active, outgoing person who loves to try new things. Today he takes his 11-month-old daughter, Tyra, to the park for the first time. Tyra is playing alone in the sandbox, when a group of toddlers joins her. At first, Tyra smiles and eagerly watches them play. But as the toddlers become more active and noisy, Tyra's smiles turn quickly to tears. She . . . reaches for Kevin, who picks her up and comforts her. But then Kevin goes a step further. After Tyra calms down, Kevin gently encourages her to play near the other children. He sits at her side, talking and playing with her. Soon Tyra is slowly creeping closer to the group of toddlers, curiously watching their moves.
>
> *[Lerner & Dombro, 2004, p. 42]*

Tyra needed Kevin. In general, anxious children (i.e., those who are high in the Big Five trait of neuroticism) are more affected by their parents' responsiveness than are easygoing children (Pauli-Pott et al., 2004). Ineffective or harsh parenting *combined with* a negative temperament creates antisocial, destructive children (Cicchetti et al., 2007). Some children naturally cope with life's challenges; others must make an effort. Thus, for example, "a shy child must control his or her fear and approach a stranger, and an impulsive child must constrain his or her desire and resist a temptation" (Derryberry et al., 2003, p. 1061).

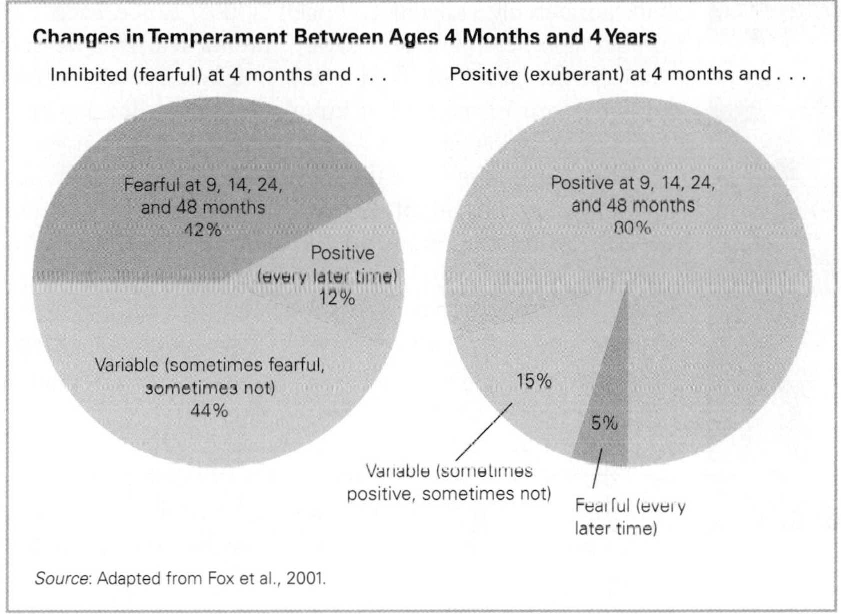

Source: Adapted from Fox et al., 2001.

FIGURE 7.1

Do Babies' Temperaments Change? The data suggest that fearful babies are not necessarily fated to remain that way. Adults who are reassuring and do not act frightened themselves can help children overcome an innate fearfulness. Some fearful children do not change, however, and it is not known whether that's because their parents are not sufficiently reassuring (nurture) or because they are temperamentally more fearful (nature).

Observation Quiz (see answer, page 204): Out of 100 4-month-olds who react positively to noises and other experiences, how many are fearful at later times in early childhood?

It's Not All Genetic

In general, most developmentalists emphasize the interaction between inherited traits and parental behavior (Kagan & Fox, 2006). Chapter 1's discussion of the research on the MAOA gene and violence touched on this point: Parents must first understand their child and then provide guidance so that inborn traits are expressed constructively, not destructively.

Many developmentalists have long warned against blaming mothers for everything that goes wrong. Now they caution against placing too much emphasis on genes, especially in infancy, because observations suggest that parenting style influences the infant's behavior as much as or more than temperament does (Roisman & Fraley, 2006). Remember that inborn temperament is evident in brain activity in the first weeks of life, and it influences behavior from childhood through old age (Kagan & Fox, 2006). It is a mistake to emphasize parental influence too much or too little; child-rearing practices and genes are both influential.

Synchrony

Synchrony is a coördinated interaction between caregiver and infant, an exchange in which they respond to each other with split-second timing. Synchrony has been described as the meshing of a finely tuned machine (Snow, 1984), an emotional "attunement" of an improvised musical duet (Stern, 1985), and a smoothly flowing "waltz" (Barnard & Martell, 1995).

synchrony A coordinated, rapid, and smooth exchange of responses between a caregiver and an infant.

In the First Few Months

Synchrony between infant and parent becomes more frequent and more elaborate as time goes on; a 6-month-old is a more responsive social partner than a 3-month-old (Feldman, 2007). Parents and infants average about an hour a day in face-to-face play, although variations are apparent from baby to baby, from time period to time period, and from culture to culture.

Detailed research reveals the mutuality of the interaction: Adults rarely smile at newborns until the infants smile at them, at which point adults grin broadly and

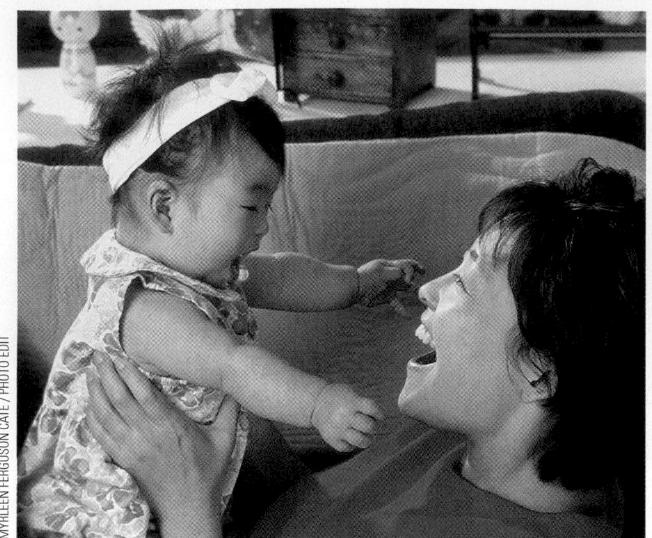

MYRLEEN FERGUSON CATE / PHOTO EDIT

Dance with Me Synchrony in action, with each one's hands, eyes, and open mouth reflecting the other's expression. The close timing of synchrony has been compared to a waltz—and these partners look as if they never miss a beat.

talk animatedly (Lavelli & Fogel, 2005). Since each baby has a unique temperament and style, parents learn to be sensitive to their particular infant (Feldman & Eidelman, 2005). Via synchrony, infants learn to read other emotions and to develop the skills of social interaction, such as taking turns and paying attention.

Although infants imitate adults, synchrony usually begins with parents imitating infants (Lavelli & Fogel, 2005). When parents detect an emotion from an infant's facial expressions and body motions and then respond, the infant learns to connect an internal state with an external expression (Rochat, 2001). Such sensitive parenting is particularly apparent in Asian cultures, perhaps because interpersonal sensitivity is crucial, and thus very small infants begin to learn it (Morelli & Rothbaum, 2007).

Suppose an infant is unhappy. An adult who mirrors the distress, and then tries to solve the problem, will teach that unhappiness is a valid emotion that can be relieved. An adult who always reacts to unhappiness by feeding the infant teaches the destructive lesson that food is the source of comfort. But if an adult's response is more nuanced (differentiating hunger, pain, boredom, or fear and responding differently to each), then the infant will learn to perceive the varied reasons for unhappiness and the many ways of responding.

When Synchrony Disappears

still-face technique An experimental practice in which an adult keeps his or her face umoving and expressionless in face-to-face interaction with an infant.

Is synchrony needed for normal development? If no one plays with an infant, how will that infant develop? Experiments using the **still-face technique** have addressed these questions (Tronick, 1989; Tronick & Weinberg, 1997). An infant is placed facing an adult, who plays with the baby while two video cameras record each partner's reactions. Frame-by-frame analysis typically reveals a sequence in which mothers synchronize their responses to the infants' movements, usually with exaggerated tone and expression, and the babies reciprocate with smiles and waving arms.

Then, on cue, the adult erases all facial expression and stares with a "still face" for a minute or two. Sometimes by 2 months, and clearly by 6 months, babies are very upset by the still face, especially from their parents (less so from strangers). Babies frown, fuss, drool, look away, kick, cry, or suck their fingers.

Babies become much more upset when exposed to the still face in front of them than when parents leave the room for a minute or two (Rochat, 2001). From a psychological perspective, this reaction is healthy: It shows that "by 2 to 3 months of age, infants have begun to expect that people will respond positively to their initiatives" (R. A. Thompson, 2006, p. 29).

➤Answer to Observation Quiz (from page 203): Out of 100 4-month-olds, 20 are fearful at least occasionally later in childhood, but only 5 are consistently fearful.

Many research studies lead to the same conclusion: A parent's responsiveness to an infant aids development, measured not only psychosocially but also biologically—by heart rate, weight gain, and brain maturation (Moore & Calkins, 2004). Much depends on the particular parent. Some rarely play with their infants, which slows down development (Huston & Aronson, 2005). Infants' brains need social interaction—an essential, expected stimulant—to develop to their fullest.

➤Response for Nurses (from page 202): It's too soon to tell. Temperament is not truly "fixed" but variable, especially in the first few months. Many "difficult" infants become happy, successful adolescents and adults.

Attachment

Toward the end of the first year, face-to-face play almost disappears. Once infants can move around and explore, they are no longer content to stay in one spot and follow an adult's facial expressions and vocalizations. Remember that, at about

BRAND X PICTURES / ALAMY

ROBERT W. GINN / ALAMY

Learning Emotions Infants respond to their parents' expressions and actions. If the moments shown here are typical, one young man will be happy and outgoing and the other will be sad and quiet.

Observation Quiz (see answer, page 206): For the pair on the left, where are their feet?

12 months, most infants can walk and talk, which changes the rhythms of their social interaction (Jaffee et al., 2001). At this time another connection, called *attachment*, overtakes synchrony.

Attachment is a lasting emotional bond that one person has with another. Attachments begin to form in early infancy, solidify by age 1, and influence a person's close relationships throughout life (see Table 7.3). In fact, according to attachment theory, adults' attachment to their parents, formed decades earlier in their childhoods, affects how they act with their own children. Humans learn in childhood how to relate to people, and those lessons echo lifelong (Grossman et al., 2005; Kline, 2008; Sroufe et al., 2005).

attachment According to Ainsworth, "an affectional tie" that an infant forms with a caregiver—a tie that binds them together in space and endures over time.

TABLE 7.3

AT ABOUT THIS TIME: Stages of Attachment

Age	Characteristics
Birth to 6 weeks	*Preattachment.* Newborns signal, via crying and body movements, that they need others. When people respond positively, the newborn is comforted and learns to seek more interaction. Newborns are also primed by brain patterns to recognize familiar voices and faces.
6 weeks to 8 months	*Attachment in the making.* Infants respond preferentially to familiar people by smiling, laughing, babbling. Their caregivers' voices, touch, expressions, and gestures are comforting, often overriding the impulse to cry. Trust (Erikson) develops.
8 months to 2 years	*Classic secure attachment.* Infants greet the primary caregiver, show separation anxiety when the caregiver leaves, play happily when the caregiver is present. Both infant and caregiver seek to be close to each other (proximity) and frequently look at each other (contact). In many caregiver–infant pairs, physical touch (patting, holding, caressing) is frequent.
2 to 6 years	*Attachment as launching pad.* Young children seek their caregiver's praise and reassurance as their social world expands. Interactive conversations and games (hide and seek, object play, reading, pretending) are common. Children expect caregivers to comfort and entertain.
6 to 12 years	*Mutual attachment.* Children seek to make their caregivers proud by learning what adults want them to learn, and adults reciprocate. In concrete operational thought (Piaget), specific accomplishments are valued by adults and children.
12 to 18 years	*New attachment figures.* Teenagers explore and make friendships on their own, using their working models of earlier attachments as a base. With more advanced, formal operational thinking (Piaget), physical contact is less important; shared ideals and goals are more influential.
18 years on	*Attachment revisited.* Adults develop relationships with others, especially romantic partnerships and parent–child relationships, that are influenced by earlier attachment patterns. Primary caregivers continue to be supportive, and adults continue to seek their praise, but they are no longer the prime source of attachment. Past insecure attachments can be repaired, although this does not always happen.

Source: Adapted from Grobman, 2008.

Lifelong Bonds Although attachment is traditionally measured at about age 1 via the Strange Situation, it builds from the first days of life and remains apparent in adulthood.

➤Answer to Observation Quiz (from page 205): The father uses his legs and feet to support his son at just the right distance for a great fatherly game of foot-kissing.

When two people are attached, they respond to each other in particular ways. Infants show their attachment through *proximity-seeking behaviors,* such as approaching and following their caregivers, and through *contact-maintaining behaviors,* such as touching, snuggling, and holding. A securely attached toddler is curious and eager to explore but maintains contact by occasionally looking back at the caregiver.

Caregivers show attachment as well. They keep a watchful eye on their baby and respond to vocalizations, expressions, and gestures. For example, many mothers or fathers, awakening in the middle of the night, tiptoe to the crib to gaze fondly at their sleeping infant. During the day, many parents instinctively smooth their toddler's hair or caress their child's hand or cheek.

Over humanity's evolutionary history, various proximity-seeking and contact-maintaining behaviors have contributed to the survival of the species. Attachment keeps toddlers near their caregivers and keeps caregivers vigilant.

Secure and Insecure Attachment

The concept of attachment was originally developed by John Bowlby (1969, 1973, 1988), a British developmentalist influenced by both psychoanalytic theory and ethology. Inspired by Bowlby's work, Mary Ainsworth, then a young American graduate student, studied the relationship between parents and infants in Uganda (Ainsworth, 1973).

Ainsworth discovered that most infants develop special attachments to their caregivers, although there are cultural differences in expression and style (IJzendoorn et al. 2006). (Ugandan mothers almost never kiss their infants; some U.S. parents kiss them repeatedly.)

In every culture, Ainsworth found some infants more securely attached than others. This variability has repeatedly been confirmed by scientists in many cultures (Cassidy & Shaver, 1999; T. Grossman et al., 2005; Sroufe, 2005; R. A. Thompson, 2006).

Attachment is classified into four types, labeled A, B, C, and D (see Table 7.4). Infants with **secure attachment** (type B) feel comfortable and confident. They are comforted by closeness to the caregiver, which provides confidence to explore. The caregiver becomes a *base for exploration,* giving assurance to venture forth. A toddler might, for example, scramble down from the caregiver's lap to play with a toy but periodically look back, vocalize a few syllables, and return for a hug.

secure attachment A relationship in which an infant obtains both comfort and confidence from the presence of his or her caregiver.

By contrast, insecure attachment (types A and C) is characterized by fear, anxiety, anger, or indifference. Insecurely attached children have less confidence. Some play independently without maintaining contact with the caregiver; this is **insecure-avoidant attachment** (type A). By contrast, an insecure child might be unwilling to leave the caregiver's lap; this is **insecure-resistant/ambivalent attachment** (type C).

insecure-avoidant attachment A pattern of attachment in which an infant avoids connection with the caregiver, as when the infant seems not to care about the caregiver's presence, departure, or return.

insecure-resistant/ambivalent attachment A pattern of attachment in which anxiety and uncertainty are evident, as when an infant becomes very upset at separation from the caregiver and both resists and seeks contact on reunion.

The fourth category (type D) is **disorganized attachment;** it has elements of the other types, but it is clearly different from them. Type D infants may shift from hitting to kissing their mothers, from staring blankly to crying hysterically, from pinching themselves to freezing in place.

disorganized attachment A type of attachment that is marked by an infant's inconsistent reactions to the caregiver's departure and return.

About two-thirds of all infants are securely attached (type B). Their mother's presence gives them courage to explore. A caregiver's departure may cause distress; the caregiver's return elicits positive social contact (such as smiling or hugging) and then more playing. A balanced reaction—being concerned about the caregiver's departure but not overwhelmed by it—reflects secure attachment.

Another one-third of infants are insecure, either indifferent (type A) or unduly anxious (type C). About 5 to 10 percent of infants fit into none of these categories and are classified as disorganized (type D).

TABLE 7.4

Patterns of Infant Attachment

Type	Name of Pattern	In Play Room	Mother Leaves	Mother Returns	Toddlers in Category (percent)
A	Insecure-avoidant	Child plays happily	Child continues playing	Child ignores her	10–20
B	Secure	Child plays happily	Child pauses, is not as happy	Child welcomes her, returns to play	50–70
C	Insecure-resistant/ambivalent	Child clings, is preoccupied with mother	Child is unhappy, may stop playing	Child is angry; may cry, hit mother, cling	10–20
D	Disorganized	Child is cautious	Child may stare or yell; looks scared, confused	Child acts oddly—may freeze, scream, hit self, throw things	5–10

Measuring Attachment

Ainsworth (1973) developed a now-classic laboratory procedure, called the **Strange Situation,** to measure attachment. In a well-equipped playroom, an infant is closely observed for eight episodes, each lasting three minutes. First, the caregiver and child are together. Then, according to a set sequence, the stranger or the caregiver enters or leaves the playroom. Infants' responses indicate which type of attachment they have formed to their caregivers. (Reactions to the caregiver indicate attachment; reactions to the stranger are influenced more by temperament than by affection.)

Strange Situation A laboratory procedure for measuring attachment by evoking infants' reactions to stress.

For research purposes, observers are carefully trained and are certified when they can clearly distinguish types A, B, C, and D. The key behaviors they focus on are the following:

- *Exploration of the toys.* A secure toddler plays happily.
- *Reaction to the caregiver's departure.* A secure toddler misses the caregiver.
- *Reaction to the caregiver's return.* A secure toddler welcomes the caregiver's reappearance.

Attachment is not always measured via the Strange Situation, especially when researchers want to study a large number of infants (Andreassen & West, 2007). Sometimes parents sort out 90 questions about their children's characteristics, and sometimes adults are interviewed extensively (according to a detailed protocol) about their relationships with their own parents.

The Attachment Experiment In this episode of the Strange Situation, Brian shows every sign of secure attachment. (*a*) He explores the playroom happily when his mother is present; (*b*) he cries when she leaves; and (*c*) he is readily comforted when she returns.

(a)

(b)

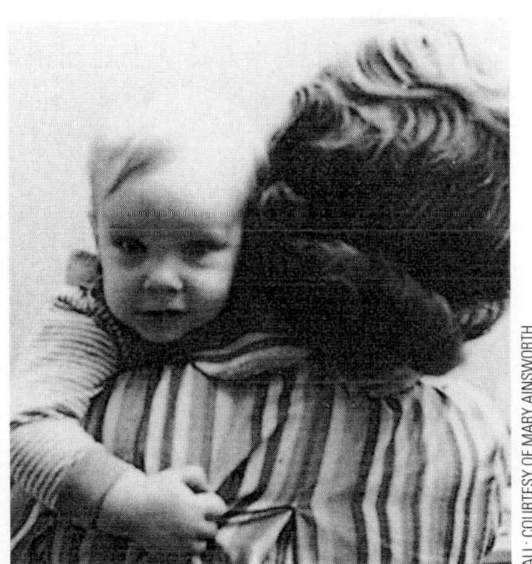

(c)

ALL: COURTESY OF MARY AINSWORTH

TABLE 7.5

Predictors of Attachment Type

Secure attachment (type B) is more likely if:

- The parent is usually sensitive and responsive to the infant's needs.
- The infant–parent relationship is high in synchrony.
- The infant's temperament is "easy."
- The parents are not stressed about income, other children, or their marriage.
- The parents have a working model of secure attachment to their own parents.

Insecure attachment is more likely if:

- The parent mistreats the child. (Neglect increases type A; abuse increases C and D.)
- The mother is mentally ill. (Paranoia increases type D; depression increases type C.)
- The parents are highly stressed about income, other children, or their marriage. (Parental stress increases types A and D.)
- The parents are intrusive and controlling. (Parental domination increases type A.)
- The parents are active alcoholics. (Alcoholic father increases type A; alcoholic mother increases type D.)
- The child's temperament is "difficult." (Difficult children tend to be type C.)
- The child's temperament is "slow to warm up." (This correlates with type A.)

Insecure Attachment and Social Setting

Early researchers expected secure attachment to "predict all the outcomes reasonably expected from a well-functioning personality" (R. A. Thompson & Raikes, 2003, p. 708). But this turned out not to be the case. Securely attached infants *are* more likely to become secure toddlers, socially competent preschoolers, academically skilled schoolchildren, and capable parents (R. A. Thompson, 2006). Many aspects of good parenting, including synchrony, correlate with secure attachment (see Table 7.5).

However, the type of attachment may change if family circumstances change. Temperament and age may also affect attachment. Many children shift in attachment status between one age and another (NICHD, 2001; Seifer et al., 2004).

The most troubled children may be those who are classified as type D. If their disorganization prevents them from developing an effective strategy for social interaction (even an avoidant or resistant one, type A or C), they may lash out. Sometimes they become hostile and aggressive, difficult for anyone to relate to (Lyons-Ruth et al., 1999). (Many of the Romanian children who were adopted after age 2, as described in Chapter 5, were type D.)

Social Referencing

Infants want to know adults' emotions. At about age 1, **social referencing** becomes evident as a child begins to look to another person for clarification or information, much as a student might consult a dictionary or other reference work. A glance of reassurance or words of caution, an expression of alarm, pleasure, or dismay—each becomes a social guide, telling toddlers how to react.

social referencing Seeking information about how to react to an unfamiliar or ambiguous object or event by observing someone else's expressions and reactions. That other person becomes a social reference.

After age 1, when infants reach the stage of active exploration (Piaget) and the crisis of autonomy versus shame and doubt (Erikson), their need to consult others becomes urgent. Toddlers search for cues in gaze and facial expressions, paying close attention to expressed emotions and watching carefully to detect intentions that explain other people's actions.

Social referencing has many practical applications. Consider mealtime. Caregivers the world over smack their lips, pretend to taste, and say "yum-yum," encouraging toddlers to eat and enjoy their first beets, liver, or spinach. For their part, toddlers become astute at reading expressions, insisting on the foods that the adults *really* like. Through this process, children in some cultures develop a taste for raw fish or curried goat or smelly cheese—foods that children in other cultures refuse.

Most everyday instances of social referencing occur with mothers. Infants usually heed their mother's wishes, expressed in tone and facial expression. This does not mean that infants are always obedient, especially in cultures where parents and children value independence. Not surprisingly, compliance has been the focus of study in the United States, where it often conflicts with independence.

For example, in one experiment, few toddlers obeyed their mother's request (prompted by the researchers) to pick up dozens of toys that they had not scattered (Kochanska et al., 2001). Their refusal indicates some emotional maturity: Self-awareness had led to pride and autonomy. The body language and expressions of some of the mothers implied that they did not really expect their children to obey.

These same toddlers, however, were quite obedient when their mothers told them not to touch an attractive toy. The mothers used tone, expression, and words to make this prohibition clear. Because of social referencing, toddlers understood the message. Even when the mothers were out of sight, half of the 14-month-olds and virtually all of the 22-month-olds obeyed. Most (80 percent) of the older toddlers seemed to agree with the mothers' judgment (Kochanska et al., 2001).

Mothers use a variety of expressions, vocalizations, and gestures to convey social information, and infants rely on them. For example, babies reflect mothers' anxiety about strangers (de Rosnay et al., 2006) and use their mother's cues to understand the differences between real and pretend eating (Nishida & Lillard, 2007).

Mothers are not the only or even the best social references. During toddlerhood, sometimes strangers are consulted more than mothers, especially about toys that the mother has not seen (Stenberg & Hagekull, 2007; Walden & Kim, 2005).

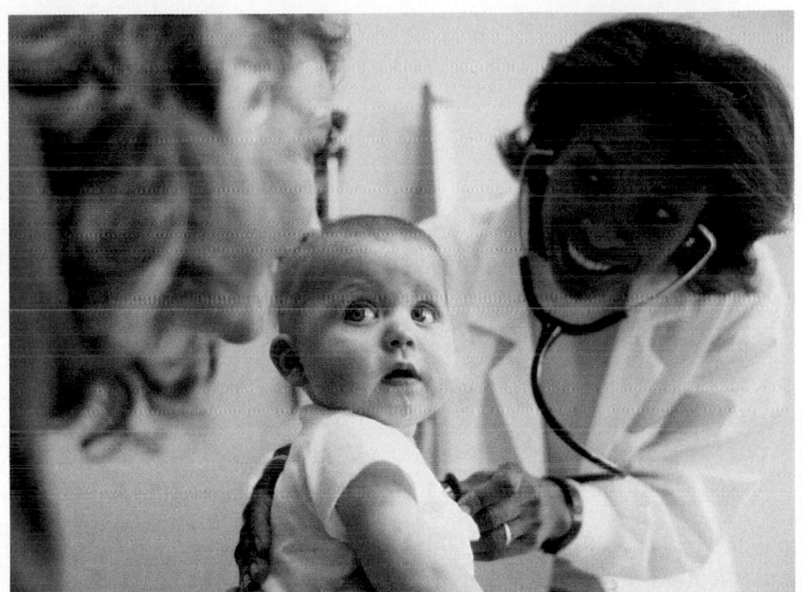
MICHAEL MALYSZKO/GETTY IMAGES

Whose Smile to Believe? Logically, the doctor is the one to watch: She has the stethoscope, and she is closer. But this baby references her mother, as any securely attached 1-year-old would.

Fathers as Social Partners

In most nations and ethnic groups, fathers spend much less time with infants than mothers do and are less involved parents (Parke & Buriel, 2006; Tudge, 2008). Although fathers' ethnotheories are one reason, mothers often act as gatekeepers, limiting fathers' interactions with their children in the stereotyped belief that child care is the special domain of mothers (Gaertner et al., 2007).

Latino Fathers

A related stereotype holds that Latino fathers are too *macho*—too assertively masculine—to be interested in child care. Several studies have refuted this view, showing that Hispanic American fathers tend to be more involved with daily child care than are fathers of other ethnic groups (Parke, 2002). In addition, when families around the world are compared, only Brazilian fathers are as actively engaged with their infants as mothers are (Tudge, 2008).

A study of more than 1,000 Latino 9-month-olds found "fathers with moderate to high levels of engagement" (Cabrera et al., 2006, p. 1203). Although many possible correlates of paternal involvement (income, education, age) were analyzed, only one significant predictor of the level of engagement was found: how happy the father was with the infant's mother. Happier husbands tend to be more involved fathers.

Comparing Fathers and Mothers

The fact is that fathers can do much to enhance their children's social and emotional development. Fathers as well as mothers naturally read their infant's emotions and then respond with synchrony, often provoking more laughter than the mothers do. Some research finds that fathers are particularly adept at helping infants modulate their anger. For instance, teenagers are less likely to lash out at friends and authorities if, as infants, they experienced a warm, responsive relationship with their fathers (Trautmann-Villalba et al., 2006).

CHROMOSOHM / SOHM / PHOTO RESEARCHERS, INC.

Up, Up, and Away! The vigorous play typical of fathers is likely to help in the infant's mastery of motor skills and the development of muscle control. (Of course, fathers must be careful not to harm fragile bones and developing brains.)

Infants may be securely attached to both parents equally, more attached to their mothers, or more attached to their fathers (Belsky et al., 2006). Close father–infant relationships can teach infants (especially boys) appropriate expressions of emotion (Boyce et al., 2006). Close relationships with infants help the men as well, reducing their risk of depression (Borke et al., 2007; Bronte-Tinkew et al., 2007).

Fathers encourage infants to explore, whereas mothers tend be more cautious and protective. "Mothers engage in more caregiving and comforting, and fathers in more high intensity play," according to several studies (Kochanska et al., 2008, p. 41). When toddlers are about to explore, they often seek their father's approval, expecting fun from their fathers and comfort from their mothers (Lamb, 2000).

In this, infants show social intelligence, because fathers play imaginative and exciting games. They move their infant's legs and arms in imitation of walking, kicking, or climbing; or play "airplane," zooming the baby through the air; or tap and tickle the baby's stomach. Mothers caress, murmur, read, or sing soothingly; combine play with caretaking; and use standard sequences such as peek-a-boo and patty-cake. In short, fathers are more proximal when it comes to stimulating body play.

Infant Day Care

You have seen that social bonds are crucial for infants. Worldwide, most infants are cared for primarily by their mothers, with most of the rest cared for by relatives, typically grandmothers. On average, only about 15 percent of infants under age 2 receive care from a nonrelative who is both paid and trained to provide it.

International Comparisons

The actual percentage of infants in day care varies markedly from nation to nation (Melhuish, 2006). Infant day care outside the home by strangers is common in France, Israel, and Sweden, where it is heavily subsidized by the government, and very scarce in India, Ethiopia, and most Latin American nations, where it is not.

In Canada, 70 percent of all children are cared for exclusively by their mothers in their first year, but in the United States, almost 80 percent are cared for by someone else as well. The reasons are many, but one of them is that Canada provides more financial support for new mothers, so more of them can afford to take time off from work to care for their babies (Côté et al., 2008).

As you will soon learn, the effects of nonmaternal care are difficult to assess, partly because cultural and economic factors affect the kind of care an infant receives. For instance, in England, a large study found that fewer than half the infants were cared for exclusively by their mothers, but almost half of those in nonmaternal care (44 percent) were cared for by grandmothers. Overall, this study found that infants in nonmaternal care were more likely to be emotionally immature later on—but that may be because grandmother care was more common when mothers were young and poor, factors that correlate with children's behavioral problems no matter who the caregiver is (Fergusson et al., 2008).

Types of Nonrelative Care

family day care Child care that occurs in the home of someone to whom the child is not related and who usually cares for several children of various ages.

More than half of all 1-year-olds in the United States are in "regularly scheduled" nonmaternal care (Loeb et al., 2004). Often this is care provided by a relative, which varies in quality and availability. Another option is **family day care,** in which children are cared for in the home of a paid nonrelative. It is called "family" care because a relatively small group of young children of many ages are together, as siblings once were in large families. Family day care may be problematic for

TABLE 7.6

High-Quality Day Care

High-quality day care during infancy has five essential characteristics:

1. *Adequate attention to each infant.* This means a low caregiver-to-infant ratio (such as two reliable adults and five infants) and, probably even more important, a small group of infants. Infants need familiar, loving caregivers; continuity of care is crucial.
2. *Encouragement of language and sensorimotor development.* Infants should receive extensive language exposure through games, songs, conversations, and positive talk of all kinds, along with easily manipulated toys.
3. *Attention to health and safety.* Good signs are cleanliness routines (e.g., handwashing before meals), accident prevention (e.g., no small objects that could be swallowed), and safe areas to explore (e.g., a clean, padded area for movement).
4. *Well-trained and professional caregivers.* Ideally, every caregiver should have a degree or certificate in early-childhood education and should have worked with children for several years. Turnover should be low, morale high, and enthusiasm evident. Good caregivers love their children and their work.
5. *Warm and responsive caregivers.* Providers should engage the children in problem solving and discussions, rather than giving instructions. Quiet, obedient children may be an indication of unresponsive care.

For a more detailed evaluation of day care, see the checklist in NICHD, 2005.

infants and toddlers because they get less attention than older children and are sometimes picked on by them (Kryzer et al., 2007).

A better option may be **center day care,** in which several paid adults care for many children in a place especially designed for the purpose. Most day-care centers group children by age, so infants and toddlers are separated from older children. Quality varies in such places, as do laws that set standards. Some U.S. states are silent on center day care for infants, others regulate it, and others forbid it.

center day care Child care that occurs in a place especially designed for the purpose, where several paid adults care for many children. Usually the children are grouped by age, the day-care center is licensed, and providers are trained and certified in child development.

In the United States, parents generally encounter a "mix of quality, price, type of care, and government subsidies" (Haskins, 2005, p. 168). Some center care is excellent (see Table 7.6), with adequate space, appropriate equipment, trained providers, and a ratio of two adults to five infants or better (de Schipper et al., 2006). Such care is hard to find. It is also quite expensive, so the families that use it are likely to have higher-than-average incomes. In some other nations whose governments provide funding, families at all income levels use center care.

The Effects of Infant Day Care

The evidence is overwhelming that good preschool education (reviewed in Chapter 9) is beneficial for young children. However, when it comes to infant day care, "disagreements about the wisdom (indeed, the morality) of nonmaternal child care for the very young remain" (NICHD, 2005, p. xiv). A major concern is that the quality of day care varies, because some caregivers look after many infants and have received only limited training (Waldfogel, 2006).

A large study in Canada found that approximately 30 percent of children were cared for by someone other than their mothers (usually relatives) in their first year. Boys from high-income families fared less well in nonmaternal care than other boys did: By age 4, they were slightly more likely to be aggressive and to have emotional problems (e.g., a teacher might note that a boy "seems unhappy"). The opposite was true for boys from low-income families: They actually benefited from nonmaternal care. No effects were found for girls. The researchers insist that no policy implications can be derived from this study, partly because care varied so much in quality, location, and provider (Côté et al., 2008).

ANN HEISENFELT / AP PHOTO

Secure Attachment Kirstie and her 10-month-old daughter Mia enjoy a moment of synchrony in an infant day-care center sponsored by a family-friendly employer, General Mills. High-quality day care and high-quality home care are equally likely to foster secure attachment between mother and infant.

Especially for Day-Care Providers (see response, page 214): A mother who brings her child to you for day care says that she knows she is harming her baby but must work out of economic necessity. What do you say?

In the United States, an ongoing longitudinal study by the Early Child Care Network of the National Institute of Child Health and Human Development (NICHD) has followed the development of more than 1,300 children from birth to age 11 (NICHD, 2005). It has found many cognitive benefits of day care, especially in language.

The social consequences were not as clear. Most analyses of the data found that secure attachment to the mother was as common among infants in center care as among infants cared for at home. Like other, smaller studies, the NICHD research confirms that infant day care, even for 40 hours a week before age 1, has much less influence on child development than does the warmth of the mother–infant relationship (NICHD, 2005).

The NICHD study has also found that infant day care seems detrimental *only* when the mother is insensitive *and* the infant spends more than 20 hours a week in a poor-quality program in which there are too few caregivers with too little training (NICHD, 2005). Again, boys were affected more than girls were. Boys who received extensive nonmaternal care became more quarrelsome and had more conflicts with their teachers than did other boys (NICHD, 2003).

No study has found that children of employed mothers develop emotional or other problems *solely* because their mothers are working outside the home. On balance, children are more likely to benefit if their mothers are employed than if they are not (Goldberg et al., 2008).

Many employed mothers make infant care their top priority. A time-use study found that mothers who worked full time outside the home spent almost as much time playing with their babies (14½ hours a week) as did mothers without outside jobs (16 hours a week) (Huston & Aronson, 2005). To make more time for their babies, the employed mothers spent half as much time on housework, less time with their husbands, and almost no time on leisure. The study concludes:

> There was no evidence that mothers' time at work interfered with the quality of their relationship with their infants, the quality of the home environment, or children's development. In fact, the results suggest the opposite. Mothers who spent more time at work provided slightly higher quality home environments.
>
> *[Huston & Aronson, 2005, p. 479]*

Infants cared for at home by a depressed mother fare worse than they would in center care (Loeb et al., 2004). Many studies find that out-of-home day care is better than in-home care if an infant's family does not provide adequate stimulation and attention (Ramey et al., 2002; Votruba-Drzal et al., 2004). The infant's temperament, the parents' ethnotheories, and the family income affect any type of care the infant receives (Crockenberg, 2003).

SUMMING UP

Infants seek social bonds, which they develop with one or several people. Parents are crucial, although much also depends on infant temperament. Synchrony begins in the early months: Infants and caregivers interact face to face, making split-second adjustments in their emotional responses to each other. Synchrony evolves into attachment, an emotional bond with adult caregivers. Secure attachment allows learning to progress; insecure infants are less confident and may develop emotional impairments. As infants become more curious and as they encounter new toys, people, and events, they use social referencing to learn whether such new things are fearsome or fun.

The emotional connections evident in synchrony, attachment, and social referencing may occur with mothers, fathers, other relatives, and day-care providers. Nations and families vary a great deal in how much nonmaternal care is provided for infants, as well as in the quality of that care. Consequences also vary, although most employed mothers still provide responsive care. Problems with later development may occur if an infant receives unresponsive care (as when too many infants have one caregiver). The quality and continuity of child care matter more than where and by whom it is provided. ■

Conclusions in Theory and in Practice

You have seen in this chapter that the first two years of life are filled with psychosocial interactions, which result from genes, maturation, culture, and caregivers. Each of the five major theories seems plausible. No single theory stands out as superior in every case.

All theorists agree that the first two years are a crucial period in a child's development: Early emotional and social development is influenced by the parents' behavior, the quality of care, cultural patterns, and inborn traits. It has not been proven whether one positive influence, such as a good day-care center, fully compensates for another, negative influence, such as a depressed mother (although parental influence is always significant).

Multicultural research has identified a wide variety of child-rearing practices in different societies. The data imply that no one event (such as toilet training, in Freud's theory) determines emotional health.

On the basis of what you have learned, you could safely advise parents to play with their infants; respond to their physical and emotional needs; let babies explore; maintain a relationship; and expect every toddler to be sometimes angry, sometimes proud, sometimes fearful. Depending on infant temperament, parental actions and attitudes may or may not have a powerful effect on later development, but they certainly can make infants happier or sadder. Synchrony, attachment, and social referencing are crucial to infant and toddler development.

Such generalities are not good enough for Jacob (the boy you met on page 192) or for any other infant who shows signs of malnutrition, delayed language, poor social skills, abnormal emotional development, insecure or disorganized attachment, or other deficits. In dealing with individual children who have problems, we need to be more specific.

Jacob was 3 years old but not talking. His psychosocial development was impaired. Looking at Table 7.7 on infant development, you can see that even at 3 months Jacob was unusual in his reactions to familiar people. All infants need one or two people who are emotionally invested in them from the first days of their life, and Jacob may have had no one. There is no indication of synchrony or attachment.

After Jacob was diagnosed with pervasive developmental disorder, his parents consulted a psychiatrist who specialized in children with psychosocial problems (Greenspan & Wieder, 2003). He showed them how to relate to Jacob, saying, "I am going to teach you how to play with your son." They learned about "floor time," four hours a day set aside to get on their son's level. They were to imitate him, act as if they were part of the game, put their faces and bodies in front of his, create synchrony even though Jacob did not initiate it. The father reports:

> We rebuilt Jacob's connection to us and to the world—but on his terms. We were drilled to always follow his lead, to always build on his initiative. In a sense, we could only ask Jacob to join our world if we were willing to enter his. . . . He would

An Eventful Time This table lists aspects of development that have been discussed in Chapters 5, 6, and 7. Throughout infancy, temperament and experience affect when and how babies display the characteristics and achievements listed here. The list is meant as a rough guideline, not as a yardstick for indicating a child's progress in intelligence or any other trait.

TABLE 7.7

AT ABOUT THIS TIME: Infancy

Approximate Age	Characteristic or Achievement
3 months	Rolls over Laughs Stays half-upright in stroller Uses two eyes together Grabs for object; if rattle in hand, can shake it Makes cooing noises Joyous recognition of familiar people
6 months	Sits up, without adult support (but sometimes using arms) Grabs and grasps objects with whole hand Babbles, listens, and responds Tries to crawl (on belly, not yet on all fours) Stands and bounces with support (on someone's lap, in a bouncer) Begins to show anger, fear, attachment
12 months	Stands without holding on Crawls well Takes a few unsteady steps Uses fingers, including pincer grasp (thumb and forefinger) Can feed self with fingers Speaks a few words (*mama, dada, baba*) Strong attachment to familiar caregivers Apparent fear of strangers, of unexpected noises and events
18 months	Walks well Runs (also falls) Tries to climb on furniture Speaks 50–100 words; most are nouns Responds to requests Likes to drop things, throw things, take things apart Recognizes self in mirror
24 months	Runs well Climbs up (down is harder) Uses simple tools (spoon, large marker) Combines words (usually noun/verb, sometimes noun/verb/noun) Can use fingers to unscrew tops, open doors Interested in new experiences and new children

> drop rocks and we would catch them. He would want to put pennies in a bank and we would block the slot. He would want to run in a circle and we would get in his way.
>
> I remember a cold fall day when I was putting lime on our lawn. He dipped his hand in the powder and let it slip through his fingers. He loved the way it felt. I took the lawn spreader and ran to the other part of our yard. He ran after me. I let him have one dip and ran across the yard again. He dipped, I ran, he dipped, I ran. We did this until I could no longer move my arms.
>
> [*Jacob's father,* 1997, *p. 62*]

Jacob's case is obviously extreme, but many infants and parents have difficulty establishing synchrony (Feldman, 2007). From the perspective of early psychosocial development, nothing could be more important than a connection like the one Jacob and his parents gradually succeeded in establishing.

> In Jacob's case it worked. He said his first word at age 3, and by age 5 . . . he speaks for days at a time. He talks from the moment he wakes up to the moment he falls asleep, as if he is making up for lost time. He wants to know everything.

➤Response for Day-Care Providers (from page 212): Reassure the mother that you will keep her baby safe and will help to develop the baby's mind and social skills by fostering synchrony and attachment. Also tell her that the quality of mother–infant interaction at home is more important than anything else for psychosocial development; mothers who are employed full time usually have wonderful, secure relationships with their infants. If the mother wishes, you can discuss ways in which she can be a more responsive mother.

> "How does a live chicken become an eating chicken? Why are microbes so small? Why do policemen wear badges? Why are dinosaurs extinct? What is French? [A question I often ask myself.] Why do ghosts glow in the dark?" He is not satisfied with answers that do not ring true or that do not satisfy his standards of clarity. He will keep on asking until he gets it. Rebecca and I have become expert definition providers. Just last week, we were faced with the ultimate challenge: "Dad," he asked: "Is God real or not?" And then, just to make it a bit more challenging, he added: "How do miracles happen?"
>
> *[Jacob's father, 1997, p. 63]*

Miracles do not always happen. Children with pervasive developmental disorder usually require special care throughout childhood; Jacob may continue to need extra attention. Nevertheless, almost all infants, almost all the time, develop strong relationships with their close family members. The power of early psychosocial development is obvious to every developmentalist and, it is hoped, to every reader of this text.

SUMMARY

Emotional Development

1. Two emotions, contentment and distress, appear as soon as an infant is born. Anger emerges with restriction and frustration, between 4 and 8 months of age, and becomes stronger by age 1.

2. Reflexive fear is apparent in very young infants. However, fear of something specific, including fear of strangers and fear of separation, does not appear until toward the end of the first year.

3. In the second year, social awareness produces more selective fear, anger, and joy. As infants become increasingly self-aware at about 18 months, emotions—specifically, pride, shame, and affection—emerge that encourage an interface between the self and others.

4. Brain maturation has an obvious impact on emotional development, although specifics are not yet known. Synesthesia (connections between senses and emotions) is apparent early in life. Self-recognition (on the mirror/rouge test) emerges at about 18 months.

5. Stress impedes early brain and emotional development. Some infants are particularly vulnerable to the effects of early care.

Theories of Infant Psychosocial Development

6. According to all five major theories, caregiver behavior is especially influential in the first two years. Freud stressed the mother's impact on oral and anal pleasure; Erikson emphasized trust and autonomy.

7. Behaviorists focus on learning; parents teach their babies many things, including when to be fearful or joyful. Cognitive theory holds that infants develop working models based on their experiences.

8. Epigenetic theory emphasizes temperament, a set of genetic traits whose expression is influenced by the environment. Specific links between inborn temperament and later personality have been found in many studies.

9. The sociocultural approach notes the impact of social and cultural factors on the parent–infant relationship. Ethnotheories shape infant emotions and traits so that they fit well within the culture. Some cultures encourage proximal parenting (more physical touch); others promote distal parenting (more talk and object play).

The Development of Social Bonds

10. Parental practices inhibit and guide a child's emotions. Ideally, a good fit develops between the parents' actions and the child's personality.

11. Sometimes by 2 months, and clearly by 6 months, infants become more responsive and social, and synchrony begins. Synchrony involves moment-by-moment interaction. Caregivers need to be responsive and sensitive. Infants are disturbed by a still face because they expect and need social interaction.

12. Attachment, measured by the baby's reaction to the caregiver's presence, departure, and return in the Strange Situation, is crucial. Some infants seem indifferent (type A—insecure-avoidant) or overly dependent (type C—insecure-resistant/ambivalent), instead of secure (type B). Disorganized attachment (type D) is the most worrisome form.

13. Secure attachment provides encouragement for infant exploration. As they play, toddlers engage in social referencing, looking to other people's facial expressions to detect what is fearsome and what is enjoyable.

14. Fathers are wonderful playmates for infants, who frequently use them as social references, learning about emotions and exploration. Male ethnotheories sometimes inhibit father involvement; mothers sometimes discourage it.

15. The impact of nonmaternal care depends on many factors. Psychosocial characteristics, including secure attachment, are influenced more by the mother's warmth than by the number of hours spent in nonmaternal care. Quality of care is crucial, no matter who provides that care.

Conclusions in Theory and in Practice

16. Experts debate exactly how critical early psychosocial development may be: Is it the essential foundation for all later growth or just one of many steps along the way? However, all infants need caregivers who are committed to them and are dedicated to encouraging each aspect of early development.

KEY TERMS

social smile (p. 188)
stranger wariness (p. 189)
separation anxiety (p. 189)
self-awareness (p. 190)
trust versus mistrust (p. 195)
autonomy versus shame and doubt (p. 195)
social learning (p. 196)
working model (p. 196)
temperament (p. 197)
Big Five (p. 198)
ethnotheory (p. 199)
proximal parenting (p. 199)
distal parenting (p. 199)
goodness of fit (p. 202)
synchrony (p. 203)
still-face technique (p. 204)
attachment (p. 205)
secure attachment (p. 206)
insecure-avoidant attachment (p. 206)
insecure-resistant/ambivalent attachment (p. 206)
disorganized attachment (p. 206)
Strange Situation (p. 207)
social referencing (p. 208)
family day care (p. 210)
center day care (p. 211)

KEY QUESTIONS

1. How would a sensitive parent respond to an infant's distress?

2. How do emotions in the second year of life differ from emotions in the first year?

3. What is known and unknown about the impact of brain maturation on emotional development?

4. What are the similarities between the psychoanalytic and the behaviorist theories of infant development?

5. What are the similarities between epigenetic and sociocultural theories of infant emotions?

6. How might synchrony affect the development of emotions in the first year?

7. Attachments are said to be lifelong. Describe an adult who is insecurely attached and explain how infant attachment could be relevant.

8. How would infants be affected by the involvement (or noninvolvement) of their fathers?

9. Why would a mother and father choose not to care for their infant themselves, 24/7?

10. What are the advantages and disadvantages of three kinds of nonmaternal infant care: relatives, family day care, and center day care?

APPLICATIONS

1. One cultural factor influencing infant development is how infants are carried from place to place. Ask four mothers whose infants were born in each of the past four decades how they transported them—front or back carriers, facing out or in, strollers or carriages, car seats or on mother's laps, and so on. Why did they choose the mode(s) they chose? What are their opinions and yours on how that cultural practice might affect infants' development?

2. Observe synchrony for three minutes. Ideally, ask the parent of an infant under 8 months of age to play with the infant. If no infant is available, observe a pair of lovers as they converse. Note the sequence and timing of every facial expression, sound, and gesture of both partners.

3. Telephone several day-care centers to try to assess the quality of care they provide. Ask about such factors as adult–child ratio, group size, and training for caregivers of children of various ages. Is there a minimum age? If so, why was that age chosen? Analyze the answers, using Table 7.6 as a guide.

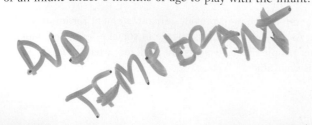

PART II The Developing Person So Far: The First Two Years

BIOSOCIAL

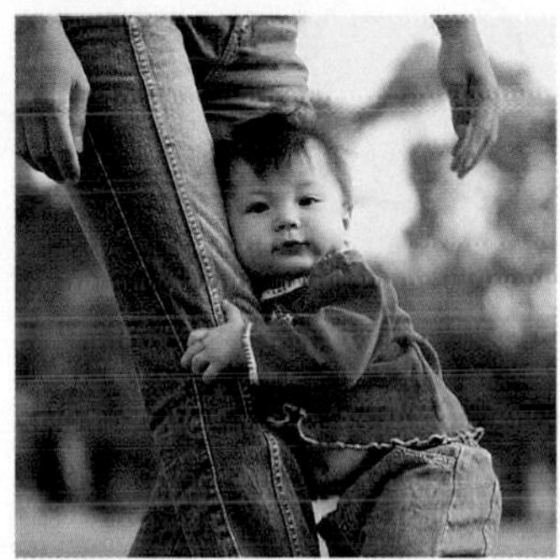

Body Changes Over the first two years, the body quadruples in weight and the brain triples in weight. Connections between brain cells grow increasingly dense, with complex neural networks of dendrites and axons. Neurons become coated with an insulating layer of myelin, sending messages faster and more efficiently, and the various states—sleeping, waking, exploring—become more distinct. Experiences that are universal (experience-expectant) and culture-bound (experience-dependent) both aid brain growth, partly by allowing pruning of unused connections between neurons.

Senses and Motor Skills Brain maturation underlies the development of all the senses. Seeing, hearing, and mobility progress from reflexes to coordinated voluntary actions, including focusing, grasping, and walking. Culture is evident in sensory and motor development, as brain networks respond to the particulars of each infant's life.

Public Health Infant health depends on immunization, parental practices (including "back to sleep"), and nutrition (ideally, breast milk). Survival rates are much higher today than they were even a few decades ago, yet in some regions of the world infant growth is still stunted because of malnutrition.

COGNITIVE

Sensorimotor Intelligence and Information Processing As Piaget describes it, during the first two years (sensorimotor intelligence) infants progress from knowing their world through immediate sensory experiences to being able to "experiment" on that world through actions and mental images. Information-processing theory stresses the links between input (sensory experiences) and output (perception). Infants develop affordances, their own ideas regarding the possibilities offered by the objects and events of the world. Recent research finds traces of memory at 3 months, object permanence at 4 months, and deferred imitation at 9 months—all much younger ages than Piaget described.

Language Interaction with responsive adults exposes infants to the structure of communication and thus language. By age 1, infants can usually speak a word or two; by age 2, language has exploded, as toddlers talk in short sentences and add vocabulary words each day. Language develops through reinforcement, neurological maturation, and social motivation.

PSYCHOSOCIAL

Emotions and Theories Emotions develop from basic newborn reactions to complex, self-conscious responses. Infants' increasing self-awareness and independence are shaped by parents, in a transition explained by Freud's oral and anal stages, by Erikson's crises of trust versus mistrust and autonomy versus shame and doubt, by behaviorism in the focus on parental responses, and by cognitive theory's working models. Much of basic temperament—and therefore personality—is inborn and apparent throughout life, as epigenetic theory explains. Sociocultural theory stresses cultural norms, evident in parents' ethnotheories that guide them in raising their infants.

The Development of Social Bonds Early on, parents and infants respond to each other by synchronizing their behavior in social play. Toward the end of the first year, secure attachment between child and parent sets the stage for the child's increasingly independent exploration of the world. Insecure attachment—avoidant, resistant, or disorganized—signifies a parent–child relationship that hinders infant learning. Infants become active participants in social interactions. Fathers and day-care providers, as well as mothers, encourage infants' social confidence.

Early Childhood

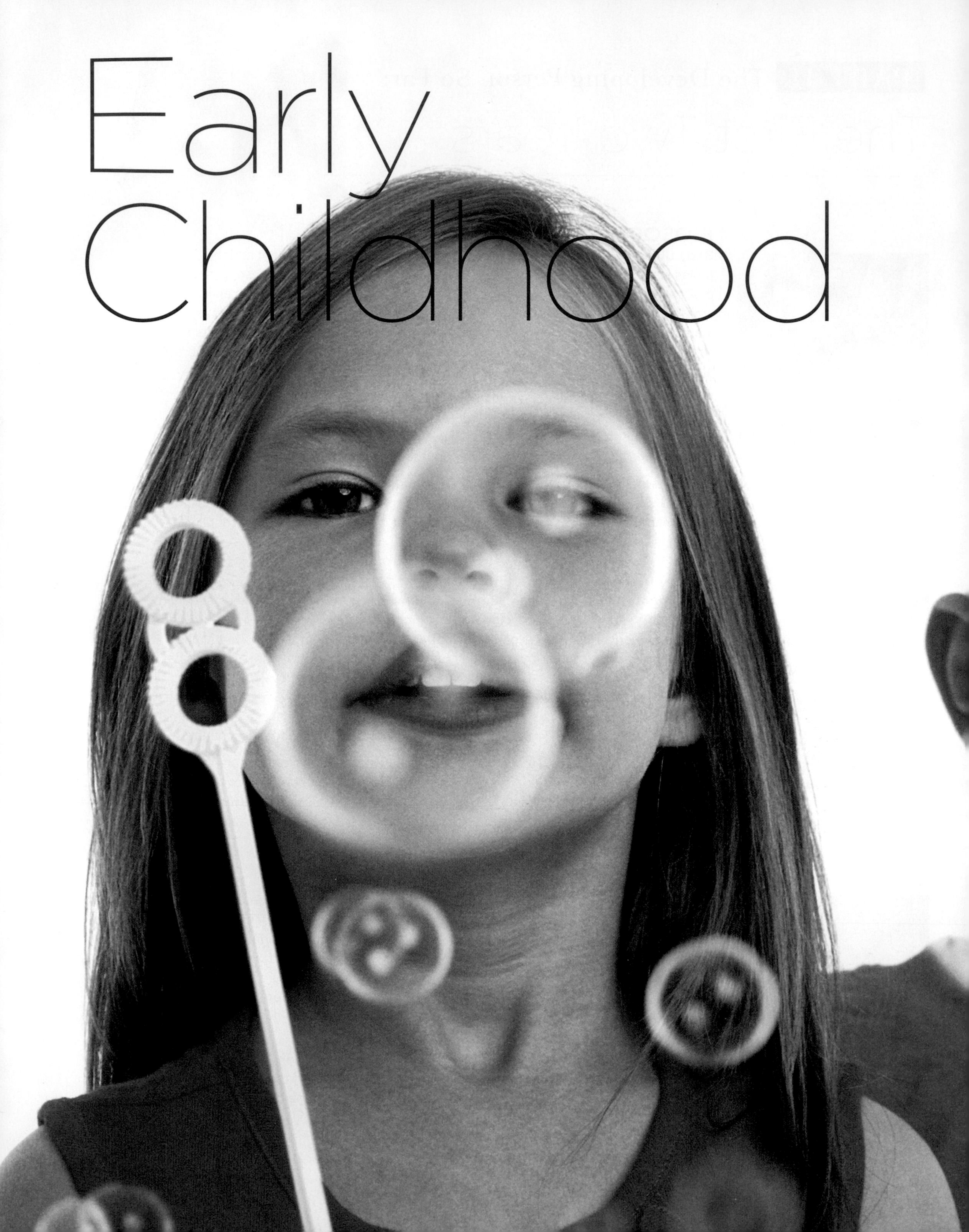

CHAPTER 8
CHAPTER 9
CHAPTER 10

PART III

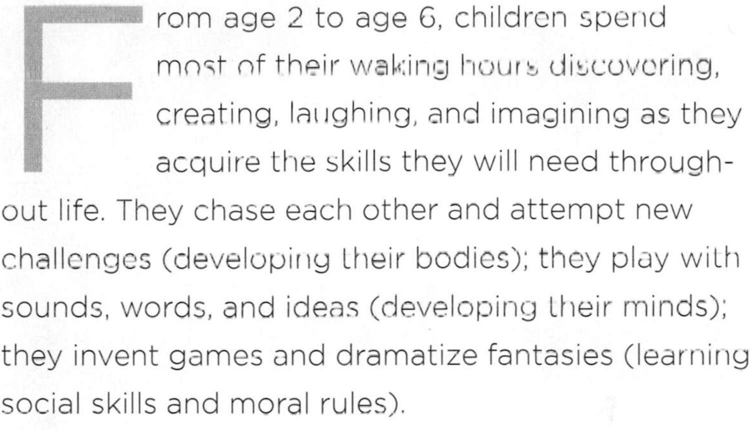

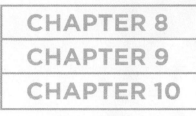

From age 2 to age 6, children spend most of their waking hours discovering, creating, laughing, and imagining as they acquire the skills they will need throughout life. They chase each other and attempt new challenges (developing their bodies); they play with sounds, words, and ideas (developing their minds); they invent games and dramatize fantasies (learning social skills and moral rules).

These years have been called *the preschool years,* but that has become a misnomer. It is now apparent that school does not necessarily mean sitting at desks in rows. Many 2- to 6-year-olds are in school of some sort, learning and playing.

These years have also been called *the play years,* since at this age growing up is a game. The young child's delight in life seems magical—whether quietly tracking a beetle through the grass or riotously turning a bedroom into a shambles. Young children's minds seem playful, too; they explain that "a bald man has a barefoot head" or that "the sun shines so children can go outside to play." However, although young children do most of their learning as they play, these are not the only play years. Developmentalists have now documented that playfulness is essential at every age.

Therefore, in this trio of chapters we now use the more traditional term *early childhood* to refer to ages 2 to 6. Early childhood is a period of extraordinary growth, learning, and play, a joyful time not only for young children but also for anyone who knows them.

8

CHAPTER OUTLINE

Early Childhood: Biosocial Development

I remember as a child leaping off the back of our couch again and again, trying to fly. My mother and brother laughed at me, although my mother also wondered whether she had made a mistake in taking me to see *Peter Pan*. An older family friend warned me that I would hurt my uterus if I jumped down from too high, too often. I didn't know what a uterus was, nor did I stop jumping until I decided that I could not fly because I had no pixie dust.

When you were 3 years old, I hope you wanted to fly like a bird, a plane, or Superman, and I hope someone kept you safe. Protection is needed, as well as appreciation of the attempt. Do you remember trying to skip, tie your shoes, or write your name? Three-year-olds try and fail, but soon practice and maturation allow them to skip, write, and do much more.

From age 2 to 6, as children grow bigger and stronger, they become more skilled at hundreds of tasks. These early childhood advances in brain and body, and the need for adult protection, are the themes of this chapter.

Body Changes

In early childhood as in infancy, the body and brain develop according to powerful epigenetic forces, biologically driven as well as socially guided, experience-expectant and experience-dependent (as explained in Chapter 5). Bodies and brains come much closer in size and function to those of adults. Compared with cute and chubby 1-year-olds, 6-year-olds are quite mature.

Growth Patterns

Just comparing a toddling 1-year-old and a cartwheeling 6-year-old makes some differences obvious. During early childhood, children become slimmer as the lower body lengthens and baby fat turns to muscle. In fact, the body mass index (or BMI, the ratio of weight to height) is lower at age 5 than at any other age in the entire life span (Guillaume & Lissau, 2002). Gone are the protruding belly, round face, short limbs, and large head that characterize the toddler. The center of gravity moves from the breastbone to the belly button, enabling cartwheels, somersaults, balancing acts, and many other motor skills. The joys of dancing, gymnastics, and pumping a swing become possible as body proportions enable new skills year by year.

MARCY MALOY / DIGITALVISION / GETTY IMAGES

Not Much Difference? The 6-year-old is only about a foot taller than her 2-year-old sister, and the width of their upper legs is almost the same. However, we perceive the older girl as much bigger than the younger one, because we notice proportions: The older girl's legs are almost twice as long, and they account for half her height.

Increases in weight and height accompany these changes in proportions. Each year from age 2 through 6, well-nourished children gain about 4½ pounds (2 kilograms) and add almost 3 inches (about 7 centimeters) to their height. By age 6, the average child in a developed nation weighs about 46 pounds (21 kilograms) and is 46 inches (117 centimeters) tall.

A typical 6-year-old:

- Weighs between 40 and 50 pounds (between 18 and 22 kilograms)
- Is at least 3½ feet tall (more than 100 centimeters)
- Looks lean, not chubby (ages 5–6 are lowest in body fat)
- Has adultlike body proportions (legs constitute about half the total height)

When many ethnic groups live together in a nation with abundant food and adequate medical care, children of African descent tend to be tallest, followed by those of European descent, then Asians, and then Latinos. However, height differences are greater *within* ethnic groups than *between* groups. Body size is especially varied among children of African descent because they are more genetically diverse than people from other continents (Goel et al., 2004).

Over the centuries, low-income families encouraged their children to eat so that they would have a reserve of fat to protect them against famine. This was lifesaving. Even today, in the poorest nations, malnourished young children are more likely to die young than are other children. They also become less capable adolescents, as shown by a recent study in Ghana. Compared with similar children who were not malnourished in early childhood, more of them were depressed, mentally impaired, or both (but fewer were delinquent) (Appoh, 2004; Appoh & Krekling, 2004).

The practice of encouraging young children to eat has recently become destructive. Many children, especially in low-income families, eat too much and become overweight. In 1975 in Brazil, for example, *undernutrition* represented two-thirds of all nutrition problems. Thirty years later, *overnutrition* had become the most common problem (Monteiro et al., 2004). The rate of overweight was twice as high among low-income Brazilians as among richer ones (Monteiro et al., 2007).

A detailed study of 2- to 4-year-olds in low-income families in New York City found many overweight children; moreover, the proportion of overweight children increased as family income fell (Nelson et al., 2004). Overweight among children also increased with age (27 percent at age 4 compared with 14 percent at age 2). This finding suggests that eating habits, not genes, were the cause. Overweight children were more often of Hispanic (27 percent) or Asian (22 percent) descent than of African (14 percent) or European (11 percent) origin.

One explanation for these ethnic differences is that a higher proportion of the Hispanic and Asian children lived with grandparents who knew firsthand the dangers of malnutrition. This possibility is supported by generational data: Hispanic and Asian American grandparents are unlikely to be obese themselves but often have overweight grandchildren (Bates et al., 2008). In the United States overall, young Latinos are twice as likely as other children to be obese (Kimbro et al., 2007).

Worldwide, an epidemic of adult heart disease and diabetes is spreading, as overfed children grow up to become overweight adults (Gluckman & Hanson, 2006). In fact, overweight children often have early symptoms of heart disease and type 2 diabetes. An article in *Lancet* (the leading medical journal in England) has predicted that by 2020, more than 228 million adults worldwide will have diabetes (more in India than in any other nation) as a result of unhealthy eating habits acquired in childhood. This article suggests that various measures to reduce childhood overeating in the United States have had only "patchwork" effect. As a result, "U.S. children could become the first generation in more than a century to have shorter life spans than their parents if current trends of excessive weight and obesity continue" (Devi, 2008, p. 105).

LAURA DWIGHT

No Spilled Milk This girl is demonstrating her mastery of the motor skills involved in pouring milk, to the evident admiration of her friend. The next skill will be drinking it—not a foregone conclusion, given the lactose intolerance of some children and the small appetites and notorious pickiness of children this age.

Observation Quiz (see answer, page 224): What three things can you see that indicate that this attempt at pouring will probably be successful?

Eating Habits

Appetite decreases between ages 2 and 6 because, compared with infants, young children need far fewer calories per pound of body weight. This is especially true for children today, who play outdoors less than their parents or grandparents did. However, instead of appreciating this natural change in appetite, many parents fret, threaten, and cajole their children into eating more than they should ("Eat all your dinner and you can have ice cream").

Nutritional Deficiencies

Although most children in developed nations consume more than enough calories, they do not always obtain adequate iron, zinc, and calcium. For example, consumption of calcium is lower than it was 20 years ago because children today drink less milk and more soda (Jahns et al., 2001). Another problem is sugar. Many cultures encourage children to eat sweets—in the form of birthday cake, holiday candy, desserts, and other treats.

Essential but Unknown Nutrients Sweetened cereals and drinks that are advertised as containing 100 percent of a day's vitamin requirements are a poor substitute for a balanced, varied diet. The main reason is their high sugar content. One of the many other reasons is that some essential nutrients have not yet been identified, much less listed on food labels. This means that eating a wide variety of foods is the only way to make sure that essential vitamins and minerals are being consumed. Fresh fruits and vegetables provide more than vitamins; they also provide other dietary essentials, not only known ones (such as fiber) but others not yet known.

Oral Health Furthermore, too much sugar and too little fiber encourage tooth decay, the most common disease of young children in developed nations; it affects more than a third of all children under age 6 in the United States (Brickhouse et al., 2008). Primary "baby" teeth are replaced by permanent teeth from about ages 6 to 10, but severe tooth decay in early childhood harms the permanent teeth (which are already formed below the baby teeth) and causes malformation of the jaw. Jaw deformities cause difficulty in chewing food and speaking properly.

Any form of malnutrition causes decay and delayed tooth growth. Thus, the state of a young child's teeth can alert adults to other health problems. National child health insurance covers dental care (Brickhouse et al., 2008).

Many preschoolers visit the dentist before age 6 if they have U.S.-born, middle-class parents, but not if their parents were born elsewhere. A study in San Francisco found that fear of the dentist was particularly common among immigrants from China, who were unlikely to take their young children for an oral health checkup (Hilton et al., 2007).

➤Answer to Observation Quiz (from page 223): The cup, the pitcher, and the person. The cup has an unusually wide opening; the pitcher is small and has a sturdy handle; and the girl is using both hands and giving her full concentration to the task.

Hazards of the "Just Right" Phenomenon

Many young children are quite compulsive about their daily routines, including meals. They insist on eating only certain foods, prepared and placed in a particular way. This rigidity, known as the "just right" or "just so" phenomenon, would be a sign of a pathological obsessive-compulsive disorder in adults but is normal and widespread among young children (Evans & Leckman, 2006). For example:

> Whereas parents may insist that the child eat his vegetables at dinner, the child may insist that the potatoes be placed only in a certain part of the plate and must not touch any other food; should the potatoes land outside of this area, the child may seem to experience a sense of near-contamination, setting off a tirade of fussiness for which many 2- and 3-year-olds are notorious.
>
> *[Evans et al., 1997, p. 59]*

Most young children's food preferences and rituals are far from ideal. (One 3-year-old I know wanted to eat only cream cheese sandwiches on white bread; one 4-year-old, only fast-food chicken nuggets.) When 1,500 parents of 1- to 6-year-olds were surveyed (Evans et al., 1997), they reported that their children's just-right phase peaked at about age 3, when the children:

Especially for Nutritionists (see response, page 227): A parent complains that she prepares a variety of vegetables and fruits, but her 4-year-old wants only French fries and cake. What should you advise?

- Preferred to have things done in a particular order or in a certain way
- Had a strong preference to wear (or not wear) certain articles of clothing
- Prepared for bedtime by engaging in a special activity, routine, or ritual
- Had strong preferences for certain foods

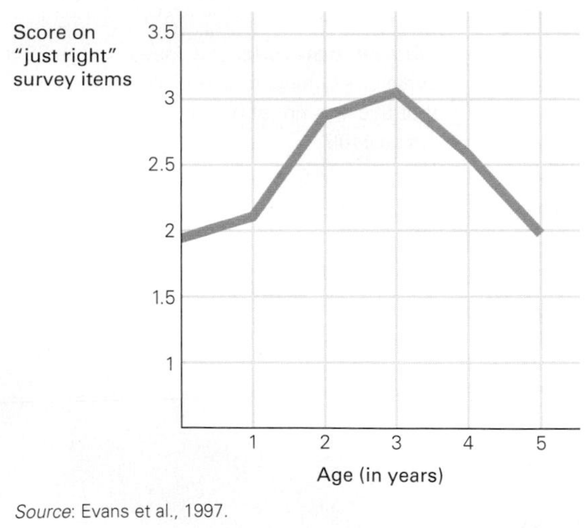

By age 6, this rigidity fades somewhat (see Figure 8.1). Another team of experts puts it this way: "Most, if not all, children exhibit normal age-dependent obsessive compulsive behaviors [which are] usually gone by middle childhood" (March et al., 2004, p. 216). Nevertheless, children of all ages, and even some adults, hold magical ideas about certain objects and routines (Evans & Leckman, 2006).

The best strategy for parents may be to be patient until the just-right obsession fades away. A child's insistence on a particular routine, a preferred pair of shoes, or a favorite cup can usually be accommodated until the child gets a little older. After all, many adults have preferred routines and engage in wishful thinking themselves, although most of them keep it in check with some rational thinking (Evans & Leckman, 2006).

Overeating is another story. Obesity is a major health problem for people of all ages, and it often begins during early childhood when the social context (television commercials, store displays, other children's eating behavior) encourages unhealthy eating and when parents do not realize the harm. Ideally, children would have only healthful foods to eat, a strategy that would protect their health lifelong (Gluckman & Hanson, 2006).

Score on "just right" survey items

Age (in years)

Source: Evans et al., 1997.

FIGURE 8.1

Young Children's Insistence on Routine This chart shows the average scores of children (who are rated by their parents) on a survey indicating the child's desire to have certain things—including food selection and preparation—done "just right." Such strong preferences for rigid routines tend to fade by age 6.

SUMMING UP

Between ages 2 and 6, children grow steadily taller and proportionately thinner, with variations depending on genes, nutrition, income, and ethnicity. Overweight is more common than underweight, especially in young children from low-income families. One reason is that adults encourage overeating, which once was protective but now may bring about the start of serious health problems. Oral health is also a concern, as many young children have cavities in their teeth. Young children usually have small appetites and picky eating habits and are often rewarded with foods that are high in sugar but low in nutrition. ■

Brain Development

Brains grow rapidly before birth and throughout infancy, as you saw in Chapter 5. By age 2, most neurons are connected to other neurons and substantial pruning of dendrites has occurred. The 2-year-old brain weighs 75 percent of what it will weigh in adulthood. (The major structures of the brain are diagrammed in Figure 8.2.)

Since most of the brain is already present and functioning by age 2, what remains to develop? The most important parts! Those functions of the brain that make us most human are the ones that develop after infancy, enabling quicker, better-coordinated, and more reflective thought (Kagan & Herschkowitz, 2005). The brain growth that occurs after infancy allows advanced language and social understanding and is a crucial difference between humans and other animals.

Speed of Thought

After infancy, proliferation of the communication pathways (dendrites and axons) results in some brain growth. However, most of the increase in brain weight (to 90 percent of adult weight by age 5) occurs because of **myelination** (Sampaio & Truwit, 2001). *Myelin* is a fatty coating on the axons that speeds signals between neurons, like insulation wrapped around electric wires to aid conduction.

The effects of myelination are most noticeable in early childhood (Nelson et al., 2006), partly because the areas of the brain that show greatest myelination during the early years are the motor and sensory areas (Kolb & Wishaw, 2008). Greater speed of thought becomes pivotal when several thoughts must occur in

myelination The process by which axons become coated with myelin, a fatty substance that speeds the transmission of nerve impulses from neuron to neuron.

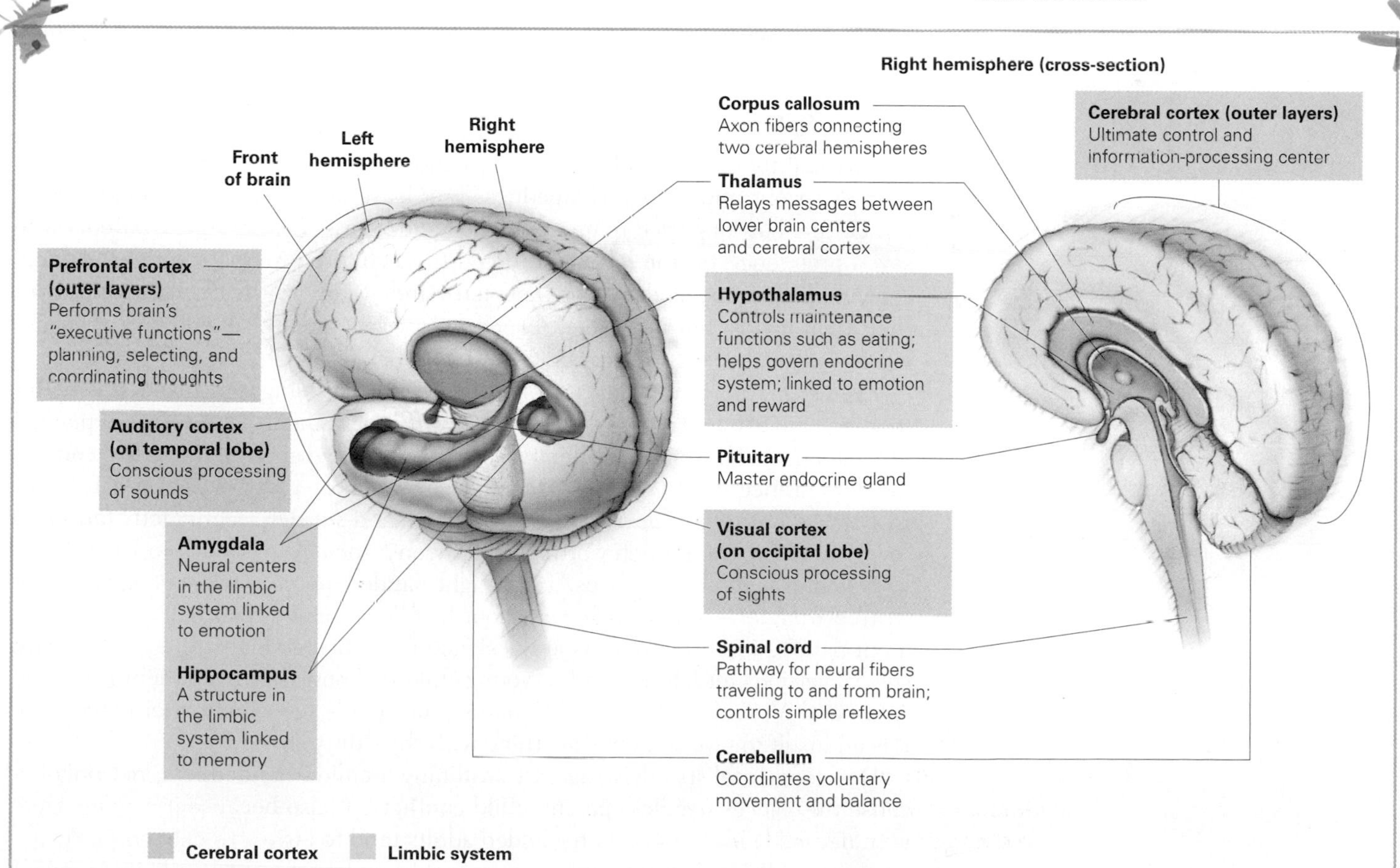

FIGURE 8.2

Connections A few of the dozens of named parts of the brain are shown here. Although each area has particular functions, the entire brain is interconnected. The processing of emotions, for example, occurs primarily in the limbic system, but many other brain areas are involved.

Especially for Early-Childhood Teachers (see response, page 228): You know you should be patient, but you feel your frustration rising when your young charges dawdle on the walk to the playground a block away. What should you do?

rapid succession. By age 6, most children can see an object and name it, catch a ball and throw it, write their ABCs in proper sequence, and so on.

Parents must still be patient when listening to young children talk, when helping them get dressed, or when watching them try to write their names. All these tasks are completed more slowly by 6-year-olds than by 16-year-olds. However, thanks to myelination, preschoolers are much quicker than toddlers, who may forget what they were doing before they finish.

Connecting the Brain's Hemispheres

One part of the brain that grows and myelinates rapidly during early childhood is the **corpus callosum**, a long, thick band of nerve fibers that connects the left and right sides of the brain. Growth of the corpus callosum makes communication between the two hemispheres more efficient, allowing children to coordinate the two sides of the brain or body. Failure of the corpus callosum to develop normally results in serious disorders and is one of many possible causes of autism (Mason et al., 2008).

corpus callosum A long, thick band of nerve fibers that connects the left and right hemispheres of the brain and allows communication between them.

To understand the significance of coordination between the two brain hemispheres, it is important to realize that the two sides of the body and of the brain do not function in identical ways. Each side specializes, so each is dominant for certain functions—the result of a process called **lateralization.** Lateralization, or "sidedness," is apparent not only in right- or left-handedness but also in the feet, the eyes, the ears, and the brain itself.

lateralization Literally, sidedness, referring to the specialization in certain functions by each side of the brain, with one side dominant for each activity. The left side of the brain controls the right side of the body, and vice versa.

Lateralization is epigenetic, prompted by genes, prenatal hormones, and early experiences. So is the maturation of the corpus callosum, which develops throughout childhood, at rates influenced by maturation and genes (Boles et al., 2008). Lateralization depends on development of the corpus callosum, which allows coordination between the two sides of the body.

The Left-Handed Child

Infants and toddlers usually prefer one hand over the other for grabbing objects such as spoons and rattles. Handedness is at least partly genetic (Goymer, 2007), but culture has long tried to impose right-handedness. For centuries, parents who saw a preference for the left hand forced their children to become right-handed. They usually succeeded in that their left-handed children learned to write with their right hands, but neurological success was incomplete: The brains of former lefties were only partly reprogrammed (Klöppel et al., 2007).

Even today, many cultures endorse the belief that being right-handed is better than being left-handed (an example of the *difference-equals-deficit error,* explained in Chapter 1). This bias is evident in language. In English, a "left-handed compliment" is insincere, and no one wants to have "two left feet" or be "out in left field." In Latin, *dexter* (as in *dexterity*) means "right" and *sinister* means "left" (and also "evil"). *Gauche,* the French word for left, means "socially awkward" in English.

Customs, including taboos, favor right-handed people. Most languages are written from left to right. Likewise, door handles, scissors, baseball mitts, instrument panels, and other objects are designed for right-handed people. (Some have special versions for lefties, but few young children know they need them.) In many Asian and African nations, the left hand is used only for wiping after defecation; it is an insult to give someone anything with that "dirty" hand.

Developmentalists advise against switching a child's handedness, not only because this causes needless parent–child conflict but also because it may interfere with natural lateralization. Left-handed adults tend to have a thicker corpus callosum, probably because growing up in a world that favors right-handedness meant that they had a greater need as children to coordinate the two sides of their bodies (Cherbuin & Brinkman, 2006). A thicker corpus callosum may be one reason a disproportionate number of artists, musicians, and sports stars are left-handed.

The Whole Brain

Through studies of people with brain damage as well as through brain imaging, neurologists have discovered how the brain's hemispheres specialize: The left half controls the right side of the body and contains areas dedicated to logical reasoning, detailed analysis, and the basics of language; the right half controls the left side of the body and contains areas dedicated to generalized emotional and creative impulses, including appreciation of most music, art, and poetry. Thus, the left side notices details and the right side grasps the big picture—a distinction that should provide a clue in interpreting Figure 8.3.

This distinction has been exaggerated, though: No one is exclusively left-brained or right-brained (except severely brain-damaged people). Every cognitive skill requires both sides of the brain, just as gross motor skills require both sides of the body (Hugdahl & Davidson, 2002). Because older children have more myelinated fibers in the corpus callosum to speed signals between the two hemispheres, they are capable of better thinking and are less clumsy.

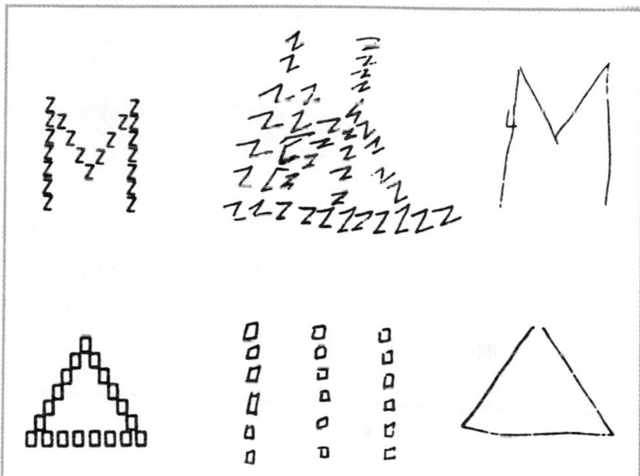

FIGURE 8.3

Copy What You See Brain-damaged adults were asked to copy the leftmost figure in each row. One person drew the middle set, another the set at the right.

Observation Quiz (see answer, page 229): Which set was drawn by someone with left-side damage and which set by someone with right-side damage?

Planning and Analyzing

You learned in Chapter 5 that the *prefrontal cortex* (sometimes called the *frontal cortex* or *frontal lobe*) is an area in the very front part of the brain's outer layer (the cortex), just behind the forehead. It "underlies higher-order cognition, including planning and complex forms of goal-directed behavior" (Luciana, 2003, p. 163).

The prefrontal cortex is crucial for humans; it is said to be the *executive* of the brain because all the other areas of the cortex are ruled by prefrontal decisions. For example, someone might feel anxious on meeting a new person whose friendship might be valuable in the future. The prefrontal cortex can calculate and plan, not letting the anxious feelings prevent a friendship from forming. Young children are much less adept at social understanding and planning, because the crucial functions of this part of the brain have not yet developed (Kolb & Whishaw, 2008).

Maturation of the Prefrontal Cortex

The frontal lobe "shows the most prolonged period of postnatal development of any region of the human brain" (Johnson, 2005, p. 210); dendrite density and myelination increase throughout childhood and adolescence (Nelson et al., 2006). Several notable benefits of maturation of the prefrontal cortex occur from ages 2 to 6:

- Sleep becomes more regular.
- Emotions become more nuanced and responsive to specific stimuli.
- Temper tantrums subside.
- Uncontrollable laughter and tears become less common.

In one series of experiments, 3-year-olds consistently made a stunning mistake (Zelazo et al., 2003). The children were given a set of cards with clear outlines of trucks or flowers, some red and some blue. They were asked to "play the shape game," putting trucks in one pile and flowers in another. Three-year-olds can do this correctly, as can some 2-year-olds and almost all older children.

➤**Response for Nutritionists** (from page 224): The nutritionally wise advice would be to offer only fruits, vegetables, and other nourishing, low-fat foods, counting on the child's eventual hunger to drive him or her to eat them. However, centuries of cultural custom make it almost impossible for parents to be wise in such cases. A physical checkup, with a blood test, may be warranted, to make sure the child is healthy.

M. MEYERSFELD / MASTERFILE

No Writer's Block The context is designed to help this South African second-grader concentrate on her schoolwork. Large, one-person desks, uniforms, notebooks, and sharp pencils are manageable for the brains and skills of elementary school children, but not yet for preschoolers.

Then the children were asked to "play the color game," sorting the cards by color. Most of them failed at this task, instead sorting by shape again. This study has been replicated in many nations; 3-year-olds usually get stuck on their initial sorting pattern (Diamond & Kirkham, 2005). Most older children, even 4-year-olds, make the switch.

When this result was first obtained, experimenters wondered whether the problem was that the children didn't know their colors; so the scientists switched the order, first playing "the color game." Most 3-year-olds did that correctly. Then, when they were asked to play "the shape game," they sorted by color again. Even with a new set of cards, such as yellow or green rabbits or boats, they still tended to sort by the criterion (either color or shape) that was used in their first trial.

Researchers are looking into many possible explanations for this surprising result (Müller et al., 2006; Yerys & Munakata, 2006). All agree, however, that something in the executive function of the brain must mature before children are able to switch from one way of sorting objects to another.

Prefrontal maturation is demonstrated in the game Simon Says, in which children are supposed to follow the leader *only* when his or her orders are preceded by the words "Simon says." Thus, when leaders touch their noses and say, "Simon says touch your nose," children are supposed to touch their noses; but when leaders touch their noses and merely say, "Touch your nose," no one is supposed to follow the example. Young children quickly lose at this game because they impulsively do what they see and are told to do. Older children are better at it because they can think before acting. (Maturation of the prefrontal cortex is also discussed in Chapters 5, 11, and 14.)

➤Response for Early-Childhood Teachers (from page 226): One solution is to remind yourself that the children's brains are not yet myelinated enough to enable them to quickly walk, talk, or even button their jackets. Maturation has a major effect, as you will observe if you can schedule excursions in September and again in November. Progress, while still slow, will be a few seconds faster in November than it was in September.

Impulsiveness and Perseveration

Neurons have two kinds of impulses: to activate or to inhibit. Each type of impulse is signaled by biochemical messages from axon to dendrite. Both activation and inhibition are necessary for thoughtful adults, who neither leap too quickly nor hesitate too long. Indeed, at the other end of the life span, a major problem with the aging brain is loss of inhibition, one consequence of which is talkativeness, or "off-target verbosity" (von Hippel, 2007). A balanced brain is most effective throughout life.

Many young children have not yet found the right balance. A 3-year-old jumps from task to task and cannot be still, even in church or any other place that requires quiet. Similarly, a young child may want a certain toy that another child has but then loses interest when the toy becomes available. Few 3-year-olds are capable of the kind of sustained attention that is pivotal for most learning in elementary school.

perseveration The tendency to persevere in, or stick to, one thought or action for a long time.

At the opposite end of the spectrum is the child who plays with a single toy for hours. **Perseveration** refers to the tendency to persevere in, or stick to, one thought or action—evident in the card-sorting study just described. It is also apparent to anyone who listens to a young child repeat one phrase or question again and again or to anyone who witnesses a tantrum if a child's favorite TV show is interrupted. That tantrum itself may perseverate: The young child's crying may become uncontrollable and unstoppable, as if the child is stuck in the emotion that triggered the tantrum.

Impulsiveness and perseveration are opposite behaviors with the same underlying cause: immaturity of the prefrontal cortex. Over the years of early childhood, brain maturation (innate) and emotional regulation (learned) decrease both impulsiveness and perseveration. Children gradually become able to pay attention when necessary (de Haan & Johnson, 2003).

As with all biological maturation, some of this is related to culture—hence the reason this chapter is called *biosocial development,* not simply *physical development.* A study of Korean preschoolers found the participants much better able to pay attention and resist perseveration than a comparable group of children in England (Oh & Lewis, 2008). One specific of this study was the shape/color task: Of the 3-year-olds, 40 percent of the Koreans but only 14 percent of the Britons successfully shifted from sorting by shape to sorting by color. The researchers explored many possible explanations, including a genetic one, but concluded that they "feel that a cultural explanation is more likely" (Oh & Lewis, 2008, p. 96). They also called for replication of the study, particularly with Korean-born children who are adopted and raised in British homes.

➤Answer to Observation Quiz (from page 227): The middle set, with its careful details, reflects damage to the right half of the brain, where overall impressions are formed. The person with left-brain damage produced the drawings that were just an M or a Δ, without the details of the tiny z's and rectangles. With a whole functioning brain, people can see both "the forest and the trees."

Emotions and the Brain

Now that we have looked at the executive functions of the prefrontal cortex, we turn to another region of the brain, called the *limbic system.* Both the expression and the regulation of emotions advance during early childhood (more about that in Chapter 10). Three major areas of the limbic system—the amygdala, the hippocampus, and the hypothalamus—are part of this advance.

The Amygdala

The **amygdala** is a tiny structure deep in the brain, named after an almond because it is about the same shape and size. It registers emotions, both positive and negative, including fear (Nelson et al., 2006). Increased activity of the amygdala is one reason some young children have terrifying nightmares or sudden terrors.

amygdala A tiny brain structure that registers emotions, particularly fear and anxiety.

Fear can overwhelm the prefrontal cortex and disrupt a child's ability to reason. If a child is scared of, say, a lion in the closet, an adult should open the closet door and tell the lion to go home, not laugh or insist that the fear is nonsense. The amygdala responds to facial expressions more than to words (Vasa & Pine, 2004). This is an aspect of social referencing, explained in Chapter 7.

Especially for Neurologists (see response, page 231): Why do many experts think the limbic system is an oversimplification?

If a child senses a parent's anxiety on entering an elevator, that child may also be fearful and cling to the parent when the elevator moves. If this sequence recurs often enough, the child's amygdala may become hypersensitive to elevators. If, instead, the parent conveys a calm attitude and makes elevator riding fun (letting the child push the buttons, for instance), the child will overcome initial feelings of fear of the strange sensations of elevator movement.

The Hippocampus

Another structure in the brain's limbic system, the **hippocampus,** is located right next to the amygdala. A central processor of memory, especially for locations, the hippocampus responds to the anxieties of the amygdala by summoning memory; it makes the child remember, for instance, that elevator riding was either scary or fun.

hippocampus A brain structure that is a central processor of memory, especially memory for locations.

Memories of location are fragile in early childhood because the hippocampus is still developing. Indeed, every type of memory has its own timetable for development (Nelson & Webb, 2003). It is possible for deep emotional memories from early childhood to interfere with verbal, rational thinking, as when a person might have a feeling of dread in some situation but not know why.

The interaction of the amygdala and the hippocampus is sometimes helpful, sometimes not, depending on the usefulness of fear and memory. Memories of past experiences are not always destructive (LaBar, 2007). Before the amygdala and hippocampus are well developed, some children are foolhardy when they should be cautious. Studies performed on some animals show that when the amygdala is surgically removed, the animals are fearless in situations that should scare them; for instance, a cat will stroll nonchalantly past monkeys—something no normal cat would do (Kolb & Whishaw, 2008).

The Hypothalamus

hypothalamus A brain area that responds to the amygdala and the hippocampus to produce hormones that activate other parts of the brain and body.

A third part of the limbic system, the **hypothalamus,** responds to (arousing) signals from the amygdala and to (usually dampening) signals from the hippocampus by producing cortisol and other hormones that activate parts of the brain and body (see Figure 8.4). Ideally, this hormone production occurs in moderation. As you remember from previous chapters, excessive cortisol (the primary stress hormone) may flood the brain and destroy part of the hippocampus. Permanent deficits in learning and memory may result.

Research has found that stress is not always harmful. Emotionally arousing experiences—meeting new friends, entering school, visiting a strange place—probably foster growth if a young child has someone or something to moderate the stress. In an experiment, brain scans and hormone measurements were taken of 4- to 6-year-olds immediately after a fire alarm. Some children were upset; some not. Two weeks later, either a friendly or a stern adult questioned them about the event. Those with higher cortisol reactions to the alarm remembered more details

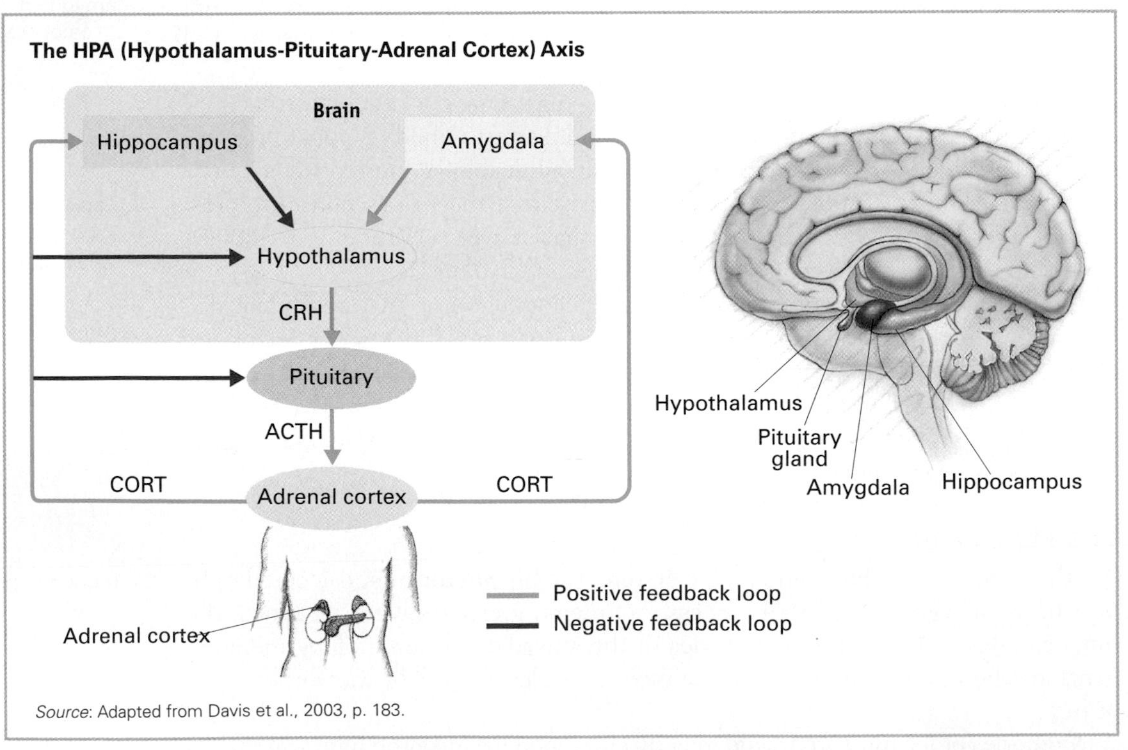

FIGURE 8.4

A Hormonal Feedback Loop This diagram simplifies a hormonal linkage, the HPA (hypothalamus-pituitary-adrenal) axis. Both the hippocampus and the amygdala stimulate the hypothalamus to produce CRH (corticotropin-releasing hormone), which in turn signals the pituitary gland to produce ACTH (adrenocorticotropic hormone). ACTH then triggers the production of CORT (glucocorticoids) by the adrenal cortex (the outer layers of the adrenal glands, atop the kidneys). Fear may either build or disappear, depending on other factors, including how the various parts of the brain interpret that first alert from the amygdala.

than did those with less stress, but the interviewer also had an effect: They remembered more with the friendly interviewer and less when the interviewer was stern (Quas et al., 2004).

Other research also finds that preschoolers remember a stressful experience better when an adult who talks to them about it is warm and attentive (Bruck et al., 2006). Thus, with the right circumstances, stress seems to facilitate memory. However, because developing brains are fragile, "prolonged physiological responses to stress and challenge put children at risk for a variety of problems in childhood, including physical and mental disorders, poor emotional regulation, and cognitive impairments" (Quas et al., 2004, p. 379).

Prolonged stress, leading to emotional and cognitive impairment, seemed to occur for the thousands of Romanian children in orphanages discussed in Chapter 5. When they saw pictures of happy, sad, frightened, and angry faces, their limbic systems were less reactive than were those of Romanian children living with their parents. The brains of these abandoned children were also less lateralized, suggesting less specialized, less efficient thinking (Parker & Nelson, 2005).

This is a likely explanation for the cognitive impairment found in a more recently institutionalized group of Romanian children. They had all lived in institutions until about age 2; then they were randomly assigned to foster homes or to continued institutional care. (Romania no longer permits wholesale international adoptions.) By age 4, those in foster homes were significantly smarter (by about 10 IQ points) than those who were institutionalized (Nelson et al., 2007). Remember from Chapter 7 that the period from age 6 to 24 months may be a crucial time for attachment, autonomy, and social emotions (specific fears, embarrassment); this research with Romanian children suggests that ages 2 to 4 may be a sensitive time for intellectual growth.

➤ **Response for Neurologists** (from page 229): The more we discover about the brain, the more complex we realize it is. Each part has specific functions and is connected to every other part.

SUMMING UP

The brain continues to mature during early childhood, with myelination occurring in several crucial areas. One is the corpus callosum, which connects the left and right sides of the brain and therefore the right and left sides of the body. Handedness becomes evident; adults should probably not try to make left-handed children switch to their right hand.

Increased myelination speeds up actions and reactions. The prefrontal cortex enables a balance between action and inhibition, allowing children to think before they act as well as to stop one action in order to begin another. As impulsiveness and perseveration decrease, children become better able to learn.

Several key areas of the brain—including the amygdala, the hippocampus, and the hypothalamus—make up the limbic system, which also matures from ages 2 to 6. The limbic system aids emotional expression and control. Children whose earlier experiences were stressful and who lacked nurturing caregivers may have impairments of their limbic systems. ■

Improved Motor Skills

Maturation of the prefrontal cortex improves impulse control, while myelination of the corpus callosum and lateralization of the brain permit better physical coordination. No wonder children move with greater speed and grace as they age from 2 to 6, becoming better able to direct and refine their actions. (Table 8.1 lists approximate ages for the acquisition of various motor skills in early childhood.)

According to a study of middle-class and working-class children in Brazil, Kenya, and the United States, young children spend the majority of their waking

TABLE 8.1

AT ABOUT THIS TIME: Motor Skills at Ages 2–6*

Approx. Age	Skill or Achievement
2 years	Run for pleasure, without falling (but bumping into things)
	Climb chairs, tables, beds, out of cribs
	Walk up stairs
	Feed self with spoon
	Draw lines, spirals
3 years	Kick and throw a ball
	Jump with both feet off the floor
	Pedal a tricycle
	Copy simple shapes (e.g., circle, rectangle)
	Walk down stairs
	Climb ladders
4 years	Catch a ball (not too small or thrown too fast)
	Use scissors to cut
	Hop on either foot
	Feed self with fork
	Dress self (no tiny buttons, no ties)
	Copy most letters
	Pour juice without spilling
	Brush teeth
5 years	Skip and gallop in rhythm
	Clap, bang, sing in rhythm
	Copy difficult shapes and letters (e.g., diamond shape, letter *S*)
	Climb trees, jump over things
	Use knife to cut
	Tie a bow
	Throw a ball
	Wash face, comb hair
6 years	Draw and paint with preferred hand
	Write simple words
	Scan a page of print, moving the eyes systematically in the appropriate direction
	Ride a bicycle
	Do a cartwheel
	Tie shoes
	Catch a ball

*Context and culture are crucial for acquisition of all these skills. For example, many 6-year-olds cannot tie shoelaces because they have no shoes with laces.

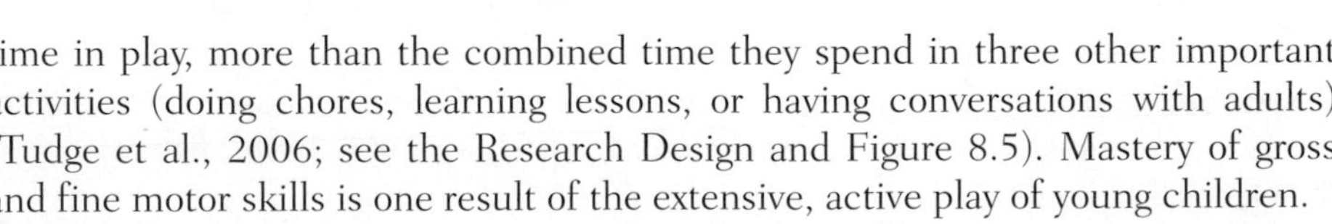

time in play, more than the combined time they spend in three other important activities (doing chores, learning lessons, or having conversations with adults) (Tudge et al., 2006; see the Research Design and Figure 8.5). Mastery of gross and fine motor skills is one result of the extensive, active play of young children.

Gross Motor Skills

Gross motor skills—which, as we defined in Chapter 5, involve large body movements—improve dramatically during early childhood. When you watch children play, you can see clumsy 2-year-olds who fall down and sometimes bump into each other, but you can also see 5-year-olds who are both skilled and graceful.

DIGITAL VISION / PUNCHSTOCK

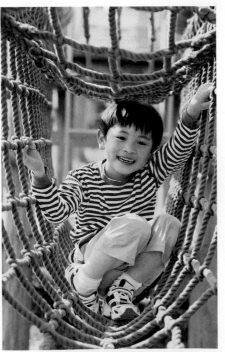

The Joy of Climbing Would you delight in climbing on an unsteady rope swing, like this 6-year-old in Japan (and almost all his contemporaries worldwide)? Each age has special sources of pleasure.

Specific Skills

Most North American 5-year-olds can ride a tricycle, climb a ladder, pump a swing, as well as throw, catch, and kick a ball. Some can skate, ski, dive, and ride a bicycle—activities that demand balance as well as coordination of both brain

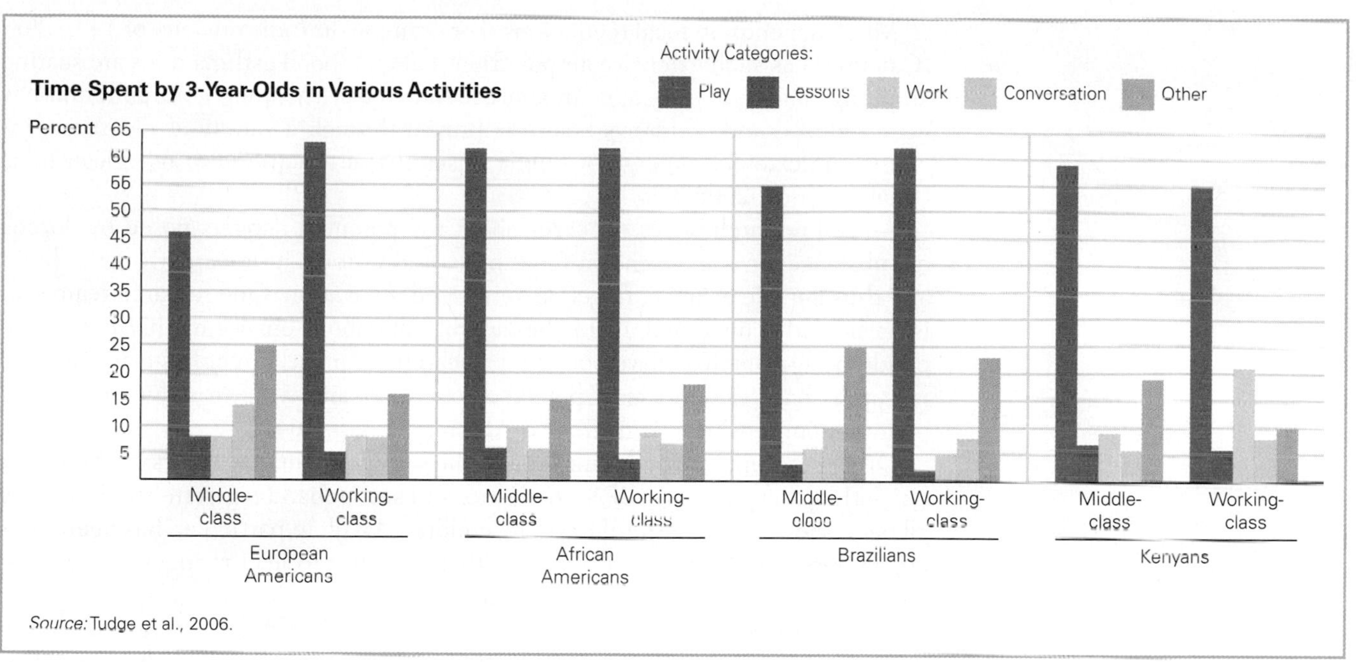

FIGURE 8.5

Mostly Playing When researchers studied 3-year-olds in the United States, Brazil, and Kenya, they found that, on average, the children spent more than half their time playing. Note the low percentages of both middle- and working-class Brazilian children in the Lessons category, which included all intentional efforts to teach children something. There is a cultural explanation: Unlike parents in Kenya and the United States, most Brazilian parents believe that children of this age should not be in organized day care.

hemispheres. In some nations, 5-year-olds swim in oceans or climb cliffs. Brain maturation, motivation, and guided practice make these skills possible.

Adults need to make sure children have safe spaces, time, and playmates; skills will follow. According to sociocultural theory, children learn best from peers who demonstrate whatever skills the child is ready to try—from catching a ball to climbing a tree. Of course, the culture and the locale influence which skills children display—some small children learn to sled, and others learn to sail.

Recent urbanization concerns many developmentalists. Compared to a century ago, when almost all children could play together in empty lots or fields without adult supervision, half the world's children now live in cities. Many of these are "megacities . . . overwhelmed with burgeoning slums and environmental problems" (Ash et al., 2008, p. 739). The next generation of young children may have few older playmates and insufficient safe space to practice motor skills.

Environmental Hazards

Environmental hazards do more harm to young, growing bodies than to older, more developed ones; they are of particular concern for urban young children, who have less opportunity to practice skills. Gone are the days when parents told their children to go out and play, expecting them safely back when hunger, weather, or nightfall brought them home. Now parents fear strangers, automobiles, and stray animals and thus keep their children inside, perhaps watching television or playing video games, but not developing gross motor skills.

Crowded, violent streets not only impede development of gross motor skills but also add to the natural fears of the immature limbic system. Meanwhile, brain and body growth are affected by the polluted air and water that characterize many cities throughout the world.

Research Design

Scientists: Jonathan Tudge and others (e.g., researchers in Brazil and Kenya).

Publication: *Child Development* (2006).

Participants: About 20 3-year-olds from each of four ethnic groups: European American and African American in Greensboro, North Carolina; Luo in Kisumu, Kenya; and European descent in Porto Alegre, Brazil. On the basis of parents' education and occupation, half the children in each group were from middle-class families and half were from working-class families.

Design: Children were observed for 20 hours each in their usual daytime activities. The child wore a wireless microphone; every 6 minutes, the observer recorded what the child was doing. Later the time was allocated among five categories: Lessons (deliberate attempts to impart information), Work (household tasks), Play (activities for enjoyment), Conversation (sustained talk with adults about things not the current focus of activity), and Other (eating, bathing, sleeping).

Major conclusion: All eight groups spent much more time playing than doing anything else. Much larger differences were found in time spent in lessons, work, and conversation.

Comment: Many features of good research are evident in this study.

Much depends on local regulations. For example, in India one city of 14 million (Calcutta) has such extensive air pollution that childhood asthma rates are soaring and lung damage is prevalent. In another Indian city (Mumbai), air pollution has been reduced and children's health improved through a variety of measures, including an extensive system of public buses that are required to use clean fuels (Bhattacharjee, 2008).

Animal research raises concerns about the potential dangers posed by dozens of substances in the air and in food, milk, and water. These can affect the brain and thus impede balance, finger dexterity, and motivation. One research team that is particularly concerned about the lack of data about environmental hazards to children suggests that "developmental researchers [must] direct basic and applied research about the effects of pollutant exposures and ways to reduce children's pollutant burdens" (Dilworth-Bart & Moore, 2006, p. 264).

Other substances—including lead in the water and air, pesticides in the soil or on clothing, bisphenol A (BPA) in plastic, and secondhand cigarette smoke—have all been shown to be harmful to young children. Lead, in particular, has been thoroughly researched. It is now apparent that exposure to lead reduces intelligence and increases behavior problems in young children.

Over the past 20 years, U.S. regulations have reduced the amount of lead in paint, gasoline, and manufacturing, and children's blood lead levels have dropped sharply. Some states (e.g., Colorado and Wyoming) have averages close to zero. In other states (e.g., Michigan and Ohio), average lead levels are still too high, defined as above 10 micrograms per deciliter of blood among children under age 6 (MMWR, May 27, 2005; MMWR, December 22, 2000). This is a community health problem, but parents can reduce lead levels in their young children by increasing the children's consumption of calcium, wiping window ledges clean of dust (which may contain lead), and making sure the children do not eat peeling chips of lead-based paint (which tastes sweet and may still be found on the walls of older buildings) (Dilworth-Bart & Moore, 2006).

Fine Motor Skills

Fine motor skills, which involve small body movements (especially those of the hands and fingers), are harder to master than gross motor skills. Pouring juice into a glass, cutting food with a knife and fork, and achieving anything more artful than a scribble with a pencil all require a level of muscular control, patience, and judgment that are beyond most 2-year-olds.

Many fine motor skills involve two hands and thus both sides of the brain: The fork stabs the meat while the knife cuts it; one hand steadies the paper while the other writes; tying shoes, buttoning shirts, pulling on socks, and zipping zippers require both hands. An immature corpus callosum and prefrontal cortex may be the underlying reason that shoelaces get knotted, paper gets ripped, and zippers get stuck. Short, stubby fingers and confusion about handedness add to the problem.

Especially for Immigrant Parents (see response, page 236): You and your family eat with chopsticks at home, but you want your children to feel comfortable in Western culture. Should you change your family's eating customs?

Schools

Traditional academic learning depended on fine motor skills as well as overall body control. Writing required finger control, reading a line of print required eye control, sitting for hours at a desk required bladder control, and so on. These are beyond most young children, so even the brightest 3-year-old is not allowed in first grade, and some slower-developing children become very frustrated by their teachers' expectations that they write neatly and cut straight.

Fine motor skills—like many other biological characteristics, such as bones, brains, and teeth—typically mature about 6 months earlier in girls than in boys.

This may be one reason girls typically outperform boys on elementary school tests of school achievement and many young girls consider boys "stupid."

It may not be that children's brain and motor skills need accelerating to adjust to traditional schools, but that the schools need adjusting to the pace of children's development. The relationship between maturation and learning is controversial. Some educators stress the need for young children to play, and others urge that early-childhood programs begin to teach the skills that children will need when they get to primary school. This issue is explored in detail in Chapter 9.

Artistic Expression

Young children are imaginative, creative, and not yet self-critical. They love to express themselves, especially if their parents applaud, display their artwork, and otherwise communicate approval. The fact that their fine motor skills are immature, and thus their expression lacks precision, is unimportant to young children. Perhaps the immaturity of the prefrontal cortex allows the imagination to flourish without the social anxiety of older children, who might say, "I can't draw" or "I am horrible at dancing."

All forms of artistic expression blossom during early childhood. Psychologists have diverse opinions about whether drawings reveal anything about children's emotions or needs (Burkitt, 2004). But there is no doubt that 2- to 6-year-olds love to dance around the room, build an elaborate tower of blocks, make music by pounding in rhythm, and put bright marks on shiny paper. In every artistic domain, from dance to sculpture, maturation of brain and body is gradual and comes with practice.

Children's artwork reflects their unique perception and cognition. For example, researchers asked young children to draw a balloon and, later, a lollipop. To adults, the drawings were indistinguishable, but the children who made the drawings were quite insistent as to which was which (Bloom, 2000) (see Figure 8.6).

Snip, Snip Cutting paper with scissors is a hard, slow task for a 3-year-old, who is just beginning to develop fine motor control. Imagine wielding blunt "safety" scissors and hoping that the paper will be sliced exactly where you want it to be.

FIGURE 8.6

Which Is Which? The child who made these drawings insisted that the one at the top left was a lollipop and the one at the top right was a balloon (not vice versa) and that the one at the bottom left was the experimenter and the one at the bottom right was the child (not vice versa).

NICOLE VILLAMORA

(a)

LAURA DWIGHT

(b)

BLEND IMAGES / ALAMY

(c)

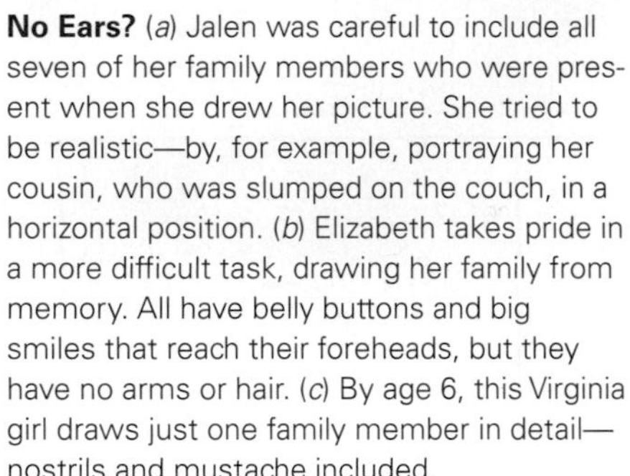

No Ears? (*a*) Jalen was careful to include all seven of her family members who were present when she drew her picture. She tried to be realistic—by, for example, portraying her cousin, who was slumped on the couch, in a horizontal position. (*b*) Elizabeth takes pride in a more difficult task, drawing her family from memory. All have belly buttons and big smiles that reach their foreheads, but they have no arms or hair. (*c*) By age 6, this Virginia girl draws just one family member in detail—nostrils and mustache included.

Maturation is also evident in children's creativity. When drawing the human figure, 2- to 3-year-olds usually draw a "tadpole"—a circle for a head with eyes and sometimes a smiling mouth, and then a line or two beneath to indicate the rest of the body. Gradually, children's drawings of people evolve from tadpoles into more human forms as fine motor skills advance.

Tadpoles are "strikingly characteristic" of children's art (Cox, 1993); they are drawn universally, in all cultures. Similarly, children worldwide seek places to climb—on rocky hillsides, playground structures, and the dining room table—imagining as they play. They like to sing, to beat rhythms, to mold clay or dirt, and so on. Creativity brings joy as well as the honing of skills.

SUMMING UP

Maturation of the brain leads to better control of the body and hence to improvement in both gross and fine motor skills. Gross motor skills develop with practice and increasing brain maturation, both progressing every year as long as young children have space to play, older children to emulate, and freedom from exposure to environmental toxins. Fine motor skills also develop, preparing children for the many requirements of formal education. ■

Injuries and Abuse

We have assumed that parents want to foster their children's development and protect them. This is true in the vast majority of families. Yet more children die from accidents and deliberate abuse than from any other cause.

In the United States, where accurate death records are kept, out of every 100,000 1- to 4-year-olds, 10.3 died accidentally, 2.5 died of cancer (the leading fatal disease at this age), and 2.4 were murdered in 2004 (U.S. Bureau of the Census, 2007).

Young children are more vulnerable to injuries and abuse than are slightly older ones, partly because they are both impulsive and dependent on others, as we have

➤**Response for Immigrant Parents** (from page 234): Children develop the motor skills that they see and practice. They will soon learn to use forks, spoons, and knives. Do not abandon chopsticks completely, because young children can learn several ways of doing things, and the ability to eat with chopsticks is a social asset.

just seen. But much of the harm done to children can be prevented, and that is our primary reason for discussing this topic in detail.

Avoidable Injury

Worldwide, injuries cause millions of premature deaths among young adults as well as children: Not until age 40 does any disease overtake accidents as a cause of mortality. Among children, 1- to 4-year-olds have five times the rate of accidental injury as 5- to 11-year-olds.

Age-related trends are apparent in the particular kinds of injuries. Teenagers and young adults are most often killed as passengers or drivers in motor-vehicle crashes. Falls are more often fatal for the very young (under 24 months) and very old (over 80 years) than for preschoolers, for whom fatal accidents are more likely to involve poison, fire, choking, or drowning.

Why do small children have so many mishaps? Immaturity of the prefrontal cortex makes young children impulsive, so they plunge into dangerous places and activities (Zeedyk et al., 2002). Unlike infants, their motor skills allow them to run, leap, scramble, and grab in a flash. Their curiosity is boundless; their impulses are uninhibited.

Injury Control

Instead of using the term *accident prevention*, public health experts prefer **injury control** (or **harm reduction**). Consider the implications of the terminology. The word *accident* implies that an injury is a random, unpredictable event; if anyone is at fault, it's likely to be a careless parent or an accident-prone child. This is called the "accident paradigm"; it implies that "injuries will occur despite our best efforts," allowing the public to feel blameless (Benjamin, 2004, p. 521).

injury control/harm reduction Practices that are aimed at anticipating, controlling, and preventing dangerous activities; these practices reflect the beliefs that accidents are not random and that injuries can be made less harmful if proper controls are in place.

Some children seem much more likely than others to move fast and take risks. Their parents may blame "accident genes," but research on twins suggests that accident proneness is more an excuse than an explanation. Usually the specific circumstances, not the child's genes, make injury more likely (Ordoñana et al., 2008). The phrase *injury control* suggests that harm can be minimized with appropriate controls. Minor mishaps are bound to occur, but serious injury is unlikely if a child falls on a safety surface instead of concrete, if a car seat protects the body in a crash, if a bicycle helmet cracks instead of a skull, if the swallowed pills come from a tiny bottle.

A Safe Leap What makes this jump safe as well as fun are the high fences on all sides of the pool, the adequate depth of the water, and the presence of at least one adult (taking the picture).

MYRLEEN FERGUSON CATE / PHOTOEDIT

Only half as many 1- to 5-year-olds in the United States were fatally injured in 2005 as in 1985, thanks to laws that govern poisons, fires, and cars. But as more households in California, Florida, Texas, and Arizona install swimming pools, drowning has become a leading cause of unintentional death for young children (Brenner et al., 2001). To prevent such deaths, laws could mandate that any body of water near a home have a high fence on all four sides, with a lock too high for a child to reach (Quan et al., 2006).

A pool-fencing ordinance in southern California was amended to allow one side of the required enclosure to be the wall of a house, with a door that could be locked. This revised attempt at injury control seemed reasonable to homeowners, builders, and legislators, but child-health professionals knew it was not adequate. The law protected trespassing children but not the family's own children or visiting children, who were able to open those doors from inside the house. For that reason, the law did not reduce California child drownings (Morgenstern et al., 2000).

Three Levels of Prevention

Injury prevention should begin long before any particular child, parent, or politician does something foolish or careless. There are three levels of prevention, which apply to every childhood health and safety issue (Tercyak, 2008):

primary prevention Actions that change overall background conditions to prevent some unwanted event or circumstance, such as injury, disease, or abuse.

secondary prevention Actions that avert harm in a high-risk situation, such as stopping a car before it hits a pedestrian.

tertiary prevention Actions, such as immediate and effective medical treatment, that are taken after an adverse event (such as illness or injury) occurs and that are aimed at reducing the harm or preventing disability.

- In **primary prevention,** the overall situation is structured to make injuries less likely. Primary prevention fosters conditions that reduce every child's chance of injury.
- **Secondary prevention** is more specific, averting harm in high-risk situations.
- **Tertiary prevention** begins after an injury, limiting the damage it causes.

In general, tertiary prevention is most visible but primary prevention is most effective (Cohen et al., 2007). To illustrate, the rate of motor-vehicle deaths has steadily decreased in the past 20 years because of all three levels of prevention. For every 100,000 infants and young children in the United States, five died as pedestrians or passengers in 1990, but only three died in 2005 (U.S. Bureau of the Census, 2007). How did each level of prevention contribute to this decline?

Especially for Urban Planners (see response, page 239): Describe a neighborhood park that would benefit 2- to 5-year-olds.

Primary prevention involves building preventive measures into the everyday environment. When it comes to motor vehicles, methods of primary prevention include sidewalks, speed bumps, pedestrian overpasses, brighter streetlights, and single-lane traffic circles (Retting et al., 2003; Tester et al., 2004). Cars have been redesigned (e.g., with better headlights and brakes) and drivers' skills improved (e.g., as a result of more frequent vision tests and stronger drunk-driving penalties).

Secondary prevention involves taking steps to reduce the dangers in high-risk situations. Improvement of street and highway safety for children calls for requiring flashing lights on stopped school buses, fencing in yards and playgrounds, refusing alcohol to teenage drivers, and insisting that young children walk with adults.

The distinction between primary prevention and secondary prevention is not clear-cut. In general, secondary prevention is more targeted, focusing on specific risk groups (e.g., young children) and proven dangers (e.g., crossing the street)

And If He Falls . . . None of these children is injured, so no tertiary prevention is needed. Photos (*b*) and (*c*) both illustrate secondary prevention, which is needed worldwide, since in every nation more children now die in accidents than from disease. A five-point car seat (the safest kind) protects the Russian child in (*b*). In photo (*a*), the metal climbing equipment with large gaps and peeling paint is hazardous. Primary prevention suggests that this "attractive nuisance" be dismantled.

MANOR PHOTOGRAPHY / ALAMY

(a)

ITAR-TASS / MARINA LYSTSEVA / LANDOV

(b)

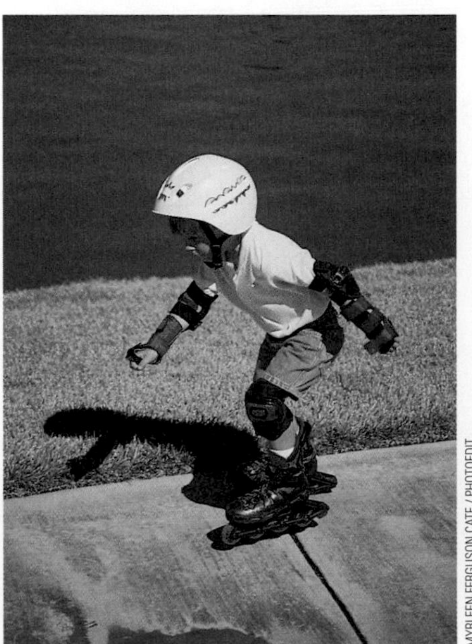
MYRLEEN FERGUSON CATE / PHOTOEDIT

(c)

rather than on the overall culture, politics, or environment. Laws requiring safety seats for child passengers are secondary prevention.

Finally, *tertiary prevention* involves measures aimed at reducing damage after injury has occurred. Laws against leaving the scene of an automobile accident, improved emergency room procedures (e.g., action to reduce brain swelling), and more effective rehabilitation after injury are examples of tertiary prevention. Speedy and well-trained ambulance teams may be especially crucial in cases of injury to children, since brain damage and bleeding can sometimes be reduced or halted, making complete recovery possible. In many European countries, tertiary prevention includes redesigning the fronts of cars so that they are less destructive to pedestrians on impact (Retting et al., 2003).

Especially for Economists (see response, page 240): In the feature below, how did Kathleen Berger's SES protect Bethany from serious harm?

a personal perspective

"My Baby Swallowed Poison"

The first strategy that most people think of to prevent injury to young children is parental education. However, public health research finds that laws that apply to everyone are more effective than education, especially if parents are not ready to learn and change or are overwhelmed by the daily demands of child care.

For example, infant car seats have saved thousands of lives. The best time to convince parents to use one in their car is before they bring their newborn home from the hospital. Use of car seats, though, is much less common when it is voluntary than when it is mandated.

As one expert explains: "Too often, we design our physical environment for smart people who are highly motivated" (Baker, 2000). But in real life, everyone has moments of foolish indifference. At those moments, automatic safety measures save lives.

I know this firsthand. My daughter Bethany, at age 2, climbed onto the kitchen counter to find, open, and swallow most of a bottle of baby aspirin. Where was I? A few feet away, nursing our second child and watching television. I did not notice what Bethany was doing until I checked on her during a commercial.

Bethany is alive and well today, but what protected her from death or serious injury? Laws limiting the number of baby aspirin per container (primary prevention), my pediatrician's advice on my first well-baby checkup to keep a bottle of syrup of ipecac on hand (secondary prevention), and my phone call to Poison Control (tertiary prevention) all contributed. I told the stranger who answered the phone, "My baby swallowed poison." He calmly asked me a few questions and then advised me to give Bethany ipecac to make her throw up the pills she had swallowed. I did, and she did. I still blame myself, but I am grateful for all three levels of prevention that protected my child.

Child Maltreatment

The next time you read news headlines about some horribly neglected or abused child, think of these words from a leading researcher in child maltreatment:

> Make no mistake—those who abuse children are fully responsible for their actions. However, creating an information system that perpetuates the message that offenders are the only ones to blame may be misleading. . . . We all contribute to the conditions that allow perpetrators to succeed.
>
> [Daro, 2002, p. 1133]

"We all contribute" in the sense that the causes of child maltreatment are multifaceted, involving not only the parents but also the neighbors, the community, the culture, and the maltreated children themselves. For example, infants are most at risk of being maltreated if they are difficult (fragile, needing frequent feeding, crying often) *and* if their mothers are depressed and do not feel in control of their lives or their infants *and* if the family is under financial stress (Bugental & Happaney, 2004).

➤**Response for Urban Planners** (from page 238): The adult idea of a park—a large, grassy open place—is not best for young children. For them, you would design an enclosed area, small enough and with adequate seating to allow caregivers to socialize while watching their children. The playground surface would have to be protective (since young children are clumsy), with equipment that encourages both gross motor skills (such as climbing) and fine motor skills (such as sandbox play). Swings are not beneficial, since they do not develop many motor skills. Teenagers and dogs should have their own designated area, far from the youngest children.

MISHAWAKA POLICE DEPARTMENT / GETTY IMAGES

Nobody Watching? Madelyn Gorman Toogood looks around to make sure no one is watching before she slaps and shakes her 4-year-old daughter, Martha, who is in a car seat inside the vehicle. A security camera recorded this incident in an Indiana department store parking lot. A week later, after the videotape was repeatedly broadcast nationwide, Toogood was recognized and arrested. The haunting question is: How much child abuse takes place that is not witnessed?

Maltreatment Noticed and Defined

Noticing is the first step. Until about 1960, people thought child maltreatment was rare and consisted of a sudden attack by a disturbed stranger. Today we know better, thanks to a pioneering study based on careful observation in one Boston hospital (Kempe & Kempe, 1978): Maltreatment is neither rare nor sudden, and the perpetrators are usually well known to the child. In fact, for young children, one or both of the child's own parents are most likely to be the abusers. That makes the situation much worse: Ongoing maltreatment, with no safe haven, is much more damaging to children than is a single brief incident, however injurious.

With this recognition came a broader definition: **Child maltreatment** now refers to all intentional harm to, or avoidable endangerment of, anyone under 18 years of age. Thus, child maltreatment includes both **child abuse,** which is deliberate action that is harmful to a child's physical, emotional, or sexual well-being, and **child neglect,** which is failure to meet a child's basic physical or emotional needs.

The more that researchers study child maltreatment, the more apparent the harmful effects of neglect become (Hildyard & Wolfe, 2002; Valentino et al., 2008). As one team wrote, "Severe neglect occurring in the early childhood years has been found to be particularly detrimental to successful adaptation" (Valentino et al., 2006, p. 483).

How frequently does maltreatment occur? It is impossible to say. Not all cases of maltreatment are noticed, not all that are noticed are reported, and not all that are reported are substantiated. Neglect is particularly likely to be ignored.

Reported maltreatment means that the authorities have been informed. Since 1993, the number of *reported* cases of maltreatment in the United States has ranged from 2.7 million to 3 million a year (U.S. Department of Health and Human Services, 2006).

Substantiated maltreatment means that a reported case has been investigated and verified (see Figure 8.7). The number of *substantiated* cases in 2005 was 900,000; in 155,000 of those cases, the victims were 2- to 5-year-olds, making the substantiated maltreatment rate in that age group about 1 maltreated child in every 70 (U.S. Department of Health and Human Services, 2008).

This 3-to-1 ratio of reported versus substantiated cases can be attributed to three factors:

- Each child is counted once, even if repeated maltreatment is reported.
- Substantiation requires proof in the form of unmistakable injuries, severe malnutrition, or a witness willing to testify. Such evidence is not always available.
- A report may be false or deliberately misleading (though less than 1 percent are).

Overall, about two-thirds of reported cases are not substantiated, but it is not known how many cases of maltreatment are not even reported. Some studies put the number at more than 10 times the reported rate. According to a confidential nationwide survey of young adults in the United States, 1 in 4 had been physically abused ("slapped, hit, or kicked" by a parent or other adult caregiver) before sixth grade and 1 in 22 had been sexually abused ("touched or forced to touch someone else in a sexual way") (Hussey et al., 2006; see the Research Design). Almost never had their abuse been reported.

child maltreatment Intentional harm to or avoidable endangerment of anyone under 18 years of age.

child abuse Deliberate action that is harmful to a child's physical, emotional, or sexual well-being.

child neglect Failure to meet a child's basic physical, educational, or emotional needs.

reported maltreatment Harm or endangerment about which someone has notified the authorities.

substantiated maltreatment Harm or endangerment that has been reported, investigated, and verified.

➤**Response for Economists** (from page 239): Children from families at all income levels have accidents, but Kathleen Berger's SES allowed her to have a private pediatrician as well as the income to buy ipecac "just in case." She also had a working phone and the education to know about Poison Control.

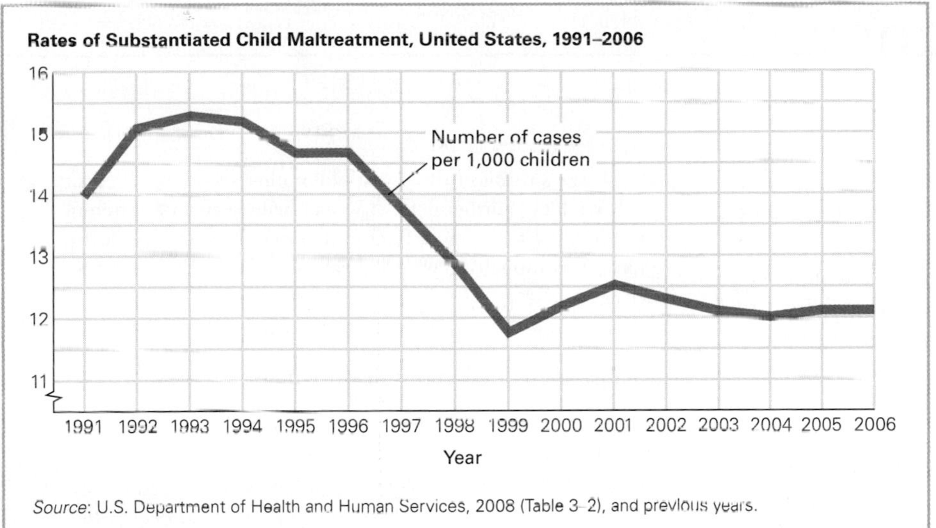

Source: U.S. Department of Health and Human Services, 2008 (Table 3–2), and previous years.

FIGURE 8.7

Still Far Too Many The number of reported and substantiated cases of maltreatment of children under age 18 in the United States is too high, but there is some good news: The rate has declined significantly from the peak in 1993.

Observation Quiz (see answer, page 243): The data point for 1999 is close to the bottom of the graph. Does that mean it is close to zero?

Research Design

Scientists: Jon Hussey and others at the University of North Carolina.

Publication: *Pediatrics* (2006).

Participants: Total of 15,197 young adults, interviewed at age 18–26 as part of the third wave of a large longitudinal study called Add Health, which began in 1995 with a representative sample of over 20,000 U.S. adolescents.

Design: Participants were asked to report, confidentially (via headphones and a computer, a method that yields more accurate answers than face-to-face or written questions do), whether their caregivers had ever maltreated them. Questions were specific (e.g., "slapped, hit, or kicked"), and participants indicated how often the behavior occurred (once, twice, or more).

Major conclusions: Maltreatment was common: One in four had been physically abused. Each type of maltreatment was associated with multiple health risks.

Comment: Although one would hope that these rates are overestimates, actual rates may be even higher, for three reasons: (1) Young adults tend to idealize their childhood; (2) the original participants were all in high school and had their parents' permission to respond to the survey; and (3) the participants in this third wave of interviews were, on average, more advantaged than those who dropped out or could not be found.

One reason for these high rates of unreported abuse may be that young adults were asked if they had *ever* been mistreated by someone who was caring for them, while most other sources report annual rates (which are lower). Another reason is that few children report their own abuse; most are not even aware that they are being maltreated until later, when they compare their experiences with those of others. Indeed, many adults who were slapped, hit, or kicked in childhood do not think of this as abuse. The authors of this study think the rates they found are *underestimates!*

Warning Signs

Often the first sign of maltreatment is delayed development, such as slow growth, immature communication, lack of curiosity, or unusual social interactions. All these difficulties may be evident even at age 1 (Valentino et al., 2006).

During early childhood, maltreated children may seem fearful, startled by noise, defensive and quick to attack, and confused between fantasy and reality. These are symptoms of **post-traumatic stress disorder (PTSD),** which was first identified in combat veterans, then in adults who had experienced some emotional injury or shock (after a serious accident, natural disaster, or violent crime, for example). PTSD is now evident in some maltreated children (De Bellis, 2001; Yehuda, 2006).

Table 8.2 (on page 243) lists signs of child maltreatment, both neglect and abuse. None of these signs are proof that a child has been abused, but whenever any of them occurs, it signifies trouble. Many nations, including the United States, require all professionals who deal with children (teachers, nurses, social workers, doctors, police officers) to report suspected maltreatment when they see any of the signs listed in the table. Not all professionals know when to be suspicious, however, as the following feature makes clear.

post-traumatic stress disorder (PTSD) An anxiety disorder that develops as a delayed reaction to having experienced or witnessed a profoundly shocking or frightening event, such as rape, war, or natural disaster. Its symptoms may include flashbacks to the event, hyperactivity and hypervigilance, displaced anger, sleeplessness, nightmares, sudden terror or anxiety, and confusion between fantasy and reality.

Especially for Nurses (see response, page 243): While weighing a 4-year-old, you notice several bruises on the child's legs. When you ask about them, the child says nothing and the parent says the child bumps into things. What should you do?

a view from science

The Neglect of Neglect

For young children, the professional most likely to suspect that a child is maltreated is a doctor or a nurse, since they are the ones who treat injuries as well as keep track of health, growth, and motor skills. Maltreatment compromises basic health in every way (Hussey et al., 2006). Abused and neglected children are often injured, sick, or hospitalized for reasons not directly related to their maltreatment (Kendall-Tackett, 2002), which gives medical personnel an additional chance to notice maltreatment.

Yet many do not. For instance, child patients are reported as maltreated three times more often in teaching hospitals (where ongoing education is part of the hospital's mission) than in regular hospitals, where "child abuse and neglect are underidentified, underdiagnosed, and undercoded" (Rovi et al., 2004, p. 589).

Can increased vigilance and a greater willingness to follow up on suspicions of neglect or abuse really make a difference? They might have for B.V., a boy in a low-income family:

> B.V., a 2-year-old male, was found lying face down in the bathtub by an 8-year-old sent to check on him. He had been placed in the bathtub by his mother, who then went to the kitchen and was absent for approximately 10 minutes. B.V. was transported by ambulance to a local hospital. He was unresponsive and had a rectal temperature of 90 degrees Fahrenheit.
>
> After medical treatment, the child's breathing resumed, and he was transported to a tertiary care hospital. B.V. remained in the pediatric intensive care unit for 9 days with minimal brain function and no response to any stimuli. He was then transferred to a standard hospital room where he died 2 days later. The mother refused to have an autopsy performed. Subsequently, the death certificate was signed by an attending physician, and cause of death was pneumonia with anoxic brain injury as a result of near-drowning.
>
> The CPS [Child Protective Services] worker advised B.V.'s mother that 10 minutes was too long to leave a 2-year-old in the bathtub unsupervised. B.V.'s mother replied that she had done it many times before and that nothing had happened.
>
> Further examination of the medical chart revealed that prior to B.V.'s death, he had a sibling who had experienced an apparent life-threatening event (previously termed a "near miss" sudden infant death syndrome). The sibling was placed on cardiac and apnea (breathing) monitors for 7 to 8 months. In addition, B.V. had been to the children's hospital approximately 2 weeks prior for a major injury to his big toe. B.V.'s toe had been severed and required numerous stitches. The mother stated that this incident was a result of the 4-year-old brother slamming the door on B.V.'s foot. Furthermore, B.V. had been seen in a different local hospital for a finger fracture the month before his death. None of the available reports indicate . . . how the finger fracture occurred.
>
> *[Bonner et al., 1999, pp. 165–166]*

No charges were filed in this death. The team notes:

> This case illustrates chronic supervisory neglect. . . . The series of suspicious events that preceded the death did not result in protective or preventive services for the family.
>
> *[Bonner et al., 1999, p. 166]*

This case is indeed a chilling example of "chronic supervisory neglect." Professionals ignored many medical signs that something was wrong—the sibling's "near-miss" SIDS, B.V.'s fractured finger and severed toe. No mention is made of the boy's weight, language, emotions, or social skills; he probably had deficits in these areas that could have raised alarm as well.

Even after B.V.'s death, the neglect of neglect continued. No help was provided for the 8-year-old who found his dying brother or for the 4-year-old who reportedly severed the toddler's toe. These children were also at high risk of maltreatment. Indeed, it could be argued that they had already been maltreated: Children are damaged by chronic feelings of helplessness and danger.

Physical abuse and neglect are most likely to be experienced by children with the following characteristics:

- Are under age 6
- Have two or more siblings
- Have an unemployed or absent father
- Have a mother who did not complete high school
- Live in a poor, high-crime neighborhood

All these risk factors were present for B.V. If his family had not been poor, he might have had a private pediatrician, who might have noticed the danger he was in. If his mother had had fewer children and a supportive husband, she might have stayed to watch him in the tub. A higher level of education might have helped her understand how to cope. Neighbors and relatives might have intervened. Medical personnel might have reported suspicions. Instead, B.V. died.

Consequences of Maltreatment

The impact of any child-rearing practice is affected by the cultural context. Certain customs (such as circumcision, pierced ears, and spanking) are considered abusive in some cultures but not in others, and their effects on children vary accordingly. Children suffer if their parents seem not to love them according to their community's standards for parental love.

TABLE 8.2

Signs of Maltreatment in Children Aged 2 to 10

Signs of Maltreatment in Children Aged 2 to 10
Injuries that do not fit an "accidental" explanation: bruises on both sides of the face or body; burns with a clear line between burned and unburned skin; "falls" that result in cuts, not scrapes
Repeated injuries, especially broken bones not properly tended
Fantasy play, with dominant themes of violence or sexual knowledge
Slow physical growth, especially with unusual appetite or lack of appetite
Ongoing physical complaints, such as stomachaches, headaches, genital pain, sleepiness
Reluctance to talk, to play, or to move, especially if development is slow
No close friendships; hostility toward others; bullying of smaller children
Hypervigilance, with quick, impulsive reactions, such as cringing, startling, or hitting
Frequent absences from school, changes of address, or new caregivers
Expressions of fear rather than joy on seeing the caregiver

Source: Adapted from Scannapieco & Connell Carrick, 2005.

Although biological and academic handicaps are substantial, deficits in a maltreated child's social skills are even more apparent. Maltreated children typically regard other people as hostile and exploitative; hence, they are less friendly, more aggressive, and more isolated than other children. The longer their abuse continues and the earlier it started, the worse their peer relationships are (Manly et al., 2001; Scannapieco & Connell-Carrick, 2005).

A life-span perspective reveals that these deficits can continue lifelong. Maltreated children may become bullies or victims or both. They tend to dissociate, that is, to disconnect their memories from their understanding of themselves (Valentino et al., 2008). Adults who were severely maltreated (physically, sexually, or emotionally) often abuse drugs or alcohol, enter unsupportive relationships,

➤Answer to Observation Quiz (from page 241): No. The number is actually 11.8 per 1,000. Note the little squiggle on the graph's vertical axis below the number 11. This means that numbers between 0 and 11 are not shown.

➤Response for Nurses (from page 241): Any suspicion of child maltreatment must be reported, and these bruises are suspicious. Someone in authority must find out what is happening so that the parent as well as the child can be helped.

REUTERS / SANJIB MUKHERJEE

Abuse or Athletics? Four-year-old Budhia Singh ran 40 miles in 7 hours with adult marathoners. He says he likes to run, but his mother (a widow who allowed his trainer to "adopt" him because she could not feed him) has charged the trainer with physical abuse. The government of India has declared that Singh cannot race again until he is fully grown. If a child, the parent, and the community approve of some activity, can it still be maltreatment?

become victims or aggressors, sabotage their own careers, eat too much or too little, and engage in other self-destructive behavior (M. G. Smith & Fong, 2004). They also have a much higher risk of emotional disorders and suicide attempts, even after other risk factors (e.g., poverty) are considered (Afifi et al., 2008).

Three Levels of Prevention, Again

Just as with injury control, there are three levels of prevention of maltreatment. The ultimate goal is to stop it before it begins—*primary prevention* that focuses on the macrosystem and exosystem (see Chapter 1). Examples of primary-prevention conditions include stable neighborhoods; family cohesion; income equality; and any measure that decreases financial instability, family isolation, and teenage parenthood.

Secondary prevention involves spotting the warning signs and intervening to keep a risky situation from getting worse. For example, insecure attachment, especially of the disorganized type (described in Chapter 7), is a sign of a disrupted parent–child relationship. Someone needs to help repair that interaction. Secondary prevention includes measures such as home visits by nurses or social workers, high-quality day care, and preventive medical treatment—all designed to help high-risk families.

Tertiary prevention includes everything intended to reduce harm when maltreatment has already occurred. Reporting and substantiating abuse are the first steps. Then someone in authority must arrange help or remove the child from the family. If hospitalization is required, that is a sign of failure: Intervention should have begun much earlier. At that point, treatment is very expensive, harm has already been done, and hospitalization itself further strains the parent–child bond (Rovi et al., 2004).

permanency planning An effort by child-welfare authorities to find a long-term living situation that will provide stability and support for a maltreated child. A goal is to avoid repeated changes of caregiver or school, which can be particularly harmful to the child.

Children need a caregiver they trust, in a safe and stable environment, whether they live with their biological parents, with a foster family, or with an adoptive family. Whenever a child is legally removed from an abusive or neglectful home and placed in foster care, federal law in the United States requires state child-welfare authorities to begin **permanency planning,** an effort to find a family who will nurture the child until adulthood (Waddell et al., 2004).

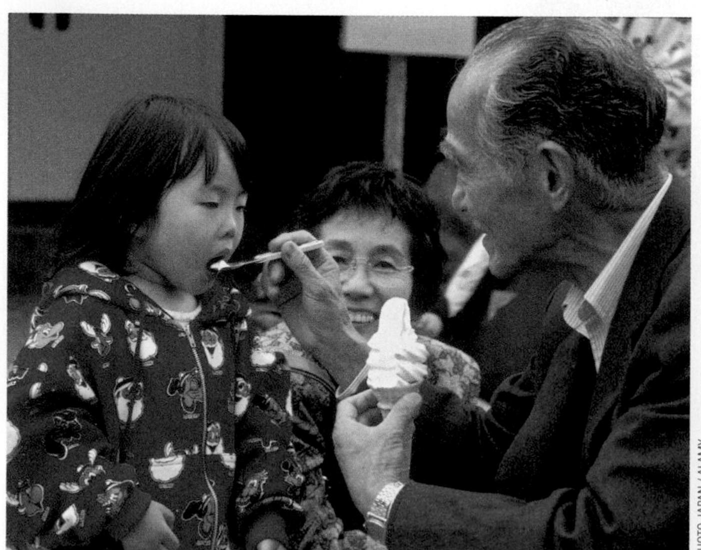

PHOTO JAPAN / ALAMY

JOACHIM LADEFOGED / VII

The Same Situation, Many Miles Apart: Fun with Grandpa Grandfathers, like those shown here in Japan and Sweden, often delight their grandchildren. Sometimes, however, they protect them—either in kinship care, when parents are designated as neglectful, or as secondary prevention before harm is evident. (The grandparents in Sweden are refugees from Iraq.)

STEPHANIE MAZE / CORBIS

Tertiary Prevention Adoption has been these children's salvation, particularly for 9-year-old Leah, clinging to her mother. The mother, Joan, has five adopted children. Adoption is generally better than foster care for maltreated children because it is a permanent, stable arrangement.

In **foster care,** children are officially removed from their parents' custody and entrusted to another adult or family (foster parents are reimbursed for the expenses they incur in meeting the children's needs). In 2005, more than half a million children in the United States were in foster care. About half of them were in a special version of foster care called **kinship care,** in which a relative—usually a grandparent—of the maltreated child becomes the foster caregiver (U.S. Department of Health and Human Services, 2004). This estimate is for official kinship care; three times as many children are informally cared for, primarily by relatives other than their parents.

foster care A legal, publicly supported system in which a maltreated child is removed from the parents' custody and entrusted to another adult or family, which is reimbursed for expenses incurred in meeting the child's needs.

kinship care A form of foster care in which a relative of a maltreated child, usually a grandparent, becomes the approved caregiver.

In the United States, most foster children are from low-income families; half are African American or Latino; and many have multiple physical, intellectual, and emotional problems (Pew Commission on Foster Care, 2004). Despite these problems, children develop better in foster care (including kinship care) than with their original abusive families if a supervising agency screens foster families effectively and provides ongoing financial support and counseling (Kenrick et al., 2006; Oosterman et al., 2007).

Many agencies do not provide adequate support. One obvious failing is that many move children from one foster home to another for reasons that are unrelated to the child's behavior or wishes. Foster children average three placements before a permanent home is found for them (Pew Commission on Foster Care, 2004). Each move increases the risk of a poor outcome (Oosterman et al., 2007).

Adoption (when an adult or couple unrelated to the child is legally granted the obligations and joys of parenthood) is the preferred permanent option. Judges and biological parents are reluctant to release children for adoption, however, and some agencies reject all but "perfect" families—those headed by a heterosexual married couple who are middle class, the same ethnicity as the child, with a mother not employed. Such families are rare.

adoption A legal proceeding in which an adult or couple unrelated to a child is granted the joys and obligations of being that child's parent(s).

Since permanency, not perfection, is the goal, most experts want such adoption restrictions loosened, courts and agencies to act quickly, and permanent guardianship allowed if adoption is impossible. Someone needs to be devoted to each and every young child, celebrating each new accomplishment, from turning somersaults to writing their name. That is how children grow best.

SUMMING UP

As they move with more speed and agility, young children encounter new dangers, becoming seriously injured more often than older children. Three levels of prevention are needed. Laws and practices should be put in place to protect everyone (primary prevention); supervision, forethought, and protective measures should be aimed at preventing mishaps (secondary prevention); and when injury occurs, treatment should be quick and effective, and changes should be made to avoid repetition (tertiary prevention).

Each year, abuse or neglect is substantiated for almost a million children in the United States. About 2 million other cases of maltreatment are reported but not substantiated, and millions more are not reported at all. Preventing maltreatment of all kinds is urgent but complex, because the source is often the family system and the cultural context, not the act of a deranged stranger. Primary prevention includes changing the social context to ensure that parents protect and love their children. Secondary prevention focuses on families at high risk—the poor, the young, the drug-addicted. In tertiary prevention, the abused child is rescued before further damage occurs. ■

SUMMARY

Body Changes

1. Children continue to gain weight and height during early childhood. Many become quite picky eaters. One reason this occurs is that many adults overfeed children, not realizing that young children are naturally quite thin.

2. Culture, income, and family customs all affect children's growth. Worldwide, an increasing number of children have unbalanced diets, eating more fat and sugar and less iron, zinc, and calcium than they need. Childhood obesity is increasingly common because children exercise less and snack more than they once did, laying the foundation for chronic adult illness.

Brain Development

3. The brain continues to grow in early childhood, weighing 75 percent of its adult weight at age 2 and 90 percent by age 5.

4. Myelination is substantial during early childhood, speeding messages from one part of the brain to another. The corpus callosum becomes thicker and functions much better. The prefrontal cortex, known as the executive of the brain, is strengthened as well.

5. Brain changes enable more reflective, coordinated thought and memory; better planning; and quicker responses. All brain functions are localized in one hemisphere or the other. Left/right specialization is apparent in the brain as well as in the body.

6. The expression and regulation of emotions are fostered by several brain areas, including the amygdala, the hippocampus, and the hypothalamus. Abuse in childhood may cause overactivity in the amygdala and hippocampus, creating a flood of stress hormones that interfere with learning.

Improved Motor Skills

7. Motor skills continue to develop, so that clumsy 2-year-olds become 6-year-olds able to move their bodies in whatever ways their culture values and they themselves have practiced. Play helps children develop the body control needed for formal education.

8. Muscle control, practice, and brain maturation are involved in the development of both gross and fine motor skills. Young children enjoy expressing themselves artistically, developing their body and finger control as well as their self-expression.

Injuries and Abuse

9. Accidents are by far the leading cause of death for children, with 1- to 4-year-olds more likely to suffer a serious injury or premature death than older children. Biology, culture, and community conditions combine to make some children more vulnerable.

10. Injury control occurs on many levels, including long before and immediately after each harmful incident, with primary, secondary, and tertiary prevention. Close supervision is required to protect young children from their own eager, impulsive curiosity.

11. Child maltreatment typically results from ongoing abuse and neglect by a child's own parents. Each year almost 3 million cases of child maltreatment are reported in the United States, almost 1 million of which are substantiated.

12. Health, learning, and social skills are all impeded by ongoing child abuse and neglect. Physical abuse is the most obvious form of maltreatment, but neglect is common and may be more harmful.

13. Foster care, including kinship care, is sometimes necessary in cases of severe abuse or neglect. Permanency planning is required because frequent changes are harmful to children. Primary and secondary prevention help parents care for their children and reduce the need for tertiary prevention.

KEY TERMS

myelination (p. 225)
corpus callosum (p. 226)
lateralization (p. 226)
perseveration (p. 228)
amygdala (p. 229)
hippocampus (p. 229)
hypothalamus (p. 230)
injury control/harm reduction (p. 237)
primary prevention (p. 238)
secondary prevention (p. 238)
tertiary prevention (p. 238)
child maltreatment (p. 240)
child abuse (p. 240)
child neglect (p. 240)
reported maltreatment (p. 240)
substantiated maltreatment (p. 240)
post-traumatic stress disorder (PTSD) (p. 241)
permanency planning (p. 244)
foster care (p. 245)
kinship care (p. 245)
adoption (p. 245)

KEY QUESTIONS

1. How are growth rates, body proportions, and motor skills related during early childhood?

2. Does low family income tend to make young children eat more or less? Explain your answer.

3. What are the crucial aspects of brain growth that occur after age 2?

4. How do emotions, and their expression, originate in the brain?

5. Why do public health workers prefer to speak of "injury control" instead of "accident prevention"?

6. What conditions are best for children to develop their motor skills?

7. What are the differences among the three kinds of prevention?

8. What are the arguments for and against laws to protect children from injury?

9. Why might neglect be worse than abuse?

10. What are the advantages and disadvantages of foster care from a nonrelative?

11. What are the advantages and disadvantages of kinship care?

APPLICATIONS

1. Keep a food diary for 24 hours, writing down what you eat, how much, when, how, and why. Then think about nutrition and eating habits in early childhood. Do you see any evidence in yourself of imbalance (e.g., not enough fruits and vegetables, too much sugar or fat, not eating when you are hungry)? Did your food habits originate in early childhood, in adolescence, or at some other time?

2. Go to a playground or other place where young children play. Note the motor skills that the children demonstrate, including abilities and inabilities, and keep track of age and sex. What differences do you see among the children?

3. Ask several parents to describe each accidental injury of each of their children, particularly how it happened and what the consequences were. What primary, secondary, or tertiary prevention measures would have made a difference?

4. Think back on your childhood and the friends you had at that time. Was there any maltreatment? Considering what you have learned in this chapter, why or why not?

9

CHAPTER OUTLINE

Early Childhood: Cognitive Development

I was one of dozens of subway riders who were captivated by a little girl, about age 3, with sparkling eyes and many braids. She sat beside a large man, her legs straight out in front of her. Her mother was standing about 6 feet to her left. The little girl repeatedly ducked her head behind the man and said, "You can't see me, Mama," unaware that her legs (in colorful, striped stockings) were constantly visible to her mother.

Like that little girl, every young child has much to learn. Young children are sometimes *egocentric*, understanding only their own perspective. Among their developing ideas is a *theory of mind*, an understanding of how minds work (as in knowing that your mother would not lose sight of you on a subway).

Researchers have found early childhood to be a time of prodigious new learning, a discovery that has changed daily life for many children. No longer merely "cared for" (as in day care or home care), young children are now taught, with educational toys, early schooling, and the like.

Examples of early learning are everywhere. The halting, simple sentences of the typical 2-year-old become the nonstop, complex outpourings of a talkative 6-year-old. Toddlers' simple block towers become elaborate cities, with tunnels, bridges, and houses designed and built by kindergartners.

How does such rapid cognitive development happen? Is it primarily through parents, or schools, or children's own maturation? This chapter describes thinking and learning from age 2 to 6, including remarkable advances in thought as well as language, and explores several explanations of how cognition in early childhood occurs.

Piaget and Vygotsky

Jean Piaget and Lev Vygotsky (introduced in Chapter 2) are justly famous for their descriptions of cognition. Their theories are "compatible in many ways" (Rogoff, 1998, p. 681), especially in what they have to say about the eager learning of young children.

Piaget: Preoperational Thinking

preoperational intelligence Piaget's term for cognitive development between the ages of about 2 and 6; it includes language and imagination (which involve symbolic thought), but logical, operational thinking is not yet possible.

For Piaget, early childhood is the second of four stages of cognition. His term for cognitive development between the ages of about 2 and 6 is **preoperational intelligence.** This stage of thinking goes beyond the sensory awareness and motor skills of infancy (sensorimotor intelligence) to include language and imagination, which involve symbolic thought. Preoperational thinking is magical and self-centered; *pre*-operational means that the child is not yet ready for logical operations (or reasoning processes) (Inhelder & Piaget, 1964).

Obstacles to Logical Operations

Piaget described four characteristics of thinking in early childhood, all of which make logic difficult: centration, focus on appearance, static reasoning, and irreversibility.

centration A characteristic of preoperational thought in which a young child focuses (centers) on one idea, excluding all others.

Centration is the tendency to focus on one aspect of a situation to the exclusion of all others. Young children may, for example, insist that lions and tigers seen at the zoo or in picture books cannot be cats, because the children "center" on the house-pet aspect of the cats they know. Or they may insist that Daddy is a father, not a brother, because they center on the role that each family member fills for them.

egocentrism Piaget's term for children's tendency to think about the world entirely from their own personal perspective.

The daddy example illustrates a particular type of centration that Piaget called **egocentrism**—literally, self-centeredness. Egocentric children contemplate the world exclusively from their personal perspective, as the little girl on the subway did.

Piaget did not equate egocentrism with selfishness. Consider, for example, a 3-year-old who chose to buy a model car as a birthday present for his mother, stubbornly convinced that she would be delighted. In fact, his "behavior was not selfish or greedy; he carefully wrapped the present and gave it to his mother with an expression that clearly showed that he expected her to love it" (Crain, 2005, p. 108).

focus on appearance A characteristic of preoperational thought in which a young child ignores all attributes that are not apparent.

A second characteristic of preoperational thought is a **focus on appearance** to the exclusion of other attributes. A girl given a short haircut might worry that she has turned into a boy. In preoperational thought, a thing is whatever it appears to be.

static reasoning A characteristic of preoperational thought in which a young child thinks that nothing changes. Whatever is now has always been and always will be.

Third, preoperational children use **static reasoning.** They assume that the world is unchanging, always in the state in which they currently encounter it. A young boy might want the television turned off while he goes to the bathroom, assuming that when he returns, he can pick up the program exactly where he left off.

irreversibility A characteristic of preoperational thought in which a young child thinks that nothing can be undone. A thing cannot be restored to the way it was before a change occurred.

The fourth characteristic of preoperational thought is **irreversibility.** Preoperational thinkers fail to recognize that reversing a process sometimes restores whatever existed before. A young child might cry because her mother put lettuce on her hamburger. Overwhelmed by her desire to have things "just right" (as explained in Chapter 8), she might reject the hamburger even after the lettuce is removed because she believes that what is done cannot be undone.

Especially for Nutritionists (see response, page 252) How can Piaget's theory help you encourage children to eat healthy foods?

Conservation and Logic

Piaget devised many experiments demonstrating the constraints on thinking that result from preoperational reasoning. A famous set of experiments involved **conservation,** the fact that the amount of something remains the same (is conserved) despite changes in its appearance.

conservation The principle that the amount of a substance remains the same (i.e., is conserved) when its appearance changes.

Suppose two identical glasses contain the same amount of liquid, and the liquid from one of these glasses is poured into a taller, narrower glass. If young children are asked whether one glass contains more liquid or both glasses contain the same amount, they will insist that the narrower glass (in which the liquid level is higher) has more.

All four characteristics of preoperational thought are evident in this mistake. Young children fail to understand conservation of liquids because they focus (*center*) on what they see (*appearance*), noticing only the immediate (*static*) condition. It does not occur to them that they could reverse the process and re-create the liquid's level of a moment earlier (*irreversibility*). (See Figure 9.1 for other examples.)

COURTESY OF KATHLEEN BERGER

Demonstration of Conservation My youngest daughter, Sarah, here at age $5\frac{3}{4}$, demonstrates Piaget's conservation-of-volume experiment. First, she examines both short glasses to be sure they contain the same amount of milk. Then, after the contents of one are poured into the tall glass and she is asked which has more, she points to the tall glass, just as Piaget would have expected. Later she added, "It looks like it has more because it's taller," indicating that some direct instruction might change her mind.

Tests of Various Types of Conservation

Type of Conservation	Initial Presentation	Transformation	Question	Preoperational Child's Answer
Volume	Two equal glasses of liquid.	Pour one into a taller, narrower glass.	Which glass contains more?	The taller one.
Number	Two equal lines of checkers.	Increase spacing of checkers in one line.	Which line has more checkers?	The longer one.
Matter	Two equal balls of clay.	Squeeze one ball into a long, thin shape.	Which piece has more clay?	The long one.
Length	Two sticks of equal length.	Move one stick.	Which stick is longer?	The one that is farther to the right.

FIGURE 9.1

Conservation, Please According to Piaget, until children grasp the concept of conservation at (he believed) about age 6 or 7, they cannot understand that the transformations shown here do not change the total amount of liquid, checkers, clay, and wood.

➤**Response for Nutritionists** (from page 250): Take each of the four characteristics of preoperational thought into account. Because of egocentrism, having a special place and plate might assure the child that this food is exclusively his or hers. Since appearance is important, food should look tasty. Since static thinking dominates, if something healthy is added (e.g., grate carrots into the cake, add milk to the soup), do it before the food is given to the child. In the reversibility example in the text, the lettuce should be removed out of the child's sight and the "new" hamburger presented.

Limitations of Piaget's Research

Notice that Piaget's tests of conservation require the child's words, not actions. When the tests of logic are simplified, children younger than 7 often succeed at them. For instance, other research has found that even 3-year-olds can distinguish appearance from reality if the test is nonverbal, as when children are asked to reach for objects rather than to talk about them (Sapp et al., 2000). In many ways, children indicate that they know something via their gestures before they can say it in words (Goldin-Meadow, 2006).

Furthermore, some young children demonstrate that they understand conservation and other logical ideas in a gamelike setting, although not in Piaget's experiments (Donaldson, 1979). For example, if a "naughty bear" rearranges one row of checkers, 4-year-olds know that the elongated line still has the same number as before. That is a very early demonstration of the concept of conservation.

Researchers now believe that Piaget underestimated conceptual ability during early childhood, just as he had underestimated it during infancy (Halford & Andrews, 2006). He relied on the children's words in an experimental setting rather than relying on nonverbal signs in a play context. As already mentioned in Chapter 6, he did not have the benefit of brain scans, which reveal more intellectual activity than behavior does.

Other aspects of Piaget's experiments to distinguish preoperational thought from the next stage (concrete operational thought) also show that he underestimated children's ability. For instance, Piaget thought that preoperational children cannot classify objects properly, in that they do not firmly grasp that dogs, cats, and cows are all kinds of animals. To some extent, Piaget was right: Many researchers have found that children are confused about the relationship between superordinate categories (such as animals), subcategories (such as dogs), and further subcategories (such as collies). (Classification is discussed further in Chapter 12.)

However, recent research finds that even 3-year-olds can classify things that they know well, such as foods, if the categories are ones they themselves often use (Nguyen & Murphy, 2003). Piaget was correct that young children do not think as logically as adults do, or even as operationally as older children do, but he did not realize how much children can understand.

Animism in Preoperational Thought

animism The belief that natural objects and phenomena are alive.

A final aspect of preoperational thought, when children see the rest of the world as similar to themselves, is called **animism,** the belief that natural objects and phenomena are alive (Piaget, 1929). Clouds, mountains, and trees are sometimes thought to have feelings, goals, and even souls. Animism is a strongly held belief for many young children, who insist that the spirit of things are active under certain circumstances (Subbotsky, 2000).

Likewise, an egocentric concept of nonhuman animals is quite common. For example, a dead bird discovered by a child might bring forth tears and require a burial ceremony. A dog might be the listener for all the wishes and worries of a child who believes that the pet understands and sympathizes. Many stories for children include animals or inanimate objects that talk and help people: These aspects of the stories are not considered unlikely by the children who hear them.

Magical happenings and magical sayings are also common in the daily lives of young children. Wishing on a star or an eyelash or saying "Cross my heart and hope to die," holding one's breath when passing a cemetery, and many more such behaviors are frequent, even if the parents belittle them as superstitions.

Many of the world's religions include beliefs that outsiders might think of as far-fetched, but adult believers are quite convinced that such "magic" is real. Tales of talking animals are found in almost every religion. Given that, it seems ill advised to criticize children because they have their own faith and interpretations that adults do not share. A childish sympathy for animals and respect for nature are, according to some people, needed correctives to the technology and materialism that are elements of many cultures (Harding, 2006).

Attempts to measure children's animism find that many children simultaneously hold rational and magical ideas (Mescheriakov, 2005). This was evident in a series of studies in the United States that explored children's understanding of death (Bering & Bjorklund, 2004). Young children saw a puppet skit about a sick mouse that was eaten by an alligator. When questioned afterward, nearly all the children asserted that the mouse was dead and would never be alive again, but most of those under age 7 thought the dead mouse still felt sick; almost all the children thought the mouse still loved his mother.

Children's understanding is inevitably affected by their culture. In the dead mouse example, children attending Catholic schools in Spain were more likely than U.S. children to believe that the dead mouse could still use its senses (Bering et al., 2005). By contrast, 4- to 6-year-olds in China more often were sure that death was irreversible, although the younger children in China were not sure that they themselves would die (Zhu & Fang, 2006).

Vygotsky: Social Learning

For many years, the magical, illogical, and self-centered aspects of cognition dominated descriptions of early childhood by researchers who were understandably influenced by Piaget. Vygotsky was the first leading developmentalist to emphasize the other side of early cognition. Young children are not always egocentric; they can be very sensitive to the wishes and emotions of others. This other side emphasizes the social aspect of young children's cognition, in contrast to Piaget's emphasis on the individual.

Children as Apprentices

Vygotsky believed that every aspect of children's cognitive development is embedded in a social context (Vygotsky, 1934/1987). Children are curious and observant. They ask questions—about how machines work, why weather changes, where the sky ends—assuming that others know the answers.

In many ways, a child is what Vygotsky called an **apprentice in thinking,** someone whose intellectual growth is stimulated and directed by older and more skilled members of society. The parents and older siblings are usually the child's teachers. If the child attends a day-care program, learning from "more capable peers" is central (C. Thompson, 2002).

apprentice in thinking Vygotsky's term for a person whose cognition is stimulated and directed by older and more skilled members of society.

According to Vygotsky, children learn because their mentors do the following:

- Present challenges
- Offer assistance (not taking over)
- Provide instruction
- Encourage motivation

Children learn to think via **guided participation** in social experiences and in explorations of their universe, with both the mentor and the child talking as well as acting. For example, children learning to draw or write or dance are quite willing to copy from one another. A child who is copied is not resentful (as an adult might be) but rather appreciates the recognition.

guided participation The process by which people learn from others who guide their experiences and explorations.

The reality that children are curious about everything, learning and remembering whatever they experience, is evidence of cognition. The ability to learn (not the measure of what is known) indicates intelligence. Vygotsky (1934/1987) said:

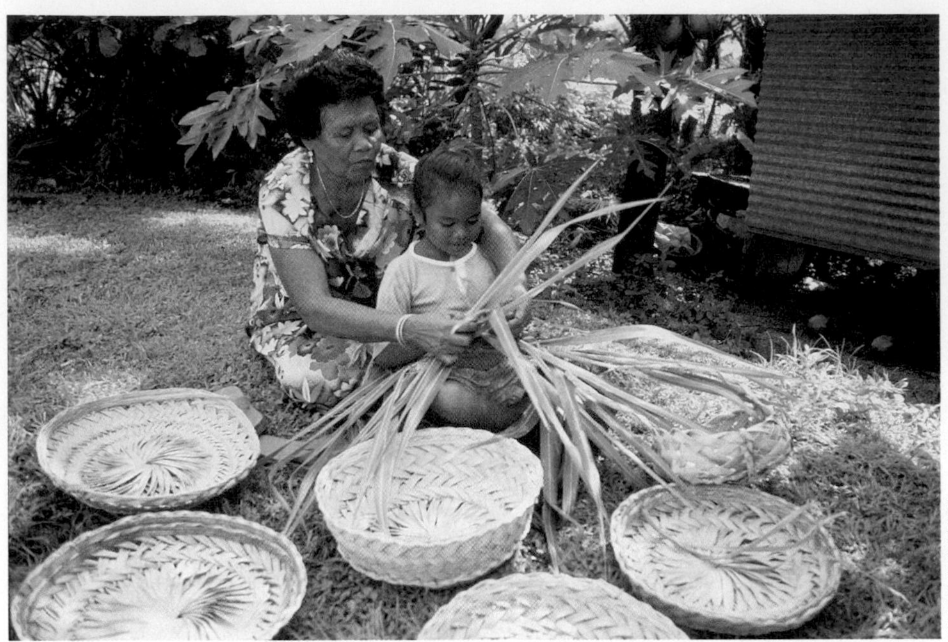
TIM ROCK / LONELY PLANET

Weaving Skills Baskets made in the Pacific island nation of Palau are known worldwide for their beauty and durability. The skills involved in weaving them are taught through scaffolding and apprenticeship.

"What children can do with the assistance of others might be in some sense even more indicative of their mental development than what they can do alone" (p. 5).

Scaffolding

zone of proximal development (ZPD) Vygotsky's term for the skills—cognitive as well as physical—that a person can exercise only with assistance, not yet independently.

scaffolding Temporary support that is tailored to a learner's needs and abilities and aimed at helping the learner master the next task in a given learning process.

As you saw in Chapter 2, Vygotsky believed that each developing individual has a **zone of proximal development (ZPD),** which includes all the skills the person can perform with assistance but cannot quite perform independently. How and when children master their potential skills depends, in part, on the willingness of others to provide **scaffolding,** or temporary sensitive support, to help them traverse that zone.

Good caregivers provide plenty of scaffolding, teaching children to look both ways before crossing the street (while holding the child's hand) or letting them stir the cake batter (perhaps stirring it a few times themselves to demonstrate the technique and to make sure the ingredients are well mixed). Scaffolding is particularly important for experiences that are directly cognitive—that is, ones that will produce better understanding of words and ideas. For example, adults reading to 3-year-olds usually provide excellent scaffolding—explaining, pointing, listening—within the child's zone of development in response to the child's needs at the moment. The sensitive reader would never tell the child to be quiet and listen but might instead prolong the session by asking the child questions.

Even in talking with a child, scaffolding is possible and helpful. Parents often answer young children's questions not with a simple answer, but with a response that builds vocabulary and understanding (Chouinard, 2007). If a child asks, "What is that?" the mother, instead of simply saying, "That is a truck," might say, "That is a kind of t-r-r…" (guiding the child to respond "truck") or "That is a garbage truck. What do you think it has inside?" As one team of researchers found in a longitudinal study, young children from age 4 to 8 whose mothers provided more scaffolding became better readers at age 8 (Dieterich et al., 2006).

Remember that children pay particular attention to other children. They are thus able to learn from someone who is slightly more competent than they are—who can provide guidance within their zone of proximal development. Children often provide scaffolding for each other. This was evident in a yearlong mentoring project that assigned third-graders to work on craft projects with preschoolers. As one older child said, "I learned how little kids think" (quoted in Fair et al., 2005, p. 229).

Older siblings can be excellent mentors. In Chiapas, Mexico, 8-year-old Tonik taught his 2-year-old sister, Katal, how to wash a doll. After several minutes of demonstrating and describing, Tonik continues:

> **Tonik:** Pour it like this. (*Demonstrates*)
> **Tonik:** Sister, pour it. (*Hands glass*)
> **Tonik:** Look! Pour it.
> **Katal:** (*Pours, with some difficulty*)
> **Tonik:** Like that. (*Approval*)
> **Katal:** (*Looks away*)
> **Tonik:** It's finished now.
>
> [*quoted in Maynard, 2002, p. 977*]

Note that when Katal looks away, Tonik wisely declares the session finished. This response encourages the learner to participate in later apprenticeships. Motivation is crucial in early education—one reason why sensitive social interaction is so powerful.

Especially for Driving Instructors (see response, page 256) Sometimes your students cry, curse, or quit. How would Vygotsky advise you to proceed?

The social learning emphasized by Vygotsky is transmitted in almost every culture through scaffolding (Gauvain, 2005). Other children, especially older siblings, play an important role in this kind of learning, too, helping children understand the behavior of their parents and other adults.

Language as a Tool

Vygotsky believed that words are pivotal in building scaffolds, developing cognition. Empirical research finds this to be the case, whether or not the child has special developmental needs (e.g., Baker et al., 2007; Philips & Tolmie, 2007). Just as a builder needs tools to construct a house, the mind needs language. Talking, listening, reading, and writing are tools to advance thought.

Language advances thinking in two ways. First, internal dialogue, or **private speech,** occurs when people talk to themselves, developing new ideas (Vygotsky, 1934/1987). Young children use private speech often, although they are sometimes unaware that they do so (Manfra & Winsler, 2006). They talk aloud to review, decide, and explain events to themselves (and, incidentally, to anyone else within earshot).

private speech The internal dialogue that occurs when people talk to themselves (either silently or out loud).

Older preschoolers use private speech more selectively and effectively, sometimes in a whisper or even without any sound. Audible or not, private speech aids cognition, so adults should allow and even encourage it (Winsler et al., 2007). Many adults themselves use private speech, sometimes writing down the ideas that emerge for later analysis.

The second way in which language advances thinking, according to Vygotsky, is by mediating the social interaction that is vital to learning. This **social mediation** function of speech occurs during both formal instruction (when teachers explain things) and casual conversation.

social mediation Human interaction that expands and advances understanding, often through words that one person uses to explain something to another.

Language used in social mediation is evident as children, guided by their mentors, learn numbers, recall memories, and follow routines. Among the cognitive tasks that are aided by words and that differentiate 6-year-olds from 2-year-olds are the abilities of the older children to do the following:

- Count objects, with one number per item (called *one-to-one correspondence*)
- Remember accurately (although false memories can confuse anyone)
- Verbalize standard experiences (called *scripts,* such as the sequence of a birthday party or a restaurant meal)

➤Response for Driving Instructors (from page 255): Use guided participation and scaffold the instruction so your students are not overwhelmed. Be sure to provide lots of praise and days of practice. If emotion erupts, do not take it as an attack on you.

Each of these cognitive accomplishments has been the subject of extensive research, and it is evident that adult instruction and verbal encouragement are crucial for all of them (e.g., Hubbs-Tait et al., 2002; Mix et al., 2002). By age 3 or 4, children's brains are mature enough to comprehend numbers, store memories, and recognize routines. Whether or not a child actually demonstrates such understanding depends on family, school, and culture. Language is a key mediator between brain potential and what children actually understand (Gelman & Kalish, 2006).

SUMMING UP

Cognition develops rapidly from age 2 to 6. Children's active search for understanding was first recognized by Piaget, who believed that young children are generally not capable of performing logical operations (which is why he called this period *preoperational*). Their egocentrism limits their understanding, and they center on only one thing at a time, focusing on appearance. Their thinking is static, not dynamic. They do not understand reversibility. Their thinking is magical and animistic, which is not necessarily bad.

Vygotsky emphasized the social and cultural aspects of children's cognition. He believed that children must be properly guided as apprentices, within their zones of proximal development. Other children as well as adults are effective mentors, providing the scaffolding that children need to help them master various skills and concepts. Language is used for private speech and social mediation, both of which are tools that help children learn. Words are particularly helpful to mediate between the child's curiosity and the mentor's knowledge. ■

Children's Theories

Both Piaget and Vygotsky realized that children actively work to understand their world. Recently, many other developmentalists have attempted to show exactly how children's knowledge develops. Children seek to explain what they experience, especially why and how people behave as they do, and many ideas about the nature of this search have been put forth (Gopnik & Schulz, 2007; Moses, 2005).

Theory-Theory

theory-theory The idea that children attempt to explain everything they see and hear by constructing theories.

One theory of cognitive development begins with the human drive to develop explanations, a drive that is especially apparent in early childhood. The term **theory-theory** stresses that children naturally try to construct theories to explain whatever they see and hear:

> More than any animal, we search for causal regularities in the world around us. We are perpetually driven to look for deeper explanations of our experience, and broader and more reliable predictions about it. . . . Children seem, quite literally, to be born with . . . the desire to understand the world and the desire to discover how to behave in it.
>
> *[Gopnik, 2007, p. 66]*

Thus, according to theory-theory, the best conceptualization of, and explanation for, mental processes in young children is that humans always seek reasons, causes, and underlying principles. Figure 9.2, with its narrative-style "recipe" for cooking a turkey, captures the essential idea of theory-theory: that children don't want logical definitions but rather explanations of various things, especially things that involve them.

A whole turkey

1 big bag full of a whole turkey (Get the kind with no feathers on, not the kind the Pilgrims ate.)
A giant lump of stuffin'
1 squash pie
1 mint pie
1 little fancy dish of sour berries
1 big fancy dish of a vegetable mix
20 dishes of all different candies; chocolate balls, cherry balls, good'n plenties and peanuts

Get up when the alarm says to and get busy fast. Unfold the turkey and open up the holes. Push in the stuffin' for a couple of hours. I think you get stuffin' from that Farm that makes it.

I know you have to pin the stuffin' to the turkey or I suppose it would get out. And get special pins or use big long nails.

Get the kitchen real hot, and from there on you just cook turkey. Sometimes you can call it a bird, but it's not.

Then you put the vegetables in the cooker—and first put one on top, and next put one on the bottom, and then one in the middle. That makes a vegetable mix. Put 2 red things of salt all in it and 2 red things of water also. Cook them to just ½ of warm.

Put candies all around the place and Linda will bring over the pies. When the company comes put on your red apron.

FIGURE 9.2

Unfold the Turkey This recipe (from *Smashed Potatoes*, edited by Jane Martel) shows many characteristics of preschool thought, among them literal interpretation of words ("Sometimes you can call it a bird, but it's not") and an uncertain idea of time ("Push in the stuffin' for a couple of hours") and quantity ("A giant lump of stuffin'").

Exactly how are explanations sought in early childhood? In one study, Mexican American mothers kept detailed diaries of every question their 3- to 5-year-olds had asked and how they themselves had responded (Kelemen et al., 2005; see the Research Design). Generally, younger children asked more questions than older children, and mothers with more years of education heard (or recorded) more questions. This study focused particularly on children's curiosity and how adults respond.

Most of the questions were about human behavior and characteristics (see Figure 9.3). For example, "Why do you give my mother a kiss?" "Why is my brother bad?" "Why do women have breasts?" and "Why are there Black kids?" Fewer questions were about nonliving things ("Why does it rain?") or objects ("Why is my daddy's car white?").

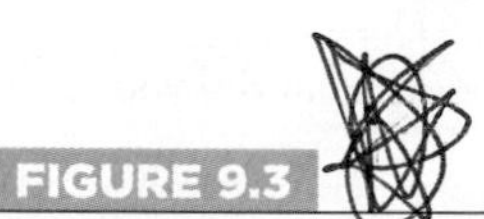

FIGURE 9.3

Questions, Questions Parents found that most of their children's questions were about human behavior—especially the parents' behavior toward the child. Children seek to develop a theory to explain things, so the question "Why can't I have some candy?" is not satisfactorily answered by "It's almost dinnertime."

Percentage of Questions Asked by 3- to 5-Year-Olds, by Domain

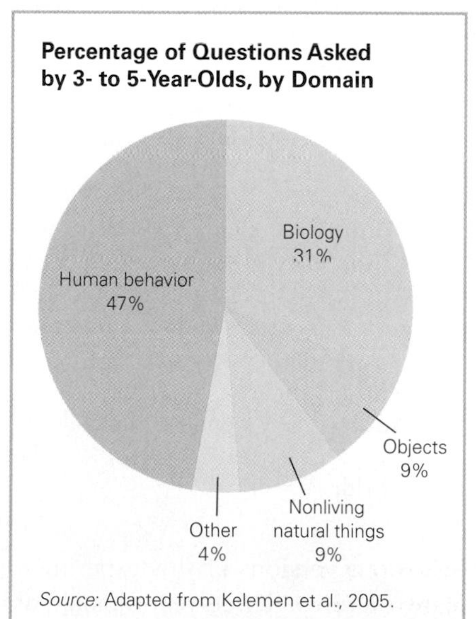

Source: Adapted from Kelemen et al., 2005.

Research Design

Scientists: Deborah Kelemen and others.

Publication: *Developmental Psychology* (2005).

Participants: A total of 48 Mexican American mothers and their 3- to 5-year-olds. Most of the women were born in Mexico and all lived in central California at the time of the study.

Design: After an initial interview, the researchers phoned the mothers every two days for two weeks to hear what "Why?" or "How?" questions the children had asked and what answers the children had been given.

Major conclusion: Children ask many questions about the purpose of things and about human behavior; they seem less curious about inanimate objects.

Comment: These families were often bilingual, immigrant, and religious. These characteristics may not have affected the results, but replication is needed to find out for sure. Ideally, children's actual questions would be tape-recorded, not simply reported by the mothers (whose reports might be distorted by unconscious biases).

Many questions concerned the underlying purpose of whatever the child observed, although parents usually responded as if children were asking about science instead. An adult might interpret a child's one-word question "Why?" to mean simply "What causes X to happen?" when the child's intended meaning might be "I want to know more about *X*" (Leach, 1997). For example, if a child asks why women have breasts, a parent, instead of talking about hormones and maturation, might say that breasts are for feeding babies. From a child's egocentric perspective, any question may really mean "How does this relate to me?" Accordingly, the parent might add that the child got his or her first nourishment from the mother's breast.

Some support for theory-theory came from a series of experiments that explored when and how 3-year-olds imitate others (Williamson et al., 2008). Children seem to assess why other people acted as they did before deciding whether they themselves should copy those actions. This is another example of a general principle: Children develop a theory about the cause of any problems they experience or about the intention underlying an adult's actions before they engage their impressive ability to imitate.

Theory of Mind

Human mental processes—thoughts, emotions, beliefs, motives, and intentions—are among the most complicated and puzzling phenomena that we encounter every day. Adults seek to understand why people fall in love, or vote as they do, or make foolish choices. Children are puzzled about a playmate's unexpected anger, a sibling's generosity, or an aunt's too-wet kiss.

To know what goes on in another's mind, people develop a "folk psychology," an understanding of others' thinking called **theory of mind.** Theory of mind typically appears rather suddenly (Wellman et al., 2001), in "an important intellectual change at about 4 years" (Perner, 2000, p. 396).

theory of mind A person's theory of what other people might be thinking. In order to have a theory of mind, children must realize that other people are not necessarily thinking the same thoughts that they themselves are. That realization is seldom possible before age 4.

Belief and Reality: Understanding the Difference

Theory of mind includes many concepts, some of which are difficult even for much older children. However, a sudden leap in understanding seems to occur at about age 4—but what exactly is it that children suddenly understand? They come to realize that thoughts may not reflect reality. This idea leads to the theory-of-mind concept that people can be deliberately deceived or fooled—an idea that is beyond most younger children, even when they themselves have been deceived.

Consider a classic experiment. An adult shows a 3-year-old a candy box and asks, "What is inside?" The child says, naturally, "Candy." But the child has been tricked:

Adult: Let's open it and look inside.
Child: Oh . . . holy moly . . . pencils!
Adult: Now I'm going to put them back and close it up again. (*Does so*) Now . . . when you first saw the box, before we opened it, what did you think was inside it?
Child: Pencils.
Adult: Nicky [friend of the child] hasn't seen inside this box. When Nicky comes in and sees it . . . what will he think is inside it?
Child: Pencils.

[adapted from Astington & Gopnik, 1988, p. 195]

Various versions of this experiment have involved thousands of children from many cultures. Three-year-olds almost always confuse what they know now with what they once thought and what someone else might think. Another way of describing this is to say that they are "cursed" by their own knowledge (Birch & Bloom, 2003), too egocentric to grasp others' perspectives.

As a result, young children are notoriously bad at deception. They play hide-and-seek by hiding in the same place time after time, or their facial expression betrays them when they tell a fib. Parents sometimes say, "I know when you are lying" and, to the consternation of most 3-year-olds, parents are usually right. (This is not true at older ages, because children become better at fooling their parents and, knowing this, parents become suspicious of the truth as well as of the lie.)

Especially for Social Scientists (see response, page 261) Can you think of any connection between Piaget's theory of preoperational thought and 3-year-olds' errors in this theory-of-mind task?

Closely related to young children's trouble with lying are their belief in fantasy (the magical thinking noted earlier) and their static reasoning (characteristic of preoperational thought), which makes it difficult for them to change their minds (remember perseveration from Chapter 8).

Contextual Influences

Recently, developmentalists have asked what, precisely, strengthens theory of mind at about age 4. Is this change more a matter of nature or of nurture, of brain maturation or of experience?

Neurological maturation is a plausible explanation. In one study, 68 children aged 2 to 5½ were presented with four standard theory-of-mind situations, including a Band-Aid box that really contained pencils (similar to the candy-box experiment just described) (Jenkins & Astington, 1996). In each situation, they were asked to perform a specific task. More than one-third of the children succeeded at all four tasks, and more than one-third failed at three or four. Age was the main factor: The 5-year-olds were most likely to succeed on all tasks, the 4-year-olds had middling success, and most 3-year-olds failed every time.

This age-related advance suggests that context is less crucial than maturation of the prefrontal cortex (Perner et al., 2002). Further evidence that the brain is the underlying reason young children do not yet understand other people's thoughts comes from children with autism. Such children may be gifted in some ways but are nonetheless impaired in social understanding, particularly theory of mind (García-Pérez et al., 2008). Their brains function differently from those of other children.

Two other influences that are affected by context are key: language and siblings. Children with greater verbal fluency (at any age) are more likely to have a theory of mind. This is partly the result of experience, especially mother–child conversations that involve thoughts and wishes (Ontai & Thompson, 2008).

When the effects of both age and language ability are taken into account, a third factor emerges: having at least one older brother or sister. One researcher estimates that, in the development of theory of mind, "two older siblings are worth about a year of chronological age" (Perner, 2000, p. 383). As they argue, agree, compete, and cooperate with their older siblings, and as their older siblings try to fool them, children realize that not everyone thinks as they do.

A study comparing theory of mind among young children in preschools in Canada, India, Peru, Samoa, and Thailand found that the Canadian 5-year-olds were slightly ahead and the Samoan 5-year-olds were slightly behind, but across cultures most 5-year-old children passed the false-belief tests (such as a culture-fair version of the pencils in the candy box) (see Figure 9.4). The researchers concluded that brain maturation was the main factor in the acquisition of theory of mind but that language, social interaction, and culture were also influential (Callaghan et al., 2005).

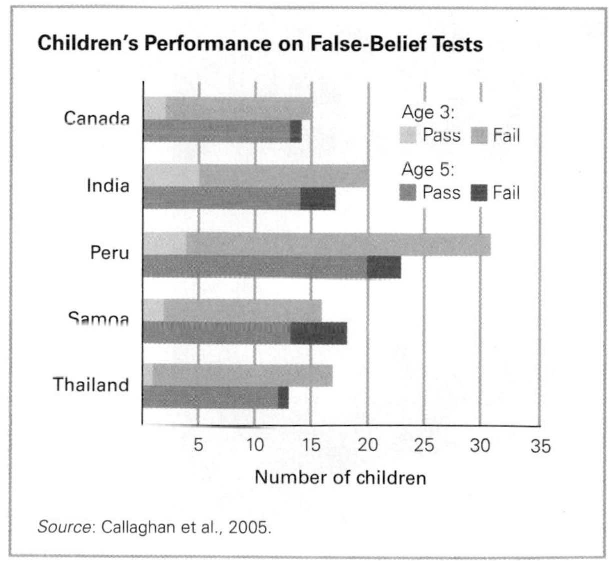

FIGURE 9.4

Few at Age 3, Most by Age 5 The advantage of cross-cultural research is that it can reveal universal patterns. Although the number of children in each group is small (from 31 3-year-olds in Peru to 13 5-year-olds in Thailand), the pattern is obvious. Something changes at about age 4 that enables most children to acquire theory of mind by age 5.

© PUNCHSTOCK

Road Rage? From their expressions, it looks as if this brother and sister may crash their toy jeep and cry, each blaming the other for the mishap. But a benefit of such sibling interactions is that they can advance theory of mind by helping children realize that people do not always think the same way.

Advances in theory of mind were also evident in a series of studies comparing children in Korea and in England. Some Korean 3-year-olds passed tests that almost no English child did. However, even for them, notable progress occurred from age 3 to 5, indicating the influence of brain maturation (Oh & Lewis, 2008).

Similar conclusions were drawn from a meta-analysis comparing 254 studies in China and North America (in which about 5,000 children were tested). The overall conclusion was that culture mattered (the Hong Kong children tended to be slowest to develop theory of mind) but that there was a strong "universal, early development of theory of mind" (Liu et al., 2008, p. 527).

Each child's logic and maturation are important (Piaget), but language, social interaction, and culture are mediators (Vygotsky) once the necessary brain structures are in place. Although 2-year-olds everywhere are simply too immature to develop theory of mind, in most cultures, sufficient "hearing and participating in conversation" occurs by age 3 to allow children to do so by age 4 (Callaghan et al., 2005, p. 382).

SUMMING UP

Scholars have recently noted that children develop theories to explain whatever they observe, and those theories do not necessarily spring from explanations given to them by adults. Children seem to be much more interested in the underlying purpose of events within the grand scheme of life; adults are more focused on immediate scientific causes. Many researchers have explored the development of theory of mind, the understanding that other people can have thoughts and ideas that are unlike one's own. Neurological maturation, linguistic competence, family context, and culture all affect the attainment of theory of mind at about age 4. ■

MICHAEL WICKES / THE IMAGE WORKS

What's That? By far the best way for a parent to teach a young child new vocabulary is by reading aloud. Ideally, the interaction should be a very social one, with much pointing and talking, as this Idaho pair demonstrate. If such experiences are part of her daily routine, this little girl not only will develop language but also will be among the first of her classmates to learn how to read.

Language

Language is pivotal to cognition in early childhood. You have already read about language involvement in private speech, social mediation, and theory of mind. In addition, language itself is the leading cognitive accomplishment of early childhood: 2-year-olds use only short, telegraphic sentences, but a few years later 6-year-olds seem able to understand and discuss almost anything (see Table 9.1).

Brain maturation, myelination, and social interaction make early childhood not only the usual time for learning language but perhaps the best time. As you remember from Chapter 1, scientists once thought that early childhood was a critical period for language learning—the *only* time when a first language could be mastered and the best time for learning a second or third language. Millions of people learn languages after age 6, however, so the critical-period hypothesis is false (Birdsong, 2006; Herschensohn, 2007).

Nonetheless, it does seem that early childhood is a *sensitive period* for language learning—for rapidly and easily mastering vocabulary, grammar, and pronunciation. Young children are sometimes called "language sponges" because they soak up every drop of language they encounter.

One scholar believes that "acquisition of a normal language is guaranteed for children up to the age of six, is steadily compromised from there until shortly after puberty, and is rare thereafter. Maturational changes in the brain . . . are plausible causes" (Pinker, 2000, p. 298). Another expert finds that there are "multiple sensitive periods . . . auditory, phonological, semantic, syntactic, and motor systems, along with the developmental interactions among these components" (Thomas & Johnson, 2008, p. 2), all of which facilitate language learning early in life.

One of the valuable traits of young children is that they talk a lot—to adults, to each other, to themselves, to their toys—unfazed by mispronunciation, misuse, stuttering, or other impediments to fluency. This is a crucial developmental asset: Language comes easily because young children are less self-conscious about what they say than are older children and adults. Egocentrism has its advantages; this is one of them.

TABLE 9.1

AT ABOUT THIS TIME: Language in Early Childhood

Approximate Age	Characteristic or Achievement
2 years	*Vocabulary:* 100–2,000 words *Sentence length:* 2–6 words *Grammar:* Plurals, pronouns, many nouns, verbs, adjectives *Questions:* Many "What's that?" questions
3 years	*Vocabulary:* 1,000–5,000 words *Sentence length:* 3–8 words *Grammar:* Conjunctions, adverbs, articles *Questions:* Many "Why?" questions
4 years	*Vocabulary:* 3,000–10,000 words *Sentence length:* 5–20 words *Grammar:* Dependent clauses, tags at ends of sentences (". . . didn't I?" ". . . won't you?") *Questions:* Peak of "Why?" questions; also many "How?" and "When?" questions
5 years	*Vocabulary:* 5,000–20,000 words *Sentence length:* Some seem unending (". . . and . . . who . . . and . . . that . . . and . . .") *Grammar:* Complex, sometimes using passive voice ("Man bitten by dog"); subjunctive ("If I were . . .") *Questions:* Include some about differences (male/female, old/young, rich/poor)

The Vocabulary Explosion

In childhood, new words are added rapidly. The average child knows about 500 words at age 2 and more than 10,000 at age 6. The *naming explosion* (explained in Chapter 6) becomes more general as verbs, adjectives, adverbs, and conjunctions are added to the thousands of nouns mastered during early childhood (Herschensohn, 2007).

Precise estimates of vocabulary size vary because contexts are diverse; some children learn four times as many words as others. For every young child, however, vocabulary builds quickly and language potential is greater than spoken vocabulary. Every normal child could become fluently bilingual given the proper circumstances.

Fast-Mapping

How does the vocabulary explosion occur? After painstakingly learning one word at a time at age 1, children develop an interconnected set of categories for words, a kind of grid or mental map, which makes speedy vocabulary acquisition possible. The process is called **fast-mapping** (Woodward & Markman, 1998) because, rather than figuring out an exact definition after hearing a word used in several contexts, children hear a word once and tentatively stick it into one of the categories on their mental language map.

fast-mapping The speedy and sometimes imprecise way in which children learn new words by tentatively placing them in mental categories according to their perceived meaning.

Like more conventional mental mapping, language mapping is not always precise. Thus, when asked where Nepal is, most people can locate it approximately ("It's in Asia"), but few can name all the countries that border it. Similarly, children quickly learn new animal names, for instance, because they can be mapped in the brain close to already-known animal names. Thus, *tiger* is easy to map if you know *lion*. A trip to the zoo facilitates fast-mapping of dozens of animal words, especially since zoos scaffold such learning by placing similar animals close together.

The benefit of knowing at least one word of a category is evident in a classic experiment. A preschool teacher taught a new word by saying, "Give me the chromium tray, not the red one" (Carey, 1985). Those children who already knew *red* quickly grasped the new word, *chromium*, and remembered it more than a week later. Those children who knew no color words did not remember the new word (a week later, they could not select a chromium object) because they were unable to map it (Mandler, 2004).

Another set of experiments began in cultures whose languages had only a few counting words: the equivalents of *one, two,* and *many.* People in such cultures were much worse at estimating quantity because they did not have the words to guide them (Gordon, 2004). Mapping and understanding a new number word, such as *nineteen,* is easier if one already knows a related word, such as *nine.*

➤Response for Social Scientists (from page 259): According to Piaget, preschool children focus on appearance and on static conditions (so they cannot mentally reverse a process). Furthermore, they are egocentric, believing that everyone shares their point of view. No wonder they believe that they had always known that the candy box held pencils and that a friend would know that, too.

Student and Teachers Children at the Lawrence, Massachusetts, YWCA show Rashon McCloud of the Boston Celtics how they use a computer to learn reading. They are participating in an NBA-sponsored program called Read to Achieve. Children are often faster than adults to catch on to technological innovations.

RAY AMATI/NBAE / GETTY IMAGES

Generally, the more linguistic clues children already have, the better their fast-mapping is (Mintz, 2005). Fast-mapping is evident even before age 2, accelerating as new words are learned because each word makes it easier to map other words (Gershkoff-Stowe & Hahn, 2007). To increase their children's vocabulary, parents should talk to their children often, adding new words that the children can map alongside ones they already understand (Hoff & Naigles, 2002). Alas, preschoolers may also map some words that their parents would rather they didn't, as I learned with my daughters.

a personal perspective

Mommy the Brat

Fast-mapping has an obvious benefit: It fosters quick acquisition of vocabulary. However, it also means that children *seem* to know words merely because they use them when, in actuality, their understanding of the words' meaning is quite limited.

Realizing that children often do not fully comprehend the meanings of words they say makes it easier to understand—and forgive—their mistakes. I still vividly recall an incident when my youngest daughter, then 4, was furious at me.

Sarah had apparently fast-mapped several insulting words into her vocabulary. However, her fast-mapping did not provide precise definitions or reflect nuances. In her anger, she called me first a "mean witch" and then a "brat." I smiled at her innocent imprecision, knowing the first was fast-mapped from fairy tales and the second from comments she got from her older sisters. Neither label bothered me, as I don't believe in witches and my brother is the only person who can appropriately call me a brat.

But then Sarah let loose an X-rated epithet that sent me reeling. Struggling to contain my anger, I tried to convince myself that fast-mapping had left her with no real idea of what she had just said.

"That word is never to be used in this family!" I sputtered.

My appreciation of fast-mapping was deepened by her response: "Then how come Rachel [her older sister] called me that this morning?"

Words and the Limits of Logic

Closely related to fast-mapping is logical extension: After learning a word, children use it to describe other objects in the same category. One child told her father she had seen some Dalmatian cows on a school trip to a farm. He understood because he remembered that she had petted a Dalmatian dog the weekend before.

Children use their available vocabulary to cover all the territory they want to talk about (Behrend et al., 2001). They try to use logic to figure out what words mean—for instance, deciding that butter is made by butterflies and birds grow from birdseed. One child, jumping on a bed, knew that to *live with* means to reside in the same home.

> **Mother:** Stop. You'll hurt yourself.
> **Child:** No I won't. (*Still jumping*)
> **Mother:** You'll break the bed.
> **Child:** No I won't. (*Still jumping*)
> **Mother:** OK. You'll just have to live with the consequences.
> **Child:** (*Stops jumping*) I'm not going to live with the consequences. I don't even know them.
>
> [*adapted from Nemy, 1998, p. B2*]

Fangs for the Memories Museums, zoos, parks, farms, factories—all provide abundant opportunities for vocabulary building and concept formation. These parents may be teaching their children not only *mountain lion* but also *habitat, carnivore,* and *incisors.*

An experiment in teaching the names of parts of objects (e.g., the spigot of a faucet) found that children learned much better if the adults named the object that had the part and then spoke of the object in the possessive (e.g., "See this butterfly? Look, this is the butterfly's thorax") (Saylor & Sabbagh, 2004). This finding shows that how a new word is presented affects the likelihood that a child will learn that word.

Young children have difficulty with words that express comparisons (such as *tall* and *short, near* and *far, high* and *low, deep* and *shallow*) because they do not understand that the meaning of these words depends on the context (Ryalls, 2000). If they have been taught that one end of the swimming pool is the deep end, children might obey parental instructions to stay out of deep puddles by splashing through every puddle they see, insisting that none of them are deep.

Words expressing relationships of place and time—such as *here, there, yesterday,* and *tomorrow*—are difficult as well. More than one child has awakened on Christmas morning and asked, "Is it tomorrow yet?" A child told to "stay there" or "come here" may not follow instructions because the terms are confusing.

One example of childlike understanding comes from Italian preschoolers who were discussing a war nearby. They seemed to understand the issues, advocating peace. But their words revealed their egocentrism. Giorgia, age 4, said, "The daddies, mommies, and children get their feelings hurt by war" (Abbott & Nutbrown, 2001, p. 123).

Acquiring Basic Grammar

Chapter 6 noted that the *grammar* of language includes the structures, techniques, and rules that are used to communicate meaning. Word order and word repetition, prefixes and suffixes, intonation and emphasis—all are part of grammar.

By age 3, English-speaking children understand many basic aspects of grammar. They know word order (subject/verb/object), saying, "I eat the apple," not any of the 23 other possible sequences of those four words. They also use plurals; tenses (past, present, and future); and nominative, objective, and possessive pronouns (*I/me/mine* or *my*). They use articles (*the, a, an*) correctly, even though the use of articles in English has many complexities.

Each aspect of language follows a particular developmental path, partly because the various parts of the brain myelinate at specific rates. Genes are generally more influential for *expressive* (spoken or written) than for *receptive* (heard or read) language. The data suggest that how much a child talks is strongly influenced by genes, while experience determines which words and grammatical constructions a child understands (Kovas et al., 2005).

overregularization The application of rules of grammar even when exceptions occur, making the language seem more "regular" than it actually is.

One charming aspect of early cognition is that young children tend to apply the rules of grammar when they should not. This tendency is called **overregularization.** For example, a rule soon learned by English-speaking children is to add a final *-s* to form the plural of a noun, so toddlers will ask for two *cookies* or more *blocks*. They apply this rule to nonsense words as well: If they are shown a drawing of an abstract shape and told it is a *wug,* and then are shown two of those shapes, they say there are two *wugs*. Many young children overregularize with that final *-s,* talking about *foots, tooths, sheeps,* and *mouses*.

Overregularization can be taken as evidence for increasing knowledge from ages 2 to 6, because many children first say words correctly and then, when they understand the rule, make overregularizing mistakes. This is particularly apparent in a language such as English, which has many exceptions to almost every rule.

For example, another simple rule is to add *-ed* to indicate words in the past tense, so children who jump today also *jumped* yesterday. Some of them also explain that they *goed* or *comed,* overregularizing because they do not yet know that these two verbs have irregular past-tense forms: *went* and *came,* respectively. Nouns are learned before verbs, and acquisition of nouns and verbs probably originates in different parts of the brain (Shapiro & Caramazza, 2003), so children who understand that they have two feet, not *feets,* might still say they *goed* to the store.

Learning Two Languages

In today's world, bilingualism is an asset. Yet language-minority children (those who speak a language that is not the dominant language of their nation) suffer unless they speak the majority language as well as the minority one.

In the United States, those who are not proficient in English tend to have lower school achievement, diminished self-esteem, and inadequate employment, as well as many other problems. Fluency in English erases these liabilities (even if a person speaks another language at home). But how and when should a second language be learned?

Tiene Identificación Lista Are you pleased or angered by this bilingual sign at a school in Chelsea, Massachusetts, that serves as a polling place on election day? In this election, voters were deciding whether or not to eliminate government funding for bilingual education. Those who favored immersion argued that signs like this one would soon become unnecessary if children were taught only in English. Those who favored bilingual education held that without it, children from minority-language families would be likely to drop out of school before mastering any language.

AP / WIDE WORLD PHOTOS

What Is the Goal?

Before exploring how and when, consider why: What is the goal of having a second language? Is a nation better off if all its citizens speak one language, or should there be more than one official language (as in Switzerland, which has three, or Canada, which has two)? Should all young children learn more than one language?

Some say no, arguing that young children need to become proficient in one, and only one, language. For instance, the "English only" advocates in the United States believe that children in that country should speak only English. Adults who hold this position argue that children who try to learn two languages might become confused and end up being semilingual rather than bilingual.

Others say yes, arguing that everyone should learn at least two languages in the language-sensitive years of early childhood. If a child lives in a home where a non-majority language is spoken yet has daily exposure to the majority language, he or she has a good start toward becoming fluent in both languages.

This second opinion has more research support. Remarkably, soon after the vocabulary explosion, many young children master two distinct sets of words and grammar, along with each language's characteristic pauses, pronunciations, intonations, and gestures (Bates et al., 2001; Mayberry & Nicoladis, 2000).

Neuroscientific research finds that young bilingual children typically site both languages in the same areas of their brains, yet manage to keep them separate. This separation allows bilingual speakers at every age to activate one language and temporarily inhibit the other, experiencing no confusion when they speak to a monolingual person (Crinion et al., 2006).

By contrast, most people who learn a second language as adults show different activation sites for each language. Sometimes they must translate from one to another as they listen and speak. A few fortunate adults who become fluent in a second language after puberty show activation in the same brain areas for both languages; these people tend to be adept at using both languages (Thomas & Johnson, 2008).

For most people, pronunciation of a second language is particularly hard to master after age 6. Actually, most young children have difficulty with pronunciation in any language. English-only children transpose sounds (*magazine* becomes *mazagine*), drop consonants (*truck* becomes *ruck*), and convert difficult sounds to easier ones (*father* becomes *fadder*), among other errors.

Pronunciation difficulties do not slow down language learning for young children (as they do for adults), however. The main reason is that, as we noted earlier, children are more receptive than expressive—they hear better than they talk. When my 4-year-old daughter asked for a "yeyo yayipop," her father said, "You want a yeyo yayipop?" She replied, "Daddy, sometimes you talk funny."

For language to develop well, young children need to be "bathed in language," as some early-childhood educators express it. The emphasis is on oral language, hearing and speaking in every situation, just as a person taking a bath is surrounded by water (Otto, 2007). The language they hear must include new words to fast-map, grammatical structures that show them how to string words together, pronunciations that they can notice and learn to repeat. Television is not a good teacher because it cannot personalize instruction; each child needs to engage with language in his or her own zone of proximal development.

Bilingualism, Cognition, and Culture

Since language is integral to culture, the debate over bilingual education is inseparable from issues of ethnic pride, identity, prejudice, and fear (Ricento, 2005). These subjective factors get in the way of objective developmental research. One group of researchers explains:

> A question of concern to many is whether early schooling [between ages 2 and 6] in English for language-minority children harms the development and/or maintenance of their mother tongue and possibly children's language competence in general. . . . [The] debate quickly and unfortunately becomes . . . hampered by extreme and emotional political positions.
>
> *[Winsler et al., 1999, p. 350]*

Research finds that bilingualism has both advantages and disadvantages for early cognition and literacy (Bialystok, 2007; Carlson & Meltzoff, 2008). Advocates for bilingual education point out, correctly, that children who speak two languages by age 5 are less egocentric in their understanding of language and more advanced in their theory of mind. Opponents point out, also correctly, that bilingual children often are less fluent in one or both languages, acquiring reading as well as other linguistic skills at a slower rate.

Especially for Immigrant Parents (see response, page 269) You want your children to be fluent in the language of your family's new country, even though you do not speak that language well. Should you speak to your children in your native tongue or in the new language?

This last fact makes many who speak the dominant language strive to have every child learn that language, putting the major burden of such learning on teachers of young children. For instance, in California, where the home language of more than half of all the children is not English, every early-childhood teacher stresses verbal expression.

Schools in all nations stress the learning of the dominant language, but minority-language parents fear that their children will make a *language shift,* becoming more fluent in the school language than in their home language (Min, 2000). Language shift occurs in almost every nation: Some language-minority children in Mexico shift to Spanish (Messing, 2007), some children from the First Nations in Canada shift to English (Allen, 2007), and so on—often to the consternation of their elders.

MARY KNOX MERRILL / THE CHRISTIAN SCIENCE MONITOR / GETTY IMAGES

Smiling Faces Sometimes Everyone in this group is an immigrant, born far from their current home in Burlington, Vermont. Jean Luc Dushime escaped the 1994 genocide in Rwanda, central Africa, when he was 14. He eventually adapted to his new language, climate, surroundings, and culture. Today he helps immigrant children make the same transition.

Some children shift in talking but not in comprehending. It is not unusual for 5-year-olds to understand their parents' language but refuse to speak it. Nor is it unusual for immigrant adults to depend on a child to serve as their spokesperson and interpreter when they deal with monolingual bureaucrats. This dependency may be a practical necessity, but it represents a role reversal that widens the generational gap between child and parent.

Language shift and role reversal are unfortunate, not only for the child and the parents but also for the society. Having many bilingual citizens is a national strength, and respect for family traditions is a bulwark against adolescent rebellion. Yet young children are preoperational: They center on the immediate status of the "foreign" language, on appearances more than past history, on parental dress and customs, not traditions and wisdom. No wonder many shift toward the dominant culture.

A dilemma is evident, for families and teachers as well as for societies. Minority-language parents are reluctant to deprive their children of their roots, heritage, and identity, yet they know that speaking, reading, and writing the dominant language are necessary for success (Suarez-Orozco & Suarez-Orozco, 2001). Adults may criticize members of their ethnic group who have "lost" their heritage language, but they also know that their children will face discrimination if they are not fluent in the dominant language.

balanced bilingual A person who is fluent in two languages, not favoring one over the other.

The best solution may be for every child to become a **balanced bilingual,** fluent in two languages, speaking both so well that no audible hint suggests the other language. Is balanced bilingualism possible? Yes. In many nations, during these sensitive years of early childhood, children readily master two or more languages.

Constant Change

The basics of language learning—the naming and vocabulary explosions, fast-mapping, overregularization, extensive practice—apply to every language a young child learns. Parents who want a child to learn two languages need to intensify the child's exposure to both, ideally before age 6. The concept of language as a social mediator that advances thinking is as relevant to learning a second language as it is to learning a first one (Lantolf, 2006). As we saw earlier, Vygotsky held that words and grammar aid cognition and skill acquisition by making scaffolding easier.

Fortunately, children have a powerful urge to communicate and a readiness to learn as much as they can. As mentioned in Chapter 1, this was dramatically illustrated by children at a boarding school for the deaf in Nicaragua (Siegal, 2004). Their teachers taught spoken Spanish and used no sign language. (This strategy is no longer common, since it is now clear that deaf children learn best if they are taught sign language from infancy. But war delayed the teachers' awareness of this finding.) However, the deaf children invented their own signs and taught them to new arrivals. Their created language flourished, as each new generation of young children added to it. The newer arrivals became more fluent than the older deaf children because they built on what had already been invented, adding new gestures.

Similarly, established languages continually change as each new generation revises it to meet current needs. In American English over the past few decades, the word *colored* was replaced by *Negro*, which gave way to *Black*, which was soon largely replaced by *African American*. Words borrowed from other languages have become basic English vocabulary—think of *salsa, loco, amour, kowtow,* and *mensch*. Some key terms in this book, *doula* and *kwashiorkor* among them, originated in other languages.

New English terms include *hip-hop*, *e-mail*, *DVD*, *spam*, *blog*, *cell* (phone), *rap* (music), *buff* (in excellent physical shape), and hundreds more. Most abbreviations used in text messaging (e.g., *pos*, *lol*, and many more) are known to children but not parents (as *pos*, "parent over shoulder," makes clear). This process is ongoing in every language: Adults who stopped learning their first language at age 5 are handicapped by their ignorance of new words if they return to their ancestral home. Everywhere, children master and modify language continually, from age 1 onward.

SUMMING UP

Children aged 2 to 6 have impressive linguistic talents. They explode into speech, from about a hundred words to many thousands, from halting baby talk to fluency. Fast-mapping and grammar are among the sophisticated devices they use, although both can backfire. No other time in the entire life span is as sensitive to language learning, especially to mastering pronunciation. Children can readily learn two languages during these years. Extensive exposure to both languages is necessary for a child to become a balanced bilingual. ■

Early-Childhood Education

A hundred years ago, children had no formal education until first grade, which is why it was called "first" and why young children were called "preschoolers." Today many 3- to 5-year-olds are in school (see Figure 9.5 for U.S. trends) not only because of changing family patterns but also because research now "documents the rapid development and great learning potential of the early years" (Hyson et al., 2006, p. 6).

Early educational institutions are referred to by various names—preschool, nursery school, day care, pre-primary—but a program's label is not a reliable indicator of its nature. All young children are active learners, but each early-childhood educational program (and sometimes each teacher) emphasizes somewhat different skills, goals, and methods (Walsh & Petty, 2007). We will consider three general categories: child-centered, teacher-directed, and intervention programs.

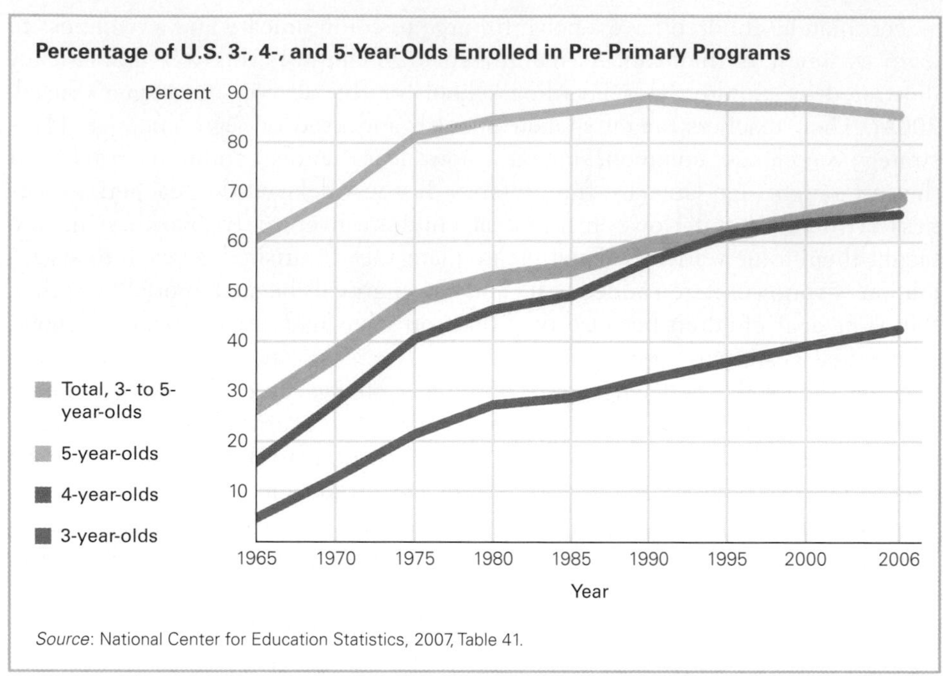

FIGURE 9.5

Changing Times As research increasingly finds that preschool education provides a foundation for later learning, more and more young children are enrolled in educational programs.

Observation Quiz (see answer, page 270): Which age group experienced the most dramatic increase in preschool attendance from 1965 to 1975?

Child-Centered Programs

Many programs are called *developmental,* or *child-centered,* because they stress children's development and growth. They emphasize children's need to follow their own interests rather than adult directions (Weikart, 1999). Many child-centered programs use a Piaget-inspired model that allows children to discover ideas at their own pace. The physical space and the materials (such as dress-up clothing, art supplies, puzzles, blocks of many sizes, and other toys) are arranged to allow self-paced exploration.

Most child-centered programs encourage artistic expression (Lim, 2004). Some educators argue that young children "are all poets" in that they are gifted in seeing the world more imaginatively than older people do. According to advocates of child-centered programs, this peak of creative vision should be encouraged; children are given many opportunities to tell stories, draw pictures, dance, and make music for their own delight (Egan & Ling, 2002).

"We teach them that the world can be an unpredictable, dangerous, and sometimes frightening place, while being careful not to spoil their lovely innocence. It's tricky."

Child-centered programs also show the influence of Vygotsky, who thought that children learn much from other children, with adult guidance (Bodrova & Leong, 2005). For example, in order to learn number skills, they play games that include math (counting objects, keeping score), follow routines that use measurements (daily calendars, schedules), and use number rules (only three children in the block corner, two volunteers to get the juice).

Montessori Schools

One type of child-centered school began a hundred years ago, when Maria Montessori opened nursery schools for poor children in Rome. She believed that children needed structured, individualized projects to give them a sense of accomplishment. They completed puzzles, used sponges and water to clean tables, traced shapes, and so on.

Like Piaget (her contemporary), Montessori (1936/1966) realized that children's thoughts and needs are different from those of adults. They learn from activities that adults might call play. Teachers gave each child tasks that dovetailed with his or her cognitive eagerness. For example, because they have a need for order, for language learning, and for using all their senses, children learned from systematic exercises that allowed them to augment their language skills as they touched and smelled various objects.

Today's **Montessori schools** still emphasize individual pride and accomplishment, presenting many literacy-related tasks (such as outlining letters and looking through books) to young children (Lillard, 2005). Many of the specifics differ from those that Montessori developed, but the underlying philosophy is the same. Children collaborate with each other and do not sit quietly while a teacher instructs them. That is what makes Montessori programs child-centered, although they do not include some activities that children enjoy (pretend play, for example).

The goal is for the children to feel proud of themselves and engaged in learning. Many aspects of Montessori's philosophy are in accord with current developmental research. That is one reason this kind of school remains popular. A study of 5-year-olds in inner-city Milwaukee who were chosen by lottery to attend Montessori programs found that they were better at prereading and early math tasks, as well as at theory of mind, than were their peers in other schools (Lillard & Else-Quest, 2006).

➤Response for Immigrant Parents (from page 266): Children learn by listening, so it is important to speak with them often. Depending on how comfortable you are with the new language, you might prefer to read to your children, sing to them, and converse with them primarily in your native language and find a good preschool where they will learn the new language. The worst thing you could do would be to restrict speech in either tongue.

Montessori schools Schools that offer early-childhood education based on the philosophy of Maria Montessori, which emphasizes careful work and tasks that each young child can do.

The Reggio Emilia Approach

Another form of early-childhood education is called the **Reggio Emilia approach** because it was inspired by a program pioneered in the Italian town of that name. Currently, 14 infant-toddler centers and 22 pre-primary schools are funded by that city, enrolling half its children age 6 or younger. Reggio Emilia programs now operate in every developed nation.

Reggio Emilia approach A famous program of early-childhood education that originated in the town of Reggio Emilia, Italy, and that encourages each child's creativity in a carefully designed setting.

In Reggio Emilia, every preschooler is encouraged to master skills that are not usually seen in North American schools until age 7 or so, such as writing and

Another Place for Children High ceilings, uncrowded play space, varied options for art and music, a glass wall revealing trees and flowers—all these features reflect the Reggio Emilia approach to individualized, creative learning for young children. Such places are rare in nations other than Italy.

Observation Quiz (see answer, page 271): How many children appear in this photograph and how many are engaged in creative expression?

using tools. However, there is no large-group instruction, with formal lessons in, say, forming letters or cutting paper. Instead "every child is a creative child, full of potential" (Gandini, 2005, p. 1), with personal learning needs and artistic drive.

Appreciation of the arts is evident not only in the children's activities but also in the presence in each school of a studio and an artist who encourages each child to be creative. This idea is evident in the architecture as well. Every Reggio Emilia school has a large central room where children gather, with floor-to-ceiling windows open to a spacious, plant-filled playground.

Big mirrors are part of the school's décor (again, with the idea of fostering individuality), and children's art is displayed on white walls and hung from high ceilings. Among the characteristics of Reggio Emilia programs are a low child/teacher ratio, ample space, and abundant materials.

One distinctive feature of the curriculum is that a small group of children become engaged in long-term projects of their choosing. Such projects foster the children's pride in their accomplishments (which are displayed for all to admire) while teaching them to plan and work together.

Teachers have 6 hours of work time each week without the children, which they spend planning activities, having group discussions, and talking to parents. Parental involvement is expected: They teach in special subject areas; meet with one another; and receive frequent reports, often with photographs, written observations, and their child's artwork. The entire town is proud of its children and schools.

Teacher-Directed Programs

Unlike the Reggio Emilia approach, teacher-directed preschool programs stress academics taught by one adult to the entire class. The curriculum includes learning the names of letters, numbers, shapes, and colors. Children are taught to listen to the teacher and sit quietly. Praise and other reinforcements are given for good behavior, and time-outs (brief separation from activities) are imposed to punish misbehavior.

In teacher-directed programs, the serious work of schooling is distinguished from the unstructured play of home. As one German boy explained:

> So home is home and kindergarten is kindergarten. Here is my work and at home is off-time, understand? My mum says work is me learning something. Learning is when you drive your head, and off-time is when the head slows down.
>
> *[quoted in Griebel & Niesel, 2002, p. 67]*

The teachers' goal is to make all children "ready to learn" when they enter elementary school. Some of these programs explicitly teach basic skills, including reading, writing, and arithmetic, perhaps via teachers asking questions that children answer together. Children practice forming letters, sounding out words, counting objects, and writing their names. If a 4-year-old learns to read, that is success. (In a child-centered program, it might arouse suspicion that the child had too little time to play.) Many teacher-directed programs were inspired by behaviorism, which emphasizes step-by-step learning and repetition.

The contrast between child-centered and teacher-directed philosophies is evident not only in lessons but also in attitudes and expectations. For instance, if one child bothers another child, should the second child tell the teacher, or should the two children work it out by themselves? If one child bites another, should the biter be isolated or reprimanded, or—as sometimes happens—should the victim be allowed to bite back? Each preschool has rules for such situations, which vary because of contrasting philosophies. In a child-centered program, the offender

➤Answer to Observation Quiz (from page 268): Attendance by 4-year-olds increased from 15 percent to 40 percent. The discussion of Head Start that follows explains why.

might be asked to think of the effect of his or her actions; in a teacher-directed program, punishment might be immediate.

➤Answer to Observation Quiz (from page 269): Eight children, and all of them are engaged in creative projects—if the boy standing at right is making music, not just noise, with that cymbal.

Head Start and Other Intervention Programs

Developmental scientists, connecting research findings and practical applications, have discovered that early childhood is a prime learning period. It is also evident that some young children learn much more than others. Five-year-olds vary dramatically in their ability to learn, talk, and even listen. The main reason is thought to be exposure to language and other learning opportunities that some parents are able to provide and others are not (Hart & Risley, 1995).

Many nations try to narrow the learning gap by offering high-quality early education. Some nations (e.g., China, France, Italy, and Sweden) make programs available to all children; others vary in what they provide (in the United States, for example, Oklahoma and some other states provide full-day kindergarten and preschool education for all children, while most other states provide a few hours a day for those who are particularly needy).

Especially for Teachers (see response, page 273) In trying to find a preschool program, what should parents look for?

In the United States, the most widespread early-childhood-education program is Project Head Start, which began in 1965 and has been funded by the federal government every year since then. This program was designed for low-income or minority children who were thought to need a "head start" on their formal education. The quality and results of Head Start programs vary from place to place. Some long-term effects are unknown, because scientific evaluation was not included in the original planning (Phillips & White, 2004).

Nevertheless, Head Start has provided half-day education for millions of 3- to 5-year-olds, boosting their social and learning skills at least temporarily and probably providing long-term benefits as well (Zigler et al., 1996). Some programs are now 6 hours long each day rather than 3, because researchers realize that the extent of learning correlates with the length of school time.

PAUL CHESLEY / STONE / GETTY IMAGES

Learning from One Another Every nation creates its own version of early education. In this scene at a nursery school in Kuala Lumpur, Malaysia, note the head coverings, uniforms, bare feet, and absence of boys. None of these elements would be found in most early-childhood-education classrooms in North America or Europe.

Observation Quiz (see answer, page 273): What seemingly universal aspects of childhood are visible in this photograph?

LAURA DWIGHT

Learning Is Fun The original purpose of the Head Start program was to boost disadvantaged children's academic skills. The most enduring benefits, however, turned out to be improved self-esteem and social skills, as is evident in these happy Head Start participants, all crowded together.

Observation Quiz (see answer, page 274): How many of these children are in close physical contact without discomfort or disagreement?

There are many problems in evaluating Head Start. Over the decades, its goals have been diffuse and varied, from lifting families out of poverty to promoting literacy, from providing dental care and immunizations to teaching standard English. Some teachers practice child-centered education and others prefer a teacher-directed approach; some consider parents part of the problem and others regard parents as allies. In any case, intervening with parents has proven difficult (Powell, 2006).

Many of the early Head Start programs had no specific curriculum or goals, which made valid evaluation impossible (Whitehurst & Massetti, 2004). An added problem has been the political turmoil that surrounds the topics of poverty, government programs, and the education of young children in the United States. Nevertheless, Head Start has survived for almost 50 years, partly because early education has been proven to be beneficial in dozens of ways. Still, the program's priorities and direction have changed continually as the political winds have shifted (Zigler & Styfco, 2004), as discussed in the following.

a view from science

Intensive Intervention

The same social imperatives that led to Head Start also led to several intensive interventions that have been well evaluated through longitudinal research. These programs have stressed cognitive development and have enrolled chidren full time for years (unlike Head Start, which was often part time). Three programs in particular (although they no longer exist in the same form) have excellent follow-up data and have inspired widespread intervention efforts (Schweinhart et al., 2005): one in Michigan, called Perry or High/Scope (Schweinhart & Weikart, 1997; Schweinhart et al., 2005); one in North Carolina, called Abecedarian (Campbell et al., 2001); and one in Chicago, called Child–Parent Centers (Reynolds, 2000; Reynolds et al., 2004).

All three programs enrolled children from low-income families for several years before kindergarten, all compared experimental groups of children with matched control groups, and all reached the same conclusion: Early education can have substantial long-term benefits, which become apparent when the children are in the third grade or later.

Children in these three programs scored higher on math and reading achievement tests at age 10 than did other children from the same backgrounds, schools, and neighborhoods. They were significantly less likely to be placed in special classes for slow or disruptive children or to repeat a year of school. In adolescence, they had higher aspirations and a greater sense of achievement and were less likely to have been abused. As young adults, they were more likely to attend college and less likely to go to jail.

All three research projects found that providing direct cognitive training (rather than simply letting children play), with specific instruction in various school-readiness skills, was useful as long as each child's needs and talents were considered. The curricular approach was a combination of child-centered and teacher-directed. Parents were engaged with the child's learning.

These programs were expensive (perhaps as much as $15,000 annually per child in 2008 dollars). However, many believe that the decreased need for special education and other social services later on eventually makes such programs a wise investment.

A study of the High/Scope program has yielded detailed comparison data in support of that belief (Schweinhart et al., 2005; see Figure 9.6). This and other studies show that children from similar low-income families who did not attend these preschool programs had more costly conditions later in life: special education (four times more expensive per student per year); unemployment (no income-tax revenue); and even imprisonment ($150,000 per inmate per year). One economist calculates that governments eventually spend at least five times more per person when children do not have the benefit of an intensive preschool program (Lynch, 2004).

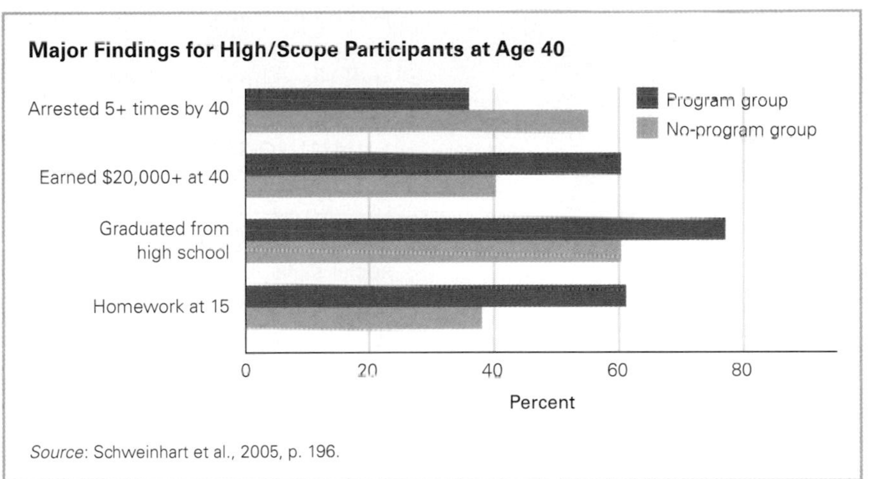

FIGURE 9.6

The Benefits of an Early Start Longitudinal research found that two years in the intensive High/Scope preschool program changed the lives of dozens of children from impoverished families. The program had a positive impact on many aspects of their education, early adulthood, and middle age. (This graph does not illustrate another intriguing finding: The girls who attended High/Scope fared much better than the boys.)

Costs and Benefits

The financial aspect of early-childhood education may be especially significant. For many early-childhood educators, Reggio Emilia is the gold standard because the child/teacher ratio is low, the physical space is luxurious, and the children seem to learn a lot; however, the cost per child for such a program is about twice that of most other types of preschool care. The town heavily subsidizes the cost; that is not the case in most other cities or nations.

Since parents pay the bulk of the cost of preschool education in the United States (except for some intervention programs), Reggio Emilia is beyond the means of most families. Child-centered programs open to all children may be feasible only in places with community support and a low birth rate (like Italy, where most families have only one child).

A key finding from all the research is that the *quality* of early-childhood education counts. Consequently, recent reauthorizations of Head Start emphasize educational quality and evaluative research (Lombardi & Cubbage, 2004).

Comparisons of programs find that the specific curricula and philosophy matter less than teachers who know how to respond to the needs of young children and have time to do so. Generally, an educational, center-based program is better than family day care or home care, but high-quality home care is better than a low-quality day-care center (Clarke-Stewart & Allhusen, 2005).

➤Response for Teachers (from page 271): Tell parents to look at the people more than the program. Parents should see the children in action and note whether the teachers show warmth and respect for each child.

➤Answer to Observation Quiz (from page 271): Three aspects are readily apparent: These girls enjoy their friendships; they are playing a hand-clapping game, some version of which is found in every culture; and, most important, they have begun the formal education that their families want for them.

➤Answer to Observation Quiz (from page 272): All five—not four (look again at the right-hand side of the photograph)!

Some characteristics of quality day care were described in Chapter 7: safety, adequate space and equipment, a low child/adult ratio, positive social interactions among children and adults, and trained staff who are likely to stay in the program. Continuity helps, for the adults as well as for the children. One of the best questions that parents comparing options can ask is, "How long has each staff member worked at this center?"

Curriculum is also important, especially by the time children reach the age of 4 or 5. Best may be programs with an emphasis on learning, reflected in a curriculum that includes extensive practice in language, fine and gross motor skills, and basic number skills. Such programs may be found in either child-centered or teacher-directed schools. As this chapter emphasizes, young children love to learn and can master many skills and ideas as long as adults do not expect them to think and behave like older children.

Beyond that, if history is a guide, new research will find additional cognitive potential among 2- to 6-year-olds and additional strategies for developing that potential. Valid evaluation (longitudinal comparisons with experimental and control groups) is still rare. Some readers of this book will undertake the research, and staff the schools, that will update our view of cognition in childhood.

SUMMING UP

Research, particularly on preschool programs for children in low-income families, has proved that high-quality early education benefits children, who improve in language, in social skills, and in prospects for the future (Clarke-Stewart & Allhusen, 2005). Many different programs, including child-centered (Montessori and Reggio Emilia) and teacher-directed programs, are available—although sometimes good programs are very expensive. Nations, states, and parents differ in what they seek from early education for their children, and programs vary in teacher preparation, curriculum, physical space, and child/adult ratios. ■

SUMMARY

Piaget and Vygotsky

1. Piaget stressed the egocentric and illogical aspects of thought during the play years. He called this stage preoperational thought because young children often cannot yet use logical operations to think about their observations and experiences.

2. Young children, according to Piaget, sometimes focus on only one thing (centration) and see things only from their own viewpoint (egocentrism), remaining stuck on appearances and on current reality. They may believe that living spirits reside in inanimate objects, a belief called animism.

3. Vygotsky stressed the social aspects of childhood cognition, noting that children learn by participating in various experiences, guided by more knowledgeable adults or peers. That guidance assists learning within the zone of proximal development, which encompasses the knowledge and skills that the child has the potential to learn.

4. According to Vygotsky, the best teachers use various hints, guidelines, and other tools to provide the child with a scaffold for new learning. Language is a bridge that provides social mediation between the knowledge that the child already has and the learning that the society hopes to impart. For Vygotsky, words are a tool for learning.

Children's Theories

5. Children develop theories, especially to explain the purpose of life and their role in it. Among these theories is theory of mind—an understanding of what others may be thinking. Notable advances in theory of mind occur at around age 4. Theory of mind is partly the result of brain maturation, but a child's language and experiences (in the family and community) also have an impact.

Language

6. Language develops rapidly during early childhood, which is a sensitive period but not a critical one for language learning. Vocabulary increases dramatically, with thousands of words added between ages 2 and 6. In addition, basic grammar is mastered.

7. Many children learn to speak more than one language, gaining cognitive as well as social advantages. Ideally, children become balanced bilinguals, equally proficient in two languages, by age 6.

Early-Childhood Education

8. Organized educational programs during early childhood advance cognitive and social skills, although specifics vary a great deal. Montessori and Reggio Emilia are two child-centered programs that began in Italy and now are offered in many nations. Behaviorist principles led to many specific practices of teacher-directed programs.

9. Head Start is a government program that generally helps low-income children. Longitudinal research on intervention programs has demonstrated that early-childhood education reduces the likelihood of later problems. Graduates of these programs are less likely to need special education and more likely to become law-abiding, gainfully employed adults, which makes preschool education a wise investment.

10. Although many types of preschool programs are successful, the quality of early education matters. Children learn best if there is a clear curriculum and if the child/adult ratio is low. The training and continuity of early-childhood teachers are also important.

KEY TERMS

preoperational intelligence (p. 249)
centration (p. 250)
egocentrism (p. 250)
focus on appearance (p. 250)
static reasoning (p. 250)
irreversibility (p. 250)
conservation (p. 250)
animism (p. 252)
apprentice in thinking (p. 253)
guided participation (p. 253)
zone of proximal development (ZPD) (p. 254)
scaffolding (p. 254)
private speech (p. 255)
social mediation (p. 255)
theory-theory (p. 256)
theory of mind (p. 258)
fast-mapping (p. 261)
overregularization (p. 264)
balanced bilingual (p. 266)
Montessori schools (p. 269)
Reggio Emilia approach (p. 269)

KEY QUESTIONS

1. Piaget is often criticized for his description of early cognition. Why is this, and is the criticism fair? (Discuss with particular reference to preoperational thought.)

2. Give an example of the process of cognition in early childhood as Vygotsky would describe it, highlighting at least three of his specific concepts.

3. What are the main similarities between Vygotsky and Piaget?

4. How would parents act differently toward their child according to whether they agreed with Piaget or with Vygotsky?

5. How does Piaget's idea of egocentrism relate to the research on theory of mind?

6. How does fast-mapping apply to children's learning of curse words?

7. How do children learn grammar without formal instruction?

8. What are the differences between child-centered and teacher-directed instruction?

9. Why is there disagreement about the extent to which Head Start benefits children?

10. Why do some cities and nations provide much better preschool education than others?

APPLICATIONS

The best way to understand thinking in early childhood is to listen to a child, as applications 1 and 2 require. If some students have no access to children, they should do application 3 or 4.

1. Replicate one of Piaget's conservation experiments. The easiest one is conservation of liquids (pictured in Figure 9.1). Work with a child under age 5 who tells you that two identically shaped glasses contain the same amount of liquid. Then carefully pour one glass of liquid into a narrower, taller glass. Ask the child which glass now contains more or if the glasses contain the same amount.

2. To demonstrate how rapidly language is learned, show a preschool child several objects and label one with a nonsense word the child has never heard. (*Toma* is often used; so is *wug*.) Or choose a word the child does not know, such as *wrench, spatula,* or the name of a coin from another nation. Test the child's fast-mapping.

3. Theory of mind emerges at about age 4, but many adults still have trouble understanding other people's thoughts and motives. Ask several people why someone in the news did whatever they did (e.g., a scandal, a crime, a heroic act). Then ask your informants how sure they are of their explanation. Compare and analyze the reasons as well as the degrees of certainty. (One person may be sure of an explanation that someone else thinks is impossible.)

4. Think about an experience in which you learned something that was initially difficult. To what extent do Vygotsky's concepts (guided participation, language mediation, apprenticeship, zone of proximal development) explain the experience? Write a detailed, step-by-step account of your learning process as Vygotsky would have described it.

10

CHAPTER OUTLINE

Early Childhood: Psychosocial Development

My daughter Bethany, at about age 5, challenged one of my students to a fight.

"Girls don't fight," he said, laughing.

"*Nobody* fights," I sternly corrected him.

We were both teaching Bethany how to express emotions, a skill considered crucial for young children. She learned well; by age 6, she no longer threatened physical fights.

But I remember that incident because I am troubled by what I said. Although the words "Nobody fights" referred to both sexes, my opposition to fighting could be seen as typical of women, sometimes called the weaker sex. Was I keeping Bethany from becoming strong and brave? Should I have encouraged her to fight and asked my student to play-fight with her, as men do with young boys? Or maybe the opposite response was needed. Perhaps I should have kept quiet, allowing my student to teach Bethany proper gender norms.

Emotional control, rough play, parenting, morality, and sex differences are all discussed in this chapter. Some aspects of these issues have been studied for decades and experts agree on them. For instance, no developmentalist doubts that bullies should be stopped, that play teaches social understanding, or that parents should guide and discipline their children. However, many topics, including sex-role development, are still controversial. It is not surprising that I still wonder whether my student's "Girls don't fight" was the right response after all.

Emotional Development

Learning when and how to express emotions (made possible as the emotional hot spots of the limbic system begin to connect to the prefrontal cortex) is the preeminent psychosocial accomplishment between ages 2 and 6 (N. Eisenberg et al., 2004). Children who master this **emotional regulation** become more capable in every aspect of their lives (Denham et al., 2003; Matsumoto, 2004).

Emotions are regulated and controlled by 6-year-olds in ways unknown to exuberant, expressive, and often overwhelmed toddlers. Children learn to be friendly to new acquaintances but not too friendly, angry but not explosive,

emotional regulation The ability to control when and how emotions are expressed.

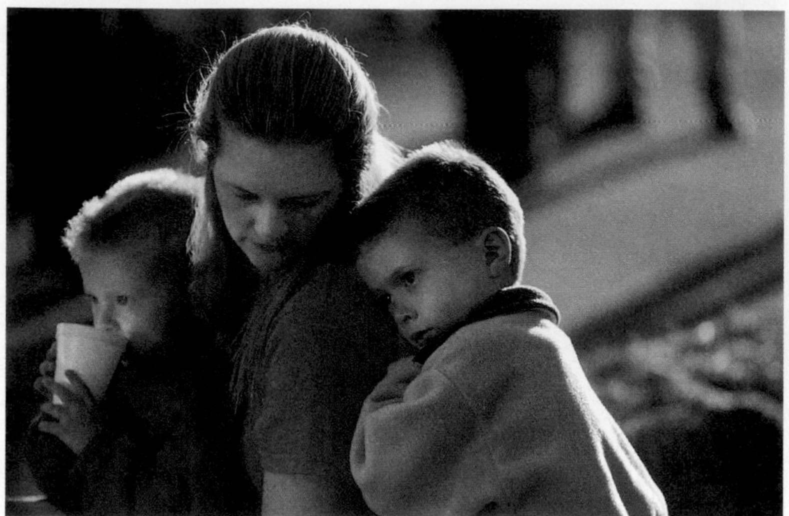
SEAN CAYTON / THE IMAGE WORKS

Close Connection Unfamiliar events often bring developmental tendencies to the surface, as with the curious boy and his worried brother, who are attending Colorado's Pikes Peak or Bust Rodeo breakfast. Their attentive mother keeps the livelier boy calm and reassures the shy one.

Observation Quiz (see answer, page 282): Mother is obviously a secure base for both boys, who share the same family and half the same genes but are different ages: One is 2 and the other is 4. Can you tell which boy is younger?

frightened by a clown but not terrified, able to distract themselves and limit their impulses if need be. (All these abilities emerge during early childhood and continue to develop throughout life.) Now we explain some specific aspects of emotional regulation.

Initiative Versus Guilt

Initiative is saying something new, extending a skill, beginning a project. Depending on the outcome (including the parents' response), children can feel either pride in their initiative or guilt about their attempt. Guilt makes them afraid to try new activities. If parents dismiss the child's emotional expressions (whether fear or excitement, anger or joy), children may not learn emotional regulation (Morris et al., 2007). They feel ashamed and then guilty for their behavior.

Usually parents encourage the 3- to 6-year-olds' natural enthusiasm, effort, and self-evaluation, which are typical at that age. During the **initiative versus guilt** stage, as Erik Erikson called his third developmental stage, self-esteem emerges from the acquisition of skills and competencies described in the previous two chapters.

initiative versus guilt Erikson's third psychosocial crisis, in which children undertake new skills and activities and feel guilty when they do not succeed at them.

self-esteem A person's evaluation of his or her own worth, either in specifics (e.g., intelligence, attractiveness) or overall.

Self-esteem is the belief in one's own ability, a personal estimate of success and worthiness. Children's beliefs about their worth are connected to parental confirmation, especially when parents remind their children of their positive accomplishments (Reese et al., 2007). ("Remember when you helped Daddy sweep the sidewalk? You made it very clean.") In contrast, parents who are too critical of their children foster low self-esteem, a belief that "the self is fundamentally flawed" (Harter, 2006, p. 529).

As self-esteem builds, children become more confident and independent, eager to begin new activities and adventures. The autonomy of 2-year-olds, often expressed as stubbornness, becomes the initiative of 5-year-olds, often seen in their self-motivated activities. In the process, children form a **self-concept,** or understanding of themselves, which encompasses not only self-esteem but also awareness of traits such as gender and size. Girls are happy to be girls, boys to be boys, and both are glad they are not babies. "Crybaby" becomes a major insult.

self-concept A person's understanding of who he or she is, in relation to self-esteem, appearance, personality, and various traits.

Pride

Erikson recognized that typical young children have immodest self-concepts, holding themselves in high self-esteem. They believe that they are strong, smart, and good-looking—and thus that any goal is quite achievable. Whatever they are (their self-concept) is also thought to be good. For instance, they believe that their nation and their religion are best, and they feel sorry for children who do not belong to their country or church.

Young children are confident that their good qualities will endure but that any bad qualities (even biological traits such as poor eyesight) will disappear with time (Lockhart et al., 2002). As one group of researchers explained:

> Young children seem to be irrepressibly optimistic about themselves. . . . Consider, for example, the shortest, most uncoordinated boy in a kindergarten class who proclaims that he will be the next Michael Jordan.
>
> [Lockhart et al., 2002, pp. 1408–1409]

The new initiative that Erikson describes is aided by a longer attention span, which is made possible by neurological maturity. Children now can focus on a task. Concentrated attention is crucial for social competence (Murphy, 2007).

Feeling proud (but not unrealistically so) is the foundation for practice and then mastery, as 4-year-olds pour juice, zip pants, or climb trees. Preschoolers predict that they can solve impossible puzzles, remember long lists of words, and control their dreams (Stipek et al., 1995; Woolley & Boerger, 2002). Naive predictions, sometimes called "protective optimism," help them try new things (Lockhart et al., 2002).

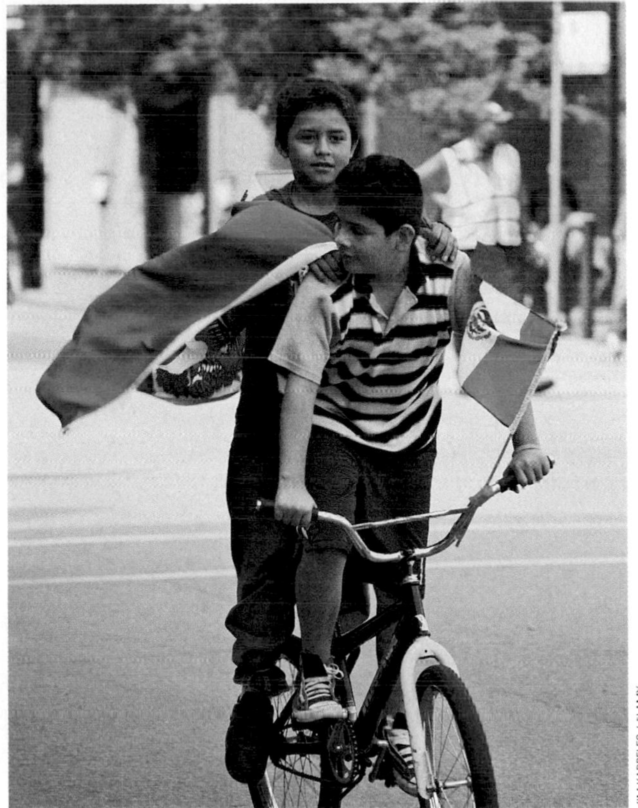

KIM KARPELES / ALAMY

Proud to Be Who They Are These two boys, riding in Chicago's Mexican Independence Day parade, seem to have found a good balance of emotional strengths: ethnic pride, friendship, and forward momentum.

Guilt and Shame

Notice that Erikson called the negative consequence of this crisis *guilt*, not shame. Generally, guilt means that people blame themselves when they do something wrong; shame means that people feel that others blame them, disapprove of them, or are disappointed in them. Erikson believed that as children develop self-awareness, they feel guilt when they realize their own mistakes. Many people believe that guilt is a more mature emotion than shame, because guilt comes from within the person (Kochanska et al., 2002; Tangney et al., 2007) whereas shame comes from outside and depends on others' awareness.

Shame can be based on what one is, rather than on something one has done. For example, shame about one's ethnic background is rooted in the belief that others devalue it. To counter such feelings, many parents of minority children (Mexican, African, or Indian American, among others) encourage ethnic pride in their children (Parke & Buriel, 2006). Both guilt and shame help children develop moral values, a topic discussed later in this chapter.

Motivation

The idea that guilt comes from within the child highlights the distinction between *intrinsic motivation* and *extrinsic motivation*. **Intrinsic motivation** occurs when people do something for the joy of doing it—as with a musician who plays for the delight of making music, even if no one else is listening. **Extrinsic motivation** comes from outside, when people do something to gain praise (or some other reinforcement) from someone else. Both are connected to emotional regulation, in that children become motivated to control their emotions, or at least the expression of them. No 5-year-old wants to cry in front of his friends; that emotion begins extrinsically but is soon internalized.

intrinsic motivation A drive, or reason to pursue a goal, that comes from inside a person, such as the need to feel smart or competent.

extrinsic motivation A drive, or reason to pursue a goal, that arises from the need to have one's achievements rewarded from outside, perhaps by receiving material possessions or another person's esteem.

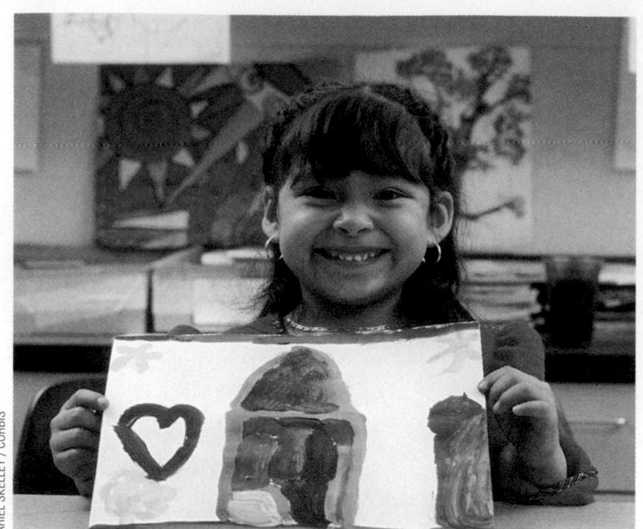

ARIEL SKELLEY / CORBIS

Happy and Colorful No wonder this 5-year-old is proud—her picture is worth framing. High self-esteem is one of the strengths of being her age. Can you imagine a 9-year-old holding an equally colorful picture so proudly?

Especially for College Students (see response, page 282): Is extrinsic or intrinsic motivation more influential in your study efforts?

Especially for Teachers (see response, page 282): One of your students tells you about playing, sleeping, and talking with an imaginary friend. Does this mean that that child is emotionally disturbed?

For the most part, preschool children are intrinsically motivated. They enjoy learning, playing, and practicing whether or not someone else wants them to. For instance, when they play a game, young children might not keep score; the fun is in playing, not winning.

The importance of intrinsic motivation is seen when children invent dialogues for their toys, concentrate on a work of art or architecture, and converse with *imaginary friends* (who exist only in the child's imagination). Imaginary friends are increasingly common from age 3 through 7, as initiative builds.

Children create imaginary friends to combat loneliness and aid emotional regulation. For example, one girl had an imaginary friend named Elephant, "7 inches tall, grey color, black eyes, wears tank top and shorts . . . plays with the child [but] sometimes is mean" (Taylor et al., 2004, p. 1178). By having an imaginary friend who is sometimes mean, this child is able to develop strategies to deal with mean people.

An Experiment in Motivation

In a classic experiment, preschool children were given markers and paper and assigned to one of three groups: (1) no award, (2) expected award (they were told *before* they had drawn anything that they would get a certificate), and (3) unexpected award (*after* they had drawn something, they heard "You were a big help" and got a certificate) (Lepper et al., 1973). Later, observers noted how often children in each group chose to draw on their own. Those who had received the expected award were less likely to draw than were those who got the unexpected award. The interpretation was that extrinsic motivation (condition 2) undercut intrinsic motivation.

This research triggered a flood of studies seeking to understand whether, when, and how positive reinforcement should be given. The consensus is that praising or paying a person after work has been done usually encourages that behavior to continue, as long as the reinforcement is based on accomplishment. However, if a substantial payment is promised in advance for something that the person already enjoys doing, the extrinsic reinforcement may backfire by diminishing intrinsic motivation (Cameron & Pierce, 2002; Deci et al., 1999).

Culture and Emotional Control

Cross-cultural research adds complexity to the development of emotional regulation. For example, children are encouraged to focus on different traits, depending on their different cultural values (Hong et al., 2000; J. G. Miller, 2004; Stubben, 2001):

- Overcome fear (United States)
- Modify anger (Puerto Rico)
- Temper pride (China)
- Control aggression (Japan)
- Be patient and cooperative (Native American communities)

Emotional regulation is valued in all cultures, but, as you see, cultures differ in the emotions that they consider most in need of control. They also differ in the ways they think emotions should be regulated (Matsumoto, 2004). Since shame indicates social awareness, cultures and families that stress social perception encourage shame and embarrassment. In some places, upholding one's family's reputation is crucial—so much so that a lack of shame signifies mental illness (Stein, 2006).

Seeking Emotional Balance

Children who have some, but not too much, shame, guilt, and other emotions are considered emotionally healthy. At every age, developmentalists seek to prevent or treat **psychopathology,** an illness or disorder (*-pathology*) of the mind (*psycho-*). Although the symptoms and the diagnosis are influenced by culture, lack of emotional regulation is universally accepted as an early sign of psychopathology in a child.

psychopathology An illness or disorder of the mind.

Externalizing and Internalizing Problems

Without adequate control, emotions are overpowering. Intense emotional reactions occur in two, seemingly opposite, ways. Some children have **externalizing problems:** Their powerful feelings burst out uncontrollably. They may externalize a feeling of rage, for example, by lashing out at other people or breaking things. Such children are sometimes called "undercontrolled."

externalizing problems Difficulty with emotional regulation that involves expressing powerful feelings through uncontrolled physical or verbal outbursts, as by lashing out at other people or breaking things.

Often the emotion that most needs control is anger because "dysregulated anger may trigger aggressive, oppositional behavior" (Gilliom et al., 2002, p. 222). Without emotional regulation, an angry child might flail at another person or lie down screaming and kicking. Such behavior is typical of a 2-year-old's temper tantrum, but most children master such overwhelming anger with time. A 5-year-old usually has more self-control, perhaps pouting and cursing, but not hitting and screaming. Whether or not the 5-year-old's curses are considered pathological depends on the culture and context.

Other people have **internalizing problems:** They are fearful and withdrawn, internalizing their emotional distress by turning it inward. They are sometimes called "overcontrolled." Again, with maturity, extreme fears and shyness diminish. The fears of a 2-year-old (e.g., of the bathtub drain, of an imaginary tidal wave, of a stranger with a missing finger) can be quite normal although not rational. Those same fears in a 6-year-old can be pathological terror, again depending on the culture. Fear of a tidal wave, for instance, is not pathological when a child has experienced the destruction caused by a tsunami.

internalizing problems Difficulty with emotional regulation that involves turning one's emotional distress inward, as by feeling excessively guilty, ashamed, or worthless.

Who's Chicken? Genes and good parenting have made this boy neither too fearful nor too bold. Appropriate caution is probably the best approach to meeting a chicken.

Both externalizing and internalizing children are unable to regulate their emotions properly, or, more precisely, are unable to regulate the *expression* of their emotions. Either they do not exercise enough self-control or they control themselves too much (Caspi & Shiner, 2006; Hart et al., 2003).

Emotional regulation is in part neurological, a matter of brain functioning. Because a child's ability to regulate emotions requires thinking before acting (deciding whether and how to display joy, anger, or fear), emotional regulation is the province of the prefrontal cortex, the executive area of the brain. As you remember from Chapter 8, the prefrontal cortex regulates those parts of the limbic system (especially the amygdala) where powerful emotions, such as fear and anxiety, form.

Normally, neurological advances in the prefrontal cortex occur at about age 4 or 5, and children become less likely to throw a temper tantrum, provoke a physical attack, or burst into giggles during prayer (Kagan & Hershkowitz, 2005). Throughout early childhood, violent outbursts, uncontrollable crying, and terrifying phobias (irrational, crippling fears) diminish. The capacity for self-control—such as not opening a present immediately if asked to wait and not expressing disappointment at an undesirable gift—becomes more evident (Carlson, 2003; Grolnick et al., 2006).

Sex Differences in Emotional Regulation

Girls are usually more advanced in emotional regulation. Although girls are better than boys at regulating externalizing emotions, they are less successful with internalizing ones. By adolescence, undercontrolled boys may be delinquents; overcontrolled girls may be anxious or depressed (Pennington, 2002).

Fighting Versus Hugging Sex differences in emotional expression become apparent toward the end of early childhood. For instance, in one study, 5-year-olds were given toy figures and heard the start of a story (Zahn-Waxler et al., 2008). In one story, two children (named Mark and Scott for the boys, Mary and Sarah for the girls) were said to start yelling at each other. Each 5-year-old was asked to use their toys to show what happened next.

Many boys responded by acting out physical aggression, with the two figures hitting and kicking each other. Boys whose behavior problems got worse between ages 5 and 9 (as rated by their teachers and parents) were most aggressive, and became even more so at age 7.

By contrast, girls were less likely to attack and more likely to have the girls in the story talk about the problem or change the subject. Curiously, those girls whose behavior problems got worse were more likely than the boys or than other girls to engage in "reparative behavior," such as hugging a girl or saying, "I'm sorry." This expression of guilt may seem to indicate maturity, but it may be a sign of internalization. As the authors explain:

> Gender-role stereotypes or exaggerations of masculine qualities (e.g., impulsive, aggressive, uncaring) and feminine qualities (submissive, unassertive, socially sensitive) are reflected not only in the types of problems males and females tend to develop but also in different forms of expression.
>
> *[Zahn-Waxler et al., 2008, p. 114]*

These researchers suggest that, for both sexes, extreme reactions predict future psychopathology (Zahn-Waxler et al., 2008).

The Brains of Boys and Girls Male and female brains differ, although the precise impact of those differences is controversial (Becker et al., 2008). Neurological and hormonal effects may make boys vulnerable to externalizing problems and girls vulnerable to internalizing ones. Normally, however, children of both sexes learn emotional regulation and are quite similar in avoiding either extreme of emotional imbalance.

Neurological damage can harm any child prenatally (if a pregnant woman is stressed, ill, or a heavy drug user) or in infancy (if an infant is chronically malnourished, injured, or frightened). As explained in earlier chapters, extreme stress can kill some neurons and stop others from developing properly. Such damage may affect the child's ability to regulate emotions, although the specific emotional dysregulation may be influenced by the child's sex. At age 5, vulnerable boys are likely to throw things and vulnerable girls to sob uncontrollably.

Caregivers and Emotional Regulation

Although inborn brain patterns are important, the quality of early caregiving also makes a difference in children's ability to regulate their emotions. Children of depressed parents are less able to regulate emotions (Forbes et al., 2006). By contrast, nurturing caregivers guide impulsive children toward emotional regulation; those children in turn become *more* competent than other children (Hane & Fox, 2006; Quas et al., 2004). Indeed, vulnerable children may have an advantage, not a handicap. Several studies find that difficult infants become more competent, intellectually and emotionally, than do typical children in kindergarten if their upbringing is unusually patient, responsive, and warm.

Negligent and inconsistent caregiving makes the problem worse (Belsky et al., 2007). This is especially evident in the emotions of maltreated 4- to 6-year-olds. Most such children (80 percent in one study) are "emotionally disregulated,"

➤Answer to Observation Quiz (from page 278): Size is not much help, since children grow slowly during these years and the heads of these two boys appear about the same size. However, emotional development is apparent. Most 2-year-olds, like the one at the right, still cling to their mothers; most 4-year-olds are sufficiently mature, secure, and curious to watch the excitement as they drink their juice.

➤Response for College Students (from page 280): Both are important. Extrinsic motivation includes parental pressure and the need to get a good job after graduation. Intrinsic motivation includes the joy of learning, especially if you can express that learning in ways others recognize. Have you ever taken a course that was not required and was said to be difficult? That was intrinsic motivation.

➤Response for Teachers (from page 280): No. In fact, imaginary friends are quite common, especially among creative children. The child may be somewhat lonely, though; you could help him or her find a friend.

becoming either indifferent or extremely angry when strangers criticize their mothers (Maughan & Cicchetti, 2002). Early neglect and abuse cause internalizing or externalizing problems that are more severe than does maltreatment that begins later in childhood (Lopez et al., 2004; Manly et al., 2001).

Experiments with lower animals show that inadequate early care causes, and is not simply correlated with, psychopathology. Highly stressed infant rats develop abnormal brain structures. However, if stressed rat pups are raised by nurturing mothers, their brains are protected by hormones elicited by their mothers, who lick, nuzzle, groom, and feed them often (J. Kaufman & Charney, 2001).

Of course, many influences affect each child. Nurture and nature interact, influencing the brain as well as behavior (Cicchetti & Curtis, 2007). The development of psychopathology in childhood is a complex process. Many causes (biological and psychosocial) sometimes lead to one disorder. The opposite occurs as well: Many disorders may result from a single cause.

Psychopathology is not the inevitable result of either inborn temperament or unresponsive caregiving. As scientists who studied 1,720 children from infancy to age 5 explain, "The fit between the child's temperament and the type of parenting the child experiences (rather than either factor alone) is predictive of children's behavioral trajectories" (Jaffee, 2007, p. 641).

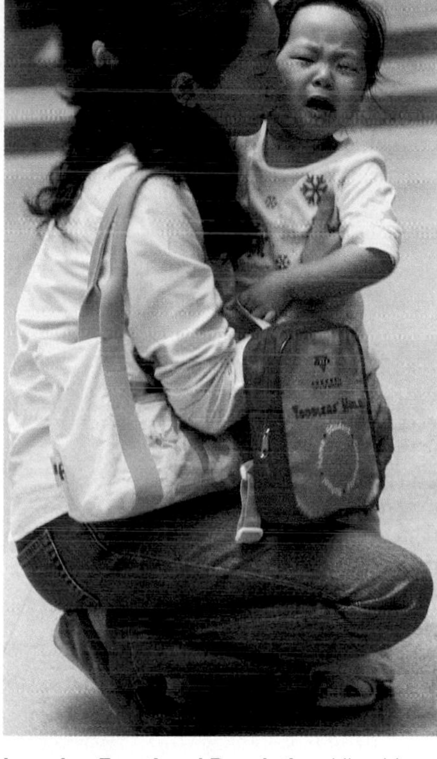
DBIMAGES / ALAMY

Learning Emotional Regulation Like this girl in Hong Kong, all 2-year-olds burst into tears when something upsets them—a toy breaks, a pet refuses to play, or it's time to go home. A mother who comforts them and helps them calm down is teaching them to regulate their emotions.

SUMMING UP

Erikson and many others find that pride, purpose, and initiative are integral components of the self-concept of young children, who typically have high self-esteem and are motivated to try new activities. Children who have difficulty with emotional regulation often develop internalizing or externalizing problems, which may be early signs of psychopathology. Boys and girls may express their emotional problems in different ways. Many factors influence the ability to regulate emotions, including genes, brain development, culture, and caregiving. ■

Play

Developmentalists believe that play is the most productive and enjoyable activity that children undertake (Elkind, 2007). Play is universal—it is apparent in every part of the world and has been for thousands of years.

Play changes between ages 2 and 6. The younger child's social play is quite simple (such as bouncing and trying to catch a ball and becoming upset if another child does not cooperate). By contrast, most 5-year-olds know how to gain entry to a play group, to manage conflict through the use of humor, to take turns, and to select and keep friends and playmates—all signs of theory of mind (see Chapter 9). The difference is the consequence of many hours of social play, which teaches children how to make, and keep, friends.

Peers and Parents

Young children play best with peers, people of about the same age and social status as themselves. Peers provide practice in emotional regulation, empathy, and social understanding (Cohen, 2006). For example, one child (about age 3) was new to peers and to preschool:

> She commanded another child, "Fall down. Go on, do what I say." When the other child stayed stalwartly on his feet, she pushed him over and was clearly amazed when he jumped up and said, "No pushing!"
>
> *[Leach, 1997, p. 474]*

In this example, the boy, with experience, had acquired a clear understanding of the rules of social play. The girl's amazement may have stemmed from having had her mother as her regular playmate—many mothers fall down on command. Fathers also follow orders. One father of a 3-year-old wrote:

> Nora casts me in the role of mommy in her pretend play as often as daddy. "Baby" is common, as is "Prince Charming" and "mermaid." I'm her go-to guy when she needs someone to sit next to at dinner or someone to sit still for a new hairstyle. . . . One day she asked me if I wanted to make valentines with her. Do I want to make valentines, Nora? Frankly? No. No, I don't. Before everyone judges me, realize that I was tired. I had made valentines with Nora every day for two weeks. Also it was November. Nora put on her serious face, looked me straight in the eye and said forcefully, "Dada, you can make a valentine for Grandma or a valentine for Nona. Those are your choices!"
>
> *[Ken, personal communication, 2008]*

Developmentalists encourage parents of both sexes to play with their children. However, children usually prefer to play with each other rather than alone or with parents. They particularly prefer playmates of the same sex, who encourage boy or girl play (Berenbaum et al., 2008).

Emotional regulation is learned best with other children. Even the most patient parent is outmatched by another child at negotiating the rules of tag, at wrestling on the grass, at pretending to be a sick baby, at fighting a dragon.

Of course, children do not always cooperate with each other. Some play groups might exclude a particular child, and some children might quit the game if they cannot have their way. Generally, however, children learn to get along. Even siblings who compete for their parents' attention may play together when parents are unavailable.

Cultural Differences in Play

All young children play, whether they are on Arctic ice or desert sand. But because play varies by culture, gender, and age, it is an ideal means for children to learn whatever social skills are required in the social context (Sutton-Smith, 1997). Particular play activities vary: Chinese children fly kites, Alaskan natives tell dreams and stories, Lapp children pretend to be reindeer, and so on. Children create dramas that reflect their culture and play games that have been passed down from older generations (Kalliala, 2006; Roopnarine et al., 1994).

Play Ball! In every nation, young children play with balls, but the specific games they play vary with the culture. Soccer is the favorite game in many countries, including Brazil, where these children are practicing their dribbling on Copacabana Beach in Rio de Janeiro.

REUTERS / SERGIO MORAES

The Ecological Context

The physical setting is one aspect of culture that shapes play. Some communities provide many toys and close supervision for children; in other places, children are left to play on their own with whatever they find. The birth rate and economic conditions in some nations give children many siblings and neighbors as playmates. They learn to play without adults but with other children of both sexes and many ages.

In Ua Pou, an island 2,000 miles southeast of Hawaii, a play group's setting is described:

> Children ranged from two to five years old. They played several hours a day without supervision while their siblings attended school nearby.
>
> The play area was potentially dangerous. A strong surf broke on the boat ramp. The large rocks on the shore were

> strewn with broken glass. The valley walls were steep and slippery. Children played on a high bridge and high, sharp, lava-rock walls. Machetes, axes, and matches were occasionally left around and young children played with these. In spite of these dangers, accidents were rare and minor. . . .
>
> Disputes were frequent but these dissipated after a few minutes. Children did not seek adults or older children to settle conflicts or direct their play.
>
> [Martini, 1994]

By contrast, in the cities of developed nations, undeveloped space is scarce and family sizes are small. Consequently, play usually occurs in child-care settings. Child-centered programs have space, playmates, toys, and adults who believe that play provides emotional and social learning (Clarke-Stewart & Allhusen, 2005).

Changing Social Circumstances

As children grow older, their play becomes more social, although culture, temperament, sex, parents, and experience all influence play at every stage (Rubin et al., 2006). One cultural shift began in technologically advanced nations and has spread worldwide: the increasing prevalence of television. Recent studies of young children's play show them using plots and characters that originated on the screen and displaying advanced sexual awareness (of such topics as oral sex) by age 6 (Kalliala, 2006). (Knowledge of sexual activities is not necessarily a sign of child abuse, as was once believed; young children may become sexually aware by watching television.) By watching adult-oriented television programs, children often become fascinated and confused about sex (Cohen, 2006; Kalliala, 2006).

Worldwide, children become more social as they grow older. This progression was first noted by an American, Mildred Parten (1932), who distinguished five kinds of play, each more interactive than the previous one:

1. *Solitary play:* A child plays alone, unaware of any other children playing nearby.
2. *Onlooker play:* A child watches other children play.
3. *Parallel play:* Children play with similar toys in similar ways, but not together.
4. *Associative play:* Children interact, observing each other and sharing material, but their play is not yet mutual and reciprocal.
5. *Cooperative play:* Children play together, creating and elaborating a joint activity or taking turns.

Children move up this sequence toward the more social forms of play as they approach age 6, when they become capable of playing games with rules. Piaget thought that rule-based play was an early manifestation of morality (Piaget, 1932).

Culture also has an effect on style of play. It is quite normal for 4-year-olds in the United States to prefer to play alone rather than with strangers (Henderson et al., 2004). Even 5-year-olds may not engage in cooperative play with unfamiliar peers in cultures that value individualism. By contrast, in some families and nations, children as young as 2 take turns, share, and otherwise engage in social play with siblings (Cohen, 2006). In China and many other nations, children are expected to play cooperatively by age 3, and most do so.

Active Play

Children need physical activity to develop muscle strength and control. They benefit from peers who provide an audience, role models, and sometimes competition. For instance, running skills develop best when children chase or race each other, not when a child runs alone.

Gross motor play is favored among young children, who enjoy climbing, kicking, running, and tumbling (Case-Smith & Kuhaneck, 2008). They may engage in active play even when parents would prefer them to be quiet. One 5-year-old boy came to his parents' bedroom every night to entertain them with an "action show," which involved elaborate jumps and acrobatics. As soon as he could, his 1-year-old brother joined in (Cohen, 2006).

Rough-and-Tumble Play

rough-and-tumble play Play that mimics aggression through wrestling, chasing, or hitting, but in which there is no intent to harm.

The most common form of active play is called **rough-and-tumble play** because it looks quite rough and because the children seem to tumble over one another. The term was coined by British scientists who studied primates in East Africa (Blurton-Jones, 1976). They noticed that monkeys often chased, attacked, rolled over in the dirt, and wrestled, quite roughly, but without hurting one another. If a young monkey wanted to play, all it had to do was come close, catch the eye of a peer, and then run a few feet, looking back. This invitation was almost always accepted, as the other monkey responded with a *play face* rather than an angry one. Puppies, kittens, and young chimpanzees similarly invite rough-and-tumble play.

When the scientists returned from Africa to their families in England, they saw that their children were like other animals—that human youngsters, like baby monkeys, enjoy rough-and-tumble play (Pellegrini & Smith, 2005). They chase, wrestle, and grab each other, developing games like tag and cops-and-robbers to guide their behavior. Rough-and-tumble play is distinguished not only by the play face but by many other expressions and gestures used by very young children to signify that their actions are "just pretend."

Rough-and-tumble play appears in every nation of the world, particularly among young males (human and otherwise) when they are allowed to play freely (Berenbaum et al., 2008). Some ecological conditions make rough-and-tumble play more likely, among them ample space and distant or absent supervision. (Even young monkeys avoid colliding with older monkeys as they chase each other.)

Although rough-and-tumble play is obviously physical, it is fun and constructive, not aggressive. It teaches children how to enter a relationship, assert themselves, and respond to someone else. Some psychologists think that it also helps the prefrontal cortex to develop—that roughhousing with each other helps children learn to regulate their emotions as well as strengthen their bodies (Pellegrini et al., 2007).

Male Bonding Sometimes the only way to distinguish aggression from rough-and-tumble play is to look at the faces. The hitter is not scowling, the hittee is laughing, and the hugger is just joining in the fun. Another clue that this is rough-and-tumble play comes from gender and context. These boys are in a Head Start program, where they are learning social skills, such as how to avoid fighting.

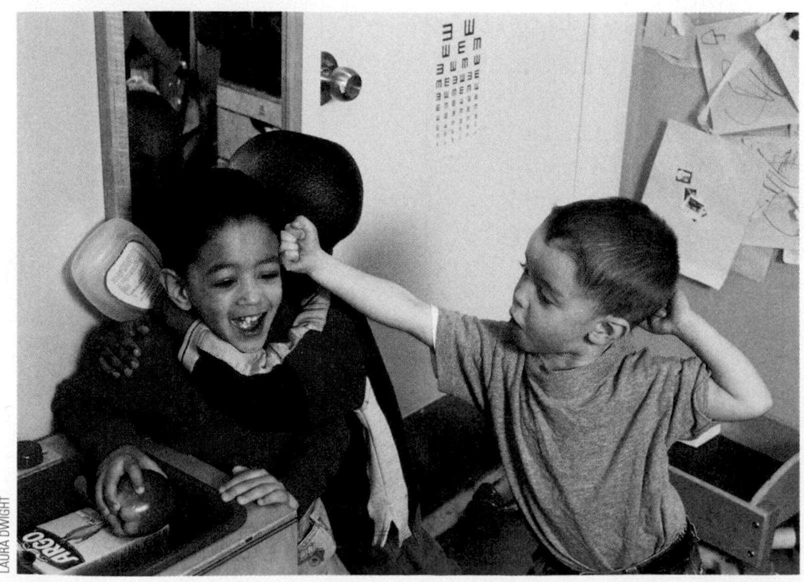
LAURA DWIGHT

During rough-and-tumble play, children are more likely to injure themselves by falling or bumping into something than to hurt one another. If adults are unsure whether they are observing a fight that should be stopped or a social activity that should continue, they should look for the play face. Children almost always smile, and often laugh, in rough-and-tumble play; they frown or scowl in real fights.

Rough-and-tumble play requires both planned provocation and self-control. Two-year-olds typically just chase and catch one another, but older children keep the play fair, long-lasting, and fun. In tag, for instance, older players set rules (which vary depending on availability of base, safety, and terrain) and then each child decides when and how far to venture. If one child is "It" for too long, another child (often a friend) makes it easy to be caught. Rough-and-tumble play also fosters caregiving, especially if a child is accidentally hurt (Reed & Brown, 2001).

Drama and Pretending

Another major type of active play that is common in early childhood is **sociodramatic play,** in which children act out various roles and plots, taking on "any identity, role, or activity that they choose. They can be mothers, babies, Cinderella, or Captain Hook. They can make tea or fly to the moon. Or they can fight, hurt others, or kill or imprison someone" (Dunn & Hughes, 2001, p. 491).

sociodramatic play Pretend play in which children act out various roles and themes in stories that they create.

Sociodramatic play allows children to do the following:

- Explore and rehearse the social roles enacted around them
- Test their ability to explain and to convince playmates of their ideas
- Practice regulating their emotions by pretending to be afraid, angry, brave, and so on
- Develop a self-concept in a nonthreatening context.

Sociodramatic play builds on pretending and social interest, both of which emerge in toddlerhood. But preschool children do more than pretend; they interact, combining their own imagination with that of others.

The beginnings of sociodramatic play are illustrated by this pair, a 3-year-old girl and a 2-year-old boy. The girl wanted to act out the role of a baby, and she persuaded the boy to play a parent.

> **Boy:** Not good. You bad.
> **Girl:** Why?
> **Boy:** 'Cause you spill your milk
> **Girl:** No. 'Cause I bit somebody.
> **Boy:** Yes, you did.
> **Girl:** Say, "Go to sleep. Put your head down."
> **Boy:** Put your head down.
> **Girl:** No.
> **Boy:** Yes.
> **Girl:** No.
> **Boy:** Yes. Okay, I will spank you. Bad boy. (*Spanks her, not hard*)
> **Girl:** No. My head is up. (*Giggles*) I want my teddy bear.
> **Boy:** No. Your teddy bear go away.
> (*At this point she asked if he was really going to take the teddy bear away.*)
>
> [*from Garvey, reported in Cohen, 2006, p. 72*]

FELICIA MARTINEZ / PHOTOEDIT, INC.

Ladies and Babies A developmental difference is visible here between the 14-month-old's evident curiosity and the 4-year-old friends' pleasure in sociodramatic play. The mother's reaction—joy at the children's imaginative play or irritation at the mess they've made—is less predictable.

Note that the girl not only directed the play but also played her part, sometimes accepting what the boy said and sometimes not. The boy took direction yet also made up his own dialogue and actions ("Bad boy!").

Compare their simple plot to the play of four boys, about age 5, in a day-care center in Finland. Joni plays the role of the evil one who menaces the other boys; Tuomas directs the drama and acts in it as well.

> **Tuomas:** And now he [*Joni*] would take me and would hang me. . . . This would be the end of all of me.
>
> **Joni:** Hands behind.
>
> **Tuomas:** I can't help it. I have to. (*The two other boys follow his example.*)
>
> **Joni:** I would put fire all around them.
> (*All three brave boys lie on the floor with hands tied behind their backs. Joni piles mattresses on them, and pretends to light a fire, which crackles closer and closer.*)
>
> **Tuomas:** Everything is lost.
> (*One boy starts to laugh.*)
>
> **Petterl:** Better not to laugh, soon we will all be dead. . . . I am saying my last words.
>
> **Tuomas:** Now you can say your last wish. . . . And now I say I wish we can be terribly strong.
> (*At that point, the three boys suddenly gain extraordinary strength, pushing off the mattresses and extinguishing the fire. Good triumphs over evil, but not until the last moment, because, as one boy explains, "Otherwise this playing is not exciting at all."*)
>
> *[adapted from Kalliala, 2006, p. 83]*

Good versus evil is a favorite theme of boys' sociodramatic play. In contrast, girls often act out domestic scenes. Such gender differences are found in many cultures. In the same day-care center where Joni piles mattresses on his playmates, the girls say their play is "more beautiful and peaceful . . . [but] boys play all kinds of violent games" (Kalliala, 2006, p. 110).

SUMMING UP

Playing with other children is a boon for children's emotional regulation, as they learn how to get along with each other. Many forms of play, including rough-and-tumble play and sociodramatic play, require social understanding and compromise. Although play is universal, the particular forms it takes vary by gender and culture. ■

Challenges for Parents

We have seen that young children's emotions and actions are affected by many factors, including brain maturation, culture, and peers. Now we focus on another primary influence on young children: their parents.

Parents tend to follow the child-rearing patterns of their own parents, unless they hated those practices—in which case they might go to the opposite extreme. It could be said that the first challenge faced by parents is the need to decide on an approach to dealing with their children—that is, on a parenting style.

Parenting Styles

Parents differ a great deal in what they believe about children and how they should act toward them. Although thousands of researchers have traced the effects of parenting on child development, the work of one person, 40 years ago, continues to be influential. Diana Baumrind (1967, 1971) studied 100 preschool children, all from California, almost all middle-class European Americans. (The cohort and cultural limitations of this sample were not obvious at the time.)

Baumrind found that parents differed on four important dimensions:

- *Expressions of warmth.* Some parents are very affectionate; others are cold and critical.
- *Strategies for discipline.* Parents vary in whether and how they explain, criticize, persuade, ignore, and punish.
- *Communication.* Some parents listen patiently; others demand silence.
- *Expectations for maturity.* Parents vary in standards for responsibility and self-control.

Especially for Political Scientists (see response, page 290): Many observers contend that children learn their political attitudes at home, from the way their parents treat them. Is this true?

Baumrind's Three Patterns of Parenting

On the basis of these dimensions, Baumrind identified three parenting styles (summarized in Table 10.1).

- **Authoritarian parenting.** The parents' word is law, not to be questioned. Misconduct brings strict punishment, usually physical (but not so harsh as to be considered abusive). Authoritarian parents set down clear rules and hold high standards. They do not expect children to give their opinions; discussion about emotions is especially rare. (One adult from such a family said that the question "How do you feel?" had only two possible answers: "Fine" and "Tired.") Authoritarian parents love their children, but they seem aloof, rarely showing affection.
- **Permissive parenting.** Permissive parents make few demands, hiding any impatience they feel. Discipline is lax, partly because permissive parents have low expectations for maturity. Instead, permissive parents are nurturing and accepting, listening to whatever their offspring say. They want to be helpful, but they do not feel responsible for shaping their children.
- **Authoritative parenting.** Authoritative parents set limits and enforce rules, yet they also listen to their children. The parents demand maturity, but they are usually forgiving (not punishing) if the child falls short. They consider themselves guides, not authorities (as authoritarian parents do) or friends (as permissive parents do).

authoritarian parenting An approach to child rearing that is characterized by high behavioral standards, strict punishment of misconduct, and little communication.

permissive parenting An approach to child rearing that is characterized by high nurturance and communication but little discipline, guidance, or control.

authoritative parenting An approach to child rearing in which the parents set limits but listen to the child and are flexible.

A fourth style, called **neglectful/uninvolved parenting,** is sometimes mistaken for the permissive style but is actually quite different (Steinberg, 2001). Neither permissive nor neglectful parents use physical punishment, but neglectful parents are strikingly unaware of what their children are doing—they seem not to care what happens to them. By contrast, permissive parents may be very involved in their children's lives, defending them from teachers' criticism, arranging play dates, and sacrificing to buy them particular toys.

neglectful/uninvolved parenting An approach to child rearing in which the parents are indifferent toward their children and unaware of what is going on in their children's lives.

TABLE 10.1

Characteristics of Parenting Styles Identified by Baumrind

Style	Characteristics				
				Communication	
	Warmth	Discipline	Expectations of Maturity	Parent to Child	Child to Parent
Authoritarian	Low	Strict, often physical	High	High	Low
Permissive	High	Rare	Low	Low	High
Authoritative	High	Moderate, with much discussion	Moderate	High	High

➤Response for Political Scientists (from page 289): There are many parenting styles, and it is difficult to determine each one's impact on children's personalities. At this point, attempts to connect early child rearing with later political outlook are speculative.

The Implications of Parenting Style

Baumrind's three-part classification, although still influential, is generally regarded as too simplistic. Among the criticisms of Baumrind's research are the following:

- Her original sample had little economic, ethnic, or cultural diversity.
- She focused more on attitudes than on daily interactions.
- She overlooked the child's contribution to parent–child relationships.
- Some authoritarian parents are very loving toward their children.
- Some permissive parents guide their children intensely, but with words, not rules. (Bornstein, 2006; Galambos et al., 2003; Lamb & Lewis, 2005; Parke & Buriel, 2006):

These and other findings about the implications of parenting style have emerged from longitudinal studies of children growing up with various types of parents. As explained in Chapter 8, parenting that is abusive or neglectful always harms children. Consequently, authoritarian parents must take care not to punish too often or too harshly, and permissive parents must not slide toward neglect. All children need parents who care about them because, no matter what their practices regarding punishment and expectations, "parental involvement plays an important role in the development of both social and cognitive competence" (Parke & Buriel, 2006, p. 437).

Beyond that, the following general long-term effects of parenting style have been reported (Baumrind, 1991; Steinberg et al., 1994):

- *Authoritarian* parents raise children who are likely to become conscientious, obedient, and quiet but not especially happy. Such children tend to feel guilty or depressed, internalizing their frustrations and blaming themselves when things don't go well. As adolescents, they sometimes rebel, leaving home before age 20.
- *Permissive* parents raise unhappy children who lack self-control, especially in the give-and-take of peer relationships. Inadequate emotional regulation makes them immature and impedes friendships, which is the main reason for their unhappiness. They tend to continue to live at home, still dependent, in early adulthood.
- *Authoritative* parents raise children who are successful, articulate, happy with themselves, and generous with others. These children are usually liked by teachers and peers, especially in the United States and other societies in which individual initiative is valued.

An especially important factor in determining parenting style is the child's temperament. Fearful and impulsive children require counterbalancing responses from their parents. Any sweeping statement about which parenting style is best will be wrong in some cases (Bugental & Grusec, 2006; Kagan & Fox, 2006).

Cultural Variations

The importance of interaction between child and context is particularly obvious when children of various ethnic groups are compared, even if all live within the same nation. Effective Chinese American, Caribbean American, and African American parents may be stricter than effective parents of northern or western European backgrounds (Chao, 2001; Hill & Bush, 2001). Sometimes such parents have been classified as authoritarian on the basis of their punishment styles, but that label may be misapplied.

A great deal depends on the parents' attitude. One study of African American mothers found that if they disapproved of spanking but did it nonetheless, their children were likely to be depressed; but this was not true if the mothers approved of spanking (McLoyd et al., 2007). Multicultural and international research has found that specific discipline methods and family rules are less important than parental warmth, support, and concern. Children from every ethnic group and every country benefit if they believe that their parents appreciate them; children everywhere suffer if they feel rejected and unwanted (Khaleque & Rohner, 2002; Maccoby, 2000).

One example of the role of culture in discipline comes from the contrast between mothers in Japan and in the United States. Japanese mothers tend to use reasoning, empathy, and expressions of disappointment to control their children more than North American mothers do. This approach may be classified as permissive, but their children typically grow up emotionally healthy, not immature and unhappy, as tends to happen in permissive U.S. families. One reason is that, regardless of parenting style, the Japanese mother–child relationship is strongly affectionate; it is called *amae,* denoting a close interpersonal bond (Rothbaum et al., 2000).

"He's just doing that to get attention."

Pay Attention Children develop best with lots of love and attention. They shouldn't have to ask for it!

Indeed, multiple cultural differences in acceptable methods of disciplining young children are apparent. For example, the proportion of Canadian parents who slap, pinch, or smack their children (Oldershaw, 2002) is half that of parents in the United States, where the Supreme Court decided in 2004 that teachers and parents could use "reasonable force" to punish children (Bugental & Grusec, 2006). That would be illegal in many other developed nations, among them Austria, Croatia, Cyprus, Denmark, Finland, Germany, Israel, Italy, Norway, and Sweden.

Especially for Parents (see response, page 294): Suppose you agree that spanking is destructive, but you sometimes get so angry at your child's behavior that you hit him or her. Is your reaction appropriate?

Values, climate, economy, and history all affect child rearing (Matsumoto & Yoo, 2006). Socioeconomic factors may be even more crucial than ethnic ones. Authoritarian parenting increases as income falls, perhaps because low-income families tend to be larger or because parents want to raise obedient children who will not challenge the police or employers later on. Parents everywhere try to raise their children to adjust to the culture they know, which may differ from the dominant culture of Baumrind's families.

Moreover, family patterns change with time, making stereotypes outdated. A multicultural study of Canadian parents found that, contrary to predictions based on U.S. research, East Asian and Caribbean immigrant parents were *less* harsh with their children than the average Canadian parent, and teachers rated their children as less aggressive than the Canadian norm (Ho et al., 2008).

Given a multicultural perspective, developmentalists hesitate to recommend any one particular style of parenting (Dishion & Bullock, 2002; J. G. Miller, 2004). That does not mean that they believe all parents function equally well—far from it. Signs of serious trouble are obvious in children's behavior, including overcontrol, undercontrol, inability to play with others, and bullying. Ineffective parenting is one possible cause of children's misbehavior, but it is not the only one.

Children, Parents, and the New Media

New challenges confront each generation of parents, and one of today's great challenges is the influence of electronic media on children. All media—the Internet, electronic games, and so on—can be harmful, especially when the content is violent (Anderson et al., 2007; Kearney et al., 2007; Smyth, 2007). However, not enough scientific research is available to draw firm conclusions about the newer media's impact on young children. Here we report on children and television, the medium that has been the focus of thirty years of research.

"Why don't you get off the computer and watch some TV?"

Children want to watch television, and parents find that TV keeps the children engaged while the parents go about their own activities. Yet six major organizations (the American Psychological Association, the American Academy of Pediatrics, the American Medical Association, the American Academy of Child and Adolescent Psychiatry, the American Academy of Family Physicians, and the American Psychiatric Association) implore parents to reduce television watching, especially among young children.

Did you notice that all six organizations have *American* in their titles? That signals the need for a cultural caution: Most research reported here has studied U.S. children and media (C. A. Anderson & Bushman, 2002; Roberts & Foehr, 2004). Readers need to ask themselves whether American media are so pervasive worldwide that they cause the same problems in every nation.

Most young children of every ethnic and economic group in the United States spend more than three hours each day using one electronic medium or another (see Table 10.2). Among young children, that medium is usually television. Almost every family owns at least two televisions, and children usually watch apart from their parents, often in their own rooms. By age 3, more than one-fourth of all children in the United States already have a television in their bedrooms, and this percentage rises as children grow older (Roberts & Foehr, 2004).

TABLE 10.2

Average Daily Exposure to Electronic Media

Age 2 to 4 Years	Hours per Day
White	3:18
Black	4:30
Hispanic	3:37
Age 5 to 7 Years	**Hours per Day**
White	3:17
Black	4:16
Hispanic	3:38

Source: Adapted from Roberts & Foehr, 2004.

The Importance of Content

What do children see? The "good guys," whether in cartoons or police dramas, hit, shoot, and kick as often as the "bad guys," yet their violence is depicted as justified.

Good guys are male and White, except in a few programs where all the characters are Black or (on Spanish-language cable channels) Latino. Females of all ethnic groups are usually depicted as victims or girlfriends, not leaders—except in girl-oriented programs that boys rarely watch. Insidious gender and racial stereotypes are still evident (Mastro et al., 2008).

Children of all ages who watch violence on television become more violent themselves (C. A. Anderson et al., 2003; Huesmann et al., 2003; Singer & Singer, 2005). They are more likely to get into fights with each other and even to break things and hurt people when they grow up. Consider the results of a longitudinal study of television watching that began with children at about age 5 and queried those same children again as adolescents (D. R. Anderson et al., 2001; see the

Video: Good, Bad, or Indifferent? A modest amount of time spent watching television and videos, especially when parents watch with their children and the content is educational, does not seem to be harmful for young children. However, the effects are not yet known for certain, because adequate longitudinal research has not yet been conducted.

"*Have some respect for my learning style.*"

Video Style Children who spend a lot of time watching television and playing video games are likely to develop a visual learning style. They get used to receiving information in the form of vivid images and brief scenes, making it harder for them to concentrate on and comprehend anything that is longer and presented in verbal form.

Research Design). Young children who watched television violence tended to become more violent, less creative, and lower-achieving teenagers.

Family Time

Many parents and older siblings are more engaged with television than with each other, and children learn from their example. Language development depends on one-to-one conversations, and emotional regulation depends on parental responsiveness. Parents and children rarely watch TV together, and, even when they do, they talk only briefly. In most families, parents and children have their own TVs, radios, and even computers, which often stay on during meals, reducing learning (Roberts & Foehr, 2004). The more television children watch, the more angry they are—a correlation that can be interpreted in many ways.

No wonder those six organizations recommend limited exposure to television. But few parents can enforce a total prohibition. (When you read about fast-mapping in Chapter 9, did you wonder why Sarah called me a brat? It was because I had momentarily unplugged the TV.) Parents can, however, limit their own and their children's video time. They can play, read, and talk with their children. Too few children know a proven fact: An animated parent can be more entertaining than Mickey Mouse.

SUMMING UP

Over the past 40 years, Diana Baumrind and most other developmentalists have found that authoritative parenting (warm, with guidance) is more effective than either authoritarian (very strict) or permissive (very lenient) parenting. Other researchers have found that uninvolved parents are the least effective of all. In any culture, children thrive when their parents appreciate them and care about their accomplishments. The children of parents who are uninvolved, uncaring, or abusive seldom become happy, well-adjusted, and high-achieving adults.

Good parenting is not achieved by following any one simple rule; children's temperaments vary, and so do cultural patterns. The media pose a particular challenge worldwide because children are attracted to colorful, fast-paced images; yet violent TV programs, in particular, lead to more aggressive behavior. Parental monitoring and limits on children's exposure to TV, accompanied by more face-to-face interaction, are recommended by every expert. ■

Research Design

Scientists: Daniel Anderson, Aletha C. Huston, Kelly L. Schmitt, Deborah L. Linebarger, and John C. Wright.

Publication: *Monographs of the Society for Research in Child Development* (2001).

Participants: A total of 570 adolescents from Massachusetts and Kansas, whose television watching and other characteristics were studied in depth (viewing diaries recorded exactly what they watched).

Design: These participants and their television viewing were first studied at age 5. As adolescents, they were asked questions about their current lives, and their high school transcripts were obtained. Researchers controlled for many factors (e.g., SES, gender, region), seeking correlations between viewing habits at age 5 and behavior at age 16 or so. Efforts were made to understand causation, not just correlation.

Major conclusion: Sixty-five correlations were found between television viewing at preschool and adolescent behavior and characteristics. Most (though not all) effects were negative, but content matters: "Marshall McLuhan appears to have been wrong. The *medium* is not the message. The *message* is the message" (p. 134).

Comment: These researchers wisely followed up on hundreds of preschoolers who had been carefully surveyed many years earlier. The result confirms the conclusions of many cross-sectional and shorter longitudinal studies: Television in the early years affects behavior in school. The other interesting result was not predicted by those most critical of TV: The content of some programs facilitates learning.

➤Response for Parents (from page 291): No. The worst time to spank a child is when you are angry. You might seriously hurt the child, and the child will associate anger with violence. You would do better to learn to control your anger and develop other strategies for discipline and for prevention of misbehavior.

Moral Development

Children develop increasingly complex moral values, judgments, and behaviors as they mature. In early childhood, as you have seen, children try to please their parents and avoid punishment, to make friends and exclude enemies. The emotional development described in this chapter, and the theory of mind described in Chapter 9, are the foundation for the self-concept and social awareness that make morality possible.

Many parents and teachers consider morality even more important than any of the other developments already described (strength, motor skills, intelligence, and so on). Perhaps for this reason, a debate rages over how children of every age internalize standards of right and wrong and how they develop virtues and avoid vices. Conflicting perspectives are taken by all five major theories of psychology (described in Chapter 2) and by many schools of philosophy, theology, and sociology. This conflict evokes the primal debate of human development, nature versus nurture:

- The "nature" perspective suggests that morality is genetic, an outgrowth of natural bonding and attachment. That would explain why young children tend to help and defend their parents, no matter what the parents do.
- The "nurture" perspective contends that culture is crucial, as children learn the values of their community. That would explain why young children admire or reject peers who eat raw fish, or hamburgers, or crickets, depending on their cultural preferences.

We have repeatedly seen that both nature and nurture are always important, but developmentalists differ as to which is more important and when (Killen & Smetana, 2007; Krebs, 2008; Turiel, 2006). Therefore, here we merely describe what is generally agreed on about moral development from age 2 to age 6. Two topics are particularly germane: the early manifestation of prosocial and antisocial behavior (including aggression) and the implications of parental methods of discipline.

Empathy and Antipathy

empathy The ability to understand the emotions and concerns of another person, especially when they differ from one's own.

antipathy Feelings of dislike or even hatred for another person.

prosocial behavior Feelings and actions that are helpful and kind but are of no obvious benefit to oneself.

antisocial behavior Feelings and actions that are deliberately hurtful or destructive to another person.

Two moral emotions are particularly likely to develop as children play with each other, choosing friends and enemies. With increasing social experiences and decreasing egocentrism, they develop **empathy,** an understanding of other people's feelings and concerns, and **antipathy,** dislike or even hatred of another person.

Empathy is not the same as sympathy, which means feeling sorry *for* someone. Rather, empathy means feeling sorry *with* someone, experiencing the other person's pain or sadness as if it were one's own. Research with mirror neurons (see Chapter 1) suggests that observing someone else may activate the same areas of the brain that are active in that person. This is how empathy works.

Ideally, empathy leads to **prosocial behavior,** helpfulness and kindness without any obvious benefit for oneself. Expressing concern, offering to share food or a toy, and including a shy child in a game or conversation are examples of prosocial behavior. Young children naturally develop friends, often many of them. Their eagerness to have friends is one reason they tell each other "I'll be your best friend" if they share candy or allow someone to join in play. The innate prosocial urge is one foundation of morality.

Antipathy can lead to **antisocial behavior,** deliberate hurtfulness or destructiveness aimed at another person (Caprara et al., 2001). Antisocial actions include verbal insults, social exclusion, and physical assaults. An antisocial 4-year-old might look another child in the eye, scowl, and then kick him hard without provocation.

By age 4 or 5—as a result of brain maturation, theory of mind, emotional regulation, and interactions with caregivers—most children can be deliberately prosocial or antisocial, with prosocial behavior generally increasing from age 3 to 6 and beyond (N. Eisenberg et al., 2004). Thus, moral emotions and moral behavior both increase.

Aggression

Regulation of emotions, development of morality, and the emergence of empathy and antipathy are nowhere more apparent than in the way children learn to deal with their aggressive impulses. The gradual control of aggression is evident on close observation of rough-and-tumble play; or in the fantasies of domination and submission that are often acted out in sociodramatic play; or in the sharing of art supplies, construction materials, and wheeled vehicles (J. D. Peterson & Flanders, 2005). Through play, children learn moral behavior—specifically, how to defend friends, cooperate with playmates, and control expression of aggression (Tremblay & Nagin, 2005).

Types of Aggression

Researchers recognize four general types of aggression, described in Table 10.3. Not surprisingly, given the moral sensibilities of children, already by age 5 children make moral judgments regarding which type of aggression is justified and which is not (Etchu, 2007). **Instrumental aggression** is very common among young children, who often seem to want something they do not have and try, without thinking, to get it. **Reactive aggression** is common as well; this type, particularly, becomes better controlled as emotional regulation increases. **Relational aggression** destroys another child's self-esteem and social networks and actually becomes more hurtful as children mature, since their esteem and social networks are more fragile.

The fourth and most ominous type is **bullying aggression.** It is fairly common in young children, but it should be stopped before they reach school age. As described in detail in Chapter 13, bullying aggression among older children is destructive for both victims and bullies.

instrumental aggression Hurtful behavior that is intended to get or keep something that another person has.

reactive aggression An impulsive retaliation for another person's intentional or accidental action, verbal or physical.

relational aggression Nonphysical acts, such as insults or social rejection, aimed at harming the social connection between the victim and other people.

bullying aggression Unprovoked, repeated physical or verbal attack, especially on victims who are unlikely to defend themselves.

Developmental Patterns

Aggression follows a developmental pattern, becoming less common, but more hurtful, with time. Infants are very aggressive; they naturally pinch, slap, and even bite others. In Richard Tremblay's dramatic words, "The only reason babies do not

TABLE 10.3

The Four Forms of Aggression

Type of Aggression	Definition	Comments
Instrumental aggression	Hurtful behavior that is aimed at gaining something (such as a toy, a place in line, or a turn on the swing) that someone else has	Often increases from age 2 to 6; involves objects more than people; quite normal; more egocentric than antisocial.
Reactive aggression	An impulsive retaliation for a hurt (intentional or accidental) that can be verbal or physical	Indicates a lack of emotional regulation, characteristic of 2-year-olds. A 5-year-old can usually stop and think before reacting.
Relational aggression	Nonphysical acts, such as insults or social rejection, aimed at harming the social connections between the victim and others	Involves a personal attack and thus is directly antisocial; can be very hurtful; more common as children become socially aware.
Bullying aggression	Unprovoked, repeated physical or verbal attack, especially on victims who are unlikely to defend themselves	In both bullies and victims, a sign of poor emotional regulation; adults should intervene before the school years. (Bullying is discussed in Chapter 13.)

kill each other is that we do not give them knives or guns" (quoted in Holden, 2000, p. 580). Fortunately, babies are weak and weaponless, so parents have time to teach self-control. One of the first moral values that children learn, universally, is to not hurt others (Krebs, 2008).

Almost all 2-year-olds are instrumentally and reactively aggressive, but the incidence of such behavior diminishes with each passing year. A 5-year-old who still attacks his or her mother is showing a lack of emotional control, which may lead to attacks on peers and externalizing problems of all kinds later in life (Moss et al., 2004).

Particularly worrisome is bullying. Children who do not learn to regulate their emotions and do not develop a moral prohibition against unprovoked harm may display bullying aggression throughout childhood, adolescence, and early adulthood (Loeber et al., 2005; Tremblay & Nagin, 2005). However, if parents teach their aggressive child to control his or her outbursts, that child will probably do well, academically and socially, displaying only average aggression by middle childhood (NICHD Early Child Care Research Network, 2004).

Parental Discipline

Many developmentalists believe that children's attachment to their parents, and then to others, is the beginning of morality. Humans protect, cooperate, and even sacrifice for each other because social groups evolved to encourage such prosocial behavior (Krebs, 2008).

LAURA DWIGHT

Parenting Style This woman is disciplining her son, who does not look happy about it.

Observation Quiz (see answer, page 299): Which parenting style is shown here?

Parents need to establish strong and affectionate bonds with their children, as already explained in Chapter 7. Beyond that, a particular issue for many developmentalists and parents is discipline, which varies a great deal from family to family and culture to culture. Ideally, parents anticipate misbehavior and guide their children toward patterns of behavior and internalized standards of morality that will help them lifelong. But parents cannot always anticipate and prevent problems.

A study of mothers and 3-year-olds during stressful times found that conflicts (including verbal disagreements) arose about every two minutes (Laible et al., 2008). Here is one example:

> **Child:** I want my other shoes.
> **Mother:** You don't need your other shoes. You wear your Pooh sandals when we go for a walk.
> **Child:** Noooooo.
> **Mother:** [*Child's name*]! You don't need your other shoes.
> **Child:** (*Cries loudly*)
> **Mother:** No, you don't need your other shoes. You wear your Pooh sandals when we go for a walk.
> **Child:** Ahhhh. Want pretty dress. (*Crying*)
> **Mother:** Your pretty dress.
> **Child:** Yeah.
> **Mother:** You can wear them some other day.
> **Child:** Noooooo. (*Crying*)
>
> [*Laible et al., 2008, pp. 442–443*]

In this study, children with secure attachments to their mothers had as many conflicts as the insecurely attached children. However, unlike the mother in the example above, their mothers were likely to compromise and explain.

Even in this simple example, as you see, complexities arise. In every nation and family, adults vary in their expectations for proper behavior. What is "rude" or "nasty" or "undisciplined" behavior in one community is often accepted, even encouraged, in another. Each family needs to decide its values and make them explicit for the child. Parents are often unaware of their ethnotheories—no wonder young children disagree, disobey, and disappoint (Bornstein, 2006; Bugental & Grusec, 2006). Parents may model moral values—such as "Do not question authority"—that they do not intend to instill in their children.

Although experts disagree about particulars, they agree that young children are eager to do what parents wish but cannot always control their bodies or their emotions. For instance, no child deliberately wets the bed, but some parents punish their children for doing so anyway. Cognitive immaturity is also inevitable, as the following explains.

a view from science

Discipline and Children's Thinking

Many developmentalists have studied the relationship between the young child's thinking and his or her behavior. Here are four reminders from Chapter 9:

1. *Remember theory of mind.* Young children gradually come to understand things from other viewpoints. Encouraging empathy ("How would you feel if someone did that to you?") increases prosocial behavior and decreases antisocial behavior.
2. *Remember emerging self-concept.* Young children are developing a sense of who they are and what they want. Adults should protect that emerging self by, for example, not forcing 3-year-olds to share. A child can learn to bring a toy to school only if other children will be allowed to play with it.
3. *Remember fast-mapping.* Young children are eager to talk and think, but they say more than they really understand. Children who "just don't listen" may have heard but not understood a command. Discussion before and after misbehavior helps children learn.
4. *Remember that young children are not logical.* Children confuse a lie and a wish because their minds are not yet logical, and they may disconnect a misdeed from the punishment. If you were spanked as a child, do you remember why?

None of this means that children should never be punished. However, parents need to consider the child's perspective. Often children attribute punishment to parental anger and rejection, not to their own misbehavior.

Parents do not necessarily think of the effects of punishment on children's moral development. For scientists, however, this is crucial. Let us now consider what children learn when their parents punish them.

Physical Punishment

Young children are slapped, spanked, or beaten more often than are children over age 6 or under age 2. Many parents remember being spanked themselves and think spanking works well. Some researchers agree; some do not (Gershoff, 2002; Larzelere & Kuhn, 2005).

However, a developmental perspective reminds us of long-term consequences. Physical punishment succeeds at the moment it is administered—spanking stops a child's misbehavior—but some longitudinal research finds that children who are physically punished are more likely to become bullies, delinquents, and then abusive adults. The moral value they learn is that "might makes right" (Jaffee et al., 2004; Straus, 1994).

Of course, many children who are spanked do not become violent adults. Spanking increases the risk, but other factors (poverty and temperament, among others) are stronger influences. Nonetheless, many developmentalists wonder why parents would take any risk with their child. Physical punishment seems to increase the possibility of long-term aggression while it increases obedience only temporarily (Amato & Fowler, 2002; Gershoff, 2002).

Psychological Control

Spanking is not the only punishment with unintended consequences. Another such method of discipline is **psychological control,** in which children's guilt and gratitude are used to control their behavior (Barber, 2002).

psychological control A disciplinary technique that involves threatening to withdraw love and support and that relies on a child's feelings of guilt and gratitude to the parents.

Consider the results of a study of an entire cohort (the best way to obtain an unbiased sample) of children born in Finland (Aunola & Nurmi, 2004). Their parents were asked 20 questions about their approach to child rearing. The following four items, which the parents rated from 1 ("Not at all like me") to 5 ("Very much like me"), measured psychological control:

1. "My child should be aware of how much I have done for him/her."
2. "I let my child see how disappointed and shamed I am if he/she misbehaves."
3. "My child should be aware of how much I sacrifice for him/her."
4. "I expect my child to be grateful and appreciate all the advantages he/she has."

The higher the parents scored on psychological control, the lower the children's math scores—and this connection grew stronger over time. Surprisingly, math achievement suffered most if parents were high in both affection and psychological control (e.g., they frequently hugged their children) (Aunola & Nurmi, 2004). Other research also finds that psychological control can depress children's achievement, creativity, and social acceptance, although affection does not always make things worse (Barber, 2002).

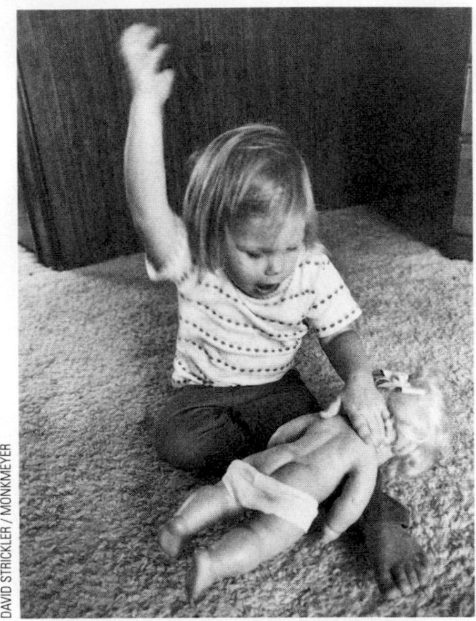

DAVID STRICKLER / MONKMEYER

Angela at Play Research suggests that being spanked is a salient and memorable experience for young children, not because of the pain but because of the emotions. Children seek to do what they have learned; they know not only how to place their hands but also that an angry person does the hitting. The only part of the lesson they usually forget is what particular misdeed precipitated the punishment. Asked why she is spanking her doll, Angela will likely explain, "She was bad."

Social Punishments

The disciplinary technique most often used in North America is the **time-out,** in which an adult requires the misbehaving child to sit quietly, without toys or playmates, for a short time (Barkin et al., 2007). The time must be brief; one minute for each year of the child's age is often suggested.

time-out A disciplinary technique in which a child is separated from other people for a specified time.

Another common practice is *induction,* in which the parents talk with the child, getting the child to understand why the behavior was wrong. Conversation helps children internalize standards, but induction takes time and patience. Since 3-year-olds confuse causes with consequences, they cannot answer an angry "Why did you do that?" nor appreciate a lengthy explanation. Simple induction ("You made him sad") is appropriate for 3-year-olds. In general, induction is recommended if the goal is an internalized standard of right and wrong (Turiel, 2006).

Methods of discipline vary in consequences and effectiveness, depending on temperament, culture, and the adult–child relationship. For example, time-out is effective *if* the child prefers to be with other people. One version of time-out for older children is suspension from school. However, if a child hates school, suspension amounts to reinforcement, not punishment. In fact, if a teacher finds teaching easier when a particular child is absent, the teacher might unconsciously provoke the child to misbehave and thus be suspended. Both the child and the teacher are thereby reinforced, not punished.

Children's personalities and parental pressures vary. As a mother, I know that patient guidance is necessary and that prevention is better than punishment, but emotions can be overwhelming. Rachel, at age 3, took a glass bottle of orange juice from the refrigerator and dropped it on the kitchen floor, where it shattered. I wanted to slap her. "Time out!" I yelled, putting her on the couch (20 feet away) until I cleaned up the mess. I needed that time-out more than she did.

Parents have powerful emotions, memories, and stresses. That's why punishment is not a simple issue. One young child who was disciplined for fighting protested, "Sometimes the fight just crawls out of me." Ideally, punishment won't "just crawl out" of the parent.

SUMMING UP

Moral development occurs throughout childhood and adolescence. During early childhood, the most powerful moral lessons are learned from other children, particularly the need to be appropriately prosocial and antisocial, with aggression controlled. Ideally, children learn to be good friends to each other, particularly avoiding unprovoked aggression. Parents discipline their children in many ways, with each method teaching lessons about right and wrong. Induction seems most likely to lead to internalized standards of morality. ■

➤**Answer to Observation Quiz** (from page 296): The authoritative style. Note the firm hold this woman has on her defiant son; he must listen (evidence that she is not permissive). Also note that she is talking to him, not hitting or yelling, and that her expression is warm (evidence that she is not authoritarian).

Becoming Boys and Girls

Identity as male or female is an important feature of a child's self-concept, a major source of self-esteem (with each gender believing that it is best) (Powlishta, 2004). The first question asked about a newborn is "Boy or girl?" Parents select gender-distinct clothes, blankets, diapers, and even pacifiers. Toddlers already know their own sex, and children become more aware of gender with every passing year (Ruble et al., 2006).

Sex and Gender

Social scientists attempt to distinguish between **sex differences,** which are the biological differences between males and females, and **gender differences,** which are culturally prescribed roles and behaviors. In theory, this seems like a straightforward separation, but, as with every nature–nurture distinction, the interaction between sex and gender makes it hard to separate the two (Hines, 2004).

sex differences Biological differences between males and females, in organs, hormones, and body type.

gender differences Differences in the roles and behavior of males and females that are prescribed by the culture.

Even 2-year-olds apply gender labels (*Mrs., Mr., lady, man*) consistently. By age 4, children are convinced that certain toys (such as dolls or trucks) are appropriate for one gender but not the other (Bauer et al., 1998; Ruble et al., 2006).

Young children confuse gender and sex. Awareness that a person's sex is a biological characteristic, not something that is determined by words, opinions, or clothing, develops gradually. It does not become firm until age 8 or so. Some little girls think that they will grow a penis when they get older, and some little boys offer to buy their mother one at the store.

Uncertainty about the biological determination of sex was demonstrated by a 3-year-old who went with his father to see a neighbor's newborn kittens. Returning home, the child told his mother that there were three girl kittens and two boy kittens. "How do you know?" she asked. "Daddy picked them up and read what was written on their tummies," he replied.

In recent years, cultural acceptance of various types of sexual orientation has increased. Some people of all ages resist the either/or, masculine or feminine, categories. Adults may be bisexual, homosexual, or "mostly straight" as well as heterosexual (Thompson & Morgan, 2008). Young children do not know such terms and may not follow gender norms, acting in ways that traditionally were considered pathological for members of their sex (Zucker, 2005). Despite the shift in the overall culture, at around age 5 children become very aware of sex and gender differences. Many psychologists wonder why.

Theories of Gender Differences

Experts as well as parents disagree about what proportion of observed male–female differences is biological (perhaps originating in hormones, brain structure,

ALAMY

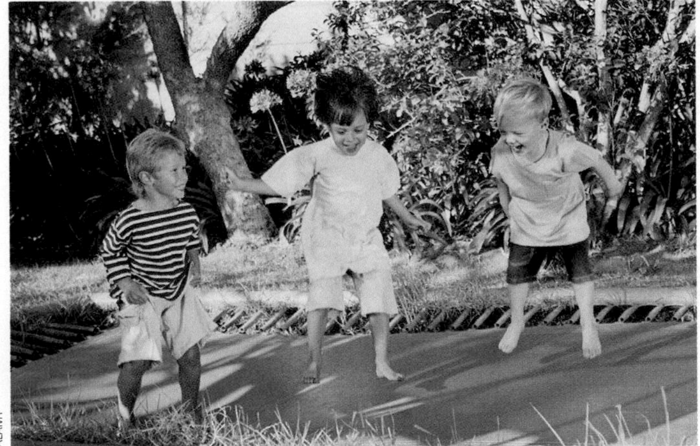

ALAMY

Biology or Culture? Could the trio in the top photo bounce on a trampoline and the three in the bottom photo all eat ice cream cones with multicolored sprinkles? If they did, would their expressions, clothes, closeness, and hair switch as well? Probably not: By age 5, dozens of differences between boys and girls are evident.

body shape) and what proportion is environmental (perhaps embedded in the culture or the family) (Leaper, 2002; Ruble et al., 2006). For example, you read earlier that girls are often ahead of boys in emotional regulation. Is that difference connected to the effect of the twenty-third pair of chromosomes on brain development, or does it arise from the fact that parents treat their sons and daughters differently?

Evidence supports both possibilities. Neuroscientists tend to look for male–female brain differences, and they find many; sociologists tend to look for male–female family and cultural patterns, and they also find many. Historians, anthropologists, political scientists, and psychologists of every perspective have likewise identified both genetic and environmental sources of male–female differences. Consider the explanations for sex or gender differences during early childhood offered by each of the five major theories.

Psychoanalytic Theory

Freud (1938) called the period from about ages 3 to 6 the **phallic stage** because he believed its central focus is the *phallus,* or penis. At about 3 or 4 years of age, said Freud, the process of maturation makes a boy aware of his male sexual organ. He begins to masturbate, to fear castration, and to develop sexual feelings toward his mother.

These feelings make every young boy jealous of his father—so jealous, according to Freud, that every son secretly wants to replace his dad. Freud called this the **Oedipus complex,** after Oedipus, son of a king in Greek mythology. Abandoned as an infant and raised in a distant kingdom, Oedipus later returned to his birthplace and, not realizing who they were, killed his father and married his mother. When he discovered what he had done, he blinded himself in a spasm of guilt.

Freud believed that this ancient story has been replayed for over two millennia because it dramatizes emotions that all boys feel about their parents—both love and hate. Every male feels guilty about the incestuous and murderous impulses that are buried in his unconscious. Boys fear that their fathers will inflict terrible punishment if their secret impulses are discovered.

In self-defense, boys develop a powerful conscience called the **superego,** which is quick to judge and punish. According to Freud, a young boy's fascination with superheroes, guns, kung fu, and the like arises from his unconscious impulse to kill his father. An adult man's homosexuality, homophobia, or obsession with punishment might be explained by an imperfectly resolved phallic stage. Later psychoanalytic theorists agree that morality originates from the clash between unconscious wishes and parental prohibitions in childhood (Hughes, 2007).

Freud offered several descriptions of the phallic stage in girls. One centers on the **Electra complex** (also named after a figure in classical mythology). The Electra complex is similar to the Oedipus complex in that the little girl wants to eliminate the same-sex parent, her mother, and become intimate with the opposite-sex parent, her father. Girls may also develop a superego, although Freud thought it weaker than in boys.

Children of both sexes cope with their guilt and fear through **identification;** that is, they ally themselves with the same-sex parent by taking on that parent's behavior and attitudes. Because they cannot actually replace their same-sex par-

phallic stage Freud's third stage of development, when the penis becomes the focus of concern and pleasure.

Oedipus complex The unconscious desire of young boys to replace their father and win their mother's exclusive love.

superego In psychoanalytic theory, the judgmental part of the personality that internalizes the moral standards of the parents.

Electra complex The unconscious desire of girls to replace their mother and win their father's exclusive love.

identification An attempt to defend one's self-concept by taking on the behaviors and attitudes of someone else.

ents, young boys copy their father's mannerisms, opinions, actions, and so on, and girls copy their mother's. Both sexes exaggerate the male or female role.

Since the middle of the twentieth century, social scientists generally have agreed that Freud's explanation of sexual and moral development "flies in the face of sociological and historical evidence" (David et al., 2004, p. 139). More recently, however, some of Freud's ideas have become more acceptable to psychologists. I have softened my criticism of Freud, as the following explains.

a personal perspective

Berger and Freud

My family's first "Electra episode" occurred in a conversation with my eldest daughter, Bethany, when she was about 4 years old:

Bethany: When I grow up, I'm going to marry Daddy.
Mother: But Daddy's married to me.
Bethany: That's all right. When I grow up, you'll probably be dead.
Mother: (*Determined to stick up for myself*) Daddy's older than me, so when I'm dead, he'll probably be dead, too.
Bethany: That's OK. I'll marry him when he gets born again.

At this point, I couldn't think of a good reply, especially since I had no idea where she had gotten the concept of reincarnation. Bethany saw my face fall, and she took pity on me:

Bethany: Don't worry, Mommy. After you get born again, you can be our baby.

The second episode was a conversation I had with my daughter Rachel when she was about 5:

Rachel: When I get married, I'm going to marry Daddy.
Mother: Daddy's already married to me.
Rachel: (*With the joy of having discovered a wonderful solution*) Then we can have a double wedding!

The third episode was considerably more graphic. It took the form of a "valentine" left on my husband's pillow by my daughter Elissa, who was about 8 years old at the time. It is reproduced here.

Finally, when my youngest daughter, Sarah, turned 5, she also expressed the desire to marry my husband. When I told her she couldn't, because he was married to me, her response revealed one more hazard of watching TV: "Oh, yes, a man can have two wives. I saw it on television."

I am not the only feminist developmentalist to be taken aback by her own children's words. Nancy Datan (1986) wrote about the Oedipal conflict: "I have a son who was once five years old. From that day to this, I have never thought Freud mistaken." Obviously, these bits of "evidence" do not prove that Freud was correct. I still think he was wrong on many counts. But I now find Freud's description of the phallic stage less bizarre than I once did.

Pillow Talk Elissa placed this artwork on my husband's pillow. My pillow, beside it, had a less colorful, less elaborate note—an afterthought. It read "Dear Mom, I love you too."

Behaviorism

In contrast to psychoanalytic theorists, behaviorists believe that virtually all roles are learned and therefore result from nurture, not nature. To behaviorists, gender distinctions are the product of ongoing reinforcement and punishment.

Some evidence supports this aspect of learning theory. Parents, peers, and teachers all reward behavior that is "gender appropriate" more than behavior that is "gender inappropriate." For example, "adults compliment a girl when she wears a dress but not when she wears pants" (Ruble et al., 2006, p. 897). According to social learning theory, children themselves notice the ways men and women behave and then internalize the standards they observe, becoming proud of themselves when they act like "little men" and "little ladies" (Bandura & Bussey, 2004; Bussey & Bandura, 1999).

The male–female distinction seems to be more significant to males than to females (Banerjee & Lintern, 2000; David et al., 2004). Boys are more often criticized for being "sissies" than girls are for being "tomboys." Fathers, more than mothers, expect their daughters to be feminine and their sons to be tough.

Behaviorists believe children learn about proper behavior not only directly (as by receiving a gender-appropriate toy or a father's praise) but also indirectly, through *social learning*. Children model their behavior particularly after that of people they perceive to be nurturing, powerful, and yet similar to themselves. For young children, those people are usually their parents. Parental attitudes about gender differences become increasingly influential as children mature (Tenenbaum & Leaper, 2002).

This theory explains why gender prejudice is particularly strong during early childhood. If a college man wants to teach young children, his classmates will probably respect him and may very well know one or more other men who made the same choice. If a 4-year-old boy says he wants the same thing, however, his peers will laugh because their experience has been quite gender-segregated. As one professor reports:

> My son came home after 2 days of preschool to announce that he could not grow up to teach seminars (previously his lifelong ambition, because he knew from personal observation that everyone at seminars got to eat cookies) because only women could be teachers.
>
> *[Fagot, 1995, p. 173]*

Thus, as young children identify with their own sex, they are reinforced (particularly by fathers and by other children) for acting in gender-specific ways (Berenbaum et al., 2008).

Cognitive Theory

Cognitive theory offers an alternative explanation for the strong gender identity that becomes apparent at about age 5. Remember that cognitive theorists focus on how children understand various ideas. Children develop concepts about their experiences. In this case, a **gender schema** is the child's understanding of sex differences (Kohlberg et al., 1983; Martin et al., 2002; Renk et al., 2006).

gender schema A cognitive concept or general belief based on one's experiences—in this case, a child's understanding of sex differences.

Young children have many gender-related experiences but not much cognitive depth. They tend to see the world in simple terms. For this reason, they categorize male and female as opposites, even when evidence contradicts such a sexist view. Nuances, complexities, exceptions, and gradations about gender (as well as about everything else) are beyond the preoperational child.

Their self-concept leads young children to a cognitive need to categorize themselves as male or female and then to behave in a way that fits their concept. For that reason, cognitive theorists see "Jill's claim that she is a girl because she is wearing her new frilly socks as a genuine expression of her gender identity" (David et al., 2004, p. 147). Similarly, a 3½-year-old boy whose aunt called him *cute* insisted that he should be called *handsome* instead (Powlishta, 2004). Obviously, he had developed gender-based categories, and he wanted others to see him as he conceptualized himself.

Cognitive and social learning theories differ in that "while both theories explain how the social reality of sex differences is internalized, social learning theory proposes that society socializes children, while cognitive developmental theory proposes that children actively socialize themselves" (David et al., 2004, pp. 139–140).

Sociocultural Theory

Proponents of the sociocultural perspective point out that many traditional cultures enforce gender distinctions with dramatic stories, taboos, and terminology. In societies where adult activities and dress are strictly separated by gender, girls and boys attend sex-segregated schools and virtually never play together. Children all over the world adopt whatever patterns of talking, behaving, and even thinking are prescribed for their sex (Leaper & Smith, 2004).

Every society has powerful values and attitudes regarding preferred behavior for men and women, but the particular tasks assigned to males and to females vary. To sociocultural theorists, this proves that society, not biology, segregates the sexes and transmits its version of proper male or female behavior (Kimmel, 2004).

To break through the restrictiveness of culture and to encourage individuals to define themselves primarily as humans, not as males or females, some parents and teachers have embraced the idea of androgyny. **Androgyny** is a balance, within one person, of traditionally masculine and feminine characteristics. To achieve androgyny, boys are encouraged to be nurturing and girls to be assertive so that both will develop less restrictive, gender-free self-concepts (Bem, 1993). This may be an admirable goal, but the fact remains that young adults who are more androgynous are not usually those with higher self-esteem or healthier self-concept (Ruble et al., 2006).

Sociocultural theory holds that parents cannot raise happily androgynous children unless their culture promotes such ideas and practices—something no culture has done. Why not? The reasons may lie buried in human nature, not sociocultural norms. That is what epigenetic theory suggests.

BJORN SVENSSON / ALAMY

BLICKWINKEL / ALAMY

Toy Guns for Boys, Cinderella for Girls
Young boys throughout the world are the ones who aim toy guns, while young girls imagine themselves as a Disney Cinderella, waiting for her handsome prince. The question is why: Are these young monks in Laos and this girl in Mexico responding to biology or to culture?

androgyny A balance, within one person, of traditionally masculine and feminine psychological characteristics.

Epigenetic Theory

We saw in Chapter 2 that epigenetic theory contends that our traits and behaviors are the result of interaction between genes and early experience—not just for each of us as individuals but for the human race as a whole. The idea that gender differences are based in genetics is supported by recent research in neurobiology, which has found dozens of biological differences between male and female brains (Hines, 2004).

Hormones Testosterone and estrogen—the hormones produced prenatally by the XY or XX fetus, respectively—cause sex differences in the brain. Remember that boys with behavior problems tend to externalize their troubles, while girls internalize; this sex difference may be neurological.

For instance, stress tends to increase testosterone in males, making them ready for "fight or flight," but it increases oxytocin (another hormone) in females, making them likely to "tend and befriend" (Taylor, 2006). Even stressed young boys are likely to punch their rivals while stressed girls seek comfort from their friends, a gender difference that may be epigenetic.

ARIEL SKELLEY / CORBIS

Trick or Treat? Any doubt about which of these children are girls and which are boys? No. Any question about whether such strict gender distinctions are appropriate at age 4? Maybe.

In nonhuman creatures, sex differences in the body and brain are legion. For example, male and female voices differ partly because of vocal control systems. In an experiment with fish, male and female hormones quickly changed the brain's impulses and altered vocalization. The researchers believe that this difference may apply to all "vocal vertebrates," including people (Remage-Healey & Bass, 2004).

Nature and Nurture Further epigenetic evidence comes from studies of homosexuals. Home videos of young children frequently reveal atypical gender patterns beginning at age 4 in those who will later be sexually attracted to people of their own sex (Rieger et al., 2008). Neither parental discipline nor rejection differed for children who later identified as heterosexual or homosexual, another result that makes sexual orientation seem more biological than sociocultural.

Although epigenetic theory stresses the biological and genetic origins of behavior, it also appreciates that environment shapes, enhances, or halts those genetic impulses. Here is one example: Girls seem to be genetically inclined to talk earlier than boys, perhaps because in prehistoric times, when women stayed behind to care for the children while the men hunted, women had to become more adept at social interaction. Consequently, female brains evolved to favor language (Gleason & Ely, 2002).

Today, women still specialize in caregiving, using language to show support and agreement, while men are still more assertive, favoring speech that is more directive, with shorter, louder sentences. Even though these are stereotypes that do not necessarily apply to a specific person, genetic adaptation of the species overall may have led to sex differences that began several millennia ago and would take centuries to change.

Researchers repeatedly find that girls tend to be more responsive to language than are boys and that mothers and daughters typically talk to each other more than do fathers and sons (Leaper, 2002; Leaper & Smith, 2004; Maccoby, 1998). Although the female advantage in language is lifelong, it is more apparent during the language-sensitive time from ages 2 to 5 than at any other age (Leaper & Smith, 2004). In the same way, all sex and gender differences may have genetic, hormonal origins that took root millions of years ago.

Gender and Destiny

The first and last of our five major theories (psychoanalytic and epigenetic) emphasize biology. A reader might use those theories to decide that, since gender-based behavior and sexual stereotypes originate in the body and brain, they are difficult to change. But the other three theories—behaviorism, cognitive theory, and sociocultural theory—all present persuasive evidence for the power of family and culture.

Thus, the five major theories lead in two opposite directions:

- Gender differences are rooted in biology.
- Children are shaped by their experiences.

Given the dynamic-systems perspective on development, both conclusions seem valid.

If children responded only to their own inclinations, some might choose behaviors, express emotions, and develop talents that are taboo—even punished—in their culture. In Western societies, little boys might put on makeup, little girls might play with guns, and both sexes might play naked outside in hot weather. Other cultures have quite different gender expectations, but no culture is without male–female distinctions.

That creates a dilemma. Since human behavior is plastic, what gender patterns *should* children learn, ideally? Answers vary among developmentalists as well as among mothers, fathers, and cultures. Was I right to correct my student who told Bethany, "Girls don't fight"?

SUMMING UP

Young boys and girls are seen as quite different, not only by parents and other adults but especially by the children themselves. Gender stereotypes are held most forcefully at about age 6. Each of the five major theories has an explanation for this phenomenon: Freud describes unconscious incestuous urges; behaviorists highlight social reinforcement; cognitive theorists describe immature categorization; sociocultural explanations focus on cultural patterns; and epigenetic theory begins with hormonal differences affecting the brain. Although each of the theories offers an explanation, they do not agree. A dynamic-systems approach recognizes that genes and culture, parents and peers, ideas and customs all interact, affecting each child. Perhaps an eclectic approach, considering all five theories, is needed to understand sex and gender differences. ■

SUMMARY

Emotional Development

1. Regulation of emotions is crucial during the play years, when children learn emotional control. Emotional regulation is made possible by maturation of the brain, particularly of the prefrontal cortex, as well as by experiences with parents and peers.

2. In Erikson's psychosocial theory, the crisis of initiative versus guilt occurs during early childhood. Children normally feel pride and self-esteem, sometimes mixed with feelings of guilt. Shame is also evident, particularly in some cultures.

3. Children are usually internally motivated to try new things during these years. Their high self-esteem makes them proud and adventuresome.

4. Both externalizing and internalizing problems indicate impaired self-control. Many severe emotional problems that indicate psychopathology are first evident during these years.

5. Boys more often manifest externalizing behaviors and girls internalizing behaviors. For both sexes, brain maturation and the quality of early caregiving affect emotional control.

Play

6. All young children enjoy playing—with other children of the same sex, if possible, alone or with parents if not.

7. The specifics of play vary by setting and culture. In contemporary cities, most children's social play occurs in day-care centers.

8. Boys are particularly likely to engage in rough-and-tumble play, learning social skills without hurting each other. Both sexes engage in dramatic play, with girls preferring more domestic, less violent themes.

Challenges for Parents

9. Three classic styles of parenting have been identified: authoritarian, permissive, and authoritative. Generally, children are more successful and happy when their parents express warmth and set guidelines. Parenting that is rejecting and uninvolved is harmful. Punishment should fit not only the age and temperament of the child but also the culture.

10. Children are prime consumers of many kinds of media, usually for several hours a day, often without their parents' involvement. Content is crucial. The themes and characters of many television programs can lead to increased aggression, as shown by longitudinal research.

Moral Development

11. The sense of self and the social awareness of the young child become the foundation for morality. This is evident in both prosocial and antisocial behavior.

12. Children develop standards for aggression. Unprovoked injury (bullying) is considered wrong by children as well as by adults.

13. Parents' choice of punishment can have long-term consequences. Physical punishment may teach lessons that parents do not want their children to learn. Other forms of punishment have long-term consequences as well.

Becoming Boys and Girls

14. Even 2-year-olds correctly use sex-specific labels, and young children become aware of gender differences in clothes, toys, future careers, and playmates. Gender stereotypes, favoritism, and segregation peak at about age 6.

15. Freud emphasized that children are attracted to the opposite-sex parent and eventually seek to identify, or align themselves, with the same-sex parent. Behaviorists hold that gender-related behaviors are learned through reinforcement and punishment (especially for males) and social modeling.

16. Cognitive theorists note that simplistic preoperational thinking leads to gender schema and therefore stereotypes. Sociocultural theorists point to the many male–female distinctions that are apparent in every society and are taught to children.

17. An epigenetic explanation notes that some sex differences result from hormones affecting brain formation. Experiences enhance or halt those neurological patterns.

18. Thus each theory has an explanation for the sex and gender differences that are apparent everywhere. Parents need to decide which differences are useful to encourage and which are destructive.

KEY TERMS

emotional regulation (p. 277)
initiative versus guilt (p. 278)
self-esteem (p. 278)
self-concept (p. 278)
intrinsic motivation (p. 279)
extrinsic motivation (p. 279)
psychopathology (p. 281)
externalizing problems (p. 281)
internalizing problems (p. 281)
rough-and-tumble play (p. 286)
sociodramatic play (p. 287)
authoritarian parenting (p. 289)
permissive parenting (p. 289)
authoritative parenting (p. 289)
neglectful/uninvolved parenting (p. 289)
empathy (p. 294)
antipathy (p. 294)
prosocial behavior (p. 294)
antisocial behavior (p. 294)
instrumental aggression (p. 295)
reactive aggression (p. 295)
relational aggression (p. 295)
bullying aggression (p. 295)
psychological control (p. 298)
time-out (p. 298)
sex differences (p. 299)
gender differences (p. 299)
phallic stage (p. 300)
Oedipus complex (p. 300)
superego (p. 300)
Electra complex (p. 300)
identification (p. 300)
gender schema (p. 302)
androgyny (p. 303)

KEY QUESTIONS

1. How can adults help children develop self-esteem?

2. What are the differences between shame and guilt?

3. What is the connection between psychopathology and emotional regulation?

4. What do children learn from rough-and-tumble play?

5. Describe the characteristics of the parenting style that seems to promote the happiest, most successful children.

6. How does moral development relate to aggression?

7. What is the connection between discipline and morality?

8. How do children change from age 2 to 6 in their male and female roles and behaviors?

9. Describe the differences among three of the five theories about the origins of sex differences.

10. List the similarities between two of the five theories about the origins of sex differences.

APPLICATIONS

1. Observe the interactions of two or more young children. Sort your observations into four categories: emotion, reasons, results, and emotional regulation. Note every observable emotion (expressed by laughter, tears, etc.), the reason for it, the consequences, and whether or not emotional regulation was likely. For example: "Anger: Friend grabbed toy; child suggested sharing; emotional regulation probable."

2. Ask three parents about punishment, including their preferred type, at what age, for what misdeeds, and by whom. Ask your three informants how they were punished as children and how that affected them. If your sources agree, find a parent (or a classmate) who has a different view.

3. Children's television programming is rife with stereotypes about ethnicity, gender, and morality. Watch an hour of children's TV, especially on a Saturday morning, and describe the content of both the programs and the commercials. Draw some conclusions about stereotyping in the material you watched, citing specific evidence (rather than merely reporting your impressions).

4. Gender indicators often go unnoticed. Go to a public place (park, restaurant, busy street) and spend at least 10 minutes recording examples of gender differentiation, such as articles of clothing, mannerisms, interaction patterns, and activities. Quantify what you see, such as baseball hats on eight males and two females or (better but more difficult) four male–female conversations, with gender differences in length and frequency of talking, interruptions, vocabulary, and so on.

PART III The Developing Person So Far: Early Childhood

BIOSOCIAL

Body Changes Children continue to grow from ages 2 to 6, but their rate of growth slows down. Normally the BMI (body mass index) is lower at about age 5 than at any other time of life. Children often become more discriminating eaters, eating too much unhealthy food and refusing to eat certain other foods altogether.

Brain Development Both the proliferation of neural pathways and myelination continue. Specific parts of the brain (including the corpus callosum, prefrontal cortex, amygdala, hippocampus, and hypothalamus) begin to connect, allowing lateralization and coordination of left and right as well as less impulsivity and perseveration. Fine motor skills, such as drawing, develop more slowly. Advances in the limbic system allow emotional control.

Injuries and Maltreatment Injury control and prevention of maltreatment are crucial, since far more children worldwide are harmed by avoidable accidents or deliberate abuse than by disease. Prevention requires that risk factors be reduced (secondary prevention) and that social changes make neglect and abuse less likely (primary prevention).

COGNITIVE

Piaget and Vygotsky Piaget stressed the young child's egocentric, illogical perspective, which prevents the child from grasping concepts such as conservation. Vygotsky stressed the cultural context, noting that children learn extensively from others. Many children develop their own theories, including a theory of mind, as they realize that not everyone thinks as they do.

Language Language abilities develop rapidly. By age 6, the average child knows 10,000 words and demonstrates extensive grammatical knowledge. Young children are quite capable of becoming balanced bilinguals if their social context is encouraging.

Early Childhood Education Young children are avid learners. Child-centered, teacher-directed, and intervention programs can all succeed.

PSYCHOSOCIAL

Emotional Development Self-esteem is usually high during early childhood. In Erikson's stage of initiative versus guilt, self-concept emerges, as does the ability to regulate emotions. Externalizing and internalizing problems signal the need to prevent later psychopathology.

Challenges for Parents Parenting styles that are warm and responsive, with much communication, are most effective in encouraging the child's self-esteem, autonomy, and self-control. Parental guidelines are needed, as is discipline. However, punishment may have long-term consequences.

Moral Development Empathy produces prosocial behavior; antipathy leads to antisocial actions. Aggression takes many forms; instrumental aggression is quite normal; bullying aggression is ominous.

Becoming Boys and Girls Children develop stereotypic concepts of sex differences (biological) and gender differences (cultural). The five major theories give contradictory explanations of nature and nurture, but all agree that sex and gender identities become increasingly salient to young children.

Middle Childhood

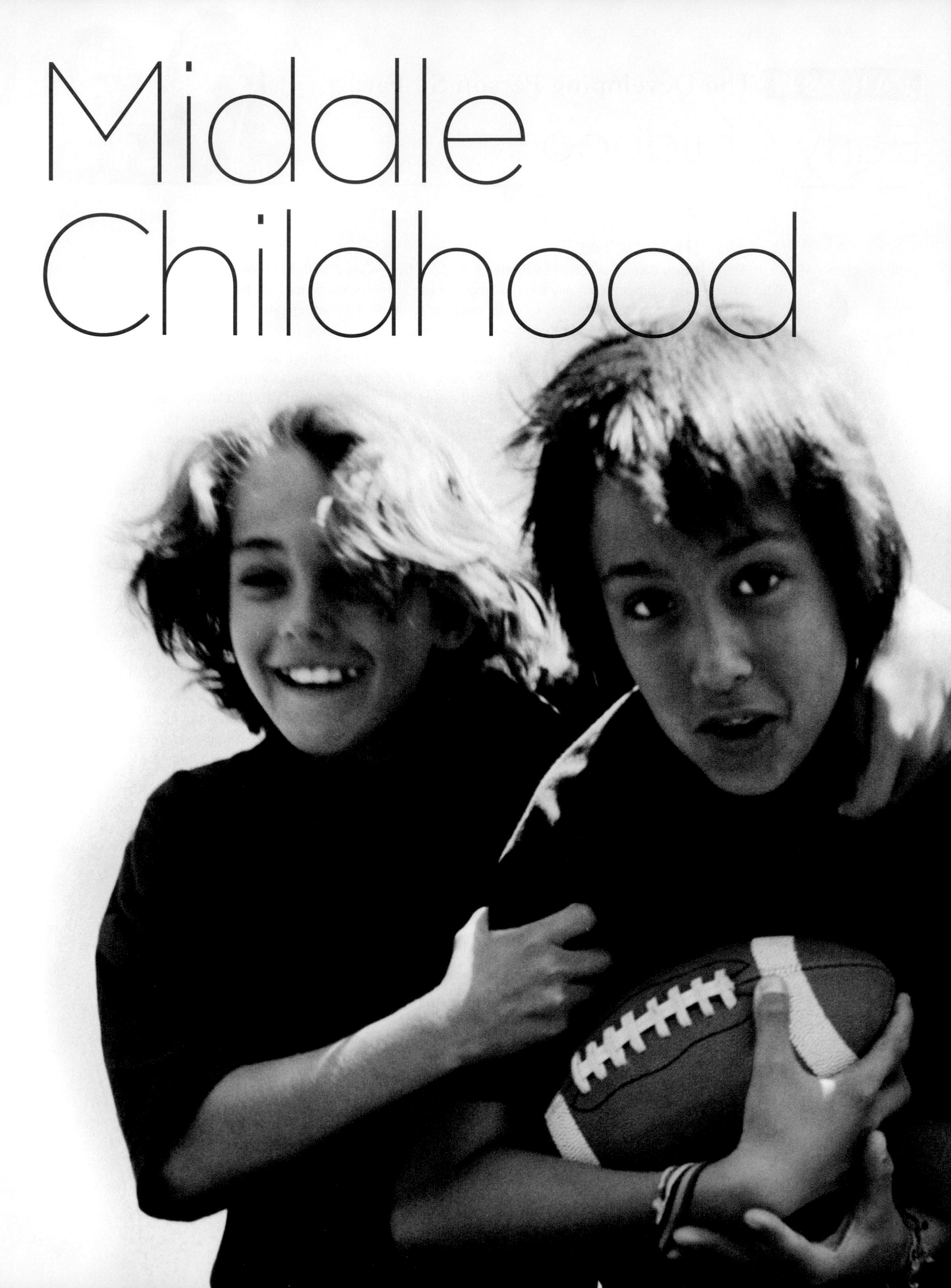

CHAPTER 11

CHAPTER 12

CHAPTER 13

PART IV

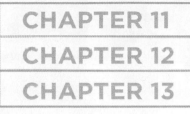

If someone asked you to pick the best years of the entire life span, you might answer like a good developmentalist, saying that every age has joys and sorrows, gains and losses. But if you were pushed to choose just one, you might select ages 7 to 11 and defend your choice persuasively. For many children, these healthy and productive years allow measured (not dramatic) growth; mastery of new athletic skills; acquisition of concepts, vocabulary, and intellectual abilities; a measure of independence from family.

In the twenty-first century, almost all children throughout the world attend school during these years, learning to read and write—abilities that open up new possibilities. Children typically appreciate their parents, make new friends, and are proud of themselves, including their nationality, gender, and ethnicity. For the most part, they are too young for the hazards of addiction, sex, and other dangers.

All this is true for many, but not all. Some school-age children struggle with special educational needs; some live in dysfunctional families; some cope with poverty and even homelessness; some contend with obesity, asthma, learning disabilities, or bullying. For them these years are the worst, not the best. The next three chapters celebrate the joys and acknowledge the difficulties of ages 7 to 11.

11

CHAPTER OUTLINE

Middle Childhood: Biosocial Development

I moved a thousand miles away from my grandparents and friends in the middle of the second grade. Entering a new school, I was self-conscious and lonely. Cynthia had a friendly smile, as well as a quick wit and red hair. More important, she talked to me; she seemed willing to be my friend.

"We cannot be friends," Cynthia said, "because I am a Democrat."

"So am I," I answered. (I knew my family believed in democracy.)

"No you're not. You are a Republican," she said.

I was stunned. We never became friends.

Neither Cynthia nor I realized that each child is unusual in some way (perhaps because of culture, family type, or, in this case, political background) and yet capable of friendship with children from other families. Cynthia must have been told something about my parents' politics that I did not know. I felt sad and rejected.

I wish that some adult had noticed my loneliness and helped us. Cynthia and I could have been good friends, but neither of us knew it.

This chapter describes not only the similarities among all school-age children but also the differences that suddenly become significant—in size, in health, in learning ability, and in almost everything else. Children make comparisons, and almost every child sometimes feels inadequate.

A Healthy Time

Genetic and environmental factors safeguard childhood. Most fatal diseases and accidents occur before age 7 or after age 12. By the school years, a measure of caution, some learned health habits, and several doses of vaccine are protective. Even during past times of high infant mortality and before immunization, school-age children were quite hardy, protected until they reached their reproductive years and could start producing the next generation.

The same factors operate today. **Middle childhood,** the period after early childhood and before adolescence (about age 7 to 11), is the healthiest period of the entire life span (see Figure 11.1). Fatal illness is very rare, and mortal injuries are unusual.

middle childhood The period between early childhood and early adolescence, approximately from ages 7 to 11.

Slower Growth, Greater Strength

The rate of growth slows down by about age 6, so school-age children do not need to adjust to dramatic body changes. That makes it easier for them to

DAVID MERCADO / REUTERS / CORBIS

Expert Eye–Hand Coordination The specifics of motor-skill development in middle childhood depend on the culture. These flute players are carrying on the European Baroque musical tradition that thrives among the poor, remote Guarayo people of Bolivia.

care for themselves—from brushing their teeth to buttoning their jackets, from making their own lunch to walking to school. Children are no longer as dependent on their families, and their bodies do not yet surprise them with the sudden and awkward increases of early adolescence.

Muscles become steadily stronger during the school years. For example, the average 10-year-old can throw a ball twice as far as a 6-year-old. Lungs are muscles, too, and their strength as well as their capacity expands. As a result, with each passing year, children can run faster and exercise longer without breathing more heavily (Malina et al., 2004).

In fact, partly because of slower growth and stronger muscles, during these years children can master almost any motor skill that doesn't require adult size. For instance, 9-year-olds can race their parents on bicycles and often win. The sports most valued by adults (such as basketball and football) require taller, bigger bodies, but school-age children are far superior to younger children in skill as well as larger in size.

Culture, motivation, and practice are crucial, of course. For instance, every schoolchild could probably learn to do a cartwheel, but few do so, because master-

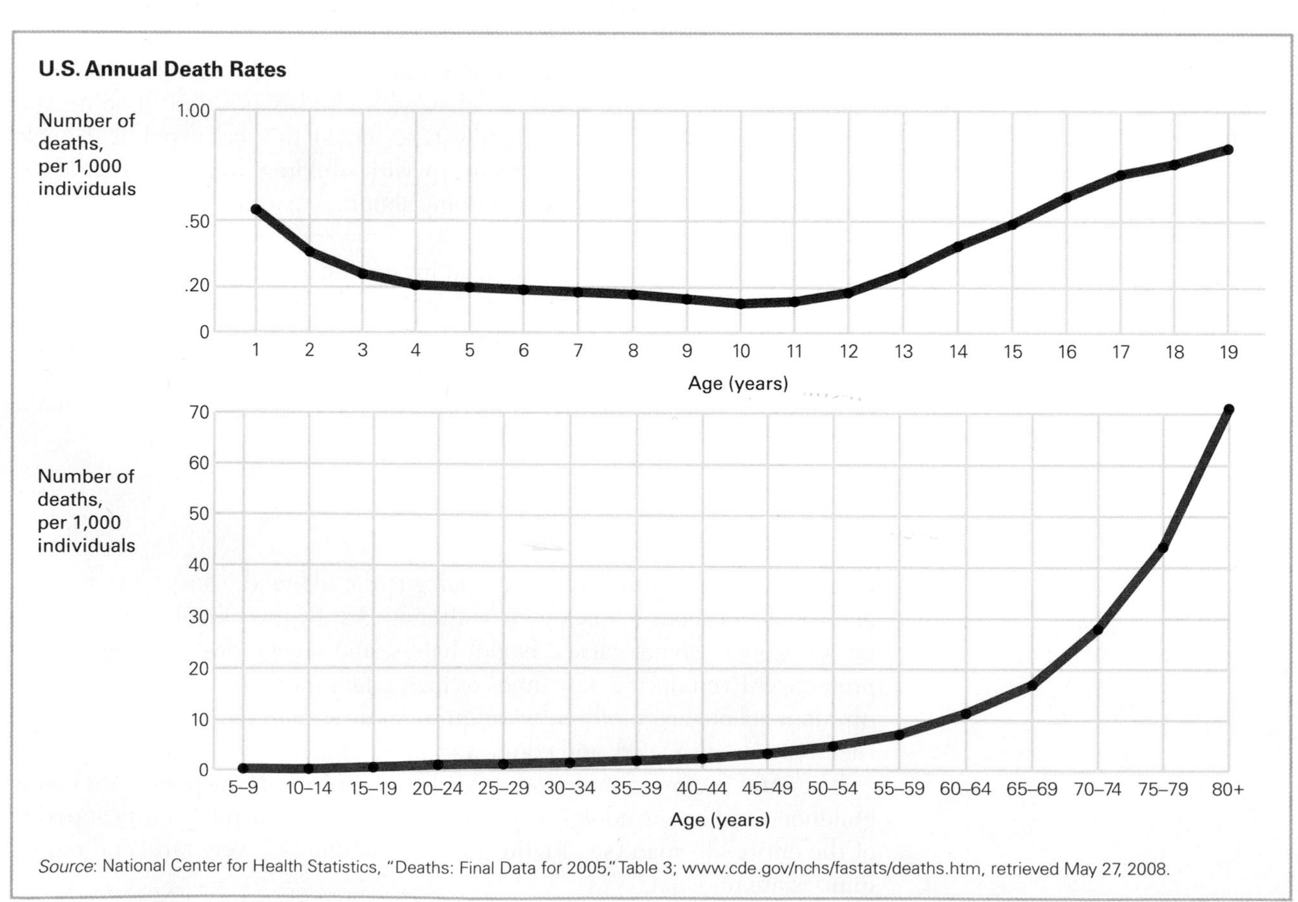

Source: National Center for Health Statistics, "Deaths: Final Data for 2005," Table 3; www.cde.gov/nchs/fastats/deaths.htm, retrieved May 27, 2008.

FIGURE 11.1

Death at an Early Age? Almost Never! Schoolchildren are remarkably hardy, as measured in many ways. These charts show that death rates for 7- to 11-year-olds are lower than those for children under 7 or over 11 and about a hundred times lower than for adults.

Observation Quiz (see answer, page 314): From the bottom graph, it looks as if ages 9 and 19 are equally healthy, but they are dramatically different in the top graph. What is the explanation for this?

ing the cartwheel takes months of practice. Similarly, eating with chopsticks is a fine motor skill attained in chopstick-using cultures by virtually all 6-year-olds (Wong et al., 2002) but by almost no school-age children in other cultures, because they do not practice this skill.

Typically, whether with chopsticks or forks, school-age children in developed nations eat enough, as their bodies grow taller and stronger. Malnutrition is unusual during these years; children are old enough to scavenge food if they need to. Usually, they just go to the kitchen to fix a snack. As the "just-right" obsession fades, children become willing to eat foods they never tried before.

Improved Medical Care

Middle childhood is a healthier time in every nation of the world than it was just 30 years ago. Immunization has reduced deaths dramatically, and serious accidents, fatal illnesses, and even minor diseases are less common.

In the United States, the improved health of school-age children is evidenced in lower prevalence of chronic illnesses, reduced exposure to environmental toxins, and fewer childhood surgeries. Hearing impairments and anemia are half as frequent as they were two decades ago, partly because both conditions are usually diagnosed and treated earlier.

Less Lead Exposure

One evident improvement is the reduced danger of exposure to lead. Elevated blood lead correlates with many disabilities (including mental retardation and hyperactivity) and especially with certain kinds of brain damage.

The widespread use of lead-free gasoline and paint has reduced blood levels of lead in children of all ages. For instance, only 1 percent of 5- to 10-year-olds had elevated lead levels in 2001, compared with almost 30 percent in 1978 (MMWR, May 27, 2005; see the Research Design).

Oral Care

Another area of improvement is oral health. Seventy years ago, many children never brushed their teeth nor saw a dentist. As a result, many of today's elderly people have lost all or most of their teeth. This problem persists in developing nations, where one sign of poverty is missing teeth.

In developed nations, most school-age children now take good care of their teeth; 75 percent of U.S. 6- to 11-year-olds have no untreated cavities (MMWR, August 26, 2005). Parents usually teach them to brush before their first adult teeth emerge (at about age 5 for girls and slightly later for boys). Experts want them to start brushing at age 2 and seeing the dentist by age 3, as Chapter 8 notes. In North America, children with poor oral health tend to have parents from nations where dentists are scarce (Chattopadhyay, 2008).

Dentists can not only protect children against tooth decay (the most common health problem for children) but can also advise children how to keep their mouths healthy. At this age, children

Research Design

Scientists: Nine scientists working for three U.S. government agencies: Environmental Protection, Housing and Urban Development, and Centers for Disease Control and Prevention.

Publication: *Mortality and Morbidity Weekly Report* (MMWR) of May 27, 2005, published by the Massachusetts Medical Society.

Participants: A large, representative U.S. sample is examined every few years as part of NHANES (the National Health and Nutrition Examination Survey). The study cited was the 1999–2002 survey, and these data were from blood tests of 6,283 people aged 6–19.

Design: Blood levels of lead were analyzed by spectrophotometry in a CDC laboratory. The cutoff for an "elevated" level was 10 μg per deciliter, a standard recognized by many public health authorities.

Major conclusion: Compared with previous NHANES data, a marked decrease in blood levels of lead was found among all groups. The decrease was attributed to "coordinated, intensive efforts" that included removing lead from gasoline, paint, and the metal used to make food cans.

Comment: This study confirmed that a public health campaign to reduce exposure to lead was succeeding. The data also reveal some problems: Children under 6 years are about 10 times more likely to have elevated lead levels than are adolescents, and rates are still relatively high among African and Latino Americans.

Back Teeth, Too Under age 5, children brush their teeth quickly and superficially, unlike this thorough, conscientious 8-year-old.

BILDERLOUNGE / SVEN SCHRADER / JUPITER IMAGES

are likely to heed such advice. However, most dentists do not counsel their young patients to avoid tobacco—the leading cause of gum disease, yellowed teeth, and bad breath among adults (Kast et al., 2008).

Children's Health Habits

As you will learn in Chapter 12, school-age children are ready and able to learn whatever adults teach them. They also follow the examples of their peers. Thus, if parents, teachers, and other children all develop good health habits, a child will almost always do the same. That fact is the basis for many special camps for children with asthma, cancer, diabetes, and other chronic illnesses: Once children spend time with others who have the same condition, they are much more amenable to taking care of themselves.

Many adult health problems can be prevented during the school years if two things occur. First, parents must be diligent in providing regular preventive care. This includes oral health (early treatment prevents later tooth loss), eye health (specific exercises can postpone the need for glasses), early intervention for spine curvature (a back brace may encourage normal growth), and immunizations. One form of child maltreatment is medical neglect, when parents do not protect their children's health.

Second, children need to learn good health habits during the school years so that their adolescent rebellion erupts in some way that does not make them sick (such as dyeing their hair green). These are the foundation years for adulthood: For example, the more regular exercise a child gets, the less likely he or she is to suffer a stroke or a heart attack decades later (Branca et al., 2007). The good health that most school-age children enjoy may either continue or be disrupted, depending on basic practices—such as eating a balanced diet, getting enough exercise and sleep, and breathing clean air. The children who are at risk of illness for economic or social reasons (such as low-income children living in crowded cities) are also the most vulnerable to illness lifelong, even if their circumstances improve in adulthood (Buckhalt et al., 2007; Dilworth-Bart & Moore, 2006).

Especially for School Nurses (see response, page 316): For the past month, a 10-year-old fifth-grade girl has been eating very little at lunch and has visibly lost weight. She has also lost interest in daily school activities. What should you do?

Physical Activity

Children often play joyfully, "fully and totally immersed" (Loland, 2002, p. 139). Beyond the sheer fun of playing, the benefits of physical activity—especially games with rules, which school-age children are now able to follow—can last a lifetime. These benefits include:

- Better overall health
- Less obesity
- Appreciation of cooperation and fair play
- Improved problem-solving abilities
- Respect for teammates and opponents of many ethnicities and nationalities

There are hazards as well:

- Loss of self-esteem as a result of criticism from teammates or coaches
- Injuries (the infamous "Little League elbow" is one example)
- Reinforcement of prejudices (especially against the other sex)
- Increases in stress (evidenced by altered hormone levels, insomnia)
- Time and effort taken away from learning academic skills

Where can children reap the benefits and avoid the hazards of active play? Three possibilities are neighborhoods, schools, and sports leagues.

➤Answer to Observation Quiz (from page 312): Look at the vertical axis. From age 1 to 20, the annual death rate is less than 1 in 1,000.

Neighborhood Games

Neighborhood play is flexible; children improvise to meet their needs. Rules and boundaries ("Out of bounds is past the tree" or "the parked truck") are adapted to the context. Stickball, touch football, tag, hide-and-seek, jump rope, and dozens of other games that involve running and catching, or kicking and jumping, can go on forever—or at least until dark. The play is active, interactive, and inclusive—ideal for children.

Modern life has made informal neighborhood games increasingly scarce. Exploding urbanization means that there are fewer open areas that are both fun and safe. For example, Mexico City had an estimated 3 million residents in 1970 and 23 million in 2008; consequently, that overcrowded city's children have less space to play.

Furthermore, many parents keep their children indoors because of "stranger danger"—although "there is a much greater chance that your child is going to be dangerously overweight from staying inside than that he is going to be abducted" (Layden, 2004, p. 96).

Indoor activities like homework, television, and video games all compete with outdoor play in every nation. Providing impoverished children in developing nations with home computers turns out to reduce exercise more than it fosters learning (Malamud & Pop-Eleches, 2008).

MOODBOARD / CORBIS

A Hand Up Neighborhood play is usually cooperative and free-form, but scenes like this one are becoming increasingly rare as the world's children have less access to open space and less time for unstructured play.

Exercise in School

When opportunities for neighborhood play are scarce, physical education in school is an especially crucial alternative. Dedicated and trained gym teachers know developmentally appropriate, cooperative games and exercises for children (Belka, 2004). However, given the way gym class is conducted in many schools, children may enjoy sports but hate physical education. One author cites an example of two children who enjoy playing in sports every weekend but have a different attitude toward sports at school:

> Their current softball unit in physical education hardly provokes any excitement. There are 18 students on each side, sides that are formed in an ad hoc manner each lesson. . . . Few students get turns to pitch, and many are satisfied playing the deepest of outfield positions in order to have minimal involvement in the game.
>
> *[Hastie, 2004, p. 63]*

As schools have come under pressure to increase reading and math knowledge (see Chapter 12), time for physical education and recess has declined. Many children share a confined play space, often spending more time waiting than moving. Many policy makers are unaware that, paradoxically, time spent in school exercise may improve academic achievement (Carlson et al., 2008).

Athletic Clubs and Leagues

Private or nonprofit clubs and organizations offer opportunities for children to play. Culture and family affect the specifics: Some children learn golf, others tennis, others boxing. Cricket and rugby are common in England and in former British colonies such as India, Australia, and Jamaica; baseball is common in Japan, the United States, Cuba, Panama, and the Dominican Republic; soccer is central in many European, African, and Latin American nations.

The best-known organized recreation program for children is Little League. Each year, 2.7 million children play baseball and softball on more than 180,000 teams in 100 countries. When it began in 1939, Little League had only three

"Just remember, son, it doesn't matter whether you win or lose— unless you want Daddy's love."

teams of boys aged 9–12. Now it includes girls, younger and older children, and 22,000 children with disabilities. Coaches usually are volunteers, typically parents, who sometimes put pressure on the children. Nonetheless, most children enjoy organized sports. One adult confesses:

> I was a lousy Little League player. Uncoordinated, small, and clueless are the accurate adjectives I'd use if someone asked politely. . . . What I did possess, though, was enthusiasm. Wearing the uniform—cheesy mesh cap, scratchy polyester shirt, old-school beltless pants, uncomfortable cleats and stirrups that never stayed up—gave me a sort of pride. It felt special and made me think that I was part of something important.
>
> [Ryan, 2005]

Belonging is important to every child, but that point raises a significant problem with organized children's sports: Many children are left out (Collins, 2003). Not all parents have the money to pay their children's fees, the time to transport them to practices and games, and the energy to support their children's teams. Children who are from poor families, who are not well coordinated, or who have disabilities are less likely to belong to sports teams—yet those are the very children who could benefit most from the exercise, since they need the strength, activity, and teamwork that sports can provide.

Indeed, especially for low-income children aged 6–11, participation in structured sports activities correlates with improved academic achievement, less delinquency, and better social relationships (Simkins et al., 2006). Ironically, in difficult economic times, sports programs for children are often the first to be cut. The opposite should be the case, if the well-being of children is the goal.

Especially for Physical Education Teachers (see response, page 318): A group of parents of fourth- and fifth-graders has asked for your help in persuading the school administration to sponsor a competitive sports team. How should you advise the group to proceed?

SUMMING UP

School-age children are usually healthy, strong, and capable. Immunizations during early childhood protect them against contagious diseases, medical care has improved, and developmental advances give them sufficient strength and coordination to take care of their own basic needs (eating, dressing, bathing). Health habits provide a foundation for health status in adulthood. Exercise is crucial, a source of joy and learning for school-age children. However, many children do not get the safe, active play or the ongoing care that they need. Neighborhood play, school physical education, and community sports leagues are all possible settings for the activity that children need, but none reaches all those who would benefit. ■

Two Common Health Problems

Most school-age children are strong and capable, as you have just seen. However, disabilities become more problematic during the school years because they interfere with crucial school learning and peer relationships.

Researchers increasingly recognize that every physical and psychological characteristic of children—including obesity, high blood levels of lead, and mental health problems—is affected by the social context and, in turn, affects that context (Jackson & Tester, 2008). Moreover, some conditions get worse during the school years, including Tourette syndrome, stuttering, and allergies. Even relatively minor problems—such as walking with a limp, wearing glasses, repeatedly having to blow one's nose, or having a visible birthmark—may make children self-conscious. For all these reasons, poor health affects every aspect of a child's life.

➤**Response for School Nurses** (from page 314): Something is wrong, and you (or the school psychologist, or both) should talk to the girl's parents. Ask whether they, too, have noticed any changes. Recommend that the child see her pediatrician for a thorough physical examination. If the girl's self-image turns out to be part of the problem, stress the importance of social support.

Any chronic condition that impairs self-esteem, limits active play, impedes focused attention, or prevents regular school attendance correlates with emotional and social problems of every kind. Here we focus on two conditions that are increasingly prevalent among schoolchildren: obesity and asthma.

Childhood Obesity

Healthy 6-year-olds tend to have the lowest **BMI,** or **body mass index** (a number expressing the relationship of height to weight), of any age group (Guillaume & Lissau, 2002). Those who are stunted (unusually short) are so because of malnutrition earlier in life, not usually at this point. Until puberty, children naturally have less body fat than they will have as adults.

Although undereating is rarely a problem during these years, overeating is (Freedman et al., 2006), as are problems with overweight and obesity. Overweight and obesity are assessed by calculating BMI. Childhood **overweight** is defined as having a BMI above the 85th percentile for age; childhood **obesity** is defined as having a BMI above the 95th percentile. Both percentiles are measured against growth charts for a reference group of children that were published by the U.S. Centers for Disease Control in 1980. A recent study indicated that the prevalence of childhood overweight and obesity may have leveled off—but at very high levels: 32 percent of children and adolescents in the United States were overweight, 16 percent were obese, and 11 percent were extremely obese (Ogden et al., 2008).

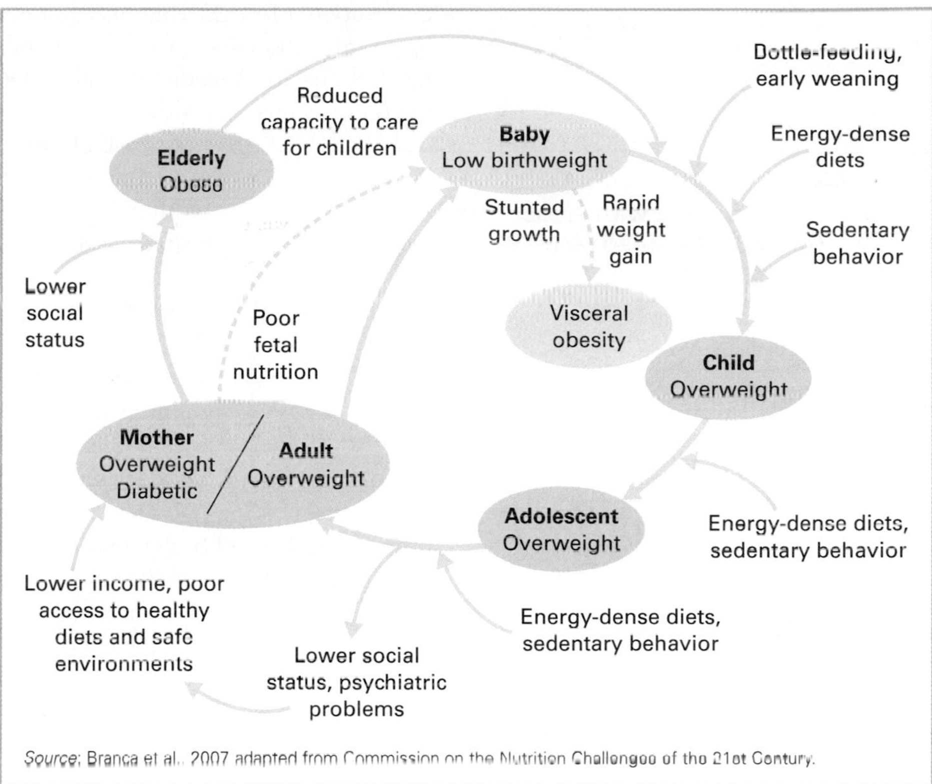

FIGURE 11.2

Inheriting Obesity This schematic diagram shows how sedentary behavior and other factors may influence, and may be influenced by, the weight status of three generations of a family.

The definitions of overweight and obesity for adults are different: a BMI between 25 and 29 for overweight and 30 or above for obesity. By that measure, two-thirds of adults in the United States, and a significant proportion of adults in every other nation, are overweight.

Within nations, eating habits influence what and how much children eat. Culture affects adults, and adults affect children. Thus, obese mothers tend to have overweight babies, whom they often overfeed. Adding to the problem, obese grandparents also overfeed their grandchildren. Obese adults rarely exercise with children, so obesity is handed down from one generation to the next (Branca et al., 2007; see Figure 11.2). Both body shape and depression are partly genetic; for that reason as well, obesity may be considered a family disease.

BMI (body mass index) A person's weight in kilograms divided by the square of height in meters.

overweight In an adult, having a BMI of 25 to 29. In a child, having a BMI above the 85th percentile, according to the U.S. Centers for Disease Control's 1980 standards for children of a given age.

obesity In an adult, having a BMI of 30 or more. In a child, having a BMI above the 95th percentile, according to the U.S. Centers for Disease Control's 1980 standards for children of a given age.

An International Problem

Childhood obesity is becoming an international problem. Historical comparisons from every nation (even China and India, where childhood obesity was once rare) find obesity "increasing at especially alarming rates in children" (Branca et al., 2007, p. 9).

Although overweight is increasing among children everywhere, the rate of increase is slowest in eastern European nations because of a recent dramatic decline in food availability. The rates are highest among groups that experienced food deprivation a few generations ago but now have ample food. In the United States, for example, low-income children and African American children have the highest rates of obesity (Freedman et al., 2006), probably because their elders, in protecting them against a health hazard that no longer exists, are overfeeding them.

TABLE 11.1

Children with Prescriptions (per 1,000 Insured, Age 19 and Under)

Medication for . . .	2001	2004	2007	2001–2007 Change (percent)
Type 2 diabetes	0.48	0.78	1.20	+151.3
High blood pressure	7.03	7.76	8.32	+18.4
Cholesterol problems	0.62	0.67	0.70	+11.6

Source: Saul, 2008.

Instead of providing protection, overfeeding now contributes to sickness. Overweight children are more likely to have asthma, high blood pressure, and elevated levels of cholesterol (especially LDL, the "bad" form of cholesterol). Furthermore, school achievement decreases, self-esteem falls, and loneliness rises, on average, as excessive weight builds (Dietz & Robinson, 2005). Obese children are more likely to die of diabetes, strokes, and liver and heart disease before old age. Many children are now being prescribed adult medicines to treat obesity-related conditions, including type 2 diabetes, high blood pressure, and cholesterol problems (see Table 11.1).

Unless the rate of childhood obesity decreases, today's children in the United States may be the first generation to die at younger ages than their parents (Devi, 2008). Similarly, in India childhood obesity follows a lethal sequence: Underweight infants become overweight children—a "thin-to-fat" pattern that often leads to diabetes in adulthood (Yajnik, 2004).

Especially for Teachers (see response, page 320): A child in your class is overweight, but you are hesitant to say anything to the parents, who are also overweight, because you do not want to insult them. What should you do?

What Causes Childhood Obesity?

To halt the epidemic of childhood obesity, we need to understand the factors that contribute to it. Researchers have focused on three major areas of concern: heredity, parenting practices, and social influences.

Heredity Some people are genetically predisposed to have a high proportion of body fat. More than 200 genes affect weight by influencing activity level, food preference, body type, and metabolic rate (Gluckman & Hanson, 2006). Two copies of a newly discovered gene (an allele called FTO) are inherited by 16 percent of all European Americans and by unknown percentages of other ethnic groups. This gene increases the likelihood of both obesity and diabetes (Frayling et al, 2007).

Parenting Practices Genes change little from one generation to the next and thus cannot have caused the marked increase in obesity. Parenting practices, however, *have* changed dramatically. Obesity is rare if infants are breast-fed for a year, if preschoolers rarely watch TV or drink soda ("pop"), and if school-age children walk or do other forms of exercise for at least an hour every day (Institute of Medicine, 2006; Patrick et al., 2004; Rhee, 2008). Each of these protective factors is much less common today than it was in past decades.

The family's eating habits have a direct impact on a child's weight. As one expert writes, "Fat runs in families but so do frying pans" (Jones, 2006, p. 1879). Fat consumption is increasing in every nation. For example, in western Europe, the average person consumed 110 grams of fat in 1960; that figure rose to 150 grams in 2005 (Branca et al., 2007). Many families eat meat every day and snack regularly on chips, cakes, and ice cream. Children are often bribed to overeat with offers of sugary or fatty treats ("You can't have any dessert until you eat everything on your plate"). Parents' efforts to keep their children from becoming obese may backfire:

> Feeding techniques that parents use to attempt to prevent overweight, including pressure and restriction, can actually promote children's overeating, training children to eat relying on external stimuli and not on internal cues such as hunger and satiety [feelings of fullness].
>
> *[Branca et al., 2007, p. 79]*

➤Response for Physical Education Teachers (from page 316): Discuss with the parents their reasons for wanting the team. Children need physical activity, but some aspects of competitive sports are better suited to adults than to children.

MICHAEL NEWMAN / PHOTO EDIT

Will She Drink Her Milk? The first word many American children learn to read is *McDonald's,* and they all recognize the golden arches. Fast food is part of almost every family's diet—one reason the rate of obesity has doubled in every age group in the United States since 1980. Even if the young girl stops playing with her straw and drinks the milk, she is learning that soda and French fries are desirable food choices.

Social Influences A third source of childhood obesity is "embedded in social policies" (Branca et al., 2007). It is governments, not individual parents, that determine the quality of school lunches; the presence or absence of soda and snack vending machines in schools; the availability and condition of parks, bike paths, and sidewalks; and the cost of fresh vegetables and fruits.

Another social factor is food advertising aimed at children. In the United States, billions of dollars are spent each year to persuade children to eat unhealthy foods. Parents are often unaware of the extent of their children's exposure to these appeals (Linn & Novosat, 2008). Such advertising is illegal in some nations, limited in others, and unrestricted in still others—and a country's rate of childhood obesity correlates with the frequency of children's exposure to food commercials on television (Lobstein & Dibb, 2005; see Figure 11.3).

Especially for Parents (see response, page 320): Suppose that you always serve dinner with the television on, tuned to a news broadcast. Your hope is that your children will learn about the world as they eat. Can this practice be harmful?

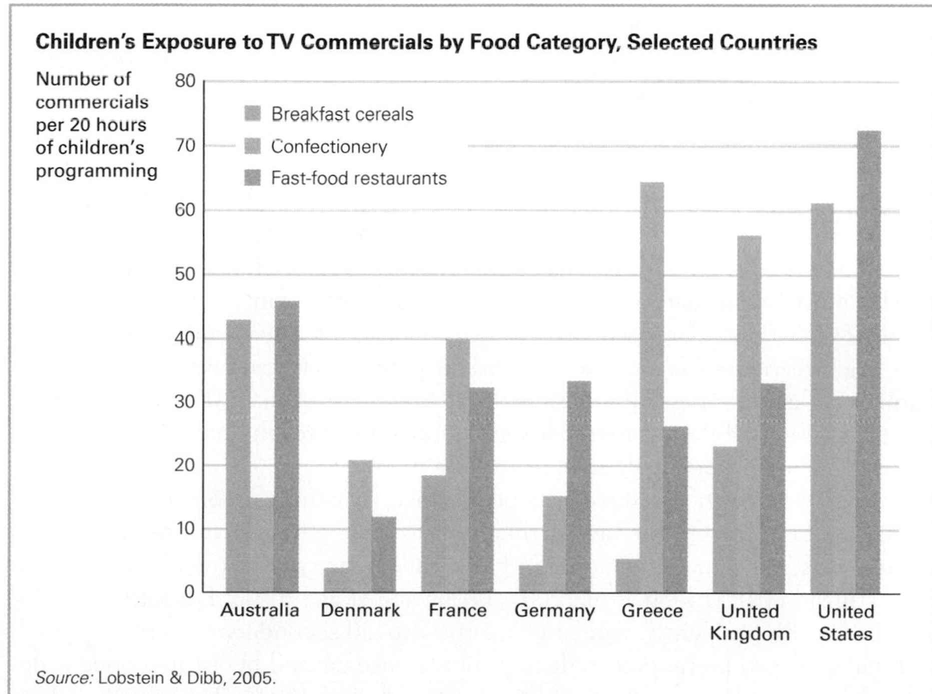

Source: Lobstein & Dibb, 2005.

FIGURE 11.3

A Greek Sweet Tooth? Regulations restricting the number of commercials in children's television programming are one reason for the national differences in exposure shown here. Equally important are cultural differences. Breakfast cereal, for instance, is heavily advertised in the United States because it is much more common in that country than elsewhere.

Most experts contend that changes in such social factors are necessary, but it is unclear which measures would markedly reduce obesity. For instance, childhood obesity correlates with hours of TV watched per day, but controlled experiments are needed to establish whether there is also a *causal* connection (Philipsen & Brooks-Gunn, 2008).

Asthma

asthma A chronic disease of the respiratory system in which inflammation narrows the airways from the nose and mouth to the lungs, causing difficulty in breathing. Signs and symptoms include wheezing, shortness of breath, chest tightness, and coughing.

Asthma is a chronic inflammatory disorder of the airways that makes breathing difficult. Although asthma affects people of every age, rates are highest among school-age children and are increasing worldwide (Bousquet et al., 2007). In the United States, asthma affects 9 percent of all children under age 18, with higher rates for Puerto Rican (19 percent) and African American (13 percent) children. These rates are about twice as high as they were in 1980 (Akinbami, 2006).

Causes of Asthma

Many researchers are studying the possible causes of asthma, including genes. Suspect alleles have been identified, but asthma has various genetic roots (Bossé & Hudson, 2007), which makes it difficult to predict who is most vulnerable.

Although genetic factors increase the risk, environment is crucial. Some experts suggest a "hygiene hypothesis"—that contemporary children are so overprotected from viruses and bacteria that they do not get the infections and childhood diseases that would strengthen their immune systems (Busse & Lemanske, 2005; Tedeschi & Airaghi, 2006). In other words, *too much* hygiene may be a problem.

Several aspects of modern life—carpets, pets inside the home, airtight windows, less outdoor play—are known to contribute to the increased rates of asthma (Tamay et al., 2007). Many allergens that trigger asthma attacks (pet dander, cigarette smoke, dust mites, cockroaches, and mold) are more concentrated in today's well-insulated homes than in the houses of a century ago.

Air pollution is also a problem. A study in Mongolia, where many people still live in sparsely populated rural areas, confirmed that asthma increases with modern city life, although poverty puts rural as well as urban Mongolians at higher risk for asthma (Viinanen et al., 2007).

Prevention of Asthma

➤**Response for Teachers** (from page 318): Speak to the parents, not accusingly (because you know that genes and culture have a major influence on body weight), but helpfully. Alert them to the potential social and health problems their child's weight poses. Most parents are very concerned about their child's well-being and will work with you to improve the child's snacks and exercise level.

The three levels of prevention discussed in Chapter 8 apply to every chronic health problem, including asthma. *Primary prevention* is the most difficult because it requires changes in the entire society. Better ventilation of schools and homes, decreased pollution, eradication of cockroaches, and construction of more outdoor play areas would make asthma less common as well as benefiting all children.

The need for primary prevention became evident during the 1996 Summer Olympics in Atlanta, Georgia. Various measures aimed at reducing traffic congestion (e.g., free mass transit) also reduced air pollution and, unexpectedly, cut the number of asthma attacks almost in half (Friedman et al., 2001). Researchers using an entirely different methodology found similar results regarding air pollution and asthma in Beijing (Pan et al., 2007).

➤**Response for Parents** (from page 319): Habitual TV watching correlates with obesity, so you may be damaging your children's health rather than improving their intellect. Your children would probably profit more if you were to make dinner a time for family conversation.

Secondary prevention reduces the occurrence of asthma among high-risk children. If asthma runs in the family, then breast-feeding babies and ridding homes of dust, pets, cockroaches, smoke, and other allergens can cut the rate of allergies and asthma in half (Elliott et al., 2007; Gdalevich et al., 2001). For asthma (as for all other health problems), regular checkups also aid secondary prevention.

Finally, *tertiary prevention* (reducing the damage caused by asthma once it develops) includes the prompt use of injections and inhalers, which markedly reduce acute wheezing and overnight hospitalizations (Glauber et al., 2001). The use of hypoallergenic materials (e.g., for mattress covers) can also reduce the rate of asthma attacks—but not by much, probably because tertiary prevention at home occurs too late (MMWR, January 14, 2005).

Children reflect their parents' attitudes, particularly regarding preventive care. Only half of a group of 8- to 16-year-olds with asthma followed their doctor's advice about medication; older, minority, and low-income children were least likely to comply, partly because their parents were also least likely to have regular contact with a medical professional (McQuaid et al., 2003). Such a lack of compliance is a major problem among older children with just about every chronic condition, including diabetes, PKU, and sickle-cell anemia. This underscores the need for developing good health habits before adolescence.

KATHY McLAUGHLIN / THE IMAGE WORKS

Pride and Prejudice In some city schools, asthma is so common that using an inhaler is a sign of prestige, as suggested by the facial expressions of these two boys. The "prejudice" is more apparent beyond the walls of this school nurse's room, in a society that allows high rates of childhood asthma to occur.

Adequate tertiary prevention occurs for less than half the children with asthma in the United States. One reason is economic: One-third of school-age children, including more than half of African American and Latino children, have no health insurance. Another reason is mistrust of doctors (most of whom are European American, high-income, older men) by parents (who are often minority, low-income young women). A third reason is that some parents do not provide timely help for their children with asthma (Sales et al., 2008). Asthma and most other health problems are best treated before an emergency, but some parents ignore health problems until they become chronic and serious.

SUMMING UP

Some children have chronic health problems that interfere with their learning in school and with their friendship formation. Among these are obesity and asthma. Both of these conditions are increasing among school-age children, and both have genetic and environmental causes. Parents' habits and care are part of the reason for these increases. Many society-wide practices and customs also affect the incidence.

Brain Development

Recall that emotional regulation, theory of mind, and left–right coordination emerge in early childhood. The maturing corpus callosum connects the two hemispheres of the brain. The prefrontal cortex—the executive part of the brain—plans, monitors, and evaluates. These developments continue in middle childhood. We look now at advances in reaction time, attention, and automatization and at ways to measure brain activity. These measurements include tests of ability and achievement that indicate whether a child is developing as expected.

Advances in Brain Functioning

Increasing myelination results "by 7 or 8 years of age, in a massively interconnected brain" (Kagan & Herschkowitz, 2005, p. 220). One consequence is a reduction in **reaction time,** the length of time it takes to respond to a stimulus. Reaction time shortens every year from birth until about age 16. Over the decades of adulthood, reaction time very slowly lengthens again. Consequently, on average, grandparents might lose to a teenage grandchild at rapid-response video games but be fairly matched with an 8-year-old.

reaction time The time it takes to respond to a stimulus, either physically (with a reflexive movement such as an eye blink) or cognitively (with a thought).

Advances in the "mental control processes that enable self-control" (Verté et al., 2005, p. 415) allow planning for the future, which is beyond the ability of the impatient younger child. Now children can analyze possible consequences before they lash out in anger or dissolve in tears, and they can figure out when a curse word seems advisable (on the playground to a bully, perhaps) and when it does not (in the classroom or at home).

Paying Attention

selective attention The ability to concentrate on some stimuli while ignoring others.

Neurological advances allow children to process different types of information in many areas of the brain at once and to pay special heed to the most important elements. **Selective attention,** the ability to concentrate on some stimuli while ignoring others, is crucial for early school competence (NICHD Early Child Care Research Network, 2003). Selective attention requires ongoing myelination and the increased production of neurotransmitters (chemical messengers). It improves noticeably at about age 7. School-age children not only notice various stimuli (which is one form of attention) but can also judge the appropriate response when several possibilities conflict (Rueda et al., 2007).

In the classroom, selective attention allows children to listen, take concise notes, and ignore distractions (all very difficult at age 6, easier by age 10). In the din of the school cafeteria, children can understand one another's gestures and expressions and respond quickly. Selective attention is also evident on the baseball diamond: Older batters ignore the other team's attempts to distract them, and alert fielders start moving into position as soon as a ball is hit their way. Selective attention underlies all the abilities that gradually mature during the school years.

automatization A process in which repetition of a sequence of thoughts and actions makes the sequence routine, so that it no longer requires conscious thought.

Automatization

Another major advance in brain function in middle childhood is **automatization,** the repetition of a sequence of thoughts and actions until it becomes automatic, or routine. At first, almost all behaviors under conscious control require careful and slow thought. After many repetitions, as neurons fire in sequence, actions become automatic and patterned. Less thinking is needed because firing one neuron sets off a chain reaction.

Neurons at Work Brain development is evident in this duet, since both singing and playing the piano require selective attention, practice, and automatization. These girls are about 9 years old; compare their proficiency with the piano banging and off-key singing of the typical preschooler.

DIGITAL VISION / GETTY IMAGES

Increased myelination and hours of practice lead to the "automatic pilot" of cognition (Berninger & Richards, 2002). Consider a child learning to read. At first, eyes (sometimes aided by a finger) focus intensely, painstakingly making out letters and sounding out each one. This sequence of actions leads to perception of syllables and then words. Eventually the process becomes so automatic that a glance at a billboard results in reading it without any intentional effort.

Automatization is apparent in the acquisition of every skill. Learning to speak a second language, to recite the multiplication tables, and to write one's name are all slow at first but then gradually become automatic. The reason for this advance is a transformation to a more efficient form of neural processing, freeing the brain for more advanced reading, speaking, computation, and writing (Berninger & Richards, 2002). Practice makes perfect (almost).

One study used brain scans to trace how children and adults understood irony. Although it was obvious from the context that a statement was ironic, children had to exert considerable mental effort (using the prefrontal cortex) to understand the words, because they take most of what they hear quite literally. By adulthood, automatization had occurred, and comprehending irony no longer took much deliberate, conscious mental effort. The prefrontal cortex was relatively inactive (Wang et al., 2006).

Measuring the Mind

Measuring developmental changes in brain functioning can be done via repeated brain scans, such as fMRI. One laboratory reported that the cortex (the top layers of the brain) is relatively thin at the beginning of childhood and then grows thicker during the school years, reaching a peak at about age 8. The brains of children who are very intelligent follow the same pattern, but the process is more pronounced: Their cortexes change from being notably thinner than average to notably thicker, and the thickening develops more slowly, particularly in the prefrontal cortex (Miller, 2006).

Intriguing research like this is difficult and expensive; this study has not yet been replicated or even fully understood. More often, mental processes are measured via children's answers to questions on standardized tests. Each child's answers are compared with those of other children who are the same age (to assess aptitude) or in the same school grade (to measure achievement).

aptitude The potential to master a specific skill or to learn a certain body of knowledge.

IQ test A test designed to measure intellectual aptitude, or ability to learn in school. Originally, intelligence was defined as mental age divided by chronological age, times 100—hence the term *intelligence quotient*, or *IQ*.

achievement test A measure of mastery or proficiency in reading, mathematics, writing, science, or some other subject.

Aptitude, Achievement, and IQ

In theory, **aptitude** is the potential to master a specific skill or to learn a certain body of knowledge. The most important aptitude for school-age children is intellectual aptitude, or the ability to learn in school. Intellectual aptitude is measured by **IQ tests** (see Figure 11.4).

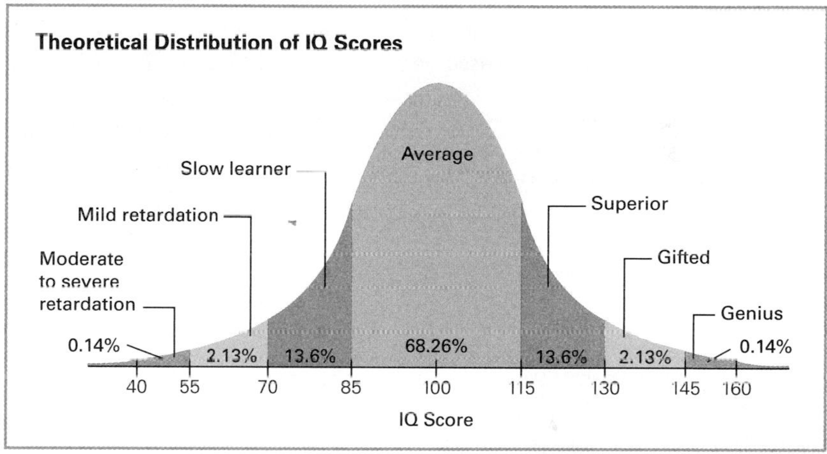

FIGURE 11.4

In Theory, Most People Are Average Almost 70 percent of IQ scores fall within the normal range. Note, however, that this is a norm-referenced test. In fact, actual IQ scores have risen in many nations; 100 is no longer exactly the midpoint. Furthermore, in practice, scores below 50 are slightly more frequent than indicated by the normal curve shown here, because severe retardation is the result not of the normal distribution but of genetic and prenatal factors.

Observation Quiz (see answer, page 325): If a person's IQ is 110, what category is he or she in?

In theory, achievement is distinct from aptitude. Achievement is not what a person *might* learn but what a person *has* learned. **Achievement tests** are taken routinely by students, as mandated in the United States by the No Child Left Behind Act (see Chapter 12), and they are used in many international assessments. Achievement is measured in reading, mathematics, writing, science, and other subjects, with norms established in each subject for children of a certain age or grade.

The words *in theory* precede those definitions because even though aptitude and achievement tests are designed to measure different characteristics, their scores are highly correlated. This is true not just for individuals but also for nations, according to a study of 46 countries (Lynn & Mikk, 2007). Both aptitude and achievement also correlate with wealth, individually and nationally (Lynn & Vanhanen, 2002).

Calculating IQ *IQ* is an abbreviation for "intelligence quotient." Originally, an IQ score was an actual quotient: Mental age (as indicated by how old children typically are when they achieve that test score) was divided by the child's actual chronological age, and the result was then multiplied by 100. Obviously, children whose test performance equals the average performance of children who are exactly the child's age have a mental age equal to their chronological age. In that case, mental age divided by chronological age equals 1, and 1 times 100 gives an IQ of 100. Thus, an IQ of 100 is exactly average.

The current method of calculating IQ is more complicated, but it is still assumed that a child's aptitude for learning increases with age, through adolescence, so dividing the score by years of age equals the IQ. For instance, an 8-year-old who answered as well as a typical 10-year-old would score at $10/8 \times 100 = 125$. In adulthood, aptitude is assumed *not* to change year by year. About two-thirds of people of all ages (calculated differently for children and adults) have an IQ between 85 and 115. Almost all (96 percent) are between 70 and 130.

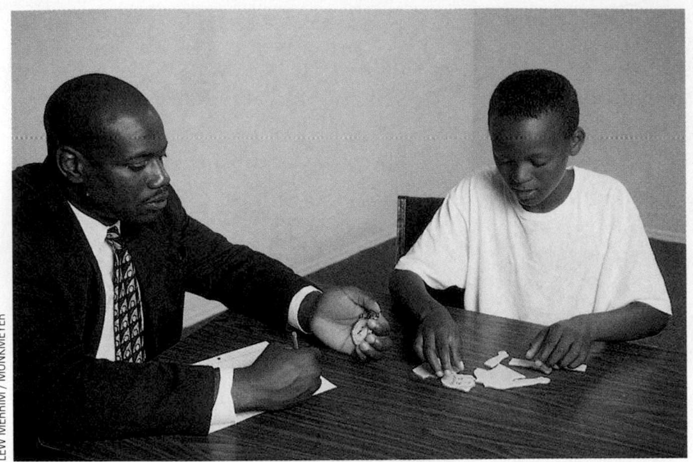
LEW MERRIM / MONKMEYER

Performance IQ This puzzle, part of a performance subtest on the Wechsler IQ test, seems simple until you try it. The limbs are difficult to align correctly, and time is of the essence. This boy has at least one advantage over most African American boys who are tested. Especially during middle childhood, boys tend to do better when their examiner is of the same sex and ethnicity.

Highly regarded and widely used IQ tests include the *Stanford-Binet* test, now in its fifth edition (Roid, 2003), and the *Wechsler* tests. There are Wechsler tests for preschoolers (the WPPSI, or Wechsler Preschool and Primary Scale of Intelligence), for adults (the WAIS, or Wechsler Adult Intelligence Scale), and for school-age children—the **WISC, or Wechsler Intelligence Scale for Children,** now in its fourth edition (Wechsler, 2003).

The WISC has 10 subtests, including tests of vocabulary, general knowledge, memory, and spatial comprehension, each of which provides a score. The Wechsler tests allow calculation of two IQ scores, one "verbal" (measured by tests of vocabulary, word problems, etc.) and the other "performance" (measured by tests that involve solving puzzles, copying shapes, etc.).

Wechsler Intelligence Scale for Children (WISC) An IQ test designed for school-age children. The test assesses potential in many areas, including vocabulary, general knowledge, memory, and spatial comprehension.

Flynn effect The rise in average IQ scores that has occurred over the decades in many nations.

Interpreting IQ Tests A child's IQ score predicts later educational attainment and then adult success. To be specific, children with high IQs usually earn good grades in school and graduate from college. As adults, they typically hold professional or managerial jobs, marry, and own homes (Sternberg et al., 2001).

The average IQs of entire nations have risen substantially—a phenomenon called the **Flynn effect,** after the researcher who first described it (Flynn, 1999). At first, the Flynn effect was doubted because IQ was thought to be totally genetic and genes don't change. But developmentalists now agree that the Flynn effect is real (Rodgers & Wänström, 2007) and believe that the reasons are environmental, including better health, smaller families, and more schooling in nations with higher scores (Flynn, 2007).

Identifying Gifted or Retarded Children A child with a very high IQ (usually above 130) may be considered unusually smart and placed in "gifted and talented" classes. In the United States, school policies and programs for such children vary from state to state. In 2004, 9 percent of children (more girls than boys) in New York State were in gifted classes; in New Mexico, only 1 percent (more boys than girls) were (National Center for Education Statistics, 2007). High IQs are as common among children in both states, but adults—voters, legislators, educators—in each state have decided to educate these children in different ways.

mental retardation Literally, slow, or late, thinking. In practice, people are considered mentally retarded if they score below 70 on an IQ test and if they are markedly behind their peers in adaptation to daily life.

Thirty years ago, the definition of **mental retardation** was straightforward: All children or adults with an IQ below 70 were classified as mentally retarded, with further subdivisions for progressively lower scores: mild retardation, 55–70; moderate retardation, 40–54; severe retardation, 25–39; profound retardation, below 25.

Historically, each of these categories signified different expectations, from "educable" (mildly retarded, able to learn to read and write) to "custodial" (profoundly retarded, unable to learn any skills). However, the mere label *mentally retarded* sometimes led parents and teachers to expect less than the child was actually capable of; consequently, the child's learning was reduced.

Furthermore, in the population as a whole, where the average IQ is 100, only about 2 percent of children score below 70; but children in many immigrant, low-income, and minority groups have an average IQ well below 100. This does not mean that they are less intelligent than other children. In fact, many immigrant children do better in school than do native-born children, in both the United States and Canada. Rather, the lower IQ scores of those children probably stem not from a lack of intellectual aptitude but from cultural bias embedded in the IQ tests. The obviously unfair result is that disproportionate numbers of those children (significantly more than 2 percent) were designated mentally retarded (Edwards, 2006; Pennington, 2002).

In an attempt to remedy that situation, one current definition of mental retardation stipulates that, in addition to having an IQ below 70, children who are designated as mentally retarded must be far behind their peers in adaptation to life. Thus, a 6-year-old who, without help, gets dressed, fixes breakfast, walks to school, and knows the names of her classmates would not be considered mentally retarded, even if she had an IQ of 65. Adaptation is often measured with the Vineland Test of Adaptive Intelligence or some other assessment tool (Venn, 2004).

Some educators prefer not to use the term *mentally retarded* at all, since most children who are slow in some areas are not slow overall. In the United States, fewer children are classified as mentally retarded than in earlier years, because more children have a specific diagnosis, such as autism or learning disability. Their overall IQ may be under 70, but labeling them mentally retarded is less helpful than other designations.

➤Answer to Observation Quiz (from page 323): He or she is average. Anyone with a score between 85 and 115 is of average IQ.

Criticisms of IQ Testing

Many developmentalists criticize IQ tests. They argue that no test can measure potential without also measuring achievement and that every test score reflects the culture of the people who wrote, administer, and take it (Armour-Thomas & Gopaul-McNicol, 1998; Cianciolo & Sternberg, 2004). Even tests designed to be culture-free (asking children to draw a person or to name their classmates) depend on cultural experiences.

Developmentalists also know that intellectual potential changes over the life span; thus, a low-IQ designation might prevent a child from fulfilliing his or her potential. A child who needs special education in an early grade might later be above average, or even gifted, like my nephew David (see Chapter 1). Like any other psychological test, an IQ test is a snapshot, providing a static, framed view of a dynamic, ever-developing brain at work.

Many measures, not simply an IQ test, are now used to indicate aptitude. If an 8-year-old cannot read, for instance, vision and hearing assessments are done; then tests of comprehension, word recognition, and phonetic skills are given to supplement the IQ test. If brain damage is suspected, tests of balance and coordination ("Hop on one foot," "Touch your nose") or of brain–eye–hand connection ("Copy this drawing of a diamond") are useful.

Even with a battery of tests, assessment may be inaccurate, especially when tests that have been standardized in the United States are used in cultures where academic intelligence is not prized (Sternberg & Grigorenko, 2004).

© OWEN FRANKEN / STOCK, BOSTON

Demonstration of High IQ? If North American intelligence tests truly reflected all aspects of the mind, children would be considered mentally slow if they could not replicate the proper hand, arm, torso, and facial positions of a traditional dance, as this young Indonesian girl does brilliantly. She is obviously adept in kinesthetic and interpersonal intelligence. Given her culture, it would not be surprising if she were deficient in the logical-mathematical intelligence required to use the Internet effectively or to surpass an American peer in playing a video game.

> Like many other Western technological inventions (such as the printing press, the sewing machine, the bicycle, and the tractor), the intelligence test (popularly known as the IQ test) has been widely exported around the world. Like tractors, intelligence tests bring with them both ostensible utility and hidden implications.
>
> *[Serpell & Haynes, 2004, p. 166]*

A more fundamental criticism concerns the very concept that there is one general thing called intelligence (often referred to as *g*, for general intelligence). Humans may have *multiple intelligences.* If they do, then using a test to find one IQ score is based on a false premise. Robert Sternberg (1996) describes three distinct types of intelligence:

- *Academic,* measured by IQ and achievement tests
- *Creative,* evidenced by imaginative endeavors
- *Practical,* seen in everyday problem solving

Other psychologists stress a kind of intelligence called *emotional intelligence,* which includes the ability to regulate one's emotions and perceptive understanding of other people's feelings. Emotional intelligence is thought to be more important than intellectual ability in determining success in adulthood (Goleman, 1995; Salovey & Grewal, 2005).

The most influential of all multiple-intelligence theories is Howard Gardner's, which originally described seven intelligences: linguistic, logical-mathematical, musical, spatial, bodily-kinesthetic (movement), interpersonal (social understanding), and intrapersonal (self-understanding). An eighth, naturalistic (understanding of nature, as in biology, zoology, or farming), and ninth, existential (asking questions about life and death), were recently added (Gardner, 1983, 1999, 2006; Gardner & Moran, 2006).

Especially for Teachers (see response, page 328): What are the advantages and disadvantages of using Gardner's eight intelligences to guide your classroom curriculum?

A person might be gifted spatially but not linguistically (a visual artist who cannot describe her work), or someone might have interpersonal but not naturalistic intelligence (a gifted clinical psychologist whose houseplants wither). Gardner's theory has been influential in education, especially with young children (e.g., Rettig, 2005); it has also been widely criticized (Kincheloe, 2004; Visser et al., 2006; Waterhouse, 2006).

According to all those (Sternberg and Goleman, as well as Gardner) who hold that humans have multiple intelligences, standard IQ tests measure only part of brain potential. If intelligence is a multifaceted jewel, then schools need to expand their curricula and tests, so that every child can shine (Williams et al., 2006).

SUMMING UP

During middle childhood, neurological maturation allows faster, more automatic reactions. Selective attention enables focused concentration in school and in play. Aptitude tests, including IQ tests, compare mental age to chronological age. Actual learning is measured by achievement tests. Determining who is gifted and who is retarded may be useful for educators, but IQ scores change much more than was originally imagined. Adaptation to circumstances is crucial, as is culture. The concept that an IQ score measures an underlying aptitude (*g*) is challenged by Robert Sternberg, Howard Gardner, and others, who believe that the brain contains not just one aptitude but many. ■

Children with Special Needs

Parents watch with pride as their offspring become smarter, taller, and more skilled. These feelings may mingle with worry when their children are not like other children. Often slowness, impulsiveness, or clumsiness is the first problem to be noticed; other problems become apparent once formal education begins.

Such problems characterize **children with special needs,** who require extra help in order to learn because of differences in their physical or mental characteristics. Many of them seem fine until they encounter the demands of primary school. One example is Billy.

children with special needs Children who, because of a physical or mental disability, require extra help in order to learn.

a personal perspective

Billy: Dynamo or Dynamite?

Billy was born full term after an uncomplicated pregnancy; he sat up, walked, and talked at the expected ages. His parents were proud of his energy and curiosity: "Little Dynamo" they called him affectionately. He began to read on schedule, and he looked quite normal. But when Billy was in third grade, his teacher, Mrs. Pease, referred him to a psychiatrist because his behavior in class was "intolerably disruptive" (Gorenstein & Comer, 2002, p. 250), as the following episode illustrates:

> Mrs. Pease had called the class to attention to begin an oral exercise: reciting a multiplication table on the blackboard. The

first child had just begun her recitation when, suddenly, Billy exclaimed, "Look!" The class turned to see Billy running to the window.

"Look," he exclaimed again, "an airplane!"

A couple of children ran to the window with Billy to see the airplane, but Mrs. Pease called them back, and they returned to their seats. Billy, however, remained at the window, pointing at the sky. Mrs. Pease called him back, too.

"Billy, please return to your desk," Mrs. Pease said firmly. But Billy acted as though he didn't even hear her.

"Look, Mrs. Pease," he exclaimed, "the airplane is blowing smoke!" A couple of other children started from their desks.

"Billy," Mrs. Pease tried once more, "if you don't return to your desk this instant, I'm going to send you to Miss Warren's office." [Billy did sit down, but before Mrs. Pease could call on anyone, Billy blurted out the correct answer to the first question she asked.]

Mrs. Pease tried again. "Who knows 3 times 7?" This time Billy raised his hand, but he still couldn't resist creating a disruption.

"I know, I know," Billy pleaded, jumping up and down in his seat with his hand raised high.

"That will do, Billy," Mrs. Pease admonished him. She deliberately called on another child. The child responded with the correct answer.

"I knew that!" Billy exclaimed.

"Billy," Mrs. Pease told him, "I don't want you to say one more word this class period."

Billy looked down at his desk sulkily, ignoring the rest of the lesson. He began to fiddle with a couple of rubber bands, trying to see how far they would stretch before they broke. He looped the rubber bands around his index fingers and pulled his hands farther and farther apart. This kept him quiet for a while; by this point, Mrs. Pease didn't care what he did, as long as he was quiet. She continued conducting the multiplication lesson while Billy stretched the rubber bands until finally they snapped, flying off and hitting two children, on each side of him. Billy let out a yelp of surprise, and the class turned to him.

"That's it, Billy," Mrs. Pease told him, "You're going to sit outside the classroom until the period is over."

"No!" Billy protested. "I'm not going. I didn't do anything!"

"You shot those rubber bands at Bonnie and Julian," Mrs. Pease said.

"But it was an accident."

"I don't care. Out you go!"

Billy stalked out of the classroom to sit on a chair in the hall. Before exiting, however, he turned to Mrs. Pease. "I'll sue you for this," he yelled, not really knowing what it meant.

[Gorenstein & Comer, 2002, pp. 250–251]

You will read more about Billy later in this chapter.

Dozens of specific diagnoses lead to classification as a child with special needs, including anxiety disorder, Asperger syndrome, attachment disorder, attention-deficit disorder, autism, bipolar disorder, conduct disorder, clinical depression, developmental delay, and Down syndrome. In the United States, two-thirds of school-age children with special needs are said to have a learning or language disability—neither of which may have been evident in earlier years, and both of which may no longer be disabilities in adulthood. Between ages 6 and 11, however, these may be noticeable handicaps.

Every special need probably begins with a biological anomaly, perhaps the extra chromosome of Down syndrome or simply an unusual allele that affects some neurological connections. But biology is only the beginning; the social context affects how disabling the condition becomes. Special needs are clearly a biosocial topic, not simply a biological one.

Developmental Psychopathology

developmental psychopathology The field that uses insights into typical development to understand and remediate developmental disorders, and vice versa.

One area within the science of development is called **developmental psychopathology,** which links the study of typical development with the study of various disorders, and vice versa. The goal is "to understand the nature, origins, and sequelae [consequences] of individual patterns of adaptation and maladaptation over time" (Davies & Cicchetti, 2004, p. 477).

Four lessons from developmental psychopathology apply to everyone:

1. *Abnormality is normal.* Most children sometimes act oddly, and children with serious disabilities are, in many respects, like everyone else.
2. *Disability changes year by year.* Someone who is severely disabled at one stage may become quite capable later on, or vice versa.
3. *Adulthood may be better or worse.* Prognosis is difficult. Many infants and children with serious disabilities that affect them psychologically (e.g., blindness)

become happy and productive adults. Conversely, some conditions become more disabling at maturity, when interpersonal skills become more important.

4. *Diagnosis depends on the social context.* According to the widely used ***Diagnostic and Statistical Manual of Mental Disorders* (DSM-IV-TR),** the "nuances of an individual's cultural frame of reference" must be considered before a diagnosis can be made (American Psychiatric Association, 2000, p. xxxiv). Perhaps psychopathology resides "not in the individual but in the adaptiveness of the relationship between individual and context" (Sameroff & MacKenzie, 2003, p. 613).

***Diagnostic and Statistical Manual of Mental Disorders* (DSM-IV-TR)** The American Psychiatric Association's official guide to the diagnosis (not treatment) of mental disorders. (*IV-TR* means "fourth edition, text revision.")

We now focus on only three of the many categories of disorders that developmental psychopathologists study: attention deficits, learning disabilities, and autistic spectrum disorders. Understanding these three can lead to a better understanding of all children.

Attention-Deficit Disorders

attention-deficit/hyperactivity disorder (ADHD) A condition in which a person not only has great difficulty concentrating for more than a few moments but also is inattentive, impulsive, and overactive.

About 10 percent of all young children have an *attention-deficit disorder* (ADD), which means they have difficulty paying attention. When ADD is accompanied by an impulse to be continually active, it is referred to as **attention-deficit/hyperactivity disorder (ADHD),** which is one of the most exasperating developmental disruptions, especially when children are impulsively active when adults want them to be quiet. Some children with ADHD are more disruptive than others, but all have three problems: They are inattentive, impulsive, and overactive. Individuals vary as to which of these three traits is most evident (Barkley, 2006).

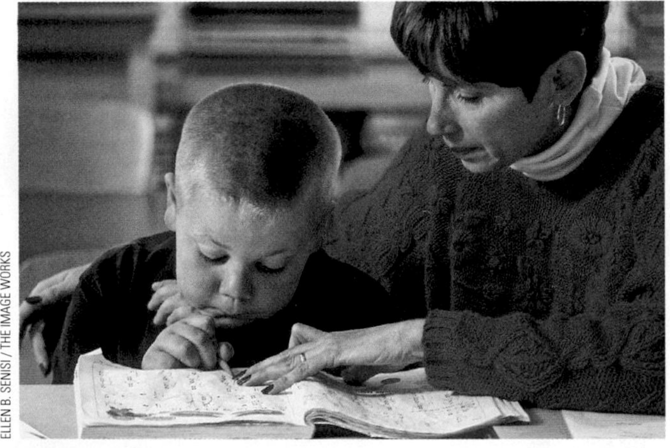

ELLEN B. SENISI / THE IMAGE WORKS

Use Your Hands A teacher helps a pupil work through a math problem. This boy has been diagnosed with mental retardation and ADHD. Note the position of her hands and his, helping him to focus his attention.

A typical child with ADHD, after sitting down to do homework, might look up, ask questions, think about playing, get a drink, fidget, squirm, tap the table, jiggle his or her legs, and go to the bathroom—and then start the whole sequence again. The difficulty may be caused by a slow-developing prefrontal cortex, an overactive limbic system, or an imbalance of neurotransmitters (Wolraich & Doffing, 2005).

Many experts and parents believe that artificial colors and preservatives in food make ADHD symptoms worse. Research that required hyperactive children to avoid additives for two weeks and then drink either placebos or beverages containing additives found that the children's impulsive behavior worsened after they consumed the additives (Eigenmann & Haenggeli, 2007). Whatever the cause, ADHD makes it hard for a child to pay attention; this difficulty often becomes a lifelong problem (Barkley, 2006).

About 5 percent of U.S. children are diagnosed with ADHD (more boys than girls, more European Americans than Latinos). One such child was Billy, the 8-year-old already described, who ran to the window when he was supposed to stay seated and who blurted out the answers without waiting to be called on. Children with ADHD often think they are being punished unfairly. Remember that Billy complained: "*I* knew that!", "I didn't do anything!", and finally "I'll sue you."

comorbidity The presence of two or more unrelated disease conditions at the same time in the same person.

Often, other disorders are comorbid with ADHD (Barkley, 2006). (**Comorbidity** means the presence of two or more unrelated disease conditions at the same time in the same person.) Some comorbid conditions may be consequences of untreated ADHD, but many disorders predate ADHD and have the same underlying cause. Among these conditions are "conduct disorder, depression, anxiety, Tourette syndrome, dyslexia, and bipolar disorder, . . . autism and schizophrenia" (Pennington, 2002, p. 163).

➤Response for Teachers (from page 326): The advantages are that all the children learn more aspects of human knowledge and that many children can develop their talents. Art, music, and sports should be an integral part of education, not just a break from academics. The disadvantage is that they take time and attention away from reading and math, which might lead to less proficiency in those subjects on standard tests and thus to criticism from parents and supervisors.

The treatment for ADHD is usually medication plus psychotherapy, as well as special education and training for parents and teachers (Barkley, 2006). Curiously, many drugs that are stimulants for adults, including amphetamines (e.g., Adderall) and methylphenidate (Ritalin), calm down children with ADHD. Prescribing drugs for children is controversial: Some fear overdosing, while others argue that refusing to prescribe drugs for ADHD is akin to withholding insulin from a diabetic. The following feature details the ongoing debate.

Especially for Health Workers (see response, page 331): Parents ask that some medication be prescribed for their kindergarten child, who they say is much too active for them to handle. How do you respond?

a view from science

Overdosing and Underdosing for ADHD

In the United States, more than 2 million children and adolescents under age 18 take prescription drugs to regulate their emotions and behavior. This rate doubled between 1987 and 1996 (Brown, 2003; Zito et al., 2003). It has leveled off in recent years but remains high, with 1 in 20 children aged 6 to 12 taking stimulants (usually for ADHD) (Vitiello et al., 2006; Zuvekas et al., 2006).

The most commonly prescribed drug is Ritalin, but at least 20 other psychoactive drugs (including Prozac, Zoloft, and Paxil) are being used to treat people of every age, including children as young as 2, for depression, anxiety, and many other conditions (Rubin, 2006). Few of these substances have been studied with children, who might respond better at higher or lower doses than those given to adults (Brown, 2003).

Many people fear that drugs are prescribed too early and too often (Rose, 2008). One writer contends:

> Squirming in a seat and talking out of turn are not "symptoms" and do not reflect a syndrome. [Such behaviors may be] caused by anything from normal childhood energy to boring classrooms or overstressed parents and teachers. We should not suppress these behaviors with drugs.
>
> *[Breggin & Baughman, 2001, p. 595]*

Most child psychologists share a concern that drugs are both underused and overused in treating children with ADHD (Angold et al., 2000; Brown, 2003). Some children who would benefit are never given medication; other children are given more medication than they need. Dosage is a particular concern, because children's weight and metabolism change continuously, so a dose that is right at age 5 might be too low at age 10. Overdosing could be especially problematic when brains and bodies are still developing.

We all have opinions about drugs: Some of us are suspicious of anything that is not natural; others believe that medication can cure almost anything (Rubin, 2006). A scientific view requires looking at evidence, not being swayed by preconceived ideas. Of course, it is impossible to be entirely objective, but many researchers, doctors, and parents try to consider the particular needs of each child rather than acting on general principles.

One group of researchers, seeking to find out whether certain drugs helped children with ADHD, began with small doses that were gradually increased until behavior improved as much as possible without side effects. After several weeks at that optimal dose, the children were given a placebo for a week. The children, parents, and teachers knew that this might occur but did not know when. Without the medication, many children's ability to function deteriorated rapidly, according to all observers. That convinced the scientists that the medication was effective (Hechtman et al., 2005).

Might childhood drug treatment for psychological problems (whether or not the origin is in the brain) have long-term consequences? This is a common fear. A particular concern is that such children will become drug dependent and will abuse chemical substances as adolescents. However, longitudinal research comparing nonmedicated and medicated children with ADHD finds the opposite: Childhood medication reduces the risk of adolescent drug abuse (Faraone & Wilens, 2003).

Far fewer children are diagnosed with ADHD in Europe than in North America. In the United States, rates of medication are highest among boys from low-income, non-Hispanic, southern households (see Table 11.2) (Martin & Leslie, 2003; Rowland et al., 2002; Witt et al., 2003; Zito et al., 2003). To a scientist, such differences suggest that culture and setting, not just biochemistry, influence diagnosis and treatment (Singh, 2008). Might girls in Kansas or London be underdiagnosed or might English-speaking boys in Mississippi be overdiagnosed? Is prejudice at work here?

TABLE 11.2

Rates of Diagnosis and Medication for ADHD

	Percent Diagnosed with ADHD	Percent of Those Diagnosed Taking Medication for ADHD
Girls	4.7	63
Boys	14.8	73
1st and 2nd grades	7.4	70
3rd, 4th, and 5th grades	12.2	72
Non-Hispanic White	10.8	76
Non-Hispanic Black	9.1	56
Hispanic	4.0	53

Source: Rowland et al., 2002.

A British writer suggests that the diagnosis of ADHD is a way for low-income families to get more public money, part of the "madhouse of modern Britain, where families of badly behaved children are rewarded by the state" (McKinstry, 2005). Such an opinion obviously reflects bias more than science, but it indicates the need for public understanding of both the problem and the efforts to solve it.

Looking at this issue from a scientific perspective means asking questions. For each child, exactly what genetic or environmental conditions foster ADHD, and what intervention is best (not just drugs, but which drug at what dose; not just family, but which child-rearing practices and family structures; not just school, but which teacher and placement)? Literally thousands of scientists in dozens of nations are seeking answers.

Ritalin was prescribed for Billy, and his parents and teacher were taught how to help him. He "improved considerably," becoming able not only to stay in his seat and complete his schoolwork but also to make friends (Gorenstein & Comer, 2002).

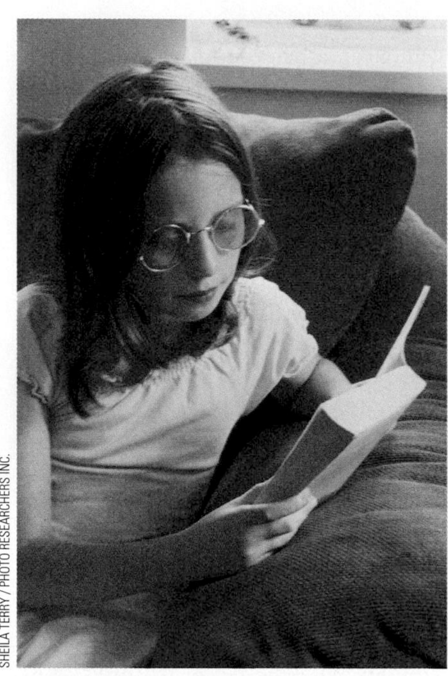

SHEILA TERRY / PHOTO RESEARCHERS INC.

Visual Aid The filters on these yellow eyeglasses seem to improve the functioning of the brain cells concerned with visual perception, helping some people with dyslexia to read.

learning disability A marked delay in a particular area of learning that is not caused by an apparent physical disability, by mental retardation, or by an unusually stressful home environment.

dyslexia Unusual difficulty with reading; thought to be the result of some neurological underdevelopment.

autism A developmental disorder marked by an inability to relate to other people normally, extreme self-absorption, and an inability to acquire normal speech.

autistic spectrum disorder Any of several disorders characterized by inadequate social skills, impaired communication, and unusual play.

Learning Disabilities

Many people have some specific **learning disability** that leads to difficulty in mastering a particular skill that most other people acquire easily. Perhaps one person is clumsy (low in kinesthetic intelligence), while another sings off key (low in musical intelligence).

A learning disability becomes problematic when a child falls markedly behind in some aspect of the school curriculum. The child may have an average or above-average IQ but "scattered" scores on subtests, scoring high on some and low on others. The child may be less capable in some areas than in others.

Learning disabilities do *not* usually result in lifelong impediments. Children typically find ways to compensate; they learn effective strategies to work around their deficiency. As an adult, such a child may function well. This seems to have been true of Winston Churchill, Albert Einstein, and Hans Christian Andersen, all of whom probably had learning disabilities as children. Conversely, an adult may feel inferior, afraid to do many things, because of childhood disability.

One common learning disability is **dyslexia,** which refers to unusual difficulty with reading. No single test accurately diagnoses dyslexia (or any other learning disability), because every academic achievement involves many skills (Sofie & Riccio, 2002). A child with a reading disability might have trouble sounding out words but might excel in other reading skills, such as comprehension and memory of printed text. Dozens of types of dyslexia have been identified.

Poor listening skills are often at the root of dyslexia. Early theories of dyslexia hypothesized that visual difficulties—e.g., reversals of letters (reading *was* instead of *saw*) and mirror writing (*b* instead of *d*)—were the origin, but more often dyslexia originates with speech and hearing problems (Pennington, 2002). An early warning occurs if a 3-year-old does not talk clearly and does not experience a naming explosion (see Chapter 6). Not only might early speech therapy improve talking, but it might also reduce or prevent later reading problems. A diagnosis might slow down later functioning, however, so care should be taken in deciding to provide therapy.

Autistic Spectrum Disorders

Autism is a disorder characterized by woefully inadequate social skills. Four decades ago, it was considered a single, rare disorder affecting fewer than 1 in 1,000 children, who experienced "an extreme aloneness that, whenever possible, disregards, ignores, shuts out anything . . . from the outside" (Kanner, 1943).

Children who developed slowly but were not so withdrawn were diagnosed as being mentally retarded or as having a "pervasive developmental disorder." Now such children are usually said to have an **autistic spectrum disorder,** which characterizes about 1 in every 150 8-year-olds (three times as many boys as girls) in the United States (MMWR, February 9, 2007).

Signs of an Autistic Spectrum Disorder There are three signs of an autistic spectrum disorder: delayed language, impaired social responses, and unusual play. Underlying all three is a kind of emotional blindness (Scambler et al., 2007). Children with any form of autism find it difficult to understand the emotions of others. Consequently, they do not want to talk, play, or otherwise interact with anyone. The problem may be a deficit in the brain's mirror neurons (see Chapter 1, Oberman & Ramachandran, 2007) that makes them feel alien, like "an anthropologist on Mars," as Temple Grandin, an educator and writer with autism, expressed it (quoted in Sacks, 1995).

Because autistic disorders cover a wide spectrum, or range, the degree of severity varies. Some children never talk, rarely smile, and often play for hours with one object (such as a spinning top or a toy train). Others, including those (like Grandin) with **Asperger syndrome,** are called "high-functioning," which means that they are unusually intelligent in some specialized area (such as drawing or geometry) and that their speech is close to normal. However, their social interaction is impaired. Still others are slow in all three areas (language, social interaction, play) but are not as severely impaired as are children with classic autism.

Some children with autistic spectrum disorder show signs in early infancy (no social smile, for example) and continue to resist social contact. Others improve by age 3 (Chawarska et al., 2007). Still others (about a fourth) start out developing normally and then deteriorate (MMWR, February 9, 2007). The most dramatic example of the latter pattern occurs in girls with *Rett syndrome*. They seem normal at first, but their brains develop very slowly and are much smaller than those of other children the same age (Bienvenu, 2005).

In other children with autism, the problem may be too much neurological activity, not too little. Their heads are large, and parts of the brain (especially the limbic system) are unusually sensitive to noise, light, and other sensations (Schumann et al., 2004). Grandin described the effect:

> Every time you take the kid into Wal-Mart, he's screaming. Well, the reason for that is that the fluorescent lights are flickering and driving him crazy, the noise in there hurts his ears, the smells overpower his nose. Wal-Mart is like being inside the speaker at a rock and roll concert.
>
> [*Medscape Psychiatry and Mental Health, 2005*]

Increased Incidence of Autism The incidence of autistic spectrum disorders may have tripled during the 1990s, as reported in California, Minnesota, and elsewhere. It is not known if this disorder is actually more common than it once was. Certainly the number of children with autistic disorders who receive special educational services has increased dramatically (Newschaffer et al., 2005). Many are quite intelligent in some ways (Dawson et al., 2007).

This increase may reflect an expanded definition of the condition, earlier diagnosis, and availability of special education (before 1980, children diagnosed as autistic were not provided special education in the United States) (Gurney et al., 2003; Parsell, 2004). This hypothesis received support from a detailed study in Texas showing that, over a six-year period, the number of children diagnosed with autism tripled in the wealthiest school districts but did not change in the poorest districts (with fewer specialists) (Palmer et al., 2005; see the Research Design).

Another possibility is that some new teratogen is harming many embryonic or infant brains. One suspect was thimerosal, an antiseptic containing mercury that is used in childhood immunizations. Many parents of autistic children first noticed their infants' impairments after their MMR (measles-mumps-rubella) vaccinations (Dales et al., 2001). This immunization hypothesis has been disproved many times. For instance, of all 500,000 children born in Denmark from 1991 to 1998,

➤Response for Health Workers (from page 329): Medication helps some hyperactive children, but not all. It might be useful for this child, but other forms of intervention should be tried first. Compliment the parents on their concern about their child, but refer them to an expert in early childhood for an evaluation and recommendations. Behavior-management techniques geared to the particular situation, not medication, will be the first strategy.

Asperger syndrome A specific type of autistic spectrum disorder, characterized by extreme attention to details and deficient social understanding.

Research Design

Scientists: Raymond Palmer, Stephen Blanchard, and David Mandall designed the study, and C. R. Jean provided critical interpretation.

Publication: *American Journal of Public Health* (2005).

Participants: All 1,040 school districts in Texas over six school years, 1994 to 2001.

Design: The school districts were sorted into tenths according to their resources: income, salaries, community wealth, proportion of disadvantaged students and so on. Within each tenth, the number of students designated as autistic was tallied each year.

Major conclusion: Increases in rate of students with autistic spectrum disorders correlated with wealth, from an increase of 300 percent in districts in the top two-tenths to no change in the bottom tenth. For every 10,000 children, 21 in the top districts and 3 in the bottom districts were designated as having autism.

Comment: These findings, covering an entire state, suggest that increases in the incidence of autism are caused by better diagnosis, greater availability of special education, and perhaps parental insistence on diagnosis and treatment.

PHANIE / PHOTO RESEARCHERS INC.

Precious Gifts Many children with autism are gifted artists. This boy attends a school in Montmoreau, France, that features workshops in which children with autism develop social, play, and learning skills.

about one-fifth never received MMR vaccinations. They were just as likely to be diagnosed with autistic spectrum disorders as those who were vaccinated (Madsen et al., 2002). Furthermore, thimerosal was removed from vaccines a decade ago, but the rates of autism are still rising.

Many other substances (pesticides, cleaning chemicals, some of the ingredients in nail polish) remain to be tested. Problems with risk analysis (explained in Chapter 4) are evident in this research, as in all research in developmental psychopathology. Scientists are not sure exactly why some children have autistic spectrum disorders or why symptoms vary. It is known, however, that the original cause of autistic spectrum disorders is biological (genes, birth or prenatal injury, perhaps chemicals), not the kind of nurture provided by the family.

Treatment of Autism Treatment to relieve symptoms of autism involves early education. Each core symptom (problems with language, social connections, and play) has been a focus of treatment.

In programs that emphasize language, one-on-one training with teachers and parents helps children learn to communicate. Usually this training involves applied behavior analysis. Data collection is followed by intervention that reinforces each step in the right direction, a method developed from behaviorism (Wolery et al., 2005).

Other programs emphasize play (Greenspan & Wieder, 2006), as with Jacob in Chapter 7. Remember that when Jacob's parents learned to play with him, his language abilities improved dramatically.

Still other programs stress attachment (Beppu, 2005). Achieving stronger parent–child bonds of attachment is a goal favored in Japan, where "successful diagnosis of high-functioning autism and Asperger syndrome has resulted in high detection rates" (p. 204). In one Japanese program, a 6-year-old boy with autism noticed his older brother pouring water and tried to take a turn. "When his mother praised him, [the boy] looked back at his mother with a smile and poured his water even more eagerly" (p. 211). According to this therapist, the boy's smile and pride were signs that he formed an attachment by connecting with his mother.

Educating Children with Special Needs

For all children with special needs, individualized instruction before age 6 can help them develop better learning strategies. Even children with severe symptoms of autism can be helped, although few ever learn to function normally (Ben-Itzchak & Zachor, 2007). For all disorders, psychologists advocate "preventive intervention rather than waiting to intervene when language and learning problems begin to cast a long and wide shadow" (Plomin, 2002, p. 59).

In the United States, children with special needs are most often first spotted by a teacher (not a parent or pediatrician), who makes a *referral,* a request for evaluation. Then other professionals observe and test the child. If they agree that the child has special needs, they discuss an **individual education plan (IEP)** with a parent (see Table 11.3). Some parents want such specialized help; others dread the social stigma of special education for their child.

This is quite different from traditional treatment. Before 1960, most children with special needs simply left school—they either dropped out or were forced out. Some were never even accepted to any school at all. That is still the case in some nations, but it changed in the United States with a 1969 law that

She Knows the Answer Physical disabilities often mushroom into additional emotional and cognitive problems. However, a disability can be reduced to a minor complication if it is recognized and if appropriate compensation or remediation is made a part of the child's education. As she signs her answer, this deaf girl shows by her expression that she is ready to learn.

ELLEN SENISI / THE IMAGE WORKS

TABLE 11.3

Laws Regarding Special Education in the United States*

PL (Public Law) 91-230: Children with Specific Learning Disabilities Act, 1969
Recognized learning disabilities as a category within special education. Before 1969, learning-disabled children received no special education or services.

PL 94-142: Education of All Handicapped Children Act, 1975
Mandated education of all school-age children, no matter what disability they might have, in the *least restrictive environment (LRE)*—which meant with other children in a regular classroom, if possible. Fewer children were placed in special, self-contained classes, and even fewer in special schools. This law required an *individual education plan (IEP)* for each child with special needs, specifying educational goals and periodic reassessment.

PL 105-17: Individuals with Disabilities Education Act [IDEA], 1990; updated 1997 and 2004
Refers to "individuals," not children (to include education of infants, toddlers, adults), and to "disabilities," not handicaps. Emphasizes parents' rights in placement and IEP.

*Other nations have quite different laws and practices, and states and school districts within the United States vary in interpretation and practice. Consult local support groups, authorities, and legal experts, if necessary.

required that all children be educated. At first, children with special needs were placed together, but neither their social skills nor their academic achievement advanced.

In response, a 1975 U.S. law called the *Education of All Handicapped Children Act* mandated that children with special needs must learn in the **least restrictive environment (LRE).** Often that meant educating them with children in the regular class, a policy called *mainstreaming.*

Some schools set aside a **resource room,** where mainstreamed children with special needs spent time with a teacher who worked individually with them. However, pulling children out of the regular classroom so that they could be in the resource room sometimes undermined their friendships and learning.

Another approach, **inclusion,** seemed more effective. Children with special needs were "included" in the general classroom, with "appropriate aids and services" (special help from a trained teacher who worked with the regular teacher).

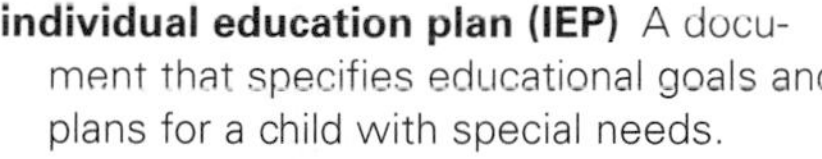

individual education plan (IEP) A document that specifies educational goals and plans for a child with special needs.

least restrictive environment (LRE) A legal requirement that children with special needs be assigned to the most general educational context in which they can be expected to learn.

resource room A room in which trained teachers help children with special needs, using specialized curricula and equipment.

inclusion An approach to educating children with special needs in which they are included in regular classrooms, with "appropriate aids and services," as required by law.

LAURA DWIGHT

Every Child Is Special One reason for a school policy of inclusion is to teach children to accept and appreciate children who have special needs. The girl with Down syndrome (in yellow) benefits from learning alongside her classmates, as they learn from her. An effective teacher treats every child as a special individual.

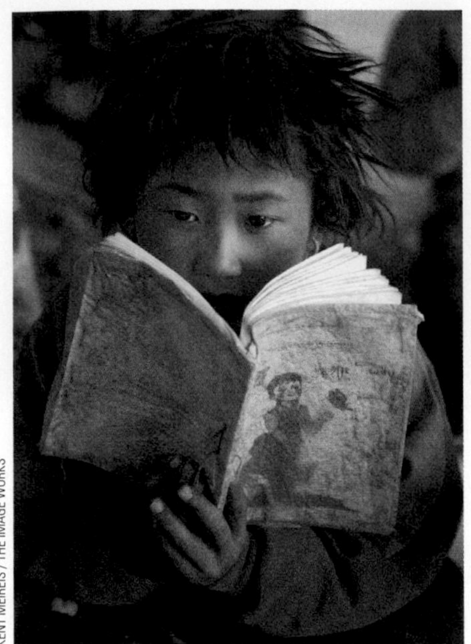

KENT MEIREIS / THE IMAGE WORKS

Culture Clash This Tibetan boy attends a Chinese school. Chinese is very difficult to learn to read, especially if it is not one's native language. He may indeed have learned to decode the printed symbols—or he may have learned to fake it.

Some adults worried that inclusion would harm the other children, but this fear proved unfounded (Kalambouka et al., 2007).

Treatment and education of children with special needs is still evolving, with marked differences in various cities, states, and nations. Compared with the United States, most other nations recognize fewer children with special needs and have fewer laws and specialized teachers for helping those children. Many cross-cultural variations are apparent, some beneficial to children and some not.

In theory, parents decide what education their children receive. This is not always the case in reality, however, partly because experts, teachers, and parents often disagree about the goals and practices of special education (Connor & Ferri, 2007; Rogers, 2007). Children with special needs typically have fewer friends and learn less than other children do, no matter what placement they are given (Wiener & Schneider, 2002), a situation that many adults seek to remedy.

SUMMING UP

Many children have special learning needs that originate in their brain development. Developmental psychopathologists emphasize that no one is typical in every way; the passage of time sometimes brings improvement and sometimes not. People with attention-deficit disorders, learning disabilities, and autistic spectrum disorders may function adequately or may have lifelong problems, depending on severity, family, school, and culture as well as on comorbid conditions. Specifics of diagnosis, prognosis, medication, and education are debatable; no child learns or behaves exactly like another, and no educational strategy is entirely successful. ■

SUMMARY

A Healthy Time

1. Middle childhood is a time of steady growth and few serious illnesses. Increasing independence and self-care allow most school-age children to be relatively happy and competent.

2. Physical activity aids health and joy in many ways. However, current environmental conditions make informal neighborhood play scarce, school physical education less prevalent, and sports leagues less welcoming for every school-age child.

Two Common Health Problems

3. Childhood obesity is a worldwide epidemic. Although genetics plays a role in body weight, less exercise and the greater availability of unhealthy food are also culprits. Many adults do not fully recognize this problem, which is one reason contemporary children are heavier than the children of the previous generation.

4. The incidence of asthma is increasing. Although the origins of asthma are genetic and the triggers are specific allergens, primary and secondary prevention have proved to be effective. This includes extending breast-feeding, increasing outdoor play, and reducing air pollution.

Brain Development

5. Brain development continues during middle childhood, enhancing every aspect of development. Myelination increases, speeding communication between neurons. The prefrontal cortex and the corpus callosum continue to mature, allowing not only analysis and planning but also selective attention and automatization.

6. IQ tests are designed to quantify intellectual aptitude. Most such tests emphasize language and logical ability and predict school achievement. IQ tests also reflect the culture in which they were created.

7. Achievement tests measure what a person has actually accomplished. Most standard achievement tests measure academic learning. Especially for assessing aptitude, measuring adaptation to daily life is crucial. This is useful in diagnosing mental retardation.

8. Critics contend that intelligence is actually manifested in multiple ways, which conventional IQ tests are too limited to measure. The concept of multiple intelligences recognizes creative and practical abilities, some of which are difficult to test.

Children with Special Needs

9. Developmental psychopathology uses an understanding of normal development to inform the study of unusual development. Four general lessons have emerged: Abnormality is normal; disability changes over time; adolescence and adulthood may make a condition better or worse; and diagnosis depends on context. Every disability has a physical and a psychological component.

10. Children with attention-deficit/hyperactivity disorder (ADHD) have potential problems in three areas: inattention, impulsiveness, and overactivity. The treatment for attention deficits is a combination of medication, home management, and education. Stimulant medication often helps children with ADHD to learn, but this treatment must be carefully monitored.

11. People with learning disabilities have unusual difficulty in mastering a specific skill that other people learn easily. The most common learning disability that manifests itself during the school years is dyslexia, unusual difficulty with reading. Children with learning disabilities can be helped if the problem is spotted early and if the assistance is individualized to suit the particular child.

12. Children with autistic spectrum disorders typically show odd and delayed language ability, impaired interpersonal skills, and unusual play. Several specific disorders, including Asperger syndrome and Rett syndrome, fall into this category. Autism may improve with intensive early education, but it never disappears entirely.

13. About 10 percent of all school-age children in the United States receive special education services. These services begin with an IEP (individual education plan) and assignment to the least restrictive environment (LRE).

14. Inclusion of children with special needs in regular education may aid the social skills of all children. However, inclusion does not meet every child's needs. Both academic and interpersonal abilities require practice, mentoring, and encouragement.

KEY TERMS

middle childhood (p. 311)
BMI (body mass index) (p. 317)
overweight (p. 317)
obesity (p. 317)
asthma (p. 320)
reaction time (p. 321)
selective attention (p. 322)
automatization (p. 322)
aptitude (p. 323)
IQ test (p. 323)
achievement test (p. 323)
Wechsler Intelligence Scale for Children (WISC) (p. 324)
Flynn effect (p. 324)
mental retardation (p. 324)
children with special needs (p. 326)
developmental psychopathology (p. 327)
Diagnostic and Statistical Manual of Mental Disorders (DSM-IV-TR) (p. 328)
attention-deficit/hyperactivity disorder (ADHD) (p. 328)
comorbidity (p. 328)
learning disability (p. 330)
dyslexia (p. 330)
autism (p. 330)
autistic spectrum disorder (p. 330)
Asperger syndrome (p. 331)
individual education plan (IEP) (p. 332)
least restrictive environment (LRE) (p. 333)
resource room (p. 333)
inclusion (p. 333)

KEY QUESTIONS

1. How does the physical growth of the school-age child compare with that of the younger child?

2. What are the main reasons for the recent increase in childhood obesity?

3. What measures to reduce asthma would benefit all children?

4. How does selective attention affect a child's ability to learn and behave?

5. What are some good uses of aptitude and achievement tests?

6. What are some misuses of intelligence tests?

7. Why was the field of developmental psychopathology created?

8. Why might parents ask a doctor to prescribe Ritalin for their child?

9. How could an adult have a learning disability that has never been spotted?

10. What are the signs of autistic spectrum disorders?

APPLICATIONS

1. Compare play spaces for children in different neighborhoods—ideally, urban, suburban, and rural areas. Note size, safety, and use. How might children's weight and motor skills be affected?

2. Developmental psychologists believe that every teacher should be skilled at teaching children with a wide variety of needs. Does the teacher-training curriculum at your college or university reflect this goal? Should all teachers take the same courses, or should some teachers be specialized? Give reasons for your opinions.

3. Internet sources vary in quality no matter what the topic, but this may be particularly true of Web sites designed for parents of children with special needs. Pick one childhood disability or disease and find several information sources on the Internet devoted to that condition. How might parents evaluate the information provided?

4. Special education teachers are in great demand. In your local public school, what is the ratio of regular to special education teachers? How many are in self-contained classrooms, resource rooms, and inclusion classrooms? What do your data reveal about the education of children with special needs in your community?

12

CHAPTER OUTLINE

Middle Childhood: Cognitive Development

At age 9, I wanted a puppy. My parents said no. I wrote a poem, promising "to brush his hair as smooth as silk" and "to feed him milk." Actually, puppies do not drink cow's milk, and I still remember these lines because my father laughed and praised my hastily written poem more than it deserved. I got Taffy, a blond cocker spaniel.

At age 10, my daughter Sarah wanted her ears pierced. I said no, it wouldn't be fair to her three older sisters, who were forced to wait until they were teenagers before I let them pierce their ears. Sarah wrote an affidavit saying that they had no objection, which each of them signed and dated. She got gold posts.

School-age children are able to master almost anything their cultural context presents: dividing fractions, surfing the Web, memorizing batting averages, and persuading their parents in whatever way works with those adults. Sarah knew that I wouldn't budge for doggerel but that signed documents from her older sisters would be persuasive.

This chapter describes this impressive cognitive development. We begin by examining how Piaget, Vygotsky, and information-processing theory describe cognition in young children. Then we turn to applications of those theories to language, reading, math, and many other topics. Not every parent encourages a child's poetry, and not every encouraged child writes poems, but culture and learning are always connected. This chapter describes how that happens.

Building on Theory

Learning is rapid in childhood. Some children, by age 11, beat their elders at chess, play music so well that adults pay to hear them, or write poems that get published. Other children live by their wits on the street or become soldiers in civil wars, learning lessons that no child should know (Grigorenko & O'Keefe, 2004).

Every theory, as Chapter 2 stressed, is practical. The dominant theories of cognition during the school years, as expressed by Jean Piaget, Lev Vygotsky, and information-processing theorists, have been used to structure education. As we describe all three approaches, think about the implications for schools, discussed at the end of this chapter.

Piaget and School-Age Children

concrete operational thought Piaget's term for the ability to reason logically about direct experiences and perceptions.

Piaget called the most important cognitive structure attained in middle childhood **concrete operational thought,** which is characterized by a collection of concepts that enable children to reason. The word *operational* comes from Latin—*operare,* "to work." Piaget uses it to emphasize practical, productive, sequential thinking. The school-age child is no longer limited by egocentrism but performs the intellectual work of logical operations.

The next stage—*formal operational thought*—is not yet attained because the child's concepts are grounded in the real world, solid and visible, like a concrete sidewalk. Formal thinking includes abstractions. For example, what is "love"? A concrete operational child might talk about hugging, kissing, and favors done; a formal operational person might talk about empathy, commitment, and sacrifice.

Piaget thought that 5- to 7-year-olds begin to understand logical concepts (Inhelder & Piaget, 1964; Piaget, 1950). Soon they apply logic in concrete situations—that is, situations that deal with visible, tangible, real things. Children thereby become more systematic, objective, scientific—and educable—thinkers.

A Hierarchy of Categories

classification The logical principle that things can be organized into groups (or categories or classes) according to some characteristic they have in common.

One crucial logical concept is **classification,** the organization of things into groups (or *categories* or *classes*) according to some characteristic that they have in common. For example, a child's parents, siblings, and cousins are part of a group called *family.* Other common classes are people, animals, toys, and food. Each class includes some elements and excludes others, and each is part of a hierarchy. Food, for instance, is the top of a hierarchy, with the next lower level including meat, grains, fruits, and so on. Most subclasses can be further divided: Meat includes poultry, beef, and pork, each of which can be even further subdivided.

It is obvious to adults who have mastered classification, but not always to children, that items at the bottom of the hierarchy belong to every higher category: Bacon is always pork, meat, and food. Adults also realize that the process does not work in reverse: Most foods are not bacon. Once they understand classification,

AP PHOTO / THE AUGUSTA CHRONICLE, CHRIS THELEN

His Science Project Concrete operational 10-year-olds like Daniel, shown here with some of his family's dairy cows, can be logical about anything they see, hear, or touch. Daniel's science experiment, on the effect of music on milk production, won first place in a Georgia regional science fair.

some children delight in writing their home address with street, city, state, nation, continent, planet, and galaxy.

Piaget devised many experiments to reveal children's developing understanding of classification. For example, an examiner shows a child a bunch of nine flowers—seven yellow daisies and two white roses (revised and published in Piaget et al., 2001). The examiner makes sure the child knows the words *flowers, daisies,* and *roses.* Then comes a revealing question: "Are there more daisies or more flowers?" Until about age 7, most children say, "More daisies." Pushed to justify their answer, the youngest children can offer no explanation. However, some 6- or 7-year-olds explain that there are more yellow ones than white ones or that, because the daisies are daisies, they aren't flowers (Piaget et al., 2001). By age 8, most children can classify objects they can see (concrete objects, not hypothetical ones). "More flowers than daisies," they say.

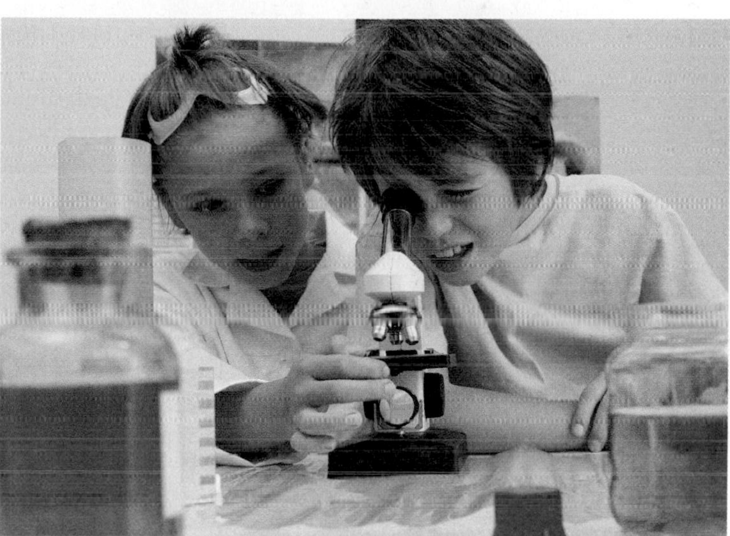

VEER

After "Gee Whiz!" After he sees the magnified image that his classmate expects will amaze him, will he analyze his observations? Ideally, concrete operational thought enables children to use their new logic to interpret their experiences.

Transitive Inference

Another example of the application of logic is the ability to grasp connections that are implied but not stated. Piaget studied *transitive inference,* the ability to figure out (infer) the unspoken link (transfer) between one fact and another.

In one example of transitive inference, a child is told, "John is taller than Jim. Jim is taller than David." Then the child is asked, "Who is taller, John or David?" Preoperational children are stumped. They cannot do this simple transitive inference, because they know only what they have been directly told. By contrast, school-age children can infer the relationship, as Piaget discovered. Later research connects transitive inference to the maturation of the hypothalamus, which reaches a crucial level at about age 7 and makes inferences and other kinds of mental logic possible (Greene et al., 2006; Heckers et al., 2004).

Transitive inference may be a prerequisite for another logical concept called *seriation,* the knowledge that things can be arranged in a logical series. Seriation is crucial for understanding the number sequence. By age 5, most children can count correctly up to 100, but they cannot correctly estimate where any particular two-digit number would be placed on a line that starts at 0 and ends at 100. Generally, this is possible by age 8 (Meadows, 2006).

Other Logical Concepts

The same flexibility is evident for other logical concepts. Remember from the experiment in Chapter 9 (in which milk is poured from one container to a container of a different shape) that younger children do not understand conservation because they are swayed by appearance. In contrast, school-age children grasp **identity,** the principle that objects remain the same even if some characteristics appear to shift. A ball is still a ball when it rolls into a hole; a child is the same person awake and asleep (some younger children think otherwise).

identity The logical principle that certain characteristics of an object remain the same even if other characteristics change.

School-age children also understand **reversibility,** the principle that after being changed, a thing may be returned to its original state. Remember that preoperational thought is static. However, by middle childhood, a child might prove conservation by using identity ("It's still the same milk") or by reversing the process (pouring the liquid back into the first container).

reversibility The logical principle that a thing that has been changed can sometimes be returned to its original state by reversing the process by which it was changed.

Reversibility is further refined by other logical principles, again demonstrating flexibility. Children understand that ice can become water again, but a cake cannot revert to flour and sugar. Reversibility is impossible in a classification hierarchy, because each level is significant; school-age children know this.

The logical abilities of the school-age child may be crucial for understanding math. Identity helps them realize that 12 plus 3 is the same as 3 plus 12 and that 15 is still 15 no matter how it was reached. Reversibility is harder to understand, but eventually it allows the realization that, if 5 times 7 equals 35, then 35 divided by 5 must be 7. In this and many other ways, logic is the foundation for understanding math.

The Significance of Piaget's Findings About Logic

Exactly what do Piaget's experiments in logic mean? Although logic is basic for math concepts, Piaget's research does *not* prove a dramatic logical shift between preoperational and concrete operational thought. Some children seem to learn logic via math, not vice versa.

Other research finds that classification appears before middle childhood (Halford & Andrews, 2006). Even infants seem to have brain networks ready to categorize what they see (Quinn, 2004), and 4-year-olds can judge whether a certain food is breakfast food, junk food, both, or neither (S. P. Nguyen & Murphy, 2003).

Similarly, transitive inference is both more complex and simpler than Piaget imagined. It requires several logical steps, not just one. Yet many birds and animals succeed at tasks measuring transitive inference (Frank et al., 2005; Wright, 2001).

Despite all these findings, Piaget's experimentation revealed something important. What develops during middle childhood is the ability to use mental categories and subcategories flexibly, inductively, and simultaneously (Meadows, 2006).

This is apparent, as already seen, with flowers and daisies or (a greater challenge) with cars, which can be classified as transportation, toys, lethal weapons, imports, consumer products, Toyotas, SUVs, and so on. Although preschool children can categorize, older children are more precise and flexible in classification, so that they are better able to separate the essential from the irrelevant (Hayes & Younger, 2004).

This movement away from egocentrism toward a more flexible logic is illustrated by research on 5- to 9-year-olds who were asked about two hypothetical boys—David, who thought chocolate ice cream was yucky, and Daniel, who found chocolate ice cream yummy. Most 5-year-olds (63 percent) thought David was wrong, and many felt he was bad or stupid as well. By contrast, virtually all (94 percent) of the 9-year-olds thought both boys could be right, and only a few were critical of David (Wainryb et al., 2004).

Vygotsky and School-Age Children

Vygotsky (1934/1994) also felt that educators should consider children's thought processes. He recognized that younger children find it difficult to understand what older children easily grasp. Vygotsky's approach was a marked improvement over the dull "meaningless acquisition" curriculum that dominated education in his day.

Vygotsky believed that an educational system based on the rote memorization of facts rendered the child "helpless in the face of any sensible attempt to apply any of this acquired knowledge" (pp. 356–357). Many developmentalists and educational reformers agreed with him and worked to change that.

The Role of Instruction

Unlike Piaget, who emphasized the child's own discovery of important concepts, Vygotsky regarded instruction as crucial. He thought that peers and teachers provide the bridge between the child's developmental potential and the needed skills and knowledge, via guided participation (see Chapter 2). In each child's *zone of proximal development* (almost-understood ideas), guidance from other people is crucial.

Confirmation of the role of social interaction and instruction comes from children who, because of their school's entry-date cutoff, are either relatively old kindergartners or quite young first-graders. Spring achievement scores of 6-year-old first-graders exceed those of kindergarten 6-year-olds who are only one month younger (Lincove & Painter, 2006; NICHD, 2007).

Additional confirmation comes from studies of the effect of high-quality teaching. There is a direct correlation between the percentage of qualified teachers in a school and children's level of learning, even when other factors (e.g., socioeconomic status, prior achievement, neighborhood) are taken into account (Wayne & Youngs, 2003). For transitive inference, schooling seems as influential as maturation (Artman & Cahan, 1999).

Remember that, for Vygotsky, formal education is only one of many contexts for learning. Children are apprentices who learn as they play together, watch television, eat dinner with their families, and engage in other daily interactions. Regarding fractions, for instance, some schoolchildren have learned the basic concepts outside school; for them, any formal instruction advances the understanding they have already acquired. But for children who don't already understand the basics, quality of instruction is crucial (Saxe, 2004).

Especially for Teachers (see response, page 342): How might Piaget's and Vygotsky's ideas help in teaching geography to a class of third-graders?

Cultural Variations: Zimbabwe and Brazil

In general, Vygotsky's emphasis on sociocultural contexts contrasts with Piaget's more maturational approach. Vygotsky believed that cultures (tools, customs, and mentors) teach people. For example, a child who is surrounded by adults who read for pleasure—and by well-stocked bookcases, daily newspapers, and store and street signs—will read more fluently than a child who has little exposure to print, even if both are taught by the same teacher in the same classroom.

Most research on children's cognition has been done in North America and western Europe, but the same patterns are apparent worldwide. In Zimbabwe, for example, children's understanding of classification is influenced not only by their age (as Piaget found) but also by factors related to society (Vygotsky's emphasis), such as the particulars of their schooling and their family's socioeconomic status (SES) (Mpofu & van de Vijver, 2000).

The most detailed international example comes from Brazil and involves the street children who sell fruit, candy, and other products to earn their living. Many have never attended school and consequently score poorly on standard math achievement tests. This is no surprise to developmentalists, who have data from numerous nations that show that unschooled children score lower in every academic area (Rogoff et al., 2005).

However, some of these young peddlers are skilled at pricing their wares and making change. Some cannot read, but they use colors and pictures to identify how many *reals* each bill is worth (Saxe, 2004). They may recalibrate selling prices daily in response to changes in the inflation rate, wholesale prices, and customer demand. These children calculate "complex markup computations . . . by using procedures that were widespread in their practice but not known to children in school" (Saxe, 1999, p. 255).

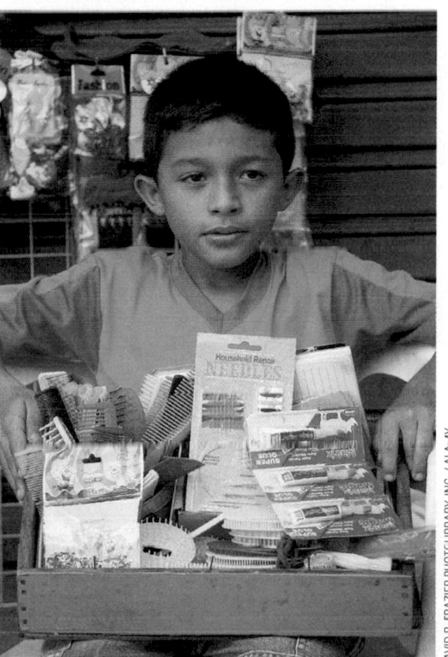

He Knows His Stuff Many child vendors, like this boy selling combs and other grooming aids on the streets of Manaus, Brazil, understand basic math and the give-and-take of social interaction; but, deprived of formal education, they know little or nothing about history and literature.

➤**Response for Teachers** (from page 341): Here are two of the most obvious ways. (1) Use logic. Once children can grasp classification and class inclusion, they can understand cities within states, states within nations, and nations within continents. Organize your instruction to make logical categorization easier. (2) Make use of children's need for concrete and personal involvement. You might have the children learn first about their own location, then about the places where relatives and friends live, and finally about places beyond their personal experience (via books, photographs, videos, and guest speakers).

Ratios and fractions, which are usually taught toward the end of middle childhood, are understood by expert street sellers. They learn math from:

- The social context
- Other sellers (especially older children)
- Daily experience

None of this would surprise Vygotsky, who believed that peers could be good mentors.

Further research in Brazil finds that school is not completely irrelevant. The best math skills were demonstrated by children who had some schooling as well as street experience (Saxe, 1991). But in every nation, math strategies taught in school are sometimes too abstract, not the ones children use in their daily lives (Meadows, 2006).

A Combined Approach

Today's educators and psychologists regard both Piaget and Vygotsky as insightful theorists, and international research confirms the merits of both theories. Our understanding of how children learn depends on "a framework that was laid down by Piaget and embellished by Vygotsky" (C. Howe, 1998, p. 207).

In other words, Piaget's appreciation that children are eager learners, trying to understand the world in ways limited by their maturation, has been extended by Vygotsky. Vygotsky realized that children learn from each other, from their culture, and from their teachers—as long as those mentors know the child's motivation, needs, and skills. In short, Piaget described universal changes; Vygotsky noted cultural impact.

Information Processing

information-processing theory A perspective that compares human thinking processes, by analogy, to computer analysis of data, including sensory input, connections, stored memories, and output.

A third, and more recent, approach to understanding cognition arises from **information-processing theory.** As you learned in Chapter 6, this approach takes its name from computer functioning. Computers receive and store vast quantities of information (numbers, letters, pixels, other coded symbols) and then use software programs to process that information.

People, too, take in large amounts of information. They use mental processes to perform three functions: search for specific units of information when needed (as a search engine does), analyze (as software programs do), and express the analysis in a format that another person (or a networked computer) can interpret.

By tracing the paths and links of each of these functions, scientists can better understand the mechanisms of learning. Information processing focuses on the specifics, not on theories but on details. It progresses from models and hypotheses to practical demonstrations (Munakata, 2006).

As you have seen, the brain gradually matures and dendrites grow. This pattern confirms the information-processing perspective, which finds no evidence for the sudden, stagelike advances suggested by Piaget. Underlying this perspective is the appreciation that the child's brain is the site of all cognition, and thus ongoing brain maturation is the foundation for advanced information processing.

Memory

As with computers, memory is crucial, according to information-processing theory. The various types of input, and many methods of storage and retrieval, affect the increasing cognitive ability of the schoolchild.

sensory memory The component of the information-processing system in which incoming stimulus information is stored for a split second to allow it to be processed. (Also called the *sensory register.*)

Sensory memory (also called the *sensory register*) is the first component of the human information-processing system. It stores incoming stimuli for a split second after being received, to allow the stimuli to be processed. To use terms first explained in Chapter 5, *sensations* are retained for a moment so that some of them can become *perceptions*. This first step of sensory awareness is already quite good in early childhood, improves slightly until about age 10, and remains adequate until late adulthood.

Working Memory Once some sensations become perceptions, the brain selects meaningful perceptions to transfer to working memory for further analysis. It is in **working memory** (also called *short-term memory*) that current, conscious mental activity occurs. Working memory improves steadily and significantly every year from age 4 to age 15 (Gathercole et al., 2004). For example, capacity increases, and sounds are remembered. These improvements are possible in part because of continuing changes in the brain. Especially significant is the increased myelination and dendrite formation in the prefrontal cortex—increases that allow the massive interconnections described in Chapter 11.

working memory The component of the information-processing system in which current conscious mental activity occurs. (Also called *short-term memory*.)

The processing of information, not mere exposure to it, is essential to getting material into working memory. Improvement in working memory during the school years includes processing advances in two crucial areas, one called the *phonological loop*, which stores sounds, and one called the *visual–spatial sketchpad*, which stores sights (Meadows, 2006). As the brain matures, children are able to use memory strategies that were inaccessible to them as young children (see Table 12.1).

The relationship between strategy and working memory was demonstrated by an experiment in which 7- and 9-year-olds memorized two lists of 10 items each (M. L. Howe, 2004). Some children had separate lists of toys and vehicles; others had two mixed lists, with toys and vehicles in both. A day later, they were asked to remember one list. Having separate lists of toys and vehicles helped the 7-year-olds a small amount, but particularly benefited the 9-year-olds. Those older children with topical lists used that organization to their advantage: They remembered many more items than did the 9-year-olds with mixed lists.

Long-Term Memory Information from working memory is transferred to **long-term memory,** which stores it for minutes, hours, days, months, or years. The capacity of long-term memory—how much information can be crammed into one

long-term memory The component of the information-processing system in which virtually limitless amounts of information can be stored indefinitely.

TABLE 12.1

Advances in Memory from Infancy to Age 11

Child's Age	Memory Capabilities
Under 2 years	Infants remember actions and routines that involve them. Memory is implicit, triggered by sights and sounds (an interactive toy, a caregiver's voice).
2–5 years	Words are now used to encode and retrieve memories. Explicit memory begins, although children do not yet use strategies. Children remember things by rote (their phone number, nursery rhymes) without truly understanding them.
5–7 years	Children realize that some things should be remembered, and they begin to use simple strategies, primarily rehearsal (repeating an item again and again). This is not a very efficient strategy, but with enough repetition, automatization occurs.
7–9 years	Children use new strategies if they are taught them. Children use visual clues (remembering how a particular spelling word looks) and auditory hints (rhymes, letters), evidence of advances in the visual–spatial sketchpad and phonological loop. They become able to take advantage of the organization of things to be remembered.
9–11 years	Memory becomes more adaptive and strategic, as children become able to learn various memory techniques from teachers and other children. They can organize material themselves, developing their own memory aids.

Source: Based on information in Meadows, 2006.

Especially for Teachers (see response, page 348): How might your understanding of memory help you teach a 2,000-word vocabulary list to a class of fourth-graders?

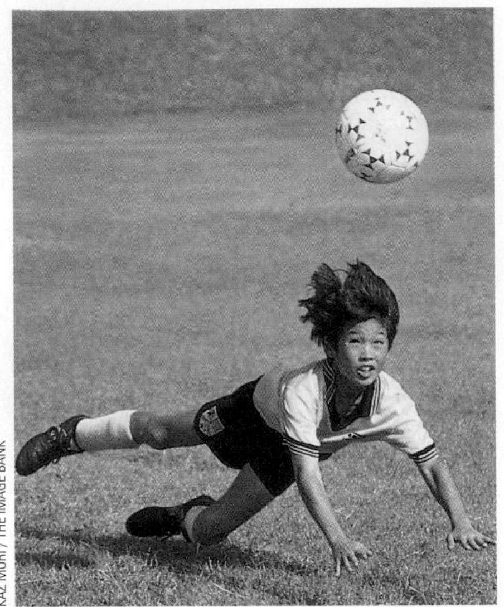

KAZ MORI / THE IMAGE BANK

Eye on the Ball This boy's concentration while heading the ball and simultaneously preparing to fall is a sign that he has practiced this maneuver enough times that he can perform it automatically. Not having to think about what to do on the way down, he can think about what to do when he gets up, such as pursuing the ball or getting back to cover his position.

knowledge base A body of knowledge in a particular area that makes it easier to master new information in that area.

control processes Mechanisms (including selective attention, metacognition, and emotion regulation) that combine memory, processing speed, and knowledge to regulate the analysis and flow of information within the information-processing system. (Also called *executive processes.*)

brain—is virtually limitless by the end of middle childhood. Together with sensory memory and working memory, long-term memory assists in organizing ideas and reactions.

Crucial to the measurement and use of long-term memory is not merely *storage* (how much material has been deposited) but also *retrieval* (how readily past learning can be brought into working memory). Retrieval is easier for some memories—especially memories of vivid, highly emotional experiences—than for others. As with adults, a child may forget or misremember some experiences (Meadows, 2006).

Speed of Thinking

Because of increasing myelination and repeated sequences of neuron firing, speed of thinking continues to increase throughout the first two decades of life (Benes, 2001); girls are generally faster thinkers than boys (Camarata & Woodcock, 2006). Repetition (pronouncing the same word, rehearsing the same dance step, adding up the same numbers) makes neurons fire in a coordinated and seemingly instantaneous sequence, and processing speed adds to the advances of repetition. That is one reason that school learning includes practice of various kinds—worksheets, reading out loud, drills.

As processes that once required hard mental labor become quick and automatic, memory capacity is freed up for additional learning. One result is that more information can be remembered, and thinking advances (Demetriou et al., 2002).

Progress from initial effort to automatization often takes years, making repetition and practice essential. Many children lose cognitive skills during the summer because the lack of daily schooling erases recent learning (K. L. Alexander et al., 2007). Even adults who leave college for a decade feel "rusty" when they return. The biggest problem with television may not be what children see but what they do not do instead of watching TV: Television crowds out reading and thus reduces repetition and achievement (Roberts & Foehr, 2004).

Knowledge

Information-processing analysis finds that the more people know, the more they can learn. Having an extensive **knowledge base,** or a broad body of knowledge in a particular subject, makes it easier to master new information in that area. The knowledge base makes thinking faster and memory better, as children link new information to already-learned material. There is an "interaction between knowledge of material to be remembered, the strategies that can be used, and the capacity of short-term memory" (Meadows, 2006, p. 97).

Adding to the knowledge base is facilitated by past experience, current opportunity, and personal motivation. That explains why school-age children's knowledge base is far greater in some domains, and far smaller in others, than their parents or teachers would like. A British study provides an example (Balmford et al., 2002; see the Research Design). Schoolchildren were asked to identify 10 out of a random sample of 100 Pokémon creatures and 10 out of 100 types of wildlife common in the United Kingdom. The 4- to 6-year-olds knew only about a third of the 20 items but could identify more living things than imaginary ones (see Figure 12.1). In contrast, 8- to 11-year-olds recognized more Pokémon creatures than living things. Memory follows peer teaching: In this cohort, many third-graders were avid collectors of Pokémon cards.

Control Processes

The mechanisms that put memory, processing speed, and the knowledge base together are called **control processes;** they regulate the analysis and flow of information within the system. Control processes include *selective attention,*

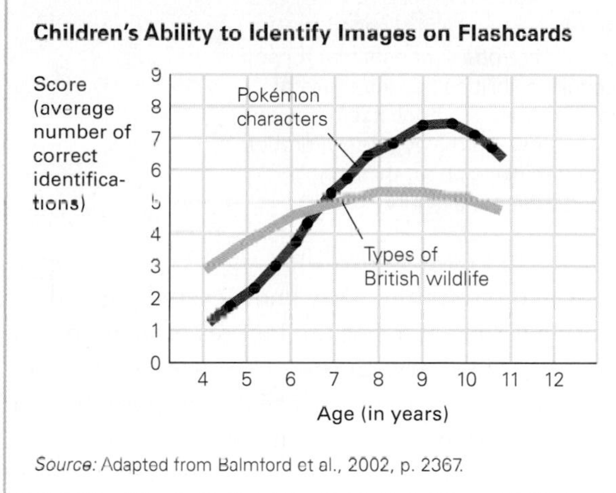

Observation Quiz (see answer, page 347): What does this graph suggest about the projected state of wildlife conservation in the United Kingdom in 2020?

FIGURE 12.1

Knowledge of the Real and the Imaginary Every child's knowledge base expands with age, but the areas of special interest tend to shift as the child grows older. At about 8 years of age, British schoolchildren's ability to identify Pokémon characters on flashcards began to surpass their ability to identify real-life animals and plants.

Research Design

Scientists: Andrew Balmford, Lizzie Clegg, Tim Coulson, and Jennie Taylor.

Publication: *Science* (2002) (a weekly journal published by the American Association for the Advancement of Science).

Participants: A total of 109 British schoolchildren, aged 4–11.

Design: Each child was asked to name 20 pictures, 10 of British wildlife (plants, mammals, invertebrates, and birds) and 10 of Pokémon characters, randomly chosen from two packs of 100. To be considered correct, the children did not have to name the genus of insect or plant (saying "beetle" was enough), but they had to do so for mammals (e.g., "badger"). Pokémon creatures had to be identified by their correct names.

Major conclusion: Children are great learners, but they do not learn much about nature. Identification increased markedly from age 4 to 8, from 32 percent to 53 percent for natural creatures, and from 7 to 78 percent for Pokémon characters.

Comment: This straightforward study is presented as a wake-up call for conservationists. The authors quote Robert Pyle: "What is the loss of a condor to a child who has never seen a wren?"

metacognition, and *emotional regulation.* These processes assume an executive role in the information-processing system. They organize, decide on, and direct operations, as the chief executive officer of a large corporation does. For that reason, control processes are also called *executive processes.*

Paying Attention When someone is able to concentrate on only the relevant part of all the material that constantly bombards the sensory memory, or uses the knowledge base to connect new information, control processes are active. A fourth-grade student listens to what the teacher is saying about the continents of the world, ignoring the classmate who might be chewing gum or tying his shoelace. That's control, the selective attention described in Chapter 11.

Control processes develop spontaneously with age, but they are also taught. Sometimes this teaching is explicit. For instance, teachers may provide spelling rules ("*i* before *e* except after *c*") and sentences to help pupils remember the notes of the treble clef ("Every Good Boy Does Fine"—E, G, B, D, F). Children can use such rules by about age 7; younger children ignore them or use them only on command (Meadows, 2006).

Sometime during middle childhood, children are able to develop their own control processes to focus their attention. We should note that cultures as well as individuals differ in what they consider worthy of attention and in how selective that attention should be.

This refinement of control processes varies by culture. For example, some cultures want single-minded concentration, as is the expectation in North American schools. Other cultures want children to learn while doing other things, as is often the case in Latin America. This latter approach is not necessarily inefficient, because "simultaneous attention may be important when learning relies on observation of ongoing events" (Correa-Chavez et al., 2005, p. 665).

Metacognition During the school years, children develop a more comprehensive form of thinking called **metacognition,** sometimes called *thinking about thinking.* Metacognition is the ultimate control process, because it allows a person to evaluate a cognitive task, determine how best to accomplish it, and then monitor his or her own performance in order to make adjustments.

metacognition "Thinking about thinking," or the ability to evaluate a cognitive task in order to determine how best to accomplish it, and then to monitor and adjust one's performance on that task.

BACHMANN / PHOTO RESEARCHERS, INC.

They've Read the Book Acting in a play based on *The Lion, the Witch, and the Wardrobe* suggests that these children have metacognitive abilities beyond those of almost any preschooler. Indeed, the book itself requires a grasp of the boundary between reality (the wardrobe) and fantasy (the witch). "Thinking about thinking" is needed in order to appreciate the allegory.

Observation Quiz (see answer, page 348): Beyond understanding the book, what are three examples of metacognition implied here? Specifically, how does the ability to memorize lines, play a part, and focus on the play illustrate metacognition?

Children under age 6 often think they know everything and are unaware of the mistakes they make or the failures of memory that are evident to adults (Meadows, 2006). In other words, their metacognition is almost nonexistent. That makes it more difficult to teach them, except by discovery and example.

Marked advances in metacognition occur when children become better aware of what they know and what they need to learn. School-age children might, for example, test themselves to judge whether they have learned their spelling words, rather than insisting (as younger children might) that they know it all (Harter, 1999).

Should metacognition be taught to children, or should it be allowed to develop spontaneously, when children are old enough? This question has been the focus of decades of research (Pressley & Hilden, 2006). Such research has looked at both discovery learning (inspired by Piaget) and explicit scaffolding (inspired by Vygotsky) from an information-processing perspective. The answer, based on research such as the study described in the following feature, is that both discovery and instruction work sometimes yet neither works all the time. Direct instruction is usually most effective during the school years, but less so earlier or later in life.

a view from science

Explicit Instruction Versus Discovery Learning

During the school years, children benefit from learning specific cognitive strategies in every academic subject (math, reading, writing, science), especially if they are given practice over weeks and months. To use the language of computers, once a program is installed, output is faster and more accurate if the operator uses the program frequently and understands its application. That works for children, too.

Controversy centers on identifying the best method for "installing" concepts in the minds of children. Some adults advocate discovery learning, saying that "experience is the best teacher" or that learning is better in "the school of hard knocks." Not so, according to information-processing theory: Children learn concepts best if they are taught directly.

A widely publicized study contrasted discovery learning with explicit instruction (Klahr & Nigam, 2004). The concept to be learned was that in order to establish cause and effect, the relevant variables must be controlled and measured one by one. This concept is basic for an understanding of the scientific method.

The researchers showed third- and fourth-graders, ages 8 to 10, an apparatus consisting of a downhill ramp connected to an uphill ramp (see Figure 12.2). There were four variables: golf ball or rubber ball, steep or shallow downhill ramp, smooth or rough ramp surface, and long or short downhill run. The object was for the participants to design experiments to best determine the effect these variables had on how far a ball would roll up the uphill ramp.

To be scientifically accurate, the experiments the children designed would have to be unconfounded—that is, they would have to test the variables one at a time, rather than combining, or confounding, them. The sample experiment depicted in Figure 12.2 is confounded, because it contrasts all four variables at once.

The children were asked, on their own, to design four experiments: two to determine the effect of run length and two to determine the effect of ramp steepness. Only 8 of the 112 children designed experiments in which the variables were unconfounded. The other 104 were then divided into two groups.

As the 52 in the direct-instruction group watched, an experimenter created pairs of demonstrations with the ramps and asked if each set would make it possible to "tell for sure" how a particular variable affected the distance traveled by the ball. After each child answered, the experimenter explained why the child was correct or incorrect, emphasizing the importance of using a design that tested a single variable at a time.

The 52 children in the discovery learning group were given an equal amount of time to create their own experiments. They worked on their own, receiving no feedback or instruction in controlling variables from the experimenters.

Then the children's understanding was assessed. They were asked to design four experiments, as before. Far more children (40 of 52) in the direct-instruction group were successful at isolating variables than were children in the discovery-learning group (12 of 52).

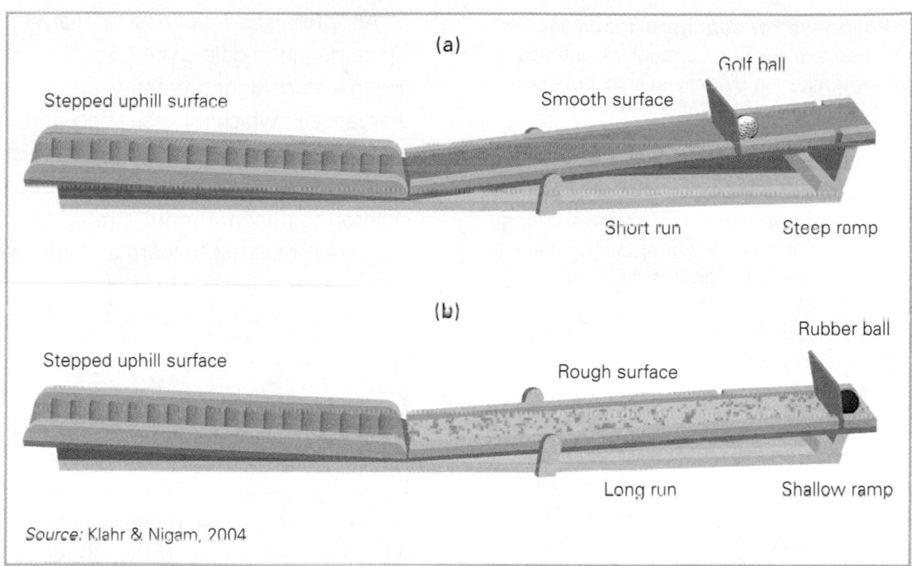

Source: Klahr & Nigam, 2004

FIGURE 12.2

Design for a Confounded Experiment On each of these two ramps, children could vary the steepness, surface, and length of the ramp, as well as the type of ball. The confounded experiment depicted here contrasts (*a*) a golf ball on a steep, smooth, short ramp with (*b*) a rubber ball on a shallow, rough, long ramp.

The next week, all the children were asked to look at two science posters, designed by 11-year-olds, that described experiments that the 11-year-olds had done but that included some flaws in design. The 104 children were then asked to suggest ways of making the posters "good enough to enter in a state-level science fair." The 40 children who had achieved their understanding of variables via direct instruction were found to be virtually as perceptive in their critiques as the 12 who had learned through discovery.

The authors of this study note that it did "not involve a difference between 'active' and 'passive' learning. In both conditions, students were actively engaged in the design of their experiments and the physical manipulation of the apparatus" (p. 663). Rather, the main difference lay in the examples and explanations provided in the direct-instruction condition but not in the discovery-learning condition.

The study's results do *not* prove that direct instruction is always best. The direct-instruction version incorporated several basics of good teaching: active participation, material to manipulate, teacher encouragement. Direct instruction does not always provide these in real-world settings. Moreover, the discovery-learning group had no way of finding out whether their discoveries were correct, unlike the many life lessons that children discover for themselves.

This research suggests, however, that discovery is not always the best method of learning, either. Piaget was mistaken when he wrote, "Each time one prematurely teaches a child something he could have discovered for himself, that child is kept from inventing it and consequently from understanding it completely" (Piaget, 1970, p. 715).

What does all this mean for teachers and parents? Probably that instruction in the form of demonstrating, explaining, and discussing various topics in some areas—perhaps morals, history, and language as well as science—can be effective during the school years. The "hard knocks" involved in finding things out for oneself are not always required.

SUMMING UP

Piaget and Vygotsky both recognized that school-age children are avid learners who actively build on the knowledge they already have. Piaget emphasized the child's own logical thinking, as the principles of classification, identity, and reversibility are understood during concrete operational thought. Research inspired by Vygotsky and the sociocultural perspective fills in Piaget's outline with details of the actual learning situation. Cultural differences can be powerful; specific instruction and practical experience make a difference.

➤Answer to Observation Quiz (from page 345): As the authors of this study observe, "People care about what they know." As their knowledge about their country's animal and plant life declines with age, these British children's concern for wildlife conservation is likely to decline, too.

➤Response for Teachers (from page 344): Children this age can be taught strategies for remembering by making links between working memory and long-term memory. You might break down the vocabulary list into word clusters, grouped according to root words, connections to the children's existing knowledge, applications, or (as a last resort) first letters or rhymes. Active, social learning is useful; perhaps in groups the students could write a story each day that incorporates 15 new words. Each group could read its story aloud to the class.

➤Answer to Observation Quiz (from page 346): (1) Memorizing extensive passages requires an understanding of advanced memory strategies that combine meaning with form. (2) Understanding how to play a part so that other actors and the audience respond well requires a sophisticated theory of mind. (3) Staying focused on the moment in the play despite distractions from the audience requires selective attention.

An information-processing analysis highlights many components of thinking that advance during middle childhood. Although sensory memory and long-term memory do not change much during these years, the speed and efficiency of working memory improve dramatically, which makes school-age children better thinkers than they had been. Another advantage for older children is that past learning results in a greater knowledge base.

In addition, control processes, such as selective attention and metacognition, enable children to become more strategic thinkers, able to direct their minds toward whatever they are motivated to learn and adults are motivated to teach. ■

Language

As you remember, many aspects of language advance rapidly before middle childhood. By age 6, children have mastered most of the basic vocabulary and grammar of their first language, and many speak a second language fluently. However, as we will now see, because school-age children have the abilities described in the chapter to this point (noted by Piaget, Vygotsky, and information-processing theorists), they advance even further in language.

Some school-age children learn as many as 20 new words a day and apply grammar rules they did not use before. These new words and applications are unlike the earlier language explosion. Increases in logic, flexibility, memory, speed of thinking, metacognition, and connections between facts enhance the learning of both first and second languages (Kagan & Herschkowitz, 2005).

RACHEL EPSTEIN / THE IMAGE WORKS

Connections Basic vocabulary is learned by age 4 or so, but the school years are best for acquiring expanded, derivative, and specialized vocabulary, especially if the child is actively connecting one word with another. With his father's encouragement, this boy in San Jose, California, will remember *Jupiter, Mars,* and the names of the other planets and maybe even *orbit, light-years,* and *solar system.*

Vocabulary

By age 5, children already know the names of thousands of objects, and they understand many other parts of speech. But school-age children are more flexible and logical in their knowledge and use of vocabulary; they can understand metaphors, prefixes and suffixes, and compound words. For example, 2-year-olds know *egg,* but 10-year-olds also know *egg salad, egg-drop soup, last one in is a rotten egg.* They understand that each of these expressions is logically connected to *egg* but is also distinct from the dozen uncooked eggs in the refrigerator. They use each expression in the appropriate contexts.

Understanding Metaphors

Metaphors, jokes, and puns are all understood much better with each year of middle childhood. The jokes of middle childhood ("What is black and white and red all over?" "Why did the chicken cross the road?") are funny only during the years when a certain mind-set is developing. That explains why they are usually not understood by very young children, and no longer funny for teenagers. Metaphors and jokes—some beyond young children, funny at age 8, but considered clichés by age 18—are evidence of increased cognitive flexibility, linguistic ability, and social awareness. Age matters.

For example, a 3-year-old said that a bald man "has a barefoot head" but could not appreciate the metaphor himself, even though his fast-mapping produced it. In contrast, most adults easily grasp the point of the T-shirt slogan, "A bald head is a solar plate for a sex machine"—signifying awareness of the social assumption that the sex drive disappears with age.

Such metaphors are only gradually understood, as linguistic sophistication advances. Many adults do not realize how difficult it can be for children (and for people from another culture) to grasp figures of speech. The humorist James Thurber remembered

> the enchanted private world of my early boyhood. . . . In this world, businessmen who phoned their wives to say they were tied up at the office sat roped to their swivel chairs, and probably gagged, unable to move or speak except somehow, miraculously, to telephone. . . . Then there was the man who left town under a cloud. Sometimes I saw him all wrapped up in the cloud and invisible. . . . At other times it floated, about the size of a sofa, above him wherever he went. . . . [I remember] the old lady who was always up in the air, the husband who did not seem able to put his foot down, the man who lost his head during a fire but was still able to run out of the house yelling.
>
> *[Thurber, 1999, p. 40]*

Especially for Parents (see response, page 350): You've had an exhausting day but are setting out to buy groceries. Your 7-year-old son wants to go with you. Should you explain that you are so tired that you want to make a quick solo trip to the supermarket this time?

Adjusting Language to the Context

One aspect of language that advances markedly in middle childhood is *pragmatics,* the practical use of language, which includes the ability to adjust one's language to communicate with varied audiences in different contexts. This ability is obvious to linguists when they listen to children talk informally with their friends and formally with their teachers or parents (never calling the latter a rotten egg).

Can You Text Me? Few adults over 40 know how to "text" anyone, but many schoolchildren quickly become masters of text messaging. Their universal use of the informal texting code—terse, ungrammatical, symbol-laden—is evidence of their ability to learn rapidly from one another.

Children are able to switch back and forth, depending on the audience, between different manners of speaking, or "codes." Each code includes variations in many aspects of language—tone, pronunciation, gestures, sentence length, idioms, vocabulary, and grammar. Sometimes the switch is between *formal code* (used in academic contexts) and *informal code* (used with friends); sometimes it is between standard or proper speech and dialect or vernacular (used on the street). Many children use a code in text messaging, with numbers (411), abbreviations (LOL), and emoticons (☺).

During middle childhood, children excel at pragmatics, using the appropriate code in each context. They not only adjust to their audience but can use logic to do so, applying grammatical rules in the classroom but not on the playground.

Children need help from teachers to become fluent in the formal code so that they will be able to communicate with educated adults from many places. The logic of grammar—when a sentence is incomplete, or whether *who* or *whom* is correct—is almost impossible to figure out without a teacher's help.

The peer group teaches the informal code, and each local community teaches dialect and pronunciation. Teachers may be exasperated, but they need to realize that there is logic embedded in the informal code as well. For example, the informal code includes demonstrating one's social awareness by using curses, slang, and "improper" grammar with some friends but not others.

Second-Language Learning and Instruction

School-age children's need to use various codes pragmatically becomes most obvious when they speak one language at home and another at school. Almost every nation's population includes many children who speak a minority language, and most of the world's 6,000 languages are never used in school. About a billion children are educated in a language other than their mother tongue; many lose fluency in their first language as an unexpected consequence. When enough children have done so, their native languages will eventually disappear. It has been predicted that about 5,000 languages will die out by 2050 (May, 2005).

English-language learner (ELL) A child who is learning English as a second language.

In the United States, 4 million students (10 percent of the school population) are **English-language learners (ELLs)** (formerly referred to as *LEP,* meaning "limited English proficiency") and thus do not yet speak English well. Many live among their co-linguists in California, Texas, New York, New Jersey, and Florida, while others are surrounded by neighbors who cannot converse with them. Many public school classes (43 percent) have at least one ELL student (Zehler et al., 2003).

A Language Shift

Middle childhood is a good time for learning a new language. Children aged 7 to 11 are eager to communicate, are logical, and have an ear (and brain) for nuances of code and pronunciation. In Canada, Israel, and many other nations, most children become fluent in two languages before puberty (DeKeyser & Larson-Hall, 2005). In other nations, including the United States, only those who do not speak the majority language are expected to become bilingual. Usually the children succeed, while their elders have a much harder time.

Many immigrants learning a new national language speak a first language that is relatively close to it. For example, those who already read and write Spanish, French, or another Romance language have a foundation for learning English, since the alphabet, many sounds, and some words are similar. Literacy and fluency in the first language make it easier to learn a second one—an example of the benefits of the knowledge base. If teachers show them how to sound out letters and recognize words that are cognates, most school-age children grasp English quickly (Carlo et al., 2004). However, children whose first language has symbol and sound systems that are markedly different from the language to be learned (e.g., Arabic and Asian children learning English) have a harder time (Snow & Kang, 2006). Linguistic discrepancies are not the only factor: Children are quite sensitive to social attitudes, especially of teachers, and that sensitivity may make them resist learning a new language. Korean immigrants to the United States learn English more rapidly than Korean immigrants to Japan learn Japanese, for reasons other than linguistic ones.

language shift A change from one language to another, which occurs not only in speaking and writing but also in the brain. A language shift is evident in many children who no longer speak or understand their mother tongue because a new language has come to dominate the linguistic areas of their brains.

Many American children, especially from Asian families, make a **language shift,** replacing their original language with English rather than becoming fluent in both languages (Tse, 2001). One reason is the connection between language and memory: concepts are remembered best in the language in which they were learned (Marian & Fausey, 2006). Many immigrant children connect English with achievement and success.

The language shift troubles many adults. Some parents send children to "heritage" language classes after school or on Saturdays. In the 1990s in the Los Angeles area, 80 Chinese heritage schools had 15,000 pupils (Liu, 2006). Parents and others fear that language loss means a loss of culture, but they know that failure to learn the dominant language is a lifelong handicap. These are both valid fears:

> Challenges of adaptation to a new language and culture for child migrants are reflected in data about their academic achievement. Language minority children are at demonstrably greater risk than native speakers of experiencing academic difficulty . . . in the United States, . . . in the Netherlands, . . . in Great Britain, . . . and in Japan.
>
> [*Snow & Kang, 2006, p. 76*]

Experts hope that all children speak and write the majority language fluently while not losing their native tongue. Children who learned the majority language from infancy should also master a second language, ideally before puberty. Few

➤Response for Parents (from page 349): Your son would understand your explanation, but you should take him along if you can do so without losing patience. You wouldn't ignore his need for food or medicine; don't ignore his need for learning. While shopping, you can teach vocabulary (does he know *pimientos, pepperoni, polenta*?), categories ("root vegetables," "freshwater fish"), and math (which size box of cereal is cheaper?). Explain in advance that you need him to help you find items and carry them and that he can choose only one item that you wouldn't normally buy. Seven-year-olds can understand rules, and they enjoy being helpful.

children in the United States accomplish this, partly because experts do not agree on the best way to reach these goals. Political controversies have made objective research difficult; no single approach has been proved to be the best (Bialystok, 2001; Hinkel, 2005; Snow & Kang, 2006).

Methods of Teaching a Second Language

Approaches range from **immersion,** in which instruction in all school subjects occurs entirely in the new language, to the opposite approach, in which children learn in their first language until the second language can be taught as a "foreign" tongue. Variations between these extremes include **bilingual education,** with instruction in two languages, and, in North America, **ESL (English as a second language)** programs in which ELL children are taught intensively and exclusively in English to prepare them for regular classes.

immersion A strategy in which instruction in all school subjects occurs in the second (majority) language that a child is learning.

bilingual education A strategy in which school subjects are taught in both the learner's original language and the second (majority) language.

ESL (English as a second language) An approach to teaching English in which all children who do not speak English are placed together in an intensive course to learn basic English so that they can be educated in the same classroom as native English speakers.

The success of any method seems to depend on the literacy of the home environment (the specific language used at home matters less than the frequency of reading, writing, and listening), the warmth and skill of the teacher, and the overall cultural context. Any method tends to fail if children feel shy, stupid, or lonely because of their language. The importance of the teacher's attitude is demonstrated by Yolanda and Paul.

a personal perspective

Two Immigrant Children

Teachers and schools can make a substantial difference in whether or not an immigrant child succeeds. Consider how two children, both Mexican American, describe their experiences with school in their adopted country.

Yolanda:

When I got here [from Mexico at age 7], I didn't want to stay here, 'cause I didn't like the school. And after a little while, in third grade, I started getting the hint of it and everything and I tried real hard in it. I really got along with the teachers. . . . They would start talking to me, or they kinda like pulled me up some grades, or moved me to other classes, or took me somewhere. And they were always congratulating me.

Paul:

I grew up . . . ditching school, just getting in trouble, trying to make a dollar, that's it, you know? Just go to school, steal from the store, and go sell candies at school. And that's what I was doing in the third or fourth grade. . . . I was always getting in the principal's office, suspended, kicked out, everything, starting from the third grade.

My fifth grade teacher, Ms. Nelson . . . she put me in a play and that like tripped me out. Like, why do you want me in a play? Me, I'm just a mess-up. Still, you know, she put me in a play. And in the fifth grade, I think that was the best year out of the whole six years. I learned a lot about the Revolutionary War. . . . Had good friends. . . . We had a project we were involved in. Ms. Nelson . . . just involved everyone. We made books, this and that. And I used to write, and wrote two, three books. Was in a book fair. . . . She got real deep into you. Just, you know, "Come on now, you can do it." That was a good year for me, fifth grade.

[quoted in Nieto, 2000, pp. 220, 249]

Note that initially, Yolanda didn't like the United States because of school, but her teachers "kind of pulled me up." By third grade she was beginning to get "the hint of it." For Paul, school was where he sold stolen candy and where his third-grade teacher sent him to the principal, who suspended him. Ms. Nelson's fifth grade was "a good year" for him, but it was too late. Soon Paul was sent to a special school, and the text suggests that he was in jail by age 18. Yolanda, in contrast, became a successful young woman.

Second-language learning remains controversial in the United States, even among immigrants who do not speak English. Cognitive research leaves no doubt that school-age children *can* learn a second language if taught logically, step by step, and that they *can* maintain their original language. The best strategies include a language-rich environment (at home and school), with ample instruction in reading, writing, and speaking (Hinkel, 2005).

GIDEON MENDEL / CORBIS

Together They Learn Thousands of children worldwide do not understand the language used in their schools because their families are refugees, asylum seekers, or immigrants. Ideally, teachers, like this one in London, use guided participation to individualize instruction as they help these children learn the new language. Note that both the teacher and the student point, listen, and speak.

The likelihood of parents, school, and culture encouraging bilingualism in children is affected by the SES of the family and of the minority group. As you remember from Chapter 1, it is difficult to separate culture and ethnicity from SES. This problem is compounded when a population speaks a non-native language. Furthermore, education is an expression of national policy. An overview finds that "language teaching has always been susceptible to political and social influences" (Byram & Feng, 2005, p. 926).

SUMMING UP

Children continue to learn language rapidly during the school years. They become more flexible, logical, and knowledgeable, figuring out the meanings of new words and grasping metaphors, jokes, and compound words. Many converse with friends using informal speech and master a more formal code to use in school. They are able to master whatever grammar and vocabulary they are taught, and they succeed at the practical task of communicating differently with friends, teachers, and family members.

Millions become proficient in a second language, a process facilitated by teachers who help them connect the new language and their original one and by peers who do not make them feel ashamed. Adults who speak and listen to each child, in school and at home, continue to help with language learning. The cultural context is crucial for making children aware of how much each language is valued by their community and nation. ■

Teaching and Learning

School-age children are great learners. Magical and egocentric thinking no longer dominate, yet 7- to 11-year-olds are not yet as resistant to authority (including teacher demands) as adolescents sometimes are.

As we have just described, school-age children develop strategies, accumulate knowledge, apply logic, and think quickly. Throughout history, children have been given new responsibility and instruction at about age 7, because that is when their bodies and brains are ready. Traditionally, this occurred at home, but now 90 percent of the world's 7-year-olds are in school.

Most parents, teachers, and political leaders believe that their children are learning what they need. In the United States (and probably in other nations as well), parents rate their children's schools higher than do nonparents in the same community, and adults in general tend to rate their local schools higher than they rate schools nationwide (Snyder et al., 2004). In the same way, many parents of home-schooled and private school children believe that public schools are worse than research finds them to be (Green & Hoover-Dempsey, 2007; Lubienski & Lubienski, 2005).

Exposure and Expectations

Important insights into the learning of all children have resulted from data on family SES. Decades of research throughout the world have found a powerful connection between academic achievement and socioeconomic status (Hauser-Cram et al., 2006; Plank & MacIver, 2003).

Children from low-income families are least likely to succeed in school, primarily because of language difficulties. Not only do they have smaller vocabularies, but their grammar is simpler (fewer compound sentences, dependent clauses, and conditional verbs) and their sentences are shorter (Hart & Risley, 1995; Hoff, 2003). They fall behind their peers first in talking, then in reading, and then in other subjects.

The information-processing perspective forces us to look at specifics of daily input that might affect the brain and thus a child's ability to learn. Possible influences abound—lead in house paint, inadequate prenatal care, lack of a nourishing breakfast, overcrowded households, few books at home, teenage parents, authoritarian child rearing . . . the list could go on and on. All of these factors correlate with low SES and less learning, but no one of them has been proven to be a major cause of poor school achievement.

There are three factors, however, that *do* appear to play an important role. One is early exposure to language. Unlike parents with higher education, many less educated parents do not speak extensively or elaborately with their children. The reasons correlate with low income (financial stress, not enough time for each child, neighborhood noise) but are not directly caused by it. Indeed, children from high-SES families who rarely hear language also do poorly in school.

In one study, researchers observed young children in their homes for three years, recording a total of 30 hours of talk per family, on average. Children in the highest-SES families heard about 2,000 words an hour, while children in the lowest-SES families heard only about 600 words per hour (Hart & Risley, 1995).

Many other studies have found a "powerful linkage" between adult linguistic input and later child output (Weizman & Snow, 2001, p. 276). Remember that dendrites in the brain grow to accommodate the child's experiences, including experience with language. This research confirms the benefits of parents talking to children.

A second factor is expectations. Many people believe that teachers' and parents' expectations are the reason some children master school subjects, whereas others do not. Research in many nations support this view (Melhuish et al., 2008; Phillipson & Phillipson, 2007; Rosenthal, 1991; Rubie-Davies, 2007).

Closely related to these microcosm expectations are the macrosystem expectations. Some cultures do not expect much of poor children, so such children are sent to schools that have far fewer resources, are given inadequate health care, and receive preparation only for low-income employment.

These three factors correlate with low SES, but the connection between them and learning is not inevitable. One of many exceptions is E. P. Jones, who won the 2004 Pulitzer Prize for his novel *The Known World* (2003). He grew up in a very poor family, headed by a single mother who was illiterate but who had high expectations for her son. Jones writes:

> For as many Sundays as I can remember, perhaps even Sundays when I was in the womb, my mother has pointed across "I" street to Seaton [school] as we come and go to Mt. Carmel [church].
>
> "You gonna go there and learn about the whole world."
>
> *[E. P. Jones, 1992/2003, p. 29]*

Many studies have confirmed that early language and adult expectations promote children's learning. This finding helps explain the lower average achievement for children of low-income families, but it is equally relevant for all children.

Influences on Curriculum

Everywhere in the world, children are taught to read, write, and do arithmetic. There are some generally accepted standards for what children can learn: Because of brain maturation and the necessity of learning in sequence, no nation teaches 6-year-olds to multiply three-digit numbers or read paragraphs fluently out loud, but every nation expects 10-year-olds to do so. Some of the sequences for reading and math are listed in Tables 12.2 and 12.3.

TABLE 12.2

Sequence of Norms and Expectations for Reading

Age	Norms and Expectations
4–5 years	Understand basic book concepts, including that English books are written from front to back, with print from left to right, and that words describe pictures.
	Recognize letters—name the letters on sight. Recognize own name.
6–7 years	Know the sounds of the consonants and vowels, including those that have two sounds (*c, g, o*). Use sounds to figure out words.
	Read simple words, such as *cat, sit, ball, jump.*
8 years	Read simple sentences out loud, 50 words per minute, including words of two syllables.
	Understand basic punctuation, consonant/vowel blends.
	Comprehend what is read.
9–10 years	Read paragraphs and chapters.
	Understand more advanced punctuation (e.g., the colon).
	Answer comprehension questions about concepts as well as facts.
	Read polysyllabic words (*vegetarian, population, multiplication*).
11–12 years	Demonstrate rapid and fluent oral reading (more than 100 words per minute).
	Comprehend paragraphs about unfamiliar topics.
	Sound out new words, figuring out meaning using cognates and context.
	Read for pleasure.
13+ years	Continue to build vocabulary, with emphasis more on comprehension than on speech.

Reading is a complex mix of skills, and children's skill at reading depends on brain maturation, education, and culture. The sequence given here is approximate; it should not be taken as a standard to measure any particular child.

TABLE 12.3

Sequence of Norms and Expectations for Math

Age	Norms and Expectations
4–5 years	Count to 20.
	Understand one-to-one correspondence of objects and numbers.
	Understand *more* and *less.*
	Recognize and name shapes.
6 years	Count to 100.
	Understand *bigger* and *smaller.*
	Add and subtract one-digit numbers.
8 years	Add and subtract two-digit numbers.
	Understand simple multiplication and division.
10 years	Add, subtract, multiply, and divide multidigit numbers.
	Understand simple fractions, percents, area and perimeter of shapes.
	Understand word problems.
12 years	Begin to use abstract concepts, such as formulas, algebra.

Math learning depends heavily on direct instruction and repeated practice, which means that some children advance more quickly than others. This list is only a rough guide, to illustrate the importance of sequence.

National Variations

The specifics of the educational curriculum vary by nation, by community, and by school subject. These variations are evident in the results of international tests, in the mix of school subjects, and in the relative power of parents, educators, and political leaders.

International Achievement Test Scores Objective assessment of curriculum might result from international, culture-neutral tests. Ideally, each nation would give the same tests, under the same conditions, to a representative group of children of a particular age and year of schooling. Such even-handed comparisons are impossible, however, because educational practices vary widely in different countries. For example, children in Scotland begin school at age 4 and thus had a three-year advantage over Russian children, who used to begin at age 7 (Mullis et al., 2004).

Because of either educational specifics or general themes of the culture, many Western nations score high in reading, as measured by the **Progress in International Reading Literacy Study (PIRLS).** In the 2006 study, most Canadian children did particularly well, and the United States ranked in the top half (Manzo, 2007a). Russian children now begin school at age 6, and in 2006 they scored at the top in the PIRLS. This result confirms some U.S. research indicating that learning in kindergarten is not simply a matter of brain maturation (Blair et al., 2007).

East Asian nations are advanced in math and science, according to another international test, the **Trends in Math and Science Study (TIMSS).** The average 10-year-old in Singapore is ahead of the top 5 percent of U.S. students in math, according to the TIMSS. Fourth-graders in Hong Kong, Japan, and Chinese Taipei (Taiwan) also do better than their counterparts in Western nations. This trend of East Asian superiority continues through high school (see Table 12.4).

Canada, England, and the United States are above average on the TIMSS, but not by much. (Poor performance has been suggested as one reason the United States has stopped participating in TIMSS; Viadero, 2007.) The lowest-ranking nations—Tunisia, Morocco, and the Philippines (not shown in the table)—do not have a long history of universal fourth-grade education. No very poor nations participated in the testing, finding it too expensive, too discouraging, or too difficult.

Progress in International Reading Literacy Study (PIRLS) Inaugurated in 2001, a planned five-year cycle of international trend studies in the reading ability of fourth-graders.

TIMSS (Trends in Math and Science Study) An international assessment of the math and science skills of fourth- and eighth graders. Although the TIMSS is very useful, different countries' scores are not always comparable, because sample selection, test administration, and content validity are hard to keep uniform.

Especially for Future Research Scientists (see response, page 356): What should you watch for in news reports about the TIMSS data?

TABLE 12.4

TIMSS Rankings of Average Math Achievement Scores of Eighth-Graders, Selected Countries*

Country	2003	1999	1995
Singapore	1	1	1
Korea	2	2	2
Hong Kong	3	3	4
Japan	4	4	3
Netherlands	5	6	6
Canada**	6	5	7
Hungary	7	8	8
Czech Republic	8	7	5
Russian Federation	9	9	9
Australia	10	10	10
United States	11	11	12
New Zealand	12	12	11
Cyprus	13	13	13
Iran	14	14	14

*Not all of the countries that participated in TIMSS (25 in 2003) are reported because most of them did not give this test in all three years. Eighth-grade rankings are given here; the fourth-grade rankings are similar, but not as much comparative data are available.

**Results for Canada are for the provinces of Ontario and Quebec only and thus are not strictly comparable with other countries' average scores.

Source: International Association for the Evaluation of Educational Achievement, 2003; http://timss.bc.edu, accessed April 25, 2007.

"Big deal, an A in math. That would be a D in any other country."

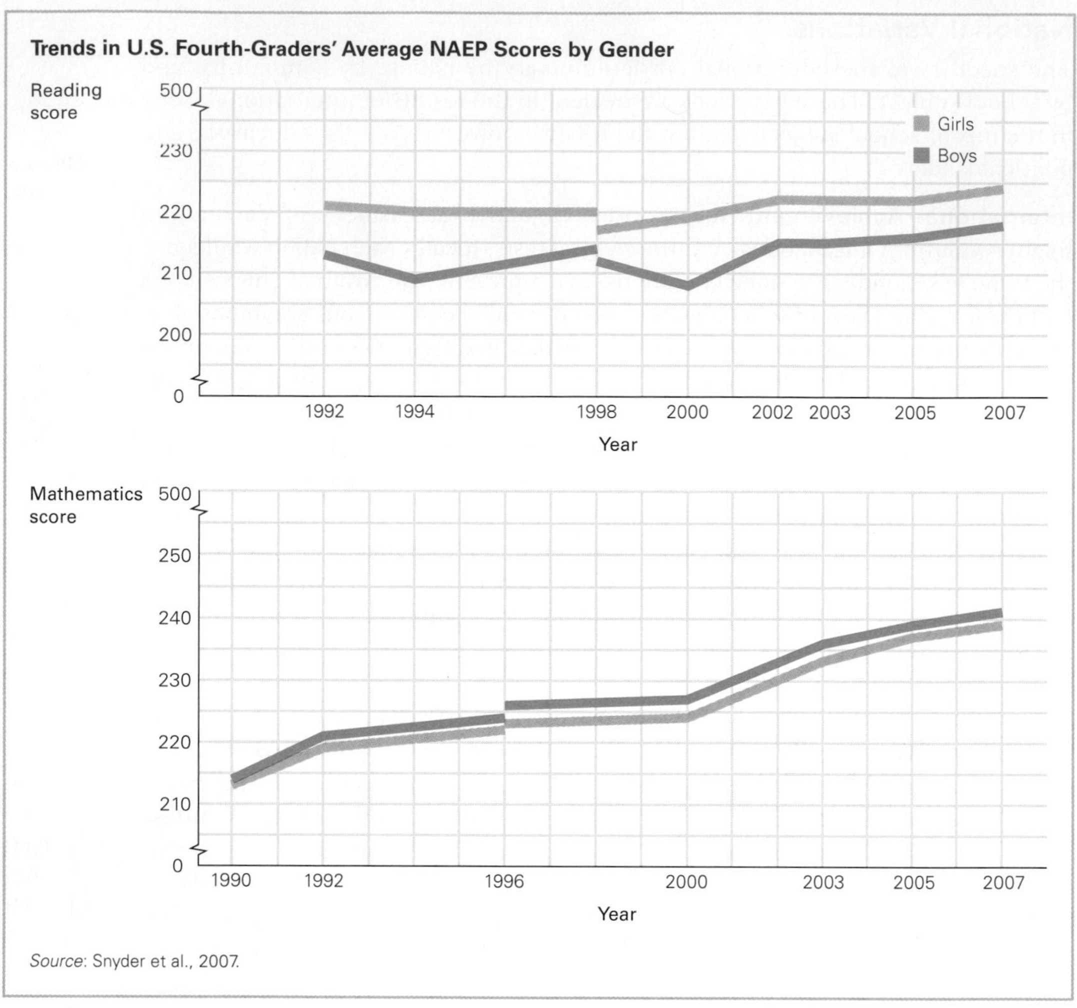

FIGURE 12.3

Not So Different Many observers assume that boys are better at math and girls are better at reading. In reality, these gender gaps are not very wide, as indicated by average scores on the annual National Assessment of Educational Progress (NAEP) tests. The maximum gender difference among fourth-graders, in reading in 2000, was just 10 points out of a possible 500. More typical are math scores, in which there was less than a one-point difference in 2007.

Gender Differences in School Performance Gender differences in performance are both confirmed and refuted by the data. Internationally, girls are slightly ahead in verbal skills and boys in math. In the United States, girls are catching up to boys in math by age 9, but boys are still a little behind in reading (see Figure 12.3). A possible reason is that processing speed develops more slowly in boys, a finding that implies the existence of differences in male and female brains (Camarata & Woodcock, 2006).

It is a fact that when it comes to overall school performance, nations differ from one another much more than boys differ from girls, and the extent of the gender spread varies. To pick two extremes found in the 2003 administration of the TIMSS, Scottish fourth-grade boys averaged 11 points higher in math than did girls, but Filipino girls averaged 9 points above Filipino boys. (In the United States, boys averaged 8 points higher.)

Compare those gender differences with the differences between the lowest- and highest-scoring nations, specifically the 255-point difference between Tunisia's 339 and Singapore's 594. Such results led one team to propose a *gender-similarities hypothesis* that males and females are similar on most measures, with very few exceptions (Hyde & Linn, 2006).

A major exception appears in the early grades, when girls typically get higher grades than boys do. In adolescence, however, girls' achievement levels tend to decrease, and relatively few females become scientists. Many reasons for this overall

➤Response for Future Research Scientists (from page 355): The next set of published results of the TIMSS is expected in 2009. As someone who knows how to think like a scientist, see if the headlines accurately reflect the data.

SHEHZAD NOORANI / PETER ARNOLD, INC.

Catching Up with the West These Iranian girls are acting out a poem they have memorized from their third-grade textbook. They attend school in a UNICEF-supported Global Education pilot project. Their child-centered classes encourage maximum participation.

difference in school performance have been suggested (Williams & Ceci, 2007): Girls approaching adolescence may wish to avoid seeming to be more intelligent than boys; girls may be less likely to persevere when material becomes confusing (Dweck, 2007); or girls may be influenced by stereotypes that linger among their role models (79 percent of teachers in U.S. public schools are women, but 53 percent of principals are men; Snyder et al., 2007).

Deciding What Children Should Learn International differences in test scores occur in part because the curriculum varies from nation to nation. For example, science has traditionally received much less emphasis in the United States than has literacy. This emphasis may be changing, as TIMSS scores may reveal.

Beyond the basics (reading, writing, and math), national differences in curriculum content are notable. For example, reasoned speaking and logical argument are taught in Russia and France but not in India (where children are expected to be quiet) or the United States (where children are expected to have opinions, not necessarily logic) (R. Alexander, 2000). Memorization is important in India but is less so in England. In some places, physical education and the arts are essential; in France, for example, every week children take physical education for three hours and arts education for more than two hours (Marlow-Ferguson, 2002).

Even nations that are geographically and culturally close to each other differ in specifics. For example, every elementary school student in Australia spends at least two hours per week studying science, but only 23 percent of students in nearby New Zealand do so (Snyder et al., 2004).

When, how, to whom, and whether second-language instruction should be provided also varies markedly from nation to nation. Within some nations, including the United States, second-language instruction varies from district to district, as already explained. Even in the same district and under the same policy, teacher quality varies, as the quotations from Yolanda and Paul illustrate and as research has confirmed (Hinkel, 2005). In other nations, including most European countries, every elementary school child learns at least one language in addition to his or her native tongue.

Religious instruction is another major variable. In some nations, every public school teaches religion. For instance, Finnish public schools require religious education—and provide parents only three choices: Lutheran, Christian Orthodox, or nonsectarian (Marlow-Ferguson, 2002).

Especially for Parents (see response, page 358): Suppose you and your school-age children move to a new community that is 50 miles from the nearest location that offers instruction in your faith or value system. Your neighbor says, "Don't worry, they don't have to make any moral decisions until they are teenagers." Is your neighbor correct?

In other nations, religious instruction is forbidden in state-sponsored schools. This is true in the United States, where 88 percent of children attend public schools; of the remainder, less than 2 percent are home-schooled and 10 percent attend a private school, most of which have a religious affiliation (Snyder et al., 2007).

Almost every nation has some private schools that are sponsored by religious groups and some that are not. Again, international variation is large. Sixteen percent of French children attend church-related schools; only 1 percent of Japanese children do (Marlow-Ferguson, 2002).

Deciding Who Determines the Curriculum Another major difference is whether the parents, the local community, the state, or the nation determines the curriculum. The following is from a minister of education in Australia:

> Education is a national priority and it is too important to be left at the mercy of state parochialism . . . with an increasingly mobile workforce, why should students and teachers be disadvantaged when they move interstate from one educational system to another?
>
> *[Bishop, quoted in Manzo, 2007b, p. 10]*

In Australia, local control of curriculum clashes with a push for national standards. The same clash is at the heart of the controversy in the United States over the **No Child Left Behind Act** of 2001, a federal law that promotes national standards for public schools. One of the most controversial aspects of educational standards is the testing that measures whether standards are being met. If schools do not meet the achievement benchmarks, parents can transfer their children out. Low-scoring schools lose funding and may have to close.

No Child Left Behind Act A U.S. law enacted in 2001 that was intended to increase accountability in education by requiring states to qualify for federal educational funding by administering standardized tests to measure school achievement.

Some states (e.g., Utah) have opted out of No Child Left Behind (NCLB), preferring their own tests and standards, even though they lose federal funds by doing so. Other states have created achievement tests that allow most schools to progress (and thus get federal funds). Most political leaders agree with the goals of NCLB (accountability and higher achievement) but not the strategies. As of this writing, revision is underway.

In the United States, a series of federally sponsored tests called the **National Assessment of Educational Progress (NAEP)** measure achievement in reading, mathematics, and other subjects. Fewer children are proficient in various skills on the NAEP than on state tests (see Figures 12.4 and 12.5), and the TIMSS shows that the NAEP may overestimate achievement (Cavanagh, 2007). Yet

National Assessment of Educational Progress (NAEP) An ongoing and nationally representative measure of U.S. children's achievement in reading, mathematics, and other subjects over time; nicknamed "the Nation's Report Card."

> local control of public schools is a hallowed tradition in American education and there has long been antipathy to the idea of a national test. . . . Some state educators say comparisons are unfair because NAEP is too rigorous and was designed to chart long-term trends, not to measure what states feel students should know.
>
> *[Vu, 2007]*

One problem with national standards, which is evident on every achievement test, is that states disagree about what they "feel children should know" and how they should learn it. Many schools (71 percent in one study) have recently cut parts of the curriculum (especially in subjects like art and music) in order to expand instruction in reading and math, in an effort to improve their chances of meeting the NCLB standards (Rentner et al., 2006).

In all these curriculum-related variations, advocating one best practice risks entanglement in ideology, politics, and culture, disconnected from the findings of educational research (Rayner et al., 2001). On their part, children do not necessarily learn what policy makers intend—or even what their own teachers teach.

➤Response for Parents (from page 357): No. In fact, these are prime years for moral education. You might travel those 50 miles once or twice a week or recruit other parents to organize a local program. Whatever you do, don't skip moral instruction. Discuss and demonstrate your moral and religious values, and help your children meet other children who share those values.

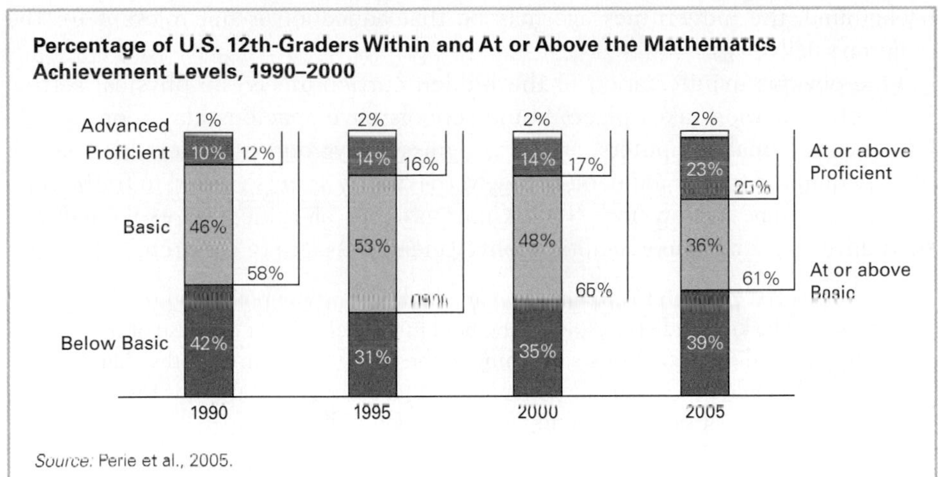

Percentage of U.S. 12th-Graders Within and At or Above the Mathematics Achievement Levels, 1990–2000

Source: Perie et al., 2005.

FIGURE 12.4

Better or Worse? Should a country's education policy emphasize helping more students become "Proficient" or better in mathematics or trying to make sure that fewer students score "Below Basic"? The United States seems to be choosing the former policy, with more resources allocated to the schools where students score high in math achievement.

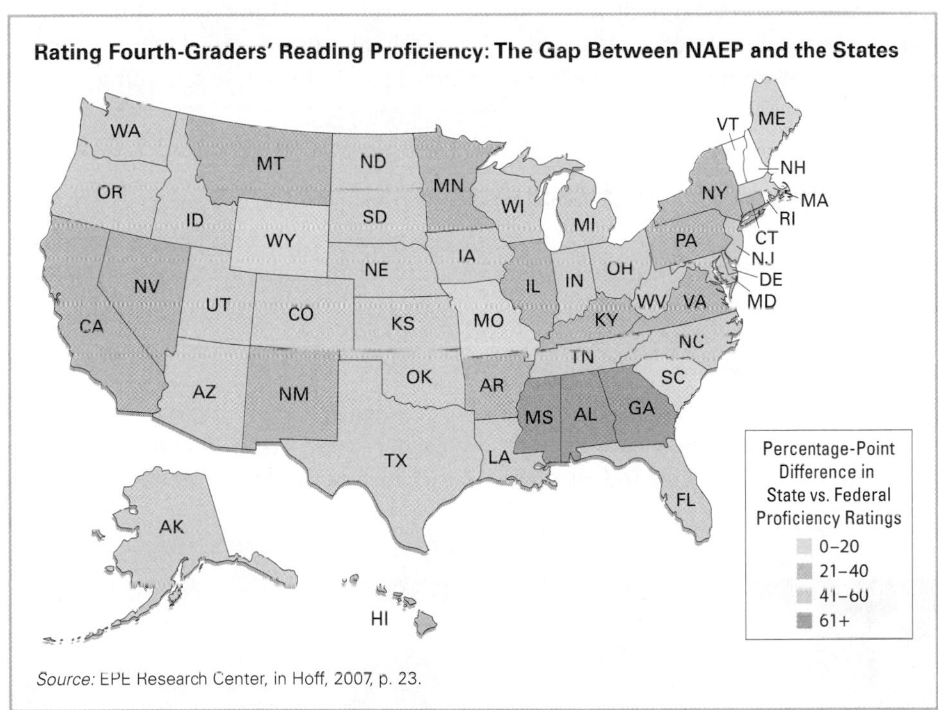

Rating Fourth-Graders' Reading Proficiency: The Gap Between NAEP and the States

Source: EPE Research Center, in Hoff, 2007, p. 23.

FIGURE 12.5

Local Standards Each state sets its own level of proficiency, which helps states in which children score low on the NAEP obtain more federal money for education. That practice may undercut high standards for student learning.

Intended, implemented, and attained curricula are three different things (Robitaille & Beaton, 2002). To complicate matters further, the official curriculum is always shadowed by a second, unspoken set of educational priorities, or a "hidden curriculum."

The Hidden Curriculum

Children inevitably absorb unrecognized lessons in school. These unofficial, unstated, or implicit rules and priorities constitute what has been called a **hidden curriculum.** The hidden curriculum makes itself known in such matters as course selection, tracking, teacher characteristics, discipline, teaching methods, sports competition, student government, and extracurricular activities. For example, if most teachers differ from most students in gender, ethnicity, or economic

hidden curriculum The unofficial, unstated, or implicit rules and priorities that influence the academic curriculum and every other aspect of learning in school.

background, the hidden message may be that education is not relevant for the children's daily lives.

One obvious manifestation of the hidden curriculum is the physical setting in which education takes place. Some schools have spacious classrooms, wide hallways, personal computers, and large, grassy playgrounds. Others have small, poorly equipped rooms and cement play yards or play streets, closed to traffic for a few hours a day. A New York State Commissioner of Education explained that such differences in school facilities convey clear messages to children:

> If you ask the children to attend school in conditions where plaster is crumbling, the roof is leaking and classes are being held in unlikely places because of overcrowded conditions, that says something to the child. . . . If, on the other hand, you send a child to a school in well-appointed [classrooms], that sends the opposite message. That says this counts. You count. Do well.
>
> *[Sobol, quoted in* Campaign for Fiscal Equity v. State of New York, *2001]*

A main reason some parents decide to educate their children at home is that they do not like the implicit learning in public schools. Home schooling is more likely when a family cannot afford private school tuition and when a married mother is not employed, so there are hidden lessons in home schooling as well (Isenberg, 2007).

Education Wars and Assumptions

As this discussion of the curriculum has demonstrated, adults differ in their beliefs about what children should learn—and how. Virtually every aspect of education is not merely debatable but has also caused bitter dispute.

The Reading Wars

Reading is a complex activity. The ability to read with speedy, automatic comprehension is the cumulative result of many earlier steps—from looking at picture books (at age 2 or earlier) to learning how to figure out unknown technical words

NAM Y. HUH / AP PHOTO

TED S. WARREN / AP PHOTO

Reading with Comprehension *(left)* Reading and math scores in third-grader Monica's Illinois elementary school showed improvement under the standards set by the No Child Left Behind Act. The principal noted a cost for this success in less time spent on social studies and other subjects. *(right)* Some experts believe that children should have their own books and be able to read them wherever and however they want. This strategy seems to be working with Josue and Cristo, two 8-year-olds who were given books through their after-school program in Rochester, Washington.

(at age 10 and beyond). Clashes over the best way to teach reading have led to "serious, sometimes acrimonious debate, fueling the well named 'reading wars'" (Keogh, 2004, p. 93).

Phonics Versus Whole Language Historically, schools used the **phonics approach** (from the root word for "sound"), in which children learn to read by learning letter-sound correspondences in order to decipher simple words. This approach seemed to be supported by behaviorism (see Chapter 2) and, more recently, by information-processing theory, which favors step-by-step instructions, with frequent repetition.

phonics approach Teaching reading by first teaching the sounds of each letter and of various letter combinations.

Piaget's theory—that children learn on their own as soon as their minds are ready—provided the rationale for another method of teaching reading, called the **whole-language approach.** For concrete operational thinkers, abstract, decontextualized memorization (as in traditional phonics) may be beyond a child's capacity. Literacy is the outcome of natural motivation to use all language skills—talking and listening, reading and writing.

whole-language approach Teaching reading by encouraging early use of all language skills—talking and listening, reading and writing.

When teachers use the whole-language approach, young children (in addition to reading) draw, talk, and write, all as part of the entire (whole) language process. They also invent their own spelling, because many languages, including English, are too variable to be spelled phonetically (see Figure 12.6).

However, unlike talking, which is experience-expectant, reading and writing are experience-dependent. Children need instruction to read and write, as Vygotsky might have argued. Beginning readers may need to be taught to translate spoken words into printed ones, and vice versa. Some children may never "discover" how to become fluent readers on their own if whole language is followed strictly.

Calling a Truce Research arising from every contemporary developmental theory has noted the uniqueness of each child as a beginning reader. Learning styles, past experiences, and motivation vary, as do language proficiency and maturation. In practical terms, this means that phonics may be essential for children who need help learning how to sound out new words. For them, targeted early instruction in letter–sound combinations may be crucial (Torgesen, 2004). Score one for phonics.

Yet for comprehension and memory, children need to make connections between concepts, not just between letters. Educators complain about a "fourth-grade slump," when many children have difficulty reading fluently with comprehension (Samuels, 2007). Phonics cannot help them with this. Rather, they are helped by reading books that are challenging and interesting and by writing about their own experiences and interests. Score one for whole language.

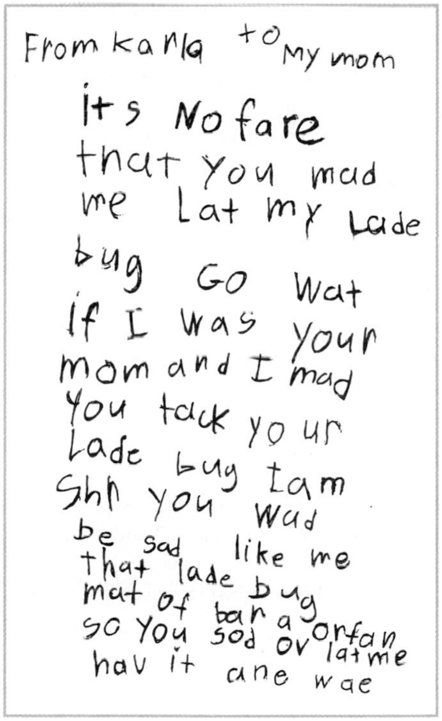

This tie points toward a truce in the reading wars. A focus on phonics need not undercut instruction that motivates children to read, write, and discuss with their classmates and their parents. For reading comprehension and fluency, phonemic awareness is a beginning, but other aspects of literacy are important as well (Muter et al., 2004). As the editors of a leading publication for teachers explain:

> In any debate on reading instruction that counterposes a focus on skills with a focus on enjoyment—or that pits phonological skills against the knowledge necessary to comprehend grade-level material—there is only one good answer: Kids need both.
>
> [*The Editors,* American Educator, *2004, p. 5*]

Fortunately, experts on the two sides in the reading wars have ended their bitter feud. Most developmentalists and many reading specialists now believe that there are "alternate pathways in learning to read" (Berninger et al., 2002, p. 295). Teachers should use both phonics and whole language (Donat, 2006). Research leaves

FIGURE 12.6

"You Wud Be Sad Like Me" Although Karla uses invented spelling, her arguments show that she is reasoning quite logically; her school-age mind is working quite well. (If you have trouble deciphering Karla's note, turn the book upside down for a translation.)

"From Karla to my mom. It's no fair that you made me let my lady bug go. What if I was your mom and I made you take your lady bug. I am sure you would be sad like me. That lady bug might have been an orphan. So you should have let me have it anyway."

little doubt that in the early grades, systematic phonics instruction "is important" (Camilli et al., 2003, p. 34), but it should not come at the expense of comprehension and pleasure.

Researchers are less sure of "the best approaches and methods of reading and writing instruction for students older than age 9 and interventions for those who are struggling readers in grades 4–12" (McCardle & Chhabra, 2004, pp. 472–473). It is known, however, that, for older children, reading instruction can and should be connected to literature, history, science, and other areas of study. An expanding knowledge base aids comprehension and helps avoid the fourth-grade slump. One teacher who knew that and taught accordingly may have saved some people's lives.

a personal perspective

Where Did You Learn *Tsunami?*

Before December 26, 2004, perhaps 1 percent of the world's population knew the word *tsunami*. I was in the other 99. Over Christmas that year, when my nephew Bill said that we should pray for the victims of the tsunami, I marveled that he could pronounce a word that I had not known until I read that day's headlines.

Even among the 1 percent who knew the word, few understood it. Some British 10-year-olds were exceptions. Their teacher, Andrew Kearny, had shown his class a video about survivors of a tsunami that struck Hawaii in the 1950s. He drew a diagram of how a tsunami is generated, which students copied into their exercise books. A girl named Tilly Smith was in that class.

> Two weeks later, Tilly was on Maikhao Beach in Phuket, Thailand, with her parents and her 7-year-old sister. Suddenly, the tide went out, leaving a wide stretch of sand where the ocean had been. Most tourists stood gawking at the disappearing ocean, but Tilly grabbed her mother's hand: "Mummy, we must get off the beach now. I think there's going to be a tsunami."
>
> Tilly's parents alerted other holiday makers nearby, then raced to tell their hotel staff in Phuket. The hotel swiftly evacuated Maikhao Beach, and minutes later a huge wave crashed onto the sand, sweeping all before it. Incredibly, the beach was one of the few in Phuket where no one was killed.
>
> *[Larcombe, 2005, p. 43]*

Tilly and her family survived for many reasons: Tilly remembered what she had learned; her parents heeded her warning; higher ground was nearby. But some credit goes to her teacher, who did more than list *tsunami* as a vocabulary word. He used examples and activities to give the concept meaning. Ten-year-olds are ready to learn and remember as long as knowledge is concrete (Piaget) and instruction includes examples and active participation (Vygotsky). This is not just good fortune, but also good education.

The Math Wars

Mathematics instruction has provoked even more controversy than instruction in reading, for at least three reasons:

1. Economic development depends on science and technology, and math is vital in both of those fields. As nations experience economic recession, STEM (science, technology, engineering, mathematics) study is seen as crucial.
2. North American and western European students are weaker in math than are students from other nations, especially East Asian nations.
3. Many children hate math and feel intimidated by it. A 2008 Google search found 81,600 sites for "math phobia."

As a result, math education is widely seen as vital yet inadequate, and that makes it vulnerable to quick solutions suggested by angry adults. That is not the best way to develop curriculum, but it is a good way to start a war.

According to one report, "U.S. mathematics instruction has been scorched in the pedagogical blaze known as the 'math wars'—a divide between those who see a need for a greater emphasis on basic skills in math and others who say students lack a broader, conceptual understanding of the subject" (Cavenagh, 2005, p. 1). This is similar to the debate over phonics vs. whole language, or direct instruction vs. discovery learning. Is there any chance of a truce?

Old and New Math Historically, math was taught by rote; children memorized number facts, such as the multiplication tables, and filled page after page of workbooks. In reaction against this approach, many educators, inspired especially by Piaget and Vygotsky, sought to make math instruction more active and engaging—less a matter of memorization than of discovery (Ginsburg et al., 1998).

This newer approach is controversial. Many parents and educators believe that children need to memorize number facts. Educators as well as mathematicians stress that math involves a particular set of rules, symbols, and processes that must be taught and that discovery can play only a limited role (Mervis, 2006).

Although math phobia may be paralyzing, high math self-confidence may not be the antidote. In the United States, 51 percent of eighth-graders are highly confident of their math ability, even though their scores on international math achievement tests are relatively low. Among 46 nations, only Israel has children with a higher level of math confidence (59 percent) than does the United States (Snyder et al., 2006). The highest math achievement scores are from Chinese Taipei (Taiwan), where relatively few (26 percent) of the students are highly confident of their math ability.

A Sequence of Skills Inspired by the information-processing approach, which looks at tiny increments in cognition, researchers have studied children day by day to understand how math understanding emerges (Siegler, 1996). Apparently, cognitive advances do not occur suddenly (in stages) and are not a matter of rote memory; rather, they occur in overlapping waves. Strategies ebb and flow, gradually becoming the standard. A child trying to add 5 and 3, for instance, begins by counting each one (probably on fingers, 1-2-3-4-5-6-7-8), and later tries a quicker strategy called "min," which involves counting up from the higher number (5 + 6, 7, 8). The min strategy is quicker than counting one by one, but a child might use min once or twice and then revert to the earlier strategy. Eventually min is used more often. Finally, adding 5 + 3 becomes automatic; children think they always knew how to do it, forgetting the waves of learning that went before.

What can teachers do to help children learn math? TIMSS experts videotaped 231 math classes in three nations—Japan, Germany, and the United States—to analyze national differences (Stigler & Hiebert, 1999). The U.S. teachers presented math at a lower level than did their German and Japanese counterparts, with more definitions but less connection to what the students had already learned. Math was a dull subject for the U.S. children, because their "teachers seem to believe that learning terms and practicing skills is not very exciting" (p. 89).

In contrast, the Japanese teachers were excited about math instruction, working collaboratively and structuring lessons so that the children developed proofs and alternative solutions, alone and in groups. Teachers used social interaction (among groups of children and groups of teachers) and sequential curricula (lessons for each day, week, and year built on previous math knowledge), often presenting the students with problems to solve in groups.

One idea that follows from information-processing theory is to make each grade of elementary school math build on the previous year's instruction. This idea is now endorsed by the National Council of Teachers of Mathematics (NCTM), an

Research Design

Scientists: NICHD Early Child Care Research Network, consisting of 29 leading child-care researchers.

Publication: *Developmental Psychology* (2004).

Participants: A total of 890 children in their second year of school in 651 elementary school classrooms. These children were part of a cohort of 1,634 children followed since birth, from 10 research sites, in various locations in the United States.

Design: Children's achievement and social outcomes were measured, as were teacher behaviors, via a structured three-hour observation in each classroom. Measures were first adjusted to reflect the children's academic and social backgrounds (e.g., SES, gender) and the teachers' backgrounds (e.g., education, ethnicity). Many factors were controlled to learn the effects of class size (which ranged from 10 to 39 students per teacher).

Major conclusions: Class size was irrelevant for many measures. Smaller classes (less than 20) were better in some ways but not all. For example, first-graders in smaller classes tended to develop better word-attack skills but were more disruptive. Their teachers were less structured but showed more warmth.

Comment: This study (cited in earlier chapters) features a large, geographically varied, longitudinal sample that allows controls for preexisting factors. However, the sample had few high-risk children (a newborn was excluded if the mother was under 19, did not speak English, or lived in an unsafe neighborhood).

influential group in the United States. For example, second-graders will learn addition, subtraction, and place value; multiplication, fractions, and decimals will be saved for the fourth grade (Mervis, 2006).

Fractions "have been downplayed" in the United States—a serious mistake, according to leaders in math education (Faulkner, quoted in Mervis, 2008, p. 1605). Some children develop a rudimentary understanding of fractions on their own, as they divide cakes, pizzas, and other things between them, trying to be fair. Other children do not already have that basic understanding. Research finds that good teachers, attuned to the children's math concepts, advance both kinds of children forward but that poor teachers help only those children who already understand the basics (Saxe, 2004).

Other Controversies

The educational landscape is filled with assumptions that are commonly held but debatable. For example, in the past 20 years adults have become convinced that children learn from homework, and many young children now bring work home. Yet some research finds that homework, if it is boring or too difficult, undermines learning instead of advancing it (Kohn, 2006).

Similarly, although many parents push for smaller class sizes, the evidence about the effect of class size is mixed (Blatchford, 2003; Hanushek, 1999; Milesi & Gamoran, 2006). Wide international variation is apparent, from a teacher–pupil ratio of 1 to 10 in Denmark to 1 to 30 in Turkey. Internationally, smaller is not necessarily better: Schools in Asian nations have large classes, yet students achieve high math and science scores (Snyder et al., 2006). Data on class size "do not lend themselves to straightforward implications for policy" (NICHD Early Child Care Research Network, 2004, p. 66; see the Research Design). Even a famous study in Tennessee, which found that smaller classes in kindergarten benefited children for several years and increased graduation rates, is open to various interpretations (Finn & Achilles, 1999; Finn et al., 2005).

Other reforms that have been strongly advocated—and strongly opposed—include raising teacher salaries; improving professional education; extending school hours; expanding the school year; creating charter schools; allowing school vouchers; and increasing sports, music classes, or silent reading. Valid, replicated, unbiased research on how beneficial each of these measures would be is thus far lacking. As one review of the impact of class size concludes:

> Reductions in class size are but one of the policy options that can be pursued to improve student learning. Careful evaluations of the impacts of other options, preferably through the use of more true experiments, along with an analysis of the costs of each option, need to be undertaken. However, to date there are relatively few studies that even compute the true costs of large class-size reduction programs, let alone ask whether the benefits . . . merit incurring the costs.
>
> *[Ehrenberg et al., 2001, p. 26]*

Similar conclusions apply for most other education reforms. Another review, this one about home schooling, charter schools, and vouchers, complains of "the difficulty of interpreting the research literature on this topic, most of which is biased and far from approaching balanced social science" (Boyd, 2007, p. 7).

The call for "evidence-based" education reforms is appreciated by all scientists, but school-based longitudinal research with valid comparison groups is almost nonexistent. A 19-member panel of experts seeking the best math curricula for the United States examined 16,000 studies but "found a serious lack of studies with adequate scale and design for us to reach conclusions" (Faulkner, quoted in Mervis, 2008, p. 1605).

Especially for School Administrators (see response, page 366): Children who wear uniforms in school tend to score higher on reading tests. Why?

Culture and Education

As you can see, many controversies regarding cognitive development as it relates to education are political more than developmental. Piaget, Vygotsky, information-processing theory (and, in earlier decades, progressive education and behavior modification) have all been used to support particular practices, sometimes for good reasons, sometimes not. To conclude this chapter, we highlight again the sometimes hidden role of culture.

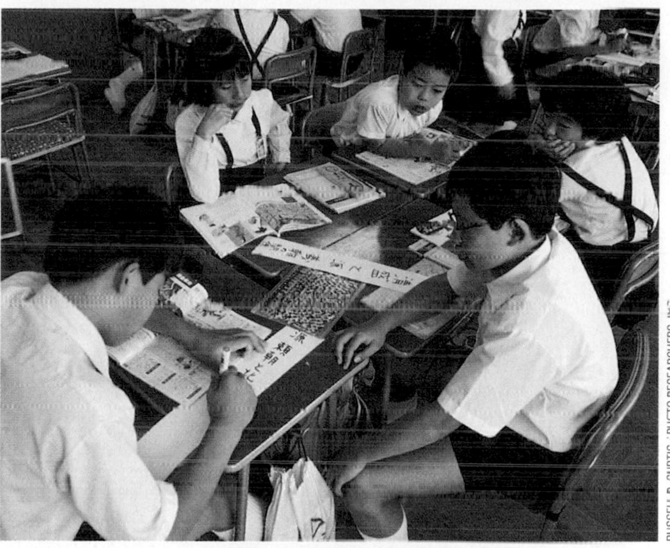

RUSSELL D. CURTIS / PHOTO RESEARCHERS, INC.

Collaborative Learning Japanese children are learning mathematics in a more structured and socially interactive way than are their North American counterparts.

Japanese Education: One Example

How good is Japanese education? Ever since Harold Stevenson first compared schoolchildren in North America and Japan (H.W. Stevenson, Chen, et al., 1993; H.W. Stevenson, Lee, et al., 1990), many American parents have envied their Japanese counterparts. Their children spend more time in school, with longer days, weeks (including Saturday mornings), and years (only one month of summer vacation). Children study both at school (and so have less free time) and at home (and so have fewer household chores). Three-fourths of them attend *juko,* private classes that supplement public school.

Similarly, many U.S. teachers envy Japanese teachers, for good reason. In Japan, teachers are respected by students and parents. In addition, teachers learn from one another; time is specifically scheduled for teachers to spend collaborating with one another (Stigler & Hiebert, 1999). Furthermore, the Japanese government funds and guides education; this involvement fosters equity and allows children who move mid-year from one region to another to lose no time in catching up with their new classmates. Absenteeism is low, and less than 2 percent of high school students leave school before graduation.

Any of these factors may explain why Japanese children score far above their U.S. peers in math and science. This contrast was among the reasons almost all members of the U.S. Congress voted for No Child Left Behind in 2001: The program anticipated that every child in the United States would eventually learn as well, and as much, as Japanese children do.

Meanwhile, in Japan, many parents and government officials have expressed disappointment with the outcomes of public education (Hosaka, 2005; Sugie et al., 2006). Some Japanese children need help developing metacognitive skills that are not taught in school, partly because large class sizes and detailed curriculum requirements make individualized attention difficult (Ichikawa, 2005). In addition, the system may sacrifice creativity and independent thought, at least according to Western critics (Kohn, 2006).

Especially for Teachers (see response, page 367): You are teaching in a school that you find too lax or too strict, or with parents who are too demanding or too uncaring. Should you look for a different line of work?

In 2002, the Japanese government eased educational and testing requirements by instituting *yutori kyoiku,* which means "more relaxed education." The required curriculum was reduced by 30 percent to allow more emphasis on learning to think rather than on memorizing facts to get high test scores (Magara, 2005). The long-term results, like the results of No Child Left Behind, are not yet known. In both cases, the legislative changes may be superficial, since the overall culture supports a particular kind of education.

Culture Clash: Self-Discipline Versus Self-Confidence

Here are excerpts from two letters to a local newspaper in British Columbia, Canada. One mother wrote:

> Our children's performances are much lower both in academic and moral areas. I noticed the children have learned very little academically. They learned to have

> self-confidence instead of being self-disciplined; learned to speak up instead of being humbled; learned to be creative instead of self-motivated; and learned to simplify things instead of organizing. All of these characteristics were not balanced, and will be the source of disadvantage and difficulties in children in this competitive society.

Another parent responded:

> She wants her children to be self-disciplined, humble, self-motivated and organized, instead of being self-confident, assertive, creative and analytic. . . . These repressive, authoritarian, "traditional" parents who hanker for the days of yore, when fresh-faced school kids arrived all neatly decked out in drab-grey uniforms and shiny lace-up leather shoes, are a menace to society.
>
> *[quoted in K. Mitchell, 2001, pp. 64–65]*

In this district, many families were immigrants from Asia (including the author of the first letter), while others, as well as almost all the school administrators and teachers, were from families that had been in Canada for generations. Similar conflicts erupt in every community that has diverse groups of families or a difference in background between the teachers and the children.

Culture Clash: Question and Response

In another Canadian community, Inuit children were taught in their native language by Inuit teachers for their first two years of school and then were taught in French or English, the majority languages, by non-Inuits.

Both groups of teachers realized that they were failing. Few Inuit children became fluent in a second language, and most dropped out before graduation. Other research finds that many aboriginals (as members of Canada's First Nations are called) become alienated from their native culture and feel depressed or even suicidal as adolescents (Chandler et al., 2003). The problem seems at first to be with bilingual education—perhaps immersion too soon or too late. But culture, not language, may actually be the pivotal factor.

A scientist using naturalistic observation found that much more than a language shift occurred when these children moved from grade 2 to grade 3 (Eriks-Brophy & Crago, 2003). The Inuit teachers encouraged group learning and cooperation, almost never explicitly judging an individual student's response. By contrast, the non-Inuit teachers often criticized behaviors that the earlier teachers had encouraged, such as group cooperation (which the non-Inuit teachers called "talking out of turn"), helping each other ("cheating"), and attempts to answer ("mistakes").

A specific example illustrates this pattern. A common routine in North American schools is called initiation/response/evaluation: The teacher asks a question, a child responds, and the teacher states whether the response is correct or not. An analysis of 14 teachers in this Inuit school found that the initiation/response/evaluation routine dominated the instruction of the non-Inuit teachers (60 percent of the time) but not that of the Inuit teachers (18 percent) (Eriks-Brophy & Crago, 2003). For example, an Inuit teacher showed a picture and asked:

> **Teacher:** This one. What is it?
> **Student:** Tutuva (*an insect*).
> **Teacher:** What is it?
> **Student:** Tutuva.
> **Teacher:** All of us, look carefully.
> **Student:** Kituquianluti (*another insect, this time correct. The teacher nodded and breathed in.*)

➤Response for School Administrators (from page 364): The relationship reflects correlation, not causation. Wearing uniforms is more common when the culture of the school emphasizes achievement and study, with strict discipline in class and a policy of expelling disruptive students.

In contrast, a non-Inuit third-grade teacher asked:

Teacher: Richard, what is this?
Richard: It is an ear.
Teacher: Good.
Teacher: Rhoda, what is this?
Rhoda: Hair.
Teacher: No. What is this?
Rhoda: Face.
Teacher: It is a face.
Rhoda: It is a face.
Teacher: Very good, Rhoda.

[*quoted in Eriks-Brophy & Crago, 2003, pp. 406–407*]

Note that the Inuit teacher never verbally evaluated the child (merely nodding and breathing to signal correctness), but the second teacher did so at least three times ("good," "no," "very good"). No wonder the children became confused and discouraged. They were unprepared to make a cultural shift as well as a language one.

Such problems can emerge anywhere. Teaching methods are the outcome of cultural beliefs, a "social system that evolves over time" (Eriks-Brophy & Crago, 2003, p. 397), often hidden from the teachers themselves. Underlying the issues that parents seize on—discipline, phonics, and math scores—are deeper issues involving culture and values.

Every child wants to learn, every teacher wants to teach, and every family wants the best for its children. This makes hidden differences in curricula and methods much harder to reconcile than more obvious cultural manifestations. No one cares if a particular child eats goat, chitlins, or whale for dinner, but people everywhere care about what their own—and their neighbors'—children learn.

Children are influenced by adult biases, even when the adults are unaware of them. To lobby for a puppy, I knew to make up a poem; Sarah knew to get signed statements endorsing pierced ears; both of us were influenced by our culture's stress on the written word. Children everywhere likewise figure out how to please their parents, their teachers, and their culture—sometimes with orations, sometimes with silent obedience, sometimes to the detriment of their own development.

BOB DAEMMRICH / THE IMAGE WORKS

Hidden Curriculum This informal, bilingual first-grade class in Acoma Pueblo, New Mexico, is a contrast to the U.S. government's nineteenth-century policy of sending all Native American children to English-only boarding schools.

Observation Quiz (see answer, page 368): What three social constructions about proper education for Pueblo children do you see?

SUMMING UP

Societies throughout the world recognize that school-age children are avid learners and that educated citizens are essential to economic development. However, schools differ in what and how children are taught. The nature and content of education raise ideological and political concerns. Examples are found in the reading wars, the math wars, debates over class size, and many other aspects of the overt and the hidden curricula.

Research finds that direct instruction (in phonics; in mathematical symbols and procedures; in the vocabulary, grammar, and syntax of second languages) is useful, even essential, if children are to master all the skills that adults want them to learn. Also crucial are motivation, pride, and social interaction. School-age children are great learners, but they cannot learn everything. Adults decide the specifics, and cultural values are apparent in every classroom. ■

➤Response for Teachers (from page 365): Nobody works well in an institution they hate, but, before quitting the profession, remember that schools vary. There is probably another school nearby that is much more to your liking and that would welcome an experienced teacher. Before you make a move, however, assess the likelihood that you could adjust to your current position in ways that would make you happier. No school is perfect, nor is any teacher.

SUMMARY

Building on Theory

1. According to Piaget, children begin concrete operational thought at about age 6 or 7. Egocentrism diminishes and logic begins. School-age children can understand classification, conservation, identity, and reversibility.

2. Vygotsky stressed the social context of learning, including the specific lessons of school and the overall influence of culture. International research finds that maturation is one factor in the cognitive development of school-age children (as Piaget predicted) and that cultural and economic forces are also influential (as Vygotsky predicted).

3. An information-processing approach examines each step of the thinking process, from input to output, using the computer as a model. Humans are more creative than computers, but this approach is useful for understanding memory, perception, and expression.

4. Memory begins with information that reaches the brain from the sense organs. Then selection processes allow some information to reach working memory. Finally, long-term memory stores some images and ideas indefinitely, retrieving some parts when needed.

5. Selective attention, a broader knowledge base, logical strategies for retrieval, and faster processing advance every aspect of cognition. Repeated practice makes thought patterns and skill sets almost automatic, so that they require little time or conscious effort.

6. Children become better at controlling and directing their thinking as the prefrontal cortex matures. Consequently, metacognition advances.

Language

7. Language learning improves in many practical ways, including expanded vocabulary, as words are logically linked together.

8. Many children learn a second language, succeeding if they are well taught. In some schools, only one language is taught.

9. Children of low SES are usually lower in linguistic skills, primarily because they hear less language and because adult expectations for their learning are low.

Teaching and Learning

10. Nations and experts agree that education is critical during middle childhood. The vast majority of the world's children now attend primary school. Schools differ in what and how they teach, especially in the hidden curriculum.

11. International assessments are useful as comparisons, partly because few objective measures of learning are available. In the United States, the No Child Left Behind Act and the National Assessment of Educational Progress attempt to raise the standard of education, with mixed success.

12. The reading wars pitted advocates of phonics against advocates of the whole-language approach. A truce has been reached, however, as research finds that phonological understanding is essential for every child who is just learning to read but that motivation and vocabulary are important as well.

13. Math learned by rote and math learned via social interaction are the two sides of the "math wars." Math and science achievement are higher in East Asian nations than elsewhere, perhaps because in those countries math lessons are sequential and interactive.

14. Cultural differences in assumptions about education are frequent, but scientific research on the best way for children to learn is scarce. For example, many people believe that children learn better in small classes, but the research is inconclusive.

KEY TERMS

concrete operational thought (p. 338)
classification (p. 338)
identity (p. 339)
reversibility (p. 339)
information-processing theory (p. 342)
sensory memory (p. 342)
working memory (p. 343)
long-term memory (p. 343)
knowledge base (p. 344)
control processes (p. 344)
metacognition (p. 345)
English-language learner (ELL) (p. 350)
language shift (p. 350)
immersion (p. 351)
bilingual education (p. 351)
ESL (English as a second language) (p. 351)
Progress in International Reading Literacy Study (PIRLS) (p. 355)
TIMSS (Trends in Math and Science Study) (p. 355)
No Child Left Behind Act (p. 358)
National Assessment of Educational Progress (NAEP) (p. 358)
hidden curriculum (p. 359)
phonics approach (p. 361)
whole-language approach (p. 361)

➤**Answer to Observation Quiz** (from page 367): The social constructions are that (1) learning colors is important, (2) children should raise their hands to be called on individually, and (3) words should be written. (Note that the Pueblo words for colors are much longer than the English equivalents—harder for first-grade readers.) Indeed, the very idea of bilingual education is a social construction, approved by most Americans but not necessarily by research.

KEY QUESTIONS

1. How do logical ideas help children understand classification?

2. According to Vygotsky, if children never went to school, how would cognitive development occur?

3. What are differences among the three kinds of memory?

4. What are the differences between language learning in early and middle childhood?

5. What are the advantages and disadvantages in teaching children who do not speak English in English-only classes?

6. How does metacognition affect the ability to learn something new?

7. What are some of the differences in education in various parts of the world?

8. Why are international tests of learning given, and what are some of the problems with such tests?

9. How might a hidden curriculum affect what a child learns?

10. Why are disagreements about curriculum and method sometimes called "wars," not merely differences of opinion?

APPLICATIONS

1. Visit a local elementary school and look for the hidden curriculum. For example, do the children line up? Why or why not, when and how? Does gender, age, ability, or talent affect the grouping of children or the selection of staff? What is on the walls? Are parents involved? If so, how? For everything you observe, speculate about the underlying assumptions.

2. Interview a 7- to 11-year-old child to find out what he or she knows *and understands* about mathematics. Relate both correct and incorrect responses to the logic of concrete operational thought.

3. What do you remember about how you learned to read? Compare your memories with those of two other people, one at least 10 years older and the other at least 5 years younger than you. Can you draw any conclusions about effective reading instruction? If so, what are they? If not, why not?

4. Talk to two parents of primary school children. What do they think are the best and worst parts of their children's education? Ask specific questions and analyze the results.

13

CHAPTER OUTLINE

Middle Childhood: Psychosocial Development

A student of mine, in New York City in 2007, drove to a garage to get a flat tire fixed.

> As I pulled up, I saw a very short boy sitting at the garage door. I imagined him to be about 8 or 9 years old and wondered why he was sitting there by himself. He directed me to park, and summoned a man who looked at my tire and spoke to the boy in a language I did not understand. This little boy then lifted my car with a jack, removed all the bolts, and fixed the flat. I was in shock. When I paid the man (who was his father), I asked how long his son had been doing this. He said about three years.
>
> *[adapted from Tiffany, personal communication, March 15, 2008]*

The International Labor Organization estimates that 218 million children throughout the world are employed, most at very low pay and some with work that destroys their health. It shocks many adults like Tiffany to learn that so many of the world's children are forced to work, in defiance of the United Nations' declaration that children have a right

> to be protected from economic exploitation and from performing any work that is likely to be hazardous or to interfere with the child's education, or to be harmful to the child's health or physical, mental, spiritual, moral, or social development.
>
> *[Convention on the Rights of the Child]*

Did this boy's work interfere with his education or development? The answer is not obvious. Some argue that family poverty and unwise family planning give rise to child labor; with so many causes, passing laws against child labor is not a solution (Basu & Pham, 1998).

Does an understanding of child development shed light on this issue? As with almost every aspect of middle childhood, details are crucial. All children need friends, families, and skills, but some peers are destructive, some families are harmful, and some skills should not be mastered. This chapter describes those details, explaining when a child's "physical, mental, spiritual, moral, or social development" is harmed. By the end of this chapter, you will know when child labor (and peer culture, bullying, self-esteem, poverty,

TUGELA RIDLEY / EPA / CORBIS

Caught in a Net Forced child labor, in which young bodies are exploited and young minds are neglected, is never beneficial. These boys are among the thousands who work in the fishing industry on Ghana's Lake Volta. Their impoverished parents gave them to fishermen, hoping that they would get some education and an apprenticeship in fishing. They are receiving neither; instead, they, like the fish they catch, are tangled in a net.

divorce, and many other influences) is harmful and when it is benign. We begin with the children themselves and then broaden our discussion to consider families, peers, and morality.

The Nature of the Child

As explained in the previous two chapters, steady growth, brain maturation, and intellectual advances make middle childhood a developmental period during which children gain independence and autonomy (see Table 13.1). They acquire an "increasing ability to regulate themselves, to take responsibility, and to exercise self-control"—all strengths that make these years a time for positive growth (Huston & Ripke, 2006, p. 9).

One simple result is that school-age children can finally care for themselves. They can not only feed themselves but make their own dinner, not only dress themselves but pack their own suitcases, not only walk to school but organize games with friends at the playground. They venture outdoors alone, with boys particularly putting some distance between themselves and home, as they engage in activities of which their parents are unaware and sometimes disapprove (Munroe & Romney, 2006). This budding independence fosters growth.

TABLE 13.1

AT ABOUT THIS TIME: Signs of Psychosocial Maturation Between Ages 6 and 11

Children are more likely to have specific chores to perform at home.
Children are more likely to have a weekly allowance.
Children are expected to tell time, and they have set times for various activities.
Children have more homework assignments, some over several days.
Children are less often punished physically, more often with disapproval or withdrawal of privileges.
Children try to conform to peer standards in such matters as clothing and language.
Children influence decisions about their after-school care, lessons, and activities.
Children use media (TV, computers, video games) without adult supervision.
Children are given new responsibility for younger children, pets, or, in some cultures, employment.
Children strive for more independence from parents.

Industry and Inferiority

One particular characteristic of school-age children, throughout the centuries and in every culture, is that they are industrious, busily and actively mastering whatever skills their culture values. Think of learning to read and add—painstaking and boring efforts, with seemingly little reward, to understand words and numbers.

For instance, how exciting can it be to slowly sound out "Jane has a dog" or to write "3 + 4 = 7" for the hundredth time? Yet school-age children busily practice reading and math: They are intrinsically motivated to read a page, finish a worksheet, memorize a spelling word, color in a map, and so on. Similarly, they enjoy collecting and categorizing and counting whatever they choose to accumulate—stamps, stickers, or seashells.

They also are ashamed about what they cannot do. Concerns about inferiority are evident in the schoolchild's ditty: "Nobody likes me. Everybody hates me. I think I'll go out and eat some worms." This lament has endured for generations because it captures, with humor that school-age children can appreciate, the self-doubt that many of them feel.

Erikson on Industry Versus Inferiority

The tension between feeling productive and feeling useless was highlighted by Erik Erikson, who noted that middle childhood is a time for learning with devoted attention and perseverance. The child "must forget past hopes and wishes, while his exuberant imagination is tamed and harnessed to the laws of impersonal things," becoming "ready to apply himself to given skills and tasks" (Erikson, 1963, pp. 258, 259). In the crisis of **industry versus inferiority** (Erikson's fourth developmental stage), children busily try to master whatever abilities their culture values.

industry versus inferiority The fourth of Erikson's eight psychosocial crises, during which children attempt to master many skills, developing a sense of themselves as either industrious or inferior, competent or incompetent.

Children judge themselves as either *industrious* or *inferior*—that is, competent or incompetent, productive or failing, winners or losers. Being productive is intrinsically joyous, and it fosters the self-control that is a crucial defense against emotional problems (Bradley & Corwyn, 2005).

Freud on Latency

Sigmund Freud described this period as **latency,** a time when emotional drives are quiet and unconscious sexual conflicts are submerged. Latency is a "time for acquiring cognitive skills and assimilating cultural values as children expand their world to include teachers, neighbors, peers, club leaders, and coaches. Sexual energy continues to flow, but it is channeled into social concerns" (P. H. Miller, 2002, p. 131).

latency Freud's term for middle childhood, during which children's emotional drives and psychosexual needs are quiet (latent). Freud thought that sexual conflicts from earlier stages are only temporarily submerged, bursting forth again at puberty.

Some experts complain that "middle childhood has been neglected at least since Freud relegated these years to the status of an uninteresting 'latency period'" (Huston & Ripke, 2006, p. 7). But current thinking is that these are extremely important years for development.

In one sense, at least, Freud was correct: Sexual impulses are quiet during these years. This is true in every culture; even when children were betrothed to each other before age 12 (rare today, but not unusual in earlier centuries), the

LINDSAY HEBBERD / WOODFIN CAMP & ASSOCIATES

Celebrating Spring No matter where they live, 7- to 11-year-olds seek to understand and develop whatever skills are valued by their culture. They do so in active, industrious ways, as described in behaviorism as well as cognitive, sociocultural, psychoanalytic, and epigenetic theories. This universal truth is illustrated here, as four friends in Assam, northeastern India, usher in spring with a Bihu celebration. Soon they will be given sweets and tea, which is the sociocultural validation of their energy, independence, and skill.

young husband and wife typically had little interaction. Everywhere, boys and girls typically choose to be with others of their sex (Munroe & Romney, 2006). Indeed, boys who post signs that read "Girls stay out" and girls who proclaim that boys are stupid and smell bad are not unusual.

Adults sometimes worry about sexual predators bothering their children. Parents warn their children not to talk to strangers and to avoid Internet chat rooms. However, few school-age children are interested in sexual advances or are seduced by strangers (Wolak et al., 2008). It is at puberty that sexual vulnerability, risk, and abuse increase significantly—a topic for the next chapter.

Self-Concept

The following self-description could have been written by many 10-year-olds:

> I'm in the fourth grade this year, and I'm pretty popular, at least with the girls. That's because I'm nice to people and can keep secrets. Mostly I am nice to my friends, although if I get in a bad mood I sometimes say something that can be a little mean. I try to control my temper, but when I don't, I'm ashamed of myself. I'm usually happy when I'm with my friends, but I get sad if there is no one to do things with. At school, I'm feeling pretty smart in certain subjects like Language Arts and Social Studies. I got As in these subjects on my last report card and was really proud of myself. But I'm feeling pretty dumb in Math and Science, especially when I see how well a lot of the other kids are doing. Even though I'm not doing well in those subjects, I still like myself as a person, because Math and Science just aren't that important to me. How I look and how popular I am are more important. I also like myself because I know my parents like me and so do other kids. That helps you like yourself.
>
> *[quoted in Harter, 1999, p. 48]*

This excerpt (from a book written by a scholar who has studied the development of children's self-concept for decades) captures the nature of school-age children. It includes *social comparison* ("especially when I see how well a lot of the other kids are doing"), *effortful control* ("I try to control my temper"), loyalty ("can keep secrets"), and appreciation from peers and parents ("I know my parents like me and so do other kids"), all of which are explained later in this chapter.

Who Knows You Best?

The child's self-concept no longer mirrors the parents' perspective. Every theory and every perceptive observer notes that school-age children recognize themselves as individuals, distinct from what their parents and teachers think of them.

One study that confirmed this began by asking questions like, "Who knows best what you are thinking? . . . how tired you are? . . . your favorite foods?" (Burton & Mitchell, 2003). Unlike 3-year-olds, who might answer, "Mommy," and rely on a parent to tell them, "Oh, you are tired, it's time for your nap," school-age children become increasingly sure of their own minds. In this study, few (13 percent) of the 5-year-olds but most (73 percent) of the 10-year-olds thought that they knew themselves better than their parents or teachers did (Burton & Mitchell, 2003).

In describing school-age children's self-concept, it is useful to distinguish between "two distinct but intimately intertwined aspects of self" (Harter, 2006, p. 508): the "I-self" and the "me-self." The I-self is the self as subject—a person who thinks, acts, and feels independently. The me-self is the self as object—a person reflected, validated, and critiqued by others (Harter, 2006).

In middle childhood, the me-self is crucial because of the new strength of **social comparison,** the measurement of one's attributes against those of

social comparison The tendency to assess one's abilities, achievements, social status, and other attributes by measuring them against those of other people, especially one's peers.

other people even when no one else explicitly makes the comparison. School-age children become much more socially aware, judging themselves as worse or better than other people in hundreds of ways. Ideally, social comparison helps children value the abilities they have and abandon the imaginary, rosy self-evaluation of preschoolers (Grolnick et al., 1997; Jacobs et al., 2002).

However, increases in self-understanding and social awareness come at a price. Self-criticism and self-consciousness tend to rise from ages 6 to 12, as self-esteem dips (Merrell & Gimpel, 1998), especially for children who live with unusual stresses (e.g., an abusive or alcoholic parent) (Luthar & Zelazo, 2003). Furthermore, self-esteem decreases as materialism increases toward the end of middle childhood (Chaplin & John, 2007). Insecure 10-year-olds may be especially likely to want the latest shoes, cell phones, and other possessions.

If children are already quite anxious and stressed, reduced self-esteem tends to lead to lower academic achievement (Pomerantz & Rudolph, 2003). This is particularly true of children who are rejected by classmates (Flook et al., 2005). A loss of self-pride in middle childhood may foreshadow emotional uncertainty and psychological stress in adolescence—not the usual path, but the one often followed by children who feel inferior (Graber, 2004).

Complications of Unrealistic Self-Esteem

Self-esteem is a tricky issue. If it is unrealistically high, it may produce less **effortful control** (which entails deliberately modifying one's impulses and emotions) and thus lower achievement (Baumeister et al., 2003); but the same consequences may occur if self-esteem is unrealistically low. Similarly, unrealistically high and low self-esteem both correlate with aggression (Sandstrom & Herlan, 2007).

effortful control The ability to regulate one's emotions and actions through effort, not simply through natural inclination.

Children who appreciate themselves and appreciate other children (i.e., when self and peers both fare well in social comparisons) tend to have more friends and to be prosocial, able to defend a friend if the occasion arises. In contrast, children who like themselves but not their peers are more likely to have few friends, to show more aggression, and to be lonelier (Salmivalli et al., 2005). In short, academic and social competence are aided by realistic evaluation of objectively measured achievement, not by unrealistically high self-esteem (Baumeister et al., 2003).

As children begin to understand that they are simultaneously similar to and different from their peers, they learn to accept themselves. As one expert explains, "Children develop feelings of self-esteem, competence, and individuality during middle childhood as they begin comparing themselves with peers" (Ripke et al., 2006, p. 261). A program that teaches anxious children to confide in friends as well as to understand their own emotions helps them develop a better self-concept; such programs have been successful not only in the United States but in many other cultures (Siu, 2007).

After-school activities, particularly sports, can provide a foundation for friendship and realistic self-esteem. Team sports are helpful in providing benefits not only for self-concept but also for academic achievement (Morris & Kalil, 2006).

Self-Esteem as an American Value

Cultural differences make self-esteem an even more complex issue. Self-esteem is not universally valued (Yamaguchi et al., 2007). Many cultures expect children to be modest. For example, Australians say that "tall poppies" are cut down, and the Japanese discourage social comparison aimed at making oneself feel superior (Toyama, 2001). Self-esteem is encouraged in the United States, but not in Angola (Guest, 2007). Although Chinese children often excel at mathematics, only 1 percent said they were "very satisfied" with their performance in that subject (Snyder et al., 2004).

Perhaps it is possible to value self-esteem too highly. Currently, in the United States, children's successes tend to be lavishly praised by adults, and report cards during middle childhood no longer have grades from A to F, but categories from excellent to "needs improvement." As a result of such efforts to protect self-esteem, U.S. children of all ages think better of themselves than they did 30 years ago. The self-esteem of college students has increased markedly (Twenge & Campbell, 2001). It is apparent that culture and cohort as well as age influence children's self-concept; the long-term effects may vary also (Heine, 2007).

Resilience and Stress

In infancy and early childhood, children depend on their immediate families for food, learning, and life itself. You read earlier in Chapter 5 about the devastation caused by infant malnutrition and about the crucial impact of the family on language learning and young children's emotional regulation. By school age, however, some children are able to escape destructive family influences by finding their own niche in the larger world.

Indeed, some children seem unscathed by their problematic, stressful environments. They have been called "resilient" or even "invincible." However, those who are familiar with recent research use the term *resilience* cautiously, if at all (see Table 13.2). As dynamic-systems theory reminds us, although some children cope better than others, none are impervious to their social context (Jenson & Fraser, 2006; Luthar et al., 2003).

TABLE 13.2

Dominant Ideas About Challenges and Coping in Children, 1965–Present

1965	All children have the same needs for healthy development.
1970	Some conditions or circumstances—such as "absent father," "teenage mother," "working mom," and "day care"—are harmful for every child.
1975	All children are *not* the same. Some children are resilient, coping easily with stressors that cause harm in other children.
1980	Nothing inevitably causes harm. Indeed, both maternal employment and preschool education, once thought to be risk factors, usually benefit children.
1985	Factors beyond the family, both in the child (low birthweight, prenatal alcohol exposure, aggressive temperament) and in the community (poverty, violence), can be very risky for the child.
1990	Risk–benefit analysis finds that some children seem to be "invulnerable" to, or even to benefit from, circumstances that destroy others. (Some do well in school despite extreme poverty, for example.)
1995	No child is invincibly resilient. Risks are always harmful—if not in educational achievement, then in emotions.
2000	Risk–benefit analysis involves the interplay among all three domains (biosocial, cognitive, and psychosocial), including factors within the child (genes, intelligence, temperament), the family (function as well as structure), and the community (including neighborhood, school, church, and culture). Over the long term, most people overcome problems, but the problems are real.
2008	The focus is on strengths, not risks. Assets in the child (intelligence, personality), the family (secure attachment, warmth), the community (good schools, after-school programs), and the nation (income support, health care) must be nurtured.

Sources: Jenson & Fraser, 2006; Luthar, 2003; Luthar et al., 2000; Maton et al., 2004; McWhinnie et al., 2008.

Resilience has been defined as "a dynamic process encompassing positive adaptation within the context of significant adversity" (Luthar et al., 2000, p. 543). Note the three parts of this definition:

resilience The capacity to adapt well to significant adversity and to overcome serious stress.

- Resilience is *dynamic,* not a stable trait. That means a given person may be resilient at some periods but not others.
- Resilience is a *positive adaptation* to stress. For example, if rejection by a parent leads a child to establish closer relationships with another adult, perhaps a grandparent or the parent of a neighbor child, that child is exhibiting resilience.
- Adversity must be *significant.* Some adversities are comparatively minor (large class size, poor vision), and some are major (victimization, neglect).

Cumulative Stress

One important discovery is that many small stresses that might be called "daily hassles" can accumulate to become major if they are ongoing. Furthermore, stresses accumulate. Almost every child can withstand one stressful event. However, several ongoing stresses make coping very difficult (Jaffee et al., 2007). Each stress can make other stresses more likely to be harmful (Fergusson & Horwood, 2003; Hammen, 2003).

One example is the noise of airplanes overhead. If a child lives near an airport, that stress happens several times a day, but just for a minute at a time. A study of 2,844 children living near three major airports found that the noise impaired the reading ability of some but not all of them (Stansfeld et al., 2005).

Another example of the impact of cumulative stress comes from research on children in New Orleans who survived Hurricane Katrina. Many experienced several stresses (see Figure 13.1) and have a much higher rate of psychological problems than they did before the hurricane hit (see Viadero, 2007).

Daily routines may build up stress. For example, a depressed mother may have little effect on her child if an emotionally stable and available father buffers her influence or if the mother herself functions well when she is with the child. However, her depression may become a significant stress if the child must, day after day, wake up and prepare for school without help, supervise and discipline younger siblings, and keep friends at a distance because the mother wants quiet.

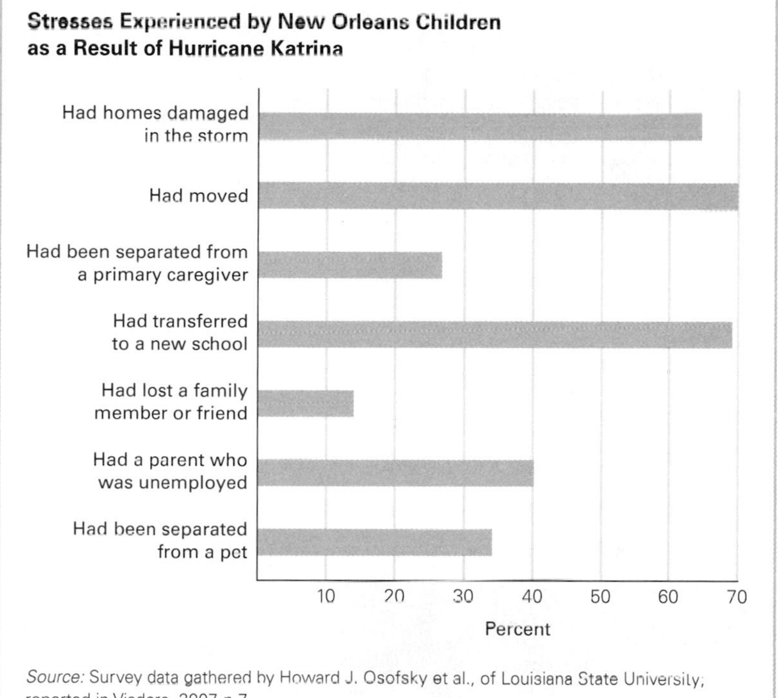

Source: Survey data gathered by Howard J. Osofsky et al., of Louisiana State University, reported in Viadero, 2007, p.7.

FIGURE 13.1

Enough Stress for a Lifetime Many children experienced more than one kind of severe stress during Hurricane Katrina and its aftermath. That disaster inflicted more stress on the children of New Orleans than most adults ever experience in their lifetime, and its long-term impact will likely be dramatic.

Gathering Strengths

A recent focus has been on the strengths within the child and community that together enable a child to thrive in difficult circumstances. One possible strength is the child's own interpretation of what is happening. In the example of the depressed family above, a child might conclude that all the family problems are the child's own fault or that the problems are somehow a blessing or simply a temporary burden that must be endured for the moment.

Another key aspect of resilience is found in children's ability to develop their own friends, activities, and skills. This is possible during the middle-childhood years and is one reason many children blossom once they are old enough to be somewhat independent. After-school activities can be a lifeline: Participation in

TIM MUELLER / THE NEW YORK TIMES / REDUX

Healing Time Children who survived Hurricane Katrina participate in a fire drill at their new charter school, Lafayette Academy in New Orleans. The resumption of school routines helps them overcome the stress they experienced in the chaos of the deadly storm.

extracurricular programs correlates with better emotional and academic functioning (NICHD Early Child Care Research Network, 2004).

To encourage resilience, community, religious, and government programs can develop extracurricular activities for all children, from 4-H to midnight basketball, from choir to Little League. Children who can choose their own activities from many possibilities are likely to find an area of competence and develop a view of themselves as industrious, not inferior.

This was apparent in a 40-year study in Hawaii that began with children born into poverty, often to parents who were alcoholic or mentally ill. In infancy, many of these children had symptoms of deprivation, and experts at the time predicted a difficult life for them (Werner & Smith, 2001).

One example was Michael, born preterm to teenage parents and weighing less than 5 pounds. He was not only from a low-income family, but he was also fatherless for the first two years of his life. His mother left him and his three younger siblings when he was eight, and his paternal grandparents became his caregivers. Yet Michael became a successful, happy, loving adult (Werner, 1979).

Michael is not the only one who defied predictions. Amazingly, about a third of the Hawaiian infants who were at high risk as babies coped well. By middle childhood, they were already finding ways to avoid family stresses, choosing instead to achieve in school, to make good friends, and to find adult mentors other than their parents. By adolescence, these children had distanced themselves from their homes. As adults, they left family problems behind (many moved far away) and established their own healthy relationships (Werner & Smith, 1992, 2001).

As was true for many of these children, school can often be an escape. An easygoing temperament and a high IQ also help (Curtis & Cicchetti, 2003), but such personal traits are not essential. In the Hawaii study, "a realistic goal orientation, persistence, and 'learned creativity' enabled . . . a remarkable degree of personal, social, and occupational success," even for children with evident learning disabilities (Werner & Smith, 2001, p. 140).

Social Support and Religious Faith

A major factor that strengthens a child's ability to deal with stress is social support. Compared with the small, homebound lives of younger children, the expanding social world of school-age children allows new possibilities (Morris & Kalil, 2006). A network of supportive relatives is a better buffer than having only one close parent (Y. Jackson & Warren, 2000). Friends help, too. Grandparents, teachers, unrelated adults, peers, and even pets can help children cope with stress (Bryant & Donnellen, 2007).

Community institutions, including churches and libraries, can be crucial sources of social support. One study concludes:

> When children attempt to seek out experiences that will help them overcome adversity, it is critical that resources, in the form of supportive adults or learning opportunities, be made available to them so that their own self-righting potential can be fulfilled.
>
> *[Kim-Cohen et al., 2004, p. 664]*

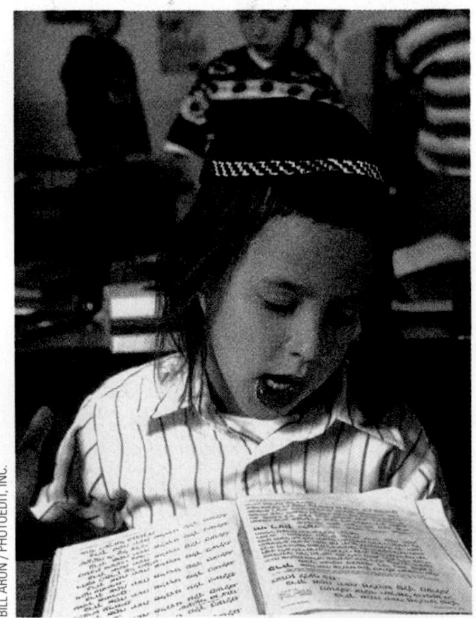

BILL ARON / PHOTOEDIT, INC.

Become Like a Child Although the particulars vary a great deal, school-age children's impulses toward industriousness, stability, and dedication place them among the most devout members of every religious faith.

A specific example is children's use of religion, which often provides social support via an adult from the same community of faith. Research shows that church

B CHILD / AP PHOTO

Grandmother Knows Best About 20,000 grandmothers in Connecticut are caregivers for their grandchildren. This 15-year-old boy and his 17-year-old sister came to live with their grandmother in New Haven after their mother died several years ago. This type of family can help children cope with stress, especially when the grandmother is relatively young and has her own house, as is the case here.

involvement particularly helps African American children in communities where social stresses and racial prejudice abound (Akiba & García-Coll, 2004). As the authors of one study explain, "The influences of religious importance and participation . . . are mediated through trusting interaction with adults, friends and parents who share similar views" (P. E. King & Furrow, 2004, p. 709).

The religious convictions of children are very diverse (Levesque, 2002), but faith itself can be psychologically protective, in part because it helps children reinterpret their experiences. Parents may provide religious guidance, but by middle childhood some children pray and attend religious services more often than their parents do.

Adults may not realize that many children (by age 8 but not at age 4) believe that prayer is communication, and they expect that prayer will make them feel better, especially when they are sad or angry (see the Research Design and Figure 13.2) (Bamford & Lagattuta, 2007). Thus, religious beliefs become increasingly useful as school-age children cope with their problems.

In accord with their self-righting impulses, children try to develop competencies. They find social supports, if not in their families then among their friends or

Research Design

Scientists: Christi Bamford and Kristin H. Lagattuta.

Publication: Not quite published! This was a poster at the Society for Research in Child Development conference, held in Boston in April 2007. All the other studies cited in this text are published, but this one is included partly to inspire young researchers.

Participants: A total of 100—20 each at ages 4, 6, and 8, and 40 college students at the University of California. Family backgrounds were equally divided between those who considered themselves very religious, somewhat religious, and not religious.

Design: Participants were shown faces depicting various emotions and picture stories of children in various situations who decided to pray. They were asked when and why people might pray as well as how they would feel afterward.

Major conclusions: Compared with younger children, 8-year-olds were more likely to believe that prayer is used for gratitude and for making something better. They also thought people would feel better after they prayed.

Comment: Exploring the religious beliefs of children is an important topic, but it is not often done in psychological research. This study is a good beginning, but culture (even for nonreligious families) affects beliefs. Replication in another nation is needed.

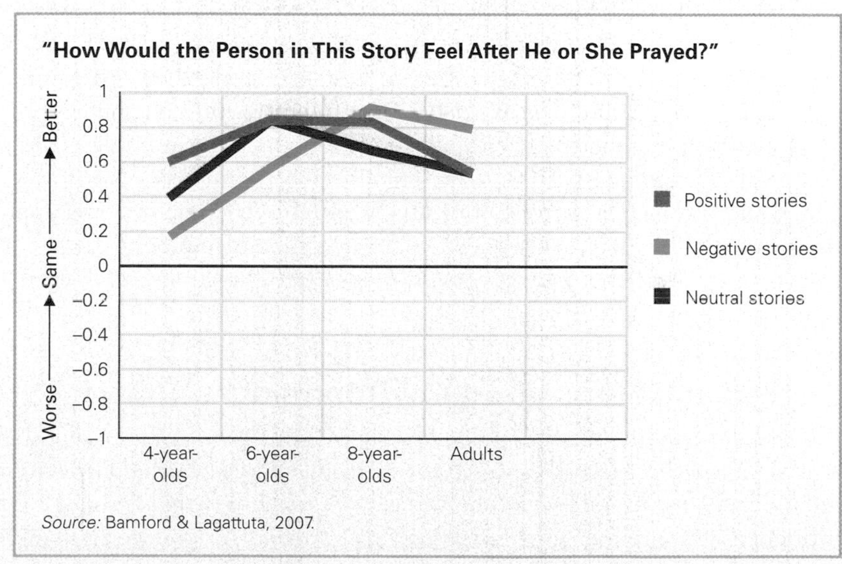

FIGURE 13.2

Help Me, God The numbers on this graph are the averages when people were asked how characters in various scenarios would feel after praying. There were only three choices: better (= 1), same (= 0), or worse (= −1). As you can see, virtually all the 8-year-olds thought prayer would make a person feel better.

unrelated adults. School success, religious faith, after-school achievements—any or all of these can help a child overcome problems. As two experts explain:

> Successful children remind us that children grow up in multiple contexts—in families, schools, peer groups, baseball teams, religious organizations, and many other groups—and each context is a potential source of protective factors as well as risks. These children demonstrate that children are protected not only by the self-righting nature of development, but also by the actions of adults, by their own actions, by the nurturing of their assets, by opportunities to succeed, and by the experience of success. The behavior of adults often plays a critical role in children's risks, resources, opportunities, and resilience.
>
> *[Masten & Coatsworth, 1998, p. 216]*

SUMMING UP

Children gain in maturity and responsibility during the school years. According to Erikson, the crisis of industry versus inferiority generates self-doubt in many school-age children. According to Freud, the relative quiet of the latency period makes it easier for children to master new skills and to absorb their culture's values.

Researchers have found that school-age children develop a more realistic self-concept than younger children. They cope by becoming more independent, using school achievement, after-school activities, supportive adults, and religious beliefs to help them overcome whatever problems they face. ■

Families and Children

No one doubts that genes affect temperament as well as ability, that peers are vital influences, and that schools and cultures affect what, and how much, children learn. Many people are also convinced that parental practices make a decided difference in how children develop. On this last point, developmental researchers have expressed doubts, suggesting that genes, peers, and communities are so powerful that there may be no room left for parents to exert influence (Harris, 1998, 2002; Ladd & Pettit, 2002; McLeod et al., 2007; O'Connor, 2002).

Especially for Scientists (see response, page 382): How would you determine whether or not parents treat all their children the same?

Some scientific data suggest that parents have little direct influence on schoolchildren. As already detailed (see Chapter 3), a substantial part of a person's behavior can be traced to heredity. This statement is based on research and statistical analysis of many traits found in monozygotic twins (genetically identical) separated at birth and raised in different homes (so that their environment is not identical) (Canli, 2006; Lykken, 2006; Plomin et al., 2002; Wright, 1999).

However, remember that nothing is entirely genetic or entirely environmental: Genes always interact with the environment, which amplifies the power of some genes and mutes the expression of others. As the dynamic-systems approach reminds us, the relationship between genes and the environment for any particular trait changes over time, with genetic influence becoming more evident, not less so, as children grow older.

Shared and Nonshared Environments

One specific finding that has made developmentalists question parental influence is that non-home effects become powerful in middle childhood because of the enlargement in the difference between the *shared environment* (e.g., household influences that are the same for two people, such as for children reared together) and the *nonshared environment* (e.g., the different friends and different teachers that two siblings have). Careful research has repeatedly found that nonshared environmental factors—particularly peers—are more influential than are shared ones during middle childhood (Hetherington et al., 1994).

Furthermore, adopted children raised in the same home seem much more influenced by their genes than by their families. By middle childhood, their personality traits and intellectual abilities differ substantially from those of their nongenetic siblings raised in the same household (Wadsworth et al., 2006). Even reading ability, obviously a learned skill, is powerfully influenced by genes.

More recent findings, however, reassert the power of parents. The analysis of shared and nonshared influences was correct, but the assumption was wrong. Children raised in the same household do *not* necessarily share the same home environment. If the family moves, if parents divorce, or if one or both lose a job, for example, every child is affected; but the impact depends on age and gender. Thus, each child is affected differently.

In addition, some nonshared influences—such as choice of school, neighborhood, or after-school activity—are directly determined by parents but are not shared, because parental income and neighborhood opportunities vary over time (Simpkins et al., 2006). Thus, these nonshared influences cannot be considered evidence for meager parental impact. In fact, parental influence is substantial.

Finally, parents' attitudes toward their children vary, so that even living in the same house with the same parents is not necessarily a shared environment, as the following study of identical twins makes clear.

a view from science

"I Always Dressed One in Blue Stuff . . ."

One way to measure family influence is to compare children of varying genetic similarity (twins, full siblings, stepsiblings, adopted children) who are raised in the same household (Reiss et al., 2000). The extent to which children share alleles (100 percent for monozygotic twins, 50 percent for full siblings, 25 percent for half-siblings, much less for unrelated individuals such as stepsiblings and adopted children) can be used to calculate how much of the variation in a trait is inherited. The remaining variation presumably arises from the environment.

This seems simple enough. However, every research design aimed at studying the links between parental behavior and child behavior is vulnerable to criticism (see Figure 13.3). Consequently, an expert team of scientists, noting the flaws in earlier research, set out to avoid such pitfalls as they compared 1,000 sets of monozygotic twins reared by their biological parents (Caspi et al., 2004).

The team assessed each child's temperament by asking the mothers and teachers to fill out a detailed, standardized checklist. They also assessed every mother's attitudes toward each child. These ranged from very positive ("my ray of sunshine") to very negative ("I wish I never had her. . . . She's a cow, I hate her") (quoted in Caspi et al., 2004, p. 153).

Many mothers described personality differences between their twins and assumed these were innate. The mothers did not realize that they themselves may have created many of these differences. For example, one mother spoke of her identical daughters:

> Susan can be very sweet. She loves babies . . . she can be insecure . . . she flutters and dances around. . . . There's not much between her ears. . . . She's exceptionally vain, more so than Ann. Ann loves any game involving a ball, very sporty, climbs trees, very much a tomboy. One is a serious tomboy and one's a serious girlie girl. Even when they were babies I always dressed one in blue stuff and one in pink stuff.
>
> *[quoted in Caspi et al., 2004, p. 156]*

Some mothers were much more cold and rejecting toward one twin than toward the other:

> He was in the hospital and everyone was all "poor Jeff, poor Jeff" and I started thinking, "Well, what about me? I'm the one's just had twins. I'm the one's going through this, he's a seven-week-old baby and doesn't know a thing about it." . . . I sort of detached and plowed my emotions into Mike.
>
> *[quoted in Caspi et al., 2004, p. 156]*

After she was divorced, this mother blamed Jeff for favoring his father: "Jeff would do anything for Don but he wouldn't for me, and no matter what I did for either of them it wouldn't be right" (p. 157). She said Mike was much more lovable.

The researchers controlled for genes, gender, age, and personality differences in kindergarten (by measuring, among other things, antisocial behavior as assessed by the children's kindergarten teachers). They found that twins whose mothers were more negative toward them tended to *become* more antisocial than their co-twin. The rejected twins were more likely to fight, steal, and hurt others at age 7 than at age 5 after all background factors were taken into account. Mothers' attitudes were obviously influential.

Many other nonshared factors—peers, teachers, and so on—are important. But this difference in identical twins confirms the popular belief: Parents matter. The assumption that parents and a home provide a completely shared environment for all their children is false. As everyone with siblings can attest, each child's family experiences are unique.

FIGURE 13.3

Improvements in Research Design Before designing a study, researchers identify the weaknesses of earlier studies so that they can consider ways of avoiding them. This chart shows the preliminary analysis made by the team that found that parents' attitudes have a direct effect on children's behavior. As they realized, "continuing refinements" in research design are always possible.

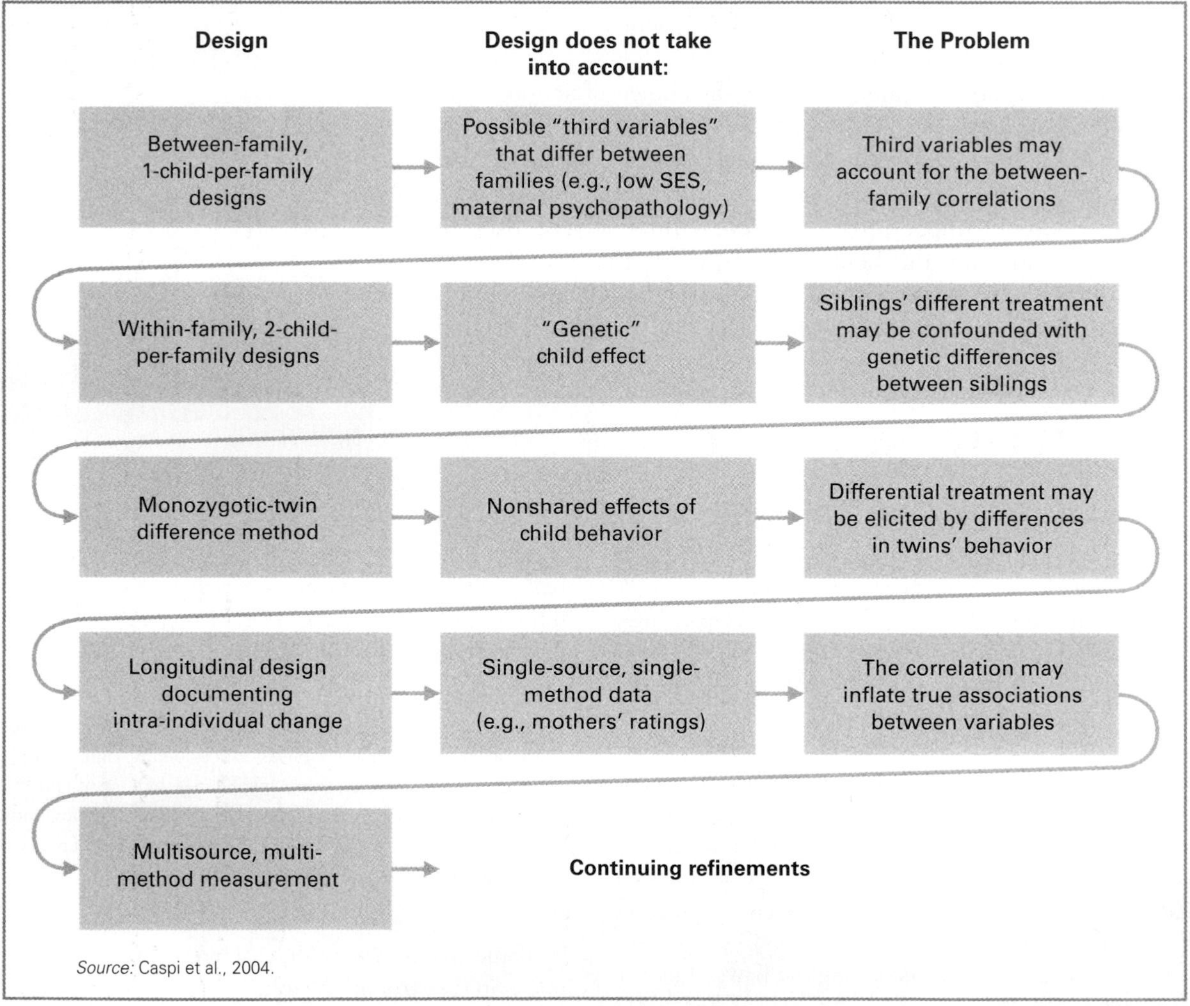

Source: Caspi et al., 2004.

➤Response for Scientists (from page 380): Proof is very difficult when human interaction is the subject of investigation, since random assignment is impossible. Ideally, researchers would find identical twins being raised together and would then observe the parents' behavior over the years.

Family Function and Structure

Exactly what do school-age children require from their families, and what factors in family structure make it likely (or unlikely) that they will get what they need? **Family structure** refers to the legal and genetic connections among related people living in the same household. **Family function** refers to the way a family works to care for its members.

The most important family function for people of all ages is to afford a safe haven of love and encouragement. Beyond that, people of various ages need different things from their families: Infants need frequent caregiving and social interaction; teenagers need both freedom and guidance; young adults need peace and privacy; the aged need respect and appreciation.

family structure The legal and genetic relationships among relatives living in the same home; includes nuclear family, extended family, stepfamily, and so on.

family function The way a family works to meet the needs of its members. Children need families to provide basic material necessities, to encourage learning, to help them develop self-respect, to nurture friendships, and to foster harmony and stability.

Functioning to Meet the Needs of School-Age Children

School-age children thrive if their families function for them in five ways:

1. *Provide basic necessities.* Children aged 6 to 11 can eat, dress, wash, and sleep without help, but someone must provide them with food, clothing, and shelter.
2. *Encourage learning.* School-age children must master academic and social skills. Families can support and guide their education.
3. *Develop self-respect.* As they become cognitively mature, school-age children become self-critical and socially aware. Families can help their children feel competent and capable.
4. *Nurture peer relationships.* School-age children need friends, and families can provide the time and opportunity to develop friendships.
5. *Ensure harmony and stability.* School-age children need protective and predictable family routines; they are particularly troubled by conflict and change.

Thus, families provide material and cognitive resources as well as emotional and social support. No family always functions perfectly, but some malfunctions are particularly harmful at various points of the life span. For instance, parental divorce is always hard on children, particularly on children who are about to enter kindergarten or middle school.

Diverse Family Structures

It is important to understand that a family, regardless of its structure, is not necessarily a household, and vice versa. As defined by the U.S. Bureau of the Census, a

KATHY MCLAUGHLIN / THE IMAGE WORKS

Meeting Her Need for Fit and Fashion A 10-year-old's rapidly growing feet frequently need new shoes, and peer pressure favors certain styles of footwear. Here, Rebekah's sisters wait and watch as their mother tries to find a boot that fits her and is fashionable.

Observation Quiz (see answer, page 385): Why isn't a salesperson helping this family find boots? And, instead of shopping for boots for Rebekah in cold weather, why didn't the mother buy her a pair the previous spring, when they were on sale?

household is composed of people who live together in the same home. One person living alone can be a household, as can nonrelatives living together. In the United States in 2005, 26 percent of households were single-person households and 6 percent were nonrelative households.

A "family household" is one that includes a least one parent and at least one child under age 18. This structure, once the norm, now accounts for less than half of the households in the United States.

Here we focus on a subset of family households, those that include a school-age child (about one-fourth of all U.S. households). We attempt to correlate family structures with the five family functions just mentioned as desirable for school-age children. The data come primarily from the United States, but the general categories are worldwide (Georgas et al., 2006).

Two Parents or One? Table 13.3 briefly describes common structures, with specific percentages estimated for families with school-age children in the United States. More than half of all school-age children live in two-parent homes as part of a **nuclear family** (a married couple and their biological offspring). Internationally, nuclear families are often headed by couples who live together but are not legally married; they *cohabit*. Depending partly on local customs, they may be con-

nuclear family A family that consists of a father, a mother, and their biological children under age 18.

TABLE 13.3

Common Family Structures (with percentages of U.S. children aged 6–11 in each family type)

Two-Parent Families (67%)

Most human families have two parents. These families are of several kinds.

1. **Nuclear family** (56%) Named after the nucleus (the tightly connected core particles of an atom), the nuclear family consists of a husband and wife and their biological offspring. About half of all families with children are nuclear.
2. **Stepparent family** (9%) Divorced fathers (Stewart et al., 2003) are particularly likely to remarry. Usually his children from a previous marriage do not live with him, but if they do, they are in a stepparent family. Divorced mothers are less likely to remarry, but when they do, the children often live with her and their stepfather. Many children spend some time in a stepparent family, but relatively few spend their entire childhood in such families.
   Blended family A stepparent family that includes children born to several families, such as the biological children from the spouses' previous marriages and the biological children of the new couple. This type of family is a particularly difficult structure for school-age children.
3. **Adoptive family** (2%) Although as many as one-third of infertile married couples adopt children, fewer adoptable children are available than in earlier decades, which means that most adoptive families have only one or two children. A single parent is sometimes an adoptive parent, but this is unusual.
4. **Polygamous family** (0%) In some nations, it is common for one man to have several wives, each bearing his children.

One-Parent Families (28%)

One-parent families are increasingly common, but they tend to have fewer children than two-parent families.

1. **Single mother, never married** (10%) Many babies (about a third of all U.S. newborns) are born to unmarried mothers, but most of these mothers intend to marry someday (Musick, 2002). Many of them do get married, either to their baby's father or to someone else. By school age, their children are often in two-parent families.
2. **Single mother—divorced, separated, or widowed** (13%) Although many marriages end in divorce (almost half in the United States, less in other nations), many divorcing couples have no children and many others remarry. Thus, only 13 percent of school-age children live with single, formerly married mothers.
3. **Single father, divorced or never married** (5%) About one in five divorced or unmarried fathers has physical custody of the children. This structure is the most rapidly increasing one in the United States, especially among divorced fathers who were actively involved in child rearing when they were married.

Other Family Types (5%)

Some children live in special versions of one- or two-parent families.

1. **Extended family** Many children live with a grandparent or other relatives as well as with one or both of their parents.
2. **Grandparents alone** For some school-age children, their one or two "parents" are their grandparents, because the biological parents are dead or otherwise unable to live with them. This family type is increasing, especially in Africa, where an epidemic of AIDS is killing many parents.
3. **Homosexual family** Some school-age children live in a homosexual family, usually when a custodial parent has a homosexual partner. Less often, a homosexual couple adopts children or a lesbian has a child. Varying laws and norms determine whether these are one- or two-parent families.
4. **Foster family** This family type is usually considered temporary, and the children are categorized by their original family structure. Otherwise, they are in one- or two-parent families depending on the structure of their foster family.

Source: Percentages are estimated from data in U.S. Bureau of the Census, 2007.

sidered married. The frequency of cohabitation varies by nation, but for school-age children, the crucial factor is whether or not they live with two biological parents who are committed to the family.

Statistics often include several other types in the two-parent category—adoptive parents, grandparents who raise children without parents, and a biological parent married to a stepparent. Although adults in these family types have less of a biological connection to the child than do parents in the nuclear family, each form can function well.

In the United States, more than one-fourth (28 percent) of all school-age children live in a **single-parent family,** with only one parent and no other adults. This is the dominant form among African Americans and includes more than half of all children in some other communities. Most American children spend some time in a single-parent family before age 18, although most also spend many years of childhood in a nuclear family.

single-parent family A family that consists of only one parent and his or her biological children under age 18.

Many Relatives in the Home The nuclear and single-parent family structures are sometimes contrasted with the **extended family,** in which children live not only with one or both of their parents but also with other relatives (usually grandparents, but often aunts, uncles, and cousins as well). Extended families are more common among low-income households, both in developed nations and developing ones (where more families are poor and more families are extended). The benefit is that expenses and responsibilities are more easily shared when everyone lives together.

extended family A family of three or more generations living in one household.

These distinctions among family types are not clear-cut, especially regarding extended families. Most nuclear and single-parent families have close connections with other relatives who live nearby, share meals, provide emotional and financial support, and otherwise function as an extended family.

Although these generalities apply particularly to North America, other nations have similar patterns. For example, especially in developing nations, extended families often have private living areas within the home for each couple and their children, as occurs in nuclear families (Georgas et al., 2006).

In some nations, the **polygamous family,** in which one man has two or more wives and may have children with each of them, is the family type for between 1 and 50 percent of the children. Overall, children do not fare as well in such families, primarily because income per child is reduced (Omariba & Boyle, 2007). Polygamy is not legal in the United States (although it still sometimes occurs), so reliable incidence data is impossible to find. Regardless of variations in laws or customs, however, worldwide the nuclear family is the most common structure.

polygamous family A family consisting of one man, several wives, and the biological children of the man and his wives.

The Homosexual Family

Reliable statistics for homosexual families are also difficult to find. According to the U.S. Bureau of the Census (2007), only 0.7 percent of households (about 1 in 140) are headed by a homosexual couple. All gay and lesbian groups, and most social scientists, consider this an underestimate. One reason it is thought to be an underestimate is that many homosexual couples are reluctant to proclaim their status. This trend seems to be reversing, as U.S. data from 2000 to 2005 show a 31 percent increase in homosexual couples declaring that they share a home (U.S. Bureau of the Census, 2002, 2007; see Table 13.4).

No official count of homosexual couples was available until 2000 because, before that, "unmarried couples" were defined by the U.S. Bureau of the Census as a cohabiting man and woman. Now that category is called "unmarried partners," and couples are allowed to specify whether they are male/female, male/male, or female/female.

➤**Answer to Observation Quiz** (from page 383): The stacks of shoeboxes indicate that this is a discount store, which has no salespeople on the floor but is a good place for a mother of three to shop for boots. And if Rebekah had gotten new boots last spring, they wouldn't fit her now.

How Many Homosexual Couples? The 31 percent increase in homosexual couples sharing a home is five times higher than the heterosexual increase, which probably means that more gay and lesbian couples have been willing to declare themselves in the past few years. It is not known how many more undeclared homosexual households there are.

TABLE 13.4

Number of Unmarried-Partner Households in the United States (officially declared)

	Male/Female	Male/Male	Female/Female	Total Homosexual Couples
2000	4,881,377	301,026	293,365	594,391
2004	5,133,637	374,397	332,799	707,196
2005	5,188,163	413,095	363,848	776,943
Increase from 2000 to 2005	306,786 (+6%)	112,069 (+37%)	70,483 (+24%)	182,552 (+31%)

Source: U.S. Bureau of the Census, 2002, 2007.

AP PHOTO / AMY CONN-GUTIERREZ

A Texas Family Two-year-old Jackson's adoptive parents have been in a committed relationship for 13 years. Their home is in Dallas, where gay couples can adopt but cannot marry.

Many gay and lesbian couples are parents, either because one of the partners was formerly married to a person of the other sex or because the couple has had a child via in vitro fertilization or adoption. Having homosexual parents seems to have no negative effects on the children (Glazer & Drescher, 2001; Shanley, 2001; Wainright et al., 2004).

The homosexual family—whether two-parent, one-parent, or multigenerational—seems to offer its children strengths and weaknesses similar to those of the heterosexual family (Herek, 2006). As adolescents, at least, children of homosexual parents have the same romantic impulses (usually heterosexual), school achievements, and psychosocial difficulties as children of heterosexual couples do. One study explains that, "regardless of family type," children are affected by the quality of their relationships with their parents, not so much by the heterosexual or homosexual nature of the parents' relationship (Wainright & Patterson, 2008, p. 124).

Connecting Structure and Function

Family structure and family function are intertwined. The crucial question is whether the family living arrangements make it more, or less, likely that several adults are devoted to the children's well-being in a stable, harmonious household.

Single-Parent and Blended Families

Especially for Single Parents (see response, page 388): You have heard that children raised in one-parent families will have difficulty in establishing intimate relationships as adolescents and adults. What can you do about this possibility?

From this perspective, single-parent families may be problematic, because these households are likely to be low-income and unstable. They are most likely to change structure as well as location (Raley & Wildsmith, 2004). Furthermore, most single mothers or fathers fill many roles besides being a parent, including wage earner, daughter or son (single parents are often dependent on their own parents), and lover (many single parents seek a new romantic relationship). Children in single-mother families "are at greatest risk," faring worse in school and in adult life than most other children (Carlson & Corcoran, 2001, p. 789).

blended family A stepparent family that includes children born to several families, such as the biological children from the spouses' previous marriages and the biological children of the new couple.

A **blended family,** the structure in which a newly married couple combine their offspring from earlier relationships, is also at risk for instability. Blended families are often categorized as nuclear families, and they have a major asset of such families: They tend to be wealthier than single-parent families. However, in blended families it is more common for older children to leave and new babies to

BILL ARON / PHOTOEDIT, INC

A Comfortable Combination The blended family—husband, wife, and children from both spouses' previous marriages—often breeds resentment, depression, and rebellion in the children. That is apparently not the case for the family shown here, which provides cheerful evidence that any family structure is capable of functioning well.

arrive, and the marriages themselves dissolve more often than do first marriages (Teachman, 2008a).

The likelihood that children will thrive in blended families depends largely on the adults' economic and emotional security. Blended families are not necessarily better for children than single-parent families, since emotional instability and added stress may outweigh the financial benefits.

Functioning Within Nuclear Families

The original nuclear family, consisting of a couple who stay married and the children they have together, tends to function best for children. On average, people who marry and stay married have personal and financial strengths that also make them better parents. Correlational statistics show that, compared with adults who never marry, married adults tend to be wealthier, better educated, healthier, more flexible, and less hostile—even before they marry.

In general, biological and adoptive parents are more dedicated to their children than are stepparents or foster parents. For these reasons, children growing up in nuclear families are more likely to have someone to teach them to brush their teeth, to read to them at bedtime, to check their homework, and so on, as well as to plan for their future by saving money for college.

As a result of parental dedication, adopted children tend to fare well in middle childhood. They are likely to have adequate self-esteem even when their adoptive parents are of another ethnicity (Juffer & van IJzendoorn, 2007).

Cultural Differences

Every family type is affected by culture (Heuveline & Timberlake, 2004). For example, many French parents are not married, but they share household and child-rearing tasks and are less likely to separate than are married adults in the United States. Thus, the cohabiting structure functions well for French children. However, in the United States, cohabiting parents are more likely to split up than are married parents. As a result, that family structure, on average, is less functional for U.S. schoolchildren (S. L. Brown, 2004).

More generally, the effect of marriage and divorce on parenthood varies not only by nation but also by ethnic group. In the United States, single parenthood is

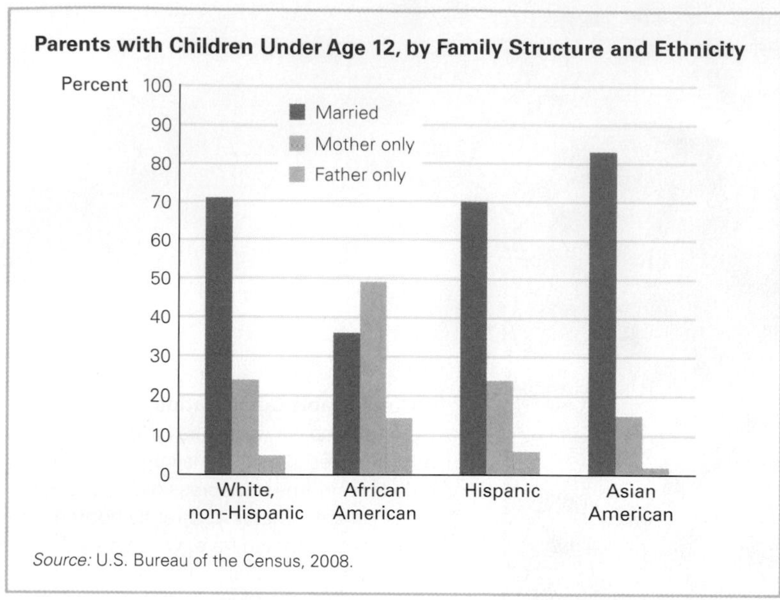

FIGURE 13.4

Fathers and Mothers Differences in structure are especially striking between African American and Asian American families with young children. Asian American families are most likely to be headed by married parents, but African American single-parent families are more than seven times more likely than Asian American ones to be headed by the father.

much more common, and more readily accepted, among African Americans. As a result, there is little social stigma for the children, and other relatives and friends are more likely to help the African American single parent than is the case in other groups (Cain & Combs-Orme, 2005; Taylor et al., 2008).

Compared with couples in other American ethnic groups, Hispanic and Asian American couples are less likely to divorce, and the fathers are typically quite concerned about their children's well-being. Children benefit from both of these correlations.

However, if divorce does occur within Hispanic and Asian families, the children may be more vulnerable than children of divorce in White, non-Hispanic families. Divorced Hispanic American fathers are *less* likely to stay involved with their children than are divorced fathers in other ethnic groups (V. King et al., 2004), and Asian fathers are less likely to seek custody of the children (see Figure 13.4). The effect of this cultural variability is unknown. Among college students, children of divorced or separated parents are more likely to wish for a close relationship with their fathers, but they are less likely to have it than are those whose fathers are still married to their mothers. This is more often the case for African Americans than for Asian Americans (Schwartz & Finley, 2005).

Every study finds exceptions to these patterns. In any family type, some children develop well and others are harmed. To learn how a family is affecting a child's development, it is "not enough to know that an individual lives in a particular family structure without also knowing what takes place within that structure" (Lansford et al., 2001, p. 850). Function, not structure, is the key aspect of a family's influence on a child.

Family Trouble

We now look at two factors that interfere with family function in every nation: low income and high conflict (Teachman, 2008b). Many families experience both, because financial stress and family fighting feed on each other. Imagine this scene.

Suppose a 6-year-old spills his milk, as every 6-year-old sometimes does. In a well-functioning, financially stable family, the parents then teach the child how to mop up a spill. They pour more milk, perhaps with a comment that encourages family harmony such as, "Everyone has an accident sometimes."

What if the 6-year-old lives in a single-parent family and that parent is already overwhelmed by unemployment, overdue rent, a baby who needs changing, and an older child who wants money for a school trip? What if the last of the food stamps bought that milk? Conflict almost inevitably erupts, with shouting, crying, and accusations (a sibling claiming, "He did it on purpose"; the 6-year-old saying, "You pushed me"; perhaps a visiting friend chiming in, "You should teach him to be careful"). As this example makes clear, poverty can make anger spill over when the milk does.

➤Response for Single Parents (from page 386): Do not get married mainly to provide a second parent for your child. If you were to do so, things would probably get worse rather than better. Do make an effort to have friends of both sexes with whom your child can interact.

Income and Children

Family income correlates with both function and structure. Directly or indirectly, all five functions are more likely to be fulfilled when the family's income is adequate (Conger & Donellan, 2007; Gershoff et al., 2007; Yeung et al., 2002). Children aged 6 to 9 show the greatest effects of family SES (Gennetian & Miller, 2002).

The Family-Stress Model To understand exactly how income affects child development, consider the *family-stress model,* which holds that the crucial question to ask about any risk factor (such as low income, divorce, unemployment) is whether or not it increases the stress on a family. In developed nations, poverty may not directly prevent children from having adequate food, clothing, and other necessities, since adults are usually able to secure at least the minimum needed. In that case, low income does not necessarily add to stress, at least in theory.

This is particularly true if the low income is temporary and the family's net worth (home ownership, investments, and so on) buffers the strain of less money earned in a particular year (Yeung & Conley, 2008). However, for many families, economic hardship is ongoing; that increases stress, which, in turn, makes adults tense and hostile toward their partners and children (Conger et al., 2002; Parke et al., 2004). Thus, the adults' stressful *reaction* to poverty is crucial.

Reaction to wealth may be a problem, too. Children in high-income families have a disproportionate share of emotional problems, which sometimes lead to adolescent drug abuse and delinquency. One reason is thought to be the stress from parental pressure on the children to excel (Luthar, 2003).

Many intervention programs aim to teach parents to be more encouraging and patient with their children (McLoyd et al., 2006). In low-income families, however, this emphasis on parental reaction may be misplaced. Poverty itself—with attendant problems such as inadequate child care, poor health, and the threat of homelessness—may be the root cause of stress. If so, raising household income and increasing net worth would help children more than focusing on problematic parenting styles and dysfunctional reactions.

Teaching Parents to Be Patient The idea that education in parenting skills may not help impoverished parents is suggested by an eight-year natural experiment (Costello et al., 2003). This study began by assessing psychopathology among 1,420 school-age children, many of whom were Native Americans. For children of every ethnicity, those from low-income households had, on average, four symptoms of mental disturbance, compared with only one symptom among the nonpoor. This finding is troubling but not surprising. Much other research has noted a link between poverty and child psychopathology (McLoyd et al., 2006).

Midway through the eight-year study, the families of about 200 children suddenly were no longer poor because a new casino began paying each Native American adult about $6,000 per year. This income was not a windfall but was expected to continue annually. Among those 200 children, the incidence of externalizing behavior (such as impulsive aggression) fell to the same levels as among the children whose families were not low-SES when the study began (Costello et al., 2003). No parental education was needed to relieve their symptoms, presumably because the raised income relieved the family stress.

Other research also suggests that reducing family financial stress directly benefits the children. In extended families that include several well-educated wage earners, the children are likely to become well educated and happy. Children in single mother households do much better if their father pays child support (J. W. Graham & Beller, 2002) or if single parents receive government subsidies (as in Austria and Iceland) (Pong et al., 2003).

Family Turbulence

Too often, harmony and stability are missing in the families of American school-age children. Harmony is not identical to stability, but the two often appear together (Buehler & Gerard, 2002; Khaleque & Rohner, 2002). Ideally, parents form a parental alliance, learning to cooperate and thus maintaining a happy, stable home (see Chapter 4).

The need for harmony explains why blended families can be problematic (Hetherington & Kelly, 2002). Jealousy, stress, and conflict arise when children share a home with unrelated children and must adjust to a new adult authority. In such situations, smooth parental alliances can take years to form.

In any family structure, children's well-being declines if family members fight, especially if parents physically or verbally abuse each other. Children may suffer harm if a fight escalates or one parent walks out and leaves the other distraught. In contrast, children may learn valuable lessons from parental disagreements that result in compromise and reconciliation (Cummings et al., 2003).

Family Transitions Every family transition affects the children, particularly during middle childhood. If family structure changes, children are more likely to quit school, leave home, and, in adolescence, use drugs, break the law, and have early sexual relationships (McLanahan et al., 2005). Unmarried mothers usually change jobs, residences, and romantic partners several times before their children are grown; such multiple transitions are particularly stressful for children (Bumpass & Lu, 2000).

Moving to a new neighborhood affects school-age children (who have a special need for continuity) more than younger or older children. Nonetheless, each year about 16 percent of all U.S. children move from one home to another, a rate three times that of adults over age 50 (U.S. Bureau of the Census, 2007). Even a move that parents consider an improvement may upset a school-age child who loses contact with friends. A move to another culture is especially hard.

Worldwide, children move more often as family income falls. Hardest hit are school-age children who are homeless or refugees. In the United States, homeless children move, on average, two to three times *a year* before moving into a shelter (Buckner et al., 1999), a major threat to their well-being.

The problems associated with moving were shown by a study in Japan, where many companies transfer junior employees repeatedly over several years. If the employee is a father, about half the time his family moves with him. Academically, this is not problematic, as there is a sequential, standard curriculum for each grade. Researchers compared children who moved with children who did not, expecting to find that daily contact with fathers had benefits for children. In fact, however, they found that the school-age children did better if they stayed put, even when their fathers were absent (Tanaka & Nakazawa, 2005). (Their mothers, however, experienced more stress—an illustration of the fact that any change affects family members differently.)

Social-Cognitive Connections In general, the child's cognitive interpretation of a negative family situation is crucial in determining how that situation affects him or her (Olson & Dweck, 2008). Some children consider the problematic family they were born into a temporary hardship and look forward to the day when they can break free and live on their own. Other children feel responsible for whatever happens in their family. This problem is called *parentification;* the child feels that he or she must be the caretaker of the parents and of younger children (Byng-Hall, 2008).

Similarly, a child's peace of mind is jeopardized if he or she is pushed to take sides in a marital dispute. Quarrels between grandparents and parents over child-rearing practices can also be harmful; this is one reason that children often fare better when grandparents do not share a residence with parents (Cain & Combs-Orme, 2005). Children can use their cognitive skills to adjust to different rules and parenting styles, but they have a much harder time when adults argue about their care in front of them: Instability and uncertainty are communicated to the children, who may have difficulty making sense of the situation.

An intriguing study of 8- to 11-year-olds assessed the impact of two related factors on children's stress levels: conflict between parents and each child's emotional reaction to the conflict. By far the more important correlate with children's psychic and academic problems was not the marital discord itself but the children's feelings of self-blame or vulnerability. When children "do not perceive that marital conflict is threatening to them and do not blame themselves" for it (El-Sheikh & Harger, 2001, p. 883), they are much less troubled (see Figure 13.5).

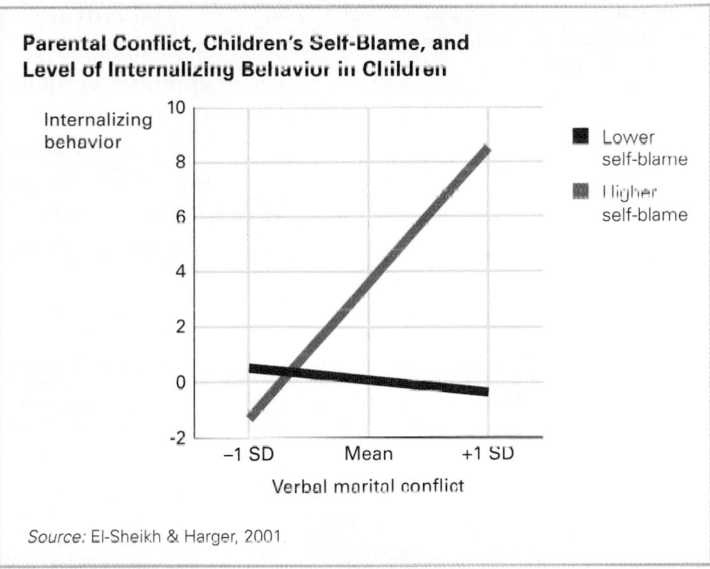

FIGURE 13.5

When Parents Fight and Children Blame Themselves Husbands and wives who almost never disagree are below the first standard deviation (–1 SD) in verbal marital conflict. Couples who frequently have loud, screaming, cursing arguments are in the highest 15 percent (+1 SD). In such high-conflict households, children are not much affected—if they do not blame themselves for the situation. However, if children do blame themselves, they are likely to have internalizing problems, such as nightmares, stomachaches, panic attacks, and feelings of loneliness.

SUMMING UP

Parents influence child development, and some families function better than others. For school-age children, families serve five crucial functions: to provide basic necessities, to encourage learning, to develop self-respect, to nurture friendships, and to provide harmony and stability. Low income, family conflict, and major life transitions interfere with these functions, no matter what the family structure.

The nuclear, two parent family is the most common, but a sizable minority of families are headed by a single parent (including one-fourth of all families of school-age children in the United States). Two-parent families tend to provide more income, stability, and adult attention, all of which have measurable benefits for children. Extended families, grandparent families, one-parent families, blended families, and adoptive families can raise successful, happy children, although each of these has its own vulnerabilities. There is no structure that inevitably harms children, and none that guarantees good family function. Adequate income, family harmony, and support for the child are crucial: These can be part of any family structure.

The Peer Group

Getting along with peers is especially important during middle childhood, "central to living a full life and feeling good" (Borland, 1998, p. 28). Difficulties with peers can cause serious problems, and being well liked is protective, especially for children from conflicted, punitive, or otherwise stressful homes (Criss et al., 2002; Rubin et al., 2006).

Peer relationships display a significant developmental progression. Younger children have friends and learn from them, but their egocentrism makes them less affected by another child's acceptance or rejection. School-age children, in contrast, are well aware of their classmates' opinions, judgments, and accomplishments.

The Culture of Children

Peer relationships, unlike adult–child relationships, involve partners who negotiate, compromise, share, and defend themselves as equals. Children learn social lessons from each other that grown-ups cannot teach because adults are from a different generation and by definition are not peers. Adults sometimes command obedience, sometimes allow dominance; but always they are much older and bigger, with the values and experiences of their own cohort, not the child's.

Remember from Chapter 1 that culture includes habits and values as well as more obvious manifestations such as clothing and food. Each age group can be said to have a culture. This is particularly true in childhood.

culture of children The particular habits, styles, and values that reflect the set of rules and rituals that characterize children as distinct from adult society.

The **culture of children** includes the particular rules and behaviors that are passed down to younger children from slightly older children without adult approval; it includes not only fashions and gestures but also values and rituals. Jump-rope rhymes, insults, and superstitions are often part of the peer culture. Even nursery games echo the culture of children. For instance, "Ring around the rosie/Pocketful of posies/Ashes, ashes/We all fall down," originated with children coping with death (Kastenbaum, 2006). (*Rosy* is short for *rosary.*)

Throughout the world, the culture of children encourages independence from adult society. By age 10, if not before, peers pity those (especially boys) whose parents kiss them in public ("mama's boy"), tease children who please the teachers ("teacher's pet," "suckup"), and despise those who betray other children to adults ("tattletale," "grasser," "snitch," "rat"). Keeping secrets from adults is part of the culture of children.

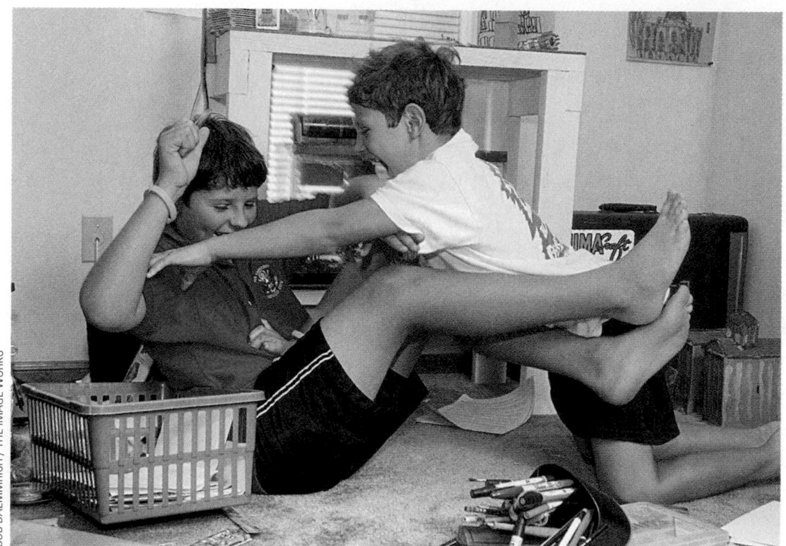

BOB DAEMMRICH / THE IMAGE WORKS

How to Play Boys teach each other the rituals and rules of engagement. The bigger boy shown here could hurt the smaller one, but he won't; their culture forbids it in such situations.

Clothing often signifies independence and peer-group membership. Many 9-year-olds refuse to wear clothes their parents buy, on the grounds that they are too loose, too tight, too long, too short, or wrong in color, style, brand, or some other aspect that is unnoticed by adults.

Since children adopt the manners and values of their peers, parents often encourage their children to form friendships with certain other children (Dishion & Bullock, 2002). This succeeds with young children, but not with older ones, some of whom prefer friends who defy authority (J. Snyder et al., 2005). Some consequences of children's preference for rebellious friends are harmless (passing a note during class), but others are not (shoplifting, spray-painting graffiti, cigarette smoking).

Gender stereotypes become more elaborate during the school years, when children much prefer to play with other children of their own sex (Ruble et al., 2006). While gender segregation is strongly maintained (especially among the boys), racial and ethnic prejudice is usually not (Nesdale, 2004). Indeed, school-age children's sense of justice and fairness helps them recognize and reject prejudice, first when it affects someone else and then when it affects them directly

KYUYA KAMAZAWA / HAGA / THE IMAGE WORKS

The Rules of the Game These young monks in Myanmar (formerly Burma) are playing a board game that adults also play, but the children have some of their own refinements of the general rules. Children's peer groups often modify the norms of the dominant culture, as is evident in everything from superstitions to stickball.

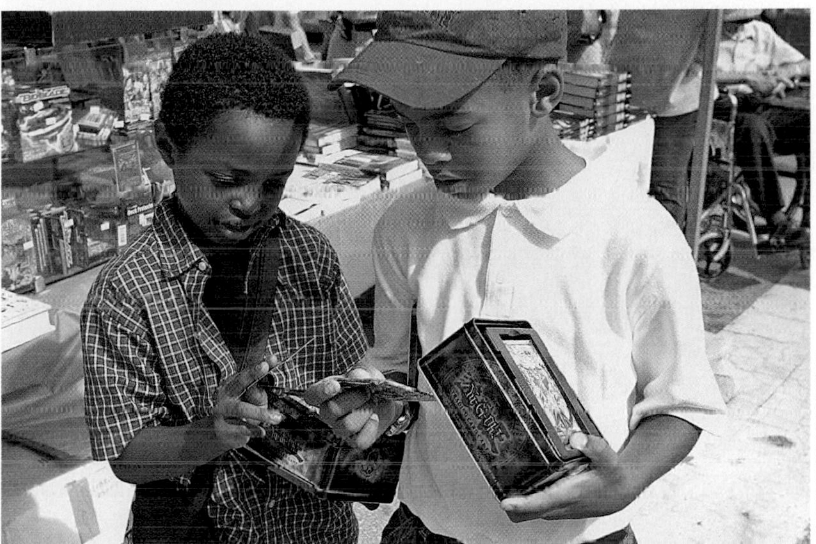

Yu-Gi-Oh The specifics vary tremendously—stamps, stickers, matchbooks, baseball cards, and many more—but the impulse to collect, organize, and trade certain items is characteristic of school-age children. For a few years, in south Florida and elsewhere, the coveted collector's item was Yu-Gi-Oh cards.

(C. S. Brown & Bigler, 2005; Killen, 2007). Children tend to identify with other children, no matter what their background.

This was evident in a survey of school-age children's attitudes about refugees. A small intervention—reading and discussing stories about refugee children—made the children's attitudes more friendly toward refugees (unlike some of their parents' attitudes) (Cameron et al., 2006). This and other studies conclude that it is quite possible for children to be proud of their ethnic, national, gender, or other group without being prejudiced against children of another group.

The culture of children is not always benign. For example, because communication with peers is a priority, children may quickly master a second language, but they may also be quick to spout curses, accents, and slang if doing so signifies being in sync (or "up," or "down") with their peers' culture.

Attitudes are affected by friends. Remember Yolanda and Paul (from Chapter 12)?

> *Yolanda:* There's one friend . . . she's always been with me, in bad or good things. . . . She's always telling me, "Keep on going and your dreams are gonna come true."
>
> *Paul:* I think right now about going Christian, right? Just going Christian, trying to do good, you know? Stay away from drugs, everything. And every time it seems like I think about that, I think about the homeboys. And it's a trip because a lot of the homeboys are my family, too, you know?
>
> *[quoted in Nieto, 2000, pp. 220, 149]*

Friendship and Social Acceptance

One value is almost universally held by school-age children—the value of friendship. Children want to be liked, and they learn faster as well as feel happier when they have friends.

Friendship

Although school-age children value acceptance by the entire peer group, personal friendship is even more important to them (Erwin, 1998; Ladd, 1999; Sandstrom & Zakriski, 2004). Indeed, if they had to choose between being popular (widely accepted by peers) but friendless (lacking emotional closeness with peers) or having close friends but being unpopular, most children would take the friends. That is a healthy choice, because friendship leads to psychosocial growth and provides a buffer against psychopathology.

A longitudinal study of peer acceptance (popularity) and close friendship (mutual loyalty) among fifth-graders found that both statuses affected social interactions and emotional health 12 years later but that having close friends was more important than being popular in this regard (Bagwell et al., 2001).

Another study found that children had about the same number of acquaintances no matter what their home backgrounds, but those from violent homes had fewer close friends and were lonelier. The researchers explained, "Skill at recruiting surface acquaintances or playmates is different . . . from the skill required to sustain close relationships," and close relationships are needed if the child is to avoid loneliness, isolation, and rejection (McCloskey & Stuewig, 2001, p. 93).

Friends and Culture Like children everywhere, these children—two 7-year-olds and one 10-year-old, of the Surma people in southern Ethiopia—model their appearance after that of slightly older children, in this case adolescents who apply elaborate body paint for courtship and stick-fighting rituals.

Observation Quiz (see answer, page 396): Are they boys or girls?

Friendships become more intense and intimate as children grow older; this is to be expected, in view of the improvement in their social cognition and effortful control. Compared with 6-year-olds, 10-year-olds demand more of their friends, change friends less often, become upset when a friendship breaks up, and find it harder to make new friends. Gender differences persist in activities (girls converse more, while boys play more games), but both boys and girls want to have best friends (Erwin, 1998; Underwood, 2004).

By age 10, most children know how to be a good friend. For example, when fifth-graders were asked how they would react if other children teased their friend, they almost all said they would ask their friend to do something fun with them and would reassure the friend that "things like that happen to everyone" (Rose & Asher, 2004).

Older children tend to choose best friends whose interests, values, and backgrounds are similar to their own. In fact, by the end of middle childhood, close friendships are almost always between children of the same sex, age, ethnicity, and socioeconomic status. This occurs not because children become more prejudiced over the course of middle childhood (they do not), but because they seek friends who understand and agree with them (Aboud & Amato, 2001; Aboud & Mendelson, 1998; Powlishta, 2004).

Popular and Unpopular Children

Some children are well liked, while others are not. Often a child's popularity changes from year to year (Kupersmidt et al., 2004; Ladd, 2005). In a study conducted over six years, researchers asked 299 children which classmates they did or did not want as playmates. Overall, about a third of the children were popular (often chosen), about half were average (sometimes chosen), and about a sixth were unpopular (often rejected), with some change in the size of each cluster from year to year. Almost every child (89 percent) changed from one cluster to another over the six years. Only 2 percent were unpopular every year, and only 6 percent were consistently popular (Brendgen et al., 2001).

Culture and cohort affect the reasons why children are liked. For example, in North American culture, shy children are not popular; in contrast, a study conducted in 1990 in Shanghai found that shy children were respected and often popular (Chen et al., 1992). Over the next 12 years, however, Chinese culture changed: Assertiveness became more valued. A new survey from the same Shanghai schools reflected this change, finding that shy children were less popular than their shy predecessors had been (Chen et al., 2005). This cultural change also meant that fewer children identified themselves as shy.

Among young children in the United States, the most popular children are "kind, trustworthy, cooperative." Particularly as children grow older (around the time of fifth grade), a new group appears: children who are "athletic, cool, dominant, arrogant, and . . . aggressive." They are feared and respected, high in social status, but not necessarily liked (Cillessen & Mayeux, 2004a, p. 147).

Another development is the emergence of three distinct types of unpopular children. Some are *neglected,* not really rejected; they are ignored but not shunned. This kind of unpopularity may not be damaging to the child, especially if he or she has a supportive family or outstanding talent (in music or the arts, say) (Sandstrom & Zakriski, 2004). If the child has even one close friend, either at school or in the neighborhood, being neglected by peers is not a problem.

The other two types of unpopular children experience active rejection. Some are **aggressive-rejected**—disliked because they are antagonistic and confrontational. Others are **withdrawn-rejected**—disliked because they are timid, withdrawn, and anxious. Children of these two types have much in common: They tend to misinterpret social situations and to lack emotional regulation, and many of them are mistreated at home (Pollak et al., 2000).

ALAMY

Loneliness Are the girls in the background whispering about the girl in the foreground loudly enough for her (but not the teacher) to hear? Perhaps this social situation is not what it appears to be, but almost every classroom has one or two rejected children, the targets of gossip, rumors, and social isolation.

Social Awareness

Interpretation of social situations (akin to emotional intelligence, discussed in Chapter 11) may be crucial for peer acceptance. **Social cognition** is the ability to understand human interactions. This ability begins in infancy (with *social referencing;* see Chapter 7) and continues to develop in early childhood (as children develop a *theory of mind;* see Chapter 9). In most cases, social cognition is well established by middle childhood. Children with impaired social cognition are likely to be rejected (Gifford-Smith & Rabiner, 2004; Ladd, 2005).

One extensive two-year study of social awareness began with 4½- to 8-year-olds. The researchers found that school-age children improve not only in social cognition but also in a related ability, effortful control (discussed earlier in this chapter). As a result of these improvements, the older children in this study had fewer emotional problems than did the younger ones, according to parents' reports (N. Eisenberg et al., 2004).

Well-liked children generally assume that social slights, from a push to an unkind remark, are accidental (Dodge et al., 2006). Therefore, a social slight does not provoke fear, self-doubt, or anger in them, as it is likely to do in rejected children. When a direct conflict occurs between themselves and another child, well-liked children think about the future of that relationship, seeking a compromise to maintain the friendship (Rose & Asher, 1999). These prosocial impulses and attitudes are a sign of social maturity, and they are rare in rejected children (Gifford-Smith & Rabiner, 2004).

aggressive-rejected Rejected by peers because of antagonistic, confrontational behavior.

withdrawn-rejected Rejected by peers because of timid, withdrawn, and anxious behavior.

social cognition The ability to understand social interactions, including the causes and consequences of human behavior.

Bullies and Victims

Almost every adult remembers isolated attacks, occasional insults, and unexpected social slights in childhood. Many adults also remember good friends who kept these incidents from escalating into bullying.

Defining Terms

Bullying is defined as repeated, systematic attacks intended to harm those who are unable or unlikely to defend themselves and who have no protective social network. Bullying occurs in every nation, in every community, and in every kind of school (religious or secular, public or private, progressive or traditional, large or small), although some schools have much less bullying than others of the same type. Bullying may be *physical* (hitting, pinching, or kicking), *verbal* (teasing, taunting, or name-calling), or *relational* (designed to destroy peer acceptance).

bullying Repeated, systematic efforts to inflict harm through physical, verbal, or social attack on a weaker person.

A key word in this definition is *repeated.* Victims of bullying typically endure shameful experiences again and again—being forced to hand over lunch money,

MICHELLE D. BRIDEWELL / PHOTOEDIT, INC.

JONATHAN NOUROK / PHOTOEDIT, INC.

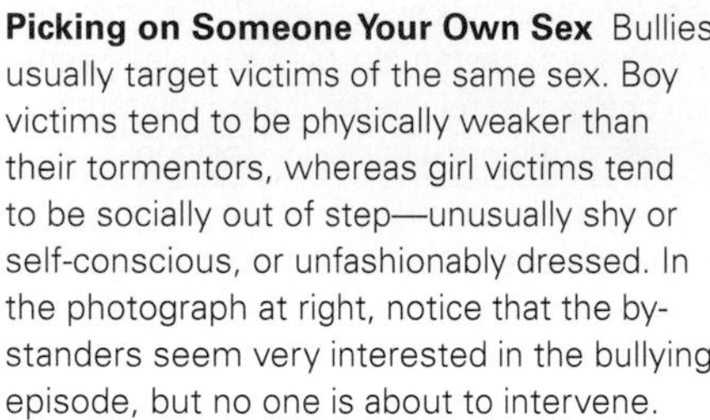

Picking on Someone Your Own Sex Bullies usually target victims of the same sex. Boy victims tend to be physically weaker than their tormentors, whereas girl victims tend to be socially out of step—unusually shy or self-conscious, or unfashionably dressed. In the photograph at right, notice that the bystanders seem very interested in the bullying episode, but no one is about to intervene.

laugh at insults, drink milk mixed with detergent, and so on, with others watching and no one defending them.

Victims of bullying tend to be "cautious, sensitive, quiet . . . lonely and abandoned at school. As a rule, they do not have a single good friend in their class" (Olweus et al., 1999, p. 15). Although it is often thought that victims are unusually ugly or impaired or odd, this is not usually the case. Victims are chosen because of their emotional vulnerability and social isolation.

Most victims are withdrawn-rejected, but some are aggressive-rejected. The latter are called **bully-victims** (or *provocative victims*) (Unnever, 2005). Bully-victims are "the most strongly disliked members of the peer group," with neither friends nor sympathizers (Sandstrom & Zakriski, 2004, p. 110).

bully-victim Someone who attacks others and who is attacked as well. (Also called *provocative victims* because they do things that elicit bullying, such as stealing a bully's pencil.)

Most bullies are *not* rejected. They have a few admiring friends (henchmen). Unless they are bully-victims, they are socially perceptive—but they lack the empathy of prosocial children. Especially over the years of middle childhood, they become skilled at avoiding adult awareness, attacking victims who can be counted on not to resist.

Boy bullies are often big; they target smaller, weaker boys. Girl bullies are often sharp-tongued; they harass shyer, more soft-spoken girls. Boys tend to use force (physical aggression), while girls tend to mock, ridicule, or spread rumors (verbal aggression). Both sexes may also use relational aggression, which becomes more common with age. With maturation, bullies become more sophisticated, using a wider variety of humiliating and hurtful tactics, including *cyberbullying* (discussed in Chapter 15).

Causes and Consequences of Bullying

Bullying may originate with a genetic predisposition or a brain abnormality, but parents, teachers, and peers usually succeed in teaching young children to restrain their aggressive impulses before middle childhood, as part of developing effortful control. However, the opposite may occur (Granic & Patterson, 2006). Families

➤Answer to Observation Quiz (from page 394): They are all girls. Boys would not be likely to stand so close together. Also, the two 7-year-olds have decorated their soon-to-be budding breasts.

that create insecure attachment, provide a stressful home life, are ineffective at discipline, or include hostile siblings tend to intensify children's aggression (Cairns & Cairns, 2001; Ladd, 2005).

The consequences of bullying can echo for years (Berger, 2007). Many victims develop low self-esteem and some explode violently; many bullies become increasingly cruel. Over time, both bullies and victims incur social costs, including impaired social understanding and relationship difficulties (Pepler et al., 2004). Even bystanders suffer (Nishina & Juvonen, 2005), liking school less. Perhaps their mirror neurons make them feel distress when they observe victimization.

Can Bullying Be Stopped?

Most victimized children find ways to halt ongoing bullying—by ignoring, retaliating, defusing, or avoiding. A study of older children who were bullied in one year but not in the next indicated that finding new friends was a crucial element in that change (P. K. Smith et al., 2004). Friendships help victims, but bullies may simply find new targets. What can be done to halt bullying altogether?

Unsuccessful Efforts: Narrow Focus on Bullies and Victims In the United States, one recent intervention produced a decrease in observed bullying but not in reported bullying (Frey et al., 2005; see the Research Design). After another much-acclaimed effort in Texas, reported bullying actually increased (Rosenbluth et al., 2004). Several studies have discovered that putting troubled students together in a therapy group or a classroom tends to increase aggression in all of them (Kupersmidt et al., 2004). Older children are particularly stuck in their patterns; some high school efforts have backfired.

Even in elementary school, well-intentioned measures, such as letting children solve problems on their own or assigning guards to the school, may make the situation worse. Teaching social cognition to victims may seem like a good idea, but the bullying problem arises from the school culture more than from any characteristics of the victims. Many antibullying projects report discouraging results (J. D. Smith et al., 2004; P. K. Smith & Ananiadou, 2003).

Successful Efforts: Involving the Entire School The more successful efforts to stop bullying do so by changing conditions in the whole school, including the behaviors of teachers and bystanders. Dan Olweus, a pioneer in antibullying efforts, advocates this *whole-school strategy*.

In 1982, after three victims of bullying in Norway killed themselves, the government asked Olweus to survey Norway's 90,000 school-age children. He reported that bullying was much more prevalent than adults realized: 14 percent of the children in grades 2–5 said that they were victims "now and then," and 10 percent admitted that they deliberately hurt other children (Olweus, 1993).

To stop the bullying, Olweus used a dynamic-systems approach, involving every segment of the school. He sent pamphlets to parents, showed videos to students, trained school staff, and increased supervision during recess. In each classroom, students discussed how to stop bullying and befriend lonely children. Bullies and their parents were counseled. Twenty months later, Olweus surveyed the children again. Bullying had been reduced by half (Olweus, 1992).

A review of all research on successful ways to halt bullying (Berger, 2007) finds the following to be true:

- The whole school must change, not just the identified bullies.
- Intervention is more effective in the earlier grades.
- Evaluation is critical. Programs that appear to be good might actually be harmful.

Research Design

Scientists: Karin S. Frey, Miriam K. Hirschstein, Jennie L. Snell, Leihua V. S. Edstron, Elizabeth MacKenzie, and Carole J. Broderick (all from The Committee on Children).

Publication: *Developmental Psychology* (2005).

Participants: All third- to sixth-graders in six schools.

Design: Confidential surveys and playground observations were conducted at six schools (three experimental and three control), both before and after interventions at the experimental schools. In the experimental schools, administrative changes (such as better supervision at recess) were coupled with a special 12-week curriculum taught by all the third- to sixth-grade teachers.

Major conclusion: Bullying is hard to stop. Playground observations found that bullying at the three control schools increased more over the school year than in the experimental schools (60 percent compared with 11 percent). However, children's attitudes and self-reported victimization did not improve.

Comment: This is good science, with experimental and control groups, before-and-after measures, observations, and questionnaires. It shows, unfortunately, that the culture of children and schools resists change.

Shake Hands or Yell "Uncle" Many schools, such as this one in Alaska, have trained peer mediators who intervene in disputes, hear both sides, take notes, and seek a resolution. Without such efforts, antagonists usually fight until one gives up, giving bullies free rein. Despite Alaska's higher rate of adolescent alcohol abuse, the state's adolescent homicide rate is lower than the national average.

This final point merits special emphasis. Some programs make a difference, some do not; only objective follow-up can tell. The best recent success was reported from a multifaceted effort that involved every school in one town over eight years. Victimization was reduced from 9 to 3 percent (Koivisto, 2004). Sustained and comprehensive effort appears to be what is needed.

Especially for Parents of an Accused Bully (see response, page 401): Another parent has told you that your child is a bully. Your child denies it and explains that the other child doesn't mind being teased.

SUMMING UP

School-age children develop their own culture, with customs that encourage them to be loyal to each other. All 6- to 11-year-olds need social acceptance and close, mutual friendships to protect against loneliness and depression.

Most children experience occasional peer rejection as well as acceptance. However, some children who are repeatedly rejected and friendless become victims of bullying. Bullying occurs everywhere, but the frequency and type depend on the school climate, on the culture, and on the child's age and gender. Efforts to reduce bullying are often not successful; a whole-school approach seems best. ■

Children's Moral Codes

A topic of great interest to many adults is the development of children's moral values. All the topics already discussed in this chapter—self-concept, parents, and peers—influence children's morality. The key question is, "Are children's morals dependent on family and culture, or can children move beyond those influences?"

Moral Questioning in Middle Childhood

One developmentalist says that ages 7 to 11 are:

> years of eager, lively searching on the part of children . . . as they try to understand things, to figure them out, but also to weigh the rights and wrongs. . . . This is the time for growth of the moral imagination, fueled constantly by the willingness, the eagerness of children to put themselves in the shoes of others.
>
> *[Coles, 1997]*

The validity of that statement is suggested by a meta-analysis of dozens of studies: Generally, children are more likely to behave prosocially in middle childhood than earlier (Eisenberg & Fabes, 1998). Another researcher finds that, in middle childhood, children are quite capable of making moral judgments, differentiating universal principles from mere conventional norms (Turiel, 2008).

A similar idea arises from the theory of *social efficacy*—that people come to believe they can affect their circumstances—and this belief then leads to action that changes the social context. Bandura writes that "the human mind is generative, reflective, proactive and creative, not merely reactive" (2006, p. 167)—naming exactly the cognitive traits that come to the fore in middle childhood. Development of these traits results in moral engagement, a drive to understand and weigh in on moral arguments. Empirical studies show that throughout middle childhood, children readily suggest moral arguments to distinguish right from wrong (Killen, 2007).

Many forces drive children's growing interest in right and wrong. These include peer culture and personal experience; for example, children in multiethnic schools are better able to argue against prejudice than are children who attend racially and ethnically homogeneous schools (Killen et al., 2006). Emotion, particularly empathy (stronger now because children are more aware of each other), is a third influential force. Intellectual maturation is a fourth, as we will now see.

Moral Reasoning

Much of the developmental research on children's morality began with Piaget's descriptions of the rules used by children as they play (Piaget, 1932/1997). This led to Lawrence Kohlberg's explanation of the various cognitive stages of morality (Kohlberg, 1963).

Kohlberg's research involved asking children and adolescents (and eventually adults) about different moral dilemmas. The story of a poor man named Heinz, whose wife was dying, serves as an example. A local druggist had the only cure for the wife's illness, an expensive drug that sold for 10 times what it cost to make.

> Heinz went to everyone he knew to borrow the money, but he could only get together about half of what it cost. He told the druggist that his wife was dying and asked him to sell it cheaper or let him pay later. But the druggist said "no." The husband got desperate and broke into the man's store to steal the drug for his wife. Should the husband have done that? Why?
>
> *[Kohlberg, 1963, p. 19]*

The crucial factor in Kohlberg's scheme is not the answer a person gives but the *reasons* for it. For instance, a person might say that the husband should steal the drug because he needs his wife to care for him, or because people will blame him if he lets his wife die, or because trying to save her life is more important than obeying the law. Each of these reasons indicates a different level of moral reasoning.

Levels of Moral Thought

Kohlberg described three levels of moral reasoning, with two stages at each level (see Table 13.5) and with clear parallels to Piaget's stages of cognition. **Preconventional moral reasoning** is similar to preoperational thought in that it is egocentric. **Conventional moral reasoning** parallels concrete operational thought in that it relates to current, observable practices. **Postconventional moral reasoning** is similar to formal operational thought because it uses logic and abstractions, going beyond what is concretely observed in a particular society.

According to Kohlberg, intellectual maturation, as well as experience, advances moral thinking. During middle childhood, children's answers shift from being primarily preconventional to being more conventional: Concrete thought and peer experiences help children move past the first two stages to the next two.

preconventional moral reasoning Kohlberg's first level of moral reasoning, emphasizing rewards and punishments.

conventional moral reasoning Kohlberg's second level of moral reasoning, emphasizing social rules.

postconventional moral reasoning Kohlberg's third level of moral reasoning, emphasizing moral principles.

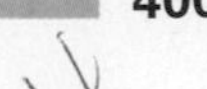

TABLE 13.5

Kohlberg's Three Levels and Six Stages of Moral Reasoning

Level I: Preconventional Moral Reasoning

The goal is to get rewards and avoid punishments; this is a self-centered level.

- *Stage One: Might makes right* (a punishment and obedience orientation). The most important value is to maintain the appearance of obedience to authority, avoiding punishment while still advancing self-interest. Don't get caught!
- *Stage Two: Look out for number one* (an instrumental and relativist orientation). Each person tries to take care of his or her own needs. The reason to be nice to other people is so that they will be nice to you.

Level II: Conventional Moral Reasoning

Emphasis is placed on social rules; this is a community-centered level.

- *Stage Three: "Good girl" and "nice boy."* Proper behavior is behavior that pleases other people. Social approval is more important than any specific reward.
- *Stage Four: "Law and order."* Proper behavior means being a dutiful citizen and obeying the laws set down by society, even when no police are nearby.

Level III: Postconventional Moral Reasoning

Emphasis is placed on moral principles; this level is centered on ideals.

- *Stage Five: Social contract.* Obey social rules because they benefit everyone and are established by mutual agreement. If the rules become destructive or if one party doesn't live up to the agreement, the contract is no longer binding. Under some circumstances, disobeying the law is moral.
- *Stage Six: Universal ethical principles.* General, universally valid principles, not individual situations (level I) or community practices (level II), determine right and wrong. Ethical values (such as "life is sacred") are established by individual reflection and may contradict egocentric (level I) or social and community (level II) values.

Criticisms of Kohlberg

Kohlberg has been criticized for not taking cultural or gender differences into account. For example, caring for family members is much more important to people in many cultures than Kohlberg seemed to recognize. Similarly, Kohlberg's original sample was all boys, which may have led him to devalue the importance of nurturance and relationships, which may be of particular moral value to girls.

In terms of children's psychosocial development, Kohlberg did not seem to recognize that although peer values differ from adult values, they may be equally valid and strong. School-age children are quite capable of questioning or ignoring adult rules that seem unfair (Turiel, 2006).

In one respect, however, Kohlberg was undeniably correct. Children use their intellectual abilities to justify their moral actions. This was shown in an experiment in which trios of children aged 8 to 18 had to decide how to divide a sum of money with another trio of children. Some groups chose to share equally; other groups were more selfish. There were no age differences in the actual decisions, but there were age differences in the arguments voiced. Older children suggested more complex rationalizations for their choices, both selfish and altruistic (Gummerum et al., 2008).

What Children Value

Many lines of research have shown that children develop their own morality, guided by peers, parents, and culture (Turiel, 2006). Some prosocial values are evident in childhood, probably originating in human genes and emotions. Among these are caring for close family members, cooperating with other children, and not hurting anyone directly (Eisenberg et al., 2006).

As children become more aware of themselves and others in middle childhood, they realize that values sometimes conflict. Concrete operational cognition, which gives them the ability to observe and to use logic, propels them to think about morality and to try to behave ethically (Turiel, 2006).

As part of growing up, children become conscious of immorality in their peers (Abrams et al., 2008) and, later, in their parents, themselves, and their culture. As their understanding increases, they also note cultural differences—of which there are many:

> On the basis of the historical and ethnographic record, we know that different people in different times and places have found it quite natural to be spontaneously appalled, outraged, indignant, proud, disgusted, guilty and ashamed by all sorts of things [such as] Islam, Christianity, Judaism, capitalism, democracy, flag burning, miniskirts, long hair, no hair, alcohol consumption, meat eating, medical inoculation . . . .
>
> [*Shweder, 1994, p. 26*]

Children initially endorse the morals of their own society, but if the culture of children conflicts with adult morality, they often choose to align themselves with peers. A child might lie to protect a friend, for instance. On a broader level, one study found that 98 percent of a group of children believed that no child should be excluded because of gender or race, even when adult society was less tolerant. The same children, however, might justify excluding another child from a friendship circle (Killen et al., 2002).

The conflict between the culture of children and that of adults is evident in the value that children place on education. Consider another comment from Paul:

> *Paul:* I try not to get influenced too much, pulled into what I don't want to be into. But mostly, it's hard. You don't want people to be saying you're stupid. "Why do you want to go to school and get a job? . . . Drop out."
>
> *[quoted in Nieto, 2000, p. 252]*

Not surprisingly, Paul later left school.

In developed nations, almost all parents value education and expect children to respect their teachers and other elders, but children do not necessarily do so (Cohen et al., 2006). Formal education may not be a universally held value, however. According to some psychologists:

> In rural Kenyan villages, the most competent children are often those viewed as having . . . accurate knowledge regarding natural herbal medicines that are used to treat parasites and other illnesses. . . . In many rural Alaska Yup'ik villages, the most competent children are often those viewed as having . . . superior hunting and gathering skills.
>
> *[Sternberg & Grigorenko, 2004, p. ix]*

As this excerpt shows, adults themselves disagree about which traits are most important for children (Heine, 2007). From a developmental perspective, it is apparent that children develop values and moral behavior during these years. Certainly parents and society have an impact.

It is also apparent that three common values among 6- to 11-year-olds are: Protect your friends, don't tell adults what is happening, and don't be too different from your peers (which can explain both apparent boredom and overt defiance, as well as standards of dress that mystify adults (such as jeans so loose that they fall off or so tight that they impede digestion). Given what we know about middle childhood, it is no surprise that children do not echo adult morality.

SUMMING UP

Moral issues are of great interest to school-age children, who are affected by their culture's standards, by their parents' wishes, and particularly by the values of their peers. Kolhberg's six stages of moral thought parallel Piaget's stages of development and suggest that the highest level of morality is a universal stance that goes beyond the norms of any particular nation. Children do seem to develop moral standards that they try to follow, although the conclusions they reach may not agree with adult standards. ■

➤Response for Parents of an Accused Bully (from page 398): The future is ominous if the charges are true. Your child's denial is a sign that there is a problem. (An innocent child would be worried about the misperception instead of categorically denying that any problem exists.) You might ask the teacher what the school is doing about bullying. Family counseling might help. Because bullies often have friends who egg them on, you may need to monitor your child's friendships and perhaps befriend the victim. Talk matters over with your child. Ignoring the situation might lead to heartache later on.

SUMMARY

The Nature of the Child

1. All theories of development acknowledge that school-age children become more independent and capable in many ways. Erikson emphasized industry, when children are busy mastering various tasks; in psychoanalytic theory, Freud described latency, when psychosexual needs are quiet.

2. Children develop their self-concept during these years, basing it on a more realistic assessment of their competence than they had in earlier years. Self-esteem that is too high may reduce effort.

3. All children are affected by any major family or peer problems they encounter. Depending partly on the child's interpretation of family problems, accumulated small stresses (daily hassles) may be more harmful than a major trauma.

4. Resilience is more likely to be found in children who have social support, independent activities, personal assets, and religious faith.

Families and Children

5. Families influence children in many ways, as do genes and peers. Each child in a family experiences different (nonshared) circumstances.

6. The five functions of a supportive family are: to satisfy children's physical needs; to encourage them to learn; to help them develop friends; to protect their self-respect; and to provide them with a safe, stable, and harmonious home.

7. The most common family structure, worldwide, is the nuclear family. Usually other relatives are nearby and supportive of nuclear families. Other structures include single-parent, stepparent, blended, adoptive, and grandparent.

8. Generally, it seems better for children to have two parents rather than one, because a parental alliance can support their development. Single-parent families and blended families have higher rates of change in residence and family composition; such changes add stress in middle childhood. Structure matters less than function.

9. Income affects family functioning. Poor children are at greater risk for emotional and behavioral problems because the stress of poverty often hinders effective parenting and because their lives are often less stable. Conflict is also harmful, even when the child is not directly involved.

The Peer Group

10. Peers are crucial in social development during middle childhood. Each cohort of children has a culture of childhood, passed down from slightly older children. Close friends are particularly helpful during these years.

11. Popular children may be cooperative and easy to get along with or may be competitive and aggressive. Much depends on the age and culture of the children.

12. Rejected children may be neglected, aggressive, or withdrawn. Aggressive and withdrawn children have difficulty with social cognition; their interpretation of the normal give-and-take of childhood is impaired.

13. Bullying is common among school-age children and has long-term consequences for bullies and victims. Bullying is hard to stop without a multifaceted, long-term, whole-school approach.

Children's Moral Codes

14. School-age children are very interested in differentiating right from wrong. The culture of children is one source of school-age morality, and so is cognitive maturity. Kohlberg described three levels of moral reasoning. When values conflict, childen often choose loyalty to peers over adult morality.

KEY TERMS

industry vs. inferiority (p. 373)
latency (p. 373)
social comparison (p. 374)
effortful control (p. 375)
resilience (p. 377)
family structure (p. 382)
family function (p. 382)
nuclear family (p. 384)
single-parent family (p. 385)
extended family (p. 385)
polygamous family (p. 385)
blended family (p. 386)
culture of children (p. 392)
aggressive-rejected (p. 395)
withdrawn-rejected (p. 395)
social cognition (p. 395)
bullying (p. 395)
bully-victim (p. 396)
preconventional moral reasoning (p. 399)
conventional moral reasoning (p. 399)
postconventional moral reasoning (p. 399)

KEY QUESTIONS

1. How does a school-age child develop a sense of self?

2. What factors make it more likely that a child will cope successfully with major stress?

3. What is the difference between family function and family structure?

4. What are the advantages and disadvantages of a stepparent family?

5. Why is a safe, harmonious home particularly important during middle childhood?

6. Which of the five functions of family for school-age children is particularly difficult for single-parent households to perform?

7. The culture of children strongly disapproves of tattletales. How does this disapproval affect bullies and victims?

8. Why might social rejection be particularly devastating during middle childhood?

9. How might bullying be reduced?

10. What moral values are held most dearly by school-age children?

APPLICATIONS

1. Go someplace where school-age children congregate, such as a schoolyard, a park, or a community center, and use naturalistic observation for at least half an hour. Describe what popular, average, withdrawn, and rejected children do. Note at least one potential conflict (bullying, rough-and-tumble play, etc.). Describe the sequence and the outcome.

2. Focusing on verbal bullying, describe at least two times when someone said a hurtful thing to you and two times when you said something that might have been hurtful to someone else. What are the differences between the two types of situations?

3. How would your childhood have been different if your family structure had been different, such as if you had (or had not) lived with your grandparents, if your parents had (or had not) gotten divorced, if you had (or had not) lived in a foster family?

PART IV The Developing Person So Far: Middle Childhood

BIOSOCIAL

A Healthy Time Growth is slower during middle childhood than in early childhood or adolescence. Exercise habits are crucial for health and happiness. Prevalent physical problems, including obesity and asthma, have genetic roots and psychosocial consequences.

Brain Development Brain maturation continues, leading to faster reactions and better self-control. Practice aids automatization and selective attention, which allow smoother and quicker action. Which specific skills are mastered depends largely on culture, gender, and inherited ability, all of which are reflected in intelligence tests. Children have many abilities not reflected in standard IQ tests.

Special Needs Many children have special learning needs. Early recognition, targeted education, and psychological support can help them, including those with autism spectrum disorders, specific learning disabilities, and attention deficit disorders.

COGNITIVE

Building on Theory Beginning at about age 7, Piaget noted, children attain concrete operational thought, including the ability to understand the logical principles of classification, identity, and reversibility. Vygotsky emphasized that children become more open to learning from mentors, both teachers and peers. Information-processing abilities increase, including greater memory, knowledge, control, and metacognition.

Language Children's increasing ability to understand the structures and possibilities of language enables them to extend the range of their cognitive powers and to become more analytical in vocabulary. Children have the cogntive capacity to become bilingual.

Education Formal schooling begins worldwide, although the specifics depend on culture. International comparisons reveal marked variations in overt and hidden curriculum, as well as in learning. The United States, with the No Child Left Behind Act, is moving toward more testing and increased emphasis on basic skills. The reading and math wars pit traditional education against a more holistic approach to learning.

PSYCHOSOCIAL

The Nature of the Child Theorists agree that many school-age children develop competencies and attitudes to defend against stress. Some children are resilient, coping well with problems and finding support in friends, family, school, religion, and community.

Families Parents continue to influence children, especially as they exacerbate or buffer problems in school and the community. During these years, families need to meet basic needs, encourage learning, foster self-respect, nurture friendship, and—most important—provide harmony and stability. Most one-parent, foster, or grandparent families are better than a nuclear family with two biological parents in open conflict, but family structure does not guarantee optimal functioning. Adequate household income and family stability benefit children of all ages, particularly in middle childhood.

Peers The peer group becomes increasingly important as children become less dependent on their parents and more dependent on friends for help, loyalty, and sharing of mutual interests. Rejection and bullying become serious problems.

Morality Moral development is notable during these years. Children behave more prosocially as their interest in right and wrong grows.

Adolescence

CHAPTER 14

CHAPTER 15

CHAPTER 16

PART V

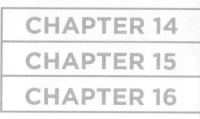

Would you ride in a car with an unskilled driver? When my daughter Bethany had her learner's permit, I tried to convey confidence. Not until a terrified "Mom! Help!" did I grab the wheel to avoid hitting a subway kiosk. I should have helped sooner, but I wasn't sure when my help was needed. It is hard to know when children become adults, able to manage without their mothers.

As an adolescent, Bethany was neither child nor adult. A century ago, puberty began at age 15 or so. Soon after that, most girls married and most boys found work. Even now, in some parts of the world, most teenage girls marry and most boys work. But not in developed countries like the United States.

It is said that *adolescence begins with biology and ends with culture*. If that is so, then adolescence once lasted a few months and now lasts more than a decade. Bodies mature earlier and social responsibilities begin later. Consequently, one observer has said that adolescence is like "starting turbo-charged engines with an unskilled driver" (Dahl, 2004, p. 17). Did I do that with Bethany?

In the next three chapters (covering ages 11–18), we begin with biology (the growth increases and other physical changes of puberty) and move toward culture (the social context). Understanding adolescence is more than an intellectual challenge: Those turbo-charged engines need skilled guidance. Get ready to grab the wheel.

14

CHAPTER OUTLINE

Adolescence: Biosocial Development

I once overheard a conversation among three teenagers, including my daughter Rachel. All three were past the awkward years, now becoming beautiful. They were discussing the imperfections of their bodies. One spoke of her fat stomach (what stomach? I could not see it), another of her long neck (hidden by her silky, shoulder-length hair), and my Rachel complained not only about a bent finger but also about her feet!

The reality that children grow into men and women is no shock to any adult. But for teenagers, heightened self-awareness often triggers surprise or even horror, joy or despair. As these three did, adolescents pay attention to details of their growth that adults may not notice. This chapter describes those details, the biosocial changes of growing bodies and emerging sexuality. We conclude with possible problems: violent death, too-early sex, and experimentation with recreational drugs.

Puberty Begins

Puberty refers to the years of rapid physical growth and sexual maturation that end childhood, eventually producing a person of adult size, shape, and sexual potential. The forces of puberty are unleashed by a cascade of hormones that produce external signs and such internal changes as the heightened emotions and sexual desires that many adolescents experience. The process normally starts between ages 8 and 14. The biological changes follow a common sequence, outlined in Table 14.1.

For girls, puberty begins with growth of the nipples and initial pubic hair, then a peak growth spurt, widening of the hips, the first menstrual period (**menarche**), final pubic-hair pattern, and full breast development. The current average age of menarche among well-nourished girls is about 12 years, 8 months (Malina et al., 2004), although variation in timing is quite normal.

For boys, the usual sequence is growth of the testes, initial pubic-hair growth, growth of the penis, first ejaculation of seminal fluid (**spermarche**), appearance of facial hair, peak growth spurt, deepening of the voice, and final pubic-hair growth (Biro et al., 2001; Herman-Giddens et al., 2001). The typical age of spermarche is just under 13 years, the same as for menarche.

Physical growth and maturation are usually complete four years after the first signs appear, although in their late teens or early 20s some individuals (usually late developers) add height, and most (especially early developers) gain more fat and muscle.

puberty The time between the first onrush of hormones and full adult physical development. Puberty usually lasts three to five years. Many more years are required to achieve psychosocial maturity.

menarche A girl's first menstrual period, signaling that she has begun ovulation. Pregnancy is biologically possible, but ovulation and menstruation are often irregular for years after menarche.

spermarche A boy's first ejaculation of sperm. Erections can occur as early as infancy, but ejaculation signals sperm production. Spermarche may occur during sleep (in a "wet dream") or via direct stimulation.

TABLE 14.1

AT ABOUT THIS TIME: The Sequence of Puberty

Girls	Approximate Average Age*	Boys
Ovaries increase production of estrogen and progesterone†	9	
Uterus and vagina begin to grow larger	9½	Testes increase production of testosterone†
Breast "bud" stage	10	Testes and scrotum grow larger
Pubic hair begins to appear; weight spurt begins	11	
Peak height spurt	11½	Pubic hair begins to appear
Peak muscle and organ growth (also, hips become noticeably wider)	12	Penis growth begins
Menarche (first menstrual period)	12½	Spermarche (first ejaculation); weight spurt begins
First ovulation	13	Peak height spurt
Voice lowers	14	Peak muscle and organ growth (also, shoulders become noticeably broader)
Final pubic-hair pattern	15	Voice lowers; visible facial hair
Full breast growth	16	
	18	Final pubic-hair pattern

*Average ages are rough approximations, with many perfectly normal, healthy adolescents as much as three years ahead of or behind these ages.

†Estrogens and testosterone influence sexual characteristics, including reproduction. Charted here are the increases produced by the gonads (sex glands). The ovaries produce estrogens and the testes produce androgens, especially testosterone. Adrenal glands produce some of both kinds of hormones (not shown).

These are the visible changes of puberty, but the entire process begins with an invisible event.

Hormones

In the months before the first signs of puberty, there is a marked increase in certain **hormones,** which are natural chemicals in the bloodstream that affect every body cell. Hormones regulate hunger, sleep, moods, stress, sexual desire, immunity, reproduction, and many other bodily functions. At least 23 hormones affect human growth and maturation. Technically, those first straggly pubic hairs are "a late event" in the process (Cameron, 2004, p. 116).

You learned in Chapter 8 that the production of many hormones is regulated deep within the brain, where biochemical signals from the hypothalamus signal another brain structure, the **pituitary,** to go into action. The pituitary produces hormones that stimulate the **adrenal glands,** which are located above the kidneys at either side of the lower back. The adrenal glands produce even more hormones.

Many of the hormones that regulate puberty follow this route, which is known as the **HPA axis** (hypothalamus–pituitary–adrenal; see Figure 14.1). Indeed, all hormones interact with each other and with the HPA axis. Abnormalities of the HPA axis in adolescence are associated with severe attention-deficit disorder, eating disorders, anxiety, and depression; all of these conditions are connected to hormones and appear for the first time or worsen at puberty (Adam & Epel, 2007; Kallen et al., 2008; Randazzo et al., 2008).

hormone An organic chemical substance that is produced by one body tissue and conveyed via the bloodstream to another to affect some physiological function.

pituitary A gland in the brain that responds to a signal from the hypothalamus by producing many hormones, including those that regulate growth and control other glands, among them the adrenal and sex glands.

adrenal glands Two glands, located above the kidneys, that produce hormones (including the "stress hormones" epinephrine [adrenaline] and norepinephrine).

HPA axis A sequence of hormone production originating in the hypothalamus and moving to the pituitary and then to the adrenal glands.

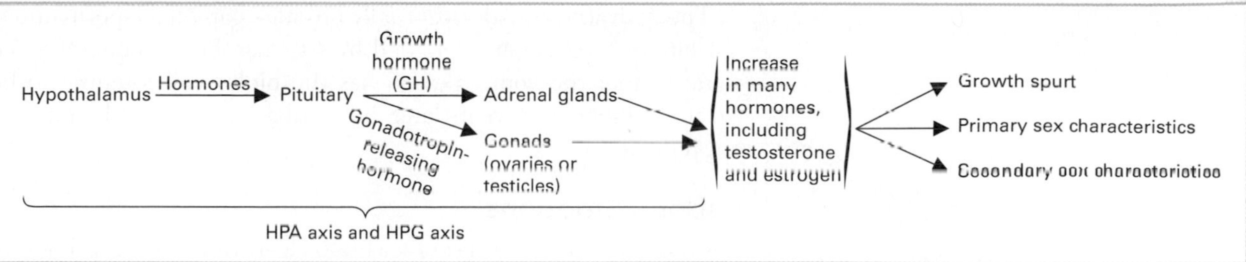

FIGURE 14.1

Biological Sequence of Puberty Puberty begins with a hormonal signal from the hypothalamus to the pituitary gland. The pituitary, in turn, signals the adrenal glands and the ovaries or testes to produce more of their hormones.

Sex Hormones

At adolescence, the pituitary also activates the **gonads,** or sex glands (ovaries in females; testes, or testicles, in males), following another sequence called the **HPG axis** (hypothalamus–pituitary–gonad). One hormone in particular, GnRH (gonadotropin-releasing hormone), causes the gonads to enlarge and dramatically increase their production of sex hormones, chiefly **estradiol** in girls and **testosterone** in boys. These hormones affect the body's entire shape and functioning, including production of other hormones that regulate stress and immunity (Young et al., 2008).

The incidence of almost every kind of psychopathology not only increases at adolescence but also begins to show marked differences between the sexes. For instance, schizophrenia is twice as common in males, and depression is twice as common in females. The sex hormones are a common explanation for these differences (Steiner & Young, 2008).

Estrogens (including estradiol) are considered female hormones, and *androgens* (including testosterone) are considered male hormones. Actually, the adrenal glands produce both in everyone. Unlike the adrenal glands, the gonads produce hormones in sex-specific ways: The ovaries produce estrogens and (possibly) much smaller quantities of testosterone, and the reverse is true of the testes. Testosterone production skyrockets in boys—up to 20 times the prepubescent level (Roche & Sun, 2003). For girls, estradiol increases to about 8 times the childhood level (Malina et al., 2004).

gonads The paired sex glands (ovaries in females, testicles in males). The gonads produce hormones and gametes.

HPG axis A sequence of hormone production originating in the hypothalamus and moving to the pituitary and then to the gonads.

estradiol A sex hormone, considered the chief estrogen. Females produce much more estradiol than males do.

testosterone A sex hormone, the best known of the androgens (male hormones); secreted in far greater amounts by males than by females.

MIKE KING / AP PHOTO

That's What Friends Are For Jennifer's preparations for her prom include a pedicure and hairstyling, courtesy of her good friends Khushbu and Meredith. In every generation and society the world over, teenagers help their same-sex friends prepare for the display rituals involved in coming of age, but the specifics vary by cohort and culture.

The activated gonads eventually produce gametes (sperm and ova), whose maturation and release are heralded by spermarche or menarche. This development signifies that the young person has the biological potential to become a parent. (Peak fertility comes years later, but ovulation and ejaculation signal the *possibility* of pregnancy.)

Sudden Emotions

The HPA axis and the HPG axis both lead from brain to body to behavior. Hormones pulsate through an adolescent's bloodstream, often erupting in some spur-of-the-moment emotional or sexual act, the kind of impulsive behavior adolescents are best known for. Teenagers may be suddenly overwhelmed by moods or lust that overtakes formerly predictable, seemingly asexual, children. Specific hormone–behavior links include the following sequences:

- Hormonal bursts lead to quick emotional extremes (despair, ecstasy).
- An increase in androgens causes sexual thoughts and a desire to masturbate.
- Testosterone at high or accelerating levels stimulates rapid arousal of emotions, especially anger.
- Fluctuating estrogen levels increase happiness, rage, and depression. For many girls, this succession of emotions occurs as estrogens rise and then fall during the menstrual cycle.

Especially for Parents of Teenagers (see response, page 412): Why would parents blame adolescent moods on hormones?

Adults probably experience these same hormonal effects. However, during puberty hormones are more erratic and powerful, less familiar and controllable, and they come in bursts, not a steady flow (Cameron, 2004; Susman & Rogol, 2004).

Furthermore, when adults have sudden changes in hormonal levels (such as during pregnancy and birth), cognitive awareness and maturation usually help control behavior. For example, a pregnant woman might find that she weeps unexpectedly, but both she and her husband usually realize that her sadness is partly hormonal. However, adolescents who fall in love might not realize that biological forces are driving their emotional attachment.

Reciprocity Between Hormones and Emotions

Hormones induce adolescents to seek sexual activity and momentary pleasure (Sato et al., 2008). But human thoughts and emotions not only result from physiological and neurological processes—they also *cause* them (Damasio, 2003). An adolescent's perceptions of how other people respond to breasts, beards, and body shapes evoke emotional reactions that, in turn, affect hormones—just as hormones affect emotions—with the particular reaction not directly tied to a specific hormone (Alsaker & Flammer, 2006).

Thus, there is a reciprocal interaction of hormones and emotions, a kind of escalating chicken-and-egg, so that hormones cause moods, which cause more hormones, which cause more intense moods, and so on. Furthermore, hormones interact with other hormones. Sex hormones, in particular, modify the levels as well as the effects of almost every other hormone (Becker et al., 2008).

This reciprocity becomes clearer with an example. Suppose a 13-year-old girl hears a lewd remark from a passing male, provoked by the sight of her developing breasts in a tight shirt. The remark might make her feel a surge of anger. That anger might cause a rise in her stress and sex hormones, which would then increase her anger and lead to a caustic retort. This kind of interaction can easily escalate, with increasing hormones and emotions, especially if the person who made the lewd remark is a teenage boy with his own hormonal impulses.

Evidence for a complex link between hormones and feelings came from a two-year study of 56 adolescents who were late to begin puberty (Schwab et al., 2001).

Doctors prescribed treatment every three months: injections of hormones (low, medium, or high doses of testosterone or an estrogen) alternating with injections of a placebo (which had no hormones). Gradually, the outward signs of puberty (breasts, lower voices, altered body size and shape) appeared.

Every three months, the researchers assessed several responses, including the level of sex hormones (measured via blood tests) and the emotions felt by the adolescents (via a questionnaire). They found an emotional shift, indirectly caused by the hormones. Over the two years, as the teenagers grew taller and developed sexually, they became happier, presumably because they were pleased about their physical development.

Especially for Doctors and Nurses (see response, page 413): When should hormones be given to an adolescent who is eager for puberty to arrive?

Surprisingly, happiness and sadness did *not* correlate with shifting hormonal levels. The teenagers did not seem emotionally aroused by the hormones in their bloodstreams—with one exception. Both boys and girls reported more anger when they had had *moderate* amounts of hormones, not the highest levels of testosterone (for the boys) or estrogens (for the girls) (Susman & Rogol, 2004).

There is a cognitive explanation for this finding. Many studies have shown that when people are aware of physiological imbalances (as might happen when high doses of hormones are given), they are better able to adjust their moods (in this case, control their anger). But when they do not connect a surge of emotion with biological shifts, they are more likely to assume that an external reason exists for their emotion; thus, they are more likely to express it.

Age and Puberty

A practical question for many parents, teachers, and children themselves is, "When will adolescence begin?" Age 11 or 12 is the most likely age of visible onset, but a rise in hormone levels is still considered normal in those as young as age 8 or as old as age 14. *Precocious puberty* (sexual development before age 8) occurs about once in 5,000 children, for unknown reasons (Cesario & Hughes, 2007). However, in most adolescents, genes, body fat, hormones, and stress all affect the age at which puberty begins (Ellis, 2004).

Both 12 The ancestors of these two Minnesota 12-year-olds came from northern Europe and West Africa. Their genes have dictated some differences between them, including the timing of puberty, but these differences are irrelevant to their friendship.

SKJOLD PHOTOGRAPHS / THE IMAGE WORKS

Genes

About two-thirds of the variation in age of puberty is genetic (van den Berg & Boomsma, 2007). Monozygotic twins are more similar in onset of puberty than same-sex dizygotic twins, who are more alike than half-sisters or half-brothers, who are more alike than nongenetic siblings of the same sex who are raised together (Ge et al., 2007).

Ethnic variations in puberty are also partly genetic. In the United States, African Americans tend to reach puberty earlier than European or Hispanic Americans do (see Figures 14.2 and 14.3). Asian Americans average several months later (Herman-Giddens et al., 2001; Malina et al., 2004).

For children of every family and ethnicity, genes on the sex chromosomes have a marked effect on age of puberty. Girls generally develop ahead of boys. In a classroom of well-nourished fifth-graders, for instance, at least one girl (XX) has already developed breasts and has grown almost to full adult height. Not until age 18 or so will her last male classmate (XY) have sprouted facial hair and grown to adult height.

These dramatic sex differences are observable. On average, girls are about two years ahead of boys in height. However, when it comes to hormonal and sexual changes that cannot be observed,

Median Age of Menarche, by U.S. Ethnic Group

Age (years)

13
12.8
12.6
12.4
12.2
12
11.8
11.6

Median age at menarche

European American girls
African American girls
Mexican American girls
Asian American girls

Source: Chumlea et al., 2003.

FIGURE 14.2

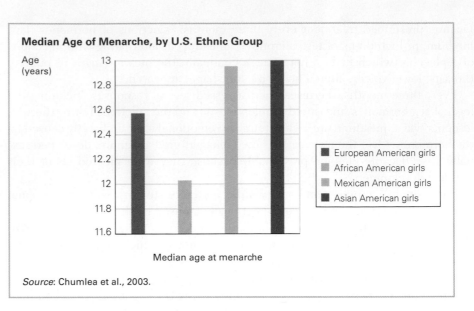

Usually by Age 13 The median age of menarche (when half the girls have begun to menstruate) differs somewhat among ethnic groups in the United States. The best signal of puberty is menarche in girls, but similar timing is apparent in boys of these ethnic groups.

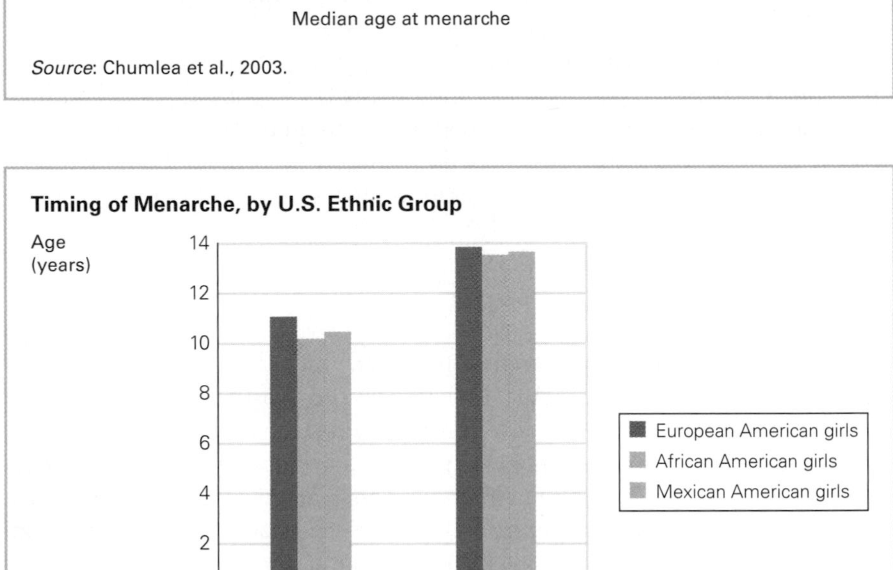

FIGURE 14.3

Almost Always by Age 14 This graph shows the age of menarche for the earliest and latest 10 percent of girls in three U.S. ethnic groups. Note that, especially for the slow developers (those in the 90th percentile), ethnic differences are very small.

Observation Quiz (see answer, page 414): At first glance, ethnic differences seem dramatic in Figure 14.2 but minimal in Figure 14.3. Why is this first glance deceptive?

girls are only a few months, not years, ahead of boys (Hughes & Gore, 2007). The discrepancy occurs because the height spurt occurs about midway in female pubescence (before menarche) but is a late event (after spermarche) for boys.

Age of puberty varies in the nations of the world, probably for genetic reasons. For instance, northern European girls are said to reach menarche at 13 years, 4 months, on average; southern European girls do so at an average age of 12 years, 5 months (Alsaker & Flammer, 2006).

Body Fat

The genetic differences noted above are apparent only when children are well fed. The amount of body fat affects the onset of puberty. Consequently, North American and European nations have not only the highest rates of childhood obesity but also the earliest ages of puberty.

Body fat also affects the age of puberty within nations. For example, puberty starts earlier in the cities of India and China than in the remote villages, probably

➤Response for Parents of Teenagers (from page 410): If something causes adolescents to shout "I hate you," to slam doors, or to cry inconsolably, parents may decide that hormones are the problem. This makes it easy to disclaim personal responsibility for the teenager's anger. However, research on stress and hormones suggests that this comforting attribution is too simplistic.

because rural children are often hungry. Puberty occurs a year earlier in the city of Warsaw than in Polish villages and 3 months earlier in Athens than in the rest of Greece (Malina et al., 2004).

Leptin and Other Hormones Some researchers believe that hormones in the food supply are one reason that puberty is occurring earlier than it did a century ago. As evidence, they point to the steroids fed to cattle to increase their bulk or to phthalates added to the plastic used in making bottles for soft drinks and water (Wang et al., 2005).

Some environmental chemicals directly affect testosterone and estrogen, and others increase fat. It could be that fat does not directly cause puberty, but rather that hormones cause weight gain, which then causes puberty (Ellison, 2002).

One hormone in particular has been implicated in the onset of puberty: **leptin,** which affects appetite. Leptin was only discovered in 1994 but is already known to increase during childhood, peaking at about age 12. Leptin levels are typically high at the onset of puberty (Rutters et al., 2008).

Curiously, leptin affects appetite in females more than in males (Geary & Lovejoy, 2008), and body fat is more closely connected to the onset of puberty in girls than in boys. Most girls weigh at least 100 pounds (45 kilograms) before their first period (Berkey et al., 2000). An interaction between leptin and female hormones is suggested by the experience of many adolescent girls, whose appetite decreases when they are "in love" and increases at the end of their menstrual cycle (when estrogen dips).

Malnutrition and Puberty In both sexes, chronic malnutrition delays puberty. Severe malnutrition in some parts of sub-Saharan Africa results in those youth being the oldest adolescents, worldwide, to reach puberty—even though their genetic cousins in North America are among the youngest.

Malnutrition probably explains why puberty did not occur until about age 17 in the sixteenth century. Undernutrition continues to delay puberty in more recent times. In the early twentieth century, the average age of menarche was 15 in Norway, Sweden, and Finland; today those nations have ample food year-round, so menarche occurs at age 12 or 13 (Tanner, 1990).

These are examples of what is called a **secular trend** in growth: Over the last two centuries, as nutrition and medical care have improved, the adolescent growth spurt has started earlier and adult height has increased. Over the twentieth century, each generation experienced puberty a few weeks earlier, and grew a centimeter or so taller, than did the preceding one (Alsaker & Flammer, 2006).

This secular trend seems to have stopped in developed nations (Roche & Sun, 2003), which may be good news for parents. Taking the gender differential into account (men average about 5 inches taller than women), today's young adults will probably not be tall enough to look down on their parents, unlike many of the youth of previous generations.

Stress

The production of many hormones is directly connected to stressful experiences via the HPA axis (Sanchez et al., 2001). Because stress affects reproductive hormones, many young women experience irregular menstruation when they leave home for college or travel abroad, and many couples find it easier to conceive when they are on vacation than when they are working.

Stress affects pubertal hormones as well, paradoxically by *increasing* (not decreasing) their production. Puberty tends to arrive earlier if a child's parents are sick, addicted, or divorced or if his or her neighborhood is violent and impoverished (Herman-Giddens et al., 2001; Hulanicka, 1999; Moffitt et al., 1992).

➤Response for Doctors and Nurses (from page 411): In very rare cases, and only when all other possible solutions (including the passage of time) have not had the desired effect. Many normal adolescents are slow to develop, and hormones affect other hormones.

leptin A hormone that affects appetite and is believed to affect the onset of puberty. Leptin levels increase during childhood and peak at around age 12.

Especially for Parents Worried About Early Puberty (see response, page 415): Suppose your cousin's 9-year-old daughter has just had her first period, and your cousin blames hormones in the food supply for this "precocious" puberty. Should you change your young daughter's diet?

secular trend The long-term upward or downward direction of a certain set of statistical measurements, as opposed to a smaller, shorter cyclical variation. As an example, over the last two centuries, because of improved nutrition and medical care, children have tended to reach their adult height earlier and their adult height has increased.

Not every scientist agrees that stress *causes* early puberty (Ellis, 2004). Since puberty is largely genetic, it could be that adults who reached puberty early were simply more likely to become young parents. Teenage parenthood correlates with less education, more anger and depression, and divorce. Consequently, the children of teenage parents would be more likely to live in conflicted, divorce-prone homes. They would experience early puberty, and that might appear to be the result of their experiences; but it could result from their genes rather than from the stress.

That argument is plausible, but evidence from longitudinal studies suggests that stress hormones do directly cause puberty. One study of 756 children, from infancy through adolescence, found that earlier puberty correlated with harsh parenting. Although parents were more likely to be harsh with their sons, the effects on puberty were evident only for their daughters, especially those girls who were most distressed (in that they cried a lot) as infants (Belsky et al., 2007). Thus nurture, combined with nature, affected puberty.

Another study found that girls who fought with their mothers *and* who lived with an unrelated man (their stepfather or their mother's boyfriend) reached puberty earlier, even when genes and weight were taken into account. The longer a girl lived with a man who was not her brother or her father, the younger she was when menarche occurred (Ellis & Garber, 2000).

Animal research confirms the role of stress. Mice, rats, and opossums become pregnant at younger ages when they live in stressful circumstances (Warshofsky, 1999). Furthermore, female mice reach puberty and sexual receptivity at younger ages when reared near unrelated adult male mice (Caretta et al., 1995; Khan et al., 2008).

Why would stress trigger puberty in girls? Logically, conflicted or stepfather families would benefit if the opposite happened—if teenagers looked and acted like children and could not reproduce. That would make them less emotional, and they would still look and act childlike, evoking protection, not lust and rivalry. That would be particularly beneficial to the children and stepparents in conflicted families. But instead the reverse occurs. One explanation comes from evolutionary theory:

> Over the course of our natural selective history, ancestral females growing up in adverse family environments may have reliably increased their reproductive success by accelerating physical maturation and beginning sexual activity and reproduction at a relatively early age.
>
> *[Ellis & Garber, 2000, p. 486]*

In other words, in past stressful times, adolescent girls could replace themselves before they died, passing on family genes. Natural selection would favor genes that postponed puberty during famine (so that newborns would not die of malnutrition) but that hastened it (so that the population could increase more readily) when the entire society was stressed or when young men left to fight other tribes or to track distant prey. These adaptations would apply particularly to females, because the survival of a community requires that many women bear and raise children. There must be some reason women become fertile before men do and become infertile at age 50 or so; perhaps the survival of the society is the explanation.

Of course, this evolutionary rationale no longer applies. Today, early sexuality and reproduction lead to social disruption, not social survival. However, the human genome has been shaped over millennia, and the onset of puberty still seems to be affected by family and neighborhood circumstances, at least for girls (Romans et al., 2003).

➤**Answer to Observation Quiz** (from page 412): The major reason is the vertical axis, which covers a total of 1½ years in Figure 14.2 and 14 years in Figure 14.3.

Too Early, Too Late

For most adolescents, only one aspect of pubertal timing is important: their friends' schedules. Puberty can enhance or diminish a person's status with peers, as well as bring personal joy or distress. When it begins makes a difference. No one wants to be early or late. Early onset is particularly hard for girls; a late start creates difficulty for boys.

➤Response for Parents Worried About Early Puberty (from page 413): Probably not. If she is overweight, her diet should change, but the hormone hypothesis is speculative. Genes are the main factor; she shares only one-eighth of her genes with her cousin.

Girls

Think about the early-maturing girl. If she has visible breasts at age 10, the boys in her class tease her; they are distressed by the sexual creature in their midst. She must fit her womanly body into a school chair designed for younger children, and she may hide her breasts in large T-shirts and bulky sweaters and refuse to undress for gym. Early-maturing girls tend to have lower self-esteem, more depression, and poorer body image than later-maturing girls (Compian et al., 2004; Mendle et al., 2007). They even exercise much less than their classmates do (Davison et al., 2007).

Early-maturing girls often have boyfriends who are several years older than they are, which adds status and protects against loneliness but also brings complications, sometimes including drug and alcohol use (Weichold et al., 2003). They are "isolated from their on-time-maturing peers [and] tend to associate with older adolescents. This increases their emotional distress" (Ge et al., 2003, p. 437).

Indeed, girls' early puberty not only correlates with drug use but also increases the risk of violent victimization (Schreck et al., 2007). Early-maturing girls are more likely to enter abusive relationships than other girls are. For all these reasons, girls are better off if they begin puberty on time or late.

Boys

Cohort is crucial for boys. In previous generations, boys tended to benefit from early puberty. Early-maturing boys who were born around 1930 often became leaders in high school and beyond (M. C. Jones, 1965). They also tended to be more successful as adults (Taga et al., 2006).

Since about 1960, however, the problems with early male maturation have outweighed the benefits. Currently, early-maturing boys are more aggressive, lawbreaking, and alcohol abusing than later maturing boys (Biehl et al., 2007; Lynne et al., 2007). For boys as well as girls, early puberty correlates with sexual activity and teenage parenthood, which in turn correlate with later depression and other psychosocial problems (B. Brown, 2004; Siebenbruner et al., 2007).

Late puberty may also be difficult, especially for boys. Slow-developing boys tend to be more anxious, depressed, and afraid of sex, at least according to research in Finland (Lindfors et al., 2007).

Ethnic Differences

Whether puberty is considered early or late depends not only on overall averages but also on the averages within one's own group. Puberty that is considered late by world norms, at age 14 or so, is not a problem if all one's peers are late as well. Well-nourished Africans tend to experience puberty a few months earlier and Asians later than Europeans, but neither is problematic within their culture and cohort.

However, ethnic differences in average age of puberty can add to intergroup tensions in multiethnic schools. In one such school, the "quiet Asian boys" were teased because they were shorter and thinner than their classmates, much to their dismay (Lei, 2003). When one larger Asian American boy fought back at an ethnic insult, he was a hero to his peers even though school authorities punished him.

Research Design

Scientists: Melissa L. Greene, Niobe Way, and Kerstin Pahl.

Publication: *Developmental Psychology* (2006).

Participants: A total of 136 high school students at a multiethnic high school in New York City.

Design: Six times over the four years of high school, students answered questionnaires about discrimination, ethnic identity, depression, and self-esteem.

Major conclusion: For all four ethnic groups (Black, Asian American, Puerto Rican, and other Latino), perceived peer discrimination had a greater impact on self-esteem than did perceived adult discrimination. The Asian Americans averaged higher levels of perceived discrimination than any other group; the African Americans were second.

Comment: This study is a welcome step toward multifaceted, multiethnic, longitudinal research on adolescents. More is needed to provide, as the researchers write, "a thorough examination of the impact of experiences of discrimination on well-being."

Late puberty is a likely explanation for the greater peer discrimination experienced by Chinese American youth in another school (Greene et al., 2006; see the Research Design). In a third multiethnic high school, Samoan students were small numerically but advanced in puberty. Perhaps as a result of their size and maturation, they were respected by their classmates of all backgrounds and were accepted as peacemakers between African American and Mexican American students (Staiger, 2006).

Such interactions illustrate the importance of physical appearance for many adolescents. Late maturers of both sexes may be troubled by their lack of development. One study of more than 3,000 Australian adolescents found that late developers had four times the rate of self-harm (cutting or poisoning themselves), an indication of serious depression (Patton et al., 2007).

SUMMING UP

Puberty usually begins between ages 8 and 14 (typically at about 11) in response to a flow of hormones that begins deep within the brain. This starts a chain reaction of hormone production from the hypothalamus to the pituitary to the adrenal and sex glands. Hormones affect the emotions as well as the physique, with adolescent outbursts caused by the combination of hormones and social reactions to visible body changes. Reciprocity between the physiological and the psychological aspects of increases in hormone levels can cause sudden anger, sadness, and lust. Many factors, including genes, body fat, and stress, affect the timing of the onset of puberty. Generally, puberty begins earlier today than in past centuries, although this secular trend appears to have stopped. Early puberty (especially for girls) or late puberty (especially for boys) is problematic. ■

Nutrition

All the changes of puberty depend on proper nourishment, yet many adolescents are deficient in their intake of necessary vitamins or minerals. One reason teenagers are likely to skip breakfast, to eat late at night, and to eat nutrition-poor foods is that shifts in their hormone levels affect their appetites.

Each generation is eating less healthfully, and so are individuals as they move through adolescence. Today's youth consume more calories (hence earlier puberty and more obesity), but they are less likely to eat a balanced diet. Currently, each cohort of adults is slightly less well nourished than the next older one: The healthiest diets are found among those over age 65. A third of the members of that age group eat vegetables at least three times a day (MMWR, March 16, 2007).

In the United States, only 19 percent of high school seniors in 2007 ate five or more servings of fruits and vegetables a day (MMWR, June 6, 2008), compared with 27 percent just a decade earlier (MMWR, August 14, 1998). As for individuals, a five-year longitudinal study in Minnesota found that eating habits worsen over the teen years (N. I. Larson et al., 2007).

Diet Deficiencies

Deficiencies of iron, calcium, zinc, and other minerals may be even more problematic during adolescence than vitamin deficiencies, since minerals are needed for bone and muscle growth. Some specifics illustrate the point.

The recommended daily dose of iron is 15 milligrams, but fewer than half of all U.S. teenagers consume that much, maybe because iron is found in green vegetables, eggs, and meat—foods that adolescents often spurn in favor of chips, sweets, and fries. Because menstruation depletes the body of iron, the incidence of anemia is greater among adolescent girls than among females of any other age or among males (Belamarich & Ayoob, 2001). Iron deficiency also puts boys at risk: Worldwide, many boys do intense physical labor or sports, and muscles need iron to grow and strengthen (Blum & Nelson-Mmari, 2004).

LEE SNIDER / THE IMAGE WORKS

What Are They Doing Here? Teenagers worldwide (like this group in Yangshuo, China) are attracted by fast-food restaurants, because the cheap food and public setting of such places make them ideal for snacking and socializing. However, the food—usually high in fat and low in nutrition—contributes to overweight and undernourishment in many of their young customers.

Calcium consumption among adolescents is also low. Although the daily recommended intake for teenagers is 1,300 milligrams, most consume less than 500 milligrams a day. About half of adult bone mass is acquired from ages 10 to 20, yet few adolescents consume enough calcium to prevent osteoporosis (fragile bones), a major cause of disability, injury, and death in late adulthood, especially among people of European descent.

One reason for the widespread calcium deficiency is that milk drinking has declined. Most North American children once drank at least a quart (about 1 liter) a day, which gave them 1,200 milligrams of calcium. In 2007, only 15 percent of U.S. ninth-graders drank even 24 ounces (¾ liter) of milk a day. Among twelfth-graders, the rates were 9 percent for girls and 19 percent for boys (MMWR, June 6, 2008).

Choices Made

Nutritional deficiencies result from the food choices that young adolescents are allowed, even enticed, to make. There is a direct link between nutritional deficiencies and the presence of vending machines in schools (Cullen & Zakeri, 2004). Fast-food establishments cluster around high schools.

Economists now advocate a "nudge" to encourage people to make better choices (Thaler & Sunstein, 2008). A nudge in the right direction, in the form of economic incentives, might eliminate vending machines.

Price is influential in food choices, especially for adolescents. At least experimentally, 10- to 14-year-olds choose healthy foods if they are cheaper than unhealthy ones (Epstein et al., 2006). However, milk and fruit juice are more expensive than fruit punch or soda. In New York City in 2008, a McDonald's salad cost four times as much as a hamburger.

Body Image

Another reason for poor nutrition is anxiety about **body image**—that is, a person's idea of how his or her body looks. Since puberty alters the entire body, it is almost impossible for teenagers to welcome every change. Unfortunately, their perceptions are distorted; they tend to focus on and exaggerate the imperfections (as did the three girls in the anecdote that opens this chapter).

body image A person's idea of how his or her body looks.

Girls go on diets because they want to be thinner, partly because boys tend to prefer to date thin girls (Halpern et al., 2005). Boys want to look taller and stronger, a concern that increases from ages 12 to 17, partly because girls value well-developed muscles in males (D. Jones & Crawford, 2005). Thus, both sexes become less happy with their own bodies at a time when the hormones of puberty increase their sexual interest.

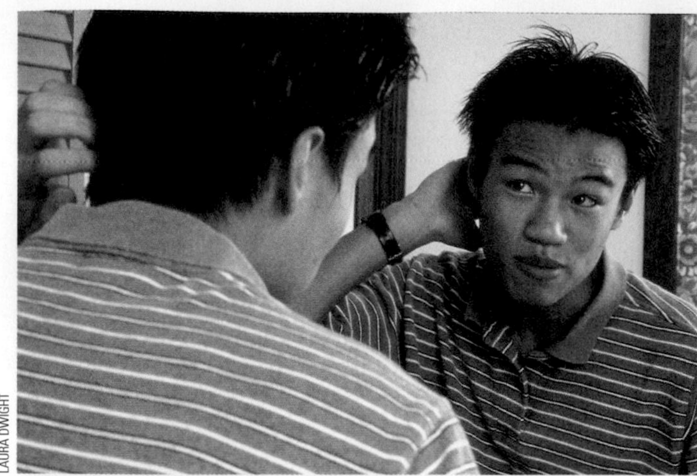
LAURA DWIGHT

Does He Like What He Sees? During adolescence, all the facial features do not develop at the same rate, and the hair often becomes less manageable. If B. T. here is typical, he is not pleased with the appearance of his nose, lips, ears, or hair.

In North America, the ideal body type and facial appearance is Anglo-Saxon. Children of ethnic minorities are bombarded by media images of celebrities and models whose faces and bodies look quite different from those their own genes have produced. Of course, few Anglo-Saxon youth achieve the ideal of beauty, either. No real woman has the proportions of a Barbie doll. Almost all young adolescents wish their bodies looked different.

Eating Disorders

One result of the widespread dissatisfaction with body image among teenagers is that many of them—mostly girls—eat erratically or ingest drugs (especially diet pills) to lose weight, and many boys take steroids to increase muscle mass. The incidence of eating disorders increases dramatically at puberty and is correlated with distorted body image, obsession with food, and suicidal depression (Bulik et al., 2008; Hrabosky & Thomas, 2008).

Individual adolescents sometimes switch from one abnormal pattern to another, from obsessive dieting to overeating to overexercising and back again, without yet having any diagnosable disorder (Henig, 2004). Here we describe the three diagnosed eating disorders: obesity, anorexia, and bulimia.

Obesity

When some adolescents see that their bodies are not as thin as they wish, they try dieting and then give up, becoming flabby and heavy instead of strong and of normal weight. A sizable minority of all U.S. teenagers are overweight, according to international standards, a higher proportion than in any other nation that has been studied (Lissau et al., 2004). This high rate occurs despite (or because of) the fact that almost two-thirds (60 percent) of all U.S. adolescent girls and almost one-third (30 percent) of the boys are trying to lose weight, according to a nationwide U.S. survey of 14,000 high school students (MMWR, June 6, 2008). In 2007, 13 percent of high school students were obese, and an additional 16 percent were overweight (MMWR, June 6, 2008).

Being overweight or obese in adolescence affects much more than just appearance. Adolescent obesity increases the risk of premature death, at least for women, partly because obese women are more likely to be suicidal (van Dam et al., 2006). Those 29 percent of obese or overweight adolescents of both sexes are also at higher risk for diabetes, heart disease, and strokes. These diseases are rarely diagnosed in adolescence, but their precursors are evident in analysis of overweight adolescents' blood (Pinhas-Hamiel et al., 2007).

Anorexia

anorexia nervosa An eating disorder characterized by self-starvation. Affected individuals voluntarily undereat and often overexercise, depriving their vital organs of nutrition. Anorexia can be fatal.

At the other extreme is **anorexia nervosa,** a disorder characterized by self-starvation. Individuals voluntarily undereat and overexercise, depriving their vital organs of nourishment. Between 5 and 20 percent of victims eventually die of the disease. The immediate cause of death is usually organ failure. In addition, many young women with anorexia are severely depressed and at risk of suicide.

According to DSM-IV-TR (American Psychiatric Association, 2000), anorexia nervosa is diagnosed when four symptoms are evident:

- Refusal to maintain a body weight that is at least 85 percent of normal for age and height
- Intense fear of weight gain

- Disturbed body perception and denial of the problem
- Absence of menstruation (in adolescent and adult females)

If someone's BMI (body mass index, explained in Chapter 11) is 18 or lower, or if she (or, less often, he) loses more than 10 percent of body weight within a month or two, anorexia is suspected.

Although anorexia may have existed in earlier centuries (think of the saints who refused all food), the disease was undiagnosed before about 1950, when some high-achieving, upper-class women in the United States grew so emaciated that they died. Soon anorexia became evident among younger women (the rate increases notably at puberty, and again at the end of adolescence), among men, and in almost every nation.

Asian, African, and Latin American young women once seemed immune to anorexia, probably because their cultures are less plagued with the obsession to be thin. Currently, although rates of undereating and overexercising are lower among these groups and among boys, no adolescent, male or female, of any ethnicity, is exempt from the risk of anorexia (Chao et al., 2008).

Nature and nurture are both precursors of anorexia. Genetic makeup can make it more likely that a person will develop anorexia: If a young woman has a close relative, especially a monozygotic twin, with this disorder or with severe depression, she is at added risk. Cultural obsession with thinness (evident not only in skinny models but also in society's concerns about the obesity epidemic) is part of the problem (Shannon, 2007).

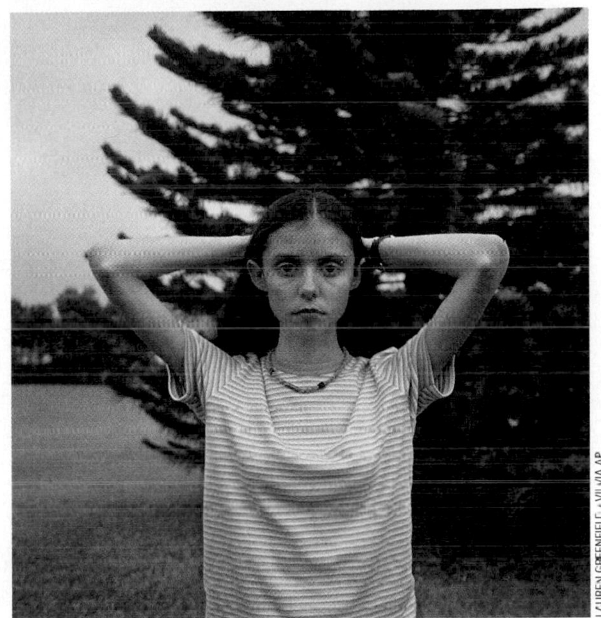

LAUREN GREENFIELD / VII VIA AP

Guess Her Age Jennifer has gained some weight since she was first admitted to an eating-disorders clinic, but she still looks younger than her years. One hypothesis about anorexia is that it stems from an unconscious desire to avoid growing up. (Jennifer is 18 years old.)

Bulimia

About three times as common as anorexia is **bulimia nervosa.** The person (again, usually female) with bulimia overeats compulsively (consuming thousands of calories within an hour or two) and then purges via induced vomiting or laxatives. Bulimia is present worldwide, in virtually every major city (Walcott et al., 2003).

bulimia nervosa An eating disorder characterized by binge eating and subsequent purging, usually by induced vomiting and/or use of laxatives.

Most people with bulimia are close to normal in weight and therefore unlikely to starve. However, they risk serious health problems, including damage to their gastrointestinal systems and cardiac arrest from electrolyte imbalance (Shannon, 2007).

Three things combine to warrant a clinical diagnosis of bulimia:

- Bingeing and purging at least once a week for three months
- Uncontrollable urges to overeat
- A distorted perception of body size

Between 1 and 3 percent of women in the United States are clinically bulimic during early adulthood (American Psychiatric Association, 2000).

Origins of Disordered Eating

Eating disorders may be the eventual outcome of the odd eating habits of many adolescents who try new diets, go without food for 24 hours (as 12 percent of U.S. high school students did in 2007), or take diet drugs (as 6 percent did) (MMWR, June 6, 2008). Although diagnosable disorders are more common after age 18, genes and childhood patterns make some teenagers vulnerable. Such individuals can be pushed from merely odd eating habits to a disorder when cultural ideals of body image are added to the stress, appetite, and sex hormones of puberty.

In all eating disorders, food consumption is disconnected from the internal cues of hunger; it serves some psychological or social need rather than any biological necessity (Shannon, 2007). It may be that:

> Parental control in child feeding may have unintended effects on the development of eating patterns; [especially with] emphasis on "external" cues in eating and decreased opportunities for the child to experience *self*-control. . . . Parental pressure to eat may result in food dislike and refusal, and restriction may enhance children's liking and consumption of restricted foods.
>
> *[J. O. Fisher & Birch, 2001, p. 35]*

Many studies have connected eating disorders to the hormonal changes of puberty, especially for girls. Early puberty, in particular, is likely to result in anxiety, poor body image, dieting, and then eating disorders (Zehr et al., 2007). Similar results to those in North America and Europe have also been found in Japan; this research suggests that eating disorders are not simply a matter of specific genes (Kaminaga, 2007) but are also connected to puberty and culture.

One family practice seems to reduce the risk of adolescent eating disorders: eating together during childhood (Franko et al., 2008). It is not known whether this occurs because family cohesion is an underlying protective factor or because family meals directly inculcate good nutritional practices.

Nonetheless, developmentalists agree that a good nutritional foundation begins with childhood habits and family examples. Many people who were overweight or underweight as infants have no weight problems as adults, but the older an overweight or underweight child is, the more likely he or she will have an eating disorder in adulthood.

SUMMING UP

All adolescents are vulnerable to poor nutrition; few are well nourished. Insufficient consumption of iron and calcium is particularly common, as fast food and nutrient-poor snacks often replace family meals. The combination of nutritional deficiencies and concern about body image may cause eating disorders, including obesity, anorexia, and bulimia. All adolescent nutrition problems have lifelong, and potentially life-threatening, consequences. ■

The Transformations of Puberty

Every body part changes during puberty. For simplicity, the study of this transformation from a child into an adult is traditionally divided into two parts: growth and sexuality. We will use that division here. We will also describe a third transformation—changes in the adolescent brain—in this chapter as they relate to changes in adolescent body rhythms and in the next chapter as they relate to adolescent cognition.

This separation is somewhat artificial, because pubescent growth always includes the interaction of these three: body, sex, and brain. However, it is also useful because it allows us to consider each of these major transformations in detail.

For example, suppose a young adolescent suddenly notices darker and thicker hair growing on his or her legs. (Everyone experiences such hair growth at puberty.) If the adolescent is female, she will probably shave her legs, feeling quite womanly. If the adolescent is male, he may search for new hair on his upper lip, his chin, and his chest, to mark his manhood. Thus, a sign of physical growth becomes a sexual marker, and then thoughts affect the reaction. (Remember from Chapter 1 that biosocial, cognitive, and psychosocial development are discussed separately for ease of understanding. All three occur simultaneously in developing persons: Our major discussion of the brain is in Chapter 15, and sexual relationships are covered in Chapter 16.)

Growing Bigger and Stronger

The first set of changes we describe is called the **growth spurt**—a sudden, uneven jump in the size of almost every part of the body, turning children into adults. Growth proceeds from the extremities to the core (the opposite of the proximal-distal growth of the prenatal and infant periods). Thus, fingers and toes lengthen before hands and feet; hands and feet before arms and legs, arms and legs before the torso.

growth spurt The relatively sudden and rapid physical growth that occurs during puberty. Each body part increases in size on a schedule: Weight usually precedes height, and growth of the limbs precedes growth of the torso.

Because the torso is the last body part to grow, many pubescent children are temporarily big footed, long-legged, and short-waisted. If young teenagers complain that their jeans don't fit, they are probably correct, even if those same jeans fit their shorter-waisted, thinner body when their parents paid for them a month before. (At least the parents had advance warning about the growth spurt when they had to buy shoes for their children in adult sizes!)

Sequence: Weight, Height, Muscles

As the bones lengthen and harden (visible on X-rays) and the growth spurt begins, children eat more and gain weight. Exactly when, where, and how much weight they gain depends on heredity, hormones, diet, exercise, and gender. Girls gain more fat than boys: By age 17, the average girl has twice the percentage of body fat of her male classmate, whose increased weight is mostly muscle (Roche & Sun, 2003).

A height spurt follows the weight spurt, burning up some fat and redistributing the rest. A year or two after the height spurt, a muscle spurt occurs. Thus, the pudginess and clumsiness of early puberty are usually gone by late adolescence. The young teenager who took nutritional supplements to increase size or strength could have simply waited a year or two.

On average, a boy's arm muscles are twice as strong at age 18 as at age 8, enabling him to throw a ball four times as far (Malina et al., 2004). A sex difference is apparent in the arm muscles (see Figure 14.4); other muscles are more gender-neutral. For instance, running speed increases over adolescence in both sexes, with boys never running much faster than girls (see Figure 14.5).

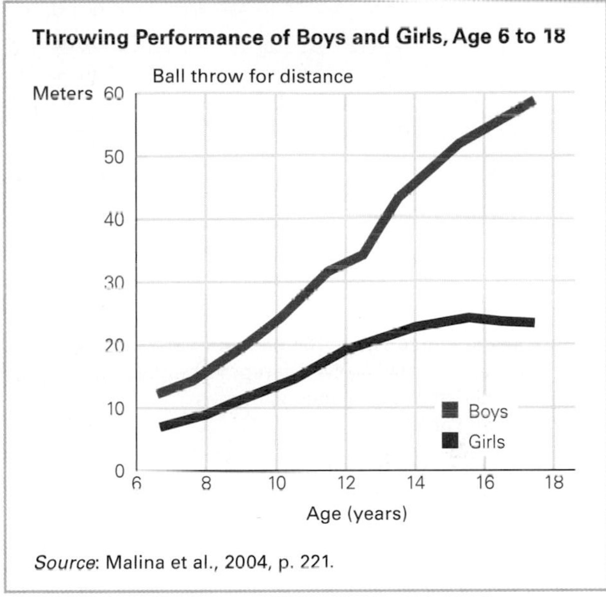

Source: Malina et al., 2004, p. 221.

FIGURE 14.4

Big Difference All children experience an increase in muscles during puberty, but gender differences are much more apparent in some gross motor skills than others. For instance, upper-arm strength increases dramatically only in boys.

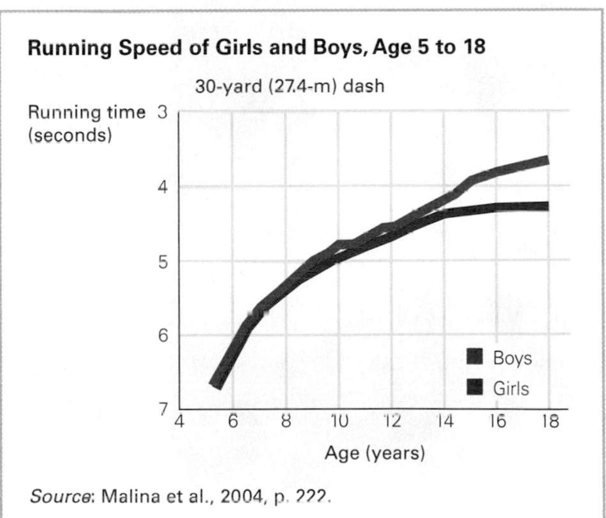

Source: Malina et al., 2004, p. 222.

FIGURE 14.5

Little Difference Both sexes develop longer and stronger legs during puberty.

Observation Quiz (see answer, page 422): At what age does the rate of increase in the average boy's muscle strength accelerate?

Organ Growth

In both sexes, organs grow and become more efficient during adolescence. Lungs triple in weight; consequently, adolescents breathe more deeply and slowly. The heart doubles in size and beats more slowly (which decreases the pulse), while blood pressure and volume both increase (Malina et al., 2004). These changes increase physical endurance, enabling many teenagers to run for miles or dance for hours.

Note that both weight and height increase *before* the growth of muscles and internal organs, which means that athletic training and weight lifting should be tailored to an adolescent's size the previous year, to protect immature muscles and organs. Sports injuries are the most common school accidents, and they increase at puberty. One reason is that, because the height spurt precedes increases in bone mass, young adolescents are more vulnerable to fractures than are adults (until old age) (Roche & Sun, 2003).

➤Answer to Observation Quiz (from page 421): About age 13. This is most obvious in ball throwing (Figure 14.4), but it is also apparent in the 30-yard dash (Figure 14.5).

Only one organ system, the lymphoid system (which includes the tonsils and adenoids), *decreases* in size, thus making teenagers less susceptible to respiratory ailments. Mild asthma, for example, often switches off at puberty (Busse & Lemanske, 2005), and teenagers have fewer colds than younger children do.

Another organ system, the skin, changes in marked ways, becoming oilier, sweatier, and more prone to acne. Hair also changes. During puberty, hair on the head and limbs (those dark leg hairs) becomes coarser and darker. New hair grows under arms, on faces, and over sex organs (pubic hair, from which puberty was named).

Visible facial and chest hair is sometimes considered a sign of manliness, although hairiness in either sex depends on genes as well as on hormones. Girls pluck or dye any facial hair they see; boys proudly shave or grow "soul patches." In these ways, both sexes are displaying sexual/cultural reactions to normal growth.

Sexual Maturation

Now we turn to the pubertal changes that are specifically sexual, as boys become men and girls become women. Sexual characteristics signify this transformation, as do many impulses.

primary sex characteristics The parts of the body that are directly involved in reproduction, including the vagina, uterus, ovaries, testicles, and penis.

secondary sex characteristics Physical traits that are not directly involved in reproduction but that indicate sexual maturity, such as a man's beard and a woman's breasts.

Sexual Body Changes

The body characteristics that are directly involved in conception and pregnancy are called **primary sex characteristics.** During puberty, every primary sex organ (the ovaries, the uterus, the penis, and the testes) increases dramatically in size and matures in function. By the end of the process, reproduction is possible, although peak fertility does not occur for either sex until about four years after puberty begins.

At the same time as maturation of the primary sex characteristics, **secondary sex characteristics** develop. Secondary sex characteristics are bodily features that do not directly affect fertility (hence they are secondary) but that signify masculinity or femininity.

One obvious secondary sexual characteristic is body shape. Younger boys and girls have very similar bodies, but at puberty, males grow taller than females and become wider at the shoulders, while girls develop breasts and a wider pelvis. Breasts and hips are often considered signs of womanhood, but neither is required for conception; thus, they are secondary, not primary, sex characteristics.

Secondary sex characteristics are important psychologically, if not biologically. Consider breasts. Many adolescent girls buy "minimizer," "maximizer," "training," or "shaping" bras, hoping that their breasts will conform to an idealized body image.

During the same years, many boys are horrified to notice a swelling around their nipples—a normal and temporary result of the erratic hormones of early puberty. If a boy's breast growth is very disturbing, drugs can reduce the swelling, although many doctors prefer to let time, rather than tamoxifen, deal with the problem (Derman et al., 2003).

Another secondary sex characteristic is a lower voice as the lungs and larynx grow. This change is more noticeable in boys, but girls' voices also deepen somewhat.

The pattern of growth at the scalp line differs for the two sexes, a secondary sex characteristic that few people notice. Instead, they notice gender markers in hair length and style, which can attain the status of a secondary sex characteristic. To become more attractive, many adolescents spend considerable time, money, and thought on their visible hair—growing, gelling, shaving, curling, straightening, highlighting, brushing, combing, styling, dyeing, wetting, drying . . .

CLEVE BRYANT / PHOTOEDIT

Male Pride Teenage boys typically feel serious pride when they first need to shave. Although facial hair is taken as a sign of masculinity, a person's hairiness is actually genetic as well as hormonal. Further evidence that the Western world's traditional racial categories have no genetic basis comes from East Asia: Many Chinese men cannot grow beards or mustaches, but most Japanese men can.

Sexual Activity

The primary and secondary sex characteristics just described are not the only manifestations of the sex hormones. Fantasizing, flirting, hand-holding, staring, displaying, and touching are all done in particular ways to reflect gender, availability, and culture. As already explained, hormones trigger thoughts and emotions, but the social context shapes thoughts into enjoyable fantasies, shameful preoccupations, frightening impulses, or actual contact.

Nature or Nurture? Regarding sex-related impulses, some experts believe that boys are more influenced by hormones and girls are more influenced by culture (Baumeister & Blackhart, 2007). Perhaps. When a relationship includes sexual intimacy, girls seem more concerned about the depth of the romance than boys do (Zani & Cicognani, 2006). Girls want their partners to say "I'll love you forever."

However, everyone is influenced by both hormones and society. All adolescents have sexual interests they did not previously have (biology), which produce behaviors that teenagers in other nations would not necessarily engage in (culture) (Moore & Rosenthal, 2006).

Girls' wish for long-term commitment may be a consequence of biology, not culture, since only girls can get pregnant. If this is so, the gender difference—girls' need for love versus boys' lust for sex—may become less apparent as advances in contraception make pregnancy less likely. The gender gap in sexual experience is narrowing in developed nations, and more widespread use of contraception may be the reason (Cherry et al., 2001).

Culture definitely affects who is likely to be a person's first sexual partner. This choice is sometimes mistakenly thought to be private and personal, or at least the result of uncontrollable biological drives, not culture. Yet culture is very influential in such matters as the age of one's first sexual partner. Most North American and European adolescents now choose partners who are about the same age as themselves (Zani & Cicognani, 2006). However, in Finland and Norway, girls tend to become sexually experienced later than boys, so boys are forced to choose older partners. In Greece and Portugal, it is girls whose first partners tend to be older (Teitler, 2002). In Nigeria, men are expected to seek inexperienced, younger teens, giving them gifts in exchange for their sexual favors. In contrast, young men in Thailand are expected to have their first sexual encounter with an older, experienced woman (World Health Organization, 2005).

AP PHOTO / CHRIS PIZZELLO

A 15-Year-Old Although she herself is very young and she is a role model for young girls, singer and *Hannah Montana* star Miley Cyrus projects an image of maturity.

Another 15-Year-Old A religious ceremony is part of the Quinceañera, a coming-of-age celebration for girls in Latino communities.

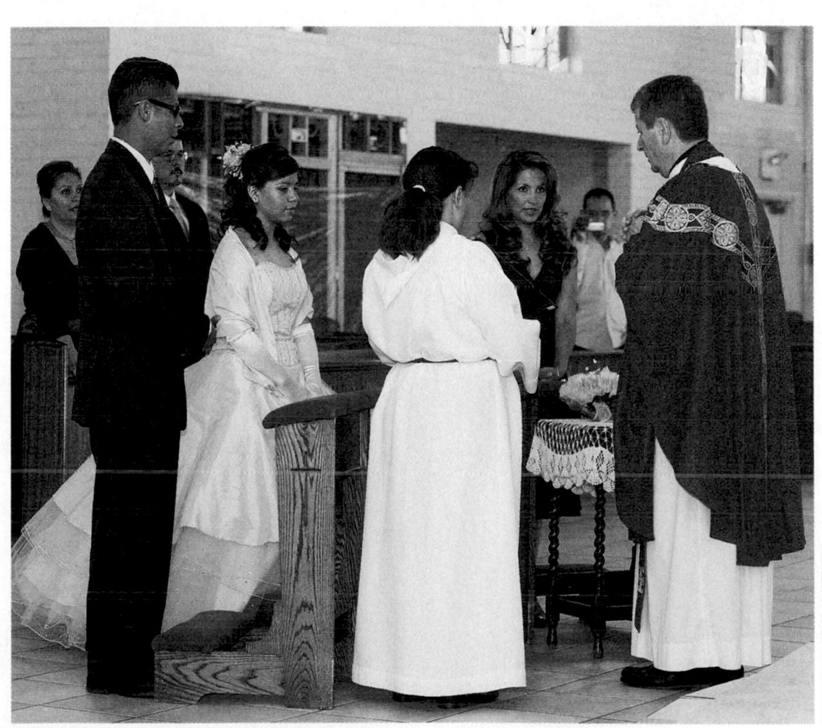
DAVID YOUNG-WOLFF / PHOTO EDIT

Religious Differences These generalities do not apply to everyone within the nations just mentioned. Subgroups as well as cohorts always differ, again for cultural reasons. One specific was found in a survey of 704 adolescents in Ghana: More 16-year-old girls than boys were sexually experienced, but those experienced girls had usually had only one partner, whereas the boys had had several. Muslim youth in Ghana were more likely to be virgins than Christian youth, who themselves were more likely to be virgins than those of neither faith (Glover et al., 2003).

As in Ghana, religious teachings affect the sexual behavior of teenagers worldwide. In a study of Jewish and Muslim adolescents in Israel and the United States, the romances of Muslim youth seldom included sexual intimacy, even in thought (Magen, 1998). One Muslim boy in Israel reported "the most wonderful and happiest day of my life":

> A girl passed our house. And she looked at me. She looked at me as though I were an angel in paradise. I looked at her, and stopped still, and wondered and marveled. . . . [Later] she passed near us, stopped, and called my friend, and asked my name and who I am. I trembled all over and could hardly stand on my feet. I used my brain, since otherwise I would have fallen to the floor. I couldn't stand it any longer and went home.
>
> *[quoted in Magen, 1998, pp. 97–98]*

KEVIN MOLONEY / THE NEW YORK TIMES / REDUX

A Daughter's Promise At a "purity ball" in Colorado, a father reads the pledge signed by his 14-year-old daughter, in which she promises that she will abstain from sex until she marries. Young adolescents who take a virginity pledge are more likely than their peers to be celibate in high school. However, they are also more likely to become parents before they graduate from college.

Changes over Time Both cohort and culture have notable effects on sexual activity. For most of the twentieth century, surveys in North America reported increasing proportions of adolescents becoming sexually active. This trend reversed in 1990. According to the Youth Risk Behavior Survey, 62.4 percent of eleventh-graders in the United States had had intercourse in 1991, but only 55.5 percent had in 2007 (Fox et al., 2005; MMWR, June 6, 2008).

Also, the double standard (with boys expected to be more sexually active than girls) has been less influential in recent decades: Since 1991, male rates of reported sexual activity have come closer to female ones (see Figure 14.6). Ethnic differences over time in high school students' sexual experience have also emerged. Rates of sexual experience since 1991 were down 14.5 percentage points (from 81 to 66.5 percent) for African Americans, down 6.3 percentage points (from 50 to 43.7 percent) for European Americans, and down 1 percentage point (from 53 to 52 percent) for Latinos (MMWR, August 1, 2008).

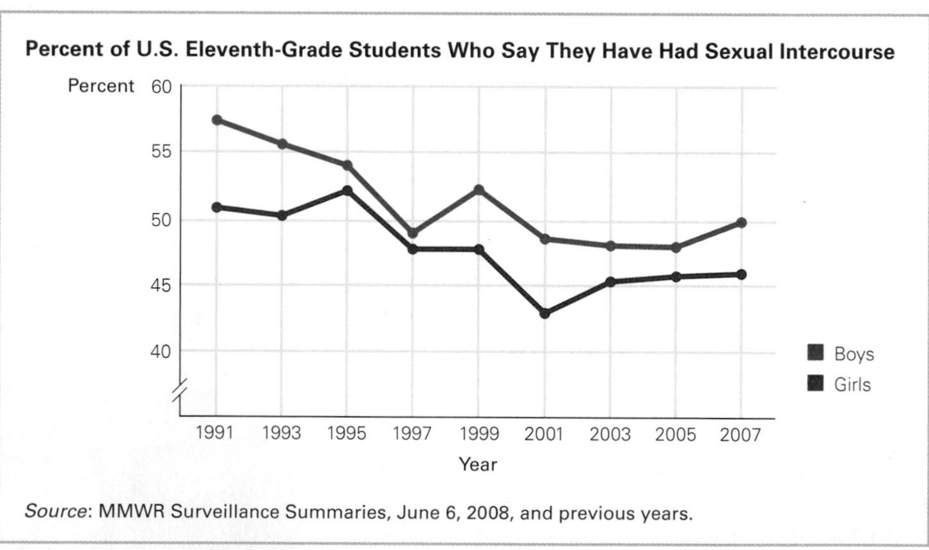

FIGURE 14.6

Boys and Girls Together Boys still tend to be somewhat more sexually experienced than girls during the high school years, but since the Youth Risk Behavior Survey began in 1991, the overall trend has been toward equality in rates of sexual activity.

All these examples demonstrate that a universal experience (rising hormones) produces another universal experience (growth of primary and secondary sex characteristics) and that these manifest themselves in many ways. Cohort and culture are always significant.

Body Rhythms

Brain activity affects body rhythms (Buzsáki, 2006). As already described, the hypothalamus and the pituitary gland regulate hormones that affect stress, appetite, sleep, and so on, following the HPA axis. The brain of every living creature responds to the environment with natural rhythms. For instance, the seasons affect reproduction (more births occur in spring), weight (more is gained in winter), and, in some species, the timing of migration and hibernation.

Furthermore, all creatures have a daily day–night cycle of biological activity that occurs approximately every 24 hours and is called the *circadian rhythm*. (*Circadian* means "about a day.") This diurnal (daily) cycle affects tiredness, hunger, alertness, elimination, body temperature, nutrient balance, blood composition, and moods. (Some people wake up cheery and others cranky, and then switch moods by nightfall.) The level of every hormone of puberty varies, depending on the time of day (Matchock et al., 2007).

The circadian rhythm is the reason jet lag affects people who fly east–west across the globe, changing time zones, but not those who fly the same distance north–south. Because of diurnal rhythms, people cannot get their recommended 60 hours of sleep per week by staying awake 24 hours for four days and then sleeping 20 hours on each of the other three days. The diurnal rise and fall of the hormone melatonin and other body chemicals make sleep elusive at some moments and impossible to postpone at others.

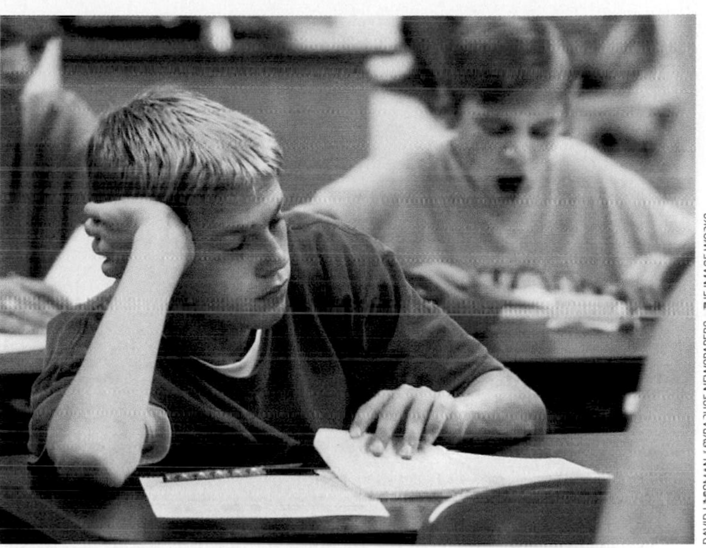

Too Early It is 8:00 A.M. on their first day of high school, and these freshmen are having trouble staying awake for orientation in their homeroom.

Puberty alters biorhythms, both seasonal and daily. Hormones from the pituitary often cause a "phase delay" in sleep–wake patterns. As a result, many teens are wide awake at midnight but half asleep all morning. Because adult brains are naturally alert in the morning and sleepy at night, social patterns set by adults may not accommodate adolescents.

In addition, some people (especially males) are naturally more alert in the evening than in the morning, a genetic trait called eveningness. Exacerbated by the phase delay of puberty, eveningness adolescents are at high risk for antisocial activities (Susman et al., 2007). Unfortunately, once their sons reach adolescence, many parents no longer supervise them, especially after midnight.

Many teenagers of both sexes naturally stay up late. They cannot fall asleep at 10:00 P.M. even if they lie in bed with their eyes closed. Nonetheless, they are forced to "rise and shine" at dawn. One consequence is wide spread sleep deprivation, as shown by the fact that teenagers seldom awaken spontaneously on weekdays (see Figure 14.7) and often "sleep in" on weekends (Andrade & Menna-Barreto, 2002).

Uneven sleep schedules (more sleep on weekends, later bedtimes, and daytime sleeping), while common, decrease well-being just as overall sleep deprivation does (Fuligni & Hardway, 2006). Girls are particularly likely to be sleep-deprived, which negatively affects their grades and happiness (Fredriksen et al., 2004). Girls lose sleep not because they are evening people (usually they are not) but because they get up earlier: They refuse to roll out of bed and go to school without allowing substantial time to get ready.

Sleep deprivation and irregular sleep schedules are associated with many other difficulties, such as falling asleep while driving, insomnia in the middle of the night, distressing dreams, and mood disorders (depression, conduct disorder, anxiety) (Carskadon, 2002b; Fredriksen et al., 2004; Fuligni & Hardway, 2006). This research suggests an obvious change in practice, but, as the following makes clear, social policies do not always follow scientific recommendations.

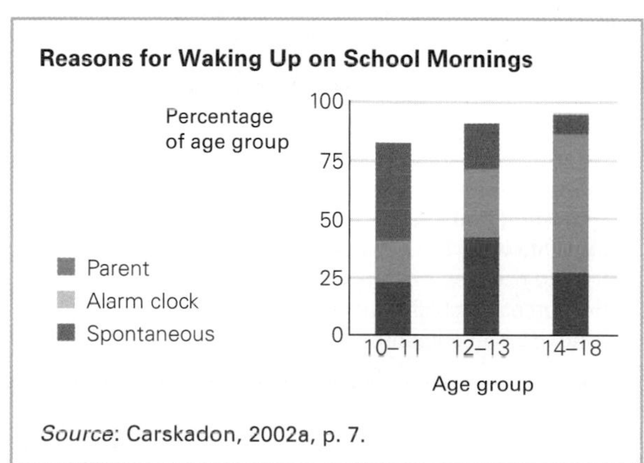

FIGURE 14.7

Sleep Deprivation Humans naturally wake up once they've had enough sleep. Few high school students wake up spontaneously on weekdays, and many sleep later on weekends than on school days. These facts suggest that most teenagers are overtired.

a view from science

Calculus at 8:00 A.M.?

Biology designs teenage bodies to be alert at midnight and tired all morning. As a result of this natural design, a teenager may sometimes fall asleep in school (see Figure 14.8). That happens because school schedules reflect the wider culture, not students' biorhythms.

Some parents fight biology. They command their wide-awake teen to "go to sleep," they hang up on classmates who phone after 10:00 P.M., they set early curfews, and they drag their offspring out of bed for school. (An opposite developmental clash occurs when parents tell their toddlers to stay in their cribs after dawn.)

Data on the phase delay of adolescence led social scientists at the University of Minnesota to ask 17 school districts to institute a later starting time for high school. Most parents were opposed. Many (42 percent) thought school for their adolescents should begin before 8:00 A.M. In fact, some (20 percent) wanted their teenagers out of the house by 7:15 A.M., as compared to only 1 percent of parents with younger children.

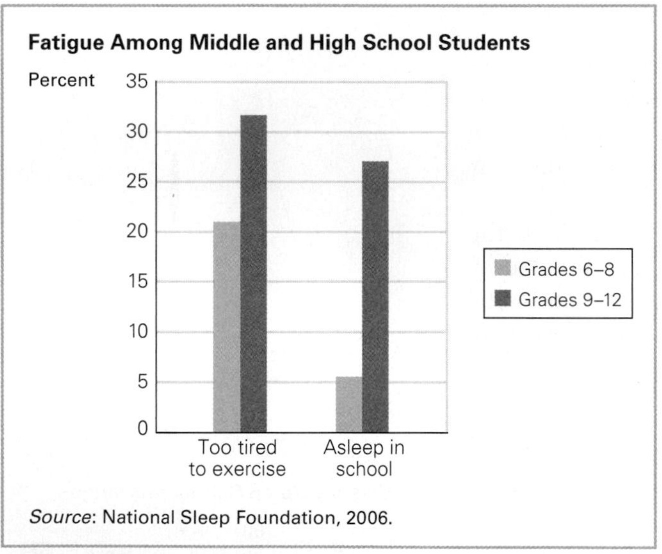

FIGURE 14.8

Dreaming and Learning? This graph shows the percentage of U.S. students who, once a week or more, fall asleep in class or are too tired to exercise. Not shown are those who are too tired overall (59 percent for high school students) or who doze in class "almost every day" (8 percent).

Members of each vocational group had their own reasons for believing that an early start was best for high-schoolers. Teachers generally thought that learning was more efficient in early morning. Bus drivers hated rush hour; cafeteria workers wanted to leave by mid-afternoon; police said teenagers should be home by 4:00 P.M.; coaches needed sports events to end before dark; employers needed to hire teens to staff the afternoon shift; community program directors wanted the gym to be available for nonschool events in the late afternoon and early evening hours (Wahlstrom, 2002).

Despite all those naysayers, one school district experimented. In Edina, Minnesota, high school classes began at 8:30 A.M. (instead of the previous 7:25 A.M.) and ended at 3:10 P.M. (instead of 2:05 P.M.). After one year, most parents (93 percent) and virtually all students approved of the new schedule. One student said, "I have only fallen asleep in school once this whole year, and last year I fell asleep about three times a week" (quoted in Wahlstrom, 2002, p. 190). The data showed fewer absent, late, disruptive, or sick students (the school nurse became an advocate) and higher grades.

Other school districts reconsidered. Minneapolis, which had started high school at 7:15 A.M., changed the starting time to 8:40 A.M. Again, attendance improved, as did the graduation rate. School boards in South Burlington (Vermont), West Des Moines (Iowa), Tulsa (Oklahoma), Arlington (Virginia), and Milwaukee (Wisconsin) voted in favor of later starting times, switching on average from 7:45 A.M. to 8:30 A.M. (Tonn, 2006). Unexpected advantages appeared: financial savings (more efficient energy use) and, at least in Tulsa, unprecedented athletic championships.

But change is hard. Researchers believe that "without a strategic approach, the forces to maintain the status quo in the schools will prevail" (Wahlstrom, 2002, p. 195). Few college students choose 8:00 A.M. classes, but high school students have no choice.

SUMMING UP

Three transformations of puberty—the growth spurt, sexual differentiation, and brain maturation—are notable. Physical growth proceeds from the extremities to the center, so the limbs grow before the internal organs. Weight precedes height, which precedes growth of the muscles and of the internal organs. Primary sex characteristics, which are connected to reproduction, and secondary sex characteristics, which signify that a person is becoming a man or a woman, develop. Both boys and girls experience an increase in sexual interest as their bodies develop and their hormone levels rise. Adolescents' sexual behavior and thoughts are powerfully affected by culture.

The brain is involved in the body's natural rhythms. A phase delay in their circadian rhythm causes teenagers to be alert late at night and sleepy in the morning. Many adolescents are sleep-deprived because adults expect them to follow adult diurnal rhythms. As a result, the risk of many problems—depression, dangerous driving, drug use, and learning difficulties—increases. ■

Health Hazards

By the end of puberty, young people are usually strong and healthy. Most 18-year-olds are capable of hard physical work, problem-free reproduction, and peak athletic performance. All the body systems, including the digestive, respiratory, circulatory, and sexual-reproductive systems, function at an optimal level. To illustrate, here is an example from the United States, which compiles quite accurate health data: 97 percent of adolescents say their health is good or excellent. Each year, fewer than 1 in 25,000 teens die of cancer, compared with 1 in 100 adults over age 65 (National Center for Health Statistics, 2007). Similar data come from every nation.

Health does not simply mean lack of disease. Growth and sexual awakening, strength and speed, emotional intensity and hormonal rushes—all of these can be quite wonderful experiences. Most adolescents enjoy their bodies. However, about 20 percent put their health in serious jeopardy, and each health risk that an adolescent takes makes it more likely that he or she will take other risks. As examples of this comorbidity, drug addicts have higher rates of violent injury, and sexually active youth risk not only sexually transmitted infections and unwanted pregnancy but also eating disorders and depression.

All of these risks peak in emerging adulthood (see the Epilogue) but often begin in adolescence. Consequently, here we look at three major health hazards for teens: injury and death, early sexual activity, and drug abuse.

Injury and Death

In every nation, as deaths due to disease decrease, the proportion of deaths that are violent (resulting from accidents, homicides, and suicides) increases. Accidents are the leading cause of death for people under age 40 on every continent, with two chilling exceptions: In Africa, the leading cause of death among youth is AIDS; in South America, homicides rank first (Blum & Nelson-Mmari, 2004). The United States is more typical: About half (46 percent) of deaths of people between ages 15 and 25 result from accidents; homicide (14 percent) is second; and suicide (13 percent) is a close third (U.S. Bureau of the Census, 2007).

DOMINIC CHAVEZ / THE DENVER POST / AP PHOTO

Twisted Memorial This wreck was once a Volvo, driven by a Colorado teenager who ignored an oncoming train's whistle at a rural crossing. The car was hurled 167 feet and burst into flames. The impact instantly killed the driver and five teenage passengers. They are among the statistics indicating that accidents, many of which result from unwise risk taking, kill 10 times more adolescents than diseases do.

Young men are particularly likely to die violently, worldwide. Accidental death rates among young men are almost as high in Canada, Mexico, and Australia as in the United States, where about one male in every 150 dies violently between his 15th and 25th birthday (National Center for Health Statistics, 2007).

Injuries requiring medical attention are so common they could be called normal. Most nations do not keep detailed age records for injury victims, but in the United States the average young man sought medical help for a serious injury twice between age 12 and age 21 and the average young woman at least once (U.S. Bureau of the Census, 2007).

Especially for Parents Worried About Their Teenager's Risk Taking (see response, page 432): You remember the risky things you did at the same age, and you are alarmed by the possibility that your child will follow in your footsteps. What should you do?

Adolescents have more injuries than any other age group. The rate is three times higher than the rate for adults aged 45 to 65. People in their late teens and early 20s also have the highest rate of violent death of any group before age 80, when accidents increase. Why this developmental pattern? Researchers have identified three causes:

1. *Body changes.* Rapid changes in size, shape, and hormone levels are unsettling. Further, many specific body chemicals (especially testosterone and MAO) trigger impulsive reactions, leading to risk taking and, often, to injury.
2. *Brain changes.* Immaturity of the cortex and the activity of the limbic system together make adolescents overrate pleasure and disregard danger when confronted with, say, drugs, sex, the police, a dare.
3. *Social context.* The 20 percent of adolescents at highest risk are those who are alienated from adults and not yet attached to families of their own.

Sex Too Soon

The second health hazard, early sexual experience, is related to the first. A community's rates of adolescent homicide and teen pregnancy are correlated. Both are also connected to the levels of poverty, deprivation, and hopelessness within a given nation (Pickett et al., 2005).

Sex can, of course, be thrilling and affirming, a bonding experience that increases the love and affection that bind people to each other. It was that kind of experience for many adolescents and young adults in past centuries, but today adolescent sex has become more hazardous, for five reasons:

1. Puberty now occurs at younger ages, triggering sexual urges. Early sexual experiences correlate with disease, depression, and drugs.
2. Most teenage mothers have no husbands to help them. Almost all teenage mothers a century ago were married; in 2005 in the United States, 83 percent were unwed.
3. Raising a child has become more complex. Thus, teenage pregnancy is no longer welcomed or expected.
4. Sexually transmitted infections are more widespread and dangerous.
5. Sexual abuse is most common in early adolescence.

The first two items on this list are explored in Chapter 16, in our main discussion of teen romance and friendship. The other three items listed—pregnancy, infections, and sexual abuse—have specific biological impacts, so we discuss them here.

SEAN SPRAGUE / THE IMAGE WORKS

No Safer? Educational posters and even intense educational programs have little proven effect on the incidence of AIDS among adolescents. This poster was displayed outside an HIV testing center in Windhoek, Namibia, a country that has one of the highest HIV infection rates in the world.

Teenage Pregnancy

There is good news about pregnancy among girls under age 18 (see Figure 14.9): It is only about half as common now as it was 20 years ago in the United States and in many other nations (U.S. Bureau of the Census, 2008). In addition, the abortion rate among teens is half what it was, use of contraceptives is higher, and intercourse is less common. Similar decreases are found in Canada, although the overall Canadian rate of teen pregnancy continues to be about half that of the United States. For girls who do get pregnant, however, the news is not so good: The health risks remain high, for themselves and their infants.

Problems for the Mother From a biological perspective, pregnancy is much more complicated for a young adolescent than for an older woman. In 2004 in the United States, the 15,000 girls under age 15 who were pregnant were at greater risk of almost every complication, including spontaneous abortion, high blood pressure, stillbirth, cesarean section, and having a low-birthweight newborn (Menacker et al., 2004).

In some nations (notably those of sub-Saharan Africa), inadequate medical care makes pregnancy the leading cause of death for teenage girls (Reynolds et al., 2006). In regions where almost everyone is malnourished, the rate of death from birth complications is almost three times higher for the youngest mothers than for older women (Blum & Nelson-Mmari, 2004). Death from birth complications almost never occurs in wealthier countries like the United States.

Pubertal hormones direct bodies to add bone, redistribute weight, and gain height while the inner organs (including the uterus) mature. Pregnancy interferes with this process, because another set of hormones directs the body to sustain new life. Nature protects the fetus, which takes essential nutrients (especially calcium and iron) from the mother. If normal pubescent growth is deflected by pregnancy, the pregnant girl becomes a shorter and sicker woman than she otherwise would have been.

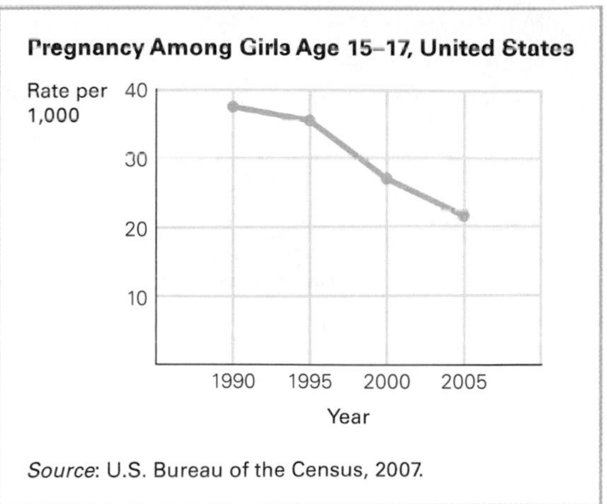

FIGURE 14.9

Fewer Children Having Children Births among teenage girls finally began to decline in the 1990s. Even more welcome is a reduction in births among girls under 15, which now occur at only 3 percent of the rate for girls age 15 to 17.

If a pregnant teenager has an abortion (as more than half of all pregnant U.S. girls under age 15 do), she avoids the medical problems of a sustained pregnancy and birth. However, she is more likely to encounter the complications of abortion than older women are, partly because she is likely to wait longer to terminate the pregnancy (MMWR, November 24, 2006). Medical assistance early in pregnancy helps avoid many problems, but many adolescents put off seeing a health care professional, hoping instead for a mistake or a miscarriage.

Problems for the Baby Babies born to young mothers are more likely to have birth complications (explained in Chapter 4) and less likely to be breast-fed. Even if they are born healthy, such babies experience more complications later on, including poor health; inadequate education; low intelligence; and anger at their family, community, and society (Borkowski et al., 2007). All these characteristics of the baby and child take a great toll on the mother and thus impede mother–child attachment.

If a teenage mother obtains good medical care, stays in school, and gets help from her family and the child's father, she is likely to be resilient, becoming a competent young woman by age 30 or so (Borkowski et al., 2007). Her children probably had a difficult first few years but adjusted, especially if she pursued her education and found a good job. Fathers can help.

However, teenage parenthood is never easy for mother, father, or child. Developmentally, it is better to postpone pregnancy until adolescent growth and emotional maturation is complete. For that reason, the drop in adolescent births is good news.

Sexual Infections

Unfortunately, the other major problem of teenage sexuality shows no signs of abating. A **sexually transmitted infection (STI)** (formerly referred to as sexually transmitted disease [STD] or venereal disease [VD]) is any infection transmitted through sexual contact, either oral or genital. Worldwide, sexually active teenagers have higher rates of the most common STIs (gonorrhea, genital herpes, and chlamydia) than any other age group (World Health Organization, 2005).

sexually transmitted infection (STI) A disease spread by sexual contact, including syphilis, gonorrhea, genital herpes, chlamydia, and HIV.

Sexual infections can damage a person's body permanently. In the United States, young persons aged 15–24 constitute only one-fourth of the sexually active population but account for half of all sexually transmitted infections (MMWR, October 20, 2006). If not treated, such infections can cause infertility and death.

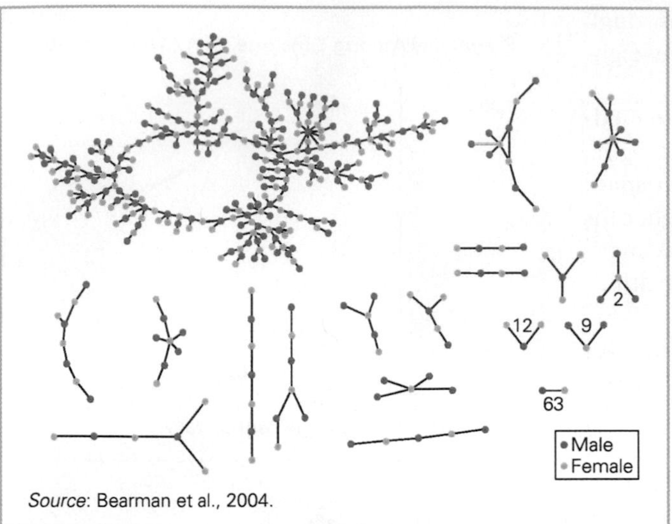

Source: Bearman et al., 2004.

FIGURE 14.10

Romantic Networks: Your Partner Becomes My Partner This is a diagram of the romances that students in one U.S. high school reported having during the preceding six months. Each dot represents romantic relationships. Patterns that occurred more than once are indicated with a number. Thus, 63 couples were still together at the end of the six-month period. Those monogamous teenagers were in the minority; most of the other students were linked to two or more romantic partners. If one person in the busy circle of relationships at the upper left had an untreated infection, it could have been transmitted to 100 other people.

Young adolescents are particularly vulnerable. If a boy has sex before age 16, or a girl has sex before age 16 with an older partner, their chance of catching an infection is twice as high as it would have been if they had waited a few years (Ryan et al., 2008).

One reason is biological. Fully developed women have some natural biological defenses against STIs; this is less true for pubescent girls, who are more likely to catch every STI they are exposed to, including AIDS (World Health Organization, 2005). In addition, for psychological reasons, young sexually active boys and girls are unlikely to seek immediate treatment or alert their partners. Furthermore, many have sexual relationships with two or more people within a short time, thus hastening the spread of infection (see Figure 14.10).

Think of it. If each person had sex with only one partner lifelong, STIs would disappear. Obviously, that is not happening.

An added complication, over and above the usual fears about confidentiality, occurs for homosexual adolescents. In some families and cultures, same-sex relationships are secret, even shameful. This makes it even more difficult for gay or lesbian teens to seek treatment than it is for heterosexual teenagers.

There are hundreds of STIs (James, 2007). We mention only two major ones here, but additional information is provided in Appendix A, pages A18–A19, and the interested reader is encouraged to consult other publications, doctors, and reliable Web sites on the topic. *Chlamydia* is the most frequently reported STI; it often begins without symptoms, yet it can cause permanent infertility. Another common STI is *human papillomavirus (HPV),* which has no immediate consequences but increases a female's risk of uterine cancer. Immunization protects against this STI, but it must occur before a girl's first intercourse—and many parents hesitate to immunize their 11- and 12-year-old daughters against a possible, sexually transmitted, infection.

Especially for Health Practitioners (see response, page 432): How might you encourage adolescents to seek treatment for STIs?

National differences in assumptions, rates, and policies regarding STIs are striking. In France, 91 percent of adolescents use contraception (usually a condom) at first intercourse (Michaud et al., 2006); not coincidentally, every French high school is required to provide students with free, confidential medical care. In contrast, far fewer Italian, German, and U.S. teenagers use condoms. For instance, in the United States, only half of sexually active high school senior girls said they had used a condom during their most recent sexual encounter (MMWR, June 6, 2008).

Parents are not the only ones who assume that STIs are not a problem. Teenagers themselves tend to be misled by appearances, not realizing that a polite, well-dressed partner could have an STI. For example, one girl in Malawi (where AIDS is epidemic) thought she was safe from infection because her partner was known to her and "my mother knows his mother" (quoted in World Health Organization, 2005, p. 11).

Sexual Abuse

We should not leave the topic of sexuality without noting that child sexual abuse is most common just after puberty. **Child sexual abuse** is any sexual activity between a juvenile (a person under a certain age, usually 16) and a person over age 18. Sexual abuse can be very destructive of development in general, not only of sexual development. Virtually every adolescent problem that can impair health (including drug abuse, eating disorders, suicide, and pregnancy) is more

child sexual abuse Any erotic activity that arouses an adult and excites, shames, or confuses a child, whether or not the victim protests and whether or not genital contact is involved.

common in adolescents who have been sexually abused. Some eventually become abusers themselves (Barbaree & Marshall, 2006).

Sex abuse is a major problem in every nation. The United Nations reports that millions of young adolescents are forced into marriage, female genital surgery, and prostitution (often across national borders) each year (Pinheiro, 2006). Exact numbers are elusive. Almost every nation has laws against child sexual abuse, and many have laws against female genital incisions, but these laws are rarely enforced. Adults often let disgust and sensationalism crowd out efforts to prevent, monitor, and eliminate sexual abuse (Davidson, 2005).

TABLE 14.2

Age and Sex Abuse: United States, 2006

Age	Number of Substantiated Victims	Percent of Maltreatment That Is Sex Abuse
Less than 1 year	445	0.4%
1–3	4,558	2.6
4–7	17,539	8.2
8–11	18,314	10.7
12–15	28,138	16.5
16–18	8,798	16.1

Source: U.S. Department of Health and Human Services, Administration on Children, Youth, and Families, 2008.

Data on substantiated childhood sexual abuse in the United States confirm that, as elsewhere, the rate is higher among 12- to 15-year-olds than among younger children (U.S. Department of Health and Human Services Administration on Children, Youth, and Families, 2006). Girls are particularly vulnerable, although boys are also at risk.

In the United States, overall rates are declining, perhaps because adolescents are becoming better informed about sexual activity (Finkelhor & Jones, 2004). Nonetheless, more than 28,000 12- to 15-year-olds were victims of proven sexual abuse in the United States in 2006 (see Table 14.2); this statistic underscores the fact that teenagers as well as younger children need protection (U.S. Department of Health and Human Services Administration on Children and Families, 2008).

Many adolescents are ignorant: Schools teach only the biology of sex and disease; peers brag and lie; and the teen media virtually never discuss healthy sexuality (Hust et al., 2008). That leaves youth to depend on adult family members for information about sex—the worst possible source for sexually abused adolescents, since most abusers are relatives (often parents) of the victims.

As with other types of child maltreatment, the consequences of sexual abuse extend far beyond the trauma of the moment or the immediate physical harm. Young people who are sexually exploited tend to fear sexual relationships and to devalue themselves lifelong. Abusers often isolate adolescents from their peers and refuse to let them socialize; thus, they are never allowed to develop healthy friendships and romances.

Drug Use and Abuse

Few adolescents imagine that our third health hazard, drug addiction, could affect them. Most experiment with drugs and experience no immediate harm or irresistible urge for more of the substance. For instance, according to the Monitoring the Future study (a nationwide annual survey of U.S. high school students that began in 1975; see the Research Design), 72 percent of high school seniors reported having used alcohol at least once in their lives, 46 percent had tried smoking cigarettes, and 42 percent had tried marijuana (Johnston et al., 2008). Figure 14.11 shows the percentage of seniors who reported having used various drugs in the past 30 days.

Adolescents enjoy doing something forbidden as well as experiencing the sensations caused by the substances. They may be particularly attracted to those sen-

Research Design

Scientists: Lloyd D. Johnston, Patrick M. O'Malley, Jerald G. Bachman, and John E. Schulenberg.

Publication: Monitoring the Future is online. Print copies are available from the National Institute on Drug Abuse, in Bethesda, Maryland.

Participants: In 2007, 48,000 students in 403 high schools, throughout the United States.

Design: Beginning in 1975, scientists from the University of Michigan surveyed adolescents each year, asking about drug use, drug availability, and personal attitudes. The basic questions have remained the same, with new drugs added (e.g., Vicodin, OxyContin). Data are reported by age, sex, ethnicity, and region.

Major conclusion: Over the 32 years of the survey, drug use declined, rose, and recently declined again. New drugs continue to appear, and sometimes old drugs become more popular again. Use is more affected by attitudes than by availability.

Comment: This study tracks many cohort changes within the United States. Interested readers should access the latest reports online. Note that other nations often show different patterns and that Monitoring the Future does not usually include high school dropouts.

sations because of their hormonal surges and the cognitive immaturity discussed in Chapter 15 (Witt, 2007).

For many adolescents, both brains and bodies push them toward new and confusing relationships and social situations. For some of those socially awkward teens, the "use of substances . . . provides a form of commerce with the social world" (Dishion & Owen, 2002, p. 489).

➤Response for Parents Worried About Their Teenager's Risk Taking (from page 428): You are right to be concerned, but you cannot keep your child locked up for the next decade or so. Since you know that some rebellion and irrationality are likely, try to minimize them by not boasting about your own youthful exploits, by reacting sternly to minor infractions to nip worse behavior in the bud, and by making allies of your child's teachers.

Variations Among Adolescents

One intriguing aspect of adolescent drug use is that it varies from group to group, which indicates that much more than biology is involved in an adolescent's decision whether or not to use drugs.

➤Response for Health Practitioners (from page 430): Many adolescents are intensely concerned about privacy and fearful of adult interference. This means your first task is to convince the teenagers that you are nonjudgmental and that everything is confidential.

National Differences in Drug Use In some nations, young adolescents drink alcohol more often than they use any other drug; in others, smoking tobacco is more common than drinking. In many places (especially eastern Europe), teenagers use both alcohol and tobacco more than in the United States; in still other places (much of the Middle East), teenagers rarely use any drugs at all (Buelga et al., 2006; Eisner, 2002).

Laws and family practices are partly responsible for these variations. For example, in many Arab nations, alcohol is strictly forbidden; in many European nations, children drink wine with dinner; in many Asian nations, anyone may smoke anywhere; in the United States, smoking is forbidden in many public places.

Overall, drug use among adolescents has decreased in the United States since 1976 (as Figure 14.11 shows), although the number of abused drugs has increased as variations like crack cocaine, ecstasy, and crystal meth have come on the scene. In Australia, over the same time period, drug use has increased.

Laws are not the only reason for variations in teenage drug use between nations or cohorts. Although most adolescents in the United States have experimented with drug use (which is illegal), most do not use drugs often. The proportion of

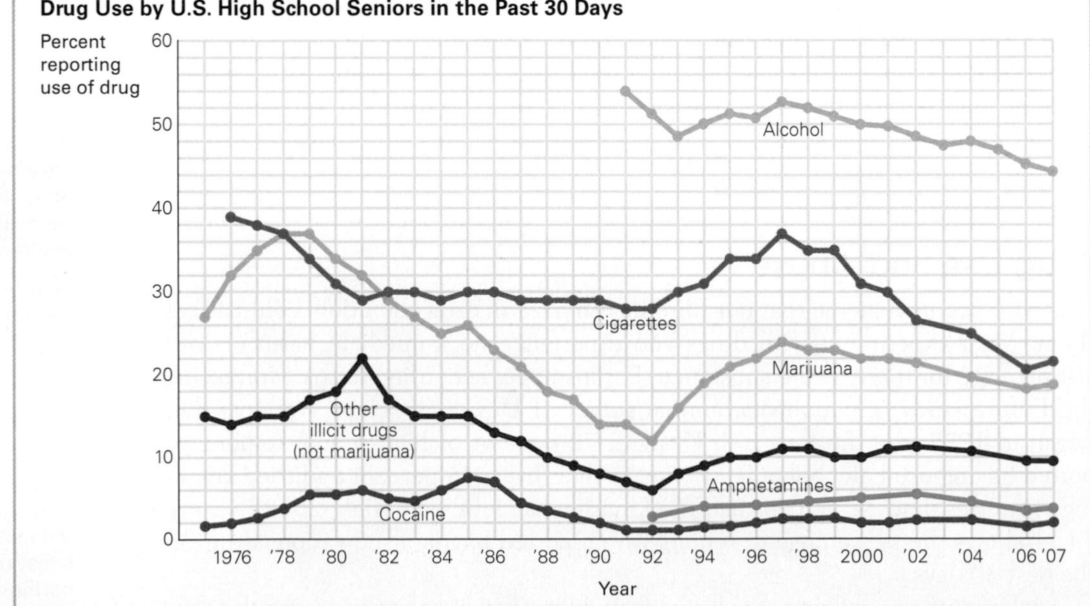

FIGURE 14.11

Rise and Fall By asking the same questions year after year, the Monitoring the Future study shows notable historical effects. It is encouraging that something in society, not in the adolescent, makes drug use increase and decrease and that the most recent data show a decline. However, as Chapter 1 emphasized, survey research cannot prove what causes change.

high school seniors who report use within the past 30 days is about half that of seniors who report ever using a drug: 44 percent for alcohol, 21 percent for cigarettes, and 19 percent for marijuana. Furthermore, a significant minority (about 20 percent) never use any drugs, usually because of religious values, not laws (C. Smith, 2005).

Although any drug use is illegal for those under age 18 in the United States, the national culture that offers consumers many choices also affects the drug market. The United States leads the world in the number of available drugs, including synthetic narcotics, which are unknown in most nations. During 2007, 10 percent of U.S. high school seniors used the synthetic narcotic Vicodin and 5 percent used OxyContin (Johnston et al., 2008).

Laws, customs, and cultures interact and change from state to state. For instance, 28 percent of high school girls in West Virginia are smokers (defined as having smoked at least one cigarette in the past 30 days), compared with 14.6 percent of high school girls in Florida (MMWR, June 6, 2008).

Nations also have markedly different rates, even nations with common boundaries (Buelga et al., 2006). For example, among 15-year-olds, 9.4 percent of the Swiss were heavy users of marijuana, compared with only 3.3 percent of Italians. Canadian youth smoke more marijuana, but fewer cigarettes, than U.S. youth do. Although marijuana is legal and widely available in the Netherlands, Dutch 15-year-olds have one of the lowest rates of heavy use (2.8 percent) of any nation (Buelga et al., 2006).

Gender Differences in Drug Use Gender differences are apparent in the use of most drugs in most nations, with boys having higher rates of use than girls. An international survey of 13- to 15-year-olds in 131 nations found that more boys than girls are smokers (except in some European nations), including three times as many boys as girls in Southeast Asia (Warren et al., 2006). According to another international survey, this one including adolescents in 31 nations, boys are almost twice as likely as girls to have tried marijuana, with 26 percent of boys and 15 percent of girls reporting use (ter Bogt et al., 2006).

Gender differences are reinforced by social constructions about proper male and female behavior. In Indonesia, for instance, 38 percent of the boys smoke cigarettes but only 5 percent of the girls do. The reasons are connected to culture, which considers smoking a marker of male identity. One boy explains, "If I don't smoke, I'm not a real man" (quoted in Ng et al., 2007).

In the United States, the Monitoring the Future study found that before 1970, more boys than girls were smokers, but then the rate among boys began to fall while the rate among girls began to rise. By the 1990s, both sexes smoked less, but a higher percentage of girls than boys smoked. In the most recent years, girls are once again somewhat less likely to be smokers than boys (Johnston et al., 2008).

Also in the United States, current rates of occasional drug use (such as trying marijuana) are close to equal for boys and girls, except that girls almost never use steroids. However, heavy use of drugs (such as daily marijuana) is about twice as prevalent among boys (Johnston et al., 2007).

Another gender difference in drug use in the United States relates to age: Among eighth-graders, the rate for girls is as high as the rate for boys, but with each succeeding year, the rate of drug use among boys increases faster than the rate among girls (Johnston et al., 2008). Age of puberty is a significant variable as well: Early developers are more likely to use drugs (Biehl et al., 2007).

Age and gender interact in another way when it comes to use of inhalants, which seem to be more attractive to young boys than to girls and older boys. Inhalants, which can be bought at hardware stores, are used by about 20 percent of

GSO IMAGES / GETTY IMAGES

JANINE WIEDEL PHOTOLIBRARY / ALAMY

The Same Situation, Many Miles Apart: Underage Drinking Like many other adolescents worldwide, these boys are tempted to try alcohol, even though they are well below the ages at which their respective countries' laws consider them mature enough to drink responsibly: 21 in most areas of the United States *(top)* and 18 in the United Kingdom *(bottom)*.

MIKA / ZEFA / CORBIS

The Emotional Message Cigarette smoking is much more common in Europe than in North America. This 15-year-old boy in Germany may be signaling his manhood with the cigarette behind his ear, and the girl, said to be just 9 years old, may be seeking to participate in his show of maturity by accepting a light.

Observation Quiz (see answer, page 436): What aspects of this scene suggest that the boy is asserting his sexuality and that the girl is actually quite young?

boys before the teen years. They are the only type of drug whose use is reported at higher rates among eighth-graders (16 percent) than among twelfth-graders (11 percent) (Johnston et al., 2008).

Harm from Drugs

Since drugs are widely used and foster peer bonding and excitement, many adolescents think adults exaggerate the harm of teen drug use. That may be, but developmentalists see many immediate and long-term consequences. Abuse, addiction, and brain damage are among "the deleterious consequences of drug use [that] appear to be more pronounced in adolescents than in adults, a difference that has been linked to brain maturation" (Moffit et al., 2006, p. 12).

One negative effect is on physical growth. All psychoactive drugs impair digestion, nutrition, and appetite. Tobacco is worst of all because it is used most often. Adolescent smokers become shorter and heavier adults. All kinds of tobacco (bidis, cigars, pipes, chewing tobacco) inhibit growth. This problem is particularly serious in India, where undernutrition is chronic and tobacco use (typically not in the form of cigarettes) is widespread (Warren et al., 2006). Since internal organs mature after the height spurt, drug-using teenagers who appear full-grown may still damage their hearts, lungs, brains, and reproductive systems.

Alcohol is the most frequently abused drug among North American teenagers. It permanently impairs memory and self-control by damaging the hippocampus and the prefrontal cortex (S. A. Brown et al., 2000; De Bellis et al., 2005; White & Swartzwelder, 2004). Experiments with lower animals suggest that slower thinking is one immediate result of alcohol use that is particularly likely among adolescent drinkers (Sircar & Sircar, 2005).

These consequences of tobacco and alcohol are fairly well known. However, many teenagers are oblivious to the dangers of marijuana. Johanna explained:

> I started off using about every other weekend, and pretty soon it increased to three to four times a week. . . . I started skipping classes to get high. I quit soccer because my coach was a jerk. My grades dropped, but I blamed that on my not being into school. . . . Finally some of my friends cornered me and told me how much I had changed, and they said it started when I started smoking marijuana. They came with me to see the substance-abuse counselor at school.
>
> *[quoted in Bell, 1998, p. 199]*

Adolescents who regularly smoke marijuana are likely to drop out of school, become teenage parents, and be unemployed (Chassin et al., 2004). Marijuana affects memory, language proficiency, and motivation (Lane et al., 2005)—all of which are especially crucial during adolescence.

But wait. Those are correlations—what about causation? Is it possible that adolescents who are not particularly clever or ambitious choose to smoke marijuana, rather than vice versa? Or maybe some third variable (such as hostile parents) is the cause of both the academic problems and the drug use.

For decades, researchers have noted that many drug-using adolescents distrust their parents, injure themselves, hate their schools, and get into trouble with the law. One hypothesis for this correlation was that the psychic strains of adolescence led to drug use. In fact, however, longitudinal research suggests that drug use causes more problems than it solves, often *preceding* anxiety disorders, depression, and rebellion (Chassin et al., 2004). Rather than lack of ambition leading to marijuana use, marijuana itself seems to destroy ambition.

Unfortunately, drugs allow momentary denial of problems (worries seem to disappear when a person is under the influence), but the problems actually get worse. If more drugs are sought to relieve anxiety about those worse problems, that leads to addiction. Like Johanna, quoted above, many adolescents do not notice when they move past use (experimenting) to *abuse* (causing harm) and then to *addiction* (needing the drug).

Most adolescent drug users are not addicts, but the authors of the Monitoring the Future study report that in 2007, 26 percent of high school seniors were binge drinkers (defined as someone who had consumed 5 or more alcoholic drinks in a row in the past two weeks), 12 percent were daily cigarette smokers, and 5 percent were daily marijuana users (Johnston et al., 2008). All these figures suggest that addiction may occur soon. In addition, the younger a person is when he or she first uses drugs, the more likely he or she is to be addicted to that drug later on (Merline et al., 2004).

Learning from Experience—or Not

With harmful drugs, as with many other aspects of living, members of the younger generation seem to have to learn things for themselves. A common phenomenon is **generational forgetting,** the idea that each new generation forgets what the previous generation learned (Chassin et al., 2004; Johnston et al., 2008).

generational forgetting The idea that each new generation forgets what the previous generation learned. As used here, the term refers to knowledge about the harm drugs can do.

Why does generational forgetting occur? One reason is that teenagers tend to distrust adults' attitudes toward drugs because adults experienced a different drug scene. The most widely used drug prevention program in U.S. schools, Project DARE (for Drug Abuse Resistance Education), features adults (usually police officers) telling students about the dangers of drugs. Perhaps because of generational forgetting, DARE has no impact on later drug use, according to several reliable studies (West & O'Neal, 2004).

Similarly, some antidrug advertisements using scare tactics (such as the one that showed eggs being broken into a hot frying pan while an announcer intoned, "This is your brain on drugs") have the opposite effect from that intended, probably because they make drugs seem exciting. Some antismoking announcements produced by cigarette companies (such as one that showed a clean-cut young person advising viewers to think before they started smoking) actually increase drug use (Block et al., 2002; Fishbein et al., 2002).

This does not mean that trying to halt early drug use is hopeless. Massive ad campaigns in Florida and California have cut adolescent smoking almost in half, in part because the publicity appealed to the young (Wakefield et al., 2003). A particularly effective ad depicted young people dumping 1,200 body bags in front of the corporate headquarters of a tobacco company to highlight the number of smoking-related deaths that occur in the United States each day (Farrelly et al., 2005). This ad worked partly because it showed adolescent rebellion against adult authority, thus appealing to the target audience.

Throughout the United States, higher prices, targeted warnings, and better law enforcement have led to a marked decline in cigarette smoking among younger adolescents. In 2007, only 7 percent of eighth-graders had smoked cigarettes in the past month, compared with 21 percent 10 years earlier (Johnston et al., 2008). Other research finds that the younger a smoker is, the more likely he or she is to quit successfully. One reason is that an increasing number of parents forbid smoking in their homes (Messer et al., 2008).

➤Answer to Observation Quiz (from page 434): The boy has a lighter in his hand, but he is using a more intimate way of sharing a light; the girl is holding her cigarette awkwardly, unlike an experienced smoker. Although it is difficult to believe that she is only 9 (as the photographer states), her plastic bracelets, her tentative posture, her hand covering her mouth, and her timid expression all suggest that she is no older than 12.

The declining U.S. rates of teenage births and abortions, as well as all the variations in drug use just described, suggest that adolescent biology is far from destiny. The emotions and sexual impulses of puberty need not be harmful. As you will see in the next two chapters, experiences of peers, guidance from elders, and application of research together have helped most young people avoid the hazards of this age period. Many adults remember the energy and sexuality of the teen years with fondness. So it should be for everyone.

SUMMING UP

Adolescence is generally a time of robust health, but also a time when poor decision making can cause serious bodily harm. Many adolescents are not yet sexually active and are not drug users. However, the rate of violent death increases at puberty, and about 20 percent of all youth are involved in dangerous and unhealthy activities. Early pregnancy takes a physiological as well as psychological toll; early sexually transmitted infections are likely to spread and may cause infertility and even death; early use of drugs may impair development of the brain and body. Variations in drug use by nation, gender, and cohort show that culture, not biology, is the reason many adolescents use illegal substances. Generational forgetting makes it more difficult for adolescents to heed adults' warnings about the hazards of early sex and drugs. Nonetheless, some prevention efforts have been successful. In the United States, the rates of adolescent pregnancy and drug use are markedly lower than those of 10 years ago. ■

SUMMARY

Puberty Begins

1. Puberty refers to the various changes that transform a child's body into an adult one. Even before the teenage years begin, biochemical signals from the hypothalamus to the pituitary gland to the adrenal glands (along the HPA axis) increase production of testosterone, estrogen, and various other hormones. These hormones cause the body to grow and change.

2. Puberty is accompanied by many emotions. Some emotional reactions, such as quick mood shifts and thoughts about sex, are directly caused by hormones. Others are caused by reactions (of others and of the young people themselves) to the bodily changes of adolescence.

3. The visible changes of puberty normally occur anytime from about age 8 to about age 14; puberty most often begins between ages 10 and 13. The young person's sex, genetic background, body fat, and level of family stress all contribute to this variation in timing.

4. Girls generally begin and end the process of puberty before boys do, although the time gap in sexual maturity is much shorter than the two-year gap in reaching peak height.

5. Adolescents who do not reach puberty at about the same age as their friends experience additional stresses. Generally (depending on culture, community, and cohort), early-maturing girls have the most difficult time of all.

Nutrition

6. To sustain body growth, most adolescents consume large quantities of food, although they do not always make healthy choices. One reason for poor nutrition is the desire to lose (or, less often, gain) weight because of anxiety about body image.

7. Although eating disorders are not usually diagnosed until early adulthood, their precursors—obesity, anorexia, and bulimia—are evident during puberty. Many adolescents eat too much of the wrong foods or too little food overall.

The Transformations of Puberty

8. The growth spurt is an acceleration of growth in every part of the body. Peak weight increase usually precedes peak height, which is then followed by peak muscle growth. The lungs and the heart also increase in size and capacity, and body rhythms (especially sleep patterns) change.

9. Sexual characteristics emerge at puberty. The maturation of primary sex characteristics means that by age 13 or so, menarche and spermarche have usually occurred, and the young person may be capable of reproducing. In many ways, the two sexes experience the same sexual maturation and impulses, although they are manifested in different ways.

10. Secondary sex characteristics are not directly involved in reproduction but do signify that the person is a man or a woman.

Body shape, breasts, voice, body hair, and numerous other features differentiate males from females. Sexual activity is influenced more by culture than by physiology.

Health Hazards

11. For about 20 percent of all adolescents, health hazards make life more difficult and sometimes shorter. The rate of violent death—accidents, homicides, and suicides—rises markedly in adolescence and reaches its highest peak by early adulthood.

12. Among the problems that adolescents face is the tendency to become sexually active before their bodies and minds are truly ready. Pregnancy before age 16 takes a physical toll on a growing girl, and STIs at any age can lead to infertility and even death.

13. Sexual abuse, which includes any sexually provocative activity that involves a juvenile and an adult, becomes most common in early adolescence. Girls are most often victims; the perpetrators are most often family members.

14. Most adolescents experiment with drugs, especially alcohol and tobacco, although such substances impair growth of the body and of the brain. Prevention and moderation are possible, but programs need to be carefully designed to avoid the effects of generational forgetting.

KEY TERMS

puberty (p. 407)
menarche (p. 407)
spermarche (p. 407)
hormones (p. 408)
pituitary (p. 408)
adrenal glands (p. 408)
HPA axis (p. 408)
gonads (p. 409)
HPG axis (p. 409)
estradiol (p. 409)
testosterone (p. 409)
leptin (p. 413)
secular trend (p. 413)
body image (p. 417)
anorexia nervosa (p. 418)
bulimia nervosa (p. 419)
growth spurt (p. 421)
primary sex characteristics (p. 422)
secondary sex characteristics (p. 422)
sexually transmitted infection (STI) (p. 429)
child sexual abuse (p. 430)
generational forgetting (p. 435)

KEY QUESTIONS

1. What aspects of puberty are under direct hormonal control?

2. What psychological responses result from the physical changes of puberty?

3. How do nature and nurture combine to enable young people to become parents?

4. Why is experiencing puberty early or late especially difficult?

5. Name three nutritional disorders and explain why adolescents are particularly vulnerable to them.

6. Why is body image particularly likely to be distorted in adolescence?

7. Why are sexually active adolescents more likely to contract STIs than are sexually active adults?

8. What are the differences between adolescent pregnancy in 1960 and 2000?

9. What are the positive and negative consequences of adolescent experimentation with drugs?

10. How and why do nations and cohorts vary in rates of adolescent drug use?

11. What can help prevent teenage drug use?

APPLICATIONS

1. Visit a fifth-, sixth-, or seventh-grade class. Note variations in the size and maturity of the students. Do you see any patterns related to gender, ethnicity, body fat, or self confidence?

2. Interview two to four of your friends who are in their late teens or early 20s about their memories of menarche or spermarche, including their memories of others' reactions. Do their comments indicate that these events are or are not emotionally troubling for young people?

3. Talk with someone who became a parent before the age of 20. Were there any problems with the pregnancy, the birth, or the first years of parenthood? Would the person recommend young parenthood? What would have been different had the baby been born three years earlier or three years later?

4. Adults disagree about the dangers of drugs. Find two people with very different opinions (e.g., a parent who would be horrified if his or her child used any drug and a parent who believes that young people should be allowed to drink or smoke at home). Ask them to explain their reasons, and write these down without criticism or disagreement. Later, present each person with the other person's arguments. What is the response? How open, flexible, and rational do the reactions seem to be? Why are beliefs about drugs so deeply held?

15

CHAPTER OUTLINE

Adolescence: Cognitive Development

It was a humid midsummer afternoon. My daughter Bethany prevailed on me to go with her to New York City's Metropolitan Museum of Art. When we climbed up to street level from the subway station, we encountered a sudden downpour. Bethany stopped and became angry—at me!

> **She:** You didn't bring an umbrella? You should have known.
> **Me:** It's OK—we'll walk quickly. It's a warm rain.
> **She:** But we'll get all wet.
> **Me:** No problem. We'll dry.
> **She:** But people will see us with our hair all wet.
> **Me:** Honey, no one cares how we look. And we won't see anyone we know.
> **She:** That's OK for you to say. You're already married.

I asked, incredulously, "Do you think you are going to meet your future husband here?"

She looked at me as if I were unbelievably stupid. "No, of course not. But people will look at me and think, 'She'll never find a husband looking like that!'"

Bethany was a gifted artist, creating paintings that still hang on my walls. She also excelled in her AP (Advanced Placement) exams, evidence of the formal abstract thinking of which adolescents are capable. Yet this incident illustrates another side of adolescent thought, called *adolescent egocentrism.*

This chapter discusses important changes in the adolescent brain and describes several aspects of adolescent cognition, including the abstract reasoning required for advanced academic courses and the intuitive, emotional thinking that is preferred by adolescents themselves. Underlying these changes is brain maturation, which helps explain adolescents' intense emotions and leads, eventually, to rational planning. The last section of this chapter discusses implications of intellectual development for middle and high school education, for those who go to college and for those who do not.

Neurological Development

As is the case with growth in the rest of the teenager's body, different parts of the brain grow at different rates (Blakemore, 2008). The limbic system (fear, emotional impulses) matures before the prefrontal cortex (planning ahead, emotional regulation). Myelination and maturation proceed from inside the brain to the cortex and from back to front (Sowell et al., 2007); accordingly, the instinctual and emotional areas develop before the reflective ones do. Furthermore, the hormones of puberty affect the amygdala (part of the limbic system) more directly than the cortex. Maturation of the cortex depends more on age and experience than on hormones.

Caution Versus Thrill Seeking

Much more interdisciplinary research is needed to integrate the neurology and psychology of adolescence. Researchers must be cautious lest "incomplete brain development [become] an explanation for just about everything about teens that adults have found perplexing, from sleep patterns to risk taking and mood swings" (Kuhn, 2006, p. 59).

As explained in Chapter 6, the fMRI, the PET, and other measures of neurological activity are expensive and complex. Furthermore, "the images generated by such methods may have a power to captivate that reaches beyond their power to explain" (Miller, 2008, p. 1413). As a result, reliable, longitudinal, multifactorial research on the brains of typical 10- to 17-year-olds is limited. Yet many scientists are understandably excited by recent discoveries about the adolescent brain. The fact that the frontal lobes (prefrontal cortex) are the last part of the brain to mature explains why many adolescents are driven by the excitement of new experiences, sensations, and peers—forgetting the caution that their parents and teachers have tried to instill (Steinberg, 2008).

Neuroscientists and developmentalists seek to understand exactly how the urge to seek emotional arousal and the capacity for logical thinking connect in the adolescent brain, as the following explains.

a personal perspective

"What Were You Thinking?"

Laurence Steinberg is a noted expert on adolescent thinking. He is also a father.

> When my son, Benjamin, was 14, he and three of his friends decided to sneak out of the house where they were spending the night and visit one of their girlfriends at around two in the morning. When they arrived at the girl's house, they positioned themselves under her bedroom window, threw pebbles against her windowpanes, and tried to scale the side of the house. Modern technology, unfortunately, has made it harder to play Romeo these days. The boys set off the house's burglar alarm, which activated a siren and simultaneously sent a direct notification to the local police station, which dispatched a patrol car. When the siren went off, the boys ran down the street and right smack into the police car, which was heading to the girl's home. Instead of stopping and explaining their activity, Ben and his friends scattered and ran off in different directions through the neighborhood. One of the boys was caught by the police and taken back to his home, where his parents were awakened and the boy questioned.
>
> I found out about this affair the following morning, when the girl's mother called our home to tell us what Ben had done. . . . After his near brush with the local police, Ben had returned to the house out of which he had snuck, where he slept soundly until I awakened him with an angry telephone call, telling him to gather his clothes and wait for me in front of his friend's house. On our drive home, after delivering a long lecture about what he had done and about the dangers of running from armed police in the dark when they believe they may have interrupted a burglary, I paused.
>
> "What were you thinking?" I asked.
>
> "That's the problem, Dad," Ben replied, "I wasn't."
>
> *[Steinberg, 2004, pp. 51, 52]*

Steinberg agrees with this last insight by his son. As he expresses it, "The problem is not that Ben's decision-making was deficient. The problem is that it was nonexistent" (Steinberg, 2004, p. 52). In his analysis, Steinberg points out a characteristic of adolescent thought: When emotions are intense, especially when one is with peers, the logical part of the brain shuts down.

This shutdown is not reflected in questionnaires that require teenagers to respond to paper-and-pencil questions regarding hypothetical dilemmas. On those tests, teenagers think carefully and answer correctly. They know the risks of sex and drugs. However,

> the prospect of visiting a hypothetical girl from class cannot possibly carry the excitement about the possibility of surprising someone you have a crush on with a visit in the middle of the night. It is easier to put on a hypothetical condom during an act of hypothetical sex than it is to put on a real one when one is in the throes of passion. It is easier to just say no to a hypothetical beer than it is to a cold frosty one on a summer night.
>
> *[Steinberg, 2004, p. 53]*

Steinberg believes that abstract questionnaires reveal insufficient information about how the brain actually works. Adolescent thinking is more variable than earlier researchers believed (Kuhn, 2006). Now that scientists realize the limitations of prior research, and neuroscientists have data from fMRI and other brain scans, new discoveries about adolescent brain functioning are on the horizon.

Ben reached adulthood safely. Some other teenagers, with less cautious police or less diligent parents, do not. Ideally, research on adolescent brains will help protect teens from their dangerous impulses (Monastersky, 2007). Parents, teachers, and authorities need to be especially careful in their guidance, to compensate for adolescents' lack of reflection. We cannot be sure that brain immaturity is behind all "troublesome adolescent behavior," but we do know that "response inhibition, emotional regulation, and organization" among teenagers are underdeveloped (Sowell et al., 2007, p. 59), all because the prefrontal cortex is not yet mature.

Does the Brain Regress in Adolescence?

You learned in Chapter 11 that the brain functions well in middle childhood, as dendrites, myelination, and the corpus callosum allow the brain to become "massively interconnected" (Kagan & Herschkowitz, 2005, p. 220). Yet you just read that the immature prefrontal cortex may be involved in much troublesome adolescent behavior. Does this mean that brain development actually regresses in adolescence?

Think about the behavior of Ben Steinberg and his friends. Eight-year-old boys would not be interested in girls at all, let alone in sneaking out at 2:00 A.M. to throw pebbles at a girl's window. If the idea did occur to them, they would think twice about it and stay in bed. In contrast, Ben and the other 14-year-olds rushed out of the house to put their pebble-throwing plan into operation.

Such behavior does not signal a regression in brain development, however. In fact, adolescents are quite capable of rational thinking. The problem is that they don't necessarily *use* that capacity before they act.

The combination of the normal sequence of brain maturation (limbic system, then cortex) and the earlier onset of puberty (perhaps because of better nutrition or greater stress) means that, for many contemporary youth, emotions rule behavior. Since the amygdala (which specializes in such quick emotional reactions as sudden anger, joy, fear, and despair) matures before the prefrontal cortex (which coordinates, inhibits, and strategizes), the complexities of social interaction and emotional restraint are beyond many teenagers (Blakemore, 2008; Compas, 2004).

The maturing limbic system makes adolescents particularly attracted to strong, immediate sensations, unchecked by the slower-maturing prefrontal cortex. For this reason,

> adolescents *like* intensity, excitement, and arousal. They are drawn to music videos that shock and bombard the senses. Teenagers flock to horror and slasher movies. They dominate queues waiting to ride the high-adrenaline rides at amusement parks. Adolescence is a time when sex, drugs, *very* loud music, and other high-stimulation experiences take on great appeal. It is a developmental period when an appetite for adventure, a predilection for risks, and a desire for novelty and thrills seem to reach naturally high levels.
>
> *[Dahl, 2004, pp. 7–8]*

When stress, arousal, passion, sensory bombardment, drug intoxication, or deprivation is extreme, the adolescent brain is overtaken by impulses that might shame adults. Teenagers brag about being so drunk they were "wasted," "bombed," "smashed," describing a state most adults try to avoid. Some teenagers choose to spend a night without sleep, a day without eating, or to exercise in pain.

The consequences of impulsive behavior may be especially severe in the twenty-first century, for two reasons:

1. Changing economic conditions mean that puberty now precedes adult employment and marriage by a decade or more. A steady job and a life partner tend to make a person more responsible; few adolescents have either.
2. Guns, drugs, and sex are now widely available to adolescents. These can turn a momentary lapse of judgment into a lethal mistake. For instance, suicides and homicides toward the end of adolescence are particularly likely to be the result of a quick impulse rather than a careful plan. Bullets allow no second thoughts.

The hormones that instigate puberty have little effect on the neurological advances necessary for adult planning and reflection (Steinberg, 2008). The parts of the brain dedicated to such functions may not become mature until years after the young person first has hormonal rushes, sexual urges, and access to weapons.

Neurological Benefits of Uneven Brain Development

Uneven brain growth in adolescence has benefits as well as hazards. With increased myelination, reactions become lightning fast, and speed is valued in many aspects of modern life. For instance, adolescent athletes are potential superstars, if wisdom and experience (ideally supplied by coaches) direct their quick reactions.

Furthermore, during adolescence, additional synaptic pruning occurs, and the dopamine system, including neurotransmitters that bring great pleasure, is very active. The joy of a first love, or a first job, or even an A on a term paper is memorable, not to be dismissed. Adults are less likely to be thrilled by such experiences.

Before the brain becomes fully mature (at about age 25), formation of new connections between synapses facilitates acquisition of new ideas, words, memories, personality patterns, and dance steps (Keating, 2004). Values acquired during adolescence are more likely to endure than those learned later, after brain links are firmly established. This is an asset if values developed during adolescence are less self-centered than those of children or more culturally attuned than those of older generations.

In short, several aspects of adolescent brain development are positive. The fact that the prefrontal cortex is still developing "confers benefits as well as risks. It helps explain the creativity of adolescence and early adulthood, before the brain becomes set in its ways" (Monastersky, 2007, p. A17). The emotional intensity of adolescents "intertwines with the highest levels of human endeavor: passion for ideas and ideals, passion for beauty, passion to create music and art" (Dahl, 2004, p. 21).

Adolescent neurological development allows contemplation of new values, which might take the form of compassion or mistrust, political participation or isolation, creativity or narrowness. As a practical application, those who care about the next generation must attend to the life lessons that adolescents are learning. Adults should provide "scaffolding and monitoring" until adolescents' brains can function well on their own and they develop proficiency in the skills they acquire (Dahl, quoted in Monastersky, 2007, p. A18).

SUMMING UP

The hormones of puberty probably cause the brain's emotional hot spots to continue to myelinate as well as to grow. Adult functioning of the prefrontal cortex depends less on specific hormones and more on age and experience; thus, it matures later. Uneven neurological development may be one reason adolescents take irrational risks and enjoy intense sensory experiences. During adolescence, emotional reactions quicken and memories endure. ■

Adolescent Thinking

Brain maturation, intense conversations, additional years of schooling, moral challenges, and increased independence all occur between ages 11 and 18. The combination propels impressive cognitive growth, as any conversation with a high school senior reveals.

Scientists disagree as to how much each of these five experiences contributes. They agree, however, that there is "enormous variability in cognitive functioning among normal adolescents, with some performing no better than third-graders on many reasoning tasks and others performing as well as or better than most adults" (Kuhn & Franklin, 2006, p. 955).

To understand any single adolescent of any age, keep this variability in mind: Although egocentrism is typically evident at the beginning of adolescence, intuition in the middle, and logic at the end, any one of these forms of cognition may appear in any adolescent at any time.

Egocentrism

During puberty, young people center many of their thoughts on themselves. In Chapter 14, you read that the physical transformations of puberty are met with anticipation, horror, and delight by the individuals who see such changes in themselves.

It is typical for young adolescents to wonder how others perceive them; to try to make sense of their conflicting feelings about their parents, school, and classmates; to think deeply (but not always realistically) about their future. One reason adolescents spend so much time talking on the phone, e-mailing, and texting is that they want to confer with close friends about every nuance of everything they have done, are doing, and plan to do next.

Young adolescents not only think intensely about themselves but also imagine what others may think about them. Together these two aspects of thought are called **adolescent egocentrism,** as first described by David Elkind (1967). This characteristic thought pattern is particularly likely in early adolescence, and it seems equally common among all youth (Beaudoin & Schonert-Reichl, 2006).

adolescent egocentrism A characteristic of adolescent thinking that leads young people (ages 10 to 13) to focus on themselves to the exclusion of others.

DAVID M. GROSSMAN / THE IMAGE WORKS

Don't Start with Me . . . All six of these Brooklyn teenagers are affected by adolescent egocentrism. They share an intense concern about how they look to other people. It is not easy to appear unique and part of a group simultaneously.

Observation Quiz (see answer, page 445): There are some obvious differences among these boys, but they have three visible characteristics in common. What are they?

Remember from Chapter 9 that *egocentric* means "self at the center." The difference between egocentrism during adolescence and the same trait during preoperational thought is that adolescents, unlike younger children, have a well-developed theory of mind (Artar, 2007). They know that other people are not necessarily thinking the same thing they are. However, their egocentrism distorts their understanding of what others may be thinking, especially about them. As one 16-year-old explained to a researcher: "My mom thinks that she was right; she couldn't understand me and what I feel. . . . That's the cause of the quarrel actually" (quoted in Artar, 2007, p. 1217). The researcher noted that, like many of her peers, this girl realized that her mother had her own thoughts, but she didn't recognize the limitations of her own thinking.

In egocentrism, adolescents regard themselves as unique, special, and much more socially significant (that is, noticed by everyone) than they actually are. Accurately imagining someone else's perspective is especially difficult when egocentrism rules (Lapsley, 1993). For example, it seems unlikely that adolescent girls are especially attracted to boys with pimples and braces, but Edgar thought so, according to his older sister:

> Now in the 8th grade, Edgar has this idea that all the girls are looking at him in school. He got his first pimple about three months ago. I told him to wash it with my face soap but he refused, saying, "Not until I go to school to show it off." He called the dentist, begging him to approve his braces now instead of waiting for a year. The perfect gifts for him have changed from action figures to a bottle of cologne, a chain, and a fitted baseball hat like the rappers wear.
>
> *[adapted from Eva, personal communication, 2007]*

Egocentrism also leads adolescents to interpret another's behavior as if it is related to themselves. A stranger's frown or a teacher's critique could make a teenager conclude that "no one likes me" and then to deduce that "I am unlovable," or even to claim that, "I can't go out in public." More positive casual reactions—a smile from a sales clerk or an extra-big hug from a younger brother—could lead to the thought that, "I am great" or "Everyone loves me," with similarly distorted self-perception.

As an aspect of egocentrism, acute self-consciousness about one's physical appearance is probably more prevalent between ages 10 and 14 than earlier or later (Rankin et al., 2004). Young adolescents would rather not stand out from their peers, hoping instead to blend in. They also believe that other people are as egocentric as they are. As one girl said:

> I am a real worrier when it comes to other people's opinions. I care deeply about what they say, think and do. If people are very complimentary, it can give you a big confidence boost, but if people are always putting you down you feel less confident and people can tell. A lot of advice that is given is "Do what you want and don't listen to anyone else," but I don't know one person who can do that.
>
> *[quoted in J. H. Bell & Bromnick, 2003, p. 213]*

personal fable An aspect of adolescent egocentrism characterized by an adolescent's belief that his or her thoughts, feelings, and experiences are unique, more wonderful or awful than anyone else's.

invincibility fable An adolescent's egocentric conviction that he or she cannot be overcome or even harmed by anything that might defeat a normal mortal, such as unprotected sex, drug abuse, or high-speed driving.

Fables

Elkind gave names to several aspects of adolescent egocentrism, among them the **personal fable** and the **invincibility fable,** which often appear together. The egocentric idea of the personal fable is that one is unique, destined to have a heroic, even legendary, life. When adolescents think they are invincible, they may be convinced that, unlike other mortals, they will not be hurt by fast driving, unprotected sex, or addictive drugs. If they take any of these risks and survive without harm, they feel special, not thankful.

NORBERT SCHWERIN / THE IMAGE WORKS

Not Me! A young woman jumps into the Pacific Ocean near Santa Cruz, California, while at a friend's birthday party. The jump is illegal, yet since 1975, 52 people have died taking that leap off these cliffs. Hundreds of young people each year decide that the thrill is worth the risk, aided by the invincibility fable and by what they think are sensible precautions. (Note that she is wearing shoes. Also note that the dog has apparently decided against risking a jump.)

For instance, one survey found that only 1 in 20 teenage cigarette smokers thought they would be smoking in five years, even though 2 out of 3 had already tried to stop and failed, and most teenage smokers become addicted to nicotine and are still smoking years later (Siqueira et al., 2001). Adolescents ignore evidence from developmental statistics, because they believe that they are exceptional, exempt from normal human vulnerability.

In every nation, those who volunteer for military service—knowing or even hoping that they will be sent into combat—are more likely to be under age 20 than over it. Young recruits take risks, in the military as well as in civilian life, more often than older, more experienced soldiers (Killgore et al., 2006). In this example, as in many others (such as addiction and violent death, described in Chapter 14), more boys than girls believe that they are invincible; they therefore take more unnecessary risks (Alberts et al., 2007).

The Imaginary Audience

Egocentrism also creates an **imaginary audience** in the minds of many adolescents, both male and female. They seem to believe that they are at center stage, with all eyes on them, and that others are as intensely interested in them as they themselves are. As a result, they are continually imagining how others might react to their appearance and behavior. Bethany did this in the story that opens this chapter, when she imagined that strangers in the museum would think about her marriage prospects when they saw her wet hair.

imaginary audience The other people who, in an adolescent's egocentric belief, are watching and taking note of his or her appearance, ideas, and behavior. This belief makes many teenagers very self-conscious.

The imaginary audience can cause teenagers to enter a crowded room as if they are the most attractive human beings alive. They might put studs in their lips or blast music for all to hear, calling attention to themselves.

The reverse is also possible: Unlike Edgar, they might avoid scrutiny lest someone notice a blemish on their chin or make fun of their braces. Many a 12-year-old balks at going to school with a bad haircut or the wrong shoes.

Many adolescents are especially concerned about the audience of their peers, who they believe are judging every visible oddity of their appearance and behavior. One girl remarked, "I would like to be able to fly if everyone else did; otherwise it would be rather conspicuous" (quoted in A. Steinberg, 1993). A 12-year-old boy said:

➤Answer to Observation Quiz (from page 443): They share gender, facial expressions, and hand positions. They are all boys; the presence of a girl or two would call for the boys to assume very different expressions and postures. Instead, they are all wearing impassive expressions, trying to look cool: No one is smiling, scowling, or clowning. None of them is touching another with his hands; although one boy is leaning on two friends' shoulders, he is careful to rest on his wrists, not his hands.

> I dress different now that I'm in middle school. I used to not care about my clothes—I'd wear whatever my mom bought for me. But now I really care [and] take time to think about it. So it bugs me when my mom yells at me for wearing jeans with holes or big shirts. It's a big deal to her if my clothes aren't clean. She thinks my teachers will think she's a bad mother or something.
>
> *[Daniel, quoted in R. Bell, 1998, p. 59]*

Note that he imagined that his mother is troubled by her own audience, which consists of the teachers in his school. It is typical to begin with the imagined reactions of other people and end by judging the cluelessness of one's own parents, as Bethany did. Of course, no one can be sure whether the audience is real and other people are actually paying attention, or what they might be thinking; but adolescents are much more self-focused and hypersensitive than are older people.

Egocentrism Reassessed

After Elkind first described adolescent egocentrism, some psychologists blamed it for every teenage problem, from drug use to pregnancy, from rebellion to apathy (Eckstein et al., 1999). A more recent wave of research has found that many adolescents do not feel invincible; in fact, some have exaggerated perceptions of risks (Mills et al., 2008).

Moreover, egocentrism "may signal growth toward cognitive maturity" (Vartanian, 2001, p. 378). Adolescents' worry about an imaginary audience may not be irrational: Their peers may really be judging them (J. H. Bell & Bromnick, 2003). For example, a 13-year-old who had moved to Los Angeles from a small town recalled:

> When I got to school the first day, everyone looked at me like I was from outer space or something. It was like, "Who's that? Look at her hair. Look at what she's wearing." That's all anybody cares about around here; what you look like and what you wear. I felt like a total outcast. As soon as I got home, I locked myself in my room and cried for about an hour. I was so lonely.
>
> *[Tina, quoted in R. Bell, 1998, p. 78]*

The phrase "all anybody cares about around here" does not apply only to Los Angeles. The same words could have been written by a young adolescent who moved from Los Angeles to a small town or by almost any adolescent who was new to a school anywhere. This girl's reaction was egocentric if she imagined more scrutiny than actually occurred, but young adolescents do sometimes reject peers who dress or act in unusual ways. At one extreme, many homosexual and transgender youth are bullied or even killed by their peers because of their unconventional behavior or appearance (Rivers, 2001).

Formal Operational Thought

In sorting through their life experiences, adolescents begin to develop logic that is no longer dependent on concrete experiences. They are now able to consider abstractions. Jean Piaget noticed and described the cognitive advance signaled by the ability to reason on the basis of "assumptions that have no necessary relation to reality" (Piaget, 1972, p. 148). He realized that cognitive processes, not just cognitive contents, can shift after childhood to a level called **formal operational thought.**

formal operational thought In Piaget's theory, the fourth and final stage of cognitive development, characterized by more systematic logical thinking and by the ability to understand and systematically manipulate abstract concepts.

One way to distinguish between formal and concrete thinking is to compare the curricula in high school and in primary school. Here are three examples:

- *Math.* Younger children multiply real numbers ($4 \times 3 \times 8$); adolescents can multiply unreal numbers, such as $(2x)(3y)$ or even $(25xy^2)(3zy^3)$.

- *Social Studies.* Younger children study other cultures by experiencing aspects of daily life—drinking goat's milk or building an igloo, for instance; adolescents can grasp concepts like "gross national product" and "fertility rate" and can figure out how these phenomena affect politics.
- *Science.* Younger students plant carrots and feed rabbits; adolescents understand that hydrogen and oxygen can combine to make water and can then test H_2O in the lab.

Piaget's Experiments

Piaget and his colleagues devised a number of tasks that demonstrate formal operational thought (Inhelder & Piaget, 1958). Successful completion of these tasks shows that "in contrast to concrete operational children, formal operational adolescents imagine all possible determinants . . . [and] systematically vary the factors one by one, observe the results correctly, keep track of the results, and draw the appropriate conclusions" (P. H. Miller, 2002).

In one experiment (diagrammed in Figure 15.1), children balance a scale by hooking weights onto the scale's arms. To master this task, a person must realize that the heaviness of the weights and their distance from the center interact reciprocally to affect balance. Therefore, a heavier weight close to the center can be counterbalanced with a lighter weight far from the center. For example, a 12-gram weight placed 2 centimeters to the left of the center might balance a 6-gram weight placed 4 centimeters to the right.

This concept was completely beyond the ability or interest of 3- to 5-year-olds. In Piaget's experiments, they randomly hung different weights on different hooks.

By age 7, children realized that the scale could be balanced by putting the same amount of weight on each arm. However, they didn't know or care that the distance from the center was important.

By age 10, at the end of their concrete operational stage, children thought about location, but they used trial and error, not logic. They succeeded with equal weights at equal distances and were pleased when they balanced different weights, but they did not figure out the formula.

AP PHOTO / TONY GUTIERREZ

A Calculated Response Texas state senator Florence Shapiro watches Jamie, a seventh-grader, solve a math problem using a graphing calculator. Many adults complain that calculators undermine learning by making math "too easy." Educators, however, welcome any tool that allows students to understand the logic of math, not simply to memorize calculations.

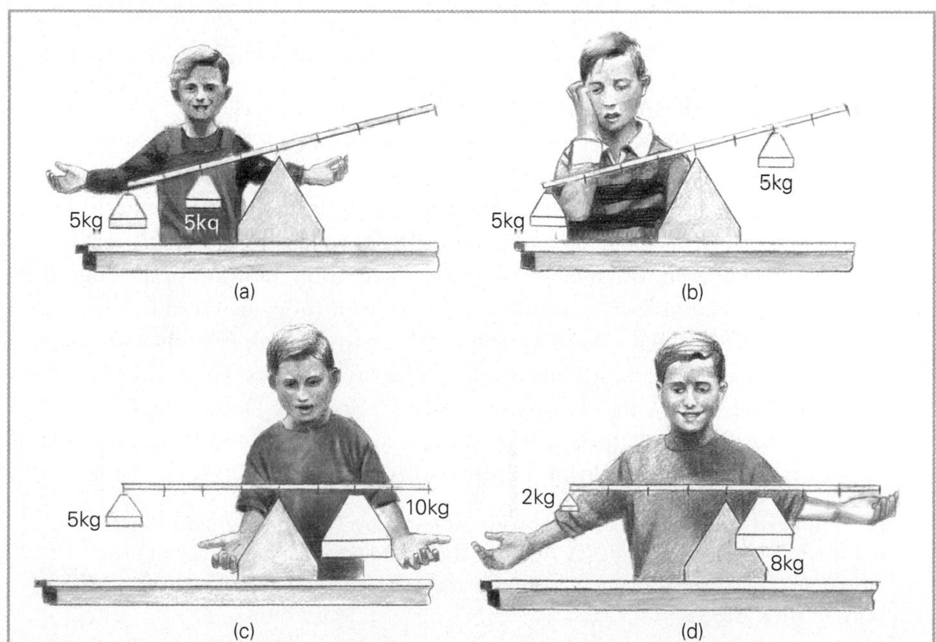

FIGURE 15.1

How to Balance a Scale Piaget's balance-scale test of formal reasoning, as it is attempted by *(a)* a 4-year-old, *(b)* a 7-year-old, *(c)* a 10-year-old, and *(d)* a 14-year-old. The key to balancing the scale is to make weight times distance from the center equal on both sides of the center; the realization of that principle requires formal operational thought.

Finally, by about age 13 or 14, some children hypothesized the reciprocal relationship between weight and distance, tested this hypothesis, and formulated the mathematical formula, solving the balance problem accurately and efficiently. Piaget attributed each of these advances to attainment of the next cognitive stage beyond concrete operations (Piaget & Inhelder, 1969).

Hypothetical-Deductive Thought

One hallmark of formal operational thought is the capacity to think of possibility, not just reality. Adolescents "start with possible solutions and progress to determine which is the real solution" (Lutz & Sternberg, 1999, p. 283). "Here and now" is only one of many alternatives, including "there and then," "long, long ago," "nowhere," "not yet," and "never." As Piaget said:

> The adolescent . . . thinks beyond the present and forms theories about everything, delighting especially in considerations of that which is not . . .
>
> *[Piaget, 1972, p. 148]*

hypothetical thought Reasoning that includes propositions and possibilities that may not reflect reality.

Tiny Elephants Adolescents are therefore primed to engage in **hypothetical thought,** reasoning about *what-if* propositions that may or may not reflect reality. For example, consider this question:

> If dogs are bigger than elephants, and
> If mice are bigger than dogs,
> Are elephants smaller than mice?

Younger children, presented with such counterfactual questions, answer no. They have seen elephants and mice, so the logic escapes them. Some adolescents answer yes. They understand what *if* means (Moshman, 2005).

Note that this is an advanced example of *transitive inference,* explained in Chapter 12. School-age children learn to do simple comparisons ("Jim is taller than David"), but they are confused when a comparison contradicts what they know. Not only are some adolescents successful at such logic, but they proudly say, "Yes, elephants are smaller than mice." As Piaget said:

> *Possibility* no longer appears merely as an extension of an empirical situation or of action actually performed. Instead, it is *reality* that is now secondary to *possibility.*
>
> *[Inhelder & Piaget, 1958, p. 251; emphasis in original]*

Conviction and Criticism Hypothetical thought transforms a person's perceptions, although not necessarily for the better. Adolescents' reflection about serious issues becomes complicated because they consider many possibilities, sometimes sidetracking logical conclusions about the immediate issues (Moshman, 2005).

For example, a survey of U.S. teenagers' religious ideas found that most 13- to 17-year-olds considered themselves religious and thought that practicing their particular faith would help them avoid hell. However, they hesitated to follow that conviction to the next logical step by trying to convince their friends to believe as they did. As one explained, "I can't speak for everybody, it's up to them. I know what's best for me, and I can't, I don't, preach" (C. Smith & Denton, 2005, p. 147).

Similarly, a high school student who wanted to keep a friend from committing suicide hesitated to judge her friend's intentions because

> to . . . judge [someone] means that whatever you are saying is right and you know what's right. You know it's right for them and you know it's right in every situation. [But] you can't know if you are right. Maybe you are right. But then, right in what way?
>
> *[quoted in Gilligan et al., 1990]*

Although adolescents are not always sure what is "right in what way," they see what is wrong. At every age, it is easier to criticize something than to create it, but criticism itself shows an advance in reasoning. Unlike younger children, adolescents do not necessarily accept current conditions. They criticize everything from the way their mother cooks spaghetti to why the Gregorian calendar, not the Chinese or Jewish one, is used to count the years. They criticize what *is*, precisely because of their hypothetical thinking.

Abstract Thinking In developing the capacity to think hypothetically, by age 14 or so adolescents become capable of **deductive reasoning,** or *top-down reasoning,* which begins with an abstract idea or premise and then uses logic to draw specific conclusions (Galotti, 2002; Keating, 2004). By contrast, **inductive reasoning,** or *bottom-up reasoning,* predominates during the school years, as children accumulate facts and personal experiences (the knowledge base) to aid their thought.

deductive reasoning Reasoning from a general statement, premise, or principle, through logical steps, to figure out (deduce) specifics. (Also called *top-down reasoning.*)

inductive reasoning Reasoning from one or more specific experiences or facts to reach (induce) a general conclusion. (Also called *bottom-up reasoning.*)

In essence, a child's reasoning goes like this: "This creature waddles and quacks. Ducks waddle and quack. Therefore, this must be a duck." This reasoning is inductive: It progresses from particulars ("waddles" and "quacks") to a general conclusion ("It's a duck"). By contrast, deduction progresses from the general to the specific: "If it's a duck, it will waddle and quack" (see Figure 15.2).

Most developmentalists agree with Piaget that adolescent thought can be qualitatively different from children's thought (Fischer & Bidell, 1998; Flavell et al., 2002; Keating, 2004; Moshman, 2005). They disagree about whether this change is quite sudden (Piaget) or more gradual (information-processing theory); about whether change results from context (sociocultural theory) or from biological changes (epigenetic theory); about whether changes occur universally in every domain (Piaget) or more selectively (all other major theories).

Many studies have found that some adolescents and adults still reason like concrete operational children, and "no contemporary scholarly reviewer of research evidence endorses the emergence of a discrete new cognitive structure at adolescence that closely resembles . . . formal operations" (Kuhn & Franklin, 2006, p. 954). In other words, logical thinking becomes more possible at adolescence, but it is probably not a separate new cognitive structure, as Piaget seemed to believe.

These criticisms of Piaget are familiar from previous chapters. There is much more cognitive variability at every age than Piaget seemed to recognize. Piaget "launched the systematic study of adolescent cognitive development" (Keating, 2004, p. 45), but his description is not the final word.

AP PHOTO / LAS CRUCES SUN-NEWS, VLADIM R CHALOUPKA

A Proud Teacher "Is it possible to train a cockroach?" This hypothetical question, an example of formal operational thought, was posed by 15-year-old Tristan Williams of New Mexico. In his award-winning science project, he succeeded in conditioning Madagascar cockroaches to hiss at the sight of a permanent marker. (His parents' logical reasoning about having 600 cockroaches living in their home is not known.)

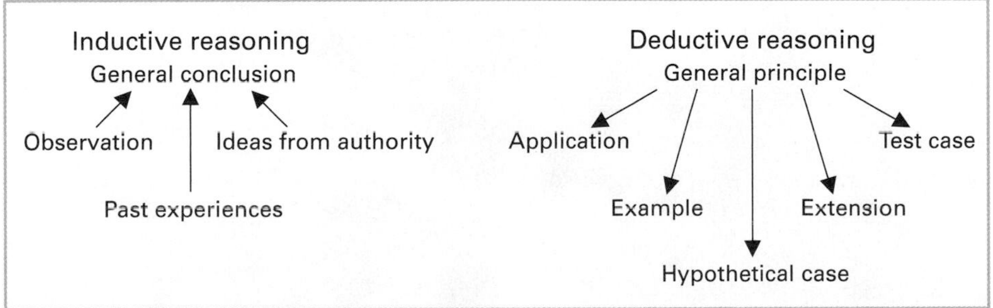

FIGURE 15.2

Bottom Up or Top Down? Children, as concrete operational thinkers, are likely to draw conclusions on the basis of their own experiences and what they have been told. This is called inductive, or bottom-up, reasoning. Adolescents can think deductively, from the top down.

Especially for Natural Scientists (see response, page 451): Some ideas that were once universally accepted, such as the belief that the sun moved around the earth, have been disproved. Is it a failure of inductive or deductive reasoning that leads to false conclusions?

Intuitive, Emotional Thought

As many developmentalists over the past three decades have shown, the fact that adolescents *can* use hypothetical-deductive reasoning does not necessarily mean that they *do* use it (Kuhn & Franklin, 2006). Adolescents find it much easier and quicker to forget about logic and follow their impulses.

Two Modes of Thinking

dual-process model The notion that two networks exist within the human brain, one for emotional and one for analytical processing of stimuli.

Advanced logical thought is counterbalanced by the increasing power of intuitive thinking. A **dual-process model** of adolescent cognition has been formulated.

Researchers are increasingly convinced that the brain has at least two distinct pathways, called *dual-processing networks.* The two processing networks have been designated by various names: intuitive/analytic, implicit/explicit, creative/factual, contextualized/decontextualized, unconscious/conscious, gist/quantitative, emotional/intellectual, experiential/rational. These terms are not interchangeable, but they all describe aspects of the same phenomenon: The mind is not one simple structure but has multiple functions and pathways (Evans, 2008).

The type of thinking described by the first half of each pair is more commonly used, preferred unless circumstances compel activation of the second, more taxing, mode. We focus here on one pair that seems especially relevant during adolescence, the intuitive/analytic pair (Gerrard et al., 2008).

intuitive thought Thought that arises from an emotion or a hunch, beyond rational explanation, and is influenced by past experiences and cultural assumptions.

analytic thought Thought that results from analysis, such as a systematic ranking of pros and cons, risks and consequences, possibilities and facts. Analytic thought depends on logic and rationality.

- **Intuitive thought** begins with a prior belief, past experience, or common assumption, rather than with a logical premise. Thoughts spring forth from memories and feelings. Intuitive cognition is quick and powerful; it feels "right."
- **Analytic thought** is the formal, logical, hypothetical-deductive thinking described by Piaget. It involves rational analysis of many factors whose interactions must be calculated, as in the scale-balancing problem. Analytic thinking requires a certain level of intellectual maturity, brain capacity, motivation, and practice.

When the two modes of thinking conflict, adults sometimes use one and sometimes the other (De Neys, 2008), but they try to coordinate them because there are "two systems but one reasoner" (De Neys & Glumicic, 2006, p. 428). Thoughts in each

BOB DAEMMRICH / THE IMAGE WORKS

Dual Processing Signs of both analysis and emotion are evident in these two girls at a school in south Texas. They are using wireless computers to study, perhaps analyzing information, formatting questions, and drawing logical conclusions. At the same time, intuitive thinking is also on display: The girls are sitting side by side for companionship and are dressed similarly, wearing shoes designed more for fashion than for walking.

mode either coexist or conflict, and *both* modes advance during adolescence. The foundation of both processes is the brain, which in adolescence allows "stronger, more effective neuronal connections" (Kuhn & Franklin, 2006, p. 957).

➤Response for Natural Scientists (from page 449): Probably both. Our false assumptions are not logically tested, because we do not realize that they might need testing.

Comparing Intuition and Analysis

Paul Klaczynski has conducted many studies comparing the thinking of children, young adolescents, and older adolescents (usually 9-, 12-, and 15-year-olds). In one study, Klaczynski (2001) presented 19 logical problems. For example:

> Timothy is very good-looking, strong, and does not smoke. He likes hanging around with his male friends, watching sports on TV, and driving his Ford Mustang convertible. He's very concerned with how he looks and with being in good shape. He is a high school senior now and is trying to get a college scholarship.
>
> *Based on this [description], rank each statement in terms of how likely it is to be true. . . . The most likely statement should get a 1. The least likely statement should get a 6.*
>
> _____ Timothy has a girlfriend.
> _____ Timothy is an athlete.
> _____ Timothy is popular and an athlete.
> _____ Timothy is a teacher's pet and has a girlfriend.
> _____ Timothy is a teacher's pet.
> _____ Timothy is popular.

Her Whole Brain Chess players like this girl, who is competing in a Connecticut championship match, must be analytic, thinking several moves ahead. But sometimes an unexpected intuitive move unnerves the opposition and leads to victory.

PETER HVIZDAK / THE IMAGE WORKS

In ranking these statements, most (73 percent) of the students made at least one analytic error. Their mistake was to rank a double statement (e.g., popular *and* athlete) as more likely than a single statement included in it (popular *or* athlete). A double statement cannot be more likely than either of its parts; therefore, those 73 percent were illogical and wrong.

This error is an example of intuitive thought: The adolescents jumped to the more inclusive statement, taking a quick, experiential leap rather than sticking to the logical task at hand.

In this study, almost all adolescents were analytical and logical on some of the 19 problems but not on others. Logical thinking improved with age and education, although not with IQ. In other words, being smarter as measured by an intelligence test did not advance logical reasoning as much as having more experience, in school and in life. Klaczynski (2001) concluded that, even though teenagers *can* use logic, "most adolescents do not demonstrate a level of performance commensurate with their abilities" (p. 854).

Preferred Conclusions What would motivate adolescents to use—or fail to use—their formal operational thinking? The students in the example above had learned the scientific method in school, and they knew that scientists use empirical evidence and deductive reasoning. But they did not always think like scientists. Why not?

Dozens of experiments and extensive theorizing have found some answers (Diamond & Kirkham, 2005; Klaczynski, 2005; Kuhn & Franklin, 2006). Essentially, logic is more difficult than intuition, and it does not always feel right. It sometimes leads people to doubt their comfortable, long-standing prejudices. Once people (of any age) reach an emotional conclusion (sometimes called a "gut feeling"), they resist changing their minds, avoiding logic that might reveal their poor judgment.

Egocentrism makes rational analysis even more difficult, as one psychologist discovered when her teenage son called late one night to be picked up from a party that had "gotten out of hand." The boy heard

> his frustrated father lament "drinking and trouble—haven't you figured out the connection?" Despite the late hour and his shaky state, the teenager advanced a lengthy argument to the effect that his father had the causality all wrong and the trouble should be attributed to other covariates, among them bad luck.
>
> *[Kuhn & Franklin, 2006, p. 966]*

sunk cost fallacy The mistaken belief that if money, time, or effort that cannot be recovered (a "sunk cost," in economic terms) has already been invested in some endeavor, then more should be invested in an effort to reach the goal. Because of this fallacy, people spend money continuing to try to fix a "lemon" of a car or sending more troops to fight a losing battle.

Common Fallacies Research confirming the difficulty of thinking scientifically comes from experiments on the **sunk cost fallacy.** The sunk cost fallacy is the mistaken assumption that, because a person has already spent money, time, or effort that cannot be recovered (a cost already "sunk"), the person should continue to spend in an effort to achieve the desired goal. People of all ages make this error, investing money to repair a "lemon" of a car, staying in a class they are failing, and so on.

An example used in the research asked people whether they would watch more of a movie they disliked if they had paid for it (e.g., on pay-per-view TV) than if it were free. People of all ages said yes (Klaczynski & Cottrell, 2004). Similarly, people of all ages are much more likely to change the channel on a movie they see in their own home, even if they expect that movie to be good, than to leave a theater showing the same film after they had paid for a ticket.

Adolescents are better than younger children at recognizing the sunk cost fallacy, realizing that "just because you made a mistake in paying to see a stupid movie, you don't need to torture yourself by watching the whole thing." But they don't necessarily act on this wisdom. Every teenager sometimes keeps on doing something (skipping school, smoking cigarettes, riding with a drunk driver) simply because once they start it is difficult to stop.

base rate neglect A common fallacy in which a person ignores the overall frequency of some behavior or characteristic (called the *base rate*) in making a decision. For example, a person might bet on a "lucky" lottery number without considering the odds that that number will be selected.

Another common fallacy is called **base rate neglect** (Barbey & Sloman, 2007), in which a person ignores statistical information about the frequency of a phenomenon and instead makes a decision on some emotional basis, such as a vivid example. For instance, a person might refuse to wear a bicycle helmet, despite statistics that show helmets save lives, until a friend is brain-damaged in an accident. Or a person might drive instead of fly after reading a story about a plane crash, ignoring statistics that airplane travel is safer. Indeed, after the terrorist attacks of 9/11, many Americans refused to fly, and highway fatalities increased.

A dual-process interpretation of such fallacies is that people prefer the easiest way to think (Barbey & Sloman, 2007). Of course, in this, as in all research, variability is evident: Logic is not universal, and yet not always absent, at adolescence.

Better Thinking

Sometimes adults define "better thinking" as a more cautious approach (as in the father's connection between "trouble" and alcohol in the excerpt above). Adults are particularly critical of the egocentrism that leads a teenager to risk future addiction by experimenting with drugs or to risk pregnancy and AIDS in order to avoid the awkwardness of using a condom.

But adults may themselves be egocentric in making such judgments, assuming that adolescents share their values. Parents want healthy, long-living children, and they conclude that adolescents miscalculate or use faulty reasoning when they make decisions that risk their lives. Adolescents, however, value social warmth and friendship. A 15-year-old who is offered a cigarette might make a rational decision to choose immediate social acceptance over the distant risk of cancer (Engels et al., 2006).

Adolescent thinking (including egocentrism) can be positive; it is not necessarily selfish or irrational (Reyna & Farley, 2006). Intuitive thinking is quick and passionate—and thus is sometimes beneficial. As one expert explains, "Zeal in adolescents can fuel positive humanistic efforts to feed the poor and care for the sick, yet it can also lead to dogmatic attitudes, intolerance . . . passions captured by a negatively charismatic figure like Adolf Hitler or Osama bin Laden" (Dahl, 2004, p. 21). Adolescents are said to "ride the waves of historical events" (B. Brown & Larson, 2002, p. 12), being noble or naive depending on the immediate context.

At every age, sometimes the best thinking is "fast and frugal" (Gigerenzer et al., 1999). Weighing alternatives, and thinking of possibilities, may become paralyzing. The systematic, analytic thought that Piaget described may be slow and costly—wasting precious time when a young person should take action.

As the knowledge base increases, thinking processes accelerate: Analysis and intuition both become more forceful. With age, thinking gains efficiency and is less likely to reach an impasse. Ideally, people use any thought process that leads to a good conclusion. It is efficient to use formal, analytic thinking in science class and to use emotional, experiential thinking (which is quicker and more satisfying) for personal issues, and this is what tends to happen in adolescence (Kuhn & Franklin, 2006). By adulthood, at least some rationality combines with emotionality.

Which mode of thinking is best when the topic is religious beliefs? Most adolescents use intuitive, not analytic, thinking for religious matters, as the following explains. Whether that is better or worse depends on one's perspective.

a view from science

Teenage Religion

As you remember from Chapter 1, scientists build on previous research or theories, replicating, extending, or disputing the work of others. Scientists question assumptions, seeking empirical evidence to verify or refute both new theories and old cultural myths. This is a formal operational approach.

Some impressionistic descriptions of teenagers and religion (e.g., Flory & Miller, 2000) emphasize cults and sects. Young congregants gather, "dressed as they are, piercings and all, and express their commitment by means of hip-hop and rap music, multimedia presentations, body modification, and anything else that can be infused with religious meaning" (Ream & Savin-Williams, 2003, p. 51).

This description evokes many emotions—the quick, intuitive responses of most adults that judge piercings and rap music to be the antithesis of true religion. Such subjective impressions, however, neither verify nor refute reality—only science does. Intuitive thought is not always correct.

A team of researchers began by "reading many published overview reports on adolescence . . . [which provided] the distinct impression that American youth simply do not have religious or spiritual lives" (C. Smith & Denton, 2005, p. 4). But, thinking like scientists, they sought evidence (see the Research Design).

The researchers found that most adolescents (71 percent) felt close to God and believed in heaven, hell, and angels. Most identified with the same religious tradition as their parents (78 percent Christian, 3 percent Jewish or Muslim). Some were agnostic (2 percent), and 16 percent said they were not religious, although many of those attended church and prayed. Less than 1 percent were unconventional (e.g., Wiccan).

Research Design

Scientist: Christian Smith (with Melinda Lundquist Denton and more than 100 other colleagues and graduate students).

Publication: *Soul Searching,* Oxford University Press (2005).

Participants: Between 2001 and 2003, in the National Study of Youth and Religion, 3,360 13- to 18-year-olds and one of their parents were interviewed by phone. A subsample of 287 were interviewed privately in person. To secure a representative sample, a random-digit-dial telephone survey of families throughout the United States was conducted to find families with at least one member between the ages of 13 and 17 who would be willing to talk.

Design: Each participant was asked questions regarding religion, school, family, sex, and drugs. Data were analyzed and reported by religious allegiance, family background, and various beliefs.

Major conclusion: Religion *is* important to most adolescents, who are much less critical or disaffected than has been portrayed.

Comment: Research on religious beliefs and development has been avoided by many scientists, partly because any conclusions are likely to be rejected by some adherents and partly because it is not easy to distinguish religious from cultural beliefs. This study is part of a new wave of research; much more needs to be published in order to understand the role of religion in development.

This study showed that adolescents' religious beliefs seemed egocentric, with faith seen as a personal tool to be used in times of difficulty (e.g., while taking an exam). Most adolescents (60 percent) said they believed that "many religions might be true." One said:

> I think every religion is important in its own respect. You know, if you're Muslim, then Islam is the way for you. If you are Jewish, well, that's great too. If you're Christian, well, good for you. It's just whatever makes you feel good about you."
>
> *[quoted in C. Smith & Denton, 2005, p. 163]*

Many respondents (82 percent) claimed that their beliefs were important to their daily life. One boy explained that religion kept him from doing "bad things, like murder or something," and one girl said:

> [Religion] influences me a lot with the people I choose not to be around. I would not hang with people that are, you know, devil worshipers because that's just not my thing, I could not deal with that negativity.
>
> *[quoted in C. Smith & Denton, 2005, p. 139]*

EPA / CORBIS

Sacred Thread Every religion has some ritual in which young people make a public commitment to their faith. These Hindu boys are receiving the *jenoi,* a sacred thread that they will wear all their lives. In this initiation ceremony, they shave their heads, wear new robes, and vow to pray three times a day and to study the Vedas, or scriptures.

The researchers doubt that "socializing with Satanists is a real issue in this girl's life" or that this boy "struggles with murderous tendencies" (C. Smith & Denton, 2005, p. 139). Although daily life in the modern United States presents many ethical issues, few adolescents reported using theology to guide them. Less than 1 percent connected religion with repentance, seeking justice, or loving one's neighbor. For most, religious beliefs were intuitive, not analytic. Religion seemed to assure individuals that they were all right (the most devout were less depressed) and occasionally served to bolster their criticisms of their parents.

What does this research imply for adults who hope to instill values in the next generation? In many ways, these data are encouraging: Most children and adolescents adhere to the faith and values of their parents.

However, the authors report that adolescent faith is often superficial and selfish, because that is what they glean from their parents. The conclusions are that teenagers need to discuss and debate and study complex spiritual issues (e.g., humankind's stewardship of the environment or the ethical relationship between rich and poor or the meaning of scriptures) to help them grasp the struggles of faith, not just the rituals of religion.

SUMMING UP

Thinking reaches heightened self-consciousness at puberty, when adolescent egocentrism may be apparent. Some young adolescents have unrealistic notions about their place in the social world, imagining themselves as invincible, unique, and the center of attention. Adults often criticize this self-awareness, but it shows a cognitive advance and may be shaped by the social context.

Piaget thought the fourth and final stage of intelligence, called formal operational thought, began in adolescence. He found that adolescents improve in deductive logic and hypothetical thinking. However, current research recognizes the dual processing of cognition: People sometimes use analytical thinking and sometimes prefer quick, intuitive reasoning. This second kind of thinking is experiential, quicker, and more intense than formal operational thought.

Because every form of thought advances during adolescence, teenagers know more, think faster, and use systematic analysis and abstract logic beyond the capability of younger children. Emotional passions, with fast and frugal thinking, may be preferred over logical, methodical thought. ■

Teaching and Learning

Given the nature of the adolescent brain and mind, what and how should teenagers be taught? Many educators, developmentalists, political leaders, and parents want to know exactly what curricula and school structures are best for 11- to 18-year-olds.

We cannot present any one answer here, because the research does not support any single answer. Various scientists, nations, and schools are trying many different strategies, some of which are based on opposite, but logical, hypotheses. We can, however, provide some definitions, facts, issues, and possibilities.

Secondary education—traditionally grades 7 through 12—is the term used to describe the school years after elementary or grade school (known as *primary education*) and before college or university (known as *tertiary education*). The importance of secondary education is widely recognized, as adults in every nation are healthier and wealthier if they have graduated from high school. Worldwide, "secondary education has [the] transformational ability to change lives for the better. . . . For young people all over the world, primary education is no longer enough" (World Bank, 2005, pp. xi–xii).

secondary education Literally the period after primary education (elementary or grade school) and before tertiary education (college). It usually occurs from about age 12 to 18, although there is some variation by school and by nation.

Even such a seemingly unrelated condition as heart disease (the leading killer worldwide) is about 50 percent more common among those who never graduated from high school than among those who graduated but never went to college (MMWR, February 16, 2007). This statistic comes from the United States, but data from every nation and every ethnic group indicate that high school graduation is a surprising boon to every aspect of health.

Partly because political leaders recognize that an educated population advances national wealth, the number of students in secondary schools is increasing rapidly. In 2004, 78 percent of the world's children received some secondary education: This included virtually all the 10- to 14-year-olds in the Americas, East Asia, and Europe; 64 percent in South Asia; and 36 percent in sub-Saharan Africa (UNESCO, 2006). Note that these are young adolescents; not all of them stay to graduate from high school. In developed nations, more than 90 percent of 16-year-olds are in school, and the rates rise each year (see Figure 15.3). About two-thirds stay to graduate.

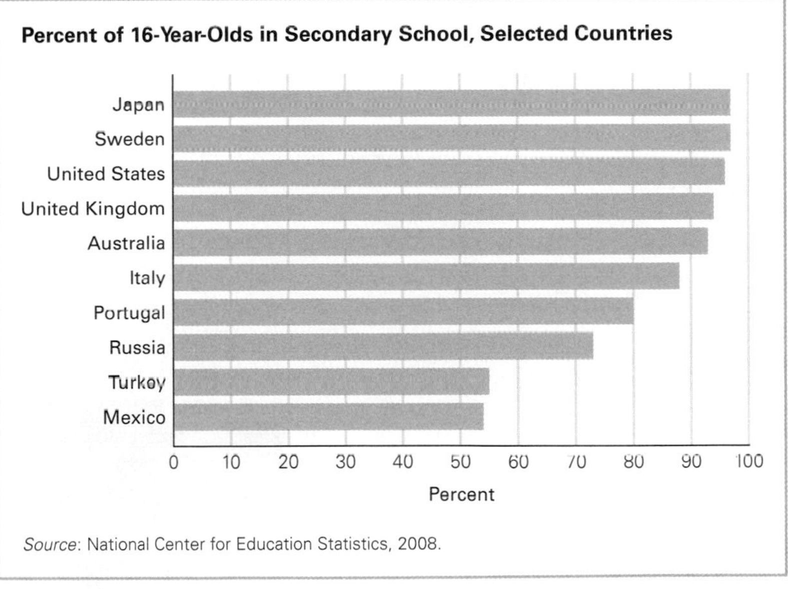

FIGURE 15.3

High School: Obligation or Privilege? In developed nations, almost every adolescent attends high school. Poorer countries, realizing that education is the key to prosperity, are striving to catch up by making secondary education more widely available.

Although almost everyone agrees that adolescents should be educated, and although no one doubts that secondary education correlates with health and wealth for individuals as well as for nations, many disagree about what and how students should be taught. No nation seems to succeed with every student.

Middle School

In the United States and many other nations, two levels of secondary education are provided for children who have completed primary school. These schools were traditionally divided into junior high schools for younger students (usually grades 7 and 8) and senior high schools for older children (usually grades 9 through 12). More recently, intermediate schools, or **middle schools,** have been established to educate children in grades 6, 7, and 8.

middle school A school for children in the grades between elementary and high school. Middle school usually begins with grade 5 or 6 and ends with grade 8.

Less Learning

During the middle school years, academic achievement often slows down and behavioral problems become more commonplace. The first year of middle school has been called the "low ebb" of learning (Covington & Dray, 2002), a time when many teachers feel ineffective (Eccles, 2004). Similar patterns of lower achievement and problem behavior occur in many places besides the United States, including Australia, when students become less conscientious about school as they age from 12 to 14 (Heaven & Ciarrochi, 2008).

Especially for Middle School Teachers (see response, page 458): You think your lectures are interesting and you know you care about your students, yet many of them cut class, come late, or seem to sleep through it. What do you do?

A child's middle school experience affects later decisions about education. "Long-term academic trajectories—the choice to stay in school or to drop out and the selection in high school of academic college-prep courses versus basic level courses—are strongly influenced by experience in grades 6–8" (Snow et al., 2007, p. 72).

Many developmentalists think that one crucial problem in middle school is that students lose close connection to teachers, partly because each teacher has dozens, sometimes hundreds, of students. Large class sizes are troublesome because throughout secondary education, bonding between students and teachers is key to student learning as well as to helping children avoid risky behavior (Crosnoe et al., 2004).

Students' relationships with one another also deteriorate in middle school, partly because they suddenly find themselves among hundreds of strangers, many older and bigger than they are. Because new middle school students have many classmates they have never seen before, first impressions become especially significant. Unfortunately, this coincides with the various physiological changes (described in Chapter 14) that make each developing person acutely self-conscious about appearance.

At puberty, friendships and peer groups are crucial for providing validation. Several studies find that aggressive and drug-using students in middle schools tend to be admired over those who are conscientious and studious—a marked difference from elementary school experience (Allen et al., 2005; Mayeux & Cillessen, 2007). To become popular, or to stay popular, many middle school students stop associating with unpopular peers (Rose et al., 2004).

ANDREW LICHTENSTEIN / CORBIS

A School Connection Middle schools are more likely to succeed when they combine high academic standards with consistent discipline and high motivation among both students and teachers. This public school in New York City's South Bronx is affiliated with the Knowledge Is Power Program, offering college preparation to students from low-income families.

Concerns about being popular may prevent many students from emulating those who are studious—the so-called geeks and nerds. Many students at this age would rather sacrifice their academic standing than risk social exclusion. This was found for math achievement in middle schools in three nations (Germany, Canada, and Israel); mathematically gifted girls were particularly likely to underachieve (Boehnke, 2008). Boys may also consider academic success to be unattractive, as James did.

a personal perspective

James, the High-Achieving Dropout

A longitudinal study in Massachusetts followed children from preschool through high school. Of all the children in the study, James was one of the most promising. In his early school years, he was an excellent reader whose mother took great pride in him—her only child. Once James entered middle school, however, the situation changed:

> Although still performing well academically, James began acting out. At first his actions could be described as merely mischievous, but later he engaged in much more serious acts, such as drinking and fighting, which resulted in his being suspended from school. He said, "The kids were definitely afraid of me but that didn't stop them" from being his friends.
>
> *[Snow et al., 2007, p. 59]*

In middle school, James felt disconnected from his teachers and counselors. He said he had "a complete lack of motivation." At the end of primary school, James planned to go to college; by tenth grade, he had left school completely. This suggests that James may have been one of the "boys who choose to emphasize their masculine identities [and] may thus actively avoid literacy activities and academic success" (Snow et al., 2007, p. 64).

Often family conflicts increase at around the time middle school begins (Shanahan et al., 2007). That happened with James. He and his abusive father blamed each other for every problem. James did not blame his mother, but she mistakenly thought that James was as self-sufficient as his physical growth made him appear. She "talked about how independent James was for being able to be left alone to fend for himself, [while] he described himself as isolated and closed off" (Snow et al., 2007, p. 59).

Conflict between parents was the issue for an eighth-grade boy in another study conducted halfway around the world, in South Korea. He says:

> I tried many times to do some studying, but when I came home, I had no place to study. The strange thing was whenever I had resolve to do homework, my mom and dad messed around the home [having an argument].
>
> *[quoted in Choi, 2005, p. 274]*

As the examples of these two boys show, the problems of young adolescents are "widespread and almost certainly multiply determined" (Snow et al., 2007, p. 63)—that is, pervasive and with many causes. A decline in achievement and motivation in middle school is not atypical (Covington & Dray, 2002), but school itself is not the only reason.

Nevertheless, many developmentalists agree that, instead of being supportive of developing egos, middle schools are "developmentally regressive" (Eccles, 2004, p. 141)—they force children to take a step backward. Think of your own middle school experience and that of your peers. A personal perspective on this issue could include you. (Send your story to Dr. Berger if you wish.)

Fear of Failure

To pinpoint the developmental mismatch between students' needs and the middle school environment, note that just when egocentrism leads young people to feelings of shame or fantasies of stardom (performing for an imaginary audience), their school schedule requires them to change rooms, teachers, and classmates every 40 minutes or so. That near-constant movement makes public acclaim, personal recognition, and even personal comfort difficult.

When extracurricular activities become competitive, fragile egos may shun the glare of attention from coaches, advisers, or other students. In middle school, grades often fall because teachers grade more harshly and students become less conscientious. Extracurricular activities that welcome all youth and catch their interest are scarce.

BOB DAEMMRICH / THE IMAGE WORKS

Isolated No More This huge lunchroom in a Texas high school could make any student sad, anxious, and lonely. Technology can help, though. This ninth-grade girl has her cell phone and MP3 player, so a potentially lonely lunch break is a happy, sociable time instead.

Research Design

Scientists: Jaana Juvonen, Adrienne Nishina, and Sandra Graham.

Publication: *Psychological Science* (2006).

Participants: A total of 2,000 middle school students from 99 classrooms in 11 Los Angeles middle schools, all low income, with ethnic diversity.

Design: Students answered questionnaires about safety, loneliness, victimization, and self-worth. Diversity was calculated by the likelihood that any two random students in a class or a school would be of the same race. Particular focus was placed on the two groups with the greatest number of students—Latino and African American.

Major conclusion: Diversity in the classrooms as well as in the schools led to less loneliness and a greater feeling of safety.

Comment: As the authors point out, "the possibility that there is safety in diversity—as opposed to safety in numbers—is an optimistic one" (p. 399). The focus on low-income Mexican and African Americans is commendable. This research needs to be extended to include, for example, Asian minority students who, according to other research, experience more bullying.

One way that young adolescents cope with stress is to blame their troubles on others—classmates, teachers, parents, governments. This may help explain the results of a study in Los Angeles: Those in more ethnically diverse schools felt safer and less lonely (Juvonen et al., 2006; see the Research Design). The researchers suggest that students who feel victimized "can attribute their plight to the prejudice of other people" rather than blame themselves for their plight (Juvonen et al., 2006, p. 398).

How can middle schools encourage rather than discourage adolescent learning? Egocentrism, intuitive thought, and logic coexist within every student. Appealing to those characteristics by providing the emotional and personal excitement of role-playing, debating, and group interaction may keep students engaged.

Many middle school reforms are currently under way, and they show varying degrees of success (Roney et al., 2004). Some research has found that "differential learning"—treating "students as individual learners" within each class—advances education in middle schools (May & Supovitz, 2006, p. 252).

Technology and Cognition

Adults have divergent perspectives regarding electronic technology and teenage cognition. Some hope that computers will be a boon to learning, creating a new generation of better-informed, technologically savvy youth. Others fear that rapid advances in technology will undercut respect for adults and schools, that egocentrism will run wild when adolescents realize how much more they know about the new technology than their parents do (Hern & Chaulk, 1997; Roschelle et al., 2000).

The advance of technology, however, is far outpacing any attempts by adults to prevent, or even reduce, its impact. A mere two decades ago, no one knew about the World Wide Web, instant messaging, chat rooms, blogs, iPods, Blackberries, or digital cameras. Yet today, teenagers are intimately acquainted with all of these technologies, even creating whole new texting "languages" to communicate with one another. In 1995, only half of all U.S. public schools had Internet capacity; now just about all of them do (see Figure 15.4; U.S. Bureau of the Census, 2007).

➤**Response for Middle School Teachers** (from page 456): Students need both challenge and involvement; avoid lessons that are too easy or too passive. Create small groups; assign oral reports, debates, and role-plays; and so on. Remember that adolescents like to hear one another's thoughts and their own voices.

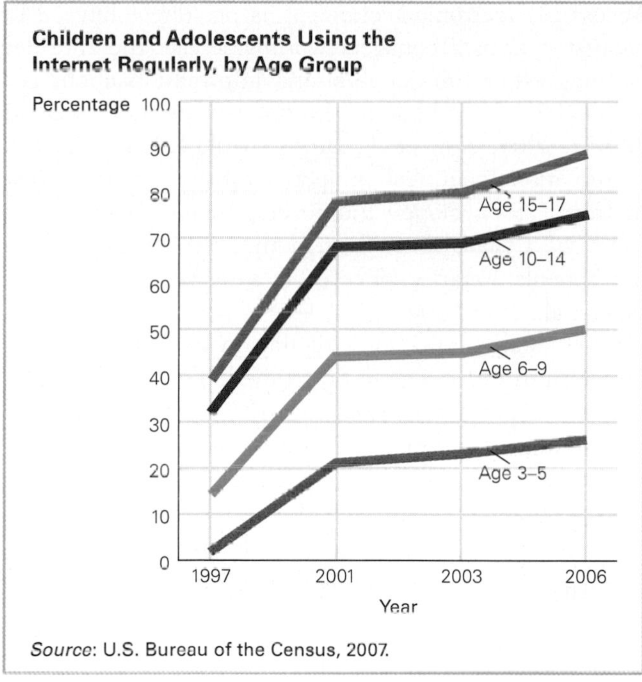

FIGURE 15.4

Logging On This graph shows the explosive increase in Internet use by children of all ages, especially teenagers, that has occurred since the mid-1990s. By age 18, almost every U.S. teenager is using the Internet at home, at school, or both, to check news, connect with friends, or find information. (Note: The data for 1997–2003 used identical questions and reliable survey methods from the annual Current Population Reports, published by the U.S. Bureau of the Census. Because CPR data for 2006 were not yet available as of this writing, the percentages given for that year are estimates and are not directly comparable with the data for other years.)

The Digital Divide

The **digital divide,** as the gap between people who have access to computers and those who do not is called, was bemoaned in the 1990s because it separated boys from girls and rich from poor (Dijk, 2005; Norris, 2001). However, in the United States and most other developed nations, the digital divide has been bridged.

digital divide The gap between people who have access to computers and those who do not, often a gap between rich and poor. In the United States and most other developed nations, this gap has now been bridged as computers have become almost universally present in schools and libraries.

In the United States, age is now the greatest divider between Internet users and nonusers. Income and ethnicity gaps in Internet use are shrinking every year, and the gender gap has all but disappeared; generational differences remain. To be specific, in 2005 (the year of the latest reliable statistics) the proportion of adolescents who used the Internet (78 percent) was by far the largest of any age group. The proportion of Internet users over age 65 was lowest (20 percent) (Snyder et al., 2006).

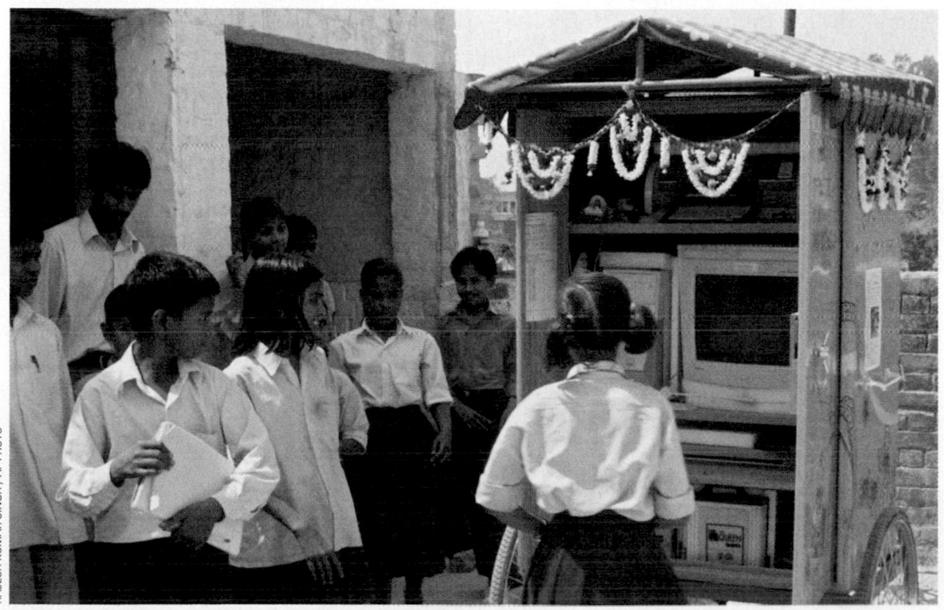

RAJESH KUMAR SINGH / AP PHOTO

Middle School Slump? These students in rural India are the same age as middle school students in developed nations, but their enthusiasm for school has not waned. One reason is that they do not take education for granted; only a select few are able to stay in school beyond age 11. Another reason may be seen here: The government is trying to upgrade the curriculum by providing traveling, Internet-connected computers.

Hello . . . . I believe that Katia has spoken for most of us when she tells us how discouraged she is. I have heard it from many other people and have heard of stagnation in other discussion groups. I am very frustrated right now. The groups I am in aren't doing much. . . . It's awfully discouraging! But think of it from the perspective that we are all part of an incredible process, a process which has never before happened in the history of humanity. We are all children, essentially "dumped" into virtual rooms with a broad topic in mind, and the rest is ultimately up to us. It's difficult! The process, like any (life, school, work, a hike, everything) has its ups and downs. That sounds kind of trite—but it's true. And it's inevitable. And it is very valuable for us as human beings. Perhaps even more so than changing the world, we are learning and growing personally, which IS indirectly shaping the future. . . . Practically speaking, I have a suggestion as to how we all can move forward from this point, and get out of the "rut."

1. Every group, think clearly and put something together in writing asking the question, "What is our ultimate goal?" I think that putting a finger on all of the objectives both practical and philosophical will be a good starting point.

2. Then, start by making a timeline to carry out those objectives—dividing them, starting small and then building it up. For example, "In the first two weeks we need to figure out a general organizational flow for our project. The week following that, we need to go into finer details and figure out what sub-groups will exist. The 4th week, we need to figure out how people will be elected and how people will carry out the tasks in each group. Blah, blah, blah."

. . . And, through time and through perseverance, it will take off! I hope that we can all move forward and get back into the fun and excitement of our work and play. I am so privileged to know all of you. I feel happy and look forward to all the years we will have together. What are all your thoughts?

Source: Quoted in Cassell et al., 2006.

FIGURE 15.5

Discouraged, But . . . You might think that the logical analysis shown in this e-mail must come from a wise adult; but, no, the writer is 14 years old. He is in India, writing to adolescents he had not met in nations he had not visited. This project joined adolescents worldwide in a junior political summit.

Access to electronic technology is no longer limited to developed nations. Teenagers worldwide use the Internet for, among other things, obtaining information about sex that their schools and parents do not provide (Borzekowski & Rickert, 2001; Gray et al., 2005; Suzuki & Calzo, 2006). An international political project involving 3,000 adolescents from 129 developed and developing nations linked all of them via e-mail, some from home and others through nearby schools, libraries, or Internet cafés (see Figure 15.5; Cassell et al., 2006).

Internationally, however, a digital divide still is evident when youth in every region are studied. Those who live in rural areas, especially without electricity, are less likely to use computers (Holderness, 2006). Battery-powered technology is narrowing the gap, although the real gap is in quality of education, and computers do not narrow that gap.

Learning via the Internet

Computers are now widely seen as essential tools for education. This view is exaggerated (children with and without computer access do equally well on various tests), but Internet use may improve reading and spatial skills (Sternberg et al., 2007). In an experiment conducted with 10- to 18-year-olds (mostly African American from low-income families) who were given free Internet access at home, those who used their computers increased both their reading scores and their school grades (Jackson et al., 2006).

Traditional research conducted before the technology explosion found that, with time, education, and experience, adolescents are likely to move past egocentric thought and think logically and deductively. The World Wide Web could either speed this development or slow it down; researchers have not yet reached a consensus either way.

Research on how adolescents use the Internet and other technology finds that most of their activity is not what teachers would call educational. Instead, it is social, as they keep in touch with friends—usually friends they know from school—via e-mail, texting, and cell phones (Greenfield et al., 2006). This social activity itself may be educational, in that many developmentalists believe that conversations and relationships advance cognition.

Many technological advances (e.g., cell phones, e-mail, texting) require social interaction, which adolescents need for cognitive growth (Subrahmanyam et al., 2006). Online communication can bring friends closer (Valkenburg & Peter, 2007). Even shy teens create screen names and engage in discussion at a distance, perhaps furthering thought and communication without the danger and intimacy of more direct contact. This may be especially important for teenagers who feel socially isolated, particularly those who are not near anyone of their sexual orientation, ethnic group, or native language.

At the same time, children can learn more about groups and cultures different from their own via chat rooms and other "virtual" contacts with people they might never meet (Tynes, 2007). Of course, such contacts are not always helpful; negative stereotypes may be reinforced rather than refuted. Nonetheless, the potential for expanding one's positive experiences is there.

The Dangers of the Internet

Many researchers are convinced that the dangers posed by the Internet are exaggerated. Sexual predators do lurk on the Internet, but most teens avoid them, just as most adults avoid distasteful Internet ads. Lonely girls at the beginning of puberty are vulnerable, but the Internet itself is not the root of their problem (Wolak et al., 2008). This is not to say that technology is always benign. The emerging hazards of Internet access include cyberbullying and self-mutilation Web sites.

Cyberbullying **Cyberbullying** occurs when one person bullies another by spreading insults and rumors by means of e-mails, text messages, or anonymous phone calls or posts embarrassing videos of the victim on the Internet (Li, 2007). The adolescents who are most likely to be involved are those who are most technologically proficient.

cyberbullying Bullying that occurs when one person spreads insults or rumors about another by means of e-mails, text messages, or anonymous phone calls or posts embarrassing videos of the victim on the Internet. (The name derives from the fact that such bullying occurs in *cyberspace,* the hypothetical environment in which digitized information is communicated over computer networks.)

Bully-victims are particularly likely to send as well as to receive insults. One study found that 23 percent of secondary school students had experienced cyberbullying and 16 percent of them said they had engaged in it (Dehue et al., 2008). Most parents were unaware of what their children were doing.

A scholar who has studied bullying in all its forms finds that cyberbullying is quite similar to other forms of bullying (Smith et al., 2008). Some observers in the popular press, however, suggest that cyberbullying is worse because its messages are accessible to all: Thinking of the imaginary audience, adolescents are sure that everyone else knows their shame (Kornblum, 2008).

Self-Mutilation Web Sites Teenagers may use the Internet to pursue an activity that they don't want adults to know about. A worrisome example of such an activity is self-mutilation, or self-injury done primarily to relieve depression and guilt (Whitlock et al., 2006). Currently, more than 400 Web sites are dedicated to "cutting," as this practice is known. Cutting is addictive, particularly for adolescent girls (Yates, 2004).

Analysis of a representative sample of 3,219 posts on cutting sites found that most were positive and helpful, allowing self-injuring adolescents to "establish interpersonal intimacy . . . , [which is] especially difficult for young people struggling with intense shame, isolation, and distress" (Whitlock et al., 2006, p. 415). The most common theme of the messages was informal support (28 percent), while many other posts described formal treatment (7 percent, usually positively) and emotional triggers (20 percent) (Whitlock et al., 2006).

Some sites, however, were negative in that they provided suggestions for concealment of the marks caused by self-injury (9 percent) or information on techniques and paraphernalia (6 percent). Here is one chilling exchange:

> Poster 1: Does anyone know how to cut deep without having it sting and bleed too much?
>
> Poster 2: I use box cutter blades. You have to pull the skin really tight and press the blade down really hard. You can also use a tourniquet to make it bleed more.
>
> Poster 3: I've found that if you press your blade against the skin at the depth you want the cut to be and draw the blade really fast it doesn't hurt and there is blood galore. Be careful, though, 'cause you can go very deep without meaning to.
>
> *[quoted in Whitlock et al., 2006, p. 413]*

Similarly, there are hundreds of Web sites directed at young people that deal with such topics as self-starvation, homophobia, violent sex, and racism. Some of them are aimed at making adolescents less vulnerable and helping them overcome their problems. Others, however, prey on adolescents' vulnerabilities and make their problems worse. In addition, Internet use, especially online gambling, may be addictive in much the same way that drug use is addictive. Adolescents are particularly vulnerable to this type of addiction (Yen et al., 2008).

Internet abuses relate to cognitive development because adolescents are often poor judges of what is rational and what is emotional. For instance, gambling thrives on base rate neglect, and self-mutilation on the sunk cost fallacy. Obviously, the Internet is a tool that adolescents must learn to use carefully.

The Transition to a New School

As you have read, developmentalists are not sure how best to teach secondary school students or how best to use the new technology for education. However, they share one insight that can help teachers and parents: Many studies have found that changes, even positive ones, are disruptive for adolescents. As a result, transitions from one school to another are difficult, usually impairing a person's ability to function and learn. Changing schools just when the growth spurt is occurring and sexual characteristics are developing is bound to create stress.

Remember from Chapter 12 that ongoing minor stresses can become overwhelming if they accumulate. This may lead to psychological problems, as one expert explains:

> A number of disorders and symptoms of psychopathology, including depression, self-injury behavior, substance abuse, eating disorders, bipolar disorder, and schizophrenia have striking developmental patterns corresponding to transitions in early and late adolescence.
>
> *[Masten, 2004, p. 310]*

Of course, the transition to middle school or high school cannot be blamed for every disorder, since hormones, body shape, sexual impulses, family, and culture also contribute. All the same, genes that predispose a person to psychopathology and thrill seeking may activate at puberty, causing havoc for those who lack emotional regulation (E. F. Walker, 2002).

The first year in a new school (middle school, high school, or college) correlates with increased bullying and decreased achievement and with the onset of depression and eating disorders. Accordingly, schools need to pay special attention to the psychological needs of new students. Schools have found many ways to do this: teaching new students in a separate area; avoiding transitions by extending elementary school to include grade 8 or even teaching kindergarten through grade 12 in a single school building; restructuring secondary schools to comprise grades 7 through 12 (as Japan recently did); and developing extensive faculty and peer support systems (such as meaningful advisee groups for new students).

One particularly effective measure to ease the transition to a new school is to strengthen the young person's support network for the change. If the adults and many of the students in a new school are notably different from those in the old school, students who are suddenly in the minority may feel alienated and worried about their academic success (Benner & Graham, 2007). It is not diversity per se that is difficult; it is suddenly finding oneself alone. Advance involvement of students and families might ease the transition, especially if new friends can quickly be found.

To strengthen the new student's network, parents can be given more choice, information, and involvement in their adolescent's education. Students can be assigned to schools in which some of their classmates are friends or at least are from the same background (Holland et al., 2007). With Mexican Americans, in particular, a program that helped new middle school students support each other, and helped their parents support them, reduced their likelihood of dropping out (Gonzales et al, 2004).

As mentioned in Chapter 12, researchers distinguish among the *intended, implemented,* and *attained* curricula of a school (Robitaille & Beaton, 2002). *Intended* curriculum refers to the content that educational leaders prescribe, *implemented* curriculum refers to what the teachers and school administrators offer, and *attained* curriculum refers to what the students learn.

Lofty intentions can lead to recrimination if the intentions are not attained. Teachers can be faulted for not implementing the curriculum, and students can be blamed for not learning what is taught.

The results of unrealized educational intentions include reduced self-esteem and motivation among both teachers and students. From a developmental perspective, this result is the opposite of what it should be. Of the three types of curricula mentioned above, attained learning is the most important; intentions and implementation should be adjusted if students are not learning as they should which often happens with students who are new to a school.

High School

As we have seen, adolescents can think abstractly, analytically, hypothetically, and logically—as well as personally, emotionally, intuitively, and experientially. The curriculum and teaching style of high school often require analytic and abstract thinking. In theory and sometimes in practice, high schools advance analytic ability. This enables students to use logic to override the "biases that not only preserve existing beliefs but also perpetuate stereotypes and inhibit development" (Klaczynski, 2005, p. 71). The question is whether too much stress is placed on logic and abstract thinking.

Most academic subjects emphasize logic, often requiring the students to make systematic deductions from laboratory experiments or historical documents. This is exactly what formal operational thinking enables adolescents to do. As a practical matter, however, the curriculum of the high school is often disconnected from the needs and requirements of three key groups: employers, colleges, and students themselves.

Focus on the College-Bound

From a developmental perspective, the fact that high schools emphasize formal thinking makes sense, since by the later years of adolescence, many students are capable of attaining that level. High school classes often assume that students have mastered formal thinking, instead of teaching them how to do it (Kuhn & Franklin, 2006).

Some nations are trying to raise their standards of education, partly so that more students will achieve the highest levels of thought. In the United States, an increasing number of high school students are enrolled in classes that are designed to be more rigorous and that require students to pass externally scored exams, either the IB (International Baccalaureate) or the AP (Advanced Placement) exam. In 2006, more than 1 million took at least one Advanced Placement class. The hope is that such classes will lead to better thinking, or at least higher achievement, though this effect has not yet been proved (McNeil, 2007; Viadero, 2006).

Winners These New York City high school girls are applauding their victory in a game that tested their factual knowledge of U.S. history. Such excitement increases motivation, but some educators worry that higher-order thinking (analysis and synthesis) may be lost in the process.

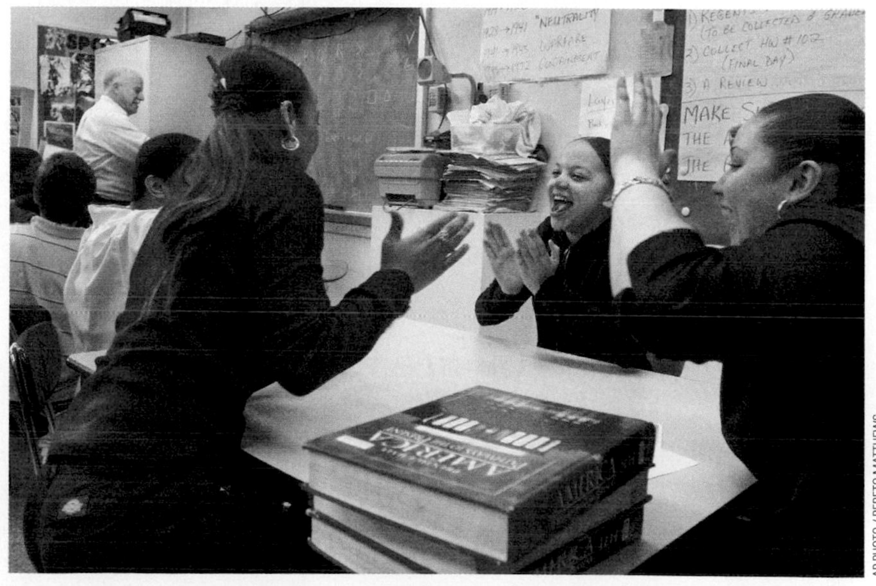

AP PHOTO / BEBETO MATTHEWS

IMAGES OF AFRICA PHOTOBANK / ALAMY

Winners, Too These boys are among the elite of Africa, studying in the physics laboratory of their high school in Kenya. (Compare their classroom with the one shown in the photograph on the preceding page.)

Observation Quiz (see answer, page 466): Although the two groups of winners are thousands of miles apart, there are three evident similarities between them. What are they?

high-stakes test An evaluation that is critical in determining success or failure. If a single test determines whether a student will graduate or be promoted, that is a high-stakes test.

Especially for High School Teachers (see response, page 466): You are much more interested in the nuances and controversies than in the basic facts of your subject, but you know that your students will take high-stakes tests on the basics and that their scores will have a major impact on their futures. What should you do?

Another manifestation of the trend toward more rigorous education is the greater number of requirements that all students must fulfill to receive an academic diploma. In many U.S. schools, no one is allowed to earn a vocational or general diploma unless the parents specifically request it (Olson, 2005). Many schools require two years of math beyond algebra, two years of laboratory science, three years of history, and four years of English. Some study of a language other than English is usually required as well, although the specific requirements vary a great deal.

In 2008, twenty-three U.S. states required students to pass a **high-stakes test** (in addition to passing a certain number of required courses) in order to graduate (*Education Week*, 2008). (Any exam for which the consequences of failing are severe is called a high-stakes test. Traditionally, such tests were used when adults sought professional licenses to go into practice as, for example, lawyers, doctors, and clinical psychologists.)

Some people consider high-stakes tests and rigorous course requirements for high school graduation to be examples of raising standards; others believe that these changes destroy learning. The fear is that teachers may be forced to "teach to the test," concentrating on rote memorization of factual information and ignoring both analysis and intuition (Nichols & Berliner, 2007).

Ironically, just when more U.S. schools are instituting high-stakes tests and requiring more courses, many East Asian nations are moving in the opposite direction (Fujita, 2000). According to a report on Chinese education,

> some prominent government officials have grown concerned that too many students have become the sort of stressed-out, test-acing drone who fails to acquire the skills—creativity, flexibility, initiative, leadership—said to be necessary in the global marketplace.
>
> *[Hulbert, 2007, p. 36]*

The same concerns have led to changes in the Korean and Japanese educational systems. The trend in Japan is toward fewer academic requirements for high school, classes five days a week instead of six, and less "examination hell," as the high-stakes tests had been called. The science adviser to the prime minister of Japan recommends more flexibility in education in order to promote more innovation. He wants students to "study whatever they are interested in" rather than to narrow their learning so as to score high on one final test (Normile, 2007).

College for All?

In the United States, one result of pushing almost all high school students to pursue an academic curriculum is that more are prepared for college. Another result is that more students drop out. Of those who do complete high school, many do not seek any further education. This category includes about one-third of high school students in the United States and at least two-thirds in most nations of the world. According to a report by the United Nations Economic and Social Council (UNESCO),

> In many parts of the world, learning contents at the secondary level are still following a pattern tailored for the 19th or early 20th century contexts, which often

> emphasizes the acquisition of academic knowledge over skills development. As the provision of secondary education expands to a wider population, there is a challenging task to diversify and adapt the curriculum to all learners of various styles and interests, especially in view of stopping dropout and school disaffection in some regions.
>
> One effort to help such students is to provide job training in schools, with courses ranging from airplane repair to secretarial skills. However, the job market is changing rapidly, so few in-school programs provide vocational skills that are needed in the workplace.
>
> *[UNESCO, 2005]*

One solution to this problem is to arrange apprenticeships, whereby students work for various local businesses and earn credits toward graduation for what they learn. Germany was the innovator in such programs, with tens of thousands of high school students in apprenticeships during the 1980s. They were guaranteed jobs if they did well.

The German apprenticeship system was successful when manufacturers needed more workers; as unemployment rates among adult workers increased, however, many employers left the program and only the most motivated students succeeded (Grollmann & Rauner, 2007). Furthermore, apprenticeship programs in Germany and elsewhere were chosen not by the students who were best suited for them but by the students whose families did not encourage them to seek higher education.

In other words, both the overt job market and family SES affected apprenticeship participation, contrary to the idea that such programs should meet the needs of the students (Lehmann, 2004). This happens elsewhere as well. According to one counselor in a Korean school designed for students who were not college-bound:

> Our students start to search for jobs when they become seniors. Most of the jobs that they end up getting are service jobs that do not require special skills. So they do not need to prepare for such jobs at an early age. What they are required to have are only two things: diploma and good appearance.
>
> *[quoted in Choi, 2005, p. 273]*

Most students aspire to college and spurn vocational education in high school. That makes sense in the twenty-first century, because more and more jobs require tertiary education. Employers provide specific training (usually much more detailed than any high school can) and hope that the newly hired employees will be able to read, think, write, and get along with other workers. Those may be the skills that high schools should focus on—skills hard to measure on a high-stakes test.

High-stakes tests are the subject of fierce debate, and students who are not college-bound are caught in the middle. In California in 2006, for example, 41,700 students (many of them from low-income Mexican American families) completed the credits for graduation but failed the state's high-stakes exam. Days before graduation, a judge ruled that the tests were discriminatory and that these students had earned their diplomas (McKinley, 2006). The state appealed and won, so none of those students were granted diplomas (Jacobson, 2006). Some went to summer school to try again; some quit.

High School Dropouts

Our discussion thus far has assumed that students want to graduate from high school. However, not every student who begins secondary school stays to finish it. Rates of children aged 11 to 18 who are enrolled in school vary from less than 20 percent in the poorest nations (such as Niger and Cambodia) to 100 percent in the richest (such as Japan and Sweden) (World Bank, 2005). Developed nations

➤Answer to Observation Quiz (from page 464): The similarities have to do with gender, uniforms, and cooperation. Sex segregation and similar garb are evident in both photographs, although they are voluntary in U.S. public schools and compulsory in many African secondary schools. Adolescents everywhere enjoy working collaboratively.

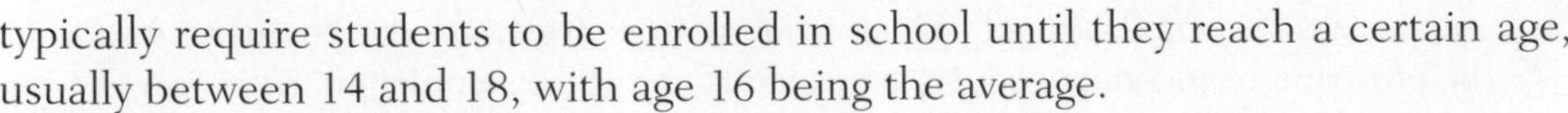

typically require students to be enrolled in school until they reach a certain age, usually between 14 and 18, with age 16 being the average.

Whenever high-stakes tests are a requisite for graduation, there is a "potential unintended consequence" that more high school students will drop out (Christenson & Thurlow, 2004, p. 36). In the 23 U.S. states that now require exit exams to graduate, fewer students do graduate (Robelen, 2006).

Dropout and graduation statistics are presented in many ways. The United States overall compares the number of students in the ninth grade with the number who do, or do not, graduate four years later. This method does not count students who take five years to graduate, or who leave school and will return, or who will earn a GED (General Education Development, formerly General Education Diploma) after scoring well on tests that measure high school learning.

By that standard, about 28 percent of U.S. students who were ninth-graders in 2004 did not graduate in 2008 (*Education Week,* 2008). Generally, girls are more likely to graduate than boys, Asian Americans more than other groups, and American Indians less than other groups (see Figure 15.6). In some major cities, including Detroit, Milwaukee, Baltimore, Los Angeles, and Nashville, fewer than half of ninth-graders go on to graduate.

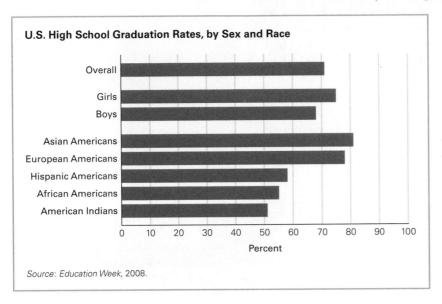

U.S. High School Graduation Rates, by Sex and Race

Overall
Girls
Boys
Asian Americans
European Americans
Hispanic Americans
African Americans
American Indians
0 10 20 30 40 50 60 70 80 90 100
Percent

Source: Education Week, 2008.

FIGURE 15.6

Almost All or Far Too Few? The 71 percent overall graduation rate is the highest in U.S. history, and higher than the rate in most other nations. All the same, three U.S. ethnic groups have graduation rates below 60 percent, and 25 nations have higher rates than the United States. School-by-school comparisons show that graduation rates depend much more on community income levels and school quality than on the ethnic makeup of the student body.

Since a high school education, including the academic skills taught in various courses, is needed for success in the future, many educators are trying to figure out how to reduce dropout rates. Some jurisdictions use tactics that do not actually benefit any of the three stakeholder groups (employers, colleges, and students), although the general public may be pleased by the apparent improvement. One deceptive practice is to use a different way of calculating dropouts—to include only those students who formally become school leavers, not those who simply stop coming to school. Another approach involves making graduation easier: With fewer requirements, more will graduate.

Taking a long view, the percentage of dropouts has gradually decreased in the United States over the past 30 years. About 90 percent of 24-year-olds have earned a high school degree of some sort, and the graduation rate in most states is inching up. The real challenge seems to be finding ways to engage students in learning.

Student Engagement

Surprisingly, students who are capable of passing their classes are as likely to drop out as those with learning disabilities. Persistence, diligence, and motivation seem to play a more crucial role than intellectual ability when it comes to earning a high school diploma (Fredricks et al., 2004). Many adolescents express boredom and unhappiness with school ("Algebra sucks," "*The Odyssey* is boring"), especially when they are complaining to their friends (Larson, 2000; Lyons, 2004). To be admired by their peers, some adolescents may appear to be detached from education. Attachment to school and assessment of self-competence typically fall in each consecutive year of high school, particularly among boys (Fredricks & Eccles, 2006; Porche et al., 2004; Wigfield et al., 1997).

➤Response for High School Teachers (from page 464): It would be nice to follow your instincts, but the appropriate response depends partly on pressures within the school and on the expectations of the parents and administration. A comforting fact is that adolescents can think about and learn almost anything if they feel a personal connection to it. Look for ways to teach the facts your students need for the tests as the foundation for the exciting and innovative topics you want to teach. Everyone will learn more, and the tests will be less intimidating for your students.

Teachers, researchers, and developmentalists describe adolescents—honor students as well as delinquents—as having "high rates of boredom, alienation, and disconnection from meaningful challenge" (Larson, 2000). That conclusion comes from a U.S. study, but similar findings have come from as far away as Australia, where teachers were asked what problems they had with their students (Little, 2005). As you can see in Figure 15.7, they reported that middle school students can be disruptive, but high school students are often disengaged.

One reason for disengagement may be that only formal operational thought is promoted in high school curricula, while egocentric and intuitive thought, which are more relational and social, are largely excluded. Schedules limit social interaction by allowing only a few minutes between classes, and school rules often prohibit students from gathering informally on school grounds before or after classes. Budget cutting often targets extracurricular activities first, which undercuts attachment to school (Fredricks & Eccles, 2006).

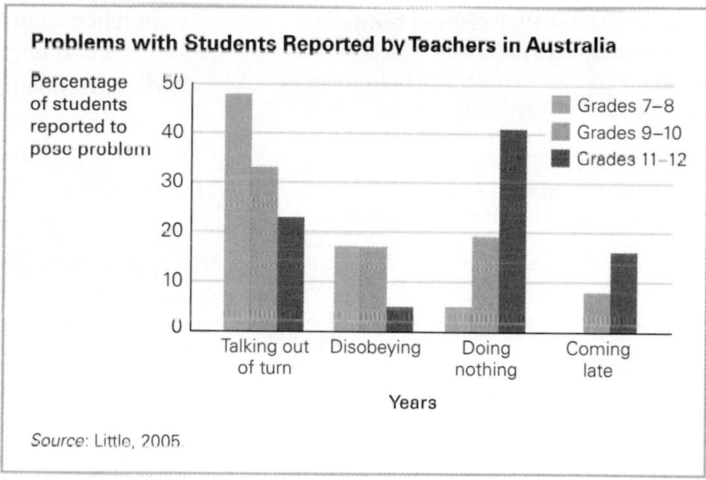

FIGURE 15.7

Teacher's Complaints Teachers around the globe concur that each adolescent age group poses its own particular set of behavioral problems in school. This chart is based on data as reported by teachers in Australia. Which is worse: a student who is actively disruptive or one who has stopped caring?

Teachers are hired for their expertise in one or more academic fields, not for their ability to relate to adolescents. They are able to model formal operational thinking—to answer complex questions about the intricacies of theoretical physics, advanced calculus, and iambic pentameter—but they are often ill equipped to deal effectively with students, especially with troubled students, who may be more likely to act impulsively. Those students are usually sent to meet with a guidance counselor, who may be responsible for hundreds of students and unable to provide the level of support that is needed. The result is that the educational system may devalue egocentric, personal, and intuitive thought to the point where some adolescents feel that they themselves are devalued.

Especially for High School Guidance Counselors (see response, page 468): Given what you know about adolescent thinking, should you spend more time helping students with college applications, with summer jobs, with family problems, or with course selection?

What can be done to encourage adolescents to be more engaged with school? While there is no single, definitive answer to this question, there are many possible avenues to explore. These include:

- *Keeping high schools small.* Extensive research suggests that 200 to 400 is the ideal number of students to have in a high school, partly because there is more opportunity for almost every student to be involved in some sort of team or club. Nevertheless, two-thirds of high school students in the United States attend schools with enrollments of over 1,000 (Snyder et al., 2006). Big schools are more economical, but they do not necessarily increase learning and motivation (Eccles et al., 2003).
- *Encouraging extracurricular activities.* There are "developmental benefits of participation in extracurricular activities for many high school adolescents" (Fredricks & Eccles, 2006, p. 712). Athletic teams elicit positive emotions and school bonding, which explains why students on such teams (including those who are not star athletes) are less prone to use drugs or alcohol, have a low incidence of depression, and earn higher grades. Overall, adolescents who are active in school clubs and on athletic teams are more likely to graduate and go to college (Mahoney et al., 2005). The same is true of students who participate in activities sponsored by nonschool groups, including religious groups (Glanville et al., 2008).
- *Reducing harassment.* School violence is decreasing in the United States, but more students fear violence than before. Setting clear rules for student behavior, rewarding students for attendance, and organizing more sporting events within (not just between) schools all reduce crime, according to a survey of Texas middle and high schools (Cheurprakobkit & Bartsch, 2005). The same study shows that measures that increase fear, such as installing metal detectors and handing out strict punishments, are more likely to increase

➤**Response for High School Guidance Counselors** (from page 467): It depends on what your particular students need; schools vary a great deal. However, all students need to talk and think about their choices and options so that they will not act impulsively. Therefore, providing information and a listening ear might be the most important thing you can spend time doing.

violence than to decrease it. Primary prevention to improve the school climate is needed because violence tends to be reduced by measures that (1) increase peer friendships, (2) strengthen teacher–student relationships, and (3) promote student involvement. Programs that teach conflict resolution have also had some success, perhaps because they make a point of accomplishing these three goals (e.g., Breunlin et al., 2002).

This list is only a start. A review of adolescent education throughout the world finds that "no culture or nation has worked out a surefire educational psychology to guarantee that every one of the youth is motivated in school" (Larson & Wilson, 2004, p. 318). Further experimentation and research are needed.

SUMMING UP

Secondary education is an integral aspect of cognitive development. However, researchers disagree about how best to teach adolescents, and different nations take very different approaches to adolescent education. Middle schools tend to be less personal, less flexible, and more tightly regulated than elementary schools, all of which may contribute to declining student achievement. Transitions are difficult for children, especially with the demands of puberty and the self-centeredness of egocentrism. Students and educators alike turn to technology—for different reasons. Most adolescents use various forms of technology every day for positive purposes, but cyberbullying and other destructive uses also occur. Parents and teachers are learning how to use technology to improve learning.

High school education can advance thinking of all kinds, including both analytic and intuitive thinking, in every domain. But it is often only formal operational thinking that is taught and tested. High-stakes testing reflects an effort to equalize achievement and increase accountability, but it may result in a less creative curriculum and increase the number of students who drop out before earning a diploma. Students who do not graduate, and even those who have apprenticeships in school, are generally not on a path toward success in the rapidly changing job market in developed nations. Essential to safe and successful secondary education are activities that encourage students to engage intellectually with ideas, with each other, and with teachers. ■

SUMMARY

Neurological Development

1. Various parts of the brain mature during puberty, each at its own rate. The neurological ideas dedicated to emotional arousal (including the amygdala) mature ahead of the areas that regulate and rationalize emotional expression (the prefrontal cortex). Consequently, many adolescents seek intense emotional experiences, untempered by rational thought.

2. The prefrontal cortex matures by early adulthood, allowing better planning and analysis. Throughout this period, ongoing myelination and experience allow faster and deeper thinking, although the ability to use reason to guide emotion is elusive.

Adolescent Thinking

3. Cognition in early adolescence may be egocentric, a kind of self-centered thinking. Adolescent egocentrism gives rise to the personal fable, the invincibility fable, and the imaginary audience.

4. *Formal operational thought* is Piaget's term for the last of his four periods of cognitive development. He tested and demonstrated formal operational thought with various experiments involving problems that students in a high school science or math class might encounter, such as figuring out how to adjust weights on a balance scale.

5. Adolescents are no longer earthbound and concrete in their thinking; they prefer to imagine the possible, the probable, and even the impossible, instead of focusing on what is real. They develop hypotheses and explore, using deductive reasoning.

6. Intuitive thinking becomes more forceful during adolescence. Few teenagers always use logic, although they are capable of doing so. Emotional, intuitive thinking is quicker and more satisfying, and sometimes better, than analytic thought.

Teaching and Learning

7. Secondary education—after primary (grade school) and before tertiary (college) education—correlates with the health and wealth of individuals and nations. Most of the world's children now receive some secondary schooling, although most do not graduate from high school.

8. In middle school, many students tend to be bored by school, difficult to teach, and hurtful to one another. One reason may be that middle schools are not structured to accommodate egocentrism or intuitive thinking.

9. Many forms of psychopathology increase at the transitions to middle school, to high school, and to college. Although transitions are always stressful, they may be particularly difficult in adolescence, when young people must also adjust to biological and family changes.

10. Adolescents use technology, particularly the Internet, more than people of any other age group. They reap many educational benefits from doing so, but there are hazards as well.

11. Education in high school seems to emphasize formal operational thinking. In the United States, the demand for more accountability has led to more AP classes and high-stakes testing. This may have unintended consequences, including a higher dropout rate.

12. Low motivation is often a problem among secondary school students. Especially in very large schools, few are actively involved in sports or other school activities that promote school bonding and thus engagement.

KEY TERMS

adolescent egocentrism (p. 443)
personal fable (p. 444)
invincibility fable (p. 444)
imaginary audience (p. 445)
formal operational thought (p. 446)
hypothetical thought (p. 448)
deductive reasoning (p. 449)
inductive reasoning (p. 449)
dual-process model (p. 450)
intuitive thought (p. 450)
analytic thought (p. 450)
sunk cost fallacy (p. 452)
base rate neglect (p. 452)
secondary education (p. 455)
middle school (p. 455)
digital divide (p. 459)
cyberbullying (p. 461)
high-stakes test (p. 464)

KEY QUESTIONS

1. Almost all neuroscientists agree about certain aspects of brain development. What are these aspects?

2. What are the reasons that the limbic system may develop before the prefrontal cortex?

3. What are some of the consequences of adolescent egocentrism?

4. What are the characteristics of formal operational thinking?

5. What are the advantages of intuitive thought?

6. How might intuition and analysis lead to opposite conclusions?

7. Why are middle schools called developmentally regressive?

8. Why are transitions a particular concern for educators?

9. What are the advantages and disadvantages of high-stakes testing?

10. What are the problems with vocational education?

11. What factors increase student engagement in high school?

APPLICATIONS

1. Describe a time when you overestimated how much other people were thinking about you. How was your mistake similar to and different from adolescent egocentrism?

2. Talk to a teenager about politics, families, school, religion, or any other topic that might reveal the way that young person thinks. Do you hear any adolescent egocentrism? Intuitive thinking? Systematic thought? Flexibility? Cite examples.

3. Think of a life-changing decision you have made. How did logic and emotion interact? What would have changed if you had given the matter more thought—or less?

4. Think back to the specific rules and the hidden curriculum (discussed in Chapter 12) of your high school. How did they affect the learning of the students in your school?

16

CHAPTER OUTLINE

Adolescence: Psychosocial Development

Our oldest daughter wore the same pair of jeans to tenth grade, day after day. She washed them each night by hand, and, at her request, I put them in the dryer very early each morning. My husband watched us both with bewilderment masked by humor, asking, "Is this some weird female ritual?" He encouraged her to wear other clothes, to no avail. Years later she explained that if she varied her clothing, her classmates would think she cared about how she looked, and then they might criticize her.

Our second daughter was 16 when she told me she had pierced her ears again. She wanted to wear more earrings at once than anyone in my generation would think of wearing. "Does this mean you'll take drugs?" I asked. She laughed at my naiveté, happy at my concern.

At age 15, our third daughter was diagnosed with Hodgkin's disease, a form of cancer. My husband and I weighed divergent opinions from four physicians, each of whom explained why his or her treatment would minimize the risk of death. Our daughter had her own priorities: "I don't care what you choose, as long as I keep my hair." (Her hair fell out temporarily, but now her health is good.)

Our youngest, in her first year of middle school, refused to wear her jacket even on the coldest days, much to her teachers' and parents' dismay. Later, when she was in high school, she offered an explanation: She had wanted her peers to think she was tough.

What strikes me now is how oblivious I was to my children's need for peer respect. I reacted as a mother, not as a wise developmentalist. As my husband said, "I knew they would become teenagers, but I didn't realize we would become parents of teenagers."

All adolescents seek respect from their peers as they seek their own identity. Although many parents are concerned about their adolescents' well-being, relatively few adolescents succumb to the dangers that adults most fear, such as drug abuse, pregnancy, suicide, jail. Instead they are caught up in things that puzzle their parents but earn respect from their friends, as my daughters did. This chapter describes the search for identity, the role of parents and peers, and the joys and potential hazards of adolescence.

Identity

Psychosocial development during adolescence is often understood as a search for a consistent understanding of oneself. Each young person wants to know "Who am I?"

identity versus role confusion Erikson's term for the fifth stage of development, in which the person tries to figure out "Who am I?" but is confused as to which of many possible roles to adopt.

identity achievement Erikson's term for the attainment of identity, or the point at which a person understands who he or she is as a unique individual, in accord with past experiences and future plans.

As Erik Erikson described it, life's fifth psychosocial crisis is **identity versus role confusion.** The complexities of finding one's own identity become the primary crisis of adolescence—a crisis in which young people struggle to reconcile their understanding of themselves as unique with their connection to their heritage (Erikson, 1968).

According to Erikson, the ultimate goal in resolving this crisis is **identity achievement.** Adolescents reconsider the goals and values set by their parents and culture, accepting some and rejecting others. With their new autonomy, they maintain continuity with their past in order to move toward their future (Chandler et al., 2003). As with all of Erikson's stages, the clash between the two extremes (here, identity versus role confusion) causes a crisis that must be resolved.

Erikson described the identity crises of Martin Luther, Mahatma Gandhi, George Bernard Shaw, and many other eminent people. He wrote biographies that focused on psychological understanding, a genre called *psychohistory.* Erikson's insights inspired many other developmentalists. Notable among them was James Marcia, who described four specific ways young people cope with this stage of life. In addition to (1) achievement and (2) role confusion, some choose (3) foreclosure, others (4) moratorium (Marcia, 1966). Over the past half-century, major psychosocial shifts have lengthened the time period of adolescence and have made it more complex (Côté, 2006; Nurmi, 2004). However, these four possible ways of coping still seem evident in the lives of contemporary youth.

Not Yet Achieved

role confusion A situation in which an adolescent does not seem to know or care what his or her identity is. (Also called *identity diffusion.*)

Role confusion is the opposite of identity achievement. It is characterized by an adolescent's lack of commitment to any goals or values, with a feeling of apathy and indifference concerning every possible role. Identity confusion is sometimes called *identity diffusion,* to emphasize that some adolescents seem diffuse, unfocused, unconcerned about their future (Phillips & Pittman, 2007).

Even the usual social demands, such as putting away clothes, making friends, completing school assignments, and thinking about college or employment, are beyond adolescents who are experiencing diffusion. Instead, it is typical for them to sleep too much, watch long hours of mind-numbing television, and turn from one romance to another with neither passion nor distress. The response to school failure, parental criticism, missed deadlines, lost papers is, "Whatever."

foreclosure Erikson's term for premature identity formation, which occurs when an adolescent adopts parents' or society's roles and values wholesale, without questioning and analysis.

Identity **foreclosure** occurs when, in order to halt the confusion, young people short-circuit their search by accepting traditional values without questioning them (Marcia, 1966; Marcia et al., 1993). They might follow roles and customs from their parents or culture, never exploring alternatives. Or they might foreclose completely on an oppositional, negative identity, again without any thoughtful questioning and without individualizing their path.

An example of foreclosure might be a boy who has always anticipated following in his father's footsteps. If his father is a doctor, he might take advanced chemistry and biology in high school; if his father is a day laborer, he might drop out of school at age 16. In Erikson's day, some girls foreclosed by choosing early marriage and motherhood in order to avoid thinking about their own future. For many young people even today, foreclosure is a comfortable shelter, a way to avoid the stress of forging a new path.

A better shelter is **moratorium,** a kind of time-out; it is considered a more mature response than foreclosure. Societies provide many moratoria that allow adolescents to postpone final identity achievement just as they are graduating from high school.

moratorium A socially acceptable way for adolescents to postpone identity achievement. Going to college is a common example.

The most obvious moratorium in North America is college, with a variety of required general courses that forestall even the need to decide about what to study. Other institutions that allow postponement of identity are the military, religious missionary work, and various internships in government, academe, and industry. All these reduce the pressure to choose one identity, offering a ready rejoinder to any older relative who urges the young person to settle down.

Adolescents in moratorium try to do what is required as student, soldier, missionary, or intern, but they consider these roles temporary, not their final identity. A new stage, called *emerging adulthood* (described in the Epilogue), is a time when many young adults aged 18 to 25 further postpone commitment.

MITCH WOJNAROWICZ / THE IMAGE WORKS

Not Just a Uniform Adolescents in moratorium adopt temporary roles to postpone achieving their final identity. High school students like these may sign up for an ROTC (Reserve Officers Training Corps) class, but few of them go on to enlist in the U.S. Marine Corps.

Four Areas of Identity Achievement

Overall, many aspects of the search for identity have become more arduous than they were when Erikson first described them (Zimmer-Gembeck & Collins, 2003). Families, societies, and adolescents themselves have shifted. Fifty years ago, the drive to become independent and autonomous was thought to be the "key normative psychosocial task of adolescence" (p. 177). Today most developmentalists believe that attainment of autonomy and identity achievement before age 18 is unlikely.

Erikson (1968) highlighted four aspects of identity: religion, sex, politics, and vocation. Terminology and emphasis have changed, yet these four domains remain important.

Religious Identity

The distinctions among role confusion, foreclosure, moratorium, and achievement are evident in religious identity, which few teenagers achieve. Some drift along, like the adolescent who said, "At the moment, religion's not that important. I guess when I get older it might become more so, but right now being with my friends and having fun and being a teenager is more important" (quoted in C. Smith, 2005, p. 159).

Other young people struggle with theological questions, with a moratorium on commitment. Many religious traditions expect some questioning during late adolescence. For example, unlike in earlier centuries when 18-year-olds made lifelong religious vows, contemporary adolescents who want to be Roman Catholic priests or nuns must first undergo years of testing and training. Likewise, the Mormon church strongly encourages young men to leave home and suspend any romantic relationships in order to perform two years of missionary work.

Similarly, a sizable minority of Amish adolescents follow a tradition known as *rumspringa* ("running around"), where they "venture out into the world" (Stevick, 2001, p. 166) for a period of exploration. Afterward they are expected to be baptized in the Amish faith, to forgo worldly temptations, and to find a spouse.

Riding in Cars with Boys This 16-year-old is having a rather mild adventure during her *rumspringa,* a period of worldly exploration for Amish youth.

COURTESY OF STICK FIGURE PRODUCTIONS

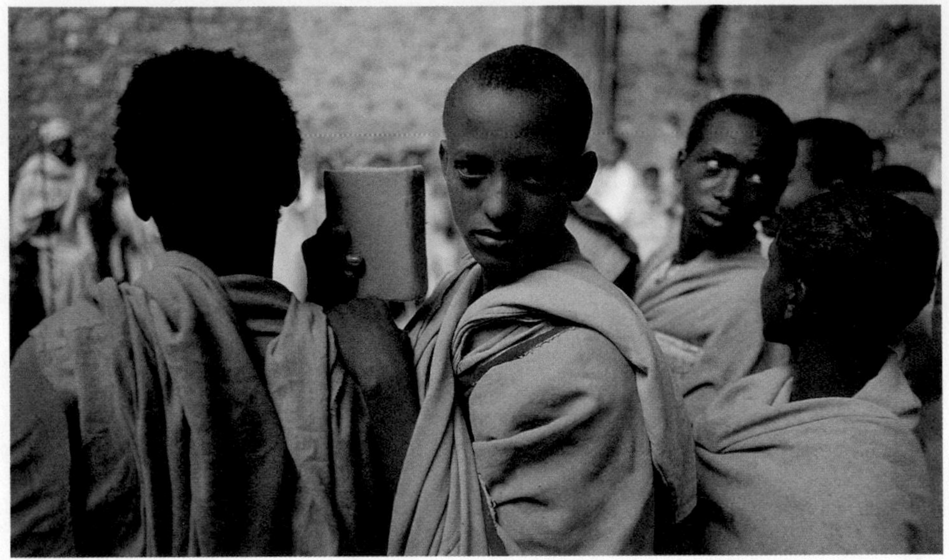
ROB HOWARD / CORBIS

A Religious Life These young adolescents in Ethiopia are studying to be monks. Their monastery is a haven in the midst of civil strife. Will the rituals and beliefs also provide them with a way to achieve identity?

Some adolescents, instead of following one of these ways to postpone commitment, foreclose on a religious identity without exploring alternatives, accepting a faith without questioning. One type of foreclosure occurs when an older teenager suddenly converts to a religion that parents might call a cult. The more common type of foreclosure is not to change religions but to become more devout than the adults seem to be.

The survey of religion highlighted in Chapter 15 found that 8 percent of the teenagers were firm believers. They often prayed, read scripture, and attended services (C. Smith, 2005). Those young people who are most active in their religions are also less likely to engage in risky activities, such as the drug use that some might consider normal exploration. This indicates that religious identity for them involves values and practices, not just a nominal identity (Sinha et al., 2007).

It is impossible to know whether these devout teenagers have foreclosed or achieved their religious identity. Time will tell. Those who foreclosed might "lose" their faith, but those who achieved a religious identity will likely deepen their commitment, not feeling threatened by those who find other paths.

Gender Identity

A half-century ago, Erikson and other psychoanalytic theorists thought of males and females as opposites (P. Y. Miller & Simon, 1980). They assumed that, although many adolescents were confused about their sexual identity, they would soon identify as men or women and adopt sex-appropriate roles (Erikson, 1968; Freud, 1958/2000).

In the past five decades, the multicultural perspective and historical circumstances have revealed the limitations of that assumption (Lippa, 2002). As you remember from Chapter 10, for social scientists *sex* and *sexual* refer to biological male and female characteristics, while *gender* refers to cultural and social characteristics that differentiate males and females (Tarrant, 2006). Accordingly, Erikson's term *sexual identity* has been replaced by **gender identity** (Denny & Pittman, 2007). Gender identity refers primarily to a person's self-definition as male or female.

gender identity A person's acceptance of the roles and behaviors that society associates with the biological categories of male and female.

Gender identity usually begins with the person's biological sex and then leads to gender role and sexual orientation, but not always (Galambos, 2004). A *gender role* refers to a behavior pattern that the culture or society considers appropriate only for men or only for women. In traditional heterosexual marriages, for example, the division of gender roles meant that homemaker was the wife's role and breadwinner was the husband's. In the workplace, the female/male division of gender roles was evident in nurse/doctor, secretary/boss, stewardess/pilot, and so on. If teenagers balked at such prescribed roles, their reaction was assumed to be a temporary phenomenon that would soon be resolved when they attained sexual identity in adulthood.

The term **sexual orientation** refers to the direction of a person's erotic desires. One meaning of *orient* is to "turn toward"; thus, sexual orientation refers to whether a person is romantically attracted to (turned on by) people of the other sex, the same sex, or both sexes. Sexual orientation can be strong or weak and can be acted upon, unexpressed, or unconscious. In Erikson's day, when scientists wrote about identity achievement, they almost always assumed that it included heterosexual orientation.

Adolescents have always experienced strong sexual drives as their hormone levels increased, and they have often been confused regarding when, how, and with whom to express those drives. That is why achieving gender identity is a complicated endeavor for teenagers of every orientation (Baumeister & Blackhart, 2007; Gilchrist & Sullivan, 2006). Some adolescents foreclose (exaggerating male or female roles), others seek a moratorium (avoiding all sexual contact), and still others move toward achievement.

Many adolescents, as they search for gender identity, switch from one version to another. In the Add Health study (see the Research Design), only a few (less than 2 percent) reported *exclusive* same-sex attraction at the first data collection, and only 11 percent of that small minority reported exclusive same-sex attraction a year later. Most had changed to exclusive other-sex attraction; one-third reported no sexual attraction at all (Udry & Chantala, 2005). (Adolescent sexuality is discussed in more detail later in this chapter.)

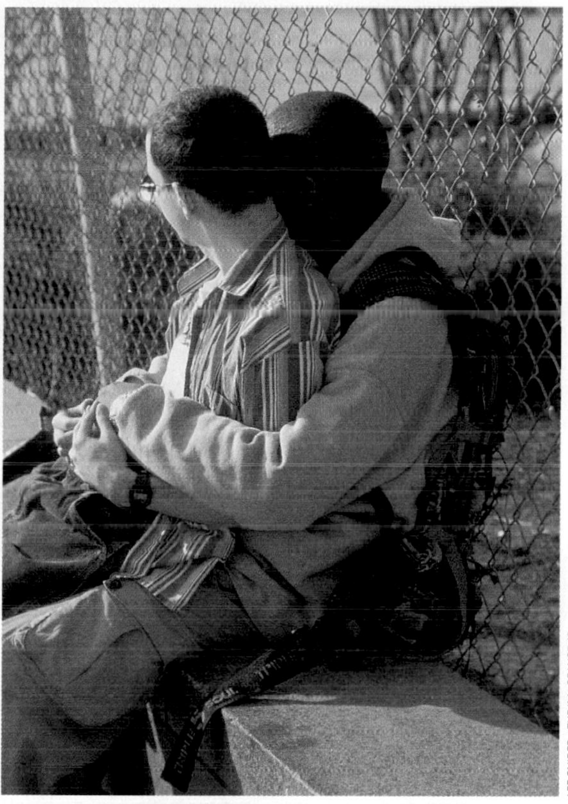
LEE SNIDER / THE IMAGE WORKS

Friendship, Romance, or Passion? Sexual identity is much more complex for today's adolescents than it once was. Behavior, clothing, and hairstyles are often ambiguous. Girls with shorn hair, boys with pierced ears, or same-sex couples embracing are not necessarily homosexual for life—and may not have a homosexual orientation at all.

sexual orientation The direction of a person's sexual and romantic attraction, whether toward others of the same sex, the opposite sex, or both sexes.

Political/Ethnic Identity

In Erikson's day, achieving political identity meant identifying with a political party. Today, once adolescents are old enough to vote—if they vote at all—they usually say they choose the person, not the party. Indeed, many adolescents seem oblivious to national and international politics (Kinder, 2006; Torney-Purta et al., 2001).

Typical of such obliviousness is a young man from Pécs, Hungary. While he was growing up, his nation revolutionized its political and economic system, replacing a Communist government with a capitalistic one. As a teenager, he heard gunfire and saw warplanes from neighboring Yugoslavia, which was being split by civil war into three new nations. Yet he neither loved nor hated communism, and he said, without irony, "There were no essential, important events in my life, only that I was born" (quoted in van Hoorn et al., 2000, p. 22).

The breakup of Yugoslavia, and this young man's statement, are examples of a shift since Erikson's time. Values and attitudes no longer spring primarily from allegiances to political parties. Instead, identity is increasingly influenced by ethnic loyalty—hence the often-used term *identity politics.* For many adolescents, ethnic identity is now one aspect of their overall identity (Phinney, 2006).

Within the United States, ethnic identity is central to many adolescents of African, Asian, and Hispanic descent, who struggle with their group's history, their parents' perspectives, and their own experiences, often combining various components of their backgrounds with their personal values. They struggle to find new

Research Design

The Add Health study is a treasure trove of data on the health of young people in the United States. It began in 1994 with a national sample of 90,000 students in grades 6–12, who answered questionnaires. Many of them were interviewed at home, studied again a year later, and then again 6 and 12 years after the original contact. The study's findings include data on school achievement, sexual activities, delinquency, career aspirations, and mental health. As of 2008, over 3,000 scientists have collected, analyzed, and published the data; thousands more will do so in the next decade.

© ED KASHI / CORBIS

© JAIPAL SINGH / EPA / CORBIS

The Same Situation, Many Miles Apart: Learning in School For these two groups of Muslim girls, the distance between their schools in Dearborn, Michigan (*left*), and Jammu, Kashmir (*right*), is more than geographical. The schools' hidden curricula teach different lessons about the roles of women.

Observation Quiz (see answer, page 479): What three differences are evident?

identities while remaining connected to their roots. Surprisingly, perhaps, gaining a strong ethnic identity does not necessarily conflict with affinity for members of other groups; in fact, quite the opposite is true (Marks et al., 2007).

The need to establish ethnic identity arises in early adolescence and peaks at about age 15 (French et al., 2006; Pahl & Way, 2006). Then ethnic identity continues to evolve, partly because social and historical circumstances continue to change. One developmentalist contends that for ethnic minorities, "the need to explore the implications of their group membership may extend the identity exploration period throughout the 20s and often beyond" (Phinney, 2006, p. 118).

Ethnicity is particularly salient for many adolescents when it is connected with religion. Indeed, the split of Yugoslavia into three nations occurred because of ethnic/religious divisions, with youth prominent in the warring groups. Each political or ethnic identity also affects language, manners, dating patterns, clothing, values, and other personal characteristics (Trimble et al., 2003).

Vocational Identity

Vocational identity in the twenty-first century is rarely achieved until age 25 or later, for a variety of reasons. One is that few teenagers can find meaningful work (Csikszentmihalyi & Schneider, 2000) and instead have jobs that do not allow for creativity, initiative, or advancement. Another is that it takes years to acquire the skills needed for many careers, so it is premature to select a vocation at age 16. A third is that most jobs are unlike those of a generation ago, so it is usually not wise for youth simply to foreclose on a vocation.

Parents still advise their adolescents as to future careers, but sometimes that advice boils down to, "Don't do what I did." In one study, for example, a boy whose father was in construction said, "I look at how hard he works and I appreciate what he does, but he always tells me 'No, you're not doing this!'" (quoted in Lehmann, 2004, p. 390).

Nonetheless, genes, social modeling, and socioeconomic status (SES) propel many adolescents toward the same vocational path their parents followed. In the same study, two boys explained their different decisions—one to become a millwright and the other to become a chemical engineer—in similar ways. The first boy said, "It's just what my family does and I just seem to enjoy working with my hands rather than working with my mind"; the other said, "I just saw my Dad doing it . . . he gets to travel all over the world" (quoted in Lehmann, 2004, p. 386). Both statements smack of foreclosure.

Two girls in this study were influenced by their mothers to avoid foreclosure. They were advised "not to be dependent" and to be "very careful," in both cases to avoid following their mothers' example of forgoing education and career because of early pregnancy (Lehmann, 2004, p. 390, 388).

Many North American parents urge their teenagers to find a part-time job while in school, hoping that this experience will introduce them to the reality of the work world and thus motivate them to study. However, a job during high school that requires 20 or more hours a week often weakens identity formation, family relationships, academic achievement, and career success (Greenberger & Steinberg, 1986; Staff et al., 2004).

Instead of learning "the value of a dollar" (a phrase adults use), many working adolescents spend their money on drugs, clothes, cars, and entertainment. For reasons not of their choosing, immigrant adolescent students in the United States are less likely to be employed than are their peers (Perreira et al., 2007). This may be one reason they tend to have higher school grades than do native born students.

SUMMING UP

Erikson's fifth psychosocial crisis, identity versus role confusion, was first described more than 50 years ago. Adolescence was thought to be the time to search for a personal identity, with identity achievement the mark of adulthood. This crisis still occurs during adolescence, and role confusion, foreclosure, and moratorium are still apparent. However, the timing has changed. The identity crisis lasts much longer, and fewer young people develop a firm sense of who they are and what path they will follow by age 18.

Furthermore, specific aspects of identity religious, political, sexual, and vocational—have taken on new forms and timetables. Sexual identity is now called gender identity, and it includes many more gender roles and sexual orientations than were previously acknowledged. Ethnic identity has become pivotal for many contemporary teenagers, who strive to incorporate their group history into current reality. Vocational identity is elusive, because the jobs available to adolescents are rarely steps toward a permanent career. ■

Relationships with Elders and Peers

The changing seas of human development are never sailed alone. At every turn, a voyager's family, friends, and community provide sustenance, directions, ballast for stability, and a safe harbor when it is time to rest. Social forces also provide a reason to move ahead or change direction. In adolescence, a time when the winds of change blow particularly strong, adults and peers are especially valuable shipmates.

The Older Generation

Adolescence is often characterized as a period of waning adult influence, during which young people distance themselves from the values and behaviors of their elders. There is some validity to this observation, but it does not always apply, and such distancing is not necessarily a good sign. In fact, when young people feel valued by their communities, trusted by teachers, and connected to parents or other adults, they are far less likely to abuse drugs, drop out of school, and take unnecessary risks (Benson, 2003; Stanton & Burns, 2003).

You Don't Listen Adolescent girls are particularly likely to accuse their mothers of not understanding them. For their part, mothers' responses vary, from anger to support and guidance.

Many people besides parents can foster a young person's healthy development throughout puberty and adolescence (Levitt et al., 2005). Members of the extended family, teachers, church leaders, and even the parents of friends can contribute to a rich social network (Parke & Buriel, 2006). "Supportive relationships with non-parent adults [are] key developmental assets predicting positive youth outcomes" (Rhodes & Roffman, 2003, p. 195).

Conflicts with Parents

Although many adults can be supportive of a teen's development, the parent–adolescent relationship is pivotal (Collins & Laursen, 2004). Disputes are common at a time when the adolescent's drive for independence clashes with the parents' customary control. The specifics depend on many factors, including the adolescent's age, gender, and culture.

Bickering Parent–adolescent conflict typically peaks in early adolescence, especially between mothers and daughters (Arnett, 1999; Granic et al., 2003; Laursen et al., 1998). Usually, it manifests as **bickering**—repeated, petty arguments (more nagging than fighting) about routine, day-to-day concerns, such as cleanliness, clothes, chores, and schedules (Eisenberg et al., 2008).

bickering Petty, peevish arguing, usually repeated and ongoing.

Few parents can resist commenting disapprovingly about dirty socks thrown on the floor or a ring through a newly pierced eyebrow, and few adolescents can calmly listen to "expressions of concern" without feeling unfairly judged. Parents want their children to be present at family dinners and to visit relatives, while teenagers just want to be with their friends. Parents notice resistance and fear the worst—addiction, jail, disappearance.

Some bickering may indicate a healthy family, since close relationships almost always include some conflict (Smetana et al., 2004). Generally, after a period when bickering occurs many times a day, parents adjust by granting more autonomy, and "friendship and positive affect [emotional state] typically rebound to preadolescent levels" (Collins & Laursen, 2004, p. 337).

Normally, teenagers adjust as well. By age 18, increased emotional maturity and reduced egocentrism bring them to appreciate their parents. However, if conflict includes "expressed hostility" from the parents, the adolescent is likely to respond with disobedience and dishonesty (Buehler, 2006), and the two generations are more likely to become distant when the teenager reaches adulthood.

"So I blame you for everything—whose fault is that?"

Neglect In Chapter 10, you learned that authoritative parenting is usually the best parenting style for school-age children and that uninvolved parenting is the worst. The same holds true for adolescents.

Although teenagers may act as if they no longer need their parents, neglect can be very destructive. Sixteen-year-old Joy's stepfather said confidently, "Teens all around here [are] doing booze and doing drugs. . . . But my Joy here ain't into that stuff" (C. Smith, 2005, p. 10).

In fact, however, Joy was smoking pot, drinking alcohol, and having sex with her boyfriend. She later reported that she "overdosed on a bunch of stuff once, pills or some prescription of my mom's—I took the whole bottle. It didn't work. I just went to sleep for a long time. . . . They never found out . . . pretty pitiful" (quoted in C. Smith, 2005, p. 12). That suicide attempt was a clear indication that she was in far worse trouble than most "teens all around here."

Independence and Culture Regarding parent–adolescent relationships, some cultures value family harmony above all else. Attempting to live up to that ideal, both generations avoid conflict; the adolescents suppress their own needs and wishes for the sake of keeping peace in the family. Developmentalists have varied responses: A high priority on family peace may be either repressive or healthy.

It could be that adolescent rebellion is a *social construction,* assumed to be necessary by middle-class Westerners but not by those of other cultures or socioeconomic status (Larson & Wilson, 2004). Or it could be that a phase of bickering followed by independence is the foundation of a healthy adulthood.

When conflict does occur, culture affects the topics of disagreement and the methods of expression. For example, Japanese youth expect autonomy in their musical choices but want parents to help them with romance; in contrast, parental interference in their love lives might make U.S. adolescents bristle (Hasebe et al., 2004). In Chile, adolescents typically obey their parents, even when they disagree, as long as they think parental authority is legitimate (Darling et al., 2008).

In every nation, family role models are influential, as the discussion of vocational identity made clear. This applies to destructive behaviors as well as to constructive ones. If older siblings are aggressive, are sexually active, or use drugs, teenagers are more likely to follow their example than to learn from their mistakes (Bank et al., 2004; Brody, 2004; East & Kiernan, 2001). Conflict with parents peaks earlier for younger siblings, another example of the power of observation of a family role model (Shanahan et al., 2007; see the Research Design).

Research Design

Scientists: Lilly Shanahan, Susan M. McHale, D. Wayne Osgood, and Ann C. Crouter.

Publication: *Developmental Psychology* (2007).

Participants: Families consisting of two siblings living with their married parents, 201 in total. The elder children were 10 to 14 years old at the start of the study, and their siblings were one to four years younger.

Design: At four intervals over five years, participants were asked about the frequency of fights with each parent in 11 domains (e.g., chores, appearance, health, relationships).

Major conclusions: Conflict peaked at about age 13 for first-born children and at about age 9 for second-born. Younger siblings had fewer conflicts overall than first-borns.

Comment: This study considers several family interaction patterns over time. Not only do younger siblings tend to follow their elder siblings (called spillover) but parents also tend to learn from experience, finding ways to avoid conflicts by the time the second child reaches puberty. Research on other types of families might show whether this pattern holds for them as well.

Closeness Within the Family

Conflict is one dimension of the parent–child relationship that is easy to notice, although it is not necessarily the most important. Another key factor that impacts the parent–child relationship is closeness, which has four specific aspects:

- Communication (Do parents and teens talk openly with one another?)
- Support (Do they rely on one another?)
- Connectedness (How emotionally close are they?)
- Control (Do parents encourage or limit adolescent autonomy?)

No developmentalist doubts that the first two, communication and support, are helpful, perhaps essential. Patterns of these set in place during childhood continue. If the patterns are positive, they provide adolescents with a buffer against some of the turbulence of the period (Cleveland et al., 2005; Collins & Laursen, 2004).

Emotional Dependency Regarding connectedness and control, consequences vary and observers differ in what they see. Consider this example, written by one of my students:

> I got pregnant when I was sixteen years old, and if it weren't for the support of my parents, I would probably not have my son. And if they hadn't taken care of him, I wouldn't have been able to finish high school or attend college. My parents also helped me overcome the shame that I felt when . . . my aunts, uncles, and especially my grandparents found out that I was pregnant.
>
> *[I, personal communication, 2004]*

➤Answer to Observation Quiz (from page 476): Facial expressions, degree of adult supervision, and head covering. (Did you notice that the Kashmiri girls wear a tight-fitting cap under their one-piece white robes?)

My student is grateful to her parents, but other observers might wonder whether her early motherhood allowed them too much control and required her to remain dependent when she should have been seeking her own identity. A study of pregnant adolescents in the United States found that in many cases (though not all) young mothers and their children fared best if the teen's parents were supportive but did not take over the care of the child (Borkowski et al., 2007).

An added complexity is that my student's parents had emigrated from South America: Cultural expectations affected her family's response to her pregnancy. In general, U.S. adolescents tend to be more dependent on their parents if they are female and from a minority ethnic group (Gnaulati & Heine, 2001). Again, this pattern could be either repressive or healthy.

parental monitoring Parents' ongoing awareness of what their children are doing, where, and with whom.

Do You Know Where Your Teenager Is? An important correlate of family closeness is **parental monitoring**—that is, parental knowledge about the child's whereabouts, activities, and companions. When monitoring is part of a warm, supportive relationship, the child is likely to become a confident, well-educated adult and to avoid drugs and risky sex (G. M. Barnes et al., 2006; Fletcher et al., 2004).

However, overly restrictive and controlling parenting correlates with depression and other disorders in teenagers, who may develop a habit of deceiving their parents. Worst of all may be *psychological control* (a threat to withdraw love and support; see Chapter 10) (Barber, 2002). Apparently, at least in the United States, adolescents need freedom in order to feel competent and loved. Parental monitoring itself may be harmful when it derives from harsh suspicion instead of from a warm connection with the adolescent (Smetana, 2008; Stattin & Kerr, 2000).

Ongoing Influence

Finding the right balance between autonomy and monitoring, between independence and support, is difficult. Each family adjusts to individual members' personalities and to cultural influences. The worst thing a parent can do is to give up and adopt the uninvolved parenting style described in Chapter 10. Even if teenagers seem oblivious or defiant, parents are still influential; this is true for all families, not only for intact, middle-class ones (B. Brown, 2005; Richardson, 2004).

One detailed study measured the self-esteem of low-income minority students in a large New York City high school. The researchers found that the school climate had little impact on self-esteem but that relationships with parents were significant. In the words of the study, "parents are a primary presence in their children's emotional lives throughout adolescence," whether they are African American, Latino, or Asian American (Greene & Way, 2005, p. 171).

Of course, genes, maturation, and friendships also affect a child's personality and activities. But parents have a decided impact through their guidance, modeling, and past decisions that affect the child (e.g., neighborhood and school choices). Children tend to follow their parents' examples in many activities, including religious involvement, drug use, and sports preferences (Rose, 2007).

Overall, ineffective parenting during childhood may produce angry, uncontrollable adolescents (Cleveland et al., 2005; Li et al., 2002). Past parenting continues to affect later behavior (Eisenberg et al., 2008). For example, one longitudinal study found a correlation between parenting style when children were in seventh grade and any problems they had (law-breaking, unprotected sex, drug use, etc.) in the eleventh grade. These researchers wrote:

> When parents permit too much freedom, they may put their young adolescents at risk for a negative peer context, but they can also put their young adolescents at risk if they are perceived as being too intrusive.
>
> *[Goldstein et al., 2005, p. 409]*

Peer Support

Parental influence is notable in childhood and at puberty. During adolescence, peer influence becomes more prominent. From hanging out with a crowd to whispering with a confidant, peers add joy to life (Tarrant et al., 2006). As one high school boy said:

> A lot of times I wake up in the morning and I don't want to go to school, and then I'm like, you know, I have got this class and these friends are in it, and I am going to have fun. That is a big part of my day—my friends.
>
> *[quoted in Hamm & Faircloth, 2005, p. 72]*

Cliques and Crowds

Adolescents organize themselves into cliques and crowds (Collins & Steinberg, 2006; Eckert, 1989), groups that help their members "bridge the gap between childhood and adulthood" (Bagwell et al., 2001, p. 26). A cluster of close friends who are loyal to one another and who exclude outsiders is called a **clique.** A **crowd** is a larger group of adolescents who share common interests, though they may not necessarily be friends.

clique A group of adolescents made up of close friends who are loyal to one another while excluding outsiders.

crowd A larger group of adolescents who have something in common but who are not necessarily friends.

A crowd may use small signs of identity (a certain brand of backpack, a particular greeting) that adults do not notice but members of other crowds do (Strouse, 1999). Crowds may be based predominantly on race or ethnicity, or on some personal characteristic or activity, such as the "brains," "jocks," "skaters," or "burnouts." Generally, the behavior of individual members is guided by the crowd's preferences in such areas as clothing, music, drugs, and school classes.

Allegiance to a crowd is much looser than to a clique. For example, a student could dress like those in a crowd (with trench coats, baggy pants, or sports shirts) but hold values unlike most of that crowd. By contrast, adolescents compare themselves with the members of their cliques, following their clique's norms rather than those of their crowd (Killeya-Jones et al., 2007).

Especially for Parents of a Teenager (see response, page 482): Your 13-year-old comes home after a sleepover at a friend's house with a new, weird hairstyle—perhaps cut or colored in a bizarre manner. What do you say and do?

Cliques and crowds provide social control and social support. They promote group standards, not directly but through criticism and social avoidance (B. Brown & Klute, 2003). Compared with primary school children, many adolescents consider appearance and style (often in opposition to adult norms) important for peer acceptance.

Choosing Friends

For many teenagers, peers become "like family," "brothers and sisters" (Way et al., 2005). In violent neighborhoods, friends not only defend against attacks but also help each other avoid physical fights. One 16-year-old boy said about his friend:

> Well, with him when I'm in an argument with somebody that disrespected me and he just comes out and backs me up and says "Yo, Chris, don't deal with that. Yo, let's just go on," you know, 'cause I could snap.
>
> *[quoted in Way et al., 2005, p. 48]*

"Snapping" is a potential danger for all adolescents, given their quick, intuitive reactions. Having a friend who says "Don't deal with that" can help them stay calm and protect them from self-destruction.

As in this example, peers can be constructive (Audrey et al., 2006; B. Brown, 2004). The adult fear of **peer pressure,** which usually means social pressure to conform to negative peer activities, ignores the other possibility—that "friends generally encourage socially desirable behaviors" (Berndt & Murphy, 2002, p. 281). Members of a clique or crowd support each other in joining sports teams, studying for exams, not smoking cigarettes, and applying to college.

peer pressure Encouragement to conform to one's friends or contemporaries in behavior, dress, and attitude; often a positive force, but usually considered a negative one, as when adolescent peers encourage one another to defy adult authority.

deviancy training Destructive peer support in which one person shows another how to rebel against authority or social norms.

Troublemakers Young people *can* lead one another into trouble, however. Collectively, peers sometimes provide **deviancy training,** in which one person shows another how to rebel against social norms (Dishion et al., 2001). Especially if adolescents believe that the most popular, most admired peers are having sex, doing drugs, or ignoring homework, they become more likely to take up the destructive behavior themselves (Rodgers, 2003). Deviancy training is a form of *social contagion:* People transmit behaviors, actions, and emotions to each other simply by being near each other.

Admiration for peers who ignore adult standards begins in early childhood. In one study, when 5-year-olds were recorded playing together without adults nearby, almost every child (87 percent) said something taboo (e.g., about sex or drugs) or anti-authority. Such talk captured the attention and often approval of the other 5-year-olds. As children mature, approval of deviancy continues; socially skilled deviants are likely to become leaders as well as delinquents later on (Snyder et al., 2008).

Selection and Facilitation To understand the impact of peers, two concepts are helpful: *selection* and *facilitation.* Teenagers select friends whose values and interests they share, abandoning friends who follow other paths. Peer selection and rejection is an active process, as adolescents test each other in various ways—confiding secrets, lending money, and so on (Way & Hamm, 2005).

Peers facilitate both destructive and constructive behaviors in one another, making it easier to do the wrong thing ("Let's all skip school on Friday") and the right thing ("Let's study together for that chemistry exam"). Peer facilitation helps individuals do things that they would be unlikely to do on their own.

Both selection and facilitation can work in any direction (Lacourse et al., 2003). One teenager joins a clique whose members smoke cigarettes and drink beer, and together they take the next step, perhaps passing around a joint at a party. Another teenager might choose friends who enjoy math puzzles, and, like Lindsay and her friends, all of them might enroll in AP calculus:

> [Companionship] makes me excited about calculus. That is a hard class, but when you need help with calculus, you go to your friends. You may think no one could be excited about calculus, but I am. Having friends in class with you definitely makes school more enjoyable.
>
> *[quoted in Hamm & Faircloth, 2005, p. 72]*

Thus, adolescents select and facilitate, choose and are chosen, encourage each other. Happy, energetic, and successful adolescents have close friends who themselves are high-achieving, with no major emotional problems. The opposite also holds: Those who are drug users, sexually active, and alienated from school choose compatible friends and provide mutual support to each other in continuing on that path (Crosnoe & Needham, 2004).

One other point about peer pressure should be made: It can be invoked to deflect, and defend against, adult criticism. When adolescents tell their parents that they must wear something or go somewhere because "everyone else is doing it," or when they break a law because someone else suggested it, they are trying to absolve themselves of responsibility (Ungar, 2000). Thus, when parents blame their teenage child's misbehavior on his or her friends, they ignore the child's own role in the peer group.

➤Response for Parents of a Teenager (from page 481): Remember: Communicate, do not control. Let your child talk about the meaning of the hairstyle. Remind yourself that a hairstyle in itself is harmless. Don't say "What will people think?" or "Are you on drugs?" or anything that might give your child reason to stop communicating.

Playing "Chicken" An interesting experiment in peer facilitation compared the risk-taking behavior of a group of adolescents (ages 13 to 16), emerging adults (ages 18 to 22), and adults (over age 24) (Gardner & Steinberg, 2005) in a video driving game called Chicken. Every so often, the video screen would flash a yellow light, indicating that soon (in one to several seconds) a wall would appear. The participants had to decide when to put on the brakes. The goal was to keep driving as long as possible but to stop before crashing into the wall. Points were gained for travel time; a crash erased all the points from that round.

The participants were randomly assigned to one of two conditions: playing alone or with two strangers of the same sex and age as themselves. When they played alone, adolescents, emerging adults, and adults all averaged one crash per 15-round session. That single crash was enough to make them wary. Adults were equally cautious when playing with peers. But when the adolescents were with peers, they became much bolder, crashing three times, on average (see Figure 16.1) (Gardner & Steinberg, 2005; Steinberg, 2007). They chose to lose points rather than to appear cautious.

Facilitation is usually mutual, not a matter of a rebel leading an innocent astray (B. Brown & Klute, 2003). In the video game experiment, each person in a three-member group of participants played 15 rounds while the other two players watched and waited for their turn. Witnessing a crash did not diminish the bystanders' willingness to take risks when it was their turn (Gardner & Steinberg, 2005).

A teenager from another study explained:

> The idea of peer pressure is a lot of bunk. What I heard about peer pressure all the way through school is that someone is going to walk up to me and say, "Here, drink this and you'll be cool." It wasn't like that at all. You'd go somewhere and everyone else would be doing it and you'd think, "Hey, everyone else is doing it and they seem to be having a good time—now why wouldn't I do this?" In that sense, the preparation of the powers that be, the lessons that they tried to drill into me, they were completely off. They had no idea what we are up against.
>
> *[quoted in Lightfoot, 1997]*

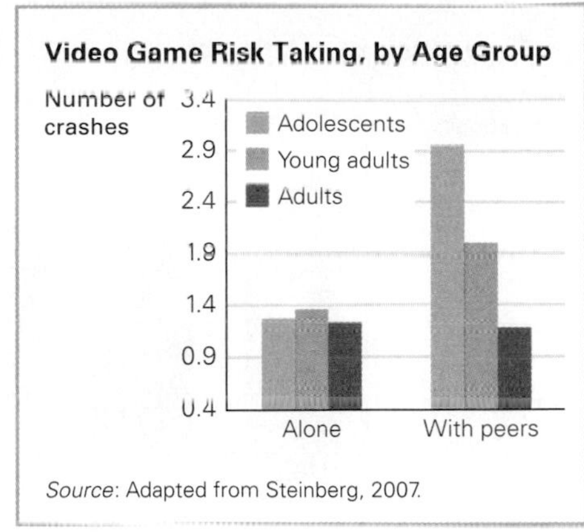

FIGURE 16.1

Admire Me Everyone wants to accumulate points in a game, earn high grades, and save money—unless one is a teenager and other teens are watching. Then a desire to obtain peer admiration by taking risks may overtake caution. At least in this game, teenage participants chose to lose points and increase crashes when other teens were present.

Immigrant Youth

Friends play a special role for immigrant adolescents. Many immigrant children become model youth, earning higher grades and having fewer emotional and behavior problems than nonimmigrants of the same ethnicity (Rumbaut & Portes, 2001; Vega et al., 2007). They may be excluded from the cliques of the native-born, but they rely on friends who are also immigrants (Azmitia et al., 2006).

Especially for Teachers of Immigrants (see response, page 485): Your immigrant students' parents never come to open-school nights or answer the written notes you send home. What should you do?

Parents Versus Peers Immigrant family members typically depend on their adolescents, who help out at home and mediate between the old and new cultures (see Figure 16.2) (Trickett & Jones, 2007; Tseng, 2004). Adolescents benefit from this arrangement, in that they gain respect within their families and experience community support, encouragement, and ethnic pride—all of which help them in a strange and sometimes hostile environment (Fuligni et al., 2005).

However, conflict can arise if the parents seek to maintain traditional practices that differ markedly from those of teenage culture (Suarez-Orozco & Suarez-Orozco, 2001). Conflict also seems to arise when the parents rely too much on their adolescents to translate and mediate between the original culture and the new one (Trickett & Jones, 2007). For one thing, these demands reduce the amount of time adolescents can spend socializing with peers.

All adolescents want to respect their parents and fit in with their peers—a sometimes impossible combination, made more difficult when the new and old cultures have different attitudes about the importance of friends (Bukowski & Adams, 2006). A parent–peer clash can occur in any family, but it is particularly common when immigrant parents expect children to silently heed their elders, while adolescents expect to follow the North American practice of expressing their disagreement and making their own choices (Collins & Steinberg, 2006).

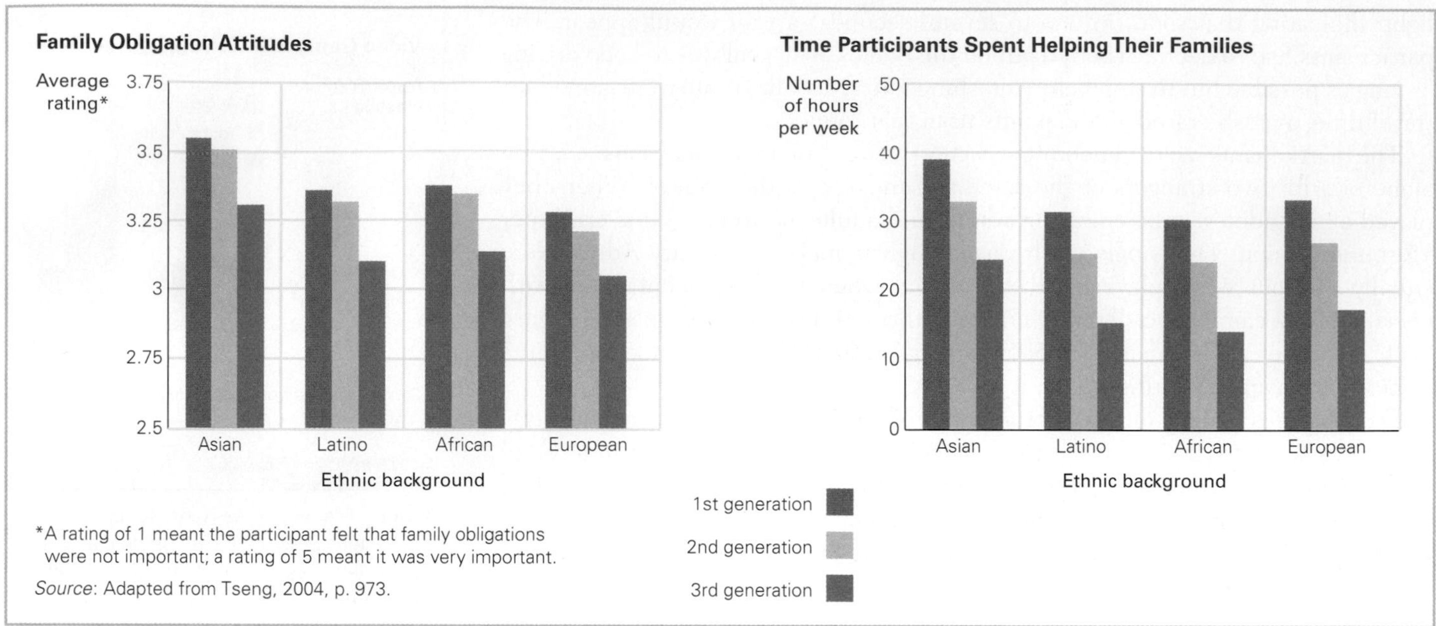

FIGURE 16.2

A Sense of Duty Nearly 1,000 U.S. college students from four ethnic groups were asked how important they thought family obligations were and how much time they spent each week helping their families (e.g., by doing household chores, translating for their parents, taking care of siblings, or working in the family business).

Observation Quiz (see answer, page 486): How many hours a week does the average first-generation immigrant college student spend helping out at home?

A Yemeni Girl in Michigan Friends may be crucial in helping adolescents and parents reconcile conflicting cultures, traditions, and desires. One example is Layla, whose family emigrated from Yemen and now lives near Detroit. At age 15, Layla was sent back to Yemen to marry her father's nephew. She later returned to her Michigan public high school and tried to keep her marriage secret (she wore no wedding ring).

Layla's high school was "both liberating and a sociocultural threat" (Sarroub, 2001, p. 390). The hidden curriculum expected teenagers to speak their minds (receiving points for participation), dress as they chose (no uniforms), and question adult authority (the student council). Equal education for both sexes is U.S. law, whereas "the gender gap in education in Yemen is among the highest in the world, with more than half of the women illiterate" (UNICEF, 2006).

What did Layla do as she tried to find her own identity? She respected her parents and adhered to the tenets of the family's Islamic faith, but she rebelled against many aspects of her heritage. For example, she was troubled that her father chewed *qaat* (a mild narcotic that is legal in Yemen but illegal in the United States), that he wanted her to wear the traditional long dresses (she wore jeans instead), and that he did not endorse her plan to get a divorce and go to college.

Layla especially resented that Yemeni tradition allowed boys more freedom than girls.

> At times Layla was confused and unhappy at home. She . . . preferred going to school where she could be with her Yemeni friends who understood her problems and with whom she could talk. "They make me feel, like, really happy. I have friends that have to deal with the same issues." . . . Layla was often angry that girls in Yemen were taken out of school. . . . She thought that the boys had been given too much freedom, much more than the girls.
>
> *[Sarroub, 2001, pp. 408–409]*

Layla is typical of many immigrant youth, who rely on friends to deal with culture clashes. Developmentalists disagree over whether the close interdependence of many immigrant families is more helpful or harmful to adolescent development. The answer probably depends on the specifics, including which issue is being dealt with, which culture is involved, and how much social support both parent and child have (Trickett & Jones, 2007).

Asian immigrant youth may particularly need friends. They tend to have lower self-esteem than do other immigrant youth, to have more family obligations, and to experience more discrimination from other teenagers (Greene & Way, 2005; Greene et al., 2006).

People of every ethnicity tend to befriend others of the same background (McPherson et al., 2001). Since friendship is particularly important during adolescence, it should not be surprising that immigrant adolescents rely on each other. For young people of every group, peers help in coping with parents, school, and one another.

SUMMING UP

Relationships with peers as well as with adults are crucial during adolescence. Parents and adolescents often bicker over small things, but parental monitoring and ongoing communication are helpful to adolescent psychosocial health. Parental neglect or excessive parental control can foster adolescent rebellion; authoritative parenting continues to be effective.

Peers aid adolescents in their search for self-esteem and maturity. Some peer groups encourage self-destructive, antisocial behavior, but more often friends help each other cope with biological, social, and emotional stresses in constructive ways. Friends, cliques, and crowds offer support for adolescents and facilitate behavior, both constructive and destructive, that individuals might not engage in alone. Immigrant adolescents are less likely to join traditional crowds and cliques, but they are aided by their friends as they try to make a place for themselves and succeed in the new culture into which their family has moved. ■

➤Response for Teachers of Immigrants (from page 483): Perhaps the parents cannot read English, or work or family obligations may prevent them from coming to school in the evening. You might ask your students to set up home visits for you at a suitable time for the parents. Then go to praise their child more than criticize.

Sexuality

No arena highlights the overlapping influences of parents, peers, and the wider community more clearly than sexuality. Human nature endows adolescents with strong sexual impulses. Societies then steer those impulses in a variety of directions—toward frightening dreams, stolen glances, pleasurable fantasies, or early pregnancy.

Much remains to be discovered about sexual activity during adolescence (B. Brown, 2006). Research ethics require parental permission before questions are asked of anyone younger than 18, and many parents refuse to let strangers ask their children about romance or sexuality. Nonetheless, some basics are known. The sex drive is strong and universal, triggered by androgens and estrogens, but sexual relationships vary in strength and expression. Some adolescents repress their sexual urges and others are obsessed by them; some 15-year-olds are married and pregnant, others have multiple partners and run from commitment. In this section, we discuss both universality and diversity.

Sequences: From Asexual to Active

Decades ago, Dexter Dunphy (1963) described the sequence of male–female relationships during childhood and adolescence:

1. Groups of friends, exclusively one sex or the other
2. A loose association of girls and boys, with public interactions within a crowd
3. Small mixed-sex groups of the advanced members of the crowd
4. Formation of couples, with private intimacies

Contemporary Patterns

Culture affects the timing and manifestation of each step on Dunphy's list, but subsequent research in many nations validates the sequence. Youth in many lands (and even the young of many species) avoid members of the other sex in childhood and are attracted to them by adulthood. This suggests that biology underlies these changes (B. Brown, 2004; Connolly et al., 2000; Weisfeld, 1999).

In modern developed nations, where puberty begins at about age 10 and marriage occurs much later, each of these four stages typically lasts several years. Same-sex groups dominate in elementary school. Same-sex friends often remain close throughout middle and high schools in the form of cliques or sports teams. Groups of same-sex friends talk about the other sex but avoid one-on-one private interaction until age 16 or later.

Early, exclusive romances are more often a sign of social trouble than maturity (B. Brown, 2004). Unlike the norm in earlier centuries and in some nations today, in North America and Europe a long-lasting commitment to one partner does not usually occur until adulthood; few people marry before age 25 or so.

Friends of Both Sexes

Contemporary adolescents often have friends of the other sex who are not their lovers. Adults sometimes worry about boy–girl contact, assuming that teenagers will have sex if adults are not nearby. They also worry about close boy–boy and girl–girl friendships, fearing homosexuality. However, many teenagers do have close, even passionate, friendships with peers of both sexes, without romantic undertones. Disruptions of such friendships can cause jealousy or depression, even though there is no sexual intimacy.

As we have seen, friends help adolescents establish their identity and join together in cliques and crowds. Adolescents also rely on friends for information and encouragement regarding romance, partly because teenage romances are often short-lived whereas friendships last for years (B. L. Barber, 2006; Collins & van Dulmen, 2006; Feiring, 1999).

Romances, Straight and Gay

The first romances appear in high school, rarely lasting more than a year. Girls claim a steady partner more often than boys do. Love is often thrilling. It is not unusual for a teenager to "fall in love" and temporarily feel unable to sleep, eat, or think.

Breakups are common; so are unreciprocated crushes. Both can be devastating, in part because often entire high school crowds are witnesses (Schwartz, 2006). Adolescents are crushed by rejection, often contemplating revenge or suicide (Fisher, 2006). In such cases, peer support can be a lifesaver.

Overall, healthy romances in later adolescence manifest a life replete with good relationships with parents and peers (Laursen & Mooney, 2007). That triple support network means that a fight with a parent, a slight from a peer, or the breakup of a romance can be taken in stride because the other two arenas provide reassurance.

For homosexual adolescents, complications slow down the formation of friendships and romantic bonds. To begin with, many do not acknowledge their sexual orientation, sometimes not even to themselves. Furthermore, national and peer cultures often make the homosexual young person feel ashamed. For example, in many Latino cultures, "adolescents who pursue same-sex sexuality are viewed by their communities as having fundamentally failed as men or women" (Diamond & Savin-Williams, 2003, p. 399).

➤Answer to Observation Quiz (from page 484): The average for all three groups is about 33 hours.

Many gay youth of every ethnicity date members of the other sex to hide their orientation (B. Brown, 2006). Past cohorts of gay youth had higher rates of clinical depression, drug abuse, and even suicide than did their heterosexual peers; it is not known if this is true for the current cohort (Savin-Williams & Diamond, 2004).

We do not even know how many youth are homosexual, heterosexual, bisexual, or asexual. In the mid-1990s, one large study of high school students in Massachusetts found only 0.5 percent who identified themselves as gay or lesbian (Garofalo et al., 1999). More recently, a large Dutch study of high school students found that 8.5 percent said they were attracted to people of the same sex as themselves (Bos et al., 2008).

The different percentages reported in these two studies may reflect culture, cohort, and specifics of the questionnaire. It may be that youth are willing to admit attraction but do not want to "identify" as any one orientation rather than another (Savin-Williams, 2005).

This latter possibility is suggested by research on adults conducted 15 years ago in the United States. As adolescents, about 10 percent of the participants had had same-sex encounters or desires, yet most of them were heterosexual adults (Laumann et al., 1994). It could be that homosexual desires are part of sexual awakening for many adolescents (only a fraction of whom report it), or it could be that many people who are bisexual as teenagers later become exclusively heterosexual.

Eleanor Maccoby (1998), an expert on gender issues, wrote that "a substantial number of people experiment with same-sex sexuality at some point in their lives, and a small minority settle into a life-long pattern of homosexuality" (p. 191). All reports find that sexual experimentation is common in adolescence, but no one knows how many people constitute that "substantial number" who "experiment with same-sex sexuality."

Retrospectively, many homosexual men report that they became aware of their sexual orientation at about age 11 but told no one until about age 17 (Maguen et al., 2002). By contrast, most girls who later identify as lesbian are oblivious to, or in denial of, their sexual urges in adolescence, perhaps because sexual self-knowledge is more difficult for girls (Baumeister & Blackhart, 2007). Many lesbians first recognize their sexual orientation in adulthood via a same-sex friendship that becomes romantic (Savin-Williams & Diamond, 2004).

Similar secrecy, awakening, and sexual confusion may occur for all youth. Many teenagers believe they have found the love of their life but soon afterward wonder how they could have been so wrong about someone. Many also worry that they are oversexed, undersexed, or deviant in some way. Research on adult sexuality finds great diversity; many adolescents do not know that there are thousands, maybe millions, of people like themselves.

© RICHARD LORD / THE IMAGE WORKS

© DONNA RANIERI / BLINKSTOCK

The Same Situation, Many Miles Apart: Teenagers in Love No matter where in the world they are, teenage couples broadcast their love in universally recognized facial expressions and body positions. Samantha and Ryan (*top*), visiting New York City from suburban Philadelphia, are similar in many ways to the teen couple (*bottom*) in Chicute, Mozambique, even though their social contexts are dramatically different.

Learning About Sex

Traditionally, intense romantic attachments in adolescence were considered a threat to normal development because they disrupted bonding between families (Coontz, 2006). Arranged childhood marriages (often to uncles or cousins), sending adolescents to monasteries or convents, chastity belts, shotgun weddings, polygamy—each of these reactions to adolescent sexuality has been considered desirable in some cultures and unnatural in others.

Today, parents and societies continue to be concerned about adolescent sexual relationships. Sex education (whether accurate or not, whether provided by parents, schools, or the media) is the most commonly used method to control adolescent sexuality. However, current messages about teenage sexuality are contradictory. Consistent and reliable guidance—about both the joys and the hazards of sex—is scarce.

For example, parents and teachers rarely discuss oral sex, even though the practice is common among adolescents (Brewster & Tillman, 2008). The lack of information leads many adolescents to conclude that as long as oral sex does not proceed to penetration, it is "safe"—a dangerously egocentric notion, given that some serious infections can be transmitted through oral sex (Kalmuss et al., 2003).

Similarly, less than half of teenagers worldwide understand how AIDS is transmitted. In South Africa, 5.5 million adults (19 percent of the population, mostly young adults) are HIV-positive—the highest number of any country in the world (UNAIDS, 2006). One reason for this high rate of infection is that, until 2003, the South African government spread misinformation about HIV/AIDS (insisting, for example, that the disease is not caused by a virus).

The opposite may be true in the United States, where young adolescents overestimate the risk of AIDS because adults invoke the fear of it in an effort to deter sexual activity among adolescents (Reyna & Farley, 2006). Throughout the world, HIV/AIDS is much better understood today than it was a decade ago. As a result, every continent has at least one nation where transmission rates are down (UNAIDS, 2006).

Learning from Peers

Adolescent sexual behavior is strongly influenced by the example of peers. Many teens discuss details of romance and sex with other members of their clique, seeking their friends' approval (Laursen & Mooney, 2007). Often, the boys brag and the girls worry about gaining a "reputation." Specifics depend on the group: All members of a clique may be virgins, or all may be sexually active.

Among contemporary U.S. teens, some church-based crowds take a "virginity pledge," vowing to postpone their first sexual intercourse until marriage. If the group considers itself a select minority and virginity is a distinguishing feature, then that becomes significant for all group members (Bearman & Brückner, 2001).

When high school crowds disperse at graduation, members who have taken a virginity pledge are more likely to marry and less likely to use contraception than are other adolescents. As a result, many become parents, but fewer are single parents (Johnson & Rector, 2004). Such findings gratify those who favor traditional patterns of sexual behavior, but they worry scientists who see a group of emerging adults at risk for early parenthood, which reduces their eventual level of education (Brückner & Bearman, 2005; Mebane et al., 2006).

Sexual experience is also strongly influenced by whether an adolescent is in an ongoing romantic relationship. Probably for this reason, physically attractive adolescents who experience early puberty are more likely to date and become sexually active, especially if they are girls who are gratified by the attention of older boys (Friedlander et al., 2007). Partners teach each other, and the lessons are not always what adults would like them to be. Ideally, before having sex, a teenage girl and boy would discuss the risks of pregnancy and sexually transmitted infections (STIs), but only about half of U.S. adolescent couples actually do so (Ryan et al., 2007).

Learning from Parents

Parents, through their monitoring, modeling, and conversation, are pivotal in every teenager's sexual decisions. However, many parents underestimate their adolescent's need for sexual information. Many parents wait to discuss sex until their child is already in a romantic relationship, and that may be too late to convey information about contraception and a shared responsibility (Eisenberg et al. 2006).

Especially for Sex Educators (see response, page 491): Suppose adults in your community never talk to their children about sex or puberty. Is that a mistake?

Furthermore, many parents know little about their adolescents' sexual activity. For example, when parents of 12-year-old girls were asked if their daughter had hugged or kissed a boy "for a long time" or hung out with older boys (both signs that sex information is urgently needed), only 5 percent said yes—but 38 percent of the daughters said yes (O'Donnell et al., 2008). Similar discrepancies are found in the responses of other adolescent–parent pairs (Guilamo-Ramos et al., 2007; Jaccard et al., 1998, 2000).

Parents also misjudge how seriously their children take their advice. One study concludes that "parent perceptions of how much credibility, trust, and accessibility they think they have established with their adolescents bear only a weak relationship to adolescent characterizations of parent credibility, trust, and accessibility" (Guilamo-Ramos et al., 2006, p. 1242).

Religious parents tend to be hesitant in talking about sex (except to warn their teens against it) (Regnerus, 2005), but religion is *not* the most significant correlate of whether parent–child conversations occur; gender and age are. Parents are more likely to talk to daughters than to sons and to older adolescents (over 15) than to younger ones. This is not good news, since young adolescent boys are most likely to heed, and need, advice about safer-sex practices (Kirby, 2001).

One problem is that parents underestimate adolescents' capacity to engage in responsible sex. For example, another study found that only 23 percent of mothers and 33 percent of fathers thought that most teenagers were capable of using a condom correctly (M. E. Eisenberg et al., 2004). In fact, however, many of these parents could learn from their teenagers: Condom use is higher among adolescents than among older adults.

Parental example may be as important as conversations. Many teens notice that their divorced parents are seeking new sexual partners. This may be why adolescents who do not live with both biological parents are more than twice as likely to begin a sexual relationship as are teens who do (Blum et al., 2000; Ellis et al., 2003). Similarly, one risk factor for becoming a teenage parent is having been born to a teenage single mother (Bonell et al., 2006).

Sex Education in School

Aware that things have changed since they were teenagers, almost all parents want other adults to provide their adolescents with up-to-date sex education, including information on safe sex and contraception (Landry et al., 2003; Yarber et al., 2005). Developmentalists agree that sex education belongs in the schools as well as in parent–child conversations, since adolescents need to learn from trusted and experienced adults before they misinform each other.

Sex education policies vary dramatically by nation. Most European schools begin sex education in elementary school, and by middle school they teach about sexual responsibility, masturbation, and oral and anal sex—subjects that are rarely covered in U.S. sex-education programs. Rates of teenage pregnancy in most European nations are less than half those in the United States, although curriculum is only one of many possible reasons. In most Asian and African nations, sex education is absent from the school curriculum, and many parents promote the double standard, warning their daughters of sexual dangers while expecting their sons to experiment (UNAIDS, 2006).

In the United States, the timing and content of sex education vary by state and community. Some schools provide comprehensive programs, offering free condoms and medical treatment, and others provide nothing at all. One recent controversy is whether abstinence should be taught as the best, or only, sexual strategy for adolescents.

Research Design

Scientists: Christopher Trenholm, Barbara Devaney, Ken Fortson, Lisa Quay, Justin Wheeler, and Melissa Clark.

Publication: Report to the U.S. Department of Health and Human Services by Mathematica Policy Research (2007).

Participants: Students in Powhatan, Virginia; Milwaukee, Wisconsin; Miami, Florida; and Clarksdale, Mississippi, were randomly assigned to be enrolled in the abstinence-only classes or not. Both groups were large enough to allow valid comparisons (1,209 in the experimental groups, 848 in the control groups).

Design: All four cities' programs were intense (more than 50 contact hours) and all began early (between ages 10 and 12). Significant differences among the four regions allowed the scientists to discover whether one version of abstinence-only education was more effective than the other and whether one population (for example, two were rural and two were urban) responded better than another. Four to six years after the programs began, students (then age 16, on average) were asked about their knowledge and behavior.

Major conclusion: No matter what the programs were, the abstinence-only curriculum had no impact on sexual experience (51 percent of both groups had had intercourse, on average, at age 14) and virtually no impact on other aspects of behavior. For example, some adults thought that abstinence-only students would not use condoms, but condom use was equal in both groups (only 9 percent of those who were sexually active never used a condom).

Comment: Neither the best hopes nor the worst fears about abstinence-only programs were confirmed. This report encourages researchers to evaluate efforts to change adolescent behavior, and its findings were one reason Congress stopped funding abstinence-only programs in 2007.

Abstinence-Only Programs The U.S. government began a massive experiment in 1998, spending about $1 billion over 10 years to promote *abstinence-only* sex education. The goal was to teach adolescents to prevent pregnancy and STIs by waiting until marriage before becoming sexually active. These programs emphasized the need for younger teens to feel confident in themselves, able to say no to sex. No information about other methods was provided, because it was feared that such knowledge might encourage teens to become sexually active.

Longitudinal evaluations conducted four to six years after the abstinence-only curriculum was launched revealed that it had had little effect. About half of students in both experimental (abstinence-only) and control groups had had sex by age 16. The number of partners and use of contraceptives were the same with and without the special curriculum (Trenholm et al., 2007; see the Research Design). Students in the control groups knew slightly more about preventing disease and pregnancy, but this knowledge did not slow down or speed up their sexual initiation.

Starting Early Adults often disagree about what children should be taught about sex, but no curriculum has dramatically affected the age at which sexual activity begins. The most effective programs start before high school, include assignments that require parent–child communication, focus on behavior and not just information, and last for years (Kirby, 2002; Weaver et al., 2006). Even so, whether or not an adolescent becomes sexually active depends more on the influences of family, peers, and culture than on information from classes, according to a nationwide, controlled study of sex education in the United Kingdom (Allen et al., 2007).

Sex education can, however, affect some specific behaviors. For example, in a Texas program, half of the ninth-graders—the experimental group—received a two-year curriculum stressing safer-sex practices as well as abstinence (Coyle et al., 2001). Teachers involved parents and provided medical referrals for students who asked for them. Three years later, a survey found that students in both groups began to have intercourse at the same age (Coyle et al., 2001). However, those in the experimental group had sex less often and used condoms more often than those in the comparison group. The researchers wonder if the program started too late: One-fourth of the ninth-graders had already had sex.

In another study, a ninth-grade boy had apparently benefited from sex education, as his five uses of "make sure" illustrate:

> I do look forward to it, if it's with a good girl, a good person. I'm going to make sure to wear protection, make sure she doesn't have a disease, make sure we know what to do if the protection doesn't work. Make sure we know the consequences of it, make sure she would know the consequences of what would happen if not everything went right.
>
> *[quoted in Michels et al., 2005, p. 594]*

This boy is atypical in that, as we have seen, emotional thinking typically speeds ahead of analytic thinking during the teen years. Will he still think the same way a few years from now, and would ongoing classroom education make a difference?

The crucial test of any aspect of sex education is not whether adolescents can learn facts (most pass multiple-choice tests) but whether their knowledge affects their behavior. As already explained in Chapter 14, rates of adolescent pregnancy and STIs are still much higher than they should be.

Sexual Behavior

Not all teenagers are having sex. Rates of adolescent sexual activity vary widely from nation to nation. In the United States in 2007, more than half of all teenagers had had sexual intercourse by age 16 (or the eleventh grade), and rates had edged up since the previous year's survey (see Figure 16.3).

Norms vary markedly within nations. In the U.S. Youth Risk Behavior Survey of high school students, the percent who said they had had intercourse was two and a half times higher in Baltimore (67 percent) than in San Francisco (26 percent) (MMWR, June 6, 2008).

A higher proportion of teenage girls in the United States give birth than do their peers in any other developed nation (eight times the rate in Japan, twice the rate in Canada and Great Britain). The reason is not because U.S. girls are having more sex but because they are less likely to use contraception than girls in the other countries. Single motherhood is becoming more common in the United States. Compared with a few decades ago, fewer teenage girls get pregnant, but those who do become pregnant experience less social pressure to marry the fathers, are less likely to have abortions, and are less likely to choose adoption. In 1960, only 13 percent of all teenage mothers in the United States were unmarried, compared with 81 percent in 2003 (U.S. Bureau of the Census, 1972, 2006).

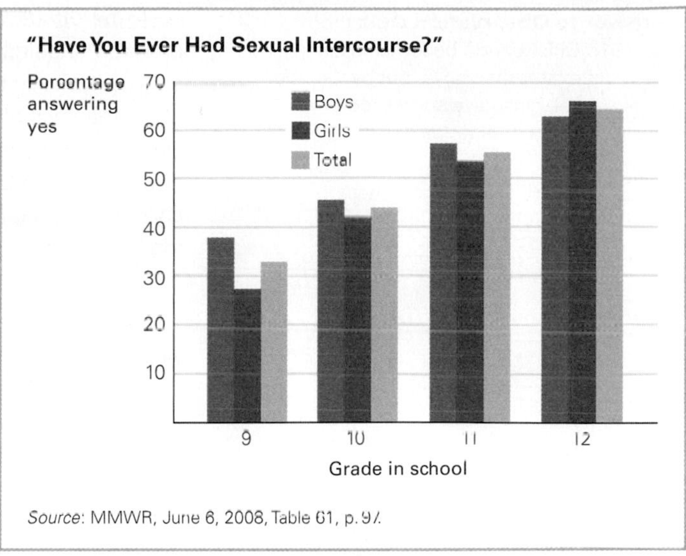

FIGURE 16.3

Is Everybody Doing It? No. About one-third of high school seniors and half of all students in grades 9 through 12, both boys and girls, are still virgins. The data for this graph are from the Youth Risk Behavior Survey, a national survey that asks the same questions of thousands of U.S. students in the ninth through twelfth grades each year. In 2007, about 14,000 students in 150 public and private schools in 44 states were surveyed.

Observation Quiz (see answer, page 492): How do boys' and girls' rates of sexual activity compare?

Other statistics are more encouraging:

- *Teen births overall have decreased dramatically in every nation.* For example, between 1960 and 2005, the adolescent birth rate in China was cut in half (reducing the United Nations' projections of the world's population by about a billion). This decline is continuing in every ethnic group within every nation. For instance, in 1991, the birth rate overall for U.S. teenagers age 15 to 17 was 39 per 1,000; in 2005, the ratio was 21 per 1,000. The largest decline among 15- to 17-year-old births was among African Americans, from 86 per 1,000 to 35—a 69 percent reduction in fourteen years (Martin et al., 2007).
- *The use of "protection" has risen.* Contraception, particularly condom use among adolescent boys, has increased markedly in most nations since 1990 (Santelli et al., 2007). The U.S. Youth Risk Behavior Survey found that 76 percent of sexually active ninth-grade boys had used a condom during their most recent intercourse (MMWR, June 6, 2008). About 20 percent of U.S. teenage couples use the pill *and* condoms, to prevent both pregnancy and infection (Manlove et al., 2003).
- *The teen abortion rate is down.* In the United States, only half as many teenagers had abortions in 2003 as in 1973 (MMWR, November 24, 2006).

These facts point to one conclusion: Although adolescent bodies and sex hormones are the same now as they have been for centuries, teenage responses to biological drives have changed dramatically. It is apparent that public policy and social norms affect even those decisions that seem to be most personal and private (Brindis, 2006; Teitler, 2002).

SUMMING UP

Adolescents have always been interested in sex, and societies have always attempted to control sexual expression. Given the earlier onset of puberty and later marriages today, adolescents are especially needful of accurate information and guidance. Parents, peers, and schools do not always teach adolescents what they need to know. Although parents are influential role models, many are slow to talk with their children about sex.

➤Response for Sex Educators (from page 489): Yes, but forgive them. Ideally, parents should talk to their children about sex, presenting honest information and listening to the child's concerns. However, many parents find it very difficult to do this because they feel embarrassed and ignorant. You might schedule separate sessions for adults over 30, for emerging adults, and for adolescents.

➤Answer to Observation Quiz (from page 491): Girls tend to become sexually active a little later than boys, but by the end of high school, girls have surpassed boys (usually because of older partners).

To be effective, sex education in school should not focus solely on abstinence and probably should begin before students become sexually active. The age at which sexual activity typically begins varies by community but may be younger than parents realize. More than half of all U.S. adolescents have experienced intercourse by age 16. There are signs that adolescent sexual behavior has become less risky than it was a decade or two ago: In the United States and worldwide, there are fewer teenage births and fewer abortions, and contraception is used more often. ■

Sadness and Anger

Adolescence is usually a wonderful time, perhaps better for current generations than for any generation before. As you have already read, identity achievement is less rushed today, parents and friends are usually helpful, and teen pregnancy and early marriage are less common. Furthermore, more teenagers are in school, fewer are malnourished, fewer use drugs, and almost none die of disease. The editor of the leading academic journal on adolescence reminds his readers that this period is more joyful than problematic (B. Brown, 2005).

comorbid A term that refers to the occurrence of two or more illnesses or disorders at the same time.

Nonetheless, for almost 20 percent of adolescents, serious troubles plague their development. Most of those problems are **comorbid,** meaning that two or more disorders ("morbidities," in medical jargon) coexist in the same person. This term was first used in Chapter 11, in the discussion of children with special needs, many of whom have multiple disorders: Comorbidity poses a difficult challenge for educators.

In adolescence, comorbidity is a challenge to life itself. A sad teenager who uses illegal drugs before age 15 is also more vulnerable to depression, unwanted pregnancy, and suicide. An angry adolescent who is, say, unusually aggressive is also at higher risk of dropping out of school, being arrested, and dying accidentally.

Distinguishing between normal moodiness and pathological problems is complex. Some emotional reactions are quite normal: Most young adolescents are less happy and angrier than they were as children. For a few, however, such emotions can become extreme, pathological, and even deadly if they are not noticed and relieved.

Depression

The general emotional trend from late childhood through adolescence is toward less confidence. A dip in self-esteem at puberty is found in every study. Ethnic differences are evident, with African Americans tending to be higher in overall self-esteem and Asian Americans lower. However, every group's average falls at puberty. Data from one cross-sequential study, shown in Figure 16.4, indicated that boys start out more confident than girls but that their self-confidence declines faster as they grow older (Jacobs et al., 2002). It is a myth that only girls, not boys, lose confidence at puberty (Barnett & Rivers, 2004).

Some studies find a rise in self-esteem over the years of secondary school and college; others do not (Fredricks & Eccles, 2002; Greene & Way, 2005; Harter, 1999). Probably the differences in the results of these studies reflect the particular population under study: Parents and peers affect self-esteem (Hall-Lande et al., 2007), and some communities are more conducive to strong relationships between teenagers and adults than are others.

Unusually low self-esteem in early adolescence is likely to continue into later adolescence. One reason is that adolescents who dislike themselves are likely to turn to drug use, early sex, and disordered eating—all of which further reduce esteem (Biro et al., 2006; Trzesniewski et al., 2006).

Sex Differences in Serious Depression

Although boys lose confidence as often as girls do at puberty, there may be sex differences in morbidity. Every study finds that girls are much more often seriously depressed than boys. For some adolescents, the sobering self-awareness that is typical in adolescence sinks to **clinical depression,** a deep sadness and hopelessness that disrupts all normal, regular activities.

The causes of clinical depression include genetic vulnerability and a depressed mother who was the adolescent's primary caregiver in infancy (Cicchietti & Toth, 1998; Murray et al., 2006). These conditions predate adolescence and occur for both sexes, but something happens at puberty to push many vulnerable children, especially the girls, into despair. The rate of clinical depression more than doubles during this time, to an estimated 15 percent, affecting about 1 in 5 girls and 1 in 10 boys (Graber, 2004).

It is not known whether the reasons for these gender differences are primarily biological, psychological, or social (Alloy & Abramson, 2007; Ge et al., 2001). Obviously, girls have different hormones from boys, but they also experience gender-specific pressures from their families, peers, and cultures. Perhaps biological and social pressures, combined with past experiences, cause some to slide into depression.

Recently, a cognitive explanation has been added to the possible reasons for girls' higher rates of depression. **Rumination**—talking about, remembering, and mentally replaying past experiences—is more common among girls than boys. If the incident replayed is unpleasant, rumination can lead to depression (Alloy et al., 2003).

Rumination may make girls sadder, but it also may protect them from lonely, impulsive actions. In fact, some people think that teenage boys are depressed as often as girls but are less likely to admit it on a questionnaire or to a therapist. Instead, they turn away from their friends, using drugs and violence instead of talk and tears. Data on suicide support this hypothesis.

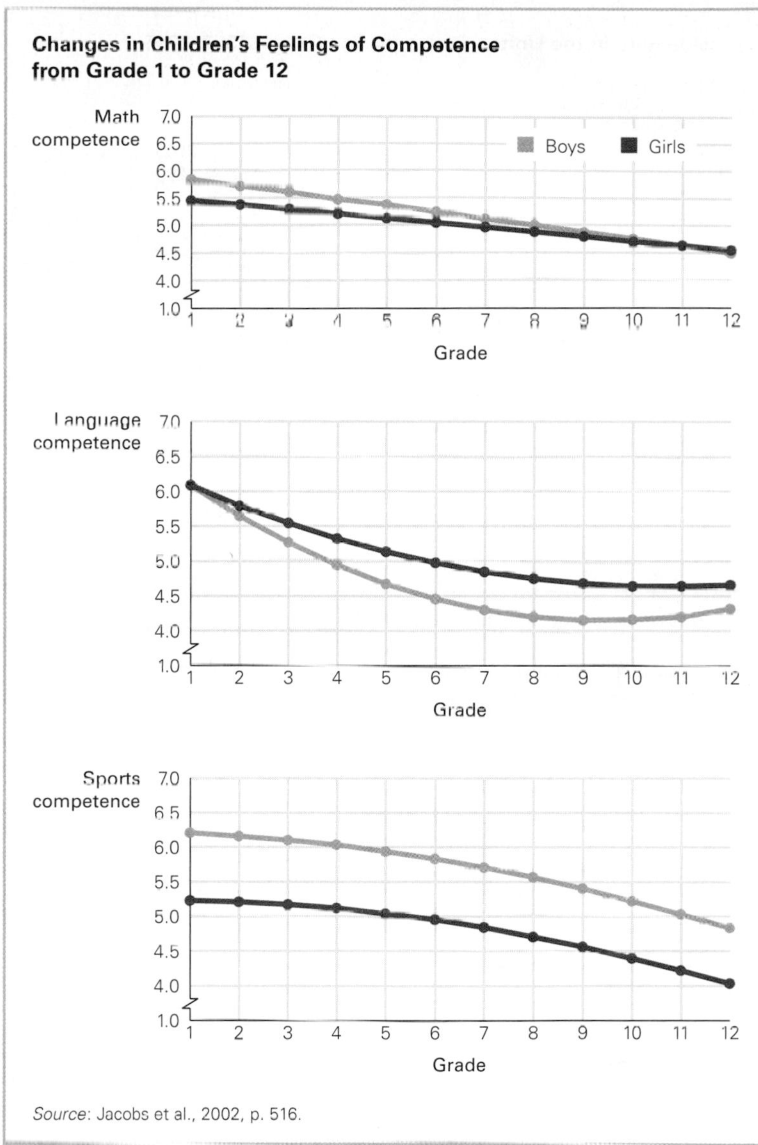

FIGURE 16.4

All the Children Are Above Average U.S. children, both boys and girls, feel less and less competent in math, language arts, and sports as they move through grades 1–12. Their scores on tests of feelings of competence could range from 1 to 7, and the fact that the twelfth-grade average was between 4 and 5 indicates that, overall, teenagers still consider themselves above average.

Suicide

Teenagers are just beginning to explore life. When trouble comes (failing a course, ending a romance, fighting with a parent), they don't always know that better days lie ahead. As you have just read, this kind of stress can lead to depression and thoughts of suicide.

Thinking about Suicide "Serious, distressing thoughts about killing oneself" is called **suicidal ideation.** This kind of thinking is most common at about age 15 (Rueter & Kwon, 2005).

The 2007 Youth Risk Behavior Survey revealed that more than one-third (36 percent) of U.S. high school girls felt so hopeless that they stopped doing some of

clinical depression Feelings of hopelessness, lethargy, and worthlessness that last two weeks or more.

rumination Repeatedly thinking and talking about past experiences.

suicidal ideation Thinking about suicide, usually with some serious emotional and intellectual or cognitive overtones.

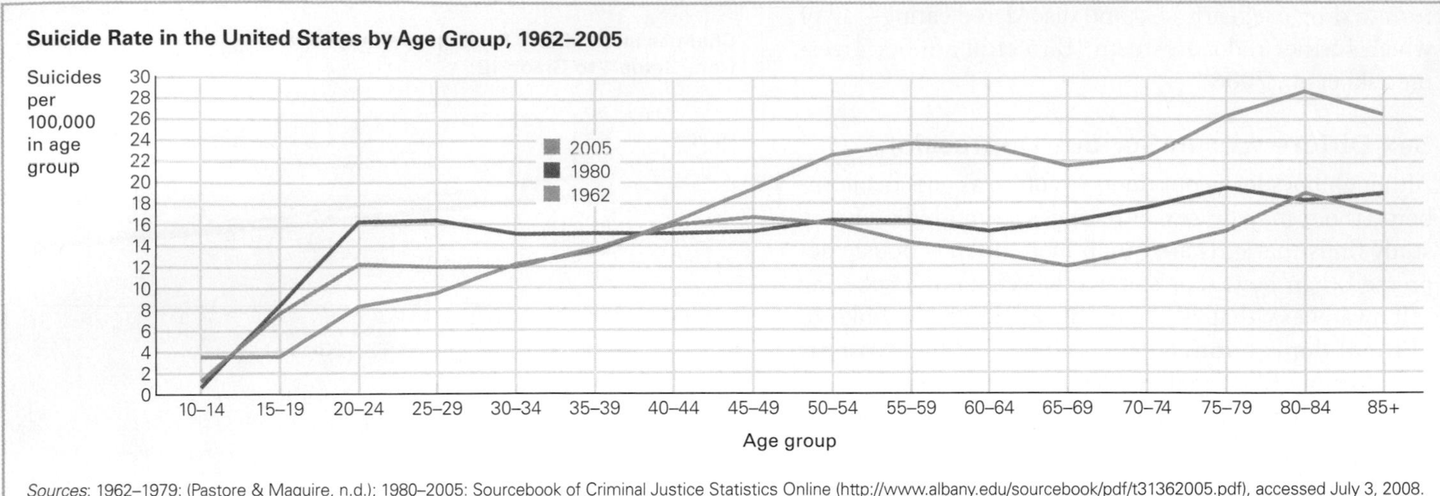

FIGURE 16.5

Much Depends on Age A historical look at U.S. suicide statistics reveals two trends, both of which were still apparent in 2005. First, older teenagers today are two times more likely to take their own lives than in 1960 but less likely than in 1980. Second, suicide rates overall are down, but they continue to be highest among elderly people age 80 and older.

Observation Quiz (see answer, page 496): In a typical cross-section of 1,000 U.S. 15- to 19-year-olds, how many committed suicide in 2005?

their usual activities for two weeks or more; one-fifth (19 percent) seriously thought about suicide. The corresponding rates for boys were 21 percent and 10 percent (MMWR, June 6, 2008).

Both sets of statistics, although they are high, actually show a reduction in suicidal ideation from previous years. Rates for suicidal ideation in 1995 were almost twice as high: 30 percent for the girls and 24 percent for the boys (MMWR, September 27, 1996).

While suicidal ideation during adolescence is common, completed suicides are not. Adolescents are *less* likely to kill themselves than adults are. Many people mistakenly think suicide is more frequent in adolescence for four reasons:

- The rate, low as it is, is much higher than it was 30 years ago (see Figure 16.5).
- Statistics on "youth" often include emerging adults aged 18 to 25, whose suicide rates are higher than those of adolescents aged 12 to 17.
- Adolescent suicides capture media attention.
- Suicide *attempts* (*parasuicides,* discussed below) may be more common in adolescence than later.

Adolescents are particularly affected when they hear about a suicide, either via media reports or from peers (Insel & Gould, 2008). That makes them susceptible to **cluster suicides,** a term for the occurrence of several suicides within a group over a brief span of time—a few weeks or months. If a high school student's "tragic end" is sentimentalized, that elicits suicidal ideation among his or her peers. This means that, whenever one teenager commits suicide, his or her friends and schoolmates are at risk.

cluster suicides Several suicides committed by members of a group within a brief period of time.

Parasuicide Instead of "attempted suicide" or "failed suicide," experts prefer the more accurate term **parasuicide,** which is defined as any deliberate action of self-harm that could have been lethal but was not. *Parasuicide* is the preferred term because emotions and confusion typically disguise the seriousness of intent, especially to adolescents. After surviving parasuicide, many adolescents wonder why they risked death.

parasuicide Any deliberate action of self-harm that could have been lethal but was not.

Internationally, rates of teenage parasuicide range between 6 and 20 percent. This wide range reflects cultural differences in frequency and in data collection. Here is one specific example: Among U.S. high school students in 2007, 9 percent of the girls and 4.5 percent of the boys said they had tried to kill themselves in the past year (MMWR, June 6, 2008; see Table 16.1). Almost one-third of those attempts were treated by a doctor or nurse. Yet the U.S. annual rate of completed suicide for ages 15 to 19 (in school or not) is about 8 per 100,000, or 0.008 percent.

TABLE 16.1

Suicidal Ideation and Parasuicide Among U.S. High School Students, 2007

		Seriously Considered Attempting Suicide (percent)	Parasuicide (Attempted Suicide) (percent)	Parasuicide Requiring Medical Attention (percent)	Actual Suicide (ages 15–19)
Overall		**14.5%**	**6.9%**	**2.0%**	Less than 0.01% (about 8 per 100,000)
Girls:	9th grade	19.0	10.5	2.6	
	10th grade	22.0	11.2	3.1	Girls: About 2 per 100,000
	11th grade	16.3	7.8	1.7	
	12th grade	16.7	6.5	1.8	
Boys:	9th grade	10.8	5.3	1.9	
	10th grade	9.3	4.9	1.0	Boys: About 11 per 100,000
	11th grade	10.7	3.7	1.4	
	12th grade	10.2	4.2	1.5	

Source: MMWR, June 6, 2008.

Adolescent Suicide Rates Four factors increase a teen's risk of suicide (Berman et al., 2006; Goldsmith et al., 2002):

- Availability of guns
- Lack of parental supervision
- Availability of alcohol and other drugs
- A culture that condones suicide

The first three factors suggest why the rate of youth suicide in North America and Europe has doubled since 1960: Adolescents have more guns, alcohol, and drugs and less supervision than they once did. It also suggests why rates have gone down in recent years, as laws restricting gun possession and reducing adolescent drinking have taken effect.

Cultural differences in attitudes toward suicide are also significant, as is shown by the fact that suicide rates vary internationally as well as state by state. Rates are higher in eastern Europe and Africa than in western Europe and South America. Rates are generally higher in the western than the eastern United States (Montana has the highest percentage of high school students who have devised a plan for suicide [18 percent], more than twice the percentage in Florida [8 percent]) (MMWR, June 6, 2008). For all these differences, culture is a plausible explanation.

Boys More than Girls Gender has a marked influence on the incidence of suicide. Although depression and parasuicide are far more common among females, completed suicide is higher for males in every nation except China. For instance, boys age 15 to 19 in the United States kill themselves four times as often as girls that age do (National Center for Health Statistics, 2007). A major reason is that males typically shoot themselves (an immediately lethal method), whereas females typically swallow pills or hang themselves (methods that allow time for intervention).

Access to deadly means may be the crucial determinant. More boys than girls have guns. For example, among 12- to 17-year-olds in California, seven times as many boys as girls own guns (Sorenson & Vittes, 2004). The importance of access may also explain why China is the only nation with more female than male suicides. Few Chinese have guns. Ingestion of lethal pesticides (many of which are illegal in the United States) is the most common means of suicide in China, and women are as likely as men are to have access to pesticides.

Another explanation of the different suicide rates for males and females is that girls ruminate, letting their friends and families know that they are depressed before they reach the despair of suicide. Boys are more likely to

Nothing to Do Compared with most other Americans, these three adolescents are at higher risk of diabetes, alcoholism, unemployment, and suicide. They live on the Rosebud Sioux Reservation in South Dakota. The suicide rate among Native American teenagers is more than three times as high as the rate for U.S. adolescents overall.

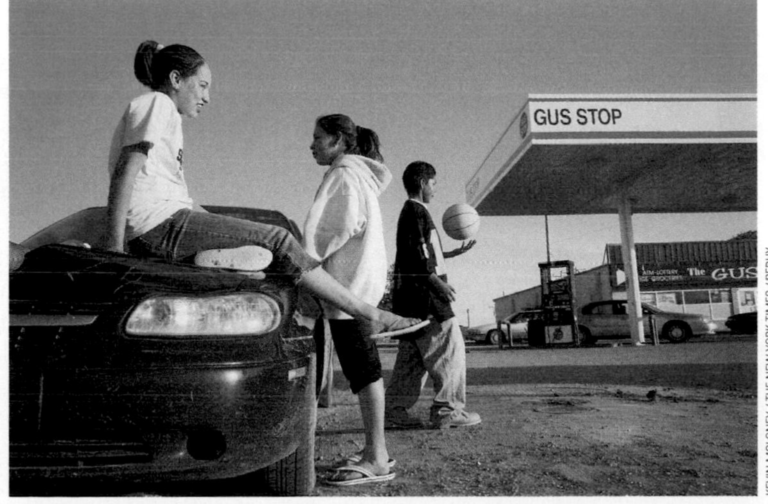

KEVIN MOLONEY / THE NEW YORK TIMES / REDUX

withdraw; their warning signs are not as obvious. Furthermore, young men somehow think it unmanly to attempt suicide and survive, so they choose more deadly methods (Aseltine & DeMartino, 2004). Consider the following.

a personal perspective

He Kept His Worries to Himself

A psychologist described an adolescent boy in these words:

> Bill is 17, a senior in high school. A good student, hard working, some would say "driven," Bill has achieved well and is hoping to go to either Harvard or Stanford next year. He is also hopeful that his college career will lead him to medical school and a career as a surgeon like his father. Bill is a tall, handsome boy, attractive to girls but surprisingly shy among them. When he socializes, he prefers to hang out in groups rather than date; in these groups, he is likely to be seen deep in introspective discussion with one girl or another. Introspection has no place on the school football team, where this past season Bill led all receivers in pass catches. Nor does he appear at all the quiet type in his new sports car, a gift from his parents on his 17th birthday. The elder of two sons, Bill has always been close to his parents, and a "good son." Perhaps for these reasons, he has been increasingly preoccupied as verbalized threats of separation and divorce become common in his parents' increasingly frequent conflicts. These worries he has kept largely to himself.
>
> *[Berman et al., 2006, pp. 43–44]*

If you were Bill's friend, would you make sure he obtained professional help? Unfortunately, Bill had no friends who were close enough to heed the warning signs. Even his parents did not realize he was troubled until

> Bill's body was brought to the local medical examiner's office; he put his father's .22-caliber handgun to his head and ended his life in an instant.
>
> *[Berman et al., 2006, p. 44]*

In retrospect, Bill had some risk factors and had shown danger signs—no close friends, male or female; his parents' conflicts; his foreclosure on his father's profession; his drive for perfection (Harvard or Stanford, football star); no older siblings to advise and comfort him. Did the gift of a sports car signify a problem, perhaps that Bill's parents provided material possessions instead of emotional closeness? Did his shyness around girls mean that he may have been worried about his sexuality? Why did his father own a handgun, and why was it loaded and accessible?

The report does not mention whether Bill's body was tested for alcohol or other drugs. Overall, about one-third of all U.S. suicides occur when a person has been drinking or taking drugs; rates of drug and alcohol use are higher for people under 30. Denial that a young person can have a problem with substance abuse may persist, even after death.

The Impact of Income and Ethnicity Wealth and education decrease the risk of many disorders, but not of suicide—quite the opposite. The reason may be news reports that typically highlight the lost potential of a suicidal adolescent (e.g., "Honor Student Kills Self"). This may encourage suicidal ideation in, say, other honor students. Or adolescents from high-SES families may be particularly hard-hit by a failing grade or a broken relationship.

Since 1990, however, rates of adolescent suicide have fallen, especially among those with more income and education. One reason may be that more adolescents are using antidepressants, and therefore fewer of them are desperately sad (Gould, 2003). A British study raised the possibility that such drugs might increase suicidal ideation (not suicide), and the U.S. Food and Drug Administration suggests that doctors treating adolescents with antidepressants be particularly alert to possible side effects in the first few months.

Such caution is always warranted; many adolescents are impulsive. However, untreated depression is a much greater risk factor than antidepressants. A meta-analysis of 27 controlled clinical trials (similar to experiments, only with participants who have a particular illness or disorder) found that antidepressants, especially when combined with cognitive-behavioral therapy, helped depressed or anxious young people far more often than they increased their suicidal ideation (Bridge et al., 2007).

➤**Answer to Observation Quiz** (from page 494): Statistically speaking, none. The rates are given per 100,000 in each age group. This means that fewer than 1 in 10,000 teens commit suicide in a year.

When U.S. statistics on adolescent suicides are reported by ethnicity, the rate within one group—African American teenage boys—is increasing, not decreasing (although it is still below the rate for European American boys). Among the many cultural hypotheses: Young Black males have fewer employment opportunities, easier access to guns, and a greater reluctance to ask for help than young males of other racial or ethnic backgrounds (Joe, 2003).

Delinquency and Disobedience

Like low self-esteem and suicidal ideation, bouts of anger are common in adolescence. Many adolescents slam doors, defy parents, and tell friends exactly how badly other teenagers (or siblings or teachers) have behaved. Some teenagers—particularly boys—"act out" by breaking laws. They steal, damage property, or injure others.

Is such behavior normal? Most developmentalists who agree with psychoanalytic theory (see Chapter 2) answer yes. A leading advocate of this view was Anna Freud (Sigmund's daughter, herself a prominent psychoanalyst), who wrote that adolescent resistance to parental authority was "welcome . . . beneficial . . . inevitable." She explained:

> We all know individual children who, as late as the ages of fourteen, fifteen or sixteen, show no such outer evidence of inner unrest. They remain, as they have been during the latency period, "good" children, wrapped up in their family relationships, considerate sons of their mothers, submissive to their fathers, in accord with the atmosphere, idea and ideal of their childhood background. Convenient as this may be, it signifies a delay of their normal development and is, as such, a sign to be taken seriously.
>
> *[A. Freud, 1958/2000, p. 263]*

Contrary to Freud, many psychologists, most teachers, and almost all parents are quite happy with well-behaved, considerate teenagers. For them, good behavior is not a sign of serious developmental problems at all. Which view is valid? Actually, both are. Adolescents vary, and understanding that fact is crucial in helping them cope with emotional stresses.

Most teenagers obey the law, and their lawfulness does not predict a later explosion or breakdown. In fact, according to a 30-year longitudinal study from

The Same Situation, Many Miles Apart: Following Tradition Adolescents worldwide flout adult conventions. Here, for instance, note the necklace on one of these boys in a Los Angeles high school (*left*) and the dyed red hair (or is it a wig?) on one of the girls in a Tokyo park (*right*). As distinctive as each of these eight rebels is, all are following a tradition for their age group—just as their parents probably did when they were adolescents.

Dunedin, New Zealand, by age 26 men who had never been arrested usually earned degrees, "held high-status jobs, and expressed optimism about their own futures" (Moffitt, 2003, p. 61).

Dozens of longitudinal studies that followed people from childhood through adulthood have now been completed. Their consensus is that increased anger during puberty is normal but that most adolescents express their anger in acceptable ways. They yell at their parents, curse at their peers, complain about school. For a minority, anger explodes, and they break something or hurt someone. That does not necessarily signal later problems. However, a small proportion of adolescents (about 7 percent, more boys than girls) are steadily aggressive throughout childhood and early adolescence (Broidy et al., 2003). They are the ones to be worried about.

Breaking the Law

juvenile delinquent A person under the age of 18 who breaks the law.

A word about terminology: **Juvenile delinquents** are lawbreakers under age 18. Some laws apply only to juveniles (for drinking, buying cigarettes, and breaking curfews) and some to everyone (for stealing, raping, and killing). Our main concern here is the more serious offenses, although we recognize that controlling minor offenses is one way to prevent major crimes.

Aggression and serious crime are more frequent during adolescence than at any other period of life. Arrest statistics in every nation reflect this, and confidential self-reports reveal that virtually every adolescent breaks the law at least once before age 20. Only about one-fourth of young lawbreakers are caught, and most of those are not arrested but are warned and released (Dodge et al., 2006).

The frequency of delinquency was evident in one study of urban seventh-graders. More than three-fourths of the sample of 1,559 (both sexes, all races, from parochial as well as public schools) had committed at least one offense (stolen something, damaged property, or hurt someone physically). Usually, however, adolescents are not chronic offenders: In the same study, less than one-third had committed five or more such acts (Nichols et al., 2006).

Gender and ethnic differences in arrest rates are dramatic. Adolescent males are arrested three times as often as females; African Americans are arrested three times as often as European Americans, who are arrested three times as often as Asian Americans (Pastore & Maguire, 2005). However, self-reports of lawbreaking show much smaller gender and ethnic differences (Dodge et al., 2006). The self-report data on girls are particularly unsettling, at least to me (see the following).

a view from science

A Feminist Looks at the Data

"Sugar and spice, and everything nice, that's what little girls are made of" was a rhyme I showed my mother soon after I learned to read, announcing, "That proves it." To my young mind, seeing those words in print proved that I was better than my older brother, who, like all little boys, was made of "snakes and snails and puppy dog tails." As my mother tells it, I have always been proud to be a girl, and then a woman.

However, as an adult scientist, I look carefully at evidence. Empirical evidence of female superiority does not withstand analysis.

A first glance at statistics suggests that adolescent girls *are* nicer than boys. For example, among U.S. high school seniors who graduated in 2003, 11 percent of the boys, but only 4 percent of the girls, had been arrested in the previous year (Pastore & Maguire, 2005). Among high school seniors who had hurt someone five or more times in the past year badly enough to need bandages or a doctor, the male–female ratio was 10 to 1 (3 percent to 0.3 percent) (Pastore & Maguire, 2005).

Expert opinion seems, at first, to confirm my early prejudices. The idea that boys are far more antisocial than girls concludes a careful review of antisocial behavior written by three men, all well-respected developmental researchers (Dodge et al., 2006).

But scientists know the difference between wishful thinking and data, and between direct and indirect aggression. Several female scholars, as well as the three men just cited, suggest that although boys are more often in physical fights, girls may prefer *relational aggression,* manifested in gossip, social exclusion, and the spreading of rumors. That would make girls' antisocial impulses less noticeable, but not necessarily less hurtful, than those of boys (Crick et al., 2001; Underwood et al., 2003).

Indeed, the data reveal that girls are not "everything nice" (Moffitt et al., 2001). The study of high school seniors cited above found that 47 percent of the girls, but only 38 percent of the boys, had gotten into five or more arguments or fights with their parents that year (Pastore & Maguire, 2005). A study of seventh-graders found that more girls than boys reported getting angry and losing self-control (Nichols et al., 2006).

This female anger does not stop at adulthood. Among heterosexual couples, women are more likely to curse, hit, and even injure their partners than men are (Archer, 2000; Moffitt et al., 2001). Reports of wife abuse are more common than reports of husband abuse for two reasons: (1) Men are generally stronger and thus more likely to seriously injure or even kill their partners in a dispute, and (2) most men hate to admit they are hurt, especially by their wives, so they keep their injuries to themselves.

I would like to reassure myself of women's goodness by citing the maternal instinct, that mothers naturally nurture and protect their children. There is some evidence for that, but there is also contrary evidence: Mothers mistreat their children at least twice as often as fathers do (U.S. Department of Health and Human Services, 2006).

How can I reconcile such findings with the belief that men are more aggressive? Females may be less likely to express anger in public, physical ways. They stab with words, not knives. Adolescent girls are less blatant in their lawbreaking and often try to talk their way out of an arrest, whereas boys are more likely to be defiant. This defiance—especially when it is physical—gives boys the reputation of being the more aggressive sex and increases their arrest rate.

In short, neither sex is "everything nice." Indeed, although girls may specialize in relational aggression in childhood and adolescence, males learn to be relationally aggressive by adulthood (Archer & Coyne, 2005). As a scientist, I realize that many men (including my brother) are quite kind—and that some "snakes and snails" are in me.

Causes of Delinquency

Two clusters of factors, one from childhood (primarily brain-based) and one from adolescence (primarily contextual), predict who is likely to commit violent crimes. Usually the brain and the social context are both necessary to make someone a serious delinquent (Dupéré et al., 2007; Lahey et al., 2003).

Persistent Offenders The first of these clusters indicates problems in brain functioning. A short attention span, hyperactivity, inadequate emotional regulation, slow language development, low intelligence, early and severe malnutrition, autistic tendencies, maternal cigarette smoking, and being the victim of severe child abuse—all of these correlate with later delinquency, although no single one of them necessarily produces it (Brennan et al., 2003).

Most of these factors are more common among boys than girls, which may be one reason for the gender difference in delinquency. Neurological impairment increases the risk that a child will become a **life-course-persistent offender** (Moffitt et al., 2001), a term for someone who breaks the law before and after adolescence as well as during it.

life-course-persistent offender A person whose disobedient and disruptive activity typically begins in childhood and continues throughout life; a career criminal.

Adolescence Only The second cluster of causes of delinquency appears in adolescence and includes risk factors that are primarily psychosocial, not biological. They include having deviant friends; having few connections to school; living in a crowded, violent, unstable neighborhood; not having a job; using drugs and alcohol; and having close relatives (especially older siblings) in jail.

Especially for Police Officers (see response, page 501): You see some 15-year-olds drinking beer in a local park when they belong in school. What do you do?

These risk factors are more prevalent among low-income, urban adolescents, but many adolescents at all income levels experience them. Any teen with these problems is at risk of becoming an **adolescence-limited offender,** someone whose criminal activity stops by age 21 (Moffitt, 1997, 2003).

adolescence-limited offender A person whose criminal activity is confined to the adolescent years, from about age 12 to 18.

AP PHOTO / DAYTONA BEACH NEWS-JOURNAL, DAVID TUCKER

Do You Know This Boy? Warren Messner fights back tears as he is sentenced in a Daytona Beach, Florida, courtroom for the 2005 beating murder of a homeless man. Messner is 16; he was sentenced to be imprisoned until he is 39. Like most teenage criminals, he was unhappy at school and broke the law with friends, three other boys who also pleaded guilty.

Adolescence-limited offenders were not perfect as children, but unlike life-course-persistent offenders, they were not the worst-behaved in their class or the first to use drugs, have sex, or be arrested. They tend to break the law with their friends, facilitated by their chosen antisocial clique. More boys than girls are in this group, but some lawbreaking cliques include both sexes. The gender gap in late-adolescent lawbreaking is narrower than it is in earlier adolescence (Moffitt et al., 2001).

By mid-adolescence, the criminal records of adolescence-limited and life-course-persistent offenders are similar. However, judges need to be aware of the differences. If adolescence-limited delinquents can be protected from various snares (such as quitting school, time in prison, drug addiction, early parenthood), they may outgrow their criminal behavior (Moffitt, 2003).

Outgrowing criminality is especially likely if a delinquent is female, lives in a harmonious two-parent family, avoids alcohol and other drugs, does well in school, is religious, and has parents who monitor activity. None of these six factors is a guarantee, but each of them reduces risk.

Adolescence-limited lawbreaking is neither inevitable nor insignificant. Antisocial behavior escalates during adolescence and can become truly dangerous to the young delinquent and to any potential victims, who are three times more likely to be other adolescents than to be adults (Baum, 2005). But it may be more plastic and less serious, in terms of life-span development, than it seems.

Human Relationships

One measure—strengthening human relationships—seems helpful in preventing crime (Heilbrun et al., 2005). Adolescents whose parents are actively involved in their lives, or young adults who are married with children, have much lower rates of violent crime than their more isolated contemporaries. Adolescents who feel connected to their teachers, who are active in their churches, or who are involved in after-school sports are less likely to break the law.

Of course, not every relationship is equally beneficial. Delinquents who learn from lawbreaking peers are more likely to be arrested again (Dishion et al., 1999; Leve & Chamberlain, 2005). Having parents who are hostile and neglectful makes serious lawbreaking more likely.

When adolescents have been arrested, *therapeutic foster care* is sometimes better than jail (Chamberlain et al., 2002). In this type of foster care, troubled and antisocial delinquents are placed in the custody of foster parents who receive extra help, training, and payment to establish a relationship with their foster child and his or her teachers. According to official police records on hundreds of delinquents in Oregon, those in therapeutic foster care are subsequently arrested only half as often as those with similar histories who are placed in traditional foster care (MMWR, July 2, 2004).

Beneficial as this program appears to be, remember that family relationships are crucial throughout adolescence. Teenagers in foster care typically have very dysfunctional birth families, but they nonetheless reach out to their relatives when they need support (Collins et al., 2008). Relatives may be helpful, even family members who were severely inadequate earlier in their lives. Every young person, delinquent or not, foster child or not, depressed or not, needs social support and tries to find it.

Overall, close relationships with supportive adults and avoidance of deviant peers help rebellious youth (adolescence-limited offenders or not) stay within bounds (J. Barnes et al., 2006; Kumpfer & Alvarado, 2003). As is evident throughout this chapter, family and friends usually help teenagers find their identity and navigate through the many difficulties they face.

SUMMING UP

Compared with people of other ages, many adolescents experience more sudden and extreme emotions that lead to powerful sadness and explosive anger. These feelings are usually expressed within supportive families, friendships, neighborhoods, and cultures that contain and channel them. For some teenagers, however, emotions are unchecked or intensified by their social contexts. This situation can lead to parasuicide (especially for girls), to minor lawbreaking (for both sexes), and, less often, to completed suicide and arrests (especially for boys). Intervention works best when it reduces the contextual risks (such as access to guns and drugs) and encourages healthy relationships between the adolescent and constructive peers and adults. ■

➤**Response for Police Officers** (from page 499): Avoid both extremes: Don't let them think this situation is either harmless or serious. You might take them to the police station and call their parents in. However, these adolescents are probably not life-course-persistent offenders; jailing them or grouping them with other lawbreakers might encourage more crime.

SUMMARY

Identity

1. Adolescence is a time for self-discovery. According to Erikson, adolescents seek their own identity, sorting through the traditions of their families and cultures.

2. Many young adolescents foreclose on their options without exploring possibilities, experience role confusion, or reach moratorium. Identity achievement takes longer for contemporary adolescents than it did half a century ago, when Erikson first described it.

3. Identity achievement occurs in many domains, including religious identity, sexual identity (now often called gender identity), political identity (often replaced by ethnic identity), and vocational identity. Each of these is sought by adolescents, although few achieve a solid identity during these years.

Relationships with Elders and Peers

4. Parents continue to influence their growing children, despite bickering over minor issues. Ideally, from age 10 to 18, communication and warmth remain high within the family, while parental control decreases and adolescents develop autonomy.

5. There are cultural differences in timing of conflicts and particulars of parental monitoring. Too much parental control, with psychological intrusiveness, is harmful, as is neglect. Parents need to grant some freedom and yet provide guidance, not an easy balance.

6. Peers can be beneficial or harmful, depending on particular friends, cliques, and crowds. Friends can lead each other astray, providing training in deviance, or can encourage each other constructively.

7. Peer pressure is evident in adolescence, but it is not the unmitigated evil that adults sometimes assume. Adolescents select their friends, who then facilitate constructive and/or destructive behavior.

8. Peers may be particularly crucial for immigrant adolescents, who often have a strong commitment to family values but who also try to adjust to new norms and customs. Most immigrant adolescents do well in school and help their families.

Sexuality

9. Misinformation about sex is common throughout the world. Parents and peers provide some sex education to adolescents, but they do not necessarily do it well. Parents are often uninformed about their children's sexual behavior.

10. In the United States, most adults want schools to teach adolescents about sex, but the specifics of the curriculum are controversial. No program (including abstinence only) has made much difference in the age at which adolescents become sexually active, although some effectively encourage protection against pregnancy and disease.

11. The teenage birth rate has fallen, and the use of contraception has increased, in every ethnic group in every nation. When teenage births do occur, the mothers are much less likely to be married than was the case 50 years ago.

Sadness and Anger

12. Almost all adolescents lose some of the confidence they had when they were children. A few individuals become chronically sad and depressed, intensifying problems they had in childhood.

13. Many adolescents think about suicide. Parasuicide is not rare, especially among adolescent girls. Few adolescents actually kill themselves; most who do so are boys. Drugs, alcohol, guns, alienation from parents and peers, and lifelong depression increase the risk of suicide.

14. Almost all adolescents become more independent and angry as part of growing up. According to psychoanalytic theory, emotional turbulence is normal during these years. Longitudinal research finds that most adolescents are not troubled and rebellious, and they nonetheless develop well.

15. Rebelliousness manifests itself in lawbreaking by almost all adolescents, but boys are more likely to be arrested for violent offenses than are girls.

16. Treatment and punishment of delinquents must take into account their history and human relationships. Adolescence-limited delinquents should be prevented from hurting themselves or others. Life-course-persistent offenders have neurological problems that start in early childhood and extend into adulthood, which makes their effective punishment less clear.

17. Relationships with others—especially with parents and teachers—are protective against serious delinquency. Therapeutic foster care is one treatment that seems effective for adolescents who have already been arrested and whose birth families are toxic.

KEY TERMS

identity versus role confusion (p. 472)
identity achievement (p. 472)
role confusion (p. 472)
foreclosure (p. 472)
moratorium (p. 473)
gender identity (p. 474)
sexual orientation (p. 475)
bickering (p. 478)
parental monitoring (p. 480)
clique (p. 481)
crowd (p. 481)
peer pressure (p. 481)
deviancy training (p. 482)
comorbid (p. 492)
clinical depression (p. 493)
rumination (p. 493)
suicidal ideation (p. 493)
cluster suicides (p. 494)
parasuicide (p. 494)
juvenile delinquent (p. 498)
life-course-persistent offender (p. 499)
adolescence-limited offender (p. 499)

KEY QUESTIONS

1. What are the differences between identity achievement and role confusion?

2. When would foreclosure or moratorium be beneficial to a teenager?

3. Give several examples of decisions a person must make in establishing gender identity.

4. Why and how do parents remain influential during their children's teen years?

5. How and when can peer pressure be helpful, and how can it be harmful?

6. Why might an adolescent want to be part of a crowd and a clique?

7. What is the usual developmental pattern of romances during adolescence?

8. What is the role of parents in adolescent children's sexuality?

9. What is the effect of various forms of sex education on adolescent sexual experience?

10. How have adolescent sexual activities changed over the past several decades?

11. Why are there gender differences in depression, suicidal ideation, and suicide?

12. What are the personal and cultural risk factors for adolescent suicide?

13. What are the similarities and differences between adolescence-limited and life-course-persistent offenders?

14. What factors make delinquency more likely, and what factors decrease the risk?

APPLICATIONS

1. Teenage cliques and crowds may be more important in large U.S. high schools than elsewhere. Interview people who spent their teenage years in U.S. schools of various sizes, or in another nation, about the peer relationships in their high schools. Describe and discuss any differences you find.

2. Locate a news article about a teenager who committed suicide. Can you find evidence in the article that there were warning signs that were ignored? Does the report inadvertently encourage cluster suicides?

3. Research suggests that most adolescents have broken the law but that few have been arrested or incarcerated. Is this true for people you know? Ask 10 of your fellow students whether they broke the law when they were under 18 and, if so, how often and in what ways. Assure them of confidentiality and ask specific questions about minor lawbreaking (e.g., drinking, skipping school) as well as actions that would be considered crimes for adults (e.g., stealing, injuring someone else). What hypothesis arises about lawbreaking in your cohort?

4. As a follow-up to Application 3, ask your fellow students about the circumstances. Was their lawbreaking done with peers or alone? What was the effect of the responses of police, parents, judges, and peers? Explain how the circumstances and responses relate to adolescent psychosocial development.

PART V The Developing Person So Far: Adolescence

BIOSOCIAL

Puberty Puberty begins adolescence, as the child's body becomes much bigger (the growth spurt) and more sexual. Both sexes experience increased hormones, reproductive potential, and primary as well as secondary sexual characteristics.

Nutrition Dietary deficiencies are common among adolescents. Eating disorders, while relatively rare, tend to begin during adolescence.

Health Hazards Brain growth, hormones, and social contexts combine to make every adolescent more interested in sexual activities, with possible hazards of early pregnancy and sexual abuse. Another hazard is drug use and abuse. In most nations, boys use more drugs than girls do. Rates of alcohol use are higher and of cigarette smoking much lower in North America than in most European and Asian nations.

COGNITIVE

Adolescent Thinking Adolescents think differently than younger children do. Piaget stressed their new ability to use abstract logic, which is part of formal operational thought. Many adolescents can think hypothetically and deductively, as they are taught to do in science classes. Elkind recognized adolescent egocentrism, as many younger teens think they are invincible or that everyone else notices what they do and wear. Many more recent scholars find that intuitive thought increases during adolescence, with emotional and experiential (or dual-process) thinking overcoming logic at times.

Teaching and Learning Secondary education promotes individual and national health and success. In middle school, grades and achievement fall, bullying increases, and many teachers and students become disenchanted. International tests find marked differences in achievement. In the United States, high-stakes tests are widely required before high school graduation.

PSYCHOSOCIAL

Identity Adolescent psychosocial development includes a search for identity, as Erikson described. Adolescents seek to forge their own identity, combining childhood experiences, cultural values, and their unique aspirations. The four contexts of identity are religion, sex, vocation, and politics/ethnicity. Few adolescents achieve identity in these four arenas; identity diffusion and foreclosure are more likely.

Relationships Families continue to be influential, despite rebellion and bickering. Adolescents seek autonomy but also rely on parental support. Friends and peers of both sexes are increasingly important.

Sexuality For heterosexual as well as homosexual youth, friends may be crucial in achieving sexual identity. About half of all U.S. teens become sexually active. Among developed nations, the United States has higher rates of teen pregnancy and less sex education.

Sadness and Anger Depression and rebellion become serious problems for some adolescents, who are at risk of suicide and violent criminality. Most lawbreaking is adolescence-limited, but some teens become life-course-persistent offenders.

है राही प्यार के
लाल

Epilogue

CHAPTER OUTLINE

Emerging Adulthood

During my senior year in high school, I applied to three colleges, each of which I had carefully chosen after listing my priorities, searching through a thick book that described hundreds of institutions, discussing my future with my family, and visiting several campuses. On the morning I was to take the College Board Achievement tests, I opened a letter from the one college I had applied to (in California) that did not require those exams. That college wanted me; they offered a small scholarship. I had never visited California or known anyone at that institution, which was 3,000 miles from my home and from the boy who had given me his fraternity pin.

No matter. I was thrilled. To my parents' distress (my mother had envisioned me at a nearby women's college), I skipped the exam, withdrew my applications to the other two colleges, and joyfully flew west the following September. By the time I was 25 years old, I had attended four colleges (I transferred back east after two years), changed majors five times, rejected the marriage offers of four young men, lived in 10 places, and started several jobs—none lasting more than 18 months. Following that period of rapid and frequent change, however, my life has changed very little.

As I think of it now, my behavior was in marked contrast to that of my grandparents, who, by age 20, had married, had a son, and bought the farm where they lived and worked the rest of their lives. My experience, however, is typical of millions of people aged 18 to 25 today. Advances in three areas in particular—globalization, technology, and medicine—have paved the way for a new developmental stage.

This new stage has caught the attention of many observers. They realize that many 18- to 25-year-olds are forging a path through life that is dramatically different from that of earlier generations. Jeffrey Arnett, struck by the fact that his students at the University of Missouri did not fit the mold of "late adolescence" or "young adulthood," began to call them **emerging adults** (Arnett, 2004). That label stuck, and it has become the term generally used to refer to the new stage.

emerging adult A person between the ages of 18 and 25. Emerging adulthood is now widely thought of as a separate developmental stage.

Emerging adulthood is distinguished by postponement of marriage and parenthood (five or more years later than in 1950, on average), attainment of education (most U.S. adults enroll in higher education, although only 39 percent complete a college degree), financial and vocational uncertainty (most still receive financial support from their parents, and few have jobs they intend to keep until they retire), and a new freedom marked by "a substantial amount of exploration and instability that are two of the defining characteristics of emerging adulthood" (Arnett, 2004, p. 39).

Your *multicultural* awareness, a frequent theme throughout this book, surely has you questioning whether this stage is universal. That is a valid query: Emerging adulthood is far more evident in developed nations than in developing ones and in higher-SES families than in lower-SES ones (Arnett, 2004). Yet the characteristics of this stage are becoming more widespread among all economic, ethnic, and national groups (e.g., Arias & Hernández, 2007). Higher education, later marriage, and financial instability are increasingly evident among 18- to 25-year-olds in China, India, Brazil, and South Africa as well as in North America, Europe, Australia, and East Asia.

This text is primarily about childhood, but, as you know, development continues throughout life. Continuity and discontinuity, nature and nurture, and the five characteristics of development (multidirectional, multidisciplinary, multicontextual, multicultural, and plastic) are evident lifelong. Accordingly, this epilogue reviews themes from Chapter 1 while touching on all three domains of development—biosocial, cognitive, and psychosocial—as they pertain to emerging adulthood.

Biosocial Development

Physical growth stops by age 18 or so, but biosocial development in emerging adulthood is marked by *multidirectional* changes. As noted earlier, "development follows many paths—up and down, stable or erratic, backtracking or leaping forward. There is evidence for simple growth, radical transformation, improvement, and decline as well as for continuity—day to day, year to year, and generation to generation. A gain and a loss may occur together, and a loss may lead to a gain, or vice versa" (p. 9).

Prime Time for Health

Emerging adults are quite strong and healthy. Traditionally, the years from 18 to 25 have been the optimal time for hard physical work, athletic achievement, and childbearing. Thanks to the three macrosystem changes already mentioned—globalization, technology, and medicine—these activities are no longer necessary. Adults are healthier than ever, but work no longer requires as much physical strength, nor do societies depend on those in their 20s to bear as many children as possible.

Low Rates of Illness

Many chronic conditions that were common a few decades ago—malnutrition, parasite infestations, and tuberculosis among them—are now unusual among young adults worldwide. Most 18-year-olds can expect to live to old age. A multicultural perspective reminds us that specifics vary (a Japanese who survives infancy can expect to live to be 90, a Nigerian only 50), but everyone who reaches adulthood can anticipate many more healthy years (United Nations, 2007).

Serious illness is rare. In a mammoth U.S. survey, 96.4 percent of emerging adults rated their health as good, very good, or excellent (National Center for Health Statistics, 2007). Similarly, 96 percent of U.S. 18- to 25-year-olds reported no limitations on their activities due to chronic health conditions, the best rate of any age group (see Figure EP.1). Disability rates vary among nations, but advances in immunization, provision of clean water, and better food distribution now make the period from age 18 to age 25 everywhere the healthiest time of adult life.

Here is more evidence of the general good health of emerging adults. By age 20, the immune system can fight off just about everything from the sniffles to cancer (Henson & Aspinall, 2003). Usually, blood pressure is normal, teeth develop no new cavities, heart rate is steady, the brain functions well, and lung capacity is as large as it will ever be. Cancer is so unusual that most diagnostic tests, such as the PSA (for prostate cancer), mammogram (for breast cancer), and colonoscopy (for colon cancer), are not recommended until after age 40. Death from disease almost never occurs during this time (Heuveline, 2002).

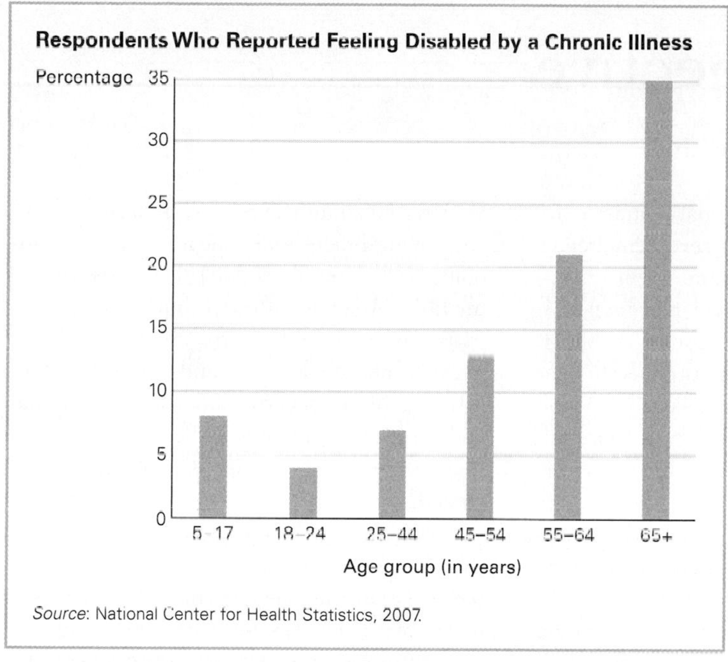

FIGURE EP.1

Strong and Independent Looking at this graph, do you wonder why twice as many 5- to 17-year-olds as 18- to 24-year-olds are said to be limited in daily activities? The answer relates to who reports the limitations. Parents answer for children; adults answer for themselves. Parents tend to be more protective, reporting that chronic conditions (mostly ADD and asthma) limit what their children can do.

Observation Quiz (see answer, page 510): At what age do half of the respondents feel disabled?

Gains and Losses in Sex and Reproduction

The sexual-reproductive system is especially vigorous during these years: The sex drive is powerful; infertility is rare; orgasm is frequent; and birth is easy, with fewer complications in the early 20s than at any other time. All these can be seen as gains that originate from biological processes. For instance, sexual-reproductive characteristics are produced by sex hormones, which peak in both sexes at about age 20 (Anis, 2007; Huang, 2007). For that reason, gains in the sexual-reproductive system in emerging adulthood result more from *nature* than *nurture*, more from biology than culture. Of course, the social context powerfully influences these natural processes, altering birth rates and encouraging sexual activity.

Falling Birth Rates Traditionally, when young couples married, a baby was born within a year or two. If that didn't occur, relatives wondered what was wrong. Indeed, with frequent unprotected intercourse, the average woman in her early 20s becomes pregnant within three months, significantly quicker than for fertile older women or teenagers just past puberty.

But as you know, that has changed: Most women in their early 20s today do not have children. Globalization, advanced technology, and modern medicine have combined to produce effective contraception, which often results in a gain in sexual pleasure and fewer pregnancies (Arnett, 2007a). The same three forces have also reduced infant mortality; new parents can now be fairly certain that each baby will survive to adulthood. People no longer need to become parents by age 20, nor do they have as many offspring as their bodies allow in the hope that some will survive.

The *multicontextual perspective* reveals a massive shift in the historical context. Centuries ago, large families were essential for survival of the species. Then, beginning in the early twentieth century, advances in public health brought about a reduction in infant mortality. The implications of that reduction were not fully understood, so large families remained the norm, births greatly exceeded deaths, and a global population explosion occurred. The world's population doubled from 3 billion in 1960 to more than 6 billion in 2000.

However, once the connection between overpopulation and poverty became widely recognized, the size of the average family shrank. The rate of population increase between 2000 and 2040 is expected to be less than half of what it was in the previous 40 years (United Nations, 2007). I have noticed the effects of the changing family size in my own life.

a personal perspective

Family Planning, My Cohort, and Me

When I was a young girl, I admired my maternal grandmother, who had 14 children. I wanted to have at least seven children of my own. I spent hours deciding what I would name them.

Thirty years later, my husband Martin and I had four children—more than most of the parents in our cohort, although not the seven I had once imagined. People are surprised to hear that we had more than two. I have been asked: "Are you Catholic or just careless?" (Answer: Neither.) "Are all your children from the same marriage?" (Answer: Yes.)

The explanation for our relatively large family seems quite logical to me. Like many members of our generation, Martin and I assumed that we would have at least two children. Bethany and Rachel were born within the first three years of our marriage.

Then the implications of globalization and overpopulation were becoming evident. We read about ZPG (zero population growth), we were concerned about our income, and we had choices when it came to contraception. In many nations, sterilization after two births was recommended: We decided against that.

We had Elissa five years later, after two of our closest friends, who planned to have no children, "gave" us their allotted share. We worried about the cost of child rearing (Martin asked, "Who will pay for braces and college?"), but Bethany and Rachel were doing well in public school (at no cost to us) and I had earned my PhD. We could afford a third.

Before Sarah, our fourth child, was conceived, ZPG was no longer a household word and my first textbook had been published. Ethical concerns about fertility had faded for our cohort, and our joint income was sufficient.

By the time Sarah was 10, the population bomb had not exploded, our children were bringing us more joy than worry, and the two oldest were self-supporting. Martin said, "I wish we had more than four." But I was past my childbearing days and I realized that our situation was already unusual: Our closest friends had only one or two children, sometimes none.

Contrary to my personal experiences, the data show that marriage and parenthood do not necessarily bring joy. Furthermore, in a massive cohort shift, many adults of my daughters' generation are single, productive, and happy. My family illustrates a number of cohort shifts: My grandparents had 19 children, 17 of whom lived to adulthood; my parents had two children; I have no grandchildren thus far.

fertility rate The average number of actual and projected births per woman in a given population.

In 90 nations, the **fertility rate**—the average number of actual and projected births per woman, currently about 2.5 worldwide—is well below the *replacement rate* (the number of births sufficient to maintain population, 2.1 births per woman). Developing as well as developed nations continue to record lower fertility rates than even a decade ago (see Figure EP.2). For example, in Egypt, the average woman had 7 offspring in 1960, 4 in 1990, 3.2 in 2000, and 2.7 today, with 1.9 projected by 2050 (United Nations, 2007). Declining birth rates and more education correlate with economic development and longer life. Thus, declining fertility is good news for human development, but it requires a shift in the social construction of what people assume is the purpose of life. Emerging adults, worldwide, are making that shift.

JUPITER IMAGES / BRAND X / ALAMY

Love Without Pregnancy Both government policy and modern contraception have changed the nature of loving relationships for young Chinese couples. This Shanghai couple may marry, they may have sex, and they may be together for 50 years or more, but they will probably have only one child.

Nations are making the shift, too. Japan, for instance, has one of the lowest fertility rates in the world (1.2), the longest life expectancy (84 years), and the highest percent of college graduates (52 percent at age 25). For the first time in its history, Japan is encouraging immigration in order to maintain population.

The Chinese government decided that lower birth rate was a cause, not merely a correlate, of economic development. Accordingly, it began to require couples to postpone marriage and limit family size. The average Chinese couple had 6 children in 1950 but has had fewer than 2 since 1990. Economic prosperity has indeed followed: The Chinese economy has grown tenfold over the past 35 years. Such coercive family-planning policies are rejected by other nations, but the Chinese experiment has shown how a loss can lead to a gain.

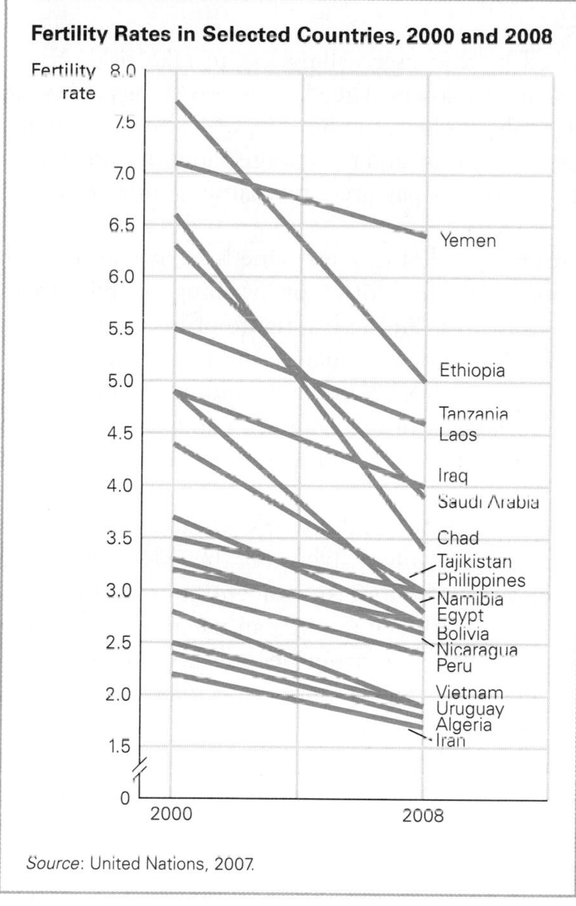

FIGURE EP.2

Fewer Children Per Woman Since the end of the twentieth century, fertility rates in a third of the world's nations, including all those in Europe, have been lower than the replacement rate. The most dramatic recent reductions have occurred in developing nations.

Observation Quiz (see answer, page 511): The source for this graph was compiled in 2006 and published in 2007, but it includes data for 2008. How can this be?

Increased Sexual Activity Globally, emerging adults are having fewer babies but more sex. Today's emerging adults have more sexual partners and engage in more sexual activity than adults who are only a few years older or than people their age once did (Pew Research Center, 2007). They are not promiscuous; most prefer to have one steady partner, then another, then another—a pattern called *serial monogamy* (Gagnon et al., 2001; Laumann & Michael, 2001; Schmookler & Bursik, 2007). Those who are most committed to each other also experience the most varied sex lives (Kaestle & Halpern, 2007).

Again, a historical perspective is useful. For most of human history, a powerful double standard prevailed: Men were expected to seek premarital sex to satisfy their biological urges, while women were expected to avoid it in order to preserve their chastity. Consequently, "good" girls were virgins when they married. The double standard affected marital sex as well: Many wives pretended to have headaches or were "frigid" when their husbands made advances; and some cultures developed the custom of genital mutilation to reduce female sexual pleasure, thus reducing pregnancies.

In developed nations, one aspect of emerging adulthood is that the double standard is disappearing. Rates of sexual activity for unmarried young women are approaching those for young men. This change in sexual activity has been accompanied by a striking change in attitudes. In the United States, a national poll found that a majority (53 percent) of people in their mid-20s believe that premarital sex is "not wrong at all," while only 18 percent of those over age 65 agree (T. W. Smith, 2005). Many emerging adults accept premarital sex as a strategy for postponing marriage—a loss or a gain, depending on one's perspective.

Do They Talk? This couple in Schenectady, New York, are in a "long-term relationship," probably years from marriage. We hope they agree about what they would do if she got pregnant, or if he found someone else, or if either was offered a great job or university scholarship in another state. Few emerging adult couples discuss such matters until they happen.

➤Answer to Observation Quiz (from page 507): Never, according to this chart, on which the vertical axis stops at 35 percent. Given the dramatic increase between the 55–64 and 65+ age groups, however, it is likely that 50 percent or more of respondents over age 80 would say that they feel disabled.

A Time for Adventure

Emerging adulthood is also marked by a greater willingness to take risks. Young adults are innovators, adventurers, and explorers. They invent new things (Einstein developed his groundbreaking ideas about physics in his 20s, while he was working at a patent office), they volunteer to fight wars and revolutions, and they are willing to uproot themselves and search for greener pastures (most immigrants are young adults).

Adventurousness has always been typical of this age. One historical example is Christopher Columbus. A book about his life (written by Washington Irving) says that Columbus arrived in Lisbon from Italy "in the full figure of his manhood" in 1470, when he was just 19. Making his living as a mapmaker, he convinced himself over the next 5 years that sailing west from Portugal would lead him to India (Irving, 1839). It took him 15 more years to convince the king and queen of Spain to finance his voyage across the Atlantic and to recruit a crew, most of whom were young adults.

edgework Occupations or recreational activities that involve a degree of risk or danger. The prospect of "living on the edge" makes edgework compelling to some individuals.

This affinity for risk taking is characteristic of **edgework**—that is, choosing an occupation or other activity because it involves living on the edge, managing stress and fear (Lyng, 2005). The joy is in the intense concentration and mastery that are required; edgework is more compelling if failure can mean disaster. Risky occupations—from firefighting to bond trading, from becoming a soldier to becoming an artist—attract young adults. To pick one in particular, most bicycle messengers in big cities are emerging adults. As one social scientist explains, "Their entire lives are wrapped inside a distinct messenger lifestyle that cherishes thrills and threats of dodging cars as they speed through the city" (Kidder, 2006).

Nonoccupational risks that could be called edgework are also common. Entering college, starting a business, filming a movie, forming a band, moving far from home, falling in love—all these are risky endeavors. The dot-com start-ups so prevalent in the early 1990s were staffed by young adults, who were less devastated than the older investors when many companies failed.

extreme sports Forms of recreation that include apparent risk of injury or death and that are attractive and thrilling as a result.

Extreme sports, in which danger and even the threat of death are part of the joy, are another recent phenomenon among emerging adults. For example, freestyle motocross was "practically invented" in the mid-1990s by Brian Deegan

On the Edge Wearing no helmet, moving against traffic, and riding a racing bike among buses and trucks—these are a thrilling combination for bicycle messengers, almost all of whom are emerging-adult men.

and Mike Metzger when they were about 20 years old (Higgins, 2006). Motocross involves riding motorcycles over barriers and off ramps, including a 50 foot high leap into "big air." As rider and cycle fall, points are gained by doing tricks with the bike, such as backward somersaults. Not surprisingly, the sport has taken a toll on these two riders:

> As a result of their longevity, Deegan and Metzger [now in their early thirties] are considered legends, graybeard veterans in a much younger man's game. . . . One has lost a kidney and broken a leg and both wrists; the other has broken arms and legs and lost a testicle. Watching them perform, many observers wonder whether they have lost their minds.
>
> *[Higgins, 2006, p. D5]*

➤Answer to Observation Quiz (from page 509): The 2008 data are projected, or estimated, on the basis of past trends. At least for the near term, fertility-rate projections (the average number of children born during a woman's lifetime) are quite accurate. The crucial element of these projections—how many children, on average, each woman has already borne—is known and will not change.

Health Risks

The example of extreme sports reminds us again that development is *multidirectional.* Gains entail losses; new freedoms are entwined with new restrictions. China is a global example: That country's dramatic economic growth is linked to restrictions on religious expression, on reproductive choice, and on occupation.

Losses accompany gains in every nation. Edgework brings excitement, but it also means that emerging adults are more likely than people of any other age to drive without a seat belt, carry a loaded gun, and abuse drugs (Reith, 2005). Worldwide, violent deaths now far exceed deaths from disease among emerging adults. We now consider two specific health hazards in which losses are connected to gains: sexually transmitted infections and drug abuse.

Sexually Transmitted Infections

Sexually transmitted infections (STIs) are one consequence of sexual freedom. As best we know, STIs have existed since the beginning of time. Laboratory tests confirm that syphilis became epidemic five centuries ago (Hayden, 2003). Most experts believe that AIDS existed long before the first diagnosis was made.

Until recently, however, most STIs were localized, not widespread. Now half of all emerging adults in the United States have had at least one STI (Lefkowitz & Gillen, 2006). Serial monogamy means that as soon as one sexual relationship ends, another may begin—and the spread of STIs is one result (Foxman et al., 2006).

Especially for Nurses (see response, page 513): When should you suspect that a patient has an untreated STI?

Globalization promotes international employment for many young adults, and technology allows rapid travel. As a result, viruses spread quickly from nation to nation. A common experience of wives in developing nations is that their husbands return home from distant work with a sexual infection (Hirsch et al., 2007; Parikh, 2007). Globalization also affects sex workers, who now have patrons from many nations (James, 2007).

Modern medicine has given us advanced contraception, yet globalization and technology (e.g., air travel) have made every sexually transmitted infection, including HIV, a widespread problem (UNAIDS, 2008). Worldwide, young adults of both sexes are STI vectors as well as victims (Cockerham, 2006). The consequences are felt by every generation. Millions of children are being raised by their grandparents because their parents have died of AIDS.

Drug Abuse

Drug abuse does not spread like a virus, but it does accompany the life patterns of many emerging adults. Fraternities and sororities, huge concerts, sporting events, and freedom from parental scrutiny, marriage, and children—all correlate with drug use and abuse (Bachmann, 2002).

FIGURE EP.3

Current Drug Use by Adolescents and Emerging Adults Most U.S. adolescents try illicit drugs (60 percent), although few of them become chronic users. In contrast, emerging adults are more likely than adolescents to have used legal drugs—alcohol and cigarettes—recently.

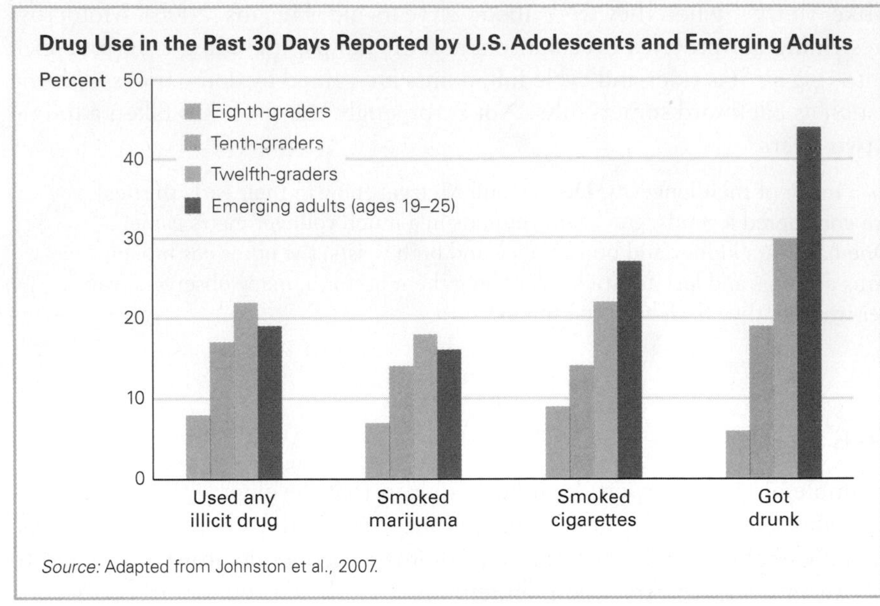

Source: Adapted from Johnston et al., 2007.

Alcohol Abuse Some drugs (such as crack and heroin) are used infrequently by high school seniors (less than 2 percent) and even more rarely by emerging adults (less than 1 percent). However, emerging adults are more likely than high school seniors to drink too much and to be addicted to cigarettes (see Figure EP.3; Johnston et al., 2007). Early drug use (before age16) is a risk factor for later use, but so are high SES, European American ethnicity, and good grades in high school (Jackson et al., 2008; Ludden & Eccles, 2007).

A longitudinal study at a large university in the U.S. Midwest found that almost everyone (83 percent), including more than a third of the former abstainers, drank excessive amounts of alcohol to celebrate their 21st birthday. Their average was 13 drinks. A substantial minority (10 percent) consumed 21 drinks—with glasses of beer, glasses of wine, and shots of liquor each counted as one drink (Rutledge et al., 2008). These "21-at-21" drinkers included as many women as men. Such binge drinking is always hazardous and sometimes fatal (Zernike, 2005).

Part of the problem is that emerging adults who abuse drugs are more likely than sober ones to be noticed by other members of their generation. Users are louder, more outgoing, and seemingly more popular, so others may be led to think that they should use drugs, too.

In one experiment, several small groups of college students were offered as much alcohol as they wanted to drink while they socialized with one another. In some groups, one student was secretly recruited in advance to drink heavily; in others, one student was assigned to drink very little; in a third condition, participants just drank as they wished. In those groups with a heavy drinker, the average student drank more than did the average student in the other two contexts. Thus, emerging adults followed the norm set by the risk takers, not by the cautious ones (reported in Miller & Carroll, 2006).

ANDREW LICHTENSTEIN / THE IMAGE WORKS

"Eggs and Kegs" Alcohol serves as a social lubricant for many young adults. In this regular ritual, college students ("eggheads") in Albany, New York, gather to drink beer until the last keg runs out, toward dawn. By then, most of them have made new friends and are tired but happy. Others, however, are sick, angry, and tearful.

The Power of Example The influence of the drug user has been made evident by other research. Young adults overestimate their peers' intake of drink and drugs, and this makes them more likely to abuse drugs. This has been shown many times with alcohol, and it also seems true for tobacco. In one study, Canadian smokers were asked to estimate the percent of people their age and sex who smoked. Emerging adults were particularly likely to guess high;

71 percent overestimated by more than 20 percentage points (Cunningham & Selby, 2007).

A *multicontextual perspective* points toward a simple way to reduce drug abuse. In the **social norms approach,** emerging adults are surveyed regarding their drug use, and the results are publicized. When emerging adults learn that most students are not excessive drug users, they reduce their own consumption. About half the colleges in the United States have surveyed alcohol use on their campuses, reported the results, and usually experienced a reduction in heavy drinking (Berkowitz, 2005; Wechsler et al., 2003). Thus, the social context is influential, but many emerging adults misjudge their context.

social norms approach A method of reducing risky behavior among emerging adults that is based on their desire to follow social norms. This approach uses surveys of emerging adults and publication of the results of those surveys to make emerging adults aware of the actual prevalence of various behaviors in their peer group.

Cognitive Development

To understand cognitive development in emerging adulthood, a *multidisciplinary approach*—with input from many disciplines—is needed. The contributions of various disciplines combine to provide a full view of the whole person. Here we work with findings from neuroscience, psychology, and sociology. A more complete picture would include information from anthropology, political science, and history as well. We begin with brain maturation, which provides the foundation for adult thinking.

Brain Maturation

As you remember, adolescent limbic systems develop before the prefrontal cortex matures. Consequently, adolescents are more likely than others to switch between two modes of thought: intuitive and logical. "Cognitive processes show very protracted transformation" (M. Taylor, 2006, p. 22), because the brain continues to mature. Adult experiences gradually sculpt brain connections, forming new dendrites while unused neurons disappear.

The experiences of emerging adults as they make practical decisions about daily life require connections between emotions and logic. As a result, "emerging adulthood truly does emerge as a somewhat crucial period of the life span," because "complex, critical, and relativizing thinking emerges only in the 20s" (Labouvie-Vief, 2006, p. 78). "Relativizing" means considering things in relation to each other. Unlike egocentric adolescents, emerging adults set priorities and consider the perspectives of many people, combining intuition and logic.

One study investigated age differences in the ways people described themselves. Researchers categorized participants' self-descriptions as *self-protective* (high in self-involvement, low in self-doubt), *dysregulated* (fragmented, overwhelmed by emotions or problems), *complex* (valuing openness and independence above all), or *integrated* (able to regulate emotions and logic). No one under age 20 was at the advanced "integrated" stage, but some adults of every age were (see Figure EP.4 on the next page). The largest shift in self-description occurred between adolescence and emerging adulthood (Labouvie-Vief, 2006). This evidence from psychology matches the evidence from neuroscience: Adults are able to use their entire brains flexibly to deal with whatever practical concerns they might have.

➤Response for Nurses (from page 511): Always. In this context, "suspect" refers to a healthy skepticism, not to prejudice or disapproval. Your attitude should be professional rather than judgmental, but you should also be aware that education, gender, self-confidence, and income do not necessarily mean that a given patient is or is not free of a sexually transmitted infection. In fact, many emerging adults are infected, often without being aware of it.

As you know, brains adapt to experiences, so it matters what particular experiences adults may have. Two of the many examples of this kind of adaptation are the cultural differences that occur in the way people approach problems and cohort differences in the reaction to technological advances (in word processing, social networking, knowledge access, and the like). One important influence on adult cognition is a college education; we will now focus on what sociological and psychological research tells us about its effects.

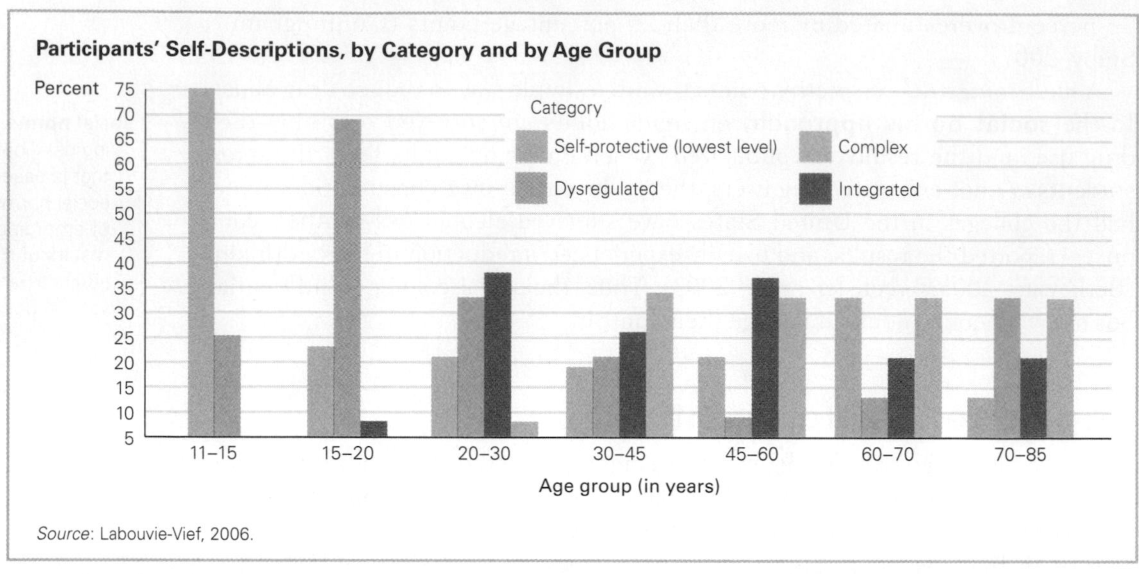

Source: Labouvie-Vief, 2006.

FIGURE EP.4

Talk About Yourself People gradually became less self-centered and less confused as they described themselves over the years of adulthood. Many adults, but no children or adolescents, achieved a level of self-acceptance at which emotions and reason were integrated.

The Culture of Higher Education

The college culture changes how people think. According to one comprehensive review:

> Compared to freshmen, seniors have better oral and written communication skills, are better abstract reasoners or critical thinkers, are more skilled at using reason and evidence to address ill-structured problems for which there are no verifiably correct answers, have greater intellectual flexibility in that they are better able to understand more than one side of a complex issue, and can develop more sophisticated abstract frameworks to deal with complexity.
>
> *[Pascarella & Terenzini, 1991, p. 155]*

Note the date on that review. College has changed since then. The most dramatic shifts are in the numbers of college students and the diversity of the student body, both of which might affect what the average student learns in college. In the first half of the twentieth century, in western Europe, Japan, and North America, fewer than 1 in every 20 young adults earned a college degree; fewer than 1 in 1,000 in the developing world graduated from college. Rates of college completion now vary from about one-half to one-fifth of emerging adults in developed nations. In many nations (not the United States), younger adults are far more likely to be college graduates than their parents (see Figure EP.5).

FIGURE EP.5

Who Graduates from College? In many developed nations, a majority of emerging adults enroll in higher education. However, only half of all U.S. college students earn a degree, compared to an average of 70 percent for all the member nations of the Organization for Economic Cooperation and Development (OECD). Japan has the lowest dropout rate: Fully 90 percent of its college students stay until they graduate.

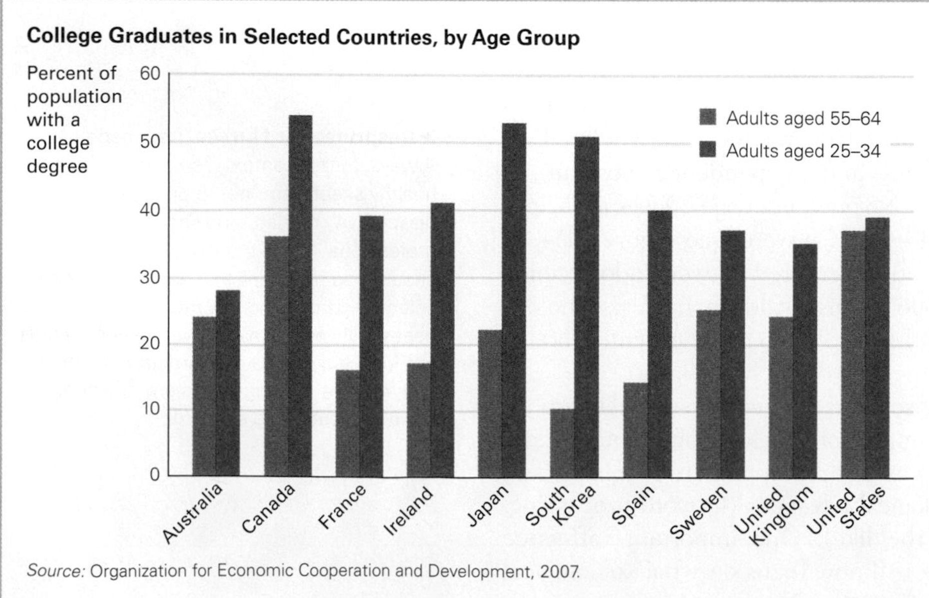

Source: Organization for Economic Cooperation and Development, 2007.

These increases are part of a worldwide trend toward more higher education. Although the proportion of the population in college is lower in South America, Africa, and Asia than in North America and Europe, the increases there are much greater than in Western nations. India is a dramatic example: At the time India became independent from Great Britain in 1948, only 100,000 students were in college. By the early twenty-first century, India had 11 million college students (Bagla, 2008).

United States? Canada? Guess Again! These students attend the University of Capetown in South Africa, where previous cohorts of Blacks and Whites would never have been allowed to socialize so freely. Such interactions foster learning.

Not only is the number of students changing, but so are their experiences, history, skills, and goals. In a reversal of the former gender breakdown, more girls than boys attend college now, and they plan on professional careers far more often than boys do (Mello, 2008). Most students are technologically savvy, having spent more hours using computers than watching television or reading. The number of personal blogs, chat rooms, and pages on Facebook.com and MySpace.com has exploded, as have music downloading, texting, virtual reality (e.g., Second Life), and interactive video games.

Fewer college students now major in the liberal arts and more specialize in business and the professions (e.g., law and medicine). Fewer of them are seeking a general education and more are focusing on financial security (see Figure EP.6). Most are employed while they are in college.

Do these changes in the social context affect cognition? Can it still be said that college makes students more flexible thinkers, "better able to understand more than one side of a complex issue"? Most of the research indicates that the answer is yes. College is still mind-altering, "a transforming element in human development"

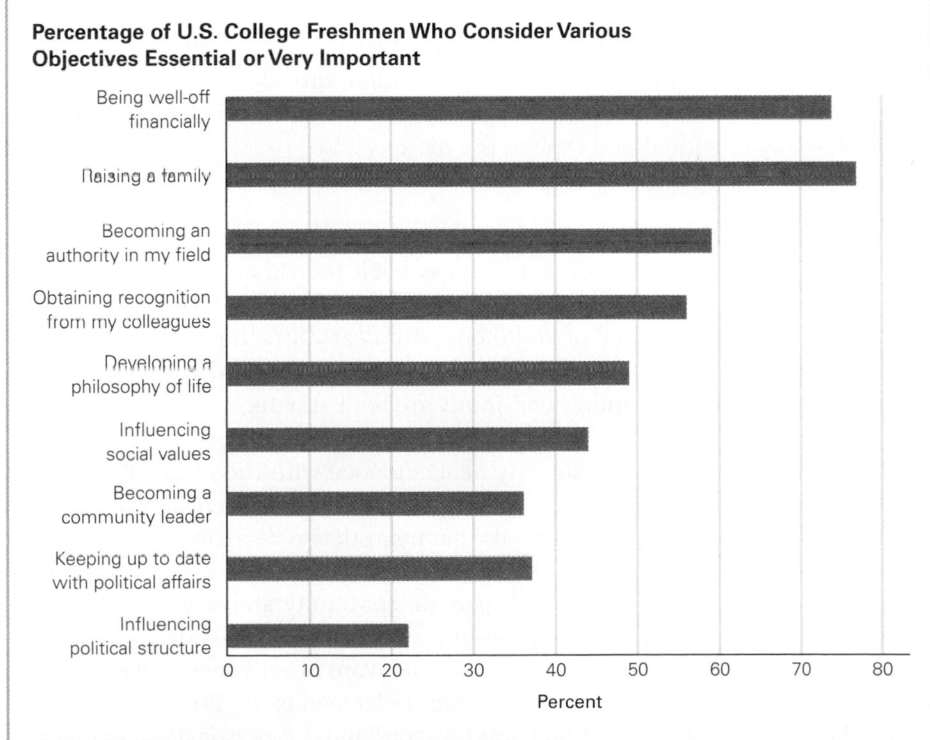

FIGURE EP.6

Personal Aspirations The American Council on Education began surveying college freshmen in 1966. Over the decades, students have gradually become more interested in their personal success and less concerned about larger issues of developing a philosophy and acting on it. For example, keeping up to date on politics was important to 58 percent in 1966 but to less than half as many (27 percent) in 1998. It rose to 36 percent in 2005.

(Benjamin, 2003, p. 11) for the millions of students who are the first in their families to attend. In fact, college may advance thinking more than it once did: "Attending college may be a consciousness-raising experience for emerging adults because they encounter new and varied people and perspectives" (Syed & Azmitia, 2008, p. 1013).

Success and satisfaction in life demonstrate the value of that cognitive advantage. Among 18-year-old high school graduates of similar backgrounds and abilities, those who go to work rather than attending college achieve less and are less satisfied (Osgood et al., 2005; Schulenberg et al., 2005). Furthermore, among children of immigrants in the United States, those who attend college are more successful, economically and intellectually, than are those who do not. Even people who begin attending community college but drop out fare better than do those with no college experience at all (Trillo, 2004).

Psychosocial Development

Plasticity is a characteristic of developmental study that is particularly relevant to understanding the psychosocial domain. That's because social development is molded in various ways by experiences.

As explained in Chapter 1, "plasticity does not mean that anyone can become anything; there are biological, brain-based, and genetic limits on every aspect of growth" (p. 19). As the preceding 12 chapters explain, experiences in childhood and adolescence impose additional limits, especially if a child has been malnourished or abused, or if an adolescent has been imprisoned or addicted. Such limits set by past experiences, as well as biological limits, are evident in emerging adulthood.

Developmentalists disagree as to exactly how powerfully early childhood experiences, or parental training, or cultural practices affect adult development. It depends partly on the individual: Some people seem to be more readily shaped by their experiences than others (Belsky et al., 2007). However, all agree that young adults sometimes defy predictions, moving off the trajectories set in their childhood and adolescence.

In emerging adulthood, the postponement of permanent family and vocational choices, and the years of education and exploration, provide a perfect context for plasticity: In such circumstances, change is likely. We now describe a few areas in which plasticity is evident and explore the reasons why.

Personality

Personality is one of the enduring aspects of each individual. As you remember from previous chapters, the origins of personality are biological, brain-based, and genetic. Personality affects all of childhood, from early attachments through adolescent depression, delinquency, and other circumstances. And yet personality is far from static: Continuity and discontinuity are both apparent in the personalities of emerging adults.

Adults try to shape their personality in accordance with the ideals of their culture. For example, among U.S. adults, longitudinal measurement of the Big Five personality traits (see Chapter 7) reveals that neuroticism decreases and conscientiousness increases (Caspi, 2000). And psychological research on personality traits of twins from age 17 to 24 finds both genetic continuity and developmental improvements: In this study, those 17-year-olds who saw life in positive terms maintained their outlook as time went on; those who were negative were likely to shift toward less worried, less anxious personalities (Blonigen et al., 2008).

Another example of the continuity and discontinuity of personality in emerging adulthood comes from research on two traits thought to be firmly genetic: inhibition and aggressiveness (Asendorpf et al., 2008). The study began with young children who ranked in the top 15 percent for these traits and followed them into emerging adulthood. The 19 children who were very aggressive at ages 4 to 6 still had that personality trait in adolescence and beyond. For example, they were more likely to have conflicts with their parents and friends, more likely to leave their jobs, less likely to complete high school (one-third had done so, compared with two-thirds of their peers), and more likely to have been arrested by age 23.

Yet these aggressive young adults had as many friends as their peers did, and they rated themselves as quite conscientious. Half of them had never been arrested as adults, and most of those who were arrested were charged with minor offenses. Only 1 of the 19 highly aggressive children had been imprisoned, and only 1 other had been arrested several times. Furthermore, careful analysis showed that the lower educational level of these 19 was not caused by their actions as emerging adults but by their earlier educational experiences, specifically having repeated several grades in childhood. Thus, it seemed likely that at least some of them would become productive and well-adjusted adults, since their childhood problems were no longer evident.

As for the emerging adults who had been inhibited as children, their prospects were very good, because "inhibited children develop into cautious, reserved adults with few signs of internalizing problems" (Asendorpf et al., 2008, p. 1007). Among the effects of this group's earlier shyness was that they were slower to secure a job, choose a career, or find a romantic partner (an assessment at age 23 found that one-third currently had partners, compared with two-thirds of their peers). However, they were no more anxious or depressed than others of their cohort, and their self-esteem was equally high. They had many friends, whom they saw often. Their tendencies that older generations might have considered negative (delayed employment and later marriage) are characteristic of emerging adults, who keep possibilities open before settling on one spouse, one career, one lifestyle.

Overall, plasticity is evident. Personality is not fixed by age 5, or 15, or 20, as it once seemed to be. Emerging adults are open to new experiences (a reflection of their adventuresome spirit), and this receptiveness allows personality shifts. The trend is toward less depression and more joy (Galambos et al., 2006).

Going to college, leaving home and becoming independent, stopping drug abuse, starting psychotherapy, searching for satisfying work and learning to do it well—all these have the potential to change the life course. This does not mean that everyone improves; some childhood experiences, genetic predispositions, and family burdens affect people lifelong. But change is possible.

A Woman Now Two young girls participate in the traditional coming-of-age ceremony in Japan. Their kimonos and hairstyles are elaborate and traditional, as is the sake (rice wine) they drink. This is part of the ceremony signifying passage from girlhood to womanhood.

Observation Quiz (see answer, page 519): At what age do you think this event occurs—15, 16, 18, or 20?

AP / WIDE WORLD PHOTOS

Intimacy

The fifth of Erik Erikson's eight stages of development, identity versus role confusion, starts in adolescence. In the past, it was also often completed in adolescence, but this is rarely the case today, as explained in Chapter 16. The seven years from ages 18 to 25 can be seen as a prolonged moratorium that allows time for exploration of sexual/gender, political/ethnic, vocation/career, and even religious identity.

Going to college, having many close friends, and avoiding permanent commitments (such as marriage and parenthood) allow emerging adults to explore all aspects of their identity. For instance, one study found that college was a useful context for discovering and developing one's own ethnic identity, not only for minorities but also for those who consider themselves White or of mixed background (Syed & Azmitia, 2008).

intimacy versus isolation The sixth of Erikson's eight stages of development. Adults seek someone with whom to share their lives in an enduring and self-sacrificing commitment. Without such commitment, they risk profound loneliness and isolation.

Then comes Erikson's sixth stage, **intimacy versus isolation.** Without intimacy, adults suffer from loneliness and isolation. Erikson explains:

> The young adult, emerging from the search for and the insistence on identity, is eager and willing to fuse his identity with others. He is ready for intimacy, that is, the capacity to commit himself to concrete affiliations and partnerships and to develop the ethical strength to abide by such commitments, even though they call for significant sacrifices and compromises.
>
> *[Erikson, 1963, p. 263]*

All intimate relationships have much in common—not only in the psychological needs they satisfy but also in the behaviors they require (Reis & Collins, 2004). Intimacy progresses from attraction to close connection to ongoing commitment. Each relationship demands some personal sacrifice, including vulnerability that brings deeper self-understanding and shatters the isolation caused by too much self-protection.

Yet emerging adults tend to avoid the intimacy of marriage and parenthood. Does this mean that they are isolated, lonely, and "suffering, selfish slackers" (Arnett, 2007b, p. 23)? Not at all.

The need for "concrete affiliations and partnerships" is as strong as ever among emerging adults, but they have found new ways to meet it. Instead of choosing one life partner, they turn to friends, lovers, and family members, who play a larger role in the emotional lives of most emerging adults now than they did 100 or even 50 years ago. Let us look briefly at these three types of relationships.

Friendships

Throughout life, friends defend against stress and provide joy (Bukowski et al., 1996; Krause, 2006). They are chosen for the very qualities (e.g., understanding, tolerance, loyalty, affection, humor) that make them good companions, trustworthy confidants, and reliable sources of support. Unlike family members, friends are earned; they choose us. Friends, new and old, are particularly crucial during emerging adulthood.

Traditionally, young men and women preferred friends of their own sex and did sex-specific activities with them. Male friendships centered on shared activities such as sports, cars, and contests (sometimes fighting with words, not weapons). Women's friendships were more intimate and emotional, involving self-disclosing talk about health, romances, and relatives. These male–female distinctions are less apparent among contemporary emerging adults. For instance, the typical emerging adult has one or two cross-sex friendships and several more nonsexual same-sex relationships (Lenton & Webber, 2006).

The common contexts of emerging adulthood today—colleges and universities, large corporations and international travel, residences far from one's original neighborhood—all foster multiple acquaintances and new friends of both sexes. Most single young adults have larger, and more supportive, friendship networks than newly married young adults once did. This is a gain in one kind of intimacy.

Romances

Worldwide, couples are marrying later than earlier cohorts did—a trend that some might consider a loss (Georgas et al., 2006). Rather than being isolated, however, many young adults not only have active romances but often live together in an arrangement called **cohabitation** (living with someone else, typically with a romantic partner). Those who cohabit usually share household expenses and daily routines as well as a bed, although they often shy away from shared income and long-term plans.

cohabitation An arrangement in which a couple live together in a committed sexual relationship but are not formally married.

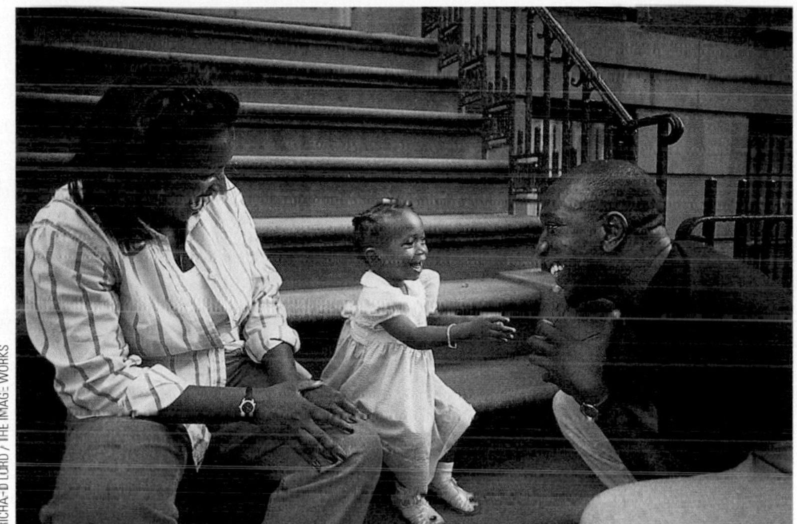
RICHARD LORD / THE IMAGE WORKS

What's Wrong with This Picture? The beaming man is a proud and responsive father, old enough to take his responsibilities seriously. A close look at his 22-month-old daughter suggests that he is doing a good job: She is delighted at the game he is playing with the ball, and he has moved his tall body way down, to be exactly at face level with her. Another fact also makes bonding easier: She is the biological child of these two young adults. So in terms of child and adult development, everything is right with this family picture—but some people might be troubled by one detail: Neither parent has a wedding ring. They have never married.

Most emerging adults in the United States, Canada, northern Europe, England, and Australia cohabit at some point. The Add Health study found that about 60 percent of a nationwide U.S. sample had cohabited by age 24 (Schoen et al., 2007). Cohabitation is increasingly common in other nations as well, although in some places it is still socially unacceptable.

Contrary to widespread belief, cohabitation does not preclude the problems that may arise after a wedding. The opposite is more likely (Cohan & Kleinbaum, 2002; Kamp Dush & Amato, 2005). Domestic violence and excessive drinking are more likely to occur among young adults who cohabit than among those who marry, and married couples are *more* likely to divorce if they had lived together before marriage. It seems as if cohabitation solves some problems for emerging adults, but it does not remedy a major developmental difficulty of our era—divorce.

Divorce is common (ending 45 percent of U.S. marriages) and difficult, not only for the partners but also for their families—their parents as well as their children. Developmentalists are working to understand these consequences in the hope of helping to alleviate them (Amato, 2000; Furstenburg & Cherlin, 1991).

➤Answer to Observation Quiz (from page 517): The most obvious clue—that the girls look like teenagers—is misleading. If you remembered that the social clock is somewhat slower in developed nations and that Asian adolescents mature relatively late, you might have guessed, accurately, that the girls are 20 years old. This is five years later than the Quinceañera, the similar occasion for Latinas, and four years later than the European American "sweet sixteen."

AP / WIDE WORLD PHOTOS

Mail-Order Bride He was looking for a woman with green eyes and reddish hair but without strong religious convictions, and he posted these criteria on a social-networking Web site. That led to an e-mail courtship and eventually marriage to "the girl of my dreams."

Family Connections

It is hard to overestimate the importance of the family at any time of the life span. Families are "our most important individual support system" (Schaie, 2002, p. 318). Although made up of individuals, a family is much more than the persons who belong to it. In dynamic synergy, children grow, adults find support, and everyone is part of an ethos that gives meaning to, and provides models for, personal aspirations and decisions.

Emerging adults are said to set out on their own, leaving their childhood home and parents behind. That is the story line, but it is not the whole truth. Parents continue to be crucial influences after age 20—more so now than earlier, since fewer emerging adults today have established their own families, secured high-paying jobs, or achieved a definitive understanding of their identity and their goals.

linked lives A term that describes the notion that family members tend to be affected by all aspects of each other's lives, from triumph to tragedy.

All members of each family have **linked lives,** meaning that the experiences and needs of family members who are at one stage of life are affected by those of members at other stages (Macmillan & Copher, 2005). Consider the current status of most parents of emerging adults. Fewer have young as well as adult children; mothers as well as fathers are employed. Parents are often financially secure: Households headed by someone aged 45 to 54 average higher incomes than those headed by someone older or younger (U.S. Bureau of the Census, 2007). Parents have always wanted to help their adult children, but now more of them can—and do.

Indeed, many emerging adults still live at home, partly because few entry-level jobs pay enough to permit independence. Specifics vary from nation to nation. Almost all unmarried young adults in Italy and Japan live with their parents, as do half those in England (Manzi et al., 2006). Fewer do so in the United States, but many parents underwrite their young-adult children's rent (Pew Research Center, 2007). In many developing nations, young adults live with their parents even after they marry and have children. Grandparents everywhere are a major source of free child care.

In the United States, about half of all emerging adults receive cash from their parents (averaging $1,000 a year) in addition to tuition, medical care, food, and other material support. Most are also given substantial gifts of time, such as help with laundry, moving, household repairs, and, if the young adult becomes a parent, child care. This assistance makes achievement (higher education, better jobs) possible (Schoeni & Ross, 2005).

The Same Situation, Many Miles Apart: Happy Young Women The British woman *(left)* and the Kenyan woman *(right)* are both developing just as their families and cultures had hoped they would. The major difference is that 23-year-old Kim is not yet married to Dave, while her contemporary already has a husband, son, and daughter.

CHRIS ROUTE / ALAMY

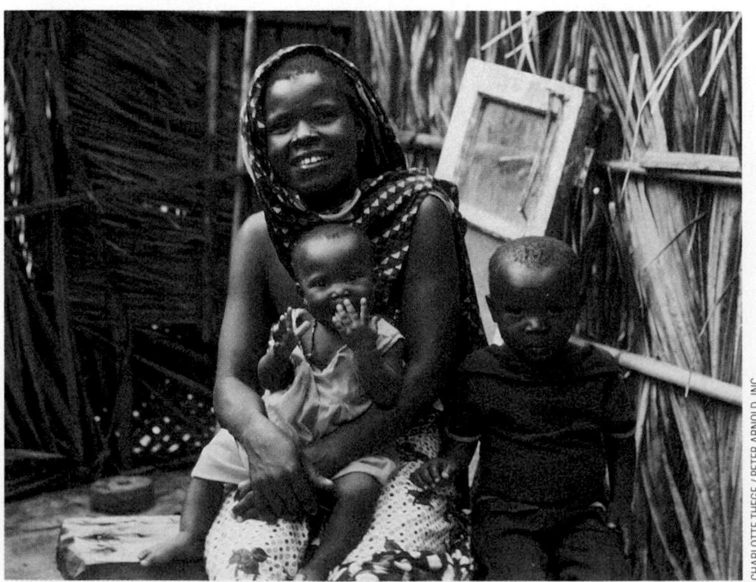

CHARLOTTE THEGE / PETER ARNOLD, INC.

This situation also highlights a problem for emerging adults who lack family support. College is costly; even with government subsidies, living expenses must be covered, and many young adults from low-income families drop out. In every nation, college graduation rates decrease as family income falls (OECD, 2007).

Emotional Health

Emerging adulthood is a prime time both for emotional health and for psychological problems.

Well-Being

Survey results suggest that psychological well-being is the dominant condition in emerging adulthood. In one U.S. study, 3,912 people were quite happy with themselves at age 18. Over the next several years, their self-esteem kept rising (see Figure EP.7; Schulenberg et al., 2005). Similarly, 404 young adults in western Canada, repeatedly questioned from ages 18 to 25, also reported increasing self-esteem (Galambos et al., 2006). This trend toward high self-esteem has become more evident over recent decades, as emerging adulthood has become the norm (Twenge et al., 2008).

One might think that the many stresses and transitions of emerging adulthood would decrease self-esteem, but the opposite seems to be true. Dealing with expected transitions successfully—especially leaving home, attending and then graduating from college, and securing a full-time job—all correlate with well-being, at least in the United States (Schulenberg et al., 2005).

Psychopathology

However, not every emerging adult benefits from independence. Some are overwhelmed by their many choices and challenges. From ages 18 to 25, "young people are coming to grips with their lives" (Galambos et al., 2006, p. 360). Some lose their grip. Average well-being increases, as just described, but so does the incidence of psychopathology (Mowbray et al., 2006; Schulenberg & Zarrett, 2006).

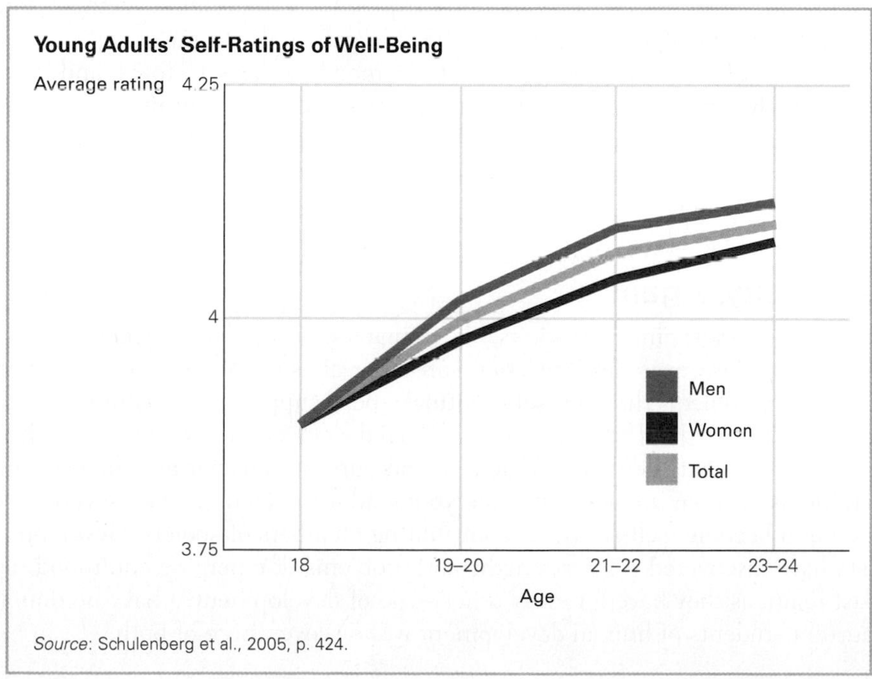

FIGURE EP.7

Worthy People This graph shows a steady increase in young adults' sense of well-being from age 18 to age 24, as measured by respondents' ratings of statements such as "I feel I am a person of worth." The ratings ranged from 1, indicating complete disagreement, to 5, indicating complete agreement. The average rating was already quite high at age 18, and it increased steadily over the years of emerging adulthood.

diathesis-stress model The view that psychological disorders, such as schizophrenia, are produced by the interaction of a genetic vulnerability (the diathesis) and stressful environmental factors and life events.

Worldwide, adults are more likely to have an episode of mental illness during emerging adulthood than during any later time. Substantial research finds that vocational, financial, and interpersonal stresses are greater in early adulthood than later on (Kessler et al., 2005). Most developmentalists accept the **diathesis-stress model** of mental illness. This model "views psychopathology as the consequence of stress interacting with an underlying predisposition (biological, psychosocial, or sociocultural) to produce a specific disorder" (Hooley, 2004, p. 204). Thus, the stresses of emerging adulthood are likely to cause problems when added to preexisting vulnerability.

Anxiety Disorders One major type of problem, evident in one-fourth of all emerging adults in the United States, is anxiety disorder, including post-traumatic stress disorder (PTSD), obsessive-compulsive disorder (OCD), and panic attacks. The manifestations of anxiety disorders are influenced by age and cultural context. In Japan, a new anxiety disorder has appeared within the last 20 years that is said to affect more than 100,000 young adults. It is called *hikikomori,* or "pull away." The sufferer stays in his (or, less often, her) room almost all the time for six months or more. Typically, a person suffering with *hikikomori* is anxious about the social and academic pressures of high school and college, and victims' parents "fear that their children won't survive without them" (M. Jones, 2005, p. 51).

It is easy to see how emerging adulthood sometimes causes anxiety disorders. Parents with only one or two children, in cultures that expect every young adult to achieve educationally, overwhelm some adolescents and young adults (Luthar, 2003). Worry about graduation and career can be intense.

Schizophrenia About 1 percent of all adults experience at least one episode of schizophrenia. They have irrational, disorganized, and bizarre thoughts, delusions, hallucinations, and emotions (American Psychiatric Association, 2000). This disorder is present in every nation. Age, gender, culture, and context affect the rates of incidence (Cantor-Graae & Selten, 2005; Kirkbride et al., 2006).

There is no doubt that schizophrenia is partly genetic. Other factors beyond heredity increase the rate of schizophrenia, including malnutrition experienced while the brain is developing (St Clair et al., 2005) and social pressure. Among immigrants, the rate of schizophrenia triples for young adults without familiar supports (Cantor-Graae & Selten, 2005; Morgan et al., 2007).

A diagnosis of schizophrenia is most common from ages 18 to 24, and males are particularly vulnerable (Kirkbride et al., 2006). Does something in the bodies, minds, or social surroundings of young men trigger schizophrenia? The diathesis-stress model suggests that the answer is yes—that is, all three are factors in the onset of schizophrenia.

Plasticity, Again

Fortunately, most emerging adults, like humans at all ages, have strengths as well as liabilities. Many overcome anxieties, substance abuse, loneliness, bizarre thoughts, and other problems through "self-righting," social support, and maturation.

Every longitudinal study of the emotional development of emerging adults finds that the links between past influences and current behavior are complex. Earlier problems have an impact, but some young adults overcome even severe deprivation and become well-adjusted, contributing members of society. Developmentalists have discovered some strengths and problems of emerging adulthood (as you just read), as they have for every other stage of development. I have no doubt that current students of human development will discover more of both.

SUMMARY

Biosocial Development

1. Emerging adults are strong and healthy, with development that is multidirectional and multicontextual. Gains and losses are apparent. The historical context has changed the developmental path for many 18- to 25-year-olds.

2. Sexual gains for emerging adults include more frequent sex and more varied experiences, as well as less fear of unwanted pregnancy. However, these gains may be offset by a loss in sexual health, as rates of sexually transmitted infections are increasing.

3. Emerging adults are creative risk takers. However, risks sometimes lead to injuries and violent deaths, partly because of edgework, extreme sports, and drug abuse.

Cognitive Development

4. Multidisciplinary research finds that, because of neurological advances, emerging adults are better able to combine logic and intuition than are younger adults.

5. College education is widespread, becoming the norm for emerging adults in many developed nations. A multicultural perspective reveals many variations in the proportion of emerging adults who enroll in college and the proportion who graduate. The diversity of students adds to the cognitive impact of the college experience.

Psychosocial Development

6. Plasticity is evident in personality changes during emerging adulthood. Although personality is affected by heredity and experience, some emerging adults shift in their attitudes and their characteristics. The general tendency is to develop whatever traits are valued within the culture.

7. Emerging adults have found many ways to satisfy their intimacy needs. More emerging adults cohabit than marry. Family supports continue to be influential, and most unmarried adults rely on an extensive network of friends and acquaintances.

8. Although most emerging adults are quite satisfied with their lives, some are troubled by severe psychic disabilities. The stresses and challenges of emerging adulthood may be overwhelming.

KEY TERMS

emerging adult (p. 505)
fertility rate (p. 508)
edgework (p. 510)
extreme sports (p. 510)
social norms approach (p. 513)
intimacy versus isolation (p. 518)
cohabitation (p. 518)
linked lives (p. 520)
diathesis-stress model (p. 522)

KEY QUESTIONS

1. What biological demands confront the typical emerging adult today, compared with 100 years ago?

2. What are three reasons the average couple has far fewer children in 2008 than in 1958?

3. What personality characteristics are likely to become more evident after age 20?

4. How has family interaction changed for emerging adults?

APPLICATIONS

1. College education is said to expand a person's understanding of other people. Tell how one college student (yourself or a friend) encountered another person whom he or she would not have met in high school, and describe how the student was affected.

2. Interview several married couples who did, and did not, cohabit, and develop a hypothesis about the impact of cohabitation on marriage.

Appendix A

Supplemental Charts, Graphs, and Tables

Often, examining specific data is useful, even fascinating, to developmental researchers. The particular numbers reveal trends and nuances not apparent from a more general view. For instance, many people mistakenly believe that the incidence of Down syndrome babies rises sharply for mothers over 35, or that even the tiniest newborns usually survive. Each chart, graph, or table in this appendix contains information not generally known.

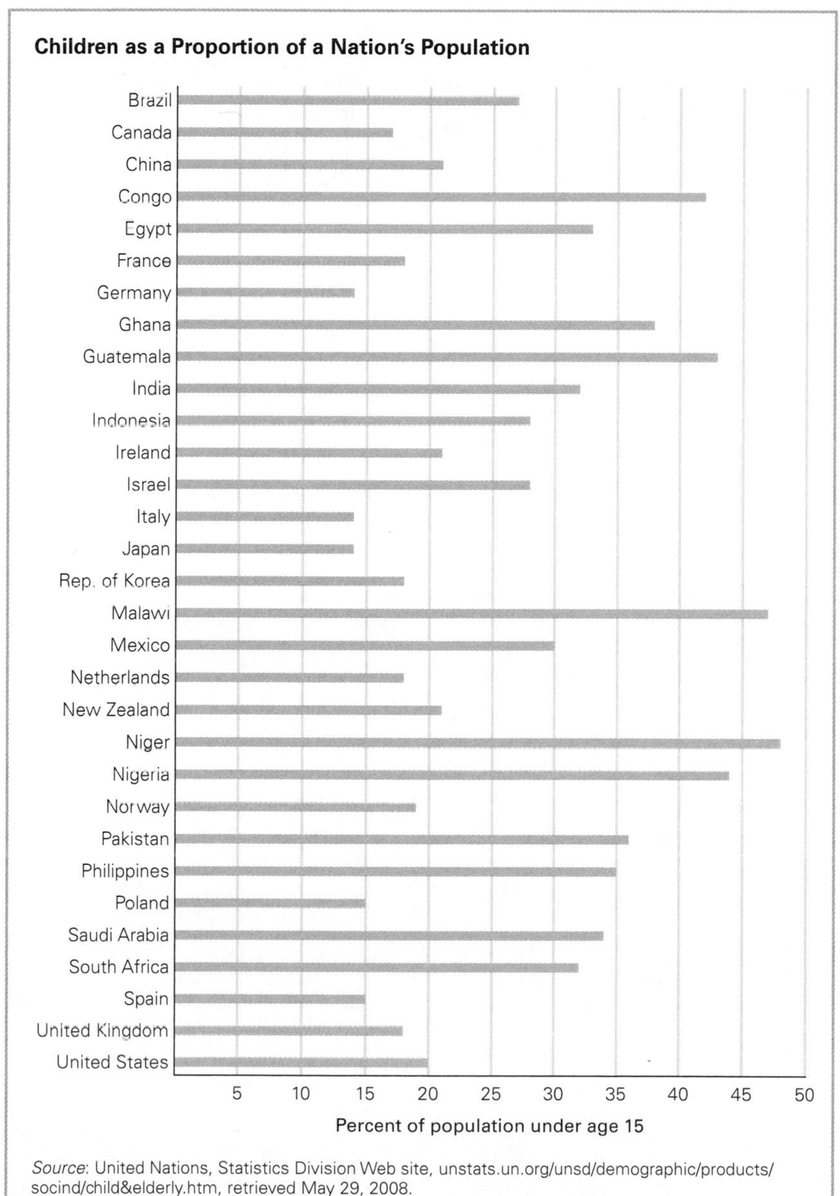

Source: United Nations, Statistics Division Web site, unstats.un.org/unsd/demographic/products/socind/child&elderly.htm, retrieved May 29, 2008.

More Children, Worse Schools? (Chapter 1)

Nations that have high birth rates also have high death rates, short life spans, and more illiteracy. A systems approach suggests that these variables are connected: For example, the Montessori and Reggio Emilia early-childhood education programs, said to be the best in the world, originated in Italy; Italy has the lowest proportion of children under 15.

Ethnic Composition of the U.S. Population (Chapter 2)

Thinking about the ethnic makeup of the U.S. population can be an interesting exercise in social comparison. If you look only at the table, you will conclude that not much has changed over the past 37 years: Whites are still the majority, Native Americans are still a tiny minority, and African Americans are still about 12 percent of the population. However, if you look at the chart, you can see why every group feels that much has changed. Because the proportions of Hispanic Americans and Asian Americans have increased dramatically, European Americans see the current non-White population at almost one-third of the total, and African Americans see that Hispanics now outnumber them. There are also interesting regional differences within the United States; for example, the state of California has the largest number of Native Americans (423,000) and the largest number of Asians (4.5 million).

Observation Quiz (see answer, page A-4): Which ethnic group is growing most rapidly?

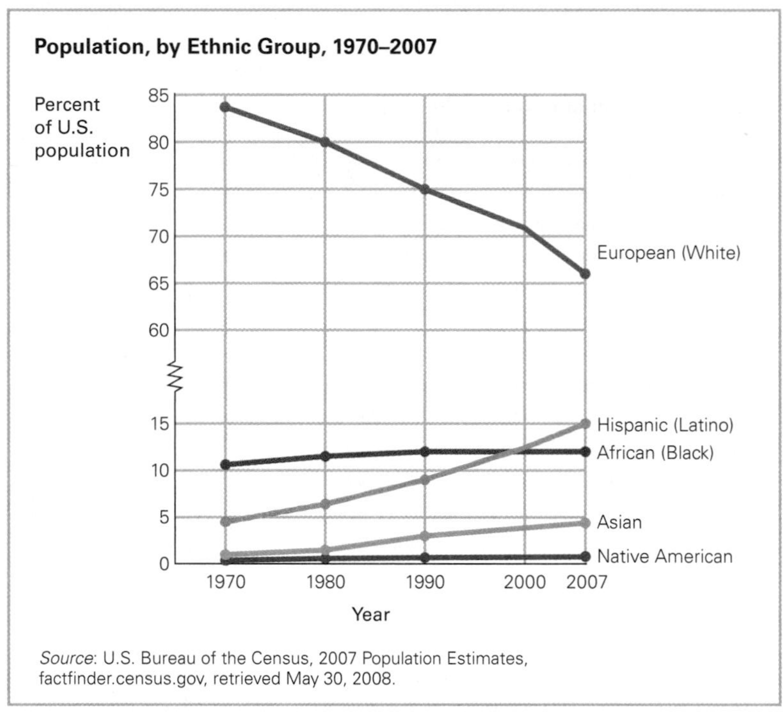

Source: U.S. Bureau of the Census, 2007 Population Estimates, factfinder.census.gov, retrieved May 30, 2008.

	Percent of U.S. population			
Ethnic origin	1970	1980	1990	2007
European (White)	83.7	80	75	66.0
African (Black)	10.6	11.5	12	12.4
Hispanic (Latino)	4.5	6.4	9	15.0
Asian	1.0	1.5	3	4.3
Native American	0.4	0.6	0.7	0.9

The Genetics of Blood Types (Chapter 3)

Blood types A and B are dominant traits, and type O is recessive. The percentages given in the first column of this chart represent the odds that a child born to the parents with the various combinations of genotypes will have the genotype given in the second column.

Genotypes of Parents*	Genotype of Offspring	Phenotype	Can Donate Blood to (Phenotype)	Can Receive Blood from (Phenotype)
AA + AA (100%) AA + AB (50%) AA + AO (50%) AB + AB (25%) AB + AO (25%) AO + AO (25%)	AA (inherits one A from each parent)	A	A or AB	A or O
AA + OO (100%) AB + OO (50%) AO + AO (50%) AO + OO (50%) AB + AO (25%) AB + BO (25%)	AO	A	A or AB	A or O
BB + BB (100%) AB + BB (50%) BB + BO (50%) AB + AB (25%) AB + BO (25%) BO + BO (25%)	BB	B	B or AB	B or O
BB + OO (100%) AB + OO (50%) BO + BO (50%) BO + OO (50%) AB + AO (25%) AB + BO (25%)	BO	B	B or AB	B or O
AA + BB (100%) AA + AB (50%) AA + BO (50%) AB + AB (50%) AB + BB (50%) AO + BB (50%) AB + BO (25%) AO + BO (25%)	AB	AB	AB only	A, B, AB, O ("universal recipient")
OO + OO (100%) AO + OO (50%) BO + OO (50%) AO + AO (25%) AO + BO (25%) BO + BO (25%)	OO	O	A, B, AB, O ("universal donor")	O only

*Blood type is not a sex-linked trait, so any of these pairs can be either mother-plus-father or father-plus-mother.
Source: Adapted from Hartl & Jones, 1999.

Odds of Down Syndrome by Maternal Age and Gestational Age (Chapter 4)

The odds of any given fetus, at the end of the first trimester, having three chromosomes at the 21st site (trisomy 21) and thus having Down syndrome is shown in the 10-weeks column. Every year of maternal age increases the incidence of trisomy 21. The number of Down syndrome infants born alive is only half the number who survived the first trimester. Although obviously the least risk is at age 20 (younger is even better), there is no year when the odds suddenly increase (age 35 is an arbitrary cut-off). Even at a maternal age of 44, less than 4 percent of all newborns have Down syndrome. Other chromosomal abnormalities in fetuses also increase with mother's age, but the rate of spontaneous abortion is much higher, so births of babies with chromosomal defects is not the norm, even for women over age 45.

Age (yrs)	Gestation (weeks) 10	35	Live Births
20	1/804	1/1,464	1/1,527
21	1/793	1/1,445	1/1,507
22	1/780	1/1,421	1/1,482
23	1/762	1/1,389	1/1,448
24	1/740	1/1,348	1/1,406
25	1/712	1/1,297	1/1,352
26	1/677	1/1,233	1/1,286
27	1/635	1/1,157	1/1,206
28	1/586	1/1,068	1/1,113
29	1/531	1/967	1/1,008
30	1/471	1/858	1/895
31	1/409	1/745	1/776
32	1/347	1/632	1/659
33	1/288	1/525	1/547
34	1/235	1/427	1/446
35	1/187	1/342	1/356
36	1/148	1/269	1/280
37	1/115	1/209	1/218
38	1/88	1/160	1/167
39	1/67	1/122	1/128
40	1/51	1/93	1/97
41	1/38	1/70	1/73
42	1/29	1/52	1/55
43	1/21	1/39	1/41
44	1/16	1/29	1/30

Source: Snijders & Nicolaides, 1996.

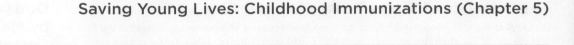

Saving Young Lives: Childhood Immunizations (Chapter 5)

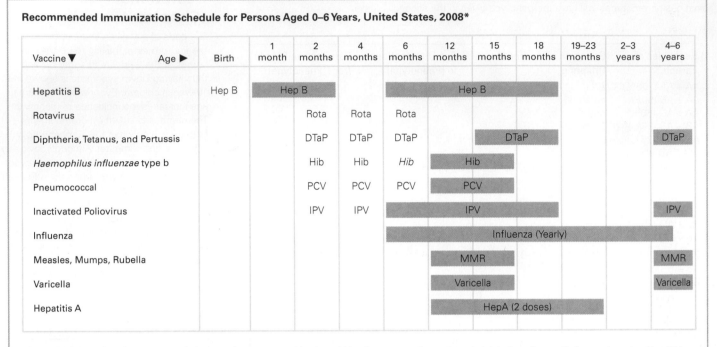

Recommended Immunization Schedule for Persons Aged 0–6 Years, United States, 2008*

<table>
<tr><th>Vaccine ▼ Age ▶</th><th>Birth</th><th>1 month</th><th>2 months</th><th>4 months</th><th>6 months</th><th>12 months</th><th>15 months</th><th>18 months</th><th>19–23 months</th><th>2–3 years</th><th>4–6 years</th></tr>
<tr><td>Hepatitis B</td><td>Hep B</td><td colspan="2">Hep B</td><td></td><td colspan="4">Hep B</td><td></td><td></td><td></td></tr>
<tr><td>Rotavirus</td><td></td><td></td><td>Rota</td><td>Rota</td><td>Rota</td><td></td><td></td><td></td><td></td><td></td><td></td></tr>
<tr><td>Diphtheria, Tetanus, and Pertussis</td><td></td><td></td><td>DTaP</td><td>DTaP</td><td>DTaP</td><td></td><td colspan="2">DTaP</td><td></td><td></td><td>DTaP</td></tr>
<tr><td>Haemophilus influenzae type b</td><td></td><td></td><td>Hib</td><td>Hib</td><td>Hib</td><td colspan="2">Hib</td><td></td><td></td><td></td><td></td></tr>
<tr><td>Pneumococcal</td><td></td><td></td><td>PCV</td><td>PCV</td><td>PCV</td><td colspan="2">PCV</td><td></td><td></td><td></td><td></td></tr>
<tr><td>Inactivated Poliovirus</td><td></td><td></td><td>IPV</td><td>IPV</td><td colspan="4">IPV</td><td></td><td></td><td>IPV</td></tr>
<tr><td>Influenza</td><td></td><td></td><td></td><td></td><td colspan="7">Influenza (Yearly)</td></tr>
<tr><td>Measles, Mumps, Rubella</td><td></td><td></td><td></td><td></td><td></td><td colspan="2">MMR</td><td></td><td></td><td></td><td>MMR</td></tr>
<tr><td>Varicella</td><td></td><td></td><td></td><td></td><td></td><td colspan="2">Varicella</td><td></td><td></td><td></td><td>Varicella</td></tr>
<tr><td>Hepatitis A</td><td></td><td></td><td></td><td></td><td></td><td colspan="4">HepA (2 doses)</td><td></td><td></td></tr>
</table>

*This chart summarizes the recommended ages or (as represented by the gold bars) age ranges for routine administration of currently licensed vaccines for children from birth to 6 years of age. For details about the schedules (including catchup schedules) for administering these vaccines, and for specific recommendations about immunizing children in certain high-risk groups, see www.cdc.gov/vaccines/recs/schedules and consult a doctor or other health-care professional.

Source: CDC Web site (cdc.gov/vaccines/recs/schedules/child-schedule), retrieved June 3, 2008.

➤**Answer to Observation Quiz** (from page A-2): Asian Americans, whose share of the U.S. population has quadrupled in the past 30 years. Latinos are increasing most rapidly in numbers, but not in proportion.

First Sounds and First Words: Similarities Among Many Languages (Chapter 6)

	Baby's word for:	
Language	Mother	Father
English	mama, mommy	dada, daddy
Spanish	mama	papa
French	maman, mama	papa
Italian	mamma	babbo, papa
Latvian	mama	te-te
Syrian Arabic	mama	baba
Bantu	ba-mama	taata
Swahili	mama	baba
Sanskrit	nana	tata
Hebrew	ema	abba
Korean	oma	apa

Which Mothers Breast-feed? (Chapter 7)

Differentiating excellent from destructive mothering is not easy, once the child's basic needs for food and protection are met. However, as the Jacob example in Chapter 7 makes clear, psychosocial development depends on responsive parent–infant relationships. Breast-feeding is one sign of intimacy between mother and infant.

Regions of the world differ dramatically in rates of breast-feeding, with the highest worldwide in Southeast Asia, where half of all 2-year-olds are still breast-fed. In the United States, factors that affect the likelihood of breast-feeding are ethnicity, maternal age, and education.

Breast-feeding Rates by Sociodemographic Factors, Among Children Born in 2004

Sociodemographic factors	Ever breast-feeding	Breast-feeding at 6 months	Breast-feeding at 12 months	Exclusive breast-feeding* at 3 months	Exclusive breast-feeding* at 6 months
U.S. national	73.8%	41.5%	20.9%	30.5%	11.3%
Sex of baby					
Male	73.6	40.8	20.0	30.7	10.8
Female	73.9	42.2	21.8	30.3	11.7
Race/ethnicity					
Native American	77.5	42.3	24.3	28.4	11.4
Asian or Pacific islander	81.7	51.8	29.1	33.4	15.8
Hispanic or Latino	81.0	45.1	24.1	30.9	11.6
African American (non-Hispanic)	56.2	26.3	11.9	20.1	7.5
European (non Hispanic)	73.9	42.5	20.8	32.6	11.8
Birth order					
First born	73.5	42.9	22.8	31.0	11.9
Not first born	74.1	39.9	18.8	29.9	10.5
Mother's age					
Less than 20	55.8	17.2	8.6	16.8	6.1
20–29	69.8	35.0	16.7	26.2	8.4
30+	77.9	48.0	24.9	34.6	13.8
Mother's education					
Less than high school	67.7	34.9	18.5	23.9	9.1
High school	65.7	32.2	16.8	22.9	8.2
Some college	75.2	40.9	18.5	32.8	12.3
College graduate	85.3	55.8	28.2	41.5	15.4
Mother's marital status					
Married	79.6	48.3	24.5	35.4	13.4
Unmarried†	60.0	25.5	12.4	18.8	6.1
Residence					
Central city	75.0	42.7	22.2	30.7	11.7
Urban	76.1	44.0	22.0	32.8	12.1
Suburban and rural	64.6	31.7	14.5	23.9	8.2

*Exclusive breast-feeding is defined in this 2006 study as only breast milk—no solids, no water, and no other liquids.
†Unmarried includes never married, widowed, separated, and divorced.
Source: Adapted from CDC's National Immunization Survey, Table 1: www.cdc.gov/breastfeeding/data/NIS_data/socio-demographic.htm, retrieved May 30, 2008.

Height Gains from Birth to Age 18 (Chapter 8)

The range of height (on this page) and weight (see page A-7) of children in the United States. The columns labeled "50th" (the fiftieth percentile) show the average; the columns labeled "90th" (the ninetieth percentile) show the size of children taller and heavier than 90 percent of their contemporaries; and the columns labeled "10th" (the tenth percentile) show the size of children who are taller than only 10 percent of their peers. Note that girls are slightly shorter, on average, than boys.

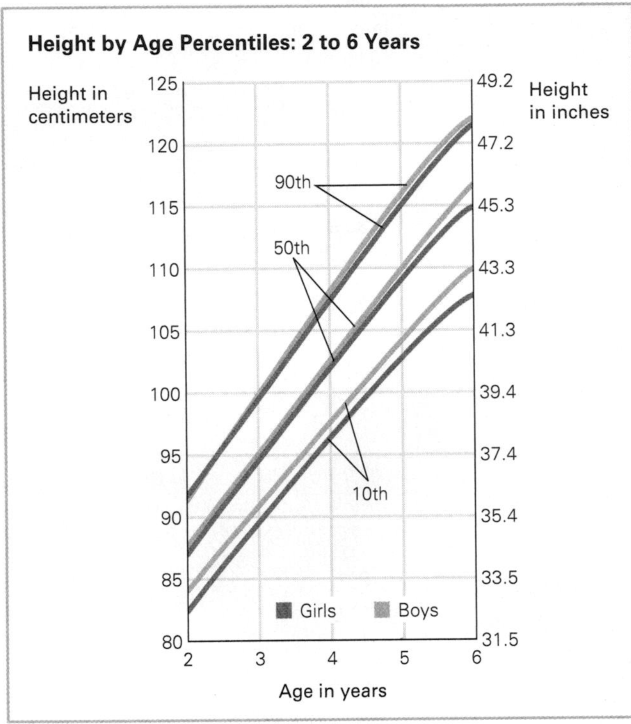

Same Data, Different Form

The columns of numbers in the table at the right provide detailed and precise information about height ranges for every year of childhood. The illustration above shows the same information in graphic form for ages 2–6. The same is done for weight ranges on page A-7. Ages 2–6 are singled out because that is the period during which a child's eating habits are set. Which form of data presentation do you think is easier to understand?

Length in Centimeters (and Inches)

AGE	Boys: percentiles 10th	50th	90th	Girls: percentiles 10th	50th	90th
Birth	47.5 (18¾)	50.5 (20)	53.5 (21)	46.5 (18¼)	49.9 (19¾)	52.0 (20½)
1 month	51.3 (20¼)	54.6 (21½)	57.7 (22¾)	50.2 (19¾)	53.5 (21)	56.1 (22)
3 months	57.7 (22¾)	61.1 (24)	64.5 (25½)	56.2 (22¼)	59.5 (23½)	62.7 (24¾)
6 months	64.4 (25¼)	67.8 (26¾)	71.3 (28)	62.6 (24¾)	65.9 (26)	69.4 (27¼)
9 months	69.1 (27¼)	72.3 (28½)	75.9 (30)	67.0 (26½)	70.4 (27¾)	74.0 (29¼)
12 months	72.8 (28¾)	76.1 (30)	79.8 (31½)	70.8 (27¾)	74.3 (29¼)	78.0 (30¾)
18 months	78.7 (31)	82.4 (32½)	86.6 (34)	77.2 (30½)	80.9 (31¾)	85.0 (33½)
24 months	83.5 (32¾)	87.6 (34½)	92.2 (36¼)	82.5 (32½)	86.5 (34)	90.8 (35¾)
3 years	90.3 (35½)	94.9 (37¼)	100.1 (39½)	89.3 (35¼)	94.1 (37)	99.0 (39)
4 years	97.3 (38¼)	102.9 (40½)	108.2 (42½)	96.4 (38)	101.6 (40)	106.6 (42)
5 years	103.7 (40¾)	109.9 (43¼)	115.4 (45½)	102.7 (40½)	108.4 (42¾)	113.8 (44¾)
6 years	109.6 (43¼)	116.1 (45¾)	121.9 (48)	108.4 (42¾)	114.6 (45)	120.8 (47½)
7 years	115.0 (45¼)	121.7 (48)	127.9 (50¼)	113.6 (44¾)	120.6 (47½)	127.6 (50¼)
8 years	120.2 (47¼)	127.0 (50)	133.6 (52½)	118.7 (46¾)	126.4 (49¾)	134.2 (52¾)
9 years	125.2 (49¼)	132.2 (52)	139.4 (55)	123.9 (48¾)	132.2 (52)	140.7 (55½)
10 years	130.1 (51¼)	137.5 (54¼)	145.5 (57¼)	129.5 (51)	138.3 (54½)	147.2 (58)
11 years	135.1 (53¼)	143.33 (56½)	152.1 (60)	135.6 (53½)	144.8 (57)	153.7 (60½)
12 years	140.3 (55¼)	149.7 (59)	159.4 (62¾)	142.3 (56)	151.5 (59¾)	160.0 (63)
13 years	145.8 (57½)	156.5 (61½)	167.0 (65¾)	148.0 (58¼)	157.1 (61¾)	165.3 (65)
14 years	151.8 (59¾)	63.1 (64¼)	173.8 (68½)	151.5 (59¾)	160.4 (63¼)	168.7 (66½)
15 years	158.2 (62¼)	169.0 (66½)	178.9 (70½)	153.2 (60¼)	161.8 (63¾)	170.5 (67¼)
16 years	163.9 (64½)	173.5 (68¼)	182.4 (71¾)	154.1 (60¾)	162.4 (64)	171.1 (67¼)
17 years	167.7 (66)	176.2 (69¼)	184.4 (72½)	155.1 (61)	163.1 (64¼)	171.2 (67½)
18 years	168.7 (66½)	176.8 (69½)	185.3 (73)	156.0 (61½)	163.7 (64½)	171.0 (67¼)

Source: These data are those of the National Center for Health Statistics (NCHS), Health Resources Administration, DHHS. They were based on studies of The Fels Research Institute, Yellow Springs, Ohio. These data were first made available with the help of William M. Moore, M.D., of Ross Laboratories, who supplied the conversion from metric measurements to approximate inches and pounds. This help is gratefully acknowledged.

Weight Gains from Birth to Age 18 (Chapter 8)

These height and weight charts present rough guidelines; a child might differ from these norms and be quite healthy and normal. However, if a particular child shows a discrepancy between height and weight (for instance, at the 90th percentile in height but only the 20th percentile in weight) or is much larger or smaller than most children the same age, a pediatrician should see if disease, malnutrition, or genetic abnormality is part of the reason.

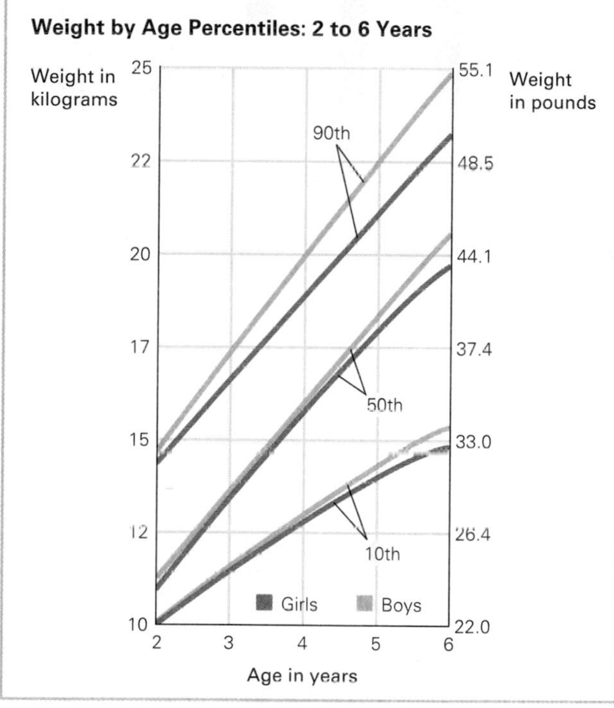

Weight in Kilograms (and Pounds)

AGE	Boys: percentiles 10th	50th	90th	Girls: percentiles 10th	50th	90th
Birth	2.78 (6¼)	3.27 (7¼)	3.82 (8½)	2.58 (5¾)	3.23 (7)	3.64 (8)
1 month	3.43 (7½)	4.29 (9½)	5.14 (11¼)	3.22 (7)	3.98 (8¾)	4.65 (10¼)
3 months	4.78 (10½)	5.98 (13¼)	7.14 (15¾)	4.47 (9¾)	5.40 (12)	6.39 (14)
6 months	6.61 (14½)	7.85 (17¼)	9.10 (20)	6.12 (13½)	7.21 (16)	8.38 (18½)
9 months	7.95 (17½)	9.18 (20¼)	10.49 (23¼)	7.34 (16¼)	8.56 (18¾)	9.83 (21¾)
12 months	8.84 (19½)	10.15 (22½)	11.54 (25½)	8.19 (18)	9.53 (21)	10.87 (24)
18 months	9.92 (21¾)	11.47 (25¼)	13.05 (28¾)	9.30 (20½)	10.82 (23¾)	12.30 (27)
24 months	10.85 (24)	12.59 (27¾)	14.29 (31½)	10.26 (22½)	11.90 (26¼)	13.57 (30)
3 years	12.58 (27¾)	14.62 (32¼)	16.95 (37¼)	12.26 (27)	14.10 (31)	16.54 (36½)
4 years	14.24 (31½)	16.69 (36¾)	19.32 (42½)	13.84 (30½)	15.96 (35¼)	18.93 (41¾)
5 years	15.96 (35¼)	18.67 (41¼)	21.70 (47¾)	15.26 (33¾)	17.66 (39)	21.23 (46¾)
6 years	17.72 (39)	20.69 (45½)	24.31 (53½)	16.72 (36¾)	19.52 (43)	23.89 (52¾)
7 years	19.53 (43)	22.85 (50¼)	27.36 (60¼)	18.39 (40½)	21.84 (48¼)	27.39 (60½)
8 years	21.39 (47¼)	25.30 (55¾)	31.06 (68½)	20.45 (45)	24.84 (54¾)	32.04 (70¾)
9 years	23.33 (51½)	28.13 (62)	35.57 (78½)	22.92 (50½)	28.46 (62¾)	37.60 (83)
10 years	25.52 (56¼)	31.44 (69¼)	40.80 (90)	25.76 (56¾)	32.55 (71¾)	43.70 (96¼)
11 years	28.17 (62)	35.30 (77¾)	46.57 (102¾)	28.97 (63¾)	36.95 (81½)	49.96 (110¼)
12 years	31.46 (69¼)	39.78 (87¾)	52.73 (116¼)	32.53 (71¼)	41.53 (91½)	55.99 (123½)
13 years	35.60 (78½)	44.95 (99)	59.12 (130¼)	36.35 (80¼)	46.10 (101¾)	61.45 (135½)
14 years	40.64 (89½)	50.77 (112)	65.57 (144½)	40.11 (88½)	50.28 (110¾)	66.04 (145½)
15 years	46.06 (101½)	56.71 (125)	71.91 (158½)	43.38 (95¾)	53.68 (118¼)	69.64 (153¼)
16 years	51.16 (112¾)	62.10 (137)	77.97 (172)	45.78 (101)	55.89 (123¼)	71.68 (158)
17 years	55.28 (121¾)	66.31 (146¼)	83.58 (184¼)	47.04 (103¾)	56.69 (125)	72.38 (159½)
18 years	57.89 (127½)	68.88 (151¾)	88.41 (195)	47.47 (104¾)	56.62 (124¾)	72.25 (159¼)

Source: Data are those of the National Center for Health Statistics, Health Resources Administration, DHHS, collected in its Health Examination Surveys.

Comparisons

Notice that the height trajectories for boys and girls on page A-6 are much closer together than the weight trajectories shown above. By age 18, the height range amounts to only about 6 inches, but there is a difference of about 65 pounds between the 10th and the 90th percentiles.

Critical Thinking Question (see answer, page A-8): How can this discrepancy between height and weight ranges be explained?

Day Care and Family Income (Chapter 9)

Note that, in both years, the wealthier families were less likely to have children exclusively in parental care and more likely to have children in center-based care.

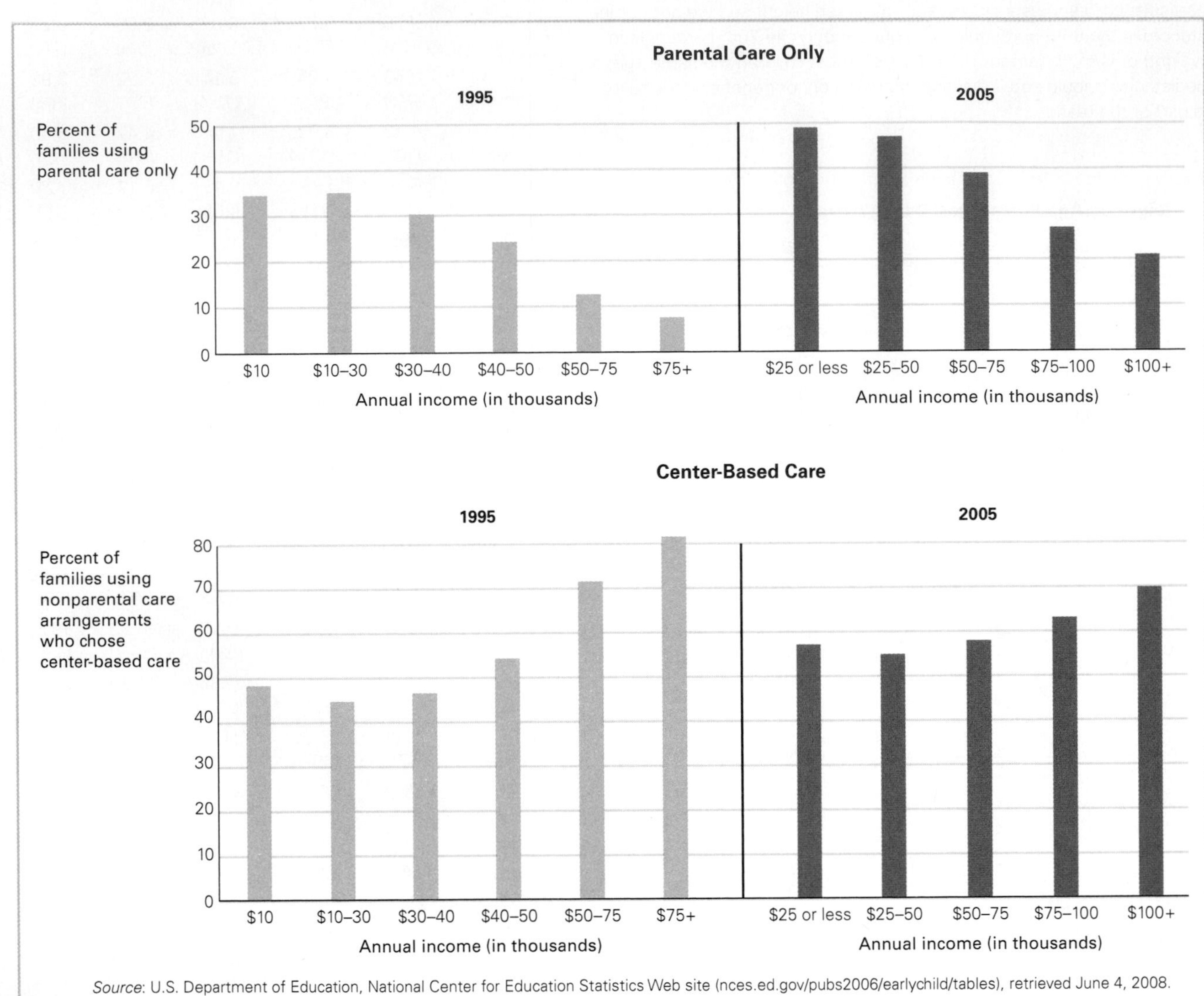

Source: U.S. Department of Education, National Center for Education Statistics Web site (nces.ed.gov/pubs2006/earlychild/tables), retrieved June 4, 2008.

➤Answer to Critical Thinking Question (from page A-7): Nutrition is generally adequate in the United States, and that is why height differences are small. But as a result of the strong influence that family and culture have on eating habits, almost half of all North Americans are overweight or obese.

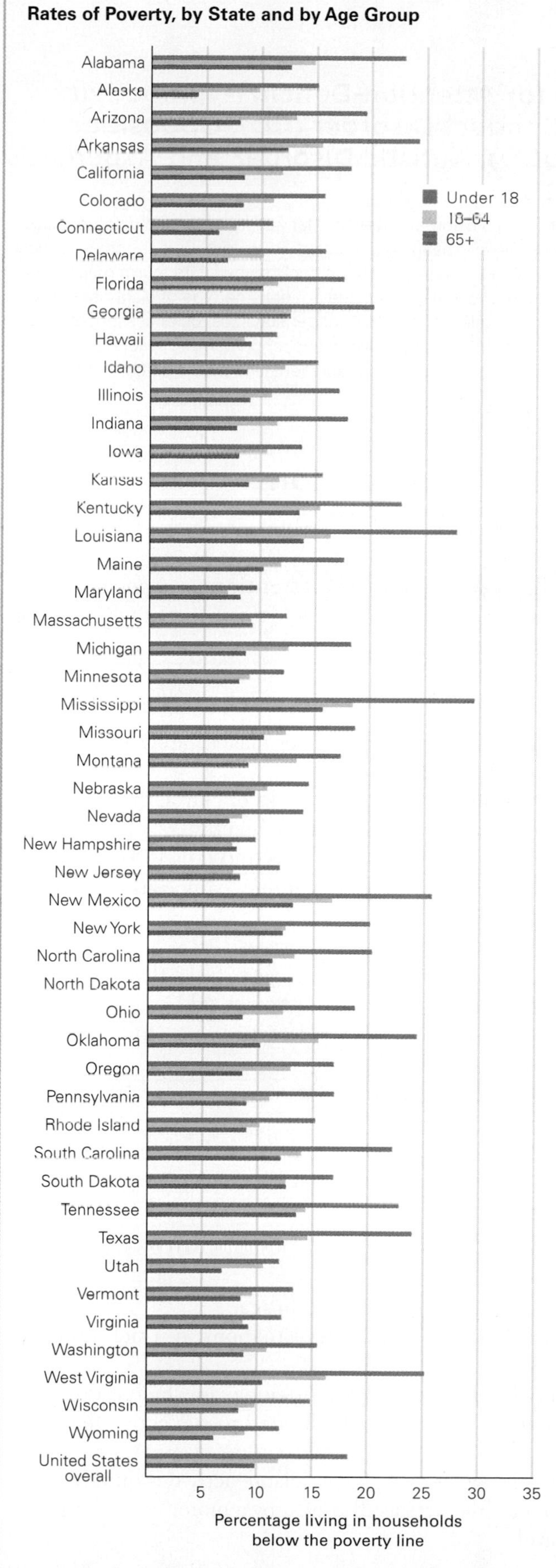

Source: U.S. Census Bureau Web site (factfinder.census.gov/servlet), retrieved June 4, 2008.

Children Are the Poorest Americans (Chapter 10)

It probably comes as no surprise that the rate of poverty is twice as high in some states as in others. What is surprising is how much the rates vary between age groups within the same state.

Observation Quiz (see answer, page A-10): In which nine states is the proportion of poor children more than twice as high as the proportion of poor people over age 65?

➤**Answer to Observation Quiz** (from page A-9): Alaska, Arizona, California, Delaware, Indiana, Michigan, Oklahoma, West Virginia, and Wisconsin.

DSM-IV-TR Criteria for Attention-Deficit/Hyperactivity Disorder (ADHD), Conduct Disorder (CD), Oppositional Defiant Disorder (ODD), Autistic Disorder, and Asperger's Disorder (Chapter 11)

The specific symptoms for these various disorders overlap. Many other childhood disorders also have some of the same symptoms. Differentiating one problem from another is the main purpose of DSM-IV-TR. That is no easy task, which is one reason the book is now in its fourth major revision and is more than 900 pages long. Those pages include not only the type of diagnostic criteria shown here but also discussions of prevalence, age and gender statistics, cultural aspects, and prognosis for about 400 disorders or subtypes, 40 of which appear primarily in childhood. Thus, the diagnostic criteria reprinted here for three disorders represent less than 1 percent of the contents of DSM-IV-TR.

Diagnostic Criteria for Attention-Deficit/Hyperactivity Disorder

A. Either (1) or (2):

(1) Six (or more) of the following symptoms of **inattention** have persisted for at least 6 months to a degree that is maladaptive and inconsistent with developmental level:

Inattention

(a) often fails to give close attention to details or makes careless mistakes in schoolwork, work, or other activities
(b) often has difficulty sustaining attention in tasks or play activities
(c) often does not seem to listen when spoken to directly
(d) often does not follow through on instructions and fails to finish schoolwork, chores, or duties in the workplace (not due to oppositional behavior or failure to understand instructions)
(e) often has difficulty organizing tasks and activities
(f) often avoids, dislikes, or is reluctant to engage in tasks that require sustained mental effort (such as schoolwork or homework)
(g) often loses things necessary for tasks or activities (e.g., toys, school assignments, pencils, books, or tools)
(h) is often easily distracted by extraneous stimuli
(i) is often forgetful in daily activities

(2) Six (or more) of the following symptoms of **hyperactivity-impulsivity** have persisted for at least 6 months to a degree that is maladaptive and inconsistent with developmental level:

Hyperactivity

(a) often fidgets with hands or feet or squirms in seat
(b) often leaves seat in classroom or in other situations in which remaining seated is expected
(c) often runs about or climbs excessively in situations in which it is inappropriate (in adolescents or adults, may be limited to subjective feelings of restlessness)
(d) often has difficulty playing or engaging in leisure activities quietly
(e) is often "on the go" or often acts as if "driven by a motor"
(f) often talks excessively

Impulsivity

(g) often blurts out answers before questions have been completed
(h) often has difficulty awaiting turn
(i) often interrupts or intrudes on others (e.g., butts into conversations or games)

B. Some hyperactive-impulsive or inattentive symptoms that caused impairment were present before age 7 years.
C. Some impairment from the symptoms is present in two or more settings (e.g., at school [or work] and at home).
D. There must be clear evidence of clinically significant impairment in social, academic, or occupational functioning.

Diagnostic Criteria for Conduct Disorder

A. A repetitive and persistent pattern of behavior in which the basic rights of others or major age-appropriate societal norms or rules are violated, as manifested by the presence of three (or more) of the following criteria in the past 12 months, with at least one criterion present in the past 6 months:

Aggression to people and animals

(1) often bullies, threatens, or intimidates others
(2) often initiates physical fights
(3) has used a weapon that can cause serious physical harm to others (e.g., a bat, brick, broken bottle, knife, gun)
(4) has been physically cruel to people
(5) has been physically cruel to animals
(6) has stolen while confronting a victim (e.g., mugging, purse snatching, extortion, armed robbery)
(7) has forced someone into sexual activity

Destruction of property

(8) has deliberately engaged in fire setting with the intention of causing serious damage
(9) has deliberately destroyed others' property (other than by fire setting)

Deceitfulness or theft

(10) has broken into someone else's house, building, or car
(11) often lies to obtain goods or favors or to avoid obligations (i.e., "cons" others)
(12) has stolen items of nontrivial value without confronting a victim (e.g., shoplifting, but without breaking and entering; forgery)

Serious violations of rules

(13) often stays out at night despite parental prohibitions, beginning before age 13 years
(14) has run away from home overnight at least twice while living in parental or parental surrogate home (or once without returning for a lengthy period)
(15) is often truant from school, beginning before age 13 years

B. The disturbance in behavior causes clinically significant impairment in social, academic, or occupational functioning.

Diagnostic Criteria for Oppositional Defiant Disorder

A. A pattern of negativistic, hostile, and defiant behavior lasting at least 6 months, during which four (or more) of the following are present:

(1) often loses temper
(2) often argues with adults
(3) often actively defies or refuses to comply with adults' requests or rules
(4) often deliberately annoys people
(5) often blames others for his or her mistakes or misbehavior
(6) is often touchy or easily annoyed by others
(7) is often angry and resentful
(8) is often spiteful or vindictive

Note: Consider a criterion met only if the behavior occurs more frequently than is typically observed in individuals of comparable age and developmental level.

B. The disturbance in behavior causes clinically significant impairment in social, academic, or occupational functioning.

Diagnostic Criteria for Autistic Disorder

A. A total of six (or more) items from (1), (2), and (3), with at least two from (1) and one each from (2) and (3):

(1) qualitative impairment in social interaction, as manifested by at least two of the following:
   (a) marked impairment in the use of multiple nonverbal behaviors such as eye-to-eye gaze, facial expression, body postures, and gestures to regulate social interaction
   (b) failure to develop peer relationships appropriate to developmental level
   (c) a lack of spontaneous seeking to share enjoyment, interests, or achievements with other people (e.g., by a lack of showing, bringing, or pointing out objects of interest)
   (d) lack of social or emotional reciprocity

(2) qualitative impairments in communication as manifested by at least one of the following:
   (a) delay in, or total lack of, the development of spoken language (not accompanied by an attempt to compensate through alternative modes of communication such as gesture or mime)
   (b) in individuals with adequate speech, marked impairment in the ability to initiate or sustain a conversation with others
   (c) stereotyped and repetitive use of language or idiosyncratic language
   (d) lack of varied, spontaneous make-believe play or social imitative play appropriate to developmental level

(3) restricted repetitive and stereotyped patterns of behavior, interests, and activities, as manifested by at least one of the following:
   (a) encompassing preoccupation with one or more stereotyped and restricted patterns of interest that is abnormal either in intensity or focus
   (b) apparently inflexible adherence to specific, nonfunctional routines or rituals
   (c) stereotyped and repetitive motor mannerisms (e.g., hand or finger flapping or twisting, or complex whole-body movements)
   (d) persistent preoccupation with parts of objects

B. Delays or abnormal functioning in at least one of the following areas, with onset prior to age 3 years: (1) social interaction, (2) language as used in social communication, or (3) symbolic or imaginative play

C. The disturbance is not better accounted for by Rett's Disorder or Childhood Disintegrative Disorder.

Diagnostic Criteria for Asperger's Disorder

A. Qualitative impairment in social interaction, as manifested by at least two of the following:
   (1) marked impairment in the use of multiple nonverbal behaviors such as eye-to-eye gaze, facial expression, body postures, and gestures to regulate social interaction
   (2) failure to develop peer relationships appropriate to developmental level
   (3) a lack of spontaneous seeking to share enjoyment, interests, or achievements with other people (e.g., by a lack of showing, bringing, or pointing out objects of interest to other people)
   (4) lack of social or emotional reciprocity

B. Restricted repetitive and stereotyped patterns of behavior, interests, and activities, as manifested by at least one of the following:
   (1) encompassing preoccupation with one or more stereotyped and restricted patterns of interest that is abnormal either in intensity or focus
   (2) apparently inflexible adherence to specific, nonfunctional routines or rituals
   (3) stereotyped and repetitive motor mannerisms (e.g., hand or finger flapping or twisting, or complex whole-body movements)
   (4) persistent preoccupation with parts of objects

C. The disturbance causes clinically significant impairment in social, occupational, or other important areas of functioning.

D. There is no clinically significant general delay in language (e.g., single words used by age 2 years, communicative phrases used by age 3 years).

E. There is no clinically significant delay in cognitive development or in the development of age-appropriate self-help skills, adaptive behavior (other than in social interaction), and curiosity about the environment in childhood.

F. Criteria are not met for another specific Pervasive Developmental Disorder or Schizophrenia.

Source: American Psychiatric Association, 2004.

Changes in Ranking of 16 Nations on Science and Math Knowledge Between Fourth and Eighth Grades (Chapter 12)

Only the 16 highest-scoring nations are included in these rankings. Many other countries, such as Chile and Morocco, rank much lower. Still others, including all the nations of Latin America and Africa, do not administer the tests on which these rankings are based. Identical rankings indicate ties between nations on overall scores. International comparisons are always difficult and often unfair, but two general conclusions have been confirmed: Children in East Asian countries tend to be high achievers in math and science, and children in the United States lose ground in science and just hold their own in math between the fourth and eighth grades.

Science Knowledge

Nation	Rank in Fourth Grade	Rank in Eighth Grade	Change in Rank
Singapore	1	1	0
Chinese Taipei	2	2	0
Japan	3	6	–3
Hong Kong	4	4	0
England	5	*	—
United States	6	9	–3
Latvia	7	18	–11
Hungary	8	7	+1
Russian Federation	9	17	–8
Netherlands	10	8	+2
Australia	11	10	+1
New Zealand	12	13	–1
Belgium	13	16	–3
Italy	14	22	–8
Lithuania	15	14	+1
Scotland	16	19	–3

Math Knowledge

Nation	Rank in Fourth Grade	Rank in Eighth Grade	Change in Rank
Singapore	1	1	0
Hong Kong	2	3	–1
Japan	3	5	–2
Chinese Taipei	4	4	0
Belgium	5	6	–1
Netherlands	6	7	–1
Latvia	7	11†	–4
Lithuania	8	13	–5
Russian Federation	9	11†	–2
England	10	*	—
Hungary	11	9	+2
United States	12	12	0
Cyprus	13	26	–13
Moldova	14	25	–11
Italy	15	19	–4
Australia	16	11	+5

*Did not participate.
†Average scale scores were tied.
Source: Trends in International Mathematics and Science Study (TIMSS), 2003, via National Center for Education Statistics Web site (nces.ed.gov/timss), retrieved June 4, 2008.

Changes in the Average Weekly Amount of Time Spent by 6- to 11-Year-Olds in Various Activities (Chapter 12)

Data can be presented graphically in many ways. The data given here were collected in the same way in 1981, 1997, and 2004, so the changes are real (although the age cutoff in 1997 was 12, not 11). What do you think would be the best way to show this information? What is encouraging and what is problematic in the changes that you see? What were children doing in 2004 that is not accounted for in this list of activities and wasn't even available in 1981?

Activity	Average Amount of Time Spent in Activity, per Week, United States			Change in Time Spent Since 1981
	In 1981	In 1997	In 2004	
School	25 hrs, 17 min.	33 hrs, 52 min.	33 hrs, 33 min.	+8 hrs, 16 min.
Organized sports	3 hrs, 5 min.	4 hrs, 56 min.	2 hrs, 28 min.	–32 min.
Studying	1 hr, 46 min.	2 hrs, 50 min.	3 hrs, 25 min.	+1 hr, 21 min.
Reading	57 min.	1 hr, 15 min.	1 hr, 28 min.	+31 min.
Being outdoors	1 hr, 17 min.	39 min.	56 min.	–21 min.
Playing	12 hrs, 52 min.	10 hrs, 5 min.	10 hrs, 25 min.	–2 hrs, 27 min.
Watching TV	15 hrs, 34 min.	13 hrs, 7 min.	14 hrs, 19 min.	–1 hr, 15 min.

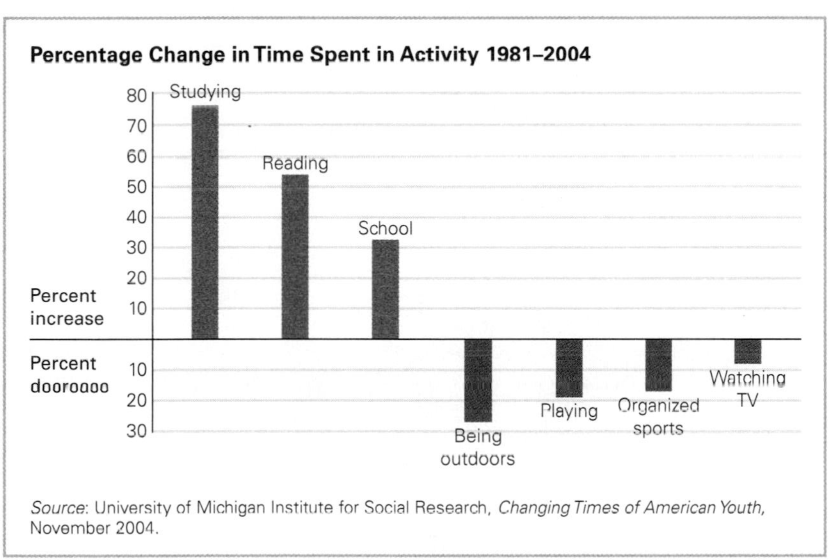

Source: University of Michigan Institute for Social Research, *Changing Times of American Youth*, November 2004.

Who Is Raising the Children? (Chapter 13)

Most children still live in households with a male/female couple, who may be the children's married or unmarried biological parents, grandparents, stepparents, foster parents, or adoptive parents. However, the proportion of households headed by single parents has risen—by 500 percent for single fathers and by almost 200 percent for single mothers. (In 2005, 52 percent of U.S. households had *no* children under age 18.)

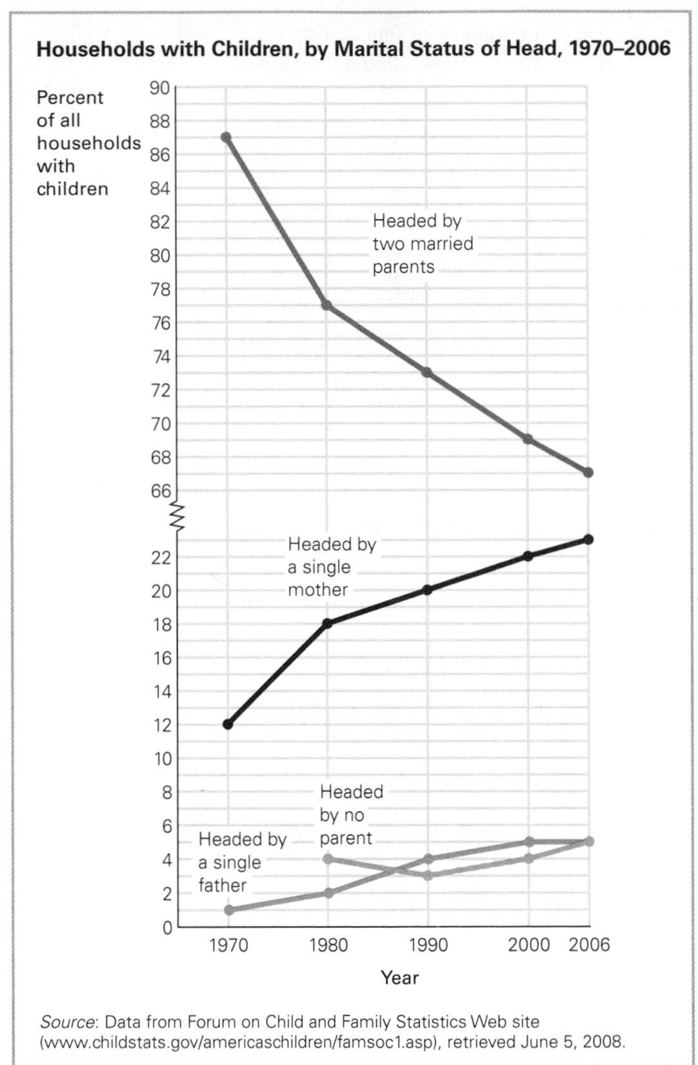

Source: Data from Forum on Child and Family Statistics Web site (www.childstats.gov/americaschildren/famsoc1.asp), retrieved June 5, 2008.

Smoking Behavior Among U.S. High School Students, 1991–2007 (Chapter 14)

The data in these two tables reveal many trends. For example, do you see that African American adolescents are much less likely to smoke than Hispanics or European Americans, but that this racial advantage is decreasing?

Percentage of High School Students Who Reported Smoking Cigarettes

Smoking Behavior	1991	1995	1999	2003	2007
Lifetime (ever smoked)	70.1	71.3	70.4	58.4	50.3
Current (smoked at least once in past 30 days)	27.5	34.8	34.8	21.9	20.0
Current frequent (smoked 20 or more times in past 30 days)	12.7	16.1	16.8	9.7	8.1

Percentage of High School Students Who Reported Current Smoking, by Sex, Ethnicity, and Grade

Characteristic	1991	1995	1999	2003	2007
Sex					
Female	27.3	34.3	34.9	21.9	18.7
Male	27.6	35.4	34.7	21.8	21.3
Ethnicity					
White, non-Hispanic	30.9	38.3	38.6	24.9	23.2
Female	*31.7*	*39.8*	*39.1*	*26.6*	*22.5*
Male	*30.2*	*37.0*	*38.2*	*23.3*	*23.8*
Black, non-Hispanic	12.6	19.2	19.7	15.1	11.6
Female	*11.3*	*12.2*	*17.7*	*10.8*	*8.4*
Male	*14.1*	*27.8*	*21.8*	*19.3*	*14.9*
Hispanic	25.3	34.0	32.7	18.4	16.7
Female	*22.9*	*32.9*	*31.5*	*17.7*	*14.6*
Male	*27.9*	*34.9*	*34.0*	*19.1*	*18.7*
Grade					
9th	23.2	31.2	27.6	17.4	14.3
10th	25.2	33.1	34.7	21.8	19.6
11th	31.6	35.9	36.0	23.6	21.6
12th	30.1	38.2	42.8	26.2	26.5

Source: MMWR (2008, June 6), Table 27.

Major Sexually Transmitted Infections: Some Basics (Chapter 14)

These and other STIs, if left untreated, may lead to serious reproductive and other health problems or even, as with HIV/AIDS and syphilis, to death. STIs can be avoided by consistently using condoms, having sex only in a relationship with an uninfected partner, or abstaining from sex.

Sexually Transmitted Infection (and Cause)	Symptoms	Treatment
Chlamydia (bacterium)	In women, abnormal vaginal discharge or burning sensation when urinating; may be followed by pain in low abdomen or low back, nausea, fever, pain during intercourse, or bleeding between menstrual periods. In men, discharge from penis or burning sensation when urinating.	Antibiotics
Genital HPV infection (virus)	The most common STI. Causes no symptoms or health problems in most people, but certain types may cause genital warts and others can cause cervical cancer in women and other cancers of the genitals in both sexes.	A vaccine is now available and is recommended for 11- and 12-year-old girls who are not yet sexually active.
Genital herpes (virus)	Blisters on or around the genitals or rectum that break and leave sores, which may take 2 to 4 weeks to heal; some people may experience fever, swollen glands, and other flu-like symptoms. Later outbreaks are usually less severe and shorter. Many people never have sores and may take years to realize they are infected. May lead to potentially fatal infections in babies and makes infected person more susceptible to HIV infection.	There is no vaccine or cure, but antiviral medications can shorten and prevent outbreaks.
Gonorrhea (bacterium)	Some men and most women have no symptoms. In men, a burning sensation when urinating; a white, yellow, or green discharge from the penis; painful or swollen testicles. In women, symptoms—pain or burning during urination, increased vaginal discharge, vaginal bleeding between periods—may be so mild or nonspecific that they are mistaken for a bladder or vaginal infection. May cause pelvic inflammatory disease (PID) in women and infertility in both sexes. Infected person can more easily contract HIV.	Antibiotics
Pelvic inflammatory disease (PID) (various bacteria)	A common and serious complication in women who have certain other STIs, especially chlamydia and gonorrhea. Pain in lower abdomen, fever, unusual vaginal discharge that may have a foul odor, painful intercourse, painful urination, irregular menstrual bleeding, and (rarely) pain in the right upper abdomen. May lead to blocked fallopian tubes, causing infertility.	Administration of at least two antibiotics that are effective against a wide range of infectious agents. In severe cases, surgery.

continued

Sexually Transmitted Infection (and Cause)	Symptoms	Treatment
HIV/AIDS (virus)	Infection with the human immunodeficiency virus (HIV) eventually leads to acquired immune deficiency syndrome (AIDS). Infection with other STIs increases a person's likelihood of both acquiring and transmitting HIV. Soon after exposure, some people have flu-like symptoms: fever, headache, tiredness, swollen lymph glands. Months or years later, when the virus has weakened the immune system, the person may experience lack of energy, weight loss, frequent fevers and sweats, yeast infections, skin rashes, short-term memory loss. Symptoms of full-blown AIDS include certain cancers (Kaposi sarcoma and lymphomas), seizures, vision loss, and coma. A leading cause of death among young adults in many nations.	There is no vaccine or cure, but antiretroviral drugs can slow the growth of the virus; antibiotics can cure some secondary infections, and various treatments are available to relieve painful or unpleasant symptoms.
Syphilis (bacterium)	Symptoms may not appear for years. *Primary stage:* One or more sores (*chancres*) a few days or weeks after exposure. *Secondary stage:* Skin rash, lesions of mucous membranes, fever, swollen lymph glands, sore throat, patchy hair loss, headaches, weight loss, muscle aches, fatigue. *Latent stage:* Primary and secondary symptoms disappear, but infection remains in the body. *Late stage (10 to 20 years after first infection):* Damage to brain, nerves, eyes, heart, blood vessels, liver, bones, and joints, progressing to difficulty coordinating muscle movements, paralysis, numbness, blindness, dementia.	Penicillin injections will kill the syphilis bacterium and prevent further damage but cannot repair damage already done.
Trichomoniasis (*Trichomonas vaginalis,* a single-celled protozoan parasite)	Most men have no symptoms, but some may temporarily have an irritation inside the penis, mild discharge, or slight burning after urination or ejaculation. Women may have a frothy, yellow-green, strong-smelling vaginal discharge and may experience discomfort during intercourse and urination; irritation and itching of the genital area; and, rarely, lower abdominal pain.	A single oral dose of metronidazole or tinidazole

Source: Compiled from CDC Fact Sheets for the various STIs, available in full online at www.cdc.gov/std/healthcomm/fact_sheets.htm; retrieved June 13, 2008.

Sexual Behaviors of U.S. High School Students, 2007 (Chapter 15)

These percentages, as high as they may seem, are actually lower than they were in the early 1990s. (States not listed did not participate fully in the survey.) The data in this table reflect responses from students in the 9th to 12th grades. When only high school seniors are surveyed, the percentages are higher. In every state, more than half of all high school seniors say they have had sexual intercourse, and about 20 percent have had four or more sex partners.

	Ever had sexual intercourse (%)			Had first sexual intercourse before age 13 (%)			Has had four or more sex partners during lifetime (%)			Is currently sexually active (%)		
State	Female	Male	Total	Female	Male	Total	Female	Male	Total	Female	Male	Total
Alaska	46.8	43.9	**45.1**	3.6	5.1	**4.4**	13.7	13.2	**13.4**	34.9	27.3	**30.9**
Arizona	44.5	47.4	**46.1**	4.1	7.2	**5.7**	12.7	18.1	**15.4**	34.3	32.8	**33.6**
Arkansas	55.3	54.8	**54.9**	5.8	12.7	**9.3**	16.1	21.0	**19.0**	42.6	37.0	**39.7**
Connecticut	41.8	43.1	**42.4**	3.7	8.2	**5.9**	9.8	15.1	**12.4**	33.3	30.2	**31.8**
Delaware	56.5	61.7	**59.3**	4.8	14.5	**9.6**	16.7	27.3	**21.8**	46.5	44.3	**45.3**
Florida	44.8	54.3	**49.5**	3.6	12.9	**8.2**	11.6	21.2	**16.4**	34.5	38.4	**36.4**
Hawaii	39.8	32.8	**36.2**	4.9	5.4	**5.1**	6.1	6.2	**6.1**	27.7	19.7	**23.6**
Illinois	48.8	51.6	**50.1**	2.8	10.6	**5.7**	12.7	18.9	**15.8**	39.8	35.2	**37.4**
Indiana	49.1	49.2	**49.1**	4.6	6.1	**5.4**	11.9	14.6	**13.3**	39.2	34.4	**37.0**
Iowa	43.6	42.9	**43.3**	3.3	4.2	**3.7**	12.8	12.5	**12.7**	35.2	31.8	**33.6**
Kansas	44.8	45.0	**45.0**	4.5	8.5	**6.5**	14.0	16.8	**15.4**	36.0	32.8	**34.4**
Kentucky	51.5	49.0	**50.3**	5.8	10.0	**7.8**	13.9	14.8	**14.4**	39.6	33.2	**36.5**
Maine	44.7	46.0	**45.4**	4.4	5.5	**5.0**	12.1	11.5	**11.8**	35.3	31.4	**33.4**
Massachusetts	43.7	45.2	**44.4**	3.6	8.6	**6.1**	10.6	14.1	**12.3**	34.0	31.4	**32.7**
Michigan	41.0	43.8	**42.4**	3.3	7.1	**5.3**	11.4	13.0	**12.2**	31.0	29.9	**30.0**
Mississippi	54.0	65.2	**59.5**	5.5	21.4	**13.3**	15.5	29.8	**22.5**	41.1	43.0	**42.3**
Missouri	53.1	50.9	**52.1**	3.2	9.7	**6.5**	12.3	18.9	**15.6**	43.7	37.2	**40.6**
Montana	46.4	44.8	**45.7**	3.4	6.8	**5.1**	12.7	14.5	**13.7**	34.8	27.6	**31.2**
Nevada	40.3	45.3	**42.8**	3.1	8.1	**5.6**	10.4	15.9	**13.1**	30.3	30.7	**30.5**
New Hampshire	44.6	44.7	**44.7**	2.6	5.6	**4.2**	10.8	12.4	**11.6**	35.7	32.4	**34.1**
New York	41.5	45.8	**43.6**	3.6	10.4	**7.0**	9.5	15.7	**12.5**	32.8	29.2	**31.1**
North Carolina	50.3	54.0	**52.1**	4.4	12.0	**8.3**	13.7	18.4	**16.1**	38.5	36.3	**37.5**
North Dakota	44.3	41.0	**42.6**	1.7	4.4	**3.0**	10.9	11.0	**10.9**	34.3	29.0	**31.6**
Ohio	44.2	44.9	**44.5**	4.1	8.5	**6.3**	11.8	16.4	**14.1**	36.3	34.2	**35.1**
Oklahoma	49.3	52.5	**50.9**	3.1	8.6	**5.8**	13.9	19.3	**16.6**	39.2	33.8	**36.5**
Rhode Island	41.4	50.1	**45.5**	2.0	10.3	**6.1**	7.4	14.6	**10.9**	31.6	34.8	**33.1**
South Carolina	48.5	54.6	**51.5**	5.6	13.7	**9.5**	14.6	21.0	**17.7**	37.3	34.5	**35.9**
South Dakota	47.1	45.9	**46.5**	1.7	6.7	**4.2**	13.7	12.9	**13.8**	37.8	30.7	**34.4**
Tennessee	50.8	58.1	**54.4**	3.0	12.0	**7.5**	11.1	22.5	**16.8**	39.3	41.4	**40.3**
Texas	51.0	54.8	**52.9**	3.6	9.7	**6.6**	13.7	20.4	**17.1**	38.8	38.7	**38.7**
West Virginia	53.0	54.1	**53.7**	4.3	8.5	**6.5**	13.6	19.4	**16.5**	42.8	40.0	**41.4**
Wisconsin	46.3	43.0	**44.6**	2.7	6.2	**4.5**	12.6	12.8	**12.7**	35.9	29.8	**32.9**
Wyoming	47.7	46.7	**47.2**	4.2	7.6	**6.0**	13.5	15.3	**14.5**	36.5	31.1	**33.7**
U.S. median	**46.3**	**46.3**	**45.9**	**3.6**	**8.5**	**6.0**	**12.6**	**15.7**	**13.8**	**35.9**	**32.8**	**34.1**

Source: MMWR (2008, June 6), Tables 62 and 64.

United States Homicide Victim and Offender Rates, by Race and Gender, Ages 14–17 (Chapter 16)

Teenage boys are more often violent offenders than victims. The ratio of victimization to offense has varied for teenage girls over the years. The good news is that rates have decreased dramatically over the past ten years for every category of adolescents—male and female, Black and White. (Similar declines are apparent for Asian and Hispanic Americans.) The bad news is that rates are still higher in the United States than in any other developed nation.

Homicide Victimization Rates per 100,000 Population for 14- to 17-Year-Olds

	Male		Female	
Year	White	Black	White	Black
1976	3.7	24.2	2.1	6.3
1981	4.3	23.0	2.4	6.0
1986	4.1	26.8	2.3	6.5
1991	8.5	71.9	2.5	9.4
1996	7.9	52.2	2.0	8.9
2001	3.8	26.3	1.4	3.9
2005	4.4	26.4	1.1	4.0

Source: U. S. Bureau of Justice Statistics Web site (www.ojp.usdoj.gov/bjs/), page revised July 11, 2007; retrieved June 6, 2008.
Tabulations based on FBI Supplementary Homicide Reports and U.S. Census Bureau, Current Population Reports.

Homicide Offending Rates per 100,000 Population for 14- to 17-Year-Olds

	Male		Female	
Year	White	Black	White	Black
1976	10.9	80.6	1.4	11.2
1981	11.6	82.9	1.2	8.1
1986	12.9	80.1	1.2	5.7
1991	22.8	214.1	1.3	10.5
1996	18.3	143.3	1.8	8.8
2001	8.2	61.0	1.0	5.1
2005	7.9	64.1	0.7	4.0

Source: U. S. Bureau of Justice Statistics Web site (www.ojp.usdoj.gov/bjs/), page revised July 11, 2007; retrieved June 6, 2008.
Tabulations based on FBI Supplementary Homicide Reports and U.S. Census Bureau, Current Population Reports. Rates include both known perpetrators and estimated share of unidentified perpetrators.

All the charts, graphs, and tables in this Appendix offer readers the opportunity to analyze raw data and draw their own conclusions. The same information may be presented in a variety of ways. On this page, you can create your own bar graph or line graph, depicting some noteworthy aspect of the data presented in the three tables. First, consider all the possibilities the tables offer by answering these six questions:

1. Are white male or female teenagers more likely to be victims of homicide?
2. These are annual rates. How many African American teens in 1,000 were likely to commit homicide in 2005?
3. Which age group is *most* likely to commit homicide?
4. Which age group is *least* likely to be victims of homicide?
5. Which age group is *almost equally* likely to be either perpetrators or victims of homicide?
6. Of the four groups of adolescents, which has shown the greatest decline in rates of both victimization and perpetration of homicide over the past decade? Which has shown the least decline?

Answers: 1. Boys—at least twice as often. 2. Less than one. 3. 18–24. 4. 0–13. 5. 35–49. 6. Black males had the greatest decline, and White females had the least (but these two groups have always been highest and lowest, respectively, in every year). *Now*—use the grid provided at right to make your own graph.

Overall Rate of Homicide by Age, 2005, United States (Chapter 16)

Late adolescence and early adulthood are the peak times for murders—both as victims and offenders. The question for developmentalists is whether something changes before age 18 to decrease the rates in young adulthood.

Age group	Victims (per 100,000 in age group)	Killers (per 100,000 in age group)
0–13	1.4	.1
14–17	4.8	9.3
18–24	14.9	26.5
25–34	11.6	13.5
35–49	5.7	5.1
50–64	2.6	1.4

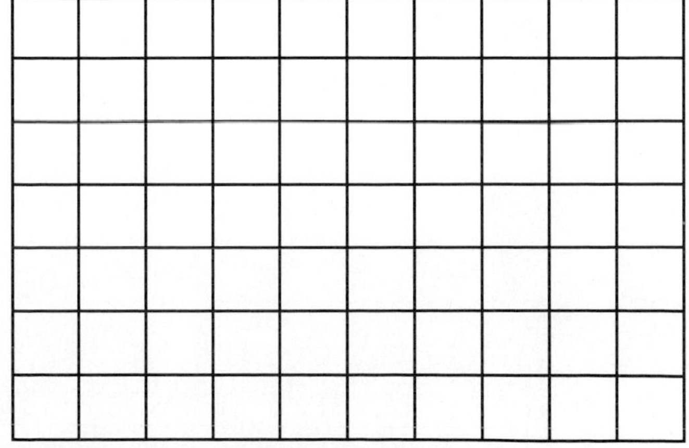

Education Affects Income (Epilogue)

Although there is some debate about the cognitive benefits of college education, there is no doubt about the financial benefits. No matter what a person's ethnicity or gender is, an associate's degree more than doubles his or her income compared to that of someone who has not completed high school. These data are for the United States; similar trends, often with steeper increases, are found in other nations.

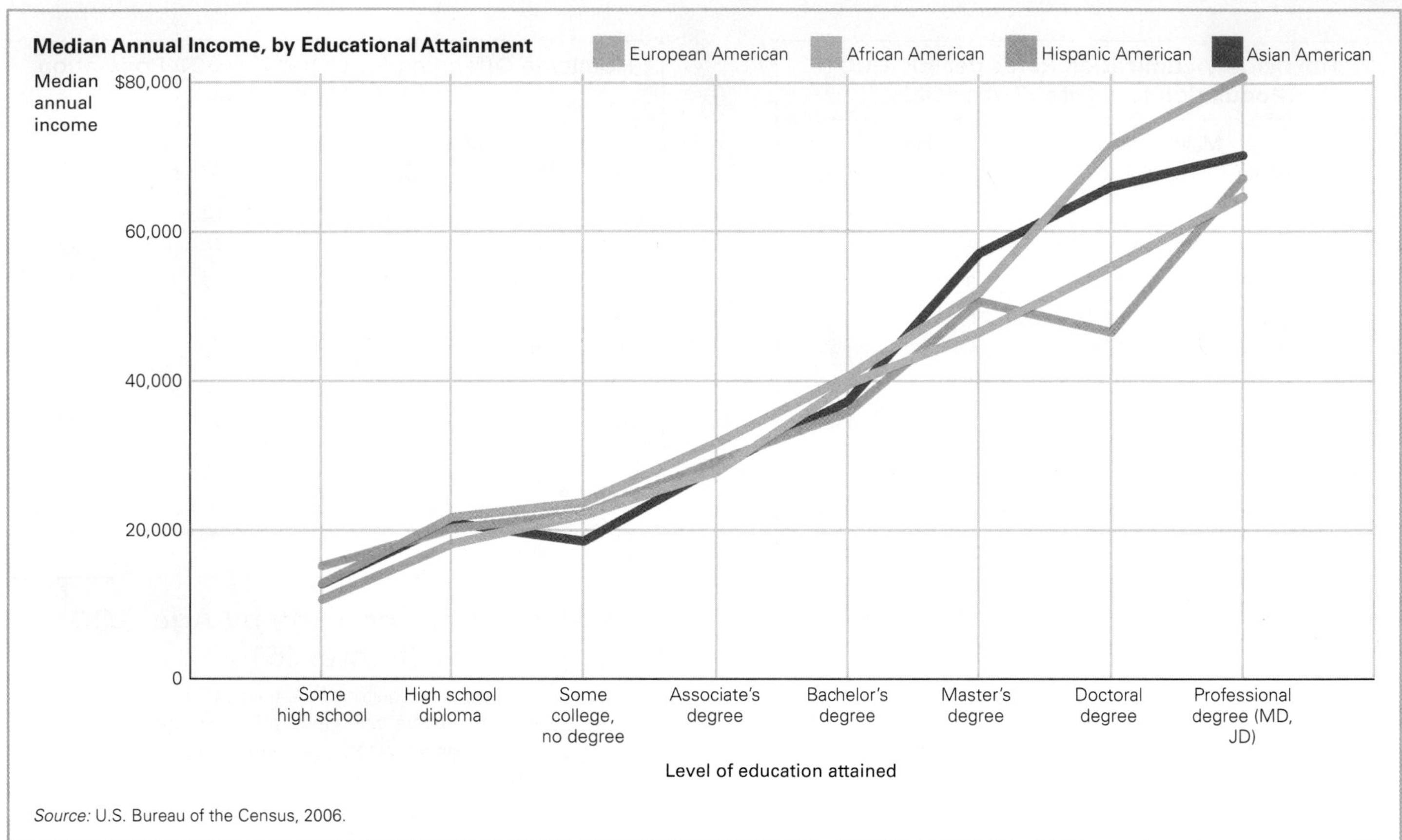

Source: U.S. Bureau of the Census, 2006.

Appendix B More About Research Methods

Appendix A provides charts and numbers that lead to questions, hypotheses, surprises, and conclusions. The Research Design boxes in every chapter illustrate some ways to study any topic and show why additional research is needed. Appendix C guides students who want to conduct an observational or experimental study.

Here Appendix B explains how to learn about any topic. It is crucial that you distinguish valid conclusions from wishful thinking. This begins with your personal experience.

Make It Personal

Think about your life, observe your behavior, and watch the people around you. Pay careful attention to details of expression, emotion, and behavior. The more you see, the more fascinated, curious, and reflective you will become. Then, as is often suggested in the Applications that appear at the end of each chapter, listen carefully and respectfully to what other people say regarding development.

Whenever you ask specific questions as part of an assignment, **remember that observing ethical standards (see Chapter 1) comes first.** *Before* you interview anyone, inform the person of your purpose and assure him or her of confidentiality. Promise not to identify the person in your report (use a pseudonym) and do not repeat any personal details that emerge in the interview to anyone (friends or strangers).Your instructor will provide further ethical guidance. If you might publish what you've learned, inform your college's Institutional Research Board (IRB).

Read the Research

No matter how deeply you think about your own experiences, and no matter how intently you listen to others whose background is unlike yours, you also need to read scholarly published work in order to fully understand whatever topic interests you. Don't believe magazine or newspaper reports; some are bound to be simplified, exaggerated, or biased.

Professional Journals and Books

Part of the process of science is that conclusions are not considered solid until they are corroborated in many studies, which means that you should consult several sources on any topic. Four **professional journals in human development** that cover all three domains (biosocial, cognitive, and psychosocial) are:

- *Developmental Psychology* (published by the American Psychological Association)
- *Child Development* (Society for Research in Child Development)
- *Developmental Review* (Elsevier)
- *Human Development* (Karger)

These journals differ in the types of articles and studies they publish, but all are well respected. Every article includes references to other recent work.

Beyond these four are literally thousands of other professional journals, each with a particular perspective or topic. To judge them, look for journals that are *peer-reviewed,* which means that scientists (other than the authors of each article) read the submissions and decided whether each should be accepted, rejected, or revised. Also consider the following details: the background of the author (research funded by corporations tends to favor their products); the nature of the publisher (professional organizations, as in the first two journals above, protect their reputations); how long the journal has been published (the volume number tells you that). Some interesting work does not meet these criteria, but these are guides to quality.

Many **books** cover some aspect of development. Single-author books are likely to present only one viewpoint. That view may be insightful, but it is limited. You might consult a *handbook,* which is a book that includes many authors and many topics. One good handbook in development, now in its sixth edition (a sign that past scholars have found it useful) is William Damon & Richard M. Lerner (eds.), *Handbook of Child Psychology* (2006), four volumes, published by Wiley.

The Internet

The **Internet** is a mixed blessing, useful to every novice and experienced researcher but dangerous as well. Every library has computers that provide access to journals and other information. Ask for help from the librarians; many are highly skilled. In addition, other students, friends, and even strangers can be helpful.

Virtually everything is on the Internet, not only massive national and international statistics but also very personal accounts. Photos, charts, quizzes, ongoing experiments, newspapers from around the world, videos, and much more are available at the click of a mouse. Every journal has a Web site, with tables of contents, abstracts, and sometimes full texts (an abstract gives the key findings; for the full text, you may need to consult the library's copy of the print version).

Unfortunately, you can spend many frustrating hours sifting through information that is useless, trash, or tangential. *Directories* (which list general topics or areas and then move you step by step in the direction you choose) and *search engines* (which give you all the sites that use a particular word or words) can help you select appropriate information. Each directory or search engine provides somewhat different lists; none provides only the most comprehensive and accurate sites. With experience and help, you will find the best sites for you, but you will also encounter some junk no matter how experienced you are.

Another problem is that anybody can put anything on the Web, regardless of its truth or fairness, so evaluate with a very critical eye everything you find. Make sure you have several divergent sources for every "fact" you find; consider who provided the information and why. Every controversial issue has sites that forcefully advocate opposite viewpoints, sometimes with biased statistics and narrow perspectives.

Here are seven Internet sites that are quite reliable:

- *www.worthpublishers.com/berger* Includes links to Web sites, quizzes, PowerPoint slides, and activities keyed to every chapter of the textbook.
- *embryo.soad.umich.edu* The Multidimensional Human Embryo. Presents MRI images of a human embryo at various stages of development, accompanied by brief explanations.
- *www.kidshealth.org* Web site on children's health, featuring a large number of articles by experts on various aspects of children's health. Sponsored by the Nemours Foundation.

- *www.cdipage.com* The Child Development Institute's Web site, with links and articles on child development and information on common childhood psychological disorders.
- *ceep.crc.uiuc.edu* Clearinghouse on Early Education and Parenting. Provides links to many education-related sites and includes brief descriptions of each.
- *site.educ.indiana.edu/cafs* Adolescence Directory online (ADOL) is an electronic guide to information on adolescent issues. It is a service of the Center for Adolescent and Family Studies at Indiana University.
- *www.cdc.gov/nchs/hus.htm* The National Center for Health Statistics issues an annual report on health trends, called "Health, United States."

Every source—you, your interviewees, journals, books, and the Internet—is helpful. Do not depend on any particular one. Especially if you use the Web, also check print resources. Avoid plagiarism and prejudice by citing every source and noting objectivity, validity, and credibility. Your own analysis, opinions, words, and conclusions are crucial.

Additional Terms and Concepts

As emphasized throughout this text, the study of development is a science. Social scientists study methods and statistics for years. Chapter 1 touches on some of these matters (observation and experiments; correlation and statistics; independent and dependent variables; experimental and control groups; cross-sectional, longitudinal, and cross-sequential research), but there is much more. A few additional aspects of research are presented here, to help you evaluate research wherever you find it.

Who Participates?

The entire group of people about whom a scientist wants to learn is called the **population.** Generally, a research population is quite large—not usually the world's entire population of almost 7 billion, but perhaps all the 4 million babies born in the United States last year, or all the 25 million Japanese currently over age 65.

The particular individuals who are studied in a specific research project are called the **participants.** They are used as a **sample** of the larger group. Ideally, a large number of people are used as a **representative sample,** that is, a sample who reflect the entire population. Every published study reports details on the sample.

Selection of the sample is crucial. Volunteers, or people with telephones, or people treated with some particular condition, are not a *random sample,* in which everyone in that population is equally likely to be selected. To avoid *selection bias,* some studies are *prospective,* beginning with an entire cluster (for instance, every baby born on a particular day) and then tracing the development of some particular characteristic.

For example, prospective studies find the antecedents of heart disease, or child abuse, or high school dropout rates—all of which are much harder to find if the study is *retrospective,* beginning with those who had heart attacks, experienced abuse, or left school. Thus, although retrospective research finds that most high school dropouts say they disliked school, prospective research finds that some who like school still decide to drop out and then later say they hated school, while others dislike school but stay to graduate. Prospective research discovers how many students are in these last two categories; retrospective research on people who have already dropped out does not.

population The entire group of individuals who are of particular concern in a scientific study, such as all the children of the world or all newborns who weigh less than 3 pounds.

participants The people who are studied in a research project.

sample A group of individuals drawn from a specified population. A sample might be the low-birthweight babies born in four particular hospitals that are representative of all hospitals.

representative sample A group of research participants who reflect the relevant characteristics of the larger population whose attributes are under study.

Research Design

Every researcher begins not only by formulating a hypothesis but also by learning what other scientists have discovered about the topic in question and what methods might be useful and ethical in designing research. Sometimes they deliberately include methods that guard against inadvertently finding the results they expect. Often the people who gather the data do not know the purpose of the research. Scientists say that these data gatherers are **blind** to the hypothesized outcome. Adult participants are sometimes "blind" as well, so that they do not, for instance, answer a survey question the way they think they should.

blind The condition of data gatherers (and sometimes participants as well) who are deliberately kept ignorant of the purpose of the research so that they cannot unintentionally bias the results.

Another crucial aspect of research design is to define exactly what is to be studied. Researchers establish an **operational definition** of whatever phenomenon they will be examining, defining each variable by describing specific, observable behavior. This is essential in quantitative research (see Chapter 1), but it is also useful in qualitative research. For example, if a researcher wants to know when babies begin to walk, does *walking* include steps taken while holding on, and is one unsteady step enough? Some parents say yes, but the usual operational definition of walking is "takes at least three steps without holding on." This operational definition allows comparisons worldwide, making it possible to discover, for example, that well-fed African babies tend to walk earlier than well-fed European babies.

operational definition A description of the specific, observable behavior that will constitute the variable that is to be studied, so that any reader will know whether that behavior occurred or not. Operational definitions may be arbitrary (e.g., an IQ score at or above 130 is operationally defined as "gifted"), but they must be precise.

Operational definitions are difficult but essential when personality traits are studied. How should *aggression* or *sharing* or *shyness* be defined? Lack of an operational definition leads to contradictory results. For instance, some say that infant day care makes children more aggressive, but others say it makes them less passive. Both statements may be equally true, depending on the operational definition. For any scientist, or any parent, operational definitions are crucial.

Reporting Results

You already know that results should be reported in sufficient detail so that another scientist can analyze the conclusions and replicate the research. Various methods, population, and research designs may produce divergent conclusions. For that reason, handbooks, some journals, and some articles are called *reviews:* They summarize past research. Often, when studies are similar in operational definitions and methods, the review is a **meta-analysis,** combining the findings of many studies to present an overall conclusion.

meta-analysis A technique of combining results of many studies to come to an overall conclusion. Meta-analysis is powerful, in that small samples can be added together to lead to significant conclusions, although variations from study to study sometimes make combining them impossible.

You also remember *statistical significance,* which indicates whether or not a particular result could have occurred by chance. Many studies report other statistics and statistical measures—all helpful to scientists as they evaluate the conclusions.

One other statistic that is often crucial is **effect size,** a way of measuring how much impact one variable has on another. Effect size ranges from 0 (no effect) to 1 (total transformation, never found in actual studies). Effect size may be particularly important when the sample size is large, because a large sample often leads to highly "significant" results (unlikely to have occurred by chance) that have only a tiny effect on the variable of interest.

effect size A way to indicate, statistically, how much of an impact the independent variable had on the dependent variable.

Some of the many statistical ways to report results are listed in Table 1.3 (page 22). An entire course devoted to statistics is part of the preparation required for most scientists. You might begin by looking at books on research methods and analysis. Clarity and integrity are always essential, especially when it comes to reporting the limitations of your research and alternative interpretations of your findings. That is how science builds.

Appendix C Suggestions for Research Assignments

The best way to study human development is to do some investigation yourself, not only by reading the textbook and expressing your ideas in speech and writing but also by undertaking some research of your own. Writing a term paper is the usual mode in most college courses: You and your instructor already know the importance of setting a deadline for each stage (topic selection, outline, first draft, final draft), of asking several readers to evaluate your paper (perhaps including other students), and of having the final version typed with references correctly cited and listed. The References, or bibliography, at the end of this text use the style established by the American Psychological Association, with a few modifications—notably, the first names of authors, instead of initials, are given, when available. Some suggestions for effective use of journals and the Internet are given in Appendix B.

The subject of human development is also ideal for more personal study, so suggestions for conducting observations, case studies, surveys, and experiments are offered here.

Learning Through Observation

Much can be learned by becoming more systematic in your observations of the people around you. One way to begin is to collect observations of ten different children, in differing contexts, during the semester. Each profile should be approximately one page and should cover the following four items:

1. *Describe the physical and social context.* You will want to describe where you are, what day and time it is, and how many people you are observing. The age and gender of those who are being observed might also be relevant. For example:

   Neighborhood playground on (street), at about 4 P.M. on (day, date), 30 children and 10 adults present.
   OR
   Supermarket at (location) on Saturday morning (day, date), about 20 shoppers present.

2. *Describe the specific child who is the focus of your attention.* Estimate age, gender, and so on of the target child and anyone else who interacts with the child. Do not ask the age of the child until after the observation, if at all. Your goal is to conduct a naturalistic observation that is unobtrusive. For example:

   Boy, about 7 years old, playing with four other boys, who seem a year or two older. All are dressed warmly (it is a cold day) in similar clothes.
   OR
   Girl, about 18 months old, in supermarket cart pushed by woman, about 30 years old. The cart is half full of groceries.

3. *Write down everything that the child does or says in three minutes.* (Use a watch with a second hand.) Record gestures, facial expressions, movements, and words. Accurate reporting is the goal, and three minutes becomes a surprisingly long time if you write down everything. For example:

   Child runs away about 20 feet, returns, and says, "Try to catch me." Two boys look at him, but they do not move. Boy frowns. He runs away and comes back in 10 seconds, stands about four feet away from the boys, and says, "Anyone want to play tag?" [And so on.]

OR
Child points to a package of Frosted Flakes cereal and makes a noise. (I could not hear if it was a word.) Mother says nothing and pushes the cart past the cereal. Child makes a whining noise, looks at the cereal, and kicks her left foot. Mother puts pacifier in child's mouth. [And so on.]

4. *Interpret what you just observed.* Is the child's behavior typical of children that age? Is the reaction of others helpful or not helpful? What values are being encouraged, and what skills are being mastered? What could have happened differently? This section is your opinion, but it must be based on the particulars you have just observed and on your knowledge of child development, ideally with specific reference to concepts (e.g., the first may be a rejected child; the second child's language development may not be encouraged).

Structuring a Case Study

A case study is more elaborate and detailed than an observation report. Select one child (ask your instructor if family members can be used), and secure written permission from the caregiver and, if the child is old enough, the child him- or herself. Explain that you are not going to report the name of the child, that the material is for your class, that the child or caregiver can stop the project at any time, and that they would be doing you a big favor in helping you learn about child development. Most people are quite happy to help in your education, if you explain this properly.

Gather Your Data

First, collect the information for your paper by using all the research methods you have learned. These methods include:

1. *Naturalistic observation.* Ask the caregiver when the child is likely to be awake and active, and observe the child for an hour during this time. Try to be as unobtrusive as possible. You are not there to play with, or care for, the child. If the child wants to play, explain that you must sit and write for now and that you will play later.

   Write down, minute by minute, everything the child does and that others do with the child. Try to be objective, focusing on behavior rather than interpretation. Thus, instead of writing "Jennifer was delighted when her father came home, and he dotes on her," you should write "5:33: Her father opened the door, Jennifer looked up, smiled, said 'dada,' and ran to him. He bent down, stretched out his arms, picked her up, and said, 'How's my little angel?' 5:34: He put her on his shoulders, and she said, 'Giddy up, horsey.'"

   After your observation, summarize the data in two ways: (a) Note the percentage of time spent in various activities. For instance, "Playing alone, 15 percent; playing with brother, 20 percent; crying, 3 percent." (b) Note the frequency of various behaviors: "Asked adult for something five times; adult granted request four times. Aggressive acts (punch, kick, etc.) directed at brother, 2; aggressive acts initiated by brother, 6." Making notations like these will help you evaluate and quantify your observations. Also, note any circumstances that might have made your observation atypical (e.g., "Jenny's mother said she hasn't been herself since she had the flu a week ago," or "Jenny kept trying to take my pen, so it was hard to write").

   Note: Remember that a percentage can be found by dividing the total number of minutes spent on a specific activity by the total number of minutes you spent observing. For example, if, during a 45-minute observation, the child played by herself for periods of 2 minutes, 4 minutes, and 5 minutes, "playing alone" would total 11 minutes. Dividing 11 by 45 yields 0.244; thus the child spent 24 percent of the time playing alone.

2. *Informal interaction.* Interact with the child for at least half an hour. Your goal is to observe the child's personality and abilities in a relaxed setting. The particular activities you engage in will depend on the child's age and temperament. Most children enjoy playing games, reading books, drawing, and talking. Asking a younger child to show you his or her room and favorite toys is a good way to break the ice; asking an older child to show you the neighborhood can provide insights.
3. *Interview adults responsible for the child's care.* Keep these interviews loose and open-ended. Your goals are to learn (a) the child's history, especially any illnesses, stresses, or problems that might affect development; (b) the child's daily routine, including play patterns; (c) current problems that might affect the child; (d) a description of the child's temperament and personality, including special strengths and weaknesses.

   You are just as interested in adult values and attitudes as in the facts; therefore, you might concentrate on conversing during the interview, perhaps writing down a few words. Then write down all you remember as soon as the interview has been completed.
4. *Testing the child.* Assess the child's perceptual, motor, language, and intellectual abilities by using specific test items you have prepared in advance. The actual items you use will depend on the age of the child. For instance, you might test object permanence in a child between 6 and 24 months old; you might test conservation in a child between 3 and 9 years old. Likewise, testing language abilities might involve babbling with an infant, counting words per sentence with a preschooler, and asking a school-age child to make up a story.

Write Up Your Findings

Second, write the report, using the following steps:

1. Begin by reporting relevant background information, including the child's birth date and sex, age and sex of siblings, economic and ethnic background of the family, and the educational and marital status of the parents.
2. Describe the child's biosocial, cognitive, and psychosocial development, citing supporting data from your research to substantiate any conclusions you have reached. Do not simply transcribe your interview, test, or observation data, although you can attach your notes as an appendix, if you wish.
3. Predict the child's development in the next year, the next five years, and the next ten years. List the strengths in the child, the family, and the community that you think will foster optimal development. Also note whatever potential problems you see (either in the child's current behavior or in the family and community support system) that may lead to future difficulties for the child. Include discussion of the reasons, either methodological or theoretical, that your predictions may not be completely accurate.

Finally, show your report to a classmate (your instructor may assign you to a peer mentor) and ask if you have been clear in your description and predictions. Discuss the child with your classmate to see if you should add more details to your report. Your revised case study should be typed and given to your professor, who will evaluate it. If you wish, send me a copy (Professor Kathleen Berger, c/o Worth Publishers, 41 Madison Avenue, New York, NY 10010).

Experiments and Surveys

As you learned in Chapter 1, experiments and surveys are wonderful ways to learn more about development, but each study needs to be very carefully designed and undertaken to avoid bias and to ensure that all the ethical considerations are taken into account. Accordingly, I recommend that an experiment or survey be undertaken by a group of students, not by an individual. Listening carefully to other opinions, using more than one person to collect data, and checking with your professor before beginning the actual study will help your results to have some validity.

If you do this, structure your work in such a way that everyone contributes and that contrary opinions are encouraged. (The normal human response is for everyone to agree with everyone else, but seeking alternate, logical explanations can move an entire group forward to deeper, more analytic thought.) You might designate one person to be the critic, or your group might spend one day designing your study and another day finding problems with the design. (Some problems simply need to be recognized and acknowledged, but some of them can be fixed by changing the design.)

Specific topics for experiments or surveys depend on your group's interests and on your professor's requirements for the course. For ideas, check this book's Subject Index or Study Guide. Since development is multidisciplinary and multicontextual, almost any topic may be relevant. Just remember to consider theory and practice, change and continuity, social interaction and cultural impact . . . and then try to limit your initial experiment or survey to one small part of this fascinating, ever-changing subject!

Glossary

A

achievement test A measure of mastery or proficiency in reading, mathematics, writing, science, or some other subject.

additive gene A gene that has several alleles, each of which contributes to the final phenotype (such as skin color or height).

adolescence-limited offender A person whose criminal activity is confined to the adolescent years, from about age 12 to 18.

adolescent egocentrism A characteristic of adolescent thinking that leads young people (ages 10 to 13) to focus on themselves to the exclusion of others.

adoption A legal proceeding in which an adult or couple unrelated to a child is granted the joys and obligations of being that child's parent(s).

adrenal glands Two glands, located above the kidneys, that produce hormones (including the "stress hormones" epinephrine [adrenaline] and norepinephrine).

affordance An opportunity for perception and interaction that is offered by a person, place, or object in the environment.

age of viability The age (about 22 weeks after conception) at which a fetus may survive outside the mother's uterus if specialized medical care is available.

aggressive-rejected Rejected by peers because of antagonistic, confrontational behavior.

allele Any of the possible forms in which a gene for a particular trait can occur.

amygdala A tiny brain structure that registers emotions, particularly fear and anxiety.

analytic thought Thought that results from analysis, such as a systematic ranking of pros and cons, risks and consequences, possibilities and facts. Analytic thought depends on logic and rationality.

androgyny A balance, within one person, of traditionally masculine and feminine psychological characteristics.

animism The belief that natural objects and phenomena are alive.

anorexia nervosa An eating disorder characterized by self-starvation. Affected individuals voluntarily undereat and often overexercise, depriving their vital organs of nutrition. Anorexia can be fatal.

anoxia A lack of oxygen that, if prolonged during birth, can cause brain damage or death to the baby.

antipathy Feelings of dislike or even hatred for another person.

antisocial behavior Feelings and actions that are deliberately hurtful or destructive to another person.

Apgar scale A quick assessment of a newborn's body functioning. The baby's color, heart rate, reflexes, muscle tone, and respiratory effort are given a score of 0, 1, or 2 twice—at one minute and five minutes after birth—and each time the total of all five scores is compared with the ideal score of 10 (which is rarely attained).

apprentice in thinking Vygotsky's term for a person whose cognition is stimulated and directed by older and more skilled members of society.

aptitude The potential to master a specific skill or to learn a certain body of knowledge.

Asperger syndrome A specific type of autistic spectrum disorder, characterized by extreme attention to details and deficient social understanding.

assisted reproductive technology (ART) A general term for the techniques designed to help infertile couples conceive and then sustain a pregnancy.

asthma A chronic disease of the respiratory system in which inflammation narrows the airways from the nose and mouth to the lungs, causing difficulty in breathing. Signs and symptoms include wheezing, shortness of breath, chest tightness, and coughing.

attachment According to Ainsworth, "an affectional tie" that an infant forms with a caregiver—a tie that binds them together in space and endures over time.

attention-deficit/hyperactivity disorder (ADHD) A condition in which a person not only has great difficulty concentrating for more than a few moments but also is inattentive, impulsive, and overactive.

authoritarian parenting An approach to child rearing that is characterized by high behavioral standards, strict punishment of misconduct, and little communication.

authoritative parenting An approach to child rearing in which the parents set limits but listen to the child and are flexible.

autism A developmental disorder marked by an inability to relate to other people normally, extreme self-absorption, and an inability to acquire normal speech.

autistic spectrum disorder Any of several disorders characterized by inadequate social skills, impaired communication, and unusual play.

automatization A process in which repetition of a sequence of thoughts and actions makes the sequence routine, so that it no longer requires conscious thought.

autonomy versus shame and doubt Erikson's second crisis of psychosocial development. Toddlers either succeed or fail in gaining a sense of self-rule over their own actions and bodies.

axon A fiber that extends from a neuron and transmits electrochemical impulses from that neuron to the dendrites of other neurons.

B

babbling The extended repetition of certain syllables, such as *ba-ba-ba*, that begins when babies are between 6 and 9 months old.

balanced bilingual A person who is fluent in two languages, not favoring one over the other.

base rate neglect A common fallacy in which a person ignores the overall frequency of some behavior or characteristic (called the *base rate*) in making a decision. For example, a person might bet on a "lucky" lottery number without considering the odds that that number will be selected.

behavioral teratogens Agents and conditions that can harm the prenatal brain, impairing the future child's intellectual and emotional functioning.

behaviorism A grand theory of human development that studies observable behavior. Behaviorism is also called *learning theory* because it describes the laws and processes by which behavior is learned.

bickering Petty, peevish arguing, usually repeated and ongoing.

Big Five The five basic clusters of personality traits that remain quite stable throughout life: openness, conscientiousness, extroversion, agreeableness, and neuroticism.

bilingual education A strategy in which school subjects are taught in both the learner's original language and the second (majority) language.

binocular vision The ability to focus the two eyes in a coordinated manner in order to see one image.

blastocyst A cell mass that develops from the zygote in the first few days after conception.

blended family A stepparent family that includes children born to several families, such as the biological children from the spouses' previous marriages and the biological children of the new couple.

blind The condition of data gatherers (and sometimes participants as well) who are deliberately kept ignorant of the purpose of the research so that they cannot unintentionally bias the results.

BMI (body mass index) A person's weight in kilograms divided by the square of height in meters.

body image A person's idea of how his or her body looks.

bulimia nervosa An eating disorder characterized by binge eating and subsequent purging, usually by induced vomiting and/or use of laxatives.

bully-victim Someone who attacks others and who is attacked as well. (Also called *provocative victims* because they do things that elicit bullying, such as stealing a bully's pencil.

bullying Repeated, systematic efforts to inflict harm through physical, verbal, or social attack on a weaker person.

bullying aggression Unprovoked, repeated physical or verbal attack, especially on victims who are unlikely to defend themselves.

C

carrier A person whose genotype includes a gene that is not expressed in the phenotype. Such an unexpressed gene occurs in half of the carrier's gametes and thus is passed on to half of the carrier's children, who will most likely be carriers, too. Generally, only when such a gene is inherited from both parents does the characteristic appear in the phenotype.

case study A research method in which one individual is studied intensively.

center day care Child care that occurs in a place especially designed for the purpose, where several paid adults care for many children. Usually the children are grouped by age, the day-care center is licensed, and providers are trained and certified in child development.

centration A characteristic of preoperational thought in which a young child focuses (centers) on one idea, excluding all others.

cerebral palsy A disorder that results from damage to the brain's motor centers. People with cerebral palsy have difficulty with muscle control, so their speech and body movements are impaired.

cesarean section A surgical birth, in which incisions through the mother's abdomen and uterus allow the fetus to be removed quickly, instead of being delivered through the vagina. (Also called *c-section* or simply *section*.)

child abuse Deliberate action that is harmful to a child's physical, emotional, or sexual well-being.

child maltreatment Intentional harm to or avoidable endangerment of anyone under 18 years of age.

child neglect Failure to meet a child's basic physical, educational, or emotional needs.

child sexual abuse Any erotic activity that arouses an adult and excites, shames, or confuses a child, whether or not the victim protests and whether or not genital contact is involved.

child-directed speech The high-pitched, simplified, and repetitive way adults speak to infants. (Also called *baby talk* or *motherese*.)

children with special needs Children who, because of a physical or mental disability, require extra help in order to learn.

chromosome One of the 46 molecules of DNA (in 23 pairs) that each cell of the human body contains and that, together, contain all the genes. Other species have more or fewer chromosomes.

classical conditioning The learning process in which a meaningful stimulus (such as the smell of food to a hungry animal) is connected with a neutral stimulus (such as the sound of a bell) that had no special meaning before conditioning. Also called *respondent conditioning*.

classification The logical principle that things can be organized into groups (or categories or classes) according to some characteristic they have in common.

clinical depression Feelings of hopelessness, lethargy, and worthlessness that last two weeks or more.

clique A group of adolescents made up of close friends who are loyal to one another while excluding outsiders.

cluster suicides Several suicides committed by members of a group within a brief period of time.

co-sleeping A custom in which parents and their children (usually infants) sleep together in the same bed.

code of ethics A set of moral principles that members of a profession or group are expected to follow.

cognitive equilibrium In cognitive theory, a state of mental balance in which people are not confused because they can use their existing thought processes to understand current experiences and ideas.

cognitive theory A grand theory of human development that focuses on changes in how people think over time. According to this theory, our thoughts shape our attitudes, beliefs, and behaviors.

cohabitation An arrangement in which a couple live together in a committed sexual relationship but are not formally married.

cohort A group of people who were born at about the same time and thus move through life together, experiencing the same historical events and cultural shifts at about the same age.

comorbidity The presence of two or more unrelated disease conditions at the same time in the same person.

comparison group/control group A group of participants in a research study who are similar to the experimental group in all relevant ways but who do not experience the experimental condition (the independent variable).

concrete operational thought Piaget's term for the ability to reason logically about direct experiences and perceptions.

conditioning According to behaviorism, the processes by which responses become linked to particular stimuli and learning takes place. The word *conditioning* is used to emphasize the importance of repeated practice, as when an athlete *conditions* his or her body to perform well by training for a long time.

conservation The principle that the amount of a substance remains the same (i.e., is conserved) when its appearance changes.

continuity Signifies developments over time that appear to persist, unchanging, from one age to the next. Parents might recognize the same personality traits in their grown children that they saw in them as infants.

control processes Mechanisms (including selective attention, metacognition, and emotion regulation) that combine memory, processing speed, and knowledge to regulate the analysis and flow of information within the information-processing system. (Also called *executive processes.*)

conventional moral reasoning Kohlberg's second level of moral reasoning, emphasizing social rules.

corpus callosum A long, thick band of nerve fibers that connects the left and right hemispheres of the brain and allows communication between them.

correlation A number indicating the degree of relationship between two variables, expressed in terms of the likelihood that one variable will (or will not) occur when the other variable does (or does not). A correlation is not an indication that one variable causes the other, only that the two variables are related.

cortex The outer layers of the brain in humans and other mammals. Most thinking, feeling, and sensing involve the cortex. (Sometimes called the *neocortex.*)

critical period A time when a particular type of developmental growth (in body or behavior) must happen. If the critical period passes without that growth, the person will never grow in that particular way.

cross-sectional research A research design that compares groups of people who differ in age but are similar in other important characteristics.

cross-sequential research A hybrid research method in which researchers first study several groups of people of different ages (a cross-sectional approach) and then follow those groups over the years (a longitudinal approach). (Also called *cohort-sequential research* or *time-sequential research.*)

crowd A larger group of adolescents who have something in common but who are not necessarily friends.

culture of children The particular habits, styles, and values that reflect the set of rules and rituals that characterize children as distinct from adult society.

cyberbullying Bullying that occurs when one person spreads insults or rumors about another by means of e-mails, text messages, or anonymous phone calls or posts embarrassing videos of the victim on the Internet. (The name derives from the fact that such bullying occurs in *cyberspace,* the hypothetical environment in which digitized information is communicated over computer networks.)

D

deductive reasoning Reasoning from a general statement, premise, or principle, through logical steps, to figure out (deduce) specifics. (Also called *top-down reasoning.*)

deferred imitation A sequence in which an infant first perceives something that someone else does and then performs the same action a few hours or even days later.

dendrite A fiber that extends from a neuron and receives electrochemical impulses transmitted from other neurons via their axons.

deoxyribonucleic acid (DNA) The molecule that contains the chemical instructions for cells to manufacture various proteins.

dependent variable In an experiment, the variable that may change as a result of whatever new condition or situation the experimenter adds. In other words, the dependent variable *depends* on the independent variable.

developmental psychopathology The field that uses insights into typical development to understand and remediate developmental disorders, and vice versa.

developmental theory A group of ideas, assumptions, and generalizations that interpret and illuminate the thousands of observations that have been made about human growth. A developmental theory provides a framework for explaining the patterns and problems of development.

deviancy training Destructive peer support in which one person shows another how to rebel against authority or social norms.

***Diagnostic and Statistical Manual of Mental Disorders* (DSM-IV-TR)** The American Psychiatric Association's official guide to the diagnosis (not treatment) of mental disorders. (*IV-TR* means "fourth edition, text revision.")

diathesis-stress model The view that psychological disorders, such as schizophrenia, are produced by the interaction of a genetic vulnerability (the diathesis) and stressful environmental factors and life events.

difference-equals-deficit error The mistaken belief that a deviation from some norm is necessarily inferior to behavior or characteristics that meet the standard.

digital divide The gap between people who have access to computers and those who do not, often a gap between rich and poor. In the United States and most other developed nations, this gap has now been bridged as computers have become almost universally present in schools and libraries.

discontinuity Signifies developments that appear quite different from those that came before. A person, or a researcher, might believe that "everything changed" when school started or when puberty began, for instance.

disorganized attachment A type of attachment that is marked by an infant's inconsistent reactions to the caregiver's departure and return.

distal parenting Caregiving practices that involve remaining distant from a baby, providing toys, food, and face-to-face communication with minimal holding and touching.

dizygotic (DZ) twins Twins who are formed when two separate ova are fertilized by two separate sperm at roughly the same time. (Also called *fraternal twins.*)

dominant–recessive pattern The interaction of a pair of alleles in such a way that the phenotype reveals the influence of one allele (the dominant gene) more than that of the other (the recessive gene).

doula A woman who helps with the birth process. Traditionally in Latin America, a doula was the only professional who attended childbirths. Now doulas are likely to work alongside a hospital's medical staff to help mothers through labor and delivery.

Down syndrome A condition in which a person has 47 chromosomes instead of the usual 46, with three rather than two chromosomes at the 21st position. People with Down syndrome typically have distinctive characteristics, including unusual facial features, heart abnormalities, and language difficulties. (Also called *trisomy-21.*)

dual-process model The notion that two networks exist within the human brain, one for emotional and one for analytical processing of stimuli.

dynamic perception Perception that is primed to focus on movement and change.

dynamic-systems approach A view of human development as an ongoing, ever-changing interaction between the physical and emotional being and between the person and every aspect of his or her environment, including the family and society.

dyslexia Unusual difficulty with reading; thought to be the result of some neurological underdevelopment.

E

eclectic perspective The approach taken by most developmentalists, in which they apply aspects of each of the various theories of development rather than adhering exclusively to one theory.

ecological-systems approach The view that in the study of human development, the person should be considered in all the contexts and interactions that constitute a life.

edgework Occupations or recreational activities that involve a degree of risk or danger. The prospect of "living on the edge" makes edgework compelling to some individuals.

effect size A way to indicate, statistically, how much of an impact the independent variable had on the dependent variable.

effortful control The ability to regulate one's emotions and actions through effort, not simply through natural inclination.

egocentrism Piaget's term for children's tendency to think about the world entirely from their own personal perspective.

Electra complex The unconscious desire of girls to replace their mother and win their father's exclusive love.

embryo The name for a developing human organism from about the third through the eighth week after conception.

embryonic period The stage of prenatal development from approximately the third through the eighth week after conception, during which the basic forms of all body structures, including internal organs, develop.

emerging adult A person between the ages of 18 and 25. Emerging adulthood is now widely thought of as a separate developmental stage.

emotional regulation The ability to control when and how emotions are expressed.

empathy The ability to understand the emotions and concerns of another person, especially when they differ from one's own.

empirical Based on observation, experience, or experiment; not theoretical.

English-language learner (ELL) A child who is learning English as a second language.

epigenetic theory An emergent theory of development that considers both the genetic origins of behavior (within each person and within each species) and the direct, systematic influence that environmental forces have, over time, on genes.

ESL (English as a second language) An approach to teaching English in which all children who do not speak English are placed together in an intensive course to learn basic English so that they can be educated in the same classroom as native English speakers.

estradiol A sex hormone, considered the chief estrogen. Females produce much more estradiol than males do.

ethnic group People whose ancestors were born in the same region and who often share a language, culture, and religion.

ethnotheory A theory that underlies the values and practices of a culture but is not usually apparent to the people within the culture.

experience-dependent brain functions Brain functions that depend on particular, variable experiences and that therefore may or may not develop in a particular infant.

experience-expectant brain functions Brain functions that require certain basic common experiences (which an infant can be expected to have) in order to develop normally.

experiment A research method in which the researcher tries to determine the cause-and-effect relationships between two variables by manipulating one (called the *independent variable*) and then observing and recording the resulting changes in the other (called the *dependent variable*).

experimental group A group of participants in a research study who experience some special treatment or condition (the independent variable).

extended family A family of three or more generations living in one household.

externalizing problems Difficulty with emotional regulation that involves expressing powerful feelings through uncontrolled physical or verbal outbursts, as by lashing out at other people or breaking things.

extreme sports Forms of recreation that include apparent risk of injury or death and that are attractive and thrilling as a result.

extremely low birthweight (ELBW) A body weight at birth of less than 2 pounds, 3 ounces (1,000 grams).

extrinsic motivation A drive, or reason to pursue a goal, that arises from the need to have one's achievements rewarded from outside, perhaps by receiving material possessions or another person's esteem.

F

family day care Child care that occurs in the home of someone to whom the child is not related and who usually cares for several children of various ages.

family function The way a family works to meet the needs of its members. Children need families to provide basic material necessities, to encourage learning, to help them develop self-respect, to nurture friendships, and to foster harmony and stability.

family structure The legal and genetic relationships among relatives living in the same home; includes nuclear family, extended family, stepfamily, and so on.

fast-mapping The speedy and sometimes imprecise way in which children learn new words by tentatively placing them in mental categories according to their perceived meaning.

fertility rate The average number of actual and projected births per woman in a given population.

fetal alcohol effects (FAE) A condition in which a child has been exposed to alcohol before birth and has some signs of fetal alcohol syndrome, including emotional and cognitive problems, but does not meet all the necessary criteria to be diagnosed with that disorder.

fetal alcohol syndrome (FAS) A cluster of birth defects, including abnormal facial characteristics, slow physical growth, and retarded mental development, that may occur in the child of a woman who drinks alcohol while pregnant.

fetal period The stage of prenatal development from the ninth week after conception until birth, during which the organs grow in size and mature in functioning.

fetus The name for a developing human organism from the start of the ninth week after conception until birth.

fine motor skills Physical abilities involving small body movements, especially of the hands and fingers, such as drawing and picking up a coin. (The word *fine* here means "small.")

Flynn effect The rise in average IQ scores that has occurred over the decades in many nations.

fMRI Functional magnetic resonance imaging, a measuring technique in which the brain's electrical excitement indicates activation anywhere in the brain; fMRI helps researchers locate neurological responses to stimuli.

focus on appearance A characteristic of preoperational thought in which a young child ignores all attributes that are not apparent.

foreclosure Erikson's term for premature identity formation, which occurs when an adolescent adopts parents' or society's roles and values wholesale, without questioning and analysis.

formal operational thought In Piaget's theory, the fourth and final stage of cognitive development, characterized by more systematic logical thinking and by the ability to understand and systematically manipulate abstract concepts.

foster care A legal, publicly supported system in which a maltreated child is removed from the parents' custody and entrusted to another adult or family, which is reimbursed for expenses incurred in meeting the child's needs.

fragile X syndrome A genetic disorder in which part of the X chromosome seems to be attached to the rest of it by a very thin string of molecules. The cause is a single gene that has more than 200 repetitions of one triplet.

G

gamete A reproductive cell; that is, a sperm or ovum that can produce a new individual if it combines with a gamete from the other sex to make a zygote.

gender differences Differences in the roles and behavior of males and females that are prescribed by the culture.

gender identity A person's acceptance of the roles and behaviors that society associates with the biological categories of male and female.

gender schema A cognitive concept or general belief based on one's experiences—in this case, a child's understanding of sex differences.

gene A section of a chromosome and the basic unit for the transmission of heredity, consisting of a string of chemicals that are instructions for the cell to manufacture certain proteins.

generational forgetting The idea that each new generation forgets what the previous generation learned. As used here, the term refers to knowledge about the harm drugs can do.

genetic counseling Consultation and testing by trained experts that enable individuals to learn about their genetic heritage, including harmful conditions that they might pass along to any children they may conceive.

genome The full set of genes that are the instructions to make an individual member of a certain species.

genotype An organism's entire genetic inheritance, or genetic potential.

germinal period The first two weeks of prenatal development after conception, characterized by rapid cell division and the beginning of cell differentiation.

gonads The paired sex glands (ovaries in females, testicles in males). The gonads produce hormones and gametes.

goodness of fit A similarity of temperament and values that produces a smooth interaction between an individual and his or her social context, including family, school, and community.

grammar All the methods—word order, verb forms, and so on—that languages use to communicate meaning, apart from the words themselves.

gross motor skills Physical abilities involving large body movements, such as walking and jumping. (The word *gross* here means "big.")

growth spurt The relatively sudden and rapid physical growth that occurs during puberty. Each body part increases in size on a schedule: Weight usually precedes height, and growth of the limbs precedes growth of the torso.

guided participation In sociocultural theory, a technique in which skilled mentors help novices learn not only by providing instruction but also by allowing direct, shared involvement in the activity. Also called *apprenticeship in thinking*.

H

habituation The process of getting used to an object or event through repeated exposure to it.

head-sparing A biological mechanism that protects the brain when malnutrition affects body growth. The brain is the last part of the body to be damaged by malnutrition.

heritability a statistic that indicates what percentage of the variation in a particular trait within a particular population, in a particular context and era, can be traced to genes.

hidden curriculum The unofficial, unstated, or implicit rules and priorities that influence the academic curriculum and every other aspect of learning in school.

high-stakes test An evaluation that is critical in determining success or failure. If a single test determines whether a student will graduate or be promoted, that is a high-stakes test.

hippocampus A brain structure that is a central processor of memory, especially memory for locations.

holophrase A single word that is used to express a complete, meaningful thought.

hormone An organic chemical substance that is produced by one body tissue and conveyed via the bloodstream to another to affect some physiological function.

HPA axis A sequence of hormone production originating in the hypothalamus and moving to the pituitary and then to the adrenal glands.

HPG axis A sequence of hormone production originating in the hypothalamus and moving to the pituitary and then to the gonads.

Human Genome Project An international effort to map the complete human genetic code. This effort was essentially completed in 2001, though analysis is ongoing.

hypothalamus A brain area that responds to the amygdala and the hippocampus to produce hormones that activate other parts of the brain and body.

hypothesis A specific prediction that is stated in such a way that it can be tested and either confirmed or refuted.

hypothetical thought Reasoning that includes propositions and possibilities that may not reflect reality.

I

identification An attempt to defend one's self-concept by taking on the behaviors and attitudes of someone else.

identity The logical principle that certain characteristics of an object remain the same even if other characteristics change.

identity achievement Erikson's term for the attainment of identity, or the point at which a person understands who he or she is as a unique individual, in accord with past experiences and future plans.

identity versus role confusion Erikson's term for the fifth stage of development, in which the person tries to figure out "Who am I?" but is confused as to which of many possible roles to adopt.

imaginary audience The other people who, in an adolescent's egocentric belief, are watching and taking note of his or her appearance, ideas, and behavior. This belief makes many teenagers very self-conscious.

immersion A strategy in which instruction in all school subjects occurs in the second (majority) language that a child is learning.

immunization A process that stimulates the body's immune system to defend against attack by a particular contagious disease. Immunization may be accomplished either naturally (by having the disease) or through vaccination (often by having an injection).

implantation The process, beginning about 10 days after conception, in which the developing organism burrows into the placenta that lines the uterus, where it can be nourished and protected as it continues to develop.

in vitro fertilization (IVF) Fertilization that takes place outside a woman's body (as in a glass laboratory dish). The procedure involves mixing sperm with ova that have been surgically removed from the woman's ovary. If the combination produces a zygote, it is inserted into the woman's uterus, where it may implant and develop into a baby.

inclusion An approach to educating children with special needs in which they are included in regular classrooms, with "appropriate aids and services," as required by law.

independent variable In an experiment, the variable that is introduced to see what effect it has on the dependent variable. (Also called *experimental variable*.)

individual education plan (IEP) A document that specifies educational goals and plans for a child with special needs.

inductive reasoning Reasoning from one or more specific experiences or facts to reach (induce) a general conclusion. (Also called *bottom-up reasoning*.)

industry versus inferiority The fourth of Erikson's eight psychosocial crises, during which children attempt to master many skills, developing a sense of themselves as either industrious or inferior, competent or incompetent.

infertility The inability to conceive after at least a year of trying to do so via sexual intercourse.

information-processing theory A perspective that compares human thinking processes, by analogy, to computer analysis of data, including sensory input, connections, stored memories, and output.

initiative versus guilt Erikson's third psychosocial crisis, in which children undertake new skills and activities and feel guilty when they do not succeed at them.

injury control/harm reduction Practices that are aimed at anticipating, controlling, and preventing dangerous activities; these practices reflect the beliefs that accidents are not random and that injuries can be made less harmful if proper controls are in place.

insecure-avoidant attachment A pattern of attachment in which an infant avoids connection with the caregiver, as when the infant seems not to care about the caregiver's presence, departure, or return.

insecure-resistant/ambivalent attachment A pattern of attachment in which anxiety and uncertainty are evident, as when an infant becomes very upset at separation from the caregiver and both resists and seeks contact on reunion.

instrumental aggression Hurtful behavior that is intended to get or keep something that another person has.

interaction effect The result of a combination of teratogens. Sometimes the risk of harm is greatly magnified when an embryo or fetus is exposed to more than one teratogen at the same time.

internalizing problems Difficulty with emotional regulation that involves turning one's emotional distress inward, as by feeling excessively guilty, ashamed, or worthless.

intimacy versus isolation The sixth of Erikson's eight stages of development. Adults seek someone with whom to share their lives in an enduring and self-sacrificing commitment. Without such commitment, they risk profound loneliness and isolation.

intrinsic motivation A drive, or reason to pursue a goal, that comes from inside a person, such as the need to feel smart or competent.

intuitive thought Thought that arises from an emotion or a hunch, beyond rational explanation, and is influenced by past experiences and cultural assumptions.

invincibility fable An adolescent's egocentric conviction that he or she cannot be overcome or even harmed by anything that might defeat a normal mortal, such as unprotected sex, drug abuse, or high-speed driving.

IQ test A test designed to measure intellectual aptitude, or ability to learn in school. Originally, intelligence was defined as mental age divided by chronological age, times 100—hence the term *intelligence quotient*, or *IQ*.

irreversibility A characteristic of preoperational thought in which a young child thinks that nothing can be undone. A thing cannot be restored to the way it was before a change occurred.

J

juvenile delinquent A person under the age of 18 who breaks the law.

K

kangaroo care A form of child care in which the mother of a low-birthweight infant spends at least an hour a day holding the baby between her breasts, like a kangaroo that carries her immature newborn in a pouch on her abdomen.

kinship care A form of foster care in which a relative of a maltreated child, usually a grandparent, becomes the approved caregiver.

knowledge base A body of knowledge in a particular area that makes it easier to master new information in that area.

kwashiorkor A disease of chronic malnutrition during childhood, in which a protein deficiency makes the child more vulnerable to other diseases, such as measles, diarrhea, and influenza.

L

language acquisition device (LAD) Chomsky's term for a hypothesized mental structure that enables humans to learn language, including the basic aspects of grammar, vocabulary, and intonation.

language shift A change from one language to another, which occurs not only in speaking and writing but also in the brain. A language shift is evident in many children who no longer speak or understand their mother tongue because a new language has come to dominate the linguistic areas of their brains.

latency Freud's term for middle childhood, during which children's emotional drives and psychosexual needs are quiet (latent). Freud thought that sexual conflicts from earlier stages are only temporarily submerged, bursting forth again at puberty.

lateralization Literally, sidedness, referring to the specialization in certain functions by each side of the brain, with one side dominant for each activity. The left side of the brain controls the right side of the body, and vice versa.

learning disability A marked delay in a particular area of learning that is not caused by an apparent physical disability, by mental retardation, or by an unusually stressful home environment.

least restrictive environment (LRE) A legal requirement that children with special needs be assigned to the most general educational context in which they can be expected to learn.

leptin A hormone that affects appetite and is believed to affect the onset of puberty. Leptin levels increase during childhood and peak at around age 12.

life-course-persistent offender A person whose disobedient and disruptive activity typically begins in childhood and continues throughout life; a career criminal.

linked lives A term that describes the notion that family members tend to be affected by all aspects of each other's lives, from triumph to tragedy.

"little scientist" The stage-five toddler (age 12 to 18 months) who experiments without anticipating the results, using trial and error in active and creative exploration.

long-term memory The component of the information-processing system in which virtually limitless amounts of information can be stored indefinitely.

longitudinal research A research design in which the same individuals are followed over time and their development is repeatedly assessed.

low birthweight (LBW) A body weight at birth of less than 5-1/2 pounds (2,500 grams).

M

marasmus A disease of severe protein-calorie malnutrition during early infancy, in which growth stops, body tissues waste away, and the infant eventually dies.

menarche A girl's first menstrual period, signaling that she has begun ovulation. Pregnancy is biologically possible, but ovulation and menstruation are often irregular for years after menarche.

mental retardation Literally, slow, or late, thinking. In practice, people are considered mentally retarded if they score below 70 on an IQ test and if they are markedly behind their peers in adaptation to daily life.

meta-analysis A technique of combining results of many studies to come to an overall conclusion. Meta analysis is powerful, in that small samples can be added together to lead to significant conclusions, although variations from study to study sometimes make combining them impossible.

metacognition "Thinking about thinking," or the ability to evaluate a cognitive task in order to determine how best to accomplish it, and then to monitor and adjust one's performance on that task.

middle childhood The period between early childhood and early adolescence, from approximately ages 7 to 11.

middle school A school for children in the grades between elementary and high school. Middle school usually begins with grade 5 or 6 and ends with grade 8.

mirror neurons Brain cells that respond to actions performed by someone else in the same way they would if the observer had done that action.

modeling The central process of social learning, by which a person observes the actions of others and then copies them.

monozygotic (MZ) twins Twins who originate from one zygote that splits apart very early in development. (Also called *identical twins*.) Other monozygotic multiple births (such as triplets and quadruplets) can occur as well.

Montessori schools Schools that offer early-childhood education based on the philosophy of Maria Montessori, which emphasizes careful work and tasks that each young child can do.

moratorium A socially acceptable way for adolescents to postpone identity achievement. Going to college is a common example.

mosaicism A condition in which an organism has a mixture of cells, some normal and some with an odd number of chromosomes or a series of missing genes.

motor skill The learned ability to move some part of the body, in actions ranging from a large leap to a flicker of the eyelid. (The word *motor* here refers to the movement of muscles.)

multifactorial Referring to a trait that is affected by many factors, both genetic and environmental.

myelination The process by which axons become coated with myelin, a fatty substance that speeds the transmission of nerve impulses from neuron to neuron.

N

naming explosion A sudden increase in an infant's vocabulary, especially in the number of nouns, that begins at about 18 months of age.

National Assessment of Educational Progress (NAEP) An ongoing and nationally representative measure of U.S. children's achievement in reading, mathematics, and other subjects over time; nicknamed "the Nation's Report Card."

nature A general term for the traits, capacities, and limitations that each individual inherits genetically from his or her parents at the moment of conception.

neglectful/uninvolved parenting An approach to child rearing in which the parents are indifferent toward their children and unaware of what is going on in their children's lives.

neuron One of the billions of nerve cells in the central nervous system, especially the brain.

No Child Left Behind Act A U.S. law enacted in 2001 that was intended to increase accountability in education by requiring states to qualify for federal educational funding by administering standardized tests to measure school achievement.

norm An average, or standard, measurement, calculated from the measurements of many individuals within a specific group or population.

nuclear family A family that consists of a father, a mother, and their biological children under age 18.

nurture A general term for all the environmental influences that affect development after an individual is conceived.

O

obesity In an adult, having a BMI of 30 or more. In a child, having a BMI above the 95th percentile, according to the U.S. Centers for Disease Control's 1980 standards for children of a given age.

object permanence The realization that objects (including people) still exist when they can no longer be seen, touched, or heard.

Oedipus complex The unconscious desire of young boys to replace their father and win their mother's exclusive love.

operant conditioning The learning process by which a particular action is followed by something desired (which makes the person or animal more likely to repeat the action) or by something unwanted (which makes the action less likely to be repeated). Also called *instrumental conditioning.*

operational definition A description of the specific, observable behavior that will constitute the variable that is to be studied, so that any reader will know whether that behavior occurred or not. Operational definitions may be arbitrary (e.g., an IQ score at or above 130 is operationally defined as "gifted"), but they must be precise.

overregularization The application of rules of grammar even when exceptions occur, making the language seem more "regular" than it actually is.

overweight In an adult, having a BMI of 25 to 29. In a child, having a BMI above the 85th percentile, according to the U.S. Centers for Disease Control's 1980 standards for children of a given age.

P

parasuicide Any deliberate action of self-harm that could have been lethal but was not.

parental alliance Cooperation between a mother and a father based on their mutual commitment to their children. In a parental alliance, the parents agree to support each other in their shared parental roles.

parental monitoring Parents' ongoing awareness of what their children are doing, where, and with whom.

parent–infant bond The strong, loving connection that forms as parents hold, examine, and feed their newborn.

participants The people who are studied in a research project.

peer pressure Encouragement to conform to one's friends or contemporaries in behavior, dress, and attitude; often a positive force, but usually considered a negative one, as when adolescent peers encourage one another to defy adult authority.

people preference A universal principle of infant perception, consisting of an innate attraction to other humans, which is evident in visual, auditory, tactile, and other preferences.

percentile A point on a ranking scale of 0 to 100. The 50th percentile is the midpoint; half the people in the population being studied rank higher and half rank lower.

perception The mental processing of sensory information when the brain interprets a sensation.

permanency planning An effort by child-welfare authorities to find a long-term living situation that will provide stability and support for a maltreated child. A goal is to avoid repeated changes of caregiver or school, which can be particularly harmful to the child.

permissive parenting An approach to child rearing that is characterized by high nurturance and communication but little discipline, guidance, or control.

perseveration The tendency to persevere in, or stick to, one thought or action for a long time.

personal fable An aspect of adolescent egocentrism characterized by an adolescent's belief that his or her thoughts, feelings, and experiences are unique, more wonderful or awful than anyone else's.

phallic stage Freud's third stage of development, when the penis becomes the focus of concern and pleasure.

phenotype The observable characteristics of a person, including appearance, personality, intelligence, and all other traits.

phenylketonuria (PKU) A genetic disorder in which a child's body is unable to metabolize an amino acid called phenylalanine. The resulting buildup of phenylalanine in body fluids causes brain damage, progressive mental retardation, and other symptoms.

phonics approach Teaching reading by first teaching the sounds of each letter and of various letter combinations.

pituitary A gland in the brain that responds to a signal from the hypothalamus by producing many hormones, including those that regulate growth and control other glands, among them the adrenal and sex glands.

placenta The organ that surrounds the developing embryo and fetus, sustaining life via the umbilical cord. The placenta is attached to the wall of the pregnant woman's uterus.

plasticity The idea that abilities, personality, and other human traits can change over time. Plasticity is particularly evident during childhood, but even older adults are not always "set in their ways."

polygamous family A family consisting of one man, several wives, and the biological children of the man and his wives.

polygenic Referring to a trait that is influenced by many genes.

population The entire group of individuals who are of particular concern in a scientific study, such as all the children of the world or all newborns who weigh less than 3 pounds.

post-traumatic stress disorder (PTSD) An anxiety disorder that develops as a delayed reaction to having experienced or witnessed a profoundly shocking or frightening event, such as rape, war, or natural disaster. Its symptoms may include flashbacks to the event, hyperactivity and hypervigilance, displaced anger, sleeplessness, nightmares, sudden terror or anxiety, and confusion between fantasy and reality.

postconventional moral reasoning Kohlberg's third level of moral reasoning, emphasizing moral principles.

postpartum depression A new mother's feelings of inadequacy and sadness in the days and weeks after giving birth.

preconventional moral reasoning Kohlberg's first level of moral reasoning, emphasizing rewards and punishments.

prefrontal cortex The area of cortex at the front of the brain that specializes in anticipation, planning, and impulse control.

preoperational intelligence Piaget's term for cognitive development between the ages of about 2 and 6; it includes language and imagination (which involve symbolic thought), but logical, operational thinking is not yet possible.

preterm birth A birth that occurs 3 or more weeks before the full 38 weeks of the typical pregnancy have elapsed—that is, at 35 or fewer weeks after conception.

primary circular reactions The first of three types of feedback loops in sensorimotor intelligence, this one involving the infant's own body. The infant senses motion, sucking, noise, and other stimuli, and tries to understand them.

primary prevention Actions that change overall background conditions to prevent some unwanted event or circumstance, such as injury, disease, or abuse.

primary sex characteristics The parts of the body that are directly involved in reproduction, including the vagina, uterus, ovaries, testicles, and penis.

private speech The internal dialogue that occurs when people talk to themselves (either silently or out loud).

Progress in International Reading Literacy Study (PIRLS) Inaugurated in 2001, a planned five-year cycle of international trend studies in the reading ability of fourth-graders.

prosocial behavior Feelings and actions that are helpful and kind but are of no obvious benefit to oneself.

protein-calorie malnutrition A condition in which a person does not consume sufficient food of any kind. This deprivation can result in several illnesses, severe weight loss, and even death.

proximal parenting Caregiving practices that involve being physically close to a baby, with frequent holding and touching.

psychoanalytic theory A grand theory of human development that holds that irrational, unconscious drives and motives, often originating in childhood, underlie human behavior.

psychological control A disciplinary technique that involves threatening to withdraw love and support and that relies on a child's feelings of guilt and gratitude to the parents.

psychopathology An illness or disorder of the mind.

puberty The time between the first onrush of hormones and full adult physical development. Puberty usually lasts three to five years. Many more years are required to achieve psychosocial maturity.

Q

qualitative research Research that considers qualities instead of quantities. Descriptions of particular conditions and participants' expressed ideas are often part of qualitative studies.

quantitative research Research that provides data that can be expressed with numbers, such as ranks or scales.

R

race A group of people who are regarded by themselves or by others as distinct from other groups on the basis of physical appearance.

reaction time The time it takes to respond to a stimulus, either physically (with a reflexive movement such as an eye blink) or cognitively (with a thought).

reactive aggression An impulsive retaliation for another person's intentional or accidental action, verbal or physical.

reflex An unlearned, involuntary action or movement emitted in response to a particular stimulus. A reflex is an automatic response that is built into the nervous system and occurs without conscious thought.

Reggio Emilia approach A famous program of early-childhood education that originated in the town of Reggio Emilia, Italy, and that encourages each child's creativity in a carefully designed setting.

reinforcement A technique for conditioning behavior in which that behavior is followed by something desired, such as food for a hungry animal or a welcoming smile for a lonely person.

relational aggression Nonphysical acts, such as insults or social rejection, aimed at harming the social connection between the victim and other people.

REM sleep Rapid eye movement sleep, a stage of sleep characterized by flickering eyes behind closed lids, dreaming, and rapid brain waves.

reminder session A perceptual experience that is intended to help a person recollect an idea, a thing, or an experience, without testing whether the person remembers it at the moment.

replication The repetition of a study, using different participants.

reported maltreatment Harm or endangerment about which someone has notified the authorities.

representative sample A group of research participants who reflect the relevant characteristics of the larger population whose attributes are under study.

resilience The capacity to adapt well to significant adversity and to overcome serious stress.

resource room A room in which trained teachers help children with special needs, using specialized curricula and equipment.

reversibility The logical principle that a thing that has been changed can sometimes be returned to its original state by reversing the process by which it was changed.

risk analysis The science of weighing the potential effects of a particular event, substance, or experience to determine the likelihood of harm. In teratology, risk analysis attempts to evaluate everything that affects the chances that a particular agent or condition will cause damage to an embryo or fetus.

role confusion A situation in which an adolescent does not seem to know or care what his or her identity is. (Also called *identity diffusion*.)

rough-and-tumble play Play that mimics aggression through wrestling, chasing, or hitting, but in which there is no intent to harm.

rumination Repeatedly thinking and talking about past experiences.

S

sample A group of individuals drawn from a specified population. A sample might be the low-birthweight babies born in four particular hospitals that are representative of all hospitals.

scaffolding Temporary support that is tailored to a learner's needs and abilities and aimed at helping the learner master the next task in a given learning process.

science of human development The science that seeks to understand how and why people of all ages and circumstances change or remain the same over time.

scientific method A way to answer questions that requires empirical research and data-based conclusions.

scientific observation A method of testing a hypothesis by unobtrusively watching and recording participants' behavior in a systematic and objective manner, in a natural setting, in a laboratory, or in searches of archival data.

secondary circular reactions The second of three types of feedback loops in sensorimotor intelligence, this one involving people and objects. Infants respond to other people, to toys, and to any other object they can touch or move.

secondary education Literally the period after primary education (elementary or grade school) and before tertiary education (college). It usually occurs from about age 12 to 18, although there is some variation by school and by nation.

secondary prevention Actions that avert harm in a high-risk situation, such as stopping a car before it hits a pedestrian.

secondary sex characteristics Physical traits that are not directly involved in reproduction but that indicate sexual maturity, such as a man's beard and a woman's breasts.

secular trend The long-term upward or downward direction of a certain set of statistical measurements, as opposed to a smaller, shorter cyclical variation. As an example, over the last two centuries, because of improved nutrition and medical care, children have tended to reach their adult height earlier and their adult weight has increased.

secure attachment A relationship in which an infant obtains both comfort and confidence from the presence of his or her caregiver.

selective adaptation The process by which humans and other species gradually adjust to their environment. This process is based on the frequency with which a particular genetic trait in a population increases or decreases over generations; that frequency depends on whether or not the trait contributes to the survival and reproductive ability of members of that population.

selective attention The ability to concentrate on some stimuli while ignoring others.

self-awareness A person's realization that he or she is a distinct individual, whose body, mind, and actions are separate from those of other people.

self-concept A person's understanding of who he or she is, in relation to self-esteem, appearance, personality, and various traits.

self-efficacy In social learning theory, the belief of some people that they are able to change themselves and effectively alter the social context.

self-esteem A person's evaluation of his or her own worth, either in specifics (e.g., intelligence, attractiveness) or overall.

self-righting The inborn drive to remedy a developmental deficit.

sensation The response of a sensory system (eyes, ears, skin, tongue, nose) when it detects a stimulus.

sensitive period A time when a certain type of development is most likely to happen and happens most easily. If that development does not occur during that sensitive period, it could still occur later. For example, early childhood is considered a sensitive period for language learning.

sensorimotor intelligence Piaget's term for the way infants think—by using their senses and motor skills—during the first period of cognitive development.

sensory memory The component of the information-processing system in which incoming stimulus information is stored for a split second to allow it to be processed. (Also called the *sensory register.*)

separation anxiety An infant's distress when a familiar caregiver leaves, most obvious between 9 and 14 months.

sex differences Biological differences between males and females, in organs, hormones, and body type.

sexual orientation The direction of a person's sexual and romantic attraction, whether toward others of the same sex, the opposite sex, or both sexes.

sexually transmitted infection (STI) A disease spread by sexual contact, including syphilis, gonorrhea, genital herpes, chlamydia, and HIV.

shaken baby syndrome A life-threatening injury that occurs when an infant is forcefully shaken back and forth, a motion that ruptures blood vessels in the brain and breaks neural connections.

single-parent family A family that consists of only one parent and his or her biological children under age 18.

small for gestational age (SGA) A term for a baby whose birthweight is significantly lower than expected, given the time since conception. For example, a 5-pound (2,265-gram) newborn is considered SGA if born on time but not SGA if born two months early. (Also called *small for dates.*)

social cognition The ability to understand social interactions, including the causes and consequences of human behavior.

social comparison The tendency to assess one's abilities, achievements, social status, and other attributes by measuring them against those of other people, especially one's peers.

social construction An idea that is built on shared perceptions, not on objective reality. Many age-related terms, such as *childhood, adolescence, yuppie,* and *senior citizen,* are social constructions.

social learning Learning that is accomplished by observing others.

social learning theory An extension of behaviorism that emphasizes the influence that other people have over a person's behavior. Even without specific reinforcement, every individual learns many things through observation and imitation of other people.

social mediation Human interaction that expands and advances understanding, often through words that one person uses to explain something to another.

social norms approach A method of reducing risky behavior among emerging adults that is based on their desire to follow social norms. This approach uses surveys of emerging adults and publication of the results of those surveys to make emerging adults aware of the actual prevalence of various behaviors in their peer group.

social referencing Seeking information about how to react to an unfamiliar or ambiguous object or event by observing someone else's expressions and reactions. That other person becomes a social reference.

social smile A smile evoked by a human face, normally evident in infants about 6 weeks after birth.

sociocultural theory An emergent theory that holds that development results from the dynamic interaction of each person with the surrounding social and cultural forces.

sociodramatic play Pretend play in which children act out various roles and themes in stories that they create.

socioeconomic status (SES) A person's position in society as determined by income, wealth, occupation, education, place of residence, and other factors.

sonogram An image of an unborn fetus (or an internal organ) produced by using high-frequency sound waves (ultrasound).

spermarche A boy's first ejaculation of sperm. Erections can occur as early as infancy, but ejaculation signals sperm production. Spermarche may occur during sleep (in a "wet dream") or via direct stimulation.

static reasoning A characteristic of preoperational thought in which a young child thinks that nothing changes. Whatever is now has always been and always will be.

still-face technique An experimental practice in which an adult keeps his or her face umoving and expressionless in face-to-face interaction with an infant.

Strange Situation A laboratory procedure for measuring attachment by evoking infants' reactions to stress.

stranger wariness An infant's expression of concern—a quiet stare, clinging to a familiar person, or sadness—when a stranger appears.

substantiated maltreatment Harm or endangerment that has been reported, investigated, and verified.

sudden infant death syndrome (SIDS) A situation in which a seemingly healthy infant, at least 2 months of age, suddenly stops breathing and dies unexpectedly while asleep.

suicidal ideation Thinking about suicide, usually with some serious emotional and intellectual or cognitive overtones.

sunk cost fallacy The mistaken belief that if money, time, or effort that cannot be recovered (a "sunk cost," in economic terms) has already been invested in some endeavor, then more should be invested in an effort to reach the goal. Because of this fallacy, people spend money continuing to try to fix a "lemon" of a car or sending more troops to fight a losing battle.

superego In psychoanalytic theory, the judgmental part of the personality that internalizes the moral standards of the parents.

survey A research method in which information is collected from a large number of people by interviews, written questionnaires, or some other means.

synapse The intersection between the axon of one neuron and the dendrites of other neurons.

synchrony A coordinated, rapid, and smooth exchange of responses between a caregiver and an infant.

T

temperament Inborn differences between one person and another in emotions, activity, and self-regulation. Temperament is epigenetic, originating in genes but affected by child-rearing practices.

teratogens Agents and conditions, including viruses, drugs, and chemicals, that can impair prenatal development and result in birth defects or even death.

teratology The study of birth defects.

tertiary circular reactions The third of three types of feedback loops in sensorimotor intelligence, this one involving active exploration and experimentation. Infants explore a range of new activities, varying their responses as a way of learning about the world.

tertiary prevention Actions, such as immediate and effective medical treatment, that are taken after an adverse event (such as illness or injury) occurs and that are aimed at reducing the harm or preventing disability.

testosterone A sex hormone, the best known of the androgens (male hormones); secreted in far greater amounts by males than by females.

theory of mind A person's theory of what other people might be thinking. In order to have a theory of mind, children must realize that other people are not necessarily thinking the same thoughts that they themselves are. That realization is seldom possible before age 4.

theory-theory The idea that children attempt to explain everything they see and hear by constructing theories.

threshold effect A situation in which a certain teratogen is relatively harmless in small doses but becomes harmful once exposure reaches a certain level (the threshold).

time-out A disciplinary technique in which a child is separated from other people for a specified time.

TIMSS (Trends in Math and Science Study) An international assessment of the math and science skills of fourth- and eighth-graders. Although the TIMSS is very useful, different countries' scores are not always comparable, because sample selection, test administration, and content validity are hard to keep uniform.

transient exuberance The great increase in the number of dendrites that occurs in an infant's brain during the first two years of life.

trust versus mistrust Erikson's first psychosocial crisis. Infants learn basic trust if the world is a secure place where their basic needs (for food, comfort, attention, and so on) are met.

23rd pair The chromosome pair that, in humans, determines the zygote's (and hence the person's) sex. The other 22 pairs are autosomes, the same whether the 23rd pair is for a male or a female.

V

very low birthweight (VLBW) A body weight at birth of less than 3 pounds, 5 ounces (1,500 grams).

visual cliff An experimental apparatus that gives an illusion of a sudden dropoff between one horizontal surface and another.

W

Wechsler Intelligence Scale for Children (WISC) An IQ test designed for school-age children. The test assesses potential in many areas, including vocabulary, general knowledge, memory, and spatial comprehension.

whole-language approach Teaching reading by encouraging early use of all language skills—talking and listening, reading and writing.

withdrawn-rejected Rejected by peers because of timid, withdrawn, and anxious behavior.

working memory The component of the information-processing system in which current conscious mental activity occurs. (Also called *short-term memory.*)

working model In cognitive theory, a set of assumptions that the individual uses to organize perceptions and experiences. For example, a person might assume that other people are trustworthy and be surprised by evidence that this working model of human behavior is erroneous.

X

X-linked Referring to a gene carried on the X chromosome. If a boy inherits an X-linked recessive trait from his mother, he expresses that trait because the Y from his father has no counteracting gene. Girls are more likely to be carriers of X-linked traits but are less likely to express them.

XX A 23rd chromosome pair that consists of two X-shaped chromosomes, one each from the mother and the father. XX zygotes become females.

XY A 23rd chromosome pair that consists of an X-shaped chromosome from the mother and a Y-shaped chromosome from the father. XY zygotes become males.

Z

zone of proximal development In sociocultural theory, a metaphorical area, or "zone," surrounding a learner that includes all the skills, knowledge, and concepts that the person is close to acquiring but cannot yet master without help.

zygote The single cell formed from the fusing of two gametes, a sperm and an ovum.

References

Abbott, Lesley, & Nutbrown, Cathy (Eds.). (2001). *Experiencing Reggio Emilia: Implications for pre-school provision.* Philadelphia: Open University Press.

Aboud, Frances E., & Amato, Maria. (2001). Developmental and socialization influences on intergroup bias. In Rupert Brown & Samuel L. Gaertner (Eds.), *Blackwell handbook of social psychology: Intergroup processes* (pp. 65–85). Malden, MA: Blackwell.

Aboud, Frances E., & Mendelson, Morton J. (1998). Determinants of friendship selection and quality: Developmental perspectives. In William M. Bukowski, Andrew F. Newcomb, & Willard W. Hartup (Eds.), *The company they keep: Friendship in childhood and adolescence* (pp. 87–112). New York: Cambridge University Press.

Abrams, Dominic, Rutland, Adam, Ferrell, Jennifer M., & Pelletier, Joseph. (2008). Children's judgments of disloyal and immoral peer behavior: Subjective group dynamics in minimal intergroup contexts. *Child Development, 79,* 444–461.

Accardo, Pasquale. (2006). Who's training whom? *The Journal of Pediatrics, 149,* 151–152.

Adam, Emma K., Klimes-Dougan, Bonnie, & Gunnar, Megan R. (2007). Social regulation of the adrenocortical response to stress in infants, children, and adolescents: Implications for psychopathology and education. In Donna Coch, Geraldine Dawson, & Kurt W. Fischer (Eds.), *Human behavior, learning, and the developing brain: Atypical development* (pp. 264–304). New York: Guilford Press.

Adam, Tanja C., & Epel, Elissa S. (2007). Stress, eating and the reward system. *Physiology & Behavior, 91,* 449–458.

Adamson, Lauren B., & Bakeman, Roger. (2006). Development of displaced speech in early mother–child conversations. *Child Development, 77,* 186–200.

Adejuyigbe, Ebunoluwa A., Odebiyi, Adetanwa I., Aina, Olabisi, & Bamiwuye, Sina. (2008). Feeding and care of low-birthweight babies in two rural communities in south-western Nigeria. *Maternal and Child Nutrition, 4,* 55–64.

Adolph, Karen E., & Berger, Sarah E. (2005). Physical and motor development. In Marc H. Bornstein & Michael E. Lamb (Eds.), *Developmental science: An advanced textbook* (5th ed., pp. 223–281). Mahwah, NJ: Erlbaum.

Adolph, Karen E., & Berger, Sarah E. (2006). Motor development. In William Damon & Richard M. Lerner (Series Eds.) & Deanna Kuhn & Robert S. Siegler (Vol. Eds.), *Handbook of child psychology: Vol. 2. Cognition, perception, and language* (6th ed., pp. 161–213). Hoboken, NJ: Wiley.

Adolph, Karen E., Vereijken, Beatrix, & Denny, Mark A. (1998). Learning to crawl. *Child Development, 69,* 1299–1312.

Adolph, Karen E., Vereijken, Beatrix, & Shrout, Patrick E. (2003). What changes in infant walking and why. *Child Development, 74,* 475–497.

Afifi, Tracie O., Enns, Murray W., Cox, Brian J., Asmundson, Gordon J. G., Stein, Murray B., & Sareen, Jitender. (2008). Population attributable fractions of psychiatric disorders and suicide ideation and attempts associated with adverse childhood experiences. *American Journal of Public Health, 98,* 946–952.

Ahmed, Saifuddin, Koenig, Michael A., & Stephenson, Rob. (2006). Effects of domestic violence on perinatal and early-childhood mortality: Evidence from North India. *American Journal of Public Health, 96,* 1423–1428.

Ainsworth, Mary D. Salter. (1973). The development of infant–mother attachment. In Bettye M. Caldwell & Henry N. Ricciuti (Eds.), *Review of child development research* (Vol. 3, pp. 1–94). Chicago: University of Chicago Press.

Akiba, Daisuke, & García Coll, Cynthia. (2004). Effective interventions with children of color and their families: A contextual developmental approach. In Timothy B. Smith (Ed.), *Practicing multiculturalism: Affirming diversity in counseling and psychology* (pp. 123–144). Boston: Pearson/Allyn and Bacon.

Akinbami, Lara J. (2006). *The state of childhood asthma, United States, 1980–2005.* National Center for Health Statistics. Retrieved July 17, 2007, from the World Wide Web: http://www.cdc.gov/nchs/data/ad/ad381.pdf

Alasuutari, Pertti, Bickman, Leonard, & Brannen, Julia. (2008). *The SAGE handbook of social research methods.* Los Angeles: SAGE.

Alberts, Amy, Elkind, David, & Ginsberg, Stephen. (2007). The personal fable and risk taking in early adolescence. *Journal of Youth and Adolescence, 36,* 71–76.

Alesina, Alberto, & Glaeser, Edward L. (2004). *Fighting poverty in the US and Europe: A world of difference.* New York: Oxford University Press.

Alexander, Karl L., Entwisle, Doris R., & Olson, Linda Steffel. (2007). Lasting consequences of the summer learning gap. *American Sociological Review, 72,* 167–180.

Alexander, Robin. (2000). *Culture and pedagogy: International comparisons in primary education.* Malden, MA: Blackwell.

Allen, Elizabeth, Bonell, Chris, Strange, Vicki, Copas, Andrew, Stephenson, Judith, Johnson, Anne, et al. (2007). Does the UK government's teenage pregnancy strategy deal with the correct risk factors? Findings from a secondary analysis of data from a randomised trial of sex education and their implications for policy. *Journal of Epidemiology & Community Health, 61,* 20–27.

Allen, Joseph P., Porter, Maryfrances R., McFarland, F. Christy, Marsh, Penny, & McElhaney, Kathleen Boykin. (2005). The two faces of adolescents' success with peers: Adolescent popularity, social adaptation, and deviant behavior. *Child Development, 76,* 747–760.

Allen, Shanley. (2007). The future of Inuktitut in the face of majority languages: Bilingualism or language shift? *Applied Psycholinguistics, 28,* 515–536.

Allis, C. David, Jenuwein, Thomas, & Reinberg, Danny (Eds.). (2007). *Epigenetics.* Cold Spring Harbor, NY: Cold Spring Harbor Laboratory Press.

Alloy, Lauren B., & Abramson, Lyn Y. (2007). The adolescent surge in depression and emergence of gender differences: A biocognitive vulnerability-stress model in developmental context. In Daniel Romer & Elaine F. Walker (Eds.), *Adolescent psychopathology and the developing brain: Integrating brain and prevention science* (pp. 284–312). New York: Oxford University Press.

Alloy, Lauren B., Zhu, Lin, & Abramson, Lyn. (2003). Cognitive vulnerability to depression: Implications for adolescent risk behavior in general. In Daniel Romer (Ed.), *Reducing adolescent risk: Toward an integrated approach* (pp. 171–182). Thousand Oaks, CA: Sage.

Alm, Bernt. (2007). To co-sleep or not to sleep. *Acta Pædiatrica, 96,* 1385–1386.

Alsaker, Françoise D., & Flammer, August (2006). Pubertal development. In Sandy Jackson & Luc Goossens (Eds.), *Handbook of adolescent development* (pp. 30–50). Hove, East Sussex, UK: Psychology Press.

Amato, Paul R. (2000). The consequences of divorce for adults and children. *Journal of Marriage & the Family, 62,* 1269–1287.

Amato, Paul R., & Afifi, Tamara D. (2006). Feeling caught between parents: Adult children's relations with parents and subjective well-being. *Journal of Marriage and Family, 68,* 222–235.

Amato, Paul R., & Fowler, Frieda. (2002). Parenting practices, child adjustment, and family diversity. *Journal of Marriage & the Family, 64,* 703–716.

American Psychiatric Association (APA). (2000). *Diagnostic and statistical manual of mental disorders: DSM-IV-TR* (4th ed.). Washington, DC: Author.

Ananth, Cande V., Demissie, Kitaw, Kramer, Michael S., & Vintzileos, Anthony M. (2003). Small-for-gestational-age births among black and white women: Temporal trends in the United States. *American Journal of Public Health, 93,* 577–579.

Anderson, Craig A., Berkowitz, Leonard, Donnerstein, Edward, Huesmann, L. Rowell, Johnson, James D., Linz, Daniel, et al. (2003). The influence of media violence on youth. *Psychological Science in the Public Interest, 4,* 81–110.

Anderson, Craig A., & Bushman, Brad J. (2002). Human aggression. *Annual Review of Psychology, 53,* 27–51.

Anderson, Craig A., Gentile, Douglas A., & Buckley, Katherine E. (2007). *Violent video game effects on children and adolescents: Theory, research, and public policy*. New York: Oxford University Press.

Anderson, Daniel R., Huston, Aletha C., Schmitt, Kelly L., Linebarger, Deborah L., & Wright, John C. (2001). Early childhood television viewing and adolescent behavior: The recontact study. *Monographs of the Society for Research in Child Development, 66*(1, Serial No. 264).

Anderson, Mark, Johnson, Daniel, & Batal, Holly. (2005). *Sudden infant death syndrome and prenatal maternal smoking: Rising attributed risk in the Back to Sleep era*. Retrieved June 23, 2005, from the World Wide Web: http://www.biomedcentral.com/1741–7015/3/4

Andrade, Miriam, & Menna-Barreto, Luiz. (2002). Sleep patterns of high school students living in Sao Paulo, Brazil. In Mary A. Carskadon (Ed.), *Adolescent sleep patterns: Biological, social, and psychological influences* (pp. 118–131). New York: Cambridge University Press.

Andrade, Susan E., Gurwitz, Jerry H., Davis, Robert L., Chan, K. Arnold, Finkelstein, Jonathan A., Fortman, Kris, et al. (2004). Prescription drug use in pregnancy. *American Journal of Obstetrics and Gynecology, 191,* 398–407.

Andreassen, Carol, & West, Jerry. (2007). Measuring socioemotional functioning in a national birth cohort study. *Infant Mental Health Journal, 28,* 627–646.

Angold, Adrian, Erkanli, Alaattin, Egger, Helen L., & Costello, E. Jane. (2000). Stimulant treatment for children: A community perspective. *Journal of the American Academy of Child & Adolescent Psychiatry, 39,* 975–984.

Anis, Tarek. (2007). Hormones involved in male sexual function. In Annette Fuglsang Owens & Mitchell S. Tepper (Eds.), *Sexual health: Vol. 2. Physical foundations* (pp. 79–113). Westport, CT: Praeger/Greenwood.

Apgar, Virginia. (1953). A proposal for a new method of evaluation of the newborn infant. *Current Researches in Anesthesia and Analgesia, 32,* 260–267.

Appoh, Lily Yaa. (2004). Consequences of early malnutrition for subsequent social and emotional behaviour of children in Ghana. *Journal of Psychology in Africa, 14,* 87–94.

Appoh, Lily Yaa, & Krekling, Sturla. (2004). Effects of early childhood malnutrition on cognitive performance of Ghanaian children. *Journal of Psychology in Africa: South of the Sahara, the Caribbean, and Afro-Latin America, 14,* 1–7.

Archer, John. (2000). Sex differences in aggression between heterosexual partners: A meta-analytic review. *Psychological Bulletin, 126,* 651–680.

Archer, John, & Coyne, Sarah M. (2005). An integrated review of indirect, relational, and social aggression. *Personality and Social Psychology Review, 9,* 212–230.

Arias, Daniel Fierro, & Hernández, Amparo Moreno. (2007). Emerging adulthood in Mexican and Spanish youth: Theories and realities. *Journal of Adolescent Research, 22,* 476–503.

Arita, Isao, Nakane, Miyuki, & Fenner, Frank. (2006, May 12). Is polio eradication realistic? *Science, 312,* 852–854.

Armour-Thomas, Eleanor, & Gopaul-McNicol, Sharon-Ann. (1998). *Assessing intelligence: Applying a bio-cultural model*. Thousand Oaks, CA: Sage.

Armson, B. Anthony. (2007). Is planned cesarean childbirth a safe alternative? *Canadian Medical Association Journal 176,* 475–476.

Arnett, Jeffrey Jensen. (1999). Adolescent storm and stress, reconsidered. *American Psychologist, 54,* 317–326.

Arnett, Jeffrey Jensen. (2004). *Emerging adulthood: The winding road from the late teens through the twenties*. New York: Oxford University Press.

Arnett, Jeffrey Jensen. (2007a). Socialization in emerging adulthood: From the family to the wider world, from socialization to self-socialization. In Joan E. Grusec & Paul D. Hastings (Eds.), *Handbook of socialization: Theory and research* (pp. 208–231). New York: Guilford Press.

Arnett, Jeffrey Jensen. (2007b). Suffering, selfish, slackers? Myths and reality about emerging adults. *Journal of Youth and Adolescence, 36,* 23–29.

Artar, Müge. (2007). Adolescent egocentrism and theory of mind: In the context of family relations. *Social Behavior and Personality, 35,* 1211–1220.

Artman, Lavee, & Cahan, Sorel. (1993). Schooling and the development of transitive inference. *Developmental Psychology, 29,* 753–759.

Aseltine, Robert H., Jr., & DeMartino, Robert. (2004). An outcome evaluation of the SOS suicide prevention program. *American Journal of Public Health, 94,* 446–451.

Asendorpf, Jens B., Denissen, Jaap J. A., & van Aken, Marcel A. G. (2008). Inhibited and aggressive preschool children at 23 years of age: Personality and social transitions into adulthood. *Developmental Psychology, 44,* 997–1011.

Ash, Caroline, Jasny, Barbara R., Roberts, Leslie, Stone, Richard, &

Sugden, Andrew M. (2008, February 8). Reimagining cities. *Science, 319,* 739.

Ashman, Sharon B., & Dawson, Geraldine. (2002). Maternal depression, infant psychobiological development, and risk for depression. In Sherryl H. Goodman & Ian H. Gotlib (Eds.), *Children of depressed parents: Mechanisms of risk and implications for treatment* (pp. 37–58). Washington, DC: American Psychological Association.

Ashman, Sharon B., Dawson, Geraldine, & Panagiotides, Heracles. (2008). Trajectories of maternal depression over 7 years: Relations with child psychophysiology and behavior and role of contextual risks. *Development and Psychopathology, 20,* 55–77.

Aslin, Richard N., & Hunt, Ruskin H. (2001). Development, plasticity, and learning in the auditory system. In Charles A. Nelson & Monica Luciana (Eds.), *Handbook of developmental cognitive neuroscience* (pp. 149–158). Cambridge, MA: MIT Press.

Astington, Janet Wilde, & Gopnik, Alison. (1988). Knowing you've changed your mind: Children's understanding of representational change. In Janet W. Astington, Paul L. Harris, & David R. Olson (Eds.), *Developing theories of mind* (pp. 193–206). New York: Cambridge University Press.

Atkinson, Janette, & Braddick, Oliver. (2003). Neurobiological models of normal and abnormal visual development. In Michelle De Haan & Mark H. Johnson (Eds.), *The cognitive neuroscience of development* (pp. 43–71). New York: Psychology Press.

Audrey, Suzanne, Holliday, Jo, & Campbell, Rona. (2006). It's good to talk: Adolescent perspectives of an informal, peer-led intervention to reduce smoking. *Social Science & Medicine, 63,* 320–334.

Auger, Nathalie, Luo, Zhong-Cheng, Platt, Robert W., & Daniel, Mark. (2008). Do mother's education and foreign born status interact to influence birth outcomes? Clarifying the epidemiological paradox and the healthy migrant effect. *Journal of Epidemiology and Community Health, 62,* 402–409.

Aunola, Kaisa, & Nurmi, Jari-Erik. (2004). Maternal affection moderates the impact of psychological control on a child's mathematical performance. *Developmental Psychology, 40,* 965–978.

Austin, Marie-Paule, Leader, Leo R., & Reilly, Nicole. (2005). Prenatal stress, the hypothalamic-pituitary-adrenal axis, and fetal and infant neurobehaviour. *Early Human Development, 81,* 917–926.

Azar, Rima, Paquette, Daniel, Zoccolillo, Mark, Baltzer, Franziska, & Tremblay, Richard E. (2007). The association of major depression, conduct disorder, and maternal overcontrol with a failure to show a cortisol buffered response in 4-month-old infants of teenage mothers. *Biological Psychiatry, 62,* 573–579.

Azmitia, Margarita, Ittel, Angela, & Brenk, Charlotte. (2006). Latino-heritage adolescents' friendships. In Xinyin Chen, Doran C. French, & Barry H. Schneider (Eds.), *Peer relationships in cultural context* (pp. 426–451). New York: Cambridge University Press.

Azrin, Nathan H., & Foxx, Richard M. (1974). *Toilet training in less than a day.* New York: Simon and Schuster.

Bachman, Jerald G. (2002). *The decline of substance use in young adulthood: Changes in social activities, roles, and beliefs.* Mahwah, NJ: Erlbaum.

Bagla, Pallava. (2008, June 13). India's education bonanza instills hope—and concern. *Science, 320,* 1415.

Bagwell, Catherine L., Schmidt, Michelle E., Newcomb, Andrew F., & Bukowski, William M. (2001). Friendship and peer rejection as predictors of adult adjustment. In William Damon (Series Ed.) & Douglas W. Nangle & Cynthia A. Erdley (Vol. Eds.), *New directions for child and adolescent development: No. 91. The role of friendship in psychological adjustment* (pp. 25–49). San Francisco: Jossey-Bass.

Baillargeon, Renée. (1994). How do infants learn about the physical world? *Current Directions in Psychological Science, 3,* 133–140.

Baillargeon, Renée. (2000). How do infants learn about the physical world? In Darwin Muir & Alan Slater (Eds.), *Infant development: The essential readings* (pp. 195–212). Malden, MA: Blackwell.

Baillargeon, Renée, & DeVos, Julie. (1991). Object permanence in young infants: Further evidence. *Child Development, 62,* 1227–1246.

Baker, Jason K., Fenning, Rachel M., Crnic, Keith A., Baker, Bruce L., & Blacher, Jan. (2007). Prediction of social skills in 6-year-old children with and without developmental delays: Contributions of early regulation and maternal scaffolding. *American Journal on Mental Retardation, 112,* 375–391.

Baker, Jeffrey P. (2000). Immunization and the American way: 4 childhood vaccines. *American Journal of Public Health, 90,* 199–207.

Baker, Susan P. (2000). Where have we been and where are we going with injury control? In Dinesh Mohan & Geetam Tiwari (Eds.), *Injury prevention and control* (pp. 19–26). London: Taylor & Francis.

Baker, Timothy B., Japuntich, Sandra J., Hogle, Joanne M., McCarthy, Danielle E., & Curtin, John J. (2006). Pharmacologic and behavioral withdrawal from addictive drugs. *Current Directions in Psychological Science, 15,* 232–236.

Baldwin, Dare A. (1993). Infants' ability to consult the speaker for clues to word reference. *Journal of Child Language, 20,* 395–418.

Balmford, Andrew, Clegg, Lizzie, Coulson, Tim, & Taylor, Jennie. (2002, March 29). Why conservationists should heed Pokémon [Letter to the editor]. *Science, 295,* 2367.

Baltes, Paul B., Lindenberger, Ulman, & Staudinger, Ursula M. (2006). Life span theory in developmental psychology. In William Damon & Richard M. Lerner (Series Eds.) & Richard M. Lerner (Vol. Ed.), *Handbook of child psychology: Vol. 1. Theoretical models of human development* (6th ed., pp. 569–664). Hoboken, NJ: Wiley.

Bamford, Christi, & Lagattuta, Kristin H. (2007, April). *Children really do "talk to god": What children know about prayer and its emotional contexts.* Poster presented at the Society for Research in Child Development, Boston, MA.

Bandura, Albert. (1977). *Social learning theory.* Englewood Cliffs, NJ: Prentice Hall.

Bandura, Albert. (1986). *Social foundations of thought and action: A social cognitive theory.* Englewood Cliffs, NJ: Prentice-Hall.

Bandura, Albert. (1997). The anatomy of stages of change. *American Journal of Health Promotion, 12,* 8–10.

Bandura, Albert. (2006). Toward a psychology of human agency. *Perspectives on Psychological Science, 1,* 164–180.

Bandura, Albert, & Bussey, Kay. (2004). On broadening the cognitive, motivational, and sociostructural scope of theorizing about gender development and functioning: Comment on Martin, Ruble, and Szkrybalo (2002). *Psychological Bulletin, 130,* 691–701.

Banerjee, Robin, & Lintern, Vicki. (2000). Boys will be boys: The effect of social evaluation concerns on gender-typing. *Social Development, 9,* 397–408.

Bank, Lew, Burraston, Bert, & Snyder, Jim. (2004). Sibling conflict and ineffective parenting as predictors of adolescent boys' antisocial behavior and peer difficulties: Additive and interactional effects. *Journal of Research on Adolescence, 14,* 99–125.

Barbaree, Howard E., & Marshall, William L. (2006). *The juvenile sex offender* (2nd ed.). New York: Guilford Press.

Barber, Bonnie L. (2006). To have loved and lost . . . adolescent romantic relationships and rejection. In Ann C. Crouter & Alan Booth (Eds.), *Romance and sex in adolescence and emerging adulthood: Risks and opportunities* (pp. 29–40). Mahwah, NJ: Erlbaum.

Barber, Brian K. (Ed.). (2002). *Intrusive parenting: How psychological control affects children and adolescents.* Washington, DC: American Psychological Association.

Barbey, Aron K., & Sloman, Steven A. (2007). Base-rate respect: From ecological rationality to dual processes. *Behavioral and Brain Sciences, 30,* 241–254.

Barinaga, Marcia. (2003, January 3). Newborn neurons search for meaning. *Science, 299,* 32–34.

Barkin, Shari, Scheindlin, Benjamin, Ip, Edward H., Richardson, Irma, & Finch, Stacia. (2007). Determinants of parental discipline practices: A national sample from primary care practices. *Clinical Pediatrics, 46,* 64–69.

Barkley, Russell A. (2006). *Attention-deficit hyperactivity disorder: A handbook for diagnosis and treatment* (3rd ed.). New York: Guilford Press.

Barnard, Kathryn E., & Martell, Louise K. (1995). Mothering. In Marc H. Bornstein (Ed.), *Handbook of parenting: Vol. 3. Status and social conditions of parenting* (pp. 3–26). Hillsdale, NJ: Erlbaum.

Barnes, Grace M., Hoffman, Joseph H., Welte, John W., Farrell, Michael P., & Dintcheff, Barbara A. (2006). Effects of parental monitoring and peer deviance on substance use and delinquency. *Journal of Marriage and Family, 68,* 1084–1104.

Barnes, Jacqueline, Katz, Ilan Barry, Korbin, Jill E., & O'Brien, Margaret. (2006). *Children and families in communities: Theory, research, policy and practice.* Hoboken, NJ: Wiley.

Barnett, Kylie J., Finucane, Ciara, Asher, Julian E., Bargary, Gary, Corvin, Aiden P., Newell, Fiona N., et al. (2008). Familial patterns and the origins of individual differences in synaesthesia. *Cognition, 106,* 871–893.

Barnett, Mark, Watson, Ruth, & Kind, Peter. (2006). Pathways to barrel development. In Reha Erzurumlu, William Guido, & Zoltán Molnár (Eds.), *Development and plasticity in sensory thalamus and cortex* (pp. 138–157). New York: Springer.

Barnett, Rosalind C., & Rivers, Caryl. (2004). *Same difference: How gender myths are hurting our relationships, our children, and our jobs.* New York: Basic Books.

Baron, Andrew Scott, & Banaji, Mahzarin R. (2006). The development of implicit attitudes: Evidence of race evaluations from ages 6 and 10 and adulthood. *Psychological Science, 17,* 53–58.

Barrett, Karen Caplovitz. (2005). The origins of social emotions and self-regulation in toddlerhood: New evidence. *Cognition & Emotion, 19,* 953–979.

Barros, Fernando C., Victora, Cesar G., Barros, Aluisio J. D., Santos, Ina S., Albernaz, Elaine, Matijasevich, Alicia, et al. (2005). The challenge of reducing neonatal mortality in middle-income countries: Findings from three Brazilian birth cohorts in 1982, 1993, and 2004. *Lancet, 365,* 847–854.

Barry, Patrick. (2007, September 8). Genome 2.0: Mountains of new data are challenging old views. *Science News, 172,* 154.

Basu, Kaushik, & Van, Pham Hoang. (1998). The economics of child labor. *American Economic Review, 88,* 412–427.

Bateman, Belinda, Warner, John O., Hutchinson, Emma, Dean, Tara, Rowlandson, Piers, Gant, Carole, et al. (2004). The effects of a double blind, placebo controlled, artificial food colourings and benzoate preservative challenge on hyperactivity in a general population sample of preschool children. *Archives of Disease in Childhood, 89,* 506–511.

Bates, Elizabeth, Devescovi, Antonella, & Wulfeck, Beverly. (2001). Psycholinguistics: A cross-language perspective. *Annual Review of Psychology, 52,* 369–396.

Bates, Gillian, Harper, Peter S., & Jones, Lesley (Eds.). (2002). *Huntington's disease* (3rd ed.). Oxford, UK: Oxford University Press.

Bates, John E., Viken, Richard J., Alexander, Douglas B., Beyers, Jennifer, & Stockton, Lesley. (2002). Sleep and adjustment in preschool children: Sleep diary reports by mothers relate to behavior reports by teachers. *Child Development, 73,* 62–74.

Bates, Lisa M., Acevedo-Garcia, Dolores, Alegria, Margarita, & Krieger, Nancy. (2008). Immigration and generational trends in body mass index and obesity in the United States: Results of the National Latino and Asian American Survey, 2002–2003. *American Journal of Public Health, 98,* 70–77.

Bateson, Patrick. (2005, February 4). Desirable scientific conduct. *Science, 307,* 645.

Bauer, Patricia J. (2006). Event memory. In William Damon & Richard M. Lerner (Series Eds.) & Deanna Kuhn & Robert S. Siegler (Vol. Eds.), *Handbook of child psychology: Vol. 2. Cognition, perception, and language* (6th ed., pp. 373–425). Hoboken, NJ: Wiley.

Bauer, Patricia J. (2007). Recall in infancy: A neurodevelopmental account. *Current Directions in Psychological Science, 16,* 142–146.

Bauer, Patricia J., & Dow, Gina Annunziato. (1994). Episodic memory in 16- and 20-month-old children: Specifics are generalized but not forgotten. *Developmental Psychology, 30,* 403–417.

Bauer, Patricia J., Liebl, Monica, & Stennes, Leif. (1998). PRETTY is to DRESS as BRAVE is to SUITCOAT: Gender-based property-to-property inferences by 4-1/2-year-old children. *Merrill-Palmer Quarterly, 44,* 355–377.

Baum, Katrina. (2005). *Juvenile victimization and offending, 1993–2003* (NCJ 209468). Washington, DC: U.S. Department of Justice, Office of Justice Programs.

Baumeister, Roy F., & Blackhart, Ginnette C. (2007). Three perspectives on gender differences in adolescent sexual development. In Rutger C. M. E. Engels, Margaret Kerr, & Håkan Stattin (Eds.), *Friends, lovers, and groups: Key relationships in adolescence* (pp. 93–104). Hoboken, NJ: Wiley.

Baumeister, Roy F., Campbell, Jennifer D., Krueger, Joachim I., & Vohs, Kathleen D. (2003). Does high self-esteem cause better performance, interpersonal success, happiness, or healthier lifestyles? *Psychological Science in the Public Interest, 4,* 1–44.

Baumrind, Diana. (1967). Child care practices anteceding three patterns of preschool behavior. *Genetic Psychology Monographs, 75,* 43–88.

Baumrind, Diana. (1971). Current patterns of parental authority. *Developmental Psychology, 4*(1, Pt. 2), 1–103.

Baumrind, Diana. (1991). The influence of parenting style on adolescent competence and substance use. *Journal of Early Adolescence, 11,* 56–95.

Bayer, Jordana K., Hiscock, Harriet, Hampton, Anne, & Wake, Melissa. (2007). Sleep problems in young infants and maternal mental and physical health. *Journal of Paediatrics and Child Health, 43,* 66–73.

Beach, Steven R. H., Wamboldt, Marianne Z., Kaslow, Nadine J., Heyman, Richard E., First, Michael B., Underwood, Lynn G., et al. (2006). *Relational processes and DSM-V: Neuroscience, assessment, prevention, and treatment.* Washington, DC: American Psychiatric Association.

Bearce, Karen Hildreth, & Rovee-Collier, Carolyn. (2006). Repeated priming increases memory accessibility in infants. *Journal of Experimental Child Psychology, 93,* 357–376.

Bearman, Peter S., & Brückner, Hannah. (2001). Promising the future: Virginity pledges and first intercourse. *American Journal of Sociology, 106,* 859–912.

Bearman, Peter S., Moody, James, & Stovel, Katherine. (2004). Chains of affection: The structure of adolescent romantic and sexual networks. *American Journal of Sociology, 110,* 44–91.

Beaudoin, Kathleen M., & Schonert-Reichl, Kimberly A. (2006). Epistemic reasoning and adolescent egocentrism: Relations to internalizing and externalizing symptoms in problem youth. *Journal of Youth and Adolescence, 35,* 999–1014.

Beck, Martha Nibley. (1999). *Expecting Adam: A true story of birth, rebirth, and everyday magic.* New York: Times Books.

Becker, Jill B., Berkley, Karen J., Geary, Nori, Hampson, Elizabeth, Herman, James P., & Young, Elizabeth (Eds.). (2008). *Sex differences in the brain: From genes to behavior.* New York: Oxford University Press.

Behne, Tanya, Carpenter, Malinda, Call, Josep, & Tomasello, Michael. (2005). Unwilling versus unable: Infants' understanding of intentional action. *Developmental Psychology, 41,* 328–337.

Behrend, Douglas A., Scofield, Jason, & Kleinknecht, Erica E. (2001). Beyond fast mapping: Young children's extensions of novel words and novel facts. *Developmental Psychology, 37,* 698–705.

Beilin, Lawrence, & Huang, Rae-Chi. (2008). Childhood obesity, hypertension, the metabolic syndrome and adult cardiovascular disease. *Clinical and Experimental Pharmacology and Physiology, 35,* 409–411.

Belamarich, Peter, & Ayoob, Keith-Thomas. (2001). Keeping teenage vegetarians healthy and in the know. *Contemporary Pediatrics, 10,* 89–108.

Belfield, Clive R., Nores, Milagros, Barnett, Steve, & Schweinhart, Lawrence. (2006). The High/Scope Perry Preschool Program: Cost benefit analysis using data from the age-40 followup. *Journal of Human Resources, 41,* 162–190.

Belizan, José M., Althabe, Fernando, Barros, Fernando C., & Alexander, Sophie. (1999). Rates and implications of caesarean sections in Latin America: Ecological study. *British Medical Journal, 319,* 1397–1402.

Belka, David. (2004). Substituting skill learning for traditional games in early childhood. *Teaching Elementary Physical Education, 15,* 25–27.

Bell, Joanna H., & Bromnick, Rachel D. (2003). The social reality of the imaginary audience: A ground theory approach. *Adolescence, 38,* 205–219.

Bell, Ruth. (1998). *Changing bodies, changing lives: A book for teens on sex and relationships* (Expanded 3rd ed.). New York: Times Books.

Belsky, Jay. (2006). Determinants and consequences of infant-parent attachment. In Lawrence Balter & Catherine S. Tamis-LeMonda (Eds.), *Child psychology: A handbook of contemporary issues* (2nd ed., pp. 53–77). New York: Psychology Press.

Belsky, Jay, Bakermans-Kranenburg, Marian J., & van IJzendoorn, Marinus H. (2007). For better and for worse: Differential susceptibility to environmental influences. *Current Directions in Psychological Science, 16,* 300–304.

Bem, Sandra Lipsitz. (1993). *The lenses of gender: Transforming the debate on sexual inequality.* New Haven, CT: Yale University Press.

Ben-Itzchak, Esther, & Zachor, Ditza A. (2007). The effects of intellectual functioning and autism severity on outcome of early behavioral intervention for children with autism. *Research in Developmental Disabilities, 28,* 287–303.

Benacerraf, Beryl R. (2007). *Ultrasound of fetal syndromes* (2nd ed.). Philadelphia: Churchill Livingstone/Elsevier.

Benes, Francine M. (2001). The development of prefrontal cortex: The maturation of neurotransmitter systems and their interactions. In Charles A. Nelson & Monica Luciana (Eds.), *Handbook of developmental cognitive neuroscience* (pp. 79–92). Cambridge, MA: MIT Press.

Benjamin, Georges C. (2004). The solution is injury prevention. *American Journal of Public Health, 94,* 521.

Benjamin, Roger. (2003). *The coming transformation of the American university.* New York: Council for Aid to Education/An Independent Subsidiary of RAND.

Benner, Aprile D., & Graham, Sandra. (2007). Navigating the transition to multi-ethnic urban high schools: Changing ethnic congruence and adolescents' school-related affect. *Journal of Research on Adolescence, 17,* 207–220.

Benson, Peter L. (2003). Developmental assets and asset-building community: Conceptual and empirical foundations. In Richard M. Lerner & Peter L. Benson (Eds.), *Developmental assets and asset-building communities: Implications for research, policy, and practice* (pp. 19–43). New York: Kluwer/Plenum.

Bentley, Gillian R., & Mascie-Taylor, C. G. Nicholas. (2000). Introduction. In Gillian R. Bentley & C. G. Nicholas Mascie-Taylor (Eds.), *Infertility in the modern world: Present and future prospects* (pp. 1–13). Cambridge, England: Cambridge University Press.

Bentley, Tanya G. K., Willett, Walter C., Weinstein, Milton C., & Kuntz, Karen M. (2006). Population-level changes in folate intake by age, gender, and race/ethnicity after folic acid fortification. *American Journal of Public Health, 96,* 2040–2047.

Beppu, Satoshi. (2005). Social cognitive development of autistic children: Attachment relationships and understanding the existence of minds of others. In David W. Shwalb, Jun Nakazawa, & Barbara J. Shwalb (Eds.), *Applied developmental psychology: Theory, practice, and research from Japan* (pp. 199–221). Greenwich, CT: Information Age.

Berenbaum, Sheri A., Martin, Carol Lynn, Hanish, Laura D., Briggs, Phillip T., & Fabes, Richard A. (2008). Sex differences in children's play. In Jill B. Becker, Karen J. Berkley, Nori Geary, Elizabeth Hampson, James P. Herman, & Elizabeth Young (Eds.), *Sex differences in the brain: From genes to behavior* (pp. 275–290). New York: Oxford University Press.

Berg, Sandra J., & Wynne-Edwards, Katherine E. (2002). Salivary hormone concentrations in mothers and fathers becoming parents are not correlated. *Hormones & Behavior, 42,* 424–436.

Berger, Kathleen Stassen. (2007). Update on bullying at school: Science forgotten? *Developmental Review, 27,* 90–126.

Bering, Jesse M., & Bjorklund, David F. (2004). The natural emergence of reasoning about the afterlife as a developmental regularity. *Developmental Psychology, 40,* 217–233.

Bering, Jesse M., Blasi, Carlos Hernández, & Bjorklund, David F. (2005). The development of 'afterlife' beliefs in religiously and secularly schooled children. *British Journal of Developmental Psychology, 23,* 587–607.

Berkey, Catherine S., Gardner, Jane D., Frazier, A. Lindsay, & Colditz, Graham A. (2000). Relation of childhood diet and body size to menarche and adolescent growth in girls. *American Journal of Epidemiology, 152,* 446–452.

Berkowitz, Alan D. (2005). An overview of the social norms approach. In Linda Costigan Lederman & Lea Stewart (Eds.), *Changing the culture of college drinking: A socially situated health communication campaign* (pp. 193–214). Cresskill, NJ: Hampton Press.

Berman, Alan L., Jobes, David A., & Silverman, Morton M. (2006). *Adolescent suicide: Assessment and intervention* (2nd ed.). Washington, DC: American Psychological Association.

Berndt, Thomas J., & Murphy, Lonna M. (2002). Influences of friends and friendships: Myths, truths, and research recommendations. In Robert V. Kail (Ed.), *Advances in child development and behavior* (Vol. 30, pp. 275–310). San Diego, CA: Academic Press.

Berninger, Virginia Wise, & Richards, Todd L. (2002). *Brain literacy for educators and psychologists.* Amsterdam: Academic Press.

Bhattacharjee, Yudhijit. (2008, February 8). Choking on fumes, Kolkata faces a noxious future. *Science, 319,* 749.

Bialystok, Ellen. (2001). *Bilingualism in development: Language, literacy, and cognition.* New York: Cambridge University Press.

Bialystok, Ellen. (2007). Acquisition of literacy in bilingual children: A framework for research. *Language Learning,* 57(Suppl. 1), 45–77.

Biehl, Michael C., Natsuaki, Misaki N., & Ge, Xiaojia. (2007). The influence of pubertal timing on alcohol use and heavy drinking trajectories. *Journal of Youth and Adolescence, 36,* 153–167.

Bienvenu, Thierry. (2005). Rett syndrome. In Merlin Gene Butler & F. John Meaney (Eds.), *Genetics of developmental disabilities* (pp. 477–519). Boca Raton, FL: Taylor & Francis.

Birch, Susan A. J., & Bloom, Paul. (2003). Children are cursed: An asymmetric bias in mental-state attribution. *Psychological Science, 14,* 283–286.

Birdsong, David. (2006). Age and second language acquisition and processing: A selective overview. *Language Learning,* 56(Suppl. 1), 9–49.

Birney, Damian P., Citron-Pousty, Jill H., Lutz, Donna J., & Sternberg, Robert J. (2005). The development of cognitive and intellectual abilities. In Marc H. Bornstein & Michael E. Lamb (Eds.), *Developmental science: An advanced textbook* (5th ed., pp. 327–358). Mahwah, NJ: Erlbaum.

Biro, Frank M., McMahon, Robert P., Striegel-Moore, Ruth, Crawford, Patricia B., Obarzanek, Eva, Morrison, John A., et al. (2001). Impact of timing of pubertal maturation on growth in black and white female adolescents: The National Heart, Lung, and Blood Institute Growth and Health Study. *Journal of Pediatrics, 138,* 636–643.

Biro, Frank M., Striegel-Moore, Ruth H., Franko, Debra L., Padgett, Justina, & Bean, Judy A. (2006). Self-esteem in adolescent females. *Journal of Adolescent Health, 39,* 501–507.

Black, Corri, Kaye, James A., & Jick, Hershel. (2005). Cesarean delivery in the United Kingdom: Time trends in the General Practice Research Database. *Obstetrics & Gynecology, 106,* 151–155.

Blair, Clancy, Knipe, Hilary, Cummings, Eric, Baker, David P., Gamson, David, Eslinger, Paul, et al. (2007). A developmental neuroscience approach to the study of school readiness. In Robert C. Pianta, Martha J. Cox, & Kyle L. Snow (Eds.), *School readiness and the transition to kindergarten in the era of accountability* (pp. 149–174). Baltimore: Brookes.

Blair, Peter S., & Ball, Helen L. (2004). The prevalence and characteristics associated with parent–infant bed-sharing in England. *Archives of Disease in Childhood, 89,* 1106–1110.

Blakemore, Sarah-Jayne. (2008). Development of the social brain during adolescence. *The Quarterly Journal of Experimental Psychology, 61,* 40–49.

Blatchford, Peter. (2003). *The class size debate: Is small better?* Maidenhead, Berkshire, England: Open University.

Block, Lauren G., Morwitz, Vicki G., Putsis, William P., Jr., & Sen, Subrata K. (2002). Assessing the impact of antidrug advertising on adolescent drug consumption: Results from a behavioral economic model. *American Journal of Public Health, 92,* 1346–1351.

Blonigen, Daniel M., Carlson, Marie D., Hicks, Brian M., Krueger, Robert F., & Iacono, William G. (2008). Stability and change in personality traits from late adolescence to early adulthood: A longitudinal twin study. *Journal of Personality, 76,* 229–266.

Bloom, Lois. (1993). *The transition from infancy to language: Acquiring the power of expression.* New York: Cambridge University Press.

Bloom, Lois. (1998). Language acquisition in its developmental context. In William Damon (Series Ed.) & Deanna Kuhn & Robert S. Siegler (Vol. Eds.), *Handbook of child psychology: Vol. 2. Cognition, perception, and language* (5th ed., pp. 309–370). New York: Wiley.

Bloom, Lois. (2000). Pushing the limits on theories of word learning. *Monographs of the Society for Research in Child Development,* 65(3, Serial No. 262), 124–135.

Blum, Deborah. (2002). *Love at Goon Park: Harry Harlow and the science of affection.* Cambridge, MA: Perseus.

Blum, Nathan J., Taubman, Bruce, & Nemeth, Nicole. (2003). Relationship between age at initiation of toilet training and duration of training: A prospective study. *Pediatrics, 111*(4, Pt. 1), 810–814.

Blum, Robert W., Beuhring, Trisha, Shew, Marcia L., Bearinger, Linda H., Sieving, Renee E., & Resnick, Michael D. (2000). The effects of race/ethnicity, income, and family structure on adolescent risk behaviors. *American Journal of Public Health, 90,* 1879–1884.

Blum, Robert Wm., & Nelson-Mmari, Kristin. (2004). Adolescent health from an international perspective. In Richard M. Lerner & Laurence D. Steinberg (Eds.), *Handbook of adolescent psychology* (2nd ed., pp. 553–586). Hoboken, NJ: Wiley.

Blurton-Jones, Nicholas G. (1976). Rough-and-tumble play among nursery school children. In Jerome S. Bruner, Alison Jolly, & Kathy Sylva (Eds.), *Play: Its role in development and evolution* (pp. 352–363). New York: Basic Books.

Bodrova, Elena, & Leong, Deborah J. (2005). High quality preschool programs: What would Vygotsky say? *Early Education and Development, 16,* 435–444.

Boehnke, Klaus. (2008). Peer pressure: A cause of scholastic underachievement? A cross-cultural study of mathematical achievement among German, Canadian, and Israeli middle school students. *Social Psychology of Education, 11,* 149–160.

Boles, David B., Barth, Joan M., & Merrill, Edward C. (2008). Asymmetry and performance: Toward a neurodevelopmental theory. *Brain and Cognition, 66,* 124–139.

Bonell, Chris, Allen, Elizabeth, Strange, Vicki, Oakley, Ann, Copas, Andrew, Johnson, Anne, et al. (2006). Influence of family type and parenting behaviours on teenage sexual behaviour and conceptions. *Journal of Epidemiology & Community Health, 60,* 502–506.

Bonner, Barbara L., Crow, Sheila M., & Logue, Mary Beth. (1999). Fatal child neglect. In Howard Dubowitz (Ed.), *Neglected children: Research, practice, and policy* (pp. 156–173). Thousand Oaks, CA: Sage.

Borke, Jörn, Lamm, Bettina, Eickhorst, Andreas, & Keller, Heidi. (2007). Father–infant interaction, paternal ideas about early child care, and their consequences for the development of children's self-recognition. *Journal of Genetic Psychology, 168,* 365–379.

Borkowski, John G., Farris, Jaelyn Renee, Whitman, Thomas L., Carothers, Shannon S., Weed, Keri, & Keogh, Deborah A. (2007). *Risk and resilience: Adolescent mothers and their children grow up.* Mahwah, NJ: Erlbaum.

Borland, Moira. (1998). *Middle childhood: The perspectives of children and parents.* London: Jessica Kingsley.

Bornstein, Marc H. (2002). Parenting infants. In Marc H. Bornstein (Ed.), *Handbook of parenting: Vol. 1. Children and parenting* (2nd ed., pp. 3–43). Mahwah, NJ: Erlbaum.

Bornstein, Marc H. (2006). Parenting science and practice. In William Damon & Richard M. Lerner (Series Eds.) & K. Ann Renninger & Irving E. Sigel (Vol. Eds.), *Handbook of child psychology: Vol. 4. Child psychology in practice* (6th ed., pp. 893–949). Hoboken, NJ: Wiley.

Bornstein, Marc H., Arterberry, Martha E., & Mash, Clay. (2005). Perceptual development. In Marc H. Bornstein & Michael E. Lamb (Eds.), *Developmental science: An advanced textbook* (5th ed., pp. 283–325). Mahwah, NJ: Erlbaum.

Bornstein, Marc H., Cote, Linda R., Maital, Sharone, Painter, Kathleen, Park, Sung-Yun, Pascual, Liliana, et al. (2004). Cross-linguistic analysis of vocabulary in young children: Spanish, Dutch, French, Hebrew, Italian, Korean, and American English. *Child Development, 75,* 1115–1139.

Bornstein, Marc H., & Lamb, Michael E. (2005). *Developmental science: An advanced textbook* (5th ed.). Mahwah, NJ: Erlbaum.

Bortz, Walter M. (2005). Biological basis of determinants of health. *American Journal of Public Health, 95,* 389–392.

Borzekowski, Dina L. G., & Rickert, Vaughn I. (2001). Adolescents, the internet, and health: Issues of access and content. *Journal of Applied Developmental Psychology, 22,* 49–59.

Bos, Henny M. W., Sandfort, Theo G. M., de Bruyn, Eddy H., & Hakvoort, Esther M. (2008). Same sex attraction, social relationships, psychosocial functioning, and school performance in early adolescence. *Developmental Psychology, 44,* 59–68.

Bossé, Yohan, & Hudson, Thomas J. (2007). Toward a comprehensive set of asthma susceptibility genes. *Annual Review of Medicine, 58,* 171–184.

Botto, Lorenzo D., Lisi, Alessandra, Robert Gnansia, Elisabeth, Erickson, J. David, Vollset, Stein Emil, Mastroiacovo, Pierpaolo, et al. (2005, March 12). *International retrospective cohort study of neural tube defects in relation to folic acid recommendations: Are the recommendations working?* Retrieved September 7, 2008, from the World Wide Web: http://www.bmj.com/cgi/content/abstract/330/7491/571

Botto, Lorenzo D., Olney, Richard S., & Erickson, J. David. (2004). Vitamin supplements and the risk for congenital anomalies other than neural tube defects. *American Journal of Medical Genetics Part C: Seminars in Medical Genetics, 125C,* 12–21.

Bouchard, Thomas J., Segal, Nancy L., Tellegen, Auke, McGue, Matt, Keyes, Margaret, & Krueger, Robert. (2004). Genetic influence on social attitudes: Another challenge to psychology from behavior genetics. In Lisabeth F. DiLalla (Ed.), *Behavior genetics principles: Perspectives in development, personality, and psychopathology* (pp. 89–104). Washington, DC: American Psychological Association.

Bousquet, Jean, Dahl, Ronald, & Khaltaev, Nikolai. (2007). Global alliance against chronic respiratory diseases. *Allergy, 62,* 216–223.

Bower, Bruce. (2006, August 12). Outside looking in: Researchers open new windows on Asperger syndrome and related disorders. *Science News, 170,* 106.

Bowlby, John. (1969). *Attachment and loss: Vol. 1. Attachment.* New York: Basic Books.

Bowlby, John. (1973). *Attachment and loss: Vol. 2. Separation: Anxiety and anger.* New York: Basic Books.

Bowlby, John. (1988). *A secure base: Clinical applications of attachment theory.* London: Routledge.

Boyce, W. Thomas, Essex, Marilyn J., Alkon, Abbey, Goldsmith, H. Hill, Kraemer, Helena C., & Kupfer, David J. (2006). Early father involvement moderates biobehavioral susceptibility to mental health problems in middle childhood. *Journal of the American Academy of Child and Adolescent Psychiatry, 45,* 1510–1520.

Boyd, William L. (2007). The politics of privatization in American education. *Educational Policy, 21,* 7–14.

Bradley, Robert H., & Corwyn, Robert F. (2005). Productive activity and the prevention of behavior problems. *Developmental Psychology, 41,* 89–98.

Branca, Francesco, Nikogosian, Haik, & Lobstein, Tim (Eds.). (2007). *The challenge of obesity in the WHO European Region and the strategies for response.* Copenhagen, Denmark: WHO Regional Office for Europe.

Brazelton, T. Berry, & Sparrow, Joshua D. (2006). *Touchpoints: Birth to 3: Your child's emotional and behavioral development* (2nd ed.). Cambridge, MA: Da Capo Press.

Breggin, Peter R., & Baughman, Fred A., Jr. (2001, January 26). Questioning the treatment for ADHD [Letter to the editor]. *Science, 291,* 595.

Brendgen, Mara, Vitaro, Frank, Bukowski, William M., Doyle, Anna Beth, & Markiewicz, Dorothy. (2001). Developmental profiles of peer social preference over the course of elementary school: Associations with trajectories of externalizing and internalizing behavior. *Developmental Psychology, 37,* 308–320.

Brennan, Patricia A., Grekin, Emily R., & Mednick, Sarnoff A. (2003). Prenatal and perinatal influences on conduct disorder and serious delinquency. In Benjamin B. Lahey, Terrie E. Moffitt, & Avshalom Caspi (Eds.), *Causes of conduct disorder and juvenile delinquency* (pp. 319–341). New York: Guilford Press.

Brenner, Ruth A., Trumble, Ann C., Smith, Gordon S., Kessler, Eileen P., & Overpeck, Mary D. (2001). Where children drown, United States, 1995. *Pediatrics, 108,* 85–89.

Bretherton, Inge, & Munholland, Kristine A. (1999). Internal working models in attachment relationships: A construct revisited. In Jude Cassidy & Phillip R. Shaver (Eds.), *Handbook of attachment: Theory, research, and clinical applications* (pp. 89–111). New York: Guilford Press.

Breunlin, Douglas C., Bryant-Edwards, Tara L., Hetherington, Joshua S., & Cimmarusti, Rocco A. (2002). Conflict resolution training as an alternative to suspension for violent behavior. *Journal of Educational Research, 95,* 349–357.

Brewster, Karin L., & Tillman, Kathryn Harker. (2008). Who's doing it? Patterns and predictors of youths' oral sexual experiences. *Journal of Adolescent Health, 42,* 73–80.

Brickhouse, Tegwyn H., Rozier, R. Gary, & Slade, Gary D. (2008). Effects of enrollment in Medicaid versus the State Children's Health Insurance Program on kindergarten children's untreated dental caries. *American Journal of Public Health, 98,* 876–881.

Bridge, Jeffrey A., Iyengar, Satish, Salary, Cheryl B., Barbe, Remy P., Birmaher, Boris, Pincus, Harold Alan, et al. (2007). Clinical response and risk for reported suicidal ideation and suicide attempts in pediatric antidepressant treatment: A meta-analysis of randomized controlled trials. *Journal of the American Medical Association, 297,* 1683–1696.

Briley, Mike, & Sulser, Fridolin (Eds.). (2001). *Molecular genetics of mental disorders: The place of molecular genetics in basic mechanisms and clinical applications in mental disorders.* London: Martin Dunitz.

Brindis, Claire D. (2006). A public health success: Understanding policy changes related to teen sexual activity and pregnancy. *Annual Review of Public Health, 27,* 277–295.

Brody, Gene H. (2004). Siblings' direct and indirect contributions to child development. *Current Directions in Psychological Science, 13,* 124–126.

Broidy, Lisa M., Nagin, Daniel S., Tremblay, Richard E., Bates, John E., Brame, Bobby, Dodge, Kenneth A., et al. (2003). Developmental trajectories of childhood disruptive behaviors and adolescent delinquency: A six-site, cross-national study. *Developmental Psychology, 39,* 222–245.

Bronfenbrenner, Urie. (1977). Toward an experimental ecology of human development. *American Psychologist, 32,* 513–531.

Bronfenbrenner, Urie, & Morris, Pamela A. (2006). The bioecological model of human development. In William Damon & Richard M. Lerner (Series Eds.) & Richard M. Lerner (Vol. Ed.), *Handbook of child psychology: Vol. 1. Theoretical models of human development* (6th ed., pp. 793–828). Hoboken, NJ: Wiley.

Bronte-Tinkew, Jacinta, Moore, Kristin A., Matthews, Gregory, & Carrano, Jennifer. (2007). Symptoms of major depression in a sample of fathers of infants: Sociodemographic correlates and links to father involvement. *Journal of Family Issues, 28,* 61–99.

Brooker, Robert J. (2009). *Genetics: Analysis & principles* (3rd ed.). New York: McGraw-Hill.

Brown, B. Bradford. (2004). Adolescents' relationships with peers. In Richard M. Lerner & Laurence D. Steinberg (Eds.), *Handbook of adolescent psychology* (2nd ed., pp. 363–394). Hoboken, NJ: Wiley.

Brown, B. Bradford. (2005). Moving forward with research on adolescence: Some reflections on the state of JRA and the state of the field. *Journal of Research on Adolescence, 15,* 657–673.

Brown, B. Bradford. (2006). A few "course corrections" to Collins & van Dulmen's "The course of true love". In Ann C. Crouter & Alan Booth (Eds.), *Romance and sex in adolescence and emerging adulthood: Risks and opportunities* (pp. 113–123). Mahwah, NJ: Erlbaum.

Brown, B. Bradford, & Klute, Christa. (2003). Friendships, cliques, and crowds. In Gerald R. Adams & Michael D. Berzonsky (Eds.), *Blackwell handbook of adolescence* (pp. 330–348). Malden, MA: Blackwell.

Brown, B. Bradford, & Larson, Reed W. (2002). The kaleidoscope of adolescence: Experiences of the world's youth at the beginning of the 21st century. In B. Bradford Brown, Reed W. Larson, & T. S. Saraswathi (Eds.), *The world's youth: Adolescence in eight regions of the globe* (pp. 1–20). New York: Cambridge University Press.

Brown, Christia Spears, & Bigler, Rebecca S. (2005). Children's perceptions of discrimination: A developmental model. *Child Development, 76,* 533–553.

Brown, Kathryn. (2003, March 14). The medication merry-go-round. *Science, 299,* 1646–1649.

Brown, Sandra A., Tapert, Susan F., Granholm, Eric, & Delis, Dean C. (2000). Neurocognitive functioning of adolescents: Effects of protracted alcohol use. *Alcoholism: Clinical and Experimental Research, 24,* 164–171.

Brown, Susan L. (2004). Family structure and child well-being: The significance of parental cohabitation. *Journal of Marriage and Family, 66,* 351–367.

Bruck, Maggie, Ceci, Stephen J., & Principe, Gabrielle F. (2006). The child and the law. In William Damon & Richard M. Lerner (Series Eds.) & K. Ann Renninger & Irving E. Sigel (Vol. Eds.), *Handbook of child psychology: Vol. 4. Child psychology in practice* (6th ed., pp. 776–816). Hoboken, NJ: Wiley.

Brückner, Hannah, & Bearman, Peter. (2005). After the promise: The STD consequences of adolescent virginity pledges. *Journal of Adolescent Health, 36,* 271–278.

Bruer, John T. (1999). *The myth of the first three years: A new understanding of early brain development and lifelong learning.* New York: Free Press.

Bryant, Brenda K., & Donnellan, M. Brent. (2007). The relation between socioeconomic status concerns and angry peer conflict resolution is moderated by pet provisions of support. *Anthrozoös, 20,* 213–223.

Bryant, Gregory A., & Barrett, H. Clark. (2007). Recognizing intentions in infant-directed speech: Evidence for universals. *Psychological Science, 18,* 746–751.

Buckhalt, Joseph A., El-Sheikh, Mona, & Keller, Peggy. (2007). Children's sleep and cognitive functioning: Race and socioeconomic status as moderators of effects. *Child Development, 78,* 213–231.

Buckner, John C., Bassuk, Ellen L., Weinreb, Linda F., & Brooks, Margaret G. (1999). Homelessness and its relation to the mental health and behavior of low-income school-age children. *Developmental Psychology, 35,* 246–257.

Buehler, Cheryl. (2006). Parents and peers in relation to early adolescent problem behavior. *Journal of Marriage and Family, 68,* 109–121.

Buehler, Cheryl, & Gerard, Jean M. (2002). Marital conflict, ineffective parenting, and children's and adolescents' maladjustment. *Journal of Marriage & Family, 64,* 78–92.

Buelga, Sofia, Ravenna, Marcella, Musitu, Gonzalo, & Lila, Marisol. (2006). Epidemiology and psychosocial risk factors associated with adolescent drug consumption. In Sandy Jackson & Luc Goossens (Eds.), *Handbook of adolescent development* (pp. 337–364). Hove, East Sussex, UK: Psychology Press.

Bugental, Daphne Blunt, & Grusec, Joan E. (2006). Socialization theory. In William Damon & Richard M. Lerner (Series Eds.) & Nancy Eisenberg (Vol. Ed.), *Handbook of child psychology: Vol. 3. Social, emotional, and personality development* (6th ed., pp. 366–428). Hoboken, NJ: Wiley.

Bugental, Daphne Blunt, & Happaney, Keith. (2004). Predicting infant maltreatment in low-income families: The interactive effects of maternal attributions and child status at birth. *Developmental Psychology, 40,* 234–243.

Bukowski, William M., & Adams, Ryan. (2006). Peers and culture: Details, local knowledge, and essentials. In Xinyin Chen, Doran C. French, & Barry H. Schneider (Eds.), *Peer relationships in cultural context* (pp. 481–486). New York: Cambridge University Press.

Bukowski, William M., Newcomb, Andrew F., & Hartup, Willard W. (Eds.). (1996). *The company they keep: Friendship in childhood and adolescence.* New York: Cambridge University Press.

Bulik, Cynthia M., Thornton, Laura, Pinheiro, Andréa Poyastro, Plotnicov, Katherine, Klump, Kelly L., Brandt, Harry, et al. (2008). Suicide attempts in anorexia nervosa. *Psychosomatic Medicine, 70,* 378–383.

Bumpass, Larry, & Lu, Hsien-Hen. (2000). Trends in cohabitation and implications for children's family contexts in the United States. *Population Studies, 54,* 29–41.

Burkitt, Esther. (2004). Drawing conclusions from children's art. *The Psychologist, 17,* 566–568.

Burton, Sarah, & Mitchell, Peter. (2003). Judging who knows best about yourself: Developmental change in citing the self across middle childhood. *Child Development, 74,* 426–443.

Buss, David M., Haselton, Martie G., Shackelford, Todd K., Bleske, April L., & Wakefield, Jerome C. (1998). Adaptations, exaptations, and spandrels. *American Psychologist, 53,* 533–548.

Busse, William W., & Lemanske, Robert F. (Eds.). (2005). *Lung biology in health and disease: Vol. 195. Asthma prevention.* Boca Raton, FL: Taylor & Francis.

Bussey, Kay, & Bandura, Albert. (1999). Social cognitive theory of gender development and differentiation. *Psychological Review, 106,* 676–713.

Butler, Merlin Gene, & Meaney, F. John. (2005). *Genetics of developmental disabilities.* Boca Raton, FL: Taylor & Francis.

Buzsáki, György. (2006). *Rhythms of the brain.* Oxford, UK: Oxford University Press.

Byard, Roger W. (2004). *Sudden death in infancy, childhood, and adolescence* (2nd ed.). Cambridge, England: Cambridge University Press.

Byng-Hall, John. (2008). The significance of children fulfilling parental roles: Implications for family therapy. *Journal of Family Therapy, 30,* 147–162.

Byram, Michael S., & Feng, Anwei. (2005). Teaching and researching intercultural competence. In Eli Hinkel (Ed.), *Handbook of research in second language teaching and learning* (pp. 911–930). Mahwah, NJ: Erlbaum.

Cabrera, Natasha J., Shannon, Jacqueline D., West, Jerry, & Brooks-Gunn, Jeanne. (2006). Parental interactions with Latino infants: Variation by country of origin and English proficiency. *Child Development, 77,* 1190–1207.

Cain, Daphne S., & Combs-Orme, Terri. (2005). Family structure effects on parenting stress and practices in the African American family. *Journal of Sociology & Social Welfare, 32,* 19–40.

Cairns, Robert B., & Cairns, Beverley D. (2001). Aggression and attachment: The folly of separatism. In Arthur C. Bohart & Deborah J. Stipek (Eds.), *Constructive & destructive behavior: Implications for family, school, & society* (pp. 21–47). Washington, DC: American Psychological Association.

Cairns, Robert B., & Cairns, Beverley D. (2006). The making of developmental psychology. In William Damon & Richard M. Lerner (Series Eds.) & Richard M. Lerner (Vol. Ed.), *Handbook of child psychology: Vol. 1. Theoretical models of human development* (6th ed., pp. 89–165). Hoboken, NJ: Wiley.

Calevo, Maria Grazia, Mezzano, P., Zullino, E., Padovani, P., & Serra, G. (2007). Ligurian experience on neonatal hearing screening. Clinical and epidemiological aspects. *Acta Pædiatrica, 96,* 1592–1599.

Callaghan, Tara, Rochat, Philippe, Lillard, Angeline, Claux, Mary Louise, Odden, Hal, Itakura, Shoji, et al. (2005). Synchrony in the onset of mental-state reasoning: Evidence from five cultures. *Psychological Science, 16,* 378–384.

Callaghan, Tara C., Rochat, Philippe, MacGillivray, Tanya, & MacLellan, Crystal. (2004). Modeling referential actions in 6- to 18-month-old infants: A precursor to symbolic understanding. *Child Development, 75,* 1733–1744.

Calvert, Karin. (2003). Patterns of childrearing in America. In Willem Koops & Michael Zuckerman (Eds.), *Beyond the century of the child: Cultural history and developmental psychology* (pp. 62–81). Baltimore: University of Pennsylvania Press.

Calvo-Merino, Beatriz, Glaser, Daniel E., Grèzes, Julie, Passingham, Richard E., & Haggard, Patrick. (2005). Action observation and acquired motor skills. An fMRI study with expert dancers. *Cerebral Cortex, 15,* 1243–1249.

Camarata, Stephen, & Woodcock, Richard. (2006). Sex differences in processing speed: Developmental effects in males and females. *Intelligence, 34,* 231–252.

Cameron, Judy, & Pierce, W. David. (2002). *Rewards and intrinsic motivation: Resolving the controversy.* Westport, CT: Bergin & Garvey.

Cameron, Judy L. (2004). Interrelationships between hormones, behavior, and affect during adolescence: Understanding hormonal, physical, and brain changes occurring in association with pubertal activation of the reproductive axis. Introduction to Part III. In Ronald E. Dahl & Linda Patia Spear (Eds.), *Adolescent brain development: Vulnerabilities and opportunities* (Vol. 1021, pp. 110–123). New York: New York Academy of Sciences.

Cameron, Lindsey, Rutland, Adam, Brown, Rupert, & Douch, Rebecca. (2006). Changing children's intergroup attitudes toward refugees: Testing different models of extended contact. *Child Development, 77,* 1208–1219.

Camilli, Gregory, Vargas, Sadako, & Yurecko, Michele. (2003). Teaching children to read: The fragile link between science and federal education policy. *Education Policy Analysis Archives, 11,* 1–52.

Campaign for Fiscal Equity v. State of New York, 719 N.Y.S.2d 475 (2001).

Campbell, Frances A., Pungello, Elizabeth P., Miller-Johnson, Shari, Burchinal, Margaret, & Ramey, Craig T. (2001). The development of cognitive and academic abilities: Growth curves from an early childhood educational experiment. *Developmental Psychology, 37,* 231–242.

Canli, Turhan. (2006). *Biology of personality and individual differences.* New York: Guilford Press.

Cantor-Graae, Elizabeth, & Selten, Jean-Paul. (2005). Schizophrenia and migration: A meta-analysis and review. *American Journal of Psychiatry, 162,* 12–24.

Caprara, Gian Vittorio, Barbaranelli, Claudio, & Pastorelli, Concetta. (2001). Prosocial behavior and aggression in childhood and pre-adolescence. In Arthur C. Bohart & Deborah J. Stipek (Eds.), *Constructive & destructive behavior: Implications for family, school, & society* (pp. 187–203). Washington, DC: American Psychological Association.

Caretta, Carla Mucignat, Caretta, Antonio, & Cavaggioni, Andrea. (1995). Pheromonally accelerated puberty is enhanced by previous experience of the same stimulus. *Physiology & Behavior, 57,* 901–903.

Carey, Susan. (1985). *Conceptual change in childhood.* Cambridge, MA: MIT Press.

Carlo, Mara S., August, Diane, McLaughlin, Barry, Snow, Catherine E., Dressler, Cheryl, Lippman, David N., et al. (2004). Closing the gap: Addressing the vocabulary needs of English-language learners in bilingual and mainstream classrooms. *Reading Research Quarterly, 39,* 188–215.

Carlson, Marcia J., & Corcoran, Mary E. (2001). Family structure and children's behavioral and cognitive outcomes. *Journal of Marriage & the Family, 63,* 779–792.

Carlson, Stephanie M. (2003). Executive function in context: Development, measurement, theory and experience. *Monographs of the Society for Research in Child Development,* 68(3, Serial No. 274), 138–151.

Carlson, Stephanie M., & Meltzoff, Andrew N. (2008). Bilingual experience and executive functioning in young children. *Developmental Science, 11,* 282–298.

Carlson, Susan A., Fulton, Janet E., Lee, Sarah M., Maynard, L. Michele, Brown, David R., Kohl, Harold W., III, et al. (2008). Physical education and academic achievement in elementary school: Data from the early childhood longitudinal study. *American Journal of Public Health, 98,* 721–727.

Carskadon, Mary A. (2002a). Factors influencing sleep patterns of adolescents. In Mary A. Carskadon (Ed.), *Adolescent sleep patterns: Biological, social, and psychological influences* (pp. 4–26). New York: Cambridge University Press.

Carskadon, Mary A. (2002b). Risks of driving while sleepy in adolescents and young adults. In Mary A. Carskadon (Ed.), *Adolescent sleep patterns: Biological, social, and psychological influences* (pp. 148–158). New York: Cambridge University Press.

Case-Smith, Jane, & Kuhaneck, Heather Miller. (2008). Play preferences of typically developing children and children with developmental delays between ages 3 and 7 years. *OTJR: Occupation, Participation and Health, 28,* 19–29.

Casey, Patrick H., Whiteside-Mansell, Leanne, Barrett, Kathleen, Bradley, Robert H., & Gargus, Regina. (2006). Impact of prenatal and/or postnatal growth problems in low birth weight preterm infants on school-age outcomes: An 8-year longitudinal evaluation. *Pediatrics, 118,* 1078–1086.

Caspi, Avshalom. (2000). The child is father of the man: Personality continuities from childhood to adulthood. *Journal of Personality and Social Psychology, 78,* 158–172.

Caspi, Avshalom, McClay, Joseph, Moffitt, Terrie, Mill, Jonathan, Martin, Judy, Craig, Ian W., et al. (2002, August 2). Role of genotype in the cycle of violence in maltreated children. *Science, 297,* 851–854.

Caspi, Avshalom, Moffitt, Terrie E., Morgan, Julia, Rutter, Michael, Taylor, Alan, Arseneault, Louise, et al. (2004). Maternal expressed emotion predicts children's antisocial behavior problems: Using monozygotic-twin differences to identify environmental effects on behavioral development. *Developmental Psychology, 40,* 149–161.

Caspi, Avshalom, Moffitt, Terrie E., Thornton, Arland, Freedman, Deborah, Amell, James W., Harrington, Honalee, et al. (1996). The life history calendar: A research and clinical assessment method for collecting retrospective event-history data. *International Journal of Methods in Psychiatric Research, 6,* 101–114.

Caspi, Avshalom, & Shiner, Rebecca L. (2006). Personality development. In William Damon & Richard M. Lerner (Series Eds.) & Nancy Eisenberg (Vol. Ed.), *Handbook of child psychology: Vol. 3. Social, emotional, and personality development* (Vol. 6, pp. 300–365). Hoboken, NJ: Wiley.

Caspi, Avshalom, Sugden, Karen, Moffitt, Terrie E., Taylor, Alan, Craig, Ian W., Harrington, HonaLee, et al. (2003, July 18). Influence of life stress on depression: Moderation by a polymorphism in the 5-HTT gene. *Science, 301,* 386–389.

Cassell, Justine, Huffaker, David, Tversky, Dona, & Ferriman, Kim. (2006). The language of online leadership: Gender and youth engagement on the internet. *Developmental Psychology, 42,* 436–449.

Cassidy, Jude, & Shaver, Phillip R. (Eds.). (1999). *Handbook of attachment: Theory, research, and clinical applications.* New York: Guilford Press.

Cavanagh, Sean. (2005, January 5). Poor math scores on world stage trouble U.S. *Education Week, 25,* 1, 18.

Cavanagh, Sean. (2007, November 13). Top-achieving nations beat U.S. states in math and science. *Education Week.*

CBS News. (2005, Feb 8). *World's smallest baby goes home: Cellphone-sized baby is discharged from hospital.* Retrieved July 15, 2008, from the World Wide Web: http://www.cbsnews.com/stories/2005/02/08/health/main672488.shtml

CDC (Centers for Disease Control and Prevention) (Ed.). (2007). *Epidemiology and prevention of vaccine-preventable diseases* (10th ed.). Washington, DC: Public Health Foundation.

Cesario, Sandra K., & Hughes, Lisa A. (2007). Precocious puberty: A comprehensive review of literature. *Journal of Obstetric, Gynecologic, & Neonatal Nursing, 36,* 263–274.

Chamberlain, Patricia, Fisher, Philip A., & Moore, Kevin. (2002). Multidimensional treatment foster care: Applications of the OSLC intervention model to high-risk youth and their families. In John B. Reid, Gerald R. Patterson, & James Snyder (Eds.), *Antisocial behavior in children and adolescents: A developmental analysis and model for intervention* (pp. 203–218). Washington, DC: American Psychological Association.

Chandler, Michael J., Lalonde, Christopher E., Sokol, Bryan W., & Hallett, Darcy. (2003). Personal persistence, identity development, and suicide: A study of Native and non-Native North American adolescents. *Monographs of the Society for Research in Child Development, 68*(2, Serial No. 273), vii–130.

Chao, Ruth K. (2001). Extending research on the consequences of parenting style for Chinese Americans and European Americans. *Child Development, 72,* 1832–1843.

Chao, Y. May, Pisetsky, Emily M., Dierker, Lisa C., Dohm, Faith-Anne, Rosselli, Francine, May, Alexis M., et al. (2008). Ethnic differences in weight control practices among U.S. adolescents from 1995 to 2005. *International Journal of Eating Disorders, 41,* 124–133.

Chaplin, Lan Nguyen, & John, Deborah Roedder. (2007). Growing up in a material world: Age differences in materialism in children and adolescents. *Journal of Consumer Research, 34,* 480–493.

Chassin, Laurie, Hussong, Andrea, Barrera, Manuel, Jr., Molina, Brooke S. G., Trim, Ryan, & Ritter, Jennifer. (2004). Adolescent substance use. In Richard M. Lerner & Laurence D. Steinberg (Eds.), *Handbook of adolescent psychology* (2nd ed., pp. 665–696). Hoboken, NJ: Wiley.

Chattopadhyay, Amit. (2008). Oral health disparities in the United States. *Dental Clinics of North America, 52,* 297–318.

Chawarska, Katarzyna, Klin, Ami, Paul, Rhea, & Volkmar, Fred. (2007). Autism spectrum disorder in the second year: Stability and change in syndrome expression. *Journal of Child Psychology and Psychiatry, 48,* 128–138.

Chen, Xinyin, Cen, Guozhen, Li, Dan, & He, Yunfeng. (2005). Social functioning and adjustment in Chinese children: The imprint of historical time. *Child Development, 76,* 182–195.

Chen, Xinyin, Rubin, Kenneth H., & Sun, Yuerong. (1992). Social reputation and peer relationships in Chinese and Canadian children: A cross-cultural study. *Child Development, 63,* 1336–1343.

Chen, Xin, Striano, Tricia, & Rakoczy, Hannes. (2004). Auditory-oral matching behavior in newborns. *Developmental Science, 7,* 42–47.

Cherbuin, Nicolas, & Brinkman, Cobie. (2006). Hemispheric interactions are different in left-handed individuals. *Neuropsychology, 20,* 700–707.

Cherry, Andrew L., Dillon, Mary E., & Rugh, Douglas (Eds.). (2001). *Teenage pregnancy: A global view.* Westport, CT: Greenwood Press.

Chess, Stella, Thomas, Alexander, & Birch, Herbert G. (1965). *Your child is a person: A psychological approach to parenthood without guilt.* Oxford, England: Viking Press.

Cheurprakobkit, Sutham, & Bartsch, Robert A. (2005). Security measures on school crime in Texas middle and high schools. *Educational Research, 47,* 235–250.

Chisholm, Kim. (1998). A three year follow-up of attachment and indiscriminate friendliness in children adopted from Romanian orphanages. *Child Development, 69,* 1092–1106.

Chiu, Chi-yue, Leung, Angela K.-y., & Kwan, Letty. (2007). Language, cognition, and culture: Beyond the Whorfian hypothesis. In Shinobu Kitayama & Dov Cohen (Eds.), *Handbook of cultural psychology* (pp. 668–688). New York: Guilford Press.

Choi, Jung-ah. (2005). New generation's career aspirations and new ways of marginalization in a postindustrial economy. *British Journal of Sociology of Education, 26,* 269–283.

Chomsky, Noam. (1968). *Language and mind.* New York: Harcourt Brace & World.

Chomsky, Noam. (1980). *Rules and representations.* New York: Columbia University Press.

Chouinard, Michelle M. (2007). Children's questions: A mechanism for cognitive development. *Monographs of the Society for Research in Child Development, 72*(1, Serial No. 286), vii-112.

Christenson, Sandra L., & Thurlow, Martha L. (2004). School dropouts: Prevention considerations, interventions, and challenges. *Current Directions in Psychological Science, 13,* 36–39.

Chronicle of Higher Education. (2008). *The almanac of higher education 2008–9.* Retrieved August 29, 2008, from the World Wide Web: http://chronicle.com/free/almanac/2008/

Chumlea, William Cameron, Schubert, Christine M., Roche, Alex F., Kulin, Howard E., Lee, Peter A., Himes, John H., et al. (2003). Age at menarche and racial comparisons in US girls. *Pediatrics, 111,* 110–113.

Cianciolo, Anna T., & Sternberg, Robert J. (2004). *Intelligence: A brief history.* Malden, MA: Blackwell.

Cicchetti, Dante, & Curtis, W. John. (2007). Multilevel perspectives on pathways to resilient functioning. *Development and Psychopathology, 19,* 627–629.

Cicchetti, Dante, Rogosch, Fred A., & Sturge-Apple, Melissa L. (2007). Interactions of child maltreatment and serotonin transporter and monoamine oxidase A polymorphisms: Depressive symptomatology among adolescents from low socioeconomic status backgrounds. *Development and Psychopathology, 19,* 1161–1180.

Cicchetti, Dante, & Toth, Sheree L. (1998). Perspectives on research and practice in developmental psychopathology. In William Damon (Series Ed.) & Irving E. Sigel & K. Ann Renninger (Vol. Eds.), *Handbook of child psychology: Vol. 4. Child psychology in practice* (5th ed., pp. 479–483). New York: Wiley.

Cillessen, Antonius H. N., & Mayeux, Lara. (2004). From censure to reinforcement: Developmental changes in the association between aggression and social status. *Child Development, 75,* 147–163.

Clarke, Ann M., & Clarke, Alan D. B. (2003). *Human resilience: A fifty year quest.* London: Jessica Kingsley.

Clarke-Stewart, Alison, & Allhusen, Virginia D. (2005). *What we know about childcare.* Cambridge, MA: Harvard University Press.

Cleveland, Michael J., Gibbons, Frederick X., Gerrard, Meg, Pomery, Elizabeth A., & Brody, Gene H. (2005). The impact of parenting on risk cognitions and risk behavior: A study of mediation and moderation in a panel of African American adolescents. *Child Development, 76,* 900–916.

Cockerham, William C. (2006). *Society of risk-takers: Living life on the edge.* New York: Worth.

Cohan, Catherine L., & Kleinbaum, Stacey. (2002). Toward a greater understanding of the cohabitation effect: Premarital cohabitation and marital communication. *Journal of Marriage & Family, 64,* 180–192.

Cohen, David. (2006). *The development of play* (3rd ed.). New York: Routledge.

Cohen, Jon. (2007, March 9). Hope on new AIDS drugs, but breast-feeding strategy backfires. *Science, 315,* 1357.

Cohen, Jon. (2007, September 7). DNA duplications and deletions help determine health. *Science, 317,* 1315–1317.

Cohen, Larry, Chávez, Vivian, & Chehimi, Sana. (2007). *Prevention is primary: Strategies* *for community well-being*. San Francisco: Jossey-Bass.

Cohen, Leslie B., & Cashon, Cara H. (2006). Infant cognition. In William Damon & Richard M. Lerner (Series Eds.) & Deanna Kuhn & Robert S. Siegler (Vol. Eds.), *Handbook of child psychology: Vol. 2. Cognition, perception, and language* (6th ed., pp. 214–251). Hoboken, NJ: Wiley.

Cohen, Lee S., Altshuler, Lori L., Harlow, Bernard L., Nonacs, Ruta, Newport, D. Jeffrey, Viguera, Adele C., et al. (2006). Relapse of major depression during pregnancy in women who maintain or discontinue antidepressant treatment. *Journal of the American Medical Association, 295,* 499–507.

Cohen, Robert, Hsueh, Yeh, Zhou, Zongkui, Hancock, Miriam H., & Floyd, Randy. (2006). Respect, liking, and peer social competence in China and the United States. In David W. Shwalb & Barbara J. Shwalb (Eds.), *New Directions for Child and Adolescent Development: Vol. 114. Respect and disrespect: Cultural and developmental origins* (pp. 53–66). San Francisco: Jossey-Bass.

Cohen, William I. (2005). Medical care of the child with Down syndrome. In Merlin Gene Butler & F. John Meaney (Eds.), *Genetics of developmental disabilities* (pp. 223–245). Boca Raton, FL: Taylor & Francis.

Cole, Michael. (2005). Culture in development. In Marc H. Bornstein & Michael E. Lamb (Eds.), *Developmental science: An advanced textbook* (5th ed., pp. 45–101). Mahwah, NJ: Erlbaum.

Coles, Robert. (1997). *The moral intelligence of children: How to raise a moral child.* New York: Random House.

Collins, Mary Elizabeth, Paris, Ruth, & Ward, Rolanda L. (2008). The permanence of family ties: Implications for youth transitioning from foster care. *American Journal of Orthopsychiatry, 78,* 54–62.

Collins, Michael F. (with Kay, Tess). (2003). *Sport and social exclusion*. London: Routledge.

Collins, W. Andrew, & Laursen, Brett. (2004). Parent-adolescent relationships and influences. In Richard M. Lerner & Laurence D. Steinberg (Eds.), *Handbook of adolescent psychology* (2nd ed., pp. 331–361). Hoboken, NJ: Wiley.

Collins, W. Andrew, & Steinberg, Laurence. (2006). Adolescent development in interpersonal context. In William Damon & Richard M. Lerner (Series Eds.) & Nancy Eisenberg (Vol. Ed.), *Handbook of child psychology: Vol. 3. Social, emotional, and personality development* (6th ed., pp. 1003–1067). Hoboken, NJ: Wiley.

Collins, W. Andrew, & van Dulmen, Manfred. (2006). "The course of true love(s) . . . ": Origins and pathways in the development of romantic relationships. In Ann C. Crouter & Alan Booth (Eds.), *Romance and sex in adolescence and emerging adulthood: Risks and opportunities* (pp. 63–86). Mahwah, NJ: Erlbaum.

Compas, Bruce E. (2004). Processes of risk and resilience during adolescence: Linking contexts and individuals. In Richard M. Lerner & Laurence D. Steinberg (Eds.), *Handbook of adolescent psychology* (2nd ed., pp. 263–296). Hoboken, NJ: Wiley.

Compian, Laura, Gowen, L. Kris, & Hayward, Chris. (2004). Peripubertal girls' romantic and platonic involvement with boys: Associations with body image and depression symptoms. *Journal of Research on Adolescence, 14,* 23–47.

Conboy, Barbara T., & Thal, Donna J. (2006). Ties between the lexicon and grammar: Cross-sectional and longitudinal studies of bilingual toddlers. *Child Development, 77,* 712–735.

Conger, Rand D., & Donnellan, M. Brent. (2007). An interactionist perspective on the socioeconomic context of human development. *Annual Review of Psychology, 58,* 175–199.

Conger, Rand D., Wallace, Lora Ebert, Sun, Yumei, Simons, Ronald L., McLoyd, Vonnie C., & Brody, Gene H. (2002). Economic pressure in African American families: A replication and extension of the family stress model. *Developmental Psychology, 38,* 179–193.

Connolly, Jennifer, Furman, Wyndol, & Konarski, Roman. (2000). The role of peers in the emergence of heterosexual romantic relationships in adolescence. *Child Development, 71,* 1395–1408.

Connor, David J., & Ferri, Beth A. (2007). The conflict within: Resistance to inclusion and other paradoxes in special education. *Disability & Society, 22,* 63–77.

Cook, Susan Wagner, Mitchell, Zachary, & Goldin-Meadow, Susan. (2008). Gesturing makes learning last. *Cognition, 106,* 1047–1058.

Coontz, Stephanie. (2006). Romance and sex in adolescence and emerging adulthood. In Ann C. Crouter & Alan Booth (Eds.), *Romance and sex in adolescence and emerging adulthood: Risks and opportunities* (pp. 87–91). Mahwah, NJ: Erlbaum.

Coovadia, Hoosen M. & Wittenberg, Dankwart F. (Eds.). (2004). *Paediatrics and child health: A manual for health professionals in developing countries* (5th ed.). New York: Oxford University Press.

Cornish, Kimberly M., Levitas, Andrew, & Sudhalter, Vicki. (2007). Fragile X syndrome: The journey from genes to behavior. In Michèle M. M. Mazzocco & Judith L. Ross (Eds.), *Neurogenetic developmental disorders: Variation of manifestation in childhood* (pp. 73–103). Cambridge, MA: MIT Press.

Correa-Chavez, Maricela, Rogoff, Barbara, & Arauz, Rebeca Mejia. (2005). Cultural patterns in attending to two events at once. *Child Development, 76,* 664–678.

Corsaro, William A., & Molinari, Luisa. (2000). Entering and observing in children's worlds: A reflection on a longitudinal ethnography of early education in Italy. In Pia Monrad Christensen & Allison James (Eds.), *Research with children: Perspectives and practices* (pp. 179–200). London: Falmer Press.

Costello, E. Jane, Compton, Scott N., Keeler, Gordon, & Angold, Adrian. (2003). Relationships between poverty and psychopathology: A natural experiment. *Journal of the American Medical Association, 290,* 2023–2029.

Côté, James E. (2006). Emerging adulthood as an institutionalized moratorium: Risks and benefits to identity formation. In Jeffrey Jensen Arnett & Jennifer Lynn Tanner (Eds.), *Emerging adults in America: Coming of age in the 21st century* (pp. 85–116). Washington, DC: American Psychological Association.

Côté, Sylvana M., Borge, Anne I., Geoffroy, Marie-Claude, Rutter, Michael, & Tremblay, Richard E. (2008). Nonmaternal care in infancy and emotional/behavioral difficulties at 4 years old: Moderation by family risk characteristics. *Developmental Psychology, 44,* 155–168.

Courage, Mary L., Reynolds, Greg D., & Richards, John E. (2006). Infants' attention to patterned stimuli: Developmental change from 3 to 12 months of age. *Child Development, 77,* 680–695.

Coutinho, Sonia Bechara, Cabral de Lira, Pedro Israel, de Carvalho Lima, Marilia, & Ashworth, Ann. (2005). Comparison of the effect of two systems for the promotion of exclusive breastfeeding. *Lancet, 366,* 1094–1100.

Covington, Martin V., & Dray, Elizabeth. (2002). The developmental course of achievement motivation: A need-based approach. In Allan Wigfield & Jacquelynne S. Eccles (Eds.), *Development of achievement motivation* (pp. 33–56). San Diego, CA: Academic Press.

Covington, Sharon N., & Burns, Linda Hammer. (2006). *Infertility counseling: A comprehensive handbook for clinicians* (2nd ed.). New York: Cambridge University Press.

Cowan, Nelson (Ed.). (1997). *The development of memory in childhood*. Hove, East Sussex, UK: Psychology Press.

Coward, Fiona. (2008, March 14). Standing on the shoulders of giants. *Science, 319,* 1493–1495.

Cox, Maureen V. (1993). *Children's drawings of the human figure*. Hillsdale, NJ: Erlbaum.

Coyle, Karin, Basen-Engquist, Karen, Kirby, Douglas, Parcel, Guy, Banspach, Stephen, Collins, Janet, et al. (2001). Safer choices: Reducing teen pregnancy, HIV, and STDs. *Public Health Reports, 116*(Suppl. 1), 82–93.

Crain, William C. (2005). *Theories of development: Concepts and applications* (5th ed.). Upper Saddle River, NJ: Prentice Hall.

Crews, Douglas E. (2003). *Human senescence: Evolutionary and biocultural perspectives*. New York: Cambridge University Press.

Crick, Nicki R., Nelson, David A., Morales, Julie R., Cullerton-Sen, Crystal, Casas, Juan F., & Hickman, Susan E. (2001). Relational victimization in childhood and adolescence: I hurt you through the grapevine. In Jaana Juvonen & Sandra Graham (Eds.), *Peer harassment in school: The plight of the vulnerable and victimized* (pp. 196–214). New York: Guilford Press.

Crinion, Jenny, Turner, R., Grogan, Alice, Hanakawa, Takashi, Noppeney, Uta, Devlin, Joseph T., et al. (2006, June 9). Language control in the bilingual brain. *Science, 312,* 1537–1540.

Criss, Michael M., Pettit, Gregory S., Bates, John E., Dodge, Kenneth A., & Lapp, Amie L. (2002). Family adversity, positive peer relationships, and children's externalizing behavior: A longitudinal perspective on risk and resilience. *Child Development, 73,* 1220–1237.

Crncec, Rudi, Wilson, Sarah J., & Prior, Margot. (2006). The cognitive and academic benefits of music to children: Facts and fiction. *Educational Psychology, 26,* 579–594.

Crockenberg, Susan C. (2003). Rescuing the baby from the bathwater: How gender and temperament (may) influence how child care affects child development. *Child Development, 74,* 1034–1038.

Crombag, Hans S., & Robinson, Terry E. (2004). Drugs, environment, brain, and behavior. *Current Directions in Psychological Science, 13,* 107–111.

Crosnoe, Robert, Johnson, Monica Kirkpatrick, & Elder, Glen H., Jr. (2004). Intergenerational bonding in school: The behavioral and contextual correlates of student–teacher relationships. *Sociology of Education, 77,* 60–81.

Crosnoe, Robert, & Needham, Belinda. (2004). Holism, contextual variability, and the study of friendships in adolescent development. *Child Development, 75,* 264–279.

Croteau, Agathe, Marcoux, Sylvie, & Brisson, Chantal. (2006). Work activity in pregnancy, preventive measures, and the risk of delivering a small-for-gestational-age infant. *American Journal of Public Health, 96,* 846–855.

Csikszentmihalyi, Mihaly, & Schneider, Barbara. (2000). *Becoming adult: How teenagers prepare for the world of work*. New York: Basic Books.

Cullen, Karen Weber, & Zakeri, Issa. (2004). Fruits, vegetables, milk, and sweetened beverages consumption and access to a la carte/snack bar meals at school. *American Journal of Public Health, 94,* 463–467.

Cummings, E. Mark, Goeke-Morey, Marcie C., & Papp, Lauren M. (2003). Children's responses to everyday marital conflict tactics in the home. *Child Development, 74,* 1918–1929.

Cunningham, John A., & Selby, Peter L. (2007). Implications of the normative fallacy in young adult smokers aged 19–24 years. *American Journal of Public Health, 97,* 1399–1400.

Curtis, W. John, & Cicchetti, Dante. (2003). Moving research on resilience into the 21st century: Theoretical and methodological considerations in examining the biological contributors to resilience. *Development & Psychopathology, 15,* 773–810.

Curtis, W. John, & Nelson, Charles A. (2003). Toward building a better brain: Neurobehavioral outcomes, mechanisms, and processes of environmental enrichment. In Suniya S. Luthar (Ed.), *Resilience and vulnerability: Adaptation in the context of childhood adversities* (pp. 463–488). New York: Cambridge University Press.

Cuskelly, Monica, Jobling, Anne, & Buckley, Susan (Eds.). (2002). *Down syndrome across the life span*. Philadelphia: Whurr.

Dahl, Ronald E. (2004). Adolescent brain development: A period of vulnerabilities and opportunities. Keynote address. In Ronald E. Dahl & Linda Patia Spear (Eds.), *Adolescent brain development: Vulnerabilities and opportunities* (Vol. 1021, pp. 1–22). New York: New York Academy of Sciences.

Dales, Loring, Hammer, Sandra Jo, & Smith, Natalie J. (2001). Time trends in autism and in MMR immunization coverage in California. *Journal of the American Medical Association, 285,* 1183–1185.

Dalman, Christina, Allebeck, Peter, Gunnell, David, Harrison, Glyn, Kristensson, Krister, Lewis, Glyn, et al. (2008). Infections in the CNS during childhood and the risk of subsequent psychotic illness: A cohort study of more than one million Swedish subjects. *American Journal of Psychiatry, 165,* 59–65.

Damasio, Antonio R. (2003). *Looking for Spinoza: Joy, sorrow, and the feeling brain*. Orlando, FL: Harcourt.

Darling, Nancy, Cumsille, Patricio, & Martinez, M. Loreto. (2008). Individual differences in adolescents' beliefs about the legitimacy of parental authority and their own obligation to obey: A longitudinal investigation. *Child Development, 79,* 1103–1118.

Daro, Deborah. (2002). Public perception of child sexual abuse: Who is to blame? *Child Abuse & Neglect, 26,* 1131–1133.

Dasen, Pierre R. (2003). Theoretical frameworks in cross-cultural developmental psychology: An attempt at integration. In T. S. Saraswati (Ed.), *Cross-cultural perspectives in human development: Theory, research, and applications* (pp. 128–165). New Delhi, India: Sage.

Datan, Nancy. (1986). Oedipal conflict, platonic love: Centrifugal forces in intergenerational relations. In Nancy Datan, Anita L. Greene, & Hayne W. Reese (Eds.), *Life-span developmental psychology: Intergenerational relations* (pp. 29–50). Hillsdale, NJ: Erlbaum.

David, Barbara, Grace, Diane, & Ryan, Michelle K. (2004). The gender wars: A self-categorization perspective on the development of gender identity. In Mark Bennett & Fabio Sani (Eds.), *The development of the social self* (pp. 135–157). Hove, East Sussex, England: Psychology Press.

Davidson, Julia O'Connell. (2005). *Children in the global sex trade*. Malden, MA: Polity.

Davies, Patrick T., & Cicchetti, Dante. (2004). Toward an integration of family systems and developmental psychopathology approaches. *Development & Psychopathology, 16,* 477–481.

Davis, Elysia Poggi, Parker, Susan Whitmore, Tottenham, Nim, & Gunnar, Megan R. (2003). Emotion, cognition, and the hypothalamic-pituitary-adrenocortical axis: A developmental perspective. In Michelle de Haan & Mark H. Johnson (Eds.), *The cognitive neuroscience of development* (pp. 181–206). New York: Psychology Press.

Davison, Kirsten Krahnstoever, Werder, Jessica L., Trost, Stewart G., Baker, Birgitta L., & Birch, Leann L. (2007). Why are early maturing girls less active? Links between pubertal development, psychological well-being, and physical activity among girls at ages 11 and 13. *Social Science & Medicine, 64,* 2391–2404.

Dawson, Michelle, Soulières, Isabelle, Gernsbacher, Morton Ann, & Mottron, Laurent. (2007). The level and nature of autistic intelligence. *Psychological Science, 18,* 657–662.

De Bellis, Michael D. (2001). Developmental traumatology: The psychobiological development of maltreated children and its implications for research, treatment, and policy. *Development and Psychopathology, 13,* 539–564.

De Bellis, Michael D., Narasimhan, Anandhi, Thatcher, Dawn L., Keshavan, Matcheri S., Soloff, Paul, & Clark, Duncan B. (2005). Prefrontal cortex, thalamus, and cerebellar volumes in adolescents and young adults with adolescent-onset alcohol use disorders and comorbid mental disorders. *Alcoholism: Clinical and Experimental Research, 29,* 1590–1600.

de Haan, Michelle. (2008). Event-related potential (ERP) measures in visual development research. In Louis A. Schmidt & Sidney J. Segalowitz (Eds.), *Developmental psychophysiology: Theory, systems, and methods* (pp. 103–126). New York: Cambridge University Press.

de Haan, Michelle, & Johnson, Mark H. (2003). Mechanisms and theories of brain development. In Michelle De Haan & Mark H. Johnson (Eds.), *The cognitive neuroscience of development* (pp. 1–18). Hove, East Sussex, England: Psychology Press.

De Lee, Joseph Bolivar. (1938). *The principles and practice of obstetrics* (7th ed.). Philadelphia: Saunders.

De Neys, Wim. (2006). Dual processing in reasoning: Two systems but one reasoner. *Psychological Science, 17,* 428–433.

De Neys, Wim, & Glumicic, Tamara. (2008). Conflict monitoring in dual process theories of thinking. *Cognition, 106,* 1248–1299.

de Rosnay, Marc, Cooper, Peter J., Tsigaras, Nicolas, & Murray, Lynne. (2006). Transmission of social anxiety from mother to infant: An experimental study using a social referencing paradigm. *Behaviour Research and Therapy, 44,* 1165–1175.

de Schipper, Elles J., Riksen-Walraven, J. Marianne, & Geurts, Sabine A. E. (2006). Effects of child-caregiver ratio on the interactions between caregivers and children in child-care centers: An experimental study. *Child Development, 77,* 861–874.

Deci, Edward L., Koestner, Richard, & Ryan, Richard M. (1999). A meta-analytic review of experiments examining the effects of extrinsic rewards on intrinsic motivation. *Psychological Bulletin, 125,* 627–668.

Dehue, Francine, Bolman, Catherine, & Völlink, Trijntje. (2008). Cyberbullying: Youngsters' experiences and parental perception. *CyberPsychology & Behavior, 11,* 217–223.

DeKeyser, Robert, & Larson-Hall, Jenifer. (2005). What does the critical period really mean? In Judith F. Kroll & Annette M. B. de Groot (Eds.), *Handbook of bilingualism: Psycholinguistic approaches* (pp. 88–108). Oxford, UK: Oxford University Press.

Demetriou, Andreas, Christou, Constantinos, Spanoudis, George, & Platsidou, Maria. (2002). The development of mental processing: Efficiency, working memory, and thinking. *Monographs of the Society for Research in Child Development, 67*(1, Serial No. 268).

Denham, Susanne A., Blair, Kimberly A., DeMulder, Elizabeth, Levitas, Jennifer, Sawyer, Katherine, Auerbach-Major, Sharon, et al. (2003). Preschool emotional competence: Pathway to social competence. *Child Development, 74,* 238–256.

Denny, Dallas, & Pittman, Cathy. (2007). Gender identity: From dualism to diversity. In Mitchell S. Tepper & Annette Fuglsang Owens (Eds.), *Sexual health: Vol. 1. Psychological foundations* (pp. 205–229). Westport, CT: Praeger/Greenwood.

Derman, Orhan, Kanbur, Nuray Öksöz, & Kutluk, Tezer. (2003). Tamoxifen treatment for pubertal gynecomastia. *International Journal of Adolescent Medicine and Health, 15,* 359–363.

Derryberry, Douglas, Reed, Marjorie A., & Pilkenton-Taylor, Carolyn. (2003). Temperament and coping: Advantages of an individual differences perspective. *Development & Psychopathology, 15,* 1049–1066.

Dershewitz, Robert A. (2002, December 28). *Another good year for immunizations*. Journal Watch Gastroenterology. Retrieved June 22, 2005, from the World Wide Web: http://gastroenterology.jwatch.org/cgi/content/full/2002/1228/11

Devi, Sharmila. (2008). Progress on childhood obesity patchy in the USA. *Lancet, 371,* 105–106.

Diamond, Adele, & Kirkham, Natasha. (2005). Not quite as grown-up as we like to think: Parallels between cognition in childhood and adulthood. *Psychological Science, 16,* 291–297.

Diamond, David M., Dunwiddie, Thomas V., & Rose, G. M. (1988). Characteristics of hippocampal primed burst potentiation in vitro and in the awake rat. *Journal of Neuroscience, 8,* 4079–4088.

Diamond, Lisa M., & Savin-Williams, Ritch C. (2003). The intimate relationships of sexual-minority youths. In Gerald R. Adams & Michael D. Berzonsky (Eds.), *Blackwell handbook of adolescence* (pp. 393–412). Malden, MA: Blackwell.

Diamond, Mathew E. (2007). Neuronal basis of perceptual intelligence. In Flavia Santoianni & Claudia Sabatano (Eds.), *Brain development in learning environments: Embodied and perceptual advancements* (pp. 98–108). Newcastle, UK: Cambridge Scholars.

Diener, Marissa. (2000). Gift from the gods: A Balinese guide to early child rearing. In Judy S. DeLoache & Alma Gottlieb (Eds.), *A world of babies: Imagined childcare guides for seven societies* (pp. 96–116). New York: Cambridge University Press.

Dieterich, Susan E., Assel, Mike A., Swank, Paul, Smith, Karen E., & Landry, Susan H. (2006). The impact of early maternal verbal scaffolding and child language abilities on later decoding and reading comprehension skills. *Journal of School Psychology, 43,* 481–494.

Dietz, Claudine, Swinkels, Sophie H. N., Buitelaar, Jan K., van Daalen,

Emma, & van Engeland, Herman. (2007). Stability and change of IQ scores in preschool children diagnosed with autistic spectrum disorder. *European Child & Adolescent Psychiatry, 16,* 405–410.

Dietz, William H., & Robinson, Thomas N. (2005). Overweight children and adolescents. *New England Journal of Medicine, 352,* 2100–2109.

DiGirolamo, Ann, Thompson, Nancy, Martorell, Reynaldo, Fein, Sara, & Grummer-Strawn, Laurence. (2005). Intention or experience? Predictors of continued breastfeeding. *Health Education & Behavior, 32,* 208–226.

Dijk, Jan A. G. M. van. (2005). *The deepening divide: Inequality in the information society.* Thousand Oaks, CA: Sage.

Dilworth-Bart, Janean E., & Moore, Colleen F. (2006). Mercy mercy me: Social injustice and the prevention of environmental pollutant exposures among ethnic minority and poor children. *Child Development, 77,* 247–265.

Dionne, Ginette, Dale, Philip S., Boivin, Michel, & Plomin, Robert. (2003). Genetic evidence for bidirectional effects of early lexical and grammatical development. *Child Development, 74,* 394–412.

DiPietro, Janet A., Hilton, Sterling C., Hawkins, Melissa, Costigan, Kathleen A., & Pressman, Eva K. (2002). Maternal stress and affect influence fetal neurobehavioral development. *Developmental Psychology, 38,* 659–668.

Dishion, Thomas J., & Bullock, Bernadette Marie. (2002). Parenting and adolescent problem behavior: An ecological analysis of the nurturance hypothesis. In John G. Borkowski, Sharon Landesman Ramey, & Marie Bristol-Power (Eds.), *Parenting and the child's world: Influences on academic, intellectual, and social-emotional development* (pp. 231–249). Mahwah, NJ: Erlbaum.

Dishion, Thomas J., McCord, Joan, & Poulin, François. (1999). When interventions harm: Peer groups and problem behavior. *American Psychologist, 54,* 755–764.

Dishion, Thomas J., & Owen, Lee D. (2002). A longitudinal analysis of friendships and substance use: Bidirectional influence from adolescence to adulthood. *Developmental Psychology, 38,* 480–491.

Dishion, Thomas J., Poulin, François, & Burraston, Bert. (2001). Peer group dynamics associated with iatrogenic effects in group interventions with high-risk young adolescents. In William Damon (Series Ed.) & Douglas W. Nangle & Cynthia A. Erdley (Vol. Eds.), *New directions for child and adolescent development: No. 91. The role of friendship in psychological adjustment* (pp. 79–92). San Francisco: Jossey-Bass.

Dodge, Kenneth A., Coie, John D., & Lynam, Donald R. (2006). Aggression and antisocial behavior in youth. In William Damon & Richard M. Lerner (Series Eds.) & Nancy Eisenberg (Vol. Ed.), *Handbook of child psychology: Vol. 3. Social, emotional, and personality development* (6th ed., pp. 719–788). New York: Wiley.

Donaldson, Margaret C. (1979). *Children's minds.* New York: Norton.

Donat, Dorothy J. (2006). Reading Their Way: A balanced approach that increases achievement. *Reading & Writing Quarterly: Overcoming Learning Difficulties, 22,* 305–323.

Dooley, Dolores, Dalla-Vorgia, Panagiota, Garanis-Papadatos, Tina, & McCarthy, Joan. (2003). *Ethics of new reproductive technologies: Cases and questions.* New York: Berghahn Books.

Doumbo, Ogobara K. (2005, February 4). It takes a village: Medical research and ethics in Mali. *Science, 307,* 679–681.

Downs, Danielle Symons, & Hausenblas, Heather A. (2007). Pregnant women's third trimester exercise behaviors, body mass index, and pregnancy outcomes. *Psychology & Health, 22,* 545–559.

Dugger, Celia W. (2006, April 30). Mothers of Nepal vanquish a killer of children. *New York Times,* pp. A1, A16.

Duncan, Greg J., & Magnuson, Katherine. (2007). Penny wise and effect size foolish. *Child Development Perspectives, 1,* 46–51.

Dunn, Judy, & Hughes, Claire. (2001). "I got some swords and you're dead!": Violent fantasy, antisocial behavior, friendship, and moral sensibility in young children. *Child Development, 72,* 491–505.

Dunphy, Dexter C. (1963). The social structure of urban adolescent peer groups. *Sociometry, 26,* 230–246.

Dupéré, Véronique, Lacourse, Éric, Willms, J. Douglas, Vitaro, Frank, & Tremblay, Richard E. (2007). Affiliation to youth gangs during adolescence: The interaction between childhood psychopathic tendencies and neighborhood disadvantage. *Journal of Abnormal Child Psychology, 35,* 1035–1045.

Dweck, Carol S. (2007). Is math a gift? Beliefs that put females at risk. In Stephen J. Ceci & Wendy M. Williams (Eds.), *Why aren't more women in science: Top researchers debate the evidence* (pp. 47–55). Washington, DC: American Psychological Association.

East, Patricia L., & Kiernan, Elizabeth A. (2001). Risks among youths who have multiple sisters who were adolescent parents. *Family Planning Perspectives, 33,* 75–80.

Eccles, Jacquelynne S. (2004). Schools, academic motivation, and stage-environment fit. In Richard M. Lerner & Laurence D. Steinberg (Eds.), *Handbook of adolescent psychology* (2nd ed., pp. 125–153). Hoboken, NJ: Wiley.

Eccles, Jacquelynne S., Barber, Bonnie L., Stone, Margaret, & Hunt, James. (2003). Extracurricular activities and adolescent development. *Journal of Social Issues, 59,* 865–889.

Eckert, Penelope. (1989). *Jocks and burnouts: Social categories and identity in the high school.* New York: Teachers College Press.

Eckstein, Daniel G., Rasmussen, Paul R., & Wittschen, Lori. (1999). Understanding and dealing with adolescents. *Journal of Individual Psychology, 55,* 31–50.

Eddleman, Keith A., Malone, Fergal D., Sullivan, Lisa, Dukes, Kim, Berkowitz, Richard L., Kharbutli, Yara, et al. (2006). Pregnancy loss rates after midtrimester amniocentesis. *Obstetrics & Gynecology, 108,* 1067–1072.

Editors. (2004). Preventing early reading failure. *American Educator, 28,* 5.

Education Week. (2008). *Diplomas count 2008: School to college: Can state P-16 councils ease the transition?* Retrieved July 25, 2008, from the World Wide Web: http://www.edweek.org/ew/toc/2008/06/05/index.html

Edwards, Oliver W. (2006). Special education disproportionality and the influence of intelligence test selection. *Journal of Intellectual & Developmental Disability, 31,* 246–248.

Egan, Kieran, & Ling, Michael. (2002). We began as poets: Conceptual tools and the arts in early childhood. In Liora Bresler & Christine Marme Thompson (Eds.), *The arts in children's lives: Context, culture, and curriculum* (pp. 93–100). Dordrecht, The Netherlands: Kluwer.

Ehrenberg, Ronald G., Brewer, Dominic J., Gamoran, Adam, & Willms, J. Douglas. (2001). Class size and student achievement. *Psychological Science in the Public Interest, 2,* 1–30.

Eigenmann, Philippe A., & Haenggeli, Charles A. (2007). Food colourings, preservatives, and hyperactivity. *Lancet, 370,* 1524–1525.

Eisenberg, Marla E., Bearinger, Linda H., Sieving, Renee E., Swain, Carolyne, & Resnick, Michael D. (2004). Parents' beliefs about condoms and oral contraceptives: Are they medically accurate? *Perspectives on Sexual and Reproductive Health, 36,* 50–57.

Eisenberg, Marla E., Sieving, Renee E., Bearinger, Linda H., Swain, Carolyne, & Resnick, Michael D. (2006). Parents' communication with adolescents about sexual behavior: A missed opportunity for prevention? *Journal of Youth and Adolescence, 35,* 893–902.

Eisenberg, Nancy, & Fabes, Richard A. (1998). Prosocial development. In William Damon (Series Ed.) & Nancy Eisenberg (Vol. Ed.), *Handbook of child psychology: Vol. 3. Social, emotional, and personality development* (5th ed., pp. 701–778). New York: Wiley.

Eisenberg, Nancy, Fabes, Richard A., & Spinrad, Tracy L. (2006). Prosocial development. In William Damon & Richard M. Lerner (Series Eds.) & Nancy Eisenberg (Vol. Ed.), *Handbook of child psychology: Vol. 3. Social, emotional, and personality development* (6th ed., pp. 646–718). Hoboken, NJ: Wiley.

Eisenberg, Nancy, Hofer, Claire, Spinrad, Tracy L., Gershoff, Elizabeth T., Valiente, Carlos, Losoya, Sandra, et al. (2008). Understanding mother-adolescent conflict discussions: Concurrent and across-time prediction from youths' dispositions and parenting. *Monographs of the Society for Research in Child Development, 73*(2, Serial No. 290), vii-viii, 1–160.

Eisenberg, Nancy, Spinrad, Tracy L., Fabes, Richard A., Reiser, Mark, Cumberland, Amanda, Shepard, Stephanie A., et al. (2004). The relations of effortful control and impulsivity to children's resiliency and adjustment. *Child Development, 75,* 25–46.

Eisner, Manuel. (2002). Crime, problem drinking, and drug use: Patterns of problem behavior in cross-national perspective. *Annals of the American Academy of Political & Social Science, 580,* 201–225.

El-Sheikh, Mona, & Harger, JoAnn. (2001). Appraisals of marital conflict and children's adjustment, health, and physiological reactivity. *Developmental Psychology, 37,* 875–885.

Elder, Glen H., Jr,, & Shanahan, Michael J. (2006). The life course and human development. In William Damon & Richard M. Lerner (Series Eds.) & Richard M. Lerner (Vol. Ed.), *Handbook of child psychology: Vol. 1. Theoretical models of human development* (6th ed., pp. 665–715). Hoboken, NJ: Wiley.

Elkind, David. (1967). Egocentrism in adolescence. *Child Development, 38,* 1025–1034.

Elkind, David. (2007). *The power of play: How spontaneous, imaginative activities lead to happier, healthier children.* Cambridge, MA: Da Capo Press.

Elliott, Leslie, Arbes, Samuel J., Jr., Harvey, Eric S., Lee, Robert C., Salo, Päivi M., Cohn, Richard D., et al. (2007). Dust weight and asthma prevalence in the National Survey of Lead and Allergens in Housing (NSLAH). *Environmental Health Perspectives, 115,* 215–220.

Ellis, Bruce J. (2004). Timing of pubertal maturation in girls: An integrated life history approach. *Psychological Bulletin, 130,* 920–958.

Ellis, Bruce J., Bates, John E., Dodge, Kenneth A., Fergusson, David M., Horwood, L. John, Pettit, Gregory S., et al. (2003). Does father absence place daughters at special risk for early sexual activity and teenage pregnancy? *Child Development, 74,* 801–821.

Ellis, Bruce J., & Bjorklund, David F. (2005). *Origins of the social mind: Evolutionary psychology and child development.* New York: Guilford Press.

Ellis, Bruce J., & Garber, Judy. (2000). Psychosocial antecedents of variation in girls' pubertal timing: Maternal depression, stepfather presence, and marital and family stress. *Child Development, 71,* 485–501.

Ellison, Peter Thorpe. (2002). Puberty. In Noël Cameron (Ed.), *Human growth and development* (pp. 65–84). San Diego, CA: Academic Press.

Engels, Rutger C. M. E., Scholte, Ron H. J., van Lieshout, Cornelis F. M., de Kemp, Raymond, & Overbeek, Geertjan. (2006). Peer group reputation and smoking and alcohol consumption in early adolescence. *Addictive Behaviors, 31,* 440–449.

Enoch, Mary-Anne. (2006). Genetic and environmental influences on the development of alcoholism: Resilience vs. risk. In Barry M. Lester, Ann Masten, & Bruce McEwen (Eds.), *Resilience in children* (Vol. 1094, pp. 193–201). New York: New York Academy of Sciences.

Epstein, Helen. (2007). *The invisible cure: Africa, the West, and the fight against AIDS.* New York: Farrar, Straus and Giroux.

Epstein, Leonard H., Handley, Elizabeth A., Dearing, Kelly K., Cho, David D., Roemmich, James N., Paluch, Rocco A., et al. (2006). Purchases of food in youth: Influence of price and income. *Psychological Science, 17,* 82–89.

Eriks-Brophy, Alice, & Crago, Martha. (2003). Variation in instructional discourse features: Cultural or linguistic? Evidence from Inuit and Non-Inuit teachers of Nunavik. *Anthropology & Education Quarterly, 34,* 396–419.

Erikson, Erik H. (1963). *Childhood and society* (2nd ed.). New York: Norton.

Erikson, Erik H. (1968). *Identity: Youth and crisis.* New York: Norton.

Erikson, Erik H. (1969). *Gandhi's truth: On the origins of militant nonviolence.* New York: Norton.

Eriksson, Birgitta Sandén, & Pehrsson, Gunnel. (2005). Emotional reactions of parents after the birth of an infant with extremely low birth weight. *Journal of Child Health Care, 9,* 122–136.

Erlandsson, Kerstin, Dsilna, Ann, Fagerberg, Ingegerd, & Christensson, Kyllike. (2007). Skin-to-skin care with the father after cesarean birth and its effect on newborn crying and prefeeding behavior. *Birth: Issues in Perinatal Care, 34,* 105–114.

Ertmer, David J., Young, Nancy M., & Nathani, Suneeti. (2007). Profiles of vocal development in young cochlear implant recipients. *Journal of Speech, Language, and Hearing Research, 50,* 393–407.

Erwin, Phil. (1998). *Friendship in childhood and adolescence.* London: Routledge.

Erzurumlu, Reha S., Guido, William, & Molnár, Zoltán (Eds.). (2006). *Development and plasticity in sensory thalamus and cortex.* New York: Springer.

Esbensen, Anna J., Seltzer, Marsha Mailick, & Greenberg, Jan S. (2007). Factors predicting mortality in midlife adults with and without Down syndrome living with family. *Journal of Intellectual Disability Research, 51,* 1039–1050.

Etchu, Koji. (2007). Social context and preschoolers' judgments about aggressive behavior: Social domain theory. *Japanese Journal of Educational Psychology, 55,* 219–230.

Evans, David W., & Leckman, James F. (2006). Origins of obsessive-compulsive disorder: Developmental and evolutionary perspectives. In Dante Cicchetti & Donald J. Cohen (Eds.), *Developmental psychopathology: Vol. 3. Risk, disorder, and adaptation* (2nd ed., pp. 404–435). Hoboken, NJ: Wiley.

Evans, David W., Leckman, James F., Carter, Alice, Reznick, J. Steven, Henshaw, Desiree, King, Robert A., et al. (1997). Ritual, habit, and perfectionism: The prevalence and development of compulsive-like behavior in normal young children. *Child Development, 68,* 58–68.

Evans, Jonathan St. B. T. (2008). Dual-processing accounts of reasoning, judgment, and social cognition. *Annual Review of Psychology, 59,* 255–278.

Eyer, Diane E. (1992). *Mother–infant bonding: A scientific fiction*. New Haven, CT: Yale University Press.

Fagan, Joseph F., Holland, Cynthia R., & Wheeler, Karyn. (2007). The prediction, from infancy, of adult IQ and achievement. *Intelligence, 35,* 225–231.

Fagot, Beverly I. (1995). Parenting boys and girls. In Marc H. Bornstein (Ed.), *Handbook of parenting: Vol. 1. Children and parenting* (pp. 163–183). Hillsdale, NJ: Erlbaum.

Fair, Cynthia, Vandermaas-Peeler, Maureen, Beaudry, Regan, & Dew, Jennifer. (2005). 'I learned how little kids think': Third-graders' scaffolding of craft activities with preschoolers. *Early Child Development and Care, 175,* 229–241.

Falk, Dean. (2004). Prelinguistic evolution in early hominins: Whence motherese? *Behavioral and Brain Sciences, 27,* 491–503, discussion 503–483.

Faraone, Stephen V., Perlis, Roy H., Doyle, Alysa E., Smoller, Jordan W., Goralnick, Jennifer J., Holmgren, Meredith A., et al. (2005). Molecular genetics of attention-deficit/hyperactivity disorder. *Biological Psychiatry, 57,* 1313–1323.

Faraone, Stephen V., & Wilens, Timothy. (2003). Does stimulant treatment lead to substance use disorders? *Journal of Clinical Psychiatry, 64,* 9–13.

Farrelly, Matthew C., Davis, Kevin C., Haviland, M. Lyndon, Messeri, Peter, & Healton, Cheryl G. (2005). Evidence of a dose-response relationship between "truth" antismoking ads and youth smoking prevalence. *American Journal of Public Health, 95,* 425–431.

Feiring, Candice. (1999). Other-sex friendship networks and the development of romantic relationships in adolescence. *Journal of Youth & Adolescence, 28,* 495–512.

Feldman, Ruth. (2007). Parent–infant synchrony and the construction of shared timing; Physiological precursors, developmental outcomes, and risk conditions. *Journal of Child Psychology and Psychiatry, 48,* 329–354.

Feldman, Ruth, & Eidelman, Arthur I. (2004). Parent–infant synchrony and the social-emotional development of triplets. *Developmental Psychology, 40,* 1133–1147.

Feldman, Ruth, & Eidelman, Arthur I. (2005). Does a triplet birth pose a special risk for infant development? Assessing cognitive development in relation to intrauterine growth and mother–infant interaction across the first 2 years. *Pediatrics, 115,* 443–452.

Feldman, Ruth, Weller, Aron, Sirota, Lea, & Eidelman, Arthur I. (2002). Skin-to-skin contact (kangaroo care) promotes self-regulation in premature infants: Sleep–wake cyclicity, arousal modulation, and sustained exploration. *Developmental Psychology, 38,* 194–207.

Fenson, Larry, Bates, Elizabeth, Dale, Philip, Goodman, Judith, Reznick, J. Steven, & Thal, Donna. (2000). Measuring variability in early child language: Don't shoot the messenger. *Child Development, 71,* 323–328.

Ferguson, Mark W. J, & Joanen, Ted. (1982, April 29). Temperature of egg incubation determines sex in *Alligator mississippiensis*. *Nature, 296,* 850–853.

Fergusson, David M., & Horwood, L. John. (2003). Resilience to childhood adversity: Results of a 12-year study. In Suniya S. Luthar (Ed.), *Resilience and vulnerability: Adaptation in the context of childhood adversities* (pp. 130–155). New York: Cambridge University Press.

Fergusson, Emma, Maughan, Barbara, & Golding, Jean. (2008). Which children receive grandparental care and what effect does it have? *Journal of Child Psychology and Psychiatry, 49,* 161–169.

Finkelhor, David, & Jones, Lisa M. (2004). *Explanations for the decline in child sexual abuse cases*. Office of Juvenile Justice and Delinquency Prevention. Retrieved August 11, 2007, from the World Wide Web: http://www.ncjrs.gov/html/ojjdp/199298/contents.html

Finn, Jeremy D., & Achilles, Charles M. (1999). Tennessee's class size study: Findings, implications, misconceptions. *Educational Evaluation and Policy Analysis, 21,* 97–109.

Finn, Jeremy D., Gerber, Susan B., & Boyd-Zaharias, Jayne. (2005). Small classes in the early grades, academic achievement, and graduating from high school. *Journal of Educational Psychology, 97,* 214–223.

Fischer, Kurt W., & Bidell, Thomas R. (1998). Dynamic development of psychological structures in action and thought. In William Damon (Series Ed.) & Richard M. Lerner (Vol. Ed.), *Handbook of child psychology: Vol. 1. Theoretical models of human development* (5th ed., pp. 467–561). New York: Wiley.

Fish, Jefferson M. (2002). The myth of race. In Jefferson M. Fish (Ed.), *Race and intelligence: Separating science from myth* (pp. 113–141). Mahwah, NJ: Erlbaum.

Fishbein, Martin, Hall-Jamieson, Kathleen, Zimmer, Eric, von Haeften, Ina, & Nabi, Robin. (2002). Avoiding the boomerang: Testing the relative effectiveness of antidrug public service announcements before a national campaign. *American Journal of Public Health, 92,* 238–245.

Fisher, Helen E. (2006). Broken hearts: The nature and risks of romantic rejection. In Ann C. Crouter & Alan Booth (Eds.), *Romance and sex in adolescence and emerging adulthood: Risks and opportunities* (pp. 3–28). Mahwah, NJ: Erlbaum.

Fisher, Jennifer O., & Birch, Leann L. (2001). Early experience with food and eating: Implications for the development of eating disorders. In J. Kevin Thompson & Linda Smolak (Eds.), *Body image, eating disorders, and obesity in youth: Assessment, prevention, and treatment* (pp. 23–39). Washington, DC: American Psychological Association.

Flavell, John H., Miller, Patricia H., & Miller, Scott A. (2002). *Cognitive development* (4th ed.). Upper Saddle River, NJ: Prentice Hall.

Fletcher, Anne C., Steinberg, Laurence, & Williams-Wheeler, Meeshay. (2004). Parental influences on adolescent problem behavior: Revisiting Stattin and Kerr. *Child Development, 75,* 781–796.

Flook, Lisa, Repetti, Rena L., & Ullman, Jodie B. (2005). Classroom social experiences as predictors of academic performance. *Developmental Psychology, 41,* 319–327.

Floor, Penelope, & Akhtar, Nameera. (2006). Can 18-month-old infants learn words by listening in on conversations? *Infancy, 9,* 327–339.

Flory, Richard W., & Miller, Donald E. (2000). *GenX religion*. New York: Routledge.

Flynn, James R. (1999). Searching for justice: The discovery of IQ gains over time. *American Psychologist, 54,* 5–20.

Flynn, James R. (2007). *What is intelligence? Beyond the Flynn effect.* New York: Cambridge University Press.

Forbes, Erika E., Fox, Nathan A., Cohn, Jeffrey F., Galles, Steven F., & Kovacs, Maria. (2006). Children's affect regulation during a disappointment: Psychophysiological responses and relation to parent history of depression. *Biological Psychology, 71,* 264–277.

Fox, Nathan A., Henderson, Heather A., Rubin, Kenneth H., Calkins, Susan D., & Schmidt, Louis A. (2001). Continuity and discontinuity of behavioral inhibition and exuberance: Psychophysiological and behavioral influences across the first four years of life. *Child Development, 72,* 1–21.

Foxman, Betsy, Newman, Mark, Percha, Bethany, Holmes, King K., & Aral, Sevgi O. (2006). Measures of sexual partnerships: Lengths, gaps, overlaps, and sexually transmitted infection. *Sexually Transmitted Diseases, 33,* 209–214.

Frank, Michael J., Rudy, Jerry W., Levy, William B., & O'Reilly, Randall C. (2005). When logic fails: Implicit transitive inference in humans. *Memory & Cognition, 33,* 742–750.

Frankenburg, William K., Dodds, Josiah, Archer, Philip, Shapiro, Howard, & Bresnick, Beverly. (1992). The Denver II: A major revision and restandardization of the Denver Developmental Screening Test. *Pediatrics, 89,* 91–97.

Franko, Debra L., Thompson, Douglas, Affenito, Sandra G., Barton, Bruce A., & Striegel-Moore, Ruth H. (2008). What mediates the relationship between family meals and adolescent health issues. *Health Psychology, 27*(Suppl. 2), S109–S117.

Frayling, Timothy M., Timpson, Nicholas J., Weedon, Michael N., Zeggini, Eleftheria, Freathy, Rachel M., Lindgren, Cecilia M., et al. (2007, May 11). A common variant in the FTO gene is associated with body mass index and predisposes to childhood and adult obesity. *Science, 316,* 889–894.

Fredricks, Jennifer A., Blumenfeld, Phyllis C., & Paris, Alison H. (2004). School engagement: Potential of the concept, state of the evidence. *Review of Educational Research, 74,* 59–109.

Fredricks, Jennifer A., & Eccles, Jacquelynne S. (2002). Children's competence and value beliefs from childhood through adolescence: Growth trajectories in two male-sex-typed domains. *Developmental Psychology, 38,* 519–533.

Fredricks, Jennifer A., & Eccles, Jacquelynne S. (2006). Is extracurricular participation associated with beneficial outcomes? Concurrent and longitudinal relations. *Developmental Psychology, 42,* 698–713.

Fredriksen, Katia, Rhodes, Jean, Reddy, Ranjini, & Way, Niobe. (2004). Sleepless in Chicago: Tracking the effects of adolescent sleep loss during the middle school years. *Child Development, 75,* 84–95.

Freedman, David S., Khan, Laura Kettel, Serdula, Mary K., Ogden, Cynthia L., & Dietz, William H. (2006). Racial and ethnic differences in secular trends for childhood BMI, weight, and height. *Obesity, 14,* 301–308.

French, Howard W. (2005, February 17). As girls 'vanish,' Chinese city battles tide of abortions. *New York Times,* p. A4.

French, Sabine Elizabeth, Seidman, Edward, Allen, LaRue, & Aber, J. Lawrence. (2006). The development of ethnic identity during adolescence. *Developmental Psychology, 42,* 1–10.

Freud, Anna. (2000). Adolescence. In James B. McCarthy (Ed.), *Adolescent development and psychopathology* (Vol. 13, pp. 29–52). Lanham, MD: University Press of America. (Reprinted from *Psychoanalytic Study of the Child,* pp. 255–278, 1958, New Haven, CT: Yale University Press)

Freud, Sigmund. (1935). *A general introduction to psychoanalysis* (Joan Riviere, Trans.). New York: Liveright.

Freud, Sigmund. (1938). *The basic writings of Sigmund Freud* (A. A. Brill, Ed.). New York: Modern Library.

Freud, Sigmund. (1964). An outline of psycho-analysis. In James Strachey (Ed. and Trans.), *The standard edition of the complete psychological works of Sigmund Freud* (Vol. 23, pp. 144–207). London: Hogarth Press. (Original work published 1940)

Frey, Karin S., Hirschstein, Miriam K., Snell, Jennie L., Van Schoiack-Edstrom, Leihua, MacKenzie, Elizabeth P., & Broderick, Carole J. (2005). Reducing playground bullying and supporting beliefs: An experimental trial of the Steps to Respect program. *Developmental Psychology, 41,* 479–491.

Friedlander, Laura J., Connolly, Jennifer A., Pepler, Debra J., & Craig, Wendy M. (2007). Biological, familial, and peer influences on dating in early adolescence. *Archives of Sexual Behavior, 36,* 821–830.

Friedman, Michael S., Powell, Kenneth E., Hutwagner, Lori, Graham, LeRoy M., & Teague, W. Gerald. (2001). Impact of changes in transportation and commuting behaviors during the 1996 Summer Olympic Games in Atlanta on air quality and childhood asthma. *Journal of the American Medical Association, 285,* 897–905.

Fries, Alison B. Wismer, & Pollak, Seth D. (2007). Emotion processing and the developing brain. In Donna Coch, Kurt W. Fischer, & Geraldine Dawson (Eds.), *Human behavior, learning, and the developing brain. Typical development* (pp. 329–361). New York: Guilford Press.

Fujita, Hidenori. (2000). Education reform and education politics in Japan. *The American Sociologist, 31*(3), 42–57.

Fuligni, Andrew J., & Hardway, Christina. (2006). Daily variation in adolescents' sleep, activities, and psychological well-being. *Journal of Research on Adolescence, 16,* 353–378.

Fuligni, Andrew J., Witkow, Melissa, & Garcia, Carla. (2005). Ethnic identity and the academic adjustment of adolescents from Mexican, Chinese, and European backgrounds. *Developmental Psychology, 41,* 799–811.

Furstenberg, Frank F., & Cherlin, Andrew J. (1991). *Divided families: What happens to children when parents part.* Cambridge, MA: Harvard University Press.

Gaertner, Bridget M., Spinrad, Tracy L., Eisenberg, Nancy, & Greving, Karissa A. (2007). Parental childrearing attitudes as correlates of father involvement during infancy. *Journal of Marriage and Family, 69,* 962–976.

Gagnon, John H., Giami, Alain, Michaels, Stuart, & de Colomby, Patrick. (2001). A comparative study of the couple in the social organization of sexuality in France and the United States. *Journal of Sex Research, 38,* 24–34.

Galambos, Nancy L. (2004). Gender and gender role development in adolescence. In Richard M. Lerner & Laurence D. Steinberg (Eds.), *Handbook of adolescent psychology* (2nd ed., pp. 233–262). Hoboken, NJ: Wiley.

Galambos, Nancy L., Barker, Erin T., & Almeida, David M. (2003). Parents do matter: Trajectories of change in externalizing and internalizing problems in early adolescence. *Child Development, 74,* 578–594.

Galambos, Nancy L., Barker, Erin T., & Krahn, Harvey J. (2006). Depression, self-esteem, and anger in emerging adulthood: Seven-year trajectories. *Developmental Psychology, 42,* 350–365.

Gall, Stanley (Ed.). (1996). *Multiple pregnancy and delivery.* St. Louis, MO: Mosby.

Gallup, Gordon G., Anderson, James R., & Shillito, Daniel J. (2002). The mirror test. In Marc Bekoff, Colin Allen, & Gordon M. Burghardt (Eds.), *The cognitive animal: Empirical and theoretical perspectives on animal cognition* (pp. 325–333). Cambridge, MA: MIT Press.

Galotti, Kathleen M. (2002). *Making decisions that matter: How people face important life choices.* Mahwah, NJ: Erlbaum.

Gandini, Leila, Hill, Lynn, Cadwell, Louise, & Schwall, Charles (Eds.). (2005). *In the spirit of the studio: Learning from the atelier of Reggio Emilia.* New York: Teachers College Press.

Gantley, M., Davies, D. P., & Murcott, A. (1993). Sudden infant death syndrome: Links with infant care practices. *British Medical Journal, 306,* 16–20.

Garbarini, Francesca, & Adenzato, Mauro. (2004). At the root of embodied cognition: Cognitive science meets neurophysiology. *Brain and Cognition, 56,* 100–106.

García-Pérez, Rosa M., Hobson, R. Peter, & Lee, Anthony. (2008). Narrative role-taking in autism. *Journal of Autism and Developmental Disorders, 38,* 156–168.

Gardner, Howard. (1983). *Frames of mind: The theory of multiple intelligences.* New York: Basic Books.

Gardner, Howard. (1999). Are there additional intelligences? The case for naturalist, spiritual, and existential intelligences. In Jeffrey Kane (Ed.), *Education, information, and transformation: Essays on learning and thinking* (pp. 111–131). Upper Saddle River, NJ: Merrill.

Gardner, Howard, & Moran, Seana. (2006). The science of multiple intelligences theory: A response to Lynn Waterhouse. *Educational Psychologist, 41,* 227–232.

Gardner, Margo, & Steinberg, Laurence. (2005). Peer influence on risk taking, risk preference, and risky decision making in adolescence and adulthood: An experimental study. *Developmental Psychology, 41,* 625–635.

Garofalo, Robert, Wolf, R. Cameron, Wissow, Lawrence S., Woods, Elizabeth R., & Goodman, Elizabeth. (1999). Sexual orientation and risk of suicide attempts among a representative sample of youth. *Archives of Pediatrics & Adolescent Medicine, 153,* 487–493.

Gathercole, Susan E., Pickering, Susan J., Ambridge, Benjamin, & Wearing, Hannah. (2004). The structure of working memory from 4 to 15 years of age. *Developmental Psychology, 40,* 177–190.

Gatzke-Kopp, Lisa M., & Beauchaine, Theodore P. (2007). Central nervous system substrates of impulsivity: Implications for the development of attention-deficit/hyperactivity disorder and conduct disorder. In Donna Coch, Geraldine Dawson, & Kurt W. Fischer (Eds.), *Human behavior, learning, and the developing brain: Atypical development* (pp. 239–263). New York: Guilford Press.

Gauvain, Mary. (2005). Scaffolding in socialization. *New Ideas in Psychology, 23,* 129–139.

Gaysina, Daria, Zainullina, Aigul, Gabdulhakov, Rail, & Khusnutdinova, Elza. (2006). The serotonin transporter gene: Polymorphism and haplotype analysis in Russian suicide attempters. *Neuropsychobiology, 54,* 70–74.

Gdalevich, Michael, Mimouni, Daniel, & Mimouni, Marc. (2001). Breast-feeding and the risk of bronchial asthma in childhood: A systematic review with meta-analysis of prospective studies. *Journal of Pediatrics, 139,* 261–266.

Ge, Xiaojia, Conger, Rand D., & Elder, Glen H., Jr. (2001). Pubertal transition, stressful life events, and the emergence of gender differences in adolescent depressive symptoms. *Developmental Psychology, 37,* 404–417.

Ge, Xiaojia, Kim, Irene J., Brody, Gene H., Conger, Rand D., Simons, Ronald L., Gibbons, Frederick X., et al. (2003). It's about timing and change: Pubertal transition effects on symptoms of major depression among African American youths. *Developmental Psychology, 39,* 430–439.

Ge, Xiaojia, Natsuaki, Misaki N., Neiderhiser, Jenae M., & Reiss, David. (2007). Genetic and environmental influences on pubertal timing: Results from two national sibling studies. *Journal of Research on Adolescence, 17,* 767–788.

Geary, Nori, & Lovejoy, Jennifer. (2008). Sex differences in energy metabolism, obesity, and eating behavior. In Jill B. Becker, Karen J. Berkley, Nori Geary, Elizabeth Hampson, James P. Herman, & Elizabeth Young (Eds.), *Sex differences in the brain: From genes to behavior* (pp. 253–274). New York: Oxford University Press.

Gelman, Susan A., & Kalish, Charles W. (2006). Conceptual development. In Deanna Kuhn & Robert S. Siegler (Series Eds.) & William Damon & Richard M. Lerner (Vol. Eds.), *Handbook of child psychology: Vol. 2. Cognition, perception, and language* (6th ed., pp. 687–733). Hoboken, NJ: Wiley.

Gennetian, Lisa A., & Miller, Cynthia. (2002). Children and welfare reform: A view from an experimental welfare program in Minnesota. *Child Development, 73,* 601–620.

Gentner, Dedre, & Boroditsky, Lera. (2001). Individuation, relativity, and early word learning. In Melissa Bowerman & Stephen C. Levinson (Eds.), *Language acquisition and conceptual development* (pp. 215–256). Cambridge, UK: Cambridge University Press.

Georgas, James, Berry, John W., van de Vijver, Fons J. R., Kagitçibasi, Çigdem, & Poortinga, Ype H. (2006). *Families across cultures: A 30-nation psychological study.* Cambridge, UK: Cambridge University Press.

Georgieff, Michael K., & Rao, Raghavendra. (2001). The role of nutrition in cognitive development. In Charles A. Nelson & Monica Luciana (Eds.), *Handbook of developmental cognitive neuroscience* (pp. 149–158). Cambridge, MA: MIT Press.

Geronimus, Arline T., Hicken, Margaret, Keene, Danya, & Bound, John. (2006). "Weathering" and age patterns of allostatic load scores among Blacks and Whites in the United States. *American Journal of Public Health, 96,* 826–833.

Gerrard, Meg, Gibbons, Frederick X., Houlihan, Amy E., Stock, Michelle L., & Pomery, Elizabeth A. (2008). A dual-process approach to health risk decision making: The prototype willingness model. *Developmental Review, 28,* 29–61.

Gershkoff-Stowe, Lisa, & Hahn, Erin R. (2007). Fast mapping skills in the developing lexicon. *Journal of Speech, Language, and Hearing Research, 50,* 682–696.

Gershoff, Elizabeth Thompson. (2002). Corporal punishment by parents and associated child behaviors and experiences: A meta-analytic and theoretical review. *Psychological Bulletin, 128,* 539–579.

Gershoff, Elizabeth T., Aber, J. Lawrence, Raver, C. Cybele, & Lennon, Mary Clare. (2007). Income is not enough: Incorporating material hardship into models of income associations with parenting and child development. *Child Development, 78,* 70–95.

Getahun, Darios, Oyelese, Yinka, Salihu, Hamisu M., & Ananth, Cande V. (2006). Previous cesarean delivery and risks of placenta previa and placental abruption. *Obstetrics & Gynecology, 107,* 771–778.

Gibbons, Ann. (2006, December 15). There's more than one way to have your milk and drink it, too. *Science, 314,* 1672a.

Gibson, Eleanor J. (1969). *Principles of perceptual learning and development.* New York: Appleton-Century-Crofts.

Gibson, Eleanor J. (1988). Levels of description and constraints on perceptual development. In Albert Yonas (Ed.), *Perceptual development in infancy* (pp. 283–296). Hillsdale, NJ: Erlbaum.

Gibson, Eleanor J. (1997). An ecological psychologist's prolegomena for perceptual development: A functional approach. In Cathy Dent-Read & Patricia Zukow-Goldring (Eds.), *Evolving explanations of development: Ecological approaches to organism-environment systems* (pp. 23–54). Washington, DC: American Psychological Association.

Gibson, Eleanor J., Gibson, James J., Smith, Olin W., & Flock, Howard. (1959). Motion parallax as a determinant of perceived depth. *Journal of Experimental Psychology, 58,* 40–51.

Gibson, Eleanor J., & Walk, Richard D. (1960). The "visual cliff." *Scientific American, 202*(4), 64–71.

Gibson, James Jerome. (1979). *The ecological approach to visual perception.* Boston: Houghton Mifflin.

Gibson-Davis, Christina M., & Brooks-Gunn, Jeanne. (2006). Couples' immigration status and ethnicity as determinants of breastfeeding. *American Journal of Public Health, 96,* 641–646.

Gifford-Smith, Mary E., & Rabiner, David L. (2004). Social information processing and children's social adjustment. In Janis B. Kupersmidt & Kenneth A. Dodge (Eds.), *Children's peer relations: From development to intervention* (pp. 61–79). Washington, DC: American Psychological Association.

Gigerenzer, Gerd, Todd, Peter M., & ABC Research Group. (1999). *Simple heuristics that make us smart.* New York: Oxford University Press.

Gilchrist, Heidi, & Sullivan, Gerard. (2006). The role of gender and sexual relations for young people in identity construction and youth suicide. *Culture, Health & Sexuality, 8,* 195–209.

Gilhooly, Mary. (2002). Ethical issues in researching later life. In Anne Jamieson & Christina R. Victor (Eds.), *Researching ageing and later life: The practice of social gerontology* (pp. 211–225). Philadelphia: Open University Press.

Gilligan, Carol, Murphy, John Michael, & Tappan, Mark B. (1990). Moral development beyond adolescence. In Charles N. Alexander & Ellen J. Langer (Eds.), *Higher stages of human development: Perspectives on adult growth* (pp. 208–225). London: Oxford University Press.

Gilliom, Miles, Shaw, Daniel S., Beck, Joy E., Schonberg, Michael A., & Lukon, JoElla L. (2002). Anger regulation in disadvantaged preschool boys: Strategies, antecedents, and the development of self-control. *Developmental Psychology, 38,* 222–235.

Gimelbrant, Alexander, Hutchinson, John N., Thompson, Benjamin R., & Chess, Andrew. (2007, November 16). Widespread monoallelic expression on human autosomes. *Science, 318,* 1136–1140.

Ginsburg, Herbert P., Klein, Alice, & Starkey, Prentice. (1998). The development of children's mathematical thinking: Connecting research with practice. In William Damon (Series Ed.) & Irving E. Sigel & K. Ann Renninger (Vol. Eds.), *Handbook of child psychology: Vol. 4. Child psychology in practice* (5th ed., pp. 401–476). New York: Wiley.

Glanville, Jennifer L., Sikkink, David, & Hernández, Edwin I. (2008). Religious involvement and educational outcomes: The role of social capital and extracurricular participation. *Sociological Quarterly, 49,* 105–137.

Glass, Roger I., & Parashar, Umesh D. (2006). The promise of new rotavirus vaccines. *New England Journal of Medicine, 354,* 75–77.

Glauber, James H., Farber, Harold J., & Homer, Charles J. (2001). Asthma clinical pathways: Toward what end? *Pediatrics, 107,* 590–592.

Glazer, Deborah F., & Drescher, Jack (Eds.). (2001). *Gay and lesbian parenting.* New York: Haworth Medical Press.

Gleason, Jean Berko, & Ely, Richard. (2002). Gender differences in language development. In Ann McGillicuddy-De Lisi & Richard De Lisi (Eds.), *Advances in applied developmental psychology: Vol. 21. Biology, society, and behavior: The development of sex differences in cognition* (pp. 127–154). Westport, CT: Ablex.

Glover, Evam Kofi, Bannerman, Angela, Pence, Brian Wells, Jones, Heidi, Miller, Robert, Weiss, Eugene, et al. (2003). Sexual health experiences of adolescents in three Ghanaian towns. *International Family Planning Perspectives, 29,* 32–40.

Gluckman, Peter D., & Hanson, Mark A. (2006). *Developmental origins of health and disease.* Cambridge, England: Cambridge University Press.

Gnaulati, Enrico, & Heine, Barb J. (2001). Separation-individuation in late adolescence: An investigation of gender and ethnic differences. *Journal of Psychology: Interdisciplinary and Applied, 135,* 59–70.

Goel, Mita Sanghavi, McCarthy, Ellen P., Phillips, Russell S., & Wee, Christina C. (2004). Obesity among US immigrant subgroups by duration of residence. *Journal of the American Medical Association, 292,* 2860–2867.

Goldberg, Wendy A., Prause, JoAnn, Lucas-Thompson, Rachel, & Himsel, Amy. (2008). Maternal employment and children's achievement in context: A meta-analysis of four decades of research. *Psychological Bulletin, 134,* 77–108.

Golden, Janet Lynne. (2005). *Message in a bottle: The making of fetal alcohol syndrome.* Cambridge, MA: Harvard University Press.

Goldin-Meadow, Susan. (2006). Nonverbal communication: The hand's role in talking and thinking. In William Damon & Richard M. Lerner (Series Eds.) & Deanna Kuhn & Robert S. Siegler (Vol. Eds.), *Handbook of child psychology: Vol. 2. Cognition, perception, and language* (6th ed., pp. 336–369). Hoboken, NJ: Wiley.

Goldin-Meadow, Susan, & Mayberry, Rachel I. (2001). How do profoundly deaf children learn to read? *Learning Disabilities Research & Practice, 16,* 222–229.

Goldsmith, Sara K., Pellmar, Terry C., Kleinman, Arthur M., & Bunney, William E. (Eds.). (2002). *Reducing suicide: A national imperative.* Washington, DC: National Academies Press.

Goldstein, Sara E., Davis-Kean, Pamela E., & Eccles, Jacquelynne S. (2005). Parents, peers, and problem behavior: A longitudinal investigation of the impact of relationship perceptions and characteristics on the development of adolescent problem behavior. *Developmental Psychology, 41,* 401–413.

Goldston, David B., Molock, Sherry Davis, Whitbeck, Leslie B., Murakami, Jessica L., Zayas, Luis H., & Hall, Gordon C. Nagayama. (2008). Cultural considerations in adolescent suicide prevention and psychosocial treatment. *American Psychologist, 63,* 14–31.

Goleman, Daniel. (1995). *Emotional intelligence.* New York: Bantam Books.

Gonzales, Nancy A., Dumka, Larry E., Deardorff, Julianna, Carter, Sara Jacobs, & McCray, Adam. (2004). Preventing poor mental health and school dropout of Mexican American adolescents following the transition to junior high school. *Journal of Adolescent Research, 19,* 113–131.

Goodwyn, Susan W., Acredolo, Linda P., & Brown, Catherine A. (2000). Impact of symbolic gesturing on early language development. *Journal of Nonverbal Behavior, 24,* 81–103.

Gopnik, Alison. (2001). Theories, language, and culture: Whorf without wincing. In Melissa Bowerman & Stephen C. Levinson (Eds.), *Language acquisition and conceptual development* (pp. 45–69). Cambridge, UK: Cambridge University Press.

Gopnik, Alison, & Schulz, Laura (Eds.). (2007). *Causal learning: Psychology, philosophy, and computation.* New York: Oxford University Press.

Gordis, Elana B., Granger, Douglas A., Susman, Elizabeth J., & Trickett, Penelope K. (2008). Salivary alpha amylase-cortisol asymmetry in maltreated youth. *Hormones and Behavior, 53,* 96–103.

Gordon, Peter. (2004, August 19). Numerical cognition without words: Evidence from Amazonia. *Science, 306,* 496–499.

Gorenstein, Ethan E., & Comer, Ronald J. (2002). *Case studies in abnormal psychology.* New York: Worth.

Goss, David A. (2002). More evidence that near work contributes to myopia development. *Indiana Journal of Optometry, 5,* 11–13.

Gottlieb, Alma. (2000). Luring your child into this life: A Beng path for infant care. In Judy S. DeLoache & Alma Gottlieb (Eds.), *A world of babies: Imagined childcare guides for seven societies* (pp. 55–90). New York: Cambridge University Press.

Gottlieb, Gilbert. (1992). *Individual development and evolution: The genesis of novel behavior.* New York: Oxford University Press.

Gottlieb, Gilbert. (2002). *Individual development and evolution: The genesis of novel behavior.* Mahwah, NJ: Erlbaum. (Original work published 1992)

Gottlieb, Gilbert. (2003). Probabilistic epigenesis of development. In Jaan Valsiner & Kevin J. Connolly (Eds.), *Handbook of developmental psychology* (pp. 3–17). Thousand Oaks, CA: Sage.

Gould, Madelyn. (2003). Suicide risk among adolescents. In Daniel Romer (Ed.), *Reducing adolescent risk: Toward an integrated approach* (pp. 303–320). Thousand Oaks, CA: Sage.

Goymer, Patrick. (2007). Genes know their left from their right. *Nature Reviews Genetics, 8,* 652–652.

Graber, Julia A. (2004). Internalizing problems during adolescence. In Richard M. Lerner & Laurence D. Steinberg (Eds.), *Handbook of adolescent psychology* (2nd ed., pp. 587–626). Hoboken, NJ: Wiley.

Gradin, Maria, Eriksson, Mats, Holmqvist, Gunilla, Holstein, Åsa, & Schollin, Jens. (2002). Pain reduction at venipuncture in newborns: Oral glucose compared with local anesthetic cream. *Pediatrics, 110,* 1053–1057.

Grady, Denise. (2007, February 6). Girl or boy? As fertility technology advances, so does an ethical debate. *New York Times.*

Graham, John W., & Beller, Andrea H. (2002). Nonresident fathers and their children: Child support and visitation from an economic perspective. In Catherine S. Tamis-LeMonda & Natasha Cabrera (Eds.), *Handbook of father involvement: Multidisciplinary perspectives* (pp. 431–453). Mahwah, NJ: Erlbaum.

Graham, Susan A., Kilbreath, Cari S., & Welder, Andrea N. (2004). Thirteen-month-olds rely on shared labels and shape similarity for inductive inferences. *Child Development, 75,* 409–427.

Granic, Isabela, Dishion, Thomas J., & Hollenstein, Tom. (2003). The family ecology of adolescence: A dynamic systems perspective on normative development. In Gerald R. Adams & Michael D. Berzonsky (Eds.), *Blackwell handbook of adolescence* (pp. 60–91). Malden, MA: Blackwell.

Granic, Isabela, & Patterson, Gerald R. (2006). Toward a comprehensive model of antisocial development: A dynamic systems approach. *Psychological Review, 113,* 101–131.

Gray, Nicola J., Klein, Jonathan D., Noyce, Peter R., Sesselberg, Tracy S., & Cantrill, Judith A. (2005). Health information-seeking behaviour in adolescence: The place of the internet. *Social Science & Medicine, 60,* 1467–1478.

Green, Christa L., & Hoover-Dempsey, Kathleen V. (2007). Why do parents homeschool? A systematic examination of parental involvement. *Education and Urban Society, 39,* 264–285.

Green, Nancy S., Dolan, Siobhan M., & Murray, Thomas H. (2006). Newborn screening: Complexities in universal genetic testing. *American Journal of Public Health, 96,* 1955–1959.

Green, Ridgely Fisk, Olney, Richard S., Reefhuis, Jennita, Botto, Lorenzo D., & Romitti, Paul A. (2008). Maternal reports of family history from the National Birth Defects Prevention Study, 1997–2001. *Genetics in Medicine, 10,* 37–45.

Greenberger, Ellen, & Steinberg, Laurence D. (1986). *When teenagers work: The psychological and social costs of adolescent employment.* New York: Basic Books.

Greene, Anthony J., Gross, William L., Elsinger, Catherine L., & Rao, Stephen M. (2006). An fMRI analysis of the human hippocampus: Inference, context, and task awareness. *Journal of Cognitive Neuroscience, 18,* 1156–1173.

Greene, Melissa L., & Way, Niobe. (2005). Self-esteem trajectories among ethnic minority adolescents: A growth curve analysis of the patterns and predictors of change. *Journal of Research on Adolescence, 15,* 151–178.

Greene, Melissa L., Way, Niobe, & Pahl, Kerstin. (2006). Trajectories of perceived adult and peer discrimination among Black, Latino, and Asian American adolescents: Patterns and psychological correlates. *Developmental Psychology, 42,* 218–238.

Greenfield, Patricia M., Gross, Elisheva F., Subrahmanyam, Kaveri, Suzuki, Lalita K., & Tynes, Brendesha. (2006). Teens on the Internet: Interpersonal connection, identity, and information. In Robert Kraut, Malcolm Brynin, & Sara Kiesler (Eds.), *Computers, phones, and the Internet: Domesticating information technology* (pp. 185–200). New York: Oxford University Press.

Greenough, William T. (1993). Brain adaptation to experience: An update. In Mark H. Johnson (Ed.), *Brain development and cognition: A reader* (pp. 319–322). Oxford, UK: Blackwell.

Greenough, William T., Black, James E., & Wallace, Christopher S. (1987).

Experience and brain development. *Child Development, 58,* 539–559.

Greenough, William T., & Volkmar, Fred R. (1973). Pattern of dendritic branching in occipital cortex of rats reared in complex environments. *Experimental Neurology, 40,* 491–504.

Greenspan, Stanley I., & Wieder, Serena. (2006). *Engaging autism: Using the floortime approach to help children relate, communicate, and think.* Cambridge, MA: Da Capo Lifelong Books.

Griebel, Wilfried, & Niesel, Renate. (2002). Co-constructing transition into kindergarten and school by children, parents, and teachers. In Hilary Fabian & Aline-Wendy Dunlop (Eds.), *Transitions in the early years: Debating continuity and progression for young children in early education* (pp. 64–75). New York: RoutledgeFalmer.

Grigorenko, Elena L., & O'Keefe, Paul A. (2004). What do children do when they cannot go to school? In Robert J. Sternberg & Elena L. Grigorenko (Eds.), *Culture and competence: Contexts of life success* (pp. 23–53). Washington, DC: American Psychological Association.

Grobman, Kevin H. (2008). *Learning & teaching developmental psychology: Attachment theory, infancy, & infant memory development.* Retrieved August 28, 2008, from the World Wide Web: http://www.devpsy.org/questions/attachment_theory_memory.html

Grollmann, Philipp, & Rauner, Felix. (2007). Exploring innovative apprenticeship: Quality and costs. *Education & Training, 49,* 431–446.

Grolnick, Wendy S., Deci, Edward L., & Ryan, Richard M. (1997). Internalization within the family: The self-determination theory perspective. In Joan E. Grusec & Leon Kuczynski (Eds.), *Parenting and children's internalization of values: A handbook of contemporary theory* (pp. 135–161). New York: Wiley.

Grolnick, Wendy S., McMenamy, Jannette M., & Kurowski, Carolyn O. (2006). Emotional self-regulation in infancy and toddlerhood. In Lawrence Balter & Catherine S. Tamis-LeMonda (Eds.), *Child psychology: A handbook of contemporary issues* (2nd ed., pp. 3–25). New York: Psychology Press.

Gros-Louis, Julie, West, Meredith J., Goldstein, Michael H., & King, Andrew P. (2006). Mothers provide differential feedback to infants' prelinguistic sounds. *International Journal of Behavioral Development, 30,* 509–516.

Gross, Jane. (2007, December 11). U.S. joins overseas adoption overhaul plan. *New York Times,* p. A29.

Grossmann, Klaus E., Grossmann, Karin, & Waters, Everett (Eds.). (2005). *Attachment from infancy to adulthood: The major longitudinal studies.* New York: Guilford Press.

Grosvenor, Theodore. (2003). Why is there an epidemic of myopia? *Clinical and Experimental Optometry, 86,* 273–275.

Guerin, Diana Wright, Gottfried, Allen W., Oliver, Pamella H., & Thomas, Craig W. (2003). *Temperament: Infancy through adolescence: The Fullerton longitudinal study.* New York: Kluwer Academic/Plenum.

Guest, Andrew M. (2007). Cultures of childhood and psychosocial characteristics: Self-esteem and social comparison in two distinct communities. *Ethos, 35,* 1–32.

Guilamo-Ramos, Vincent, Jaccard, James, Dittus, Patricia, & Bouris, Alida M. (2006). Parental expertise, trustworthiness, and accessibility: Parent–adolescent communication and adolescent risk behavior. *Journal of Marriage and Family, 68,* 1229–1246.

Guillaume, Michele, & Lissau, Inge. (2002). Epidemiology. In Walter Burniat, Tim J. Cole, Inge Lissau, & Elizabeth M. E. Poskitt (Eds.), *Child and adolescent obesity: Causes and consequences, prevention and management* (pp. 28–49). New York: Cambridge University Press.

Gummerum, Michaela, Keller, Monika, Takezawa, Masanori, & Mata, Jutta. (2008). To give or not to give: Children's and adolescents' sharing and moral negotiations in economic decision situations. *Child Development, 79,* 562–576.

Gurney, James G., Fritz, Melissa S., Ness, Kirsten K., Sievers, Phillip, Newschaffer, Craig J., & Shapiro, Elsa G. (2003). Analysis of prevalence trends of autism spectrum disorder in Minnesota. *Archives of Pediatrics & Adolescent Medicine, 157,* 622–627.

Gustafson, Kathryn E., Bonner, Melanie J., Hardy, Kristina K., & Thompson, Robert J., Jr. (2006). Biopsychosocial and developmental issues in sickle cell disease. In Ronald T. Brown (Ed.), *Comprehensive handbook of childhood cancer and sickle cell disease: A biopsychosocial approach* (pp. 431–448). New York: Oxford University Press.

Guzell, Jacqueline R., & Vernon-Feagans, Lynne. (2004). Parental perceived control over caregiving and its relationship to parent–infant interaction. *Child Development, 75,* 134–146.

Hack, Maureen, Flannery, Daniel J., Schluchter, Mark, Cartar, Lydia, Borawski, Elaine, & Klein, Nancy. (2002). Outcomes in young adulthood for very-low-birth-weight infants. *New England Journal of Medicine, 346,* 149–157.

Hagerman, Randi Jenssen, & Hagerman, Paul J. (2002). *Fragile X syndrome: Diagnosis, treatment, and research* (3rd ed.). Baltimore: Johns Hopkins University Press.

Halford, Graeme S., & Andrews, Glenda. (2006). Reasoning and problem solving. In William Damon & Richard M. Lerner (Series Eds.) & Deanna Kuhn & Robert S. Siegler (Vol. Eds.), *Handbook of child psychology: Vol. 2. Cognition, perception, and language* (6th ed., pp. 557–608). Hoboken, NJ: Wiley.

Hall-Lande, Jennifer A., Eisenberg, Marla E., Christenson, Sandra L., & Neumark-Sztainer, Dianne. (2007). Social isolation, psychological health, and protective factors in adolescence. *Adolescence, 42,* 265–286.

Halpern, Carolyn Tucker, King, Rosalind Berkowitz, Oslak, Selene G., & Udry, J. Richard. (2005). Body mass index, dieting, romance, and sexual activity in adolescent girls: Relationships over time. *Journal of Research on Adolescence, 15,* 535–559.

Hamerton, John L., & Evans, Jane A. (2005). Sex chromosome anomalies. In Merlin Gene Butler & F. John Meaney (Eds.), *Genetics of developmental disabilities* (pp. 585–650). Boca Raton, FL: Taylor & Francis.

Hamilton, Brady E., Martin, Joyce A., & Ventura, Stephanie J. (2007). Births: Preliminary data for 2006. *National Vital Statistics Reports, 56*(7), 1–18.

Hamm, Jill V., & Faircloth, Beverly S. (2005). The role of friendship in adolescents' sense of school belonging. *New Directions for Child and Adolescent Development, 107,* 61–78.

Hammen, Constance. (2003). Risk and protective factors for children of depressed parents. In Suniya S. Luthar (Ed.), *Resilience and vulnerability: Adaptation in the context of childhood adversities* (pp. 50–75). New York: Cambridge University Press.

Hammond, Christopher J., Andrew, Toby, Mak, Ying Tat, & Spector, Tim D.

(2004). A susceptibility locus for myopia in the normal population is linked to the PAX6 gene region on chromosome 11: A genome-wide scan of dizygotic twins. *American Journal of Human Genetics, 75,* 294–304.

Hane, Amie Ashley, & Fox, Nathan A. (2006). Ordinary variations in maternal caregiving influence human infants' stress reactivity. *Psychological Science, 17,* 550–556.

Hanna, Jacob, Wernig, Marius, Markoulaki, Styliani, Sun, Chiao-Wang, Meissner, Alexander, Cassady, John P., et al. (2007, December 21). Treatment of sickle cell anemia mouse model with iPS cells generated from autologous skin. *Science, 318,* 1920–1923.

Hanushek, Eric A. (1999). The evidence on class size. In Susan E. Mayer & Paul E. Peterson (Eds.), *Earning and learning: How schools matter* (pp. 131–168). Washington, DC: Brookings Institution Press/Russell Sage Foundation.

Harding, Stephan. (2006). *Animate earth: Science, intuition and Gaia.* Totnes, Devon, UK: Green Books.

Harjes, Carlos E., Rocheford, Torbert R., Bai, Ling, Brutnell, Thomas P., Kandianis, Catherine Bermudez, Sowinski, Stephen G., et al. (2008, January 18). Natural genetic variation in Lycopene Epsilon Cyclase tapped for maize biofortification. *Science, 319,* 330–333.

Harlow, Harry F. (1958). The nature of love. *American Psychologist, 13,* 673–685.

Harlow, Harry Frederick. (1986). *From learning to love: The selected papers of H. F. Harlow* (Clara Mears Harlow, Ed.). New York: Praeger.

Harris, Judith Rich. (1998). *The nurture assumption: Why children turn out the way they do.* New York: Free Press.

Harris, Judith Rich. (2002). Beyond the nurture assumption: Testing hypotheses about the child's environment. In John G. Borkowski, Sharon Landesman Ramey, & Marie Bristol-Power (Eds.), *Parenting and the child's world: Influences on academic, intellectual, and social-emotional development* (pp. 3–20). Mahwah, NJ: Erlbaum.

Harris, Paul L. (2000). On not falling down to earth: Children's metaphysical questions. In Karl Sven Rosengren, Carl N. Johnson, & Paul L. Harris (Eds.), *Imagining the impossible: Magical, scientific, and religious thinking in children* (pp. 157–178). New York: Cambridge University Press.

Harrison, Paul J., & Weinberger, Daniel R. (2005). Schizophrenia genes, gene expression, and neuropathology: On the matter of their convergence. *Molecular Psychiatry, 10,* 40–68.

Hart, Betty, & Risley, Todd R. (1995). *Meaningful differences in the everyday experience of young American children.* Baltimore: Brookes.

Hart, Daniel, Atkins, Robert, & Fegley, Suzanne. (2003). Personality and development in childhood: A person-centered approach. *Monographs of the Society for Research in Child Development, 68*(Serial No. 272), vii–109.

Harter, Susan. (1998). The development of self-representations. In William Damon (Series Ed.) & Nancy Eisenberg (Vol. Ed.), *Handbook of child psychology: Vol. 3. Social, emotional and personality development* (5th ed., pp. 553–618). New York: Wiley.

Harter, Susan. (1999). *The construction of the self: A developmental perspective.* New York: Guilford Press.

Harter, Susan. (2006). The self. In William Damon & Richard M. Lerner (Series Eds.) & Nancy Eisenberg (Vol. Ed.), *Handbook of child psychology: Vol. 3. Social, emotional, and personality development* (6th ed., pp. 505–570). Hoboken, NJ: Wiley.

Hartl, Daniel L., & Jones, Elizabeth W. (1999). *Essential genetics* (2nd ed.). Sudbury, MA: Jones and Bartlett.

Hartmann, Donald P., & Pelzel, Kelly E. (2005). Design, measurement, and analysis in developmental research. In Marc H. Bornstein & Michael E. Lamb (Eds.), *Developmental science: An advanced textbook* (5th ed., pp. 103–184). Mahwah, NJ: Erlbaum.

Hasebe, Yuki, Nucci, Larry, & Nucci, Maria S. (2004). Parental control of the personal domain and adolescent symptoms of psychopathology: A cross-national study in the United States and Japan. *Child Development, 75,* 815–828.

Haskins, Ron. (2005). Child development and child-care policy: Modest impacts. In David B. Pillemer & Sheldon Harold White (Eds.), *Developmental psychology and social change: Research, history, and policy* (pp. 140–170). New York: Cambridge University Press.

Hassold, Terry J., & Patterson, David (Eds.). (1999). *Down syndrome: A promising future, together.* New York: Wiley-Liss.

Hastie, Peter A. (2004). Problem-solving in teaching sports. In Jan Wright, Lisette Burrows, & Doune MacDonald (Eds.), *Critical inquiry and problem-solving in physical education* (pp. 62–73). London: Routledge.

Hauser-Cram, Penny, Warfield, Marji Erickson, Stadler, Jennifer, & Sirin, Selcuk R. (2006). School environments and the diverging pathways of students living in poverty. In Aletha C. Huston & Marika N. Ripke (Eds.), *Developmental contexts in middle childhood: Bridges to adolescence and adulthood* (pp. 198–216). New York: Cambridge University Press.

Hayden, Deborah. (2003). *Pox: Genius, madness, and the mysteries of syphilis.* New York: Basic Books.

Haydon, Jo. (2007). *Genetics in practice: A clinical approach for healthcare practitioners.* Hoboken, NJ: Wiley.

Hayes, Brett K., & Younger, Katherine. (2004). Category-use effects in children. *Child Development, 75,* 1719–1732.

Hayes, Rachel A., & Slater, Alan. (2008). Three-month-olds' detection of alliteration in syllables. *Infant Behavior & Development 31,* 153–156.

Heath, Andrew C., Madden, Pamela A. F., Bucholz, Kathleen K., Nelson, Elliot C., Todorov, Alexandre, Price, Rumi Kato, et al. (2003). Genetic and environmental risks of dependence on alcohol, tobacco, and other drugs. In Robert Plomin, John C. DeFries, Ian W. Craig, & Peter McGuffin (Eds.), *Behavioral genetics in the postgenomic era* (pp. 309–334). Washington, DC: American Psychological Association.

Heaven, Patrick C. L., & Ciarrochi, Joseph. (2008). Parental styles, conscientiousness, and academic performance in high school: A three-wave longitudinal study. *Personality and Social Psychology Bulletin, 34,* 451–461.

Hechtman, Lily, Abikoff, Howard B., & Jensen, Peter S. (2005). Multimodal therapy and stimulants in the treatment of children with attention-deficit/hyperactivity disorder. In Euthymia D. Hibbs & Peter S. Jensen (Eds.), *Psychosocial treatments for child and adolescent disorders: Empirically based strategies for clinical practice* (2nd ed., pp. 411–437). Washington, DC: American Psychological Association.

Heckers, Stephan, Zalesak, Martin, Weiss, Anthony P., Ditman, Tali, & Titone, Debra. (2004). Hippocampal activation during transitive inference in humans. *Hippocampus, 14,* 153–162.

Heilbrun, Kirk, Goldstein, Naomi E. Sevin, & Redding, Richard E. (Eds.). (2005). *Juvenile delinquency: Prevention, assessment, and intervention*. New York: Oxford University Press.

Heine, Steven J. (2007). Culture and motivation: What motivates people to act in the ways that they do? In Shinobu Kitayama & Dov Cohen (Eds.), *Handbook of cultural psychology* (pp. 714–733). New York: Guilford Press.

Hemminki, Kari, Sundquist, Jan, & Lorenzo Bermejo, Justo. (2008). Familial risks for cancer as the basis for evidence-based clinical referral and counseling. *The Oncologist, 13,* 239–247.

Henderson, Heather A., Marshall, Peter J., Fox, Nathan A., & Rubin, Kenneth H. (2004). Psychophysiological and behavioral evidence for varying forms and functions of nonsocial behavior in preschoolers. *Child Development, 75,* 251–263.

Henig, Robin Marantz. (2004, November 30). Sorry. Your eating disorder doesn't meet our criteria. *New York Times Magazine,* pp. 32–37.

Henson, Sian M., & Aspinall, Richard J. (2003). Ageing and the immune response. In Richard J. Aspinall (Ed.), *Aging of organs and systems* (pp. 225–242). Boston: Kluwer Academic.

Herek, Gregory M. (2006). Legal recognition of same-sex relationships in the United States: A social science perspective. *American Psychologist, 61,* 607–621.

Herman-Giddens, Marcia E., Wang, Lily, & Koch, Gary. (2001). Secondary sexual characteristics in boys: Estimates from the National Health and Nutrition Examination Survey III, 1988–1994. *Archives of Pediatrics & Adolescent Medicine, 155,* 1022–1028.

Hern, Matt, & Chaulk, Stu. (1997). The internet, democracy and community: another.big.lie. *Journal of Family Life, 3*(4), 36–39.

Hernandez-Reif, Maria, Diego, Miguel, & Field, Tiffany. (2007). Preterm infants show reduced stress behaviors and activity after 5 days of massage therapy. *Infant Behavior & Development, 30,* 557–561.

Herschensohn, Julia Rogers. (2007). *Language development and age*. New York: Cambridge University Press.

Hertenstein, Matthew J., & Campos, Joseph J. (2001). Emotion regulation via maternal touch. *Infancy, 2,* 549–566.

Hetherington, E. Mavis, & Kelly, John. (2002). *For better or for worse: Divorce reconsidered*. New York: Norton.

Hetherington, E. Mavis, Reiss, David, & Plomin, Robert (Eds.). (1994). *Separate social worlds of siblings: The impact of nonshared environment on development*. Hillsdale, NJ: Erlbaum.

Heuveline, Patrick. (2002). An international comparison of adolescent and young adult mortality. *Annals of the American Academy of Political and Social Science, 580,* 172–200.

Heuveline, Patrick, & Timberlake, Jeffrey M. (2004). The role of cohabitation in family formation: The United States in comparative perspective. *Journal of Marriage & Family, 66,* 1214–1230.

Hewlett, Barry S., Lamb, Michael E., Shannon, Donald, Leyendecker, Birgit, & Schölmerich, Axel. (1998). Culture and early infancy among central African foragers and farmers. *Developmental Psychology, 34,* 653–661.

Hibbeln, Joseph R., Davis, John M., Steer, Colin, Emmett, Pauline, Rogers, Imogen, Williams, Cathy, et al. (2007). Maternal seafood consumption in pregnancy and neurodevelopmental outcomes in childhood (ALSPAC study): An observational cohort study. *Lancet, 369,* 578–585.

Higgins, Matt. (2006, August 5). Risk of injury is simply an element of motocross. *New York Times,* p. D5.

Higuchi, Susumu, Matsushita, Sachio, Muramatsu, Taro, Murayama, Masanobu, & Hayashida, Motoi. (1996). Alcohol and aldehyde dehydrogenase genotypes and drinking behavior in Japanese. *Alcoholism: Clinical and Experimental Research, 20,* 493–497.

Hildyard, Kathryn L., & Wolfe, David A. (2002). Child neglect: Developmental issues and outcomes. *Child Abuse & Neglect, 26,* 679–695.

Hill, Nancy E., & Bush, Kevin R. (2001). Relationships between parenting environment and children's mental health among African American and European American mothers and children. *Journal of Marriage and Family, 63,* 954–966.

Hillier, Dawn. (2003). *Childbirth in the global village: Implications for midwifery education and practice*. New York: Routledge.

Hillman, Richard. (2005). Expanded newborn screening and phenylketonuria (PKU). In Merlin Gene Butler & F. John Meaney (Eds.), *Genetics of developmental disabilities* (pp. 651–664). Boca Raton, FL: Taylor & Francis.

Hilton, Irene V., Stephen, Samantha, Barker, Judith C., & Weintraub, Jane A. (2007). Cultural factors and children's oral health care: A qualitative study of carers of young children. *Community Dentistry and Oral Epidemiology, 35,* 429–438.

Hinds, David A., Stuve, Laura L., Nilsen, Geoffrey B., Halperin, Eran, Eskin, Eleazar, Ballinger, Dennis G., et al. (2005, February 18). Whole-genome patterns of common DNA variation in three human populations. *Science, 307,* 1072–1079.

Hines, Melissa. (2004). *Brain gender*. Oxford, England: Oxford University Press.

Hinkel, Eli. (2005). *Handbook of research in second language teaching and learning*. Mahwah, NJ: Erlbaum.

Hirsch, Jennifer S., Meneses, Sergio, Thompson, Brenda, Negroni, Mirka, Pelcastre, Blanca, & del Rio, Carlos. (2007). The inevitability of infidelity: Sexual reputation, social geographies, and marital HIV risk in rural Mexico. *American Journal of Public Health, 97,* 986–996.

Ho, Caroline, Bluestein, Deborah N., & Jenkins, Jennifer M. (2008). Cultural differences in the relationship between parenting and children's behavior. *Developmental Psychology, 44,* 507–522.

Hobbes, Thomas. (1997). *Leviathan: Authoritative text, backgrounds, interpretations* (Richard E. Flathman & David Johnston, Eds.). New York: Norton. (Original work published 1651)

Hoehl, Stefanie, Reid, Vincent, Mooney, Jeanette, & Striano, Tricia. (2008). What are you looking at? Infants' neural processing of an adult's object-directed eye gaze. *Developmental Science, 11,* 10–16.

Hoekstra, Rosa A., Bartels, Meike, & Boomsma, Dorret I. (2007). Longitudinal genetic study of verbal and nonverbal IQ from early childhood to young adulthood. *Learning and Individual Differences, 17,* 97–114.

Hofer, Myron A. (2006). Psychobiological roots of early attachment. *Current Directions in Psychological Science, 15,* 84–88.

Hoff, David J. (2007). Not all agree on meaning of NCLB proficiency. *Education Week, 26*(33), 1, 23

Hoff, Erika. (2003). The specificity of environmental influence: Socioeconomic status affects early vocabulary development via maternal speech. *Child Development, 74,* 1368–1378.

Hoff, Erika, & Naigles, Letitia. (2002). How children use input to acquire a lexicon. *Child Development, 73,* 418–433.

Holden, Constance. (2000, July 28). The violence of the lambs. *Science, 289,* 580–581.

Holden, Constance. (2006, June 30). An evolutionary squeeze on brain size. *Science, 312,* 1867b.

Holderness, Bill. (2006). Toward bridging digital divides in rural (South) Africa. In David Buckingham & Rebekah Willett (Eds.), *Digital generations: Children, young people, and new media* (pp. 251–272). Mahwah, NJ: Erlbaum.

Holland, Janet, Reynolds, Tracey, & Weller, Susie. (2007). Transitions, networks and communities: The significance of social capital in the lives of children and young people. *Journal of Youth Studies, 10,* 97–116.

Hollich, George J., Hirsh-Pasek, Kathy, Golinkoff, Roberta Michnick, Brand, Rebecca J., Brown, Ellie, Chung, He Len, et al. (2000). Breaking the language barrier: An emergentist coalition model for the origins of word learning. *Monographs of the Society for Research in Child Development, 65*(3, Serial No. 262), v-123.

Hong, Ying-yi, Morris, Michael W., Chiu, Chi-yue, & Benet-Martinez, Veronica. (2000). Multicultural minds: A dynamic constructivist approach to culture and cognition. *American Psychologist, 55,* 709–720.

Hooley, Jill M. (2004). Do psychiatric patients do better clinically if they live with certain kinds of families? *Current Directions in Psychological Science, 13,* 202–205.

Hormann, Elizabeth. (2007). Sleeping with your baby: A parent's guide to co-sleeping. *Birth, 34,* 355–356.

Horn, Ivor B., Brenner, Ruth, Rao, Malla, & Cheng, Tina L. (2006). Beliefs about the appropriate age for initiating toilet training: Are there racial and socioeconomic differences? *The Journal of Pediatrics, 149,* 165–168.

Hosaka, Toru. (2005). School absenteeism, bullying, and loss of peer relationships in Japanese children. In David W. Shwalb, Jun Nakazawa, & Barbara J. Shwalb (Eds.), *Applied developmental psychology: Theory, practice, and research from Japan* (pp. 283–299). Greenwich, CT: Information Age.

Howe, Christine. (1998). *Conceptual structure in childhood and adolescence: The case of everyday physics.* London: Routledge.

Howe, Mark L. (2004). The role of conceptual recoding in reducing children's retroactive interference. *Developmental Psychology, 40,* 131–139.

Hrabosky, Joshua I., & Thomas, Jennifer J. (2008). Elucidating the relationship between obesity and depression: Recommendations for future research. *Clinical Psychology: Science and Practice, 15,* 28–34.

Huang, Jannet. (2007). Hormones and female sexuality. In Annette Fuglsang Owens & Mitchell S. Tepper (Eds.), *Sexual health: Vol. 2. Physical foundations* (pp. 43–78). Westport, CT: Praeger/Greenwood.

Hubbard, Raymond, & Lindsay, R. Murray. (2008). Why *p* values are not a useful measure of evidence in statistical significance testing. *Theory and Psychology, 18,* 69–88.

Hubbs-Tait, Laura, Culp, Anne McDonald, Culp, Rex E., & Miller, Carrie E. (2002). Relation of maternal cognitive stimulation, emotional support, and intrusive behavior during Head Start to children's kindergarten cognitive abilities. *Child Development, 73,* 110–131.

Huesmann, L. Rowell, Moise-Titus, Jessica, Podolski, Cheryl-Lynn, & Eron, Leonard D. (2003). Longitudinal relations between children's exposure to TV violence and their aggressive and violent behavior in young adulthood: 1977–1992. *Developmental Psychology, 39,* 201–221.

Hugdahl, Kenneth, & Davidson, Richard J. (Eds.). (2002). *The asymmetrical brain.* Cambridge, MA: MIT Press.

Hughes, Judith M. (2007). *Guilt and its vicissitudes: Psychoanalytic reflections on morality.* New York: Routledge.

Hughes, Sonya M., & Gore, Andrea C. (2007). How the brain controls puberty, and implications for sex and ethnic differences. *Family & Community Health, 30*(Suppl. 1), S112–S114.

Hulanicka, Barbara. (1999). Acceleration of menarcheal age of girls from dysfunctional families. *Journal of Reproductive & Infant Psychology, 17,* 119–132.

Hulbert, Ann. (2007, April 1). Re-education. *New York Times Magazine,* pp. 34ff.

Husain, Nusrat, Bevc, Irene, Husain, M., Chaudhry, Imram B., Atif, N., & Rahman, A. (2006). Prevalence and social correlates of postnatal depression in a low income country. *Archives of Women's Mental Health, 9,* 197–202.

Hussey, Jon M., Chang, Jen Jen, & Kotch, Jonathan B. (2006). Child maltreatment in the United States: Prevalence, risk factors, and adolescent health consequences. *Pediatrics, 118,* 933–942.

Hust, Stacey J. T., Brown, Jane D., & L'Engle, Kelly Ladin. (2008). Boys will be boys and girls better be prepared: An analysis of the rare sexual health messages in young adolescents' media. *Mass Communication and Society, 11,* 3–23.

Huston, Aletha C., & Aronson, Stacey Rosenkrantz. (2005). Mothers' time with infant and time in employment as predictors of mother–child relationships and children's early development. *Child Development, 76,* 467–482.

Huston, Aletha C., & Ripke, Marika N. (2006). Middle childhood: Contexts of development. In Aletha C. Huston & Marika N. Ripke (Eds.), *Developmental contexts in middle childhood: Bridges to adolescence and adulthood* (pp. 1–22). New York: Cambridge University Press.

Hyde, Janet Shibley, & Linn, Marcia C. (2006, October 27). Gender similarities in mathematics and science. *Science, 314,* 599–600.

Hyson, Marilou, Copple, Carol, & Jones, Jacqueline. (2006). Early childhood development and education. In William Damon & Richard M. Lerner (Series Eds.) & K. Ann Renninger & Irving E. Sigel (Vol. Eds.), *Handbook of child psychology: Vol. 4. Child psychology in practice* (6th ed., pp. 3–47). Hoboken, NJ: Wiley.

Ichikawa, Shin'ichi. (2005). Cognitive counseling to improve students' metacognition and cognitive skills. In David W. Shwalb, Jun Nakazawa, & Barbara J. Shwalb (Eds.), *Applied developmental psychology: Theory, practice, and research from Japan* (pp. 67–87). Greenwich, CT: Information Age.

IJzendoorn, Marinus H. Van, Bakermans-Kranenburg, Marian J., & Sagi-Schwartz, Abraham. (2006). Attachment across diverse sociocultural contexts: The limits of universality. In Kenneth H. Rubin & Ock Boon Chung (Eds.), *Parenting beliefs, behaviors, and parent-child relations: A cross-cultural perspective* (pp. 107–142). New York: Psychology.

Inhelder, Bärbel, & Piaget, Jean. (1958). *The growth of logical thinking from childhood to adolescence: An essay on the construction of* *formal operational structures*. New York: Basic Books.

Inhelder, Bärbel, & Piaget, Jean. (1964). *The early growth of logic in the child*. New York: Harper & Row.

Insel, Beverly J., & Gould, Madelyn S. (2008). Impact of modeling on adolescent suicidal behavior. *Psychiatric Clinics of North America, 31,* 293–316.

Institute of Medicine, Committee on Food Marketing and the Diets of Children and Youth. (2006). *Food marketing to children and youth: Threat or opportunity?* Washington, DC: National Academies Press.

International Association for the Evaluation of Educational Achievement. (2003). *TIMSS & PIRLS International Study Center*. Retrieved June 25, 2008, from the World Wide Web: http://timss.bc.edu/

Irving, Washington. (1839). *The life and voyages of Christopher Columbus*. Boston: Marsh, Capen, Lyon, and Webb.

Irwin, Scott, Galvez, Roberto, Weiler, Ivan Jeanne, Beckel-Mitchener, Andrea, & Greenough, William. (2002). Brain structure and the functions of FMR1 protein. In Randi Jenssen Hagerman & Paul J. Hagerman (Eds.), *Fragile X syndrome: Diagnosis, treatment, and research* (3rd ed., pp. 191–205). Baltimore: Johns Hopkins University Press.

Isenberg, Eric J. (2007). What have we learned about homeschooling? *Peabody Journal of Education, 82,* 387–409.

Iverson, Jana M., & Fagan, Mary K. (2004). Infant vocal-motor coordination: Precursor to the gesture-speech system? *Child Development, 75,* 1053–1066.

Izard, Carroll E., Fine, Sarah, Mostow, Allison, Trentacosta, Christopher, & Campbell, Jan. (2002). Emotion processes in normal and abnormal development and preventive intervention. *Development & Psychopathology, 14,* 761–787.

Jaccard, James, Dittus, Patricia J., & Gordon, Vivian V. (1998). Parent–adolescent congruency in reports of adolescent sexual behavior and in communications about sexual behavior. *Child Development, 69,* 247–261.

Jaccard, James, Dittus, Patricia J., & Gordon, Vivian V. (2000). Parent–teen communication about premarital sex: Factors associated with the extent of communication. *Journal of Adolescent Research, 15,* 187–208.

Jackson, Kristina M., Sher, Kenneth J., & Schulenberg, John E. (2008). Conjoint developmental trajectories of young adult substance use. *Alcoholism: Clinical and Experimental Research, 32,* 723–737.

Jackson, Linda A., von Eye, Alexander, Biocca, Frank A., Barbatsis, Gretchen, Zhao, Yong, & Fitzgerald, Hiram E. (2006). Does home internet use influence the academic performance of low-income children? *Developmental Psychology, 42,* 429–435.

Jackson, Richard J. J., & Tester, June. (2008). Environment shapes health, including children's mental health. *Journal of the American Academy of Child & Adolescent Psychiatry, 47,* 129–131.

Jackson, Yo, & Warren, Jared S. (2000). Appraisal, social support, and life events: Predicting outcome behavior in school-age children. *Child Development, 71,* 1441–1457.

Jacob's father. (1997). Jacob's story: A miracle of the heart. *Zero to Three, 17,* 59–64.

Jacobs, Janis E., Lanza, Stephanie, Osgood, D. Wayne, Eccles, Jacquelynne S., & Wigfield, Allan. (2002). Changes in children's self-competence and values: Gender and domain differences across grades one though twelve. *Child Development, 73,* 509–527.

Jacobson, Linda. (2006, June 7). Latest decision keeps Calif. exit-exam law as graduations near. *Education Week, 25*(39), 25.

Jaffe, Eric. (2004). Mickey Mantle's greatest error: Yankee star's false belief may have cost him years. *Observer, 17*(9), 37.

Jaffee, Sara, Caspi, Avshalom, Moffitt, Terrie E., Belsky, Jay, & Silva, Phil. (2001). Why are children born to teen mothers at risk for adverse outcomes in young adulthood? Results from a 20-year longitudinal study. *Development & Psychopathology, 13,* 377–397.

Jaffee, Sara R. (2007). Sensitive, stimulating caregiving predicts cognitive and behavioral resilience in neurodevelopmentally at-risk infants. *Development and Psychopathology, 19,* 631–647.

Jaffee, Sara R., Caspi, Avshalom, Moffitt, Terrie E., Polo-Tomas, Monica, Price, Thomas S., & Taylor, Alan. (2004). The limits of child effects: Evidence for genetically mediated child effects on corporal punishment but not on physical maltreatment. *Developmental Psychology, 40,* 1047–1058.

Jaffee, Sara R., Caspi, Avshalom, Moffitt, Terrie E., Polo-Tomás, Monica, & Taylor, Alan. (2007). Individual, family, and neighborhood factors distinguish resilient from non-resilient maltreated children: A cumulative stressors model. *Child Abuse & Neglect, 31,* 231–253.

Jahns, Lisa, Siega-Riz, Anna Maria, & Popkin, Barry M. (2001). The increasing prevalence of snacking among U.S. children from 1977 to 1996. *Journal of Pediatrics, 138,* 493–498.

James, Raven. (2007). Sexually transmitted infections. In Annette Fuglsang Owens & Mitchell S. Tepper (Eds.), *Sexual health: Vol. 4. State-of-the-art treatments and research* (pp. 235–267). Westport, CT: Praeger/Greenwood.

Jansson, Ulla-Britt, Hanson, M., Sillen, Ulla, & Hellstrom, Anna-Lena. (2005). Voiding pattern and acquisition of bladder control from birth to age 6 years—A longitudinal study. *Journal of Urology, 174,* 289–293.

Jenkins, Jennifer M., & Astington, Janet Wilde. (1996). Cognitive factors and family structure associated with theory of mind development in young children. *Developmental Psychology, 32,* 70–78.

Jenson, Jeffrey M., & Fraser, Mark W. (2006). *Social policy for children & families: A risk and resilience perspective*. Thousand Oaks, CA: Sage.

Joe, Sean. (2003). Implications of focusing on black youth self-destructive behaviors instead of suicide when designing preventative interventions. In Daniel Romer (Ed.), *Reducing adolescent risk: Toward an integrated approach* (pp. 325–332). Thousand Oaks, CA: Sage.

Johnson, Dana E. (2000). Medical and developmental sequelae of early childhood institutionalization in Eastern European adoptees. In Charles A. Nelson (Ed.), *The Minnesota symposia on child psychology: Vol. 31. The effects of early adversity on neurobehavioral development* (pp. 113–162). Mahwah, NJ: Erlbaum.

Johnson, Kirk A., & Rector, Robert. (2004). *Adolescents who take virginity pledges have lower rates of out-of-wedlock births*. The Heritage Foundation. Retrieved November 29, 2006, from the World Wide Web: http://www.heritage.org/Research/Family/upload/63285_1.pdf

Johnson, Mark H. (2005). Developmental neuroscience, psychophysiology and genetics. In Marc H. Bornstein & Michael E. Lamb (Eds.), *Developmental science: An advanced textbook* (5th ed., pp. 187–222). Mahwah, NJ: Erlbaum.

Johnson, Mark H. (2007). The social brain in infancy: A developmental cognitive neuroscience approach. In Donna Coch, Kurt W. Fischer, & Geraldine Dawson (Eds.), *Human behavior, learning, and the developing brain. Typical development* (pp. 115–137). New York: Guilford Press.

Johnson, Scott P., Bremner, J. Gavin, Slater, Alan, Mason, Uschi, Foster, Kirsty, & Cheshire, Andrea. (2003). Infants' perception of object trajectories. *Child Development, 74,* 94–108.

Johnston, Lloyd D., O'Malley, Patrick M., Bachman, Jerald G., & Schulenberg, John E. (2006). *Monitoring the Future national survey results on drug use, 1975–2006: Volume II: College students and adults ages 19–45* (NIH Publication No. 06–5884). Bethesda, MD: National Institute on Drug Abuse.

Johnston, Lloyd D., O'Malley, Patrick M., Bachman, Jerald G., & Schulenberg, John E. (2007). *Monitoring the Future national survey results on drug use, 1975–2006. Volume I: Secondary school students* (NIH Publication No. 07–6205). Bethesda, MD: National Institute on Drug Abuse.

Johnston, Lloyd D., O'Malley, Patrick M., Bachman, Jerald G., & Schulenberg, John E. (2008). *Monitoring the Future national results on adolescent drug use: Overview of key findings, 2007* (NIH Publication No. 08–6418). Bethesda, MD: National Institute on Drug Abuse.

Jones, Chandra R., & Devoe, Lawrence D. (2005). Maternal nutrition for normal intrauterine growth. In Jatinder Bhatia (Ed.), *Perinatal nutrition: Optimizing infant health and development* (pp. 53–76). New York: Dekker.

Jones, Diane, & Crawford, Joy. (2005). Adolescent boys and body image: Weight and muscularity concerns as dual pathways to body dissatisfaction. *Journal of Youth and Adolescence, 34,* 629–636.

Jones, Edward P. (2003). *Lost in the city: Stories.* New York: Amistad. (Original work published 1992)

Jones, Emily J. H., & Herbert, Jane S. (2006). Exploring memory in infancy: Deferred imitation and the development of declarative memory. *Infant and Child Development, 15,* 195–205.

Jones, Ian. (2006). Why do women experience mood disorders following childbirth? *British Journal of Midwifery, 14,* 654–657.

Jones, Maggie. (2006, January 15). Shutting themselves in. *New York Times Magazine,* pp. 46–51.

Jones, Mary Cover. (1965). Psychological correlates of somatic development. *Child Development, 36,* 899–911.

Jones, Steve. (2006, December 22). Prosperous people, penurious genes. *Science, 314,* 1879.

Juffer, Femmie, & van IJzendoorn, Marinus H. (2007). Adoptees do not lack self-esteem: A meta-analysis of studies on self-esteem of transracial, international, and domestic adoptees. *Psychological Bulletin, 133,* 1067–1083.

Juvonen, Jaana, Nishina, Adrienne, & Graham, Sandra. (2006). Ethnic diversity and perceptions of safety in urban middle schools. *Psychological Science, 17,* 393–400.

Kaestle, Christine Elizabeth, & Halpern, Carolyn Tucker. (2007). What's love got to do with it? Sexual behaviors of opposite-sex couples through emerging adulthood. *Perspectives on Sexual and Reproductive Health, 39,* 134–140.

Kagan, Jerome. (2002). *Surprise, uncertainty, and mental structures.* Cambridge, MA: Harvard University Press.

Kagan, Jerome. (2007). A trio of concerns. *Perspectives on Psychological Science, 2,* 361–376.

Kagan, Jerome, & Fox, Nathan A. (2006). Biology, culture, and temperamental biases. In William Damon & Richard M. Lerner (Series Eds.) & Nancy Eisenberg (Vol. Ed.), *Handbook of child psychology: Vol. 3. Social, emotional, and personality development* (6th ed., pp. 167–225). Hoboken, NJ: Wiley.

Kagan, Jerome, & Herschkowitz, Elinore Chapman. (2005). *Young mind in a growing brain.* Mahwah, NJ: Erlbaum.

Kagan, Jerome, & Snidman, Nancy C. (2004). *The long shadow of temperament.* Cambridge, MA: Belknap Press.

Kagitcibasi, Cigdem. (2003). Human development across cultures: A contextual-functional analysis and implications for interventions. In T. S. Saraswati (Ed.), *Cross-cultural perspectives in human development: Theory, research, and applications* (pp. 166–191). New Delhi, India: Sage.

Kahana-Kalman, Ronit, & Walker-Andrews, Arlene S. (2001). The role of person familiarity in young infants' perception of emotional expressions. *Child Development, 72,* 352–369.

Kalambouka, Afroditi, Farrell, Peter, Dyson, Alan, & Kaplan, Ian. (2007). The impact of placing pupils with special educational needs in mainstream schools on the achievement of their peers. *Educational Research, 49,* 365–382.

Källén, Bengt. (2004). Neonate characteristics after maternal use of antidepressants in late pregnancy. *Archives of Pediatric and Adolescent Medicine, 158,* 312–316.

Kallen, Victor L., Tulen, Joke H. M., Utens, Elisabeth M. W. J., Treffers, Philip D. A., De Jong, Frank H, & Ferdinand, Robert F. (2008). Associations between HPA axis functioning and level of anxiety in children and adolescents with an anxiety disorder. *Depression and Anxiety, 25,* 131–141.

Kalliala, Marjatta. (2006). *Play culture in a changing world.* Maidenhead, England: Open University Press.

Kalmuss, Debra, Davidson, Andrew, Cohall, Alwyn, Laraque, Danielle, & Cassell, Carol. (2003). Preventing sexual risk behaviors and pregnancy among teenagers: Linking research and programs. *Perspectives on Sexual and Reproductive Health, 35,* 87–93.

Kaminaga, Moyuru. (2007). Pubertal development and eating disorders. *Japanese Journal of Developmental Psychology, 18,* 206–215.

Kamlin, C. Omar F., O'Donnell, Colm P. F., Davis, Peter G., & Morley, Colin J. (2006). Oxygen saturation in healthy infants immediately after birth. *Journal of Pediatrics, 148,* 585–589.

Kamp Dush, Claire M., & Amato, Paul R. (2005). Consequences of relationship status and quality for subjective well-being. *Journal of Social and Personal Relationships, 22,* 607–627.

Kanner, Leo. (1943). Autistic disturbances of affective contact. *Nervous Child, 2,* 217–250.

Kapoor, Amita, Dunn, Elizabeth, Kostaki, Alice, Andrews, Marcus H., & Matthews, Stephen G. (2006). Fetal programming of hypothalamo-pituitary-adrenal function: Prenatal stress and glucocorticoids. *Journal of Physiology, 572*(Pt. 1), 31–44.

Kapornai, Krisztina, & Vetró, Ágnes. (2008). Depression in children. *Current Opinion in Psychiatry, 21,* 1–7.

Karpov, Yuriy V., & Haywood, H. Carl. (1998). Two ways to elaborate Vygotsky's concept of mediation. *American Psychologist, 53,* 27–36.

Kast, Kelly R., Berg, Rob, Deas, Ann, Lezotte, Dennis, & Crane, Lori A.

(2008). Colorado dental practitioners' attitudes and practices regarding tobacco-use prevention activities for 8- through 12-year-old patients. *Journal of the American Dental Association, 139,* 467–475.

Kastenbaum, Robert. (2006). *Death, society, and human experience* (9th ed.). Boston: Allyn and Bacon.

Kato, Shingo, Hanabusa, Hideji, Kaneko, Satoru, Takakuwa, Koichi, Suzuki, Mina, Kuji, Naoaki, et al. (2006). Complete removal of HIV-1 RNA and proviral DNA from semen by the swim-up method: Assisted reproduction technique using spermatozoa free from HIV-1. *Aids, 20,* 967–973.

Kaufman, Joan, & Charney, Dennis. (2001). Effects of early stress on brain structure and function: Implications for understanding the relationship between child maltreatment and depression. *Development & Psychopathology, 13,* 451–471.

Kazdin, Alan E. (2001). *Behavior modification in applied settings* (6th ed.). Belmont, CA: Wadsworth/Thomson Learning.

Kearney, Paul, & Pivec, Maja. (2007). Sex, lies and video games. *British Journal of Educational Technology, 38,* 489–501.

Keating, Daniel P. (2004). Cognitive and brain development. In Richard M. Lerner & Laurence D. Steinberg (Eds.), *Handbook of adolescent psychology* (2nd ed., pp. 45–84). Hoboken, NJ: Wiley.

Kedar, Yarden, Casasola, Marianella, & Lust, Barbara. (2006). Getting there faster: 18- and 24-month-old infants' use of function words to determine reference. *Child Development, 77,* 325–338.

Kelemen, Deborah, Callanan, Maureen A., Casler, Krista, & Perez-Granados, Deanne R. (2005). Why things happen: Teleological explanation in parent–child conversation. *Developmental Psychology, 41,* 251–264.

Keller, Heidi, Lamm, Bettina, Abels, Monika, Yovsi, Relindis, Borke, Jörn, Jensen, Henning, et al. (2006). Cultural models, socialization goals, and parenting ethnotheories: A multicultural analysis. *Journal of Cross-Cultural Psychology, 37,* 155–172.

Keller, Heidi, Yovsi, Relindis, Borke, Joern, Kartner, Joscha, Jensen, Henning, & Papaligoura, Zaira. (2004). Developmental consequences of early parenting experiences: Self-recognition and self-regulation in three cultural communities. *Child Development, 75,* 1745–1760.

Keller, Meret A., & Goldberg, Wendy A. (2004). Co-sleeping: Help or hindrance for young children's independence? *Infant and Child Development, 13,* 369–388.

Kelley, Sue A., Brownell, Celia A., & Campbell, Susan B. (2000). Mastery motivation and self-evaluative affect in toddlers: Longitudinal relations with maternal behavior. *Child Development, 71,* 1061–1071.

Kellman, Philip J., & Arterberry, Martha E. (2006). Infant visual perception. In William Damon & Richard M. Lerner (Series Eds.) & Deanna Kuhn & Robert S. Siegler (Vol. Eds.), *Handbook of child psychology: Vol. 2. Cognition, perception, and language* (6th ed., pp. 109–160). Hoboken, NJ: Wiley.

Kelly, Michelle M. (2006). The medically complex premature infant in primary care. *Journal of Pediatric Health Care, 20,* 367–373.

Kempe, Ruth S., & Kempe, C. Henry. (1978). *Child abuse.* Cambridge, MA: Harvard University Press.

Kendall-Tackett, Kathleen. (2002). The health effects of childhood abuse: Four pathways by which abuse can influence health. *Child Abuse & Neglect, 26,* 715–729.

Kennedy, Colin R., McCann, Donna C., Campbell, Michael J., Law, Catherine M., Mullee, Mark, Petrou, Stavros, et al. (2006). Language ability after early detection of permanent childhood hearing impairment. *New England Journal of Medicine, 354,* 2131–2141.

Kenrick, Jenny, Lindsey, Caroline, & Tollemache, Lorraine (Eds.). (2006). *Creating new families: Therapeutic approaches to fostering, adoption, and kinship care.* London: Karnac Books.

Keogh, Barbara K. (2004). The importance of longitudinal research for early intervention practices. In Peggy D. McCardle & Vinita Chhabra (Eds.), *The voice of evidence in reading research* (pp. 81–102). Baltimore: Brookes.

Kessler, Ronald C., Berglund, Patricia, Demler, Olga, Jin, Robert, & Walters, Ellen E. (2005). Lifetime prevalence and age-of-onset distributions of DSM-IV disorders in the National Comorbidity Survey Replication. *Archives of General Psychiatry, 62,* 593–602.

Khaleque, Abdul, & Rohner, Ronald P. (2002). Perceived parental acceptance–rejection and psychological adjustment: A meta-analysis of cross-cultural and intracultural studies. *Journal of Marriage & the Family, 64,* 54–64.

Khan, Ayesha, Bellefontaine, Nicole, & deCatanzaro, Denys. (2008). Onset of sexual maturation in female mice as measured in behavior and fertility: Interactions of exposure to males, phytoestrogen content of diet, and ano-genital distance. *Physiology & Behavior, 93,* 588–594.

Khawaja, Marwan, Jurdi, Rozzet, & Kabakian-Khasholian, Tamar. (2004). Rising trends in cesarean section rates in Egypt. *Birth: Issues in Perinatal Care, 31,* 12–16.

Kidder, Jeffrey L. (2006). "It's the job that I love": Bike messengers and edgework. *Sociological Forum, 21,* 31–54.

Killen, Melanie. (2007). Children's social and moral reasoning about exclusion. *Current Directions in Psychological Science, 16,* 32–36.

Killen, Melanie, Lee-Kim, Jennie, McGlothlin, Heidi, & Stangor, Charles. (2002). How children and adolescents evaluate gender and racial exclusion. *Monographs of the Society for Research in Child Development, 67*(4, Serial No. 271).

Killen, Melanie, Margie, Nancy Geyelin, & Sinno, Stefanie. (2006). Morality in the context of intergroup relationships. In Melanie Killen & Judith G. Smetana (Eds.), *Handbook of moral development* (pp. 155–183). Mahwah, NJ: Erlbaum.

Killen, Melanie, & Smetana, Judith. (2007). The biology of morality: Human development and moral neuroscience. *Human Development, 50,* 241–243.

Killeya-Jones, Ley A., Costanzo, Philip R., Malone, Patrick, Quinlan, Nicole Polanichka, & Miller-Johnson, Shari. (2007). Norm-narrowing and self- and other-perceived aggression in early-adolescent same-sex and mixed-sex cliques. *Journal of School Psychology, 45,* 549–565.

Killgore, William D. S., Vo, Alexander H., Castro, Carl A., & Hoge, Charles W. (2006). Assessing risk propensity in American soldiers: Preliminary reliability and validity of the Evaluation of Risks (EVAR) scale-English version. *Military Medicine, 171,* 233–239.

Kim-Cohen, Julia, Moffitt, Terrie E., Caspi, Avshalom, & Taylor, Alan. (2004). Genetic and environmental processes in young children's resilience and vulnerability to socioeconomic deprivation. *Child Development, 75,* 651–668.

Kimbro, Rachel Tolbert, Brooks-Gunn, Jeanne, & McLanahan, Sara. (2007). Racial and ethnic differentials in overweight and obesity among 3-year-old children. *American Journal of Public Health, 97,* 298–305.

Kimmel, Michael S. (2004). *The gendered society* (2nd ed.). New York: Oxford University Press.

Kincheloe, Joe L. (2004). *Multiple intelligences reconsidered*. New York: Peter Lang.

Kinder, Donald R. (2006, June 30). Politics and the life cycle. *Science, 312,* 1905–1908.

King, Pamela Ebstyne, & Furrow, James L. (2004). Religion as a resource for positive youth development: Religion, social capital, and moral outcomes. *Developmental Psychology, 40,* 703–713.

King, Valarie, Harris, Kathleen Mullan, & Heard, Holly E. (2004). Racial and ethnic diversity in nonresident father involvement. *Journal of Marriage & Family, 66,* 1–21.

Kirby, Douglas. (2001). *Emerging answers: Research findings on programs to reduce teen pregnancy*. Washington, DC: The National Campaign To Prevent Teen Pregnancy.

Kirby, Douglas. (2002). Effective approaches to reducing adolescent unprotected sex, pregnancy, and childbearing. *Journal of Sex Research, 39,* 51–57.

Kirkbride, James B., Fearon, Paul, Morgan, Craig, Dazzan, Paola, Morgan, Kevin, Tarrant, Jane, et al. (2006). Heterogeneity in incidence rates of schizophrenia and other psychotic syndromes: Findings from the 3-center ÆSOP study. *Archives of General Psychiatry, 63,* 250–258.

Kitzinger, Sheila. (2001). *Rediscovering birth*. New York: Simon & Schuster.

Klaczynski, Paul A. (2001). Analytic and heuristic processing influences on adolescent reasoning and decision-making. *Child Development, 72,* 844–861.

Klaczynski, Paul A. (2005). Metacognition and cognitive variability: A dual-process model of decision making and its development. In Janis E. Jacobs & Paul A. Klaczynski (Eds.), *The development of judgment and decision making in children and adolescents* (pp. 39–76). Mahwah, NJ: Erlbaum.

Klaczynski, Paul A., & Cottrell, Jennifer M. (2004). A dual-process approach to cognitive development: The case of children's understanding of sunk cost decisions. *Thinking & Reasoning, 10,* 147–174.

Klahr, David, & Nigam, Milena. (2004). The equivalence of learning paths in early science instruction: Effects of direct instruction and discovery learning. *Psychological Science, 15,* 661–667.

Klassen, Terry P., Kiddoo, Darcie, Lang, Mia E., Friesen., Carol, Russell, Kelly, Spooner, Carol, et al. (2006). *The effectiveness of different methods of toilet training for bowel and bladder control* (AHRQ Publication No. 07–E003). Rockville, MD: Agency for Healthcare Research and Quality.

Klaus, Marshall H., & Kennell, John H. (1976). *Maternal–infant bonding: The impact of early separation or loss on family development*. St. Louis, MO: Mosby.

Kline, Kathleen Kovner. (2008). *Authoritative communities: The scientific case for nurturing the whole child*. New York: Springer.

Klöppel, Stefan, Vongerichten, Anna, Eimeren, Thilo van, Frackowiak, Richard S. J., & Siebner, Hartwig R. (2007). Can left-handedness be switched? Insights from an early switch of handwriting. *Journal of Neuroscience, 27,* 7847–7853.

Klug, William, Cummings, Michael, Spencer, Charlotte, & Palladino, Michael. (2008). *Concepts of genetics* (9th ed.). San Francisco: Pearson/Benjamin Cummings.

Kochanska, Grazyna, Aksan, Nazan, Prisco, Theresa R., & Adams, Erin E. (2008). Mother–child and father–child mutually responsive orientation in the first 2 years and children's outcomes at preschool age: Mechanisms of influence. *Child Development, 79,* 30–44.

Kochanska, Grazyna, Coy, Katherine C., & Murray, Kathleen T. (2001). The development of self-regulation in the first four years of life. *Child Development, 72,* 1091–1111.

Kochanska, Grazyna, Gross, Jami N., Lin, Mei-Hua, & Nichols, Kate E. (2002). Guilt in young children: Development, determinants, and relations with a broader system of standards. *Child Development, 73,* 461–482.

Kohlberg, Lawrence. (1963). The development of children's orientations toward a moral order: I. Sequence in the development of moral thought. *Vita Humana, 6,* 11–33.

Kohlberg, Lawrence, Levine, Charles, & Hewer, Alexandra. (1983). *Moral stages: A current formulation and a response to critics*. New York: Karger.

Kohn, Alfie. (2006). *The homework myth*. Cambridge, MA: Da Capo Lifelong Books.

Koivisto, Maila. (2004). A follow-up survey of anti-bullying interventions in the comprehensive schools of Kempele in 1990–98. In Peter K. Smith, Debra Pepler, & Ken Rigby (Eds.), *Bullying in schools: How successful can interventions be?* (pp. 235–249). New York: Cambridge University Press.

Kolb, Bryan, & Whishaw, Ian Q. (2003). *Fundamentals of human neuropsychology* (5th ed.). New York: Worth.

Kolb, Bryan, & Whishaw, Ian Q. (2008). *Fundamentals of human neuropsychology* (6th ed.). New York: Worth.

Konner, Melvin. (2007). Evolutionary foundations of cultural psychology. In Shinobu Kitayama & Dov Cohen (Eds.), *Handbook of cultural psychology* (pp. 77–105). New York: Guilford Press.

Koolhaas, Jaap M., de Boer, Sietse F., & Buwalda, Bauke. (2006). Stress and adaptation. *Current Directions in Psychological Science, 15,* 109–112.

Koops, Willem. (2003). Imaging childhood. In Willem Koops & Michael Zuckerman (Eds.), *Beyond the century of the child: Cultural history and developmental psychology* (pp. 1–18). Philadelphia: University of Pennsylvania Press.

Kornblum, Janet. (2008, July 15). Cyberbullying grows bigger and meaner with photos, video. *USA Today*.

Kovas, Yulia, Hayiou-Thomas, Marianna E., Oliver, Bonamy, Dale, Philip S., Bishop, Dorothy V. M., & Plomin, Robert. (2005). Genetic influences in different aspects of language development: The etiology of language skills in 4.5-year-old twins. *Child Development, 76,* 632–651.

Krause, Neal. (2006). Social relationships in late life. In Robert H. Binstock & Linda K. George (Eds.), *Handbook of aging and the social sciences* (6th ed., pp. 181–200). Amsterdam: Elsevier.

Krcmar, Marina, Grela, Bernard, & Lin, Kirsten. (2007). Can toddlers learn vocabulary from television? An experimental approach. *Media Psychology, 10,* 41–63.

Krebs, Dennis L. (2008). Morality: An evolutionary account. *Perspectives on Psychological Science, 3,* 149–172.

Krentz, Ursula C., & Corina, David P. (2008). Preference for language in early infancy: The human language bias is not speech specific. *Developmental Science, 11,* 1–9.

Krieger, Nancy, Chen, Jarvis T., Waterman, Pamela D., Rehkopf, David H., & Subramanian, S. V. (2005). Painting a truer picture of U.S. socioeconomic and racial/ethnic health inequalities: The Public Health Disparities Geocoding Project. *American Journal of Public Health, 95,* 312–323.

Krueger, Robert F., & Markon, Kristian E. (2006). Reinterpreting comorbidity: A model-based approach to understanding and classifying psychopathology. *Annual Review of Clinical Psychology, 2,* 111–133.

Kruk, Margaret E., Prescott, Marta R., & Galea, Sandro. (2008). Equity of skilled birth attendant utilization in developing countries: Financing and policy determinants. *American Journal of Public Health, 98,* 142–147.

Kryzer, Erin M., Kovan, Nikki, Phillips, Deborah A., Domagall, Lindsey A., & Gunnar, Megan R. (2007). Toddlers' and preschoolers' experience in family day care: Age differences and behavioral correlates. *Early Childhood Research Quarterly, 22,* 451–466.

Kuhn, Deanna. (2006). Do cognitive changes accompany developments in the adolescent brain? *Perspectives on Psychological Science, 1,* 59–67.

Kuhn, Deanna, & Franklin, Sam. (2006). The second decade: What develops (and how). In William Damon & Richard M. Lerner (Series Eds.) & Nancy Eisenberg (Vol. Ed.), *Handbook of child psychology: Vol. 2. Cognition, perception, and language* (6th ed., pp. 953–993). Hoboken, NJ: Wiley.

Kuller, Jeffrey A., Strauss, Robert A., & Cefalo, Robert C. (2001). Preconceptional and prenatal care. In Frank W. Ling & W. Patrick Duff (Eds.), *Obstetrics and gynecology: Principles for practice* (pp. 25–54). New York: McGraw-Hill.

Kumpfer, Karol L., & Alvarado, Rose. (2003). Family-strengthening approaches for the prevention of youth problem behaviors. *American Psychologist, 58,* 457–465.

Kupersmidt, Janis B., Coie, John D., & Howell, James C. (2004). Resilience in children exposed to negative peer influences. In Kenneth I. Maton, Cynthia J. Schellenbach, Bonnie J. Leadbeater, & Andrea L. Solarz (Eds.), *Investing in children, youth, families, and communities: Strengths-based research and policy* (pp. 251–268). Washington, DC: American Psychological Association.

LaBar, Kevin S. (2007). Beyond fear: Emotional memory mechanisms in the human brain. *Current Directions in Psychological Science, 16,* 173–177.

Labouvie-Vief, Gisela. (2006). Emerging structures of adult thought. In Jeffrey Jensen Arnett & Jennifer Lynn Tanner (Eds.), *Emerging adults in America: Coming of age in the 21st century* (pp. 59–84). Washington, DC: American Psychological Association.

Lacourse, Eric, Nagin, Daniel, Tremblay, Richard E., Vitaro, Frank, & Claes, Michel. (2003). Developmental trajectories of boys' delinquent group membership and facilitation of violent behaviors during adolescence. *Development & Psychopathology, 15,* 183–197.

Ladd, Gary W. (1999). Peer relationships and social competence during early and middle childhood. *Annual Review of Psychology, 50,* 333–359.

Ladd, Gary W. (2005). *Children's peer relations and social competence: A century of progress.* New Haven, CT: Yale University Press.

Ladd, Gary W., & Pettit, Gregory S. (2002). Parenting and the development of children's peer relationships. In Marc H. Bornstein (Ed.), *Handbook of parenting: Vol. 5. Practical issues in parenting* (2nd ed., pp. 269–309). Mahwah, NJ: Erlbaum.

Lahey, Benjamin B., Moffitt, Terrie E., & Caspi, Avshalom (Eds.). (2003). *Causes of conduct disorder and juvenile delinquency.* New York: Guilford Press.

Laible, Deborah, Panfile, Tia, & Makariev, Drika. (2008). The quality and frequency of mother–toddler conflict: Links with attachment and temperament. *Child Development, 79,* 426–443.

Lamb, Michael E. (1982). Maternal employment and child development: A review. In Michael E. Lamb (Ed.), *Nontraditional families: Parenting and child development* (pp. 45–69). Hillsdale, NJ: Erlbaum.

Lamb, Michael E. (2000). The history of research on father involvement: An overview. In H. Elizabeth Peters, Gary W. Peterson, Suzanne K. Steinmetz, & Randal D. Day (Eds.), *Fatherhood: Research, interventions, and policies* (pp. 23–42). New York: Haworth Press.

Lamb, Michael E. (Ed.). (2004). *The role of the father in child development* (4th ed.). Hoboken, NJ: Wiley.

Lamb, Michael E., & Lewis, Charlie (2005). The role of parent–child relationships in child development. In Marc H. Bornstein & Michael E. Lamb (Eds.), *Developmental science: An advanced textbook* (5th ed., pp. 429–468). Mahwah, NJ: Erlbaum.

Lamm, Bettina, Keller, Heidi, Yovsi, Relindis D., & Chaudhary, Nandita. (2008). Grandmaternal and maternal ethnotheories about early child care. *Journal of Family Psychology, 22,* 80–88.

Landry, David J., Darroch, Jacqueline E., Singh, Susheela, & Higgins, Jenny. (2003). Factors associated with the content of sex education in U.S. public secondary schools. *Perspectives on Sexual and Reproductive Health, 35,* 261–269.

Lane, Scott D., Cherek, Don R., Pietras, Cynthia J., & Steinberg, Joel L. (2005). Performance of heavy marijuana-smoking adolescents on a laboratory measure of motivation. *Addictive Behaviors, 30,* 815–828.

Lansford, Jennifer E., Ceballo, Rosario, Abbey, Antonia, & Stewart, Abigail J. (2001). Does family structure matter? A comparison of adoptive, two-parent biological, single-mother, stepfather, and stepmother households. *Journal of Marriage & the Family, 63,* 840–851.

Lantolf, James P. (2006). Sociocultural theory and L2: State of the art. *Studies in Second Language Acquisition, 28,* 67–109.

Lapsley, Daniel K. (1993). Toward an integrated theory of adolescent ego development: The "new look" at adolescent egocentrism. *American Journal of Orthopsychiatry, 63,* 562–571.

Larcombe, Duncan. (2005). Content matters: Sometimes even more than we think. *American Educator, 29,* 42–43.

Larson, Nicole I., Neumark-Sztainer, Dianne, Hannan, Peter J., & Story, Mary. (2007). Trends in adolescent fruit and vegetable consumption, 1999–2004: Project EAT. *American Journal of Preventive Medicine, 32,* 147–150.

Larson, Reed W. (2000). Toward a psychology of positive youth development. *American Psychologist, 55,* 170–183.

Larson, Reed W., & Wilson, Suzanne. (2004). Adolescence across place and time: Globalization and the changing pathways to adulthood. In Richard M. Lerner & Laurence D. Steinberg (Eds.), *Handbook of adolescent psychology* (2nd ed., pp. 299–330). Hoboken, NJ: Wiley.

Larzelere, Robert E., & Kuhn, Brett R. (2005). Comparing child outcomes of physical punishment and alternative disciplinary tactics: A meta-analysis. *Clinical Child and Family Psychology Review, 8,* 1–37.

Laumann, Edward O., Gagnon, John H., Michael, Robert T., & Michaels, Stuart.

(1994). *The social organization of sexuality: Sexual practices in the United States*. Chicago: University of Chicago Press.

Laumann, Edward O., & Michael, Robert T. (2001). Setting the scene. In Edward O. Laumann & Robert T. Michael (Eds.), *Sex, love, and health in America: Private choices and public policies* (pp. 1–38). Chicago: University of Chicago Press.

Laursen, Brett, Coy, Katherine C., & Collins, W. Andrew. (1998). Reconsidering changes in parent–child conflict across adolescence: A meta-analysis. *Child Development, 69,* 817–832.

Laursen, Brett, & Mooney, Karen S. (2007). Individual differences in adolescent dating and adjustment. In Rutger C. M. E. Engels, Margaret Kerr, & Håkan Stattin (Eds.), *Friends, lovers, and groups: Key relationships in adolescence* (pp. 81–92). Hoboken, NJ: Wiley.

Lavelli, Manuela, & Fogel, Alan. (2005). Developmental changes in the relationship between the infant's attention and emotion during early face-to-face communication: The 2-month transition. *Developmental Psychology, 41,* 265–280.

Layden, Tim. (2004, November 15). Get out and play! *Sports Illustrated, 101,* 80–93.

Leach, Penelope. (1997). *Your baby & child: From birth to age five* (3rd ed.). New York: Knopf.

Leaper, Campbell. (2002). Parenting girls and boys. In Marc H. Bornstein (Ed.), *Handbook of parenting: Vol. 1. Children and parenting* (2nd ed., pp. 189–225). Mahwah, NJ: Erlbaum.

Leaper, Campbell, & Smith, Tara E. (2004). A meta-analytic review of gender variations in children's language use: Talkativeness, affiliative speech, and assertive speech. *Developmental Psychology, 40,* 993–1027.

Lefkowitz, Eva S., & Gillen, Meghan M. (2006). "Sex is just a normal part of life": Sexuality in emerging adulthood. In Jeffrey Jensen Arnett & Jennifer Lynn Tanner (Eds.), *Emerging adults in America: Coming of age in the 21st century* (pp. 235–255). Washington, DC: American Psychological Association.

Lehmann, Wolfgang. (2004). "For some reason, I get a little scared": Structure, agency, and risk in school–work transitions. *Journal of Youth Studies, 7,* 379–396.

Lehn, Hanne, Derks, Eske M., Hudziak, James J., Heutink, Peter, van Beijsterveldt, Toos C. E. M., & Boomsma, Dorret I. (2007). Attention problems and attention-deficit/hyperactivity disorder in discordant and concordant monozygotic twins: Evidence of environmental mediators. *Journal of the American Academy of Child and Adolescent Psychiatry, 46,* 83–91.

Lei, Joy L. (2003). (Un)necessary toughness?: Those "loud black girls" and those "quiet Asian boys". *Anthropology & Education Quarterly, 34,* 158–181.

Lenneberg, Eric H. (1967). *Biological foundations of language*. New York: Wiley.

Lenton, Alison, & Webber, Laura. (2006). Cross-sex friendships: Who has more? *Sex Roles, 54,* 809–820.

Leonard, Christiana M. (2003). Neural substrate of speech and language development. In Michelle De Haan & Mark H. Johnson (Eds.), *The cognitive neuroscience of development* (pp. 127–156). New York: Psychology Press.

Lepage, Jean-François, & Théoret, Hugo. (2006). EEG evidence for the presence of an action observation-execution matching system in children. *European Journal of Neuroscience, 23,* 2505–2510.

Lepper, Mark R., Greene, David, & Nisbett, Richard E. (1973). Undermining children's intrinsic interest with extrinsic reward: A test of the "overjustification" hypothesis. *Journal of Personality & Social Psychology, 28,* 129–137.

Lerner, Claire, & Dombro, Amy Laura. (2004). Finding your fit: Some temperament tips for parents. *Zero to Three, 24,* 42–45.

Lerner, Richard M., Theokas, Christina, & Bobek, Deborah L. (2005). Concepts and theories of human development: Historical and contemporary dimensions. In Marc H. Bornstein & Michael E. Lamb (Eds.), *Developmental science: An advanced textbook* (5th ed., pp. 3–43). Mahwah, NJ: Erlbaum.

Leve, Leslie D., & Chamberlain, Patricia. (2005). Association with delinquent peers: Intervention effects for youth in the juvenile justice system. *Journal of Abnormal Child Psychology, 33,* 339–347.

Levesque, Roger J. R. (2002). *Not by faith alone: Religion, law, and adolescence*. New York: New York University Press.

Levitt, Mary J., Levitt, Jerome, Bustos, Gastón L, Crooks, Noel A., Santos, Jennifer D., Telan, Paige, et al. (2005). Patterns of social support in the middle childhood to early adolescent transition: implications for adjustment. *Social Development, 14,* 398–420.

Lewin, Kurt. (1943). Psychology and the process of group living. *Journal of Social Psychology, 17,* 113–131.

Lewis, Lawrence B., Antone, Carol, & Johnson, Jacqueline S. (1999). Effects of prosodic stress and serial position on syllable omission in first words. *Developmental Psychology, 35,* 45–59.

Lewis, Michael. (1997). *Altering fate: Why the past does not predict the future*. New York: Guilford Press.

Lewis, Michael, & Brooks, Jeanne. (1978). Self-knowledge and emotional development. In Michael Lewis & L. A. Rosenblum (Eds.), *Genesis of behavior: Vol. 1. The development of affect* (pp. 205–226). New York: Plenum Press.

Lewis, Michael, & Ramsay, Douglas. (2005). Infant emotional and cortisol responses to goal blockage. *Child Development, 76,* 518–530.

Lewis, Pamela, Abbeduto, Leonard, Murphy, Melissa, Richmond, Erica, Giles, Nancy, Bruno, Loredana, et al. (2006). Psychological well-being of mothers of youth with fragile X syndrome: Syndrome specificity and within-syndrome variability. *Journal of Intellectual Disability Research, 50,* 894–904.

Li, De-Kun, Willinger, Marian, Petitti, Diana B., Odouli, Roxana, Liu, Liyan, & Hoffman, Howard J. (2006). Use of a dummy (pacifier) during sleep and risk of sudden infant death syndrome (SIDS): Population based case-control study. *British Medical Journal, 332,* 18–21.

Li, Qing. (2007). New bottle but old wine: A research of cyberbullying in schools. *Computers in Human Behavior, 23,* 1777–1791.

Li, Xiaoming, Stanton, Bonita, Galbraith, Jennifer, Burns, James, Cottrell, Lesley, & Pack, Robert. (2002). Parental monitoring intervention: Practice makes perfect. *Journal of the National Medical Association, 94,* 364–370.

Lieu, Tracy A., Ray, G. Thomas, Black, Steven B., Butler, Jay C., Klein, Jerome O., Breiman, Robert F., et al. (2000). Projected cost-effectiveness of pneumococcal conjugate vaccination of healthy infants and young children. *Journal of the American Medical Association, 283,* 1460–1468.

Lightfoot, Cynthia. (1997). *The culture of adolescent risk-taking*. New York: Guilford Press.

Lillard, Angeline, & Else-Quest, Nicole. (2006, September 29). Evaluating Montessori education. *Science, 313,* 1893–1894.

Lillard, Angeline Stoll. (2005). *Montessori: The science behind the genius.* New York: Oxford University Press.

Lim, Boo Yeun. (2004). The magic of the brush and the power of color: Integrating theory into practice of painting in early childhood settings. *Early Childhood Education Journal, 32,* 113–119.

Lincove, Jane Arnold, & Painter, Gary. (2006). Does the age that children start kindergarten matter? Evidence of long-term educational and social outcomes. *Educational Evaluation and Policy Analysis, 28,* 153–179.

Lindfors, Kaj, Elovainio, Marko, Wickman, Sanna, Vuorinen, Risto, Sinkkonen, Jari, Dunkel, Leo, et al. (2007). Brief report: The role of ego development in psychosocial adjustment among boys with delayed puberty. *Journal of Research on Adolescence, 17,* 601–612.

Lindsay, Geoff. (2000). Researching children's perspectives: Ethical issues. In Ann Lewis & Geoff Lindsay (Eds.), *Researching children's perspectives* (pp. 3–20). Philadelphia: Open University Press.

Linn, Susan, & Novosat, Courtney L. (2008). Calories for sale: Food marketing to children in the twenty-first century. *Annals of the American Academy of Political and Social Science, 615,* 133–155.

Lippa, Richard A. (2002). *Gender, nature, and nurture.* Mahwah, NJ: Erlbaum.

Lissau, Inge, Overpeck, Mary D., Ruan, W. June, Due, Pernille, Holstein, Bjorn E., & Hediger, Mary L. (2004). Body mass index and overweight in adolescents in 13 European countries, Israel, and the United States. *Archives of Pediatrics & Adolescent Medicine, 158,* 27–33.

Little, Emma. (2005). Secondary school teachers' perceptions of students' problem behaviours. *Educational Psychology, 25,* 369–377.

Little, Peter (Ed.). (2002). *Genetic destinies.* Oxford, England: Oxford University Press.

Liu, David, Wellman, Henry M., Tardif, Twila, & Sabbagh, Mark A. (2008). Theory of mind development in Chinese children: A meta-analysis of false-belief understanding across cultures and languages. *Developmental Psychology, 44,* 523–531.

Liu, Ping. (2006). Community-based Chinese schools in Southern California: A survey of teachers. *Language, Culture and Curriculum, 19,* 237–246.

Lobstein, T., & Dibb, S. (2005). Evidence of a possible link between obesogenic food advertising and child overweight. *Obesity Reviews, 6,* 203–208.

Lockhart, Kristi L., Chang, Bernard, & Story, Tyler. (2002). Young children's beliefs about the stability of traits: Protective optimism? *Child Development, 73,* 1408–1430.

Loeb, Susanna, Fuller, Bruce, Kagan, Sharon Lynn, & Carrol, Bidemi. (2004). Child care in poor communities: Early learning effects of type, quality, and stability. *Child Development, 75,* 47–65.

Loeber, Rolf, Lacourse, Eric, & Homish, D. Lynn. (2005). Homicide, violence, and developmental trajectories. In Richard Ernest Tremblay, Willard W. Hartup, & John Archer (Eds.), *Developmental origins of aggression* (pp. 202–222). New York: Guilford Press.

Loland, Sigmund. (2002). *Fair play in sport: A moral norm system.* London: Routledge.

Lombardi, Joan, & Cubbage, Amy Stephens. (2004). Head Start in the 1990s: Striving for quality through a decade of improvement. In Edward Zigler & Sally J. Styfco (Eds.), *The Head Start debates* (pp. 283–295). Baltimore: Brookes.

López, Frank A. (2006). ADHD: New pharmacological treatments on the horizon. *Journal of Developmental & Behavioral Pediatrics, 27,* 410–416.

Lopez, Nestor L., Vazquez, Delia M., & Olson, Sheryl L. (2004). An integrative approach to the neurophysiological substrates of social withdrawal and aggression. *Development & Psychopathology, 16,* 69–93.

Lubienski, Sarah Theule, & Lubienski, Christopher. (2005). *A new look at public and private schools: Student background and mathematics achievement.* Retrieved September 4, 2007, from the World Wide Web: http://www.pdkintl.org/kappan/k_v86/k0505lub.htm

Lucast, Erica K. (2007). Informed consent and the misattributed paternity problem in genetic counseling. *Bioethics, 21,* 41–50.

Luciana, Monica. (2003). Cognitive development in children born preterm: Implications for theories of brain plasticity following early injury. *Development and Psychopathology, 15,* 1017–1047.

Luciana, Monica. (2003). The neural and functional development of human prefrontal cortex. In Michelle de Haan & Mark H. Johnson (Eds.), *The cognitive neuroscience of development* (pp. 157–179). New York: Psychology Press.

Ludden, Alison Bryant, & Eccles, Jacquelynne S. (2007). Psychosocial, motivational, and contextual profiles of youth reporting different patterns of substance use during adolescence. *Journal of Research on Adolescence, 17,* 51–88.

Ludington-Hoe, Susan M., Johnson, Mark W., Morgan, Kathy, Lewis, Tina, Gutman, Judy, Wilson, P. David, et al. (2006). Neurophysiologic assessment of neonatal sleep organization: Preliminary results of a randomized, controlled trial of skin contact with preterm infants. *Pediatrics, 117,* e909–923.

Luthar, Suniya S. (2003). The culture of affluence: Psychological costs of material wealth. *Child Development, 74,* 1581–1593.

Luthar, Suniya S., Cicchetti, Dante, & Becker, Bronwyn. (2000). The construct of resilience: A critical evaluation and guidelines for future work. *Child Development, 71,* 543–562.

Luthar, Suniya S., D'Avanzo, Karen, & Hites, Sarah. (2003). Maternal drug abuse versus other psychological disturbances: Risks and resilience among children. In Suniya S. Luthar (Ed.), *Resilience and vulnerability: Adaptation in the context of childhood adversities* (pp. 104–129). New York: Cambridge University Press.

Luthar, Suniya S., & Zelazo, Laurel Bidwell. (2003). Research on resilience: An integrative review. In Suniya S. Luthar (Ed.), *Resilience and vulnerability: Adaptation in the context of childhood adversities* (pp. 510–549). New York: Cambridge University Press.

Lutz, Donna J., & Sternberg, Robert J. (1999). Cognitive development. In Marc H. Bornstein & Michael E. Lamb (Eds.), *Developmental psychology: An advanced textbook* (4th ed., pp. 275–311). Mahwah, NJ: Erlbaum.

Lykken, David T. (2006). The mechanism of emergenesis. *Genes, Brain & Behavior, 5,* 306–310.

Lynch, Robert G. (2004). *Exceptional returns: Economic, fiscal, and social benefits of investment in early childhood development.* Washington, DC: Economic Policy Institute.

Lyng, Stephen (Ed.). (2005). *Edgework: The sociology of risk taking.* New York: Routledge.

Lynn, Richard, & Mikk, Jaan. (2007). National differences in intelligence and educational attainment. *Intelligence, 35,* 115–121.

Lynn, Richard, & Vanhanen, Tatu. (2002). *IQ and the wealth of nations.* Westport, CT: Praeger.

Lynne, Sarah D., Graber, Julia A., Nichols, Tracy R., Brooks-Gunn, Jeanne, & Botvin, Gilbert J. (2007). Links between pubertal timing, peer influences, and externalizing behaviors among urban students followed through middle school. *Journal of Adolescent Health, 40,* 181.e7–181.e13.

Lyons, Linda. (2004, June 8). *Most teens associate school with boredom, fatigue.* Retrieved September 15, 2007, from the World Wide Web: http://www.galluppoll.com/content/?ci=11893&pg=1

Lyons-Ruth, Karlen, Bronfman, Elisa, & Parsons, Elizabeth. (1999). IV. Maternal frightened, frightening, or atypical behavior and disorganized infant attachment patterns. *Monographs of the Society for Research in Child Development, 64*(3, Serial No. 258), 67–96.

Maas, Carl, Herrenkohl, Todd I., & Sousa, Cynthia. (2008). Review of research on child maltreatment and violence in youth. *Trauma Violence Abuse, 9,* 56–67.

Maccoby, Eleanor E. (1998). *The two sexes: Growing up apart, coming together.* Cambridge, MA: Belknap Press of Harvard University Press.

Maccoby, Eleanor E. (2000). Parenting and its effects on children: On reading and misreading behavior genetics. *Annual Review of Psychology, 51,* 1–27.

MacKay, Andrea P., Berg, Cynthia J., King, Jeffrey C., Duran, Catherine, & Chang, Jeani. (2006). Pregnancy-related mortality among women with multifetal pregnancies. *Obstetrics & Gynecology, 107,* 563–568.

Macmillan, Ross, & Copher, Ronda. (2005). Families in the life course: Interdependency of roles, role configurations, and pathways. *Journal of Marriage and Family, 67,* 858–879.

Madsen, Kreesten Meldgaard, Hviid, Anders, Vestergaard, Mogens, Schendel, Diana, Wohlfahrt, Jan, Thorsen, Poul, et al. (2002). A population-based study of measles, mumps, and rubella vaccination and autism. *New England Journal of Medicine, 347,* 1477–1482.

Magara, Keiichi. (2005). Children's misconceptions: Research on improving understanding of mathematics and science. In David W. Shwalb, Jun Nakazawa, & Barbara J. Shwalb (Eds.), *Applied developmental psychology: Theory, practice, and research from Japan* (pp. 89–108). Greenwich, CT: Information Age.

Magen, Zipora. (1998). *Exploring adolescent happiness: Commitment, purpose, and fulfillment.* Thousand Oaks, CA: Sage.

Maguen, Shira, Floyd, Frank J., Bakeman, Roger, & Armistead, Lisa. (2002). Developmental milestones and disclosure of sexual orientation among gay, lesbian, and bisexual youths. *Journal of Applied Developmental Psychology, 23,* 219–233.

Mahler, Margaret S., Pine, Fred, & Bergman, Anni. (1975). *The psychological birth of the human infant: Symbiosis and individuation.* New York: Basic Books.

Mahmoud, Adel. (2004, July 9). The global vaccination gap. *Science, 305,* 147.

Mahoney, Joseph L., Larson, Reed W., & Eccles, Jacquelynne S. (Eds.). (2005). *Organized activities as contexts of development. Extracurricular activities, after-school and community programs.* Mahwah, NJ: Erlbaum.

Malamud, Ofer, & Pop-Eleches, Cristian. (2008). *General education vs. vocational training: Evidence from an economy in transition.* Social Science Research Network. Retrieved August 3, 2008, from the World Wide Web: http://ssrn.com/abstract=1161038

Malina, Robert M., Bouchard, Claude, & Bar-Or, Oded. (2004). *Growth, maturation, and physical activity* (2nd ed.). Champaign, IL: Human Kinetics.

Malinger, Gustavo, Lev, Dorit, & Lerman-Sagie, Tally. (2006). Normal and abnormal fetal brain development during the third trimester as demonstrated by neurosonography. *European Journal of Radiology, 57,* 226–232.

Malone, Fergal D., Canick, Jacob A., Ball, Robert H., Nyberg, David A., Comstock, Christine H., Bukowski, Radek, et al. (2005). First-trimester or second-trimester screening, or both, for Down's syndrome. *New England Journal of Medicine, 353,* 2001–2011.

Mandler, Jean Matter. (2004). *The foundations of mind: Origins of conceptual thought.* Oxford, England: Oxford University Press.

Mandler, Jean M. (2007). On the origins of the conceptual system. *American Psychologist, 62,* 741–751.

Manfra, Louis, & Winsler, Adam. (2006). Preschool children's awareness of private speech. *International Journal of Behavioral Development, 30,* 537–549.

Mange, Elaine Johansen, & Mange, Arthur P. (1999). *Basic human genetics* (2nd ed.). Sunderland, MA: Sinauer Associates.

Manlove, Jennifer, Ryan, Suzanne, & Franzetta, Kerry. (2003). Patterns of contraceptive use within teenagers' first sexual relationships. *Perspectives on Sexual and Reproductive Health, 35,* 246–255.

Manly, Jody Todd, Kim, Jungmeen E., Rogosch, Fred A., & Cicchetti, Dante. (2001). Dimensions of child maltreatment and children's adjustment: Contributions of developmental timing and subtype. *Development & Psychopathology, 13,* 759–782.

Mann, Ronald D., & Andrews, Elizabeth B. (Eds.). (2007). *Pharmacovigilance* (2nd ed.). Hoboken, NJ: Wiley.

Manzi, Claudia, Vignoles, Vivian L., Regalia, Camillo, & Scabini, Eugenia. (2006). Cohesion and enmeshment revisited: Differentiation, identity, and well-being in two European cultures. *Journal of Marriage and Family, 68,* 673–689.

Manzo, Kathleen Kennedy. (2006, October 4). Scathing report casts cloud over 'Reading First'. *Education Week, 26*(6), 1.

Manzo, Kathleen Kennedy. (2007a, November 30). America idles on international reading test. *Education Week.* 27(14), 11.

Manzo, Kathleen Kennedy. (2007b, March 14). Australia grapples with national content standards. *Education Week, 26*(27), 10.

Mao, Amy, Burnham, Melissa M., Goodlin-Jones, Beth L., Gaylor, Erika E., & Anders, Thomas F. (2004). A comparison of the sleep-wake patterns of cosleeping and solitary-sleeping infants. *Child Psychiatry and Human Development, 35,* 95–105.

March, John S., Franklin, Martin E., Leonard, Henrietta L., & Foa, Edna B. (2004). Obsessive-compulsive disorder. In Tracy L. Morris & John S. March (Eds.), *Anxiety disorders in children and adolescents* (2nd ed., pp. 212–240). New York: Guilford Press.

Marcia, James E. (1966). Development and validation of ego-identity status. *Journal of Personality & Social Psychology, 3,* 551–558.

Marcia, James E., Waterman, Alan S., Matteson, David R., Archer, Sally L., & Orlofsky, Jacob L. (1993). *Ego identity: A handbook for psychosocial research.* New York: Springer-Verlag.

Marcus, Gary. (2004). *The birth of the mind: How a tiny number of genes creates the complexities of human thought.* New York: Basic Books.

Marian, Viorica, & Fausey, Caitlin M. (2006). Language-dependent memory in bilingual learning. *Applied Cognitive Psychology, 20,* 1025–1047.

Marks, Amy Kerivan, Szalacha, Laura A., Lamarre, Meaghan, Boyd, Michelle J., & Coll, Cynthia García. (2007). Emerging ethnic identity and interethnic group social preferences in middle childhood: Findings from the Children of Immigrants Development in Context (CIDC) study. *International Journal of Behavioral Development, 31,* 501–513.

Marlow, Neil, Wolke, Dieter, Bracewell, Melanie A., & Samara, Muthanna. (2005). Neurologic and developmental disability at six years of age after extremely preterm birth. *New England Journal of Medicine, 352,* 9–19.

Marlow-Ferguson, Rebecca (Ed.). (2002). *World education encyclopedia: A survey of educational systems worldwide* (2nd ed.). Detroit, MI: Gale Group.

Marschark, Marc, & Spencer, Patricia Elizabeth (Eds.). (2003). *Oxford handbook of deaf studies, language, and education.* Oxford, England: Oxford University Press.

Martin, Andres, & Leslie, Douglas. (2003). Trends in psychotropic medication costs for children and adolescents, 1997–2000. *Archives of Pediatrics & Adolescent Medicine, 157,* 997–1004.

Martin, Carol Lynn, Ruble, Diane N., & Szkrybalo, Joel. (2002). Cognitive theories of early gender development. *Psychological Bulletin, 128,* 903–933.

Martin, Joyce A., Hamilton, Brady E., Sutton, Paul D., Ventura, Stephanie J., Menacker, Fay, Kirmeyer, Sharon, et al. (2007). Births: Final data for 2005. *National Vital Statistics Reports, 56*(6), 1–104.

Martin, Joyce A., Hamilton, Brady E., Ventura, Stephanie J., Menacker, Fay, & Park, Melissa M. (2002, February 12). Births: Final data for 2000. *National Vital Statistics Reports, 50*(5).

Martini, Mary. (1994). Peer interactions in Polynesia: A view from the Marquesas. In Jaipaul L. Roopnarine, James Ewald Johnson, & Frank H. Hooper (Eds.), *Children's play in diverse cultures* (pp. 73–103). Albany, NY: State University of New York Press.

Martino, Steven C., Collins, Rebecca L., Elliott, Marc N., Strachman, Amy, Kanouse, David E., & Berry, Sandra H. (2006). Exposure to degrading versus nondegrading music lyrics and sexual behavior among youth. *Pediatrics, 118,* e430–441.

Marx, Jean. (2007, January 19). Trafficking protein suspected in Alzheimer's disease. *Science, 315,* 314.

Mascolo, Michael F., Fischer, Kurt W., & Li, Jin. (2003). Dynamic development of component systems of emotions: Pride, shame, and guilt in China and the United States. In Richard J. Davidson, Klaus R. Scherer, & H. Hill Goldsmith (Eds.), *Handbook of affective sciences* (pp. 375–408). Oxford, England: Oxford University Press.

Mason, Robert A., Williams, Diane L., Kana, Rajesh K., Minshew, Nancy, & Just, Marcel Adam. (2008). Theory of mind disruption and recruitment of the right hemisphere during narrative comprehension in autism. *Neuropsychologia, 46,* 269–280.

Masten, Ann S. (2004). Regulatory processes, risk, and resilience in adolescent development. In Ronald E. Dahl & Linda Patia Spear (Eds.), *Adolescent brain development: Vulnerabilities and opportunities* (Vol. 1021, pp. 310–319). New York: New York Academy of Sciences.

Masten, Ann S., & Coatsworth, J. Douglas. (1998). The development of competence in favorable and unfavorable environments: Lessons from research on successful children. *American Psychologist, 53,* 205–220.

Masten, Carrie L., Guyer, Amanda E., Hodgdon, Hilary B., McClure, Erin B., Charney, Dennis S., Ernst, Monique, et al. (2008). Recognition of facial emotions among maltreated children with high rates of post-traumatic stress disorder. *Child Abuse & Neglect, 32,* 139–153.

Mastro, Dana E., Behm-Morawitz, Elizabeth, & Kopacz, Maria A. (2008). Exposure to television portrayals of Latinos: The implications of aversive racism and social identity theory. *Human Communication Research, 34,* 1–27.

Matchock, Robert L., Dorn, Lorah D., & Susman, Elizabeth J. (2007). Diurnal and seasonal cortisol, testosterone, and DHEA rhythms in boys and girls during puberty. *Chronobiology International, 24,* 969–990.

Maton, Kenneth I., Schellenbach, Cynthia J., Leadbeater, Bonnie J., & Solarz, Andrea L. (Eds.). (2004). *Investing in children, youth, families, and communities: Strengths-based research and policy.* Washington, DC: American Psychological Association.

Matsumoto, David. (2004). Reflections on culture and competence. In Robert J. Sternberg & Elena L. Grigorenko (Eds.), *Culture and competence: Contexts of life success* (pp. 273–282). Washington, DC: American Psychological Association.

Matsumoto, David. (2007). Culture, context, and behavior. *Journal of Personality, 75,* 1285–1320.

Matsumoto, David, & Yoo, Seung Hee. (2006). Toward a new generation of cross-cultural research. *Perspectives on Psychological Science, 1,* 234–250.

Maughan, Angeline, & Cicchetti, Dante. (2002). Impact of child maltreatment and interadult violence on children's emotion regulation abilities and socioemotional adjustment. *Child Development, 73,* 1525–1542.

May, Henry, & Supovitz, Jonathan A. (2006). Capturing the cumulative effects of school reform: An 11-year study of the impacts of America's choice on student achievement. *Educational Evaluation and Policy Analysis, 28,* 231–257.

May, Philip A., Gossage, J. Phillip, Brooke, Lesley E., Snell, Cudore L., Marais, Anna-Susan, Hendricks, Loretta S., et al. (2005). Maternal risk factors for fetal alcohol syndrome in the Western Cape Province of South Africa: A population-based study. *American Journal of Public Health, 95,* 1190–1199.

May, Stephen. (2005). Language policy and minority language rights. In Eli Hinkel (Ed.), *Handbook of research in second language teaching and learning* (pp. 1055–1073). Mahwah, NJ: Erlbaum.

Mayberry, Rachel I., & Nicoladis, Elena. (2000). Gesture reflects language development: Evidence from bilingual children. *Current Directions in Psychological Science, 9,* 192–196.

Mayeux, Lara, & Cillessen, Antonius H. N. (2007). Peer influence and the development of antisocial behavior. In Rutger C. M. E. Engels, Margaret Kerr, & Håkan Stattin (Eds.), *Friends, lovers, and groups: Key relationships in adolescence* (pp. 33–46). Hoboken, NJ: Wiley.

Maynard, Ashley E. (2002). Cultural teaching: The development of teaching skills in Maya sibling interactions. *Child Development, 73,* 969–982.

Mazzocco, Michèle M. M., & Ross, Judith L. (2007). *Neurogenetic developmental disorders: Variation of manifestation in childhood.* Cambridge, MA: MIT Press.

McAdams, Dan P., & Pals, Jennifer L. (2006). A new big five: Fundamental principles for an integrative science of personality. *American Psychologist, 61,* 204–217.

McCardle, Peggy, & Chhabra, Vinita. (2004). The accumulation of evidence: A continuing process. In Peggy D. McCardle & Vinita Chhabra (Eds.), *The voice of evidence in reading research* (pp. 463–478). Baltimore: Brookes.

McCloskey, Laura Ann, & Stuewig, Jeffrey. (2001). The quality of peer relationships among children exposed to family violence. *Development & Psychopathology, 13,* 83–96.

McConkie-Rosell, Allyn, & O'Daniel, Julianne. (2007). Beyond the diagnosis: The process of genetic counseling. In Michèle M. M. Mazzocco & Judith L. Ross (Eds.), *Neurogenetic developmental disorders: Variation of manifestation in childhood* (pp. 367–389). Cambridge, MA: MIT Press.

McCrae, Robert R., & Costa, Paul T. (2003). *Personality in adulthood: A five-factor theory perspective* (2nd ed.). New York: Guilford Press.

McDonald, Candice, Lambert, Jack, Welz, Tanya, Nayagam, Daya, Poulton, Mary, Aleksin, Devi, et al. (2007). Why are children still being infected with HIV? Experiences in the prevention of mother-to-child transmission of HIV in south London. *Sexually Transmitted Infections, 83,* 59–63.

McIntyre, Donald A. (2002). *Colour blindness: Causes and effects*. Chester, UK: Dalton.

McKelvie, Pippa, & Low, Jason. (2002). Listening to Mozart does not improve children's spatial ability: Final curtains for the Mozart effect. *British Journal of Developmental Psychology, 20,* 241–258.

McKinley, Jesse. (2006, May 10). Two setbacks for exit exams taken by high school seniors. *New York Times,* p. A21.

McKinstry, Leo. (2005). *Not ill—Just naughty*. The Spectator. Retrieved July 22, 2007, from the World Wide Web:http://www.spectator.co.uk/archive/features/13287/not-ill-just-naughty.thtml

McKusick, Victor A. (2007). Mendelian Inheritance in Man and its online version, OMIM. *American Journal of Human Genetics, 80,* 588–604.

McLanahan, Sara, Donahue, Elisabeth, & Haskins, Ron (Eds.). (2005). *The future of children: Marriage and child wellbeing*. Washington, DC: Brookings Institution.

McLeod, Bryce D., Wood, Jeffrey J., & Weisz, John R. (2007). Examining the association between parenting and childhood anxiety: A meta-analysis. *Clinical Psychology Review, 27,* 155–172.

McLoyd, Vonnie C., Aikens, Nikki L., & Burton, Linda M. (2006). Childhood poverty, policy, and practice. In William Damon & Richard M. Lerner (Series Eds.) & K. Ann Renninger & Irving E. Sigel (Vol. Eds.), *Handbook of child psychology: Vol. 4. Child psychology in practice* (6th ed., pp. 700–775). Hoboken, NJ: Wiley.

McLoyd, Vonnie C., Kaplan, Rachel, Hardaway, Cecily R., & Wood, Dana. (2007). Does endorsement of physical discipline matter? Assessing moderating influences on the maternal and child psychological correlates of physical discipline in African American families. *Journal of Family Psychology, 21,* 165–175.

McNeil, Michele. (2007, May). Rigorous courses, fresh enrollment. *Education Week, 26*(36), 28–31.

McPherson, Miller, Smith-Lovin, Lynn, & Cook, James M. (2001). Birds of a feather: Homophily in social networks. *Annual Review of Sociology, 27,* 415–444.

McQuaid, Elizabeth L., Kopel, Sheryl J., Klein, Robert B., & Fritz, Gregory K. (2003). Medication adherence in pediatric asthma: Reasoning, responsibility, and behavior. *Journal of Pediatric Psychology, 28,* 323–333.

McWhinnie, Chad, Abela, John R. Z., Hilmy, Nora, & Ferrer, Ilyan. (2008). Positive youth development programs: An alternative approach to the prevention of depression in children and adolescents. In John R. Z. Abela & Benjamin L. Hankin (Eds.), *Handbook of depression in children and adolescents* (pp. 354–373). New York: Guilford Press.

Meadows, Sara. (2006). *The child as thinker: The development and acquisition of cognition in childhood* (2nd ed.). New York: Routledge.

Mebane, Felicia E., Yam, Eileen A., & Rimer, Barbara K. (2006). Sex education and the news: Lessons from how journalists framed virginity pledges. *Journal of Health Communication, 11,* 583–606.

Medscape Psychiatry & Mental Health. (2005). *Autism first-hand: An expert interview with Temple Grandin, PhD*. Retrieved September 3, 2007, from the World Wide Web: http://www.medscape.com/viewarticle/498153

Melhuish, Edward, & Petrogiannis, Konstantinos. (2006). An international overview of early childhood care and education. In Edward Melhuish & Konstantinos Petrogiannis (Eds.), *Early childhood care and education: International perspectives* (pp. 167–178). London: Routledge.

Melhuish, Edward C., Phan, Mai B., Sylva, Kathy, Sammons, Pam, Siraj-Blatchford, Iram, & Taggart, Brenda. (2008). Effects of the home learning environment and preschool center experience upon literacy and numeracy development in early primary school. *Journal of Social Issues, 64,* 95–114.

Mell, Loren K., Ogren, David S., Davis, Robert L., Mullooly, John P., Black, Steven B., Shinefield, Henry R., et al. (2005). Compliance with national immunization guidelines for children younger than 2 years, 1996–1999. *Pediatrics, 115,* 461–467.

Mello, Zena R. (2008). Gender variation in developmental trajectories of educational and occupational expectations and attainment from adolescence to adulthood. *Developmental Psychology, 44,* 1069–1080.

Meltzoff, Andrew N. (2007). 'Like me': A foundation for social cognition. *Developmental Science, 10,* 126–134.

Meltzoff, Andrew N., & Moore, M. Keith. (1999). A new foundation for cognitive development in infancy: The birth of the representational infant. In Ellin Kofsky Scholnick, Katherine Nelson, Susan A. Gelman, & Patricia H. Miller (Eds.), *Conceptual development: Piaget's legacy* (pp. 53–78). Mahwah, NJ: Erlbaum.

Menacker, Fay, Martin, Joyce A., & MacDorman, Marian F. (2004, November 15). Births to 10–14-year-old mothers, 1990–2002: Trends and health outcomes. *National Vital Statistics Reports, 53*(7).

Mendle, Jane, Turkheimer, Eric, & Emery, Robert E. (2007). Detrimental psychological outcomes associated with early pubertal timing in adolescent girls. *Developmental Review, 27,* 151–171.

Merline, Alicia C., O'Malley, Patrick M., Schulenberg, John E., Bachman, Jerald G., & Johnston, Lloyd D. (2004). Substance use among adults 35 years of age: Prevalence, adulthood predictors, and impact of adolescent substance use. *American Journal of Public Health, 94,* 96–102.

Merlino, Joseph P., Jacobs, Marilyn S., Kaplan, Judy Ann, & Moritz, K. Lynne (Eds.). (2007). *Freud at 150: Twenty-first*

century essays on a man of genius. Lanham, MD: Rowman & Littlefield.

Merrell, Kenneth W., & Gimpel, Gretchen A. (1998). *Social skills of children and adolescents: Conceptualization, assessment, treatment*. Mahwah, NJ: Erlbaum.

Merriman, William E. (1999). Competition, attention, and young children's lexical processing. In Brian MacWhinney (Ed.), *The emergence of language* (pp. 331–358). Mahwah, NJ: Erlbaum.

Mervis, Jeffrey. (2006, May 19). Well-balanced panel to tackle algebra reform. *Science, 312,* 982a.

Mervis, Jeffrey. (2008, March 21). Expert panel lays out the path to algebra—and why it matters. *Science, 319,* 1605.

Mescheriakov, B. G. (2005). Psychometric approach to child animism. *Cultural-Historical Psychology, 1,* 70–86.

Mesquita, Batja, & Leu, Janxin. (2007). The cultural psychology of emotion. In Shinobu Kitayama & Dov Cohen (Eds.), *Handbook of cultural psychology* (pp. 734–759). New York: Guilford Press.

Messer, Karen, Trinidad, Dennis R., Al-Delaimy, Wael K., & Pierce, John P. (2008). Smoking cessation rates in the United States: A comparison of young adult and older smokers. *American Journal of Public Health, 98,* 317–322.

Messing, Jacqueline. (2007). Multiple ideologies and competing discourses: Language shift in Tlaxcala, Mexico. *Language in Society, 36,* 555–577.

Michaud, Pierre-Andre, Chossis, Isabelle, & Suris, Joan-Carles. (2006). Health-related behavior: Current situation, trends, and prevention. In Sandy Jackson & Luc Goossens (Eds.), *Handbook of adolescent development* (pp. 284–307). Hove, East Sussex, UK: Psychology Press.

Michels, Tricia M., Kropp, Rhonda Y., Eyre, Stephen L., & Halpern-Felsher, Bonnie L. (2005). Initiating sexual experiences: How do young adolescents make decisions regarding early sexual activity? *Journal of Research on Adolescence, 15,* 583–607.

Mikulincer, Mario, & Goodman, Gail S. (2006). *Dynamics of romantic love: Attachment, caregiving, and sex*. New York: Guilford Press.

Milesi, Carolina, & Gamoran, Adam. (2006). Effects of class size and instruction on kindergarten achievement. *Educational Evaluation and Policy Analysis, 28,* 287–313.

Miller, Greg. (2005, May 13). Reflecting on another's mind. *Science, 308,* 945–947.

Miller, Greg. (2006, March 31). The thick and thin of brainpower: Developmental timing linked to IQ. *Science, 311,* 1851.

Miller, Greg. (2008, June 13). Growing pains for fMRI. *Science, 320,* 1412–1414.

Miller, Joan G. (2004). The cultural deep structure of psychological theories of social development. In Robert J. Sternberg & Elena L. Grigorenko (Eds.), *Culture and competence: Contexts of life success* (pp. 111–138). Washington, DC: American Psychological Association.

Miller, Orlando J., & Therman, Eeva. (2001). *Human chromosomes* (4th ed.). New York: Springer.

Miller, Patricia H. (2002). *Theories of developmental psychology* (4th ed.). New York: Worth Publishers.

Miller, Patricia Y., & Simon, William. (1980). The development of sexuality in adolescence. In Joseph Adelson (Ed.), *Handbook of adolescent psychology* (pp. 383–407). New York: Wiley.

Miller, Suzanne M., McDaniel, Susan H., Rolland, John S., & Feetham, Suzanne L. (Eds.). (2006). *Individuals, families, and the new era of genetics: Biopsychosocial perspectives*. New York: Norton.

Miller, William R., & Carroll, Kathleen. (2006). *Rethinking substance abuse: What the science shows, and what we should do about it*. New York: Guilford Press.

Mills, Britain, Reyna, Valerie F., & Estrada, Steven. (2008). Explaining contradictory relations between risk perception and risk taking. *Psychological Science, 19,* 429–433.

Mills, James L., McPartlin, Joseph M., Kirke, Peadar N., Lee, Young J., Conley, Mary R., Weir, Donald G., et al. (1995). Homocysteine metabolism in pregnancies complicated by neural-tube defects. *Lancet, 345,* 149–151.

Min, Pyong Gap. (2000). Korean Americans' language use. In Sandra Lee McKay & Sau-ling Cynthia Wong (Eds.), *New immigrants in the United States: Readings for second language educators* (pp. 306–332). Cambridge, UK: Cambridge University Press.

Mintz, Toben H. (2005). Linguistic and conceptual influences on adjective acquisition in 24- and 36-month-olds. *Developmental Psychology, 41,* 17–29.

Mitchell, Katharyne. (2001). Education for democratic citizenship: Transnationalism, multiculturalism, and the limits of liberalism. *Harvard Educational Review, 71,* 51–78.

Mix, Kelly S., Huttenlocher, Janellen, & Levine, Susan Cohen. (2002). *Quantitative development in infancy and early childhood*. New York: Oxford University Press.

MMWR. (1996, September 27). Youth risk behavior surveillance—United States, 1995. *MMWR Surveillance Summaries, 45*(SS-4), 1–83.

MMWR. (1998, August 14). Youth risk behavior surveillance—United States, 1997. *MMWR Surveillance Summaries, 47*(SS-3).

MMWR. (2000, December 22). Blood lead levels in young children—United States and selected states, 1996–1999. *Morbidity and Mortality Weekly Report, 49,* 1133–1137.

MMWR. (2002, April 5). Alcohol use among women of childbearing age—United States, 1991–1999. *Morbidity and Mortality Weekly Report, 51*(13), 273–276.

MMWR. (2002, September 13). Folic acid and prevention of spina bifida and anencephaly: 10 years after the U.S. public health service recommendation. *MMWR Recommendations and Reports, 51*(RR13), 1–3.

MMWR. (2003, June 13). Varicella-related deaths—United States, 2002. *Morbidity and Mortality Weekly Report, 52,* 545–547.

MMWR. (2004, July 2). Therapeutic foster care for the prevention of violence: A report on recommendations of the Task Force on Community Preventive Services. *MMWR Recommendations and Reports,* 53(RR10), 1–8.

MMWR. (2004, October 15). Newborn screening for cystic fibrosis: Evaluation of benefits and risks and recommendations for state newborn screening programs. *MMWR: Recommendations and Reports,* 53(RR13), 1–36.

MMWR. (2005, January 14). Reducing childhood asthma through community-based service delivery—New York City, 2001–2004. *Morbidity and Mortality Weekly Report, 54,* 11–14.

MMWR. (2005, February 4). Quickstats: Pregnancy, birth, and abortion rates for teenagers aged 15–17 years—United States, 1976–2003. *Morbidity and Mortality Weekly Report, 54*(4).

MMWR. (2005, May 27). Blood lead levels—United States, 1999–2002. *Morbidity and Mortality Weekly Report, 54,* 513–516.

MMWR. (2005, August 26). Surveillance for dental caries, dental sealants, tooth retention, edentulism, and enamel fluorosis—United States, 1988–1994 and 1999–2002. 54(3), 1–44.

MMWR. (2006, June 9). Youth risk behavior surveillance—United States, 2005. *MMWR Surveillance Summaries, 55*(SS05), 1–108.

MMWR. (2006, October 20). STD-prevention counseling practices and human papillomavirus opinions among clinicians with adolescent patients—United States, 2004. *Morbidity and Mortality Weekly Report,* 55(41), 1117–1120.

MMWR. (2006, November 24). Abortion surveillance—United States, 2003. *MMWR Surveillance Summaries,* 55(SS11), 1–32.

MMWR. (2007, January 12). Table II: Provisional cases of selected notifiable diseases, United States, weeks ending January 6, 2007 and January 7, 2006 (1st Week) *Morbidity and Mortality Weekly Report,* 56(1), 12–20.

MMWR. (2007, February 9). Prevalence of autism spectrum disorders—Autism and Developmental Disabilities Monitoring Network, six sites, United States, 2000. *MMWR Surveillance Summaries,* 56(SS01), 1–11.

MMWR. (2007, February 16). Prevalence of heart disease—United States, 2005. *Morbidity and Mortality Weekly Report,* 56(06), 113–118.

MMWR. (2007, March 16). Fruit and vegetable consumption among adults—United States, 2005. *Morbidity and Mortality Weekly Report,* 56(10), 213–217.

MMWR. (2007, June 8). Assisted reproductive technology surveillance—United States, 2004. *Morbidity and Mortality Weekly Report Surveillance Summaries,* 56(SS06), 1–22.

MMWR. (2008, January 18). School-associated student homicides—United States, 1992–2006. *Morbidity and Mortality Weekly Report,* 57(2), 33–36.

MMWR. (2008, February 29). Outbreak of measles—San Diego, California, January–February 2008. *Morbidity and Mortality Weekly Report,* 57(8), 203–206.

MMWR. (2008, April 11). Prevalence of self-reported postpartum depressive symptoms—17 states, 2004–2005. *Morbidity and Mortality Weekly Report,* 57(14), 361–366.

MMWR. (2008, June 6). Youth risk behavior surveillance—United States, 2007. *MMWR Surveillance Summaries,* 57(SS04), 1–131.

Moffitt, Terrie E. (1997). Adolescence-limited and life-course-persistent offending: A complementary pair of developmental theories. In Terence P. Thornberry (Ed.), *Developmental theories of crime and delinquency* (pp. 11–54). New Brunswick, NJ: Transaction.

Moffitt, Terrie E. (2003). Life-course-persistent and adolescence-limited antisocial behavior: A 10-year research review and a research agenda. In Benjamin B. Lahey, Terrie E. Moffitt, & Avshalom Caspi (Eds.), *Causes of conduct disorder and juvenile delinquency* (pp. 49–75). New York: Guilford Press.

Moffitt, Terrie E., Caspi, Avshalom, Belsky, Jay, & Silva, Phil A. (1992). Childhood experience and the onset of menarche: A test of a sociobiological model. *Child Development, 63,* 47–58.

Moffitt, Terrie E., Caspi, Avshalom, & Rutter, Michael. (2006). Measured gene–environment interactions in psychopathology: Concepts, research strategies, and implications for research, intervention, and public understanding of genetics. *Perspectives on Psychological Science, 1,* 5–27.

Moffitt, Terrie E., Caspi, Avshalom, Rutter, Michael, & Silva, Phil A. (2001). *Sex differences in antisocial behaviour: Conduct disorder, delinquency, and violence in the Dunedin longitudinal study.* New York: Cambridge University Press.

Monastersky, Richard. (2007, January 12). Who's minding the teenage brain? *Chronicle of Higher Education, 53,* A14–A18.

Monteiro, Carlos A., Conde, Wolney L., & Popkin, Barry M. (2004). The burden of disease from undernutrition and overnutrition in countries undergoing rapid nutrition transition: A view from Brazil. *American Journal of Public Health, 94,* 433–434.

Monteiro, Carlos A., Conde, Wolney L., & Popkin, Barry M. (2007). Income-specific trends in obesity in Brazil: 1975–2003. *American Journal of Public Health, 97,* 1808–1812.

Montessori, Maria. (1966). *The secret of childhood* (M. Joseph Costelloe, Trans.). Notre Dame, IN: Fides. (Original work published 1936)

Moore, Celia L. (2002). On differences and development. In David J. Lewkowicz & Robert Lickliter (Eds.), *Conceptions of development: Lessons from the laboratory* (pp. 57–76). New York: Psychology Press.

Moore, Ginger A., & Calkins, Susan D. (2004). Infants' vagal regulation in the still-face paradigm is related to dyadic coordination of mother–infant interaction. *Developmental Psychology, 40,* 1068–1080.

Moore, Keith L., & Persaud, Trivedi V. N. (2003). *The developing human: Clinically oriented embryology* (7th ed.). Philadelphia: Saunders.

Moore, Keith L., & Persaud, Trivedi V. N. (2007). *The developing human: Clinically oriented embryology* (8th ed.). Philadelphia: Saunders/Elsevier.

Moore, Susan, & Rosenthal, Doreen. (2006). *Sexuality in adolescence: Current trends* (2nd ed.). New York: Routledge.

Morelli, Gilda A., & Rothbaum, Fred. (2007). Situating the child in context: Attachment relationships and self-regulation in different cultures. In Shinobu Kitayama & Dov Cohen (Eds.), *Handbook of cultural psychology* (pp. 500–527). New York: Guilford Press.

Morgan, Craig, Kirkbride, James, Leff, Julian, Craig, Tom, Hutchinson, Gerard, McKenzie, Kwame, et al. (2007). Parental separation, loss and psychosis in different ethnic groups: A case-control study. *Psychological Medicine, 37,* 495–503.

Morgan, Ian G. (2003). The biological basis of myopic refractive error. *Clinical and Experimental Optometry, 86,* 276–288.

Morgan, Kirstie, & Hayne, Harlene. (2007). Nonspecific verbal cues alleviate forgetting by young children. *Developmental Science, 10,* 727–733.

Morgenstern, Hal, Bingham, Trista, & Reza, Avid. (2000). Effects of pool-fencing ordinances and other factors on childhood drowning in Los Angeles County, 1990–1995. *American Journal of Public Health, 90,* 595–601.

Morris, Amanda Sheffield, Silk, Jennifer S., Steinberg, Laurence, Myers, Sonya S., & Robinson, Lara Rachel. (2007). The role of the family context in the development of emotion regulation. *Social Development, 16,* 361–388.

Morris, Pamela, & Kalil, Ariel. (2006). Out-of-school time use during middle childhood in a low-income sample: Do combinations of activities affect achievement and behavior? In Aletha C. Huston & Marika N. Ripke (Eds.), *Developmental contexts in middle childhood: Bridges to adolescence and adulthood* (pp. 237–259). New York: Cambridge University Press.

Moses, Louis J. (2005). Executive functioning and children's theories of mind. In

Bertram F. Malle & Sara D. Hodges (Eds.), *Other minds: How humans bridge the divide between self and others* (pp. 11–25). New York: Guilford Press.

Moshman, David. (2005). *Adolescent psychological development: Rationality, morality, and identity* (2nd ed.). Mahwah, NJ: Erlbaum.

Moss, Ellen, Cyr, Chantal, & Dubois-Comtois, Karine. (2004). Attachment at early school age and developmental risk: Examining family contexts and behavior problems of controlling-caregiving, controlling-punitive, and behaviorally disorganized children. *Developmental Psychology, 40,* 519–532.

Moster, Dag, Lie, Rolv T., Irgens, Lorentz M., Bjerkedal, Tor, & Markestad, Trond. (2001). The association of Apgar score with subsequent death and cerebral palsy: A population-based study in term infants. *Journal of Pediatrics, 138,* 798–803.

Mottl-Santiago, Julie, Walker, Catherine, Ewan, Jean, Vragovic, Olivera, Winder, Suzanne, & Stubblefield, Phillip. (2008). A hospital-based doula program and childbirth outcomes in an urban, multicultural setting. *Maternal & Child Health Journal, 12,* 372–377.

Mowbray, Carol T., Megivern, Deborah, Mandiberg, James M., Strauss, Shari, Stein, Catherine H., Collins, Kim, et al. (2006). Campus mental health services: Recommendations for change. *American Journal of Orthopsychiatry, 76,* 226–237.

Mpofu, Elias, & van de Vijver, Fons J. R. (2000). Taxonomic structure in early to middle childhood: A longitudinal study with Zimbabwean schoolchildren. *International Journal of Behavioral Development, 24,* 204–212.

Müller, Ulrich, Dick, Anthony Steven, Gela, Katherine, Overton, Willis F., & Zelazo, Philip David. (2006). The role of negative priming in preschoolers' flexible rule use on the dimensional change card sort task. *Child Development, 77,* 395–412.

Mullis, Ina V. S., Martin, Michael O., Gonzalez, Eugenio J., & Chrostowski, Steven J. (2004). *TIMSS 2003 international mathematics report: Findings from IEA's Trends in International Mathematics and Science Study at the eighth and fourth grades.* Chestnut Hill, MA: TIMSS & PIRLS International Study Center, Lynch School of Education, Boston College.

Munakata, Yuko. (2006). Information processing approaches to development. In William Damon & Richard M. Lerner (Series Eds.) & Deanna Kuhn & Robert S. Siegler (Vol. Eds.), *Handbook of child psychology: Vol. 2. Cognition, perception, and language* (6th ed., pp. 426–463). Hoboken, NJ: Wiley.

Munroe, Robert L., & Romney, A. Kimbal. (2006). Gender and age differences in same-sex aggregation and social behavior: A four-culture study. *Journal of Cross-Cultural Psychology, 37,* 3–19.

Murphy, Kevin, & Delanty, Norman. (2007). Sleep deprivation: A clinical perspective. *Sleep and Biological Rhythms, 5,* 2–14.

Murphy, Laura M. Bennett, Laurie-Rose, Cynthia, Brinkman, Tara M., & McNamara, Kelly A. (2007). Sustained attention and social competence in typically developing preschool-aged children. *Early Child Development and Care, 177,* 133–149.

Murray, Erin K., Ricketts, Sue, & Dellaport, Jennifer. (2007). Hospital practices that increase breastfeeding duration: Results from a population-based study. *Birth, 34,* 202–211.

Murray, Lynne, Halligan, Sarah L., Adams, Gillian, Patterson, Paul, & Goodyer, Ian M. (2006). Socioemotional development in adolescents at risk for depression: The role of maternal depression and attachment style. *Development and Psychopathology, 18,* 489–516.

Musick, Kelly. (2002). Planned and unplanned childbearing among unmarried women. *Journal of Marriage & Family, 64,* 915–929.

Muter, Valerie, Hulme, Charles, Snowling, Margaret J., & Stevenson, Jim. (2004). Phonemes, rimes, vocabulary, and grammatical skills as foundations of early reading development: Evidence from a longitudinal study. *Developmental Psychology, 40,* 665–681.

Nakamura, Suad, Wind, Marilyn, & Danello, Mary Ann. (1999). Review of hazards associated with children placed in adult beds. *Archives of Pediatrics and Adolescent Medicine, 153,* 1019–1023.

Narberhaus, Ana, Segarra, Dolors, Caldú, Xavier, Giménez, Monica, Junqué, Carme, Pueyo, Roser, et al. (2007). Gestational age at preterm birth in relation to corpus callosum and general cognitive outcome in adolescents. *Journal of Child Neurology, 22,* 761–765.

National Academy of Sciences, Institute of Medicine. (2008). *Science, evolution, and creationism.* Washington, DC: National Academies Press.

National Center for Education Statistics. (2007). *Digest of Education Statistics.* Retrieved June 5, 2008, from the World Wide Web: http://nces.ed.gov/programs/digest/d07/tables/dt07_041.asp

National Center for Health Statistics. (2000, September 21). Deaths: Final data for 1999. *National Vital Statistics Reports, 49*(8).

National Center for Health Statistics. (2007). Births: Final data for 2005. *National Vital Statistics Reports, 56*(6), 1–104.

National Center for Health Statistics. (2007). *Health, United States, 2007, with chartbook on trends in the health of Americans* (DHSS Publication No. 2007–1232). Hyattsville, MD: Author.

National Center for Health Statistics. (2008). *Deaths: Final data for 2005.* U.S. Department Of Health And Human Services. Retrieved June 15, 2008, from the World Wide Web: http://www.cdc.gov/nchs/data/nvsr/nvsr56/nvsr56_10.pdf

National Research Council and Institute of Medicine. (2000). *From neurons to neighborhoods: The science of early childhood development.* Washington, DC: National Academy Press.

National Sleep Foundation. (2006). *Summary findings of the 2006 Sleep in America poll.* Retrieved July 17, 2008, from the World Wide Web: http://www.sleepfoundation.org/atf/cf/%7BF6BF2668-A1B4-4FE8-8D1A-A5D39340D9CB%7D/2006_summary_of_findings.pdf

Neal, David T., Wood, Wendy, & Quinn, Jeffrey M. (2006). Habits—A repeat performance. *Current Directions in Psychological Science, 15,* 198–202.

Neave, Nick. (2008). *Hormones and behaviour: A psychological approach.* New York: Cambridge University Press.

Nelson, Charles A., de Haan, Michelle, & Thomas, Kathleen M. (2006). *Neuroscience of cognitive development: The role of experience and the developing brain.* Hoboken, NJ: Wiley.

Nelson, Charles A., III, Thomas, Kathleen M., & de Haan, Michelle. (2006). Neural bases of cognitive development. In William Damon & Richard M. Lerner (Series Eds.) & Deanna Kuhn & Robert S. Siegler (Vol. Eds.), *Handbook of child psychology: Vol. 2. Cognition, perception, and language* (6th ed., pp. 3–57). Hoboken, NJ: Wiley.

Nelson, Charles A., & Webb, Sara J. (2003). A cognitive neuroscience perspective on early memory development. In Michelle de Haan & Mark H. Johnson (Eds.), *The cognitive neuroscience of development* (pp. 99–126). New York: Psychology Press.

Nelson, Charles A., III, Zeanah, Charles H., Fox, Nathan A., Marshall, Peter J., Smyke, Anna T., & Guthrie, Donald. (2007, December 21). Cognitive recovery in socially deprived young children: The Bucharest Early Intervention Project. *Science, 318,* 1937–1940.

Nelson, Jennifer A., Chiasson, Mary Ann, & Ford, Viola. (2004). Childhood overweight in a New York City WIC population. *American Journal of Public Health, 94,* 458–462.

Nelson, Katherine. (2007). *Young minds in social worlds: Experience, meaning, and memory.* Cambridge, MA: Harvard University Press.

Nemy, Enid (with Alexander, Ron). (1998, November 2). Metropolitan diary. *New York Times,* p. B2.

Nesdale, Drew. (2004). Social identity processes and children's ethnic prejudice. In Mark Bennett & Fabio Sani (Eds.), *The development of the social self* (pp. 219–245). Hove, East Sussex, England: Psychology Press.

Nesselroade, John R., & Molenaar, Peter C. M. (2003). Quantitative models for developmental processes. In Jaan Valsiner & Kevin J. Connolly (Eds.), *Handbook of developmental psychology* (pp. 622–639). Thousand Oaks, CA: Sage.

Newman, Stuart A., & Müller, Gerd B. (2006). Genes and form: Inherency in the evolution of developmental mechanisms. In Eva M. Neumann-Held & Christoph Rehmann-Sutter (Eds.), *Genes in development: Rereading the molecular paradigm* (pp. 38–73). Durham, NC: Duke University Press.

Newschaffer, Craig J., Falb, Matthew D., & Gurney, James G. (2005). National autism prevalence trends from United States special education data. *Pediatrics, 115,* e277–282.

Newton, Christopher R., McBride, Joanna, Feyles, Valter, Tekpetey, Francis, & Power, Stephen. (2007). Factors affecting patients' attitudes toward single- and multiple-embryo transfer. *Fertility and Sterility, 87,* 269–278.

Ng, Nawi, Weinehall, Lars, & Öhman, Ann. (2007). 'If I don't smoke, I'm not a real man'—Indonesian teenage boys' views about smoking. *Health Education Research, 22,* 794–804.

Nguyen, Huong Q., Jumaan, Aisha O., & Seward, Jane F. (2005). Decline in mortality due to varicella after implementation of varicella vaccination in the United States. *New England Journal of Medicine, 352,* 450–458.

Nguyen, Simone P., & Murphy, Gregory L. (2003). An apple is more than just a fruit: Cross-classification in children's concepts. *Child Development, 74,* 1783–1806.

NICHD Early Child Care Research Network. (2001). Child care and children's peer interaction at 24 and 36 months: The NICHD study of early child care. *Child Development, 72,* 1478–1500.

NICHD Early Child Care Research Network. (2003). Does amount of time spent in child care predict socioemotional adjustment during the transition to kindergarten? *Child Development, 74,* 976–1005.

NICHD Early Child Care Research Network. (2003). Do children's attention processes mediate the link between family predictors and school readiness? *Developmental Psychology, 39,* 581–593.

NICHD Early Child Care Research Network. (2004). Trajectories of physical aggression from toddlerhood to middle childhood. *Monographs of the Society for Research in Child Development, 69*(Serial No. 278), vii-129.

NICHD Early Child Care Research Network. (2004). Does class size in first grade relate to children's academic and social performance or observed classroom processes? *Developmental Psychology, 40,* 651–664.

NICHD Early Child Care Research Network. (2004). Are child developmental outcomes related to before- and after-school care arrangements? Results from the NICHD Study of Early Child Care. *Child Development, 75,* 280–295.

NICHD Early Child Care Research Network (Ed.). (2005). *Child care and child development: Results from the NICHD study of early child care and youth development.* New York: Guilford Press.

NICHD Early Child Care Research Network. (2007). Age of entry to kindergarten and children's academic achievement and socioemotional development. *Early Education and Development, 18,* 337–368.

Nichols, Sharon L., & Berliner, David C. (2007). *Collateral damage: How high-stakes testing corrupts America's schools.* Cambridge, MA: Harvard Education Press.

Nichols, Tracy R., Graber, Julia A., Brooks-Gunn, Jeanne, & Botvin, Gilbert J. (2006). Sex differences in overt aggression and delinquency among urban minority middle school students. *Journal of Applied Developmental Psychology, 27,* 78–91.

Nielsen, Mark. (2006). Copying actions and copying outcomes: Social learning through the second year. *Developmental Psychology, 42,* 555–565.

Nielsen, Mark, Suddendorf, Thomas, & Slaughter, Virginia. (2006). Mirror self-recognition beyond the face. *Child Development, 77,* 176–185.

Nieto, Sonia. (2000). *Affirming diversity: The sociopolitical context of multicultural education* (3rd ed.). New York: Longman.

Nigg, Joel T. (2006). *What causes ADHD? Understanding what goes wrong and why.* New York: Guilford Press.

Nishida, Tracy K., & Lillard, Angeline S. (2007). The informative value of emotional expressions: 'Social referencing' in mother–child pretense. *Developmental Science, 10,* 205–212.

Nishina, Adrienne, & Juvonen, Jaana. (2005). Daily reports of witnessing and experiencing peer harassment in middle school. *Child Development, 76,* 435–450.

Normile, Dennis. (2007, April 13). Japan picks up the 'innovation' mantra. *Science, 316,* 186.

Norris, Pippa. (2001). *Digital divide: Civic engagement, information poverty, and the internet worldwide.* New York: Cambridge University Press.

Nurmi, Jari-Erik. (2004). Socialization and self-development: Channeling, selection, adjustment, and reflection. In Richard M. Lerner & Laurence D. Steinberg (Eds.), *Handbook of adolescent psychology* (2nd ed., pp. 85–124). Hoboken, NJ: Wiley.

O'Connor, Thomas G. (2002). The 'effects' of parenting reconsidered: Findings, challenges, and applications. *Journal of Child Psychology & Psychiatry, 43,* 555–572.

O'Connor, Thomas G., Rutter, Michael, Beckett, Celia, Keaveney, Lisa, Kreppner, Jana M., & English & Romanian Adoptees Study Team. (2000). The effects of global severe privation on cognitive competence: Extension and longitudinal follow-up. *Child Development, 71,* 376–390.

O'Doherty, Kieran. (2006). Risk communication in genetic counselling: A discursive approach to probability. *Theory & Psychology, 16,* 225–256.

O'Donnell, Lydia, Stueve, Ann, Duran, Richard, Myint-U, Athi, Agronick, Gail, Doval, Alexi San, et al. (2008). Parenting practices, parents' underestimation of daughters' risks, and alcohol and sexual behaviors of urban girls. *Journal of Adolescent Health, 42,* 496–502.

O'Rahilly, Ronan R., & Müller, Fabiola. (2001). *Human embryology & teratology* (3rd ed.). New York: Wiley-Liss.

Oberman, Lindsay M., & Ramachandran, Vilayanur S. (2007). The simulating social mind: The role of the mirror neuron system and simulation in the social and communicative deficits of autism spectrum disorders. *Psychological Bulletin, 133,* 310–327.

Oddy, Wendy H. (2004). A review of the effects of breastfeeding on respiratory infections, atopy, and childhood asthma. *Journal of Asthma, 41,* 605–621.

OECD (Organisation for Economic Co-operation and Development). (2008). *Education at a glance 2008: OECD indicators.* Paris: OECD Publications.

Ogden, Cynthia L., Carroll, Margaret D., & Flegal, Katherine M. (2008). High body mass index for age among US children and adolescents, 2003–2006. *Journal of the American Medical Association, 299,* 2401–2405.

Oh, Seungmi, & Lewis, Charlie. (2008). Korean preschoolers' advanced inhibitory control and its relation to other executive skills and mental state understanding. *Child Development, 79,* 80–99.

Oldershaw, Lynn. (2002). *A national survey of parents of young children.* Toronto, ON, Canada: Invest in Kids.

Olson, Kristina R., & Dweck, Carol S. (2008). A blueprint for social cognitive development. *Perspectives on Psychological Science, 3,* 193–202.

Olson, Lynn. (2005, June 22). States raise bar for high school diploma. *Education Week, 24*(41), 1, 28.

Olson, Steve. (2004, September 3). Making sense of Tourette's. *Science, 305,* 1390–1392.

Olweus, Dan. (1992). Bullying among schoolchildren: Intervention and prevention. In Ray DeV. Peters, Robert Joseph McMahon, & Vernon L. Quinsey (Eds.), *Aggression and violence throughout the life span* (pp. 100–125). Thousand Oaks, CA: Sage.

Olweus, Dan. (1993). Victimization by peers: Antecedents and long-term outcomes. In Kenneth H. Rubin & Jens B. Asendorpf (Eds.), *Social withdrawal, inhibition, and shyness in childhood* (pp. 315–341). Hillsdale, NJ: Erlbaum.

Olweus, Dan, Limber, Sue, & Mahalic, Sharon F. (1999). *Bullying prevention program.* Boulder, CO: Center for the Study and Prevention of Violence, Institute of Behavioral Science, University of Colorado at Boulder.

Omariba, D. Walter Rasugu, & Boyle, Michael H. (2007). Family structure and child mortality in sub-Saharan Africa: Cross-national effects of polygyny. *Journal of Marriage and Family, 69,* 528–543.

Ombelet, Willem. (2007). Access to assisted reproduction services and infertility treatment in Belgium in the context of the European countries. *Pharmaceuticals Policy and Law, 9,* 189–201.

Ontai, Lenna L., & Thompson, Ross A. (2008). Attachment, parent–child discourse and theory-of-mind development. *Social Development, 17,* 47–60.

Oosterman, Mirjam, Schuengel, Carlo, Slot, N. Wim, Bullens, Ruud A. R., & Doreleijers, Theo A. H. (2007). Disruptions in foster care: A review and meta-analysis. *Children and Youth Services Review, 29,* 53–76.

Ordoñana, Juan R., Caspi, Avshalom, & Moffitt, Terrie E. (2008). Unintentional injuries in a twin study of preschool children: Environmental, not genetic, risk factors. *Journal of Pediatric Psychology, 33,* 185–194.

Orshan, Susan A. (2008). *Maternity, newborn, and women's health nursing: Comprehensive care across the lifespan.* Philadelphia: Wolters Kluwer/Lippincott Williams & Wilkins.

Osgood, D. Wayne, Ruth, Gretchen, Eccles, Jacquelynne S., Jacobs, Janis E., & Barber, Bonnie L. (2005). Six paths to adulthood: Fast starters, parents without careers, educated partners, educated singles, working singles, and slow starters. In Richard A. Settersten, Jr., Frank F. Furstenberg, Jr., & Rubén G. Rumbaut (Eds.), *On the frontier of adulthood: Theory, research, and public policy* (pp. 320–355). Chicago: University of Chicago Press.

Otto, Beverly. (2008). *Literacy development in early childhood: Reflective teaching for birth to age eight.* Upper Saddle River, NJ: Prentice Hall.

Pahl, Kerstin, & Way, Niobe. (2006). Longitudinal trajectories of ethnic identity among urban Black and Latino adolescents. *Child Development, 77,* 1403–1415.

Palmer, Raymond F., Blanchard, Stephen, Jean, Carlos R., & Mandell, David S. (2005). School district resources and identification of children with autistic disorder. *American Journal of Public Health, 95,* 125–130.

Pan, Xiaochuan, Yue, Wei, He, Kebin, & Tong, Shilu. (2007). Health benefit evaluation of the energy use scenarios in Beijing, China. *Science of The Total Environment, 374,* 242–251.

Pang, Jenny W. Y., Heffelfinger, James D., Huang, Greg J., Benedetti, Thomas J., & Weiss, Noel S. (2002). Outcomes of planned home births in Washington State: 1989–1996. *Obstetrics & Gynecology, 100,* 253–259.

Parikh, Shanti A. (2007). The political economy of marriage and HIV: The ABC approach, "safe" infidelity, and managing moral risk in Uganda. *American Journal of Public Health, 97,* 1198–1208.

Park, D. J. J., & Congdon, Nathan G. (2004). Evidence for an "epidemic" of myopia. *Annals, Academy of Medicine, Singapore, 33,* 21–26.

Parke, Ross D. (2002). Fathers and families. In Marc H. Bornstein (Ed.), *Handbook of parenting: Vol. 3: Being and becoming a parent* (2nd ed., pp. 27–73). Mahwah, NJ: Erlbaum.

Parke, Ross D., & Buriel, Raymond. (2006). Socialization in the family: Ethnic and ecological perspectives. In William Damon & Richard M. Lerner (Series Eds.) & Nancy Eisenberg (Vol. Ed.), *Handbook of child psychology: Vol. 3. Social, emotional, and personality development* (6th ed., pp. 429–504). Hoboken, NJ: Wiley.

Parke, Ross D., Coltrane, Scott, Duffy, Sharon, Buriel, Raymond, Dennis, Jessica, Powers, Justina, et al. (2004). Economic stress, parenting, and child adjustment in Mexican American and European American families. *Child Development, 75,* 1632–1656.

Parker, Susan W., & Nelson, Charles A. (2005). The impact of early institutional rearing on the ability to discriminate facial expressions of emotion: An event-related potential study. *Child Development, 76,* 54–72.

Parsell, Diana. (2004, November 13). Assault on autism. *Science News, 166,* 311–312.

Parten, Mildred B. (1932). Social participation among pre-school children. *The Journal of Abnormal and Social Psychology, 27,* 243–269.

Pascarella, Ernest T., & Terenzini, Patrick T. (1991). *How college affects students: Findings and insights from twenty years of research.* San Francisco: Jossey-Bass Publishers.

Pascual-Leone, Alvaro, & Torres, Fernando. (1993). Plasticity of the sensorimotor cortex representation of the reading finger in Braille readers. *Brain, 116,* 39–52.

Pastore, Ann L., & Maguire, Kathleen. (2005). *Sourcebook of criminal justice statistics, 2003* (NCJ 208756). Rockville, MD: Justice Statistics Clearinghouse/NCJRS.

Pastore, Ann L., & Maguire, Kathleen. (n.d.). *Sourcebook of criminal justice statistics online.* Retrieved August, 1, 2008, from the World Wide Web: http://www.albany.edu/sourcebook/pdf/t31362005.pdf

Paterson, David S., Trachtenberg, Felicia L., Thompson, Eric G., Belliveau, Richard A., Beggs, Alan H., Darnall, Ryan, et al. (2006). Multiple serotonergic brainstem abnormalities in sudden infant death syndrome. *Journal of the American Medical Association, 296,* 2124–2132.

Patrick, Kevin, Norman, Gregory J., Calfas, Karen J., Sallis, James F., Zabinski, Marion F., Rupp, Joan, et al. (2004). Diet, physical activity, and sedentary behaviors as risk factors for overweight in adolescence. *Archives of Pediatrics & Adolescent Medicine, 158,* 385–390.

Patton, George C., Hemphill, Sheryl A., Beyers, Jennifer M., Bond, Lyndal, Toumbourou, John W., McMorris, Barbara J., et al. (2007). Pubertal stage and deliberate self harm in adolescents. *Journal of the American Academy of Child & Adolescent Psychiatry, 46,* 508–514.

Paul, David, Leef, Kathleen, Locke, Robert, Bartoshesky, Louis, Walrath, Judy, & Stefano, John. (2006). Increasing illness severity in very low birth weight infants over a 9-year period. *BMC Pediatrics, 6,* 2.

Pauli-Pott, Ursula, Mertesacker, Bettina, & Beckmann, Dieter. (2004). Predicting the development of infant emotionality from maternal characteristics. *Development & Psychopathology, 16,* 19–42.

Pellegrini, Anthony D., Dupuis, Danielle, & Smith, Peter K. (2007). Play in evolution and development. *Developmental Review, 27,* 261–276.

Pellegrini, Anthony D., & Smith, Peter K. (Eds.). (2005). *The nature of play: Great apes and humans.* New York: Guilford Press.

Pennington, Bruce Franklin. (2002). *The development of psychopathology: Nature and nurture.* New York: Guilford Press.

Pepler, Debra, Craig, Wendy, Yuile, Amy, & Connolly, Jennifer. (2004). Girls who bully: A developmental and relational perspective. In Martha Putallaz & Karen L. Bierman (Eds.), *Aggression, antisocial behavior, and violence among girls: A developmental perspective* (pp. 90–109). New York: Guilford Press.

Perfetti, Jennifer, Clark, Roseanne, & Fillmore, Capri-Mara. (2004). Postpartum depression: Identification, screening, and treatment. *Wisconsin Medical Journal, 103,* 56–63.

Perie, Marianne, Grigg, Wendy S., & Dion, Gloria S. (2005). *The nation's report card: Mathematics 2005* (NCES 2006–453). Washington, DC: U.S. Department of Education, National Center for Education Statistics.

Perner, Josef. (2000). About + belief + counterfactual. In Peter Mitchell & Kevin John Riggs (Eds.), *Children's reasoning and the mind* (pp. 367–401). Hove, England: Psychology Press.

Perner, Josef, Lang, Birgit, & Kloo, Daniela. (2002). Theory of mind and self-control: More than a common problem of inhibition. *Child Development, 73,* 752–767.

Perreira, Krista M., Harris, Kathleen Mullan, & Lee, Dohoon. (2007). Immigrant youth in the labor market. *Work and Occupations, 34,* 5–34.

Persaud, Trivedi V. N., Chudley, Albert E., & Skalko, Richard G. (1985). *Basic concepts in teratology.* New York: Liss.

Peterson, Jordan B., & Flanders, Joseph L. (2005). Play and the regulation of aggression. In Richard Ernest Tremblay, Willard W. Hartup, & John Archer (Eds.), *Developmental origins of aggression* (pp. 133–157). New York: Guilford Press.

Pettit, Gregory S. (2004). Violent children in developmental perspective: Risk and protective factors and the mechanisms through which they (may) operate. *Current Directions in Psychological Science, 13,* 194–197.

Pew Commission on Children in Foster Care. (2004). *Safety, permanence and well-being for children in foster care.* Retrieved June 23, 2007, from the World Wide Web: http://pewfostercare.org/research/docs/FinalReport.pdf

Pew Research Center. (2007). *A portrait of "Generation Next": How young people view their lives, futures and politics.* Pew Research Center. Retrieved August 26, 2007, from the World Wide Web: http://people press.org/reports/pdf/300.pdf

Philips, Sharon, & Tolmie, Andrew. (2007). Children's performance on and understanding of the Balance Scale problem: The effects of parental support. *Infant and Child Development, 16,* 95–117.

Philipsen, Nina, & Brooks-Gunn, Jeanne. (2008). Overweight and obesity in childhood. In Thomas P. Gullotta & Gary M. Blau (Eds.), *Handbook of childhood behavioral issues: Evidence-based approaches to prevention and treatment* (pp. 125–146). New York: Routledge/Taylor & Francis.

Phillips, Deborah A., & White, Sheldon H. (2004). New possibilities for research on Head Start. In Edward Zigler & Sally J. Styfco (Eds.), *The Head Start debates* (pp. 263–278). Baltimore: Brookes.

Phillips, Tommy M., & Pittman, Joe F. (2007). Adolescent psychological well-being by identity style. *Journal of Adolescence, 30,* 1021–1034.

Phillipson, Sivanes, & Phillipson, Shane N. (2007). Academic expectations, belief of ability, and involvement by parents as predictors of child achievement: A cross-cultural comparison. *Educational Psychology, 27,* 329–348.

Phinney, Jean S. (2006). Ethnic identity exploration in emerging adulthood. In Jeffrey Jensen Arnett & Jennifer Lynn Tanner (Eds.), *Emerging adults in America: Coming of age in the 21st century* (pp. 117–134). Washington, DC: American Psychological Association.

Piaget, Jean. (1929). *The child's conception of the world* (Joan Tomlinson & Andrew Tomlinson, Trans.). New York: Harcourt, Brace and Company.

Piaget, Jean. (1932). *The moral judgment of the child* (Marjorie Gabain, Trans.). London: K. Paul, Trench, Trubner & Co.

Piaget, Jean. (1950). *The psychology of intelligence* (Malcolm Piercy and D. E. Berlyne, Trans.). London: Routledge & Paul.

Piaget, Jean. (1952). *The origins of intelligence in children.* (M. Cook, Trans.). Oxford, England: International Universities Press.

Piaget, Jean. (1954). *The construction of reality in the child* (Margaret Cook, Trans.). New York: Basic Books.

Piaget, Jean. (1962). *Play, dreams and imitation in childhood* (C. Gattegno & F. M. Hodgson, Trans.). New York: Norton. (Original work published 1945)

Piaget, Jean. (1970). *The child's conception of movement and speed* (G. E. T. Holloway and M. J. Mackenzie, Trans.). New York: Basic Books.

Piaget, Jean. (1972). *The psychology of intelligence*. Totowa, NJ: Littlefield. (Original work published 1950)

Piaget, Jean. (1997). *The moral judgment of the child* (Marjorie Gabain, Trans.). New York: Simon and Schuster. (Original work published 1932)

Piaget, Jean, & Inhelder, Bärbel. (1969). *The psychology of the child*. New York: Basic Books.

Piaget, Jean, Voelin-Liambey, Daphne, & Berthoud-Papandropoulou, Ioanna. (2001). *Problems of class inclusion and logical implication* (Robert L. Campbell, Ed. & Trans.). Hove, East Sussex, England: Psychology Press. (Original work published 1977)

Pickett, Kate E., Mookherjee, Jessica, & Wilkinson, Richard G. (2005). Adolescent birth rates, total homicides, and income inequality in rich countries. *American Journal of Public Health, 95,* 1181–1183.

Pin, Tamis, Eldridge, Beverley, & Galea, Mary P. (2007). A review of the effects of sleep position, play position, and equipment use on motor development in infants. *Developmental Medicine & Child Neurology, 49,* 858–867.

Pinborg, Anja, Loft, Anne, & Nyboe Andersen, Anders. (2004). Neonatal outcome in a Danish national cohort of 8602 children born after in vitro fertilization or intracytoplasmic sperm injection: The role of twin pregnancy. *Acta Obstetricia et Gynecologica Scandinavica, 83,* 1071–1078.

Pineda, David A., Palacio, Luis Guillermo, Puerta, Isabel C., Merchán, Vilma, Arango, Clara P., Galvis, Astrid Yuleth, et al. (2007). Environmental influences that affect attention deficit/hyperactivity disorder: Study of a genetic isolate. *European Child & Adolescent Psychiatry, 16,* 337–346.

Pinhas-Hamiel, Orit, Lerner-Geva, Liat, Copperman, Nancy M., & Jacobson, Marc S. (2007). Lipid and insulin levels in obese children: Changes with age and puberty. *Obesity, 15,* 2825–2831.

Pinheiro, Paulo Sèrgio (Ed.). (2006). *World report on violence against children*. Geneva, Switzerland: United Nations.

Pinker, Steven. (1999). *Words and rules: The ingredients of language*. New York: Basic Books.

Pinker, Steven. (2007). *The stuff of thought: Language as a window into human nature*. New York: Viking.

Piontelli, Alessandra. (2002). *Twins: From fetus to child*. London: Routledge.

Pizer, Ginger, Walters, Keith, & Meier, Richard P. (2007). Bringing up baby with baby signs: Language ideologies and socialization in hearing families. *Sign Language Studies, 7,* 387–430.

Plank, Stephen B., & MacIver, Douglas J. (2003). Educational achievement. In Marc H. Bornstein, Lucy Davidson, Corey L. M. Keyes, & Kristin Moore (Eds.), *Well-being: Positive development across the life course* (pp. 341–354). Mahwah, NJ: Erlbaum.

Plomin, Robert. (2002). Behavioural genetics in the 21st century. In Willard W. Hartup & Rainer K. Silbereisen (Eds.), *Growing points in developmental science: An introduction* (pp. 47–63). Philadelphia: Psychology Press.

Plomin, Robert, DeFries, John C., Craig, Ian W., & McGuffin, Peter. (2003). *Behavioral genetics in the postgenomic era*. Washington, DC: American Psychological Association.

Plomin, Robert, Happé, Francesca, & Caspi, Avshalom. (2002). Personality and cognitive abilities. In Peter McGuffin, Michael J. Owen, & Irving I. Gottesman (Eds.), *Psychiatric genetics and genomics* (pp. 77–112). New York: Oxford University Press.

Plutchik, Robert. (2003). *Emotions and life: Perspectives from psychology, biology, and evolution*. Washington, DC: American Psychological Association.

Polanczyk, Guilherme, & Rohde, Luis Augusto. (2007). Epidemiology of attention-deficit/hyperactivity disorder across the lifespan. *Current Opinion in Psychiatry, 20,* 386–392.

Pollack, Harold, & Frohna, John. (2001). A competing risk model of sudden infant death syndrome incidence in two U.S. birth cohorts. *Journal of Pediatrics, 138,* 661–667.

Pollak, Seth D., Cicchetti, Dante, Hornung, Katherine, & Reed, Alex. (2000). Recognizing emotion in faces: Developmental effects of child abuse and neglect. *Developmental Psychology, 36,* 679–688.

Pomerantz, Eva M., & Rudolph, Karen D. (2003). What ensues from emotional distress? Implications for competence estimation. *Child Development, 74,* 329–345.

Pong, Suet-ling, Dronkers, Jaap, & Hampden-Thompson, Gillian. (2003). Family policies and children's school achievement in single- versus two-parent families. *Journal of Marriage and Family, 65,* 681–699.

Porche, Michelle V., Ross, Stephanie J., & Snow, Catherine E. (2004). From preschool to middle school: The role of masculinity in low-income urban adolescent boys' literacy skills and academic achievement. In Niobe Way & Judy Y. Chu (Eds.), *Adolescent boys: Exploring diverse cultures of boyhood* (pp. 338–360). New York: New York University Press.

Posner, Michael I., Rothbart, Mary K., Sheese, Brad E., & Tang, Yiyuan. (2007). The anterior cingulate gyrus and the mechanism of self-regulation. *Cognitive, Affective & Behavioral Neuroscience, 7,* 391–395.

Powell, Douglas R. (2006). Families and early childhood interventions. In William Damon & Richard M. Lerner (Series Eds.) & K. Ann Renninger & Irving E. Sigel (Vol. Eds.), *Handbook of child psychology: Vol. 4. Child psychology in practice* (6th ed., pp. 548–591). Hoboken: Wiley.

Powlishta, Kimberly. (2004). Gender as a social category: Intergroup processes and gender-role development. In Mark Bennett & Fabio Sani (Eds.), *The development of the social self* (pp. 103–133). Hove, East Sussex, England: Psychology Press.

Pratt, Thomas, & Price, David J. (2006). Dual roles of transcription factors in forebrain morphogenesis and development of axonal pathways. In Reha S. Erzurumlu, William Guido, & Zoltán Molnár (Eds.), *Development and plasticity in sensory thalamus and cortex* (pp. 19–41). New York: Springer.

Pressley, Michael, & Hilden, Katherine. (2006). Cognitive strategies: Production deficiencies and successful strategy instruction everywhere. In William Damon & Richard M. Lerner (Series Eds.) & Deanna Kuhn & Robert S. Siegler (Vol. Eds.), *Handbook of child psychology: Vol. 2. Cognition, perception, and language* (6th ed., pp. 511–556). Hoboken, NJ: Wiley.

Pruden, Shannon M., Hirsh-Pasek, Kathy, Golinkoff, Roberta Michnick, &

Hennon, Elizabeth A. (2006). The birth of words: Ten-month-olds learn words through perceptual salience. *Child Development, 77,* 266–280.

Purves, Dale, Augustine, George J., Fitzpatrick, David, Hall, William C., LaMantia, Anthony-Samuel, McNamara, James O., et al. (Eds.). (2004). *Neuroscience* (3rd ed.). Sunderland, MA: Sinauer Associates.

Quan, Linda, Bennett, Elizabeth E., & Branche, Christine M. (2007). Interventions to prevent drowning. In Lynda S. Doll, Sandra E. Bonzo, James A. Mercy, & David A. Sleet (Eds.), *Handbook of injury and violence prevention* (pp. 81–96). New York: Springer.

Quas, Jodi A., Bauer, Amy, & Boyce, W. Thomas. (2004). Physiological reactivity, social support, and memory in early childhood. *Child Development, 75,* 797–814.

Quill, Elizabeth. (2008, March 14). Blood-matching goes genetic. *Science, 319,* 1478–1479.

Quinn, Alexander E., Georges, Arthur, Sarre, Stephen D., Guarino, Fiorenzo, Ezaz, Tariq, & Graves, Jennifer A. Marshall. (2007, April 20). Temperature sex reversal implies sex gene dosage in a reptile. *Science, 316,* 411.

Quinn, Paul C. (2004). Development of subordinate-level categorization in 3- to 7-month-old infants. *Child Development, 75,* 886–899.

Raikes, Helen, Alexander Pan, Barbara, Luze, Gayle, Tamis-LeMonda, Catherine S., Brooks-Gunn, Jeanne, Constantine, Jill, et al. (2006). Mother-child bookreading in low-income families: Correlates and outcomes during the first three years of life. *Child Development, 77,* 924–953.

Raley, R. Kelly, & Wildsmith, Elizabeth. (2004). Cohabitation and children's family instability. *Journal of Marriage & Family, 66,* 210–219.

Ramchandani, Paul, Stein, Alan, Evans, Jonathan, & O'Connor, Thomas G. (2005). Paternal depression in the postnatal period and child development: A prospective population study. *Lancet, 365,* 2201–2205.

Ramey, Craig T., Ramey, Sharon Landesman, Lanzi, Robin Gaines, & Cotton, Janice N. (2002). Early educational interventions for high-risk children: How center-based treatment can augment and improve parenting effectiveness. In John G. Borkowski, Sharon Landesman Ramey, & Marie Bristol-Power (Eds.), *Parenting and the child's world: Influences on academic, intellectual, and social-emotional development* (pp. 125–140). Mahwah, NJ: Erlbaum.

Randazzo, William T., Dockray, Samantha, & Susman, Elizabeth J. (2008). The stress response in adolescents with inattentive type ADHD symptoms. *Child Psychiatry & Human Development, 39,* 27–38.

Rankin, Jane L., Lane, David J., Gibbons, Frederick X., & Gerrard, Meg. (2004). Adolescent self-consciousness: Longitudinal age changes and gender differences in two cohorts. *Journal of Research on Adolescence, 14,* 1–21.

Rauscher, Frances H., & Shaw, Gordon L. (1998). Key components of the Mozart effect. *Perceptual & Motor Skills, 86*(3, Pt. 1), 835–841.

Rauscher, Frances H., Shaw, Gordon L., & Ky, Catherine N. (1993, 14 Oct). Music and spatial task performance. *Nature, 365,* 611.

Rayco-Solon, Pura, Fulford, Anthony J., & Prentice, Andrew M. (2005). Differential effects of seasonality on preterm birth and intrauterine growth restriction in rural Africans. *American Journal of Clinical Nutrition, 81,* 134–139.

Rayner, Keith, Foorman, Barbara R., Perfetti, Charles A., Pesetsky, David, & Seidenberg, Mark S. (2001). How psychological science informs the teaching of reading. *Psychological Science in the Public Interest, 2,* 31–74.

Read, Jennifer S., & The Committee on Pediatric AIDS. (2007). Diagnosis of HIV-1 infection in children younger than 18 months in the United States. *Pediatrics, 120,* e1547–1562.

Ream, Geoffrey L., & Savin-Williams, Ritch C. (2003). Religious development in adolescence. In Gerald R. Adams & Michael D. Berzonsky (Eds.), *Blackwell handbook of adolescence* (pp. 51–59). Malden, MA: Blackwell.

Reece, E. Albert, & Hobbins, John C. (Eds.). (2007). *Handbook of clinical obstetrics: The fetus & mother handbook* (2nd ed.). Malden, MA: Blackwell.

Reed, Tom, & Brown, Mac. (2001). The expression of care in the rough and tumble play of boys. *Journal of Research in Childhood Education, 15,* 104–116.

Reese, Elaine, Bird, Amy, & Tripp, Gail. (2007). Children's self-esteem and moral self: Links to parent-child conversations regarding emotion. *Social Development, 16,* 460–478.

Regnerus, Mark D. (2005). Talking about sex: Religion and patterns of parent–child communication about sex and contraception. *Sociological Quarterly, 46,* 79–105.

Reilly, Sheena, Eadie, Patricia, Bavin, Edith L., Wake, Melissa, Prior, Margot, Williams, Joanne, et al. (2006). Growth of infant communication between 8 and 12 months: A population study. *Journal of Paediatrics and Child Health, 42,* 764–770.

Reis, Harry T., & Collins, W. Andrew. (2004). Relationships, human behavior, and psychological science. *Current Directions in Psychological Science, 13,* 233–237.

Reiss, David, Neiderhiser, Jenae M., Hetherington, E. Mavis, & Plomin, Robert. (2000). *The relationship code: Deciphering genetic and social influences on adolescent development.* Cambridge, MA: Harvard University Press.

Reith, Gerda. (2005). On the edge: Drugs and the consumption of risk in late modernity. In Stephen Lyng (Ed.), *Edgework: The sociology of risk taking* (pp. 227–246). New York: Routledge.

Remage-Healey, Luke, & Bass, Andrew H. (2004). Rapid, hierarchical modulation of vocal patterning by steroid hormones. *Journal of Neuroscience, 24,* 5892–5900.

Renk, Kimberly, Donnelly, Reesa, McKinney, Cliff, & Agliata, Allison Kanter. (2006). The development of gender identity: Timetables and influences. In Kam-Shing Yip (Ed.), *Psychology of gender identity: An international perspective* (pp. 49–68). Hauppauge, NY: Nova Science.

Rentner, Diane Stark, Scott, Caitlin, Kober, Nancy, Chudowsky, Naomi, Chudowsky, Victor, Joftus, Scott, et al. (2006). *From the capital to the classroom: Year 4 of the No Child Left Behind Act.* Washington, DC: Center on Education Policy.

Rettig, Michael. (2005). Using the multiple intelligences to enhance instruction for young children and young children with disabilities. *Early Childhood Education Journal, 32,* 255–259.

Retting, Richard A., Ferguson, Susan A., & McCartt, Anne T. (2003). A review of evidence-based traffic engineering measures designed to reduce pedestrian–motor vehicle crashes. *American Journal of Public Health, 93,* 1456–1463.

Reyna, Valerie F., & Farley, Frank. (2006). Risk and rationality in adolescent decision making: Implications for theory, practice, and public policy. *Psychological Science in the Public Interest, 7,* 1–44.

Reynolds, Arthur J. (2000). *Success in early intervention: The Chicago child–parent centers.* Lincoln, NE: University of Nebraska Press.

Reynolds, Arthur J., Ou, Suh-Ruu, & Topitzes, James W. (2004). Paths of effects of early childhood intervention on educational attainment and delinquency: A confirmatory analysis of the Chicago Child-Parent Centers. *Child Development, 75,* 1299–1328.

Reynolds, Heidi W., Wong, Emelita L., & Tucker, Heidi. (2006). Adolescents' use of maternal and child health services in developing countries. *International Family Planning Perspectives, 32*(1), 6–16.

Rhee, Kyung. (2008). Childhood overweight and the relationship between parent behaviors, parenting style, and family functioning. *Annals of the American Academy of Political and Social Science, 615,* 12–37.

Rhodes, Jean E., & Roffman, Jennifer G. (2003). Nonparental adults as asset builders in the lives of youth. In Richard M. Lerner & Peter L. Benson (Eds.), *Developmental assets and asset-building communities: Implications for research, policy, and practice* (pp. 195–209). New York: Kluwer/Plenum.

Ricento, Thomas. (2005). Considerations of identity in L2 learning. In Eli Hinkel (Ed.), *Handbook of research in second language teaching and learning* (pp. 895–910). Mahwah, NJ: Erlbaum.

Richardson, Rick, & Hayne, Harlene. (2007). You can't take it with you: The translation of memory across development. *Current Directions in Psychological Science, 16,* 223–227.

Richardson, Rhonda A. (2004). Early adolescence talking points: Questions that middle school students want to ask their parents. *Family Relations, 53,* 87–94.

Ridley, Matt. (1999). *Genome: The autobiography of a species in 23 chapters.* London: Fourth Estate.

Rieger, Gerulf, Linsenmeier, Joan A. W., Gygax, Lorenz, & Bailey, J. Michael. (2008). Sexual orientation and childhood gender nonconformity: Evidence from home videos. *Developmental Psychology, 44,* 46–58.

Riordan, Jan (Ed.). (2005). *Breastfeeding and human lactation* (3rd ed.). Sudbury, MA: Jones and Bartlett.

Ripke, Marika N., Huston, Aletha C., & Casey, David M. (2006). Low-income children's activity participation as a predictor of psychosocial and academic outcomes in middle childhood and adolescence. In Aletha C. Huston & Marika N. Ripke (Eds.), *Developmental contexts in middle childhood: Bridges to adolescence and adulthood* (pp. 260–282). New York: Cambridge University Press.

Rivers, Ian. (2001). The bullying of sexual minorities at school: Its nature and long-term correlates. *Educational and Child Psychology, 18,* 32–46.

Rizzolatti, Giacomo, & Craighero, Laila. (2004). The mirror-neuron system. *Annual Review of Neuroscience, 27,* 169–192.

Rizzolatti, Giacomo, & Sinigaglia, Corrado. (2008). *Mirrors in the brain: How our minds share actions and emotions* (Frances Anderson, Trans.). New York: Oxford University Press.

Robelen, Erik W. (2006, June 20). Exit exams found to depress H. S. graduation rates. *Education Week, 25*(41), 30.

Roberts, Brent W., Kuncel, Nathan R., Shiner, Rebecca, Caspi, Avshalom, & Goldberg, Lewis R. (2007). The power of personality: The comparative validity of personality traits, socioeconomic status, and cognitive ability for predicting important life outcomes. *Perspectives on Psychological Science, 2,* 313–345.

Roberts, Donald F., & Foehr, Ulla G. (2004). *Kids and media in America: Patterns of use at the millennium.* New York: Cambridge University Press.

Roberts, Leslie. (2007, October 26). Battling over bed nets. *Science, 318,* 556–559.

Robins, Lee N., Helzer, John E., & Davis, Darlene H. (1975). Narcotic use in Southeast Asia and afterward: An interview study of 898 Vietnam returnees. *Archives of General Psychiatry, 32,* 955–961.

Robitaille, David F., & Beaton, Albert E. (Eds.). (2002). *Secondary analysis of the TIMSS data.* Boston: Kluwer.

Rochat, Philippe. (2001). *The infant's world.* Cambridge, MA: Harvard University Press.

Roche, Alex F., & Sun, Shumei S. (2003). *Human growth: Assessment and interpretation.* Cambridge, UK: Cambridge University Press.

Rodgers, Joseph. (2003). EMOSA sexuality models, memes, and the tipping point: Policy & program implications. In Daniel Romer (Ed.), *Reducing adolescent risk: Toward an integrated approach* (pp. 185–192). Thousand Oaks, CA: Sage.

Rodgers, Joseph Lee, & Wänström, Linda. (2007). Identification of a Flynn Effect in the NLSY: Moving from the center to the boundaries. *Intelligence, 35,* 187–196.

Rogers, Chrissie. (2007). Experiencing an 'inclusive' education: Parents and their children with 'special educational needs'. *British Journal of Sociology of Education, 28,* 55–68.

Rogoff, Barbara. (1998). Cognition as a collaborative process. In William Damon (Series Ed.) & Deanna Kuhn & Robert S. Siegler (Vol. Eds.), *Handbook of child psychology: Vol. 2. Cognition, perception, and language* (5th ed., pp. 679–744). New York: Wiley.

Rogoff, Barbara. (2003). *The cultural nature of human development.* New York: Oxford University Press.

Rogoff, Barbara, Correa-Chávez, Maricela, & Cotuc, Marta Navichoc. (2005). A cultural/historical view of schooling in human development. In David B. Pillemer & Sheldon H. White (Eds.), *Developmental psychology and social change: Research, history and policy* (pp. 225–263). New York: Cambridge University Press.

Roid, Gale H. (2003). *Stanford-Binet intelligence scales* (5th ed.). Itasca, IL: Riverside.

Roisman, Glenn I., & Fraley, R. Chris. (2006). The limits of genetic influence: A behavior-genetic analysis of infant–caregiver relationship quality and temperament. *Child Development, 77,* 1656–1667.

Romans, Sarah E., Martin, J. M., Gendall, Kelly, & Herbison, G. Peter. (2003). Age of menarche: The role of some psychosocial factors. *Psychological Medicine, 33,* 933–939.

Roney, Kathleen, Brown, Kathleen M., & Anfara, Vincent A., Jr. (2004). Middle-level reform in high- and low-performing middle schools: A question of implementation? *Clearing House, 77,* 153–159.

Roopnarine, Jaipaul L., Johnson, James E., & Hooper, Frank H. (Eds.). (1994). *Children's play in diverse cultures.* Albany, NY: State University of New York Press.

Roschelle, Jeremy M., Pea, Roy D., Hoadley, Christopher M., Gordin, Douglas N., & Means, Barbara M. (2000). Changing how and what children learn in school with computer-based technologies. *The Future of Children, 10*(2), 76–101.

Rose, Amanda J., & Asher, Steven R. (1999). Children's goals and strategies in response to conflicts within a friendship. *Developmental Psychology, 35,* 69–79.

Rose, Amanda J., & Asher, Steven R. (2004). Children's strategies and goals in response to help-giving and help-seeking tasks within a friendship. *Child Development, 75,* 749–763.

Rose, Amanda J., Swenson, Lance P., & Waller, Erika M. (2004). Overt and relational aggression and perceived popularity: Developmental differences in concurrent and prospective relations. *Developmental Psychology, 40,* 378–387.

Rose, Richard J. (2007). Peers, parents, and processes of adolescent socialization: A twin-study perspective. In Rutger C. M. E. Engels, Margaret Kerr, & Håkan Stattin (Eds.), *Friends, lovers, and groups: Key relationships in adolescence* (pp. 105–124). Hoboken, NJ: Wiley.

Rose, Steven. (2008, January 31). Drugging unruly children is a method of social control [Correspondence]. *Nature, 451,* 521.

Rosenbluth, Barri, Whitaker, Daniel J., Sanchez, Ellen, & Valle, Linda Anne. (2004). The Expect Respect project: Preventing bullying and sexual harassment in US elementary schools. In Peter K. Smith, Debra Pepler, & Ken Rigby (Eds.), *Bullying in schools: How successful can interventions be?* (pp. 211–233). New York: Cambridge University Press.

Rosenthal, Miriam K. (1991). The relation of peer interaction among infants and toddlers in family day care to characteristics of the child care environment. *Journal of Reproductive and Infant Psychology, 9,* 151–167.

Rothbart, Mary K., & Bates, John E. (2006). Temperament. In William Damon & Richard M. Lerner (Series Eds.) & Nancy Eisenberg (Vol. Ed.), *Handbook of child psychology: Vol. 3. Social, emotional, and personality development* (6th ed., pp. 99–166). Hoboken, NJ: Wiley.

Rothbaum, Fred, Pott, Martha, Azuma, Hiroshi, Miyake, Kazuo, & Weisz, John. (2000). The development of close relationships in Japan and the United States: Paths of symbiotic harmony and generative tension. *Child Development, 71,* 1121–1142.

Rovee-Collier, Carolyn. (1987). Learning and memory in infancy. In Joy Doniger Osofsky (Ed.), *Handbook of infant development* (2nd ed., pp. 98–148). New York: Wiley.

Rovee-Collier, Carolyn. (1990). The "memory system" of prelinguistic infants. In Adele Diamond (Ed.), *The development and neural bases of higher cognitive functions* (Vol. 608, pp. 517–542). New York: New York Academy of Sciences.

Rovee-Collier, Carolyn. (2001). Information pick-up by infants: What is it, and how can we tell? *Journal of Experimental Child Psychology, 78,* 35–49.

Rovee-Collier, Carolyn, & Hayne, Harlene. (1987). Reactivation of infant memory: Implications for cognitive development. In Hayne W. Reese (Ed.), *Advances in child development and behavior* (Vol. 20, pp. 185–238). San Diego, CA: Academic Press.

Rovi, Sue, Chen, Ping-Hsin, & Johnson, Mark S. (2004). The economic burden of hospitalizations associated with child abuse and neglect. *American Journal of Public Health, 94,* 586–590.

Rowland, Andrew S., Umbach, David M., Stallone, Lil, Naftel, A. Jack, Bohlig, E. Michael, & Sandler, Dale P. (2002). Prevalence of medication treatment for attention deficit-hyperactivity disorder among elementary school children in Johnston County, North Carolina. *American Journal of Public Health, 92,* 231–234.

Rozin, Paul. (2007). Food and eating. In Shinobu Kitayama & Dov Cohen (Eds.), *Handbook of cultural psychology* (pp. 391–416). New York: Guilford Press.

Rubie-Davies, Christine M. (2007) Classroom interactions: Exploring the practices of high- and low-expectation teachers. *British Journal of Educational Psychology, 77,* 289–306.

Rubin, Kenneth H., Bukowski, William M., & Parker, Jeffrey G. (2006). Peer interactions, relationships, and groups. In William Damon & Richard M. Lerner (Series Eds.) & Nancy Eisenberg (Vol. Ed.), *Handbook of child psychology: Vol. 3. Social, emotional, and personality development* (6th ed., pp. 619–700). Hoboken, NJ: Wiley.

Rubin, Lawrence C. (2006). *Psychotropic drugs and popular culture: Essays on medicine, mental health and the media.* Jefferson, NC: McFarland.

Ruble, Diane, Alvarez, Jeanette, Bachman, Meredith, Cameron, Jessica, Fuligni, Andrew, García Coll, Cynthia, et al. (2004). The development of a sense of "we": The emergence and implications of children's collective identity. In Mark Bennett & Fabio Sani (Eds.), *The development of the social self* (pp. 29–76). Hove, East Sussex, England: Psychology Press.

Ruble, Diane N., Martin, Carol Lynn, & Berenbaum, Sheri. (2006). Gender development. In William Damon & Richard M. Lerner (Series Eds.) & Nancy Eisenberg (Vol. Ed.), *Handbook of child psychology: Vol. 3. Social, emotional, and personality development* (6th ed., pp. 858–932). Hoboken, NJ: Wiley.

Rueda, M. Rosario, Rothbart, Mary K., Saccomanno, Lisa, & Posner, Michael I. (2007). Modifying brain networks underlying self regulation. In Daniel Romer & Elaine F. Walker (Eds.), *Adolescent psychopathology and the developing brain: Integrating brain and prevention science* (pp. 401–419). Oxford, UK: Oxford University Press.

Rueter, Martha A., & Kwon, Hee-Kyung. (2005). Developmental trends in adolescent suicidal ideation. *Journal of Research on Adolescence, 15,* 205–222.

Ruffman, Ted, Slade, Lance, Sandino, Juan Carlos, & Fletcher, Amanda. (2005). Are A-not-B errors caused by a belief about object location? *Child Development, 76,* 122–136.

Rumbaut, Rubén G., & Portes, Alejandro (Eds.). (2001). *Ethnicities: Children of immigrants in America.* Berkeley, CA and New York: University of California Press and the Russell Sage Foundation.

Russell, Mark. (2002, January 25). South Korea: Institute helps spread use of vaccines in Asia. *Science, 295,* 611–612.

Rutledge, Patricia C., Park, Aesoon, & Sher, Kenneth J. (2008). 21st birthday drinking: Extremely extreme. *Journal of Consulting and Clinical Psychology, 76,* 511–516.

Rutter, Michael. (2006). The psychological effects of early institutional rearing. In Peter J. Marshall & Nathan A. Fox (Eds.), *The development of social engagement: Neurobiological perspectives* (pp. 355–391). New York: Oxford University Press.

Rutter, Michael, & O'Connor, Thomas G. (2004). Are there biological programming effects for psychological development? Findings from a study of Romanian adoptees. *Developmental Psychology, 40,* 81–94.

Rutters, Femke, Nieuwenhuizen, Arie G., Vogels, Neeltje, Bouwman, Freek, Mariman, Edwin, & Westerterp-Plantenga, Margriet S. (2008). Leptin-adiposity relationship changes, plus behavioral and parental factors, are involved in the development of body weight in a Dutch children. *Physiology & Behavior, 93,* 967–974.

Ruys, Jan H., de Jonge, Guus A., Brand, Ronald, Engelberts, Adèle, C., &

Semmekrot, Ben A. (2007). Bed-sharing in the first four months of life: A risk factor for sudden infant death. *Acta Pædiatrica, 96,* 1399–1403.

Ryalls, Brigette Oliver. (2000). Dimensional adjectives: Factors affecting children's ability to compare objects using novel words. *Journal of Experimental Child Psychology, 76,* 26–49.

Ryan, Michael J. (2005, June 8). *Punching out in Little League*. Boston Herald. Retrieved September 11, 2005, from the World Wide Web: http://news.bostonherald.com/blogs/rapSheet/index.bg?mode=viewid&post_id=190

Ryan, Suzanne, Franzetta, Kerry, Manlove, Jennifer, & Holcombe, Emily. (2007). Adolescents' discussions about contraception or STDs with partners before first sex. *Perspectives on Sexual and Reproductive Health, 39,* 149–157.

Ryan, Suzanne, Franzetta, Kerry, Manlove, Jennifer S., & Schelar, Erin. (2008). Older sexual partners during adolescence: Links to reproductive health outcomes in young adulthood. *Perspectives on Sexual and Reproductive Health, 40,* 17–26.

Rymer, Russ. (1994). *Genie: A scientific tragedy*. New York: Harper Perennial.

Saarni, Carolyn, Campos, Joseph J., Camras, Linda A., & Witherington, David. (2006). Emotional development: Action, communication, and understanding. In William Damon & Richard M. Lerner (Series Eds.) & Nancy Eisenberg (Vol. Ed.), *Handbook of child psychology: Vol. 3. Social, emotional, and personality development* (6th ed., pp. 226–299). Hoboken, NJ: Wiley.

Sacks, Oliver W. (1995). *An anthropologist on Mars: Seven paradoxical tales*. New York: Knopf.

Sadeh, Avi, Raviv, Amiram, & Gruber, Reut. (2000). Sleep patterns and sleep disruptions in school-age children. *Developmental Psychology, 36,* 291–301.

Saffran, Jenny R., Werker, Janet F., & Werner, Lynne A. (2006). The infant's auditory world: Hearing, speech, and the beginnings of language. In William Damon & Richard M. Lerner (Series Eds.) & Deanna Kuhn & Robert S. Siegler (Vol. Eds.), *Handbook of child psychology: Vol. 2. Cognition, perception, and language* (pp. 58–108). Hoboken, NJ: Wiley.

Sakata, Mariko, Utsu, Masaji, & Maeda, Kazuo. (2006). Fetal circulation and placental blood flow in monochorionic twins. *The Ultrasound Review of Obstetrics & Gynecology, 6,* 135–140.

Sales, Jessica, Fivush, Robyn, & Teague, Gerald W. (2008). The role of parental coping in children with asthma's psychological well-being and asthma-related quality of life. *Journal of Pediatric Psychology, 33,* 208–219.

Salkind, Neil J. (2004). *An introduction to theories of human development*. Thousand Oaks, CA: Sage.

Salmivalli, Christina, Ojanen, Tiina, Haanpaa, Jemina, & Peets, Katlin. (2005). "I'm OK but you're not" and other peer-relational schemas: Explaining individual differences in children's social goals. *Developmental Psychology, 41,* 363–375.

Salovey, Peter, & Grewal, Daisy. (2005). The science of emotional intelligence. *Current Directions in Psychological Science, 14,* 281–285.

Sameroff, Arnold J., & MacKenzie, Michael J. (2003). Research strategies for capturing transactional models of development: The limits of the possible. *Development & Psychopathology, 15,* 613–640.

Sampaio, Ricardo C., & Truwit, Charles L. (2001). Myelination in the developing human brain. In Charles A. Nelson & Monica Luciana (Eds.), *Handbook of developmental cognitive neuroscience* (pp. 35–44). Cambridge, MA: MIT Press.

Samuels, S. Jay. (2007). The DIBELS tests: Is speed of barking at print what we mean by reading fluency? *Reading Research Quarterly, 42,* 563–566.

Sanchez, Maria del Mar, Ladd, Charlotte O., & Plotsky, Paul M. (2001). Early adverse experience as a developmental risk factor for later psychopathology: Evidence from rodent and primate models. *Development & Psychopathology, 13,* 419–449.

Sandstrom, Marlene J., & Herlan, Rebecca D. (2007). Threatened egotism or confirmed inadequacy? How children's perceptions of social status influence aggressive behavior toward peers. *Journal of Social & Clinical Psychology, 26,* 240–267.

Sandstrom, Marlene J., & Zakriski, Audrey L. (2004). Understanding the experience of peer rejection. In Janis B. Kupersmidt & Kenneth A. Dodge (Eds.), *Children's peer relations: From development to intervention* (pp. 101–118). Washington, DC: American Psychological Association.

Santelli, John S., Lindberg, Laura Duberstein, Finer, Lawrence B., & Singh, Susheela. (2007). Explaining recent declines in adolescent pregnancy in the United States: The contribution of abstinence and improved contraceptive use. *American Journal of Public Health, 97,* 150–156.

Santesso, Diane L., Schmidt, Louis A., & Trainor, Laurel J. (2007). Frontal brain electrical activity (EEG) and heart rate in response to affective infant-directed (ID) speech in 9-month-old infants. *Brain and Cognition, 65,* 14–21.

Sapp, Felicity, Lee, Kang, & Muir, Darwin. (2000). Three-year-olds' difficulty with the appearance–reality distinction: Is it real or is it apparent? *Developmental Psychology, 36,* 547–560.

Sarroub, Loukia K. (2001). The sojourner experience of Yemeni American high school students: An ethnographic portrait. *Harvard Educational Review, 71,* 390–415.

Sato, Satoru M., Schulz, Kalynn M., Sisk, Cheryl L., & Wood, Ruth I. (2008). Adolescents and androgens, receptors and rewards. *Hormones and Behavior, 53,* 647–658.

Saul, Stephanie. (2008, July 26). Weight drives the young to adult pills, data says. *New York Times*.

Savin-Williams, Ritch C. (2005). *The new gay teenager*. Cambridge, MA: Harvard University Press.

Savin-Williams, Ritch C., & Diamond, Lisa M. (2004). Sex. In Richard M. Lerner & Laurence D. Steinberg (Eds.), *Handbook of adolescent psychology* (2nd ed., pp. 189–231). Hoboken, NJ: Wiley.

Saw, Seang-Mei, Cheng, Angela, Fong, Allan, Gazzard, Gus, Tan, Donald T. H., & Morgan, Ian. (2007). School grades and myopia. *Ophthalmic and Physiological Optics, 27,* 126–129.

Saxe, Geoffrey B. (1991). *Culture and cognitive development: Studies in mathematical understanding*. Hillsdale, NJ: Erlbaum.

Saxe, Geoffrey B. (1999). Sources of concepts: A cultural-developmental perspective. In Ellin Kofsky Scholnick, Katherine Nelson, Susan A. Gelman, & Patricia H. Miller (Eds.), *Conceptual development: Piaget's legacy* (pp. 253–267). Mahwah, NJ: Erlbaum.

Saxe, Geoffrey B. (2004). Practices of quantification from a socio-cultural perspective. In Andreas Demetriou & Athanassios Raftopoulos (Eds.), *Cognitive developmental change: Theories, models and measurement* (pp. 241–263). New York: Cambridge University Press.

Saylor, Megan M., & Sabbagh, Mark A. (2004). Different kinds of information affect word learning in the preschool years: The case of part-term learning. *Child Development, 75,* 395–408.

Scambler, Douglas J., Hepburn, Susan L., Rutherford, Mel, Wehner, Elizabeth A., & Rogers, Sally J. (2007). Emotional responsivity in children with autism, children with other developmental disabilities, and children with typical development. *Journal of Autism and Developmental Disorders, 37,* 553–563.

Scannapieco, Maria, & Connell-Carrick, Kelli. (2005). *Understanding child maltreatment: An ecological and developmental perspective.* New York: Oxford University Press.

Schafer, Graham. (2005). Infants can learn decontextualized words before their first birthday. *Child Development, 76,* 87–96.

Schaffer, H. Rudolph. (2000). The early experience assumption: Past, present, and future. *International Journal of Behavioral Development, 24,* 5–14.

Schaie, K. Warner. (2002). The impact of longitudinal studies on understanding development from young adulthood to old age. In Willard W. Hartup & Rainer K. Silbereisen (Eds.), *Growing points in developmental science: An introduction* (pp. 307–328). New York: Psychology Press.

Schardein, James L. (1976). *Drugs as teratogens.* Cleveland, OH: CRC Press.

Schellenberg, E. Glenn, Nakata, Takayuki, Hunter, Patrick G., & Tamoto, Sachiko. (2007). Exposure to music and cognitive performance: Tests of children and adults. *Psychology of Music, 35,* 5–19.

Schick, Brenda, de Villiers, Peter, de Villiers, Jill, & Hoffmeister, Robert. (2007). Language and theory of mind: A study of deaf children. *Child Development, 78,* 376–396.

Schmookler, Terra, & Bursik, Krisanne. (2007). The value of monogamy in emerging adulthood: A gendered perspective. *Journal of Social and Personal Relationships, 24,* 819–835.

Schoen, Robert, Landale, Nancy S., & Daniels, Kimberly. (2007). Family transitions in young adulthood. *Demography, 44,* 807–820.

Schoeni, Robert F., & Ross, Karen E. (2005). Material assistance from families during the transition to adulthood. In Richard A. Settersten, Jr., Frank F. Furstenberg, Jr., & Rubén G. Rumbaut (Eds.), *On the frontier of adulthood: Theory, research, and public policy* (pp. 396–416). Chicago: University of Chicago Press.

Schön, Daniele, Boyer, Maud, Moreno, Sylvain, Besson, Mireille, Peretz, Isabelle, & Kolinsky, Régine. (2008). Songs as an aid for language acquisition. *Cognition, 106,* 975–983.

Schreck, Christopher J., Burek, Melissa W., Stewart, Eric A., & Miller, J. Mitchell. (2007). Distress and violent victimization among young adolescents: Early puberty and the social interactionist explanation. *Journal of Research in Crime and Delinquency, 44,* 381–405.

Schulenberg, John, O'Malley, Patrick M., Bachman, Jerald G., & Johnston, Lloyd D. (2005). Early adult transitions and their relation to well-being and substance use. In Richard A. Settersten, Jr., Frank F. Furstenberg, Jr., & Rubén G. Rumbaut (Eds.), *On the frontier of adulthood: Theory, research, and public policy* (pp. 417–453). Chicago: University of Chicago Press.

Schulenberg, John, & Zarrett, Nicole R. (2006). Mental health during emerging adulthood: Continuity and discontinuity in courses, causes, and functions. In Jeffrey Jensen Arnett & Jennifer Lynn Tanner (Eds.), *Emerging adults in America: Coming of age in the 21st century* (pp. 135–172). Washington, DC: American Psychological Association.

Schumann, Cynthia Mills, Hamstra, Julia, Goodlin-Jones, Beth L., Lotspeich, Linda J., Kwon, Hower, Buonocore, Michael H., et al. (2004). The amygdala is enlarged in children but not adolescents with autism; the hippocampus is enlarged at all ages. *Journal of Neuroscience, 24,* 6392–6401.

Schwab, Jacqueline, Kulin, Howard E., Susman, Elizabeth J., Finkelstein, Jordan W., Chinchilli, Vernon M., Kunselman, Susan J., et al. (2001). The role of sex hormone replacement therapy on self-perceived competence in adolescents with delayed puberty. *Child Development, 72,* 1439–1450.

Schwartz, Jeffrey, & Begley, Sharon. (2002). *The mind and the brain: Neuroplasticity and the power of mental force.* New York: Regan Books.

Schwartz, Pepper. (2006). What elicits romance, passion, and attachment, and how do they affect our lives throughout the life cycle? In Ann C. Crouter & Alan Booth (Eds.), *Romance and sex in adolescence and emerging adulthood: Risks and opportunities* (pp. 49–60). Mahwah, NJ: Erlbaum.

Schwartz, Seth J., & Finley, Gordon E. (2005). Fathering in intact and divorced families: Ethnic differences in retrospective reports. *Journal of Marriage and Family, 67,* 207–215.

Schweinhart, Lawrence J., Montie, Jeanne, Xiang, Zongping, Barnett, W. Steven, Belfield, Clive R., & Nores, Milagros. (2005). *Lifetime effects: The High/Scope Perry Preschool study through age 40.* Ypsilanti, MI: High/Scope Press.

Schweinhart, Lawrence J., & Weikart, David P. (1997). *Lasting differences: The High/Scope preschool curriculum comparison study through age 23.* Ypsilanti, MI: High/Scope Educational Research Foundation.

Sciutto, Mark J., & Eisenberg, Miriam. (2007). Evaluating the evidence for and against the overdiagnosis of ADHD. *Journal of Attention Disorders, 11,* 106–113.

Sears, Robert R., Maccoby, Eleanor E., & Levin, Harry. (1976). *Patterns of child rearing.* Stanford, CA: Stanford University Press.

Sebastián-Gallés, Núria. (2007). Biased to learn language. *Developmental Science, 10,* 713–718.

Seifer, Ronald, LaGasse, Linda L., Lester, Barry, Bauer, Charles R., Shankaran, Seetha, Bada, Henrietta S., et al. (2004). Attachment status in children prenatally exposed to cocaine and other substances. *Child Development, 75,* 850–868.

Senghas, Ann, Kita, Sotaro, & Özyürek, Asli. (2004, September 17). Children creating core properties of language: Evidence from an emerging sign language in Nicaragua. *Science, 305,* 1779–1782.

Serageldin, Ismail. (2002, April 5). World poverty and hunger—The challenge for science. *Science, 296,* 54–58.

Serpell, Robert, & Haynes, Brenda Pitts. (2004). The cultural practice of intelligence testing: Problems of international export. In Robert J. Sternberg & Elena L. Grigorenko (Eds.), *Culture and competence: Contexts of life success* (pp. 163–185). Washington, DC: American Psychological Association.

Shahin, Hashem, Walsh, Tom, Sobe, Tama, Lynch, Eric, King, Mary-Claire, Avraham, Karen, et al. (2002). Genetics of congenital deafness in the Palestinian population: Multiple connexin 26 alleles with shared origins in the Middle East. *Human Genetics, 110,* 284–289.

Shanahan, Lilly, McHale, Susan M., Osgood, Wayne, & Crouter, Ann C.

(2007). Conflict frequency with mothers and fathers from middle childhood to late adolescence: Within- and between-families comparisons. *Developmental Psychology, 43,* 539–550.

Shanley, Mary Lyndon. (2001). *Making babies, making families: What matters most in an age of reproductive technologies, surrogacy, adoption, and same-sex and unwed parents.* Boston: Beacon Press.

Shannon, Joyce Brennfleck (Ed.). (2007). *Eating disorders sourcebook: Basic consumer health information about anorexia nervosa, bulimia nervosa, binge eating, compulsive exercise, female athlete triad, and other eating disorders* (2nd ed.). Detroit, MI: Omnigraphics.

Shapiro, Kevin, & Caramazza, Alfonso. (2003). Grammatical processing of nouns and verbs in left frontal cortex? *Neuropsychologia, 41,* 1189–1198.

Sharma, Monica. (2008). Twenty-first century pink or blue: How sex selection technology facilitates gendercide and what we can do about it. *Family Court Review, 46,* 198–215.

Shattuck, Paul T. (2006). The contribution of diagnostic substitution to the growing administrative prevalence of autism in US special education. *Pediatrics, 117,* 1028–1037.

Sheffield, Ellyn G., & Hudson, Judith A. (2006). You must remember this: Effects of video and photograph reminders on 18-month-olds' event memory. *Journal of Cognition and Development, 7,* 73–93.

Shepard, Thomas H., & Lemire, Ronald J. (2004). *Catalog of teratogenic agents* (11th ed.). Baltimore: Johns Hopkins University Press.

Shevell, Tracy, Malone, Fergal D., Vidaver, John, Porter, T. Flint, Luthy, David A., Comstock, Christine H., et al. (2005). Assisted reproductive technology and pregnancy outcome. *Obstetrics & Gynecology, 106,* 1039–1045.

Shirilla, Joan J., & Weatherston, Deborah (Eds.). (2002). *Case studies in infant mental health: Risk, resiliency, and relationships.* Washington, DC: Zero to Three.

Shweder, Richard A. (1994). Are moral intuitions self-evident truths? *Criminal Justice Ethics, 13,* 24–32.

Siebenbruner, Jessica, Zimmer-Gembeck, Melanie J., & Egeland, Byron. (2007). Sexual partners and contraceptive use: A 16-year prospective study predicting abstinence and risk behavior. *Journal of Research on Adolescence, 17,* 179–206.

Siegal, Michael. (2004, September 17). Signposts to the essence of language. *Science, 305,* 1720–1721.

Siegel, Larry. (2006). *Post-publication peer reviews: Correlation is not causation.* American Academy of Pediatrics. Retrieved September 11, 2007, from the World Wide Web: http://pediatrics.aappublications.org/cgi/eletters/118/2/e430#2217

Siegler, Robert S. (1996). *Emerging minds: The process of change in children's thinking.* New York: Oxford University Press.

Silverman, Wendy K., & Dick-Niederhauser, Andreas. (2004). Separation anxiety disorder. In Tracy L. Morris & John S. March (Eds.), *Anxiety disorders in children and adolescents* (2nd ed., pp. 164–188). New York: Guilford Press.

Simpkins, Sandra D., Fredricks, Jennifer A., Davis-Kean, Pamela E., & Eccles, Jacquelynne S. (2006). Healthy mind, healthy habits: The influence of activity involvement in middle childhood. In Aletha C. Huston & Marika N. Ripke (Eds.), *Developmental contexts in middle childhood: Bridges to adolescence and adulthood* (pp. 283–302). New York: Cambridge University Press.

Singer, Dorothy G., & Singer, Jerome L. (2005). *Imagination and play in the electronic age.* Cambridge, MA: Harvard University Press.

Singer, Lynn T., Arendt, Robert, Minnes, Sonia, Farkas, Kathleen, Salvator, Ann, Kirchner, H. Lester, et al. (2002). Cognitive and motor outcomes of cocaine-exposed infants. *Journal of the American Medical Association, 287,* 1952–1960.

Singer, Wolf. (2003). The nature–nurture problem revisited. In Ursula M. Staudinger & Ulman Lindenberger (Eds.), *Understanding human development: Dialogues with lifespan psychology* (pp. 437–447). Dordrecht, The Netherlands: Kluwer.

Singh, Gopal K., & Siahpush, Mohammad. (2006). Widening socioeconomic inequalities in US life expectancy, 1980–2000. *International Journal of Epidemiology, 35,* 969–979.

Singh, Ilina. (2008). ADHD, culture and education. *Early Child Development and Care, 178,* 347–361.

Singh, Leher. (2008). Influences of high and low variability on infant word recognition. *Cognition, 106,* 833–870.

Sinha, Jill W., Cnaan, Ram A., & Gelles, Richard J. (2007). Adolescent risk behaviors and religion: Findings from a national study. *Journal of Adolescence, 30,* 231–249.

Siqueira, Lorena M., Rolnitzky, Linda M., & Rickert, Vaughn I. (2001). Smoking cessation in adolescents: The role of nicotine dependence, stress, and coping methods. *Archives of Pediatrics & Adolescent Medicine, 155,* 489–495.

Sircar, Ratna, & Sircar, Debashish. (2005). Adolescent rats exposed to repeated ethanol treatment show lingering behavioral impairments. *Alcoholism: Clinical and Experimental Research, 29,* 1402–1410.

Siu, Angela F. Y. (2007). Using friends to combat internalizing problems among primary school children in Hong Kong. *Journal of Cognitive and Behavioral Psychotherapies, 7,* 11–26.

Skinner, B. F. (1957). *Verbal behavior.* New York: Appleton-Century-Crofts.

Skirton, Heather, & Patch, Christine. (2002). *Genetics for healthcare professionals: A lifestage approach.* Oxford, UK: Bios.

Slobin, Dan I. (2001). Form–function relations: How do children find out what they are? In Melissa Bowerman & Stephen C. Levinson (Eds.), *Language acquisition and conceptual development* (pp. 406–449). Cambridge, UK: Cambridge University Press.

Smedley, Audrey, & Smedley, Brian D. (2005). Race as biology is fiction, racism as a social problem is real: Anthropological and historical perspectives on the social construction of race. *American Psychologist, 60,* 16–26.

Smetana, Judith G. (2008). "It's 10 o'clock: Do you know where your children are?" Recent advances in understanding parental monitoring and adolescents' information management. *Child Development Perspectives, 2,* 19–25.

Smetana, Judith G., Metzger, Aaron, & Campione-Barr, Nicole. (2004). African American late adolescents' relationships with parents: Developmental transitions and longitudinal patterns. *Child Development, 75,* 932–947.

Smith, Christian (with Denton, Melinda Lundquist). (2005). *Soul searching: The religious and spiritual lives of American teenagers.* Oxford, UK: Oxford University Press.

Smith, Gordon C. S., Shah, Imran, Pell, Jill P., Crossley, Jennifer A., & Dobbie, Richard. (2007). Maternal obesity in early pregnancy and risk of spontaneous and elective preterm deliveries: A retrospective cohort study. *American Journal of Public Health, 97,* 157–162.

Smith, J. David, Schneider, Barry H., Smith, Peter K., & Ananiadou, Katerina. (2004). The effectiveness of whole-school antibullying programs: A synthesis of evaluation research. *School Psychology Review, 33,* 547–560.

Smith, Margaret G., & Fong, Rowena. (2004). *The children of neglect: When no one cares.* New York: Brunner-Routledge.

Smith, Peter K., & Ananiadou, Katerina. (2003). The nature of school bullying and the effectiveness of school-based interventions. *Journal of Applied Psychoanalytic Studies, 5,* 189–209.

Smith, Peter K., Mahdavi, Jess, Carvalho, Manuel, Fisher, Sonja, Russell, Shanette, & Tippett, Neil. (2008). Cyberbullying: Its nature and impact in secondary school pupils. *Journal of Child Psychology and Psychiatry, 49,* 376–385.

Smith, Peter K., Pepler, Debra J., & Rigby, Ken. (2004). *Bullying in schools: How successful can interventions be?* New York: Cambridge University Press.

Smith, Tom W. (2005). Generation gaps in attitudes and values from the 1970s to the 1990s. In Richard A. Settersten, Jr., Frank F. Furstenberg, Jr., & Rubén G. Rumbaut (Eds.), *On the frontier of adulthood: Theory, research, and public policy* (pp. 177–221). Chicago: University of Chicago Press.

Smyth, Joshua M. (2007). Beyond self-selection in video game play: An experimental examination of the consequences of massively multiplayer online role-playing game play. *CyberPsychology & Behavior, 10,* 717–727.

Snow, Catherine E. (1984). Parent–child interaction and the development of communicative ability. In Richard L. Schiefelbusch & Joanne Pickar (Eds.), *The acquisition of communicative competence* (pp. 69–107). Baltimore: University Park Press.

Snow, Catherine E., & Kang, Jennifer Yusun. (2006). Becoming bilingual, biliterate, and bicultural. In William Damon & Richard M. Lerner (Series Eds.) & K. Ann Renninger & Irving E. Sigel (Vol. Eds.), *Handbook of child psychology: Vol. 4. Child psychology in practice* (6th ed., pp. 75–102). Hoboken, NJ: Wiley.

Snow, Catherine E., Porche, Michelle V., Tabors, Patton O., & Harris, Stephanie Ross. (2007). *Is literacy enough? Pathways to academic success for adolescents.* Baltimore: Brookes.

Snow, David. (2006). Regression and reorganization of intonation between 6 and 23 months. *Child Development, 77,* 281–296.

Snyder, James, Schrepferman, Lynn, McEachern, Amber, Barner, Stacy, Johnson, Kassy, & Provines, Jessica. (2008). Peer deviancy training and peer coercion: Dual processes associated with early onset conduct problems. *Child Development, 79,* 252–268.

Snyder, James, Schrepferman, Lynn, Oeser, Jessica, Patterson, Gerald, Stoolmiller, Mike, Johnson, Kassy, et al. (2005). Deviancy training and association with deviant peers in young children: Occurrence and contribution to early-onset conduct problems. *Development & Psychopathology, 17,* 397–413.

Snyder, Thomas D., Dillow, Sally A., & Hoffman, Charlene M. (2008). *Digest of education statistics: 2007.* National Center for Education Statistics. Retrieved July 26, 2008, from the World Wide Web: http://nces.ed.gov/pubsearch/pubsinfo.asp?pubid=2008022

Snyder, Thomas D., Tan, Alexandra G., & Hoffman, Charlene M. (2004). *Digest of education statistics, 2003* (NCES 2005025). Washington, DC: U.S. Government Printing Office.

Snyder, Thomas D., Tan, Alexandra G., & Hoffman, Charlene M. (2006). *Digest of education statistics, 2005* (NCES 2006–030). Washington, DC: National Center for Education Statistics.

Society for Research in Child Development (SRCD). (2007, March). *Ethical standards for research with children.* Retrieved March 23, 2008, from the World Wide Web: http://www.srcd.org/ethicalstandards.html

Soderstrom, Melanie. (2007). Beyond babytalk: Re-evaluating the nature and content of speech input to preverbal infants. *Developmental Review, 27,* 501–532.

Soekadar, Surjo R., Haagen, Klaus, & Birbaumer, Niels. (2008). Brain–computer interfaces (BCI): Restoration of movement and thought from neuroelectric and metabolic brain activity. In Armin Fuchs & Viktor K. K. Jirsa (Eds.), *Coordination: Neural, behavioral and social dynamics* (pp. 229–252). New York: Springer.

Sofie, Cecilia A., & Riccio, Cynthia A. (2002). A comparison of multiple methods for the identification of children with reading disabilities. *Journal of Learning Disabilities, 35,* 234–244.

Sorenson, Susan B., & Vittes, Katherine A. (2004). Adolescents and firearms: A California statewide survey. *American Journal of Public Health, 94,* 852–858.

Sowell, Elizabeth R., Thompson, Paul M., & Toga, Arthur W. (2007). Mapping adolescent brain maturation using structural magnetic resonance imaging. In Daniel Romer & Elaine F. Walker (Eds.), *Adolescent psychopathology and the developing brain: Integrating brain and prevention science* (pp. 55–84). Oxford, UK: Oxford University Press.

Spandorfer, Philip R., Alessandrini, Evaline A., Joffe, Mark D., Localio, Russell, & Shaw, Kathy N. (2005). Oral versus intravenous rehydration of moderately dehydrated children: A randomized, controlled trial. *Pediatrics, 115,* 295–301.

Spelke, Elizabeth S. (1993). Object perception. In Alvin I. Goldman (Ed.), *Readings in philosophy and cognitive science* (pp. 447–460). Cambridge, MA: MIT Press.

Spickard, Paul R. (2007). *Almost all aliens: Immigration, race, and colonialism in American history and identity.* New York: Routledge.

Sroufe, L. Alan, Egeland, Byron, Carlson, Elizabeth A., & Collins, W. Andrew. (2005). *The development of the person: The Minnesota study of risk and adaptation from birth to adulthood.* New York: Guilford Press.

St Clair, David, Xu, Mingqing, Wang, Peng, Yu, Yaqin, Fang, Yourong, Zhang, Feng, et al. (2005). Rates of adult schizophrenia following prenatal exposure to the Chinese famine of 1959–1961. *Journal of the American Medical Association, 294,* 557–562.

Staff, Jeremy, Mortimer, Jeylan T., & Uggen, Christopher. (2004). Work and leisure in adolescence. In Richard M. Lerner & Laurence D. Steinberg (Eds.), *Handbook of adolescent psychology* (2nd ed., pp. 429–450). Hoboken, NJ: Wiley.

Staiger, Annegret Daniela. (2006). *Learning difference: Race and schooling in the multiracial metropolis.* Stanford, CA: Stanford University Press.

Stansfeld, Stephen A., Berglund, Birgitta, Clark, Charlotte, Lopez-Barrio, Isabel, Fischer, Paul, Öhrström, Evy, et al. (2005). Aircraft and road traffic noise and children's cognition and health: A cross-national study. *Lancet, 365,* 1942–1949.

Stanton, Bonita, & Burns, James. (2003). Sustaining and broadening intervention effect: Social norms, core values, and parents. In Daniel Romer (Ed.), *Reducing adolescent risk: Toward an integrated approach* (pp. 193–200). Thousand Oaks, CA: Sage.

Stanton, Cynthia K., & Holtz, Sara A. (2006). Levels and trends in cesarean birth in the developing world. *Studies in Family Planning, 37,* 41–48.

Stattin, Håkan, & Kerr, Margaret. (2000). Parental monitoring: A reinterpretation. *Child Development, 71,* 1072–1085.

Stein, Arlene. (2006). *Shameless: Sexual dissidence in American culture*. New York: New York University Press.

Steinberg, Adria. (1993). *Adolescents and schools: Improving the fit*. Cambridge, MA: Harvard Education Letter.

Steinberg, Laurence. (2001). We know some things: Parent–adolescent relationships in retrospect and prospect. *Journal of Research on Adolescence, 11,* 1–19.

Steinberg, Laurence. (2004). Risk taking in adolescence: What changes, and why? In Ronald E. Dahl & Linda Patia Spear (Eds.), *Adolescent brain development: Vulnerabilities and opportunities* (Vol. 1021, pp. 51–58). New York: New York Academy of Sciences.

Steinberg, Laurence. (2007). Risk taking in adolescence: New perspectives from brain and behavioral science. *Current Directions in Psychological Science, 16,* 55–59.

Steinberg, Laurence. (2008). A social neuroscience perspective on adolescent risk-taking. *Developmental Review, 28,* 78–106.

Steinberg, Laurence, Lamborn, Susie D., Darling, Nancy, Mounts, Nina S., & Dornbusch, Sanford M. (1994). Over-time changes in adjustment and competence among adolescents from authoritative, authoritarian, indulgent, and neglectful families. *Child Development, 65,* 754–770.

Steiner, Meir, & Young, Elizabeth A. (2008). Hormones and mood. In Jill B. Becker, Karen J. Berkley, Nori Geary, Elizabeth Hampson, James P. Herman, & Elizabeth Young (Eds.), *Sex differences in the brain: From genes to behavior* (pp. 405–426). New York: Oxford University Press.

Stenberg, Gunilla, & Hagekull, Berit. (2007). Infant looking behavior in ambiguous situations: Social referencing or attachment behavior? *Infancy, 11,* 111–129.

Stern, Daniel N. (1985). *The interpersonal world of the infant: A view from psychoanalysis and developmental psychology*. New York: Basic Books.

Sternberg, Betty J., Kaplan, Karen A., & Borck, Jennifer E. (2007). Enhancing adolescent literacy achievement through integration of technology in the classroom. *Reading Research Quarterly, 42,* 416–420.

Sternberg, Robert J. (1996). *Successful intelligence: How practical and creative intelligence determine success in life*. New York: Simon & Schuster.

Sternberg, Robert J., & Grigorenko, Elena (Eds.). (2004). *Culture and competence: Contexts of life success*. Washington, DC: American Psychological Association.

Sternberg, Robert J., Grigorenko, Elena L., & Bundy, Donald A. (2001). The predictive value of IQ. *Merrill-Palmer Quarterly, 47,* 1–41.

Stevenson, Harold W., Chen, Chuansheng, & Lee, Shin-ying. (1993, January 1). Mathematics achievement of Chinese, Japanese, and American children: Ten years later. *Science, 259,* 53–58.

Stevenson, Harold W., Lee, Shin-ying, Chen, Chuansheng, Stigler, James W., Hsu, Chen-Chin, & Kitamura, Seiro. (1990). Contexts of achievement: A study of American, Chinese, and Japanese children. *Monographs of the Society for Research in Child Development,* 55(1–2, Serial No. 221), 1–123.

Stevick, Richard A. (2001). The Amish: Case study of a religious community. In Clive Erricker & Jane Erricker (Eds.), *Contemporary spiritualities: Social and religious contexts* (pp. 159–172). London: Continuum.

Stewart, Susan D., Manning, Wendy D., & Smock, Pamela J. (2003). Union formation among men in the U.S.: Does having prior children matter? *Journal of Marriage and Family, 65,* 90–104.

Stigler, James W., & Hiebert, James. (1999). *The teaching gap: Best ideas from the world's teachers for improving education in the classroom*. New York: Free Press.

Stipek, Deborah, Feiler, Rachelle, Daniels, Denise, & Milburn, Sharon. (1995). Effects of different instructional approaches on young children's achievement and motivation. *Child Development, 66,* 209–223.

Stokstad, Erik. (2003, December 12). The vitamin D deficit. *Science, 302,* 1886–1888.

Straus, Murray A. (with Donnelly, Denise A.). (1994). *Beating the devil out of them: Corporal punishment in American families*. New York: Lexington Books.

Streissguth, Ann. (2007). Offspring effects of prenatal alcohol exposure from birth to 25 years: The Seattle Prospective Longitudinal Study. *Journal of Clinical Psychology in Medical Settings, 14,* 81–101.

Streissguth, Ann P., & Connor, Paul D. (2001). Fetal alcohol syndrome and other effects of prenatal alcohol: Developmental cognitive neuroscience implications. In Charles A. Nelson & Monica Luciana (Eds.), *Handbook of developmental cognitive neuroscience* (pp. 505–518). Cambridge, MA: MIT Press.

Stright, Anne Dopkins, Gallagher, Kathleen Cranley, & Kelley, Ken. (2008). Infant temperament moderates relations between maternal parenting in early childhood and children's adjustment in first grade. *Child Development, 79,* 186–200.

Strouse, Darcy L. (1999). Adolescent crowd orientations: A social and temporal analysis. In Jeffrey A. McLellan & Mary Jo V. Pugh (Eds.), *The role of peer groups in adolescent social identity:*

Stubben, Jerry D. (2001). Working with and conducting research among American Indian families. *American Behavioral Scientist, 44,* 1466–1481.

Suarez-Orozco, Carola, & Suarez-Orozco, Marcelo M. (2001). *Children of immigration*. Cambridge, MA: Harvard University Press.

Subbotsky, Eugene. (2000). Causal reasoning and behaviour in children and adults in a technologically advanced society: Are we still prepared to believe in magic and animism? In Peter Mitchell & Kevin John Riggs (Eds.), *Children's reasoning and the mind* (pp. 327–347). Hove, UK: Psychology Press.

Subrahmanyam, Kaveri, Smahel, David, & Greenfield, Patricia. (2006). Connecting developmental constructions to the internet: identity presentation and sexual exploration in online teen chat rooms. *Developmental Psychology, 42,* 395–406.

Sue, Christina A., & Telles, Edward E. (2007). Assimilation and gender in naming. *American Journal of Sociology, 112,* 1383–1415.

Suellentrop, Katherine, Morrow, Brian, Williams, Letitia, & D'Angelo, Denise. (2006, October 6). Monitoring progress toward achieving maternal and infant Healthy People 2010 objectives—19 states, Pregnancy Risk Assessment Monitoring System (PRAMS), 2000–2003. *MMWR Surveillance Summaries,* 55(SS09), 1–11.

Sufang, Guo, Padmadas, Sabu S., Fengmin, Zhao, Brown, James J., & Stones, R. William. (2007). Delivery settings and caesarean section rates in China. *Bulletin of the World Health Organization, 85,* 755–762.

Sugie, Shuji, Shwalb, David W., & Shwalb, Barbara J. (2006). Respect in Japanese childhood, adolescence, and society. *New Directions for Child and Adolescent Development, 114,* 39–52.

Sun, Min, & Rugolotto, Simone. (2004). Assisted infant toilet training in a Western family setting. *Journal of Developmental & Behavioral Pediatrics, 25,* 99–101.

Suomi, Steven J. (2002). Parents, peers, and the process of socialization in primates. In John G. Borkowski, Sharon Landesman Ramey, & Marie Bristol-Power (Eds.), *Parenting and the child's world: Influences on academic, intellectual, and social-emotional development* (pp. 265–279). Mahwah, NJ: Erlbaum.

Susman, Elizabeth J., & Rogol, Alan. (2004). Puberty and psychological development. In Richard M. Lerner & Laurence D. Steinberg (Eds.), *Handbook of adolescent psychology* (2nd ed., pp. 15–44). Hoboken, NJ: Wiley.

Sutton-Smith, Brian. (1997). *The ambiguity of play.* Cambridge, MA: Harvard University Press.

Suzuki, Lalita K., & Calzo, Jerel P. (2004). The search for peer advice in cyberspace: An examination of online teen bulletin boards about health and sexuality. *Journal of Applied Developmental Psychology, 25,* 685–698.

Syed, Moin, & Azmitia, Margarita. (2008). A narrative approach to ethnic identity in emerging adulthood: Bringing life to the identity status model. *Developmental Psychology, 44,* 1012–1027.

Taga, Keiko A., Markey, Charlotte N., & Friedman, Howard S. (2006). A longitudinal investigation of associations between boys' pubertal timing and adult behavioral health and well-being. *Journal of Youth and Adolescence, 35,* 401–411.

Talge, Nicole M., Neal, Charles, & Glover, Vivette. (2007). Antenatal maternal stress and long-term effects on child neurodevelopment: How and why? *Journal of Child Psychology and Psychiatry, 48,* 245–261.

Tallandini, Maria Anna, & Scalembra, Chiara. (2006). Kangaroo mother care and mother–premature infant dyadic interaction. *Infant Mental Health Journal, 27,* 251–275.

Tamay, Zeynep, Akcay, Ahmet, Ones, Ulker, Guler, Nermin, Kilic, Gurkan, & Zencir, Mehmet. (2007). Prevalence and risk factors for allergic rhinitis in primary school children. *International Journal of Pediatric Otorhinolaryngology, 71,* 463–471.

Tamis-LeMonda, Catherine S., Bornstein, Marc H., & Baumwell, Lisa. (2001). Maternal responsiveness and children's achievement of language milestones. *Child Development, 72,* 748–767.

Tamis-LeMonda, Catherine S., Way, Niobe, Hughes, Diane, Yoshikawa, Hirokazu, Kalman, Ronit Kahana, & Niwa, Erika Y. (2008). Parents' goals for children: The dynamic coexistence of individualism and collectivism in cultures and individuals. *Social Development, 17,* 183–209.

Tanaka, Yuko, & Nakazawa, Jun. (2005). Job-related temporary father absence (Tanshinfunin) and child development. In David W. Shwalb, Jun Nakazawa, & Barbara J. Shwalb (Eds.), *Applied developmental psychology: Theory, practice, and research from Japan* (pp. 241–260). Greenwich, CT: Information Age.

Tang, Chao-Hsiun, Wang, Han-I, Hsu, Chun-Sen, Su, Hung-Wen, Chen, Mei-Ju, & Lin, Herng-Ching. (2006). *Risk-adjusted cesarean section rates for the assessment of physician performance in Taiwan: A population-based study.* BioMed Central. Retrieved April 27, 2007, from the World Wide Web: http://www.biomedcentral.com/1471–2458/6/246

Tangney, June Price, Stuewig, Jeff, & Mashek, Debra J. (2007). Moral emotions and moral behavior. *Annual Review of Psychology, 58,* 345–372.

Tanner, James Mourilyan. (1990). *Foetus into man: Physical growth from conception to maturity* (Rev. and enl. ed.). Cambridge, MA: Harvard University Press.

Tarrant, Mark, MacKenzie, Liam, & Hewitt, Lisa A. (2006). Friendship group identification, multidimensional self-concept, and experience of developmental tasks in adolescence. *Journal of Adolescence, 29,* 627–640.

Tarrant, Shira. (2006). *When sex became gender.* New York: Routledge.

Tarter, Ralph E., Vanyukov, Michael, Giancola, Peter, Dawes, Michael, Blackson, Timothy, Mezzich, Ada, et al. (1999). Etiology of early age onset substance use disorder: A maturational perspective. *Development & Psychopathology, 11,* 657–683.

Tay, Marc Tze-Hsin, Au Eong, Kah Guan, Ng, C. Y., & Lim, M. K. (1992). Myopia and educational attainment in 421,116 young Singaporean males. *Annals, Academy of Medicine, Singapore, 21,* 785–791.

Taylor, Margot J. (2006). Neural bases of cognitive development. In Ellen Bialystok & Fergus I. M. Craik (Eds.), *Lifespan cognition: Mechanisms of change* (pp. 15–26). New York: Oxford University Press.

Taylor, Marjorie, Carlson, Stephanie M., Maring, Bayta L., Gerow, Lynn, & Charley, Carolyn M. (2004). The characteristics and correlates of fantasy in school-age children: Imaginary companions, impersonation, and social understanding. *Developmental Psychology, 40,* 1173–1187.

Taylor, Ronald D., Seaton, Eleanor, & Dominguez, Antonio. (2008). Kinship support, family relations, and psychological adjustment among low-income African American mothers and adolescents. *Journal of Research on Adolescence, 18,* 1–22.

Taylor, Shelley E. (2006). Tend and befriend: Biobehavioral bases of affiliation under stress. *Current Directions in Psychological Science, 15,* 273–277.

Teachman, Jay. (2008a). Complex life course patterns and the risk of divorce in second marriages. *Journal of Marriage and Family, 70,* 294–305.

Teachman, Jay D. (2008b). The living arrangements of children and their educational well-being. *Journal of Family Issues, 29,* 734–761.

Tedeschi, Alberto, & Airaghi, Lorena. (2006). Is affluence a risk factor for bronchial asthma and type 1 diabetes? *Pediatric Allergy and Immunology, 17,* 533–537.

Teitler, Julien O. (2002). Trends in youth sexual initiation and fertility in developed countries: 1960–1995. *Annals of the American Academy of Political & Social Science, 580,* 134–152.

Tenenbaum, Harriet R., & Leaper, Campbell. (2002). Are parents' gender schemas related to their children's gender-related cognitions? A meta-analysis. *Developmental Psychology, 38,* 615–630.

ter Bogt, Tom, Schmid, Holger, Gabhainn, Saoirse Nic, Fotiou, Anastasios, & Vollebergh, Wilma. (2006). Economic and cultural correlates of cannabis use among mid-adolescents in 31 countries. *Addiction, 101,* 241–251.

Tercyak, Kenneth P. (2008). Editorial: Prevention in child health psychology and the Journal of Pediatric Psychology *Journal of Pediatric Psychology, 33,* 31–34.

Tester, June M., Rutherford, George W., Wald, Zachary, & Rutherford, Mary W. (2004). A matched case-control study evaluating the effectiveness of speed humps in reducing child pedestrian injuries. *American Journal of Public Health, 94,* 646–650.

Thaler, Richard H., & Sunstein, Cass R. (2008). *Nudge: Improving decisions about health, wealth, and happiness.* New Haven, CT: Yale University Press.

Thelen, Esther, & Corbetta, Daniela. (2002). Microdevelopment and dynamic systems: Applications to infant motor development. In Nira Granott & Jim Parziale (Eds.), *Microdevelopment: Transition processes in development and learning* (pp. 59–79). New York: Cambridge University Press.

Thelen, Esther, & Smith, Linda B. (2006). Dynamic systems theories. In William Damon & Richard M. Lerner (Series Eds.) & Richard M. Lerner (Vol. Ed.), *Handbook of child psychology: Vol. 1. Theoretical models of human development* (6th ed., pp. 258–312). Hoboken, NJ: Wiley.

Thomas, Michael S. C., & Johnson, Mark H. (2008). New advances in understanding sensitive periods in brain development. *Current Directions in Psychological Science, 17,* 1–5.

Thompson, Christine. (2002). Drawing together: Peer influence in preschool-kindergarten art classes. In Liora Bresler & Christine Marme Thompson (Eds.), *The arts in children's lives: Context, culture, and curriculum* (pp. 129–138). Dordrecht, The Netherlands: Kluwer.

Thompson, Elisabeth Morgan, & Morgan, Elizabeth M. (2008). "Mostly straight" young women: Variations in sexual behavior and identity development. *Developmental Psychology, 44,* 15–21.

Thompson, Ross A. (2006). The development of the person: Social understanding, relationships, conscience, self. In William Damon & Richard M. Lerner (Series Eds.) & Nancy Eisenberg (Vol. Ed.), *Handbook of child psychology: Vol. 3. Social, emotional, and personality development* (6th ed., pp. 24–98). Hoboken, NJ: Wiley.

Thompson, Ross A., & Nelson, Charles A. (2001). Developmental science and the media: Early brain development. *American Psychologist, 56,* 5–15.

Thompson, Ross A., & Raikes, H. Abigail. (2003). Toward the next quarter-century: Conceptual and methodological challenges for attachment theory. *Development & Psychopathology, 15,* 691–718.

Thurber, James. (1999). The secret life of James Thurber. In James Thurber (Ed.), *The Thurber carnival.* New York: Harper Perennial. (Original work published 1945)

Tishkoff, Sarah A., & Kidd, Kenneth K. (2004). Implications of biogeography of human populations for 'race' and medicine. *Nature Genetics, 36,* S21–S27.

Tluczek, Audrey, Koscik, Rebecca L., Modaff, Peggy, Pfeil, Darci, Rock, Michael J., Farrell, Philip M., et al. (2006). Newborn screening for cystic fibrosis: Parents' preferences regarding counseling at the time of infants' sweat test. *Journal of Genetic Counseling, 15,* 277–291.

Tomasello, Michael. (2001). Perceiving intentions and learning words in the second year of life. In Melissa Bowerman & Stephen C. Levinson (Eds.), *Language acquisition and conceptual development* (pp. 132–158). Cambridge, UK: Cambridge University Press.

Tomasello, Michael. (2006). Acquiring linguistic constructions. In William Damon & Richard M. Lerner (Series Eds.) & Deanna Kuhn & Robert S. Siegler (Vol. Eds.), *Handbook of child psychology: Vol. 2. Cognition, perception, and language* (6th ed., pp. 255–298). Hoboken, NJ: Wiley.

Tomasello, Michael, Carpenter, Malinda, & Liszkowski, Ulf. (2007). A new look at infant pointing. *Child Development, 78,* 705–722.

Tonn, Jessica L. (2006, March 22). Later high school start times: A reaction to research. *Education Week,* 25(28), 5, 17.

Torgesen, Joseph K. (2004). Preventing early reading failure—and its devastating downward spiral. *American Educator, 28,* 6–9, 12–13, 17–19, 45–47.

Torney-Purta, Judith, Lehmann, Rainer, Oswald, Hans, & Schulz, Wolfram. (2001). *Citizenship and education in twenty-eight countries: Civic knowledge and engagement at age fourteen.* Amsterdam: International Association for the Evaluation of Educational Achievement.

Toyama, Miki. (2001). Developmental changes in social comparison in preschool and elementary school children: Perceptions, feelings, and behavior. *Japanese Journal of Educational Psychology, 49,* 500–507.

Trautmann-Villalba, Patricia, Gschwendt, Miriam, Schmidt, Martin H., & Laucht, Manfred. (2006). Father-infant interaction patterns as precursors of children's later externalizing behavior problems: A longitudinal study over 11 years. *European Archives of Psychiatry and Clinical Neuroscience, 256,* 344–349.

Tremblay, Richard E., & Nagin, Daniel S. (2005). Developmental origins of physical aggression in humans. In Richard Ernest Tremblay, Willard W. Hartup, & John Archer (Eds.), *Developmental origins of aggression* (pp. 83–106). New York: Guilford Press.

Trenholm, Christopher, Devaney, Barbara, Fortson, Ken, Quay, Lisa, Wheeler, Justin, & Clark, Melissa. (2007). *Impacts of four Title V, Section 510 abstinence education programs final report.* U.S. Department of Health and Human Services. Retrieved August 22, 2007, from the World Wide Web: http://www.mathematica-mpr.com/abstinencereport.asp

Trickett, Edison J., & Jones, Curtis J. (2007). Adolescent culture brokering and family functioning: A study of families from Vietnam. *Cultural Diversity and Ethnic Minority Psychology, 13,* 143–150.

Trillo, Alex. (2004). Somewhere between Wall Street and El Barrio: Community college as a second chance for second-generation Latino students. In Philip Kasinitz, John H. Mollenkopf, & Mary C. Waters (Eds.), *Becoming New Yorkers: Ethnographies of the new second generation* (pp. 57–78). New York: Russell Sage.

Trimble, Joseph, Root, Maria P. P., & Helms, Janet E. (2003). Psychological perspectives on ethnic and racial psychology. In Guillermo Bernal, Joseph E. Trimble, Ann Kathleen Burlew, & Frederick T. Leong (Eds.), *Racial and ethnic minority psychology series: Vol. 4. Handbook of racial & ethnic minority psychology* (pp. 239–275). Thousand Oaks, CA: Sage.

Tronick, Edward. (2007). *The neurobehavioral and social-emotional development of infants and children.* New York: Norton.

Tronick, Edward Z. (1989). Emotions and emotional communication in infants. *American Psychologist, 44,* 112–119.

Tronick, Edward Z., & Weinberg, M. Katherine. (1997). Depressed mothers and infants: Failure to form dyadic states of consciousness. In Lynne Murray & Peter J. Cooper (Eds.), *Postpartum depression and child development* (pp. 54–81). New York: Guilford Press.

Trzesniewski, Kali H., Donnellan, M. Brent, Moffitt, Terrie E., Robins, Richard W., Poulton, Richie, & Caspi, Avshalom. (2006). Low self-esteem during adolescence predicts poor health, criminal behavior, and limited economic prospects during adulthood. *Developmental Psychology, 42,* 381–390.

Tsai, James, Floyd, R. Louise, & Bertrand, Jacquelyn. (2007). Tracking binge drinking among U.S. childbearing-age women. *Preventive Medicine: An International Journal Devoted to Practice and Theory, 44,* 298–302.

Tsao, Feng-Ming, Liu, Huei-Mei, & Kuhl, Patricia K. (2004). Speech perception in infancy predicts language development in the second year of life: A longitudinal study. *Child Development, 75,* 1067–1084.

Tse, Lucy. (2001). *"Why don't they learn English?" Separating fact from fallacy in the U.S. language debate.* New York: Teachers College Press.

Tseng, Vivian. (2004). Family interdependence and academic adjustment in college: Youth from immigrant and U.S.-born families. *Child Development, 75,* 966–983.

Tudge, Jonathan. (2008). *The everyday lives of young children: Culture, class, and child rearing in diverse societies.* New York: Cambridge University Press.

Tudge, Jonathan R. H., Doucet, Fabienne, Odero, Dolphine, Sperb, Tania M., Piccinini, Cesar A., & Lopes, Rita S. (2006). A window into different cultural worlds: Young children's everyday activities in the United States, Brazil, and Kenya. *Child Development, 77,* 1446–1469.

Turiel, Elliot. (2006). The development of morality. In William Damon & Richard M. Lerner (Series Eds.) & Nancy Eisenberg (Vol. Ed.), *Handbook of child psychology: Vol. 3. Social, emotional, and personality development* (6th ed., pp. 789–857). Hoboken, NJ: Wiley.

Turiel, Elliot. (2008). Thought about actions in social domains: Morality, social conventions, and social interactions. *Cognitive Development, 23,* 136–154.

Twenge, Jean M., & Campbell, W. Keith. (2001). Age and birth cohort differences in self-esteem: A cross-temporal meta-analysis. *Personality and Social Psychology Review, 5,* 321–344.

Twenge, Jean M., Konrath, Sara, Foster, Joshua D., Campbell, W. Keith, & Bushma, Brad J. (2008). Egos inflating over time: A cross-temporal meta-analysis of the narcissistic personality inventory. *Journal of Personality, 76,* 875–902.

Twomey, John G. (2006). Issues in genetic testing of children. *MCN: The American Journal of Maternal/Child Nursing, 31,* 156–163.

Tynes, Brendesha M. (2007). Internet safety gone wild? Sacrificing the educational and psychosocial benefits of online social environments. *Journal of Adolescent Research, 22,* 575–584.

U.S. Bureau of the Census. (1972). *Statistical abstract of the United States: 1972* (93rd ed.). Washington, DC: U.S. Government Printing Office.

U.S. Bureau of the Census. (2002). *Statistical abstract of the United States, 2001: The national data book* (121st ed.). Washington, DC: U.S. Department of Commerce.

U.S. Bureau of the Census. (2006). *Statistical abstract of the United States: 2007* (126th ed.). Washington, DC: U.S. Government Printing Office.

U.S. Bureau of the Census. (2007). *Statistical abstract of the United States: 2008* (127th ed.). Washington, DC: U.S. Department of Commerce.

U.S. Census Bureau. (2007). *Vital statistics, by country: 2006 and 2010.* U.S. Census Bureau. Retrieved April 14, 2008, from the World Wide Web: http://www.census.gov/compendia/statab/tables/08s1305.xls

U.S. Department of Health and Human Services. (2004). *Trends in the well-being of America's children and youth, 2003* (No. 017–022–01571–4). Washington, DC: U.S. Government Printing Office.

U.S. Department of Health and Human Services, Administration on Children, Youth and Families. (2006). *Child maltreatment 2004.* Washington, DC: U.S. Government Printing Office.

U.S. Department of Health and Human Services, Administration on Children, Youth and Families. (2008). *Child maltreatment 2006.* Washington, DC: U.S. Government Printing Office.

Udry, J. Richard, & Chantala, Kim. (2005). Risk factors differ according to same-sex and opposite-sex interest. *Journal of Biosocial Science, 37,* 481–497.

UNAIDS. (2006). *Report on the global AIDS epidemic 2006.* Geneva, Switzerland: World Health Organization

UNAIDS. (2008). *UNAIDS annual report 2007: Know your epidemic* (UNAIDS/08.21E/JC1535E). Geneva, Switzerland: Author.

Underwood, Marion K. (2003). *Social aggression among girls.* New York: Guilford Press.

Underwood, Marion K. (2004). Gender and peer relations: Are the two gender cultures really all that different? In Janis B. Kupersmidt & Kenneth A. Dodge (Eds.), *Children's peer relations: From development to intervention* (pp. 21–36). Washington, DC: American Psychological Association.

UNESCO. (2005). *Education for all: Global monitoring report 2006: Literacy for life.* Paris: United Nations Educational, Scientific and Cultural Organization.

UNESCO. (2006). *Global education digest 2006: Comparing education statistics across the world* (UIS/SD/06–01). Montreal, Canada: UNESCO Institute for Statistics.

Ungar, Michael T. (2000). The myth of peer pressure. *Adolescence, 35,* 167–180.

UNICEF (United Nations Children's Fund). (2006). *The state of the world's children 2007: Women and children: The double dividend of gender equality.* New York: UNICEF.

United Nations. (2007). *World population prospects: The 2006 revision* (Vols. 1–3). New York: United Nations, Department of Economic and Social Affairs.

United Nations Development Programme. (2008). *Human development report 2007/2008: Fighting climate change: Human solidarity in a divided world.* Retrieved April 5, 2008, from the World Wide Web: http://hdr.undp.org/en/media/hdr_20072008_en_indicator_tables.pdf

United Nations World Food Programme. (2007). *World hunger series: Hunger and health.* London: Earthscan.

Unnever, James D. (2005). Bullies, aggressive victims, and victims: Are they distinct groups? *Aggressive Behavior, 31,* 153–171.

Valentino, Kristin, Cicchetti, Dante, Rogosch, Fred A., & Toth, Sheree L. (2008). True and false recall and dissociation among maltreated children: The role of self-schema. *Development and Psychopathology, 20,* 213–232.

Valentino, Kristin, Cicchetti, Dante, Toth, Sheree L., & Rogosch, Fred A. (2006). Mother–child play and emerging social behaviors among infants from maltreating families. *Developmental Psychology, 42,* 474–485.

Valera, Eve M., Faraone, Stephen V., Murray, Kate E., & Seidman, Larry J.

(2007). Meta-analysis of structural imaging findings in attention-deficit/hyperactivity disorder. *Biological Psychiatry, 61,* 1361–1369.

Valkenburg, Patti M., & Peter, Jochen. (2007). Preadolescents' and adolescents' online communication and their closeness to friends. *Developmental Psychology, 43,* 267–277.

Valsiner, Jaan. (2006). Developmental epistemology and implications for methodology. In William Damon & Richard M. Lerner (Series Eds.) & Richard M. Lerner (Vol. Ed.), *Handbook of child psychology: Vol. 1. Theoretical models of human development* (6th ed., pp. 166–209). Hoboken, NJ: Wiley.

van Dam, Rob M., Willett, Walter C., Manson, JoAnn E., & Hu, Frank B. (2006). The relationship between overweight in adolescence and premature death in women. *Annals of Internal Medicine, 145,* 91–97.

van den Berg, Stéphanie M., & Boomsma, Dorret I. (2007). The familial clustering of age at menarche in extended twin families. *Behavior Genetics, 37,* 661–667.

van Hof, Paulion, van der Kamp, John, & Savelsbergh, Geert J. P. (2008). The relation between infants' perception of catchableness and the control of catching. *Developmental Psychology, 44,* 182–194.

Van Hoorn, Judith Lieberman, Komlosi, Akos, Suchar, Elzbieta, & Samelson, Doreen A. (2000). *Adolescent development and rapid social change: Perspectives from Eastern Europe.* Albany, NY: State University of New York Press.

van IJzendoorn, Marinus H., Bakermans-Kranenburg, Marian J., & Sagi-Schwartz, Abraham. (2006). Attachment across diverse sociocultural contexts: The limits of universality. In Kenneth H. Rubin & Ock Boon Chung (Eds.), *Parenting beliefs, behaviors, and parent–child relations: A cross-cultural perspective* (pp. 107–142). New York: Psychology.

Vartanian, Lesa Rae. (2001). Adolescents' reactions to hypothetical peer group conversations: Evidence for an imaginary audience? *Adolescence, 36,* 347–380.

Vasa, Roma A., & Pine, Daniel S. (2004). Neurobiology. In Tracy L. Morris & John S. March (Eds.), *Anxiety disorders in children and adolescents* (2nd ed., pp. 3–26). New York: Guilford Press.

VBAC.com. (n.d.). *Birth Trends.* Retrieved April 5, 2008, from the World Wide Web: http://www.vbac.com/birthtrends.html

Vega, William A., Chen, Kevin W., & Williams, Jill. (2007). Smoking, drugs, and other behavioral health problems among multiethnic adolescents in the NHSDA. *Addictive Behaviors, 32,* 1949–1956.

Venn, John J. (Ed.). (2004). *Assessing children with special needs* (3rd ed.). Upper Saddle River, NJ: Pearson.

Verona, Sergiu. (2003). Romanian policy regarding adoptions. In Victor Littel (Ed.), *Adoption update* (pp. 5–10). New York: Nova Science.

Verté, Sylvie, Geurts, Hilde M., Roeyers, Herbert, Oosterlaan, Jaap, & Sergeant, Joseph A. (2005). Executive functioning in children with autism and Tourette syndrome. *Development & Psychopathology, 17,* 415–445.

Viadero, Debra. (2006, February 15). Scholars warn of overstating gains from AP classes alone. *Education Week* 25(23), 14.

Viadero, Debra. (2007, April 5). Long after Katrina, children show symptoms of psychological distress. *Education Week, 26*(32), 7.

Viinanen, Arja, Munhbayarlah, S., Zevgee, T., Narantsetseg, L., Naidansuren, Ts, Koskenvuo, M., et al. (2007). The protective effect of rural living against atopy in Mongolia. *Allergy, 62,* 272–280.

Viltart, Odile, & Vanbesien-Mailliot, Christel C. A. (2007). Impact of prenatal stress on neuroendocrine programming. *ScientificWorldJournal, 7,* 1493–1537.

Visser, Beth A., Ashton, Michael C., & Vernon, Philip A. (2006). Beyond g: Putting multiple intelligences theory to the test. *Intelligence, 34,* 487–502.

Vitiello, Benedetto, Zuvekas, Samuel H., & Norquist, Grayson S. (2006). National estimates of antidepressant medication use among U.S. children, 1997–2002. *Journal of the American Academy of Child & Adolescent Psychiatry, 45,* 271–279.

Vogler, George P. (2006). Behavior genetics and aging. In James E. Birren & K. Warner Schaie (Eds.), *Handbook of the psychology of aging* (6th ed., pp. 41–55). Amsterdam: Elsevier.

von Hippel, William. (2007). Aging, executive functioning, and social control. *Current Directions in Psychological Science, 16,* 240–244.

Votruba-Drzal, Elizabeth, Coley, Rebekah Levine, & Chase-Lansdale, P. Lindsay. (2004). Child care and low-income children's development: Direct and moderated effects. *Child Development, 75,* 296–312.

Vouloumanos, Athena, & Werker, Janet F. (2007). Listening to language at birth: Evidence for a bias for speech in neonates. *Developmental Science, 10,* 159–164.

Vu, Pauline. (2007). *Lake Wobegon, U.S.A.* Pew Research Center. Retrieved July 27, 2007, from the World Wide Web: http://pewresearch.org/pubs/403/lake-wobegon-usa

Vygotsky, Lev S. (1986). *Thought and language* (Alex Kozulin, Ed. & Eugenia Hanfmann & Gertrude Vakar, Trans.). Cambridge, MA: MIT Press. (Original work published 1934)

Vygotsky, Lev S. (1987). *Thinking and speech* (Robert W. Rieber & Aaron S. Carton, Eds. & Norris Minick, Trans. Vol. 1). New York: Plenum Press. (Original work published 1934)

Vygotsky, Lev S. (1994). Principles of social education for deaf and dumb children in Russia (Theresa Prout, Trans.). In Rene van der Veer & Jaan Valsiner (Eds.), *The Vygotsky reader* (pp. 19–26). Cambridge, MA: Blackwell. (Original work published 1925)

Vygotsky, Lev S. (1994). The development of academic concepts in school aged children (Theresa Prout, Trans.). In Rene van der Veer & Jaan Valsiner (Eds.), *The Vygotsky reader* (pp. 355–370). Cambridge, MA: Blackwell. (Original work published 1934)

Waddell, Charlotte, Macmillan, Harriet, & Pietrantonio, Anna Marie. (2004). How important is permanency planning for children? Considerations for pediatricians involved in child protection. *Journal of Developmental & Behavioral Pediatrics, 25,* 285–292.

Wadsworth, Sally J., Corley, Robin, Plomin, Robert, Hewitt, John K., & DeFries, John C. (2006). Genetic and environmental influences on continuity and change in reading achievement in the Colorado Adoption Project. In Aletha C. Huston & Marika N. Ripke (Eds.), *Developmental contexts in middle childhood: Bridges to adolescence and adulthood* (pp. 87–106). New York: Cambridge University Press.

Wahlstrom, Kyla L. (2002). Accommodating the sleep patterns of adolescents within current educational structures: An uncharted path. In Mary A. Carskadon (Ed.), *Adolescent sleep patterns: Biological, social, and psychological influences* (pp. 172–197). New York: Cambridge University Press.

Wailoo, Michael, Ball, Helen L., Fleming, Peter, & Ward Platt, Martin. (2004). Infants bed-sharing with mothers.

Archives of Disease in Childhood, 89, 1082–1083.

Wainright, Jennifer L., & Patterson, Charlotte J. (2008). Peer relations among adolescents with female same-sex parents. *Developmental Psychology, 44,* 117–126.

Wainright, Jennifer L., Russell, Stephen T., & Patterson, Charlotte J. (2004). Psychosocial adjustment, school outcomes, and romantic relationships of adolescents with same-sex parents. *Child Development, 75,* 1886–1898.

Wainryb, Cecilia, Shaw, Leigh A., Langley, Marcie, Cottam, Kim, & Lewis, Renee. (2004). Children's thinking about diversity of belief in the early school years: Judgments of relativism, tolerance, and disagreeing persons. *Child Development, 75,* 687–703.

Wakefield, Melanie, Flay, Brian, Nichter, Mark, & Giovino, Gary. (2003). Effects of anti-smoking advertising on youth smoking: A review. *Journal of Health Communication, 8,* 229–247.

Walcott, Delores D., Pratt, Helen D., & Patel, Dilip R. (2003). Adolescents and eating disorders: Gender, racial, ethnic, sociocultural and socioeconomic issues. *Journal of Adolescent Research, 18,* 223–243.

Walden, Tedra A., & Kim, Geunyoung. (2005). Infants' social looking toward mothers and strangers. *International Journal of Behavioral Development, 29,* 356–360.

Waldfogel, J. (2006). What do children need? *Public Policy Research, 13,* 26–34.

Walker, Elaine F. (2002). Adolescent neurodevelopment and psychopathology. *Current Directions in Psychological Science, 11,* 24–28.

Walsh, Bridget A., & Petty, Karen. (2007). Frequency of six early childhood education approaches: A 10-year content analysis of early childhood education journal. *Early Childhood Education Journal, 34,* 301–305.

Wang, A. Ting, Lee, Susan S., Sigman, Marian, & Dapretto, Mirella. (2006). Developmental changes in the neural basis of interpreting communicative intent. *Social Cognitive and Affective Neuroscience, 1,* 107–121.

Wang, Richard Y., Needham, Larry L., & Barr, Dana B. (2005). Effects of environmental agents on the attainment of puberty: Considerations when assessing exposure to environmental chemicals in the National Children's Study. *Environmental Health Perspectives, 113,* 1100–1107.

Warren, Charles W., Jones, Nathan R., Eriksen, Michael P., & Asma, Samira. (2006). Patterns of global tobacco use in young people and implications for future chronic disease burden in adults. *Lancet, 367,* 749–753.

Warshofsky, Fred. (1999). *Stealing time: The new science of aging.* New York: TV Books.

Washington, Harriet A. (2006). *Medical apartheid: The dark history of medical experimentation on Black Americans from colonial times to the present.* New York: Doubleday.

Waterhouse, Lynn. (2006). Multiple intelligences, the Mozart effect, and emotional intelligence: A critical review. *Educational Psychologist, 41,* 207–225.

Watson, John B. (1928). *Psychological care of infant and child.* New York: Norton.

Watson, John B. (1998). *Behaviorism.* New Brunswick, NJ: Transaction. (Original work published 1924)

Waxman, Sandra R., & Lidz, Jeffrey L. (2006). Early word learning. In William Damon & Richard M. Lerner (Series Eds.) & Deanna Kuhn & Robert S. Siegler (Vol. Eds.), *Handbook of child psychology: Vol. 2. Cognition, perception, and language* (6th ed., pp. 299–335). Hoboken, NJ: Wiley.

Way, Niobe, Gingold, Rachel, Rotenberg, Mariana, & Kuriakose, Geena. (2005). Close friendships among urban, ethnic-minority adolescents. In Niobe Way & Jill V. Hamm (Eds.), *The experience of close friendships in adolescence* (Vol. 107, pp. 41–59). San Francisco: Jossey-Bass.

Way, Niobe, & Hamm, Jill V. (Eds.). (2005). *The experience of close friendships in adolescence.* San Francisco: Jossey-Bass.

Wayne, Andrew J., & Youngs, Peter. (2003). Teacher characteristics and student achievement gains: A review. *Review of Educational Research, 73,* 89–122.

Weatherston, Deborah J. (2002). The red coat: A story of longing for relationships, past and present. In Joan J. Shirilla & Deborah Weatherston (Eds.), *Case studies in infant mental health: Risk, resiliency, and relationships* (pp. 187–200). Washington, DC: Zero to Three.

Weaver, Chelsea M., Blodgett, Elizabeth H., & Carothers, Shannon S. (2006). Preventing risky sexual behavior. In John G. Borkowski & Chelsea M. Weaver (Eds.), *Prevention: The science and art of promoting healthy child and adolescent development* (pp. 185–214). Baltimore: Brookes.

Wechsler, David. (2003). *Wechsler intelligence scale for children—Fourth edition (WISC-IV).* San Antonio, TX: The Psychological Corporation.

Wechsler, Henry, Nelson, Toben F., Lee, Jae Eun, Seibring, Mark, Lewis, Catherine, & Keeling, Richard P. (2003). Perception and reality: A national evaluation of social norms marketing interventions to reduce college students' heavy alcohol use. *Quarterly Journal of Studies on Alcohol, 64,* 484–494.

Weichold, Karina, Silbereisen, Rainer K., & Schmitt-Rodermund, Eva. (2003). Short-term and long-term consequences of early versus late physical maturation in adolescents. In Chris Hayward (Ed.), *Gender differences at puberty* (pp. 241–276). New York: Cambridge University Press.

Weikart, David P. (Ed.). (1999). *What should young children learn? Teacher and parent views in 15 countries.* Ypsilanti, MI: High/Scope Press.

Weikum, Whitney M., Vouloumanos, Athena, Navarra, Jordi, Soto-Faraco, Salvador, Sebastian-Galles, Nuria, & Werker, Janet F. (2007, May 25). Visual language discrimination in infancy. *Science, 316,* 1159.

Weisfeld, Glenn E. (1999). *Evolutionary principles of human adolescence.* New York: Basic Books.

Weizman, Zehava Oz, & Snow, Catherine E. (2001). Lexical output as related to children's vocabulary acquisition: Effects of sophisticated exposure and support for meaning. *Developmental Psychology, 37,* 265–279.

Wellman, Henry M., Cross, David, & Watson, Julanne. (2001). Meta-analysis of theory-of-mind development: The truth about false belief. *Child Development, 72,* 655–684.

Werner, Emmy E. (1979). *Cross-cultural child development: A view from the planet Earth.* Monterey, CA: Brooks/Cole.

Werner, Emmy E., & Smith, Ruth S. (1992). *Overcoming the odds: High risk children from birth to adulthood.* Ithaca, NY: Cornell University Press.

Werner, Emmy E., & Smith, Ruth S. (2001). *Journeys from childhood to midlife: Risk, resilience, and recovery.* Ithaca, NY: Cornell University Press.

Wertsch, James V. (1998). *Mind as action.* New York: Oxford University Press.

Wertsch, James V., & Tulviste, Peeter. (2005). L. S. Vygotsky and contemporary developmental psychology. New York: Routledge.

West, Sheila, & Sommer, Alfred. (2001). Prevention of blindness and priorities for the future. *Bulletin of the World Health Organization, 79,* 244–248.

West, Steven L., & O'Neal, Keri K. (2004). Project D.A.R.E. outcome effectiveness revisited. *American Journal of Public Health, 94,* 1027–1029.

White, Aaron M., & Swartzwelder, H. Scott. (2004). Hippocampal function during adolescence: A unique target of ethanol effects. In Ronald E. Dahl & Linda Patia Spear (Eds.), *Adolescent brain development: Vulnerabilities and opportunities* (Vol. 1021, pp. 206–220). New York: New York Academy of Sciences.

Whitehurst, Grover J., & Massetti, Greta M. (2004). How well does Head Start prepare children to learn to read? In Edward Zigler & Sally J. Styfco (Eds.), *The Head Start debates* (pp. 251–262). Baltimore: Brookes.

Whitfield, Keith E., & McClearn, Gerald. (2005). Genes, environment, and race: Quantitative genetic approaches. *American Psychologist, 60,* 104–114.

Whitlock, Janis L., Powers, Jane L., & Eckenrode, John. (2006). The virtual cutting edge: The internet and adolescent self-injury. *Developmental Psychology, 42,* 407–417.

Wiener, Judith, & Schneider, Barry H. (2002). A multisource exploration of the friendship patterns of children with and without learning disabilities. *Journal of Abnormal Child Psychology, 30,* 127–141.

Wigfield, Allan, Eccles, Jacquelynne S., Yoon, Kwang Suk, Harold, Rena D., Arbreton, Amy J. A., Freedman-Doan, Carol, et al. (1997). Change in children's competence beliefs and subjective task values across the elementary school years: A 3-year study. *Journal of Educational Psychology, 89,* 451–469.

Willatts, Peter. (1999). Development of means–end behavior in young infants: Pulling a support to retrieve a distant object. *Developmental Psychology, 35,* 651–667.

Williams, Wendy M., Blythe, Tina, White, Noel, Li, Jin, Gardner, Howard, & Sternberg, Robert J. (2002). Practical intelligence for school: Developing metacognitive sources of achievement in adolescence. *Developmental Review, 22,* 162–210.

Williams, Wendy M., & Ceci, Stephen J. (2007). Introduction: Striving for perspective in the debate on women in science. In Stephen J. Ceci & Wendy M. Williams (Eds.), *Why aren't more women in science: Top researchers debate the evidence* (pp. 3–23). Washington, DC: American Psychological Association.

Williamson, Rebecca A., Meltzoff, Andrew N., & Markman, Ellen M. (2008). Prior experiences and perceived efficacy influence 3-year-olds' imitation. *Developmental Psychology, 44,* 275–285.

Wilson-Costello, Deanne, Friedman, Harriet, Minich, Nori, Siner, Bonnie, Taylor, Gerry, Schluchter, Mark, et al. (2007). Improved neurodevelopmental outcomes for extremely low birth weight infants in 2000–2002. *Pediatrics, 119,* 37–45.

Wingert, Pat. (2007, March 5). The baby who's not supposed to be alive. *Newsweek,* 59.

Winsler, Adam, Díaz, Rafael M., Espinosa, Linda, & Rodríguez, James L. (1999). When learning a second language does not mean losing the first: Bilingual language development in low-income, Spanish-speaking children attending bilingual preschool. *Child Development, 70,* 349–362.

Winsler, Adam, Manfra, Louis, & Díaz, Rafael M. (2007). "Should I let them talk?": Private speech and task performance among preschool children with and without behavior problems. *Early Childhood Research Quarterly, 22,* 215–231.

Wishart, Jennifer G. (2007). Socio-cognitive understanding: A strength or weakness in Down's syndrome? *Journal of Intellectual Disability Research, 51,* 996–1005.

Witherington, David C., Campos, Joseph J., & Hertenstein, Matthew J. (2004). Principles of emotion and its development in infancy. In Gavin Bremner & Alan Fogel (Eds.), *Blackwell handbook of infant development* (Paperback ed., pp. 427–464). Malden, MA: Blackwell.

Witt, Ellen D. (2007). Puberty, hormones, and sex differences in alcohol abuse and dependence. *Neurotoxicology and Teratology, 29,* 81–95.

Witt, Whitney P., Riley, Anne W., & Coiro, Mary Jo. (2003). Childhood functional status, family stressors, and psychosocial adjustment among school-aged children with disabilities in the United States. *Archives of Pediatrics & Adolescent Medicine, 157,* 687–695.

Wolak, Janis, Finkelhor, David, Mitchell, Kimberly J., & Ybarra, Michele L. (2008). Online "predators" and their victims: Myths, realities, and implications for prevention and treatment. *American Psychologist, 63,* 111–128.

Wolery, Mark, Barton, Erin E., & Hine, Jeffrey F. (2005). Evolution of applied behavior analysis in the treatment of individuals with autism. *Exceptionality, 13,* 11–23.

Wolraich, Mark L., & Doffing, Melissa A. (2005). Attention deficit hyperactivity disorder. In Merlin Gene Butler & F. John Meaney (Eds.), *Genetics of developmental disabilities* (pp. 783–807). Boca Raton, FL: Taylor & Francis.

Wong, Sheila, Chan, Kingsley, Wong, Virginia, & Wong, Wilfred. (2002). Use of chopsticks in Chinese children. *Child: Care, Health & Development, 28,* 157–161.

Wood, Alex, & Joseph, Stephen. (2007). Grand theories of personality cannot be integrated. *American Psychologist, 62,* 57–58.

Wood, Alexis C., Saudino, Kimberly J., Rogers, Hannah, Asherson, Philip, & Kuntsi, Jonna. (2007). Genetic influences on mechanically-assessed activity level in children. *Journal of Child Psychology and Psychiatry, 48,* 695–702.

Woodward, Amanda L., & Markman, Ellen M. (1998). Early word learning. In William Damon (Series Ed.) & Deanna Kuhn & Robert S. Siegler (Vol. Eds.), *Handbook of child psychology: Vol. 2. Cognition, perception and language* (5th ed., pp. 371–420). New York: Wiley.

Woolley, Jacqueline D., & Boerger, Elizabeth A. (2002). Development of beliefs about the origins and controllability of dreams. *Developmental Psychology, 38,* 24–41.

World Bank. (2005). *Expanding opportunities and building competencies for young people: A new agenda for secondary education.* Washington, DC: Author.

World Health Organization (WHO). (2000). *New data on the prevention of mother-to-child transmission of HIV and their policy implications—Conclusions and recommendations.* Retrieved September 3, 2005, from the World Wide Web: http://www.who.int/child-adolescent-health/New_Publications/CHILD_HEALTH/MTCT_Consultation.htm

World Health Organization. (2003). *World atlas of birth defects* (2nd ed.). Geneva, Switzerland: Author.

World Health Organization. (2005). *Sexually transmitted infections among adolescents: Issues in adolescent health and development.* Geneva, Switzerland: Author.

Wright, Barlow C. (2001). Reconceptualizing the transitive inference ability: A framework for existing and future research. *Developmental Review, 21,* 375–422.

Wright, Dave, Bradbury, Ian, Cuckle, Howard, Gardosi, Jason, Tonks, Ann, Standing, Sue, et al. (2006). Three-stage contingent screening for Down syndrome. *Prenatal Diagnosis, 26,* 528–534.

Wright, Lawrence. (1999). *Twins: And what they tell us about who we are.* New York: Wiley.

Yajnik, Chittaranjan S. (2004). Early life origins of insulin resistance and type 2 diabetes in India and other Asian countries. *Journal of Nutrition, 134,* 205–210.

Yamaguchi, Susumu, Greenwald, Anthony G., Banaji, Mahzarin R., Murakami, Fumio, Chen, Daniel, Shiomura, Kimihiro, et al. (2007). Apparent universality of positive implicit self-esteem. *Psychological Science, 18,* 498–500.

Yarber, William L., Milhausen, Robin R., Crosby, Richard A., & Torabi, Mohammad R. (2005). Public opinion about condoms for HIV and STD prevention: A midwestern state telephone survey. *Perspectives on Sexual and Reproductive Health, 37,* 148–154.

Yates, Tuppett M. (2004). The developmental psychopathology of self-injurious behavior: Compensatory regulation in posttraumatic adaptation. *Clinical Psychology Review, 24,* 35–74.

Yehuda, Rachel (Ed.). (2006). *Annals of the New York Academy of Sciences: Vol. 1071. Psychobiology of posttraumatic stress disorder: A decade of progress.* Boston: Blackwell.

Yen, Ju-Yu, Ko, Chih-Hung, Yen, Cheng-Fang, Chen, Sue-Huei, Chung, Wei-Lun, & Chen, Cheng-Chung. (2008). Psychiatric symptoms in adolescents with internet addiction: Comparison with substance use. *Psychiatry and Clinical Neurosciences, 62,* 9–16.

Yerys, Benjamin E., & Munakata, Yuko. (2006). When labels hurt but novelty helps: Children's perseveration and flexibility in a card-sorting task. *Child Development, 77,* 1589–1607.

Yeung, Melinda Y. (2006). Postnatal growth, neurodevelopment and altered adiposity after preterm birth—From a clinical nutrition perspective. *Acta Paediatrica, 95,* 909–917.

Yeung, W. Jean, & Conley, Dalton. (2008). Black–White achievement gap and family wealth. *Child Development, 79,* 303–324.

Yeung, W. Jean, Linver, Miriam R., & Brooks-Gunn, Jeanne. (2002). How money matters for young children's development: Parental investment and family processes. *Child Development, 73,* 1861–1879.

Young, Elizabeth A., Korszun, Ania, Figueiredo, Helmer F., Banks-Solomon, Matia, & Herman, James P. (2008). Sex differences in HPA axis regulation. In Jill B. Becker, Karen J. Berkley, Nori Geary, Elizabeth Hampson, James P. Herman, & Elizabeth Young (Eds.), *Sex differences in the brain: From genes to behavior* (pp. 95–105). New York: Oxford University Press.

Zahn-Waxler, Carolyn, Park, Jong-Hyo, Usher, Barbara, Belouad, Francesca, Cole, Pamela, & Gruber, Reut. (2008). Young children's representations of conflict and distress: A longitudinal study of boys and girls with disruptive behavior problems. *Development and Psychopathology, 20,* 99–119.

Zani, Bruna, & Cicognani, Elvira. (2006). Sexuality and intimate relationships in adolescence. In Sandy Jackson & Luc Goossens (Eds.), *Handbook of adolescent development* (pp. 200–222). Hove, East Sussex, UK: Psychology Press.

Zeck, Willibald, Walcher, Wolfgang, Tamussino, Karl, & Lang, Uwe. (2008). Adolescent primiparas: Changes in obstetrical risk between 1983–1987 and 1999–2005. *The Journal of Obstetrics and Gynaecology Research, 34,* 195–198.

Zeedyk, M. Suzanne, Wallace, Linda, & Spry, Linsay. (2002). Stop, look, listen, and think? What young children really do when crossing the road. *Accident Analysis & Prevention, 34,* 43–50.

Zehler, Annette M., Fleischman, Howard L., Hopstock, Paul J., Stephenson, Todd G., Pendzick, Michelle L., & Sapru, Saloni. (2003). *Descriptive study of services to LEP students and LEP students with disabilities: Vol. 1. Research report.* Arlington, VA: Development Associates.

Zehr, Julia L., Culbert, Kristen M., Sisk, Cheryl L., & Klump, Kelly L. (2007). An association of early puberty with disordered eating and anxiety in a population of undergraduate women and men. *Hormones and Behavior, 52,* 427–435.

Zeifman, Debra, Delaney, Sarah, & Blass, Elliott M. (1996). Sweet taste, looking, and calm in 2- and 4-week-old infants: The eyes have it. *Developmental Psychology, 32,* 1090–1099.

Zelazo, Philip David, Müller, Ulrich, Frye, Douglas, & Marcovitch, Stuart. (2003). The development of executive function in early childhood. *Monographs of the Society for Research in Child Development, 68*(3, Serial No. 274), 11–27.

Zernike, Kate. (2005, March 12). Drinking game can be a deadly rite of passage. *New York Times.*

Zhu, Li-qi, & Fang, Fu-xi. (2006). Preschool children's understanding of death. *Chinese Journal of Clinical Psychology, 14,* 91–93.

Zigler, Edward, & Styfco, Sally J. (Eds.). (2004). *The Head Start debates.* Baltimore: Brookes.

Zigler, Edward F., Kagan, Sharon Lynn, & Hall, Nancy Wilson (Eds.). (1996). *Children, families, and government: Preparing for the twenty-first century.* New York: Cambridge University Press.

Zimmer-Gembeck, Melanie J., & Collins, W. Andrew. (2003). Autonomy development during adolescence. In Gerald R. Adams & Michael D. Berzonsky (Eds.), *Blackwell handbook of adolescence* (pp. 175–204). Malden, MA: Blackwell.

Zito, Julie Magno, Safer, Daniel J., dosReis, Susan, Gardner, James F., Magder, Laurence, Soeken, Karen, et al. (2003). Psychotropic practice patterns for youth: A 10-year perspective. *Archives of Pediatrics & Adolescent Medicine, 157,* 17–25.

Zucker, Kenneth J. (2005). Gender identity disorder in children and adolescents. *Annual Review of Clinical Psychology, 1,* 467–492.

Zuvekas, Samuel H., Vitiello, Benedetto, & Norquist, Grayson S. (2006). Recent trends in stimulant medication use among U.S. children. *American Journal of Psychiatry, 163,* 579–585.

Name Index

Subject Index